CRITICAL SURVEY
OF
POETRY

CRITICAL SURVEY

OF

POETRY

Second Revised Edition

Volume 3

Hans Magnus Enzensberger - Gerard Manley Hopkins

Editor, Second Revised Edition
Philip K. Jason
United States Naval Academy

Editor, First Edition, English and Foreign Language Series
Frank N. Magill

SALEM PRESS, INC.
Pasadena, California   Hackensack, New Jersey

Editor in Chief: Dawn P. Dawson
Managing Editor: Christina J. Moose
Developmental Editor: Tracy Irons-Georges
Research Supervisor: Jeffry Jensen
Acquisitions Editor: Mark Rehn
Photograph Editor: Philip Bader
Manuscript Editors: Sarah Hilbert, Leslie Ellen Jones,
Melanie Watkins, Rowena Wildin
Assistant Editor: Andrea E. Miller
Research Assistant: Jeff Stephens
Production Editor: Cynthia Beres
Layout: Eddie Murillo

∞ The paper used in these volumes conforms to the American National Standard for Permanence of Paper for Printed Library Materials, Z39.48-1992(R1997).

Library of Congress Cataloging-in-Publication Data
Critical survey of poetry / Philip K. Jason, editor.—2nd rev. ed.
p. cm.
Combined ed. of: Critical survey of poetry: foreign language series, originally published 1984, Critical survey of poetry: supplement, originally published 1987, and Critical survey of poetry: English language series, rev. ed. published 1992. With new material. Includes bibliographical references and index.
ISBN 1-58765-071-1 (set : alk. paper) — ISBN 1-58765-074-6 (v. 3 : alk. paper) —
1. Poetry—History and criticism—Dictionaries. 2. Poetry—Bio-bibliography. 3. Poets—Biography—Dictionaries. I. Jason, Philip K., 1941 - .

PN1021 .C7 2002
809.1′003—dc21
2002008536

First Printing

PRINTED IN THE UNITED STATES OF AMERICA

CONTENTS

COMPLETE LIST OF CONTENTS

VOLUME 1

VOLUME 2

VOLUME 3

VOLUME 4

VOLUME 5

VOLUME 6

VOLUME 7

VOLUME 8

POETRY AROUND THE WORLD

RESEARCH TOOLS

INDEXES

CRITICAL SURVEY

OF

POETRY

HANS MAGNUS ENZENSBERGER

Born: Kaufbeuren, Germany; November 11, 1929

PRINCIPAL POETRY

Verteidigung der Wölfe, 1957

Landessprache, 1960

Museum der modernen Poesie, 1960

Gedichte: Die Entstehung eines Gedichts, 1962

Blindenschrift, 1964

Poems, 1966

Poems for People Who Don't Read Poems, 1968

Gedichte, 1955-1970, 1971

Mausoleum: Siebenunddreissig Balladen aus der Geschichte des Fortschritts, 1975 (*Mausoleum: Thirty-seven Ballads from the History of Progress*, 1976)

Der Untergang der Titanic: Eine Komödie, 1978 (*The Sinking of the Titanic: A Poem*, 1980)

Beschreibung eines Dickichts, 1979

Die Furie des Verschwindens: Gedichte, 1980

Dreiunddreissig Gedichte, 1981

Diderot und das dunkle Ei: Eine Mystifikation, 1990

Zukunftsmusik, 1991

Selected Poems, 1994

Hans Magnus Enzensberger, 1995

Gedichte, 1950-1995, 1996

Kiosk: Neue Gedichte, 1995 (*Kiosk*, 1997)

Gedichte, 1999 (6 volumes)

Leichter als Luft: Moralische Gedichte, 1999 (*Lighter than Air: Moral Poems*, 2000)

OTHER LITERARY FORMS

Hans Magnus Enzensberger has worked in a wide variety of literary forms. His doctoral dissertation, *Clemens Brentanos Poetik* (1961; Clemens Brentano's poetics), completed in 1955, is a central piece of Brentano scholarship. As the founder and editor (now coeditor) of the leftist journal *Kursbuch* (begun in 1965), Enzensberger exercised a substantial influence as a cultural critic on several fronts. Versed in eight languages, he has been a prolific translator of foreign poets and an astute editor of their works. He has written numerous essays and nonfiction works on politics, poetics, and social issues, as well as experimental fiction, drama, and works for radio and television.

ACHIEVEMENTS

Hans Magnus Enzensberger has significantly influenced the course of German intellectual life and letters since he first appeared on the scene in 1957, and his works have been published in many languages. His career has been distinguished by several honors and literary awards. In 1956, he received the Hugo-Jacobi Prize; in 1962, the literary prize of the Union of German Critics for his critical poems; and in 1963, the treasured Georg Büchner Prize. In 1967, the city of Nuremberg honored him with its cultural award for having represented Germany "in a manner so urgently necessary to counteract the clichéd image of neo-German fanaticism within the Federal Republic." Also in 1967, he received the Etna-Taormina International Poetry Prize. In 1982 he won the Premio Pasolini, in 1985 the Heinrich Böll Prize, and in 1987 the Bavarian Academy of Fine Arts Award.

BIOGRAPHY

The eldest of three brothers, Hans Magnus Enzensberger was born in the Bavarian Allgäu and grew up in a middle-class home in Nuremberg. He attended high school from 1942 to 1945, but in 1945, he was inducted into the Volkssturm for militia "cleanup" duty. After the war, he served as an interpreter and bartender for the Royal Air Force, earning his keep as well through the black market. He completed his secondary schooling (the *Abitur*) in 1949 and spent the next five years studying literature, languages, and philosophy in Erlangen, Freiburg, Hamburg, and Paris. His work on Brentano's poetry concluded his university studies. He was later employed as a radio editor in Stuttgart and as a visiting professor in Ulm. In 1957, he traveled to the United States and Mexico; in the same year, he published his first book of poems, *Verteidigung der Wölfe* (defense of the wolves). Returning from Mexico, Enzensberger settled first in Norway. Two years later, a stipend took him to Italy, and later he became a reader for Suhrkamp, the large publishing house in Frankfurt. His second volume of poems, *Landessprache* (country talk), met with great critical acclaim, as did his anthology of modern poetry, *Museum der modernen Poesie* (1960; museum of modern poetry). Several awards and distinctions followed. Enzensberger continued to travel, in 1963 to the Soviet Union and in 1965 to South America, spending the year between these journeys in Frankfurt, where he taught as a visiting professor of poetics. In 1965, he moved from Tjörne to West Berlin and founded the journal *Kursbuch*. In the same year he became a professor of poetry at the University of Frankfurt. He was commissioned by the Goethe Institute of the Federal Republic of Germany to conduct lecture tours in 1966 and 1967 to Athens, Ankara, and New Delhi. He went to Wesleyan University as a fellow at the Center for Advanced Studies in 1967 but soon relinquished his fellowship in protest against the Vietnam War. He later traveled through America and the Far East, eventually spending several months in Cuba, where he began work on the epic poem he completed nine years later, *The Sinking of the Titanic*. He traveled to Spain in 1971 with a camera team and held lectures in Japan in 1973, at the behest of the Goethe Institute. He later returned to Berlin, and then to Munich, where he founded and edited the journal *Trans-Atlantik* (1980-1982). In his seventh decade, Enzensberger remained a committed social critic of postwar German society and is regarded as one of Germany's most important literary figures.

ANALYSIS

Hans Magnus Enzensberger stepped onto the literary scene as Germany's angry young man in the 1950's, a time when the Federal Republic of Germany (West Germany) was cashing in on its economic miracle. Enzensberger's anger, which would continue to fuel his verse, was directed against a world controlled by an inhumane technologized civilization and the repressive machinery of power, be it government or industry, politics or the military, or even the mass media of the "consciousness industry." As an independent, abrasive political poet and polemicist, he stands in the tradition of Heinrich Heine and Bertolt Brecht. Gottfried Benn's influence, evident from the beginning, has become more pronounced since the early 1970's. Enzensberger remains the defender of freedom against authority and power, seeking "revision, not revolution."

Enzensberger makes a systematic effort to relate theory and praxis by combining aesthetic and political re-

flections in his literary works. He fuses literature and history, or historical documentation and literary "fiction," referring to this mixture as *Faktographien* (factographs). Though his concept of literature rests decidedly upon a political commitment, this is never so explicit in his poetry as to be reducible to a platform of positions. Although Enzensberger, like Brecht, is conscious of the functional value of poetry, its social utility, his aesthetic is fraught with ideological reservations. He rejects monolithic philosophies and political dogmatism, and his position can perhaps be best described as an enlightened and critical skepticism.

EARLY POETRY

Looking for the larger contours in the development of Enzensberger's poetry, it is instructive to speak of three different phases. The first phase includes the volumes *Verteidigung der Wölfe*, *Landessprache*, and *Blindenschrift* (braille). Here, Enzensberger tried to "determine the situation, not to offer prognoses or horoscopes." He sharply criticized current conditions, revealing an aesthetic intelligence and an artistic mastery that had at its command a legion of traditional and modern forms and literary techniques. As a political poet in the vein of Heine and Brecht, Enzensberger did much to resuscitate the political poem. Finally, this phase of his poetry demonstrates his rebellious anger and scorn, as well as his dogmatic skepticism.

In these early volumes, one finds a mixture of Brecht's "public" and Benn's "private" poetry. From Brecht, Enzensberger learned the nature of political poetry and how to put it across, while from Benn he learned a basic method of composition, the notion of "prismatic infantilism," the use of concatenated imagery. Enzensberger's satire is often in the vein of W. H. Auden. In *Blindenschrift*, in particular, Enzensberger exhibits a strong concentration on particulars, a new sort of detail, along with lyrical grace and simplicity.

THE 1960'S AND 1970'S

In Enzensberger's second phase, his poetry receded into the background. These were the years (roughly from 1965 to the early 1970's) when Enzensberger pursued political theory and action and, at one point, polemically called the whole industry of literature into question. He devoted himself to "factual" literature, to the documentary form then very much in vogue in West

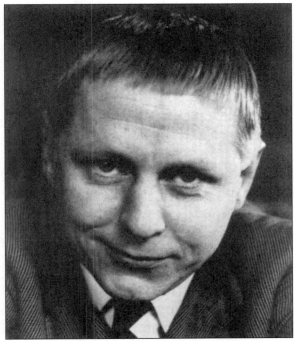

Hans Magnus Enzensberger (© Lütfi Özkök)

Germany. He concentrated as well on polemical essays that came to make his *Kursbuch* so controversial.

In the early 1970's, however, Enzensberger returned to poetry. This shift coincided with a renewed interest in the study of history, explicit in recent volumes such as *Mausoleum, The Sinking of the Titanic,* and *Die Furie des Verschwindens* (the fury of passing). Here, Enzensberger understands and portrays history in its dialectical dimensions. He locates and concentrates on historical moments during which "the exploitation of science [becomes] the science of exploitation." Frequently, his poetic history of scientific and technological progress focuses on instances of moral regression. It is particularly in these respects that Enzensberger's "philosophy of life" has come to resemble that of Gottfried Benn.

THE SINKING OF THE TITANIC

One of Enzensberger's finest works is his epic poem *The Sinking of the Titanic,* which he himself translated into English in 1980. This poem reveals much about Enzensberger's attitudes toward poetry, toward history, and toward his own growth and change during the last decade.

Enzensberger began writing *The Sinking of the Titanic* while in Cuba in 1968-1969 but finished it much later, in 1977, in Berlin, after having lost the original manuscript during one of his many travels. While tracing the history of a work's composition is often the task of scholarly research, here it is made part of the poem itself. Enzensberger weaves an intricate and polychromatic fabric in his text, creating a kind of space-time continuum in which the catastrophe of the *Titanic* and his writing about it are simultaneously enacted and represented, explicated and documented, anticipated and recalled, on the various primary, secondary, and tertiary stages which the thirty-three cantos and the sixteen interpolated poems provide.

The structure of the work, as well as its subtitle, "A Comedy," refer directly to Dante's *La divina commedia* (c. 1320; *The Divine Comedy*). Enzensberger fuses different historical moments and psychological states to form the distinctive texture of the poem: the historical incident of the 1912 catastrophe; the watershed years of twentieth century German history, from 1918 to 1945; the time of the poem's composition, from 1968 to 1977; temporal excursions to the sixteenth, seventeenth and nineteenth centuries, and to some unspecified future; geographical excursions to the Netherlands, Italy, Havana, and Berlin—all of these are portals through which Enzensberger guides the reader, back and forth. The poet and the reader become eyewitnesses, seeing ideas in motion, people in motion, history re-created.

The power of Enzensberger's poetic imagination creates a fascinating and compelling simultaneity of historical experience and event, fictional vision and scenario. In asides and innuendos, he brings technical issues and compositional problems to the surface of his text. At other times, the tenor of his reflection registers disappointment and resignation, as when he recalls the failure of misguided actions: "Everything we did was wrong./ And so everything was wrong/ that we thought." At other times, he injects ironic self-mockery and persiflage: "A good comrade/ I was not./ Instead of writing about sugar,/ about Socialism on an island,/ I fished dead survivors and dead fatalities,/ nonpartisan-like and half a century too late,/ out of the black water."

The intricate configuration of the poem revolves around the *Titanic* as a commonplace symbol for the demise of modern civilization. At the same time, it is important to remember that commonplaces do not sit well with Enzensberger; he is much keener on contradictions, on the "integration of ambivalences," to use a phrase of Gottfried Benn. Consequently, Enzensberger uses one canto (the sixteenth) to display the hollowness and malleability of the very object that provides his central metaphor—the *Titanic*. This canto is a piece of ironic sophistry, the poetry of the disillusioned Left, and is, like everything else, part of the cargo of Enzensberger's fated ship.

History, being "an invention for which reality provides the stuff," becomes present as it is reenacted in the mind. The twenty-eighth canto concludes: "these people sinking before me, with me, after me, are telephoning/ with one another in my forty-six-thousand-gross-tonnage-head." Enzensberger's poetic figuration of historical fact locates the moving forces of history within the momentum of collective fictions; at the same time he exposes the radical internalization of contemporary paranoia. Enzensberger, reluctant to "tell the truth," tells instead the truth about truth in this poem. The multiplicity of voices which speak through this work belong not only to the survivors and heirs of the *Titanic*, to those who died tragically then and who die (and live) tragically now, not only to the books, films, and other commercial enterprises (including the poet's own) which profit from the catastrophe of the *Titanic* but also to the socially and economically exploited, to radicals with misgivings, and to Enzensberger as he thought and wrote in 1968 as well as Enzensberger as he thought and wrote in 1977. The questions raised by Enzensberger in *The Sinking of the Titanic* will continue to echo in his readers's heads: "How was it in reality? How was it in my poem?/ *Was* it in my poem?"

In 1958, Alfred Andersch said of Enzensberger that he had written "what has been absent in Germany since Brecht: the great political poem." Since that time, Enzensberger's poetry has undergone considerable change, but it has never lacked an underlying political commitment. Enzensberger has shown that "political poetry" need not be artistically retrograde; indeed, for him, a poem is political to the extent that its language constitutes resistance against repression and a means of emancipation from debilitating social forces.

LIGHTER THAN AIR

This collection of lyric meditations, published in 1999, displays Enzensberger in a lighter mode, as the title suggests. The volume consists of seventy lyric meditations, combining caustic wit with humor as Enzensberger comments on everything from useless products to the inconsequential existence of humankind. Although lighter than some of his other fare, these poems remain concerned with the themes that have always occupied Enzensberger's attention. Enzensberger is typically satiric and sarcastic in his outrage at moral injustices, social inanities, and human self-absorption, as in "Equisetum," which elevates a lowly horsetail to a level of moral superiority over human beings as the plant "bid[es] its time,/ simpler than we are, and hence/ unvanquishable."

OTHER MAJOR WORKS

LONG FICTION: *Der kurze Sommer der Anarchie: Buenaventura Durruits Leben und Tod*, 1972; *Wo warst du, Robert?*, 1998 (*Where Were You, Robert?*, 2000; also as *Lost in Time*, 2000).

PLAYS: *Das Verhör von Habana*, pr., pb. 1970 (*The Havana Inquiry*, 1974); *Die Tochter der Luft: Ein Schauspiel, nach dem spanischen des Calderón de la Barca*, pr., pb. 1992; *Voltaires Neffe: Eine Fälschung in Diderots Manier*, pb. 1996.

NONFICTION: *Clemens Brentanos Poetik*, wr. 1955, pb. 1961; *Brentanos Poetik*, 1961; *Einzelheiten*, 1962 (*The Consciousness Industry: On Literature, Politics, and the Media*, 1974); *Einzelheiten II: Poesie und Politik*, 1963; *Politik und Verbrechen*, 1964 (*Politics and Crime*, 1974); *Politische Kolportagen*, 1966; *Deutschland, Deutschland unter anderem*, 1967; *Staatsgefährdende Umtriebe*, 1968; *Freisprüche: Revolutionäre vor Gericht*, 1970; *Palaver: Politische Überlegungen, 1967-1973*, 1974; *Der Weg ins Freie: Fünf Lebensläufe*, 1975; *Raids and Reconstructions: Essays on Politics, Crime, and Culture*, 1976; *Critical Essays*, 1982; *Politische Brosamen*, 1982 (*Political Crumbs*, 1990); *Ach Europa! Wahrnehmungen aus sieben Landern: Mit einem Epilog aus dem Jahre*

2006, 1987 (*Europe, Europe: Forays into a Continent*, 1989); *Dreamers of the Absolute: Essays on Politics, Crime, and Culture*, 1988; *Mittelmass und Wahn: Gesammelte Zerstreuungen*, 1988 (*Mediocrity and Delusion: Collected Diversions*, 1992); *Die grosse Wanderung*, 1992; *Aussichten auf den Bürgerkrieg*, 1993; *Civil War*, 1994; *Civil Wars: From L.A. to Bosnia*, 1994; *Diderots Schatten: Unterhaltungen, Szenen, Essays*, 1994; *Deutschland, Deutschland unter anderm: Äusserungen sur Politik*, 1996; *Requiem für eine romantische Frau: Die Geschichte von August Bussman und Clemens Brentano*, 1996; *Baukasten zu einer Theorie der Medien: Kritische Diskurse zur Pressefreiheit*, 1997; *Zickzack: Aufsätze*, 1997 (*Zig Zag: The Politics of Culture and Vice Versa*, 1997).

CHILDREN'S LITERATURE: *Esterhazy: Eine Hasengeschichte*, 1993 (*Esterhazy: The Rabbit Prince*, 1994; with Irene Dische); *Der Zahlenteufel: Ein Kopfkissenbuch für Alle, die Angst vor der Athematik haben*, 1997 (*The Number Devil: A Mathematical Adventure*, 1998).

EDITED TEXTS: *Gedichte, Erzählungen, Briefe*, 1958; *Museum der modernen Poesie*, 1960; *Allerleirauh: Viele schöne Kinderreime*, 1961; *Gedichte*, 1962; *Poesie*, 1962; *Vorzeichen: Fünf neue deutsche Autoren*, 1962; *Gespräche mit Marx und Engels*, 1973.

TRANSLATIONS: *Gedichte*, 1962 (of William Carlos Williams); *Geisterstimmen: Übersetzungen und Imitationen*, 1999.

MISCELLANEOUS: *Der fliegende Robert: Gedichte, Szenen, Essays*, 1992.

BIBLIOGRAPHY

Demetz, Peter. *Postwar German Literature: A Critical Introduction*. New York: Pegasus, 1970. This basic text remains a useful examination of German postwar authors in the context of their times.

Enzensberger, Hans Magnus. *Hans Magnus Enzensberger in Conversation with Michael Hulse and John Kinsella*. London: Between the Lines, 2002. A lengthy interview with Enzensberger, a career sketch, a comprehensive bibliography, and excerpts from critics and interviewers.

Falkenstein, Henning. *Hans Magnus Enzensberger*. Berlin: Colloquium-Verlag, 1977. A brief biography, in German.

Fischer, Gerhard, ed. *Debating Enzensberger: "Great Migration" and "Civil War."* Tübingen: Stauffenberg, 1996. Papers delivered at the 1995 Sydney German Studies Symposium. Includes bibliographical references.

Kilian, Monika. *Modern and Postmodern Strategies: Gaming and the Question of Morality—Adorno, Rorty, Oyotard, and Enzensberger*. New York: Peter Lang, 1998. Examines the debate between modern and postmodern thought, including the postmodern notion that "universalizing strategies of modern thought are cognitively and morally wrong," with reference to these German writers. Bibliography, index.

Natan, Alex, and B. Keithsmith, eds. *Essays on Lehmann, Kasack, Nossack, Eich, Gaiser, Böll, Celan, Bachmann, Enzensberger, East German Literature*. Vol. 4 in *German Men of Letters Literary Essays*. New York: Berg, 1987. A collection of twelve essays, including analysis of Enzensberger in English.

Rim, Byung-Hee. *Hans Magnus Enzensberger: Ein Paradigma der deutschen Lyrik seit Mitte der 1950er Jahre*. New York: Peter Lang, 2000. An examination of Enzensberger's poetics. In German.

Schickel, Joachim, ed. *Über Hans Magnus Enzensberger*. Frankfurt am Main, Germany: Suhrkamp, 1970. A hefty biography (more than three hundred pages), including a bibliography of works by and about Enzensberger. In German.

Richard Spuler;
updated by Christina J. Moose

LOUISE ERDRICH

Born: Little Falls, Minnesota; June 7, 1954

PRINCIPAL POETRY
Jacklight, 1984
Baptism of Desire, 1989

OTHER LITERARY FORMS

Like many other American Indian writers, Louise Erdrich writes in various genres: short fiction, novels, memoirs, and children's literature. She has published a series of novels exploring the lives of American Indians, usually of mixed heritage, from her own Chippewa tribe. Starting with *Love Medicine* (1984) and extending through *Last Report on the Miracles at Little No Horse* (2001), Erdrich has created an imaginative territory that has been compared to William Faulkner's Yoknapatawpha County. In addition to this "family" of novels, Erdrich coauthored, with her husband Michael Dorris, *The Crown of Columbus* (1991).

As the mother of six children, Erdrich developed an interest in children's literature and has published books for children, including *Grandmother's Pigeon* (1996) and *The Birchbark House* (1999), which she also illustrated. Her memoir, *The Blue Jay's Dance: A Birth Year* (1995), is an account of her own pregnancy and the birth of one of her daughters.

Louise Erdrich (Michael Dorris)

ACHIEVEMENTS

Louise Erdrich's major achievements have been in fiction. Early in her career, she was awarded first prize in the 1982 Nelson Algren fiction competition, for "The World's Greatest Fisherman." This short story became a chapter in *Love Medicine*, which won the National Book Critics Circle Award for best work of fiction in 1984. *The Beet Queen* (1986) won first prize at the 1987 O. Henry Awards, as well as a National Book Critics Circle Award nomination. *The Antelope Wife* (1998) won the World Fantasy Award for best novel in 1999. In 2001, her novel *The Last Report on the Miracles at Little No Horse* was nominated for a National Book Award.

She has also been awarded a number of fellowships: She was a Johns Hopkins University teaching fellow in 1978, a MacDowell Colony fellow in 1980, a Yaddo Colony fellow in 1981, a Dartmouth College visiting fellow in 1981, a National Endowment for the Arts fellow in 1982, and a Guggenheim fellow in 1985-1986.

BIOGRAPHY

Louise Erdrich was born in Little Falls, Minnesota, the daughter of Ralph Louis, a German American teacher with the Bureau of Indian Affairs (BIA), and Rita Joanne, her French and Chippewa mother, also a teacher in the BIA school. The first of seven children, Erdrich told author Joseph Bruchac she grew up "not thinking about [her mixed blood], everybody knowing you were a mixed-blood in town. You'd go to the [Turtle Mountain] reservation to visit sometimes and sometimes you'd go to your other family. It really was the kind of thing you just took for granted." Erdrich's parents fostered her creativity. In her interview with Bruchac, she said, "Both my mom and dad were encouraging. . . . I had that kind of childhood where I didn't feel art was something strange."

Erdrich grew up in Wahpeton, North Dakota, not far from Turtle Mountain reservation, where her grandfather Pat Tourneau had been tribal chairman. Erdrich moved away from Wahpeton to enter Dartmouth College in 1972, the first year it admitted women. At Dartmouth, Erdrich met her future husband and collaborator, Michael Dorris, the newly hired chair of the Native American Studies department. Between receiving her B.A. and entering The Johns Hopkins University M.A. program, Erdrich worked at a series of what she called "really crazy jobs," among which were beet weeder, waitress, psychiatric aide, signaler for a construction gang, lifeguard, and poetry teacher for the North Dakota Arts Council. These jobs provided her with practical experience in the world, which she later incorporated into her writing.

Erdrich's return to Dartmouth as writer in residence brought her into contact with Michael Dorris. They began exchanging poems and stories, collaborated on "The World's Greatest Fisherman," and married in 1981. They had six children: Reynold (died in 1991), Jeffrey, Madeline, Persia, Pallas, and Aza. The Erdrich-Dorris marriage was extraordinary in many respects. They collaborated fully on writing projects, although only *The Crown of Columbus* bears both names. Erdrich told Joseph Bruchac: "Michael and I are truly collaborators in all aspects of writing and life. It's very hard to separate the writing and the family life and Michael and I as people."

Erdrich's separation from Dorris was followed by the tragedy of his suicide in 1997. Erdrich settled in Minneapolis with three of her children and began operating Birchbark Books, a bookstore. She continued to write and publish fiction and children's books but not poetry. "Being a fiction writer," she told interviewer Laura Coltelli, is "closer to the oral tradition of sitting around and telling stories."

ANALYSIS

Erdrich's interest in writing can be traced to her childhood and her heritage. She told *Writer's Digest* contributor Michael Schumacher, "People in [Native American] families make everything into a story. . . . People just sit and the stories start coming, one after another. I suppose that when you grow up constantly hearing the stories rise, break, and fall, it gets into you somehow." Her parents encouraged her writing: "My father used to give me a nickel for every story I wrote, and my mother wove strips of construction paper together and stapled them into book covers. So at an early age I felt myself to be a published author earning substantial royalties."

Although most of her characters and themes grow out of her background as a Native American woman who grew up off the reservation, the writings of Louise Erdrich not only reflect her multilayered, complex backgrounds–she is both Turtle Mountain Chippewa and European American—but also confound a variety of literary genre and cultural categories. In her fiction and poetry she plainly regards the survival of American Indian cultures as imperative. She prescribes the literary challenge for herself and other contemporary Native writers in her essay "Where I Ought to Be: A Writer's Sense of Place," published in a 1985 issue of *The New York Times Book Review:* In the light of enormous loss, they must tell the stories of contemporary survivors while protecting and celebrating the cores of cultures left in the wake of catastrophe.

Erdrich's themes tend to focus on abandonment and return, pleasure and denial, failure, and absurdity. She raises virtually all the issues important to an understanding of the human condition: accidents of birth and parentage, falling in love, generosity, greed, psychological damage, joy, alienation, vulnerability, differentness, parenting, aging, and dying.

JACKLIGHT

The meanings of this volume radiate outward and circle back to the title poem. Instead of being trapped by the hunters' jacklights, the animals in Louise Erdrich's poem lure the hunters into the woods: "And now they take the first steps, not knowing/ how deep the woods are and lightless." This poem's themes are typical of Erdrich: her knowledge of the natural world's wisdom, an awareness of the contentious interaction between humans and animals, and a prophetic sense that human beings need the healing power nature offers.

Following the title poem, section 1, "Runaways," explores the theme of return, most often to the natural world. Erdrich details a "quest for one's own background" in the work. She describes mixed-blood American Indians like herself searching "to discover where we are from." In "Indian Boarding School," the children running away from their off-reservation schools speak collectively that "Home's the place we head for in our sleep." In "Rugaroo," an alcoholic man's search is so dogged that "He blew up with gas./ And now he is the green light floating over the slough." As the title poem prophesied, there is a return to the natural world and a haunting transformation.

Section 2, entitled "Hunters," pursues the theme of the interaction between the human world and the natural, human beings having forgotten, for the most part, links with the natural world. "The Woods" presents a first-person speaker who has made the move back to the woods and who invites her lover to join her: "now when I say *come,*/ and you enter the woods,/ hunting some creature like the woman I was,/ I surround you." An integration is made, but it is bizarre and somewhat threatening: "When you lay down in the grave of a slashed tree,/ I cover you, as I always did;/ this time you do not leave." The following poem removes the threat as the speaker directly addresses her husband: "Again I see us walking into the night trees,/ irreversible motion, but the branches are now lit within." There is more companionship here, less seduction. This poem is clearly a response to the "Jacklight" poem, taking up its challenge and discovering new powers: "Husband, by the light of our bones we are going."

"Captivity" uses the narrative of Mary Rowlandson, who was captured by the Wampanoag Indians in 1676. At first repulsed by her male captor, Rowlandson will not eat the food he offers. Later, she witnesses a tribal ritual: "He led his company in the noise/ until I could no longer bear/ the thought of how I was." The poem concludes with her entreaty to the earth "to admit me/ as he was."

Section 3, a sequence of poems, is entitled "The Butcher's Wife," with the central character a powerful woman, Mary Kroger. These are narrative poems dealing chiefly with non-Native American material, although Kroger is a midwesterner and aware of what the land was like before white incursions. In the poem "Clouds," Kroger says, "Let everything be how it could have been, once:/ a land that was empty and perfect as clouds." When her husband dies, Kroger goes through a transformation: "Widowed by men, I married the dark firs." Kroger has answered the call of "Jacklight." By "marrying" the woods she has discovered unexpected powers. "At certain times," she says, "I speak in tongues."

Erdrich concludes *Jacklight* with Indian oral narratives. In "The Strange People," for example, she uses a story about the antelope. As in "Jacklight," Erdrich narrates this poem from the point of view of the animal. Initially, the antelope doe is attracted by the hunter whose "jacklight/ fills my eyes with blue fire." Though she is killed by the hunter she does not die. A trickster figure, she becomes "a lean gray witch/ through the bullets that enter and dissolve." He is no match for her, and she leaves in the morning to return to the woods.

"Turtle Mountain Reservation" closes the volume and is dedicated to Erdrich's Chippewa grandfather. This Grandpa "hitchhikes home" and comes at last to the swamp and the woods, "his hands/ that have grown to be the twisted doubles/ of the burrows of mole and badger." He *is* the woods. The speaker recognizes that she too comes from "Hands of earth, of this clay." This book of poems is, indeed, a return to her roots for Erdrich.

BAPTISM OF DESIRE

The Roman Catholic Church teaches that there are three forms of baptism: fire, water, and desire. Any of these will establish the necessary condition for salvation to occur. In her second book of poems, Erdrich focuses on desire and forms a powerful metaphor for the union of the physical and the spiritual. Subjects from her first book of poems reappear in her second. The reader recognizes Mary Kroger, for example, and also the American Indian trickster figure Potchikoo. For the most part, however, Erdrich explores new material, primarily religious but also deeply connected to her own experience as a woman, a wife, and a mother.

The most striking poem in the volume is "Hydra," which composes part 2 and appears to be Erdrich's statement about her coming into her own as a creative being. The critic Amy Adelstein states that "Erdrich draws on the ambivalent imagery of the serpent as seducer and an initiator into the sacred mysteries." From an American Indian perspective, the hydra or snake is Erdrich's power animal, her guide and the activator of her poetic imagination: "Snake of the long reach, the margin,/ The perfect sideways motion/ I have imitated all my life./ Snake of hard hours, you are my poetry." So compelling is this "Hydra" that it explains Erdrich's ability to write poems during pregnancy, childbirth, and the early years of her various children. In her notes to this volume she says that most of the poems were written during periods of sleeplessness brought on by her pregnancies.

RELIGIOSITY

Some readers prefer the religious poems to the more domestic ones. The critic Annie Finch states that they are "lush in imagery, fascinating in their suggestiveness, refreshing, often, in their very privacy." Erdrich achieves this privacy through persona poems in some cases. "The Visit," in the voice of Mary, the Mother of Jesus, takes up the subject of the Immaculate Conception or the virgin birth. Erdrich's poem begins with the stark statement, "It was not love. No flowers or ripened figs/ were in his hands." Mary was told she was to become the Mother of God, but this was no romantic proposition. What about Joseph, Mary's husband-to-be? "What could he do but fit the blades/ of wood together into a cradle?"

In "Avila," Erdrich writes in the voice of Saint Teresa of Avila's brother speaking to his sister. The opening imagery is vivid and direct, the question shocking: "Sister, do you remember our cave of stones,/ how we entered from the white heat of afternoons,/ chewed seeds, and plotted one martyrdom/ more cruel than the last?" He refers to the disasters of the Children's Crusade to free the Holy Land from Muslim rule.

"Sacraments," a long seven-part poem, is equally compelling. Erdrich discards the definitions given by the Catechism for a more private perspective. In the poem on Holy Orders, for instance, she begins: "God, I was not meant to be the isolate/ cry in this body./ I was meant to have your tongue in my mouth." The speaker longs for union with her God, but the rendering is more in the vein of the fifteenth century Hindu poet Mīrā Bāī than of traditional Christianity.

DOMESTIC SPIRITUALITY

Erdrich discovers the spiritual element in caring for her children. In "Sunflowers" a mother and father tend to their children at night. After soothing the children, changing diapers, and providing milk, the parents return to bed and dream of "a field of sunflowers," which, like humans, are profoundly phototropic, turning their heads to the light, "to the bronze/ face of the old god/ who floats over us and burns." The spirituality here is primitive, even pagan, and much in tune with Erdrich's heri-

tage as American Indian. The children are like the flowers, a connection suggested but not underlined by Erdrich. Amy Adelstein comments on this suggestiveness as a trait of Erdrich's poems. She says, "It is in a dreamlike, suggestive state that the metamorphosis of shapes and identities and the confounding of time and space occur, approximating the ritual of baptism."

"Ritual," the last poem in *Baptism of Desire*, details a mother's duties as protector of her children: "I bind the net beneath you with the tendons of my wrist." Then she returns to sleep beside her husband, their bed covered with a quilt depicting "the twelve-branched tree of life." She uses this tree as metaphor for their union, which grows and spreads as a tree does, "Until the slightest twigs scrape at the solid frost-blue/ of the floor of heaven."

OTHER MAJOR WORKS

LONG FICTION: *Love Medicine*, 1984 (revised and expanded, 1993); *The Beet Queen*, 1986; *Tracks*, 1988; *The Crown of Columbus*, 1991 (with Michael Dorris); *The Bingo Palace*, 1994; *Tales of Burning Love*, 1996; *The Antelope Wife*, 1998; *The Last Report on the Miracles at Little No Horse*, 2001.

NONFICTION: *The Blue Jay's Dance: A Birth Year*, 1995.

CHILDREN'S LITERATURE: *Grandmother's Pigeon*, 1996 (illustrated by Jim LaMarche); *The Birchbark House*, 1999.

BIBLIOGRAPHY

Bak, Hans. "Circles Blaze in Ordinary Days." In *Native American Women in Literature and Culture*, edited by Susan Castillo and Victor M. P. Da Rosa. Porto, Portugal: Fernando Pessoa University Press, 1997. Hans Bak writes an extensive analysis of the *Jacklight* poems and sees Erdrich's first book of poetry as having a different appeal from *Baptism of Desire*. He terms that appeal its "hybrid" or "amphibious" quality in that Erdrich draws upon both aspects of her heritage, the German American and the Chippewa.

Chavkin, Allan, ed. *The Chippewa Landscape of Louise Erdrich*. Tuscaloosa: University of Alabama Press, 1998. Collects original essays focusing on Erdrich's writings that are rooted in the Chippewa experience. Premier scholars of Native American literature investigate narrative structure, signs of ethnicity, the notions of luck and chance in Erdrich's narrative cosmology, and her use of comedy in exploring American Indian's tragic past.

Chavkin, Allan, and Nancy Feyl, eds. *Conversations with Louise Erdrich and Michael Dorris*. Jackson: University Press of Mississippi, 1994. This is a collection of twenty-five interviews with the couple and includes an interview with Joseph Bruchac.

Hafen, Jane P. "Sacramental Language: Ritual in the Poetry of Louise Erdrich." *Great Plains Quarterly* 16 (1996): 147-155. Hafen, a Taos Pueblo Indian, examines Erdrich's books of poetry together. In them, she finds evidence of the oral culture and a blending of rituals from the Chippewa and European-American religious traditions. Erdrich's poetry reveals her individual voice and personal experience while at the same time connecting to the rituals of her mixed-blood heritage.

Ludlow, Jeannie. "Working (In) the In-Between: Poetry, Criticism, Interrogation, and Interruption." *Studies in American Indian Literature* 6 (Spring, 1994): 24-42. Ludlow writes a sophisticated literary analysis of Joy Harjo's "The Woman Hanging from the Thirteenth Floor Window" and Louise Erdrich's "Lady in the Pink Mustang" from *Jacklight*. She finds Erdrich's poem potentially more empowering.

Wong, Hertha Dawn. *Louise Erdrich's Love Medicine: A Casebook*. London: Oxford University Press, 1999. Presents documents relating to the historical importance of *Love Medicine*, representative critical essays, and excerpts from several interviews with Erdrich and Michael Dorris.

Claire Keyes,
updated by Sarah Hilbert

Sergei Esenin

Born: Konstantinovo, Russia; October 3, 1895
Died: Leningrad, U.S.S.R.; December 28, 1925

Principal poetry

Radunitsa, 1915 (All Soul's Day, 1991)
Goluben', 1918 (Azure, 1991)
Ispoved' khuligana, 1921 (*Confessions of a Hooligan*, 1973)
Pugachov, 1922
Stikhi skandalista, 1923
Moskva kabatskaia, 1924
"Cherni chelovek," 1925
Persidskie motivi, 1925
Rus' sovetskaia, 1925
Strana sovetskaia, 1925
Anna Snegina, 1925
Sobranie sochinenii, 1961-1962 (5 volumes)

Other literary forms

Sergei Esenin wrote little besides poetry. Some autobiographical introductions and a few revealing letters are helpful in analyzing his poetry. The short story "Bobyl i druzhok" and the tale "Yar" are rarely mentioned in critical discussion of Esenin's work, but his theoretical treatise "Kliuchi Marii" (1918; the keys of Mary) helps to explain his early revolutionary lyrics. This economically written, perceptive study traces the religious origins of various aspects of ancient Russian culture and art.

Achievements

Perhaps the most controversial of all Soviet poets, Sergei Esenin is certainly also one of the most popular, among both Russian émigrés and Soviet citizens. The popularity of his poetry never diminished in the Soviet Union, despite a period of twenty-five years during which his work was suppressed and his character defamed. Officially, Esenin was labeled the "Father of Hooliganism," and his works were removed from public libraries and reading rooms. In the early 1950's, however, his reputation was fully rehabilitated, and his poems are now widely available in the Soviet Union. Today, Esenin rivals Aleksandr Blok, Vladimir Mayakovsky, and even Alexander Pushkin as the most popular of all Russian poets. Indeed, every reprinting of the five-volume edition of his poems originally issued in 1961 has sold out in a matter of days.

Although Esenin welcomed and supported the 1917 October Revolution, he soon began to have second thoughts. He did not like the transformation that was taking place in the rural areas, and he longed for the traditional simple peasant life and the old "wooden Russia." His flamboyant lifestyle, his alcoholism, and his dramatic suicide eventually brought him the scorn of the Soviet authorities.

The most important representative of the Imaginist movement in Russian poetry, Esenin at his best achieved a distinctive blend of deep lyricism, sincerity, melancholy, and nostalgia. Calling himself "the last poet of the village," Esenin used folk and religious motifs, images of nature, and colorful scenes from everyday village life, which he painted with a natural freshness and beauty. His disappointment with his own life, his unhappy marriages, and his apprehensions concerning the changes he saw at every hand—all are reflected in the mood of unfulfilled hope and sadness which pervades his poetry.

BIOGRAPHY

Sergei Aleksandrovich Esenin was born in the small village of Konstantinovo, since renamed Esenino in the poet's honor, in the fertile Ryzan province. His parents were poor farmers, and because his mother had married against the will of her parents, the Titovs, the couple received no support from their families. Esenin's father had to go to Moscow, where he worked in a butcher shop, in order to send home some money. When he stopped sending the money, his wife had no other choice but to find work as a live-in servant. Her parents at last decided to help and took the young boy to live with them.

Esenin's grandfather, Feodor Andreevich Titov, belonged to a religious sect known as the Old Believers; he frequently recited religious poems and folk songs, and he approached life with an optimistic vigor. Esenin's grandmother sang folk songs and told her grandson many folktales. Both grandparents adored the young Esenin, who lived a happy and relatively carefree life. They left a great impression on the young boy.

From 1904 to 1909, Esenin attended the village school, where, with little effort, he was graduated with excellent marks. His grandfather Titov decided that Esenin should become a teacher and sent him to the church-run Spas-Klepiki pedagogical school from 1909 to 1912. At first, Esenin was extremely unhappy in the new surroundings; he even ran away once and walked forty miles back to his grandparents' home. Eventually, however, he became reconciled to his fate, and he was noticed by his teachers and peers for the unusual ease with which he wrote poetry. The boy with the blond, curly hair became self-confident and even boastful, which made him unpopular with some of his fellow students.

At the age of sixteen, after his graduation in 1912, Esenin decided not to continue his studies at a teacher's institute in Moscow. Instead, he returned to his grandparents' home and devoted his life to poetry. He was happy to be free to roam aimlessly through the fields and the forests, and his early poems reflect his love for animals and for the rural landscape. Although he also used religious themes in his early poems, Esenin was probably not very religious, certainly not as devoted as his grandfather. He was, however, very familiar with the religious traditions of the Old Believers and with the patriarchal way of life.

Esenin realized that in order to become known as a poet, he had to move to a big city. In 1912, he moved to Moscow, taking a job in the butcher's shop where his father worked. He disliked the job but soon found work as a bookstore clerk, where he was happier. Esenin also joined the "Surikov Circle," a large group of proletarian and peasant writers.

Esenin lost his job in the bookstore, but in May of 1913, he became a proofreader in a printing shop. The work strengthened his interest in the labor movement, and though he never completely accepted the ideology of the Social Revolutionary Party, he distributed illegal literature and supported other revolutionary activities. In order to learn more about history and world literature, Esenin took evening courses at the Shaniavski People's University in Moscow. With his goal of becoming a great poet, he recognized the need to broaden his education.

The foremost Russian writers of the time, however, lived in St. Petersburg rather than in Moscow, and in March of 1915, Esenin moved to Petrograd (as

St. Petersburg was known between 1914, when Russia went to war against Germany, and 1924, when it became Leningrad). Upon his arrival, Esenin went to see Aleksandr Blok, who helped the young "peasant" and introduced him to well-known poets such as Zinaida Gippius, Feodor Sologub, and Vyacheslav Ivanov and to novelists such as Ivan Bunin, Aleksandr Kuprin, and Dimitri Merezhkovsky. The young poet Anatoly Mariengof became Esenin's intimate friend. Esenin was appointed as an editor of the political and literary journal *Severnie Zapiski*, an appointment that brought him in contact with other writers and intellectuals. Through the help of a fellow peasant poet, Nikolai Klyuyev, Esenin met the publisher M. V. Averyanov, who published Esenin's first volume of poems, *All Soul's Day*, in 1915.

In the autumn of 1915, Esenin was drafted into the army, which for him was a tragedy. He agonized in the dirty barracks and under the commands of the drill sergeant. Eventually, he succeeded in being transferred to the "Commission of Trophies," a special unit for artists, but he neglected his duties so flagrantly that he was ordered to a medical unit stationed near the czar's residence in Tsarskoe Selo. The czarina discovered that the young poet was stationed nearby and invited him to the court to read his poetry. Esenin was flattered, but he also carried in his heart a deep hatred for the monarchy. Under some still unclear circumstances, Esenin left Tsarskoe Selo before February of 1917, and in 1918 he published his second volume of poetry, *Azure*.

In August of 1917, Esenin married Zinaida Raikh, who was then working as a typist for a newspaper published by the Socialist Revolutionary Party. The marriage ended in divorce in October, 1921, following the birth of two children. Raikh, who subsequently became a famous actress, married the great theatrical director Vsevolod Meyerhold. Esenin maintained ties with Raikh until the end of his life, and the dissolution of his first marriage established the pattern that was to mark his last years.

In 1918, however, Esenin was hopeful and ambitious, on the verge of fame. In March of 1918, he again moved to Moscow and continued to write optimistic, mythical poetry about the future of Russia. He tried to understand the revolution, although he abhorred the suf-

fering it brought. In late 1918, during a visit to his native Konstantinovo, Esenin observed the passivity of the peasants. With the poem "Inonia," he tried to incite them to positive action.

During this period, Esenin, with several minor poets such as Mariengof, formed a literary movement known as Imaginism. The Imaginists (*imazhinisty*) had been inspired by an article about the Imagist movement in English and American poetry, founded by Ezra Pound. Except for the name, however, and—more important—the doctrine that the image is the crucial component of poetry, there was little connection between Pound's Imagism and the Russian Imaginism. For Esenin, the movement encouraged liberation from the peasant themes and mythical religiosity of his early verse. In addition, as is evident in the Imaginist manifesto of 1919, the movement was useful in attracting publicity, of which Esenin was very conscious.

In the fall of 1921, at a studio party, Esenin met the well-known American dancer Isadora Duncan, who was giving a series of dance recitals in Russia. Although Esenin spoke no English and Duncan knew only a few phrases in Russian, they found enough attraction in each other for Esenin to move immediately into Duncan's apartment. The turbulence of the relationship became notorious. In 1922, Duncan needed to raise money for her new dancing school in Moscow. She wanted to give a series of dance recitals in Western Europe and in the United States, but she also realized the difficulties she and Esenin would face in the United States if they were not legally married. On May 2, 1922, they were married, and Esenin became the first (and the only legal) husband of Isadora Duncan.

America disappointed Esenin. He could not communicate, and even Prohibition did not slow down his acute alcoholism. In America, he was seen merely as the husband of Isadora Duncan, not as a famous Russian poet. The skyscrapers could not replace the gray sky over the Russian landscape. After a nervous breakdown, Esenin returned alone to Russia, and when Duncan returned some time later, he refused to live with her again.

After his return to the Soviet Union, Esenin became increasingly critical of the new order. He was never able to accept the atmosphere of cruelty and destruction during the civil war, and the ruthless law of vengeance carried out by many fanatics, even after the war, was criminal in his eyes. It was difficult for Esenin both as an individual and as a poet to conform to Lenin's NEP (new economic policy) period. To some extent, he regarded this difficulty as a personal failure and reacted to it with spells of depression alternating with outbursts of wild revelry. He styled himself a "hooligan," and he excused his heavy drinking, drug-taking, barroom brawls, blasphemous verse, and all-night orgies as fundamentally revolutionary acts.

At the same time, Esenin saw himself as a prodigal son. He yearned for motherly love, the healing touch of nature, and the peaceful countryside. In 1924, he returned to his native village, but he could not find the "wooden Russia" which he had once glorified in his poems. "Rus' sovetskaia" (Soviet Russia), his famous poem of 1925, expresses his isolation in his own country. The revolution had not fulfilled Esenin's dreams of a rural utopia, and he, "the last poet of the village," was among its victims.

From September, 1924, until February of 1925, Esenin visited Baku and the Crimea, a trip which resulted in the publication of the collection *Persidskie motivi* (Persian motifs). In 1925, he married Sofya Tolstaya, one of Leo Tolstoy's granddaughters. The marriage was predictably unhappy; Esenin's deteriorating health caused him to be admitted repeatedly to hospitals. He managed to write the somewhat autobiographical long poem *Anna Snegina*, which describes the fate of the prerevolutionary people in the new Soviet society. The poor reception of the poem and the harsh criticism it provoked devastated Esenin.

The poet began to mention suicide more frequently. Even though his physical health improved, Esenin remained very depressed. In December of 1925, he left his wife in Moscow and went to Leningrad, where he stayed at the Hotel Angleterre. He was there for several days and was frequently visited by friends. On December 27, Esenin cut his arm and in his own blood wrote his last poem, "Do svidan'ia, drug moi, do svidan'ia . . ." ("Good-bye, My Friend, Good-bye"); later that day, Esenin gave the poem to friends (who neglected to read it) and showed the cut to them, complaining that there was no ink in his room. In the early hours of December 28, the poet hanged himself on a radiator pipe.

Esenin's widow arrived the next day and took her husband's body in a decorated railroad car to Moscow. In Moscow, thousands of people waited for the arrival of the train. Fellow writers and artists carried the coffin from the train station to its temporary resting place in a public building, where thousands more paid their last respects. Esenin was buried on the last day of 1925.

ANALYSIS

Sergei Esenin's poetry can be divided into two parts: first the poetry of the countryside, the village, and the animals and, second, the primarily postrevolutionary poetry of *Moskva kabatskaia* (Moscow the tavern city) and of *Rus' sovetskaia*. Generally, the village poetry is natural and simple, while many of the later poems are more pretentious and affected. The mood of country landscapes, the joys of village life, and the love for and of animals is created with powerful melodiousness. The poet's sincere nostalgia for "wooden Russia" is portrayed so strongly, that it becomes infectious. Esenin creates idylls of the simple Russian village and of country life with the freshness of a skilled painter, yet the musicality of his verse is the most characteristic quality of Esenin's poetry. His simple, sweet, and touching early lyrics are easy to understand and are still loved by millions of readers in the Soviet Union.

As a "peasant poet," Esenin differed from some other Russian peasant poets of the time, such as Nikolai Klyuyev and Pyotr Oreshin. Esenin stressed primarily the inner life of the peasant, while the others paid more attention to the peasants' environment. His peasants are free of material things, even though they are part of their environment, while in the work of other peasant poets, *things* are preeminent.

Esenin's early poems chiefly employ the vocabulary of the village; they reveal the influence of the *chastushki*, the popular folk songs widely heard in any Russian village. When he arrived in Petrograd, Esenin presented himself as "the poet of the people"; dressed in a peasant blouse adorned with a brightly colored silk cord, he chanted his poems about harvests, rivers, and meadows.

When Esenin moved to Petrograd, he began to learn the sophisticated techniques of the Symbolists, particularly from Aleksandr Blok. Esenin was able to create a complete picture of a landscape or a village with a single image. He continued, however, to maintain the melancholy mood and the sadness which would always be typical of his poetry.

At the time of his suicide, Esenin was still quite popular, both in the Soviet Union and among Russian émigrés. Beginning in 1926, the State Publishing House published Esenin's collected works in four volumes, but many poems were missing from this edition. By that time, the "morally weak Eseninism" had been officially denounced. In 1948, a one-volume selection of Esenin's poetry was published, and it sold out immediately. By the early 1950's, Esenin was again fully rehabilitated, and in 1961, a five-volume edition appeared, which has since been reprinted several times. According to Soviet critics, Esenin's tremendous popularity can be explained by the fact that his poetry was consonant with the feelings of the Russian people during the most difficult days in their history.

ALL SOUL'S DAY AND AZURE

Though not free of the melancholy typical of Esenin's work, his first collection, *All Soul's Day*, radiates happiness as well. These early poems express the joy of village life, the poet's love for his homeland, and the pleasures of youth; even the colors are light and gay: blue, white, green, red. Esenin employs religious themes and Christian terminology, but the poems are more pantheistic, even pagan, than Christian. *All Soul's Day* was well received by the critical Petrograd audience, and this response immeasurably boosted Esenin's confidence. The poet was only twenty years old when he proved his mastery of the Russian language.

Esenin's second collection, *Azure*, appeared after the revolution, in 1918, but the majority of the poems were written during World War I. These poems reflect Esenin's uncertainty concerning the future, although he did accept and praise the October Revolution. He visualized the revolution as a glorious cosmic upheaval leading to a resurrection of Russia and its rural roots. The style, mood, and vocabulary of *Azure* reveal the influence of Blok and Klyuyev.

While there was no doubt that Esenin was initially on the side of the Bolsheviks, his vision of the revolution was a highly individual one. He saw a return to peasant communities and to a primitive democratic simplicity.

The threatening industrialization and the technological development of the mysterious electricity, the hidden source of power, which he witnessed later, horrified him. Three long poems with religiously symbolic titles, which were part of the *Azure* cycle, reflect this attitude: "Preobrazhenie" ("Transfiguration") "Prishestvie" ("The Coming"), and "Inonia."

The well-known poem "Inonia" reflects with particular clarity Esenin's wish for a peasant utopia, an anticapitalist, agricultural republic that could resist the industrial giants. Esenin saw himself as the prophet of a new religion that had to overcome the peasants' traditional Christianity in order to bring about a happy, rural, socialist paradise. By 1920, however, Esenin realized that the results of the revolution were slowly destroying his "rural Russia," and he saw himself as "the last poet of the village."

PUGACHOV

During this period of growing disillusionment, Esenin began to forsake the simplicity and the rural spirit of his early verse, although folk elements never disappeared from his work. Among the most significant of his more experimental Imaginist poems was the long dramatic poem *Pugachov*, published in 1922. This unfinished verse-drama exhibits the unusual metaphors and verbal eccentricities which were characteristic of the Imaginists. The hero of Esenin's poem, the Cossack leader of a peasant rebellion in the 1770's, is highly idealized and bears little resemblance to the historical Pugachev. In contrast to Pushkin, who treated the same subject in his novella *Kapitanskaya dochka* (1836; *The Captain's Daughter*, 1883), Esenin passionately sympathized with Pugachev and his peasants. He also drew parallels between Pugachev's revolt and the October Revolution: In his view, both had failed because of man's egotism and his unwillingness to sacrifice for the common good.

"STRANA NEGODIAEV"

In 1922 and 1923, Esenin wrote another dramatic poem, partially during his trip to the the United States and Western Europe and partially after his return. "Strana negodiaev" (the country of scoundrels), influenced by Western cinema, marked a departure from the Imaginist style of *Pugachov*. In it, Esenin abandoned striking imagery in favor of a rather crude realistic style.

He never completed the poem, however, realizing that it was a failure. In the poem, Esenin refers to America as a greedy trap in which deceit is the key to survival; at the same time, he acknowledges the industrial achievement of the West. In sympathizing with the anti-Soviet hero of this dramatic poem, Esenin confirmed that he had lost much of his enthusiasm for the revolution.

MOSKVA KABATSKAIA

Indeed, by 1923, Esenin saw himself as lost in his own country. He did not reject the revolution itself but the results of the revolution. He was already notorious for his alcoholism, his orgiastic lifestyle, and his escapades around Moscow. His most decadent poems were included in the collection *Moskva kabatskaia*. In these poems, he confessed that he would have become a thief if he had not been a poet, and he exposed all his vices. These poems reflect Esenin's disappointment with himself, with love, and with religion. The critics accused him of wallowing in filth.

The poet of the village and the countryside became overshadowed in the 1920's by the alcoholic of *Moskva kabatskaia*. Esenin's manner became harsher, reflecting the worsening crisis of his life. Gentle laments for the passing of the idealized countryside were replaced by nostalgia for lost youth and the search for a home. Esenin largely abandoned the devices cultivated by the Imaginists, returning to the materials of his early verse yet handling them in a new manner—stark, assured, despairing.

With the poems of *Moskva kabatskaia*, Esenin sought to reconcile himself with the new Russia. In the celebrated poem "Rus' sovetskaia," he admits that he is too old to change, and he fears that he will be left behind by younger generations. In a mixture of resignation and defiance, he accepts the new order and resolves to continue writing poetry not by society's standards but by his own.

PERSIDSKIE MOTIVI

Although Esenin never visited Persia, during his visit to Baku and the Caucasus in 1925, he wrote a cycle of short poems entitled *Persidskie motivi*. Technically, the poems are well written, but Esenin's love lyrics addressed to different girls, in which genuine nostalgia mingles with superficiality and a lack of conviction, suggest that the poet was nearing a dead end.

ANNA SNEGINA

In 1925, Esenin also published the long autobiographical poem *Anna Snegina*, written during his stay in Batum. The poem describes a love affair set in a Russian village during the Civil War. Soviet critics, however, were not interested in decadent love affairs; they expected poetry promoting the revolutionary spirit. Esenin was not able to produce this; he remained the anachronistic dreamer of a rural utopia. In his eyes, Soviet society had no need of him nor of his poetry.

OTHER MAJOR WORKS

NONFICTION: "Kliuchi Marii," 1918.

BIBLIOGRAPHY

Davis, J. *Esenin: A Biography in Memoirs, Letters, and Documents*. Ann Arbor, Mich.: Ardis, 1982. Davis culls the autobiographical material from the poet's work and complements it with biographical commentaries, shedding light on various aspects of Esenin's life. These materials, in turn, shed light on his poetry.

De Graaff, Frances. *Sergei Esenin: A Biographical Sketch*. The Hague: Mouton, 1966. In his valuable study of Esenin's life and poetry, De Graaff combines biography with the poet's works, bolstering his observations with citations from many poems, in Russian and English, and providing an extensive bibliography.

McVay, Gordon. *Esenin: A Life*. Ann Arbor, Mich.: Ardis, 1976. In this most definitive biography of Esenin in English, the author encompasses the poet's entire life, including his tragic death by suicide, about which McVay chronicles the events in detail. The book offers brief analyses of Esenin's works along with copious illustrations.

Mariengof, Anatoli. *A Novel Without Lies*. Translated by Jose Alaniz. Chicago: Ivan R. Dee, 2000. A detailed memoir of Mariengof's association with Esenin and the literary avant-garde of the 1920's.

Prokushev, Yuri. *Sergei Esenin: The Man, the Verse, the Age*. Moscow: Progress, 1979. In this biography of Esenin by a Russian scholar, Prokushev offers the Russian point of view about the poet and his poetry. The emphasis is on the biographical details. It is somewhat tinted ideologically, stressing Esenin's often failed efforts to adapt to the Soviet reality, his love for Russia, and the realistic aspects of his poetry. Despite its politically motivated slant, the book is full of interesting observations.

Thurley, Geoffrey. Introduction to *Confessions of a Hooligan*. Cheadle: Hulme, 1973. A book of translations of Esenin's poems about his struggle against alcoholism. In the introduction Thurley examines circumstances that led to the writing of these poems.

Visson, Lynn. *Sergei Esenin: Poet of the Crossroads*. Würzburg, Germany: Jal-Verlag, 1980. Visson undertakes a thorough, expert analysis of the stylistic features of Esenin's poetry, with extensive quotations from the poems, in Russian and in English, offering penetrating insights into the artistic merits of Esenin's poetry and gauging the scope of his contribution to Russian poetry.

Rado Pribic;
bibliography updated by Vasa D. Mihailovich

MARTÍN ESPADA

Born: Brooklyn, New York; 1957

PRINCIPAL POETRY

The Immigrant Iceboy's Bolero, 1982

Trumpets from the Islands of Their Eviction, 1987, expanded 1994

Rebellion Is the Circle of a Lover's Hands = Rebelión es el giro de manos del amante, 1990

City of Coughing and Dead Radiators: Poems, 1993

Imagine the Angels of Bread: Poems, 1996

A Mayan Astronomer in Hell's Kitchen: Poems, 2000

OTHER LITERARY FORMS

Although Martín Espada is known primarily as a poet, he also has edited two collections, *Poetry like Bread: Poets of the Political Imagination from Curbstone Press* (1994) and *El Coro: A Chorus of Latino and Latina Poetry* (1997); translated the poetry of Clemente Soto Vélez in *The Blood That Keeps Singing: Selected Poems of Clemente Soto Vélez* (1991; with Camilo Pérez-Bustillo); and published one collection of essays in *Zapata's Disciple: Essays* (1998).

ACHIEVEMENTS

Martín Espada has garnered many honors, including a Massachusetts Artists Foundation Fellowship (1984), a National Endowment for the Arts (NEA) Fellowship (1986 and 1992), the PEN/Revson Foundation Fellowship (1989) and Paterson Poetry Prize (1991) for *Rebellion Is the Circle of a Lover's Hands*, the Lilly Teaching Fellowship (1994-1995), the PEN/Voelcker Award for Poetry (1994), and a Massachusetts Cultural Council Artist Grant (1996). In 1997, he won an American Book Award for poetry with *Imagine the Angels of Bread*. The collection also was a finalist for the National Book Critics Circle Award. His collection of essays *Zapata's Disciple* won the 1999 Independent Publisher Book Award in the category of creative nonfiction/memoir.

BIOGRAPHY

Born in 1957, in Brooklyn, New York, to a Puerto Rican father and a Jewish mother, Martín Espada grew up in Brooklyn. His father, Frank Espada, became active in the Civil Rights movement during the 1950's. He was a leader in the Puerto Rican community of New York City. Devoting his life at the time to the cause of civil rights for all minorities, Frank Espada had to put his creative impulses on hold. Years later, he became a noted photographer. At a young age, Martín Espada learned about the need to fight against injustice. During the 1960's, his father took his young son to protest meetings and rallies. This was Frank Espada's way of educating Martín to the political and social struggle that minorities must wage against prejudice, racism, and indifference.

He began writing poetry when he was fifteen. Espada has stated that he found writing to be even more important than sleeping. Some of the odd jobs that Espada held as a young man include a bindery worker, a groundskeeper for a minor league baseball ballpark, a night desk clerk, and a bouncer in a bar. Each of these experiences allowed him to witness the difficulties which people of color encounter on a daily basis in the United States. The many diverse settings helped him to be what Espada calls a "spy." He made the most of being a keen observer. The "mental notes" he made eventually were turned into poems. In 1981, Espada was graduated from the University of Wisconsin at Madison with a B.A. in history. He then went on to earn his law degree from Boston's Northeastern University School of Law in 1985. After earning his law degree, Espada worked as a tenant lawyer near Boston in Chelsea, Massachusetts. He was a supervisor for a legal-aid office, Su Clinica Legal, that served a clientele of primarily Spanish-speaking residents. In 1991, his wife, Katherine, gave birth to a son. Espada has been an English professor on the faculty of the University of Massachusetts at Amherst since 1993.

ANALYSIS

Martín Espada has committed himself to living a life that does not take the status quo as the way things have to be. As a lawyer, he fought the system in order to make life better for those who are less fortunate. In his poetry, Espada has continued to shed light on the injustices that have been done especially to the Latino immigrants who have come to the United States in search of a better life. Influenced by the activist Chilean poet Pablo Neruda, Espada is a political poet in the best sense of the term. He does not write easy slogans to make himself and his audience merely feel better. He understands the immense responsibility he has shouldered in writing poems that take on sensitive topics. Espada's poetry not only challenges the audience, but it also challenges the poet. He must rise above the temptation to compose mere propaganda. Coming from a Puerto Rican heritage, Espada was made well aware by the majority population at any early age not only how corrosive prejudice can be to the minority being brutalized but also how it sours an entire country.

THE IMMIGRANT ICEBOY'S BOLERO AND TRUMPETS FROM THE ISLANDS OF THEIR EVICTION

For his first collection, Espada included photographs taken by his father. The title poem speaks to his father's journey to the United States. As a boy of nine,

Frank Espada had to work as an ice boy. It was his job to carry large blocks of ice up the stairs of tenement buildings. Because of this heavy lifting, his back was permanently injured. The poem is a moving account of how much pressure a young Frank Espada was under as he attempted to make it in a new and hostile environment. Espada included Spanish translations of his poems for his second collection. In the poem "Tiburon," Espada uses the image of a shark consuming a fisherman in order to reflect on the relationship between the United States and Puerto Rico. In 1987, an expanded edition was published which included a select number of poems from *The Immigrant Iceboy's Bolero*. The title poem of *Trumpets from the Islands of Their Eviction* shows the struggle with which Puerto Ricans are constantly faced in order to be heard by the Anglo world around them. Espada opens the poem with images that give voice to the plight of immigrants coming from Puerto Rico:

Martín Espada (© Miriam Berkley)

At the bar two blocks away,
immigrants with Spanish mouths
hear trumpets
from the islands of their eviction.
The music swarms into the barrio
of a refugee's imagination,
along with predatory squad cars
and bullying handcuffs.

REBELLION IS THE CIRCLE OF A LOVER'S HANDS

Once again Espada includes a Spanish translation of each poem. He writes eloquently about how what may seem personal is really also political. Individuals who go about their everyday lives working and trying to do right by their families are given a voice by a caring poet. In the short lyric poem "Latin Night at the Pawnshop," Espada expresses his concern for an entire Latin culture through the experience of finding musical instruments relegated to a pawnshop. The poem opens with the image of an "apparition of a salsa band." Instruments such as a "Golden trumpet," a "silver trombone," a "tambourine," and some "maracas," all have "price tags dangling." Espada sees these price tags as comparable to a "city morgue ticket/on a dead man's toe." The strength of this collection can be found in how Espada can take seemingly inconsequential incidents and show them to be representative of a larger offense or crime that has be done to a culture that has vibrancy and exists under the nose of the Anglo-American world.

IMAGINE THE ANGELS OF BREAD

In his fifth poetry collection, Espada celebrates what has been called "the bread of the imagination, the bread of the table, and the bread of justice." The political and the personal are brilliantly wedded in a number of autobiographical poems. The poet conjures up images of family bonds, the smells of a particular neighborhood, and the lessons learned from various menial jobs. The title poem is inhabited by many elements including compassion and rage, reality and visions. Espada states that "This is the year that squatters evict landlords," and that "this is the year/ that shawled refugees deport judges/ who stare at the floor." Even though there are so many injustices of the past, the poet believes that maybe this will be the year that all the wrongs will be put right. Espada recognizes that after all the rage is vented that

there must be hope for a better future. It is no wonder that this collection won the American Book Award for poetry in 1997.

A MAYAN ASTRONOMER IN HELL'S KITCHEN

As with his earlier collections, Espada continues in *A Mayan Astronomer in Hell's Kitchen* to speak eloquently for the downtrodden, for those who have not as of yet been able to share in the American Dream. Divided into three sections, the collection opens with a section, "A Tarantula in the Bananas," that concerns the plight of Puerto Ricans in this country. The first poem, "My Name Is Espada," delineates the value of a family name and how it has survived throughout history. The word *espada* literally means "sword in Spain." In the poem, the poet also relates a personal history of his name:

Espada: sword in Puerto Rico, family name of bricklayers
who swore their trowels fell as leaves from iron trees;
teachers who wrote poems in galloping calligraphy;
saintcarvers who whittled a slave's gaze and a
    conqueror's beard;
shoemaker spitting tuberculosis, madwoman
dangling a lantern to listen for the cough;
gambler in a straw hat inhabited by mathematical angels;
preacher who first heard the savior's voice
bleeding through the plaster of the jailhouse;
dreadlocked sculptor stunned by visions of birds,
sprouting wings from his forehead, earthen wings in the
    fire.

No matter what struggle is at hand for a person of color, a Puerto Rican, a member of the Espada family, it is possible to find strength in heritage, in a family name. Espada concludes the first section with a short poem entitled "What Francisco Luis Espada Learned at Age Five, Standing on the Dock." The lesson learned by young Francisco was that "Sometimes/ there's a/ tarantula/ in the/ bananas."

The second section, "A Mayan Astronomer in Hell's Kitchen," includes some of Espada's most touching poems to date. There are two poems specifically dedicated to his wife, Katherine Espada. There is humor as well as poignancy in "I Apologize for Giving You Poison Ivy by Smacking You in the Eye with the Crayfish at the End of My Fishing Line." Out of ignorance, the poet injures Katherine. He was born in Brooklyn and ignorant about how to fish, what crayfish are, and how dangerous poison ivy can be to a person's skin. The poem is humorous, touching, and also speaks to a cultural divide. The last section of *A Mayan Astronomer in Hell's Kitchen*, "A Library of Lions," contains the most overtly political poems of the collection. The last poem, "The River Will Not Testify," details how seventeenth century Puritans butchered Native Americans. Espada writes with conviction about human dignity. Never pandering to a cause at the expense of the language, Espada has fashioned a gripping body of work that illuminates the human condition.

OTHER MAJOR WORKS

NONFICTION: *Zapata's Disciple: Essays*, 1998.

TRANSLATION: *The Blood That Keeps Singing: Selected Poems of Clemente Soto Vélez*, 1991 (with Camilo Pérez-Bustillo).

EDITED TEXTS: *Poetry like Bread: Poets of the Political Imagination from Curbstone Press*, 1994, expanded 2000; *El Coro: A Chorus of Latino and Latina Poetry*, 1997.

BIBLIOGRAPHY

Bartlett, Ellen J. "Law and Language Are His Weapons." *The Boston Globe*, August 8, 1990, p. 41. Fleshes out how Espada believes in using the law and words to make a difference in the lives of those who are less fortunate.

Browning, Sarah. "Give Politics a Human Face: An Interview with Lawyer-Poet-Professor Martín Espada." *Valley Advocate*, November 18, 1993. Espada speaks to the importance of keeping poetry relevant to the everyday lives of people and that anyone who wishes to become a writer should remember to stay involved in the world. Poetry can be political without falling into the trap of being no more than mere propaganda.

Campo, Rafael. "Why Poetry Matters." *The Progressive* 63 (April, 1999): 43-44. Campo's review of Espada's collection of essays *Zapada's Disciple* makes the point that Espada writes in order to shed light on the world around him. Whether writing poetry or prose, he finds it impossible to shy away from the undecorated truth.

Espada, Martín. "The Politics of Advocacy: Three Poems." *Hopscotch: A Cultural Review* 2 (2001): 128-133. Espada discusses three of his poems ("Ezequiel," "The Poet in the Box," and "Circle Your Name") and how merely writing about a worthy topic is not enough to have a successful poem. He makes the point that all good poets still must find the precise words for each poem. A strong poem works because both subject matter and language successfully have been wedded together.

Fink, Thomas. "Visibility and History in the Poetry of Martín Espada." *Americas Review* 25 (1999): 202-221. Fink details Espada's involvement in the Puerto Rican independence movement and how his heritage impacts the poetry he writes. The richness and in-your-face quality of Espada's poetry makes him one of the most important poets writing in English.

Gonzalez, Ray. "A Poetry of Legacy: An Interview with Martín Espada." *The Bloomsbury Review*, July/August, 1997, pp. 3+. Espada reveals how the historical past, his father, and the birth of his own son have been influential in shaping his poetry, how he sees his role as a political poet.

Keene, John R. Review of *City of Coughing and Dead Radiators*. *MELUS* 21 (Spring, 1996): 133-135. Keene reinforces how vital a poet such as Espada is on the American literary landscape. In this collection, Espada is able to balance weighty topics with the perfect choice of words. Keene marvels at how Espada can accomplish this without ever sounding hollow or pedantic.

Ratiner, Steven. "Poetry and the Burden of History: An Interview with Martín Espada." *The Christian Science Monitor*, March 6, 1991, pp. 16+. In this interview as in others, Espada points to the fact that a poet can also be a historian. The poet can put a "human face" on history, on monumental events. While important issues must be confronted directly by the poet, Espada believes that a poem suffers if the poet was overwhelmed by anger. The correct tone is of preeminent importance to Espada.

Ullman, Leslie. "To Speak on Behalf." *The Kenyon Review* 14 (Summer, 1992): 174-187. Ullman reviews collections by Cornelius Eady (*The Gathering of My*

Name), Lucille Clifton (*Quilting: Poems, 1987-1990*), Julie Fay (*Portraits of Women*), and Martín Espada (*Rebellion Is the Circle of a Lover's Hands*). Although each of these poets comes to his or her poetry from a unique reference point, Ullman finds that these poets have something very much in common. All these poets in their own ways bear witness to the human experience, to something larger than themselves.

Jeffry Jensen

SIR GEORGE ETHEREGE

Born: Maidenhead(?), England; c. 1635
Died: Paris(?), France; c. May 10, 1691

PRINCIPAL POETRY

The New Academy of Complements, 1669
A Collection of Poems, Written upon Several Occasions, 1673
The Works of Sir George Etherege: Containing His Plays and Poems, 1704
The Works of Sir George Etherege: Plays and Poems, 1888 (A. Wilson Verity, editor)
Restoration Carnival, 1954 (V. De Sola Pinto, editor)
Poems, 1963 (James Thorpe, editor)

OTHER LITERARY FORMS

Sir George Etherege is primarily known not for his poetry but for his plays. He wrote three comedies, all typical representatives of the risqué wit of Restoration comedy. His first comedy, *The Comical Revenge: Or, Love in a Tub* (1644), however, tended to rely more heavily on farce and burlesque than on wit for its comic effect. His second comedy, *She Would if She Could*, followed in 1668. The play which firmly established Etherege's reputation, *The Man of Mode: Or, Sir Fopling Flutter*, appeared in 1676. The play's characters, particularly the rake Dorimant, the comic lover Sir Fopling Flutter, and the witty Harriet, are among the most memorable in Restoration comedy.

ACHIEVEMENTS

Sir George Etherege's reputation as an accomplished dramatist is, without question, secure. In modern times, however, his poetry has been little noticed. This lack of recognition is puzzling in view of the fact that in his own age Etherege's poetry enjoyed a great deal of popularity. Many of his short lyrics were set to music by the best composers of the time, notably Henry Purcell. James Thorpe, Etherege's modern editor, points out that his poems can be found in fifty contemporary manuscripts and in 150 printed books. Although he is seldom recognized as a poet today, in his own time Etherege was considered as accomplished as the earls of Dorset and Buckingham and Thomas Sedley, Etherege's best friend, all of whom are much more frequently anthologized. His "soft lampoons," as one fellow poet expressed it, were "the best of any man." He was noted especially for his concise expression and confident control of metaphor, and for these reasons he clearly deserves the attention of the modern reader.

Critics often speak of a particular writer as "a man of his times," and this epithet certainly applies to Etherege. His poems can be best understood and appreciated by viewing them as near-perfect reflections of the age in which he was writing. Restoration tastes, recorded so vividly in the drama of the period, emphasized wit, elegance, and sophistication, qualities which characterize Etherege's poems. If one had to characterize Etherege's poems in one word, the best choice would be "effortless." Like so many of his Restoration contemporaries, particularly his friend Sedley, Etherege mastered an art of stylish ease and naturalness. There are no jagged edges to his poetry, no profound explorations of troublesome personal questions. Instead, the reader encounters traditional, familiar themes, graced by a polished elegance.

BIOGRAPHY

The details of Sir George Etherege's early life are sketchy. The year of his birth is tentatively identified as 1635, and not much is known of his early youth. Following the production of his first two comedies, Etherege began a sporadic diplomatic career. In 1668 he served as secretary to Sir Daniel Harvey in Turkey but returned to England three years later. Following the production of *The Man of Mode* in 1676, Etherege's life was noteworthy only for numerous drunken brawls and for his fathering a child out of wedlock. Later, he was sent to The Hague by Charles II. In 1680 he was knighted, as rumor would have it after purchasing the title so that he could marry a wealthy widow. In 1685 he was sent to Ratisbon, in what is now West Germany, by James II. His diplomatic career in Ratisbon degenerated into a dissolute life of gambling and more drunken tavern brawling. To his squalor can be added sloth and negligence, since, during his diplomatic career in Ratisbon, Etherege never bothered to learn German, and left his records in chaos for others to sort out. He died in 1691, probably in Paris.

From these biographical facts it is presumed that Etherege was not an admirable man. What is clear, at least, is that the accounts of trickstering, gaming, drinking, loving, and debauchery found in his plays and in some of his poetry are authoritative. Etherege was truly the embodiment of the "Restoration rake."

ANALYSIS

Of the approximately thirty poems in Sir George Etherege's canon, the majority focus on the game of love, the prominent theme of his comedies. Etherege delights in investigating the wooing, the rejecting, and the successes and failures which characterize the game. In the true spirit of Restoration poetry, however, these investigations are never conducted in a personal mode; Etherege is not interested in examining love philosophically or personally. He is most often objective and detached, sometimes bemused, but never intensely involved in his subject matter. Consequently, his investigations of love appear in conventional, readily recognizable forms: the pastoral dialogue, the *carpe diem* theme, the "forsaken mistress" theme, and the satire based on standard Horatian and Juvenalian forms. Despite the variety of his forms, Etherege's poetic intent remains constant: to depict the game of love in all its manifestations, joyful or sorrowful, poignant or ludicrous.

"SONGS"

With this theme in mind, perhaps Etherege's most significant poem is one of his "Songs," which appears in his play *She Would if She Could*. In this song Gatty

confesses her love for Courtall. Following her song, Gatty is chided by her sister for her frank admission of affection; her sister feels she should dissemble. In this episode one can find many of the implicit themes of Etherege's poetry in a nutshell. The rules of the game of love call for pretense rather than sincere declaration of love. To heed this warning is to play the game successfully.

PASTORAL POEMS

Etherege occasionally wrote in the pastoral mode, loosely following a long tradition of poetry which utilizes the theme of rural bliss in uncluttered, paradisiacal settings. The artificiality of pastoral paradises was congenial to his poetic tastes since he apparently never desired to explore anything of topical, immediate significance. Instead, he preferred the timeless world of the pastoral and its often inherent paradox of unhappiness amid pastoral perfection. In his "Song: Shepherd! Why so dull a lover?" the poet exhorts the passive, lethargic shepherd to "lay your pipe a little by" and spring into action lest a life of loving pass him by. Etherege's other attempts at the pastoral, however, are bittersweet, even tragic.

In his "Song: When Phillis watched her harmless sheep," sung by Aurelia and her lady-in-waiting Letitia in Etherege's play *The Comical Revenge*, the poet opens in a rural paradise where the shepherdess Phillis happily occupies her time keeping guard over her sheep. Trouble brews, however, when "her silly heart did go astray," and her sheep, symbolizing her lost innocence and bliss, scatter. By the poem's end the rejected Phillis wishes only to die. Thus, Etherege creates a tension between the bliss of rural retirement and the quickness with which such happiness can vanish. His exploitation of this tension is not intended, however, to carry with it any didactic message of the need to free one's life from the tyranny of love's transitoriness. Readers are meant to pity Phillis and to consider that such pain might be inflicted on them, but not necessarily to gird against the caprices of fate.

The identical theme is found in "When first Amintas charmed my heart," sung to Harriet by her lady-in-waiting, Busy, in Etherege's play, *The Man of Mode*. Again, pastoral bliss is threatened when Amintas steals the shepherdess's heart. In this poem, however, Etherege's message is slightly more allegorically constructed. While the shepherdess dallies with Amintas, a pack of wolves that symbolizes the evils of a lack of responsibility devours her "heedless sheep." The shepherdess, who narrates her own sad tale, views the wolves' attack as a foreshadowing of her own lost happiness with Amintas as she concludes ominously, "And all will now be made a prey." Again, Etherege's message is simply the inevitable transitoriness of happiness.

The themes of these two poems afforded Etherege ample opportunity to use his poetry to expound further on the necessity of protecting oneself and others from love's destructive transitoriness. He felt no urge, however, to moralize. His sole poetic impulse was to examine the game of love from all sides. Only the playing of the game matters—a game at which no one wins.

Carpe diem theme

Two of Etherege's poems focus specifically on the *carpe diem* theme, a favorite in the seventeenth century, especially among the Sons of Ben and the Cavalier poets. In "To a Lady, Asking Him How Long He Would Love Her," which, as James Thorpe mentions, was probably influenced by Abraham Cowley's "Inconstancy," the lady Cloris has just asked her lover if he can pledge to her his endless love. The lover gives her the traditional answer that because all life is transitory, he can make no such guarantee. In the spirit of the *carpe diem* tradition, however, he urges her not to be sad but to anticipate their future bliss together, limited though it may be. This poem is noteworthy because it is one of the few times Etherege ventures forth from his amorality to assert a message of warmth. The poem concludes with the lover addressing his mistress: "Cloris, at worst you'll in the end/ But change your lover for a friend." In his other *carpe diem* poem, entitled simply "Song," however, his message is typically amoral. In an effort to charm his mistress out of her reticence, he compares her kisses to "those cordials which we give/ To dying men, to make them live." His motive is clear: to bedazzle his mistress into succumbing to his desires.

Lament of the suitor

Counterbalanced by his two pastoral poems, wherein it is the ladies Cloris and Phillis who suffer love's rejection, are his poems which center on the laments of suitors, heartlessly spurned by their cold mistresses. Like the ludicrous lover in *The Man of Mode*, Sir Fopling Flutter, who luxuriates in his role as rejected suitor ("I sigh! I sigh!"), Etherege's poetic suitors seemingly enjoy their defeats. In his "Voiture's Urania," an imitation of a sonnet by the French poet Vincent Voiture, the rejected lover virtually revels in his despondency: "I bow beneath her tyranny." There is no trace of a resolve on the lover's part to overcome his defeat, but merely a decadent wish to pine: "Hopeless I languish out my days." The masochistic lover surfaces also in "Silvia," which, as Thorpe points out, was perhaps Etherege's most popular poem. Silvia's heartlessness is traditionally depicted: "With a frown she can kill." The poem is noteworthy, however, for its exercise of irony. With typical Restoration wit, Etherege has written the poem in a bouncy anapestic meter, the sprightliness of which ironically undermines the sadness the lover is expressing. Thus, Etherege's game of love is frequently one in which rejection can serve as an energizing force. An equally accomplished poem is his "Song," artfully constructed in two stanzas, wherein the first stanza depicts the wooing lover as a singing voice, while the second stanza portrays the mistress as a lute who, he hopes, will "tune her strings to love's discourse."

Feminine beauty

In his continuing investigation of the game of love, Etherege also wrote two poems in the tradition of praising feminine beauty. "To a Lady Who Fled the Sight of Him," influenced, as Thorpe points out, by a Horatian ode, glorifies the beautiful lady whose natural grace and beauty, like Diana's, are sufficient to ward off lust and sexuality. Etherege's commonplace treatment of this tradition, however, is superseded in his poem "To a Very Young Lady." In this poem the girl's beauty is compared to the rising sun, and the poet wonders how mortals will be able to view the splendor of her beauty's sun as it reaches its noon. Implicit in his praise of the girl's beauty, however, is the inevitability that her beautiful sunrise and glorious noon will eventually become a fading sunset in which the splendor of her beauty will vanish. As is so often the case with Etherege's poetry, this implicit message is not intended as a moral mandate to discourage the lady from worldly preoccupations. If anything, the poet's intent is to remind her uncharitably and with no small trace of cruelty that at any time an "untimely frost" can decay "early glories."

MISOGYNIST THEMES

This hint of misogyny, ironically embedded in a poem praising feminine beauty, bursts forth with greater intensity in his "Song: Ladies, though to your conquering eyes," which appears in his play *The Comical Revenge*. In this poem Etherege steps out of his normally cool, detached tone to deliver an angry message to ladies who enjoy spurning their suitors. He snarls, "Then wrack not lovers with disdain/ Lest love on you revenge their pain." Similarly, in a "Song" which appears in a tavern scene in *The Comical Revenge*, the message is clearly stated that men should stay away from aloof women as they are only good for wasting one's time. Instead, men are instructed to "Make much of every buxom girl/ Which needs but little courting." Finally, in his "Song: To happy youths," which, as Thorpe notes, was patterned after Juvenal's Sixth Satire, Etherege's misogyny is most evident. He warns youth that happiness can be attained only through avoidance of women. No matter how beautiful the woman, he warns, "The snake's beneath the flower." In these three poems, the game of love has lost its charm for Etherege. Tender flirtation and wanton affection are replaced by crudeness and even cruelty toward the woman. Once again, however, no moral message is intended in the poet's disgust. These dark looks at love merely express a temporary loss of a desire to play the game, not a realization of the emptiness of such pursuits.

An uncharacteristic work among Etherege's love poems is "The Divided Heart," in which the poet is worried that his mistress, Celia, will not always be as faithful as she is now. "The Divided Heart" stands alone stylistically as Etherege's only experiment in the courtly tradition of love poetry. It is written in a consciously elegant, stylized manner, which differs from his usual effortless, easy style. On the opposite end of the spectrum is "The Imperfect Enjoyment," which, as Richard E. Quaintance believes, belongs to a genre initiated by Ovid: A lover, initially frustrated by the reluctance of his mistress, is overjoyed when she suddenly becomes receptive to his sexual advances. At the critical moment, however, he is unable to perform the sex act, and again he is left to languish in frustration. Not surprisingly, the genre underwent a modest revival during the Restoration. In Etherege's poem the lover concludes that none of this would have happened if his mistress had been "less fair." Although the poem is not bawdy, the low comedy of the lover's misfortunes is far removed from the lofty, stylized elegance of "The Divided Heart" and is yet another indication of the diversity with which Etherege explores the game of love.

SATIRIC POETRY

In addition to the many poems in which he investigated the game of love, Etherege tried his hand occasionally at satire. Like his love poems, his satires are not didactic attempts at exposing and reforming the hypocrisies of humankind but merely exercises in light, frivolous ridicule. The fervor with which people can become involved in card games is mocked in his poem "A Song on Basset," and the reader is tempted to wonder whether Alexander Pope had read it prior to his account of the game of ombre in *The Rape of the Lock* (1714). Etherege also composed four satires on John Sheffield, the earl of Mulgrave, the first and most noteworthy of which is entitled "Ephelia to Bajazet." Bajazet is the earl of Mulgrave, who, according to Thorpe, was so extraordinarily ugly that he verged on the grotesque. To compound the absurdity of the man, he was insufferably vain as well. The forsaken Ephelia mourns her rejection at the hands of her cruel Bajazet. Again, one can detect no reforming impulse in the satire, only ridicule. Etherege leaves the decision up to the reader as to who is the more ludicrous: the grotesque, loathsome Mulgrave or the pitiably absurd forsaken mistress who would lament the loss of such an undesirable scoundrel.

Perhaps his most intriguing satire, "A Prologue Spoken at the Opening of the Duke's New Playhouse," reflects Etherege's concern as a dramatist with the problems of having to pander to the public's taste. In this satire, the speaker is a typical Restoration theater owner who proclaims his delight in catering to the extravagant, even vulgar tastes of his audiences. Much of his defense of his pandering centers on his metaphor comparing a play to a kept woman. Just as the woman demands increasingly ornate surroundings, so also do the play and the theater demand more ostentation to appeal to their audiences. The poem is noteworthy as a reflection of Etherege's concern that the dramatists of the period were being increasingly pressured to construct their plays as vulgar extravaganzas.

In both his love poetry and his satires, Etherege accurately reflects the poetic tastes of the Restoration. His poems are witty, sophisticated, detached—without a trace of personal investment. His investigations of love are sometimes poignant, sometimes comic, sometimes sympathetic, sometimes arrogant. At no point, however, does Etherege allow a moral tone to creep into his poetry. He does not demand that the reader consider the moral responsibilities of love, only the game-playing itself. Effortless shaping of his poetry, not didactic content, was Etherege's chief goal, and he accomplished it as successfully as any of his more famous Restoration contemporaries.

OTHER MAJOR WORKS

PLAYS: *The Comical Revenge: Or, Love in a Tub*, pr., pb. 1664; *She Would if She Could*, pr., pb. 1668; *The Man of Mode: Or, Sir Fopling Flutter*, pr., pb. 1676.

NONFICTION: *The Letterbook of Sir George Etherege*, 1928 (Sybil Rosenfeld, editor); *Letters of Sir George Etherege*, 1973.

BIBLIOGRAPHY

Boswell, Eleanore. "Sir George Etherege." *The Review of English Studies: A Quarterly Journal of English Literature and the English Language* 7 (1931): 207-209. Offers some new information on Etherege's life, particularly during his diplomatic stay at Ratisbon.

Etherege, George, Sir. *The Poems of Sir George Etherege*. Edited by James Thorpe. Princeton, N.J.: Princeton University Press, 1963. This collection is included in secondary sources because the preface by James Thorpe provides some useful insights into Etherege's poetry. Notes that in his own time, Etherege was a poet of consequence, his poems being frequently copied. Thorpe remarks that although Etherege chose conventional themes, he nevertheless gave an edge to them in his poems.

Huseboe, Arthur R. *Sir George Etherege*. Boston: Twayne, 1987. A useful volume on Etherege's works, including background information on his life and the times in which he lived. Chapter 5 comments on his poetry and mentions that in his time Etherege's poems were widely known, but not so today. Discusses his love poems, including those that were also songs, and poems of praise.

Mann, David D. *A Concordance to the Plays and Poems of Sir George Etherege*. Westport, Conn.: Greenwood Press, 1985. A valuable resource for Restoration scholars. Includes approximately thirty poems written between 1663 and 1688. Discusses Etherege's use of language and allusions in the introduction. Cites Bracher's comments on Etherege as a man with a "shrewd eye for pretense and hypocrisy."

_____. *Sir George Etherege: A Reference Guide*. Boston, Mass.: G. K. Hall, 1981. A guide to bibliographical resources on Etherege.

Scott-Kilvert, Ian, ed. *British Writers*. Vol. 2. New York: Charles Scribner's Sons, 1979. The entry on Etherege lists him under Restoration court poets. Contains concise, useful background information and extracts from some of his important poems, illustrating his "simplicity and entire lack of self-consciousness." Praises Etherege for his craftsmanship and says he is at his best in his lyrics.

Thorpe, James E., ed. *Poems of George Etherege*. Princeton, N.J.: Princeton University Press, 1963. More than seventy pages of notes and bibliographical references enhance this standard edition of the poems.

Young, Douglas M. *The Feminist Voices in Restoration Comedy: The Virtuous Women in the Play-Worlds of Etherege, Wycherley, and Congreve*. Lanham, Md.: University Press of America, 1997. Sir George Etherege, William Wycherley, and William Congreve introduce into their play-worlds major female characters who demand independence from and equality with their male counterparts. Young focuses on each of these major female characters and how they fit into the social and marital relationships typically found in English Restoration society.

Elizabeth J. Bellamy;
bibliography updated by the editors

WILLIAM EVERSON

Brother Antoninus
Born: Sacramento, California; September 10, 1912
Died: Santa Cruz, California; June 3, 1994

PRINCIPAL POETRY

These Are the Ravens, 1935
San Joaquin, 1939
The Masculine Dead, 1942
X War Elegies, 1943
The Waldport Poems, 1944
War Elegies, 1944
The Residual Years, 1945
Poems MCMXLII, 1945
The Residual Years, 1948
The Privacy of Speech: Ten Poems in Sequence,
  1949
The Crooked Lines of God, 1959
The Year's Declension, 1961
The Hazards of Holiness, 1962
The Blowing of the Seed, 1966
Single Source, 1966
*The Achievement of Brother Antoninus: A Compre-
  hensive Selection of His Poems with a Critical
  Introduction*, 1967
The Rose of Solitude, 1967
Poems of Nineteen Forty Seven, 1968
The Springing of the Blade, 1968
The Residual Years: Poems, 1934-1948, 1968
Man-Fate, 1974
The Veritable Years: 1949-1966, 1978
The Masks of Drought, 1980
*Eastward the Armies: Selected War Poems, 1935-
  1942*, 1980
Renegade Christmas, 1984
*In Medias Res: Canto One of an Autobiographi-
  cal Epic, Dust Shall Be the Serpent's Food*,
  1984
The High Embrace, 1986
Mexican Standoff, 1989
The Blood of the Poet, 1994
The Integral Years: Poems, 1966-1994, 2000

OTHER LITERARY FORMS

Never hesitant about admitting his literary indebtedness to Robinson Jeffers, since it was Jeffers's poetry that seized him as a youth and helped him realize his own vocation as a poet, William Everson has written numerous introductions to recent reprinted editions of Jeffers's work, as well as a critical study, *Robinson Jeffers: Fragments of an Older Fury* (1968). Like his older mentor, Everson is intensely interested in the West as landscape and California as region, and he explores both of these concerns, as subject matter and sources for art, in *Archetype West: The Pacific Coast as a Literary Region* (1976). The importance of regional identity, as well as what he perceives to be the artist's responsibility in portraying as honestly as possible the disparity between the inner (human) and the outer (natural) landscapes, has been the central focus of many of Everson's essays and lectures over the past thirty years—many of which are contained in *Earth Poetry* (1980) and *Birth of a Poet* (1982).

ACHIEVEMENTS

The most dramatic poet of the Western landscape since Robinson Jeffers, William Everson has always provoked extreme responses from his audience—either intense admiration for his painful, self-probing and self-revealing confessionalism, or intense dislike for the extremely visceral histrionics of his verse and his voice on the reading platform. In like manner, neither his poetry nor his life has ever been lukewarm. Indeed, it is difficult to consider his art as separate from his life, since his poetry has been personal from the beginning of his career; it was not until his third book of poems, *The Masculine Dead*, however, that he broke noticeably away from Jeffers and into the intensely confessional verse for which he would become known. While Robert Lowell is usually acknowledged as the first American poet since Hart Crane to advance the art of the sequence, and as the harbinger of the modern confessional mode of poetry, Everson had actually been developing the sequence form and the confessional voice since 1939, twenty years before Lowell's *Life Studies* (1959) was published. Using his literal self as a symbol of the modern predicament, Everson has, as he says in *Birth of a Poet*, "spent the greater part of my life trying to probe down through the negative factors to find the living root which makes me what I am."

Probing down into himself to discover his "living root" has meant, in a national sense, discovering the American character. During World War II, having taken his stand as a pacifist and having suffered the consequent three-and-a-half years of incarceration in Oregon and California camps for conscientious objectors, Everson wrote some of the most incisive and forceful antiwar poetry ever to be produced in America or abroad. This did not go unnoticed, for it led to the national publication of an edition of his selected poems, *The Residual Years* (1948), as well as a Guggenheim Fellowship in 1949.

While Everson's entry into the Dominican Order in 1951, at which time he became Brother Antoninus, may have hurt his public following (for one poet had dropped out of sight nominally and thus publicly, and another one began to emerge), the confessional tenor of the poet's verse was intensified with his eventual entry into the "dark night of the soul" and Jungian psychoanalysis. Gradually, Brother Antoninus received greater public recognition than William Everson had: He was nominated for the Pulitzer Prize in 1959, awarded the Commonwealth Club of California Silver Medal in 1968 for *The Rose of Solitude*, and sponsored to give public readings of his work not only throughout America but also in Dublin, London, Hamburg, Berlin, Munich, Rome, and Paris. He became, in short, world-renowned as the Dionysian monk who wrote dithyrambic and explicit poetry celebrating the sexual conjunction of man and woman and God. At the height of his career, however, Brother Antoninus confused his audience as Everson once had; he abruptly left the Dominican Order in 1969, and became William Everson once again.

Also a master printer, Everson's hand-printed, limited edition of Jeffers's *Granite & Cypress* (1975) was chosen by Joseph Blumenthal, in his exhibition "The Printed Book in America" (1977), as one of the seventy best-made books in the history of American printing. Everson was also cowinner of the Shelley Memorial Award for poetry in 1977 and a winner of an NEA grant in 1981.

BIOGRAPHY

William Oliver Everson, born September 10, 1912, in Sacramento, California, was the second of three chil-

dren and the first son of Lewis and Francelia Everson. It is noteworthy that Everson was the first son of his family because throughout his career he has stressed (in his poetry, in some autobiographical essays, and quite specifically in his unpublished autobiography, "Prodigious Thrust") that an Oedipal complex is a key factor in his own psychology, in his strained relationship with his father, and in his relationship with the women in his life. Everson's mother, almost twenty years younger than his father, had been Catholic but was forced to leave the Church in order to marry the man she loved (a fact of increasing importance to the poet later in his life when he converted to Catholicism). Everson's father was a Norwegian emigrant and had been an itinerant printer, musician, and bandmaster until, with a wife and children, he settled in Selma, California, in 1914, and there established the Everson Printery in 1920. As a boy, Everson looked to his mother for support, confidence, and emotional understanding, while growing increasingly intimidated, resentful and—he has said—even hateful of his father, a taciturn and self-professed atheist who believed Christianity and faith in an afterlife were below the dignity of enlightened minds. In short, from infancy, Everson was exposed to—and often torn between—the extreme differences of his parents' dispositions and sensibilities.

Everson's first poetic attempts were love poems he wrote to his high school sweetheart, beginning in his junior year. In his senior year, he wrote topical poems for the Selma High School yearbook, *The Magnet*. After graduation (June, 1931), he enrolled in Fresno State College the following fall but remained there only one semester, during which time he had what might be called his first "literary" poem, "The Gypsy Dance" (blatantly derived from Edgar Allan Poe's "The Bells," with its strict trochaic meter and long lines), published in *The Caravan*, the Fresno State College literary magazine. Unable to find anything in college interesting enough to keep him, he returned to his parents' home (December, 1932) and remained there, while working at a local cannery, until June, 1933, when he entered the Civilian Conservation Corps (CCC). Except for short leaves of absence, Everson remained in the CCC camp for a year, but he felt intellectually deficient and painfully isolated, so he returned to Fresno State in the fall of

1934. This time he remained enrolled for the entire academic year, and he found something that was not only interesting but also inspiring: the poetry of Robinson Jeffers. It was after this discovery that he decided to be the first poet of the San Joaquin Valley.

In 1935, again living in his parents' home, Everson had his first collection of poems, *These Are the Ravens*, published. Although the poems in the volume were not very remarkable, at twenty-three he had begun a lifelong career that would encompass much more than the San Joaquin Valley. Everson married Edwa Poulson, the young woman to whom he had written the love poems in high school, in May, 1938; they settled on a small farm outside Selma, she teaching elementary school and he writing his poetry and tending the vineyard which surrounded their home. Despite the fact that he was content with his domestic life, the threat of America's involvement in the war being waged in Europe set the tenor of much of the poetry contained in his next two published volumes, *San Joaquin* (1939) and *The Masculine Dead* (1942). In 1940, Everson's mother died; in the same year, he was forced by the Selective Service Act to take a stand on the war, and he registered as a conscientious objector. Thus, in 1943, the poet was incarcerated in a Civilian Public Service (CPS) camp for conscientious objectors in Waldport, Oregon, where he would be instrumental in establishing the Waldport School of Fine Arts and the United Press, both precursors of the later San Francisco Renaissance.

Everson remained incarcerated, with the exception of short leaves of absence, for almost three years, during which time his father died, and he and his wife agreed to a divorce because she had fallen in love with another man; thus he lost all his familial connections with his home back in the valley. In August, 1946, two months after being released from a CPS camp in Weaverville, California, where he had been transferred earlier that year, Everson met and fell in love with Mary Fabilli, an artist and Catholic, recently divorced herself. They were married in the summer of 1948, a year that was also important for Everson because the first national publication of a volume of his selected poetry was issued (*The Residual Years*) and because on Christmas Eve of that year he converted to Catholicism. Paradoxically, the Church refused to recognize the Eversons'

marriage because both had been married previously and Mary had been married in a Catholic ceremony; in short, their marriage was annulled, they separated in May, 1949, and Everson was baptized in July. A month before his baptism, he was awarded a Guggenheim Fellowship which would enable him to write with financial support for a year; the stipend lasted only ten months, however, and shortly thereafter Everson entered a Catholic Worker House in Oakland, California, where he would remain for fourteen months. In June, 1951, he entered the Dominican Order at St. Albert's College in Oakland, as a *donatus*, and there he was given the name Brother Antoninus.

From *The Crooked Lines of God* (poems written between 1949 and 1954) through *The Hazards of Holiness* (1962), the poems of Brother Antoninus emerge as a tortuous series of twists and turns as he struggles, because of his vows of celibacy, in the embrace of Thanatos (that is, the death-urge of the self). In 1960, however, he fell in love with Rose Tunnland, a Catholic divorcé and mother of three children; it was out of this intense love relationship and the breaking of his vows that *The Rose of Solitude* emerged. Partly out of guilt but mostly out of a difference in personalities, this relationship was ended in 1963, but in 1965 the poet fell in love with another woman, Susanna Rickson, again broke his vows, and this time made the painful decision to leave the Dominican Order. So, in December, 1969, Brother Antoninus concluded a poetry-reading (at the University of California, Davis) by stripping off his monk's habit and walking off the platform as William Everson once again. He married Susanna six days later, and they lived at Stinson Beach until, in 1971, Everson became poet in residence at the University of California, Santa Cruz.

ANALYSIS

Always a poet of extremes, from the beginning of his career William Everson has expressed both need and fear, compulsion and revulsion, toward those things in his life most important to him. Much of the tension in his poetry seems to arise from his mind knowing what his heart would like to deny—that is, all is transitory, all is mutable, and there is no permanent security in life. Indeed, the major recurrent theme throughout his canon is that of thwarted love. While this is certainly not a unique theme, nor one limited to modern consciousness, Everson's attempt to understand and confessionally explain the ongoing internal war that he suffers (between his heart and mind) leads him, in psychological terms, to his encounter with and ultimate victory over the personal shadow-side of consciousness, and to repeated sought-after encounters with the anima or feminine side. In fact, it is the feminine side in his own consciousness, as well as that embodied in woman, for which he expresses both the greatest need and, paradoxically, the greatest fear throughout his career.

THESE ARE THE RAVENS

In the 1930's the world was a fearful place for young Everson, as he composed his first collection of poetry, *These Are the Ravens*; even nature, which he would consistently portray as feminine, seemed hostile and malignant. In his earliest poem, "First Winter Storm," the speaker is one who hunkers indoors, afraid of the unknown and ominous unpredictability of the elemental life force that moves outside his walls ("I felt the fear run down my back/ And grip me as I lay"). Humans, in this early volume, are rendered more or less passive in the face of nature's seemingly conscious enmity toward all of life, and this human condition is indicative of the poet's own relation to the world of adulthood and experience. Everson was seventeen when the Depression hit rock bottom in 1929; he had had no career plans when he was graduated from high school in 1931; he had not prepared to go to college, and his first term there proved fruitless; he had returned to his parents' home to live, but back there he realized that he had become a disappointment to his father; he had enlisted in the Civilian Conservation Corps and remained in the CCC camp for a year; he had then returned to Fresno State for a year, discovered the poetry of Jeffers, and made a lifelong decision to be a poet.

Unable to support himself while pursuing his chosen vocation, however, he had again moved in with his parents, and he would remain with them until his marriage, three months before his twenty-sixth birthday in 1938. Yet, because he had been unable to break away from his dependence upon his parents, he grew, as he wrote in "Prodigious Thrust," into "the full status of his ambivalence with the father-hunger and father-fear, the mother-hunger and mother-fear at war within him."

AMBIVALENCE IN POETRY

The "ambivalence" he suffered manifested itself in his inability to identify with the masculine or feminine in his own personality. The constant dark moodiness he experienced he attributed to his agnatic heritage (stemming, that is, from his masculine precursors), and this he eschewed because he believed it to be related to male savagery and patriarchal dominance. In "I Know It as the Sorrow" for example, Everson attempts to explain the "ache" in his blood, and his recurrent "waking as a child weeping in the dark for no reason," as a psychic condition he has inherited and for which he is not, therefore, responsible. This "sorrow," he says, lies in "the secret depths" of his soul; however, while he may not be responsible for his temperament, the "warriors" of the past which he calls up, as well as their "women/ Shivering in the cliff-wind," are integral to *his* own perspective of life. In short, at the a priori level he views the masculine as dominant, savage, and strong, and the feminine as receptive, docile, and weak. In "Fish-Eaters," again, Everson recalls his progenitors, the males among whom are "giants roaring with mirth," and the females who are "withered women" who know "no strength but the lips held mutely over the teeth." Although he vehemently eschews his *masculine* heritage—stating, at the conclusion of "Fish-Eaters," that "I find no hunger for the sword"—what he implicitly praises in heroic terms is the very thing he denounces—that is, the assertiveness of the male libido.

THEMATIC TREATMENT OF WOMEN

By consistently portraying women as weak and passive creatures, while at the same time portraying men pejoratively as the exact opposite, Everson leaves himself neither gender with which to identify; in other words, by dividing himself from both his father and his mother, from the patrilineal and matrilineal inheritances, he divides himself. He becomes, therefore, the "watcher" in "Who Sees Through the Lens" (*San Joaquin*), a man who spends his nights staring through a telescope up at the stars, a man "fixed in the obsession of seeking, the dementia for knowing," and a man so determined to understand and explain the meaning of life that he intellectually vivisects his own being for understanding. Whereas his "cold mind needles the rock" of stars at night, during the day he divides his mind from his body as he "fumbles the sleeping seed, pokes at the sperm." This seeker is reminiscent of Jeffers's Barclay, in *The Women at Point Sur* (1929), filled with a kind of self-loathing for the corruptibility of his flesh; thus he denies his body for the monomaniacal glorification of his intellect—until, that is, his alienation becomes too painful to bear and he then strives to submerge his consciousness in sexual ecstasy. Significantly, it is in "Who Sees Through the Lens" that Everson for the first time categorizes woman as receptacle and comforter for the male's intellectual frustration—a role she will be forced to play often throughout the poet's career. After he describes the "watcher," therefore, the poet beseeches him to "give over;/ Come star-bruised and broken back to the need;/ Come seeking the merciful thighs of the lover." It is between the feminine thighs, in short, that surcease may be found for the intellectual man; indeed, she offers him a momentary, mindless oblivion which he both desires and fears.

Woman, like everything else in life for Everson, is not to be trusted with his heart, as she changes and thus forbids his dependency upon her. He is, he says in "Abrasive," "torn by the wars of perpetual change," and he finds that one side of his psyche longs "to slip yielding and drowned in an ocean of silence,/ Go down into some abstract and timeless norm of reality,/ Shadow the eyes, the uneasy heart, and be done." Yet, while woman can grant him the momentary oblivion of consciousness, as well as the anodyne for his "uneasy heart," another side of his nature scoffs at such a need and reminds his heart that "the sun makes a fool of you," for this symbol of the masculine principle flaunts life's transitions, "shocking with seasons" those individuals who search for stasis.

PROTECTING VULNERABILITY

Although Everson married Edwa Poulson in 1938, and in a sense fulfilled his emotional needs while suffering his own mental chiding for succumbing to the belief that a commitment such as marriage could last, he wrote no poems to or about his wife or his love for her; instead, he wrote such poems as "The Illusion" (*The Masculine Dead*), wherein he denigrates those people who sit in the comfort of their homes, surrounding themselves with the security of a family, while all around them people are being destroyed by the unpredictable, as "they pitch

and go down with the blood on their lips,/ With the blood on the broken curve of their throats,/ With their eyes begging." What he, in his heart, wanted desperately to believe possible (that, for example, emotional security could be sustained), he found himself unable to accept intellectually; therefore, he kept his wife at a distance, for she was part of "the illusion" that made him emotionally vulnerable.

In his life Everson took definite steps to minimize his vulnerability. He had a vasectomy, which he explains in "The Sides of a Mind" (*The Masculine Dead*) as his attempt to avoid guilt for the pain life would inflict upon his children ("each shiver of pain they ever felt/ Would ripple in to the moment of my act,/ And I will not yield"). As he writes in *Earth Poetry*, another step he took was that of subordinating his marriage to his career: "The mistake I made . . . in regard to being an artist . . . was when I married I sacrificed the inner viability of my marriage to my career . . . I denied the primacy of her person. By reducing her to an object and sacrificing that object even to a school of thought, I denied the reality of the situation."

IN CRITIQUE OF MASCULINE AGGRESSION

When the Selective Service Act was instituted in 1940, and when America's involvement in World War II seemed imminent, Everson took yet another self-protective step by registering as a conscientious objector. Throughout *The Masculine Dead*, which was inspired by the moral revulsion he felt over the war being waged in Europe, Everson continued to denounce his father's world of masculine and militaristic aggression. In "The Sides of a Mind," he describes himself, a poet, sitting at a table and struggling to articulate some comprehensible explanation for the confusion and destruction in the world; suddenly a political activist bursts into his room and criticizes his physical passivity: "We have time no longer for the seeds of your doubt./ We have time only for man and man/ Facing together the brute confusion of the stubborn world." Because the poet is unable to embrace his father's ethics and values (as a young man, for instance, his father had been beaten and jailed for his efforts to establish a typographical union), he learns to embrace the old man's disappointment as a testament to his own, the son's, authenticity: "Father, whatever you hoped for," he says in the second section of the poem, "I am not what you wanted./ I sit hunched in a room."

What he once viewed as weakness, consequently, he now views as virtue in the feminine; furthermore, in "The Presence," he suggests that an individual and nation are corrupted by such a thing as war only insofar as the feminine psychic principle is corrupt. What he views as "the presence" is primal, savage and masculine, as it "stoops in the mind, hairy and thick," destroying "norms" and "modes of arrest" when it becomes actively motivating in the conscious mind. By this "presence," he maintains, women "will be used" if they relinquish their "precepts of will" ("Throwing their bellowing flesh on the tool/ That eases the rutting sow"). By taking the pacifistic stand against the war, therefore, Everson chose to accept for himself what he saw as the traditionally feminine response to life, as he states in "Now in These Days": He will "wait in these rooms," he vows, accepting "the degradation of slavery and want" imposed upon him in a camp for conscientious objectors.

"The Chronicle of Division"

In January, 1943, Everson was conscripted and sent to a camp in Waldport, Oregon. He would remain incarcerated for three years, during which time he composed his longest sequential and confessional poem, "The Chronicle of Division" (*The Residual Years*). While this poem describes poignantly and incisively the human deprivation suffered by men locked up for their beliefs, the underpinning and gradually overriding focus is on the psychological condition of men without women. Paradoxically, while it had been the feminine temperament that Everson had espoused and embraced as a necessary response to what he perceived as a war caused by *masculine* aggression and warmongering, it was the feminine embodied in his wife which proved to be the most devastating to him. Because there had been no "primacy" in the relationship (and he gradually came to see his vasectomy as a testament to this), and because of the indefinite length of their separation, Everson's wife fell in love with another man and (in a letter) requested a divorce.

While the poet deals with the consequent pain and feelings of rejection he experiences, throughout the poem, he discovers something within himself which is more awesome than the loss of his marriage and home:

He discovers the capacity to kill, as he suddenly realizes that he desires to strangle his wife, "Till the plunging features/ Bulge and go black,/ And all his old hurt/ Lies healed on the bed." The disconcerting irony in this is immediately apparent to him, for he is locked up because he refuses to kill and yet finds within himself the *desire* to murder punitively; "the presence," then, "hairy and thick," hunkers in himself. Unable to accept this shadow-side of his consciousness, he attempts to purge himself of all his past familial and regional associations, believing that he might thereby conjoin his "divisible selves,/ Ill-eased with each other."

The "woman within"

With the war ended and his release from the CPS camp guaranteed in 1946, he began immediately to direct his attention, in "The Fictive Wish" (*The Residual Years*), to an introspective search for that "woman within," that woman "of his," whom he might learn to know well enough to recognize outside himself were he confronted by her. It is not surprising that Everson describes this woman in strictly physical and sexual terms, with "her breast" the "ease of his need,/ And the thigh a solace. . . ." Two months after being released from the camp, he met and fell in love with Mary Fabilli, a Catholic divorcé who had been recently betrayed by her husband and was also suffering the pain of rejection. In short, because of chance similarities in their respective pasts, and because he was actively searching for the woman "of his," Everson could truthfully feel about Mary, as he was to write in "Prodigious Thrust," that "I knew her before I met her."

Three months after being released from his confinement in the CPS camp Everson wrote "The Blowing of the Seed," to Mary and about the cathartic and rejuvenating power of their love. It is apparent that the woman has quickly become his "other self" and the nurturer of his "huge hope"; she "broke" his loneliness, he tells her, and she freed his "isolate heart." Not only has Mary allowed him to come "up out of darkness," allowed his courage to burst out of a "cold region" of "ash," but her love for him has caused a new ascendancy of his masculine ego; consequently, Everson makes a one-hundred-and-eighty-degree turn in attitude, abandons his "feminine," passive demeanor and voices a traditional drive toward male primacy, wrenching their relationship into the age-old equation of strong male and weak female. Clearly this "new" attitude, voiced with a Dionysian and dithyrambic intensity, is Everson's way of compensating for the debilitating vulnerability and ultimate rejection he suffered with the break-up of his first marriage *and* with the treatment and alienation he suffered because of his moral position against the war. In other words, what he denied for almost ten years (that is, male aggression, libidinal masculinity, and male primacy), he affirms in "The Blowing of the Seed"; after all, the intellectual denial of the traditionally patriarchal world had involved an immense price and overwhelming nakedness emotionally, psychologically, and spiritually. While he attempts to continue writing with masculine bravado in his next poem, "The Springing of the Blade," trying to be a Whitmanesque singer of fecundity, he finds himself "strung" in "the iron dimension," his term for the past and its ineradicable cleavages and losses. Again he finds his capacity to love thwarted by his inability to live in face of the inevitable threats of infidelity that living entails—that is, the infidelity of time to life, of the real to the ideal, of the body to the spirit, and of the heart to the mind.

Although Everson and Mary Fabilli were married, their love was thwarted by another factor as well: She was a Catholic and he was not. He felt, as he expresses in "The First Absence," increasingly fearful of her possible abandonment of him; and as she began to attend religious services more frequently than she had before their marriage, he began to accompany her. Believing, therefore, that by converting to Catholicism he could secure, as he says in "The Quarrel," the "necessary certitude to start anew," he decided to do what was necessary to be baptized a Catholic. What was necessary was not what he expected, for the Church refused to recognize their marriage because it had not granted the annulment of Mary's first marriage; in short, they were forced to separate. Left alone, Everson was again compelled to face his own incompleteness, was again forced to face life without the emotional security of his union with another; thus, in "In the Dream's Recess," he pleads to God: "Give me the cleansing power!/ . . . Make me clean!" He needed strength now, to face his own vulnerability, and to face the inferior shadow-side of his own personality: "The sullied presence crouches in

my side,/ And all is fearful where I dare not wake or dream."

THE CROOKED LINES OF GOD AND THE HAZARDS OF HOLINESS

Not surprisingly, after Everson decided to become Brother Antoninus, a *donatus* in the Dominican Order, he set out with a convert's zealousness to denounce, in *The Crooked Lines of God*, all that he had been and believed secularly. In "The Screed of the Flesh," for example, he eschews the fleshly life he had lived with his two wives; in fact, he goes so far in his zealotry as o fictionalize his past persona as one who "gloried self,/ Singing the glory of myself." To anyone familiar with the poet's pre-Catholic verse, it is apparent that, to the contrary, Everson spent very little time "singing the glory" of himself or of his life, for his verse is tortured by self-analysis, doubt, and distrust. Obviously he intends for his conversion to purify his life and obliterate his past errors and losses, and because woman, with her tempting "merciful thighs," has hurt him the most, he claims, in "A Penitential Psalm," that his "corruptness" is his only through inheriting his mother's (and, before her, Eve's) "iniquities": "in sin did my mother conceive me!" Delegating the responsibility for his own shadow-side to another, however, could not last; thus, after his zealousness had been worn down by six years of celibacy and three years of almost total creative barrenness, in *The Hazards of Holiness* Brother Antoninus's central poetic subject becomes his "dark night of the soul," as well as his contention with the shadow-side of his consciousness.

The terse, almost truncated and imageless poetic lines throughout *The Hazards of Holiness* exemplify a period in his life when, as expressed in "Saints," there is "No thing. Not anything," and the poet pleads to God: "Do something!/ Kiss or kill/ But move me!" Very similar to the pantheistical god in "Circumstance," a pre-Catholic poem in *San Joaquin*, who "hears not, nor sees," in "You, God," the supreme deity in this period of the poet's life is a "God of death,/ Great God of no-life." In "Jacob and the Angel," the man of the flesh and earth, Esau, becomes emblematic of Everson, and Jacob (Antoninus) must wrestle with his dark brother for supremacy—even in the face of the fact that God has apparently abandoned the celibate monk despite all his earlier confessions and self-denials. "But I?" the poet asks in "Sleep-Tossed I Lie," where he questions the value of his barrenness, bitterly imagining lovers locked in passion in the night beyond the walls of his monastery. As a result of his torturous introspection, and out of the pain he suffers for the denial of the flesh, he laments: "Long have I lain,/ Long lain, and in the longing/ Fry." Again, in "Black Christ," he cries out of his barrenness, "Kill me./ . . . I beg thy kindness." Importantly, though, in the last poem of *The Hazards of Holiness*, "In Savage Wastes," a breakthrough is achieved, and the poet shows a lessening of his desire to retreat any longer into contemplation of a distant Celestial City. Instead, he affirms that "I [shall] go forth/ And return to the ways of man," no longer willing to deny his essential humanness, "And will find my God in the thwarted love that breaks between us!" With his new attitude, then, his quest for meaning and wholeness leads Brother Antoninus out of a ten-year period of celibacy and into a relationship with Rose Tunnland, to and about whom he wrote *The Rose of Solitude*.

THE ROSE OF SOLITUDE

After learning to embrace his fleshly, Esau-like nature, the poet begins to praise woman as the means through which the polarities of his psyche may be balanced and possibly synthesized, and through which he may be permitted to move closer to God. Brother Antoninus believes that, both emotionally and physically, he has been resurrected through the love for Rose ("I dream the dawn of the longest night: The one resurrection"); furthermore, all the poems in *The Rose of Solitude* attest to the victory of Eros (love directed toward self-realization) over Thanatos (the instinctual desire for death, as it was expressed throughout *The Hazards of Holiness*). The poet tells his reader, in "The Kiss of the Cross," that "She brought me back./ . . . I was brought back alive." Out of his desire for a sustained equipoise between the mind and the heart, the spirit and the flesh, while at the same time questioning the rightness of breaking his vows of celibacy, he pleads: "O Christ & Lady/ Save me from my law!" Ultimately, however, Brother Antoninus becomes with Rose like the proverbial tree that can reach heaven only if its roots have penetrated hell, as he indicates in "Immortal Strangeness":

> When we fell—
>   on the hard floor
>   in the harsh dark,
>   on the bitter boards—,
> When we fell
> We rose.

In short, the conjunction of Christ with woman at the symbolic level, conjoined at the actual level by the act of love, reveals the *felix culpa*; furthermore, the poet has come to believe that, in spite of Catholic dogma and monastic strictures, Eros and the Christ-force are nonexclusive, and so the disparity between his human needs and the mode of his existence begins to dissolve.

The relationship with Rose ended in separation (she fell in love with another man, the poet has said in several interviews), but in 1965, nearly two years before the publication of *The Rose of Solitude*, Brother Antoninus met and fell in love with Susanna Rickson, to whom he wrote and dedicated "Tendril in the Mesh" (*Man-Fate*), the last poem he was to write as a monk. His love for her fuses mythologies: "Kore! Daughter of dawn! Persephone! Maiden of twilight!/ . . . In the node of your flesh you drip my flake of bestowal." Through her, furthermore, he witnesses the conjunction of Eros and Christ: "Dark God of Eros, Christ of the buried blood,/ Stone-channeled beast of ecstasy and fire. . . ." At the end of the first public reading of this poem on December 7, 1969, the poet formally left the Dominican Order.

MAN-FATE

A painful period of self-doubt followed for almost five years, chronicled in *Man-Fate*. In "The Gash," for instance, the poet says, "To covet and resist for years, and then/ To succumb, is a fearsome thing." To compensate for the vulnerability and alienation he feels, Everson sets out consciously to discover a *masculine* persona as powerful as that of Antoninus. While it is a slow birth back to what he calls, in "The Challenge," his "basic being," he makes a decision about the "garb" of his ethos and new identity in "The Scout." Reflecting upon the fact that his monk's habit is being worn by someone else in the monastery, he says that now "I assume the regalia of the Old West:/ Beads, buckskin and bearclaws. . . ." This new persona, he believes, will be his "sentinel," as he states in "The Black Hills," just as his habit had been, standing between him and the outside world of chance and abrasion. While this may be true, the primal and stereotypically male "regalia" also noticeably prevents the integration of his anima or feminine side into his consciousness, as the reader witnesses in *The Masks of Drought*.

THE MASKS OF DROUGHT

After being hired in 1971 as poet in residence at the University of California, Santa Cruz, Everson began to experience a lessening of his poetic output, writing only one or two poems a year for eight years. While this "drought" was certainly one he was fighting, *The Masks of Drought* was inspired by two other droughts, the literal California drought in 1977 and 1978 and the poet's sexual impotence. Throughout the volume the latter is not only objectified but intensified by the former, as in "Kingfisher Flat," in which the poet, lying beside his wife at night, thinks of the creek outside their home as objectifying the blocked flow of his own sexuality: "The starved stream/ Edges its way through dead stones,/ Noiseless in the night." Like the rattlesnake, in "Rattlesnake August," who when "Fate accosts—/ Licks his lip and stabs back," Everson stabs back at his age, at his physical condition, and at nature (his symbol of the feminine and her power to cause his impotence). In "Cutting the Firebreak," the poet says he is "one" with his "mad scythe" when he cuts down weeds; furthermore, the reason he and his phallic instrument are "mad" is understood when he tells the reader, in the last two lines of the poem, that the wild flowers he cuts down are, to his mind, "All the women in my life/ Sprawled in the weeds—drunk in death." In "Chainsaw," Everson goes into the woods with his saw, "the annihilate god" (and, like the earlier scythe, another phallic symbol), intending to cut down three alders, symbols of the feminine, with "woman-smooth bark,/ . . . naked skin."

Everson is attempting to impose himself upon nature, by enacting the old Western code of manhood that stressed participation insofar as it led to nature's *submission*, but what happens throws him into an acute awareness of his human condition and folly: the third tree bucks back, kicks the saw's chain against his leg, tears his pants, but misses his flesh entirely. Nevertheless, dazed by the near catastrophe, Everson imagines his leg's truncation, a "pitiful stump," for "Something is fin-

ished,/ Something cleanly done," and this imagined "absence" becomes distorted, transformed into a bitter reminder of the actual loss—his sexual virility. Gradually, however, he realizes the "folly" of the impulse that sent him to the woods in the first place: that is, his need to assert his maleness upon the femaleness of nature to prove his virility. He acknowledges his foolishness and begins to accept his human limitations.

Although he says, in "Spotfire," that—between the extremes of his own nature—"I have seen my heart's fate/ Shaped in the balance,/ And know what I am," the last poem he composed for *The Masks of Drought*, "Moongate," indicates that he has still not realized a "balance" between his masculine and feminine sides. After staying up late one night and reflecting upon all the losses in his life, Everson says that a "sudden yearn of unrealization" then "clutches" his heart, and this causes him to feel that "a dream awaits me, back in bed,/ And I turn to take it up." Significantly, in the dream he recounts in the poem he finds himself with Edwa, back in the time before the first traumatic loss and betrayal he suffered for loving a woman. Suddenly a fox, clearly meant to represent Everson's vocation and the pursuit of success therein, darts into the poet's focus, and *he* abandons Edwa for his pursuit of "the illusive one." As he runs "urgently" up river, he hears the steps of someone behind him; when he turns he sees a "strange woman" who "cannot see" what it is that Everson pursues, but nevertheless, he says, "What I see she follows." After seeing her, he returns to his chase until "dusk draws down" and he can no longer follow the fox; importantly, it is only *now*, when he can go no further, that he turns to face the anima image again: "And her eyes are shining, shining." Everson stated in an interview that he intended to write a sequel to this poem, and in the next poem he would have the "strange woman" move out in front of him while the fox falls behind. It is noteworthy that the fox in "Moongate" is male.

THE INTEGRAL YEARS

While Everson's pre-Catholic poetry was published in *The Residual Years* (1948) and the Catholic poetry he wrote as Brother Antoninus was published in *The Veritable Years*, the poetry written since his departure from the Dominican Order appeared in one volume titled *The Integral Years*. Smaller collections that are included in the trilogy's third volume have already been published: *Man-Fate, The Masks of Drought, Renegade Christmas,* and *Mexican Standoff*. Also included in *The Integral Years* are poems that have been published in limited editions: *In Medias Res* and "Skald" (1984), the first two cantos of an autobiographical epic titled *Dust Shall be the Serpent's Food: The Engendering Flood*.

Suffering for many years the increasingly debilitating effects of Parkinsonism, Everson's poems find their way onto the page much more slowly than they once did. Yet throughout *The Residual Years, The Veritable Years,* and the early movements of *The Integral Years,* the poet has ceaselessly affirmed and reaffirmed—by means of his own life and poetic witness—the human capacity for successful self-renewal and self-creation. Indeed, like most great artists, Everson has created more than courageous life-affirming assertions; he has created powerful and enduring testaments to the inexhaustible will of the human spirit to transcend mundane, gender-specific identity and realize the integrated, whole self androgynous.

Other major works

NONFICTION: *Friar Among Savages: Father Luis Cáncer,* 1958 (as Brother Antoninus); *Robinson Jeffers: Fragments of an Older Fury,* 1968; *Archetype West: The Pacific Coast as a Literary Region,* 1976; *Earth Poetry,* 1980; *Birth of a Poet,* 1982; *William Everson, on Writing the Waterbirds and Other Presentations: Collected Forewords and Afterwords, 1935-1981,* 1983; *The Excesses of God: Robinson Jeffers as a Religious Figure,* 1988; *Dust Shall Be the Serpent's Food: The Engendering Flood, 1990; Naked Heart: Talking on Poetry, Mysticism, and the Erotic,* 1992; *Take Hold upon the Future: Letters on Writers and Writing, 1938-1946,* 1994; *Prodigious Thrust,* 1996.

MISCELLANEOUS: *William Everson: The Light the Shadow Casts, Five Interviews with William Everson Plus Corresponding Poems,* 1996 (Clifton Ross, editor)

Bibliography

Bartlett, Lee, ed. *Benchmark and Blaze: The Emergence of William Everson.* Metuchen, N.J.: Scare-

crow Press, 1979. A collection of twenty-two critical appraisals of the poetry and printing of Everson-Antoninus, this work provides an excellent overview of the poet-printer's distinguished career and accomplishments. Presented here are appraisals by such writers as Robert Duncan, Ralph J. Mills, Jerome Mazzaro, William Stafford, Kenneth Rexroth, and Albert Gelpi.

_____. *William Everson.* Boise, Idaho: Boise State University Press, 1985. This brief monograph provides a useful introduction to the major phases of the poet's life, his movement from Everson to Antoninus and back to Everson. Strangely, however, Bartlett focuses more on Everson's accomplishments as a master printer than his achievements as a poet. Discussion of Everson's poems, in fact, is seldom present here; where present, it is little more than paraphrase.

_____. *William Everson: The Life of Brother Antoninus.* New York: New Directions, 1988. Although informative about Everson's relationship with Kenneth Rexroth in the early 1950's, as well as about Everson's place in the San Francisco Renaissance, Bartlett's study provides only cursory readings of Everson's poems and no discussion at all of the poet's second marriage to Mary Fabilli, the relationship that served as a catalyst for Everson's conversion to Catholicism. Contains an excellent bibliography.

Carpenter, David A. "William Everson: Peacemaker with Himself." *Concerning Poetry* 13, no. 1 (1982): 19-34. This study provides a useful analysis of the archetypal struggle apparent in Everson's life and poetry between the Dionysian and Apollonian impulses, that is, between the flesh and the spirit, and the poet's lifelong struggle between the two in his search for a lasting synthesis of them.

_____. *The Rages of Excess: The Life and Poetry of William Everson.* Bristol, Ind.: Wyndham Hall Press, 1987. A critical biography that is weighted with too many long passages from Everson's poems, this essentially Jungian study attempts to interpret the poet's complex psychology and life via close analysis of the poetic canon and vice versa. Noteworthy here are the close, detailed discussions of Everson's long poems, such as his *Chronicle of Division* and *Tendril in the Mesh*. Good bibliography.

Everson, William. *William Everson: The Light the Shadow Casts*. Edited and introduced by Clifton Ross. Berkeley, Calif.: New Earth Publications, 1996. Five interviews with Everson with corresponding poems. Offers invaluable insight into the life and work of the poet.

Houston, James D., et al. *The Death of a Poet: Santa Cruz Writers, Poets, and Friends Remember William Everson*. Austin, Tex.: W. Thomas Taylor, 1994. A collection of biographical essays about Everson originally published in the *Metro Santa Cruz* in 1994 following Everson's death.

David A. Carpenter;
bibliography updated by the editors

SIR RICHARD FANSHAWE

Born: Ware Park, Hertfordshire, England; June, 1608
Died: Madrid, Spain; June 16, 1666

PRINCIPAL POETRY

"Il pastor fido," "The Faithful Shepherd," with an Addition of Divers Other Poems, 1648 (translation of Giambattista Guarini's poem and original poetry)
Selected Parts of Horace, 1652 (translation)
The Lusiad, 1655 (translation of Luís de Camões's epic)
The Shorter Poems and Translations, 1964
The Poems and Translations of Sir Richard Fanshawe, 1997, 1999 (2 volumes; Peter Davidson, editor)

OTHER LITERARY FORMS

With the exception of one essay and English versions of two Spanish plays, Sir Richard Fanshawe's published writings are all poems: either original verse or translations from Latin, Italian, Spanish, and Portuguese. Both the essay and the plays are undistinguished. No collected edition of Fanshawe's works exists, but most of the poetry is available in modern texts. Geoffrey Bullough edited *The Lusiad* (1963), N. W. Bawcutt collected both printed and manuscript material in *The Shorter Poems and Translations* (1964), and J. H. Whitfield's *Il pastor fido* prints the original Italian and Fanshawe's English on facing pages. *The Cyclopedia of English Literature* (1847) reprints two poems found nowhere else.

Two extraliterary works throw considerable light on the man and his times: *The Memoirs of Anne, Lady Fanshawe,* written in 1676 and edited by John Loftis (1979), gives a fond wife's view of her husband's private and public life, *Original Letters and Negotiations of His Excellency Sir Richard Fanshaw,* published in two volumes (1724), records his years as ambassador to Spain.

ACHIEVEMENTS

Sir Richard Fanshawe's reputation as a poet is small. He wrote only a few poems in English; they demonstrate a good ear for sound and a good eye for images, but the canon is too small to be of major importance. Fanshawe put more effort into translations, which in the 1640's and 1650's expanded English literary horizons by introducing European classics and by prompting poetic experimentation. Besides translating Latin poets such as Horace and Vergil, Fanshawe rendered into English many poems and plays from the Italian, Spanish, and Portuguese. He translated authors (such as Luis de Góngora, Luis de Camões, and Giambattista Guarini) who, like himself, were courtiers, soldiers, and diplomats as well as poets. He preferred the genres that appealed to an aristocratic audience: the sonnet, the epic, pastoral verse drama, and plays of intrigue.

Translation, however, is a sandy foundation for literary fame. If one translates works that later lose international stature, the translator's fame declines as well. If one renders acknowledged classics, translators of the next generation will offer more "modern" versions. Fanshawe's translations suffered both fates. His well-done translations of Guarini's *Il pastor fido* (1590; *The Faithful Shepherd*) and Camões's *Os Lusíadas* (1572; *The Lusiads*) are little remarked because the originals are now scarcely read. Fanshawe did fine versions of Horace's odes and Vergil's *Aeneid* (c. 29-19 B.C.E.), but modern readers of these Roman poets can easily find equally adept translations in contemporary idiom. No wonder, then, that Fanshawe's name appears only in the most thorough literary histories and anthologies.

If Fanshawe lacks a popular reputation, he preserves one among period specialists. They acknowledge his importance in helping open English literature to foreign influence. They also point out that Fanshawe began a new emphasis in translating the spirit more than the literal sense of a work. Finally, they testify to the fluidity and grace of Fanshawe's verse, which maintains a measure of Elizabethan lyricism amid the bombast and brittleness of much interregnum literature.

BIOGRAPHY

Sir Richard Fanshawe would have made the perfect hero for a nineteenth century historical novel. His life was shaped by the events of the English Civil War (1640-1660). King Charles I's disputes with the Puritans over church ritual and with Parliament over taxation brought two decades of rebellion, a regicide, and a Commonwealth government under Oliver Cromwell. Fanshawe's social class and ideals ensured that he would remain faithful to the Royalist cause and that he would spare neither expense nor energy in defense of monarchy. The war years brought Fanshawe dramatic and romantic adventures, a courageous and ardent wife, and a series of important political posts. He was, in Alfred Harbage's phrase, "royal quixote and married lover."

Fanshawe was born in 1608, the son of Sir Henry Fanshawe, third Remembrancer to James I. At fifteen, Fanshawe entered Jesus College, Cambridge, where he excelled at classical languages. Three years later he went to the Inner Temple to study law but found it a less agreeable subject. Two early poems record his fidelity to the Muse of poetry and to aristocratic ideals. A tour of France and Spain in the early 1630's allowed Fanshawe to indulge his love of languages and to prepare for a diplomatic career. The tour was rewarded: From 1635 to 1638 he served as secretary to the English ambassador in Spain.

The eruption of civil war in 1640 brought Fanshawe into the royal army. Quartered at Oxford in 1643, he met Anne Harrison, seventeen years younger and the daughter of an impoverished knight. Fanshawe married her in 1644 and was appointed secretary of war to Prince Rupert. For the next two years the newlyweds followed the prince's court around England and to the Channel Islands.

When the Puritan capture of Charles led to a lull in the fighting, the Fanshawes settled in London. In 1648, Fanshawe brought out his translation of *Il pastor fido* and other poems. Soon thereafter, the imprisoned Charles asked Fanshawe to carry letters to the Queen in France. Back now on active service, Fanshawe became treasurer of the navy and recruited Royalist soldiers in Ireland. When Cromwell invaded Ireland after the execution of Charles, the Fanshawes barely escaped. Entering the service of Charles II, Fanshawe led an embassy to Spain to seek financial aid. In 1651, Fanshawe was captured at the Battle of Worcester and imprisoned at Whitehall. Two months later, Anne successfully petitioned for her husband's release on grounds of his ill health.

Sir Richard Fanshawe (© Michael Nicholson/Corbis)

Fanshawe's enforced leisure in prison and on parole allowed him to turn his attention to literature. In the next six years, he produced the rest of his major works: translations of Horace's odes, of Camões's epic, and of two Spanish plays; he also rendered John Fletcher's *The Faithful Shepherdess* into Latin. The death of Oliver Cromwell (1658) and the restoration of Charles II (1660), however, turned Fanshawe's energies to politics again. Knighted in 1660 and elected to Parliament in 1661, Fanshawe rapidly received a series of major appointments: ambassador to Portugal, 1662; privy councillor, 1663; and ambassador to Spain, 1664. Fanshawe served in Madrid for two years before being recalled after a controversial negotiation of a commercial treaty. While preparing to return, Fanshawe was stricken with a fever and died. Anne took him on a final European crossing, bringing his body back to Hertfordshire for burial.

Fanshawe's life is vividly recorded in Anne's memoirs. She obviously loved her husband dearly and admired his every action, from his reading poetry as he walked to his sacrificing of his personal fortune for the Royalist cause. Her book describes Fanshawe as a brave soldier, a worthy courtier, the "tendrest husband imaginable," and a reserved man who revealed "the thought of his heart" only to his wife. Together they had survived battle, imprisonment, exile, and shipwreck as the winds of war blew them around England and across Europe. Anne's devotion to her husband more than matched his loyalty to the Stuart kings. The Fanshawes remain one of the remarkable couples in English literary history.

ANALYSIS

Sir Richard Fanshawe's reputation rests almost entirely on his translations, but he did write some creditable original poems, published in 1648, including "An Ode upon Occasion of His Majesty's Proclamation in the Year 1630" (1630), "The Saint's Encouragement" (1643), and "The Royalist" (1646). These three poems' topicality almost consigns them to social history, though they are charming pieces, skillfully contrived. Two poems, one of advice for Prince Charles "Presented to his Highness, *in the West*, Ann. Dom. 1646" and "The Rose," are among his better adaptations—translations so free as to be arguably Fanshawe's own, although acknowledged as translations. In all these poems, one sees traits that make him a dedicated and successful translator rather than a memorable original poet. His success as translator can best be seen in *The Faithful Shepherd* and *The Lusiad*.

"AN ODE UPON OCCASION OF HIS MAJESTY'S PROCLAMATION IN THE YEAR 1630"

In "An Ode upon Occasion of His Majesty's Proclamation in the Year 1630," the collegiate Fanshawe responds to a 1630 edict in which Charles I urged gentlemen to mind their rural estates and stop migrating to an overcrowded London. A survey of European countries torn by wars leads to one central image: England is like that "blest isle" to which Jove had chained the dove of peace while he fought to take over the heavens. What follows paints a picture of England's gentlemen and beautiful ladies healthfully at home in their natural country environment. The poem, as John Buxton points out in *A Tradition of Poetry* (1967), is written in one of Fanshawe's peculiar stanzaic adaptations, the Sapphic. The classical Sapphic was a quantitative stanza consist-

ing of three eleven-syllable lines followed by one of five syllables. The Sapphic tended to stay off balance, with a concentration of long syllables near the center of the lines and the short final line heightening the impression of asymmetry. The effect resembles sprung rhythm. Fanshawe adapts Sappho by using accentual rhythm and by shortening and regularizing the lines; three tetrameters precede a dimeter. In "An Ode upon Occasion of His Majesty's Proclamation in the Year 1630," the tetrameters of the early stanzas are as predictably regular as the wars that plagued Europe. Only the dimeters preserve the effect of syncopated rhythm. When, however, he comes to the four stanzas imaging England as Jove's blest isle, he "springs" the rhythm so that the most energetic and original rhythms of the poem coincide with its celebration of England's dynamic peacefulness. As a translator, Fanshawe habitually adapted stanzaic patterns in this way, not duplicating the original but finding an appropriate English analogue.

Young Fanshawe's metrical insights proved to be more acute, however, than his political ones. Within the decade, his country's "White Peace" had changed to war. Yet the national pride evident in his support for Charles's proclamation remains as a crucial factor in two other original poems, "The Saint's Encouragement" and "The Royalist." Although both evidence the Cavalier spirit of Royalists whose king had not yet been defeated, the earlier song has a lighter tone than the latter.

"THE SAINT'S ENCOURAGEMENT"

In "The Saint's Encouragement," written early in the war, Fanshawe's speaker is a Puritan "saint" addressing his fellow rebels and urging them to fight on. The poem's nine stanzas undercut his encouraging words in heavy-handed ways. Fanshawe's Puritan promises to maintain liberty by "prisonments and plunders," brags of victories that were historical defeats, and indirectly indicates that Puritan fears are well-founded. Fanshawe thus derides the motives the Puritans used to justify the war, but the poem shows little thematic growth. What makes it memorable are two technical devices—its meter and its refrain. Ostensibly, each eight-line stanza consists of two ballad stanzas butted together. The effect of the doubling is to rush one through alternating three- and four-stress lines at a pace no balladeer could maintain. What Fanshawe has done is re-create the helter-skelter tempo of the medieval poulter's measure, a meter in which lines of twelve and fourteen syllables alternate in couplets. The singsong clumsiness of poulter's measure had been mocked from Geoffrey Chaucer's Sir Topas on, and thus the poem's very meter mocks the Puritan cause. The refrain, "the clean contrary way," enhances the fun. The rebels successively "fight for the king," frighten cavaliers, "stand for peace and truth," and get carried to heaven, "the clean contrary way."

"THE ROYALIST"

"The Saint's Encouragement" employs techniques of ridicule that only a cavalier sure of impending victory would dare use. By 1646, however, when Fanshawe wrote "The Royalist," the situation had changed. Four years of civil war had proven the parliamentary armies a real danger to Charles, now "distressed" and "beggared." Fanshawe's drinking song captures the tension with which Charles's loyalists lived. Its four eight-line stanzas eschew the metrical jokes of the earlier war poem; iambic tetrameter lines rhyme alternately. Its singer concentrates his energy fighting off grief with bowls of potent sack: "A sorrow dares not show its face/ When we are ships and sack's the sea." The ship image need not be apt, only feisty. "Pox on this grief, hang wealth, let's sing," the speaker continues. For more than half the poem such rebellious outbursts alternate with sentimental reminders that Royalists share the poverty of their king. Gradually, the singer's rebelliousness settles into the wistful, fantastic cast of alcoholic euphoria.

Although Fanshawe's Royalist found reality hard to accept in 1646, the poet profited from war's challenges. "An Ode upon Occasion of His Majesty's Proclamation in the Year 1630" succeeds because it concentrates a naïve patriotism in one exquisite image; "The Saint's Encouragement" succeeds because it cleverly expresses an oversimple political faith. "The Royalist," however, succeeds precisely because it does not simplify the tensions which Charles I's followers endured.

"PRESENTED TO HIS HIGHNESS" AND "THE ROSE"

In these original poems, Fanshawe relies on popular thinking for themes and images but creates his own pattern and situation. In poems such as "Presented to His Highness" and "The Rose," this reliance borders on translation. In "Presented to His Highness," Fanshawe notes the source "out of which this is taken," Robert Buchanan's poem honoring James I, then virtually translates the Latin, adapting whatever needs changing to fit England's current civil "self-hurt." The poem is the sort of advice disguised as praise that modern psychologists call "positive reinforcement" and that Renaissance handbooks called courtesy—tactful encouragement that a Royalist owed his prince.

"The Rose" differs from the poems previously discussed in treating love instead of politics. Its two versions so freely adapt such a conventional theme that editors and critics variously list it as original, translated from Guarini, or translated from Don Luis de Góngora y Argote. Fanshawe takes Góngora's sonnet "Vana Rose" and embroiders it with strange bright images from Guarini and other Renaissance writers. "Blushing," "virgin," "wardrobe," and "perfume" image the rose as a lovely young girl to whom the poem teaches a sober lesson: "Thou'rt wondrous frolic being to die so soon." "The Rose" shares the strengths of Fanshawe's original poems: metric sensitivity, colorful diction, a graceful central image. Yet in its short eighteen lines (or fourteen lines in the alternate version), Fanshawe embeds images that work oddly with the central one. "Some clown's course lungs" can "poison thy sweet flower" by tearing it with a "careless plough." The image of ploughing as impregnating underlies the conceit, but the mixed metaphor gets even more eccentric when Fanshawe identifies those who would pluck the rose as "Herods." Most of these images do not occur in Góngora's stark sonnet. Whether such changes make the poem luxuriant translation or multilevel allegory is arguable. Fanshawe's translations of love themes do tend to heighten the sensual elements.

GUARINI'S THE FAITHFUL SHEPHERD

In original poems and adaptations, Fanshawe was not a strongly original thinker. He was, however, a polished metrist with an eye for an image and an ear for the distinctive music of each language—qualities ideal in a translator. He had a personal affinity for Horace's genial wit and his Vergil sparkles with sensuous detail, but his translations of Guarini's pastoral and Camões's epic are his most impressive works, the first for grace and melody, the second for boldness. Guarini and Camões provided thoughts, images, sounds, and structures which

Fanshawe transposed into English, preserving the very different characters of the original yet heightening elements important to his countrymen.

Guarini's *The Faithful Shepherd* offered his sophisticated Italian audience the excitement of a good soap opera and the psychological comforts of an analyst's couch—both in six thousand lines of melodious verse. It is fine closet drama, designed not for the stage but for leisurely reflection. Delicate characters who prize each other more than life face separation, jealousy, the decrees of an apparently malignant deity, and the machinations of more worldly characters, while the audience shares their emotional stretchings and remains secure that all will come out right. What occupies Guarini most is the array of psychological questions rising out of the situations. These range from the effectiveness of cosmetics to the meaning of dreams, from the pleasures of the hunt to the purpose behind obscure divine commands. The lengthy set speeches of closet drama allow him to present different perspectives on such questions, especially those concerning love. These speculations run through his pale, pastel landscape in bright little spills and waterfalls of poetry.

For "royal quixote and married lover" such poetry's appeal must be immediate. Fanshawe's dedication claims that *The Faithful Shepherd* relates to the exiled Prince Charles's situation. To Royalists, dialogues such as those of old Montano and Titiro, who counsel each other to preserve faith in impossible dreams, would be as memorable as subtle insights into the psychology of romantic love.

To capture the spirit of Guarini's melodious language, Fanshawe used five devices. He changed meter, added a rhyme scheme, condensed, modernized some references, and transposed decorative figures much as one might rearrange knickknacks on a shelf. Geoffrey Bullough, in "Sir Richard Fanshawe and Guarini," adds that Fanshawe tended to replace abstractions with concrete images. This tendency was perhaps Fanshawe's personal quirk, perhaps his judgment that Guarini's pastels needed more color for English tastes. Each of the other devices, however, brought the English closer to the spirit of the Italian than duplication could have done. As a translator, Fanshawe passed beyond competence into genius.

His choice of rhyme and meter, for example, minimizes differences between the two languages. An inflected language such as Italian is so naturally rich in rhymes that Guarini could achieve small ripples of rhyme without establishing a formal scheme. Since uninflected English is relatively rhyme-poor, Fanshawe accentuates what rhymes it has by ending lines with them. To achieve the sense of a rush of words, Guarini avoided a set metrical pattern and limited end-stops. Fanshawe chose to discipline English's relatively rougher sounds by using a definite meter: the iambic pentameter line that his audience's ear expected in high drama. He managed the effect of a rush of words, however, by varying the placement of his pauses:

> for he
> Who is still wrangling with his Destinie
> And his malignant fortune, becomes hoarse,
> And loses both his singing and discourse.

Fanshawe further enhances the effect of a rush of song by freely moving to passages of rhymed octometer or even shorter lines.

His other adaptations of Guarini evidence a similar care for the spirit of the original. An inflected language inevitably translates into more words in an uninflected one. Judicious cutting, especially of repetitious rhetorical figures, keeps Fanshawe's *The Faithful Shepherd* close to the original's length. Fanshawe was ready to abandon those figures which had gone out of fashion. Though his contemporaries admired a plainer, less ornamented style than some flamboyant predecessors had, to abandon ornament altogether would have suited neither Fanshawe, Guarini, nor their audiences. In fact, one is struck by Fanshawe's ability to reproduce the Italian poet's figure in passages of stichomythia and in the Echo passage, which relies upon puns. At times, Fanshawe moves rather than abandons a rhetorical device; he may cut a catalog from one of Mirtillo's set speeches, then insert a similar catalog into his next speech. The result is a beautifully naturalized piece of poetry: rich but not cloying, smooth and melodious, tighter and more concrete than the original but wide enough for the psychological and philosophical musings of its charming hero and heroine or of its mild villain and villainess. Fanshawe's verse is like a muted verbal watercolor rather than an oil on canvas.

CAMÕES'S THE LUSIADS

When one compares *The Faithful Shepherd* with Fanshawe's translation of *The Lusiads*, one sees the justice of Voltaire's assertion that the Portuguese epic comes from Fanshawe's hand "bold, harsh, and unpoetical." The difference, however, may not be a sign of carelessness in the translator but rather of the fineness of his ear. In adapting Camões, Fanshawe used an approach different from that which he took with Guarini.

The Portuguese epic describes Vasco da Gama's epochal voyage around the Cape of Good Hope and on to Calicut (modern Calcutta), India. En route, da Gama stops at various ports and details much of the history of brave and adventurous Portugal, especially the wars by which it drove the Moors from Iberia. *The Lusiads* is a thoroughly masculine epic, a nine-thousand-line exercise in the passionate patriotism of a small but courageous country. Da Gama possesses all the virtues of a military leader and some of a diplomat's tact—traits necessary for peacefully expanding trade and coexisting more or less respectfully with alien cultures. Camões's narrative, however, unlike Guarini's pastoral, has little room for reflectiveness. What there is instead, Camões conveys in three ways. First, he uses a machinery of pagan gods (apparently under the rule of the Christian God) who fight for or against da Gama's success. Yet Venus and Bacchus serve more often to tie *The Lusiads* to classical tradition than to justify God's ways to man. Second, Camões sometimes juxtaposes episodes whose political-science lessons are contradictory—leaving the reader to wrestle with implicit ambiguity. Third, Camões himself steps into the narrative to reflect upon the significance of a political maneuver, to hold Portugal up to other nations as an example, and to complain about bad government—or pray for better. More frequent than poetic musings, however, are judgments; instead of imagination's pale washes, the reader sees logic's black-and-white and bright primary colors. These qualities Fanshawe chooses to heighten in his translation.

Thus, he retains the *ottava rima* of the original; its natural split into sestet and couplet are ideally suited for describing a situation or painting a picture, then making a brief transition to another situation or picture. Fanshawe does not cut down the pale flowers of rhetoric; rather, he creates newer, more exotic ones. He does not explain historical background but instead leaves the non-Portuguese reader struggling—at times, drowning—in da Gama's ocean, without the explanatory rafts that would keep him afloat during certain obscure episodes. Fanshawe is often metrically rough and grammatically awkward, simply omitting the small words which English substitutes for inflections.

Claiming in his dedication that history teaches, Fanshawe seems to have expended considerable energy on Camões's political commentaries. Otherwise, his best passages are those describing martial splendor, color, and pageantry, lamenting the fate of poets, predicting the glory of a small nation's future, or judging the rightness of causes. Fanshawe also devotes much attention to a purely physical—although married—sensuality with which Venus, in Canto IX, rewards patience, obedience, and uncommon bravery.

Fanshawe's poems, original or translated, are rarely read today. His political science has become obsolete, and his Royalism looks naïve in the twentieth century. Yet his loyalty, his personal love of color, his attention to sound and image—and the sweet humility that enables him to capture spirits as diverse as Camões and Guarini—remain as models for minor poets and major translators of any day.

Robert M. Otten

OTHER MAJOR WORKS

TRANSLATIONS: *Fida pastora*, 1658 (of John Fletcher's play *The Faithful Shepherdess*); *Querer por solo querer, To Love Only for Love Sake*, 1670 (of Antonio de Mendoza's play); *Fiestas de Aranjuez*, 1671.

NONFICTION: *Original Letters and Negotiations of His Excellency Sir Richard Fanshaw*, 1724 (2 volumes).

BIBLIOGRAPHY

Cordner, Michael. "Dryden's 'Astraea Redux' and Fanshawe's 'Ode.'" *Notes and Queries* 31 (September, 1984): 341-342. An examination of Fanshawe's "An Ode upon Occasion of His Majesty's Proclamation in the Year 1630." Cordner studies this work as it relates to Fanshawe's Royalist politics, the political situation in seventeenth century England and, in particular, Oliver Cromwell's achievements and England's political relations to France. Of interest to the Fanshawe scholar only.

Davidson, P. R. K., and A. K. Jones. "New Light on Marvell's 'The Unfortunate Lover'?" *Notes and Queries* 32 (June, 1985): 170-172. A discussion of a newly discovered collection of Fanshawe's miscellaneous letters, papers, and literary notes probably originally compiled in Madrid in the 1660's. Among the findings examined are verses presumed to be from his later "Latin Poems" and several epigrams. The "Prophetic Epigram" of 1648 is presented in its original Latin and translated. This work is of interest to the Fanshawe scholar only.

Fanshawe, Anne, and Anne Halkett. *The Memoirs of Lady Anne Halkett and Lady Ann Fanshawe*. Edited by John Loftis. New York: Oxford University Press, 1980. Lady Anne Fanshawe's memoirs offer exceptional insights into the life and work of her husband. Sir Richard's diplomatic duties to the court of James I and James II are well chronicled as is the couple's life during Sir Richard's tenure as England's ambassador to Spain and Portugal. Loftis includes comprehensive chronologies, annotated bibliographies, and an index.

Graham, Judith Hanson. "Sir Richard Fanshawe's Works as Public Poetry." *Dissertation Abstracts International* 46 (July, 1985): 157A. This is the first work to explore the relationship between Fanshawe's literature and his fierce Royalist politics. Graham carefully examines the content, form, and style of Fanshawe's poetry and convincingly argues that Fanshawe intended to affect the politics of the age through his poetry. Graham offers a new and valid approach to understanding Fanshawe.

Martindale, Charles. "Unlocking the Word-Hoard: In Praise of Metaphrase." *Comparative Criticism: A Yearbook* 6 (1984): 47-72. This dense, complex work applies various translation theories to the literary forms utilized by Fanshawe and such contemporaries as John Milton and John Dryden in their translations of classical literature. Martindale's study is best appreciated by the advanced Fanshawe scholar.

Elizabeth Spalding Otten;
bibliography updated by the editors

KENNETH FEARING

Born: Oak Park, Illinois; July 28, 1902
Died: New York, New York; June 26, 1961

PRINCIPAL POETRY

Angel Arms, 1929
Poems, 1935
Dead Reckoning: A Book of Poetry, 1938
Collected Poems, 1940
Afternoon of a Pawnbroker and Other Poems, 1943
Stranger at Coney Island and Other Poems, 1948
New and Selected Poems, 1956
Complete Poems, 1993

OTHER LITERARY FORMS

Kenneth Fearing had a relatively successful career as a writer of mystery and detective fiction, combining an ability to fashion a complex plot that concentrated on a character trapped within the labyrinth of a large city or organization with a strong sense of the psychology of a relatively innocent man driven to commit murder. His novels are set in the streets of Manhattan and reflect the desperation of the Depression and the paranoia of the Cold War. Among his most enduring works are *The Hospital* (1939), which covers an incident from multiple points of view, *Dagger of the Mind* (1941), which examines the motives of an artist/killer from within the mind of the protagonist, and his most powerful book, *The Big Clock* (1946), which follows a man who is a witness to a crime for which he is being framed. The exceptional narrative tension of *The Big Clock* and the depth of revelation that makes the narrator especially compelling became the essential elements of the film version directed by John Farrow in 1948 and the remake called *No Way Out* (1987), which starred Kevin Costner.

ACHIEVEMENTS

During the Depression, Kenneth Fearing was recognized as a major American writer, but although he has been almost completely ignored by scholars since the 1950's and is largely unknown even to literate Americans, his poetry has scarcely been dated by the passage of time. His concern for the failure of official versions of anything to confront reality, his deep skepticism about socially sanctioned standards of "success," his recognition that urban life could provide extraordinary energy as well as desperate loneliness, and his development of a laconic, terse voice that joined common American speech with an arch tone derived from centuries-old practices of ironic styles permitted him to produce a kind of poetry that is still engaging and relevant. He was an innovative artist whose work was admired by Ezra Pound, who published him in the magazine *Exiles* in the mid-1920's. Fearing anticipated some of the rhythmic methods and structural devices of poets such as Allen Ginsberg and Robert Creeley, while extending Carl Sandburg's feeling for the proletariat into the decades when it became apparent that Sandburg's optimism was no longer justified. In his examinations of psychic survival in a world where absurdity was overcoming reality, Fearing was a pioneer whose initial reports are an accurate and chilling rendering of the twentieth century city as a landscape of desolation.

BIOGRAPHY

Kenneth Fearing was an approximate contemporary of Ernest Hemingway, born in 1902 in the modestly prosperous suburb of Oak Park, Illinois, where Hemingway spent his childhood, and dying just days before Hemingway's suicide in 1961. Unlike Hemingway, however, Fearing was almost exclusively a man of the city. His public schooling and matriculation at the University of Wisconsin were designed to prepare him for a professional life similar to that of his father, who was a successful attorney in Chicago. Even at the University of Wisconsin, however, Fearing displayed aspects of the artistic temperament which mingled with his ability to handle the routines of an advertising copywriter and editor for various newspapers and magazines. His friend the poet Carl Rakosi remembers him there with a "great shock of uncut, unkempt hair . . . a low gravelly voice like Humphrey Bogart . . . always a heavy drinker who did his writing at night [and] slept all morning, skipping classes." A man on the fringe of his time, he was the focus of "admirers basking in his bohemian boldness." After completing his bachelor's degree in 1924, he worked briefly as an apprentice journalist in Chicago before moving to New York, where he settled in the celebrated

artistic quarter of Greenwich Village in lower Manhattan.

Fearing spent most of the 1920's continuing his campus unconventionality, holding dead-end jobs as a salesman and clerk while gradually connecting with political and aesthetic movements in the city's subculture. In 1927, he began a career as a writer for public relations firms while working as a freelance journalist. Through the 1930's, he contributed stories to pulp magazines and wrote editorials for several newspapers while writing poetry steadily. His first collection of poems, *Angel Arms*, was published in 1929, and Fearing completed two other books of poems during the decade of the Depression. During this time, he was awarded a fellowship in creative writing by the Guggenheim Foundation and had begun to attend writers' conferences and give readings, but his success as a poet—his collected poems were published by New Directions in 1940—did not deter him from a venture into fiction in 1939 with *The Hospital*, a novel whose multinarrative scheme was typical of his experimental approach to problems of structure. The almost immediate commercial success of this work enabled Fearing to turn his attention to fiction as the center of his writing life, but although he worked steadily through the 1940's and 1950's in this mode, he also produced poems continuously until the mid-1950's. Yet, as critic M. L. Rosenthal recalled, Fearing was already "neglected in the postwar repressive backwash well underway in the late forties."

Fearing's most successful novel, *The Big Clock*, was the source of a fine film in 1948, but after *Loneliest Girl in the World* (1951), his work was not particularly successful either critically or commercially. By the time he died of cancer in 1961, he had almost completely vanished from view as a writer. A small revival of interest in his writing began in the decade of the 1990's, but his poetry is almost entirely absent from most standard anthologies, he is ignored by the academy, and critical interest remains at a very low level.

ANALYSIS

In the rather unlikely but not inconceivable event that the detective-protagonists of Dashiell Hammett (notably Sam Spade) and Raymond Chandler (particularly Philip Marlowe) had been impelled to express their thoughts and reactions in poetic form, the result might well have resembled the work of Kenneth Fearing. Like them, he lived close to the dark underside of society—a loner who had been around, knew what unpleasant activities even well-meaning people were capable of, and instinctively sympathized with the bottom dogs who always seemed to draw a club when they needed a spade for a flush. He shared their instinctive desire to try to make sense of a world that seemed chaotic and dangerous, where decent people struggled hopelessly and ruthless, brutal ones often thrived, and he knew that his poetry—like their efforts to set some small thing right—was unlikely to accomplish much. Nevertheless, in spite of the semicynical tone of his work, he avoided a slide into nihilism by the continued effort of the work itself. Spade and Marlowe are fictional detectives who often think like poets. Fearing was a poet with the sensibility of the hard-boiled private eye, and his language—sometimes coarse, sometimes literary, usually sardonic, laconic, or even mordant—is a reflection of the *film noir* world he took as his subject: a world where sunlight was notably absent, dark shadows threatened to engulf everyone, claustrophobia was nearly constant, and the night seemed endless.

ANGEL ARMS

In the early stages of his career, Fearing resembled his Midwestern compatriot Carl Sandburg, but while Sandburg's affirmative *The People, Yes* (1936) expressed a belief that the common man would be triumphant, even in his first poems Fearing was more cautious, suggesting that the best one could hope for would be "the people . . . maybe." His first subjects were people from the working class—"nifties, yeggs, and thirsties," as he put it in the street slang of the 1930's—and his close identification with their situations enabled him to capture their conditions of existence without condescension. In *Angel Arms*, his first book, the initial poem, called "St. Agnes' Eve," is a reduction of John Keats which depicts a man, awakened by gunfire at night, who gets out of bed "to scratch his stomach and shiver on the cold floor." Other poems depict a homeless woman, Minnie Spohr, rummaging "among the buckets at midnight"; a group of friends, "Andy and Jerry and Joe," drifting through the city, directionless, who "didn't know what we wanted and there was nothing to say"; a

woman of the street seen in desperate dignity, "Hilda in white/ Hilda sad./ Hilda forgiving the lover who martyr'd her"; and Blake and his office coworkers, whose limited possibilities have not prevented them from feeling the excitement of life in the high-energy zone of the city:

> They liked to feel the city, away below them, stretch out
> and breathe.
> They liked the Metropolitan's red eye, and Broadway.
> They liked to hear liners on the river baying at the sky.
> They liked it all.

"THE DRINKERS" AND "AMERICAN RHAPSODY (2)"

Fearing's most effective poem in this series is "The Drinkers," a precursor of William Carlos Williams's *Pictures from Brueghel* (1962), in which men in "Gonzetti's basement on MacDougal," a Greenwich Village dive, are likened to figures in a painting by Franz Hals, *Flemish Drinkers or Burghers of Antwerp*. Fearing's description is simple, straightforward, and direct, the details evoking the ethos of alienation that is one of his central subjects: "Four men drinking gin, three of them drunk. Outside is the street that sleeps and screams."

Although he never really lost his sympathy for people down and out in an "unreal city," Fearing's focus shifted from his early portraits of what was then considered "the proletariat" to poems that were designed as satirical comments on the false promises of consumerist society—promises that were close to outright lies in the midst of the Depression. He made the logical assumption that if most people were fundamentally decent, then some outside agency must be responsible for the massive neurosis he detected—a conclusion that was consistent with the political position of many left-wing artists during the 1930's. Fearing remained totally independent during his life and had as much scorn for Communist organizations as for any other, but his poems caught the contradictions in the American economic system with devastating effect. In "American Rhapsody (2)" from *Poems*, Fearing describes a man arranging a rendezvous in which the couple might "pretend, even alone, we believe the things we say," and then turns a date into a social tableau, connecting the rot in the world around them to the couple's relationship:

You be the mother and go out and beg for food; I'll be a merchant, the man you approach, a devoted husband, famous as a host; the merchant can be a jobless clerk who sleeps on subway platforms then lies dead in potter's field; the clerk can be a priest, human, kindly, one who enjoys a joke; the priest can be a lady in jail for prostitution and the lady can be a banker who has his troubles too.

MEANING AMID SOCIAL FAILURE

In "Portrait (2)" from the characteristically named collection *Dead Reckoning*, Fearing compiles a litany of names—officious-sounding law firms, medical authorities, and well-known products—to form a hollow facade covering "nothing," a word he repeats three times at the core of the portrait. The emptiness of useless accomplishment is carried further in the first poem from "The Agency," a section in the *Collected Poems*. In "Agent No. 174 Resigns," the "agent" is a symbol for a citizen who, like Herman Melville's Bartleby, has decided to stop cooperating with "the agency," which is a figure for the institutions of organized society. This idea is explored further in the obviously named "Portrait of a Cog" and in "Yes, the Agency Can Handle That," in which Fearing suggests that some cosmic agency has been presented as a fix for everything, but that in reality, all the essential human needs are unmet. The poem concludes with the mordant, undermining irony that Fearing often employs: "And there is no mortal ill that cannot be cured by a little money, or lots of love, or by a friendly smile; no."

It was not much of an extension for Fearing to carry the implications of social failure into a stance that paralleled the position being developed by existentialist thinkers in Europe just prior to and immediately after World War II. The pyramid of duplicity that he develops in poems such as "Dear Beatrice Fairfax:" which concludes, "It takes a neat, smart, fast, good, sweet doublecross/ To doublecross the gentleman who doublecrossed the gentleman who doublecrossed/ Your doublecrossing, doublecrossing, doublecross friend" ultimately drains every action of meaning. Thus he tends to generalize, as in "Beware" (from *Afternoon of a Pawnbroker and Other Poems*), "Damn near anything leads to trouble,/ Someone is always, always stepping out of line." With this increasingly bleak outlook, Fearing was on the verge of the absurdist predicament that postulates nihilism or suicide as the only possible course in a world where nothing has any significance. His solution, in his work, was to celebrate the exhilarating, impersonal energy of the city as an almost living entity, fascinating to experience and dangerously exciting to try to master. The early poem "They Liked It" conveys this feeling, as does "Invitation," with its defiant proclamations of intent beginning, "We will make love, when the hospitals are quiet and the blue police car stops to unload prisoners," and concluding, "We will be urged by the hunger of the live. . . . We will be aroused, we will make love, we will dream, we will travel through endless spaces, and we will smile across the room." Fearing adopted the existentialist idea that even in a meaningless universe, the attempt to create meaning is ultimately meaningful. For him, this meant that the *way* of saying something could be a method for making the statement valid or viable, and his work both echoed some of the innovative styles of his contemporaries and anticipated the poetics of writers in the second half of the twentieth century.

One can see the modernist dictum postulated by Ezra Pound, "Make it new," operating in poems such as "Jack Knuckles Falters," which uses quotes from a condemned man as recorded in a tabloid in the manner of John Dos Passos; in abrupt parenthetical insertions skewing the rhythms in "Jake" in the style of E. E. Cummings, as well as in a use of expostulations and nonsense expressions in "Dirge" reminiscent of Cummings ("And wow he died as wow he lived,/ Going whop to the office and blooie home to sleep and biff got married and bam had children and oof got fired,/ Zowie did he live and zowie did he die"). A kind of surrealist imagery more typical in painting or European poetry occurs in "Nocturne" with lines such as "giant pillars, filled with spiral stairs, upholding towers of sculptured night/ Where pure ether tides unroll in corridors that have no end and rise in mist." While this type of experimental use of language is not frequent in Fearing, it is part of a spectrum of possibility that he used to establish meaning through the creative use of language. Similarly, although Fearing rarely wrote like Dylan Thomas, the poem "Denouement" uses direct address ("Sky, be blue, and more than blue; wind, be flesh and blood; flesh and blood be deathless") and nouns as verbs in rhythms that anticipate some of Thomas's work. Established forms such as the dramatic monologue are given a contemporary flavor in "Readings, Forecasts, Personal Guidance" and "Afternoon of a Pawnbroker." In his more original work with form, Fearing used a long line in a kind of bridge between Walt Whitman and Allen Ginsberg, and he anticipated Ginsberg's use of repetition in "Howl" with poems such as "Dance of the Mirrors," which uses "You" as a basic unit for variation and return, and "If Money," which manipulates why, what, where, and who in a fairly intricate scheme. Even the tight texture and elliptic syntax of Robert Creeley is forecast by "Flophouse":

> Out of the frailest texture, somehow, and by some means
>   from
> the shabbiest odds and ends,
> If that is all there is;
> In some way, of even the shaken will,
> If, now, there is nothing else left,
> Now and here in the pulse and breath.

STRANGER AT CONEY ISLAND

The combination of Fearing's range of modernist techniques combined with the dry vernacular of the hip city dweller on the rough edges of life evokes an era without containing the poet entirely within that era. Toward the latter part of his life, Fearing began to move beyond what Kenneth Rexroth called the belief that "Western Civilization was already dead on its feet, a walking corpse bled of all value." Without actually suggesting how it might come to pass, Fearing envisioned a transcendent passage to another mode of existence. As early as "Debris" he mused on "this life," which he called "insane but true," but offered an image of serenity and renewal: "While mist rises from the cool valleys,/ And somewhere in fresh green hills there is the singing of a bird." Or in "Requiem" (1938) he could foresee a future "day like this, with motors streaming through the fresh parks, the streets alive with casual people,/ And everywhere, on all of it, the brightness of the sun." His last book, *Stranger at Coney Island and Other Poems*, was described by Jerome Rothenberg as a poetic sequence in which Fearing's concern for vision and magic led to "an almost continuous play on the abnormal (haunted) nature of the 'real.'" Such poems as "Lanista," "Elegy,"

"Museum," and "This Day" from that collection project a kind of reflective confidence that the current state of social disorder could be replaced by some new and more affirmative way of living in which people might be seen "confidently waiting for the sun that will surely rise," as in the close of "Museum."

The sardonic cynic's tone that Fearing perfected was an authentic expression of his feelings of disgust with many facets of American society, but his initial identification with what Rexroth calls "the impoverished stratum of the underworld" never subsided. An accomplished literary professional and a heartland populist as well, Fearing produced poetry that was essentially unencumbered by figures of decoration that submerge a voice in a period and drain it of authority through excessive concern with the temporarily fashionable. Fearing's voice remains an effective instrument for rendering the qualities of life in the twentieth century. As M. L. Rosenthal perceptively describes him, he was "boisterously witty, alcoholic and mordant in his dead-accurate Flaubertian hostility to cruelty and cant."

OTHER MAJOR WORKS

LONG FICTION: *The Hospital*, 1939; *Dagger of the Mind*, 1941 (also known as *Cry Killer!*); *Clark Gifford's Body*, 1942; *The Big Clock*, 1946; *John Barry*, 1947 (in collaboration with Donald Friede and Henry Bedford-Jones, collectively as Donald F. Bedford); *Loneliest Girl in the World*, 1951 (also known as *The Sound of Murder*); *The Generous Heart*, 1954; *The Crozart Story*, 1960.

BIBLIOGRAPHY

Barnard, Rita. *The Great Depression and the Culture of Abundance: Kenneth Fearing, Nathanael West, and Mass Culture in the 1930's*. New York: Cambridge University Press, 1995. The author analyzes the political and social views of Fearing and West and relates them to the history of American literature and popular culture. Includes bibliographical references and index.

Burke, Kenneth. "Two Kinds of Against." *The New Republic* 82 (June 26, 1935): 198-199. A theoretical analysis of Fearing's poetry, comparing it to that of Whitman and Cummings in particular. Good on

Fearing's main themes and revealing in terms of his social interests.

Dahlberg, Edward. Introduction to *Poems*, by Kenneth Fearing. New York: Dynamo Press, 1935. Dahlberg is one of the most eccentrically interesting critics of American literature, and his singular style is perfectly suited to examining Fearing's own peculiarities. This is a good overview of Fearing's work to that time, a sympathetic response to the poet's goals that is still timely.

Deutsch, Babette. "Flooded with the Immediate Age." *The Nation* 149 (August 19, 1939): 201-202. An essay that contends that Fearing is an ideal spokesman for his age. Deutsch considers his poetry in technical terms, concentrating on tone and rhythm in particular.

Dupee, F. W. "Sinister Banalities." *The New Republic* 103 (October 28, 1940): 597. An essay that examines Fearing as a satirist, claiming that the poet is a representative of the "Left" and showing how he uses some of the techniques T. S. Eliot introduced in *The Waste Land* (1922).

Jerome, Judson. "Ten Poets: Rare to Overdone." *The Antioch Review* 17 (March, 1957): 135-144. A balanced evaluation that identifies some of Fearing's stylistic limitations while indicating an appreciation for his development of a poetic persona in his work.

Rosenthal, David. "The Collected Poems of Kenneth Fearing." *Village Voice Literary Supplement* 53 (March, 1987): 4. One of the few examples of a late twentieth century response to Fearing's writing, this is an essay that might augur and encourage a revival of interest in Fearing's work through its shrewd evaluation of the elements of modernism that Fearing employed.

Rosenthal, M. L. "Don Kenneth and the Racket." *The Nation* 184 (January 19, 1957): 64-65. From one of the best critics to consider Fearing's poetry, this essay is an extension of the material Rosenthal developed in his book on American poets of the Depression. Very good on Fearing's use of comic modes, his creation of an individual voice, and his dissection of the American social system.

Leon Lewis;
bibliography updated by the editors

JAMES FENTON

Born: Lincoln, England; April 25, 1949

PRINCIPAL POETRY

Our Western Furniture, 1968
Put Thou Thy Tears into My Bottle, 1969
Terminal Moraine, 1972
Vacant Possession: Poems, 1978
A German Requiem, 1980
The Memory of War: Poems, 1968-1982, 1982
Children in Exile, 1983
Out of Danger, 1993

OTHER LITERARY FORMS

James Fenton is almost as well known as a journalist as he is as a poet. He began work in 1970 as a freelance writer, and in 1971 he joined the British weekly journal *New Statesman*. He went to Vietnam and Cambodia in 1973, and his poetic account of the turmoil was published in *The Memory of War: Poems, 1968-1982* and in prose in *All the Wrong Places: Adrift in the Politics of Asia* (1988). In 1983 he published *You Were Marvelous*, an account of his life as a journalist in Germany and a theatrical critic in London. He continued to be a contributor to the press, discussing literary subjects and sometimes political matters. His collection of essays, *The Snap Revolution*, appeared in 1986, and *The Strength of Poetry*, his lectures while professor of poetry at Oxford University from 1995 to 1999, were published in 2001.

ACHIEVEMENTS

James Fenton's greatest contribution to the world of letters may lie in the fact that he has shown that art and the real world of politics are not separate from each other and that the artist can be an important public commentator on the world. In 1968 Fenton's first year at Oxford, he won the Newdigate Prize, the most important literary award available to undergraduates. His first collection, *Terminal Moraine*, won a Gregory Award. He became a fellow of the Royal Society of Literature in 1983. In 1984 he won the Geoffrey Faber Memorial Prize. In 1994 he became the Oxford Professor of Poetry. Known as a leading poet in Great Britain, he contributed regularly to *The New York Review of Books*.

BIOGRAPHY

James Martin Fenton was born to an Anglican theologian and priest, John Charles Fenton, and Mary Hamilton Fenton; he was born in Lincoln in northern England and educated in part at the famous boys' school Repton in Derbyshire. He went to Magdalen College, Oxford, in 1967. Wanting to broaden his knowledge, he switched his course of study from English to philosophy, psychology, and physiology, and this interest in scientific subjects shows up occasionally in his poetry.

Although he had distinguished himself as a poet at Oxford, he graduated with a third-class degree. However, he was able to find work as a journalist in London, where he soon joined the important leftist journal *New Statesman*. In 1972 he published his first volume of poems, *Terminal Moraine*. He won a Gregory Award for the book and used the money to finance a freelance writing trip to the Cambodian war zone. In Vietnam and Cambodia he reported for British newspapers on the Vietnam War but also began to write poetry about this Eastern world of exotic beauty and nightmarish violence.

In 1976 he returned to England and became a political correspondent for the *New Statesman*. In 1978 his work in Germany led to his poem "A German Requiem." In 1979 he became the drama critic for the London *Sunday Times* but continued to write poetry, if sparingly, throughout his periods of journalistic employment. In 1982 he had his greatest success with *The Memory of War*, a series of poems set mostly in the Far East. However well known he became as a war poet, he had another side to his art, which he showed in *Children in Exile*, in which many of the poems read like nonsense, with touches of the comic and the sinister.

In the mid-1990's he became the Oxford Professor of Poetry. He had traveled to interesting and sometimes dangerous parts of the world and had written poetry about his times abroad. Living just outside Oxford, he continued to involve himself in journalism, in serious literary criticism, and public broadcasting, with a steady, if

James Fenton (© Joyce Ravid)

modest, pursuit of poetry, often directly related to politics and public life in general.

ANALYSIS

James Fenton's public reputation is firmly connected to his "occasional" poems based in twentieth century political chaos. The "occasional" poem is a form with a long history in English literature, in which a historical incident is used as a basis for the work; John Dryden (1631-1700) was a master of the form. Fenton's use of a historical event, however, is less formal and more emotional than Dryden's, and there is a strong sense of humanizing the "occasional," making those works attractive to a contemporary audience. Fenton does, however, have several other distinct and attractive subjects for his art.

"IN A NOTEBOOK"

Three poems from *The Memory of War* are examples of Fenton's reaction to war in Cambodia, "In a Notebook," "Cambodia," and "Dead Soldiers." "In a Notebook" is in two sections, the first describing the idyllic village life before the war reaches the Cambodian people. *"There was a river overhung with trees/ With wooden houses built along its shallows/ From which the morning sun drew up a haze.*" These passages are printed in italics and juxtaposed against the brutal truth of a later time: Some of the lines are the same, picked out of the earlier passage; again, "There was a river overhung with trees" but with a difference: "The villages are burnt," and the speaker is "afraid, reading this passage now,/ That everything I knew has been destroyed," and "most of [his] friends are dead." Fenton does not judge but simply reports the facts of disaster.

"CAMBODIA"

"Cambodia" is even more terse and uncommitted, a short poem of five sets of couplets: "One man shall smile one day and say goodbye./ Two shall be left, two shall be left to die./ One man shall give his best advice./ Three men shall pay the price." The numbers laconically mount until "One man to five. A million men to one./ And still they die. And still the war goes on."

"DEAD SOLDIERS"

"Dead Soldiers" is distanced from the slaughter, as the poet recalls a drunken meal "When His Excellency Prince Norodom Chantaraingsey/ Invited [him] to lunch on the battlefield." The tension between the ambition of the narrator, a correspondent eager to get a good interview, and the political cynicism of the participants involves the "Jockey Cap," the brother of the infamous Pol Pot, who caused the murder of millions of his fellow Cambodians. Jockey Cap is proud to show that he is in "the know:" "did they show you the things they do/ With the young refugee girls?" Time passes, and the correspondent begins to realize that the war is simply a business; "It was a family war," and "there were villains enough." It is a sour, frank exploration of the higher levels of political corruption, indifference, and cruelty, ripe with irony and punning asides.

"A GERMAN REQUIEM"

The exploration of twentieth century political disasters is not always expressed in the hard-boiled language of the war correspondent; it can look quite innocent. "A German Requiem" is a poem about forgetting as a way to survive after World War II. A group of German widows, once or twice a year, takes a bus, the "Widow's Shuttle," to visit the graves of their war dead. In nine short sections, the women are viewed, picking and choosing with great care what they want to remember. "It is not your memories which haunt you./ It is not what you have written down./ It is what you have forgotten, what you must forget." Some of the memories have lugubrious twists to them. The town suffered so much destruction, so much death that the women "unscrewed the name-plates from the shattered doorways/ And carried them away with the coffins." Some memories elicit self-pity; "Oh, if I were to begin, if I were to begin to tell you/ The half, the quarter, a mere smattering of what we went through!" This is a guilty nation, perhaps, but there is a limit: "But come. Grief must have its term? Guilt too, then." Germany's responsibility for the war is never mentioned. "Nothing more need be said, and it is better that way—." This interest in commenting upon the cruelties of twentieth century politics is a constant in Fenton's career. It can also be seen in "Jerusalem" and "Tiananmen" in the volume *Out of Danger*.

"GOD, A POEM"

Always enthusiastic about the poetry of W. H. Auden, Fenton has been called the "second Auden," in large part because of his poetry of enormous sophistication, wit, and charm. He is most like Auden in his poems of whimsical, surrealistic angst, in which the metaphors, the similes, and the general settings strike of a slightly manic comic frenzy. "God, a Poem" from *Children in Exile* counts upon the novelty of a god who is sufficiently present to comment upon the narrator's concerns but not much help otherwise. Indeed, the language used by this questionable deity makes his powers somewhat suspect:

> Oh he *said:* "If you lay off the crumpet
> I'll see you alright in the end.
> Just hang on until the last trumpet.
> Have faith in me, chum—I'm your friend."

This intimate, slangy salesman of salvation is a long way from the God of Christian forgiveness, and when pressed too far about his promise of eternal life, his demotic dismissal of responsibility is very clear. "'I'm sorry, I must have been pissed—/ Though your name rings a sort of a bell. You/ Should have guessed that I do not exist.'"

"THE EMPIRE OF THE SENSELESS"

"The Empire of the Senseless," section 5 of *The Memory of War*, consists of five poems of nonsense, reminiscent not only of Auden but also of Lewis Carroll, often at his most aggressive. Much of it is simply fun, with the pleasure coming from the singular freshness of the oddly skewed descriptions, as in "The Kingfisher's Boxing Gloves": "The alligator yawns and heaves a sigh./ Between its teeth, black as an upright grand,/ The mastik bird performs its dentistry."

This kind of edgy horseplay is only part of a piece of Fenton's improvisational flair in poetry. He includes some "found" poetry, arbitrary bits of prose found in odd places, and in "Exempla" (from *The Memory of War*) flirts with the idea of bringing science and scientific language into poetry. This sort of experiment is not always successful aesthetically, but it makes for lively interludes in his books.

"NOTHING" AND "OUT OF DANGER"

Fenton is not simply a clever poet; he is also a lyric poet of considerable power. If he seems to write more of failed love than triumph, he does it with intense, if reluctant, reticent feeling. "Nothing," from *Children in Exile*, is plangent acceptance of failed love: "I take a jewel from a junk-shop tray/ And wish I had a love to buy it for./ Nothing I choose will make you turn my way." The desperation of the situation makes the lover unable to work, read, or write; "Nothing I am will make you love me more." It is reminiscent of the depressed love laments of Sir Thomas Wyatt and Henry Howard Surrey, seventeenth century English courtier poets.

"Out of Danger" displays Fenton's sexual passion. It is a love poem, after the fact, of reassurance to the loved one that all is over, and that no longer is she subject to the dangers of the love affair, the jealousy, the excesses of love. "I was cruel, I was wrong—/ Hard to say and hard to know./ You do not belong to me./ You are out of danger now—."

OTHER MAJOR WORKS

NONFICTION: *You Were Marvelous*, 1983; *The Snap Revolution*, 1986; *All the Wrong Places: Adrift in the Politics of Asia*, 1988; *Leonardo's Nephew*, 1998; *The Strength of Poetry*, 2001.

TRANSLATION: *Rigoletto*, 1982 (of Francesco Maria Piave's libretto).

EDITED TEXTS: *The Original Michael Frayn: Satirical Essays*, 1983; *Cambodian Witness: The Autobiography of Someth May*, 1987; *Underground in Japan*, 1992.

BIBLIOGRAPHY

Grant, Damian. "The Voice of History in British Poetry, 1970-1984." *Etudes-Anglaise* 38, no. 2 (April-June, 1985): 158-179. A commentary on Fenton's historical poems and the various kinds thereof in the context of similar themes in other British poetry of the period.

Hulse, Michael. "The Poetry of James Fenton." *The Antigonish Review* 58 (Summer, 1984): 93-102. A general commentary on Fenton's poetry up to the early 1980's.

Kerr, Douglas. "James Fenton and Indochina." *Contemporary Literature* 35 (Fall, 1994): 476-491. A discussion of the nature of Fenton's experience in the Far East and the poetry and prose arising from that experience.

Parker, Ian. "Auden's Heir." *The New Yorker*, July 25, 1994, pp. 62-68. Fenton has been able to make use of certain elements in Auden's work; a discussion of how he does it with success without being accused of imitation by critics.

Robinson, Alan. "James Fenton's Narratives: Some Reflections on Postmodernism." *Critical Quarterly* 29 (Spring, 1987): 81-93. Fenton's poems often have a strong narrative shape; Robinson examines that aspect of his work in the light of contemporary critical definitions.

Stark, Ellen-Kreger. "An American's Confession: On Reading James Fenton's *Out of Danger*." *Critical Quarterly* 36 (Summer, 1994): 106-110. A discussion of Fenton's use of the narrator and the nature of the confessional aspect in some of these poems.

Charles H. Pullen

LAWRENCE FERLINGHETTI

Born: Yonkers, New York; March 24, 1919

PRINCIPAL POETRY

Pictures of the Gone World, 1955, revised 1995 (with eighteen new poems)
A Coney Island of the Mind, 1958

Starting from San Francisco, 1961
An Eye on the World: Selected Poems, 1967
The Secret Meaning of Things, 1969
Tyrannus Nix?, 1969
Back Roads to Far Places, 1971
Open Eye, Open Heart, 1973
Who Are We Now?, 1976
Landscapes of Living and Dying, 1979
A Trip to Italy and France, 1981
Endless Life: The Selected Poems, 1981
Over All the Obscene Boundaries: European Poems and Transitions, 1984
These Are My Rivers: New and Selected Poems, 1955-1993, 1993
A Far Rockaway of the Heart, 1997
San Francisco Poems, 1998
How to Paint Sunlight: Lyric Poems and Others, 1997-2000, 2001

OTHER LITERARY FORMS

Early in his career, Lawrence Ferlinghetti was very much interested in the French Symbolist poets, and in

Lawrence Ferlinghetti

1958 City Lights published his first and only translation of French poetry: *Paroles*, by Jacques Prévert. His translations of pieces by an Italian poet, Pier Paolo Pasolini, appeared in 1986 as *Roman Poems*. Ferlinghetti has rarely published anything except poetry in book form, although he has written many critical and review articles that have appeared in both magazines and newspapers. Even his prose works—*Her* (1960) and *The Mexican Night* (1970)—sound so much like his poetry that it is questionable whether one should actually call them prose. He published another novel, *Love in the Days of Rage*, in 1988.

Ferlinghetti's two books of plays, *Unfair Arguments with Existence* and *Routines*, were published by New Directions in 1963 and 1964, respectively. His interest in the theater and oral poetry led to various filmings and recordings of his readings. The two best-known of Ferlinghetti's performances, "Tyrannus Nix?" and "Assassination Raga," are preserved in both film and record. *Leaves of Life: Drawing from the Model* (1983), published under the pseudonym Mendes Monsanto, is a collection of his drawings.

ACHIEVEMENTS

In 1957, Lawrence Ferlinghetti first received national attention as a result of the "Howl" obscenity trial. At that time, Ferlinghetti was recognized not as a poet but as the publisher and distributor of Allen Ginsberg's *Howl and Other Poems* (1956). After winning the controversial trial, Ferlinghetti received enough attention to boost his own collection of poems, *A Coney Island of the Mind*, into a best-seller position. His name became strongly associated with the new, or "Beat," poetry being developed on the West Coast. Since then, Ferlinghetti has been recognized as a poet of movements and protests.

Being often antigovernment in his responses, Ferlinghetti has gone so far as never to accept government grants for either his own writing or the City Lights publishing house. Nevertheless, he received a National Book Award nomination in 1970 for *The Secret Meaning of Things*, the *Library Journal* Notable Book of 1979 citation for *Landscapes of Living and Dying* in 1980, and the 1986 Silver Medal for poetry from the Commonwealth Club of California for *Over All the Obscene Boundaries*. In 1977, the city of San Francisco paid tribute to Ferlinghetti by honoring him at the Civic Art Festival—the first time a poet was so recognized. The City of Rome awarded him a poetry prize in 1993, and San Francisco not only named a street in his honor in 1994 but also named him the city's first poet laureate in 1998. In 2000, Ferlinghetti was a joint winner, with film critic Pauline Kael, of the National Book Critics Circle's Ivan Sandrof Award for Lifetime Achievement. Furthermore, in 2001, City Lights Bookseller and Publishers was designated an official landmark.

Ferlinghetti is noted for the many public readings he has given in support of free speech, nuclear disarmament, antiwhaling, and so on. Often overlooked by critics, Ferlinghetti has remained an active voice speaking for the American people against many institutions and practices—government, corporate, and social alike—that limit individual freedom; he stands out as a poet and a true individual.

BIOGRAPHY

Lawrence Ferlinghetti—born in Yonkers, New York, in 1919—was the youngest of five sons of Charles and Clemence Ferlinghetti. Several months before Lawrence's birth, Charles Ferlinghetti died unexpectedly of a heart attack and Lawrence's mother, Clemence, suffered a breakdown as a result. She was unable to care for Lawrence and was eventually institutionalized at the state hospital in Poughkeepsie, New York.

After these humble and tragic beginnings, it is ironic that Lawrence was taken and cared for by his mother's well-to-do uncle, Ludwig Mendes-Monsanto, and his wife, Emily, in their Manhattan home. It is also ironic that American-born Lawrence Ferlinghetti learned French as his first language. In fact, throughout his childhood he actually believed himself to be French, having been taken in by his great-aunt Emily, who left her husband and returned to France, her homeland. Lawrence spent the first five years of his life in Strasbourg with Emily, whom he refers to as his "French mother." Emily was eventually persuaded to return to New York to rejoin Ludwig, but the reunion lasted only for a short time. Lawrence—who knew himself only as Lawrence Ferling Monsanto—was placed in an orphanage for seven months. Eventually Emily reclaimed him and took him away, after leaving Ludwig again. This time they remained in New York.

Emily took on work as a French tutor for the daughter of the very wealthy Presley and Anna Lawrence Bisland. Emily and Lawrence lived in a small room in the third floor servants' area until one day Emily mysteriously disappeared, whereupon Lawrence was adopted by the Bislands.

The Bislands had had a son who died in early childhood. His name—and Mrs. Bisland's maiden name—was Lawrence, her father having founded Sarah Lawrence College near Bronxville. Mr. Bisland was also a man of letters, with a profound interest in contemporary literature, although his experiences included being one of the last men to ride the Chisholm trail on the last of the great cattle drives. The Bislands were aristocratic, adventuresome, cosmopolitan, but also creative in spirit. In fact, Ferlinghetti maintains that Presley Bisland's writings gave him the idea that being an author was a dignified calling.

At the age of ten, Ferlinghetti was told about his natural mother, Clemence Ferlinghetti, whom he met one traumatic Sunday afternoon. He was given the choice to go with her, whom he considered a stranger, or to stay with the Bislands. He chose to stay. Unknown to Ferlinghetti, the Bislands had arranged to send him away to school. A few weeks later he found himself boarding with a family named Wilson in one of New York City's rougher neighborhoods. Their son Bill, being older, became a hero to young Ferlinghetti. Lawrence joined the Boy Scouts and went to baseball and football games and was far less lonely than he had been at the Bisland mansion.

At the age of sixteen, Lawrence began to write poetry. His stepsister, Sally Bisland, gave him a book of Charles Baudelaire in translation. Ferlinghetti remembers it as the first collection of poems he read from cover to cover. He was then sent to a private high school, Mount Hernon, near Greenfield, Massachusetts. In his senior year, Mrs. Bisland took him for the first of a series of visits to see his natural mother and brothers at their home in Ossining.

Ferlinghetti attended college at the University of North Carolina at Chapel Hill and was graduated in 1941, after which he joined the Navy and served in World War II. It was while he was in the Navy that he received a telegram from Central Islip State Hospital saying that Emily Monsanto, Lawrence's "French mother," had died, having listed Ferlinghetti as her only living relative. This was the first he had heard of her since she had left him with the Bislands when he was ten.

In World War II, Ferlinghetti was on one of the primary Naval sub chasers coming in for the Normandy invasion. Later, in 1945, on the first day of the U.S. occupation of Japan, his ship landed there. Eventually he was able to visit Nagasaki, where he witnessed the aftermath of the atomic bombing of that city. The devastation he witnessed left an indelible impression.

After his discharge from the Navy, Ferlinghetti returned to New York City and lived in Greenwich Village, taking on work as a mail clerk for *Time* magazine. His interest in poetry revived, and he returned to Columbia University under the G.I. Bill, receiving his M.A. degree in 1947. That summer Presley Bisland died. Soon afterward, Ferlinghetti left for Paris, where he met many literary figures. He completed work on a thesis and was awarded a degree from the Sorbonne. He also wrote a novel, which was rejected by Doubleday. In 1949, Ferlinghetti returned to America for a two-week visit with Mrs. Bisland. In 1951, both she and Ferlinghetti's natural mother died. In the same year, after several trips back and forth between Europe and the United States, Ferlinghetti married Selden Kirby-Smith, who was known as Kirby. They moved to San Francisco, where Ferlinghetti wrote articles for *Art Digest* and book reviews for the *San Francisco Chronicle.*

Influenced greatly by Kenneth Rexroth and Kenneth Patchen, who both lived in San Francisco, Ferlinghetti soon came to be considered a political poet. He was published in Peter Martin's magazine *City Lights* and eventually the two men collaborated to open the City Lights Bookstore in 1953. In 1955, the same year that Ferlinghetti's first book of poetry, *Pictures of the Gone World,* was published under the City Lights imprint, Peter Martin sold Ferlinghetti his interest in the store. At about that time, Ferlinghetti became acquainted with James Laughlin, president of the publishing house New Directions. It was through Laughlin that Ferlinghetti's second book of poems, *A Coney Island of the Mind,* became a best-seller.

Allen Ginsberg came into Ferlinghetti's life from the East, bringing a poem titled "Howl" with him. Fer-

linghetti was impressed with Ginsberg and published *Howl and Other Poems.* It was this book that caused Ferlinghetti to be arrested, the charge against him being that he printed and sold obscene writings. He was eventually cleared, and, partly because of the publicity, City Lights flourished.

Although Ferlinghetti and his wife Kirby were divorced in the early 1970's, their marriage had been relatively stable; in 1962 a daughter, Julie, was born, and in 1963 a son, Lorenzo. During the 1960's Ferlinghetti traveled to South and Central America, to Europe, and to the Soviet Union, giving poetry readings whenever possible. In 1974 he met Paula Lillevand; they moved in together in 1978, but they parted two years later.

Ferlinghetti first took LSD in 1967, the poem "Mock Confessional" resulting from that experience. Throughout the 1970's and 1980's Ferlinghetti remained actively interested in political and environmental matters, his poetry inevitably reflecting his political and social concerns. During these years he traveled extensively in Europe and sometimes in Latin America, giving readings of his poems.

In 1977 Ferlinghetti took up drawing, an interest he had left behind some twenty years earlier, and soon he was painting as well. His expressionist-style works were displayed in a formal exhibition in the mid-1980's in the Bay area, and another show was organized in Berlin in 1990. He continued to edit volumes of City Lights anthologies throughout the 1990's. Ferlinghetti also collaborated in a video, directed by Christopher Felver, called *The Coney Island of Lawrence Ferlinghetti,* released in 1996. In it, the poet acts in autobiographical vignettes, tours places of particular meaning to him, reads his poetry, and expounds on his artistic philosophy and political views.

ANALYSIS

Lawrence Ferlinghetti's poetry may be looked on as a kind of travelog in which he has subjectively recorded choice experiences or montages from experience—often jazzlike or free-associative. For Ferlinghetti, "reality" itself becomes metaphorical, something he endows with mythical import, although he is not a poet given to hidden meanings. While his poetry is largely autobiographical, an adequate analysis of his poetry is possible without thorough biographical knowledge; Ferlinghetti's poetry is not excessively self-contained.

A CONEY ISLAND OF THE MIND

Whereas Ferlinghetti's poems are for the most part historical, or autobiographical, Ferlinghetti the man is a myth, appearing as a cult hero, one of the original Beats. Sometimes a martyr to a cause, Ferlinghetti will occasionally insert his political ideologies into a poem for no apparent reason other than that they seem to fit his role. Halfway through the sometimes absurd, sometimes delightful poem "Underwear," Ferlinghetti overextends his metaphor by becoming politically involved:

> You have seen the three-color pictures
> with crotches encircled
> to show the areas of extra strength
> and three-way stretch
> promising full freedom of action
> Don't be deceived
> It's all based on the two-party system
> which doesn't allow much freedom of choice

The reader is often seduced, but behind Ferlinghetti's seemingly spoken voice, full of American colloquialisms, is an intellect schooled in the classics, highly knowledgeable of literature, past and present—a voice full of allusions. Rather surprisingly, Ferlinghetti makes many direct references to greater works of literature by borrowing lines to suit his own purposes. Even the title of Ferlinghetti's best-selling book *A Coney Island of the Mind* is taken from Henry Miller's *Into the Night Life* (1947). One repeatedly discovers lines and phrases such as T. S. Eliot's "Let us go then you and I" and "Hurry up please it's time" ironically enlisted for use in such poems as "Junkman's Obbligato." Ferlinghetti frequently employs fragments from literature without alerting his audience to his borrowing. In the poem "Autobiography" he states, "I read the Want Ads daily/ looking for a stone a leaf/ an unfound door"—an oblique reference to Thomas Wolfe's opening in *Look Homeward, Angel* (1929). He makes even more esoteric references to W. B. Yeats's "horsemen" in poems such as "Reading Yeats I Do Not Think" and again in "Autobiography." In "Assassination Raga" one finds a variation on Dylan Thomas's "The force that through the green fuse drives the flower." In its stead, Ferlinghetti writes of "The force that through the red fuze/ drives the bullet"—the poem being in honor of Robert Kennedy and read in Nourse Auditorium, San Francisco, June 8, 1968, the day Kennedy was buried after having been assassinated during his presidential campaign in Los Angeles.

In his role as a subjective historian and political rebel, Ferlinghetti never orates with so much pomp as to raise himself above his audience. In his meager "Charlie Chaplin" manner—Chaplin being a persona to whom he continuously compares himself in poems such as "Constantly Risking Absurdity," "In a Time of Revolution for Instance," and "Director of Alienation"—Ferlinghetti is just as capable of making fun of himself as he is of satirizing various institutions and aspects of society.

"DOG"

Whereas some poets seek to find metaphorical reflections of themselves in nature, Ferlinghetti rarely looks there for inspiration. Furthermore, being more fond of philosophy than of drama, Ferlinghetti projects a sense of conflict mainly through his own personal quest—for his true self. His feelings of alienation and the quest for environmental constants that do not restrict one's freedom are depicted in the poem "Dog," which begins: "The dog trots freely in the street/ and sees reality/ and the things he sees/ are bigger than himself. . . ." As the poem progresses the reader comes to understand that this is an ordinary stray dog—and also Ferlinghetti in a stray-dog suit. "And the things he sees/ are his reality/ Drunks in doorways/ Moons on trees. . . ." The dog keeps on going with a curiosity that demands diversity from experience.

Ferlinghetti goes deeper, allowing the reader also to don a dog suit, to see "Ants in holes/ Chickens in Chinatown windows/ their heads a block away." Thus the reader learns that he is roaming the streets of San Francisco. The dog trots past the carcasses that are hung up whole in Chinatown. At this point the reader learns that he "would rather eat a tender cow/ than a tough policeman/ though either might do." The reader has already been told that the dog does not hate cops; he merely has no use for them.

Here the reader begins to wonder whether being stray is conditional on having no preferences. Is the dog a Democrat or a Republican? The reader later learns that this dog is at least "democratic." Ferlinghetti does deal with unusual specifics as the dog trots past the San Francisco Meat Market, and keeps going: "past the Romeo Ravioli Factory/ and past Coit's Tower/ and past Congressman Doyle of the Unamerican Committee.´. . ." Here Ferlinghetti manages to make a political statement that is alien to a dog's perspective. This "Unamerican Committee" is obviously something that Ferlinghetti the Beat poet has recognized—not the Ferlinghetti in the dog suit. The Ferlinghetti in the dog suit says that ultimately "Congressman Doyle is just another/ fire hydrant/ to him." Thus the reader knows how the Ferlinghetti in a dog suit might treat Congressman Doyle—symbolically or not. A few lines earlier, Ferlinghetti alludes to Dylan Thomas by labeling the dog "a sad young dog" (see Thomas's *Portrait of the Artist as a Young Dog*, 1940): The dog appears to be metaphorical of all poets and artists, especially Ferlinghetti himself.

Ferlinghetti proceeds to declare that a dog's knowledge is only of the senses. His curiosity already quite obvious, the day becomes:

> a real live
> > barking
> > > democratic dog
> engaged in real
> > > free enterprise
> with something to say
> > > about ontology
> something to say
> > > about reality.

In this segment, a major change can be noted: Ferlinghetti has abandoned flush left margins. Beginning with the line "barking," Ferlinghetti demonstrates a new-found freedom through his staggered, free-form typography. The poem continues, and the dog himself trots more freely, cocking his head sideways at street corners "as if he is just about to have/ his picture taken/ for Victor Records." His ear is raised, and it is suggested that he embodies a question mark as he looks askew into the "great gramophone of puzzling existence," waiting and looking, just like Ferlinghetti, for an answer to everything—and it all sounds like poetry.

A FAR ROCKAWAY OF THE HEART

In 1997, nearly forty years after *A Coney Island of the Mind*, Ferlinghetti published a volume whose title insists that it be taken as a companion piece to the earlier work: *A Far Rockaway of the Heart*. Its 101 poems revealed that both the poet's strengths and his weaknesses were in full force as he approached his eightieth birthday. The colloquial diction is as easy as ever, but its novelty is somewhat tarnished; the wide-ranging quotation from and reference to the words of other poets is as masterful as ever, and all the more impressive as the common literary canon has all but disappeared from the cultural landscape. A number of critics noted that Ferlinghetti's styles, themes, and techniques seemed barely to have changed over the long course of his career, yet the poet himself begins the volume acknowledging this fact:

> Everything changes and nothing changes
> Centuries end
>
> and all goes on
> as if nothing
> ever ends
> As clouds still stop in mid-flight
> like dirigibles caught in cross-winds
>
> And the fever of savage city life
> still grips the streets. . . .
>
> It's as if those forty years just vanish.

Perhaps it is presumptuous of the poet to proclaim his own timelessness. Yet perhaps his ongoing social and political concerns are timeless because in forty years, little has occurred to remedy the ills he sees around him, and the world goes on as absurd—and as beautiful—as ever.

OTHER MAJOR WORKS

LONG FICTION: *Her*, 1960; *Love in the Days of Rage*, 1988.

PLAYS: *Unfair Arguments with Existence*, pb. 1963; *Routines*, pb. 1964.

NONFICTION: *The Mexican Night*, 1970; *Literary San Francisco*, 1980 (with Nancy J. Peters); *Leaves of Life: Drawing from the Model*, 1983 (as Mendes Mensanto).

TRANSLATIONS: *Selections from "Paroles" by Jacques Prévert*, 1958; *Roman Poems*, 1988 (of Pier Paolo Pasolini).

BIBLIOGRAPHY

Cherkovski, Neeli. *Ferlinghetti: A Biography*. Garden City, N.Y.: Doubleday, 1979. Reviews the wrenching dislocations of Ferlinghetti's childhood, his stint in the U.S. Navy, his studies at Columbia and in Paris, and the development of his artistic and political commitments, always emphasizing the theme of the poet's search for a self. Cherkovski's writing style is uninspired, but the book still manages to provide much information that will be of interest to students of Ferlinghetti. Illustrated with photographs. Provides a primary and a secondary bibliography; indexed.

Felver, Christopher. *Ferlinghetti Portrait*. Salt Lake City, Utah: Gibbs Smith, 1998. Primarily a pictoral work with some poetry. Contains Ferlinghetti's autobiographical poem.

Ferlinghetti, Lawrence. *The Cool Eye: Lawrence Ferlinghetti Talks to Alexis Lykiard*. Exeter, Devon, England: Stride, 1993. A transcription of an interview with some biographical information.

Kherdian, David. *Six Poets of the San Francisco Renaissance: Portraits and Checklists*. Fresno, Calif.: Giligia Press, 1967. Kherdian provides a bio-bibliography of six poets operating in the San Francisco area in the 1960's. Chief among them is Ferlinghetti, who operates the City Lights Bookshop in San Francisco, which continues to be a mecca for readers seeking foreign or avant-garde literature. For all students.

Kush, S. S., videographer and ed. *Ferlinghetti, City Lights, and the Beats in San Francisco: From the Margins to the Mainstream*. Video. 5 cassettes. San Francisco: Cloud House Poetry Archives, 1996. Ferlinghetti's life as a publisher of the Beats, younger writers influenced by the Beat movement, and a lecture by Ferlinghetti. Nine hours covering a key period in the history of twentieth century American poetry and one of its major avatars.

Meltzer, David. *The San Francisco Poets*. New York: Ballantine Books, 1971. Meltzer provides interviews with six modern poets whose vision is curiously shaped by their avant-garde life in San Francisco. A must for any student of the San Francisco poetry movement of the 1960's. Includes a bibliography.

Silesky, Barry. *Ferlinghetti: The Artist in His Time*. New York: Warner Books, 1990. A chatty biography, written with the informality and punchiness of a popular-magazine article. Based on extensive interviews with Ferlinghetti and his associates. Silesky leaves critical appraisal of the poetry to numerous poets and critics interviewed in the book's final chapter; they include Allen Ginsberg, Robert Creeley, Paul Carroll, Ralph Mills, Diane Wakoski, and Gary Snyder. Features a selected bibliography, an index, and photographs.

Skau, Michael. *"Constantly Risking Absurdity": Essays on the Writings of Lawrence Ferlinghetti*. Troy, N.Y.: Whitston, 1989. A brief monograph, illustrated, on Ferlinghetti's works.

Smith, Larry R. *Lawrence Ferlinghetti, Poet-at-Large*. Carbondale: Southern Illinois University Press, 1983. This well-written book has one particularly interesting feature: a multicolumned chronology that parallels events in Ferlinghetti's personal life, his writing achievements, and City Lights publishing history. After presenting a "biographic portrait," Smith argues that Ferlinghetti is best placed within a European rather than American literary tradition. Smith provides a thoughtful treatment of Ferlinghetti's poetic themes and devices, and surveys the prose writings and drama as well. Contains photographs, notes, a selected bibliography, and an index.

John Alspaugh,
updated by Leslie Ellen Jones

EDWARD FIELD

Born: Brooklyn, New York; June 7, 1924

PRINCIPAL POETRY

Stand Up, Friend, with Me, 1963
Variety Photoplays, 1967
A Full Heart, 1977
Stars in My Eyes, 1978
New and Selected Poems from the Book of Life, 1987

Counting Myself Lucky: Selected Poems, 1963-1992, 1992

A Frieze for a Temple of Love, 1998

OTHER LITERARY FORMS

Edward Field's most important works, aside from his poetry, are the novels he wrote in collaboration with Neil Derrick under the collective pseudonym of Bruce Elliot. The most successful of these works was the novel *Village* (1982), a chronicle of life over many decades in Greenwich Village, New York.

Field also edited an anthology titled *A Geography of Poets* (1979), which was a notable effort to showcase the works of poets from all over the United States. In 1992 Field, collaborating with Gerald Locklin and Charles Stetler, edited *A New Geography of Poets*.

ACHIEVEMENTS

In 1962, Edward Field was given the Lamont Award for *Stand Up, Friend, with Me*, his first collection of poems, and was subsequently awarded a Guggenheim Fellowship. He received the Shelley Memorial Award from the Poetry Society of America in 1974 and a Lambda Literary Award in 1992 for *Counting Myself Lucky: Selected Poems, 1963-1992*. The American Academy of Arts and Letters awarded Field its Prix de Rome.

BIOGRAPHY

Born in Brooklyn to Jewish parents five years before the beginning of the Great Depression, Edward Field remained intimately associated with New York City for most of his life. His poetry frequently alludes to a childhood in which the young Field longed for a father's love which he believed was denied to him. Field's comment is telling: "when I look back on childhood/ (That four psychiatrists haven't been able to help me bear the thought of)/ There is not much to be glad for. . . ." One of six children, Edward appears to have felt neglected by his parents and to have been regarded with hostility or contempt by his peers. Trained in music from an early age, Field played cello in a musical trio made up of members of his family. In 1942, while working at a Manhattan department store, Field met First Lady Eleanor Roosevelt, an occasion he was to commemorate in 2001 in the same building (now the Mid-Manhattan Library) at a reading of his own work.

Field joined the Army Air Corps in 1942 and flew twenty-five bomber missions, during which, he reported, "five planes had been destroyed by flak under me." In March of 1943, while still undergoing his military training, he was given a Red Cross package containing, among other things, an anthology of poetry. As he later wrote, "This was a bombshell. I knew immediately that I was going to be a poet." He left the military with the rank of second lieutenant, and back in New York, Field sought to pursue his education under the G.I. Bill. He gradually came to realize that university life was not what he had hoped for and left New York University in 1948. With one thousand dollars in savings, he sailed for France. On the ship he met a poet named Robert Friend, whom Field later credited as having introduced him to the fundamentals of modern poetry.

Remaining in Paris until the spring of 1949, Field enjoyed associating with Friend and with other members of the artistic community. Visiting London, he met poet Stephen Spender and saw T. S. Eliot. Field, though low on funds, then went to Greece, where he found himself comfortable enough to write some of the first poems he was later to publish. By 1950 he was back in New York.

Upon his return to the United States, Field felt keenly the atmosphere of repression which contrasted so strongly with the environments of Paris and Greece. The social intolerance which shaped many aspects of Cold War attitudes threatened his liberty. As a nonconformist, homosexual, and Jew, he was revolted by this intolerance, and he sought to cope with his intense anxiety by embarking upon a long sequence of various psychological therapies.

In 1955 Field met Frank O'Hara, whose poems and attitude toward poetry were helpful to him. Field continued to write while working in offices and endeavoring to develop skills as an actor. A major event occurred in his poetic life when, in 1963, he was awarded the Lamont Award for his first book of poems, *Stand Up, Friend, with Me*. From that time on, Field led the life of a recognized literary figure. After the publication of his first book in 1963, he received a Guggenheim Fellowship to travel abroad.

He published his second book of poetry, *Variety Photoplays*, in 1967. The success of *Stand Up, Friend, with Me* had made it possible for Field to earn money by giving readings of his poetry, and he began to enjoy a measure of financial security. His life was complicated at this time by the illness of his companion Neil Derrick, whose deteriorating eyesight made him increasingly dependent upon Field, who soon began to collaborate with his friend in the writing of fiction. After Field published *A Full Heart*, his third book of poetry, in 1977, he and Derrick published their first novel, *The Potency Clinic*, in 1978, using the collective nom de plume of Bruce Elliot.

Recognizing that the New York literary establishment was exercising a domineering influence on American poetry, Field sought to balance the situation in 1979 by publishing an anthology of American poetry titled *A Geography of Poets*. His next project was another collaboration with Neil Derrick, and in 1982 appeared *Village* by Bruce Elliot, a novel about life in Greenwich Village from 1845 to 1975. This novel was a best-seller.

In 1987 the Sheep Meadow Press issued *New and Selected Poems*, with poems from previous volumes supplemented by twenty-seven new ones. *Counting Myself Lucky: Selected Poems, 1963-1992* was published by the Black Sparrow Press, which also issued *A Frieze for a Temple of Love*, a collection of poems to which is added an eighty-one-page text titled "The Poetry File," a mixture of memoir, gossip, and observations on poetry.

ANALYSIS

Field's poetry is distinguished by its casualness, a characteristic he cultivated deliberately in a reaction to the obscurity of much modern poetry. His verse tends to be conversational in tone, syntax, and vocabulary, and usually nothing is concealed. It is easy for the reader to forget that Field is a trained musician and actor, yet perhaps these forms of competence contribute to the power which sometimes emerges in his work.

STAND UP, FRIEND, WITH ME

Field's poetic voice represents the casually personal, often responding to incongruities and offering a city-dweller's bemusement at the persistence of nature. In his first book of poetry, for example, he describes goats, donkeys, a porcupine, and a walrus. He illustrates his own experience with plants in the city. In "Tulips and Addresses," he describes how he acquired some discarded tulip bulbs and carried them about with him for months before he found a home. He concludes:

Now I am living on Abingdon Square, not the Ritz
  exactly, but a place
And I have planted the tulips in my window box:
Please God make them come up, so that everyone who
  passes by
Will know I'm there, at least long enough to catch my
  breath,
When they see the bright red beautiful flowers in my
  window.

A similar note sounds in "The Garden," where, after describing the exotic plants he has sprouted from seed in his home, he celebrates his participation in this collection of living things: "We have formed a colony in a strange land/ Planting our seeds and making ourselves at home."

The dominant note is the assertion of the importance of the unaffectedly personal, a theme announced in the volume's prologue, where, beginning with an image of the universe, Field zooms in on the surface of the earth,

Edward Field (Academy of American Poets)

quickly focusing on New York and then upon "this house, upstairs and through the wide open door/ Of the front bedroom with a window on the world," concluding, "Look, friend, at me."

VARIETY PHOTOPLAYS

This collection includes a number of treatments of Hollywood films. According to poets Charles Stetler and Gerald Locklin, "Field has discovered and exploited the full mythological potential of old movies." These poems have such titles as "Curse of the Cat Woman," "Frankenstein," "Bride of Frankenstein," and "The Life of Joan Crawford," and they offer colloquial résumés of Hollywood movies and themes. Each is a sort of dramatic monologue, a self-contained entertainment. Field's poems in fact often present comical moments which dramatize small events, as in "Plant Poems," where he assumes the persona of a scientist:

> As the leading agronomist
> in the Kharkov Agricultural
> Institute
> I want to announce the discovery
> that plants feel as we do
>
> . . . .
>
> and when you chop up a lettuce
> it is saying Ouch.

A FULL HEART

The publication in 1977 of *A Full Heart* drew fire from reviewer M. L. Rosenthal, a literary critic and editor of William Butler Yeats. Rosenthal strongly objected to what he saw as the "indefatigably prosaic" dimension of Field's poetry, a dimension which Field himself was later to defend by explaining, "I use a local New York syntax, a kind of Jewish syntax that New Yorkers use in everyday life," and "it seems to me that poetry should be easier to read than prose." Since much of *A Full Heart* presents Field's coming to terms with his most important personal relationships, Rosenthal found this casually phrased confessional mode self-indulgent and facile.

The poem "A Full Heart" describes Field's Polish immigrant mother and her sisters, "loving women" whose burdened and unappreciated lives included only the most modest consolations. "Gone Blind" describes the impact upon Field of his companion's blindness; it concludes: "Gone blind/ he has brought me light." "Visiting Home"

is a long reflection upon the poet's relationship with his parents, and this meditation ends with an acceptance which, if qualified, has a tone of resolution: "I am my father's son./ Even if I can't stand it, still/ I am."

Despite Field's normal aversion to symbolism or implication, the poem "Sharks" reads very much like an exercise in the figurative. Although Field was enjoying a reasonable prosperity as literary man, he was over fifty by this time, and perhaps this poem is an anticipation of future vulnerability:

> Especially at evening
> everyone knows the sharks come in
> when the sun makes puddles of blood on the sea
> and the shadows darken.
>
> It is then, as night comes on
> the sharks of deep water
> approach the shore
> and beware, beware, the late swimmer.

A FRIEZE FOR A TEMPLE OF LOVE

This volume consists of three sections: a collection of Field's verse from 1993 to 1997, a long poem titled "Silver Wings: Notes for a Screenplay," and a largely prose conclusion titled "The Poetry File." The short poems included in the first section fall generally into two groups, the first of which continues the Fieldian theme of demonstrating poetic freedom by focusing on sexuality and bodily functions, and the second of which acknowledges the approach of death. Both groups include expressions of Field's abiding resentment of his parents, as he remarks in "The Spirit of '76," "My parents have faded away at last./ I survived you two sickos, just,/ but it's a relief to say thanks, and goodbye." Reflecting upon mortality in the final stanza of "Death Mask," Field writes:

> Life
>   a lazy buzz
> then
>   the quick sting.
>
> A long inward breath,
>   then
> the sudden
>   exhaling.

These lines carry an echo of Emily Dickinson's "I Heard a Fly Buzz When I Died," and the metaphors, unusual in Field's poems, suggest that the poet is deliberately connecting with a tradition he has long disavowed. Other passages in the book seem to reiterate Field's independence of that tradition.

In "Living Will," Field explains to Neil Derrick's sister his preparations for death, but he makes it clear that he has not yet surrendered, for the poem ends: "May death take me/ only as I put down/ the last word."

"Silver Wings: Notes for a Screenplay" is a narrative based upon Field's military service and love affairs as recalled fifty years later, and "The Poetry File," though mostly in prose, is a valuable compilation of Field's views about his own poetry and that of his contemporaries.

OTHER MAJOR WORKS

LONG FICTION: *The Potency Clinic*, 1978 (with Neil Derrick, under the name "Bruce Elliot"); *Village*, 1982 (with Neil Derrick, under the name "Bruce Elliot"); *The Office*, 1987 (with Neil Derrick, under the name "Bruce Elliott").

EDITED TEXTS: *A Geography of Poets*, 1979; *A New Geography of Poets*, 1992 (with Gerald Locklin and Charles Stetler).

CHILDREN'S LITERATURE: *Magic Words: Poems*, 1998.

BIBLIOGRAPHY
Crow, Kelly. "Time for Recalling the Departed and Reuniting the Long-Lost Related." *The New York Times*, June 24, 2001, p. 6. A report on a reading by Field at the Mid-Manhattan Library, a building in which, when the building housed a department store, Field worked as a junior employee in 1942. Crow describes Field's reading style (". . . he discarded the microphone . . . and . . . bellowed") and records Field's description of Eleanor Roosevelt, whom he had met in the same building nearly sixty years earlier.

Field, Edward. "The Poetry File." The concluding section of *A Frieze for a Temple of Love*. Santa Rosa, Calif.: Black Sparrow Press, 1998. This collection of miscellaneous observations on poetry and poets provides a good perspective on Field's insights and de-

velopment as a poet. Always in the entertainer mode, Field tosses in a substantial amount of gossip as well.

Goldgar, Harry. "The Poets' Selections: Two Distinguished American Poets Offer Worthwhile Volumes." *St. Petersburg Times*, July 5, 1987, p. 7D. In a review of two poetry volumes, including Field's *New and Selected Poems*, Field's friend Goldgar comments with enthusiasm upon the poet's "plainspeaking, gut-feeling, anti-establishment" works, praising their "accessibility" and lack of inhibition. Field had briefly been in residence at Eckerd College in St. Petersburg, Florida.

Stetler, Charles, and Gerald Locklin. "Edward Field, Stand-Up Poet." *The Minnesota Review* 9, no. 1 (1969). This essential article by two of Field's fellow poets celebrates his role in what the authors call "a full-scale renaissance of the Oral Tradition." Stetler and Locklin are particularly enthusiastic about Field's "movie poems" and the way they have "shaped or recorded patterns of our emotional lives." Associating Field's aesthetic with the media theory of Marshall McLuhan, this article explains how Field's poetry, especially in actual performance, escapes the limitations of the printed page.

Robert W. Haynes

ANNE FINCH

Countess of Winchelsea

Born: Sydmonton, Hampshire, England; April, 1661
Died: London, England; August 5, 1720

PRINCIPAL POETRY
Miscellany Poems, on Several Occasions, 1713
The Poems of Anne, Countess of Winchelsea, 1902
Selected Poems of Anne Finch, Countess of Winchelsea, 1979
The Anne Finch Wellesley Manuscript Poems, 1998

OTHER LITERARY FORMS
On the rare occasions when Anne Finch worked in other genres, she wrote in verse, such as in her two

plays, the unproduced closet dramas *The Triumphs of Love and Innocence* (wr. c. 1685-1690, pb. 1902) and *Aristomenes: Or, The Royal Shepherd* (wr. c. 1688-1691, pb. 1713). The former is a tragicomedy, the latter a tragedy. She also wrote an epilogue to Nicholas Rowe's 1714 *The Tragedy of Jane Shore*, which was spoken by the actress playing the title role.

ACHIEVEMENTS

When Anne Finch's *Miscellany Poems, on Several Occasions* appeared in 1713 ("Written by a Lady," according to the title page of the first printing, though later printings gave her name), it was only the third volume of poetry by a woman to have been published in the eighteenth century, and she was one of the first women to devote a lifetime to writing poetry. Contemporary social strictures and prejudices notwithstanding, Finch was acknowledged by London's male literary circles, many of her poems were included (albeit usually anonymously) in leading publications, and Alexander Pope and Jonathan Swift celebrated her in commendatory verses.

During her long career, she wrote in a variety of poetic forms, including elegies, pastorals, satires, verse epistles, beast fables, ballads, and occasional poetry, and though her output was mainly in the Restoration and Augustan neoclassic traditions, the poems often transcended prevailing conventions of subject, form, and theme. In her nature poems, for example, she anticipated the Romantic movement, and in many works she introduced a feminine sensibility, giving voice to a socially and educationally marginalized sex and presenting, perhaps for the first time, portraits of love and marriage from a woman's perspective.

BIOGRAPHY

Anne Finch was born in southern England to Sir William and Anne (Haslewood) Kingsmill, whose families were landed gentry with royal connections. Both parents died before Anne was three, and she and two siblings lived, at various times, with a stepfather, uncle, and grandmother. Unusual for the time, Sir William in his will set aside money for the support and education not only of his son and heir but also of his daughters. Young Anne thus had a substantive education in English poetry and drama, and also in the classics and foreign languages. She

benefited, too, from living in London with her paternal grandmother, a wealthy, strong-willed woman (who twice brought Chancery suits in behalf of Anne and her sister).

In 1683, at age twenty-one, Anne joined the household of the duchess of York (Mary of Modena, Italian second wife of the duke of York, heir to the throne) and the next year wed Colonel Heneage Finch, a soldier who was part of the duke of York's retinue. By all accounts, this was a happy and loving marriage. Her husband through the decades actively supported her writing, requesting that she write poems for him, editing and transcribing them, and compiling manuscripts for private circulation.

In 1685, when the duke of York became King James II, the couple remained part of the court circle, but when James was deposed three years later, Colonel Finch stayed loyal to the Stuart cause and refused to swear allegiance to the new monarchs, William and Mary. Thus estranged from court and politics, Anne and Heneage Finch retreated to the country seat—Eastwell Park in Kent—of his nephew, the earl of Winchelsea, where they lived a kind of self-imposed exile for many years, though occasionally visiting London or the spa at Tunbridge Wells, where Anne sought relief from her unremitting neurotic complaints.

While in Kent, Finch continued to write poems (using the pseudonym Ardelia), and whereas she kept her work secret at court, in her country exile she circulated poems in manuscript among acquaintances. She first appeared in print in 1701, when her Pindaric ode "The Spleen" was published. After his nephew died, in 1712, and Colonel Finch succeeded to the title, the couple moved permanently to London. There the countess, though still suffering from melancholy and depression, continued to write poetry and came to know leading writers of the period, including Pope, Rowe, and Swift, as well as John Gay, Matthew Prior, and Thomas Warton. In 1719, Swift in "Apollo Outwitted" praised her poetry and at the same time teased her for being so modest, playfully urging her to publish more often. At the age of fifty-nine, Finch died at her London home.

ANALYSIS

During the eighteenth century, after her death, Anne Finch was recalled primarily as the author of "The

Spleen," widely admired as an exemplar of the then popular Pindaric ode form. In the nineteenth century, attention shifted to her nature poetry, primarily as a result of William Wordsworth's 1815 remark in his supplementary essay to the preface of *Lyrical Ballads* (originally published, 1798):

> . . . excepting the nocturnal 'Reverie of Lady Winchelsea,' and a passage or two in the 'Windsor Forest' of Pope, the poetry of the period intervening between the publication of the 'Paradise Lost' and 'The Seasons' does not contain a single new image of esteemed nature, and scarcely presents a familiar one from which it can be inferred that the eye of the Poet had been steadily fixed upon his object, much less that his feelings had urged him to work upon it in the spirit of genuine imagination.

As a result of this praise, Finch was regarded for more than a century almost solely as a pre-Romantic nature poet, but in the mid-twentieth century critics started to consider her as more of a mainstream neoclassical writer. Still another canonical shift occurred late in the twentieth century, when Finch was recognized as an early feminist voice.

"THE INTRODUCTION"

This poem, with which Finch opened manuscripts of her work that circulated among friends, is a poignant presentation in heroic couplets of the subservient place of women, particularly the plight of one who sought recognition and acceptance as a poet. Anticipating the censure she could expect by so-called Witts—men who achieved their reputations "only by finding fault"—Finch says they would call her lines "insipid, empty, uncorrect." They would condemn them simply because "they're by a Woman writt," and because "a woman that attempts the pen" is "an intruder on the rights of men." Such men tell women that they should desire just "Good breeding, fassion, dancing, dressing, play." Finch argues that women are not innately inferior, but rather are "Education's, more than Nature's fools" and recalls Old Testament women who functioned as public poets. At the end, she stoically withdraws "with contracted wing," determining to be content sharing her work with "some few friends." Two other poems in which Finch also deals with the obstacles confronting a woman poet

are "The Appology" and the fablelike "Mercury and the Elephant."

"THE PETITION FOR AN ABSOLUTE RETREAT"

In the lengthy, discursive "The Petition for an Absolute Retreat," one of her two major nature poems, Finch's indebtedness to other seventeenth century poets is apparent: Andrew Marvell's view of the natural world as a haven, Henry Vaughan's mysticism, and Robert Herrick's straightforwardly simple style. Finch's poem is dedicated to the countess of Thanet (called Arminda in the poem), a country friend whose presence in a work celebrating rural privacy and seclusion as means of spiritual renewal suggests that Finch requires female companionship, perhaps an alter ego, to sustain her muse.

The poem also expresses her desire for a husband to share the retreat, a "*Partner* suited to my Mind," who will eschew "Fame and Splendor, Wealth and Pride" and will not let business, wars, or other matters separate them. Despite the opening paean to an "Absolute Retreat" in a remoteness "That the World may ne'er invade," Finch is not calling for a permanent, solitary, spartan isolation in her halcyon eden, and she recognizes that retreat cannot halt the debilitating passage of time. The plethora of classical allusions, an idealized rather than a realistic portrayal of nature, and the elegiac rather than descriptive style place the poem firmly in the Augustan tradition, with only slight pre-Romantic qualities.

"A NOCTURNAL REVERIE"

Of Finch's more than two hundred poems, fewer than ten are principally about external nature, and the best of these are "The Petition for an Absolute Retreat" and "A Nocturnal Reverie." The latter, whose fifty lines comprise one sentence, is noteworthy for its descriptive concreteness and specificity, from an opening that echoes the start of the fifth act of William Shakespeare's *The Merchant of Venice* (pr. c. 1596-1597) to the close, when dawn comes and "Our Cares, our Toils, our Clamours are renew'd," bringing the speaker's respite to an end. Like animals, the poet feels freer at night, but this is a "shortliv'd Jubilee," for "Morning breaks, and All's confused again." Whereas her contemporary poets engage mainly in vague generalizing, Finch in this poem evokes the senses: She describes a returning stray horse coming so close that "torn up Forage in his Teeth we hear" and refers to cattle "unmolested" and other animals also at peace while "Tyrant-*Man* do's sleep," establishing a typically Romantic rivalry between man and nature. On the other hand, stereotypical epithets, a tribute to a friend midway through the poem, and a reflective, almost gothic melancholy make "A Nocturnal Reverie" closer to such eighteenth century standards as John Pomfret's "The Choice" (1700) and Thomas Warton the Younger's *Pleasures of Melancholy* (1747) than to James Thomson's *The Seasons* (1726-1730), an Augustan Age touchstone for nature poetry.

"THE TREE"

Because the tree provides her with "delightful Shade" and "cool Shadows," the poet is indebted to it. She notes that birds, which it shelters, reward it with their music; travelers, who use it for protection from storms, thank it with their praise; and the shepherd, whom it shields from scorching sun, "Tunes to thy dancing Leaves his Reed." The poet pays her debt by wishing that the tree will stand for ages, "Untouch'd by the rash Workman's hand" until it dies naturally, when "fierce Winds," not an ax, will fell the dead tree, after which it will "like ancient Heroes, burn,/ And some bright Hearth be made thy Urn." By not naming any species, Finch universalizes the tree, so it exemplifies the Arcadian nature-versus-man theme that is central to the poem, which feminist critics also interpret as presenting a feminized landscape menaced by masculine intrusion.

"TO THE NIGHTINGALE"

"To the Nightingale," in Finch's 1713 *Miscellany Poems, on Several Occasions* along with "A Nocturnal Reverie," "The Tree," and "The Spleen," uses the bird as an emblem of lyric poetry, which had been a common practice among Renaissance writers, including Thomas Dekker, John Lyly, Thomas Middleton, and Sir Philip Sidney. Beginning by invoking the bird as muse, the speaker wants her song to be as free as the bird's, because poets are at their best "when unconfin'd" by tradition and rules. However, "Cares," presumably the world around her, weigh her down and their "Thoughts molest," so she decides that escape to the bird's lyric world is a futile hope, and like her peers she must be satisfied writing poems that "Criticize, reform, or preach," that is, embrace the prevailing neoclassical poetic practices. Because she is a woman, Finch knows that she faces even greater obstacles than do her male counterparts, and the

realization is part of her problem. This poem of unrequited aspirations anticipates structurally as well as thematically John Keats's "Ode to a Nightingale" (1819) and Percy Bysshe Shelley's "To a Skylark" (1820).

"THE SPLEEN"

In her occasional poems, Finch usually utilizes neoclassical poetic devices that obscure the contemporary autobiographical elements. Among these works are "A Letter to Dafnis April: 2d 1685," a brief verse epistle to her husband; "To Mr. F. Now Earl of W.," also about her marriage; and the epistle "To My Sister Ogle, Decbr 31, 1688" and "A Poem for the Birth-day of the Right Honble the Lady Catherine Tufton." Primary in this group is "The Spleen," which was first published in 1701 and remained popular for a century, in large part because of its subject: Finch's lifelong struggle with melancholy, depression, and other neuroses, which at the time were collectively called "the spleen," an affliction somewhat more common among women than among men.

Widespread attention first focused upon the illness when Robert Burton's *The Anatomy of Melancholy* was published in three volumes in 1621, and poems dealing with melancholy proliferated, including John Milton's "Il Penseroso" (c. 1631), Matthew Green's "The Spleen," Robert Blair's "The Grave" (1743), and Thomas Gray's "Elegy Written in a Country Churchyard" (1751). However, "The Spleen"—a Pindaric ode in an irregular strophic pattern of 150 lines—is the most detailed treatment, so precise and accurate in its details that it was utilized as a text by eighteenth century medical practitioners.

Finch starts by describing the protean quality of the ailment's manifestations: "A Calm of stupid Discontent"; rage; "Panick Fear." She then laments how "On Sleep intruding dost thy Shadows spread," causing terror, bad dreams, and delusions. She recalls that Brutus "Was vanquish'd by the *Spleen*" and tells of how it changes an "Imperious *Wife*" into a servile woman and affects fools as well as "Men of Thoughts refin'd." Turning to herself, she laments its destructive force on her poetry ("I feel my Verse decay, and my crampt Numbers fail"). Following her clinical examination of the illness, she tells of how people pretend to suffer from the affliction to excuse wayward behavior and concludes with a grudging stoic recognition of the futility of attempting to conquer the debilitating illness.

OTHER MAJOR WORKS

PLAYS: *The Triumphs of Love and Innocence*, wr. c. 1685-1690, pb. 1902; *Aristomenes: Or, The Royal Shepherd*, wr. c. 1688-1691, pb. 1713.

BIBLIOGRAPHY

Brower, Reuben A. "Lady Winchelsea and the Poetic Tradition of the Seventeenth Century." *Studies in Philology* 42 (1945): 61-80. In this influential article, Brower places Finch's poetry firmly in the eighteenth century tradition and distances her from the Romantics. He considers her nature poems as products of her early years and demonstrates their similarity to seventeenth century Metaphysical poetry.

Hinnant, Charles H. *The Poetry of Anne Finch: An Essay in Interpretation*. Newark: University of Delaware Press, 1994. In this first comprehensive study of Finch's poetry, Hinnant examines her work in relation to that of Augustan contemporaries and nineteenth century Romantics, and also considers her as an early feminist writer. He provides detailed explications of many poems, usefully balancing his interpretations with those of others.

McGovern, Barbara. *Anne Finch and Her Poetry: A Critical Biography*. Athens: University of Georgia Press, 1992. This first full-length life of Finch focuses upon her "historical place" and "displacement" (as McGovern puts it) among her contemporaries, "and particularly on the methods by which she developed a poetic identity for her own artistic liberation." Of value is an appendix of twelve uncollected poems from a manuscript at Wellesley College in Massachusetts.

McGovern, Barbara, and Charles H. Hinnant, eds. *The Anne Finch Wellesley Manuscript Poems*. Athens: University of Georgia Press, 1998. Fifty-three previously unpublished Finch poems from a manuscript at Wellesley College in Massachusetts are printed in this volume with useful critical commentary and annotations. Since Finch wrote many of these poems in the last two decades of her life, their availability makes possible a reevaluation of her career.

Mallinson, Jean. "Anne Finch: A Woman Poet and the Tradition." In *Gender at Work: Four Women Writers of the Eighteenth Century*, edited by Ann Messinger.

Detroit: Wayne State University Press, 1990. A consideration of Finch as one of the first English women poets to surmount the barriers of sexual prejudice and forge a career that was accepted and applauded by contemporary male counterparts.

Reynolds, Myra, ed. *The Poems of Anne, Countess of Winchelsea*. Chicago: University of Chicago Press, 1902. This volume, with a useful introduction, reprints what is included in the 1713 *Miscellany* as well as some works from manuscript sources. Though supplemented by the publication of the Wellesley manuscript poems, it remains a standard source.

Rogers, Katharine, ed. *Selected Poems of Anne Finch, Countess of Winchelsea*. New York: Ungar, 1979. The first collection of Finch poems since the 1902 edition edited by Myra Reynolds, this selection of almost seventy representative poems is prefaced by an introductory essay that explicates the poems, places them in their eighteenth century context, and considers Finch as an early woman poet of consequence.

Gerald H. Strauss

FIRDUSI

Born: Near Tús, Iran; between 932 and 941
Died: Near Tús, Iran; between 1020 and 1025

PRINCIPAL POETRY

Shahnamah, c. 1010

OTHER LITERARY FORMS

Although the only surviving work by Firdusi is the *Shahnamah* (the book of kings), another long poem titled *Yusuf u Zulaikha* (Joseph and Zulaikha), detailing the story of the biblical character Joseph and Potiphar's wife, has been attributed to Firdusi. This poem, however, is not Firdusi's and belongs to a much later period. Other verses scattered in various anthologies of the classical period have been ascribed to the poet, but none of these fragments can be assigned to him with certainty. These fragments have been collected and studied by H. Ethé in his *Firdûsî als Lyriker* (1872-1873).

ACHIEVEMENTS

The names of Firdusi and his *Shahnamah* became synonymous with the national epic of Iran. With the birth of the discipline of Orientalism, this book was brought to the West through translations and in turn influenced Western authors such as Matthew Arnold, who based his "Sohrab and Rustum" on it. Thus, Firdusi's poem was established as an important work in world literature.

BIOGRAPHY

Little factual information is available concerning Firdusi's life. The character of the poet is overgrown by a thicket of tales which sprang up around him shortly after his death. His first name was Hasan, or Ahmad, or Mansūr, the latter being more commonly used. He was born in or around the city of Tús in northeastern Iran, possibly in a village called Bāzh. His date of birth is given as any year between 932 and 941. His father was a country gentleman of the *dihqān* class, the rural landowners. Firdusi's youth was spent in circumstances of financial ease. When still young, he versified individual heroic tales, but it was not until the age of thirty-five or forty that he systematically attempted the versification of one of the existing prose *Shahnamahs* of his time, spending between twenty and thirty-five years of his life on this project. During this time, he completed at least two redactions of his work, one in 994-995 and the other in 1009-1010.

Apparently Firdusi was hoping to offer his great epic to a king whom he considered worthy of it. Thus, when he finished the first redaction, he kept it for nearly twenty years before finally offering it to King Mahmūd of Ghazna in the hope of receiving some reward. During this time, the poet had grown old and destitute. It would be incorrect to assume that Firdusi began his project with the intention of offering the finished product to King Mahmūd or even for the sake of financial gain: From references to the project scattered throughout the epic, it is clear that he began the work at least twenty years before Mahmūd ascended the throne. That the poet was relatively young and financially secure when he began his versification of individual stories is evident from the introduction to the story of Bīzhan and Manīzha, in which he paints a picture of himself as a young and affluent country gentleman.

In the middle of his great project, however, his life had already changed for the worse. He was old, tired, and poor. When he submitted his poem, completed in 1010 or 1011, the court disregarded his great effort.

It is known from references within his poem that Firdusi lost a son, who was about thirty-seven years old at the time of his death and probably not very loving toward his father. The classical Persian sources refer to a daughter of the poet as well, but Firdusi himself mentions nothing about her. Firdusi lived some ten or fifteen years after his disappointment with the court of Mahmūd, busying himself with making corrections to and insertions in the text of his poem, and finally dying in 1020 or 1025.

Whereas dependable historical data about Firdusi's life are difficult to unearth, a wealth of folklore concerning him exists in the classical accounts of his life. This folk biography of the poet exists not only in the living oral tradition but also within the classical Persian texts. The contents of the classical Persian sources recounting the biography of the poet demonstrate standard folk motifs. They further disregard historical facts by telling of Firdusi's meeting with famous persons long dead when the poet was born. These texts seem to be largely retellings, in courtly prose, of the stories circulating about the poet in the oral tradition of the period of their composition.

According to these sources, the poet began the versification of the *Shahnamah* so that he could supply his daughter with an adequate dowry out of the reward he expected to obtain for it. When he finished the work, he had it transcribed in seven volumes and took it to the court of King Mahmūd. There, with the help of a great minister, he presented it and it was accepted by the king, who promised the poet sixty thousand gold coins, or one coin per verse. Yet the monarch paid Firdusi only twenty thousand silver coins in the end. The reason for this change of heart on the part of the king was that Firdusi was accused of heresy by those who wished him ill. Firdusi, bitterly disappointed, went to the bath, and on coming out, bought a drink of sherbet and divided the money between the bath man and the sherbet seller. Knowing, however, that he had thus insulted the king, he fled the capital, taking his poem with him. Firdusi sought refuge with a noble Iranian prince, and in his palace he composed a satire of one hundred or more couplets on King Mahmūd, which he inserted as a preface to the *Shahnamah*. When he recited this satire to his host, the prince, a prudent man, told him: "Mahmūd is my liege-lord, sell me these one hundred satirical verses for one thousand coins each." The poet agreed, and the prince took possession of the verses and destroyed them. Of the one hundred verses, it is said, only six remain. This account, however, is inconsistent with the fact that the entire text, showing every sign of authenticity, remains.

After this episode, Firdusi retired to his native city of Tús, where he lived his last years in the company of his daughter. Meanwhile, the king had a change of heart and decided to send the poet his just reward. As the camels bearing the royal reward were entering the city through one gate, however, the corpse of Firdusi was being borne forth through another. Such is the account of the classical Persian texts.

ANALYSIS

The national saga of Iran, which constitutes an ethnic history of the Iranians, existed in written form long before the time of Firdusi. Sagas of this type formed a genre of classical Persian literature, both in verse and in prose, which were known by the generic name *Shahnamah*. Firdusi chose an existing prose *Shahnamah* to versify during his long poetic career. He included in his narrative other relevant tales from the oral tradition, creating a coherent narrative detailing the national saga of Iran in verse. His masterful verse gradually replaced the original prose work, and in time the term *Shahnamah* came to be applied exclusively to his poem.

SHAHNAMAH

The *Shahnamah* is a long epic poem which in the great majority of manuscripts comprises between forty-eight thousand and fifty-two thousand distichs. In some later manuscripts the number of distichs reaches fifty-five thousand or more. The *Shahnamah* is composed in the meter of *mutaqarib*, which is made of a line of eight feet in two hemistichs. Whereas the hemistichs of each line have end rhyme, successive lines do not rhyme with one another. As in the case of all other classical Persian poetry, a regular caesura exists between hemistichs. The *mutaqarib* meter, although used in the work of pre-

Firdusian poets in different kinds of narrative poetry, came to be almost exclusively reserved for epic poems after Firdusi. The *Shahnamah* has been repeatedly published in Iran, Europe, and India, and has been translated either in whole or abridged form into many languages.

The narrative of the *Shahnamah* can be divided into three parts. The first, a mythological section, begins with the reign of the first king, Kayūmars, and deals with a dynasty of primordial rulers, or demigods, who function as creative kings or culture heroes. They either invent some useful item or teach men a new craft. This group of kings, possibly based on an ancient class of old Iranian gods, are called the *Pīshdādīs* (the ancient creators).

The second part of the epic deals with a series of kings called the *Kayāniyān*. The rule of this group constitutes the purely legendary section of the *Shahnamah*. As all creative activities have already been dealt with by the *Pīshdādīs*, the *Kayāniyān* dynasts mark the beginning of the legendary and the heroic section. Their reign is filled with great wars and lofty deeds of heroes and kings. In this section, men become the main figures of the tales. Although the men encountered in these stories are heroic, or idealized, they are nevertheless completely human, lacking the creative powers of the demigods of the previous section. While they may be sorcerors, makers of illusions, they are not divine.

The third part of the *Shahnamah* is the semihistorical section, which narrates an idealized version of the reign of historical monarchs who ruled Iran from roughly the sixth century B.C.E. to the Arab conquest in the seventh century C.E. Incorporating a version of the medieval Alexander romances, of which Alexander of Macedonia is the central figure, this semihistorical section is comparatively lacking in action and includes much didactic verse. Recounting the tales which sprang up around the characters of certain historical monarchs of this period, it ends with an account of the fall of the Sasanid Empire (224-641 C.E.) and the Muslim conquest of Iran.

One gets the impression that in composing the narrative of the first two parts, the mythical and the heroic/legendary section, the poet exercised his imagination to a greater extent than when working with the semihistorial section. Scholars such as W. L. Hanaway have suggested that this feature of the *Shahnamah* results from a greater availability of detailed material relating to the historical monarchs of Iran at the time of its composition. The availability of this detailed material limited the extent to which the poet could exercise his imagination. Firdusi repeatedly states that he tried to remain faithful to the sources from which he was working. As a result of his faithfulness to these sources, Hanaway observes, he became more of a historian than an epic poet. In one instance at the end of a long episode in the reign of King Anūshīravān and his grand vizier Būzarjumihr, just before he began to compose the legend of the invention of the game of chess, Firdusi writes:

Thanks be to the lord of the sun and of the moon
That I was finally rescued from Būzarjumihr and the king.
Now that this boring task has come to an end
Let us begin to relate the tale of Chess.

Thus, the poet seems to have been restricted by a text, one which bored him, but to which he remained faithful.

Amin Banani has observed that Firdusi is in a sense the historian of his race. Firdusi often specifies the source from which he obtained his information, a habit which enables scholars to distinguish between the tales which have an oral origin and those which are based on written sources. The *Shahnamah* narrates, in chronological order, the progression and the evolution of the concept of kingship in the context of the Iranian legendary history. Individual kings may fall, but the line of kings continues uninterrupted. In the course of the steady progression of the institution, kings evolve from divine priest-kings/culture heroes (such as Jamshīd) to monarchs who rule by divine grace through their royal glory (called *farr* in the epic).

A motif that runs through the poem is that of the royal person who is recognized and restored to his rightful place. Sometimes it is a hero who helps establish the new king. The central hero of the epic, Rustam, is one such protector of king and crown. At other times, the king is restored through the efforts of more obscure persons, such as shepherds or blacksmiths. Yet as G. M. Wickens observes, "at no point in the vast cavalcade are we in any serious doubt that the true line of kingship, as distinct from individual kings, will survive." Exploits of individual heroes, such as Rustam's mortal battle with his son Suhrāb, his battles with demons, and the tale of his seven trials, are couched in the overriding motif of the protection of the crown.

Similarly, there is a recurring dramatic tension between good and evil, legitimacy and illegitimacy, and Iranian and non-Iranian. It is in this context that the tale of the perpetuation of the institution of kingship is told. This dramatic tension in the epic is heightened by a skillful use of characterization. There are, as Banani has pointed out, no archetypes in the *Shahnamah*. Every character is so minutely developed that he ceases to be a hero in the abstract and develops instead into an individual with a well-defined pattern of behavior. Through this characterization, "the goodness of the best is possible and the evil of the most wretched is not incredible." Thus, there is no fairy-tale world of black and white, or absolute good and absolute evil, in Firdusi's poem.

Because of its size, the *Shahnamah* is not easily manageable as an object of literary criticism. It should be remembered that the two great classical epics of the Western world, the *Iliad* (c. 800 B.C.E.) and the *Odyssey* (c. 800 B.C.E.), together comprise no more than approximately twenty-seven thousand lines. The *Shahnamah's* great length, as well as its relative linguistic inaccessibility, have made it a poor candidate for literary criticism. Thus, Firdusi's poem still remains virtually virgin territory for critical analysis.

BIBLIOGRAPHY

Banani, Amin. "Ferdowsi and the Art of Tragic Epic." In *Islam and Its Cultural Divergence*, edited by G. L. Tikku. Urbana: University of Illinois Press, 1971. A short critical examination of Firdusi's *Shahnamah*.

Clinton, Jerome W. *In the Dragon's Claws: The Story of Rostam and Esfandiyar*. Washington, D.C.: Mage, 1999. Clinton's translation of the tale of the epic hero king Rostam includes genealogical tables of the royal heroes of Shahnamah.

Hanaway, W. L. "The Iranian Epics." In *Heroic Epic and Saga*, edited by Felix J. Oinas. Bloomington: Indiana University Press, 1978. Provides an introduction to the history of epic poetry in Iran.

Jackson, Abraham V. Williams. *Early Persian Poetry, from the Beginnings Down to the Time of Firdausi*.

New York: Macmillan, 1920. An early survey of the Persian poetic tradition that Firdusi embraced for epic poem *Shahnamah*.

Levy, Reuben, trans. *The Epic of the Kings: "Shah-nama," the National Epic of Persia*. 2d ed. Costa Mesa, Calif.: Mazda, 1996. Among the recent abridged translations of the epic, this one contains a foreword by Ehsan Yarsater, a preface by Amin Banani, and an introduction by Dick Davis.

Nöldeke, Theodor. *The Iranian National Epic: Or, The Shahnamah*. Translated by Leonid Bogdanov. Philadelphia: Porcupine Press, 1979. A critical study of Firdusi's *Shahnamah* and its historical and cultural background.

Rypka, Jan. *History of Iranian Literature*. Edited by Karl Jahn. Dordrecht, Netherlands: D. Reidel, 1968. A broad history and analysis of Iranian literature.

Wilkinson, J. V. S. *The "Shah-namah" of Firdausi*. London: Oxford University Press, 1931. Wilkinson outlines the structure of Firdusi's epic with sketches of principal stories and twenty-four illustrations from a fifteenth century manuscript in Persian owned by the Royal Asiatic Society.

Yohannan, John D. *Persian Poetry in England and America: A Two-Hundred-Year History*. Delmar, N.Y.: Caravan Books, 1977. A history of the translation, interpretation, and influence of Persian poetry in England and America.

Mahmoud Omidsalar;
bibliography updated by Mabel Khawaja

Edward FitzGerald

Born: Near Woodbridge, Suffolk, England; March 31, 1809
Died: Merton, Norfolk, England; June 14, 1883

Principal poetry

Salámán and Absál, 1856
Rubáiyát of Omar Khayyám, 1859, revised 1868, 1872, 1879

Other literary forms

Although Edward FitzGerald's reputation as a poet rests on the *Rubáiyát of Omar Khayyám*, he was a gifted writer in other forms. In 1851 FitzGerald published a philosophical dialogue called *Euphranor: A Dialogue on Youth*, and in 1852 he produced a collection of aphorisms titled *Polonius: A Collection of Wise Saws and Modern Instances*. FitzGerald's *Six Dramas of Calderón* in 1853 began his series of free translations of drama, which included his *Agamemnon* of 1865, *Oedipus Rex* in 1880-1881, and *Oedipus at Colonus* in 1880-1881.

Achievements

Edward FitzGerald's essential achievement is unique in the history of English literature. His *Rubáiyát of Omar Khayyám* is nominally a translation, but out of hundreds of separate short poems by a relatively minor Persian poet of the twelfth century, FitzGerald fashioned a beautifully unified poem in English. It is written with such power of expression, splendor of diction, and perfection of poetic music that it has long been recognized not only as an essentially original contribution to English poetry but also as one of the greatest poems in the language. FitzGerald's contemporary Charles Eliot Norton expressed the view that the *Rubáiyát* had all the merits of a great original poem and that it was unique among translations for its value as English poetry. This view has come to be universal, and the distinguished scholar Cecil Y. Lang wrote in 1968 that FitzGerald's *Rubáiyát* was "surely the most popular poem in the English language."

Biography

Edward FitzGerald was born in a Jacobean mansion in rural Suffolk, England. His parents were cousins and came from what was then one of the wealthiest families in Great Britain. As FitzGerald grew up, he developed a great dislike for the arrogance, ostentation, and formality of manners which he associated with wealth, but his part of the family fortune allowed him to live life on his own eccentric and creative terms throughout most of his adult years. FitzGerald's mother, Mary Frances Fitz-Gerald, was a proud and dominating woman, and Fitz-Gerald's relations with her were always difficult.

If FitzGerald's character was in part shaped by wealth and a troubled relationship with his mother, his early years also gave him a love for the quiet scenery of Suffolk, which would stay with him throughout his life. In 1818 FitzGerald was sent to the King Edward VI Grammar School in Bury St. Edmunds. There, he received a fine classical education and developed a number of important friendships. In 1826 FitzGerald went to the University of Cambridge, where he was an undisciplined but happy student who showed again his great gift for making friends. Among his many friends at Cambridge was the future novelist William Makepeace Thackeray.

After graduating from Cambridge in 1830, FitzGerald traveled briefly to Paris, spent time in London, Southampton, and Cambridge, and eventually made his way back to Suffolk. His family's wealth made it unnecessary for him to pursue a career, and for the next two decades or so FitzGerald mostly lived the quiet life of a country gentleman, developing his serious interests in art, music, literature, and gardening. He also became and would remain throughout his life a prolific and brilliant correspondent. During these years FitzGerald was friends with and corresponded with a broad range of distinguished writers, including Thomas Carlyle; Thackeray; Alfred, Lord Tennyson; Frederick Tennyson; the scholar James Spedding; and the poet Bernard Barton.

Although FitzGerald's letters during this period show him to be a writer of great accomplishment, and it is evident that men of Carlyle's and Thackeray's stature respected his intellect and taste, he contributed nothing official to English literature between 1830 and 1850. In 1844, however, he met a young scholar of Eastern languages named Edward Cowell who, by late 1852, was teaching FitzGerald Persian. In 1856 Cowell found a fifteenth century manuscript of Omar Khayyám in the Bodleian Library at Oxford. Cowell sent FitzGerald a transcript of this manuscript, and in 1859 appeared the first version of FitzGerald's *Rubáiyát of Omar Khayyám*.

Before the *Rubáiyát*, FitzGerald's publications had been few, eccentric, and unsuccessful. Despite its beautiful prose, his *Euphranor* of 1851 went mostly unnoticed. His book of aphorisms, *Polonius*, fared little better. His very free versions of the dramas of Pedro Calderón de la Barca as well as his highly original translation of the Persian *Salámán and Absál* had little critical or popular success. At first, the *Rubáiyát* did little better. By 1861, however, it began to be recognized in

literary circles, and eventually it would be published in three more editions during FitzGerald's lifetime.

FitzGerald remained preoccupied with the *Rubáiyát* throughout the rest of his life, but he also produced important, if very personal, versions of the works of Aeschylus and Sophocles. FitzGerald's quiet later years were marked by a constant stream of wonderful letters, increasing (though lovable) eccentricity of behavior, and a great interest in sailing and the simple life of the fishermen of his home county. He died while visiting friends in Norfolk on June 14, 1883. He was seventy-four.

ANALYSIS

Edward FitzGerald's place in English poetry is based on his *Rubáiyát of Omar Khayyám*. Despite this poem's nominal status as a translation, it has long been recognized as an essentially original contribution to English literature. Whatever may be the merits of the original Persian poems from which the *Rubáiyát* derives, the structure, diction, prosody, music, and movement of FitzGerald's poem belong to the English language and to FitzGerald himself. Moreover, even the ideas of the poem are given a unity, force, character, and application which have much more to do with FitzGerald than with Omar.

FITZGERALD AS "TRANSLATOR"

FitzGerald produced during his literary career translations of Greek tragedies, Spanish plays, and Persian poems. In all of these works, his approach is the same: He leaves out what he wishes to leave out. He conflates and changes originals as it suits him. He dresses the altered frames of his materials in his own highly personal style, and he emphasizes that which interests him and dismisses or changes that which does not. FitzGerald was always completely honest about this. When the publisher of the *Rubáiyát* spoke of the translation as being faithful, FitzGerald insisted that it was anything but that. In fact, FitzGerald always treated the works from which his translations derive as "sources" rather than "originals." He is little more concerned with being faithful to Omar than William Shakespeare was worried about being faithful to his sources.

FitzGerald's freedom and originality in dealing with Omar's poetry may best be seen in the fact that there is actually no coherent work called the *Rubáiyát* written by the Persian poet. The word *rubáiyát* in Persian is simply the plural form of the word for short poem or epigram. What Omar actually wrote—or was credited with—were roughly 750 individual short poems, each of which was a poem unto itself. Indeed, in Persian manuscripts, Omar's quatrains or epigrams are arranged merely alphabetically, based on the first letter in the first line of each quatrain poem. FitzGerald's earliest version of the *Rubáiyát* contains 75 stanzas, while his last version contains 101 stanzas. In all of his five versions of the poem, Omar's epigrams have become true stanzas in a highly structured and unified whole. Thus, FitzGerald chose only those poems which he wanted to use and then imposed a unity upon them which never existed in the original. Moreover, FitzGerald was very free with the original individual poems of Omar. In his final *Rubáiyát*, FitzGerald has forty-nine stanzas that roughly paraphrase actual Omar poems; his other fifty-two stanzas are composites of more than one Omar poem, or they do not derive from Omar at all.

THEMES AND MEANINGS

FitzGerald's *Rubáiyát* is a powerful meditation on and passionate questioning of the meaning of human life and the nature of the cosmos. For FitzGerald's Omar, the essential fact of life is life's brevity. Human beings are surrounded by darkness and death. There is great pathos in this, but the shortness and essential sadness of human life make momentary joy all the more important and cherishable. Also, it is only in such joys as love, retirement into gardens, flowers, poetry, and most of all, wine that the essence of true life is known. For FitzGerald's Omar, neither worldly greatness nor religious doctrine has any real value or meaning. Worldly greatness is an illusion, and religious doctrine is futile. The universe is ruled by a dark, unknowable force, perhaps a god, but if this god exists, it moves and acts in deeply mysterious ways, without regard for humans and beyond human understanding.

In FitzGerald's *Rubáiyát*, human beings exist only for a brief moment, and it is crucial that this moment be spent in vital, sensuous life rather than in empty speculation. In certain sections of the poem, FitzGerald makes Omar question a very Christian-sounding religion in a sharply sardonic and even satiric spirit. These sections were both shocking and stimulating to FitzGerald's contemporaries, and perhaps they will always have that sort of power for many readers. It is tempting to describe the

vision of the *Rubáiyát* as a kind of hedonistic epicurean nihilism, but that is too simple. Somehow, the poem is neither so dark nor so grim as its themes would suggest. This is in part because of the sheer verbal and musical beauty of the poem, but it is also because basic human life and momentary joy are treated in the poem as having great value and pathos precisely because they are surrounded by death, unknowable mystery, and cosmic darkness.

STRUCTURE AND STYLE

One of the most outstanding features of FitzGerald's *Rubáiyát* is its essential unity. FitzGerald achieves this by organizing his poem so that it begins with morning, the new year, and life and moves toward night, the close of the year, and death. Also, the stanzas of the poem are connected by repeated imagery, themes, and even grammar and syntax in such a way as to create a sense of movement within coherent unity. Moreover, the various sections of the poem, each composed of several stanzas, form coherent arguments that are then linked by logic and rhetoric so as to form a powerful whole.

The imagery of the poem is at once simple, exotic, and effective. FitzGerald's wine cups, roses, moons, gardens, taverns, deserts, lovers, birds, and wine all combine in such a way as to communicate with passionate directness, while creating an exotic sense of an imaginative Persia that haunts the mind. The *Rubáiyát* is a remarkably easy poem to read, but it creates a sense of richness and resonance.

The diction and general style of the *Rubáiyát* are a remarkable combination of simplicity and sensuousness. FitzGerald's mode of expression often has an almost eighteenth century clarity and compactness:

> Myself when young did eagerly frequent
> Doctor and Saint, and heard great argument
>   About it and about; but evermore
> Came out by the same door where in I went.

Yet this directness is combined with a tenderness and richness of music that are equally typical of FitzGerald:

> I sometimes think that never blows so red
> The Rose as where some buried Caesar bled;
>   That every Hyacinth the Garden wears
> Dropped in her Lap from some once lovely
>   Head.

Finally, in addition to structure, imagery, and diction, there is the distinctive stanza of the poem. FitzGerald's stanza, very loosely derived from Omar's quatrain form, consists of four lines of iambic pentameter, rhyming *aaxa*. This stanza was new to English, and FitzGerald's mastery of it created a distinctive prosodic and musical effect that accounts for much of the *Rubáiyát*'s magic.

RECEPTION AND HISTORICAL IMPORTANCE

When FitzGerald first published the *Rubáiyát* in 1859, it went almost totally unnoticed. By 1861, however, the poem was beginning to find readers among Pre-Raphaelite writers and artists. Dante Gabriel Rossetti, Algernon Charles Swinburne, and John Ruskin praised the poem, and it soon became popular in both England and the United States. By 1900 it was an acknowledged classic of English poetry, and it was published in hundreds of editions between 1870 and 1920.

Its historical importance lies in two spheres, one intellectual, the other poetic. Intellectually, FitzGerald's *Rubáiyát* was a compelling expression of religious doubt in a great age of religious doubt. FitzGerald raised many of the same questions that poets such as Matthew Arnold, James Walter Thomson, Thomas Hardy, and A. E. Housman raised, but he invested those doubts with a pathos and tenderness that were uniquely attractive. Poetically, FitzGerald's poem spoke a sensuous, rich, and exotic language that appealed to and influenced not only the Pre-Raphaelite poets between 1860 and 1880 but also the aesthete and decadent poets at the end of the nineteenth century.

OTHER MAJOR WORKS

NONFICTION: *Euphranor: A Dialogue on Youth*, 1851.

TRANSLATIONS: *Six Dramas of Calderón*, 1853 (of Pedro Calderón de la Barca); *Agamemnon*, 1865 (of Aeschylus); *Oedipus Rex*, 1880-1881 (of Sophocles); *Oedipus at Colonus*, 1880-1881 (of Sophocles).

MISCELLANEOUS: *Polonius: A Collection of Wise Saws and Modern Instances*, 1852.

BIBLIOGRAPHY

Alexander, Doris. *Creating Literature Out of Life: The Making of Four Masterpieces*. University Park, Pa.: The Penn State University Press, 1996. This excellent book contains a fascinating account of how FitzGerald created the *Rubáiyát*. Emphasizes the psychological crises in FitzGerald's life that created the energies necessary to turn a "translation" into a work of original genius.

Bowra, Maurice. *In General and Particular*. New York: World Publishing, 1964. This collection of essays devotes one long essay to FitzGerald that deals sensitively and incisively with both his life and the *Rubáiyát*. It is particularly good on FitzGerald's qualities as a translator and on the style of the *Rubáiyát*.

France, Peter, ed. *The Oxford Guide to Literature in English Translation*. New York: Oxford University Press, 2000. Provides an invaluable account of all of FitzGerald's translations, in which the *Rubáiyát* and his other works are compared with other translations of the same originals and placed within the history of translation.

Martin, Robert Bernard. *With Friends Possessed: A Life of Edward FitzGerald*. New York: Atheneum, 1985. The standard biography of FitzGerald, a brilliant account of his life and work; particularly strong on his psychological character, his friendships, his literary achievement, his life in Suffolk, and his letters.

Richardson, Joanna. *Edward FitzGerald*. London: Longman's, 1960. A brief but very useful study of FitzGerald. Contains a good overview of his life, a balanced and reliable account of the *Rubáiyát*, and an especially strong section on FitzGerald as letter writer.

Phillip B. Anderson

ROLAND FLINT

Born: Park River, North Dakota; February 27, 1934
Died: Kensington, Maryland; January 2, 2001

PRINCIPAL POETRY
And Morning, 1975
The Honey and Other Poems for Rosalind, 1976 (limited edition chapbook)
Say It, 1979

Resuming Green: Selected Poems, 1965-1982, 1983

Sicily, 1987 (limited edition chapbook)

Stubborn, 1990

Hearing Voices, 1991 (limited edition chapbook; with William Stafford)

Pigeon, 1991

Pigeon in the Night, 1994 (selected poems with Bulgarian/English translation)

Easy, 1999

OTHER LITERARY FORMS

Beginning in the 1980's, Roland Flint developed a keen interest in the poetry of Bulgaria, visiting the country a number of times and working in the United States to establish an audience for such work. In addition to the 1994 bilingual edition of his own poetry, *Pigeon in the Night*, Flint helped translate three volumes of Bulgarian poetry: Boris Khristov's *Words and Graphite* (1991; with Betty Grinberg) and *The Wings of the Messenger* (1991; with Grinberg and Lyubomir Nikolov) and Lyubomir Nikolov's *Pagan* (1992; with Viara Tcholakova).

ACHIEVEMENTS

Roland Flint won the Corcoran Gallery award in poetry in 1976 and earned a National Endowment for the Arts Fellowship in 1981. *Stubborn* (1990) was selected for the National Poetry Series. Flint also received the Maxwell Anderson Award from the University of North Dakota in 1993 and Maryland State Arts Council grants in 1989 and 1993. He was Maryland's poet laureate from 1995 to 2000.

BIOGRAPHY

One of six children born to a North Dakota potato farmer who had lost the family farm early during the Depression, Roland Henry Flint spent his formative years working strenuous farm jobs. Such physically demanding work taught Flint toughness and discipline but also connected him to the cycles of the living earth, to its physical beauty and its harshness. After his first try at college proved unsuccessful, he enlisted in the Marines and served in Korea just after the war. Walking guard duty by an ammunition dump one Christmas night, he resolved with epiphanic clarity that when he returned stateside he would take college seriously. After earning

his B.A. from the University of North Dakota-Grand Forks in 1958, where he wrote his first poems, he received his master's degree from Marquette University in 1960 and then his doctorate from the University of Minnesota in 1968. In both postgraduate positions he taught and grew to love the dynamics of a classroom and the opportunity to explore the craft of writing with students. He joined the faculty of Georgetown University in 1968 and taught literature and creative writing with distinction, retiring in 1997.

Although he published poetry in journals for more than twenty years, he did not release his first volume until his early forties. Flint often quoted James Wright: "I want poetry to be beautiful, but if it doesn't speak of the hell in our lives, it leaves me cold." Although Flint's poetry frequently centers on the simple joys of his daily life and the emotional support of his second wife, his two daughters, and his two stepsons, Flint drew from his own private pain to shape his most effective poetry, confessional mediations about growing up in rural poverty (including a suicide attempt at age fourteen) and the difficult relationship he maintained with his disciplinarian father; about his first marriage, which ended in divorce in 1973; and about the deaths of his brother and both his parents. However, the centering emotional trauma of Flint's life was the 1972 death of his six-year-old son Ethan David, killed by a car. Although long reluctant to address directly in interviews questions about his son's death, Flint's poetry, whatever the subject, is centrally about that adjustment process. As he often advised his writing students, "Push it where it hurts. That's where the poems are." After retiring from Georgetown, Flint concentrated on his duties as Maryland's poet laureate until his declining health forced him to resign that appointment in October, 2000. Almost three months later, he died of cancer at home at the age of sixty-six.

ANALYSIS

The achievement of Roland Flint's poetry is its remarkable accessibility. Although he was a career academic (teaching for more than thirty years at Georgetown University), Flint's poetry is not marked by the heavy-handed intellectual embroidery, lexical experimenting, obscure symbols, and erudite allusions that put so much contemporary poetry out of reach of a large audience.

Reflecting perhaps his rural upbringing on the Great Plains or his early dissatisfactions with higher education (he dropped out of college his first try), Flint's poetry is, as he often described it, "user-friendly," poetry intended to be read within public forums rather than treated to classroom analysis. During his five-year stint as Maryland's poet laureate (1995-2000), Flint worked tirelessly to bring poetry to audiences across his state not often exposed to it: rural schools, retirement homes, prisons, business clubs, private homes, and even local cable and national talk show audiences. With a rich, engaging voice, he was known for spellbinding readings. Because his poetry itself celebrates the ordinary miracles of daily life as well as the pain and the wonder drawn from Flint's own emotional experiences, audiences are compelled by such honesty and directness. By forsaking the posture of imperial poet, Flint imbues his poetry with a most affective intimacy and vulnerability.

Not surprisingly, such intimacy is achieved via a poetic line that dispenses with the intrusive play of anticipated rhythm and strict rhyme. What Flint offers instead is a blank-verse line that sounds its musical best when read aloud in subtle manipulations of sound and line length that create a sophisticated pace to poetry that sounds deceptively simple, even conversational. He often described his work as "common feelings captured in uncommon language," poetry within the colloquial range that defined the midcentury work of poets such as Theodore Roethke (the subject of Flint's doctorate), James Wright (a friend and colleague at the University of Minnesota), and William Stafford (an early mentor and eventual collaborator).

AND MORNING

Roland Flint's first collection is haunted by what he does not directly treat: the death of his son (the title puns on morning/mourning). Flint acknowledges only that upon reaching midlife, he finds himself "broken, permanently/ in some ways I did not devise/ and may not speak of." The poems are each pressured by time, by the perplexing drama of mortality and the quick moment of translation from presence to absence. Deaths and funerals, illness and accidents, violence and bad luck haunt the narrative line of poem after poem.

"Heads of the Children" recalls the verbal abuse of Flint's father and the anger Flint himself directed at his own son—it is the unspoken pain of the poem that the reader understands that this recollection is part of the grieving process of the father for his now-dead son. Flint speaks of his need for consolation, for his Christian upbringing to give logic to events that appear to be paradoxically both shattering and pointless. A preacher, he says, "just opens his mouth/ and there is that parabola/ draining into peace." Yet Flint's poetry refuses the simple surrender to grief. The collection moves in its two stunning closing poems to solutions. In "Wheel," Flint observes his wife and daughter awkwardly fashion a gift-cup for him out of clay and compares such a clumsy process to his own writing and argues that in language he has found a way to fashion, perhaps awkwardly, moments of clarity from painful experience. In the simple quatrain of the volume's closing poem, "And Morning In," Flint offers a simple image: a rooster on a fence post crowing to the sunrise, "I'm up again/ and so are you," a strategy of embracing each morning as opportunity despite (or perhaps because of) the knowledge of mortality. It is Flint's characteristic achievement to draw from the natural world an accessible image that so easily becomes a suggestive symbol.

SAY IT

As the bold title suggests, the poems gathered in *Say It* refuse self-pity and negotiate strategies for adjusting to the bewildering time-bound world defined in *And Morning* (1975). Each piece is cast in straightforward and undecorated blank verse, the language accessible and immediate. For the first time, Flint directly treats the death of his son, but the emphasis here is on recovery and spiritual resurrection. In "Shim" Flint recounts sharing a drunken embrace with a woman, a stranger at a wedding reception. Although he discounts the possibility of any affair, he calls the embrace an act of love that caught them both at an inexplicable moment of mutual need, and he reassures the woman, "today I'm here to give you balance." The title itself refers to a home-repair process of filling cracks, usually with putty. Restoring fractures metaphorically relates to the repair work Flint is undertaking on his heart.

Other poems celebrate the unsuspected richness of the simplest moments: the first blush of sunrise, the call of an early spring bird, a bowl of late-morning oatmeal, the gift of two jars of honey. In "Say It" Flint summarizes this strategy by recalling the terror when a bug crawled into his ear as he slept. Later he claims the invading bug had whispered an urgent message, "*listen*": "the brown, ugly, implacable bug saying/ pay attention." That the instrument of such an epiphany, the resolution to take in every moment of the ordinary world, would be a repulsive bug suggests how the most repellant events can trigger such splendid resolve.

Flint then moves into a cycle of prose poems, intensely felt quasi parables, that highlight such moments when the unadorned world unexpectedly teaches lessons rich with emotional import. The closing section is a potpourri of recovery poems, Flint recalling a wonderful afternoon with Ethan, relishing the scent of a student who wears the same perfume as his long-dead grandmother, watching a man on his way to Mass stealing a ripe apple from a neighbor's yard, trying to explain the mystery of why his houseplants exploded in fecundity under a neighbor's care. In the closing piece, "Jog," Flint accepts the "ghosts" that have become his life" but humbly asks God *to go on blessing [his] life.* That humane resolution, of course, risks sentimentality and cliché. Yet, given Flint's devastating experience, such a prayer fixes the poet's determination to accept hard experience and to demand nevertheless the right to live in permanent expectation of surprise and delight.

STUBBORN

More than ten years later, Flint finds delight elusive and grief stubborn. Poems in his third major collection exist within that difficult balance. For example, in the opening poem, "A Letter Home," Flint admits to his mother with matter-of-fact directness that nearly forty years earlier he had clumsily tried to commit suicide. She had surprised him as he struggled trying to hang himself with a towel, and he had lied elaborately. He now offers no rationale for the action save his growing awareness even then of how random and pointless death seemed. Yet the poem closes with a difficult gesture of gratitude: "Thank God you came in when you did/ mother, for the life you gave/ what it's been, what it will be."

In the centerpiece poem, "Stubborn," Flint recounts an afternoon's drive when he chanced upon a small boy apparently lost. Stopping to help he eventually finds the distraught parents who say only that somehow the boy had gotten out of the house. The implications of such

carelessness for Flint are devastating. Barely restraining his tears, he tells the father about his own son's accident, but the father, indifferent to such pain, barely responds. Flint turns to his poetry—"go and write/ do what has been given to do"—to shape his grief into a prayer that the small boy might have the life his own son never had.

In the closing poem, "Sicily," Flint decides that life must be lived within a "permanent radius of risk," amid recovery from and expectation of catastrophe, like living beneath a volcano. Although he relishes the unearned joys of nature and of poetry itself, he acknowledges as well the deep grief in his heart and how, as much as he wants to accept the implications of a Christian afterlife, the closest he can come is the simple gesture of remembering those he has lost already. Thus even when he celebrates unexpected moments of joy, grand and small—cutting firewood, sharing whiskey with friends, listening as a child to his parents make love, or watching cats and grackles—he knows inevitably that everything curves toward death.

PIGEON

Pigeon represents a radical departure in tone and style for Flint. Forsaking the intimacy of first-person narrative, here Flint fashions for himself a third-person poetic persona: He calls himself "Pigeon" or simply "p." With often biting wit, Flint irreverently adopts the guise of a bird that is everyday and ordinary and clumsy in flight and whose beauty must be appreciated only after accepting its evident ugliness. Each characteristic comes to be part of Flint's own self-deprecating dissection of his roles as husband, poet, and teacher. The poetic line itself playfully toys with rhymes and rhythms and even typography. The titles serve as first lines, further disrupting the reading process and demanding a lighter approach.

To be sure, Flint still treats those stubborn griefs—the persistent tick of time, the inevitable experience of mortality, the onset of creaking bones and forgetfulness—but here Flint cannot resist undercutting the evident tragedy of such experiences with a poetic line that refuses to take itself seriously. It is as if the persona of the pigeon allows Flint a respite from poetry otherwise engaged in the sobering business of living amid catastrophe. At one point, Pigeon receives a phone call bearing bad medical news about his brother, and Flint acknowledges later when he recalls his dead son that he "can't quite hang on to pigeon when/ The night bores in like this." Yet Flint moves by volume's close to a difficult gesture of thanksgiving, appropriately on Thanksgiving morning, when Pigeon gives thanks for the remarkable wonder of the simplest gifts: his children, his wife, "the fat bird in the oven," and, perhaps most important, the fact that he woke up that morning to give thanks at all.

EASY

There is a valedictory feel to what proved to be Flint's last published volume, *Easy*, the feeling of a man who has come to terms at last with the difficult realities of his life, a poet looking back on his own emotional life and his achievement as a chronicler of that experience. In "Little Men Who Come Blindly," Flint watches a father testily instruct his young son on the mechanics of bike-riding and how the child handles such hurting and decides with a wisdom born of experience that there is nothing he could do, except write about it, extending to the reader what he knows he cannot say to the father, a caution to remember how stunningly brief life can be and how persistent rebuke can prove.

Set against poems that lovingly recollect friends and family now dead ("Tom" is a particularly poignant lyric on the first spring after his brother's death) are brief moments the poet has caught that remind the reader, amid so much catastrophe, of the stunning, fragile miracle of beauty. Yet it is supremely love that Flint offers as resolution. The title poem lingers on every element of an ordinary evening meal between Flint and his wife; Flint extends the promise of such intimacy by using third-person pronouns. The poem is executed with long lines rich with long vowel sounds and in-line punctuation that force the reader to slow down and relish the lingering evening. It is a remarkable moment of comfort and ease secured, Flint's longtime readers understand, amid a lifetime rocked by the unpredictable intrusion of chance. This is finally the role of the poet, which Flint acknowledges in his closing "Prayer": to remind readers that sorrow is never the last word, that joy is always a moment away, and that, without trivializing its cutting stroke, death alone justifies relishing every moment. If "Any day's writing may be the last," he gives humble thanks to a Lord, who must be in charge of such evident chaos, for giving him the gift of writing: "The work is all."

OTHER MAJOR WORKS

POETRY TRANSLATIONS: *Words and Graphite*, 1991 (of Boris Khristov's volume of poetry *Dumi i grafiti*; with Betty Grinberg); *The Wings of the Messenger*, 1991 (of Khristov's poetry; with Grinberg and Lyubomir Nikolov); *Pagan*, 1992 (of Nikolov's poetry; with Vyara Tcholakova).

BIBLIOGRAPHY

Ackerson, Duane. "Roland (Henry) Flint." In *Contemporary Poets, Sixth Edition*, edited by Thomas Riggs. New York: St. James Press, 1996. Provides extensive biographical information and examines the theme of love and loss in *Stubborn*.

Barnes, Bart. "Professor Roland Flint Dies; Maryland Poet Laureate." *The Washington Post*, January 5, 2001, p. B8. After Flint's death, a colleague writes, "Flint's great gift and subtle art was to speak in what seemed to be his own voice."

Bernard, J. D. "Surviving Grief: The Poetry of Roland Flint." *POET LORE* 76, no. 2 (1981). A critical examination of such poems as "And Morning," "Jog," and "Say It."

Gariepy, Jennifer. "Roland (Henry) Flint." In *Contemporary Authors*, Vol. 153, edited by Terrie M. Rooney. Detroit: Gale, 1997. Contains basic biographical information and a list of publications.

Kaganoff, Penny. Review of *Stubborn*, by Roland Flint. *Publishers Weekly* 237, no. 17 (April 27, 1990): 57. Kaganoff believes Flint's strongest poems are those in which he confronts mortality with his mind as well as his heart.

Joseph Dewey

J. V. FOIX

Born: Sarría, Spain; January 28, 1893
Died: Barcelona, Spain; January 29, 1987

PRINCIPAL POETRY

Gertrudis, 1927
KRTU, 1932

Sol, i de dol, 1936

Les irreals omegues, 1948

On he deixat les claus . . . ?, 1953

Del "Diari 1918," 1956

Onze nadals i un cap d'any, 1960

L'estrella d'en Perris, 1963

Desa aquests llibres al calaix de baix, 1964

Obres poètiques, 1964

Quatre nus, 1964

Darrer comunicat, 1970

Tocant a mà, 1972

Antologia poètica, 1973

Obres completes, 1974-1990 (4 volumes)

Quatre colors aparien el món . . . , 1975

OTHER LITERARY FORMS

In addition to his poetry, J. V. Foix published a number of works that are impossible to define in terms of conventional genres. Typical of his idiosyncratic manner are his "letters" to Clara Sobirós and Na Madrona Puignau, both invented personages. The Sobirós missive, which appropriately heads both the *Obres poètiques* and the first volume of the *Obres completes*, is a veritable manifesto of Foix's aesthetics. In "Na Madrona," he combines commentaries on contemporary events with a peculiar expression of concern for the ills of his society. In a third epistle, written in 1962 and addressed to Joan Salvat-Papasseit, that most engagé of Catalan poets, Foix, while amicably vindicating the honesty of his own convictions, conveys to his former associate the warm sympathy of a kindred soul, rising, at long last, above all the differences in temperament and upbringing that poisoned their relationship. In *Allò que no diu La vanguardia* (1970; what *La vanguardia* does not say)—the reference is to the noted Barcelonese newspaper—Foix parodies the reporter's jargon, distorting the idiom of the short bulletin and the somewhat longer newspaper column until he attains a magnificent absurdity. In still another vein, he devised a tale of fantasy, *La pell de la pell* (1970; skin's skin), complete with outlandish apparitions and magical transformations of time and place; there are infernal links between this work and *Noranta set notes sobre ficcions poncianes* (1974; ninety-seven notes on fictions à la Ponç), a congeries of paragraph-length meditations and aphorisms, inspired by the paintings of his friend, Joan Ponç.

In *Catalans de 1918* (1965; Catalans of 1918), an ingenuous Foix becomes the James Boswell of a forgotten era. In an intriguing admixture of memoirs and character sketches, he evokes the *Zeitgeist* of the decade between 1910 and 1920. Through autobiographical tidbits (reminiscences—deliciously recounted—of associations, confrontations, collaborations, casual acquaintances, and chance encounters), he introduces an entire gallery of famous and not-so-famous Catalans: revered masters, friends, and colleagues. Foix takes special care to recapture not only the speech of the personages in question but also the ambience which provides an appropriate foil for their cameo appearances. Worthy, too, of special attention is Foix's prolific and influential output as a journalist during the period preceding the Spanish Civil War (1917-1936). The numerous articles he contributed to *La publicitat*, a biweekly newspaper he directed from 1931 to 1936, stand out as especially significant, for they attest sensibilities keenly attuned to the critical issues of the day. A select sample of these articles appears in a collection titled *Els lloms transparents* (1969; transparent loins), edited by Gabriel Ferrater.

ACHIEVEMENTS

The domain of the Catalan language comprises most of the eastern sector of the Iberian Peninsula (Catalonia proper, that is, and the Valencian region), the Balearic Isles, the Republic of Andorra, and, to a lesser extent, the French territories of Cerdagne and Roussillon. The Catalan-speaking people, today some eight million strong, boast their own distinctive Romance tongue, a time-honored cultural heritage, and a brilliant literary tradition which goes back to the dawning of the Middle Ages. Thanks to a dramatic resurgence (commonly called the Renaixença) which began in the early 1830's, Catalan literature and art are flourishing today more vigorously than ever, despite the cataclysmic convulsions brought about by the Spanish Civil War and the repressive measures imposed by the Franco regime.

Together with a number of distinguished contemporary writers, painters, sculptors, and avant-garde artists of all types (Salvador Espriu, Joan Oliver, Mercé Rodoreda, Josep M. Subirachs, Joan Miró, Salvador Dalí, and Antoni Tàpies, to name but a representative few), J. V. Foix stands out as a worthy champion of the best that Catalan culture has to offer to Western civilization. Few Catalan writers can vie with Foix in devotion to motherland, erudition, breadth of vision, and sheer genius for bringing to fruition the highest potential of the Renaixença. Though worlds apart from Espriu in the ultimate resolution and implication of a truly personal and original poetic, Foix, like Espriu, strikes a happy balance between, on the one hand, aesthetic sophistication and avant-garde exploration, and, on the other hand, a sound understanding of the solid, broad infrastructure of the living language of his society. What has earned Foix a rank of special distinction is, above all, his unique talent for articulating through poems, through essays, and, indeed, through his urbane lifestyle and cosmopolitan outlook, the canons of a staunch Catalanism, founded upon the principles of moderation and tolerance, transcending chauvinism and partisan affiliation of any kind—canons formulated by Joan Maragall, Foix's illustrious turn-of-the-century predecessor, a thinker who oriented his ideals toward the prospect of a Catalan autonomy within the context of pan-Iberian federalism.

Cognizant of Foix's venturesome, indefatigable quest for ever-novel approaches to the creative process, and of his pursuit of what Northrop Frye and Carlos Bousoño have called, in reference to other writers, the "encyclopedic form" or the *pupila totalizadora*, and what Arthur Terry has termed, apropos of Foix himself, the *visió còsmica*, some of the more perceptive readers of Foix (Enrique Badosa, Patricia Boehne, Gabriel Ferrater, Pere Gimferrer, Albert Manent, David Rosenthal, and Terry, among others) have drawn parallels between him and such luminaries of twentieth century literature as Ezra Pound, T. S. Eliot, Federico García Lorca, and Fernando Pessoa. Indeed, Foix can mold into a collage of macrocosmic proportions strains issuing from both within and without the mainstream of the autochthonous tradition, techniques borrowed from the *stilnovisti* as well as from the Futurists and the Surrealists, echoes recaptured from the writers of ancient Greece as well as from homegrown classics (Ramon Llull, Ausiàs March, Jordi de Sant Jordi). Foix's overall production, then, projects the epiphany of an innovator endowed with a scrupulous social conscience. His stirring voice frequently has to cry out in order to bemoan the poet's personal anguish and that of many of his fellow citizens,

who, though never having left their own country, have suffered from the malaise which Paul Ilie has perceptively diagnosed as "inner exile."

Because of the prejudicial policies of the centralist Spanish government, limited Catalan readership, and other inimical circumstances, Foix, like practically all of his Catalan colleagues, does not enjoy the wide recognition he justly deserves. He does not lack, however, the enthusiastic acclaim of well-informed critics at home and abroad. His name occupies, as it should, a prominent place in the standard histories and anthologies of Catalan literature. He attracted the attention of numerous scholars, and a sizable body of his work has been translated into Castilian, English, French, and Italian. Foix is held in high esteem by the younger Catalan literati, and his influence is detectable among them, especially in the works of Gabriel Ferrater and Pere Gimferrer, outstanding poets in their own right.

In 1961, Foix was elected to the Catalan Academy (the Institut d'Estudios Catalans), and in 1973, on the occasion of his eightieth birthday, he was awarded the Premi d'Honor de les Lletres Catalanes. On that occasion, two prestigious magazines, *Destino* and *Serra d'Or*, dedicated special issues to him, and his friends published an homage anthology (*Antologia poètica*).

BIOGRAPHY

Josep Arseni Vicenç Foix i Mas ("Foix" rhymes with *gauche*), or J. V. Foix, was born of peasant stock. His father came from Torrents de Lladurs, a town in the province of Lérida (Western Catalonia). The second of three children—he shared the household with two sisters—he received the usual schooling and exhibited an unusual, precocious interest in Catalan culture and literary studies. His formal education came to an abrupt end in 1911 after an unsuccessful bout with the study of law. Other occupations were to absorb the young Foix's attention. Following in his father's footsteps, Foix worked in earnest to build for himself a reputation as the premier *pâtissier* in his native town.

In retrospect, Foix presented the intriguing figure of a man with two private lives: One belongs to the bourgeois merchant, who plods a course marked by the work ethic leading to material rewards; the other pertains to the genuine artist fully devoted to a métier that thrives on the values of the spirit. Foix plied his trade by day and wrote at a feverish pace by night. The first fifteen years of his career (beginning, approximately, in the year 1915) were years of particularly intense activity. In his book *Catalans de 1918*, he provides a captivating account of his numerous sessions in libraries, his contacts with the many aspiring authors of his generation who later became his intimate friends and with established scholars and literati—Fabra, Mosén Jacinto Verdaguer, d'Ors, Carner, and Riba—who were all engaged in the epic task of shaping the future of Catalan culture. From 1917 on, various journals of the avant-garde mushroomed in Barcelona, and Foix contributed articles to all of them and directed some. Himself a central figure of the intelligentsia, he became acquainted with the prominent personalities who were creating a stir in the literary and artistic circles of the Catalan metropolis: Paul Éluard, Federico García Lorca, Tristan Tzara, Dalí, Miró, Luis Buñuel. Foix relished playing the part of a cultural middleman of sorts, an aesthetician at large. In this role, he introduced, in 1925, the first exhibitions of Dalí and Miró.

Foix's creative surge paralleled and in some cases even anticipated the artistic renewal experienced throughout Europe in the mid-1920's. While the revolutionary tendencies which were fermenting on the Continent were making their sensational impact in Catalonia, especially through the movements of Futurism and Surrealism, and García Lorca was publishing *Romancero gitano, 1924-1927* (1928), Foix was reaping in *Gertrudis* the first fruit of a protracted labor. By 1930, he had completed the main components of those books which many years later would reach the printing press under the titles *KRTU, Del "Diari 1918," Sol, i de dol* (alone and in mourning), *Catalans de 1918*, and even some items of *Les irreals omegues* (the unreal omegas).

The advent of the Republic in 1931 and the subsequent five years of autonomy, which encouraged high hopes for the future of Catalan nationhood, enhanced Foix's consciousness of his civic responsibilities. Though he shunned direct involvement in politics, he acquitted himself brilliantly of his self-imposed duties as ideologue in *Revolució catalanista* (1934; the Catalan revolution), a book he coauthored with his friend Josep Carbonell. As a representative of the emerging Catalan state, he attended two international conventions of the PEN Club, held in Belgrade and in Dubrovnik in the early 1930's.

The civil war struck hard at the hopes of those who, like Foix, had set their hearts on tolerance and constructive dialogue. The abolition of the Catalan press, after Franco's victory, brought Foix's journalistic career to a standstill, but censorship could not dry up the fountainhead of his inspiration or stint the vitality of his poetic voice—which, fortunately, found an outlet in numerous books published after the Spanish Civil War. Following Franco's death, Foix had the satisfaction of witnessing a revitalized Catalonia, autonomous once again. He died in Barcelona, Spain, on January 29, 1987.

ANALYSIS

By 1930, J. V. Foix had developed the mainstays of his craft upon which he would effect countless variations. In particular, he had perfected his favored techniques of antithesis: the old opposed to the new, the familiar articulated with the exotic, reason contravened by *follia*, fantastical narratives counterbalanced by references to the workaday world, Arcadia admixed with veristic depictions of the Catalan landscape. Other quintessential traits of Foix's resourcefulness readily come to mind: his lyric élan, his profuse language contained within exquisite conciseness of form elaborated to an adamantine luster, his play on perspectivism and the effects of trompe l'oeil, inviting analogies with the visual arts (especially with paintings of Giorgio de Chirico, Dali, Yves Tanguy, René Magritte, Miró). Foix's associations with the Buñuel of *Un Chien andalou* (1928) and *L'Âge d'or* (1930) fostered, no doubt, his strong penchant for transforming into devices of literature sudden shifts of focus, flashbacks and flash-forwards, telescopings and superimpositions of images, panoramic shots, foreshadowings, fadeouts, and other cinematic techniques.

Through his mimesis of the oneiric experience, Foix unfolds the wide horizons of a kaleidoscopic, constantly changing universe: He evokes a dreamlike world in a state of flux, brings about mutations upon a protean imagery, develops into full-fledged personal myths symbols rooted in the subconscious. In the final analysis, however, the universe he envisages remains, as Terry has perceptively pointed out, strikingly unified—paradoxical and mysterious though its unity may be. It is because of his convictions concerning an absolute order which governs all things and also because of his compelling drive toward explorations beyond well-trodden paths that Foix, despite his obvious indebtedness to the champions of Surrealism, is not merely another epigone of that movement.

Foix is a bold exponent of the avant-garde, "a poet, magician, speculator of the word," to use his own words, an "investigator of poetry." In his reflections on his own work, Foix employs distinctive terminology–*alliberament* (liberation), "el risc de la investigació estética" (the risk of aesthetic research), "un joc gairebé d'atzar" (a game of chance, just about), "l'exercici de la facultat de descobrir" (the exercise of the skill of making discoveries)—in order to describe his exploratory, "investigative" imagination. Though keenly aware of the pitfalls lurking in his risky ventures as an avant-garde artist, Foix will not accept a road map or even, at times, general bearings from the Surrealists or from other revered masters. He insists on sallying forth, on his own, into uncharted realms of the imagination, so allured is he by prospects of serendipitous innovations and by the intuition of elusive *sobiranes certeses* (sovereign certainties).

"WITHOUT SYMBOLISM"

Thus do Foix's, and the reader's, literary adventures begin. At the outset, the author dazzles the reader with an array of colors, odors, sounds, and other sensory perceptions. He frequently projects himself into the persona of the passionate lover, engulfed in one of his usual reveries about his femme fatale. Typical is the prose poem from *Gertrudis*, "Sense simbolisme" ("Without Symbolism"), in which a lover embarks upon a first-person account of a doomed amatory episode. "I abandoned the horse," says the lover, for a start, "that, by the most beauteous blinking of his eyelids, had converted the sun into an ornament for his forehead, and I made sure to take this ornament along with me that night—a very special lantern which guided me, faithfully, to Gertrude's garden." The lover finds his *amada* "tooting" his name "to the pretty cadence of a popular fox-trot." His attempt to embrace her is foiled by "the viscosity of a precise ray of moonlight." Ensuing scenes have the disjointedness of a dream. The sight of Gertrude's tresses stimulates a train

of heady olfactory impressions: "The intense odor of the acacias anesthetized us so that we felt on the verge of a fainting spell. By sheer will power, I managed, though, to collect all the odors and enclose them in a case held shut by a ring studded with genuine jewels; and I felt at once revived by my audaciousness at this happy stroke of luck."

Lucky, however, the lover is not, as he soon discovers. In bold images of the type which Carlos Bousoña has labeled *visión*, Gertrude is shown as literally reaching for the stars: "She would unhook the stars one by one and would rinse them, with a shuddering of the infinite, in a pond half green, half silver, and would release them to the toads. . . ." This is clearly the high point of the episode. In contrast with a superwoman endowed with the might of a demiurge, the lover could not be cast in a more demeaning and ridiculous role. He is left to "harmonize" the "infamous croakings" of those denizens of stagnant waters "with the aid of a system of pedals that my beloved, with foresight, had providently arranged." He tries again, to no avail, to possess his beloved.

The distressed lover has little else to do but contemplate his fall from Earthly Paradise. Cognizant of the "heavy threat of the moon," he searches for his horse. The animal, now completely immersed in darkness, its eyes plastered over with "the stimulant of black tar," carries the lover and Gertrude to the rim of an abyss. Another odor—this time the unpleasant smell of the bramble bush—impels him to make a third try for that reward which, once again, proves unattainable. Overwhelmed by gloomy concerns—"torn asunder by fright" when assailed by various nightmarish flashes—the protagonist abandons the horse and tries to return home by taxi, but ends up, instead, in an unknown village. In his last fantasies, he feels a perverse pleasure in "purifying" himself "by gulping down as in a milk shake the smoke of all the chimneys in the neighborhood" and, finally, "in taking refuge beneath the crust of the large cities in order to capture the melody that the people's leaden footsteps create in homage to my littleness."

What order, one may ask, can ever transpire from the lover's stream of consciousness? At issue here is the recognition that "Without Symbolism" (the title proves to be obviously ironic) abounds in symbols which Foix cleverly disguises as principles of an overall design. Design, then, is the fountainhead of that order which an attentive reader will gradually intuit in Foix's composition. In effect, this intriguing piece evolves, organically, from a masterfully carried-out process that enhances the suggestiveness even as it fulfills the potential of a fundamental binary schema. This simple schema stems, in turn, from the atavistic opposition between male and female. To the exaltation of an apotheosized Gertrude, Foix counterposes the debasement of an antihero at the edge of annihilation. If the one shines in all of her stellar splendor, the other lurks in the darkness of the netherworld.

"THE PARTISANS OF THE SUN"

Foix, who in another prose poem, "The Partisans of the Sun," constructs a personal mythology upon the antagonism between two primeval races—the partisans of the sun, who live in the open and gather at daybreak, and their adversaries, the cave dwellers, who come out only by moonlight—is well aware of the tension between two fields of symbols, the chthonian and the uranic, to borrow the terminology which Rupert C. Allen, Gustavo Correa, and others have employed in their illuminating studies of García Lorca: Definitely uranic is the portrayal of Gertrude in the accouterments of a *donna angelicata*, and unmistakably chthonian the depiction of the lover's persona with the demeanor of a fallen angel. What may interest the reader is the affinity between Foix's and García Lorca's respective versions of stock symbols—the horse, the moon, and various elements of nature—versions which often involve an intermingling of the heavenly and earthly spheres, as when (to mention but a few illustrations from Foix) Gertrude from her lofty position casts the stars into the lowly pond, the menacing moon hangs "heavily" down upon the fate of the lover, and the horse loses its association with the sun in order to become a demoniac figure, as lurid as such a common representation of human libido ought to be.

Affinities of this kind detract nothing from the fierce independence and the original genius of the two writers in question. A striking aspect of Foix's innovative spirit is the ambivalent treatment he accords to the Gertrude-lover dyad as a latter-day manifestation of the age-old courtly love tradition, one of the many aspects of medieval literature that has never ceased to fascinate Foix.

Insofar as he expatiates upon leitmotifs of the quasi-canonized damsel and the virtually doomed young gallant, Foix exhibits a faithful adherence to that tradition. A closer reading, though, brings to light telltale signs of distortions characteristic of parody and even of the burlesque. As he dwells upon the veritable chasm that separates the distant, disdainful *belle dame sans merci* and her mournful admirer who stews in the juices of his own morbid passion, Foix appears less interested in revitalizing worn-out topics than in elaborating in his own rendition of the ridiculous Don Juan *manqué*, much in the grotesque vein which Ramón del Valle-Inclán had developed into a new art form in his revolutionary *esperpentos* of the early 1920's. Foix is quite successful in reconciling the conventions of the past with the fashionable trends of his day. Tradition? Yes, but only up to a point. Not for anything does he declare in one of his more renowned sonnets: "I am excited by what is new and enamored by what is old."

SOL, I DE DOL

With *Sol, i de dol*, Foix's attention shifted directly to the refinement of the outer form of poetry. This sequence of seventy splendid sonnets evinces a control, balance, and precision that many would consider possible only in an author of the classical Renaissance—the Renaissance that the historical and political circumstances of the fifteenth and sixteenth centuries did not allow Catalan literature to experience.

Foix reached the zenith of his mastery, however, in the most complex of his literary modes, which, since it extends toward the farthest stretches of poetic signification, appropriately may be labeled "contextual." Most commonly found in *Les irreals omegues, On he deixat les claus . . . ?* (where did I leave the keys . . . ?), and *Desa aquests llibres al calaix de baix* (these books in the bottom drawer), the "contextual" composition exhibits, instead of a title, an epigraph or a rubric in prose, ranging from three to fifteen lines, followed by a section in verse of variable length, which constitutes the body of the poem proper. By the intertextual articulation of the epigraph (the "pretext," one may say) with the verse component (that is, the "text" proper), Foix creates a "con-text" rich in metaphysical, ethical, and aesthetic connotations. It is not unusual for Foix to challenge his readers to round out the context with their own insights into historical circumstances, merely hinted at either through clues interspersed within the composition itself or by the date included at the end of the piece. Thus, Foix tries to raise the consciousness of his readers about important social issues, even as he engages their full participation in the re-creation of the poem itself.

"I WAS RIDING AT FULL GALLOP AROUND THE CITY WALLS, PURSUED BY A THRONG OF SUPERSTITIOUS COALMONGERS"

Civic consciousness, social concern, and a sense of moral outrage are fully evident in Foix's poem "I Was Riding at Full Gallop Around the City Walls, Pursued by a Throng of Superstitious Coalmongers." The broad period the author specifies in the dating of the composition (July, 1929, to October, 1936) was one of the most turbulent in Spanish history. Brutalized victims of a religiosity of the worst kind, foisted upon them by a reactionary Big Brother, Foix's *carboners* (coalmongers) have little to do with the *carboneros* whose naïve, innocent, blind faith Unamuno y Jugo secretly admired. To Foix, they are the agents of blind passion, an unthinking multitude as loathsome to him as are their victimizers. The poem calls to mind the unctuousness and bigotry of some, the animosity and resentment of many, and the tensions which seethed within the masses until they exploded in the conflagration of 1936, and Foix's persona cannot but cry out in consternation: "Give me a lamp: — Where is my horse?/ Give me stone-hard coals and luminous pebbles/ Give me night walls in lunar cities." At the end of the poem, the persona attains the dubious distinction of speaking as a prophet of sorts, vexed by suspicions of an ominous handwriting on the wall; thus, Foix—with the prescience of García Lorca's *Poeta en Nueva York* (wr. 1929-1930, pb. 1940; *Poet in New York*, 1940, 1955), Pablo Neruda's *España en el corazón* (1937; *Spain in the Heart*, 1946), and Pablo Picasso's painting *Guernica* (1937)—cries out against man's inhumanity to man and warns of the danger that humankind will bring on itself the dreadful wrath of the gods.

OTHER MAJOR WORKS

SHORT FICTION: *Allò que no diu La vanguardia*, 1970; *La pell de la pell*, 1970.

NONFICTION: *Revolució catalanista*, 1934 (with Josep Carbonell); *Catalans de 1918*, 1965; *Els lloms transparents*, 1969; *Noranta set notes sobre ficcions poncianes*, 1974.

MISCELLANEOUS: *Obres completes*, 1974-1990 (4 volumes; includes his epistles).

BIBLIOGRAPHY

Boehne, Patricia J. *J. V. Foix*. Boston: Twayne, 1980. An introductory biographical study and critical analysis of selected works by Foix. Includes bibliographic references and an index.

Cocozzella, Peter. Review of *Tocant a mà*, by J. V. Foix, edited by Joan R. Veny-Mesquida. *World Literature Today* 68, no. 1 (Winter, 1994): 107. Cocozzella provides a summary in English of Veny-Mesquida's introduction in Catalan to *Tocant a mà*. Complementing positivistic analysis with the insights provided by current literary theory, Veny-Mesquida, in a substantial introduction of some eighty pages, calls upon foreign and homegrown pundits—Norman Friedmann, Gerald Prince, Carles Miralles, Maurici Serrahima, Enric Sulla, Ferrater, and Gimferrer, among others—to help him shed light on Foix's engrossing masterpieces.

Gimferrer, Pere. *La poesia de J. V. Foix*. Barcelona: Edicions 62, 1997. Critical interpretation of selected works by Foix. Published in Catalan.

Peter Cocozzella;
bibliography updated by the editors

JEAN FOLLAIN

Born: Canisy, France; August 29, 1903
Died: Quai des Tuileries, France; March 10, 1971

PRINCIPAL POETRY

La Main chaude, 1933
Chants terrestres, 1937
Ici-bàs, 1941
Usage du temps, 1943
Exister, 1947
Les Choses données, 1952
Territoires, 1953

Objets, 1955

Des heures, 1960

Appareil de la terre, 1964

D'après tout, 1967 (*Après Tout: Poems by Jean Follain*, 1981)

Transparence of the World, 1969

Espaces d'instants, 1971

Présent Jour, 1978

OTHER LITERARY FORMS

In addition to his poetry, Jean Follain wrote several nonfiction works, notable among which are *Collège* (1973), an account of his secondary-school experiences in the years immediately following World War I, and a history of Peru, *Pérou* (1964).

ACHIEVEMENTS

Jean Follain was the recipient of several awards for his poetic achievements, including the Mallarmé (1939), the Blumenthal (1941), the Capri (1958), and the Grand Prix de Poésie of the French Academy (1970). He was also made a Chevalier in the French Legion of Honor.

BIOGRAPHY

Jean René Follain was born in Canisy, Normandy, France, on August 29, 1903. His maternal grandfather was a notary and his paternal grandfather was a school-teacher. His father was a professor at the Collège de Saint-Lô, located in a neighboring town. Follain was to study at this institution, where he was awarded a prize for excellence in philosophy, and subsequently wrote one of his finest prose works, *Collège*, about his experiences there.

In 1921, Jean Follain began his law studies at the law school at Caen and was graduated with honors. As a student, he was also interested in the history of the nineteenth century. In 1923, he went to Paris on a probationary basis with a lawyer and in 1927 became a member of the Paris bar and practiced law until 1952.

Meanwhile, Follain became a part of the group of poets and painters that formed around the review *Sagesse*, founded by Fernand Marc, where he published his first poems. There he met André Salmon, Pierre Reverdy, Pierre MacOrlan, Léon-Paul Fargue, Guegen, Armen Lubin, Max Jacob, Pierre Minet, Madeleine Is-

rael, Georges Duveaux, and Alfred Gaspart. In 1932, he collaborated with several of these writers to publish in literary journals such as *Dernier Carre*, *Feuillets inutiles*, and *Montparnasse*. His first poems were published in the *Nouvelle Revue française*, *Commerce*, *Europe*, and *Cahiers du sud*. Follain married Madeleine Denis, a painter, in 1934.

In 1952, Follain quit the bar to become a court magistrate in Charleville, where he remained until 1961. Between 1957 and 1967, he traveled quite extensively all over the world to countries such as Thailand, Japan, Brazil, Peru, the United States, the Ivory Coast, and Senegal. In 1969, he made a film for educational television called *Canisy, vu par Jean Follain* (Canisy, as seen by Jean Follain), directed by Michel Nicoletti.

Follain was killed accidentally by a car on March 10, 1971, on the Tuileries quay. He had enjoyed an active and distinguished literary career, serving as president of the Friends of Rimbaud; president of the selection committees for the Cazes Prize, the Max Jacob Prize, and the Deux Magots Prize; and assistant secretary general of the French PEN Club.

ANALYSIS

Jean Follain has been hailed as one of the great secret voices of the twentieth century. He addressed humanity's search for a total union between the known surroundings of a fleeting earthly life and the unknown, absolute finalities of death, space, and time. He succeeded in integrating a world of directly observable facts with the complexities of experiences and powers beyond human control. His ability to communicate this message by choosing the proper words and by realizing their full semantic value and power in their proper placement in a sentence constitutes his greatest poetic achievement. Three major collections of Follain's poetry, *La Main chaude* (the hot hand), *Chants terrestres* (terrestrial songs), and *Exister* (to exist), each introduce a theme or a stylistic component essential to the understanding of Follain's art and repeated in later works.

La Main chaude introduced Follain's concept of poetry as a continuum of incongruous events, the role of memory, and the ever-present village of Normandy where he spent his youth. *Chants terrestres* presents Follain's preoccupation with words: word choice, syntax, the play

Jean Follain (Courtesy of French Cultural Services)

of sound, and the power of evocation. *Exister* introduces stylistic patterns that were established for the first time in Follain's poetry and that persisted in later volumes.

LA MAIN CHAUDE

La Main chaude is composed of poems whose titles are rather surprising and completely unrelated to one another. They include "Poème glorieux" (glorious poem), "L'Épicier" (the grocer), "Mets" (food), "La Digestion aux cannons" (the digestion of cannons), "La Place publique en été" (the public square in summer), "Ode à l'amour juvenile" (ode to young love), "À la dame du temps de Borgia" (to the lady of Borgia's time), "Milords" (milords), "Les Belles noyées" (the beautiful drowned ones), "Combat singulier de seigneurs dans la campagne" (the singular combat of lords in the country), and "Appel aux soldats roux" ("Appeal to the Red-haired Soldiers"). At first glance each poem seems to be a disparate fragment sharing no unity of leitmotif or style with the other poems.

The objective of this collection is to conjure the sense of specific recollections of places, occasions, and objects. Although the poems refer to simple evocations, the familiar is suddenly juxtaposed to unexpected or incongruous words or happenings which shatter known and assumed relationships. The harmony of the collection, then, is achieved from the unity of contrasting spectacles.

Follain's intention in constructing the poems in this manner is not to distort language but to convey the message that the world as perceived and the world of visions are one. He creates a web with simple words whose meanings are unclear. He then compares the web he has created to the Normandy countryside of his youth, where echoes can be discerned from unclear depths and where lights shining on objects create an impression of uncertainty as to whether the lights are illuminating the objects or the grouping of the objects is creating the lights.

Memory has a special role in these poems. It is not simply a link between the past and the present. According to Follain, memory is distinct from the past on which it draws, and is what makes the past a key to the mystery that stays with us and does not change: the present. The different evocations presented in the various poems of this collection concern the mystery of the present. They recall the concrete details of his youth in Normandy and give them their form, both luminous and removed at the same time. Simultaneously, the form gives the evocations the aura of a ceremony, another of Follain's preoccupations. He compares the evocations of this poetry collection to an unchanging ceremony heralding some inexorable splendor. For Follain, it is a fulfillment not only of a need for ceremony but also of a fondness for the ceremonious, in which each isolated detail is an evocation of the procession of an immeasurable continuum.

CHANTS TERRESTRES

The collection *Chants terrestres* takes its name from the poem "Chants terrestres" in the collection *La Main chaude*. As in the earlier collection, the poems in *Chants terrestres* bear titles that seem unrelated to one another. They include "La Dame à crieurs de pâtés" (the lady at the pâté-vendor's), "L'Adieu du diplomate" (the diplomat's farewell), and "Le Gant rouge" (the red glove). Again, it is not possible to speak of a unifying thread among the individual poems with regard to a structural plan, a rhythmical pattern, or conventional poetic themes such as nostalgia, death, or regret.

These poems, however, are a testimony to Follain's preoccupation with words. As always, the evocations in the poems reflect his tendency to recall the beloved memories of his native village of Canisy in Normandy. He constructs a world with seemingly simple words which encompass the most minute instances of his life, perpetually in search of the elusive reality of things. Nature and humanity in their most universally accepted forms are seized in sentences in which their substance and truth defy classification or definition. Objects become stratified, and the precision of the lines of verse gives life to inert words so that they, too, become objects. Human life becomes stratified as well. Follain constructs it layer by layer, piece by piece, in such a way that the reader is never really able to distinguish the importance of the events discussed because the most obscure, abandoned, and minute details surface to haunt him in these poems.

EXISTER

In the collection *Exister*, thematic and structural patterns begin to emerge for the first time. In these poems, Follain shows that the emotions experienced in the activities of daily life give rise to complexities or contradictions and can be transcended through disengaged contemplation.

The themes are few and recurring: daily life (especially from Follain's childhood) in contact with the power of time, and the possibility of overcoming its restrictions—work, illness, and violence—through the transcendental forces of love, religion, and contemplation. The style is stark, austere, and simple. Rhetorical devices are seldom used. The depth and power of the text depends on the reader's ability to become an active participant and interpreter of its message on many levels. This is consistent with the goal of modern poetry since Arthur Rimbaud.

STRUCTURAL PATTERNS

Two major and several minor structural patterns emerge. The first major structural pattern deals with emotion and can be presented as follows: emotional response, reversal of emotion, suppression of emotion. For example, in "L'Amirauté" (the admiralty), the first section presents a world which excludes the observer: The windows do not give light, the weather is bad, the town is alien, the building is seen from the exterior. The second section is a complete reversal of the darkness and pessimism of the first part: The building is a place of

shelter; it is attractively furnished and comes to be associated with the heart. The second part, then, cancels the initial emotion, and the rest of the poem avoids further emotional reactions. The third section of the poem presages death. The emphasis, however, is on the time of passage into death and not on the physical or mental destruction of the person. The vocabulary is abstract, and there is no evocation of suffering. The fourth part of the poem moves to a totally intellectual level.

This pattern recurs in many other poems of this collection and in subsequent collections. For example, in "L'Amitié" (friendship), pride and human contact are replaced by the frustration of departure and then by detached observation of the external world. In "L'Enfant au tambour" (the child with the drum), the threat of death and the oppressiveness of the garden are succeeded by a contempt for war and by a return to the original scene from an intellectual perspective. In "L'Appel du chevalier" (the call of the chevalier), the boy's tedious work gives way to the heroism of the past and then to a suppression of emotion and consciousness in sleep. This irrelevance of emotion is later evidenced in the poem "Postures" (situations), from the collection *Des Heures*.

The second major structural pattern which emerges in Follain's poetry is as follows: immediate, nonimmediate, conflict, solitude, harmony, essential, partial harmony. The manifestations of this pattern, however, vary from poem to poem. In the poem "L'Amirauté," it is constructed in the following way: The first section presents a self-contained world which can be easily comprehended by the reader. The second section shows this immediate perception to be only partially valid, and the interplay of elements beyond the observable plays an important role in this section. The poem ends with a shift to the sphere of the timeless and unconditional truth which is beyond the perceived world, in this case, religion. The opposing elements become reconciled.

Examples of the shift from the immediate include the introduction of the elemental forces of wind and night in "L'Appel du chevalier"; the inscription of the hours in the wearing out of the damask in "Paysage des deux ouvriers" (landscape of two laborers); and the wild nature surrounding the enclosure in "Amis d'Austerlitz" (friends from Austerlitz).

Another variation is the sudden interruption of one human activity by another one—for example, work after love in "Indifference du bricoleur" (the handyman's indifference), "Chanson de la maîtresse du boulanger" (song of the baker's mistress), "La Brodeuse d'abeilles" (the embroiderer of the bees); or the inverse, love after work, as in "L'Empailleur d'oiseaux" (the taxidermist of birds) and "L'Anecdote" (the anecdote).

Yet another technique is the intrusion of psychological elements after establishing an introduction based on the tangible and the concrete, as in "Métaphysique" (metaphysics) and "L'Histoire" (the story). Conflict and solitude appear in many forms. They include the violence of passion and conflict in the kisses of "Les Portraits" (the portraits); solitude in "L'Ennui" (boredom) and "L'Enfant de l'amour" (the love child); torture in "La Matière" ("Matter"); separation in "L'Empailleur d'oiseaux"; the destruction of the flower in "Domaine d'ombre" (the domain of shadow); the duel in "Le Vin du soir" (evening wine); and abandonment in "La Créature" (the creature).

SEARCH FOR HARMONY

These examples bear witness to the inadequacy of human attempts to live in harmony with the rest of humankind. Harmony or unity may be achieved in a variety of ways. They include love in "Des Hommes" (men); gentleness in "Le Pain" (the loaf); beauty in "La Pyramide" ("The Pyramid"); familiarity in "Parler seul" ("Speech Alone"); benevolence in "La Vie domestique" ("Domestic Life"); reciprocal influence in "L'Existence" ("Existence"); and a communion between nature and the senses in "La Bête" ("The Beast"). Other variations, however, may occur. At times, the reference to harmony is indirect. For example, in "L'Asie" ("Asia"), the man is eating soup.

At first glance, this does not seem to be a universal portrayal of harmony, but it must he noted that in Follain's poetry, food and drink are synonymous with peaceful human interaction. In other cases, conflict and harmony may appear in the same poem—for example, the moans of passion and the soft sounds in "Les Jardins" (the gardens); the conflict between darkness and flames and the harmony which arises from the unity of friends in "Les Amis d'Austerlitz." In still other cases, conflict and solitude are present in the same poem, such as in "Le Vin du soir," as is partial harmony and total harmony (such as compassion and marriage) in "Les Devoirs" (duties), or the loyalty and cooperation between the father and the daughter and the union between the daughter and the leaf (in "Aux Choses lentes," to slow things).

DEATH

The essential is often represented by references to death (as in "Existence"), which is then linked to the world or universe (as in "Les Portraits," "Le Vin du soir," and "Ineffable de la fin," ineffable to the end), or to religion (as in "Balances," balances, and "Le Pas," the step), or to eternity (as in "Natures mortes," still lifes, and "Les Journaliers," the day laborers), or to timelessness (as in "Le Secret," "The Secret"). This structural pattern directly reflects Follain's sensitivity to man's need to integrate his earthly surroundings with the absolutes of death, religion, space, and time.

"LA BRODEUSE D'ABEILLES"

Again, there is a certain variation and flexibility among the elements of the pattern. For example, in the poem "La Brodeuse d'abeilles," the introductory lines present the theme of physical love. The succeeding lines then place the theme of solitude alongside the theme of passion. Follain's intention here is to show the multidimensional aspect of life, represented by people or objects. In this case, it is clearly communicated that the reader cannot perceive this person in a solely physical context. The poem appeals to his sensitivity and depth of perception and comprehension as well as his ability to integrate the deeper meanings of the relationship between two opposing concepts. In this poem, the ability to shift the perspective of the relationship leads to a coherent conclusion of the text. It is suggested that a union or harmony may be attained on an aesthetic level between the *brodeuse* and the physical world represented here by her clothing, her jewelry, and other outward manifestations. This can be realized, however, only when the element of passion or direct physical contact is eliminated entirely.

"ENFANTEMENT"

There are also different rates of progress among the various elements which constitute the pattern. For example, the poem "Enfantement" (child-birth) shows some deviation from the order and progress of the pattern. It begins with the contact with the inaccessible and then moves to the tangible, accessible environment of the city. The person is introduced first and then the description of the city is given. Also, the reversal of emotion precedes rather than coincides with the shift from the immediate. Another example occurs in the poem "Le Sapeur" (the sapper). The progression begins normally from calm observation to the agitation of the fish, which reverses the emotional tone. Next, there is a shift to the remote in terms of the fish being nonhuman and being caught. The next element to be introduced, however, has nothing to do with union or harmony. It shifts back to concrete details, which then leads to the nonimmediate, as represented by the sound of the church bells.

SUBTHEMES

Other, simpler patterns also exist. They appear less uniformly but still serve to indicate general tendencies. The first pattern traces the development from the depiction of the exterior world as a setting for humankind to the presentation of a single person and then to the intangible represented by the soul or God. This pattern occurs in "L'Amirauté," "Domaine d'ombre," and "L'Haine en été" (hate in summer). The development of this pattern is often linked to another one: the introduction of a woman who allows the escape from the immediate, the reference to the soul allowing the reduction of emotional tone and the introduction of the dimension of unity. The latter element of this pattern is especially important because it allows the extension of the poem beyond a point which might otherwise have been final. An example of this occurs in "Apparition de la vieille" (the appearance of the old woman). The harmony brought about by the return of the old woman from the childhood stories seems sufficient to conclude the poem, but a more satisfying conclusion is created by the shift to the intangible—memory—as a culmination of the movement from the person to the objects associated with her. The same occurs in "Les Uns et les autres" (the ones and the others). The expected conclusion was one which would have preserved the severity of the last lines of verse. Instead, however, it ends with a reference to love, after depicting nature, people, and objects. The effect of this tendency is quite compatible with other aspects of Follain's writing—that is, to show a decrease of man's involvement with the exterior world.

The second pattern which emerges is that the poems tend to move from a restrictive view of the world to one which permits penetration into the normally inaccessible, thereby reducing the incommunicability with the world. For example, in "L'Ennui," the poet penetrates into the interior of the body with the song; the body underneath the clothes in "La Mémoire" (the memory) and "Aux choses lentes"; the invisible heart in "L'Amirauté"; and the knowledge of secrets in "Paysage des deux ouvriers."

The third observation to be made is that the poems tend to move from the temporal to the atemporal, which bridges the past and the present.

Finally, the senses alluded to appear in an order of decreasing materialism: touch, sound, sight, scent. At times, this order motivates the harmonious conclusion of the poem—for example, the intense stare in "Aux Choses lentes" or the peaceful visual conclusion of "Pathétique" in contrast to the noise presented in the introduction. Scent is especially associated with the intangible and the essential, as in "Métaphysique" and "La Journée en feu" (the day on fire).

Follain aims at recording the flow of life rather than imposing a form on it. His writing reflects his perception of the duality of life. There is a double inclination to address the known objects of the world and then to subject them to a more abstract vision, thereby giving the reader access to the essential and intangible, which allows him to reconcile these two tendencies. Stylistically, the reader must realize that the patterns underlying Follain's poetry do not impose absolute constraints of any kind. The reader is not able to predict accurately what the succeeding line of verse will say. That is because the images and concepts which constitute the text cannot be construed as examples of a single topic. Follain's poetry overflows with semantic excess; the meaning of the lines is not exhausted by their structural relationships. This allows space within the poem for the unpredictable and the spontaneous, thus freeing language and experience from automatization and compelling the reader to take an active part in the creation of meaning.

OTHER MAJOR WORKS

NONFICTION: *Paris*, 1935; *L'Épicerie d'enfance*, 1938; *Canisy*, 1942 (English translation, 1981); *Chef-lieu*, 1950; *Pérou*, 1964; *Collège*, 1973; *Selected Prose*, 1985.

BIBLIOGRAPHY

Gavronsky, Serge, ed. *Poems and Texts: An Anthology of French Poems.* New York: October House, 1969. Translations of selected poems and interviews with Ponge, Follain, Guillevic, Frénaud, Bonnefoy, Du-Bouchet, Roche, and Pleynet.

Guillevic, Eugène, with Lucie Albertini. *Avec Jean Follain.* Paris: PAP, 1993. A brief recollection and commentary on Follain by fellow poet Guillevic. In French.

Marks, Elaine. *French Poetry from Baudelaire to the Present.* New York: Dell, 1962. Provides a historical background to Follain's work. Includes bibliographic references.

Thomas, Jean-Jacques. *Poeticized Language: The Foundations of Contemporary French Poetry.* University Park: Pennsylvania State University Press, 1999. A historical study of French poetry that offers some background and insight into the works of Follain. Includes bibliographical references and index.

Anne Laura Mattrella;
bibliography updated by the editors

CAROLYN FORCHÉ

Born: Detroit, Michigan; April 28, 1950

PRINCIPAL POETRY

Gathering the Tribes, 1976
The Country Between Us, 1981
The Angel of History, 1994

OTHER LITERARY FORMS

Carolyn Forché has provided translations of the poems of Central American writers Claribel Alegría (*Flowers from the Volcano,* 1982; *Sorrow,* 1999) and, working with William Kulik, Robert Desnos (*Selected Poems of Robert Desnos,* 1991). In addition, she wrote the text for a series of photographs of El Salvador, covering the period from 1979 to 1982, in *El Salvador: The Work of Thirty Photographers* (1983). Her essays, reviews, and poems have appeared in major publications, including *The New York Times Book Review, The Atlantic Monthly, Ms., American Poetry Review, The New Yorker, Antaeus,* and *Virginia Quarterly Review.* Forché edited the influential anthology *Against Forgetting: Twentieth-Century Poetry of Witness* (1993) and coedited *Writing Creative Nonfiction: Instruction and Insights from Teachers of the Associated Writing Programs* (2001).

ACHIEVEMENTS

Carolyn Forché's poems focus on people—her ancestors, her childhood friends, Native Americans, and Salvadorans, to name a few—and emphasize place—often Detroit, the Southwest, or Central America. Her commitment to speaking for those who have been silenced, whether for economic, ethnic, racist, or political reasons, has won for her many readers and much critical acclaim. Her first book, *Gathering the Tribes,* concerning a girl's initiation into adulthood, received the Yale Series of Younger Poets Award in 1975. Her second, *The Country Between Us,* concerning a young woman's development of a social conscience, was the Lamont Selection of the Academy of Poets (1981) and won the Poetry Society of America's Alice Fay di Castagnola Award. The commitment to politics that surfaced clearly in the second volume is also evident in *El Salvador: The Work of Thirty Photographers,* in many of her essays, and in her work-in-progress. She has received numerous awards for her poetry and various fellowships, including a National Endowment for the Arts Fellowship (1977), and a John Simon Guggenheim Memorial Fellowship (1978). In 1994, *The Angel of History* received *The Los Angeles Times* Book Award for poetry. Forché also received the Edita and Ira Morris Hiroshima Foundation for Peace and Culture Award for 1998, which was presented to her in recognition of her work on behalf of human rights and the preservation of memory and culture.

Forché has been a member of several literary organizations, including the International Association of Poets, Playwrights, Editors, Essayists, and Novelists (PEN) and the Academy of American Poets, and of political and government groups such as Amnesty International, the Institute for Global Education, and the Commission on United States-Central American Relations.

BIOGRAPHY

Born in 1950 to Michael Joseph Forché, a tool and die maker, and Louise Nada Sidlosky Forché, a homemaker, Carolyn Louise Forché, the oldest of seven children, spent her first five years in Detroit, Michigan, before moving to the suburbs with her family. With the encouragement of her mother, Forché began writing poems at nine, often as an escape, much like daydreaming. At eighteen, she published her first poem, "Artisan Well," in the October, 1968, issue of *Ingenue*.

At Justin Morrill College, an experimental college of Michigan State University, she attracted the attention of several professors, who became mentors and encouraged her writing. In 1970 and again in 1971 she won first prize in Michigan State University's poetry competition. At college she majored in creative writing and minored in English literature and French but also took courses in international relations, philosophy, and history. In addition to French she studied Russian, Spanish, Serbo-Croatian, and Tewa (Pueblo Indian)—perhaps following an interest generated by her Slavic-speaking relatives. After receiving her B.A. in 1972, she entered the M.F.A. program at Bowling Green State University in Ohio; she received her master's degree in 1975. Her M.A. thesis, "Secret Histories," suggests the direction that her poetry would take: the chronicling of the lives of those who have been forgotten.

As a student she worked on the poems that formed her first collection, *Gathering the Tribes*, and she completed it at age twenty-four. The collection was well received, entering its third printing only a year after its publication. She then turned her attention to the period involving Vietnam. In high school she and her working-class friends had been supportive of the war, but in college she joined the antiwar movement. She struggled to understand Vietnam partly because her first husband, whom she married when she was nineteen, was psychologically scarred by the war and partly because her political conscience had been stimulated by Terrence Des Pres's *Survivors: An Anatomy of Life in the Death Camps* (1976), which she had read while convalescing from viral meningitis in 1976. She made Des Pres's acquaintance, and the two writers entered into a correspondence that lasted until his death in 1987. His last work, *Praises and Dispatches* (1988), explores the relationship between poetry and politics, a subject that is of importance in understanding Forché's poems.

During the 1970's, Forché developed an interest in Central America. Working on the translation of the poems of Claribel Alegría, she traveled to Spain in 1977 to consult the exiled poet. There she met a number of Latin American writers and began to learn about the region's human rights problems. Returning to California, she taught English at San Diego State University but also worked for Amnesty International. When she received a Guggenheim Fellowship, Leonel Gomez, Alegría's nephew, suggested that she use it to travel in El Salvador; other friends, however, suggested Paris. Gomez argued, "Do you want to write poetry about yourself the rest of your life?" Answering in the negative, she chose El Salvador. From 1978 to 1980, as a journalist and human rights activist reporting to Amnesty International, she traveled in El Salvador, witnessing the poverty of the peasants, the ill health of the children, the rural hospitals where operations were often performed without anesthesia, and also the luxurious homes of the military. During this period the notorious death squads were be-

Carolyn Forché (© Jerry Bauer)

coming active, and she learned about the missing people and the torture of political dissidents. Once back in the United States, she lectured and wrote articles concerning her experiences, following the Salvadorans' plea: "Document it. . . . go back and tell them what you've seen." Her poems on El Salvador are included in *The Country Between Us*, which gained for Forché a reputation as a political poet. Perhaps that designation is not, or should not be, unusual, for as Forché points out, "History and politics affect everyone's life, everywhere, always."

As she had after her first collection, she again took a hiatus from poetry, explaining that reflection and solitude were necessary for writing poetry and the political situation allowed her neither. Instead she turned to writing a series of essays on places she had visited. The first, on El Salvador, appeared in *American Poetry Review* in 1981, and she planned additional essays on Lebanon and on Northern Ireland. While in Lebanon, she presented a series of news documentaries on Beirut (parts of which reminded her of Detroit) for National Public Radio's program *All Things Considered*.

Forché was married on December 27, 1984, to Henry E. Mattison, a photographic correspondent with *Time* magazine whose assignments included Nicaragua, El Salvador, Lebanon, and South Africa. They were together in South Africa but left in 1986 for the birth of their son, Sean Christophe, for they did not want their child to be born under the apartheid system.

In 1974 Forché began to teach English and writing or became a writer in residence at various universities, including Michigan State University, San Diego State University, the University of Virginia, New York University, Vassar College, and Columbia University. In 1989, she settled at George Mason University, which became her academic home.

ANALYSIS

In her first collection, *Gathering the Tribes*, Carolyn Forché recounts the experiences of her youth and maturation, focusing on places and people of importance to her development. She writes of her grandmother and Michigan but also of Teles Goodmorning (a Pueblo Indian) and the Southwest, claiming a spiritual kinship. Her second volume, *The Country Between Us*, is

marked by a similar emphasis on places and people, but this time the place is often El Salvador or Czechoslovakia and the people are victims of oppression.

The first volume charts the growth of a child entering adulthood, and the second completes the process, chronicling the development of a social conscience with an emphasis on commitment and responsibility. Criticized for being an activist poet, Forché counters, "There is no such thing as a nonpolitical poetry." Her belief that "we are, as a species, now careening toward our complete destruction with ever-greater velocity" explains her political involvement and her commitment to speak out.

GATHERING THE TRIBES

In *Gathering the Tribes*, Forché links the process of her maturation to the influence of specific people and places. These poems display a strong sense of place, whether it be the Michigan of her childhood, the Wakhan region of northern Afghanistan, or the Pueblo villages of New Mexico. Yet there is also a strong sense of dislocation: Her Slavic ancestors left their homeland; the narrator can never be part of the Southwest. Thus strong bonds between people are essential; the tribes must be gathered together. The people whom she cherishes might be her Slavic ancestors, her childhood friends, or those she considers spiritual ancestors—the Indians of the Southwest. It is often women who provide guidance—her peasant grandmother; the Indians Rosita and Alfansa; the narrator's lover, Jacynthe. Reinforcing the prominent position of women in the collection are many domestic images, such as bread making and pea shelling, and images drawn from nature and the natural cycles. This emphasis on women has led to questions about Forché's position on the women's movement; she responds, "I think any intelligent woman would have to consider herself a feminist."

Gathering the Tribes is divided into three parts. The first, "Burning the Tomato Worms," focuses primarily on the narrator's Slavic ancestors and their history, including their probable forced migration from northern Afghanistan, across Turkey, to the region where Russia borders Czechoslovakia. The poems suggest a connection between the past of the ancestors and the present of the narrator's girlhood. In other words, her life is a continuation of their lives, especially that of the peasant grandmother, Anna. The poems are imbued with Anna's wisdom and knowledge of the Old World's folkways and folklore, knowledge that the narrator needs: "Grandma, come back, I forgot/ How much lard for these rolls" ("The Morning Baking"). Throughout the poems, there is a transference of the past to the present. Eventually the narrator becomes, in a sense, her grandmother: "But I'm glad I'll look when I'm old/ Like a gypsy dusha hauling milk."

The strong bond between the speaker and her grandmother is evident in the central poem "Burning the Tomato Worms." The poem is set in the Midwest, with its "ploughed land" and "horse-breath weather," reminding the narrator of her deceased grandmother Anna. The narrator is directly linked to her grandmother's ancestors:

> Before I was born, my body as snowfat
> Crept over Wakhan
> As grandfathers spat into fires and thawed
> Their tarpaulin
> Sending crackled paths of blood
> Down into my birth.

She inherits these memories and those of her grandmother's youth in Eastern Europe, when political oppression forced her family to leave home:

> When time come
> We go quick
> I think
> What to take.

Carrying nothing but the bare essentials, the grandmother eventually settled in Michigan.

It is Anna who, "shelling snow peas" with Uzbek hands that once were "known for weaving fine rugs," teaches the narrator and guides her, relying on Old World maxims such as "Eat bread and salt and speak the truth." Anna wants the speaker to confront "something/ That was sacred and eternal." The meaning of this "something" is left ambiguous until the final section of the poem, when the reader understands that the grandmother is leading the speaker to an acceptance of the natural cycles of life. Her grandmother shapes the speaker's life, yet the narrator is not frozen to the past but is part of the present and future. Her life is a counterbalance to her grandmother's death. Thus the poem tells of the younger

woman's sexual awakening and ends with a transferring of life from the grandmother to the speaker.

Just as the first part of *Gathering the Tribes* examines the influence of Forché's biological ancestors, the second, "Song Coming Toward Us," shows the influence of her spiritual forebears, primarily the Indians of the Southwest. The bonds are again clear: "What has been/ and what is becoming/ are all of the same age" ("Calling Down the Moose"). The Indians, such as Alfansa (in "Alfansa") and Rosita ("Mientras Dure Vida, Sobra el Tiempo"), are her teachers, just as her grandmother was. This section ends with "Plain Song," which expresses her acceptance of her eventual death, since death, like sex, is part of the natural cycle:

> When it happens, let the birds come.
> Let my hands fall without being folded.
>
> . . . .
>
> Close my eyes with coins, cover
> my head with agave baskets
> that have carried water.

The final section, "The Place That Is Feared I Inhabit," draws predominantly on Forché's personal experiences rather than on her ancestors. The poems chronicle the development of the narrator's sexuality, from her infatuation with Joey, a childhood boyfriend, in "Taproot" and "This Is Their Fault" to a more adult understanding of sexuality as a young mother in "Year at Mudstraw," followed by a sense of disillusionment in "Taking Off My Clothes"; here the speaker voices the suspicion that her lover cannot appreciate her, just as he could not appreciate a Ming bowl. One of the final poems, "Kalaloch," presents a lesbian relationship against the backdrop of nature. The first few stanzas of the erotic poem focus on Jacynthe and the speaker's stay at the coast, where they gather mussels, pick berries, and watch the fog and the tide at day and the moon and the campfire at night. Their love is as natural as the setting in which it is expressed.

THE COUNTRY BETWEEN US

If *Gathering the Tribes* can be said to chronicle an initiation into adulthood, Forché's second volume, *The Country Between Us*, explores the responsibilities and commitments of that adulthood. The catalyst for this collection was Forché's stay in El Salvador. Eight of the poems in the volume have to do with that experience, and the first section of the volume is dedicated to Oscar Romero, the archbishop who, in 1980, was murdered as he said Mass in San Salvador. Yet Vietnam and Czechoslovakia are also highlighted in this collection. As in the first collection, people are central. Included are a steelworker troubled by Vietnam; a woman with whom the speaker shared childhood dreams and who now lives in a trailer with her husband and children, wondering what happened to her life; Terrence Des Pres, Forché's confidant and mentor; a dissident from Eastern Europe; and a political in El Salvador.

The prose poem "The Colonel," the most frequently quoted piece in *The Country Between Us*, is autobiographical, like much of Forché's work, and is based on an encounter with a Salvadoran military officer. At first, the evening described seems unexceptional, even ordinary. The speaker and her friend have dinner (lamb, wine, and fruit) with the colonel and his wife. Typical household items such as newspapers, a pet dog, and a television set make the setting comfortable and tranquil—yet the broken glass embedded in the wall surrounding the compound suggests otherwise. The family's activities—one child files her nails, the other goes out for the evening, the wife serves coffee—are also familiar. Nevertheless, the horror of the situation is soon apparent. The colonel dumps a sackful of human ears on the dining table, emphasizing his intolerance for human rights activists:

> He spilled many ears on the table. They were like dried peach halves. There is no other way to say this. He took one of them in his hands, shook it in our faces, dropped it into a water glass. It came alive there. I am tired of fooling around he said.

While the colonel might have power now, the poem suggests that the situation will not last: "Some of the ears on the floor caught this scrap of his voice. Some of the ears on the floor were pressed to the ground." The ears assume a life of their own and a memory, and they will be avenged.

While the volume's first part, "In Salvador, 1978-80," focuses on that country, the second, "Reunion," examines oppression found elsewhere: Turkey ("Expatriot"), Czechoslovakia ("Letter from Prague, 1968-78"),

and the United States with its economic oppression. In "As Children Together," Victoria and the speaker grow up together and speak of their girlish dreams; Victoria envisions herself in Montreal, living a romantic life filled with flowers, "a satin bed, a table/ cluttered with bottles of scent." She wants desperately to escape her parents' house with "its round tins of surplus flour,/ chipped beef and white beans, relief checks," where her father whittles aimlessly on soap cakes. Victoria becomes promiscuous and eventually marries a serviceman, who returns from Vietnam "broken/ cursing holy blood at the table/ where nightly a pile of white shavings/ is paid from the edge of his knife." Her life, a legacy of Vietnam and poverty, is circumscribed by the trailer in which she lives. Still, the poem ends on a note of hope. One of the girls, the speaker, has broken the cycle: "If you read this poem, write to me./ I have been to Paris since we parted."

In "Joseph," the character of that name, the narrator's childhood companion and first boyfriend, has also lost his dreams. His life now consists of working in the steel mill, meeting women in bars ("You take her panties to your face/ and it is all you have and all/ your father had and all your brothers"), and fishing. The narrator recognizes the emptiness of his working-class life: "It is not enough, the fish,/ the white heads of beer, your winnings." His youth held a promise that was not fulfilled because of the oppression of poverty. Now the gap between the two former friends prevents communication.

The final part of the collection, "Ourselves or Nothing," contains one long poem of the same title, dedicated to Terrence Des Pres. The poem suggests the importance of remembering, of not letting "Belsen, Dachau, Saigon, Phnom Penh/ and the one meaning Bridge of Ravens,/ Sao Paulo, Armagh, Calcutta, Salvador" be forgotten, and the importance of not remaining behind the "cyclone fence," of not hovering "in a calm protected world like/ netted fish, exactly like netted fish." It is crucial to become involved, for, as the poem concludes, "It is either the beginning or the end/ of the world, and the choice is ourselves/ or nothing."

THE ANGEL OF HISTORY

In *The Angel of History*, Forché's ambition and accomplishment reach new heights. Read either as a single, long poem or a sequence of related poems, this dazzling volume breaks away from the techniques of her earlier work. Forché's own comment, in her notes to the volume, says it best:

> The first-person, free-verse, lyric-narrative poem of my earlier years has given way to a work which has desired its own bodying forth: polyphonic, broken, haunted, and in ruins, with no possibility of restoration.

There may be some overstatement here; something that is fragmentary is not necessarily in ruins. However, the ruined moral landscape that Forché's persona annotates is projected with a "terrible beauty." Through the voice (or voices) of the recording angel, the poet absorbs and releases visions and echoes of the disasters that humans of the twentieth century have wrought upon themselves. Readers are forced to witness and respond to the Holocaust, to Hiroshima, and to genocide in Latin America. At once angry and compassionate, devastated and distanced, the angel forces the reader to accept the harsh reality and guides the reader toward a thin but luminous possibility of redemption. Forché's poem is like the bell in "The Garden Shukkei-en," devastated by the atomic bomb though since restored: "It is the bell to awaken God that we've heard ringing."

Forché has been praised by some critics for her ability to blend the political with a personal poetic mode. Yet others disagree, claiming that Forché is too much a part of her poems and that her poetic diction is unsuited to her subject. Forché counters that all subjects should be appropriate for poetry and that she has a responsibility to speak as a witness: "In my own life, the memory of certain of those who have died remains in very few hands. I can't let go of that work if I am of that number." Forché includes the political in her work, but, most important, she never forgets that she is writing poetry, poetry that is lyrical, honest, sensual, tender, courageous, and intelligent.

OTHER MAJOR WORKS

NONFICTION: *El Salvador: The Work of Thirty Photographers*, 1983 (text for photographs).

TRANSLATIONS: *Flowers from the Volcano*, 1982 (of Claribel Alegría); *Selected Poems of Robert Desnos*, 1991 (with William Kulik); *Sorrow*, 1999, (of Claribel Alegría).

EDITED TEXT: *Against Forgetting: Twentieth-Century Poetry of Witness*, 1993; *Writing Creative Nonfiction: Instruction and Insight from Teachers of the Associated Writing Programs*, 2001 (with Philip Gerard).

BIBLIOGRAPHY

Bedient, Calvin. "Poetry and Silence at the End of the Century." *Salmagundi*, no. 111 (Summer, 1996): 195-207. Bedient compares *The Angel of History* with Charles Wright's *Chickamauga* and T. S. Eliot's *The Waste Land*.

Bogan, Don. "The Muses of History." *The Nation* 24 (October, 1994): 464-469. This brief but careful reading of *The Angel of History* attends to its structure and tone. Bogan sets Forché's work alongside James Fenton's collection *Out of Danger*.

Doubiago, Sharon. "Towards an American Criticism: A Reading of Carolyn Forché's *The Country Between Us*." *The American Poetry Review* 12 (January/February, 1983): 35-39. Doubiago faults other critics who have no tolerance for a political message in poetry and suggests that any aesthetic has a political basis. She argues that Forché's work points to the need for "a new poetic ethic."

Forché, Carolyn. Interview by David Montenegro. *The American Poetry Review* 17 (November/December, 1988): 35-40. Forché discusses a number of issues, including her work-in-progress, the influence of her grandmother on her poetry, her childhood, and Vietnam. She defends her incorporation of historical and political concerns into her poetry.

Gleason, Judith. "The Lesson of Bread." *Parnassus: Poetry in Review* 10 (Spring/Summer, 1982): 9-21. Gleason finds Forché effective in transmitting the horror of El Salvador in *The Country Between Us*, but also effective in suggesting a hope for the future by the use of the image of bread making in this volume and in *Gathering the Tribes*.

Greer, Michael. "Politicizing the Modern: Carolyn Forché in El Salvador and America." *The Centennial Review* 30 (Spring, 1986): 125-135. Greer presents a useful critical discussion of the eight Salvadoran poems in *The Country Between Us*, showing how Forché employs modernist poetics to examine political events. The vocabulary drawn from literary theory might prove an obstacle to the uninitiated reader of this article.

Ostriker, Alicia. "Beyond Confession: The Poetics of Postmodern Witness." *American Poetry Review* 30, no. 2 (March/April, 2001): 35-39. Offers a look at what is likely to be called the poetics of postmodern witness by examining the title poem of Adrienne Rich's *An Atlas of the Difficult World*, Forché's *The Angel of History*, and Sharon Doubiago's *South American Mi Hija*. Ostriker notes how "the fragmentary quality of Forché's writing registers the way consciousness cracks under the weight" of witnessed horrors.

Barbara Wiedemann;
updated by Philip K. Jason

UGO FOSCOLO

Born: Zante, Ionian Isles, Greece; February 6, 1778
Died: Turnham Green, near London, England; September 10, 1827

PRINCIPAL POETRY

Bonaparte liberatore, 1797
Poesie, 1803
Dei sepolcri, 1807 (*On Sepulchres*, 1835, 1971)
Le grazie, 1848

OTHER LITERARY FORMS

Ugo Foscolo is best known for his *Ultime lettere di Jacopo Ortis* (1802; *Last Letters of Jacopo Ortis*, 1970), an epistolary novel written after the Treaty of Campoformio (October 17, 1797), in which Napoleon Bonaparte ceded Venice to the Austrians. Napoleon's action shocked Foscolo, who had previously written an ode entitled "A Bonaparte liberatore" ("To the Liberator Bonaparte"). In this autobiographical novel written in the form of letters from the student Jacopo Ortis to his friend Lorenzo Alderani, eroticism and politics (of a strong anti-Gallic strain) are merged. In the same year, Foscolo wrote a tragedy, *Tieste* (1797), in the style of

Vittorio Alfieri, the success of which owed much to its revolutionary democratic spirit.

Between 1804 and 1805, while in France, Foscolo began work on an Italian translation of Laurence Sterne's *A Sentimental Journey* (1768). This translation was finished in 1813 in Pisa and was published concurrently with an autobiographical work, *Notizie intorno a Didimo Chierico* (1813; news about Didimo Chierico). On January 22, 1809, in support of his nomination for a professorship at Pavia University, Foscolo published an important work titled *Dell'origine e dell'ufficio della letteratura* (about the origin and function of literature), in which he promotes a sociohistorical approach to literature.

Among Foscolo's most important nonlyric works are the tragedies *Aiace* (pr. 1811) and *Ricciarda* (pr. 1813). *Aiace* was not successful at its premiere but today is considered one of Foscolo's best works. Foscolo's *Epistolario* (1949-1970; letters) is outstanding, from both a literary and a political standpoint, and is characterized by sincerity even in the most intimate matters. In Switzerland, Foscolo published his speeches under the title *Della servitu d'Italia* (1823; on the servitude of Italy), a work which shows Foscolo's pessimism concerning the then-fermenting Risorgimento, the movement for the unification of Italy.

From 1816 until his death in 1827, Foscolo lived in England and dedicated himself to producing scholarly, critical works such as *Saggi sul Petrarca* (1821; *Essays on Petrarch*, 1823) and *Discorso sul testo e su le opinioni diverse prevalenti intorno alla storia e alla emendazione critica della "Commedia" di Dante* (1825). Through these works, Foscolo helped to initiate in Italy a modern critical awareness of the psychological and sociohistorical background of literature.

ACHIEVEMENTS

Ugo Foscolo was a man of strong commitment and even stronger will, never afraid to follow the path of truth in the pursuit of the ideals he held worthy. Like many Italian writers from Petrarch and Dante on, Foscolo brought a strong thread of classical culture to the Romanticism which dominated the entire European scene during the early 1800's. His personal experiences and his cultural background became the raw material from which he worked all of his life. Foscolo's writings, in some sense, summed up much of the achievement and many of the trends of Italian literature of his day (the critical studies of Dante, Petrarch, and Boccaccio are notable in this respect), and he stood as a significant milestone for writers of succeeding generations. His burial at the Church of Santa Croce in Florence, where he is entombed among the greatest figures of Italian literary and political history, suggests his place in Italian culture and letters.

BIOGRAPHY

Niccolò Ugo Foscolo was born to parents of mixed heritage; his mother, Diamantina Spaty, was Greek, while his father, Andrea Foscolo, was Venetian. When Foscolo was ten years old, his father died. He and his mother then moved to Venice, where he stayed until 1797, during which time he began to attend political and literary gatherings such as those of the Countess Isabella Teotochi. In this period, he developed an admiration for the revolutionary doctrines of Jean-Jacques Rousseau, Vittorio Alfieri, and Robespierre while attending classes taught by Melchiorre Cesarotti at Padua University.

In 1797, because of his political ideas, Foscolo was forced to flee to Bologna, where he received the nomination of honorary lieutenant for the French army in Italy. He performed this role as a strict republican until the infamous Treaty of Campoformio, which caused Foscolo to hate Bonaparte so much that he moved to Milan, where he lived from 1797 to 1815. In Milan, Foscolo made the acquaintance of Vincenzo Monti and Giuseppe Parini, and he also pursued love affairs with Teresa Pickler, Isabella Roncioni, and the Countess Antonietta Fagnani Arese.

When, in 1798, the second coalition of the Austrians and Russians reconquered northern Italy from Napoleon (who was at that time in Egypt), Foscolo fought against this action under General Jean-Étienne Championnet, but his open aspiration for Italian independence provoked great hostility from the French. Nevertheless, he went to France for two years (1804-1806) and made the acquaintance of the famous Italian writer Alessandro Manzoni, as well as an English girl, Fanny Emerytt, by whom he had a daughter, Floriana. Returning to Milan in 1806, Foscolo pursued more love affairs and dedi-

cated himself to various writing activities. In 1812, after the presentation of his second tragedy, *Aiace*, in which certain characters were seen as anti-French, the poet was forced to flee to Florence. There, Foscolo involved himself in the circle of the countess of Albany until the Austrians took Milan in 1813. Unable to pledge allegiance to the Austrian government, Foscolo went into voluntary exile in Switzerland in 1815. One year later, he moved to England, where he collaborated in the publication of magazines and journals, gave classes in literature, and was reunited with his daughter, Floriana. He quickly exhausted Floriana's savings, some three thousand pounds, and remained deeply in debt until his death in 1827. Only in 1871 was his body brought to Florence and buried, as requested in his will, in the Church of Santa Croce, next to the tombs of Michelangelo, Machiavelli, Alfieri, and Galileo.

Foscolo's achievements were acknowledged during his lifetime, but it was only after his death that his writings were fully recognized as a milestone in Italian literature. He succeeded in detaching himself from the regionalism of his predecessors. From political realism, he went on to pessimism, though he never espoused the fatalism expressed by his younger contemporary Giacomo Leopardi; Foscolo's was a dynamic pessimism which organized his heroic and lyric behavior. If the function of poetry, as Natalino Sapegno states in his *Disegno storico della letteratura italiana* (1973), is to discover amid the contradictions of this earthly life that universal harmony by which man restores his own existence, Foscolo, amid a troubled life, found support in his art and created a personal vision of the sublime.

ANALYSIS

The Romantic movement dominated Italian literature during the first half of the nineteenth century, and Ugo Foscolo, along with other writers, such as Vincenzo Monti and Alessandro Manzoni, was part of it, though at a rather different level. Foscolo's personal life and his involvement in the political, social, and literary history of Italy are closely meshed in his poetry.

"SONETTI"

Foscolo's twelve sonnets (known collectively as the "Sonetti"), which combine the strength of Dante and the melancholy of Petrarch, have much in common with his novel *Last Letters of Jacopo Ortis:* the oppressive influence of Fate on politics and personal life, hints of suicide, the pleasures and despair of love, and a sense of hostility against the invaders of Italy. There is in these sonnets, however, a new sense of nature, a more ironic and melancholic approach to the political problems of Italy, and a more lyric treatment of autobiographical themes such as love, exile, death of loved ones, and exhortations to achieve glory through poetry.

In the sonnet "Te nudrice alle muse" ("You Nurturer of the Muses"), addressed to Italy, Foscolo complains about the proposed abolition of the Latin language, a proposal made by the legislature of the Cisalpina Republic. This sonnet at first appears to be academic and traditional in structure, theme, and style, reflecting the influence of Alfieri and the neoclassical literary forms of the late eighteenth century. There is, nevertheless, an innovative element in this sonnet: the first use by Foscolo of a technique, later perfected in *On Sepulchers*, by which the various sections of a poem are related by larger, "historical" logic rather than by conventional syntactic logic. The two quatrains of this sonnet refer to the past, while, without any apparent connective tissue, the tercets ironically address Italy on the inconveniences that would be caused by the abolition of the Latin language. The logic which related quatrains and tercets reflects the overlying concept that there can be no contemporary Italian language and culture without reference to the language and culture of the past.

The sonnet "E tu?" ("And You?") also contrasts quatrains and tercets: The quatrains have an *abba-abba* rhyme scheme and are historical in content, while the tercets rhyme *aba-cbc* and are erotic in theme and mood. The poet starts by using heroic, quasi-Ossianic terminology to recall the medieval fights in Florence; then, in a more lyric fashion, he praises Florence as the dwelling place of his beloved.

"Ne più" ("Never Again"), another sonnet from this collection, speaks of the tragedy of the exiled Foscolo. The poet, though Italian by birth and education, will never be able to forget that he was born of a Greek mother in the luminous and wooded Zacinto, and that his poetry echoes Homer and Theocritus. Foscolo recalls his island and the myths of Venus and Ulysses with

a surge of melody in full rhymes. The first statement nostalgically affirms that he will never again set foot on the sacred shore of his native island and, unlike Ulysses, will not be granted burial in his native land. The last tercet, however, brings the consolation that, if not his body, at least his song will return to Zacinto: Poetry will be his means of immortality.

The Foscolo of the "Sonetti" reaches a climax of poetic inspiration when he turns from history and mythology to treat his personal life or naturalistically perceived objects. A vein of melancholy emerges in sonnets such as "Perché taccia il rumor di mia catena" ("To Hush the Clangor of My Chain"), "Forse perché della fatal quiete" ("Perhaps Because of the Fateful Quiet"), and "Un dì, s'io non andrò sempre fuggendo" ("One Day, Should I Not Always Flee"). In these sonnets, for example, there are autobiographical references to his unfortunate love for the Florentine Isabella Roncioni and to the death of his brother John, which reminds him of his exile.

The sonnet "Perhaps Because of the Fateful Quiet" is a dialogue with the evening; it moves in a thickly harmonious structure from the proposal of the theme through a central part to the conclusion. Its merit, as Foscolo himself said, lies in producing, through a broken structure, the same effects that musicians achieve through dissonance and painters achieve through shading. The poem starts with monosyllables and bisyllables, pauses at the fourth line in perfect lyric hendecasyllables until the eighth line, and then begins again the tormented rhythmic pattern. In a fashion reminiscent of Edward Young and Giuseppe Parini, Foscolo writes of the evening that is dear to him because it is the image of death; it keeps the secret paths of his heart, promising rest for his ever-warring spirit.

"To Louise Pallavicini Fallen from a Horse" and "To the Healed Friend"

During the same years in which these sonnets were composed (1800-1802), Foscolo also wrote two *odi:* "A Luigia Pallavicini caduta da cavallo" ("To Louise Pallavicini Fallen from a Horse") and "All'amica risanata" ("To the Healed Friend"), for Antonietta Fagnani Arese. These two odes praise the beauty of and virtually deify the two women to whom they are dedicated. The autobiographical elements and controlled poetic expertise of the sonnets continue in these odes, which are additionally characterized by literary eclecticism and imagery drawn from pagan mythology.

The first ode describes a fall which the beautiful Louise took from a horse and expresses the wish that she will recover and become more beautiful than before. The whole poem is supported by mythic prototypes: Venus stung on the foot while leaning over the dead body of Ado, the "bath of Pallas," the intervention of Neptune against the enraged horse, and finally the fall of Diana into the volcano Etna, followed by her recovery. Though the poem's structure (eighteen stanzas of six lines each) is taken from Carlo Frugoni, and its imagery is inherited from poets such as Ludovico Ariosto, Poliziano, and Alfieri, Foscolo proves his mastery of form, style, and imagination by achieving a certain degree of seriousness in a lyric genre which in eighteenth century Italy had a rather light, occasional status. In Foscolo's work, goddesses care for human suffering and exchange feelings of love with mortal creatures. The highly artificial tone characteristic of occasional verse does not diminish the sense of beauty and serenity which this ode evokes, foreshadowing Foscolo's more mature work in *Le grazie*.

The second ode, usually viewed in relation to the passionate letters which Foscolo wrote to Antonietta Fagnani Arese, is, by contrast, carefully controlled in emotion. The process of deification is more stylized here than in the ode to Louise Pallavicini. The poet begins with a description of the healing of his beloved, again using mythological allusions. The deification reaches its climax when the poet declares that his verses will be the woman's salvation from death and from the jealousy of others. The conclusion reiterates the mood of the earlier sonnet to his native island, "Ne più mai toccherò le sacre sponde" ("I Will Never Touch Again the Sacred Shore") and anticipates the poem *Le grazie* with a recollection of the spirit of Sappho and the sound of Greek poetry. As in the first ode, Foscolo contemplates evil and death only to distance himself from them, to aspire to a higher sense of beauty and eternity.

ON SEPULCHERS

In considering *On Sepulchers*, Giovanni Getto, in *La composizione dei "Sepolcri" di Ugo Foscolo* (1977), observes that the three images—suggesting nature, civilization, and death—which are presented at the beginning of the poem, represent the complex symbol of *On Sepulchers's* entire figurative world. The poem draws together all the poetic motifs of Foscolo's earlier work into a new and powerful synthesis. The dialectic of this poem is, ultimately, between death and immortality. If the evils of this life cannot be avoided, immortality may be attained through memory, as evidenced by burial monuments, for after death the hero will obtain at least this measure of glory. In the various shadings of *On Sepulchers*, Foscolo continuously fuses images and contrasting tones and creates the highly individual syntax which distinguishes his verse.

On Sepulchers is infused with a sense of melancholy, mystery, and historicism. After evoking life, nature, poetry, and hopes broken by death, Foscolo blames the new Napoleonic law for having placed in the same tomb the bones of great men and those of thieves. He remembers then the sensible pagan rituals in honor of the virtuous dead, contrasting them with the superstitious rites of Christianity, which are characterized by a fear of the next world. He then passes to a historical vision in praise of Florence, where Dante and the parents of Petrarch were born, and where Machiavelli, Michelangelo, and Galileo are buried in Santa Croce. The sense of heroism and of the regeneration of the Italian nation comes from a tie between the living and the dead. This is why the heroic spirits of the past inspired Homer, especially the spirit of Hector, the greatest and most unfortunate of all heroes.

For Foscolo, poetry was one of the most pure and significant achievements of humankind. His translations from Homer in the period preceding the composition of *On Sepulchers* inspired him to celebrate the heros of the past in order to unite former times with the present in an ineffable harmony. The occasional, the meditative, the narrative, and the fantastic impulses all converge in this poem. Unlike *Last Letters of Jacopo Ortis*, which echoes the Titanism of Alfieri, and unlike the "Sonetti," which expresses the solitude and the horror of Foscolo's life, *On Sepulchers* testifies to the poet's liberation from his past passions. From the beginning, the reader of *On Sepulchers* has in front of his eyes not a bare tomb but a sepulcher comforted by the tears of the living, because "Hope, the last Goddess, flees the sepulchers." From reason to fantasy, from the past to the present, from the dead to the living, from autobiographical references to the recollection of the great poets and heroes of the past, Foscolo develops his themes like a symphony. The initial rhetorical question in *On Sepulchers*, in which the desolation of death is clearly stated, is finally transformed into the attitude that all people worthy of glory, such as Hector, will have the "honor of tears as long as the sun will shine over human afflictions."

LE GRAZIE

The interrelationship between poetry and the other arts, while present in Foscolo's earlier poetry, becomes central in *Le grazie*. The vision of poetry which eternalizes heroism through emulation of living people, as found in *On Sepulchers*, is here replaced with that of beauty, which educates the human spirit to reveal the secret consonance of the universe.

Aldo Vallone, in *Le Grazie nella storia della poesia foscoliana*, has remarked that the neoclassicism of *On Sepulchers* becomes for Foscolo in *Le grazie* the natural way of composing poetry. The expressive elements contained in this ambitious allegorical and didactic poem, which remained unfinished at Foscolo's death, reveal his absolute mastery of his material. By technical devices such as the usage of certain prepositions, of narrative sections, and of repetition of key words, Foscolo suggests at one moment the shading of the verse, while at another moment he reestablishes equilibrium among the various segments of the poem, producing an effect of musical lyricism.

Composing *Le grazie* while at the villa Bellosguardo, near Florence, Foscolo was inspired by the Venus of Canova and the statuary group of the Graces. The poem also reveals the influence of the neoclassical aesthetics of Johann Joachim Winckelmann, and marks Foscolo's passage from pure to critical lyric. This is not to say that there is any lack of images or lyric pleasure; on the contrary, critical and poetic thoughts are here combined. The philosophical intuition of reality as harmony goes side by side with passion and melancholy.

In the tradition of Homer and Callimachus, three hymns compose *Le grazie*. The first hymn is dedicated to Venus, Goddess of Beauty, the second to Vesta, Goddess of the Hearth, and the third to Pallas, Goddess of the Arts. According to *Le grazie*, aesthetics were born in Greece, and with them civilization began. Italy became the major theater of civilization, and there music, dance, lyric language, greatness of mind, and physical beauty gave rebirth to the Graces—that is, to Harmony. This concept is presented in the second hymn and poetically developed by the image of a sacrifice made by three of the women Foscolo loved: Nencini, with a harp; Martinetti, with a honeycomb; and Bignami, with a swan. The last hymn takes the reader to the middle of an ocean on an ethereal Earth. Pallas, in fact, weaves a veil which exalts youth, love, hospitality, maternal affection, and filial piety. With this veil, she covers the Graces so that they can protect themselves from passion.

The form of the three hymns seems to be less impetuous than that of *On Sepulchers*: Dissonances are softened, and the verse has a smoother and less luminous modulation.

OTHER MAJOR WORKS

LONG FICTION: *Ultime lettere di Jacopo Ortis*, 1802 (*Last Letters of Jacopo Ortis*, 1970).

PLAYS: *Tieste*, pr. 1797; *Aiace*, pr. 1811; *Ricciarda*, pr. 1813.

NONFICTION: *Orazione a Bonaparte pel Congresso di Lione*, 1802; *Dell'origine e dell'ufficio della letteratura*, 1809; *Notizie intorno a Didimo Chierico*, 1813; *Essay on the Present Literature of Italy*, 1818; *Saggi sul Petrarca*, 1821 (*Essays on Petrarch*, 1823); *Della servitù d'Italia*, 1823; *Discorso sul testo e su le opinioni diverse prevalenti intorno alla storia e alla emendazione critica della "Commedia" di Dante*, 1825; *Discorso storico sul testo del "Decamerone,"* 1825; *On the New Dramatic School in Italy*, 1826; *Epistolario*, 1949-1970 (7 volumes).

TRANSLATIONS: *La chioma di Berenice*, 1803 (of Callimachus's poetry); *Esperimenti di traduzione della "Iliade" di Omero*, 1807 (of Homer's *Iliad*); *Viaggio sentimentale di Yorick lungo la Francia e l'Italia*, 1813 (of Laurence Sterne's *A Sentimental Journey*).

BIBLIOGRAPHY
Cambon, Glauco. *Ugo Foscolo: Poet of Exile*. Princeton, N.J.: Princeton University Press, 1980. A critical study of the works of Foscolo. Includes an index.

Franzero, Charles Marie. *A Life in Exile: Ugo Foscolo in London, 1816-1827*. London: Allen, 1977. A biography focusing on Foscolo's life in London.

Matteo, Sante. *Textual Exile: The Reader in Sterne and Foscolo*. New York: P. Lang, 1985. A study of Foscolo and Laurence Sterne. Substantial bibliography.

O'Neill, Tom. *Of Virgin Muses and of Love: A Study of Foscolo's Dei sepolcri*. Dublin: Irish Academic Press, 1981. Includes bibliographical references and index.

Radcliff-Umstead, Douglas. *Ugo Foscolo*. New York: Twayne, 1970. An introductory biography and critical analysis of selected works by Foscolo. Includes bibliographic references.

Rosenfeld, Erika Kay. *An Evaluation of Foscolo's "The Graces" Based on an Original Translation*. Thesis. New York: Columbia University, 1976. Reprint. Ann Arbor, Mich.: University Microfilms, 1981. A rare English-language scholarly study of *Le grazie*.

Adriano Moz;
bibliography updated by the editors

GIROLAMO FRACASTORO

Born: Verona, Republic of Venice (now in Italy); c. 1478

Died: Incaffi, near Verona, Republic of Venice; August 6, 1553

PRINCIPAL POETRY

Syphilis sive morbus Gallicus, 1530 (*Syphilis: Or, A Poetical History of the French Disease*, 1686)

Ioseph, wr. c. 1540-1545, pb. 1555 (*The Maiden's Blush: Or, Joseph*, 1620)

Opera omnia, 1555 (includes *In obitu M. Antonii Turrii Veronensis, Ioseph*, and other poetry)

OTHER LITERARY FORMS

Foremost among Girolamo Fracastoro's prose work is the treatise *Syphilis* (wr. 1553, pb. 1939). Other scientific pieces include *Homocentricorum sive de stellis* (1538; homocentricity on the stars), *De causis criticorum dierum libellus* (1538), *De sympathia et antipathia rerum* (1546; on the attraction and repulsion of things), *De contagionibus et contagiosis morbis et eorum curatione* (1546; *De contagione et contagiosis morbis et eorum curatione*, 1930), and *De vini temperatura* (1534). Also of interest are three Humanistic dialogues: *Naugerius sive de poetica dialogus* (1549; English translation, 1924), and the unfinished "Turrius sive de intellectione dialogus" and "Fracastorius sive de anima dialogus," which were published posthumously in the *Opera omnia* of 1555.

A play, *La Venexiana* (the Venetian, or Venetian comedy), was discovered in 1928 by Emilio Lovarini, deciphered from manuscript miscellany collected in 1780 by Iacopo Morelli. No other text is known, and no mention was made of the play in its time, although it seems to have been written after 1509. The work was published in 1950 in a bilingual edition with introduction and English translation by Matilde Valenti Pfeiffer. A pseudonym, Hieronymous Zarello, was applied to the work, but the Fracastoro expert Girlando Lentini attested its authenticity in his August, 1948, article, "Non piu anonima la Venexiana," in the *Giornale di Sicilia*. The play was published twice by Lovarini, in 1928 and in 1947. The work has been described by Pfeiffer as "one of the earliest character plays in world literature." Its alternation of long and short episodes during the course of four days and its shift of place and mood anticipate the dramaturgy of William Shakespeare. In five acts, its six characters convey the vulnerability of romantic love. The play moves quickly; the characters are quaint and boldly drawn; the language is unusually pithy and droll. It is a rare document of Venetian life, as its epigraph avers: "Non fabula non comedia ma vera historia" ("Neither fable, nor comedy, but real history").

Another work, "Apocalisse" (apocalypse), extant among Fracastoro's manuscripts as late as 1700, is now lost. W. Parr Greswell notes as well that Fracastoro's "Citriorum epigrammata" and many of his smaller pieces are lost. In referring to Fracastoro's accumulated writings, it is important to note Murray Bundy's observation that "little attempt has ever been made to establish a critical text or to determine chronology."

ACHIEVEMENTS

Girolamo Fracastoro was a Renaissance man in the finest sense of the term. As poet, scholar, scientist, and physician, he embodied the essence of sixteenth century curiosity and Humanistic commitment. Greswell states that "perhaps the productions of no other modern poet have been more commended by the learned, than those of Fracastoro."

Fracastoro's research and writing on infectious diseases drew attention in 1530 when he determined the origin of an epidemic of syphilis in Naples at the time of Charles VIII. It is generally believed that Fracastoro named the disease after the amorous shepherd of Greek mythology, who was punished by the sun god for his infidelity. (Other sources assert that the word derives from *sifilide*, a term in common usage in the local dialect.) A later work, *De contagione et contagiosis morbis et eorum curatione*, dealing with typhus, tuberculosis, and syphilis, developed the concept of infection by transfer of minute organisms from diseased individuals to healthy ones.

In *De sympathia et antipathia rerum* (on the attraction and repulsion of things), Fracastoro discussed a concept of *simpatia* different from that of his Humanist contemporaries. For him, it was a *species spiritualis* that unified the world, a cosmological principle which was to be studied naturalistically, one which applied to both anthropological and aesthetic concepts. This concentration of research is also present in *De causis criticorum dierum libellus* (on the causes of critical days). Fracastoro's emphasis in this treatise was so advanced (he located the causes of disease in microorganisms rather than in astral or numerological relationships) as to cause his biographer, Bruno Zanobio, to comment that "the traditional position of philosophy is turned upside down: philosophy is such to the extent that it investigates not abstract but concrete nature."

Fracastoro was renowned as a physician, but his knowledge of astronomy, literature, and philosophy reflected the comprehensive talents of the learned men of his time. Familiar with the new theories made possible by the use of the telescope, he criticized the employment of epicycles and deferents in astronomy and was the first to use the geographical term "pole" when referring to the magnetic extremes of the Earth. In his work *Homo-*

Girolamo Fracastoro

centricorum sive de stellis, Fracastoro declared that experience was the only valid scientific method, and he furnished illustrations of the movements of celestial bodies, their orbits, the seasons, and the various types of days (civil, solar, and sidereal). The work was apparently known to Giordano Bruno, who included Fracastoro as one of the interlocutors in Bruno's dialogue *De l'infinito universo et mondi* (1583; *Of the Infinite Universe and Worlds*, 1950). The biographer Roberto Massalongo went so far as to assert that the work "paved the way" for the great theories of Nicholas Copernicus. Indeed, Fracastoro was read carefully in the nineteenth century by Alexander von Humboldt, who considered Fracastoro's geological investigations significant enough to classify him with Leonardo da Vinci as a scientist far in advance of his time.

BIOGRAPHY

Depending upon the source, the birth of Girolamo Fracastoro (who signed himself Hieronymous Fracastorius in his Latin writings) can be traced to 1478, 1482, 1483, or 1484. There is no controversy, however, concerning his origin. He was born into a very ancient and honorable patrician family, the son of Paolo Philippo and Camilla dei Mascarelli, of a wellborn family of Vicenza. An esteemed ancestor, Aventino Fracastoro, was a celebrated physician of Scala and a gentleman of Verona; he died in 1368, and his tomb in the Church of San Fermo must have been a constant reminder to the young Girolamo of his noble lineage.

Two oddities regarding Fracastoro's birth and early years have been noted by numerous biographers. At birth, his lips were so tightly sealed that a surgeon's knife was required to separate them. Julius Caesarus Scaliger referred to the event in one of the twenty-seven epigrams in his *Altars in Honor of Fracastoro* (1554), relating that the god of medicine and poetry, Apollo himself, intervened at Fracastoro's birth to create a mouth for the poet. The other extraordinary event was the death of his mother (some say his nurse), who was struck and killed by lightning while holding the young Fracastoro in her arms. There is no further record of the effects of these events upon the young poet. Reports agree, however, that his intellect was early noted and that no expense was spared regarding his education.

Fracastoro entered the University of Padua as an adolescent and exhibited a desire to master every science that occupied his attention, demonstrating a singularly advanced proficiency in mathematics. In addition, he studied literature, astronomy (astrology at that time), medicine, and philosophy, the last with Nicolo Leonico Tomeo and Pietro Pomponazzi. Pomponazzi was a tutor in Aristotle, Averroës, and Alexander of Aphrodisias, and received considerable attention for a paper he wrote which was incorrectly interpreted as calling into question the immortality of the soul.

Upon receiving his degree in 1502, Fracastoro became an instructor in logic and also served as *conciliarius anatomicus*, giving lectures on medicine and anatomy. It was at this time that he met a young medical student named Nicholas Copernicus. Other colleagues and acquaintances who were to play roles in his literary activities were Alessandro Farnese (later Pope Paul III), Gaspar Contarenus and Ercole Gonzaga (later made cardinals), Giovanni Matteo Giberti (subsequently Bishop of Verona), Pietro Bembo (dedicatee of his most significant work of poetry and personal secretary to Pope Leo X), Andreas Navagero (dedicatee of Fracastoro's work on poetics and a national historian and ambassador), and the brothers Marcus Antonius, Joannes Baptista, and Raymundo della Torre (all utilized as characters in Fracastoro's literary "dialogues").

Fracastoro married young, possibly in 1500; his wife, Elena, who was apparently five years older than her husband, died in 1540. They had five children, four sons and one daughter, only two of whom survived their father. During the period of national strife after the League of Cambria, Fracastoro took refuge in the Republic of Venice, where he enjoyed the patronage of General Alviano, serving as personal physician and as an instructor in the informal academy that Alviano had established in Podenone. Niccolò Machiavelli commented on the precarious situation of the Venetian and Veronese states at this time. German, Spanish, French, and Swiss troops were all garrisoned in the area at one time or another, and plague was rampant. Soon after the defeat of the Venetian forces, Fracastoro retired to the villa in Incaffi and alternated residence between there and Verona, some fifteen miles distant. The villa was a peaceful retreat, frequented regularly by writers, scientists, philosophers, and artists. Fracastoro himself has described it in the eulogy for Marcus Antonius della Torre:

> Here acts, absolv'd from modish fashion's school
> Nor moves in measur'd steps, nor stands by rule
> But drinks at pleasure, and reclines at ease
> No laws to trammel, no fops to tease.

Between the years 1509 and 1530, Fracastoro actively practiced medicine and continued his research in botany, cosmography, and infectious diseases. Fracastoro was an eminent physician, serving Catherine de Médicis, and was once called to serve as court physician to Marguerite of Navarre. The early version of *Syphilis: Or, A Poetical History of the French Disease* (not to be confused with Fracastoro's treatise on the same subject) was completed by 1525, and Fracastoro's retirement to study and to write coincides with its publication in 1530 (his first work to issue from a printing press). By that time, he was no longer happy to be recognized primarily as a physician, though it was in this capacity that he was subsequently called upon by Pope Paul III (Alessandro Farnese) to serve as medical adviser (*medicus conductus et stipendiatus*) to the Council of Trent in 1545.

At the time, the pope was very concerned about both security and the political ramifications of holding the Council in Trent; his preference was Bologna. Fracastoro's assessment of the danger of epidemic convinced the authorities of the wisdom of the change. Fracastoro's influence on the decision to move the council from Trent to Bologna suggests the stature of his professional opinion. In 1546, Fracastoro was made a canon of Verona. Though always interested in politics, he never held public office.

Fracastoro died of cerebral apoplexy on August 6, 1553. He had predicted such a death, which occurred without the attendance of either physician or priest. Earlier, he had saved the life of a nun who was suffering from the same affliction by application of a remedy of his own devising. Ironically, his servants failed to understand his motions calling for medical aid in his own case, and he is said to have died quite resigned to his fate. Though there is some controversy concerning his place of burial, his body reputedly rests in the ruins of the parish church of Saint Eufemia, near the villa in Incaffi; the church itself has been destroyed. Soon after his death, an effigy in bronze was placed in the Benedictine cloister near Verona. In Verona itself, south of the Porta Vittoria, is a *cimitero* with monuments to the city's greatest citizens. Fracastoro's name can be found most prominently over the alcove designated number one. In 1559, a statue of Fracastoro by Danese Cataneo was erected in the Piazza dei Signiori, near those of Catullus, Napos, Macer, Vitruvius, and Dante.

ANALYSIS

Girolamo Fracastoro flourished in the atmosphere of the Italian Renaissance, when the diminished influence of theological study gave way to an increased interest in science and nature. The contemplative attitude was gradually replaced by a more aggressive operative one. Nature was viewed as an autonomous reality with its own laws before which supernatural intervention was of minimal use. Man was forced to rely on his capacity for progressive understanding of the principles that regulated the natural world.

SYPHILIS

Such were the ideas that made up the narrative poem *Syphilis*, upon which rests Fracastoro's literary fame. Written in 1521 and dedicated to Pietro Bembo, the poem consists of thirteen hundred verses in Latin hexameter (not verses in the contemporary sense of stanzas, but blocks of copy in his handwritten manuscript); in the words of Bruno Zanobio, it "represents a magnificent paradigm of formal sixteenth century virtuosity in refined Latin of a didactic quality reminiscent of Vergil's *Georgics*" (37-30 B.C.E.). The work reveals the author's early concept of *seminaria* (microorganisms), a concept which he derived from the pre-Socratic philosopher Democritus by way of the *semina morbi* of Lucretius's *De rerum natura* (c. 55 B.C.E.), available to Fracastoro in a 1515 translation by his friend Andreas Navagero.

It is significant to note the exercise of poetic license in the application of some scientific terms. Meter altered the use of terminology in these cases: *contages* was used for *contagio* (contact or touch); *seminaria* for *semina* (seeds); *achores* for *pustula* (sores, infections). This was the case earlier, when Lucretius used *pestilitas* for *pestilentia* (pestilence or plague). Fracastoro's *seminaria* differ from traditional *semina*, however, and it is difficult to know if the author foresaw the actual existence of microbes. The inability at the time to distinguish between organic and inorganic and the belief in spontaneous generation would probably have prevented Fracastoro from assigning to his *seminaria* the characteristics of microorganisms as they are known today.

Fracastoro developed the concept further in a prose treatise, also entitled *Syphilis*, which was completed in 1553 but not published until 1939. Zanobio interprets Fracastoro's work on syphilis to be his new premise for the construction of a philosophy of nature: "Nature creates and destroys and gives misery and happiness, and it is useless to appease the gods. Science, whose power alone can give joy, dictates man's actions." Fracastoro's most significant contribution to the scientific side of syphilography was *De contagione et contagiosis morbis et eorum curatione*, published sixteen years after the poem *Syphilis*. Leona Baumgartner and John F. Fulton observe that in his concept of animate contagion, Fracastoro was "a precursor of Pasteur and Koch."

The poem *Syphilis* was an immediate success and earned extravagant praise from many sides. Bembo announced that the work equaled that of Lucretius and Vergil. Jacopo Sannazzaro, a contemporary and a cruel critic of anyone who threatened to challenge his own supremacy, commented that it surpassed his *De partu virginium* (1527; of Virgin birth), a work twenty years in process. It was neither the first nor the last poem on the subject, but it was the longest, the most serious, the most eloquent, and by far the best publicized.

An early version of the poem was completed by 1521; the date has been established through Fracastoro's mention of Pope Leo as still alive (the pope died in 1522). The author first presented the work to its dedicatee, Bembo, in a two-book version. Bembo suggested changes, among which was the deletion of a myth on the origin of mercury as a remedy. He thought it too obvious an imitation of Aristaeus in Vergil's *Georgics*. Fracastoro rejected most of the suggested changes but did expand the work to three books.

The earliest extant version, published in 1530, is referred to as the "Verona text." In this text, two verses are omitted, while the lines beginning "Quo tandem . . ." and "Aetheris inuisas . . ." have been entered, apparently in Fracastoro's own hand, on the "authorized" or "Rome text" of the following year. This change is not found in other contemporary editions, and there were no other changes in seven subsequent editions published in the author's lifetime. The omitted lines are not included in the *Opera omnia* of 1555, but are in the one of 1574. The poem is found in more than one hundred editions; it has appeared many times in Latin editions, eleven Latin versions of which are in the *Opera omnia*. Many bilingual editions exist, with several editions in English. It has appeared in six languages.

SYPHILIS, BOOK 1

The first book begins with a consideration of the "varied chances of things" which appear responsible for the dread disease. The author observes "how number governs moved things and things moving," a possible reference to the theories of Pythagoras and Heraclitus. Fracastoro, as a protobacteriologist, determines that the "origin of the affliction" is to be found in the air; the *semina morbi* (diseased seeds) are *semina coeli* (germs of the heavens). References to seeds, germs, atoms, and corpuscles can be traced to the writings of Lucretius and Epicurus, but Fracastoro makes the observation that this affliction strikes only the *humanum genus* (human race), Vergil's *ingens genus*, the race having mind and reason.

"Into Italy, it broke with the Frenchmen's war and after them it was named [*morbus Gallicus*]." Although the disease did not at that time carry the onus of immorality it subsequently assumed, it was referred to by the Italians as "the French disease," by the French as "the Neapolitan evil," by the Germans and English as "the French pox and Bordeaux evil," in Holland and North Africa as "the Spanish pox," in Portugal as "the Castilian disease," in Persia and Turkey as "the Christian disease," in Russia as "the Polish disease," and in Poland as "the German disease."

Italy at the time of the poem's composition was torn by conflicts with Louis XII of France and Maximilian of Germany. The country was suffering from plague, famine, and war. It is not surprising, then, that the author should designate Mars as influential in the country's misfortunes: "Venus and Mars the dire/ Against all humans, planets would conspire/ . . . when they converge at some spot in the skies." Giovanni Boccaccio in his *Decameron* (c. 1348-1353) had referred to the influence of celestial bodies which resulted in the Black Death. Guy de Chauliac, a famous fourteenth century French surgeon, had attributed the plague to the conjunction of Saturn and Mars on March 22, 1345, in the fourteenth degree of Aquarius: "Two centuries before this, in the skies/ Saturn and Mars would lock their silent cars." Fracastoro himself drew an astrological parallel to the syzygy of the same planets in the sign of Cancer: "Jupiter calls a congress of the stars/ Evoking Saturn and the war god Mars . . . he calls the Crab . . . to open the double doors of heaven's halls." By the "god's decree . . . to the air is this new poison given, the effluvium of homicide." With the introduction of Sirius, the air carries "the seeds of poison everywhere." Here, the author invents a new god who has no basis in classical mythology and is indeed a fictitious character offering prophecy. Such an expediency was often resorted to by fifteenth and sixteenth century writers.

Fracastoro, however, writes as a physician, a man of science, and he proceeds to reveal the difficulties of his investigation. The halting speech of the poet results from the delay with which the heavens confront the scientist as he seeks to link the disease to the things that cause it. "Making no advance," he fears that much "hangs on the play of chance." As he proceeds to "comb the symptoms," he finds that the disease is at home both in hovel and in court. Its symptoms are never quite the same. "Its form and seed vary everywhere/ Knowing no bounds and limits, peoples, states . . . it flashes through the air." He does, however, ascertain that it survives four months of incubation, "shutting the moon's disc four times." In order to delineate more dramatically this "hideous leprosy," Fracastoro describes the personal plight of a handsome youth of Brescia: "Gone is the brilliance of his youth and spring/ Dying by inches his soul sinks. . . ." This graphic depiction is extended to include the suffering of Fracastoro's native land as well as the personal grief he feels with the premature death of his friend Marcus Antonius della Torre. Wright refers to this final section of book 1 as "some of the finest verse ever done by Fracastoro, indeed by any Latin poet of the period." The following invocation to Italy has been deemed by Mario Truffi as the equal of Petrarch and Giacomo Leopardi:

> Dear land, my land, that only yesterday
> Hoped for the happiness of peace profound.
> O soil of heroes! God's land! Holy ground,
> Where is your ancient treasure? Torn away.
> Your breasts, prodigious for Adige's flood,
> Gave you fecundities so passing good.
> Today, O Italy, what colors drear
> Depict your suffering, your ills, your fear?
> Trembling are all the strings of my poor lute
> To tell of your misfortunes, but are mute.
> Garda, go hide your shame amidst your reeds.
> Laurels no longer seek your water's needs.

Fracastoro demonstrates dramatic concern on many levels. One analogy connects the desolate River Adige and Lake Garda, into which it flows near his home, with the desecrated blood of his nation: "The Adige bathes in new sterility, having lost its ancient force." Another parallel is drawn between the decline of the country and the death of della Torre: "Noble Anthony passes and naught can save him from the tomb, still in the bloom of spring, O Italy!" Fracastoro finally resorts again to the poetic muse to save his country: "The mellow lyre of old Catullus hand/ Might stir your woods again, O Fatherland." This allusion to classical poetry would not have been lost on the author's contemporaries. Bembo related that the work "makes me think the soul of Vergil has passed into [Fracastoro]."

SYPHILIS, BOOK 2

Book 2 includes, as did book 1, the customary encomiums to Bembo ("armed in his humility, whose sheer ability is equal to the grandest name") and to Pope Leo X ("Prince, whose fame is more than great"), that they might turn a willing ear to the poet's voice. It also pays tribute to Sannazzaro, the "Christian Vergil," as "Fornello's god, a new poet's voice/ That made old Vergil's epic heart rejoice."

Soon, "in fear and trembling," Fracastoro "takes up his pen" to prescribe medication and treatment. His prescriptions are many and varied—some, clearly, dated folk remedies and others still in use today. One of the first is "Spain's ornament, the pride of Italy," the lemon tree. "Beloved of Venus," it acquired its power through the tears Venus shed for Adonis, which were "shut within the golden rind a gift/ Of heav'nly virtues, energetic, swift." There follow in rapid succession both exotic and common reliefs: myrrh of Arabia, frankincense from Libya, and apopanax from the Nile, as well as cinnamon, bittercress, cassia, cucumber, turpeth, saffron, mint, thyme, ladysmantle, briony, chicory, hartstongue, and hops, these last as common "pharmacopia of the day." In addition, one finds salves and ointments made from oil, wool fat, honey, goose fat, linseed paste, starwort, and narcissus. Other applications include copper and potassium nitrates and oxides of lead, antimony, and storax. Considering that bloodletting was also part of the cure, the activities prescribed are strange: hunting, a form of tennis, and wood chopping—"Be active if you wish to keep alive."

The use of mercury is traced at this point to a mythological origin. The Syrian shepherd Ilceo has incurred the wrath of Diana and Phoebus for killing a favorite deer. He has been stricken with a disease for which no remedy exists under the sun. The goddess Calliroe appears to him, however, and directs him to a nymph, Lipare, who leads him to a cave below Mount Etna wherein is found a stream in which flows a liquid metal (quicksilver). It is interesting to note that this substance, mercury, was known for its medicinal properties to Aristotle as *arguron chuton*, and to Pliny as *argentum vivum*. Such treatment was also applied in the intervening centuries by Rhazes and Avicenna.

The Ilceo myth probably represented a nonclassical reference for Fracastoro. The name is not found elsewhere, and Bembo thought it a poor choice of material. It is of interest to note, however, that it is this section of the work that Greswell chose to excerpt in the *Memoirs of Angelus Politianus, Joannes Picus of Mirandula, Actius Sincerus Sannazzarius, Pietrus Bembus, Hieronymous Fracastorius, and the Amalthei* (1801). Wright observes that the author's language becomes less poetic in the closing section of the book, after the telling of the myth, as Fracastoro relates the therapeutic marvels of the common herbs as skin treatment.

SYPHILIS, BOOK 3

Truffi finds the third book to be the "best from the poetic side." In this section, Fracastoro praises Christopher Columbus for his explorations in the New World ("yoking the mountains in a mighty quest"); Fracastoro was the first to use Columbus's achievement as poetic material. Fracastoro's Columbus desperately invokes the moon to reveal land to him and his fatigued mariners. There then appears a sea nymph, who directs him to the island of Ofiri (Haiti, scene of the first European landing in the Americas on December 6, 1492). The sailors anger the gods by shooting forest birds sacred to Apollo, whereupon they are cursed. This episode parallels scenes in the *Odyssey* (c. 800 B.C.E.) and in Vergil's *Aeneid* (29-19 B.C.E.). The remedy for their affliction is to be found in "seeking aid from the same forest they profaned."

The "aborigines" whom they encounter on the island are descendants of the Atlanteans, the cursed remnants of an ancient race, who are afflicted with a disease which demonstrates "a living path/ Of what the gods invented in their wrath." Fracastoro relates their plight through the legend of Sifilo (Syphilis). During a particularly long and devastating drought, Syphilis, a shepherd for King Ilceo, inveighed against the sun god and instead venerated King Ilceo. Syphilis advocated similar conduct on the part of others until they, "braving gods, denying gods, devastating temples fair," convinced Ilceo of

his own glory, and the King, in "mad joy and blinded thus, commanded that each state receive him as a god." It was at this point that the "island paradise received the evil of a subtle seed. . . . He who wrought this outrage was the first, and after him this malady is called Syphilis, and even the King escaped not its attack."

Upon consultation, the nymph America advised a sacrifice. Initially, Syphilis was designated, but through the intercession of Juno (recalling the legend of Iphigenia and the biblical story of Isaac), a substitution was made—in this case, a black cow's blood to appease Terra (Tellus, Latin deity of the earth) and a white heifer to change Juno's mood. The blood of the beast created "fecund seeds in Tellus's vast breast," which became the *lignum-sanctum* (Guaiacum tree) from which was extracted the syphilis cure: "the lignumsanctum you must/ Cull, lest disaster fall on every one/ For a bird-murder and an outraged sun." Thus, it was determined that "Every year a shepherd symbolizes/ The victim; ancient are the sacrifices." The author ends his work by appealing to Apollo (and to Bembo) that his poem be remembered, "as descendants may one day wish to read of signs and appearance of the disease."

Again, it should be noted that there was in Fracastoro's time no hint of immorality involved with the disease. To the contrary, Fracastoro asserts in his poem that the disease "hatched from a poison that no vice has wrought," though he does refer to it as venereal (from Latin *venereus*, love) in the prose adaptation written later.

NAUGERIUS SIVE DE POETICA DIALOGUS

In *Naugerius sive de poetica dialogus*, the focus of Fracastoro's aesthetics is revealed. According to Zanobio, Fracastoro determined that neither content nor form rendered the essence of the poetic but rather "intuition, the universal present in all things and expressing itself in the judgment that regulates them." Bundy sees this as "the view of a pagan of the Renaissance quite in sympathy with the frank aestheticism of the majority of contemporary [1924] artists." John Addington Symonds praised Fracastoro's writing from a literary standpoint, suggesting that it "recalls the purity of phrase of Catullus." Bundy further notes that Fracastoro's use of the dialogue is Ciceronian in both form and substance, in that Fracastoro employed the later Latin variation on

Plato of using less dramatic, more real characters, as did Fracastoro's contemporaries Giovanni Pontano, Sperone Speroni, Antonio Minturno, and Gimabattisto Gyraldus. Ciceronian as well is the "absence of philosophical first principles directing the course of the dialogue; [Fracastoro] is frankly eclectic rather than a great original thinker."

Fracastoro's *Naugerius sive de poetic dialogus* not only presents a theory of the poetic but presents it as "consummate art" itself. According to Bundy, "The symmetry, the beauty of external form, illustrates the ideal which he sets forth." Bundy further asserts that in this work Fracastoro was one of the first writers of the Renaissance to formulate in elegant manner a concept close to Aristotle's intentions in his *Poetics* (c. 334-323 B.C.E.) and that *Naugerius sive de poetica dialogus* "is one of a few Renaissance treatises which insists upon an aesthetic standard." Wilmer Cave Wright has commented that to be immortal, one needs only to write a treatise telling poets what the aim of poetry is. The poets, of course, will not read the work, but it will be mandatory reading for all subsequent historians of criticism.

THE "MINOR POEMS"

Of Fracastoro's works of poetry other than *Syphilis*, Truffi notes "the poem on the death of della Torre, that to G. B. della Torre, to Rainerio, to Bishop Giberti, to Marguerite de Valois (Queen of Navarre), to Francesco della Torre, to Alessandro Farnese, to Pope Guilio III and minor poems all praiseworthy for their purity of style and classicity of verse." The eulogies for Marcus Antonius della Torre are included in various versions of the collected works; the "minor poems" are less commonly available. Henry Wadsworth Longfellow included two of them in his anthology *The Poets and Poetry of Europe* (1896), commenting that Fracastoro wrote "A few poems in the mother tongue which show liveliness and facility of poetical composition." One, "To a Lady," retains the familiar hexameter and identifies the woman's "all perfect symmetry" as the eternal model of beauty wherein love finds its future home. In "Homer," the Horatian motto *ut pictura poesis* is employed by the author to indicate how, through the depiction of "sunny banks and grottoes cold," Homer became "the first great painter of scenes of old." Francastoro is said to have written a madrigal, "Madrigal al sonno" (to slumber), on

the occasion of his wife's death. The "Madrigal al sonno" is a hymn on the power of narcotics to alleviate suffering, written in the vernacular and lacking the weight of Fracastoro's Latin verse. "Alcon seu de cura canum venaticorum" (Alcon, or: how to take care of dogs for the hunt) is a short poem about the training of dogs for the hunt, known to have been among Fracastoro's favorite pastimes. The poem is included only in works appearing later than the sixteenth century, and Emilio Barbarani rejects it as spurious, mainly because it was not included in the volume of the author's poetry which was organized in 1555.

As a major writer of the Italian Renaissance, Fracastoro exhibits the comprehensive thinking of the period. He was equally at ease in the speculative and in the applied fields of science and art. Though securely based in the classical form of his predecessor, Vergil, Fracastoro's poetry embraced common topics and rendered them with grace and sensitivity. His versatility lends a particular vitality to his writing that will assure his work a permanent place in the respect and esteem of future generations.

OTHER MAJOR WORKS

PLAY: *La Venexiana*, wr. after 1509, pb. 1928, 1947 (English translation, 1950).

NONFICTION: *De vini temperatura*, 1534; *De causis criticorum dierum libellus*, 1538; *Homocentricorum sive de stellis*, 1538; *De sympathia et antipathia rerum*, 1546; *De contagionibus et contagiosis morbis et eorum curatione*, 1546 (*De contagione et contagiosis morbis et eorum curatione*, 1930); *Naugerius sive de poetica dialogus*, 1549 (English translation, 1924); *Syphilis*, wr. 1553, pb. 1939.

MISCELLANEOUS: *Opera omnia*, 1555, 1574 (includes "Turrius sive de intellectione dialogus" and "Fracastorius sive de anima dialogus").

BIBLIOGRAPHY

Baumgartner, Leona, and John F. Fulton. *A Bibliography of the Poem "Syphilis sive Morbus Gallicus" by Girolamo Fracastoro of Verona*. New Haven, Conn.: Yale University Press, 1935. A bibliography of editions in Latin including the *Opera omnia* and translations into Italian, English, French, and German.

Bundy, Murray W. Introduction to *Naugerius, Sive de poetica dialogus*, by Girolamo Fracastoro. Urbana: University of Illinois Press, 1924. Includes brief biographical and historical details.

Gould, Stephen Jay. "Syphilis and the Shepherd of Atlantis." *Natural History* 109, no. 8 (October, 2000): 38-42. Gould discusses the "Syphilis sive morbus Gallicus" by Fracastoro and the genome of syphilis.

Greswell, W. Parr. *Memoirs of Angelus Politianus, Joannes Picus of Mirandula, Actius Sincerus Sannazzarius, Pietrus Bembus, Hieronymous Fracastorius, and the Amalthei.* 2d ed. London: Cadell & Davies, 1805. Contains translations from the poetical works, notes, and observations of Fracastoro.

Hudson, Margaret M., and Robert S. Morton. "Fracastoro and Syphilis: Five Hundred Years On." *The Lancet* 348, no. 9040 (November 30, 1996): 1495-1496. The authors pay tribute to the physician who spread knowledge of the origin, clinical details, and available treatments of syphilis throughout a troubled Europe.

Pearce, Spencer. "Nature and Supernature in the Dialogues of Girolamo Fracastoro." *The Sixteenth Century Journal* 27, no. 1 (Spring, 1996): 111. Fracastoro was one of the first philosophers of nature during the Italian Renaissance. In his dialogues, Fracastoro attempts to construct a philosophical anthropology in which man's supernatural vocation may be accommodated within the rational framework of a philosophy of nature.

Pfeiffer, Matilde Valenti. Introduction to *La Venexiana.* New York: S. F. Vanni, 1950. Pfeiffer's introduction offers some historical information on the discovery of the play and Emilio Lovarini's conjecture that the play was written by Fracastoro.

H. W. Carle;
bibliography updated by the editors

PHILIP FRENEAU

Born: New York, New York; January 2, 1752
Died: Near Freehold, New Jersey; December 18, 1832

PRINCIPAL POETRY

"The Rising Glory of America," 1772 (with H. H. Brackenridge)
The American Village, 1772
"The British Prison-Ship," 1781
The Poems of Philip Freneau: Written Chiefly During the Late War, 1786
A Journey from Philadelphia to New-York, by Robert Slender, Stocking Weaver, 1787
Poems Written Between the Years 1786 and 1794, 1795
Poems Written and Published During the American Revolutionary War, 1809
A Collection of Poems . . . Written Between the Year 1797 and the Present Time, 1815
The Poems of Philip Freneau, 1902-1907 (3 volumes; F. L. Patee, editor)
Poems of Freneau, 1929 (H. H. Clark, editor)
The Last Poems of Philip Freneau, 1945 (Lewis Leary, editor)

OTHER LITERARY FORMS

Philip Freneau is best remembered today for his poems. In his own time, however, such was hardly the case. Freneau's contemporaries knew him best for his satirical, sometimes vituperative essays. Freneau first used his satirical skills as a prose writer in *Father Bombo's Pilgrimage to Mecca* (1770), which he wrote with Hugh Henry Brackenridge while the two were undergraduate classmates at Princeton (then College of New Jersey). In the introduction to the 1975 edition of the book, Michael D. Bell argues convincingly that this brief volume, more than half of which is by Freneau, is the first American novel.

After the outbreak of the American Revolution, Freneau put his satirical pen to work for American independence by contributing prose (and some poetry) to Brackenridge's *United States Magazine* in 1779. During 1781 and 1782, he helped Francis Bailey publish *Freeman's Journal*, a liberal and, of course, anti-British newspaper. During 1790 and 1791, he edited the *Daily Advertiser* in New York. Freneau's next publishing venture is what some would consider his most famous; others would call it his most notorious. From October of 1791 until October of 1793, he edited *The National Ga-*

zette in Philadelphia, which was at that time the center of the national government. In this newspaper, Freneau supported Jeffersonian politics and opposed the Federalist position of John Fenno's *United States Gazette*, which operated under the financial control of Alexander Hamilton, the principal voice of Federalism.

Following Thomas Jefferson's temporary withdrawal from politics which concurred with loss of financial support for *The National Gazette*, Freneau returned to his New Jersey estate and set up a press of his own. There he published almanacs, yet another newspaper, *The Jersey Chronicle*, and the second collection of his poetry (1795). In 1797, he and his expanding family relocated in New York, where Freneau began one more newspaper, *The Time Piece and Literary Companion* (March, 1797, to March, 1798). In his later years, he made contributions to such other newspapers as Charleston's *City Gazette* (1788-1790, and also 1800-1801), the Philadelphia *Aurora* (1799-1800), the *New-York Weekly Museum* (1816), and Trenton's *True American* (1821-1824).

Philip Freneau (Library of Congress)

ACHIEVEMENTS

Philip Freneau's contribution to the development of American satirical journalism is considerable. In *The Political Activities of Philip Freneau* (1902), Samuel E. Forman presents a scholarly discussion of Freneau's role in the political arena of the early American republic. While serving as secretary of state, Jefferson declared that Freneau's *National Gazette* "has saved our constitution, which was galloping fast into monarchy" (*The Writings of Thomas Jefferson*, edited by Paul L. Ford, 1892). In his "Tomo Cheeki, the Creek Indian," a series of essays written for the *Jersey Chronicle* and printed on his own press at Mt. Pleasant, New Jersey, Freneau celebrated the unsullied national life of the American Indian, which contrasted sharply with the corrupted, unnatural life of whites transplanted from Europe. He also used his newspapers to condemn slavery and to advance temperance (not abstinence, but control).

Freneau's major contribution to American letters, however, is his poetry. He has been called the poet of the American Revolution, the first American poet of any real significance, the father of American poetry, and the first herald of Romanticism in America. None of these titles is entirely correct. Although he styled himself poet of the Revolution by publishing the fourth collection of his poems in 1809 as *Poems Written and Published During the American Revolutionary War* (two-thirds of the poems in the volume have nothing to do with the war), Freneau must share the title of poet of the Revolution with at least one other poet, Phillis Wheatley, America's first black to publish a book. Her *Poems on Various Subjects, Religious and Moral* appeared in 1773 and contains many poems which predict the movement toward independence; Wheatley continued to devote her pen to American independence in succeeding years by publishing such substantial poems as "To His Excellency General Washington" and "Liberty and Peace."

Certainly, Freneau can no longer be considered America's first significant poet but must join the growing list of poets whose reputations continue to be reclaimed or to be established for the first time. These recently recognized early American poets now include Anne Bradstreet, Edward Taylor, and Phillis Wheatley, as well as Freneau. The existence of this enlarged list of important early American poets assuredly calls into question the notion that Freneau is the Father of American poetry. Despite Lewis Leary's assertion, however, that "in the strict sense he had no descendants" (*Soundings: Some Early American Writers*, 1975), Freneau does participate significantly in the American experience of nature and in the struggle for freedom and identity, as well as in America's awakening Romanticism. Even though Freneau founded no school of poetry, his poems display characteristics and foreshadowings of Edgar Allan Poe, Ralph Waldo Emerson, James Fenimore Cooper, and Herman Melville.

Although Freneau must share several of his formerly attributed titles, he is no less significant as a writer of good poetry. To be sure, he is a transitional figure, but his significance does not begin and end as a figure of transition. This critical commonplace, that Freneau was a transitional figure and nothing more, may have predisposed many to find Freneau's poetic ideas desultory and inconsistent. Perhaps these readers have not yet discovered how to read Freneau, for as Richard C. Vitzthum has ably shown in his provocative and balanced work, *Land and Sea: The Lyric Poetry of Philip Freneau* (1978), Freneau created personal and highly internalized poetic symbols, thereby manifesting his most significant contribution to the Romantic movement. Freneau's poetry is, indeed, intensely personal, and when the keys to this personal intensity are revealed, his poems speak a universal tongue.

BIOGRAPHY

Shortly after Philip Morin Freneau was born, the family moved from New York City to Mt. Pleasant, New Jersey, where Freneau reached adolescence. Even though his father died in 1767, his mother Agnes managed to send her son to Princeton, then known as the College of New Jersey, in 1768. Freneau's classmates included such notables as Hugh Henry Brackenridge and James Madison; also in attendance during Freneau's tenure were William Bradford (later attorney general of the United States) and Aaron Burr. The curriculum of the college at that time was not structured to prepare men for the ministry but was designed to shape cultured gentlemen; in a word, Freneau was not trained to be a dogmatist, a factor which was to have profound significance on his development as a poet.

After leaving Princeton, Freneau tried teaching for a time, first in Flatbush, Long Island, and later at Somerset Academy in Maryland, where his former college classmate, Brackenridge, was principal. For the next two years, from 1773 to 1775, it is believed that Freneau studied theology. Later in 1775, while in New York, the poet wrote and published patriotic, satirical poems about the British; the first, short version of the gothic poem "The House of Night" also appeared that year. From 1776 to 1778, he lived and traveled in the Virgin and Caribbean islands. In July, 1778, while attempting to return to the United States, Freneau was taken prisoner by the British but was soon released. During the next two years, the young author wrote poems and essays for Brackenridge's *United States Magazine*. On May 25, 1780, Freneau shipped out on the *Aurora* from Philadelphia and found himself taken prisoner by the British a second time. This occasion was not destined to be the relatively uneventful one of his first capture. Indeed, he was kept a prisoner for almost two months and later wrote about the cruelty shown him and other prisoners in "The British Prison-Ship," which he published as a broadside in 1781.

For the next few years, Freneau sailed as supercargo or captain of several ships sailing from the American mainland to various islands of the Caribbean. In 1786, Francis Bailey, formerly publisher of Brackenridge's *United States Magazine*, printed the first edition of Freneau's collected poems, *The Poems of Philip Freneau: Written Chiefly During the Late War*. As was the case with his fourth poetry collection, only about half of these poems actually address issues of the war. In 1788, Bailey came out with a second collection, *The Miscellaneous Works*, this volume including both poetry and prose.

By 1790, however, Freneau was back on land, where he married Eleanor Forman, whom he had been courting for several years. The following October the Freneaus moved to Philadelphia, where the poet had been invited to serve in two capacities: as a part-time translator for the State Department under Jefferson and as editor of the *National Gazette*. Freneau carried out the duties of these two positions with energy and distinction for the next two years; following the financial collapse of *The National Gazette*, brought on in large part by an epidemic of yellow fever in Philadelphia, the Freneaus returned to Mt. Pleasant. There the poet set up his own press, published much poetry and prose, and apparently tried farming for a while. By 1802, in order to support his family better, Freneau had returned to sea, probably as a captain. He stopped sailing for good, however, in 1807 at the time of Jefferson's Embargo Act. Later, in 1809 and then again in 1815, he supervised the printing of several collections of his poems. He and his family lost their home to fire in 1818 with the unfortunate result that many of his manuscripts and letters were destroyed. In 1824, the family moved to a small farm near Freehold, New Jersey, where the poet died in 1832 in a snowstorm while apparently trying to find his way back to his home.

ANALYSIS

Philip Freneau's poetry gave rise to no school, and it fired no tradition. At all points, however, it celebrates the American quest for freedom—freedom of the individual to choose a political and intellectual identity, to pursue creative and artistic imagination, and to discover religious and/or spiritual commitment. Even America's rugged natural terrain seemed to promise limitless possibilities of achieving social and cultural independence. The principal subjects of Freneau's poems, then, include politics, the imagination, theology, and nature. His poems reveal the inner struggle of a man who refused to settle into the security of dogma (whether of a particular church or of societal codes) and who determined to find his own explanations for the human predicament. This determination to search for his own answers anticipates the attitude of later writers from the American Renaissance to the present day.

POLITICAL POETRY

Jefferson's statement that Freneau "saved our constitution" readily identifies the trenchant role this citizen of the new republic played in politics. In addition to his numerous, biting essays which strike out against British cruelties and Hamilton's Federalism, Freneau wrote poetry dealing with various controversial political issues. In "The British Prison-Ship," Freneau exposes British inhumanity to American prisoners. Among Freneau's many political poems is a particularly strong indictment of slavery; "To Sir Toby" is as forceful a condemnation of traffic in human cargo as any of its time. After isolating the central motive for the practice of slavery—greed—the poet then describes the plight of the innocent victims of this avarice as the unwitting and certainly unwilling participants in a veritable hell on earth. In this description, Freneau makes effective use of his classical training; the pictures of the black man's torture call up horrible scenes "that Vergil's pencil drew." The captains of the slave ships become "surly Charons," while the slave masters who put to torture the new ranks of "ghosts" are "beasts, . . . Plutonian scourges, and despotic lords."

THE IMAGINATION

Freneau's poems on the force of the imagination may seem to be light-years away from his political poetry; such, however, is hardly the case. His poems on politics and the imagination merely represent two sides of the same coin whose mint is freedom. Those poems dealing with politics address problems of freedom in the actual world; those centering on the imagination treat of the ideal world produced by artistic creativity whose freedom is apparently boundless. It is fitting that one of this poet's earliest works is devoted entirely to the subject of the imagination; "The Power of Fancy" was composed in 1770 while Freneau was still an undergraduate at Princeton. In this piece, the young poet delineates the fancy as "regent of the mind," the mental faculty which derives its power from divine inspiration. By the power of fancy, the mind can set out on a cosmic journey, exploring distant stars, the moon, and even hell. From this journey through the cosmos, the fancy then takes the poet out into the Atlantic and on to such exotic sites as the Caribbean, the Pacific, and the Mediterranean. In the final lines of the poem, the young Freneau calls the fancy "the muses' pride" wherein "reside/ Endless images of things." These images are of "Ideal objects such a store,/ The universe could hold no more."

The sort of imagination Freneau describes in "The Power of Fancy" clearly owes much to Plato's theory of ideal forms; it is the function of the poet, so Freneau maintains, to tap this realm of forms for his own poetic images. The fancy then serves the poet as a mode of memory and is closely aligned with Lockean associative psychology. The view of the fancy or imagination that Freneau advances in this poem looks back rather than forward; it more nearly approximates the operation of the imagination explored by Mark Adenside in *The Pleasures of Imagination*, an immensely popular book-length poem first printed in English in 1744, than it points ahead toward the Romantics of the early nineteenth century. The mode of fancy that Freneau depicts in "The House of Night," however, looks to the future; written some nine years later than "The Power of Fancy," this poem suggests an affinity for some of the poems of John Keats. In the later poem, Freneau maintains that the power of fancy can in sleep play a "wild delusive part so well/ you lift me into immortality,/ Depict new heavens, or draw scenes of hell"; Keats's immortal nightingale sings a similar strain.

Other Romantic elements occur in "The House of Night," especially those projecting gothicism. Freneau achieves some gothic effects by use of the element of surprise. At one point in this poem about a young man's encounter with the personification of death (a gothic effect in itself), for example, the youth (as persona) describes darkness in terms of Apollo and his chariot of the sun. Rather than a blazing chariot, "darkness rode/ In her black chariot." Some lines of the poem strongly suggest Poe. Seduced by Death into attending him as he approaches his own "death," the youth describes his predicament in unsettling lines. In such phrases as "sad chamber," languishing "in despair," and breathing "loathsome air," one might fully expect to find Poe's "The Raven" or in such short stories as his "The Fall of the House of Usher" or "Ligeia."

THEOLOGY AND NATURE

The power of the imagination enabled Freneau to explore much more than his tendency to create strange, even perverse images and characters; indeed, he appears to pursue in his poetry the construction of a personal theology. This pursuit is always punctuated by the poet's awestruck fascination for and appreciation of nature. These last two important subjects of Freneau's poetry, theology and nature, can therefore most profitably be examined together.

The pictures Freneau draws of nature are not always attractive. "The Hurricane" depicts an actual storm at sea which befell Freneau on a voyage to Jamaica in 1784. The poem opens with this arresting couplet: "Happy the man who, safe on shore,/ Now trims, at home, his evening fire." Rather than being safe and enjoying the warmth of the hearth, Freneau finds himself exposed to a merciless cold storm at sea. At one point, he presents a vividly terrifying image of the small ship on whose fragile deck burst "mountains . . . on either side." He draws a picture of "death and darkness," which engulf the ship with tempests raging "with lawless power"; in such a pass, "What friendship can . . . be/ What comfort?" The dark and doom of this unhappy predicament foreshadow the destruction of Ishmael's ship, the *Pequod*, in *Moby Dick* (1851).

The contrast the poet establishes in "The Hurricane" between the security of the land and the peril of the sea is identified by Richard C. Vitzthum as a major key to the personal symbolism that Freneau develops in his poems; but while "The Wild Honey Suckle" and "The Indian Burying Ground," both wholly landlocked poems, do develop less precarious scenes, these poems of the land also resound with poignant notes of regret at life's transience. "The Wild Honey Suckle" celebrates the beauty of that plant's white flower which is nevertheless doomed to a brief span of life. The lives of men correspond to the short duration of the flower; indeed, from birth to death, as Freneau writes in one of the most effective couplets in American literature, "The space between, is but an hour,/ The frail duration of a flower." "The Indian Burying Ground" describes the somber, sitting position of the dead, but Freneau sees promise of great spiritual and intellectual hope in such a posture. To him, the sitting position bespeaks "the nature of the soul,/ Activity, that knows no rest." Although "life is spent," so the poet explains, the old ideas which supported and breathed life into these honored dead are not gone.

"ON THE UNIVERSALITY AND OTHER ATTRIBUTES OF THE GOD OF NATURE"

The one poem of the Freneau canon which most clearly articulates his attitudes toward his religious consciousness is the often-overlooked piece "On the Universality and Other Attributes of the God of Nature."

Written in 1815 when Freneau was sixty-three, the poem represents a crystallization of his theology. It is arranged into seven quatrains of iambic tetrameters. A reading aloud reveals that its fairly regular rhythm echoes common speech; the only variations of the iambic pattern occur in the occasional trochees and one spondee (in the twentieth line). In each case where a variation occurs, the word "all" appears and always receives a primary stress (emphasized word or syllable); "all" recurs fourteen times. These variations do indeed prevent the rhythm from becoming monotonous, thus holding the listener's attention.

The variations accomplish more, however, than merely hold one's attention. To be sure, Freneau's repeated use of the word "all" underscores the poem's emphasis on the universal; the persistence of this word then serves as a sort of incremental repetition which restates the poem's concern with the universal attributes of God in each of the seven stanzas; "all" appears twice in the first two, only once in the next two, but twice again in the fifth, and then three times each in the climactic sixth and seventh stanzas, establishing a pattern which enhances the meaning of the poem. The poem opens with the rhetorical question, "All that we see, about, abroad,/ What is it all, but nature's God?" The next couplet maintains that this God of nature may be seen in His meaner works of the earth, such as human beings, animals, and plants, as well as in the heavens: "In meaner works discover'd here/ No less than in the starry sphere." Implicit in these lines is the idea of the Great Chain of Being, whereby creation may be viewed as a great ladder, the lowest rungs of which include elements of inanimate matter while the highest hold the higher animals, and finally man himself, closest to God; but more seems to be at work here.

In 1785 or 1786, Freneau came across a book by the Swedish scientist, mystic, and scholar of the Bible, Emanuel Swedenborg; the poet records his experience of reading Swedenborg in the poem "On a Book Called Unitarian Theology." He remarks that God "Illumes all Nature" and "Bids towards itself all trees and plants aspire." Swedenborg had himself outlined in his *Principia rerum naturalium* (1734) an elaborate doctrine of series and degrees which he claimed accounted for each distinct link in a universal chain stretching from inorganic substance to man and thence to God. Regarding this doctrine of degrees, Freneau appears to have changed his mind little between 1786 and 1815.

In the second stanza, Freneau asserts that God "lives in all, and never stray'd/ A moment from the works he made." If one includes the notion of an "absentee God" as a necessary tenet of a Deist, then at this point Freneau clearly denies his sympathy with Deism. The God whom he describes "Bespeaks a wise creating cause;/ Impartially he rules mankind." This last line suggests Freneau's strong support of religious freedom, for an impartial God is hardly selective about how He is worshiped. The poet expresses his unqualified commitment to religious freedom in "On the Emigration to America" (written in 1784) in which he describes the political and religious conditions in Europe as "half to slaves consigned"; Europe herself is a place "Where kings and priests enchain the mind." In "Reflections on the Gradual Progress of Nations from Democratical States to Despotic Empires" (written in 1799), he quips of priests per se that they "hold the artillery of the sky."

The last stanza of "On the Universality and Other Attributes of the God of Nature" contains one of the simplest and at the same time one of the finest lines in American poetry. The line states the thesis on which Freneau bases his theology: "He all things into *being* loved." In the Swedenborg piece, he draws a parallel picture of God as "One Power of Love" who "Warms into life the changeful race of man." This idea of God as a God of warmth and love is far distant from the cold, Deistic Clockmaker who left his machine to run itself down. Freneau's God, who is by virtue of his "attributes divine" unlimited and therefore universal or ubiquitous, brings into existence "all things"; this achievement He brings about out of unselfish love. "Things" take on form, then, as less perfect renderings of Him. Freneau's God "never stray'd/ A moment from the works he made." Quite contrary to the Deist Clockmaker, the poet's God "still presides" over all he has created, and "For them in life, or death provides."

The line, "He all things into *being* loved," then, is hardly simple. Contained within its eight syllables is the whole of Freneau's sophisticated and humanitarian theology. Although his identification of God as "of Nature" seems to align him with Deism (or, as some would undoubtedly hold, with pantheism), his insistence on a God of love denies this classification. His assertion that God provides for all in death may suggest to some a belief in an afterlife of heavenly bliss. Such is not the case, however, for in one of his last poems, "On Observing a Large Red-streak Apple," Freneau defines the afterlife of the apple as the "youngsters . . . three or four" which will rise "from your core." This sort of afterlife whereby continuation is accomplished through successive generations resembles more closely Greco-Roman ideas of afterlife than it does Deism. Surely Freneau's classical training served him in arriving at his position. It is probably more accurate to label Freneau a unitarian than a Deist, though one senses that he would himself resist all labels.

Certainly his theology is liberal and not limited by dogma. So, also, his attitudes toward politics, the creative imagination, and nature are unencumbered by a dogmatic or didactic perspective. Rather, his poems describe the career of a man who found the world about him fascinating and who consequently used his poetry to record his experience of that world. Freneau's poetry is intensely personal, heralding the individuality which characterizes Poe, Nathaniel Hawthorne, Emerson, Melville, Henry David Thoreau, and Walt Whitman.

OTHER MAJOR WORKS

LONG FICTION: *Father Bombo's Pilgrimage to Mecca*, 1770.

NONFICTION: *Letters on Various Interesting and Important Subjects*, 1799 (republished in 1943, by H. H. Clark).

MISCELLANEOUS: *The Miscellaneous Works of Mr. Philip Freneau Containing His Essays and Additional Poems*, 1788; *The Prose of Philip Freneau*, 1955 (Philip M. Marsh, editor).

BIBLIOGRAPHY

Andrews, William D. "Philip Freneau and Francis Hopkinson." In *American Literature, 1764-1789: The Revolutionary Years*, edited by Everett Emerson. Madison: University of Wisconsin Press, 1977. The writings of Freneau and Hopkinson are examined as expressions of the political events of the time, particularly the war for independence. Freneau's bitter invective is contrasted with Hopkinson's witty urbanity, and Freneau's dedication to poetry as art is contrasted with Hopkinson's view of poetry as a hobby. Suggested readings and an index are included.

Elliott, Emory. "Philip Freneau: Poetry of Social Commitment." In *Revolutionary Writers: Literature and Authority in The New Republic, 1725-1810*. New York: Oxford University Press, 1982. Elliott examines Freneau as a poet-teacher of morality. His changing directions are understood as moves to strengthen power of instruction through poetic forms. Several poems are analyzed to illustrate Freneau's faith in poetry as social commitment. Supplemented by notes, a select bibliography, and an index.

Leary, Lewis. "Philip Freneau." In *Major Writers of Early American Literature*, edited by Everett Emerson. Madison: University of Wisconsin Press, 1972. From early political verse, to flights of fancy, Freneau was caught between destructive forces. After the Revolutionary War, his talents were released for light verse and humorous satire. As he grew older, his poems grew bitter and disillusioned. Although not a great poet, he had talent. Complemented by a bibliography and an index.

McWilliams, John P., Jr. *The American Epic: Transforming a Genre, 1770-1860*. Cambridge, England: Cambridge University Press, 1989. This book uses Freneau's reaction to Timothy Dwight's *The Conquest of Canaan* to show contemporary criticism of attempts to write the American epic. Although Freneau did not himself attempt an epic poem, his influence on others to make the attempt was considerable. Includes notes and an index.

Pearce, Roy Harvey. "Antecedents: The Case of Freneau." In *The Continuity of American Poetry*. Princeton, N.J.: Princeton University Press, 1961. This brief, important assessment of Freneau, who hoped to make poetry from democratic dogma, deplores his turn from positive exposition to verse as a weapon of invective, attacking opponents of democracy. He lost his audience after the American Revolution, and his poetry found no place in the hearts of his countrymen.

Ronnick, Michele Valerie. "A Note on the Text of Philip Freneau's 'Columbus to Ferdinand': From Plato to Seneca." *Early American Literature* 29, no. 1 (1994): 81. A discussion of Freneau's "Columbus to Ferdinand" as it was first published in *United States Magazine* with two lines that were left out of all subsequent editions.

Tichi, Cecelia. *New World, New Earth: Environmental Reform in American Literature from the Puritans Through Whitman.* New Haven, Conn.: Yale University Press, 1979. Arguing that early American writers were keenly conscious of environmental concerns, Tichi draws on the work of many great authors, including Freneau, whom Tichi presents as one who used his poetry to approach problems of comprehending environmental reform with visionary ideals, mundane with sublime experience. Contains notes and an index.

Wertheimer, Eric. "Commencement Ceremonies: History and Identity in 'The Rising Glory of America,' 1771 and 1786." *Early American Literature* 29, no. 1 (1994): 35. An examination of the thematic obsession with imperial beginnings in the poem "The Rising Glory of America" by Freneau and Henry Brackenridge.

John C. Shields;
bibliography updated by the editors

ROBERT FROST

Born: San Francisco, California; March 26, 1874
Died: Boston, Massachusetts; January 29, 1963

PRINCIPAL POETRY
A Boy's Will, 1913
North of Boston, 1914
Mountain Interval, 1916
Selected Poems, 1923
New Hampshire: A Poem with Notes and Grace Notes, 1923
West-Running Brook, 1928
Collected Poems, 1930
A Further Range, 1936
Collected Poems, 1939
A Witness Tree, 1942
A Masque of Reason, 1945
Steeple Bush, 1947
A Masque of Mercy, 1947
Complete Poems, 1949
How Not to Be King, 1951
In the Clearing, 1962
The Poetry of Robert Frost, 1969

OTHER LITERARY FORMS

Although the majority of Robert Frost's published work is poetry, it is worth noting that he published a one-act play titled *A Way Out*, in 1929. By this point in his career, Frost had established himself as a fine narrative poet capable of both monologue and dialogue within the poetic narrative mode and with a strong visual mind capable of creating powerful dramatic situations. While Frost never made a serious effort to adapt these dramatic strengths to the stage, much of his poetic success lies with his sense of stage and dramatic persona. His only other literary publications include letters, particularly to his friend Louis Untermeyer, and lectures in which he discusses in detail his own work and poetic theory. He recorded many of his poems on records and film.

ACHIEVEMENTS

Perhaps the most successful of American poets, Robert Frost reached a large and diversified readership almost immediately after the publication of *North of Boston*. He sustained both popular and critical acclaim throughout his entire career, which spanned fifty years and ended with his death in 1963, shortly after the publication of his last collection, *In the Clearing*. He is the only writer to have won the Pulitzer Prize for Poetry four times (in 1924 for *New Hampshire*, in 1931 for the first *Collected Poems*, in 1937 for *A Further Range*, and in 1943 for *A Witness Tree*). He was nominated for the Nobel Prize in 1950 upon publication of the *Complete Poems*, but did not receive it, perhaps because the two preceding Nobel Prizes had been awarded to Americans: T. S. Eliot in 1948 and William Faulkner in 1949. Frost earned other awards, such as the Frost Medal, awarded by the Poetry Society of America (1941), an

Robert Frost (Library of Congress)

Academy of American Poets Fellowship (1953), and the Bollingen Prize (1963). He was also appointed the United States' Poet Laureate Consultant in Poetry (1958-1959).

Few American poets have laid claim to both an enormous critical and popular reputation. Much of Frost's contribution to American literature came from his ability to speak in poetic but plain language to both common people and scholars and to observe ordinary occurrences with irony and wit. If modern American poetry began with Walt Whitman and Emily Dickinson and evolved through Edgar Lee Masters, Robinson Jeffers, and Edward Arlington Robinson, Frost's poetry is the culmination, combining all elements of poetic craft and modern themes. Frost liberated American poets by proving the potential success of traditional forms, even during a period when form was giving way to free verse under the influence of T. S. Eliot and Ezra Pound.

Frost's most important contribution may be as the model for a clearly identifiable twentieth century *American* poet. Unlike the expatriate Americans, Frost never lost touch with American persistence, folk humor, plain

speech, and attachment to the land. His pragmatic, clever intelligence never became pedantic, never abstract, condescending, or introverted, but remained full of mischief and horseplay. In both his poetry and his public image, although his private life was different, Frost embodied the American ideals of rugged gentleness, quiet reflection, and an unconquerable spirit. His poetry is compassionate without falling into sentimentality, and positive without being naïve.

BIOGRAPHY

A native of New Hampshire and a graduate of Harvard University, Robert Lee Frost's father, William Prescott Frost, moved to San Francisco in 1873 to escape post-Civil War bitterness against the South. Shortly before his untimely death at thirty-five, William Prescott requested that he be buried in New England. Fulfilling this request, Robert, his sister Jeanie Florence, and their mother accompanied the casket across the country to Massachusetts. Because they could not afford the return trip, the Frosts settled in Salem, New Hampshire, when Robert was eleven years old. In 1892 Robert Frost was graduated as co-valedictorian from Lawrence High School and entered Dartmouth College to study law. He dropped out, however, before completing his first semester, spending the following two years working at odd jobs and writing poetry. In 1894 he published his first poem, "My Butterfly," and became engaged to Elinor White, with whom he had shared the valedictorian honor. After his marriage in 1895, Frost helped his mother run a small private school, studied for two years at Harvard, then moved to Derry, New Hampshire, for a life of farming. Between 1900 and 1905 Frost raised poultry and wrote most of the poems that would constitute his first two volumes; after 1905 he taught school in Plymouth, New Hampshire, and in 1912 he sailed for England with Elinor and his two children, where he collected and published *A Boy's Will* and *North of Boston*. By the time the Frosts returned to New York in 1915, *North of Boston* had become an enormous critical and popular success, and Frost spent the next year, and indeed most of his life, in the limelight giving readings and lectures.

Because Frost is so strongly identified as a New England poet whose poems are inextricably rooted in the land of New Hampshire and Vermont, readers expect a high correlation between the events of his life and the resultant poetry. While Frost certainly invested most of his life in New England, there is a surprising dichotomy between his biography and his poetic themes. His family life was tragic because premature death beset many of its members. His father died of tuberculosis, his mother of cancer. He lost his sister; two of his children died in infancy; his married daughter died in childbirth; and his son committed suicide. While being operated on for cancer, his wife died of a heart attack. In spite of his long wait for recognition and the private disasters which befell him, however, Frost's poetry is free from bitterness and from any direct personal references. Instead of writing about his own experiences, as so many modern American poets have done, Frost wrote about the process of discovery and the relationship between people and their surroundings.

Frost's particular world was New England, but his landscapes are metaphorical, not specific; his speech universal, not regional; and his themes archetypal, not autobiographical. His official biographer, Lawrance Thompson, unveiled many shocking characteristics of Frost's personality—including jealousy and vindictiveness—but, much to Frost's credit, his art rises above these frailties and speaks not of pettiness but of deep matters of the heart.

ANALYSIS

The most distinctive characteristic of Robert Frost's work is elusiveness. Frost operates on so many levels that to interpret his poems confidently on a single level frequently causes the reader to misunderstand them completely. This elusiveness makes Frost one of the most interesting and continually intriguing American poets. He teaches the joys of discovering what lies beneath the veil, and readers grow to appreciate how he has cleverly masked what seems so intuitively obvious.

The veils themselves are constructed of technical devices such as symbol, rhyme, stanzation, imagery, and dramatic situation, and they are rooted in language play, which Frost uses to effect sleight-of-hand tricks. He is a magician whose devices are so artful that readers usually cannot see how he transforms one theme into another; they may be delighted with the effect, yet they

cannot help wondering how they have been tricked so completely.

Because Frost's poems operate on so many levels, it is possible for almost everyone to find his own beliefs about life reflected in his poetry. Optimists can argue that Frost understands the complexities of life while still affirming man's ability to make creative choices which determine his future. Realists can argue that Frost is not an optimist, although, having acknowledged that doubt is more prevalent than faith, he still derives pleasure from the process of living life in the present. Skeptics can point out Frost's irony, noting that he affirms nothing but the dualities and contradictions of life and human nature. Each type of reader has interpreted Frost correctly; one must consider all levels of Frost's poems before being certain of any particular meaning. Because Frost writes about familiar experiences in what appears to be conversational language, the overwhelming impulse is to accept what he says at face value.

The fact that most readers seem to see their own beliefs reflected in Frost's poetry certainly accounts for his popular success, but this point also raises some serious questions about his poetic achievement. If his poems advance no universal truths, Frost may well be accused of having no philosophy—of being too vague and complex for any clear interpretation to be derived from his works. "Stopping by Woods on a Snowy Evening" is only one of many examples of a poem which has been read with many contradictory interpretations. Readers have variously explained its meaning, ranging from the serenity of a snowy night to the virtues of duty to the lure of death to self-mockery. A critic who reads Frost moralistically, believing that "Stopping by Woods on a Snowy Evening" is a lesson about keeping promises, has fallen into Frost's trap. Readers must be exceedingly careful not to impose their own ideas on the poems or to blindly accept any interpretations.

The place to begin an explication of Frost's poetry is with the narrative persona and dramatic situation, for it is here that Frost draws the reader into the poems and begins his illusions. Only a few of his poems have no dramatic context—most of his celebrated ones do, such as "Mending Wall," "Two Tramps in Mud Time," "Death of the Hired Man," "West-Running Brook," "Tree at My Window," "Two Look at Two"—and except for such very short lyrical poems as "Nothing Gold Can Stay," the dramatic context offers the surest chance of discovering Frost's themes.

"AFTER APPLE-PICKING"

In "After Apple-Picking," for example, a great deal can be established about the dramatic situation, the dramatic moment, and the narrative persona. The reader knows that the narrator has been harvesting apples, perhaps in great numbers, and that he is now "done" with apple-picking. He has collected his apples in barrels, one of which remains unfilled, and the narrator speculates that there may be a few apples left unpicked, although he does not know for certain. His ladder, long and two-pointed, is in the tree where he has left it, and it points "toward heaven still."

In these first six lines, Frost has already begun his sleight of hand by introducing some facts within the dramatic situation which seem extraneous to the poem's development. For example, why does he describe a "two-pointed" ladder when it does not make any difference what kind of ladder it is as long as the narrator can reach the apples with it? Why does he say that it is "sticking" toward heaven? These details of course help to bring the poem alive, but as part of the dramatic situation they add implications far beyond their descriptive use. Heaven is not simply a direction; if it were, Frost could have said "skyward," or not said anything at all since it is obvious that a ladder which sticks through a tree must be pointing up. The empty barrel is similarly suggestive: Readers want to know whether it is empty because somebody miscalculated the number of barrels needed, whether the narrator simply quit before the job was "done," or whether there is a more sinister suggestion that something which should have been filled is empty. Both the ladder and the barrel are facts within the dramatic situation, but they are more than simple details because they raise questions which fall outside the realm of the poem. The reader should be careful to recognize that these questions arise only if he wishes to read the ladder and barrel as suggestive. Clearly, however, Frost did not place them in the poem by accident and therefore they are important. The same kind of suggestiveness can be found in phrases throughout the poem: "winter sleep," "pane of glass," "my dreaming," "cellar bin," "rumbling sound," "cider-apple heap," "woodchuck," and "human sleep."

Complicating the dramatic moment, the narrator tells some things about himself which help to explain why he has left the barrel empty. Readers know that the time is late fall because it is the end of apple-picking season and the beginning of winter sleep. Readers also know that the narrator is tired as he remembers visions which he saw "this morning through a pane of glass" and as he recognizes what form his dreaming is about to take. The morning world of "hoary grass" was strange to him, and as the ice pane melted, the narrator intentionally let it fall and break. Now, at the end of the day, he is embarking upon a nightmare of apples; his ladder sways precariously as the boughs bend. He is no longer safe in the apple tree where he had once been certain of his purpose; now, it is the source of his fears. Too many apples "rumble" into the cellar, a place beneath the earth, in the opposite to that direction in which the ladder is pointing. What worries the narrator most is that some of the good apples "not bruised or spiked" will end up in the "cider-apple heap," a place which offends the narrator's sense of justice. Just as readers want to know why the barrel was left unfilled, the narrator asks why good apples which he let fall by accident are sent to the heap. If readers can understand why he is so troubled by this, they will know a great deal more about the poem's meaning.

With his typical magic, however, Frost sets the reader up to accept the easy explanation as he tempts him to explain the narrator's anxieties merely as a fear of failure to do his job properly. Frost has planted a host of potentially misleading elements which encourage conventional interpretations. The ladder, with its image of outstretched arms, implores heaven, perhaps even suggesting Jacob's ladder. Because apples have such a strong traditional association with the story of the Garden of Eden, one might also conclude that apples represent the narrator's fall into mortal existence—his banishment from the grace of God. He has not, himself, sinned but carries the burden of original sin, and even though he has done the best he can with his life—he has dutifully picked apples until the very end—he is still plagued by nightmares. He knows that he has let slip from his grasp some apples which went undeservedly to the cider-apple heap; it is he who has condemned them to unworthy destruction by the apple grinder, and it occurs to him that his destiny might be similar to one of the good apples that is banished to destruction by chance. The narrator, then, is plagued by two doubts: The first is his own failure to fulfill all his earthly obligations, knowing that time is running out for him ("essence of winter sleep is on the air"); the second is a fear that there is no ultimate mercy—fallen apples like fallen men are disposed of indiscriminately. The hoary world he saw through the pane of glass (with its biblical allusion: "For now we see through a glass, darkly; but then face to face") was the image of life and death, and of his own mortality.

Frost has gone to a great deal of trouble to establish this as the proper reading: The narrator is frightened by the thought of death because he is uncertain whether he has satisfied his earthly duties. A simple moralistic conclusion might be that people should work harder before finding themselves, like the narrator, on the verge of death without salvation. Frost first offered the reader those suggestive objects, then presented a narrator filled with visions, dreams, and sleep, and finally, he produced a dozen highly recognizable and traditional biblical symbols. Why should not "After Apple-Picking" (and "Stopping by Woods on a Snowy Evening," for that matter) be interpreted as a poem about the virtues of steadfastness and singleness of purpose? Yet, one cannot read the poem only at that level; Frost has effected a sleight of hand. Any good magician must continually remind the audience that this is not reality; it is, indeed, a magic show where they have come to be fooled. If Frost wants readers to catch on, he has to provide some means for them to spot the trickery. With Frost's poetry, the price of admission to the magic show is high, and there are no easy explanations as to how the trick is performed, but Frost usually plays fair and gives the reader important clues.

One of the clues in "After Apple-Picking" is the use of personal pronouns. In line 16, and throughout the poem, the narrator continually refers to himself as "I," but in line 37 he shifts to say "one" ("one can see what will trouble this sleep of mine"). He could have said "*I* can see," but there is that deliberate shift to "one," who can be no one else but the reader, and Frost might as well have said "you" can see. All along, the reader has been thinking that the narrator is troubled about his

sleep because he is unprepared for death, but now he begins to suspect that this interpretation is incorrect. "This sleep of *mine*" is not the sleep the reader originally understood, and the narrator corrects the misconception by adding, "whatever sleep it is." The reader believed it was death, and for good reason: Again tricked into it, the reader has fallen into the poem's message.

The "one" who can see the narrator's sleep is not the reader but the woodchuck who could "say" whether "it's like his long sleep or just some human sleep." In reality, the woodchuck could not *say* anything, nor could the woodchuck fear death because of any failure to fulfill religious obligations. The narrator can speak of and fear death, unsure of salvation, but not the woodchuck. Even more trickily, the narrator projects or imagines what the woodchuck's long sleep is ("as I describe its coming on"); so readers have the woodchuck, who cannot possess human vision, telling the narrator only what the narrator imagines and ascribes to the animal. It is through *imagination* that man conceives death, just as the reader has used his imagination to create the symbols in the poem. So moments of life may be misinterpreted to create concepts of death. For Frost, human imagination is the trickster, not death, and men often use it to torment themselves about a mortality which they have fabricated.

THEME OF EARTHLY EXISTENCE

This theme of "After Apple-Picking" reflects Frost's larger world view and helps to account for the frequent misreading of his poems. Even though "After Apple-Picking" seems to be concerned with death, Christian fate, redemption, and the virtuous life—abstract ideas about the afterlife—Frost is much more concerned with earthly existence. He seldom speaks of anywhere else, and when he does, it is always in terms of how one is on earth. Frost neither believes nor disbelieves in religious or philosophical abstractions; yet, time and again, readers insist that he is promoting one view or the other. Frost's code, both in his art and in his public life, is an appreciation of wit and irony; Frost the magician is also the most appreciative audience of life's magic show, and it is important to remember that when there is a strong presence of a narrative persona, the poem is most likely to turn ironic. Frost is most ironic toward himself, and he becomes most poignant when he sees that he has become his own victim in the magic show. In "Birches," for example, the narrator is searching for connections which he does not fully understand, while in "At Woodward's Gardens," a remarkably similar poem, the narrator is more amused by a much too clever comparison between people and monkeys. By comparing these two poems, readers have an illustration of how, when the narrator is aloof and haughty, and when he is able to be more of an observer than a participant, the irony is weakened. When the narrator is as much the audience as the magician, however, the poems reverse themselves as the narrator, himself, comes to appreciate life's sleight of hand.

DRAMATIC SITUATION AND NARRATIVE PERSONA

Many of Frost's most popular and critically acclaimed poems employ what might be called "sleight of tongue." Notice how, when the narrator in "After Apple-Picking" says "this sleep of *mine*," he is also saying "this sleep of *mind*"; in "Tree at My Window," when the narrator says "not all their *light tongues* could be profound," he is not only referring to an image of leaves blowing on the tree but also to the process of photosynthesis which nourishes the plant. In his celebrated sonnet "Design," Frost mixes a set of provocative objects (spider web, delicate white flower, moth) within a dramatic situation, and for twelve lines asks a traditional poetic question which in traditional sonnet fashion will be answered in the couplet. Instead of giving an answer, however, Frost proffers another question which is keyed to the various uses of the parts of speech and the equivocal meanings of the words "design" and "appall." Similarly, in "Stopping by Woods on a Snowy Evening," Frost establishes a dramatic situation with an involved narrator, offers a solution to the dramatic question in line 15 ("And miles to go before I sleep"), then reverses the entire tone of the poem by repeating the line to give it a different meaning.

In the longer poems, dramatic situation and narrative persona are the important elements of irony, while in the shorter poems rhyme and stanzation provide the clues. The poems written in couplets are more playful and bemused than they are ironic because, in the cynical twentieth century, it was difficult for poets to sustain through couplets the solemnity which irony demands. A single couplet or triplet judiciously placed can create exactly the right ironic effect, but an entire poem in couplets tends toward ridicule rather than the reverse. Knowing this, Frost works to overcome the effect, but his couplet poems tend to reflect longing or sadness and are, in fact, more sincere than ironic. Curiously, some of the most ironic poems are those which use triple and quadruple rhyme schemes, such as "Stopping by Woods on a Snowy Evening" and "After Apple-Picking." The least ironic are those with an *abcb* structure; these poems present such personal and impossible questions that no answer is acceptable, and thus there is no irony. The impossibility of his question allows the narrator to be distanced from the dramatic tension, and the absence of personal involvement reduces the narrator's commitment to discovery. Comparing "Stopping by Woods on a Snowy Evening" to "Come In," two very similar poems, the reader can see that the rhyme scheme of "Come In" does not permit as strong a potential for a shift in tone as does the *aaba* of "Stopping by Woods on a Snowy Evening." The locked third line in the *aaba* form allows the narrator much less chance of escaping, and because the fourth line returns the poem to the first two, the narrator must turn internally to the poem for a resolution.

More adaptable to irony than the *abcb* stanzation are the alternating quatrains, octaves, and sonnets, but these are more openly philosophical and convey a sense of pleasant discovery rather than deep involvement. The narrator feels good about his discovery, as in "Two Tramps in Mud Time" and "Design," and these poems tend to contain elements of irony without making any final ironic statement. The forms in which Frost is most consistently ironic are stanzas with framed segments (such as *abba*, *abca*, *abbba*, *aaba*). In the longer, rhymed poems, such as "The Grindstone" and "After Apple-Picking," and in the four-line strophic poems, such as "Stopping by Woods on a Snowy Evening" and "Choose Something Like a Star," the ironic tone is strong, especially when Frost begins shortening lines, as in "Fire and Ice," and altering the number of syllables per line. Without ever reading the poem, one could speculate that "After Apple-Picking" is ironic because of the framed segments (such as the opening six lines), enjambment, shortened lines (line 2 following the long first line, and lines 14 and 16), and the double and triple rhymes (lines

5-6 and lines 14-16, for example). With this combination of techniques, there is little doubt that one cannot accept the poem at face value.

More important than the technical devices for discovering Frost's irony and major themes is the presence of "opposites," which set up patterns of reversal. Frost frequently presents "pairs" of contrasting personas, ideas, images, or symbols, such as in "Tree at My Window," where man faces nature with only a curtain between; in "Two Look at Two," where identical pairs confront each other; in "West-Running Brook," "Home Burial," and "Death of the Hired Man," where husband and wife take opposite views; in "Two Tramps in Mud Time," where the narrator faces the lumberjacks in a confrontation of vocation and avocation; and perhaps most famously in "Mending Wall," where narrator and neighbor, pine and apple trees, civilized man and savage, father and son, light and dark, ego and alter ego square off against each other with yet another barrier—the wall—between them.

"Mending Wall"

Most of the "opposite" poems use some kind of physical barrier to identify territory, and the wall in "Mending Wall" has been consciously constructed in violation of nature which "doesn't love the wall." To the narrator, the wall serves no useful purpose and is only an annoying reminder of his neighbor's foolish platitudes and the inability of the neighbors to communicate except once a year at spring mending time. Before the narrator built a wall, he would want to know what he "was walling in or walling out," but there is a more important question implied: If there were no wall, would he and his neighbor still be opposites? Because the narrator knows that the answer is "yes," and because he is deliberately antagonistic ("Spring is the mischief in me, and I wonder if I could put a notion in his head"), the presence of the wall is a purely academic argument for the narrator. The wall is unnatural—nature wants it down and topples it every winter—just as the wife in "West-Running Brook" thinks it is unnatural that the brook runs west instead of east like all the other country brooks. Fred, her husband, however, knows that there is a more important issue: not one of "opposites" or dualities but one of "contraries." He says that "our life runs down in sending up the clock" and extends this comparison to the sun,

which runs down in sending up the brook. The ultimate question is, What sends up the sun? What happens when the water flings backward on itself in a movement toward the source? There is *something* sending up the sun; *something* that does not love a wall. The persistence of "unnatural" barriers, like the wall, the brook, the apples, and the curtain in "Tree at My Window," reminds the narrator that he cannot explain the existence of contraries any more than his neighbor can explain why good fences make good neighbors, but he does know that in contraries lie the secrets of living; that through the self-conscious process of witnessing contraries one is most likely to discover one's own life's forces rather than any profound secrets of life.

Unlike the English Romantic poets and "nature poets" with whom he is frequently compared, Frost does not look to nature for an affirmation of life, for solace, or for a road to self-discovery. For Frost, man is alone in the world, unable to answer questions about God and death but having some control over his earthly destiny. For Frost, who is not a fatalist or a determinist, who believes things happen neither for good nor evil but simply occur, who does not fear death nor embrace promises of heaven, the only way is "to go by contraries," making creative choices, accepting paradoxes, questioning walls and brooks.

Through wit and irony people can remind themselves that much of their fallibility is self-induced; that they trick themselves and then despair when they think their manufactured illusions have become reality. They have not. Good fences do not necessarily make good neighbors; brooks do not wave at human beings in any annunciation; death does not come as a thrush, or a snowy night, or a spider.

"Fire and Ice"

In "Fire and Ice," the entire doctrine of "Opposites" and irony is at work, and this poem, perhaps most directly of all his work, illustrates Frost's themes and techniques. Arranged as a single stanza of nine lines (in framed segments), the poem establishes the opposites of fire and ice, hot and cold, love and hate, and centers on the middle (fifth) line of the poem. Fire is presented in the first four lines, ice in the last four. The center line asks, "But *if* it had to perish twice," and that becomes the ironic key. Whether the world will be destroyed a second time makes no difference to Frost's narrator; it is a moot question reserved for the gullible reader who interprets "After Apple-Picking" as a Christian manifesto. Frost is much more concerned with the power of hate, an opposite of love, which he says "will suffice," but one must not be tricked by that simple explanation either, to conclude that man is beset by hate any more than he is pursued by death. It "would suffice," if readers wanted it to, just as the woodchuck "would say" if he were asked, but the world does not have to "perish twice" except as one fears destruction, and readers do not have to ask the woodchuck, and one does not have to stoop to hate. "Some say the world will end in fire," but not Frost.

During an age when the thrust of literature has been to question illusion and reality, and to lament the lonely plight and desperation of the isolated man in an overwhelming universe, Frost presents a more positive vision, rooted in the American search for the good life. Human beings may struggle to discover their tormented spirit, but they are also capable of creative choices and of accepting contraries and uncertainties. Frost delights in the mysteries of life without being burdened by debilitating responsibilities for them, and while human beings might not become the conquerors of the universe, neither are they suppressed by it, and in that Frost rejoices.

OTHER MAJOR WORKS

PLAY: *A Way Out*, pb. 1929 (one act).

NONFICTION: *The Letters of Robert Frost to Louis Untermeyer*, 1963 (with a commentary by Untermeyer); *The Record of a Friendship*, 1963 (Margaret Bartlett, editor); *Selected Letters of Robert Frost*, 1964 (Lawrance Thompson, editor); *Selected Prose*, 1966 (Hyde Cox and Edward C. Lathem, editors).

BIBLIOGRAPHY

Burnshaw, Stanley. *Robert Frost Himself*. New York: George Braziller, 1986. Written by someone who had been an almost lifelong friend of Frost, this very personal biography is in part an attempt to redress the balance skewed in the definitive Lawrance Roger Thompson work. Includes a chronology, extensive notes, an accurate index, and a revealing collection of illustrations.

Faggen, Robert. *Robert Frost and the Challenge of Darwin*. Ann Arbor: University of Michigan Press, 1997. With copious evidence amassed for his argument, Faggen depicts Robert Frost as a poet of the first order and among the most challenging of the moderns. Frost is placed as our chief poet of the scientific and the skeptical turn of mind.

Gerber, Philip L. *Robert Frost*. Rev. ed. Boston: Twayne, 1982. This series is designed as a collection of first references of which this volume is a solid member. Begins with an objective biographical overview and follows with substantial chapters on technique, themes, theories, and accomplishments. Includes a chronology, extensive notes and references, a select bibliography, and an index.

Lathem, Edward Connery. *Robert Frost: A Biography*. New York: Holt, Rinehart and Winston, 1981. Condenses the three-volume "authorized" biography by Lawrance Roger Thompson into one volume, intended for the general reader. Without question the most meticulously researched and minutely recorded study of Frost, which many reviewers have judged personally biased. Solid on facts, this volume contains judgments which must be used with caution. It has no notes and a limited bibliography.

Meyers, Jeffrey. *Robert Frost: A Biography*. Boston: Houghton Mifflin, 1996. Meyers shapes a long life into a vivacious character study based on the conflicts that seemed to drive Frost as well as do him damage. Includes bibliographical references and an index.

Poirier, Richard. *Robert Frost: The Work of Knowing*. New York: Oxford University Press, 1977. This substantial scholarly work refrains from partial judgments and presents a balanced view of the man and his work. Although it contains a biographical chapter, it concentrates mostly on the writings, which it analyzes lucidly. Contains a chronology of writings, an index, and a limited bibliography.

Potter, James L. *The Robert Frost Handbook*. University Park: Pennsylvania State University Press, 1980. A basic and the widely used resource on Frost, this work is indispensable for both first readers and scholars. Contains chronologies of both life and works, guides to various approaches to the poems, discussions of various literary and cultural contexts, and technical analyses, as well as a complete annotated bibliography and an index.

Pritchard, William H. *Frost: A Literary Life Reconsidered.* New York: Oxford University Press, 1984. This measured, sophisticated, detailed approach to Frost's life and work is another attempt to correct Thompson's view. Unlike many scholarly biographies, this one is good for browsing, enjoyable for the general reader. Includes full notes and an index.

Thompson, Lawrance Roger, and R. H. Winnick. *Robert Frost: A Biography.* New York: Holt, Rinehart and Winston, 1982. A one-volume, condensed version of an exhaustive, three-volume authorized biography originally published between 1966 and 1976.

Walton Beacham;
bibliography updated by the editors

ROY FULLER

Born: Failsworth, Lancashire, England; February 11, 1912

Died: London, England; September 27, 1991

PRINCIPAL POETRY

Poems, 1939
The Middle of a War, 1942
A Lost Season, 1944
Epitaphs and Occasions, 1949
Counterparts, 1954
Brutus's Orchard, 1957
Collected Poems, 1936-1961, 1962
Buff, 1965
New Poems, 1968
Off Course, 1969
To an Unknown Reader, 1970
Song Cycle from a Record Sleeve, 1972
Tiny Tears, 1973
An Old War, 1974
From the Joke Shop, 1975
The Joke Shop Annexe, 1975

An Ill-Governed Coast: Poems, 1976
Poor Roy, 1977
The Other Planet, 1979
Re-treads, 1979
The Reign of Sparrows, 1980
More About Tompkins and Other Light Verse, 1981
The Individual and His Times: Selected Poems, 1982
House and Shop, 1982
As from the Thirties, 1983
Upright Downfall, 1983 (with Barbara Giles and Adrian Rumble)
Mianserin Sonnets, 1984
Subsequent to Summer, 1985
New and Collected Poems, 1934-1984, 1985
Outside the Cannon, 1986
Consolations, 1987
Available for Dreams, 1989
Last Poems, 1993

OTHER LITERARY FORMS

Roy Fuller was a competent novelist and may well be considered a poet-novelist, much like Thomas Hardy. His principal novels are *The Second Curtain* (1953), *The Perfect Fool* (1963), *My Child, My Sister* (1965), and *The Carnal Island* (1970). He wrote several children's novels, including *Savage Gold: A Story of Adventure* (1946) and *With My Little Eye: A Mystery Story for Teenagers* (1948). He also edited *Byron for To-day* (1948) and *Fellow Mortals* (1981), an anthology of animal verse. His autobiography was issued in a number of volumes: *Souvenirs* (1980), *Vamp Till Ready: Further Memoirs* (1982), and *Home and Dry: Memoirs III* (1984), reissued in complete form as *The Strange and the Good: Collected Memoirs* (1989).

ACHIEVEMENTS

Roy Fuller was honored for his literary accomplishments, becoming a Fellow of the Royal Society of Literature and a Companion of the British Empire in 1970. In that year he won the Queen's Gold Medal for Poetry. Two years previously he had won the Duff Cooper Memorial Prize for his *New Poems*, and in 1980 he received the Society of Authors Cholmondeley Award. Finally, in 1990 he was awarded an honorary doctorate of letters by the University of Kent at Canterbury.

BIOGRAPHY

Roy Broadbent Fuller was the elder son of Leopold Charles Fuller of Oldham, England, an industrial town in Lancashire, in the northwest of England, and of Nellie Broadbent. His father was manager of a rubber-proofing mill but died when Roy Fuller was only eight. Two years later his mother and her two sons moved to Blackpool, a nearby seaside town, where Fuller received his education at Blackpool High School. He left there at age sixteen, the minimum leaving age then being fourteen, and was articled (apprenticed) to a local firm of solicitors (attorneys). He became briefly involved in left-wing politics and always retained left-wing sympathies. His northern upbringing, with its culture of wry, anti-establishment humor, became one of the distinguishing features of his poetic voice.

He completed his articles in 1934, passing the necessary exams to qualify him as a lawyer. He moved south for his first post, at a law firm in Ashford, Kent, in the southeast of England. There he met Kathleen Smith, whom he married in 1936. Their only child, John, was born January 1, 1937. Later John was to become a well-known poet and academic in his own right. Just before the outbreak of World War II in 1939, the family moved to London, where Roy Fuller joined the Woolwich Building Society, one of the largest mortgage lending societies in the United Kingdom.

In 1941 he enlisted in the Royal Navy, in which he served until 1946. He was one of the first technicians to work with the recently installed systems of radar. In 1942 he was posted to Kenya, an experience which propelled him into writing poetry in a much more systematic way than before, though he had published a largely unnoticed volume of poems in 1939. His two volumes written during the war, *The Middle of a War* (1942) and *A Lost Season* (1944), brought him to public attention. In 1944 he was relocated back to London, becoming a lieutenant in the Royal Navy volunteer reserve. He worked at the Admiralty as a technical adviser to the director of naval air radio.

Fuller then resumed his legal career with the Woolwich, remaining with it until his retirement. He wrote several legal volumes on Building Society law and from 1958 to 1969 served as chairman of the legal advice panel of the Building Societies Association. On his re-tirement in 1969 he was made director of the Woolwich, a post he held until his death, and vice president of the Building Societies Association.

Fuller was thus one of the few modern poets who have systematically and successfully pursued a career outside the academic or artistic world. His commercial role did not prevent him from writing profusely or from becoming a respected poet, novelist, essayist and reviewer. Between 1945 and 1969 he wrote seven adult and two children's novels, produced six volumes of poetry, and edited three volumes of other people's poetry. Shortly before his retirement, he was voted professor of poetry at Oxford University, a post he held until 1973.

He continued to be extremely active after his retirement, not only writing poetry and another novel and producing a lengthy series of memoirs, but also as a governor of the British Broadcasting Corporation (BBC) and as a member of the Arts Council as chairman of its literature panel. He also served as chairman of the Poetry Book Society. He continued to live in London until his death in 1991.

ANALYSIS

Roy Fuller was respected as an accomplished poet and man of letters, who sought not only to raise the technical standards of poetry in his day but also to reinstate its moral voice and significance in a culture that he saw as constantly betraying itself. As a poet he fought against cultural sloppiness, using a voice typical of the great British ironists such as Alexander Pope and Lord Byron, but perhaps with more self-deprecation and sensitivity than most ironists.

THE WAR POET

Fuller's first volume of verse, titled merely *Poems*, attracted little notice. Two poems in it, however, are worthy of note: "To M. S. Killed in Spain" and "To My Brother." Both reflect the growing sense of war in the Europe of the late 1930's, his friend killed in the Spanish Civil War, and his brother touring Nazi Germany. The latter poem's central image is an edition of Alexander Pope's poems his brother had given him, Pope becoming symbolic of the ordered world Fuller feels is now shattering. Its influence is that of W. H. Auden, a poet he continued to admire for his intelligence, discipline, and formal skills.

It is in his war poetry that Fuller first found his true voice, ironically, as World War II produced very few British poets of note. In contrast to World War I, World War II was not shocking. Fuller's depiction of it reflects personal boredom, the squalid world of military quarters and docks, and good-byes. The experience that really opened him was his being drafted to East Africa. The impact of a foreign culture and landscape forced his poetry to assume a new directness, as did the experience of living in close quarters with very ordinary young men, with the need to communicate in terms of their concrete realities.

"The Green Hills of Africa" depicts both a native village in striking detail and the debilitating effect of modern civilization. A similar pessimism informs "The Plains." Again, a masterful ability to depict a scene with a few vivid images is followed by a train of thought on the tawdriness of the cycle of killing and being killed. In the wake of the lion come the jackals and vultures. His concern for the animals is paralleled by his concern for the Africans. The narrative "Teba" shows the contradictions of a rapidly evolving society. Fuller's anti-idealism is again reflected in "The Petty Officers' Mess," possibly the most accomplished poem in the two volumes of war poetry. Fuller proceeds with an image of caged monkeys, through sailors' arguments to wider political questions, then ironically reduces these back again to the level of the monkeys' own scrapes and fights.

THE 1950'S

Returning to civilian life, Fuller wrote his next volume, *Epitaphs and Occasions*. His "Dedicatory Epistle" shows a new, easy ironic tone and verse form using iambic tetrameter couplets influenced by Pope and Auden. For all its lightness of tone, however, there is a note of purpose:

> The poet now must put verse back
> Time and again upon the track
> That first was cut by Wordsworth when
> He said that verse was meant for men.

This mixture of tautness, technical brilliance, ironic tone, and yet artistic seriousness was shared by a number of younger poets in the 1950's, particularly Donald Davie and Philip Larkin. The group came to be known as the Movement, representing a reaction to the florid Romanticism and gesturing of Dylan Thomas and other poets of the 1930's and 1940's.

Similar poems are "Meditation," often anthologized with its throwaway ending:

> . . . perhaps we shall, before
> Anything really happens, be safely dead.

In "Obituary to R. Fuller," actually quoted at his memorial service forty-two years later, his self-deprecation is comic. "The Divided Life Released" talks of the reality of wartime life and the unrealities of postwar suburban life, a dichotomy parallel to that of the poet and the lawyer, which Fuller managed to come to terms with creatively.

Counterparts (1954) and *Brutus's Orchard* (1957) followed, both containing powerful poems that break through the typical understatement, self-deprecating irony, and avoidance of emotion typical of the Movement style. "Rhetoric of a Journey" continues the theme of the uprooted, divided poet, but anchors it far more autobiographically in a moving statement. "Ten Memorial Poems," on Fuller's mother's death, is a confessional series, in places reminiscent of Alfred, Lord Tennyson's *In Memoriam* (1850). The feeling is that of the poet coming to full maturity in his control, depth, and focus.

"Images of Autumn" expresses Fuller's feeling of cultural helplessness. Poetry is no longer a public art form; the public no longer can hear the poet, who is now unheard and invisible. What is particularly difficult is that the poet is not writing just out of personal need but because he desires revelation of some "social truths." "Poet and Reader" closes with:

> All art foresees a future,
> Save art which fails to weigh
> The sadness of the creature,
> The limit of its day,
> Its losing war with nature.

Such rejection forces him into self-regarding stances: "Poem out of Character" is typical. It finishes by deconstructing his own poetry as gesture in the face of universal truth.

In "Elementary Philosophy," the despair of a godless philosophy is heard in tones that echo Thomas Hardy. Another of Hardy's themes, and also William Butler Yeats's, is the growing dichotomy of body and mind. From the middle of *Brutus's Orchard*, Fuller becomes much more aware of his own sexuality as he feels his body aging. "The Perturbation of Dreams" and "Mythological Sonnets" are powerful expressions of midlife angst.

THE 1960'S

"Faustian Sketches," the final section of Fuller's *Collected Poems, 1936-1961* (1962), continues this awareness. In "On the Mountain" his own failing physical powers are symbolized by the decline and fall of the Roman Empire. The ironic surface tones of the earlier poems give way to deeper and more tragic ironies, with the poet's full range of emotions being engaged. The sonnet sequence *Meredithian Sonnets*, which closes the *Collected Poems*, well illustrates this.

Buff (1965) contains Fuller's third sonnet sequence, *The Historian*, which contains thirty-five sonnets, ranging over the ironies of history. "All history is the history of pain," he wrote elsewhere. "To X" is another sequence, of roundels this time, a difficult traditional form.

The decade began for Fuller with a recognition of his pivotal place in modern British poetry, with his *Collected Poems*; it closed with his *New Poems* (1968), published shortly before his retirement from his business duties. Many of the poems in this volume are concerned with art and the artist. "Those of Pure Origin" is a striking, long philosophical poem, inspired by a quotation from the German poet Friedrich Hölderlin. Its clear, relaxed voice and well-controlled stanzaic free verse seem a model for philosophic discussion in verse.

LATER YEARS

Fuller's retirement merely released him into a prolific old age, although not adding unduly to his reputation. The same self-deprecating tone is heard in "To an Unknown Reader" in *Tiny Tears* (1973): "a whole lifetime's remorseful exposure/ Of a talent falling short of its vision?" He continues to experiment in verse form; "At T. S. Eliot's Memorial Service" is written in couplets first used by Tennyson in "Locksley Hall."

From the Joke Shop (1975) probably illustrates best how prolific Fuller continued to be. It contains sixty-three poems written between late summer and early spring. Every poem is composed of three-line iambic stanzas, but the run-on lines and verses annul any sense of a mechanical form. The collection contains many poems reminiscent of "In Memoriam" and shows Fuller as a man of culture, not breaking any new territory in terms of what he has to say, but very stimulating in the flexibility of his poetic voice. "The Joke Shop" is his poetic imagination, with its need to "amuse" an audience.

If poems are jokes, they are also sparrows. Fuller sees himself as a minor poet in *The Reign of Sparrows* (1980). What is striking here is the technical brilliance he has achieved, from cinquains to elegiac pindarics, as well as the ability to find significance in the most trivial everyday event. *Subsequent to Summer* (1985) continues the formal brilliance in this sequence of forty-nine quasi sonnets, each poem consisting of seven unrhymed couplets. It is effortless verse, philosophical poetry at its best. This fascination with the sonnet is akin to Robert Lowell's. In *Available for Dreams* (1989) there is a tremendous variety of sonnet forms, becoming almost free verse, just as in Lowell's diary-like *Life Studies* (1959).

After Fuller's death, his son John discovered a large number of unpublished poems, which he edited as *Last Poems* (1993). The American poet Wallace Stevens features prominently: Fuller's autumnal flowering has often been compared to that of Stevens, as to Yeats and Hardy. The final section, *Later Sonnets from the Portuguese* (echoing Elizabeth Barrett Browning's sequence), consists of some forty-four sonnets.

Fuller is praised for sustaining the quality of British poetry during the relatively lean period of 1950-1960. He went on to outwrite all the other Movement poets, using his intelligence, wit, and formal skills to make significant comments on the cultural and everyday life of the later part of the twentieth century. He may not take the reader out of that life, but he does fully engage with it in significant detail.

OTHER MAJOR WORKS

LONG FICTION: *The Second Curtain*, 1953; *Fantasy and Fugue*, 1954 (pb. in the United States as *Murder in Mind*, 1986); *Image of a Society*, 1956; *The Ruined Boys*, 1959 (pub. in the United States as

That Distant Afternoon, 1957); *The Father's Comedy*, 1961; *The Perfect Fool*, 1963; *My Child, My Sister*, 1965; *The Carnal Island*, 1970; *Stares*, 1990.

NONFICTION: *Owls and Artificers: Oxford Lectures on Poetry, 1969-1970*, 1971; *Professors and Gods: Last Oxford Lectures on Poetry*, 1973; *Souvenirs*, 1980; *Vamp Till Ready: Further Memoirs*, 1982; *Home and Dry: Memoirs III*, 1984; *The Strange and the Good: Collected Memoirs*, 1989; *Spanner and Pen: Post-war Memoirs*, 1991.

CHILDREN'S LITERATURE: *Savage Gold: A Story of Adventure*, 1946; *With My Little Eye: A Mystery Story for Teenagers*, 1948; *Catspaw*, 1966; *Seen Grandpa Lately?*, 1972; *The World Through the Window: Collected Poems for Children*, 1989.

EDITED TEXTS: *Byron for To-day*, 1948; *New Poems*, 1952 (with Clifford Dyment and Montagu Slater); *Supplement to New Poetry*, 1964; *Fellow Mortals*, 1981.

MISCELLANEOUS: *Questions and Answers in Building Society Law and Practice*, 1949; *The Building Societies Acts: Great Britain and Ireland, 1957-1961*, 1962.

BIBLIOGRAPHY

Austin, Allan E. *Roy Fuller*. Boston: Twayne, 1979. This compact volume contains chapters on early, middle, and late poetry up to *From the Joke Shop*. An excellent, comprehensive volume.

Orr, Peter, ed. *The Poet Speaks*. London: Routledge & Kegan Paul, 1966. Fuller proves forthright in talking both about himself and his work.

Powell, Neil. *Roy Fuller: Writer and Society*. Manchester, England: Carcanet, 1995. A full biographical account of Fuller's life and writings with a lengthy bibliography.

Smith, Steven E. *Roy Fuller: A Bibliography*. Aldershot, England: Scolar Press, 1996. A good bibliography with a full index.

Tolley, A. T., ed. *Roy Fuller: A Tribute*. Ottawa, Ont.: Carleton University Press, 1993. A far-ranging collection of biographical pieces celebrating Fuller's life and assessing his contribution to modern literature.

David Barratt

ALICE FULTON

Born: Troy, New York; January 25, 1952

PRINCIPAL POETRY

Anchors of Light, 1979
Dance Script with Electric Ballerina, 1983
Palladium, 1986
Powers of Congress, 1990
Sensual Math, 1995
Felt, 2001

OTHER LITERARY FORMS

Alice Fulton has published her essays in journals, as well as a collection of essays, *Feeling as a Foreign Language: The Good Strangeness of Poetry* (1999). Her short story "Queen Wintergreen" was published in *The Best American Short Stories, 1993*, and she has made her poetry and stories available on the Internet. She has also contributed to audio recordings of her poetry accompanied by music, such as *Poets in Person: American Poets and Their Art* (1991), *I Will Breathe a Mountain: A Cycle from American Women Poets* (1991), *Turbulence: A Romance* (1997), *Mail: from Daphne and Apollo Remade* (2000), and *Turns and Turns into the Night* (2001).

Alice Fulton (© Hank De Leo, courtesy of W. W. Norton)

ACHIEVEMENTS

Alice Fulton has been published in many poetry anthologies since 1982. She has also won numerous honors, including fellowships from the MacDowell Colony, the Millay Colony, the Michigan Society of Fellows, the Yaddo Colony, the Bread Loaf Writers' Conference, the Guggenheim Foundation, and the John D. and Catherine T. MacArthur Foundation. She won the Emily Dickinson Award from the Poetry Society of America in 1980; an Academy of American Poets prize in 1982; the Rainer Maria Rilke Award in 1984; the Consuelo Ford Award "Terrestrial Magnetism" from the Poetry Society of America in 1984; National Poetry Series award in 1985; the Society of Midland Authors Poetry Award for their National Poetry Series Competition in 1985; a Society of Midland Authors Award in 1987; a Bess Hokin Prize from *Poetry* magazine in 1989; the Ingram Merrill Foundation Award in 1990; the Robert Chasen Poetry Prize from Cornell University; a Henry Russel Award from the University of Michigan in 1990; the Elizabeth Matchett Stover award from *Southwest Review* in 1994; and the Editor's Prize in Fiction from the *Missouri Review* in 1997.

BIOGRAPHY

Born in 1952 in Troy, New York, Alice Fulton attended Catholic schools in her hometown. She began writing poetry during the 1970's. She received her bachelor of arts degree in creative writing from Empire State College in Albany, New York, in 1978 and in 1982 her master of fine arts degree from Cornell University, where she had studied with A. R. Ammons. She married artist Hank De Leo in 1980.

In 1983, she became an assistant professor of English at the University of Michigan, where she was promoted to William Wilhartz Professor in 1986, associate professor in 1990, and full professor in 1992. Fulton has also been a visiting professor of creative writing at both Vermont College (1987) and at the University of California, Los Angeles (1991). During the 1990's, Fulton served as a judge for many poetry writing prizes, including the National Book Award, the Lamont Prize, the Akron Poetry Prize, and the Walt Whitman Award. She and De Leo make their home in Ypsilanti, Michigan. Active on the Web, Fulton maintains a homepage accessible through the Web site for the University of Michigan at Ann Arbor, English Department.

ANALYSIS

Like both Emily Dickinson and Annie Dillard, Alice Fulton is an explorer of the mind, individuality, societal roles, and ultimately the cosmos. Fulton is sometimes even called a postmodern Dickinson because of her dense vocabulary, her spasmodic pace, and her mingling of the personal and the abstract. Fulton also shares with Dickinson a view of poetry as the play of the mind. Words are tried on like dresses to offer new explanations for old situations. With only a vocabulary and a different grammar, Fulton holds up old verities to new light: Like Dickinson, she "tell[s] the truth but tell[s] it slant." With this technique, Fulton casts societal suppositions and inherited myths into different frames as she goes about with a new vocabulary, making the familiar unfamiliar and strangely making the unfamiliar familiar. Questions become more important than answers in her vocabulary for a world ever more unstable, fragmented, and formless. Like Dickinson, she seeks to redefine life by emphasizing the periphery, thereby rearranging the focus of the reader's attention; the expected is never there.

Although Dillard operates in a different genre (fiction), Fulton, like Dillard, wants to go beyond the seen and the normal to relocate herself in a larger milieu that reaches beyond time and currency. To place herself in a different sphere as she redefines her world, Fulton uses different references for her explorations. She uses terms from chaos theory, fractal forms, and Heisenberg's theory of indeterminacy to map out the concealed elements of life that shape people because poems, as she said in 1986, "are linguistic models of the world's working [and] our knowledge of form includes the new concept of manageable chaos, along with the ancient categories of order and chaos." Alice Fulton, poet, is like a fish noticing and defining water for the first time. To this end, in her essay "Inconvenient Knowledge" (1997, 1998), she calls for writers to "become cultural outsiders. . . . Imagination [poetry] is the transfiguring force . . . pressing against cultural assumptions in order to reinvent them."

Another common element that Fulton shares with Dickinson and Dillard, besides their pushing against type, is an association with Catholicism. Although Dickinson is seen as a prototype of the New England Protestant, she actually spent much household time talking with the Irish workers employed with her family. Because of these conversations, she dropped her negative attitude toward Catholicism. In fact, the pallbearers for her coffin were the family's Irish Catholic workmen. Dillard, also born a Protestant of Calvinist origins, converted to Catholicism in her adult life, and Fulton was born Catholic with Irish ancestors.

Like other poets in the line of writers who do not produce the norm and follow tradition, Fulton has to be read and reread. Her poems present spaces that lyrical poetry has overlooked. In a course description of Fulton's course English 535, "Postmodern Fractal Poetics: Writing in Three Dimensions," which appeared online at the University of Michigan's Web site, Fulton provides her own, best guide to her poetics:

> Fractal poetics is composed of the disenfranchised aspects, the dark matter of Tradition: its blind spots, recondite spaces, and recursive fields. . . . [I]t exists on a third ground between "high" and "low" terrain, resistant to those classifications. . . . Fractal poetics has dispensed with fidelity to the "normal" and the "natural," to "simplicity" and "sincerity." Instead of reproducing speech, the poem makes a sound-unto-itself; its music is not so much voiced as built. . . . The disjunctive shifts of fractal poetry . . . are akin to nonlinear interactions [an allusion to mathematics] in which the value of the whole cannot be predicted by summing the strength of its parts. A fractal poem might contain purposely insipid or flowery lines that would be throwaways if taken out of context. When juxtaposed with other inclusions, however, these debased lines establish a friction or frame greater than their discrete presence would predict."

"FIX"

In "Fix" Fulton reaffirms her ties to Dickinson. She comments on science and natural forces, as does Dickinson, but the clearest parallel is contained in her first line, "There is no caring less," which she repeats three other times throughout the course of the poem. The line is metrically identical to the opening lines of

Dickinson's poems; it is also stylistically identical, making a seemingly uncomplicated, blanket statement about the nature of things without obvious justification. It is a thoroughly ambiguous sentiment, devoid of any clear meaning, and it is this ambiguity that works to Fulton's advantage as she explores the various ramifications of there being "no caring less" throughout the poem. However, despite the different meanings she tries on—which lead the reader to view the idea through the screen of the universe's indifference to humanity, the apathy of the "you" she addresses in the beginning of the poem, and her own devotion to the same—what is left at the poem's conclusion is still a statement that can be played with semantically any number of ways, but it does not provide closure. There clearly exists "no caring less," but at the final moment both subject and object are absent.

"THE ORTHODOX WALTZ"

"The Orthodox Waltz" is a slow, smoky poem, full of suggestion and implication. In this, as in her other poems, Fulton feels no need to provide her reader with background information, preferring to begin *in medias res* and allowing the readers to sort out the situation for themselves. The poem is a metaphor for the typical pattern of courtship; it is a dance and a highly orthodox one at that, as the man leads and the woman must follow. However, although the man may lead, there is a necessary give-and-take in such a dance, and each party seeks response from the other in order to continue. This highly complex back-and-forth action is symbolized in part by Fulton's description of the man's actions:

> He kept his ear pressed
> like a safecracker's
> stethoscope against
> her head, kept his
> recombinant endearments
> tumbling toward a click.

It is this "click" that is the necessary culmination of courtship, the connection of two people that enables them to edge past the first hesitant phase and form a relationship. So often, Fulton points out, this is a step that must finally be taken alone, without the approbation or input of others, as the woman in her poem is distracted by her partner's "clasp and lust-/ spiel" from all her mother's years of good advice.

"MAIDENHEAD"

"Maidenhead" is one of Fulton's longer poems, and one of her more complex as well. Into it she weaves Dickinson, her likewise reclusive aunt, the Catholic school she attended, and her white graduation dress, which she compares to Dickinson's. She identifies herself at seventeen as markedly different from the rest of the girls in her school; she sits alone reading Dickinson on the bus and is teased on account of her aunt, while the other girls read wedding magazines and sunbathe. In this poem, as in others, Fulton freely uses imagery relating to science and nature:

> There's an optical effect,
> *interference*,
> I think it's called, that puts the best
> light on a gem's flaws
>
> . . . .
>
> wave trains of light collide
> from aberrations
>
> . . . . .
>
> There is a lace
> of nerves, I've learned, a nest of lobe and limbic
> tissue around the hippocampus, which on magnetic
>   resonance
> imaging resembles a negative of moth.

She ties such imagery predominantly to her thoughts on the inner workings of Dickinson's and her aunt's troubled minds; at times she directly addresses Dickinson, commenting on how she compares to her aunt. In addition to this, she also uses imagery relating to Catholicism, mentioning the nuns at her high school changing their habits, the uniform she is forced to wear every day, the different connotations of a veil, and the stitches in her newly-made white dress that are "so uncatholic and so - / made for me." It is a poem in which Fulton feels no remorse about simply moving on without any clear transition to another subject, returning only later and just as suddenly.

"CASCADE EXPERIMENT"

In "Cascade Experiment," Fulton's growing unease with received religious information, where "childhood catechisms all had heaven," leads her to search for answers in science:

> Because faith creates its verification
> and reaching you will be no harder than believing
> in a planet's caul of plasma
> or interacting with a comet.

Yet by line 28, she is calling herself "an infidel of amplitude" as she "discard[s] and enlarge[s]" both received religion and received science. She recognizes that science, like religion, permits only some information to be known. Other information, such as the "thirteen species/ of whiptail lizards composed entirely of females/ stay undiscovered due to bias/ against such things existing." If Fulton is to discover the truth of the world for herself, she will have to become an independent, passionate explorer, who will "meet the universe halfway . . . move toward what/ looks to us like nothing."

"CHERRY BOMBS"

The knowledge that young girls learn as they grow (or perhaps that which they are born knowing) about their growing up, whether they wish to acknowledge the information or not, is the central idea in "Cherry Bombs." That future is almost set like the "Lilt perms . . . [into] an unfixable forever" that the poet does not want. She rejects the future war planned for her with its "training bras," "GI Joe advances," the combat of "Labor," and "monuments for women/ dead of children." Like Dillard in *An American Childhood* (1987), the poet wants to be herself as she defines herself. "No one could make me/ null and void," she vows at age five, as her childhood quickly passes.

"FUZZY FEELINGS"

Just as all people live multiple lives as multiple people, Fulton shows herself as one of the rest of us, layered. In "Fuzzy Feelings," she is a dental patient, a consumer of the popular magazine *Glamour*, a sister, and an aunt, thinking of events occurring at the moment, a few moments ago, and last year that blend together in some unplanned pattern and texture. The blending begins in the dentist's chair as Fulton stares at the ceiling, waiting for her dental work to begin. Her staring leads to thoughts of nature's colors mixed with the colors in the office, without a perceivable break. Interspersed are words from the dentist, "sinking one into another" while Fulton "fak[es] Lamaze and ancient mantras" to take her out of the chair and out of the room and away from dental pain. Her mind takes her to questions about sex that she read in the magazine while waiting for her appointment and to thoughts of the world's textures.

However, the thoughts of being somewhere else, home, lead her to the emotional pain from the death of her niece, her sister Sandy's child. This kind of pain cannot be stopped by Novocaine. It is too deep, too strong. It hinders her sister Sandy from being layered; she is just pain. To hide the pain that identifies her on only one layer, Sandy "blends some body/ veil into herself. Gets ready to flex/ the verbal abs and delts and hopes/ she won't be up till dawn." Like Fulton, who will have "a refined smile" and "a headache" when she leaves the dental office, Sandy will hide "The fissures= = [the] vacancies inside." Both Fulton and her sister strive for some kind of "grace" in living despite the pain: "Right now I'm trying to open wide." The multiple meanings of the images and the abstractions in the poem lead the reader to a visual picture, more poignant because of the poet's lack of straight narration and tone about the events. The pain is always interior, whatever the cause.

OTHER MAJOR WORKS

NONFICTION: *Feeling as a Foreign Language: The Good Strangeness of Poetry*, 1999.

BIBLIOGRAPHY

Fulton, Alice. "Interview with Alice Fulton." Interview by Christanne Miller." *Contemporary Literature* 38, no. 4 (Winter 1997): 585-615. Examines the norms for current poetry and the movements away from those norms.

Keller, Lynn. "The 'Then Some Inbetween': Alice Fulton's Feminist Experimentalism." *American Literature* 71, no. 2 (1999): 311-340. Explores Alice Fulton's nonalignment with any particular school of poetry and discusses the problems for poet and reader with her of lack of a traditional identity.

Miller, Cristanne. "'The Erogenous Cusp' or Intersections of Science and Gender in Alice Fulton's Poetry." *Feminist Measures: Soundings in Poetry and Theory.* Ann Arbor: University of Michigan Press, 1994. Miller explores Fulton's use of quantum physics to reinvent poetic discourse.

_____. "Questioning Authority in the Late Twentieth Century." In *Marianne Moore: Questions of Authority.* Cambridge, Mass.: Harvard University Press, 1995. Fulton is placed in a tradition with Emily Dickinson and Marianne Moore.

_____. "Wonder Stings Me More than the Bee." *Emily Dickinson International Society Bulletin* 8, no. 2 (1996): 10-11. Fulton is discussed as a descendant of the nineteenth century poet Emily Dickinson via the Fulton poem whose title comes from a Dickinson letter. The implicit idea is the lack of clear boundaries in life, despite societal attempts to maintain them.

Petoskey, Barbara. "Crossing Boundaries." *LSAmagazine,* Fall, 1995, 30-31. The author discusses the ways that Fulton works with her colleagues from different disciplines at the University of Michigan and offers poetry courses that appeal to a broad range of students.

Carol Lawson Pippen

G

TESS GALLAGHER

Tess Bond

Born: Port Angeles, Washington; July 21, 1943

PRINCIPAL POETRY

Stepping Outside, 1974
Instructions to the Double, 1976
Under Stars, 1978
Portable Kisses, 1978
On Your Own, 1978
Willingly, 1984
Amplitude: New and Selected Poems, 1987
Moon Crossing Bridge, 1992
The Valentine Elegies, 1993
Owl-Spirit Dwelling, 1994
My Black Horse: New and Selected Poems, 1995
Portable Kisses Expanded, 1993

OTHER LITERARY FORMS

Tess Gallagher made her primary reputation as a poet, although she authored a televison play, *The Wheel* (1970), early in her career. Gallagher turned to writing prose in the 1980's, probably because of the influence of her husband, writer Raymond Carver. In 1982 she wrote the screenplay *The Night Belongs to the Police*, and in 1985 she coauthored with Carver *Dostoevsky: A Screenplay*. In 1986 Gallagher published *The Lover of Horses and Other Stories* along with *A Concert of Tenses: Essays on Poetry*. Afterward she published *At the Owl Woman Saloon* (1997), and *Soul Barnacles: Ten More Years with Ray* (2000).

Her body of work also includes contributions as a columnist to *American Poetry Review* and poems, short stories, and essays to such prominent periodicals as *Antaeus, Ironwood, Missouri Review, The New Yorker*, and the *North American Review*.

ACHIEVEMENTS

Gallagher is noted for her sensitive portrayal of family life as well as insightful, almost mystical exploration of personal issues, particularly grief. At their best, her works meld the ordinary with the evocative, producing work which is emotionally and philosophically profound. Although some have found Gallagher's work occasionally self-centered, she is generally considered one of the United States' best contemporary poets.

From almost the beginning of her writing career, she won some prestigious awards: two from the National Endowment for the Arts (1976, 1981), a CAPS grant from the New York State Arts Council (1976), and the Elliston Award (1976). In 1978 Gallagher was awarded the Voertman Award and a fellowship from the Guggenheim Foundation. *American Poetry Review* honored her as having the "best poems of 1980." She won the Governor's Award from the state of Washington in 1984, 1986, and 1987. In 1988 she was awarded a New York State arts grant and in 1990 the Maxine Cushing Gray Foundation Award.

BIOGRAPHY

Tess Gallagher was born Tess Bond, the oldest of five children. Her father worked as a logger, and her mother was a homemaker. Gallagher went to Washington University in St. Louis, where she studied under poet Theodore Roethke the semester before he died. Gallagher worked three jobs to fund her college education, a sacrifice that ultimately exhausted her, so that she dropped out before earning a degree. In 1963 she married Lawrence Gallagher, but they divorced in 1968. When he left for Vietnam, Gallagher realized that, despite being reared to marry and have children, she wanted to be an artist and needed solitude to do achieve her goal. By the time her husband returned, "something penetrated the dream of our lives. . . . [I]t had somehow vanished, the idea of having children." She wanted to write so much that she ended her marriage to do it. Subsequently, she married Michael Burkard in 1973; they were divorced in 1977. Later, she met writer Raymond Carver, with whom she lived with for eleven years. They married two months before his death, a death that inspired some of her best work.

Gallagher eventually earned both a bachelor's degree and a master's degree at the University of Washington. She entered the Iowa Writers' Workshop and was awarded the master of fine arts degree from the University of Iowa in 1974. To support her writing, Gallagher held academic positions at St. Lawrence University (1974-1975), Kirkland College in New York (1975-1977), the University of Montana (1977-1979), and the University of Arizona (1979-1980). From 1980 to 1990, she was associate professor of English and coordinator of the creative writing program at Syracuse University. She also briefly taught at Willamette University in 1981. A new development in her poetry, one she did not feel she could communicate to her students, plus a need for more solitude for reading and writing impelled Gallagher to relinquish her tenure at Syracuse and live on savings until a three-year Lyndhurst grant enabled her to write *At the Owl Woman Saloon*. During 1996-1997, Gallagher was the Edward F. Arnold Visiting Professor of English at Whitman College, and in 1998 she was

Tess Gallagher (© Jim Heynen)

poet in residence at Bucknell University. She was honored as a distinguished alumna at the University of Washington.

ANALYSIS

Tess Gallagher's poetry is like a double- or even triple-exposed photograph: It contains layer after layer. Her poetry epitomizes the title of her early volume *Instructions to the Double* in that it expresses multiplicity of meaning. A major difference between *Instructions to the Double* and later work is that the persona of Tess Gallagher gradually fades from her later poems, absolving her of an early charge of self-absorption. Gallagher writes of relationships, love, grief, and memory in and of themselves, as well as specific memories. She writes of her Northwest childhood in a working-class family, her parents, lovers, and particularly her dead husband, writer Raymond Carver. Most of her relationship poems are set in the Northwest, with boats, forests, and birds mysteriously in concert.

Gallagher's strength comes from extracting spiritual lessons from ordinary items or events, as in her "View from an Empty Chair." In this way, she deals in Emersonian correspondences. However, she takes correspondences a step further by eventually including the dead in the correspondence between humanity and nature. In "Tableau Vivant" the dead reflect on those mourning them. Some poems simply blend the living and dead. "Inside the Known" contains a narrator who confuses the self with not only her shadow but also a corpse. "With Stars" blends childhood memory with stars with the dead. This combining of the living with the dead and nature informs many, if not most, of the elegiac poems in *Moon Crossing Bridge*. In her later work, Gallagher's romantic sensibility becomes mystical in its understanding and attempt to portray the ineffable.

INSTRUCTIONS TO THE DOUBLE

Instructions to the Double, Gallagher's first significant publication, established her as an original and contemporary voice, contemporary—and confessional—in that she writes of her familial relationships, societal expectations of women, and a final acceptance of herself. The originality of her collection lies in its skillful use of doubles—a body's impression on a burnt mattress, reflections of people in eyes, glass, and water—all of which suggested a hidden, static quality. This quality becomes progressively ghostly as the characters she writes about seem still present, such as "the ballerina closing the halo/ of her partner's arms" in "Zero," the photographs in "Time Lapse with Tulips," or memories of those dead. "Even now," the poet of "Coming Home" says, "he won't stay out of what I have/ to say to you."

These resonances are made even more poignant by the metaphorical "doubling." The ballerina's partner's arms are both a halo and a zero, the red tulips in a photograph are also tulips in a Mason jar, a widow's expression is like that of a worried wife's gaze toward the sea, anticipating her husband's return. Then the doubles themselves double, creating associations and memories which spin into infinity, as water creates wakes and snails leave silver trails.

UNDER STARS

Gallagher's next volume, *Under Stars*, continues a passionate lyricism but is less personal and more social. The first section contains poems about joy and pain in Ireland. In this sense, they are poems of place. "Disappearances in the Guarded Sector" evokes the political turmoil in Belfast. "The Ballad of Ballymote" captures the wry sensibility and speech rhythms of the Irish. Gallagher makes the connection with the Irish so real and intimate that the second section, containing poems about family and lovers, flows naturally from the first section. This connection is expressed in the last lines of the title poem, "Under Stars," a double tribute to a lover and to universal kinship:

> Again I walk into the wet grass
> toward the starry voices. Again, I
> am the found one, intimate, returned
> by all I touch on the way.

"The Same Kiss After Many Years" deviates in subject matter in that for most of the poem, parents comment on their grown children's last visit but end with a surprising "Kiss me/ let's forget them," a happy tribute to older lovers.

WILLINGLY

Critics consider *Willingly* to contain some of Gallagher's best and worst work. Her better poems in this volume are not about herself but are nonetheless filtered through her consciousness, such as "Conversation with a Fireman from Brooklyn" and "Black Silk." In both poems another person is featured, but the "I" reflects on the others' behavior. "Each Bird Walking" details a man's emotions washing his dying mother—his embarrassment, his recognition of the role reversal and mortality—so compellingly that the "I" cannot stand to hear more and echoes the mother's phrase, "That's good, that's enough." A series about the life, dying, and death of Gallagher's father movingly depicts life's fragility. In "3 A.M. Kitchen: My Father Talking," she captures so well the language and resignation of a worn-out laborer, that the skill demonstrated in the poem illustrates the father's impact on the author. Some poems in *Willingly* have been called "unrealized" ("Not There") and, conversely, "slack" ("I Save Your Coat, But You Lose It Later"). The poems in *Willingly* signify a change in Gallagher's development in that most of them are narratives, with beginnings, middles, and ends, prefiguring the short stories she was to write later.

AMPLITUDE

Amplitude consists of selected poems from Gallagher's previous volumes, amplified by twenty-six new, unclassified poems. One finds that the best of her "old," earliest poems mark a private, somewhat self-absorbed voice. The book then follows her artistic and personal maturation as she moves from issues of self-identity and sexuality into attempts to fuse the individual with the communal. This attempt is particularly evident in a few of the new poems, where she again attempts public poetry by setting them in San Salvador. "That Kind of Thing" contrasts the irony of a luxury hotel and the indifference of a foreign aid official with the desperately poor. "In Maceio" is gently self-deprecating as Gallagher relates the story of a woman who kept thrusting into her arms flowers that had stood on a podium and that Gallagher intended to throw out.

The strongest new poems deal with the loss of those whom Gallagher loved and the resulting grief. "Small Garden Near a Field" addresses her dead brother and moves through their shared memories to the present, when she decides to drive by the house they lived in, though it and the neighborhood have deteriorated so as to "push back/ the goodness of the past so it doesn't cry out. . . ." "The Hands of the Blind Man" is equally powerful as it catalogs small, simple pleasures until the stunning last two lines, "yet never did anyone in the dark/ leave hands on me as you." In these new poems of love, loss, and grief, Gallagher is at her best. The San Salvador poems seem limp and could be rewritten as prose.

MOON CROSSING BRIDGE

Considered Gallagher's best work, *Moon Crossing Bridge* focuses her themes of love, loss, and the connection between the living and dead into one elegiac attempt to grieve Raymond Carver's death. In *Moon Crossing Bridge*, Gallagher also tries to capture the ineffable, beating her head against that barrier that prevents the living from knowing what happens to the dead. She does this using surrealism and a compression of syntax and image that result in a brilliant, pinpointed desperation.

An example of this scintillation is "Valentine Delivered by a Raven." In it, a leftover holly berry becomes a valentine, a raven the dead's keeper and messenger. In the last lines, the speaker dissolves into fog as the raven "flaps away on my love's errand," an image suggesting the yearning to dissolve and join the departed. This need to join her beloved results sometimes in a certain confusion over whether she is touching the living husband or his corpse ("Un Extrano"). However, the desire to join him recurs skillfully in her blending of Eastern and Western cultures (in "Moon Crossing Bridge"), past and present (in "Embers"), and her insistence on both, instead of an either/or choice ("Yes"). All express Gallagher's need for union and her attempt to scale divisions. The tortured focus of *Moon Crossing Bridge* expresses grief chronicled by the paradox of language trying to reach beyond the limits of both itself and life and somehow succeeding.

MY BLACK HORSE

This book contains twenty-three new poems as well as selections from Gallagher's previous works. These address her themes of grief and family but are infused with maturity, particularly in "Don't Wipe Your Madness Off Me," a poem that compassionately deals with balancing tensions between a sibling and his aging mother. "Laughter and Stars" is a stunning tribute to her husband's last night, coupled with regret at not realizing the moment more fully. The poems in this volume are notable for delineating Gallagher's artistic maturity.

OTHER MAJOR WORKS

SHORT FICTION: *The Lover of Horses and Other Stories*, 1986; *At the Owl Woman Saloon*, 1997.

SCREENPLAY: *The Night Belongs to the Police*, 1982; *Dostoevsky: A Screenplay*, 1985 (with Raymond Carver).

TELEPLAY: *The Wheel*, 1970.

NONFICTION: *A Concert of Tenses: Essays on Poetry*, 1986; *Soul Barnacles: Ten More Years with Ray*, 2000.

BIBLIOGRAPHY

Harris, Peter. "Poetry Chronicle. An Extravagant Three: New Poetry by Mitchell, Hoagland, and Gallagher." *Virginia Quarterly Review* 71, no. 4 (1995): 656. This review of *Moon Crossing Bridge* pronounces the book as "great souled" and "reckless," Gallagher's "greatest achievement" to date. Harris praises the poet's willingness to open herself and plunge into the nuances of grief. The poems' associations of the present with memories compress past, present, and future until, like one of the poems in the collection, Gallagher is "never alone," never without the presence of her late husband. This compression goes so far as to eroticize death, fusing life and death into "a shadow soaked in love." Gallagher's 1984 essay, "The Poem as a Reservoir for Grief," foretells *Moon Crossing Bridge* in that its grief poems are "a kind of live-in church."

McFarland, Ron. *Tess Gallagher*. Boise, Idaho: Boise University Press, 1995. This fifty-page volume contains a succinct summary of Gallagher's life and canon. It is particularly helpful in creating a standing for measuring the worth of a contemporary poet in mid-career. The conclusion is reflective and surprising in that it exposes a case of plagiarism in recent Gallagher scholarship. This short book is an effective and honest reference for an overview of Gallagher's work.

Monaghan, Peter. "Tess Gallagher Shares Her Passions for Poetry, the Precision of Language, and the Prose of Raymond Carver." *The Chronicle of Higher Education* 43, no. 40 (June 13, 1997): B8-B9. Gallagher discusses writing poetry and teaching the fiction of her late husband, Carver.

Sterne, Melvin. "Rough Road to Writing Fame for UW Alumna Tess Gallagher" *The Daily University of Washington*, March, 2000. An article preceding Gallagher's 2000 speaking engagement, this article stresses the "dark years" of her early life, her fame, and her famous relationship with Raymond Carver. It also emphasizes the contemporary years, in which "the link is ongoing" with Carver, as she lives in Port Angeles, where she writes and cares for her aging mother.

Mary Hanford Bruce

BRENDAN GALVIN

Born: Everett, Massachusetts; October 20, 1938

PRINCIPAL POETRY

The Narrow Land, 1971
The Salt Farm, 1972
No Time for Good Reasons, 1974
The Minutes No One Owns, 1977
Atlantic Flyway, 1980
Winter Oysters, 1983
Seals in the Inner Harbor, 1986
Wampanoag Traveler, 1989
Great Blue: New and Selected Poems, 1990
Early Returns: Poems from 1963 to 1983, 1992
Saints in Their Ox-Hide Boat: A Poem, 1992
Sky and Island Light: Poems, 1996
Hotel Malabar: A Narrative Poem, 1998
The Strength of a Named Thing: Poems, 1999

OTHER LITERARY FORMS

Brendan Galvin has written critical articles on Theodore Roethke, a number of reviews, and the controversial essay "The Mumbling of Young Werther: Angst by Blueprint in Contemporary Poetry" (published in *Ploughshares* in 1978). He has also published several short stories. His translation of *Women of Trachis* by Sophocles appeared in 1998.

ACHIEVEMENTS

In Brendan Galvin's work, a hard-won accuracy of statement and description stands in place of fashionable "poetic" ambiguities. His writing makes that of most other poets seem sloppy and vague. Galvin wrestles a clarity from language that makes attempts to paraphrase his lines not only futile but also ridiculous. The experience of his poetry is *in* the language; the experience *is* the language. Fresh diction and imagery are his hallmark, as are highly imaginative yet precisely appropriate figures of speech.

Galvin has refined his gift for language in many ways. Denotative accuracy and connotative subtlety are reinforced by his finely tuned sense of rhythm and sound. His lines break cleanly, splitting where meaning divides or where hesitation is a necessary part of the reader's experience. Almost every feature of Galvin's craft is functional. In his disciplined poems, "free verse" is a solved riddle. Galvin has known what to do with this freedom; there is little chance of mistaking his work for prose broken up into lines.

Galvin seems to have a special territory that he has made his own and in which he has no rival among his contemporaries. His ability to bring his gifts to bear upon rendering a close look at a particular object, especially a natural object (or process), is unparalleled in his time. He has fashioned a distinct poetic idiom, alternately tart and tender, for this task of giving his readers a new chance to see the natural world and to feel themselves in it.

Galvin has given such an alert and sensitive account of the region he knows best—the coastal Northeast and particularly Cape Cod—that it has become truly known and almost mythically real. The animals of the shore and sea, the birds above, the climate and landscape, the cultural temperature of the small New England town—these are Galvin's province, and his song is the perfect translation of its wide range of sensations into language. To his lyric achievements he has added three book-length poems that assure his place as a major storyteller in verse. Galvin's achievement has been recognized by the Charity Randall Citation from the International Poetry Forum, the first O. B. Hardison Poetry Prize from the Folger Shakespeare Library (1991), and National Endowment for the Arts and Guggenheim Fellowships.

BIOGRAPHY

Brendan James Galvin was born in the Boston suburb of Everett, Massachusetts, and has maintained a strong identification with the history and flavor of New England. He received a B.S. degree in natural science from Boston College in 1960; one finds evidence of the trained eye of the informed naturalist everywhere in his work. Shifting to English studies in graduate school, Galvin earned an M.A. from Northeastern University in 1964, where he also began his teaching career.

In 1965, Galvin enrolled in a course of study at the University of Massachusetts that would lead to an M.F.A. in creative writing in 1967 and a Ph.D. in 1970. Although he had dabbled in poetry since the late 1950's, it was only after 1964 that Galvin charged himself with the serious pursuit of poetic excellence. The early results were impressive; he had two poems published in the *Atlantic Monthly* in 1965. Still, Galvin's published output was small until 1970, after which a creative explosion seems to have occurred.

The late 1960's were busy years, busy in ways that allowed for poetry to be germinated if not harvested in publication. In 1968 Galvin married Ellen Baer, and the couple has raised two children. A one-year position at Slippery Rock State College in Pennsylvania (1968-1969) would inevitably cause some temporary dislocation of sensibility for a man so attuned to the Massachusetts coast. With the 1969-1970 academic year, Galvin began his long association with Central Connecticut State College. The chance for settled employment and the completion of his doctoral work seems to have freed Galvin's energies. His dissertation, which involved a close reading of Theodore Roethke's poems through the lens of Kenneth Burke, was also a stimulus to Galvin's direction as a poet. Of the poets of his generation, Galvin is the heir apparent to Roethke as a precise and loving recorder of the natural world. Much of what Galvin records is the Cape Cod area, where his Irish immigrant grandfather settled, known to Galvin from childhood. It is there that he would spend some part of each year.

Galvin's first two collections were chapbooks published in limited editions. These slim volumes of the early 1970's introduced some of his recurring motifs: the country-city dichotomy, the close observation of nature, the pain of history, the ethos of the New England town or neighborhood, the entrance into fantasy or dream. Galvin's first full-length collection, *No Time for Good Reasons*, recapitulated and extended these interests and revealed Galvin to be a most inventive fashioner of imagery and figures of speech. The same year that this gathering of ten years' work was published, Galvin won a fellowship from the National Endowment for the Arts. By now a tenured professor at Central Connecticut, Galvin had made for himself a secure position as a poet-teacher-critic but only the beginning of a national reputation.

In 1975-1976, Galvin took over William Meredith's courses at Connecticut College in New London as a visiting professor. By the next year, his second major collection, *The Minutes No One Owns*, was receiving acclaim. In it, Galvin's voice and vision grew more distinctly his own, and his range of subjects grew broader.

Galvin hit full stride and wider recognition with his next two collections: *Atlantic Flyway* and *Winter Oysters* both received Pulitzer Prize nominations, the latter making the short list. *Seals in the Inner Harbor*, easily as strong a collection as the Pulitzer nominees, rounded out a miraculous period of steady achievement and continued Galvin's tendency toward a greater openness, a fuller release of personality, begun in the preceding book.

Wampanoag Traveler represents a change of pace. This is Galvin's first book-length poem, a sustained narrative-meditation in the form of fourteen letters by an imaginary eighteenth century naturalist, Loranzo Newcomb.

In the consolidating gesture of *Great Blue: New and Selected Poems* (1990), the map of Galvin's dedicated journey of more than twenty-five years revealed the highest promontory of achievement. Yet, many of Galvin's critics (Dave Smith, George Garrett, and Thomas Reiter are among the exceptions) have not known how to deal with this poet for whom words really matter and for whom nature is not merely an abstract idea or a stirring in the blood. In the volumes that followed through the 1990's, Galvin's art climbed from strength to strength. After retiring from his post at Central Connecticut State University, Galvin continued his prolific output, shuttling between visiting writer posts around the country and his home in Truro, Massachusetts.

ANALYSIS

Brendan Galvin's work has been called passionless. The charge is groundless but understandable. The human figure, the domestic drama, does not loom in the forefront of Galvin's work. That is not to say that his books are not peopled, but certainly he has given less attention to the themes of love, sex, family, and self than is customary. Galvin often treats nature, the town and city, and humankind in the aggregate. Moreover, much of his work on animals—birds in particular—seems to be at man's expense: Direct or implicit contrasts between human life and animal life are made to man's disadvantage—"no bird violates another/ with the inflections of small print."

For Galvin, man is only one center of interest in the universe he moves through, and not necessarily the most important one. Through Galvin's work, one comes to learn that there is a passion in beholding the rest of creation, that his acts of attention—whether the subject be a heron, a thunderstorm, or "The First Night of Fall"—are more than intellectual exercises. There is a passionate humility and what might be called a passionate objectivity. There is a passionate giving of the full resources of his art to something other than himself. There is a passion felt, by the alert reader, seeping through the pressure that would control it. There is a passion in the acts of language that so rarely stoop to the mere naming of passions. There is a passion that leads the thing observed and the observer to become intertwined: "A small event at a time,/ sleep comes to the weedy pond/ at the top of your mind." There is drama enough, too, in the small events that Galvin records so well. Small or large, the events to which he is attentive diminish, with sanity, the human ego: "I know the wind and more/ is beating down the centuries,/ and while I sit the tides go on/ rearranging the earth."

In three of Galvin's earlier books, there is a recurring character named Bear who is, one assumes, the more earthbound side of the poet's nature. Galvin's Bear is another version of the metaphor found in Delmore Schwartz's "The Heavy Bear Who Goes with Me," for while Schwartz seems only embarrassed and victimized by the body's clumsy pursuit of its appetites, Galvin has a friendly feeling toward the pull of the instinctual. He records, sympathetically, Bear's difficulties with artists, intellectuals, high-toned women, and all of the mind's

subtleties. Bear seems to have the last word; something about him is more anchored in this world than in the world of abstraction, even while this world remains a mystery. Bear's senses do not fail him, but *mind* gets in the way.

"THE ENVY OF INSTINCT"

In a poem called "The Envy of Instinct" (from *The Minutes No One Owns*), Galvin develops the theme of man's separation from the rest of nature, a theme that he never leaves for long. The poem begins with the speaker asking, "Earth, air, or water,/ which are we natural to?" The problem is that there is no easy answer. Is a steel and glass skyscraper man's natural habitat? The speaker is out running in his paltry human way, "one foot/ before another." It is as if this human running were not the real thing or were an activity that the human animal was not—or was no longer—fit for. The runner knows that before he reached this place "a deer clicked off/ the distance like a caliper." Such movement, he realizes, is true running.

Under the strain of this now unnatural exercise, the runner seems to break down into his more primitive animal parts:

> My heart beats red
> as the pouch
> of a horny frigate bird.
> My lungs are sponges
> working for more air.

The speaker wonders which of the many distinctions between man and the lower orders is the crucial one: speech, perhaps, or the complexity of his nervous system. He is amazed at the freedom that the absence of reason allows. A bird he sees skimming along the shore "could go without reason/ to Venezuela tomorrow." By contrast, the complexity of human life is felt to be a series of unsatisfactory compromises, a collection of disparate and trivial indulgences of the mind.

The poem concludes with an earnest yet comic longing for "the energy ants save the world with." Galvin would store it up until he had enough of it to redirect natural history so that man became a properly subordinate phase, not a thing unto himself: "A decimal at a time, to carry off/ whole silos, nudging the origin/ of species my way."

"RUNNING"

In another poem of the same volume, "Running," the speaker is reduced by exhaustion to the status of a mere physical presence. The keen celebrant of nature, observing while he runs, seems to be casting off his human difference and becoming suffused with the essential physicality of existence. One might think of Eugene O'Neill's *The Emperor Jones* (1921) turned into a true comedy. Galvin's skill at capturing this process is impressive: "By mile four/ I'm only the framework a breeze passes through." At the end of the run, there is a chant of victory in the blood, a half-silly song of belonging: ". . . my pulse begins its/ shorebird glossolalia. It says/ dowitcher coot yellow-legs/ brant bufflehead knot." The catalog of birds' names is a self-mocking description of the runner's delirium as well as that echo in the blood that joins him, for the moment, to his fellow creatures.

"THE WINTER RUNNER"

An earlier poem, "The Winter Runner" (*No Time for Good Reasons*), gives the man-in-nature interest a mythic dimension. This poem is told in the third person, depicting the runner (an American Indian, perhaps, or a hunter) as a small figure crossing a richly evocative terrain that changes constantly. There is no war between the mind and the body here, but rather a vital harmony. Galvin finds just the right words to bring mind and object together: "the low hills afterthoughts/ between the sky and sea." Looking over the runner's shoulder, the reader shares direct sensory experience: "the orange, thumbnail tip of sun/ and last fruits of day: eelgrass softening/ from tan to plum." This poem is distanced in a bygone golden age; even though the imagination can recreate it, such a state is an illusive goal for contemporary man. That is Galvin's complaint.

"PITCH PINES"

"Pitch Pines" (*Atlantic Flyway*) illustrates Galvin's naturalist's eye and conservationist impulse in both theme and language. The poem begins by sketching the unpromising appearance of trees that are "blown one sided/ by winds salted out of the northeast." The unusual use of "salted" in this passage is characteristic of Galvin's spare diction, gaining richness through compression and suggestion. These pines are derelicts of trees, with "limbs flaking and dying/ to ribs, to antlers and spidery twigs,/ scaly plates slipping off the trunks."

The sharp picture is accompanied by a sharpness of sounds; plosive consonants–*b, k, p, g, t,* and *d*—allowing the reader to hear the branches breaking and striking the ground.

Nothing about the pitch pines is hopeful. They are "blamed for a history of cellar holes" and they "thin out by dropping sour needles/ on acid soil." Although the sound patterns are less aggressive here, one should note the high density of repeated sounds in these phrases: in "history of cellar holes" the bonding on *h, s, r,* and *l* sounds is accompanied by a pleasant modulation of vowels; in "dropping sour needles/ on acid soil" the *d, r, s,* and *l* links are carried along Galvin's movement up and down the vowel scale. Galvin's skillful manipulation of sounds and rhythms continues as he describes the result of the pines' pollination: "a shower/ that curdles water to a golden scum."

At this point, the poem's perspective becomes historical. John Brereton, the reader is told, had known a Cape Cod "timbered to its shores/ with hardwoods." The demand for buildings and ships, however, began the process of denuding the cape. The swamp cedars were "split to shakes" or used for foundations "while sheep cropped/ elm and cherry sprouts/ and plows broke the cleancut fields." Birch, maple, elm, beech, and oak were all put to use as firewood for various enterprises, notably the iron and glass industries, "till the desert floundered/ out of the backlands and knocked/ on the rear door of towns." Only the ugly, useless pitch pines were left, unlikely survivors of the "brushfire" of progress.

"Pitch Pines" raises the question of the price of progress, but it does so in a way that avoids the usual harangue associated with such subjects. The facts, as Galvin selects and presents them, are left to speak for themselves, and they speak with an eloquence born of restraint. The tenacious pitch pines are a stunted note of hope; they remind readers that whatever they see around them in nature is *what is left* after the toll of man's actions has been taken. (One might compare this poem to Galvin's earlier "Ward's Grove," in which the rhetoric is more heated; the poem includes the splendid simile of "the oil derrick offshore like Triton's middle finger.")

In "Pitch Pines," Galvin alludes to John Brereton (or Brierton) and Bartholomew Gosnold, two Englishmen who followed Giovanni Verrazano's path across the Atlantic and in May, 1602, founded a short-lived colony on an island off Cape Cod. Brereton's *True Relation of the Discovery of the North Part of Virginia* is the record of that voyage. In imagining Brereton's view "from Bartholomew Gosnold's deck," Galvin reveals not only his growing interest in regional history but also his love of names. An opportunity to get the sounds of "Bartholomew Gosnold" into a poem is not to be missed. This historical interest is felt elsewhere in *Atlantic Flyway:* in "Homage to Henry Beston," in two poems about old maps, and, in terms of family, in the Irish American focus of "1847" and "Himself."

"DEFENDING THE PROVINCES"

Atlantic Flyway contains some of Galvin's most imaginative poems of small-town life. "Shoveling Out" and "Hometown" evoke a bracing nostalgia for the flavor of growing up in these comfortable places where a mixture of boredom and dread gives life a special balance: "we lived with that town/ like a man lives with a trick heart" ("Hometown"). Most of these poems of the small town, like much of Galvin's achievement, use the device of the catalog or inventory. Item by item, his strategic accumulation of telling details reaches out for a total vision: The parts are important, but the whole is more than their sum.

Galvin's vision of the small town is particularly clear in "Defending the Provinces." This poem begins with a contrast between the scale of city and town. The paralysis induced by the city's infinite range of choices is set against the security of the small town's confined and simpler patterns. Galvin presents the image of a man spinning around on a city street corner with a "shopping bag in each fist." His dizzying, anonymous dance (perhaps the bags are hiding liquor bottles) takes him "through all the compass points/ until he falls." The speaker may fall on the Main Street of his town, but this street only allows the choice of north or south, and the townspeople "know my name/ and drive me home."

Galvin then identifies the small-town ethos with the sixteenth century art of Pieter Brueghel (the elder), noted for his country landscapes and his renderings of peasant life and folk wisdom. The city's representative becomes Jackson Pollock, the nonrepresentational twentieth century artist noted for his frenzied canvases produced by dripping the paint and allowing for random effects.

Clearly enough, Galvin is no partisan of cities. As cultural meccas, he finds them sterile. As places for human interaction, he finds them lacking in human scale and warmth. If the values of a small town in New England are provincial, a defense of the provinces is one that he is willing to undertake. Still, he admits that the logic of the case is limited. There are certain, seemingly trivial, things that people simply "have to know" in order to appreciate the town—and if they know them, they do not need the argument. A brief catalog of the things one has to know includes: "You have to know/ what a Chrysler marine engine/ is doing in the Widow Wood's front yard." Knowing such things, one belongs; and belonging, after all, is what matters.

The poem goes on to celebrate, in an affectionately humorous vein, the provincial outlook itself. Readers hear how the townsfolk tout the good weather and excuse the bad, or even glorify it: "Next day, since it makes a good story, we will say/ we saw minnows swimming in roadside puddles." Galvin gives his readers a special brand of boosterism, talking about "skies the color of Boy Scout Troops" in a way the Chamber of Commerce people would if only they could. He asks readers to join him in writing the president, requesting the evacuation of "the Big Apple" so that it can be planted with kudzu. Then all Americans, including the lost city-dwellers, can make a return to the small town. Here, cleansed and ready to experience provincial epiphanies, they will be able to see and relate how "one star/ over the bay seemed to move closer."

NO TIME FOR GOOD REASONS AND THE MINUTES NO ONE OWNS

Galvin's poetry of place is not only a poetry of landscape and nature description; it is also a poetry of community. In poems such as "Rookie's Place" and "Stealing the Christmas Greens" (*No Time for Good Reasons*), Galvin presents uncannily accurate slices of small-town life. The reader who attends to this group of poems—"The Paper Route" and "Assembling a Street" are others—will find a large cast of small-town characters and a judicious selection of scenes and events presented with loving patience. In many of these poems, Galvin asserts or suggests the special kind of shared knowledge that defines a community and that outsiders can only misunderstand or patronize.

From *The Minutes No One Owns*, "Jumping the Grave-Sized Hole" not only presents Galvin's characteristic social archaeology of the New England town but also presents the problem of the outsider—summer people, progress, and suburbanization—that threatens the bonds of time-won intimacies and thus the essence of the town. While Galvin's impulse is to value and protect that sense of community, he realizes that the other side of closeness is closed-ness, the easy falling into small-mindedness and prejudice. "Them" deals with those others, the minorities who remain strangers even within the town itself.

Winter Oysters and
Seals in the Inner Harbor

Poems such as "August," "General Confession of the Ex-King of Hamburg," and "Mrs. McCandless" (all from *Winter Oysters*) reveal Galvin's ability to etch the contrasting values and styles of native and summer people, intrusions of progress, and the carefully balanced sense of community. "Rural Mailboxes" (from *Seals in the Inner Harbor*) expresses once again Galvin's understanding of the mixed private and public identities of small-town New England life as he imagines the "tinny speech" which spreads gossip among the isolated icons of privacy.

Each of these poems combines the wit, bite, and tenderness that so often mate in Galvin's work, although the proportions change from poem to poem. Almost every line suggests more than it literally says, but there is never a loss of clarity. The closed range of experience in Galvin's small towns allows people some sense of mastery over their condition that is lacking in city life. They can develop reliable habits that will serve them almost as well as instinct serves the creatures of the sky and sea that Galvin has studied so carefully. The journey of the mind in a poem like "The Old Trip by Dream Train" (*Atlantic Flyway*) is reminiscent of Galvin's treatment of the migratory patterns and the homing instincts of birds, a subject that occupies his attention in many poems. The seeming freedom of birds' flight, the majestic range, however, is another matter. In "The Migrants" and "The Birds," Galvin provides a humbling perspective too often masked by our homocentric habits of mind. In "Transmigration" (*Winter Oysters*), one of Galvin's most ambitious poems, that dream of birds' flight is imaginatively realized.

Galvin's largely successful search for clarity is a difficult enterprise. The songs he sings and the songs he echoes are songs that everyone needs to relearn. In part, the resourceful poet works like the title creature in "The Mockingbird" (*Winter Oysters*), who knows that when "the voices fill you,/ you must say nothing wrong,/ but follow them back/ through the day, going phrase/ by phrase over hills. . . ." Over the years and through his many poems and collections, Galvin has been slowly putting together a viable myth: The myth of a vigorous, inspiring, forgiving world in which we may be permitted to thrive if we behave honorably and respectfully. Yet, in Galvin's work, this myth does not seem like a pagan dream, an impossible return to a version of man in a nature that never was. Galvin leads the reader to feel fully engaged and ready to carry that energy of engagement out of the poems and back to the world, having fitted the lens of Galvin's vision to his eye.

Great Blue and Saints in Their Ox-Hide
Boat

The general direction of Galvin's career may be reflected in the general pattern of *Great Blue: New and Selected Poems*. The progress of the poems here is from sky to sea to land, and from man as a social, historical, and economic creature to explorations of the individual psyche. A pivotal poem in this progress is the title poem of *Seals in the Inner Harbor*, a poem in which a comprehensive vision of the connectedness of things is economically, powerfully, and yet gently and humorously, evoked. There is another progression as well: a progress of shifting genre emphasis from lyric to meditative-narrative to dramatic.

In fact, Galvin's next effort after *Great Blue* is a book-length poem (his second), at once narrative and dramatic. *Saints in Their Ox-Hide Boat* deepens Galvin's penetration into his Irish roots as he gives voice to the exploits of his sixth-century namesake, Brendan the Navigator. Informed by history but in no way shackled by it, Galvin creates the characters of Saint Brendan and his monks, voicing the physical hardships of their journey, imagining their meditations on man's relationship to God, conjuring the hallucinations fostered by their long and hazardous voyage. Alternately pious and playful, this story in verse once again shows Galvin's mastery of a vigorous and rigorous poetic diction that is never merely or falsely poetic.

HOTEL MALABAR AND SKY AND ISLAND LIGHT

Just as ambitious, though different in almost every other way, is *Hotel Malabar*. Conveyed through several first-person narrators, this novel in verse mixes espionage and contemporary history in a dark vision of late twentieth century America. Galvin examines the corruption and deceit that underpin imperialist intentions.

Sky and Island Light brings readers once again the Galvin who is a master at evocation of place. Ireland, the Outer Hebrides, the Orkneys, the Shetland Islands, and familiar Cape Cod are the main locales that his artistry first inhabits, then reveals. Perhaps as a consequence of his own aging, many of these poems deal with time's passage and with loss. Yet the pulse of life and the joy of beholding is everywhere, as is the characteristic firmness of diction and felt form.

THE STRENGTH OF A NAMED THING

In *The Strength of a Named Thing*, Galvin mostly stays at home, doing what he does best. The title of this collection suggests it all: Named things are Galvin's meat, and the names themselves are his seasoning. The essential human project of naming things that lies behind the earliest speech is the miracle that poets endlessly celebrate. Crows, bats, slugs, scallops, fish, birds of all sorts, shifts in light, shades of weather, increments of seasons, vegetation, geological features, these are the subjects or supporting details of Galvin's most distinctive poems. Man is a part of all this—but only a part. Galvin's poetry helps one to know this, to feel it to be true. One learns, as the subjects of "Young Owls" do, "how nothing in this world/ gets out of its life alive." Readers are led to bless this gift of life that they share: "You could be/ the least tern who plucks/ the edge of the sea's potlatch,/ or the egret in its pool/ like your spirit's sudden cry at sloughed confusion" ("The Birds"). In the clear beholding that Galvin's art provides, an interchange takes place and our crippling separateness vanishes.

OTHER MAJOR WORKS

TRANSLATION: *Women of Trachis*, (1998, of Sophocles).

BIBLIOGRAPHY

Callahan, Mary. "Singing What's Out There." *Boston College Magazine* 47 (Winter, 1988): 37-41. This personality profile offers material on Galvin's schooling, his work habits, and his inspirations and prejudices. Galvin admits proudly to consulting reference books to indulge his passion for accuracy. He believes in a poet's need for obsessions. Galvin's own "How I Wrote It" follows, with commentaries on the creative process behind four of his poems.

Christina, Martha, ed. *Outer Life: The Poetry of Brendan Galvin*. Bristol, R.I.: Ampersand Press, 1991. This first collection of essays on Galvin's work is remarkable for the high standard of critical prose and critical insight. Contributors include Thomas Reiter (on *Wampanoag Traveler*), Peter Makuck, and Neal Bowers. The latter's "Outside In: Brendan Galvin's Poetry" views Galvin's work as a precursor to the "new formalism" in its attempt to avoid "an absurd self-involvement." Bowers uses New England countryman Robert Frost as a foil to highlight Galvin's temperament and method.

Garrett, George. "This Business of Getting the World Right: The Poetry of Brendan Galvin." *Three Rivers Poetry Journal* 19-20 (1982): 7-18. This engaging appreciation presents important biographical material and includes Galvin's own comments elicited by interview. Garrett stresses Galvin's integrity and helps readers to find the poet in the work. He considers the ways in which "the discipline, method, and the language of the sciences" combine in Galvin's art.

Kitchen, Judith. "Simplicities." *Georgia Review* 52, no. 2 (Summer, 1998): 341-361. Part of this omnibus review attends to Galvin's *Sky and Island Light*, making an excellent case for Galvin's importance as a writer who can set intensely observed natural detail in the context of human history so that one informs the other. A fine appreciation not only of this book's virtues but also of Galvin's work as a whole.

Makuck, Peter. "Galvin's Outer Reaches." *Texas Review* 8 (Fall/Winter, 1987): 38-58. This comprehensive overview pays special attention to Galvin's humor, his love of the odd word, and his attachment to marginalized people (victims, immigrants). Makuck explores the design and coherence of several collections, tracing how the poet has set increasingly greater risks for himself. These include the movement toward formal sequences and long, even book-length, poems, as well as the imaginative re-creation of the past.

Paradis, Philip. "A Conversation with Brendan Galvin." *Tar River Poetry* 27 (Fall, 1987): 1-12. This interview begins with comments on the proper (and improper) relationship between poet and critic, then goes on to explore the importance of the image to the genesis and texture of Galvin's poems. Paradis has Galvin describe his writing habits, his attitude regarding poetic diction, and the influence of other poets on his own development. The interview reveals Galvin's commitment to a writing life unencumbered by theory, fashion, or coterie.

Smith, R. T. "The Light Through the Trees." In *Spreading the Word: Editors on Poetry*, edited by Stephen Corey and Warren Slesinger. Columbia, S.C.: Bench Press, 2001. Smith writes about the features of a particular poem, "May Day," and what led him to choose it for an issue of *Shenandoah*. Smith attends to the poem's imagery, its quality of observation, its "rich ambivalence," and its formal virtuosity. A fine appreciation of a representative Galvin poem.

Philip K. Jason,
updated by Jason

FEDERICO GARCÍA LORCA

Born: Fuentevaqueros, Spain; June 5, 1898
Died: Víznar, Spain; August 19, 1936

PRINCIPAL POETRY

Libro de poemas, 1921
Canciones, 1921-1924, 1927 (*Songs*, 1976)
Romancero gitano, 1924-1927, 1928 (*The Gypsy Ballads of García Lorca*, 1951, 1953)
Poema del cante jondo, 1931 (*Poem of the Gypsy Seguidilla*, 1967)
Llanto por Ignacio Sánchez Mejías, 1935 (*Lament for the Death of a Bullfighter*, 1937, 1939)
Primeras canciones, 1936

Poeta en Nueva York, 1940 (*Poet in New York*, 1940, 1955)
Diván del Tamarit, 1940 (*The Divan at the Tamarit*, 1944)

OTHER LITERARY FORMS

The publisher Aguilar of Madrid issued a one-volume edition of Federico García Lorca's works, compiled and annotated by Arturo del Hoyo, with a prologue by Jorge Guillén and an epilogue by Vicente Aleixandre. In addition to the poetry, it includes García Lorca's plays, of which the tragic rural trilogy *Bodas de sangre* (pr. 1933, pb. 1935; *Blood Wedding*, 1939), *Yerma* (pr. 1934; English translation, 1941), and *La casa de Bernarda Alba* (wr. 1936; pr., pb. 1945; *The House of Bernarda Alba*, 1947) are world famous and represent García Lorca's best achievement as a poet become director-playwright. In order to portray all the facets of García Lorca's artistic personality, the Aguilar edition also includes his first play, *El maleficio de la mariposa* (pr. 1920, pb. 1957; *The Butterfly's Evil Spell*, 1963); an example of his puppet plays, *Los títeres de Cachiporra: La tragicomedia de don Cristóbal y la señá Rosita* (wr. 1928, pr. 1937; *The Tragicomedy of Don Cristóbal and Doña Rosita*, 1955); selections from *Impresiones y paisajes* (1918; impressions and landscapes), García Lorca's first published prose works, in which his genius is already evident in the melancholic, impressionistic style used to describe his feelings and reactions to the Spanish landscape and Spanish life; several short prose pieces and dialogues; a number of lectures and speeches; a variety of representative letters to friends; texts of newspaper interviews; poems from the poet's book of suites; fifteen of his songs; and twenty-five of his drawings.

Although the Aguilar edition reflects a consummate artist, still missing from its pages are a number of other works: a five-act play, *El público* (fragment, wr. 1930, pb. 1976; *The Audience*, 1958), and the first part of a dramatic biblical trilogy titled "La destrucción de Sódoma" (wr. 1936; the destruction of Sodom), on which García Lorca was working at the time of his death. Lost are "Los sueños de mi prima Aurelia" (the dreams of my cousin Aurelia) and "La niña que riega la albahaca y el príncipe preguntón" (the girl who waters the sweet basil flower and the inquisitive prince), a puppet play presented in Granada on January 5, 1923. "El sacrificio de Ifigenia" (Iphigenia's sacrifice) and "La hermosa" (the beauty) are titles of two plays whose existence cannot be substantiated.

Reportedly, García Lorca also collected a group of poems titled "Sonetos del amor oscuro" (sonnets of dark love), the title suggesting to certain critics the poet's preference for intimate masculine relationships. Until the 1960's, most of the works evaluating García Lorca centered on the events of his life and death and were only interspersed with snatches of literary criticism. Since his death, thematic and stylistic studies by such noted scholars as Rafael Martínez Nadal, Gustavo Correa, Arturo Barea, Rupert C. Allen, and Richard L. Predmore have served to illuminate García Lorca's symbolic and metaphorical world.

ACHIEVEMENTS

The typically Spanish character of his plays and poetry, enhanced by rich and daring lyrical expression, have made Federico García Lorca one of the most universally recognized poets of the twentieth century. His tragic death in 1936 at the hands of the Falange, the Spanish Fascist Party, in the flower of his manhood and literary creativity, merely served to further his fame.

The first milestone of García Lorca's short but intense career was the publication of *The Gypsy Ballads of García Lorca*, which solidly established his reputation as a fine poet in the popular vein. His dark, brooding, foreboding ballads of Gypsy passion and death captured the imagination and hearts of Spaniards and foreigners, Andalusians and Galicians, illiterate farmers and college professors. Critics saw in García Lorca's poems the culmination of centuries of a rich and diverse Spanish lyric tradition. For example, Edwin Honig has noted that García Lorca's poetry took its inspiration from such diverse sources as the medieval Arabic-Andalusian art of amorous poetry; the early popular ballad; the Renaissance synthesis in Spain of classical traditions, as exemplified by the "conceptist" poetry of Luis de Góngora y Argote; and the *cante jondo*, or "deep song," of the Andalusian Gypsy.

Living in an era of vigorous cultural and literary activity, called by many Spain's second golden age, García Lorca clearly maintained his individuality. His innate

Federico García Lorca (AP/Wide World Photos)

charm and wit, his strong and passionate presence, his *duende*, or "soul," as a performer of Andalusian songs and ballads, and his captivating readings of his own poetry and plays drew the applause and friendship of equally talented writers and artists, such as Rafael Alberti, Pedro Salinas, Jorge Guillén, Vicente Aleixandre, Salvador Dalí, and Luis Buñuel.

The poet reached the peak of his popular success in the late 1920's. Both his *Songs* and *The Gypsy Ballads of García Lorca* were published to great critical acclaim. In the same period, he delivered two memorable lectures, the first at the *cante jondo* festival organized jointly with composer Manuel de Falla in Granada, and the second at the festival in honor of Góngora's tercentenary. His play *Mariana Pineda* (pr. 1927, pb. 1928; English translation, 1950) was produced in Barcelona, and the following year he founded and published the literary journal *Gallo*. Despite these achievements, however, García Lorca suffered a grave spiritual crisis, to which he alludes in his correspondence but never really clarifies. This crisis led him to reevaluate his artistic output and turn to new experiences and modes of expression.

The result of García Lorca's soul-searching can be seen in his later works, especially *Poet in New York* and *Lament for the Death of a Bullfighter*. In the former, García Lorca fully unleashes his imagination in arabesques of metaphor which on first reading appear incomprehensible. *Poet in New York* is a difficult and frequently obscure work that has been viewed as a direct contrast to his earlier poetry. Yet, as Predmore has so painstakingly demonstrated, these poems extend rather than depart from García Lorca's established preference for ambiguous and antithetical symbolism.

The two threads that run throughout García Lorca's work are the themes of love and death: They lend a poetic logic and stability to what may otherwise appear chaotic and indecipherable. A study of these themes in García Lorca's poetry and plays reveals a gradual evolution from tragic premonition and foreboding, through vital passion repressed and frustrated by outside forces, to bitter resignation and death. Throughout his life, García Lorca's constant companion and friend was death. The poet Antonio Machado described this intimacy with death in his lament for García Lorca:

> He was seen walking with Her, alone,
> unafraid of her scythe.
>
> . . . .
>
> Today as yesterday, gypsy, my Death,
> how good to be with you, alone
> in these winds of Granada, of my Granada.

García Lorca's gift of imagination, his genius for metaphor and volatile imagery, and his innate sense of the tragic human condition make him one of the outstanding poets of the twentieth century. With his execution in Granada in 1936 at the outbreak of the Spanish Civil War, the frustrated personas of his poetry and plays, who so often ended their lives in senseless tragedy, materialized in his own person. In García Lorca, life became art and art became life. Combining the experience of two cultures, he addressed in both, the Andalusian and the American man's primal needs and fears within his own interior world.

BIOGRAPHY

Federico García Lorca was born on June 5, 1898, in Fuentevaqueros, in the province of Granada. His father, Don Federico García Rodríguez, was a well-to-do landowner, a solid rural citizen of good reputation. After his first wife died, Don Federico married Doña Vicenta Lorca Romero, an admired schoolteacher and a musician. García Lorca was very fond of his mother and believed that he inherited his intelligence and artistic bent from her and his passionate nature from his father. It was in the countryside of Granada that García Lorca's poetic sensibility took root, nourished by the meadows, the fields, the wild animals, the livestock, and the people of that land. His formative years were centered in the village, where he attended Mass with his mother and absorbed and committed to memory the colorful talk, the folktales, and the folk songs of the *vega* (fertile lowland) which would later find a rebirth in the metaphorical language of his poetry and plays.

In 1909, his family moved to Granada, and García Lorca enrolled in the College of the Sacred Heart to prepare for the university. This was the second crucial stage in his artistic development: Granada's historical and literary associations further enriched his cultural inheritance from the *vega* and modified it by adding an intellectual element. García Lorca wanted to be a musician and composer, but his father wanted him to study law. In 1915, he matriculated at the University of Granada, but he never was able to adapt completely to the regimentation of university studies, failing three courses, one of them in literature. During the same period, he continued his serious study of piano and composition with Don Antonio Segura. García Lorca frequented the cafés of Granada and became popular for his wit. In 1916 and 1917, García Lorca traveled throughout Castile, Léon, and Galicia with one of his professors from the university, who also encouraged him to write his first book, *Impresiones y paisajes*. He also came into contact with important people in the arts, among them Manuel de Falla, who shared García Lorca's interest in traditional folk themes, and Fernando de los Ríos, an important leader in educational and social reforms, who persuaded García Lorca's father to send his son to the University of Madrid.

In 1919, García Lorca arrived in Madrid, where he was to spend the next ten years at the famous Residencia de Estudiantes, in the company of Rafael Alberti, Jorge Guillén, Pedro Salinas, Gerardo Diego, Dámaso Alonso, Luis Cernuda, and Vicente Aleixandre. There García Lorca published his first collection of poems, *Libro de poemas*, and became involved with the philosophical and literary currents then in vogue. In 1922, García Lorca returned to Granada to conduct with Manuel de Falla a "Festival of Cante Jondo."

The years from 1924 to 1928 were successful but troubled ones for García Lorca, marked by moments of elation followed by depression. During these years, García Lorca developed a close friendship with Salvador Dalí and spent several summers with the Dalí family at Cadaqués. He published his second book of poems, *Songs*, in 1927 and in that same year saw the premiere of *Mariana Pineda* in Barcelona and Madrid. In December of 1927, García Lorca participated in the famous Góngora tricentennial anniversary celebrations in Seville, where he delivered one of his most famous lectures, "The Poetic Image in Don Luis de Góngora." Gradually, García Lorca's fame spread, and his *The Gypsy Ballads of García Lorca* became the most widely read book of poems to appear in Spain since the publication of Gustavo Adolfo Bécquer's *Rimas* in 1871. During the period from May to December of 1928, García Lorca suffered an emotional crisis which prompted him to leave Spain to accompany Fernando de los Ríos to New York. After spending nine months in the United States, a stay that included a visit to Vermont, García Lorca returned to Spain by way of Cuba with renewed interest and energy for his work. The clearest product of this visit was *Poet in New York*, one of his greatest books of poems, published four years after his death.

Upon his return to Madrid in 1930, García Lorca turned his focus increasingly to the dramatic. In 1932, under the auspices of the Republic's Ministry of Education, García Lorca founded La Barraca, a university theater whose aim was to bring the best classical plays to the provinces. In the same period, he saw the successful staging of *Blood Wedding* and *El amor de don Perlimplín con Belisa en su jardín* (pr. 1933, pb. 1938; *The Love of Don Perlimplín for Belisa in His Garden*, 1941). His achievements in Spain were capped by another trip to the New World, this time to Argentina, where *Blood Wedding, Mariana Pineda,* and *La*

zapatera prodigiosa (pr. 1930, pb. 1938; *The Shoemaker's Prodigious Wife*, 1941) were staged and received with great enthusiasm. The years 1934 and 1935 saw the writing of the *Lament for the Death of a Bullfighter* and the premieres of at least four new plays. By 1936, García Lorca had decided to return to Granada for the celebration of his name day and also to bide his time until the political turmoil in Madrid abated. During his stay, the civil war broke out, and amid the fighting between the Nationalist and the Popular forces in Granada, García Lorca was detained and executed on August 19, 1936, in the outskirts of Víznar. His body was thrown into an unmarked grave.

ANALYSIS

In imagery that suggests an "equestrian leap" between two opposing worlds, Federico García Lorca embodies a dialectical vision of life, on the one hand filled with an all-consuming love for man and nature and, on the other, cognizant of the "black torso of the Pharaoh," the blackness symbolizing an omnipresent death unredeemed by the possibility of immortality. The tension between these two irreconcilable forces lends a tautness as well as a mystery to much of his poetry.

"ELEGÍA A DOÑA JUANA LA LOCA"

A recurring theme throughout García Lorca's work which is expressive of this animating tension is that of thwarted love, repressed by society or simply by human destiny and ending inevitably in death. This obsession with unfulfilled dreams and with death is evident in the poet's first collection. In a moving elegy to the Castilian princess Juana la Loca titled "Elegía a doña Juana la Loca," García Lorca details in fifteen stanzas the lamentable fate of a woman driven to madness by her unrequited love for her husband, Felipe el Hermoso. Throughout the poem, García Lorca addresses her as a red carnation in a deep and desolate valley, to whom Death extended a bouquet of withered roses instead of flowers, verses, and pearl necklaces. Like other great tragic heroines of Spanish literature, such as Isabel de Segura and Melibea, and those of García Lorca's own creative imagination, she is a victim of fate.

The themes of violent passion and death, later more fully expressed in *The Gypsy Ballads of García Lorca,* are latent in the description of Juana as a princess of the red sunset, the color of blood and fire, whose passion is like the dagger, whose distaff is of iron, whose flax is of steel. Here, metallic substances are symbols of death; Juana lies in her coffin of lead, and within her skeleton, a heart broken into a thousand pieces speaks of her shattered dreams and frustrated life.

"BALLAD OF THE LITTLE SQUARE"

In contrast to the bleak symbolism of these works, children and their world interested and delighted García Lorca, and he futilely sought in their charm and innocence a respite from the anguish of existence. In another poem from his first collection, "Balada de la placeta" ("Ballad of the Little Square"), the poet is listening to children singing. In a playful dialogue, the children ask the poet what he feels in his red, thirsty mouth; he answers, "the taste of the bones of my big skull." The poet's consciousness of death's presence mars his contemplation of youthful fun. Although he might wish to lose himself in the child's world, he clearly recognizes in a later poem, "Gacela de la huida" ("Gacela of the Flight"), that the seeds of death are already sown behind that childish exterior: "No one who touching a newborn child can forget the motionless horse skulls." Still, he tries to reject the physical destruction, the putrefaction of death which he so vividly describes in "Gacela de la muerte oscura" ("Gacela of the Dark Death") and in the *Lament for the Death of a Bullfighter.*

"THE SONG OF THE HORSEMAN"

García Lorca was a master of the dramatic ballad, full of mystery, passion, and dark, sudden violence. His tools were simple words and objects culled from everyday living, that contrasted with and intensified the complex emotions underlying the verse. García Lorca's mastery of the ballad form is exemplified in "Canción de jinete" ("The Song of the Horseman"), from *Songs.* The horseman's destination is the distant city of Córdoba. Although he knows the roads well and his saddlebags are packed with olives, he fatalistically declares that he will never reach Córdoba. García Lorca never tells a story outright; he makes his audience do the work. Thus, Death is looking at the horseman from the towers of Córdoba, as he cries "Ay! How long the road! Ay! My valiant pony! Ay! That death should wait me before I reach Córdoba." How? Why? Who? Where? These questions are left to the imagination.

"SOMNAMBULE BALLAD"

It is through the figure of the Andalusian Gypsy that García Lorca best conveys his personal vision of life. With his characteristic techniques of metaphorical suggestion and dramatic tension, enriched by an artist's palette of colors, García Lorca in *The Gypsy Ballads of García Lorca* treats his usual subject matter of love and death, passion and destruction, with great lyrical fantasy. The refrain "Green, how much I want you green" establishes the enchanted atmosphere of the famous "Romance sonambulo" ("Somnambule Ballad"), where everything possesses the greenish cast of an interior world: "Green wind, green flesh, green hair." The best known of García Lorca's ballads, it only implies the story behind the death of a pair of lovers: his the result of a wound that runs from his chest to his throat, hers from drowning in the sorrow of having waited for him so long in vain.

The themes of passion and violence are underscored by the theme of liberty, denied to the lovers by fate and a false social order. The Gypsy girl's death is already intimated in the first stanza, where she is described as having a shadow on her waist, with green flesh, hair of green, and eyes of cold silver that cannot see. On a first reading, the two lines "The ship upon the sea/ and the horse in the mountain," which precede the description, seem to be a discordant and senseless addition to the narrative. To understand their function, the reader must see them in relation to the theme of liberty. Man is imprisoned by his passions, by destiny, death, a sense of honor, and social institutions. In contrast, the images of the ship upon the sea and the horse in the mountain suggest total freedom. The horse, which in García Lorca's work often represents male virility, prefigures the Gypsy's attainment of the freedom that is his by nature. The image of the ship, on the other hand, has a long tradition of symbolizing liberty, especially in the Romantic period; its interpretation here, as such, is logical and expected. The description of the stars as white frost and the mountain as a filching cat foreshadows the violence of the characters' deaths.

Thus, "Somnambule Ballad" offers a profusion of surrealistic and seemingly disconnected images governed by a vigorous inner logic. In this, it is representative of García Lorca's finest works. The repetition of key images—of green, cold silver, the moon, water, and the night—unifies the poem. The Gypsy girl and the Gypsy are together in death and cannot hear the pounding of the drunken Civil Guard on the door. Death has granted them freedom, and all is as it should be: "The ship upon the sea, and the horse on the mountain." Using the local color and ambience of Gypsy life, García Lorca gives voice to his own frustrations and those of man in general. Fettered by passion, destiny, and social norms, man's only escape is through death.

POET IN NEW YORK

The strange poems of *Poet in New York* are the work of a mature poet. In New York, García Lorca, who had loved life in all its spontaneity, who had grieved over the death of gypsies, their instinctive and elemental passions suffocated, was confronted with the heartless, mechanized world of the urban metropolis. In *Poet in New York*, the Gypsy is replaced by the black man, whose instinctive impulses and strengths are perverted by the white man's civilization and whose repression and anguish is embodied in the figure of the great King of Harlem in a janitor's suit. The blood of three hundred crimson roses that stained the Gypsy's shirt in "Somnambule Ballad" now flows from four million butchered ducks, five million hogs, two thousand doves, one million cows, one million lambs, and two million roosters.

The disrespect for life in this landscape of vomiting and urinating multitudes is portrayed in the death of a cat, within whose little paw, crushed by the automobile, García Lorca sees a world of broken rivers and unattainable distances. Alone, alienated, and frustrated in his endeavors, man cannot appeal to anyone for help, not even the Church, which in its hypocrisy and heathen materialism betrays the true spirit of Christianity. The poet sees death and destruction everywhere. His own loneliness and alienation, described in "Asesinato" ("Murder"), recall the haunting words and melody of the *cante jondo:* "A pinprick to dive till it touches the roots of a cry."

LAMENT FOR THE DEATH OF A BULLFIGHTER

Considered by many to be García Lorca's supreme poetic achievement, the *Lament for the Death of a Bullfighter* is the quintessence of the Spanish "tragic sense of life." In this lament, García Lorca incorporated aspects of a long poetic tradition and revitalized them through his own creativity. Based on a true incident, as were most of García Lorca's poems, the elegy was written upon the death of his good friend Ignacio, an intellectual and a bullfighter, who was gored by a bull and died in August of 1934. The bullfight is elevated by García Lorca to a universal level, representing man's heroic struggle against death. Death, as always in García Lorca's poetry, emerges triumphant, yet the struggle is seen as courageous, graceful, meaningful.

The elegy is divided into four parts: "La cogida y la muerte" ("The Goring and the Death"), "La sangre derrameda" ("The Spilling of the Blood"), "Cuerpo presente" ("The Body Present"), and "Alma ansente" ("Absent Soul"). In general, the poem moves from the concrete to the abstract, from report to essay, from the specific to the general. Part 1 describes the events, the chaos, the confusion, the whole process of death in a series of images appealing to all the five senses. Phones jangle, the crowd is mad with grief, the bulls bellow, the wounds burn. What dominates is the incessant and doleful bell, reminding the poet, with each repetition of "at five o'clock in the afternoon," of the finality of death, worming its way into Ignacio's being, hammering its way into the public mind and into the poet's consciousness. The macabre sights and smells of death are detailed in all their colorful goriness: the white sheet, a pail of lime, snowy sweat, yellow iodine, green gangrene. Time ceases for Ignacio as all the clocks show five o'clock in the shadow of the afternoon. Refusing to look at Ignacio's blood in the sand, García Lorca vents his anger and frustration at seeing all that beauty, confidence, princeliness, strength of body and character, wit, and intelligence slowly seeping out as the moss and the grass open with sure fingers the flowers of Ignacio's skull.

The poet's initial reaction of shock and denial slowly softens into gradual acceptance. Utilizing the slower Alexandrine meter in "The Body Present," García Lorca contemplates the form of Ignacio laid out on a sterile, gray, cold stone. The finality of death is seen in the sulphur yellow of Ignacio's face and in the rain entering his mouth in the stench-filled silence. García Lorca cannot offer immortality. He can only affirm that man must live bravely, and that death, too, will one day cease to exist. Hence, he tells Ignacio to sleep, fly, rest: Even the sea dies. Death, victorious, challenged only by the value of Ignacio's human experience, is dealt with in the last part.

By autumn, the people will have forgotten Ignacio, robbed by death and time of the memory of his presence. Only those like the poet, who can look beyond, will immortalize him in song.

Lament for the Death of a Bullfighter expresses the fundamental attitude of the Spaniard toward death: One must gamble on life with great courage and heroism. Welcoming the dark angels of death, the "toques de bordón" or the black tones of the guitar, the poet is paradoxically affirming life. This is man's only consolation.

García Lorca's evolution as a poet was characterized throughout by this movement toward an all-encompassing death. Synthesizing a variety of themes and poetic styles and forms, García Lorca embodied, both in his life and in his verse, modern man's struggle to find meaning in life despite the overwhelming reality of physical and spiritual death.

OTHER MAJOR WORKS

PLAYS: *El maleficio de la mariposa*, pr. 1920 (*The Butterfly's Evil Spell*, 1963); *Mariana Pineda*, pr. 1927, pb. 1928 (English translation, 1950); *Los títeres de Cachiporra: La tragicomedia de don Cristóbal y la señá Rosita*, wr. 1928, pr. 1937 (*The Tragicomedy of Don Cristóbal and Doña Rosita*, 1955); *El paseo de Buster Keaton*, pb. 1928 (*Buster Keaton's Promenade*, 1957); *La doncella, el marinero y el estudiante*, pb. 1928 (*The Virgin, the Sailor, and the Student*, 1957); *Quimera*, wr. 1928, pb. 1938 (*Chimera*, 1944); *El público*, wr. 1930, pb. 1976 (fragment; *The Audience*, 1958); *La zapatera prodigiosa*, pr. 1930 (*The Shoemaker's Prodigious Wife*, 1941); *Así que pasen cinco años*, wr. 1931, pb. 1937 (*When Five Years Pass*, 1941); *El amor de don Perlimplín con Belisa en su jardín*, pr. 1933 (*The Love of Don Perlimplín for Belisa in His Garden*, 1941); *Bodas de sangre*, pr. 1933 (*Blood Wedding*, 1939); *Yerma*, pr. 1934 (English translation, 1941); *Doña Rosita la soltera: O, El lenguaje de las flores*, pr. 1935 (*Doña Rosita the Spinster: Or, The Language of the Flowers*, 1941); *El retablillo de don Cristóbal*, pr. 1935 (*In the Frame of Don Cristóbal*, 1944); *La casa de Bernarda Alba*, wr. 1936, pr., pb. 1945 (*The House of Bernarda Alba*, 1947).

NONFICTION: *Impresiones y paisajes*, 1918.

MISCELLANEOUS: *Obras completas*, 1938-1946 (8 volumes); *Obras completas*, 1954, 1960; *Obras completas*, 1973.

BIBLIOGRAPHY

Gibson, Ian. *Federico García Lorca*. New York: Pantheon Books, 1989. A monumental biography which goes to the heart of García Lorca's genius with brilliant prose and telling anecdotes. Meticulously reconstructs the poet's periods in New York, Havana, and Buenos Aires. Vividly re-creates the café life of Spain in the 1930's and the artistic talents that were nurtured there. Evokes the landscapes of Granada, Almeria, Cuba, and Argentina celebrated in the poetry.

Johnston, David. *Federico García Lorca*. Bath, England: Absolute, 1998. Johnston explains that García Lorca, rather than celebrating, is more concerned with deconstructing the essentials of Spain's culture of difference. He claims that the poet's most radical ultimate intention was the deconstruction of a civilization and the redefinition of the individual's right to be, not through the language of ethics or of the law, but in terms of a natural imperative.

Morris, C. Brian. *Son of Andalusia: The Lyrical Landscapes of Federico García Lorca*. Nashville, Tenn.: Vanderbilt University Press, 1997. In six chapters and an epilogue, Morris identifies the presence of Andalusian legends, traditions, songs, and beliefs in García Lorca's life and works.

Soufas, C. Christopher. *Audience and Authority in the Modernist Theater of Federico García Lorca*. Tuscaloosa: University of Alabama Press, 1996. A systematic study of all García Lorca's finished plays and provisional sketches presented in chronological order with attention to their effect on the viewing public. Relates Lorca's work to that of other avant-garde dramatists of the 1920's and 1930's.

Stainton, Leslie. *Lorca: A Dream of Life*. New York: Farrar, Straus and Giroux, 1999. Stainton, an American scholar who lived in Spain for several years, writes of García Lorca's homosexuality, his left-wing political views, and his artistic convictions. Her detailed account is strictly chronological. García Lorca's work is described but not analyzed.

Katherine Gyékényesi Gatto;
bibliography updated by Elaine Laura Kleiner

GARCILASO DE LA VEGA

Born: Toledo, Spain; 1501
Died: Nice, France; October 13, 1536

PRINCIPAL POETRY

Las obras de Boscán y algunas de Garcilasso de la Vega repartidas en quatro libros, 1543

Las obras del excelente poeta Garcilasso de la Vega, 1569

Obras del excelente poeta Garci Lasso de la Vega con anotaciones y enmiendas del Licenciado Francisco Sánchez . . . , 1574

Obras de Garci Lasso de la Vega con anotaciones de Fernando de Herrera, 1580

Garcilaso de la Vega: Natural de Toledo, Principe de los Poetas Castellanos, 1622 (*The Works of Garcilaso de la Vega Surnamed the Prince of Castilian Poets*, 1823)

Obras de Garcilaso de la Vega, ilustradas con notas, 1765

Works: A Critical Text with a Bibliography, 1925

Garcilaso de la Vega: Obras completas, Edición de Elías L. Rivers, 1964

Garcilaso de la Vega y sus comentaristas: Obras completas del poeta acompañadas de los textos íntegros de los comentarios de El Brocense, Fernando de Herrera, Tamayo y Vargas y Azara, 1966

OTHER LITERARY FORMS

Garcilaso de la Vega is remembered only for his poetic works.

ACHIEVEMENTS

Garcilaso de la Vega revolutionized Castilian poetry, playing a unique role in Spanish literature and achieving a notable place in European literature as well. In accomplishing this poetic revolution, Garcilaso may rightly be called the first modern Spanish poet. Although the fifteenth century in Spain had seen efforts to introduce into Castilian poetry the Italian hendecasyllable, attempts such as those of the Marquis of Santillana, who composed a collection of "Sonetos fechos al itálico modo" (sonnets made in the Italian way), had not been successful. Equally unsuccessful had been the use of a non-Italianate hendecasyllabic line by the fifteenth century poets Juan de Mena and Francisco Imperial.

Garcilaso's perfection of the Castilian hendecasyllable, successful cultivation of both Italianate verse forms and metrical innovations, and his use of classical models, all contributed to a poetry of intimate sentiment, delicate metaphor, conceptual content, and musicality. Religious themes, so important in the poetry of even the late Middle Ages in Spain, are completely absent in his verse, which crystallized the introduction into Spain of the essentially secular values of the Renaissance. From fifteenth century Spanish poetry, Garcilaso retained a certain predilection for wordplay, along with the favorable influence of the Catalan poet Ausias March. While at times expressively manipulating syntax, Garcilaso created a poetic diction soon regarded as a model of lucid simplicity for the Spanish language.

In international terms, Garcilaso is also notable for having preceded by many years the introduction of Italianate forms and sentiment into both English and French poetry. His use of pastoral poetry to express interiorized sentiments, of interest to the student of comparative literature, also represents a notable contribution to the development of this international literary mode.

Garcilaso's poetry, all of which was published posthumously, was rapidly accorded classic status, and editions of his poems with copious annotation and commentary appeared within the sixteenth century. The first of these was the edition by the esteemed scholar Francisco Sánchez de las Brozas, initially published in 1574. The important poet Fernando de Herrera first published his annotated edition in 1580. Additional annotated editions were published by other editors in the seventeenth and eighteenth centuries. The 1543 edition included most of the sonnets currently known to be Garcilaso's or attributed to him, all the other poems in Italian meters, and one poem in a traditional Castilian verse form. Subsequent editions have gradually been enlarged by adding more sonnets, other compositions in Castilian verse forms, and several Latin poems, as well as some letters and the poet's will. Virtually all dating of his compositions is conjectural, and the numbers commonly as-

Garcilaso de la Vega (© Corbis)

signed to specific poems do not correspond to their presumed order of composition.

Garcilaso's poetry in some sense became the model and inspiration for virtually all poetry written during the nearly two centuries of Spain's Golden Age, and for much of Spanish poetry up to the present day. Although the traditional Castilian verse forms were championed by poets such as Cristóbal de Castillejo and his followers in the sixteenth century, the influence and acceptance of Garcilaso's innovations was so pervasive that it has been said that every Spanish poet "carries his Garcilaso inside himself." Garcilaso's own compositions in the traditional verse forms—and his Latin poetry—illuminate the development of his Spanish poetry in the new style but are not themselves of primary interest in defining or understanding his art. The poetical canon left by Garcilaso provided the inspiration and basis for both of the somewhat antithetical schools or styles of poetry that were to evolve later in the Golden Age. The statement of ideas without metaphorical adornment and Garcilaso's retention of wordplay and puns from medieval Spanish poetry evolved ultimately into the dense, conceptual style exemplified by Francisco de Quevedo, while Garcilaso's manipulation of word order, sense of color, and

use of metaphor were reflected in Luis de Góngora y Argote's hyperbatons, polychromatic palette, and extravagant imagery.

Garcilaso pioneered the use of six distinct verse forms in Spanish poetry. The Spanish sonnet, composed of fourteen hendecasyllabic lines divided into two quatrains and two tercets, possessed a fundamentally different structure from the sonnet subsequently developed in English by William Shakespeare. The *estancia* combined lines of eleven and seven syllables in a pattern established in the poem's first strophe and then repeated in the subsequent strophes. The *lira*, so called because of its use in an ode whose first line contained this word (meaning "lyre"), was a particular form of the *estancia*, which became standardized. The *tercetos* consisted of three-line stanzas of eleven-syllable lines, with the first and third lines rhyming, and the middle line rhyming with the first and third lines of the next stanza. The *octava real* was a stanza of eight hendecasyllabic lines, rhyming *abababcc*. Garcilaso also introduced into Spanish the use of blank verse.

BIOGRAPHY

Garcilaso de la Vega's brief but active life might serve as a model for that of the multitalented "Renaissance man." Born in 1501 of a family with influence in the court of Ferdinand and Isabella and with several well-known authors in its antecedent generations, Garcilaso died in 1536 of wounds received in Provence while he was fighting for Emperor Charles V.

Garcilaso entered the Emperor's service in 1519 or 1520, was first wounded in battle in 1521, and he participated in several important campaigns, for which he was awarded the prestigious Order of Saint James in 1523. During his accompaniment of the court in the subsequent years of the decade, his friendship with the poet Juan Boscán developed. This relationship was of profound significance for Garcilaso's literary career; when, for example, his friend Boscán was persuaded by the Venetian ambassador to employ the Italian hendecasyllable in Castilian verse, Garcilaso did likewise, changing Spanish poetry forever. It has been suggested that his sonnets 31 and 38 were written in this period.

In 1525, Garcilaso married Doña Elena de Zúñiga, a lady-in-waiting to Charles V's sister, Princess Leonore.

The following year, he met and became infatuated with Isabel Freyre, who came to Spain from Portugal with Doña Isabel de Portugal when the latter married Charles V. Although his marital relationship apparently never saw expression in his poetry, Garcilaso's love for Isabel Freyre, seemingly unrequited, became a central poetic theme. The "Canción primera" ("First Ode") and sonnets 2, 15, and 27, probably from this period, express the poet's emotional state and his amorous devotion to an unnamed lady. The first numbered of his "Canciones en versos castellanos" ("Songs in Castilian Verse Forms"), on the occasion of "his lady's marriage," was presumably composed in response to Isabel Freyre's wedding. While with the retinue of Charles V in Italy, where the monarch had gone in 1529 or 1530 to receive the Imperial crown, Garcilaso apparently composed his "Canción cuarta" ("Fourth Ode") and sonnet 6, perhaps reflecting his anguish over the affair with Isabel.

In 1531, however, Charles V withdrew his favor, banishing Garcilaso to a small island in the Danube River because he had persisted in supporting a marriage opposed by the royal family. Sonnets 4 and 9 and the "Canción tercera" ("Third Ode") reflect the poet's unhappiness during this period. Thanks to the intervention of the duke of Alba, however, the island confinement was altered to banishment to Naples, where the poet gained a position of confidence with the viceroy, earned the praise of Cardinal Bembo, and, as reflected in his sonnets 14, 19, and 33 and in the famous "Canción quinta, a la flor de Gnido" ("Fifth Ode, To the Flower of Gnido"), made the acquaintance of several other important Neapolitan literary figures. During this period, he also studied the classics and met the expatriate Spanish author Juan de Valdés, who mentioned Garcilaso in his *Diálogo de la lengua* (wr. c. 1535, pb. 1737; dialogue of the language). Garcilaso's "Egloga segunda" ("Second Eclogue"), probably composed shortly after his brief trip to Spain and return to Naples in 1533, praises the House of Alba, while the "Egloga primera" ("First Eclogue") and sonnet 10, both apparently composed during the period 1533-1534, reflect the death at that time of Isabel Freyre. It is reasonable to assume that during this time in Naples, the poet composed his several Latin poems and stopped composing in the old Castilian verse forms.

During the years 1535 and 1536, Garcilaso returned to the Emperor's service. Sonnets 32 and 35 suggest that Garcilaso was wounded in an encounter with the Moors in an expedition to Tunis in 1535. With the Emperor's entourage in Sicily after returning from Tunis, Garcilaso composed his "Elegía primera" ("First Elegy"), for the recent death of the brother of the duke of Alba, and the "Elegía segunda" ("Second Elegy"), addressed to his friend Boscán. The "Egloga tercera" ("Third Eclogue"), generally regarded as the poet's last work, was written when Garcilaso was again part of the Emperor's court and in full favor, as Charles V decided to move against the French. It was while participating in this campaign that the poet was killed.

Juan Boscán, Garcilaso's lifelong friend, gathered Garcilaso's poems, intending to publish them with his own. Upon Boscán's death in 1542, his widow carried out the project, realizing its publication in 1543.

ANALYSIS

While Garcilaso de la Vega took much inspiration from Italian and classical models, he did not merely imitate them; rather, he assimilated and transformed these influences in the development if his own distinctive poetic voice.

"SECOND ECLOGUE"

This development is particularly evident in Garcilaso's eclogues. The "Second Eclogue," his longest composition, fully initiated the pastoral mode in his poetry. The poem possesses a balanced structure in which motifs and differing stanzaic forms—*tercetos, estancias, rima al mezzo* (interior rhyme)—are arranged in a symmetrical pattern centered on lines 766 through 933, which portray in dialogic form a chance encounter between the shepherd Albanio and Camila, his childhood playmate, who has earlier rejected his translation of their childhood friendship into love. On being rejected once more by Camila, after his hopes have been raised, Albanio goes mad. This central scene is preceded by a prologue in which Albanio laments his sad state; by several *estancias* inspired by Horace's *Beatus ille*; and by a section of dialogue between Albanio and Salicio in which Albanio recounts the story of his love for Camila, her negative response, and his present desire to kill himself. The dialogue, modeled upon an episode in Jacopo

Sannazzaro's *Arcadia* (1501-1504), is punctuated by an exchange in Petrarchan *rima al mezzo* in which Camila the huntress appears at the fountain where she first rejected Albanio and recalls the unpleasant incident.

Following the central scene between Camila and Albanio, a passage in *rima al mezzo* presents the struggle of Salicio and Nemoroso, another shepherd, to control the crazed Albanio. The following passage is in *tercetos*; with Albanio subdued, Nemoroso tells Salicio that Severo, a sage enchanter who had cured him, has come to Alba and can cure Albanio of his love woes. A brief dialogic *rima al mezzo* then leads to a lengthy panegyric by Nemoroso to the House of Alba. A short dialogue in *estancias* reaffirms the certainty of Albanio's eventual cure, and as dusk falls, the two shepherds discuss their leave-taking and the disposition of Albanio.

The "Second Eclogue" departs from the refinement of Vergilian bucolics and displays characteristics that separate it from the more perfected form that Garcilaso was to achieve in his "First Eclogue" (which, despite its designation, was composed *after* the "Second Eclogue"). The tranquility and idealization of nature and human feelings are disturbed by a number of familiar or rustic expressions and proverbs, concentrated in the dialogue between Albanio and Salicio that precedes Camila's appearance. These exchanges acquire an almost comic character that has caused some critics to regard them as constituting a dramatic farce in themselves. The poet engagingly steps outside the poetic conventions of the pastoral mode by having Albanio question Salicio's advice with the query, "Who made you an eloquent philosopher/ being a shepherd of sheep and goats?" There is a considerable amount of jocularity elsewhere in exchanges between Albanio and Salicio and in Nemoroso's initial resistance to helping Salicio subdue the crazed Albanio. Although it has been assumed that Albanio represents Garcilaso's friend and mentor the duke of Alba, a number of details suggest that Albanio is more plausibly Bernardino de Toledo, the duke's younger brother, whose death in 1535 occasioned Garcilaso's "First Elegy." Though somewhat distracting, these elements contribute to the originality of Garcilaso's poetic creation.

The "Second Eclogue" is also rich in conceits and various forms of wordplay. Some of these devices are reminiscent of Petrarch, while others have their antecedents in Castilian poetry of the fifteenth century. In its representation of Albanio's love as an anguished state, the poem recalls the Petrarchan influence evident in Garcilaso's earlier works.

"FIRST ECLOGUE"

In his "First Eclogue," Garcilaso attained perfect balance and equilibrium, a consistent and refined tone, idiom, and sentiment, and the definitive expression of the central amorous relationship in his life, the love for Isabel Freyre. A four-stanza prologue and dedication to the duke of Alba introduces two shepherds, again Salicio and Nemoroso, who lament respectively and in succession, each in twelve stanzas, their disappointments in love. The two successive speeches are separated by a one-stanza transition, and culminated by a single stanza conclusion, so that the poem as a whole comprises thirty fourteen-line stanzas.

In the two shepherds and their lamentations, the poet has represented himself ("Salicio" is an anagram of Garcilaso, while "Nemoroso" is a coinage based on the Latin root *nemus*, closely related in meaning to Spanish *vega*, a meadow) and expressed in a perfectly balanced duality the two essential elements of his relationship with Isabel Freyre: its failure, followed by her marriage to another, and her death. The lamentations begin at daybreak and end as the sun sets and the shepherds return with their flocks. Unity is achieved in the use of a single verse form throughout, the *estancia* (here a fourteen-line stanza of eleven- and seven-syllable lines); in the two shepherds' embodiment of the poet; and in the restriction of the action to a single day's time. Without calling attention to itself, an exquisite and seemingly effortless design governs the entire poem, which in its structure is similar to that of Vergil's "Eighth Eclogue."

The poem's opening six lines establish the delicacy and balance of the pastoral mode, exemplifying Garcilaso's expressive manipulation of word order to yield consonance of form and meaning. The first two lines, "The sweet lamentation of two shepherds/ Salicio jointly and Nemoroso," introduce the duality of the shepherds, separating and balancing them at the beginning and end of the poetical line. Here, the use of the first of many carefully positioned modifiers begins to create the idealized, gentle, tender ambience that defines the eclogue. The opening lines contain no active verbs, instead using infinitives, participles, and verbs of being. This construction suggests that the sheep are forgetful of their grazing, attentive rather to the shepherds' "savory song," a dreamlike oblivion and perfect harmony between nature and man. In an abrupt change, the next line addresses the duke of Alba, expressively heightening the contrast between the idyllic pastoral environment and the affairs of state or martial concerns that preoccupy the dynamic man of action.

The evocation of the duke's military activities in the succeeding stanzas touches a theme that was an important part of the poet's life and that finds expression in other of his poems, most notably the "Second Elegy." This poem, apparently written to Boscán from Sicily in 1535, expresses the poet's distaste for the petty politics of the emperor's retinue. Garcilaso depicts himself as a tender lover trapped in Mars's service, envying Boscán's tranquil, secure family life, and scorning the hypocrisy and ambition of those who surround the "African Caesar." The poem's opening lines, remarking on Vergil's presence in Sicily, through Aeneas, confirm Garcilaso's active awareness of Vergil during this period.

The stanza of the "First Eclogue" which connects the dedication to the duke with the beginning of Salicio's lament returns to the idyllic natural setting. A characteristic hyperbaton represents the gradually rising sun, first rising above the waves, then above the mountains, and finally directly revealed at the beginning of the stanza's third line to introduce at daybreak the reclining Salicio. The pasture in which the shepherd is at his ease is crossed by a gurgling brook whose pleasant sound harmonizes with the music of the shepherd's sweet complaint. Assonant rhyme in addition to the usual consonantal rhyme, and internal rhyme in one verse, lend the passage a delicate musicality. As the clear brook flows unimpeded and burbling to accompany the shepherd's song, so too does the stanza, continuous, unimpeded, and without rigorous syntax.

The stanza that begins Salicio's complaint, addressed to the absent Galatea, who has not returned his love, is reminiscent of the plaints of several of Vergil's shepherds and provides a strident contrast to the sonorous passage preceding it. The shepherd first berates Galatea

as harder than marble to his complaints and colder than ice to the fire that consumes him. The bitterness of these sentiments becomes death in the absence of the one who could give him life with her presence, then shame and embarrassment at his own pathetic state, then incredulity at the lady's refusal to command a soul that has always given itself to her, until it dissolves in the stanza's last line in the flowing tears bidden to emerge abundantly and without sorrow. This final line becomes a refrain at the end of the remainder of Salicio's stanzas, with the exception of the last one. Following stanzas contrast the permanence of the shepherd's sorry state with the daily changes of a delicately evoked nature, questioning the justice of his situation and reproachfully recalling his lady's falseness and deception.

While Salicio's unrequited love for Galatea recalls Garcilaso's disappointment in his love for Isabel Freyre, the shepherd Nemoroso's lament for his lost love, Elisa, recalls Garcilaso's mourning at Isabel's death. Nemoroso's lament confirms in a general way, though without many specific borrowings, Garcilaso's profound familiarity with Petrarch and his ability to equal or surpass the Italian model in his own poetry. Nemoroso's theme, the loved one's death, is also traditionally regarded as the subject of Garcilaso's famous sonnet 10, "Oh dulces prendas, por mi mal halladas" (O sweet favors, found to my woe), and sonnet 25. Sonnet 10, expressing the poet's grief on finding a token of his departed love, and contrasting the joy that love once brought him with the sadness it presently causes, is reminiscent of both Vergil and Petrarch. The sonnet is recalled in the "First Eclogue" when Nemoroso describes the consoling tears engendered by a lock of Elisa's hair, always kept at his bosom.

Nemoroso's song begins with an evocation of nature, distilled into select details each refined with adjectival description into exquisite perfection ("running, pure, crystalline waters," "green field," "fresh shade"). The natural setting is self-contained, turned in upon itself and vaguely anthropomorphic as green ivy winds its way among trees that see themselves reflected in the water. The harmony between man and his thoughts and an idealized natural surrounding is disturbed only by the suggestion of present sadness and by the last line's reference to joy-filled memories, implying that joy is past.

The following stanzas recall the happy times the lovers shared and mourn their brevity; in imagery that anticipates the Baroque violence of Góngora, the shepherd expresses his passion, his rage, and his desolation. In the final stanza of Nemoroso's lament, anger and despondency yield to a quiet prayer to the now-divine loved one to hasten the coming of the shepherd's death so that they may enjoy tranquilly together and without fear of loss the eternal fields, mountains, rivers, and shaded flowery valleys of the third sphere. Natural beauty is thus raised to a cosmic plane; in Salicio's plaint, the imagery that concludes the lament recalls its opening lines.

The dreamlike poetic moment of the two shepherds' lamentations is ended in the eclogue's final stanza. Looking at the pink clouds and sensing the creeping shadows that reverse the process of sunrise described at the poem's opening, the two shepherds awaken from their reverie and conduct their sheep home, step by step. So, too, does the reader leave an exquisite and incomparably evoked poetic world of true sentiment, delicate appreciation of nature, and harmony between man and his surroundings, representative of Garcilaso's enduring contribution to Spanish literature.

BIBLIOGRAPHY

Cammarata, Joan. *Mythological Themes in the Works of Garcilaso de la Vega*. Potomac, Md.: Studia Humanitatis, 1983. A critical analysis of Garcilaso's use of folklore and mythology. Includes bibliographical references and index.

Fernández-Morera, Dario. *The Lyre and the Oaten Flute: Garcilaso and the Pastoral*. London: Tamesis, 1982. A critical study of selected works by Garcilaso. Includes bibliographical references and index.

Ghertman, Sharon. *Petrarch and Garcilaso*. London: Tamesis, 1975. Ghertman analyzes and compares the linguistic styles of Francesco Petrarca and Garcilaso.

Heiple, Daniel L. *Garcilaso de la Vega and the Italian Renaissance*. University Park: Pennsylvania State University Press, 1994. Heiple analyzes Garcilaso's work and its place in the history of Italian renaissance literature. Includes bibliographical references and index.

Keniston, Hayward, ed. *Garcilaso de la Vega*. New York: Kraus Reprint, 1967. A critical study of Garcilaso's life and works. Includes bibliographical references and index.

Theodore L. Kassier;
bibliography updated by the editors

GEORGE GASCOIGNE

Born: Cardington, England; c. 1539
Died: Stamford, England; October 7, 1577

PRINCIPAL POETRY

A Hundreth Sundrie Flowres Bounde Up in One Small Poesie, 1573 (poetry and prose; revised as *The Posies of George Gascoigne*, 1575)
The Fruites of Warre, 1575
The Steele Glas, a Satyre, 1576
The Complaynt of Phylomene, 1576 (a companion piece to *The Steele Glas, a Satyre*)
The Grief of Joye, 1576

OTHER LITERARY FORMS

The first two volumes of George Gascoigne's poetry also contain many of his most popular prose works. Among these is "Certayne Notes of Instruction Concerning the Making of Verse" (found in *The Posies of George Gascoigne*), an important work of literary criticism, and said to be the first of its kind in the English language. Also found in the early volumes are a number of full-length plays, all types never before presented in English, as well as some interesting masques and royal entertainments.

Gascoigne also experimented with fictional and nonfictional narrative. One of these works, *The Spoyle of Antwerpe* (1576), is a rare example for the times of detailed and honest journalistic reporting about the war. *The Discourse of the Adventures Passed by Master F. J.* (found in *A Hundreth Sundrie Flowres Bounde Up in One Small Poesie*) is a work of prose fiction which has received considerable attention from scholars and critics. Also among these works are several long didactic prose pieces that are moralistic in tone.

ACHIEVEMENTS

George Gascoigne tried his hand at many forms of literature, with an innovator's quick eye for literary forms not used before in England or in English. Writing as a gifted amateur at the court of Queen Elizabeth and turning near the end of his life toward writing as a profession, Gascoigne presented a notable list of first achievements. He wrote the first work of English literary criticism and presented in England the first ancient Greek tragedy and the first translation from Italian prose comedy. His verse satire *The Steele Glas*, itself an important early example of social satire, was the first English poem (not including translations) which employed nondramatic blank verse.

Gascoigne was also innovative in narrative modes, presenting in *The Discourse of the Adventures Passed by Master F. J.* what many call the first work of prose fiction in English. For a time he was followed by a school of imitators, including George Whetstone and Nicholas Breton. Gascoigne seldom brought his work to a fine polish, however, and this lack of finish together with an archaic style in diction and meter have produced a modern assessment that his works are valuable merely for their innovative literary attempts, rather than their actual achievements.

This opinion has undergone some welcome revaluation. Recent critics have stressed Gascoigne's serious commitment to moral themes, his patriotic determination to form a distinctively English practice in poetry (analogous to the contemporary French movement sponsored by the poets of the Pléiade), and his verve for realistic detail and psychologically valid observation of human nature. Gascoigne is a transitional figure whose work helped to extend English poetic resources and so led to the "flowering" of the New Poetry of the 1580's and 1590's. This fact was recognized to some extent by his own age: The preface to Edmund Spenser's *The Shepheardes Calender* of 1579 refers to Gascoigne as "the very chief of our late rymers." In addition, Gascoigne offers many Elizabethan poetic "voices," selecting his own preferred emphases among the range of options in style and convention available to poets during the Tudor period from Thomas Wyatt through John Donne (Gascoigne presents interesting points of comparison with both of these poets). A reassessment

suggests a moral poetry of strength, verve, and self-perception; an amatory and social poetry of frankness, witty playfulness, and realism; an adroit and sensitive portrayal of first- and third-person personas; and a commitment throughout to extend the formal and linguistic resources of the English poetic medium.

BIOGRAPHY

A common mode of discussing personal lives in medieval and Renaissance literature is the exemplum, a device whereby figures from history or literature typify human virtues or vices such as heroism, devotion, or greed. As if conditioned by a habitual way of reading experience, many lives of actual sixteenth century literary figures fulfilled a seemingly fictionalized pattern, glossed by Richard Helgerson in his book *The Elizabethan Prodigals* (1976). The life of George Gascoigne provides a fine example of this "pattern of prodigality," in which youthful folly is coupled with writings in such "vain" literary forms as amatory verse. Gascoigne discusses his wasted youth and later reformation in many prefaces and poems, and although his efforts to reform were aimed at very practical financial goals, they were

George Gascoigne (Hulton Archive)

doubtless also sincere. Among Gascoigne's most important poems, in fact, are introspective accounts of his poor record of worldly successes.

Gascoigne began life from a secure position in a wealthy if litigious family of landed gentry. Like many other young Elizabethan gentlemen of means, he discontinued his formal education (in law) to pursue advancement at court, where he soon exhausted his patrimony and yet found no position. In addition, his reputation was sullied by various legal disputes and by a series of troubles over the legality of his marriage in 1561, as a man in his early years, to Elizabeth Bacon Breton, a much older widow with attractive property. By 1565, with friends at court but no chance of success there, the poet began to search for a means of making a living. He renewed his legal studies at Gray's Inn, where he spent most of his time in literary efforts; soon he had relocated in the country for an unsuccessful try at farming.

Gascoigne turned in 1571 to a new project for recouping his fortunes: He volunteered as a soldier in the Netherlands' campaign to aid William, Prince of Orange, against the Spanish. He returned briefly in 1572 to oversee the publication of an anonymous version of his collected writings, *A Hundreth Sundrie Flowres Bounde Up in One Small Poesie*. In mid-term of the same year, he was unexpectedly named a member of parliament from Midhurst (aided by the well-timed presentation of a dramatic masque at a wedding for a member of the family of Lord Montagu). In an anonymous letter, however, his creditors appealed to prevent his being seated, charging him with manslaughter, spying, and atheism, as well as with being "a common Rymer and a deviser of slaunderous Pasquelles againste divers personnes of greate callinge." Gascoigne returned quickly to the Holland wars, where he proved to be a capable leader but found little advancement of his fortunes, and where he learned the grim realities of war, expressed effectively in his poem "Dulce Bellum Inexpertis" ("War Is Sweet to Those with No Experience of It").

Gascoigne returned to England in 1574, to face the disastrous reception of *A Hundreth Sundrie Flowres Bounde Up in One Small Poesie:* Copies had been confiscated because of charges of libel and immorality. Gascoigne undertook an entire change in his manner

of life and his career as a writer, and finally his fortunes began to turn. A cleaned-up and reorganized version of his writings, *The Posies of George Gascoigne*, was a success, helped by the poet's repentant and revealing prefaces. Concurrently, he published his other serious, moralistic writings; he gained important patronage; and he found a promising position with William Cecil, minister to the Queen. While his career was on the mend, he fell ill in 1576. He died in October, 1577, probably not quite forty years of age and, for the first time in many years, in good hopes for worldly comfort and a secure reputation as an Elizabethan writer, civil servant, and gentleman.

If the poet's difficulties benefited him, they did so by stimulating a vein of honest introspection. In addition, they urged the poet to create consciously his literary career. Gascoigne posed successfully as an aspiring Renaissance man, a virtuoso equally skilled in arms or letters. Gascoigne is certainly not the most important or the most successful of the Elizabethan poets. The critic John Buxton has rightly observed of him that "when greatness was within his reach he allowed himself to be distracted." Yet Gascoigne is not the dull moralist and clumsy, love lyricist of received literary-historical opinion. In poetic technique he has the verve of an experimentalist and the skill of a virtuoso, although without achieving the final polish of succeeding poets. His lasting achievement, however, may rest in his sensitive but tough-minded portrayals of a series of personae, all expressing in one way or another his own effort to interpret, for himself as much as for others, a meaning for his life.

ANALYSIS

Linked to the pattern of reformed prodigality which shaped the poet's life, two personas are often reflected in George Gascoigne's writings, one a young courtier and the other a newly reformed moralist, "a man of middle-yeares, who hath to his cost experimented the vanities of youth, and to his perill passed them: who hath bought repentence deare, and yet gone through with the bargaine." The brash, witty young writer of society verse is interesting in comparison with and contrast to other Elizabethans writing in Italianate modes of amatory poetry. In the best poems, the middle-aged moralistic persona is interesting, too. Gascoigne made a lifelong profound study of his "master," Geoffrey Chaucer (as he calls him in the *Certayne Notes of Instruction Concerning the Making of Verse*). Gascoigne's ability to portray interesting and subtle personae most likely derives from his study of the first important vernacular poet in English.

Elizabethan poets were creators of artifice. Gascoigne intensified the efforts of his generation of poets—notably Barnabe Googe, Thomas Howell, George Turberville, and others—to extend the stylistic and linguistic potential of English as a poetic medium. A confirmed patriot in diction, Gascoigne preferred older, native words, striving for a Chaucerian effect, as Vere Rubel has shown in her *Poetic Diction in the English Renaissance* (1941). Similarly, as Rubel also shows, Gascoigne sought vigor and range in his vocabulary and made extensive use of figurative language from contemporary rhetoric, to create new or startling effects. He does not, however, often achieve the well-wrought and compressed effects of a more careful stylist such as Sir Philip Sidney; his rather loose syntax and conversational narration seem also to have been borrowed from Chaucer.

For Gascoigne, the key to a poem's effectiveness (and the first point in his "Certayne Notes of Instruction Concerning the Making of Verse") is "to grounde it upon some fine invention." The poet means here a clever, new, or indirect idea of how to accomplish the poem's aim—an invented story, an unusual comparison, or a studied hyperbole, but never anything trite or obvious. This emphasis on "invention" points to another feature of Gascoigne's poetry, especially his social and amatory poetry: These poems were written in response to quite specific circumstances, daily occasions calling for social dialogue or for personal expression. Poetry was a favored medium of social exchange in Elizabethan high society.

Following a seminal article by Yvor Winters, many modern critics have found that Gascoigne reacted against much Elizabethan poetry. Such critics rightly note in him a preferred speaker who is a somewhat rustic, folksy fellow, honest and direct. In presenting studied personas and enjoying conscious artifice, however, Gascoigne places himself in the main current of Elizabethan poetic practice. Actually, the poet's opposition to styles current in his age is more apparent than real. Especially for modern readers, who are suspicious of elegance in poetry, Gascoigne's effect of forthright, direct speech seems "natural," obscuring the degree of artifice and mannerism underlying its creation.

Similarly, in his love poetry Gascoigne is often described as opposing the popular currents of Italianate Petrarchism which produced the "golden" New Poetry of the 1580's and 1590's. Indeed, many Elizabethan sonneteers borrowed from Petrarch and other Italian poets an elevated, passionate tone, a language of superlatives, and an idealistic devotion to the beloved. Italian poetry also offered other choices, however, and Gascoigne, like Sir Thomas Wyatt before him, found in Italian models clever, witty indirectness, worldly-wise or Cavalier compliment, and a tone sometimes boastful, sometimes insulting, but seldom simply refined. Where Wyatt's persona expresses a high-minded moral resolve and rejects the amatory mores which ensnare him, however, Gascoigne's attitudes in the amatory poems are less moral. In his youthful poetry he delights in verbal and social play for its own sake. In a slightly cynical, worldly way, he portrays the very real court society in which he lived—with such flair, in fact, that commentators in his age and in the twentieth century have read him as writing *romans à clef*, relating actual events involving real personalities of the day.

Gascoigne also sought to extend the range and power of vernacular poetry by exploring a variety of poetic lines and stanzas. His "Certayne Notes of Instructions Concerning the Making of Verse" describes many verse forms, identifying their characteristic uses and effects. Here Gascoigne shows sound judgment; for one, he opposes the common use of the term "sonnet" to mean any short, songlike poem, preferring the meaning accepted today. On the other hand, some less forward-looking aspects of Gascoigne's practices in form and meter require comment. As other poets of the generation before Spenser and Sidney did, Gascoigne often uses the long line of twelve or fourteen syllables, with obvious, unmodulated meters. Long verses had first become popular for their handiness in translating Latin epic meters; they gave what was thought to be a stately effect and allowed for ease of line-for-line translation. The main forms are the "fourteener," rhymed iambic couplets of fourteen syllables each, and "the commonest sort of verse which we use now adayes," a couplet made of a twelve-syllable line followed by a fourteen-syllable line. (Gascoigne calls this "Poulter's measure," after the dairyman's habit of giving two extra eggs when a second dozen was bought.) Long verses resist compression of language and, moreover, tend to pause heavily in mid-line, with a sing-song effect. The jog-trot of these meters was increased by the preference of the poets of Gascoigne's generation for monosyllabic words and for a regularized iambic stress, with the heavy stresses evenly strong and the light stresses evenly light. The old-fashioned, obvious effects of these meters have obscured Gascoigne's other poetic values for many readers. As he matured, his metrical touch lightened and he used the longer lines less frequently.

"GASCOIGNES MEMORIES"

Gascoigne's virtuoso talent is strikingly shown in five poems grouped together as "Gascoignes Memories." Upon his return in 1566 to Gray's Inn, five friends had challenged him to a verse-writing contest. Each was assigned a different theme, a proverb or a familiar Latin saying, for expansion and comment. In one weekend Gascoigne produced five poems, 258 lines in all. Each has a unique verse structure, and all were composed on horseback without pen and paper—indeed a feat of memory. The most difficult verse form is seen in the poem on the theme *Sat cito, si sat bene* ("No haste but good," as the poet translates it), written in seven sonnets linked by repeated lines. In addition, the poems vary in tone and style, showing here the conversationality of proverbs, there an urbane polish. Each of the five poems meditates on the youthful poet's wasted time at court; they predict his later, mature voice of didactic seriousness which, without self-pity, works toward honest self-perception. In these same poems, however, Gascoigne performs a feat of brilliant poetic improvisation.

VERSE-MAKING AND INVENTION

The young writer of society verse similarity took delight in his skill at verse-making, which was closely tied to actual uses in court society. In Gascoigne's amatory poetry, one senses specific, real events, real lovers, and real affairs. In Elizabethan high society, fashionable amatory play did not necessarily imply actual *affaires*

d'amour. Poems of amatory praise could gain remunerative recognition for their aspiring authors from quite proper court ladies—including the Queen. Men and women typically paired off for a variety of social interactions, playing at pleasant amatory fictions. It is precisely these conventional social exchanges which Gascoigne manipulates with zest and skill.

One poem discusses the ill chance of the loser in a contest with another man for a woman's kiss. "Three Sonnets in Sequence" were written in a woman's copy of Lucius Apuleius's *The Golden Ass* (c. 150), a copy given by "her David" to "his Berzabe." Riddles in verse are propounded (but not solved). An amusing exchange of poems is made on the occasion of a dinner attended by a woman, her husband, her brother, her old lover, and a hopeful new suitor (the poem's speaker).

"Invention" is at the heart of these poems. A clever "invention" is analogous in poetic *content* (that is, in the poem's concept of what to say in order to respond effectively to a given social or amatory occasion) to the skillful realization of poetic language and form. The amatory poems praising court ladies strikingly show this element. Indeed, the poems "In Prayse of Brydges, Nowe Lady Sandes" and "In Prayse of a Gentlewoman Who Though She Were Not Very Fayre, Yet Was She as Hard Favored as Might Be" follow precisely the poet's suggestions in the "Certayne Notes of Instruction Concerning the Making of Verse" to "finde some supernaturall cause whereby [one's] penne might walke in the superlative degree" or "to aunswere for any imperfection that shee hath." The poem praising Bridges explains a birthmark on the lady's forehead as the scar of a wound made by jealous Cupid.

Gascoigne handles the Petrarchan amatory conventions with verve and with something of a showman's skill. Italianate verse supplied rich material for his own independent uses, pulled out of any original context, although the poems reproduce neither Petrarch's idealism nor his refined tone. Thus, in "Gascoignes Anatomie," the poet describes a lover's physical appearance feature by feature. The unkempt hair, hollow eyes, wan cheeks, and trembling tongue are familiar, stereotyped details, but piled on with a characteristic exuberance. Another poem, "Gascoignes Passion," plays cleverly on Petrarchan contradictions, finding opportunity for unusual comparisons and inventive wordplay ("I live in love, even so I love to live"). One of the cleverest amatory poems is "Gascoignes Araignement," in which the speaker is accused of unjust flattery by Beauty in a court of law. The poem is Cavalier in tone and very successful in its use of a shorter, eight-syllable line.

The amatory poems tend to hint at underlying stories. This tendency is heightened by the many prose headnotes which give the occasions of their composition. (Probably to disguise his own participation in many social events—or to display his facility in creating personae—Gascoigne presented the first short poems in *A Hundreth Sundrie Flowers Bounde Up in One Small Poesie* anonymously). This potential for narrative is inherent in Petrarchan conventions and may indeed have been consciously adapted by Gascoigne from similar headnotes in sixteenth century editions of Petrarch's sonnets—Gascoigne's autograph appears on the title page of a copy of an edition by Giovanni Gesualdo. Since Petrarch's poems trace his love for Laura *in vito* and *in morte*, these explanatory notes serve to narrate the story of the poet's love.

Gascoigne twice tried his hand at an extended linking of amatory poems to tell a story. The less complex attempt is "The Delectable History of Sundry Adventures Passed by Dan Bartholomew of Bathe." The affair opens with three poems of "triumph" at the protagonist's attaining "the bathe of perfect blisse" in love. Immediately, however, there follow his "Dolorous Discourses" upon being jilted, then a series of increasingly despairing poems culminating in "His Last Wyll and Testament" and "His Farewell." The narrative success of these poems is heightened by the use of "the Reporter," a third-person narrator whose interspersed verse comments add an objective yet sympathetic context for the poet-persona's writings.

THE DISCOURSE OF THE ADVENTURES PASSED BY MASTER F. J.

The Discourse of the Adventures Passed by Master F. J. refines this technique. Here the place of "the Reporter" is taken, in prose, by a friend who tells the circumstances of the protagonist's writing a series of love poems considerably after the time when they were written. This narrator's commentary on the young poet's inexperience creates the sort of rich context which the Dan

Bartholomew sequence lacks. The tale tells of the first love affair of F. J., with an experienced married woman, in a country house in the north of England. F. J. learns something of society and a good deal about himself. The narrator relates all this with sympathy and humor from the knowing perspective of a man who has rejected amatory folly but understands its pathos, idealisms, and delusions. He is, presumably, Gascoigne himself, looking back on his days of writing love poetry.

Although *The Discourse of the Adventures Passed by Master F. J.* is usually cited as prose fiction, it contains some of Gascoigne's most interesting amatory poems. The narrator's commentary includes critical assessments of the poems and explains poetic devices and intentions. Many of the poems are frankly adulterous—for example, F. J.'s "Frydayes Breakefast," which tells of a morning's lovemaking. The poems are "inventive"; the daring poem opening "Beautie shut up thy shop" claims that the mistress's beauty excels all others, leaving other men's ladies to seem like painted and trussed-up shopwares left behind once the genuine article has been sold. Such poems are questionable from any point of view requiring propriety or seriousness of content. Characteristically, however, Gascoigne defends them, including them among the "pleasant" poems of *The Posies of George Gascoigne* on the grounds of their "rare invention and Method before not commonly used."

In sum, Gascoigne's amatory *vers de société* is characterized by virtuoso display and clever, unusual content. The poet evokes a real world of social interplay and witty poetic exchanges. The narrative of *The Discourse of the Adventures Passed by Master F. J.* also suggests what Gascoigne can do when writing introspectively, as he often does on moral topics. In spite of the conservatism of his preferred theme of reformed youthful folly, Gascoigne handles it in his best poems with a perception and honesty which modern readers can appreciate. Although this reformed persona is often profoundly disillusioned, he still respects important values which are rare in a society whose snares have led him astray. In the important poem "Gascoignes Wodmanship," for example, this recognition leads to a double vision which balances the poet's sense of his own failings against those of his world, which in many ways has failed *him*. Such a persona makes an effective medium for satire.

THE STEELE GLAS, A SATYRE

It is thus significant to observe that Gascoigne's long satirical commentary on the corruptions of his times, *The Steele Glas*, is not merely objective. Its opening compares the speaker himself to the nightingale of myth, its tongue (his art) silenced by detractors and by worldly obstacles. This unusual opening frames the poem in the context of personal experience. Moreover, it helps the poet define his genre for his reader: His voice, like the bird's, is mournful and halting; like the bird "closely cowcht" in a thicket, he is a covert observer of men. Gascoigne also observes himself, in a well-known passage of self-description explained by this marginal gloss: "He which wil rebuke other mens faults, shal do wel not to forget hys owne imperfections."

As a central device, the satirist presents images in two mirrors, one of steel which cannot falsify and one of crystal which sees into the soul. The social satire is conveyed by an immense variety of examples of abuses of human potential or social responsibility; yet Gascoigne intersperses visionary descriptions of an ideal political state to counter an all-critical attitude. The ideas here are traditional, urging renewal of a hierarchical social order and attributing social corruptions to such cardinal sins as lust and greed. The Chaucerian language and vivid heaping of details from contemporary life create a distinctive English flavor. As Ronald Johnson comments on *The Steele Glas*, "At no one place is Gascoigne's perception unusually keen; breadth of vision rather than depth recommends the poem to us."

The most perceptive of the poems of personal analysis is "Gascoignes Wodmanship." As mentioned above, the poem mixes a satirist's awareness of society's faults with an introspective man's recognition of personal failings. The speaker's follies are portrayed with humor and sympathy. Thus the tone is at once serious, ironic, and bemused. Like many of the amatory poems, this one is based on a controlling "invention" supplied by an event in the poet's experience. While a guest of Lord Grey of Wilton, Gascoigne has poor luck in hunting, which he seeks to excuse by describing how "he shoots awrie almost at every marke" which he aims at in life. The metaphor of hunting is suspenseful and significant as well, because skill at hunting was a distinguishing accomplishment for an Elizabethan gentleman. The poem's main theme is the fleeting value of the goals for which the poet has aimed—favor at court, amatory pleasures, soldierly reputation. Something deeper is also suggested: In part, the poet has failed because his own morality prevents him from playing the games of society; ironically, his own codes of behavior make him unlikely to enjoy the world's rewards. "Gascoignes Wodmanship" is didactic and yet metaphorically and technically innovative, combining social satire with personal introspection and achieving an exemplary economy of style and control of tone.

A HUNDRETH SUNDRIE FLOWRES BOUNDE UP IN ONE SMALL POESIE

A final type of poetry with which Gascoigne had success is the lyrical, songlike short poem. The maker of heavy fourteeners could also write lyrics for music: A tailnote to "Gascoignes Good Nyghte" in *A Hundreth Sundrie Flowres Bounde Up in One Small Poesie* lists eight poems which "have verie sweete notes adapted unto them." Among the most attractive of his writings is an original psalm, "Gascoignes Good Morrow," which expresses the pleasure of simple piety in direct language and a subtle stanza form. For a song with amatory content, "Of all the byrds that I do know," a charming melody was given in John Bartlett's *Booke of Ayres* (1606). This song was composed to praise a lady named "Phillip"—clearly a pseudonym, for "Philip" was a stock name for a sparrow, as "Tom" is for a male cat. Likening the woman to a pet bird is lightly amusing, though teasingly salacious in its implication; for example, she is always on call for sexual play. In his songs, as in other forms, Gascoigne shows a virtuoso's talent for evoking a range of themes and effects; he handles the deceptively simple language of the form with skill.

Also in the form of a song is "Gascoignes Lullabie," the one among his short poems which has received, as it deserves, the most attention. Renouncing love, the speaker sings "as women do" to lull to sleep the lusts of youth. In an order assigned by the Elizabethan psychology of desire, they are his vanished youth itself and then his "gazing eyes" (which seek out feminine beauty), his "wanton will" (which impels him to desire), and his "loving boye" (a euphemism for his male potency). The poem's rich meaning results, in part, from the disarming music of the lullaby itself, which makes accepting the rigors of age seem ironically easy. Moreover, the central metaphor is significantly inappropriate in one sense, as babies, not old men, are to be sung to sleep; *within* the older man there remain, hidden, "full many babes" of youth's impulses which are not easily stilled. By the end, singing the poem serves as a frail distraction for the old man from still-active youthful urges. Treasuring what he must abandon, then, with some grimness the speaker resolves to "welcome payne, let pleasure passe." This poem shows Gascoigne at his best. A governing metaphor, used as an "invention" around which the poem is built, provides richness of meaning and depth of feeling, accomplished with an ease which renders unobtrusive the artifice of the poem's language and verse form.

OTHER MAJOR WORKS

LONG FICTION: *The Discourse of the Adventures Passed by Master F. J.*, 1573 (revised as *The Pleasant Fable of Ferdinando Jeronimi and Leonora de Valasco*, 1575).

PLAYS: *Jocasta*, pr. 1566 (with Francis Kinwelmershe; translation of Lodovico Dolce's play *Giocasta*); *Supposes*, pr. 1566 (translation of Ludovico Ariosto's *I suppositi*); *A Devise of a Maske for the Right Honorable Viscount Mountacute*, pr. 1572; *The Glasse of Government*, pb. 1575; *The Princely Pleasures at Kenelworth Castle*, pr. 1575 (with others); *The Tale of Hemetes the Heremyte*, pr. 1575, pb. 1579.

NONFICTION: "Certayne Notes of Instruction Concerning the Making of Verse," 1575; *The Spoyle of Antwerpe*, 1576; *The Droomme of Doomes Day*, 1576; *A Delicate Diet, for Daintiemouthde Droonkardes*, 1576.

BIBLIOGRAPHY

Adams, Robert P. "Gascoigne's 'Master F. J.' as Original Fiction." *Publications Modern Language Association* 73 (1958): 315-326. Adams argues convincingly that *The Discourse of the Adventures Passed by Master F. J.* be read as a work of imaginative art and not as a disguised autobiography. Supplemented by a bibliography.

Bowman, Silvia E. *George Gascoigne*. New York: Twayne, 1972. A fascinating and informative survey, with specific comparisons of Gascoigne and Petrarch and a discussion of *The Steele Glas* as satire. "The Love Lyrics," *The Discourse of the Adventures Passed by Master F. J.*, and Gascoigne's three plays are also discussed. Supplemented by a chronology, notes, a select bibliography, and an index.

Bradner, Leiclster. "Point of View in George Gascoigne's Fiction." *Studies in Short Fiction* 3 (1965): 16-22. Bradner discusses the roles of the narrators in "Dan Bartholomew of Bath" and the two versions of *The Discourse of the Adventures Passed by Master F. J.* Supplemented by a bibliography.

Hughes, Felicity A. "Gascoigne's Poses." *Studies in English Literature, 1500-1900* 37, no. 1 (Winter, 1997): 1-19. Hughes questions the claim that in *The Posies* Gascoigne corrected his writings in conformity with the wishes of censors who found his writing offensive. Gascoigne did not succumb to the pressure. His "revised" edition of 1575 is no cleaner than the first edition, and it represents an attempt to brazen it out with the censors rather than placating them.

Prior, Roger. "Gascoigne's Posies as a Shakespearian Source." *Notes and Queries* 47, no. 4 (December, 2000): 444-449. Gascoigne wrote a masque to celebrate the 1572 double wedding of a son and daughter of Anthony Browne, first Viscount Montague, and two children of Sir William Dormer. Prior draws many parallels between this masque, published in Gascoigne's collection *The Posies* and William Shakespeare's *Romeo and Juliet*.

Prouty, C. T. *George Gascoigne: Elizabethan Courtier, Soldier, and Poet*. New York: Benjamin Bloom, 1942. A valuable study that places the life and work of Gascoigne in a historical context. Provides a useful discussion of Gascoigne as dramatist, court poet, narrator, and moralist. Three chapters are devoted to Gascoigne's life. Supplemented by an index, a bibliography, and appendices.

Schelling, Felix E. *The Life and Writings of George Gascoigne*. New York: Russell & Russell, 1967. A very useful survey of Gascoigne's life and work and an excellent source of biographical information. Supplemented by a bibliography, an index, and an appendix which contains four previously—to 1967—not printed poems.

Winters, Yvor. "The Sixteenth Century Lyric: Part I." *Poetry* 53 (February 5, 1939): 258-272 and "The Sixteenth Century Lyric: Part II." *Poetry* 53 (March 6, 1939): 320-325. The two essays by the well-known poet separate sixteenth century poetry into two schools, Petrarchan and expository, and argue that Gascoigne is the best of the expository poets of his age. Supplemented by a bibliography.

Richard J. Panofsky;
bibliography updated by the editors

THÉOPHILE GAUTIER

Born: Tarbes, France; August 30, 1811
Died: Paris, France; October 23, 1872

PRINCIPAL POETRY

Poésies, 1830 (English translation, 1973)
Albertus: Ou, l'Âme et le péché, 1833 (enlarged ed. of *Poésies*; *Albertus: Soul and Sin*, 1909)
La Comédie de la mort, 1838 (*The Drama of Death*, 1909)
España, 1845
Poésies complètes, 1845
Émaux et camées, 1852, 1872 (*Enamels and Cameos*, 1900)
Dernières Poésies, 1872

OTHER LITERARY FORMS

Théophile Gautier was an immensely prolific writer with a widely diversified range of interests and concerns. Although he considered himself primarily a poet, he earned his living as a journalist for some forty years, contributing art, theater, and literary criticism to various newspapers and journals. Gautier's art criticism is often eloquent and perceptive, anticipating the achievement of Charles Baudelaire. As an art critic, Gautier is notable for his early and passionate defense of such contrasting contemporary painters as Eugène Delacroix and Jean-Auguste-Dominique Ingres and for introducing the French public to the works of such Spanish masters as Bartolomé Murillo, Diego de Velázquez, Jose de Ribera, Francisco de Zurbarán, and Francisco de Goya. Gautier's theater criticism is especially voluminous, and, although only a small part of it is of continuing interest for its wit and stylistic verve, it is a remarkable quotidian document of the Parisian theatrical scene of the mid-nineteenth century. In addition to theater criticism, Gautier wrote a number of plays—some as a collaborator—none of which holds the stage today, even as a curiosity. More successful were his scenarios for a number of popular ballets, including the enduring favorite *Giselle: Ou, Les Wilis* (1841; *Giselle: Or, The Wilis*, 1970).

Of greater interest are Gautier's works of literary criticism. *Les Grotesques* (1844; *The Grotesques*, 1900) is a collection of studies of then little-known French authors of the fifteenth through the mid-seventeenth centuries, originally published as a series of individual newspaper articles under the collective title "Exhumations littéraires." The authors discussed (among them François Villon, Cyrano de Bergerac, and Théophile de Viau) were generally ignored or considered as *naïfs* in the early part of the nineteenth century, and Gautier played an important role in the rise of their reputations. Additionally, Gautier wrote several perceptive, if somewhat biased, appreciations (amounting to monographs) of such contemporaries as Gérard de Nerval, Honoré de Balzac, and Baudelaire, and he began *Histoire du Romantisme* (*History of Romanticism*, 1900), which remained unfinished because of his death but was published posthumously in 1874.

Gautier was also a passionate traveler, and he left a number of perceptive and entertaining travelogues of visits to Spain, Italy, the Middle East, and Russia. In the best tradition of travel literature, these works are more than simple guidebooks; they are accounts of the intellectual and spiritual voyages of an artist through the sometimes exotic sensibilities of foreign cultures.

The most significant literary genre to which Gautier contributed other than poetry was fiction—not only novels but also a considerable number of short stories, tales, and novellas. Many of these shorter works were originally published in newspapers and journals, and they typically deal with the fantastic (a popular subgenre of

Théophile Gautier (Hulton Archive)

the early nineteenth century, exemplified by the tales of E. T. A. Hoffmann and Edgar Allan Poe) or present exotic evocations of the Orient (not the Far East, as the modern reader might assume; for Gautier, the Orient was the Middle East). Of particular note is an early collection of tales, *Les Jeunes-France: Romans goguenards* (1833; liberally translated as "the new French generation," a title referring to a popular name accorded to the second generation of French Romantic writers and painters). Significantly, Gautier was one of the first Romantics to cast a critical look at Romanticism, and three of the six tales in *Les Jeunes-France* are delightful out-and-out parodies of Romantic emotional excess and literary paraphernalia.

Gautier also wrote three novels: *Mademoiselle de Maupin* (1835-1836; *Mademoiselle de Maupin: A Romance of Love and Passion*, 1887), *Le Roman de la momie* (1856; *The Romance of the Mummy*, 1863), and *Le Capitaine Fracasse* (1863; *Captain Fracasse*, 1880). To some extent, all three are variations of the popular historical romance as exemplified by the novels of Sir

Walter Scott or, in France, by Alfred de Vigny's 1826 novel, *Cinq-Mars* (English translation, 1847). *The Romance of the Mummy* is somewhat overburdened by minute technical detail, a quality that, along with a plot of more than usual improbability, has relegated the work to almost complete oblivion. *Mademoiselle de Maupin* is, on the other hand, possibly the best-known title in the Gautier canon. Its titular heroine (loosely based on an actual seventeenth century personality) is bisexual, not only an accomplished singer but also an adroit swordswoman who frequently dons male attire. The novel has been criticized for the flatness of its two other major characters, Albert and Rosette, as well as for a seeming reversal in the development of the heroine. Gautier quickly divested himself of the traditional apparatus of the historical novel and used the work as a vehicle for the exploration of the problem of identity: In one sense, the union of male and female in the person of the heroine serves as a metaphor for human perfection.

Finally, in *Captain Fracasse* (another manifestation of the early nineteenth century predilection for the early seventeenth century, the age of Louis XIII and Richelieu), in the tradition of Vigny's *Cinq-Mars* and Alexandre Dumas's *Les Trois Mousquetaires* (1844; *The Three Musketeers*, 1846), Gautier again appropriated the apparatus and structure of the historical romance, in which complications are typically happily resolved. Gautier endows this "literary machine" with a number of ironic twists that play with the idea of the illusions and uncertainties of human existence, undermining the assumptions of the genre even as he demonstrates a dazzling mastery of its conventions. *Captain Fracasse* is considered by many critics as Gautier's prose masterpiece.

ACHIEVEMENTS

Théophile Gautier was one of the most influential, as well as one of the few successful, poets of the second generation of French Romantics. His early poetry clearly demonstrates his debt to the greats of the first generation, but it did not take long for Gautier to establish his own voice and develop his own aesthetic (eclectic as it was). By mid-century, Gautier had become a leading literary figure, influential in his own right. His formulation of the theory of *l'art pour l'art* (art for art's sake), in which the value of art is determined solely by its capacity to create beauty, regardless of ethical or utilitarian considerations, was profoundly influential and produced ramifications beyond the borders of France (a major instance being the Aesthetic movement of late nineteenth century England, represented by such writers as Walter Pater, Algernon Charles Swinburne, and Oscar Wilde).

As the doctrine of art for art's sake eliminated ethics and social function as criteria for the making and criticism of art, it also tempered the vague notion of "imagination" with a concept of art as craft and discipline. In one literary review, Gautier was to state: "Art is beauty, the eternal invention of detail, the correct choice of words, the painstaking care of execution; the word 'poet' literally signifies 'maker.'. . . Everything which is not well made does not exist." As the prime spokesman for this reexamination of aesthetic principles, he evolved a concept in which literature might emulate the plastic arts (particularly sculpture) by being "chiseled," "polished," and "objective." This notion was strongly advocated in Gautier's final verse collection, *Enamels and Cameos*, but it was more consistently developed and perfected by the generation of poets who succeeded Gautier, the Parnassians (particularly Charles-Marie Leconte de Lisle and José-María de Heredia).

No major poet was more generous in acknowledging a debt to Gautier than was Charles Baudelaire. The latter's masterpiece, *Les Fleurs du mal* (1857; *Flowers of Evil*, 1909), was dedicated to Gautier: "the impeccable poet, the perfect magician . . . my very dear and most venerated master and friend." Certain of Baudelaire's concepts of the feminine ideal, death, and the "spleen of Paris" are easily traced back to the poetry of Gautier. There are similar debts in the works of such poets as Paul Verlaine, Stéphane Mallarmé, and Paul Valéry.

Not the least of Gautier's accomplishments was purely personal, for he was renowned for his friendships with many of the leading cultural and artistic personalities of his day, including Victor Hugo, Delacroix, Nerval, Baudelaire, Hippolyte Taine, the Goncourt brothers, and Maxime Du Camp. At Gautier's death, more than eighty poets from all over Europe contributed to a commemorative volume of poems in recognition of his place in French letters and his passionate commitment to art and beauty.

Assessing Gautier's poetic achievement is problematic. If he was overpraised by his contemporaries and no longer seems the "impeccable poet" of Baudelaire's dedication to Gautier in *Flowers of Evil*, he is surely underestimated today. His place as a transitional figure is clear; the influence of both his poetry and his ideas upon the course of French literature is undeniable; his influence outside his native country in the nineteenth century was not inconsiderable. In the history of Western culture, few have argued as eloquently as Gautier the notion that art is man's supreme achievement, ennobling him, lifting him above the petty pursuits and scarring disappointments of human existence.

BIOGRAPHY

Pierre Jules Théophile Gautier was born on August 30, 1811, in Tarbes, a small town in southern France at the foot of the Pyrenees. His father, a minor government official, was transferred with his family from this provincial home on the frontier of Spain to the cosmopolitan bustle of Paris in 1814, when Gautier was not quite three years old. Tarbes made an indelible impression upon Gautier, who himself traced his wanderlust and his perpetual fascination with the exotic to a desire to recapture the idealized world of his early life at Tarbes.

In Paris, after an unsuccessful attempt to conform to the regimen of a boarding school, Gautier was enrolled as a day pupil at the Collège Charlemagne. There, his scholastic career prospered. His parents, particularly his father, were strongly supportive of their son's interests, and Gautier was encouraged to develop an early talent for sketching by studying art in the studio of the painter Louis Édouard Rioult. Gautier's years of study in the studio were to be of the greatest importance in his development as a writer.

While enrolled at the Collège Charlemagne and simultaneously studying with Rioult, Gautier met and befriended the precocious young writer Gérard de Nerval (who published his first collection of poetry at the age of seventeen and, in his twentieth year, published a translation of *Faust* much admired by Johann Wolfgang von Goethe). Nerval was one of the chief organizers of the pro-Romantic claque that was to attend the premiere of Victor Hugo's drama *Hernani* at the Théâtre-Français on February 25, 1830, and he enlisted Gautier's assistance as the head of a subsquad of Hugo supporters. The evening was destined to become a watershed in French theatrical history; it served to mark the "official" recognition of the Romantic movement in France. Gautier left a warm and lively account of that evening, which the French refer to as the "battle of *Hernani*." The long-haired, outrageously attired young Romantics (Gautier would be known throughout his life for the *gilet rouge*, or red waistcoat, he wore that evening) applauded and cheered their hero, Hugo, while the old-guard neoclassicists hissed him down. The performance could barely proceed for the noise and interruptions, but somehow the new Romanticism triumphed.

Gautier and Nerval soon became involved with a group of young literary hopefuls who together formed a literary club, the *petit cénacle* (so called to distinguish it from the original *Cénacle* of the first-generation Romantics: Hugo, Alphonse de Lamartine, Alfred de Vigny, and Alfred de Musset). This "little club" was a flamboyant and colorful group, most of the members of which are now forgotten. In July, 1830, under the influence of his fellow members, Gautier's first collection of verse, *Poésies*, appeared, containing poems which were clearly imitative of the established poets of the first generation. It was not long, however, before Gautier began to write poetry and fiction critical of Romantic excess, and both *Albertus* and the short-fiction collection *Les Jeunes-France* are examples of this ironic, satirical vein.

The life span of the *petit cénacle* was quite short, but another, even more Bohemian and intellectually stimulating, "club" developed around a group of writers and artists who took up communal living in a slum area near the Louvre, in a cul-de-sac called the Impasse du Doyenné. Among Gautier's comrades there were Nerval, Delacroix, Dumas, and Arsène Houssaye (the future director of the Théâtre-Français). It was among these artists that Gautier composed *The Drama of Death, Mademoiselle de Maupin*, and *Les Jeunes-France*, and his years among them were to mark the end of the more carefree, youthful stage of his career.

It soon became necessary for Gautier to take on the burden of providing for the financial security and comfort not only of himself but also of a number of dependents (including, at one time or other, his father and two sisters, two mistresses—Eugénie Fort and Ernesta Grisi—and three illegitimate children). In 1836, he accepted the post of art and theater critic for the Parisian newspaper *La Presse* (his first article was devoted to some paintings of Delacroix), thus inaugurating a long and often wearisome career as a journalist. Over the years, he contributed to several leading newspapers and journals, including *Le Figaro, Le Moniteur universel*, and *Le Revue des deux mondes*. Although he became a highly influential critic, Gautier never really enjoyed the work, ever resenting the time lost from the composition of poetry.

In 1840, Gautier made a trip to Spain on a quasi-business venture to buy rare books and artifacts to be resold at higher prices in France. The enterprise turned out to be a financial disaster, but it proved to be an inspirational gold mine for the poet—the travel book *Voyage en Espagne* (1843; *Wanderings in Spain*, 1853) and a collection of verse, *España*, were derived from this experience. The trip tempered Gautier's rather idealistic vision of Spain, but it failed to cure him of his desire to travel. Future travels took him to Italy, the Middle East, North Africa, and, twice, to Russia. Each major trip resulted in a travel book, which, besides serving the purpose of a guidebook, served as a record of Gautier's perceptions and personal development.

During the last twenty years of his life, Gautier was involved with a number of mistresses, most seriously with Ernesta Grisi, the famous contralto, who was mother of his two daughters. Gautier had earlier become infatuated with Ernesta's sister, the celebrated ballerina Carlotta Grisi. His love for Carlotta was unrequited, but they remained lifelong friends; for her, he created the title roles in the ballets *Giselle* and *La Péri* (1843). It was Ernesta, however, who provided the background of domestic peace in which Gautier could work freely. He soon became a Parisian literary lion and received the title of Chevalier de la Légion d'Honneur. He became a favorite of the literary salons, particularly those of Madame Sabatier, of the actress Rachel (Elisa Felix), and of Princess Mathilde. The last named was to prove a most generous friend and benefactor, appointing Gautier as her personal librarian at a time of great financial difficulty for the poet, who was nearly destitute and suffering from the privations of the Franco-Prussian War.

Over the years, Gautier developed many binding friendships both within and outside the literary world and became well respected for his affection, concern, even-temperedness, and generosity. Rarely has a literary figure received such tributes for both artistic and personal qualities. The most important artistic endeavor of his last twenty years was the composition of a final collection of poems, *Enamels and Cameos*. After contending with a variety of illnesses, including several heart attacks, Gautier died in Paris at the age of sixty-one and was buried in the cemetery of Montmartre.

ANALYSIS

The typical twentieth century critical estimation is that Théophile Gautier is a transitional figure in French poetry, although this was not the judgment of his own time, for he was highly, perhaps extravagantly, praised by his contemporaries. Today, Gautier is often viewed as a second-generation Romantic whose earliest work is excessively imitative of the previous generation and whose mature work anticipates the poetic achievement of later, greater poets and of entire literary schools. It is a curiosity that Gautier is better known today as a spokesman for an aesthetic doctrine, art for art's sake—which he never systematized and only fitfully realized—than for his poetry itself.

That particular aesthetic was years in developing. If Gautier was incapable, even to the end, of setting aside all the Romantic "baggage" of his early years, there always existed in him a detached, ironic, objective observer who bridled at subscribing wholeheartedly to Romantic subjectivity or Romantic political and social involvement. The idea that a work of art should exist in a vacuum, as some kind of cold, clear object without reference to extraneous and irrelevant religious, political, and social meanings, was first clearly stated in Gautier's work in the preface to the novel *Mademoiselle de Maupin*. This concept of art for art's sake was not original with Gautier, who was himself uncomfortably conscious of the vagueness of such grand abstractions as beauty, form, and art: In subsequent pronouncements, he attempted to grapple with these abstractions and to concretize them. For all this, Gautier was still a child of the Romantic era (a fact he would fondly recall until his death), and as a boy of nineteen, he exuberantly entered the literary scene, consciously treading in the giant footsteps of the noted first-generation French Romantic poets: Hugo, Lamartine, Vigny, and Musset.

POÉSIES

Gautier's first book of verse, *Poésies*, is characterized by a precocious formal virtuosity. Stock Romantic themes, such as love and the impermanence of life, abound in this first collection, although as early as the second edition of 1833 (which enlarged the scope of *Poésies* from forty to sixty poems), the detached, satiric observer characteristic of Gautier's mature verse can be detected—most notably in the long narrative poem "Albertus: Ou, l'Âme et le péché" ("Albertus: Soul and Sin"), after which the 1833 collection is named. With typical Romantic whimsy and ambiguity, Gautier termed the poem a "theological legend." The work recounts the tale of a witch who, by transforming herself into a beautiful woman, lures the titular hero into selling his soul for a single night of pleasure. Upon sealing the bargain, she reverts to her normal state and drags Albertus off to a witches' Sabbath. The discovery of the hero's mangled body in a forest clearing the following morning presumably demonstrates the wages of sin.

Even a brief summary suffices to indicate the customary Romantic fascination with the occult, the macabre, and the grotesque. In this poem, however, Gautier, much in the manner of Goethe and Lord Byron (to whom "Albertus" is unmistakably indebted), casts an ironic glance back on the clichés and excesses of Romanticism, the enthusiastic abandon that often merely gave way to bathos. In spite of the evident enjoyment and skill with which he creates the Romantic milieu (certain passages give early witness to Gautier's undeniable descriptive genius), there is at the same time an ironic undercutting of the emotional atmosphere of Romantic horror. Gautier would refer to "Albertus" and to *The Drama of Death* as examples of his *maladie gothique* (gothic illness). While acknowledging their descriptive verve and the formal and prosodic talent they evidence, a modern reader is likely to view these early works as occasionally enjoyable compendia of motifs and preoccupations of the Romantic era.

THE DRAMA OF DEATH

The Drama of Death (a miscellany of fifty-six poems composed between 1832 and 1838) possesses, as do all

Gautier's collections to some extent, no particular thematic unity. Like *Poésies, The Drama of Death* displays the poet's mastery of a variety of verse forms; also noteworthy are the early glimpses of Gautier's developing aesthetic, particularly in the poems concerning Michelangelo, Petrarch, Albrecht Dürer, and Raphael, which celebrate the enduring triumphs of art. Other poems, especially the three-part title poem, confirm Gautier's obsession with death. Some of these death poems are somberly eloquent in their struggle to balance the states of being and nonbeing; more often, they demonstrate a morbid fascination with the gruesome physical mutation caused by death or the idea of animate interment, such as "Le Ver et la trépassée" ("The Worm and the Dead Woman"), which is cast as a ghoulish dialogue between a young bride-to-be, mistakenly buried alive, and a worm, her rather unexpected spouse. Indeed, the theme of death pervades Gautier's œuvre, but in early Gautier works, one might describe it as an obsession, often purely physical, without resolution. The psychology of this obsession was of tremendous consequence for Gautier's aesthetic, ultimately leading him to prefer the enduring to the mutable—to prefer, as he stated, "marble to flesh"—and to value art over life itself.

"IN DESERTO"

The mature phase of Gautier's career as a poet began with the collection of forty-three miscellaneous poems titled *España*. This collection was viewed as a kind of poetic companion volume to the 1843 travelogue *Wanderings in Spain:* Both convey the traveler-poet's absorption in the topography and the art and culture of the Iberian Peninsula; both relate a search for the ideal (which Spain had always represented to Gautier) tempered by experience. Gautier's descriptive genius, the immense technical vocabulary characteristic of his entire canon, more consistently comes to the fore in this collection than in any of its predecessors.

The poem "In deserto" (in the desert) subtly exemplifies Gautier's growing mastery of his art while revealing the contradictions that often distinguish his poetic practice from his poetic theory. Through a rapid accumulation of images, Gautier paints a vivid portrayal of the stark central wilderness of Spain. Each subsequent image is calculated to reinforce the effect of aridity and

desolation. In the first ten lines, there is a topographical description of a wasteland of rocky mountains and stretches of desert, rendered in a technical vocabulary capable of fine distinction: "Les monts aux flancs zébrés de tuf, d'ocre et de marne/ . . . le grès plein de micas papillotant aux yeux/ . . . L'ardente solfatare avec la pierre-ponce" (The mountainsides striped like the zebra in tuff, ochre and marl/ . . . Sandstone replete with mica sparkling to the eye/ . . . The glowing volcanic vent with its pumice stone).

The sun rises to a noonday glare over a world incongenial to the gentle, fragile forms of life:

> Là, point de marguerite au coeur étoilé d'or
> Point de muguet prodigue égrenant son trésor;
> Là, point de violette ignorée et charmante,
> Dans l'ombre se cachant comme une pâle amante;
> (There, no daisy with heart of golden stars
> No lavish lily of the valley stringing out its pearls,
> There, no charming and unnoticed violet
> Hiding in the shadows like some pale lover.)

In this landscape, only the smooth-skinned viper and the scaly lizard are at home. In a final image, a solitary eagle is seen atop a mountain peak, silhouetted against the raw and riotous colors of sunset. The effect of the whole is of a photograph focused to the sharpest clarity, and if this were the sum of Gautier's intention, the poem would be an unqualified success. Instead, he chooses to complicate the effect by the inclusion of a single metaphor. It seems as if Gautier were uncomfortable with the sharp, objective lines of the photographic image, and a subjective note is introduced when, suddenly, a narrator appears to remark that the rocks, boulders, and sandy expanses "are less arid and dead to vegetation/ Than my rocklike heart to all feeling." The reader recognizes the comparison immediately as a rather overworked, sentimental image pieced together from conventional Romantic vocabulary.

In the midst of a hard-edged descriptive "composition of place," this subjective note is a solitary leftover of what John Ruskin would term the "pathetic fallacy," in which the external world appears as a projection of the poet's inner reality. Is the unusual and stark position of the image so early in the poem (one would conventionally expect it in the conclusion) a coup of perception or a miscalculation? Does it, perhaps, signal some realization on the poet's part of a certain "inhumanness" in an aesthetic that increasingly stresses surface and gesture over the subjectivity of inner meaning? To a modern reader, this "rocklike heart" probably seems gratuitous, and the poem as a whole discloses the Gautier whom critic Wallace Fowlie calls a "prisoner of appearances," restricted in his role as "spectator of the visible world of objects, landscapes, and animals." That it was perplexing for Gautier to "look within" is a characteristic made more clear in another poem from *España*, "À Zurbarán."

"À ZURBARÁN"

Gautier frequently required the stimulus of some existing artifact for poetic inspiration. He developed for this purpose the concept of the *transpostion d'art*, in which an art object (a painting, a piece of statuary, even a building) could be created anew in words, recomposed, as it were, by the poet. Some of Gautier's finest achievements are in this genre. "À Zurbarán," for example, is a powerful evocation, not of a single canvas by the sixteenth century Spanish master, but of that superascetic religiosity which thrived in the age of the Inquisition and which imbues so much of Francisco de Zurbarán's work. Thus, Gautier singles out Zurbarán's monks and penetrates to the very essence of their spirituality, formed by the harsh discipline of fasting, hair shirts, and flagellation. The poet is dumbstruck by the display:

Croyez-vous donc que Dieu s'amuse à voir souffrir
Et que ce meurtre lent, cette froide agonie
Fassent pour vous le ciel plus facile à s'ouvrir?
(Do you then believe that God is amused by suffering,
And that this prolonged death, this gelid agony
Will make the gates of heaven more easy to open?)

Along with the poet's sense of revulsion, however, is a recognition of the strange, unearthly strength in the physical presence of these ascetics: "Pourtant quelle énergie et quelle force d'âme/ Ils avaient, ces chartreux, sous leur pâle linceul" (All the same, what energy, what spiritual power/ They had, those brothers, beneath their colorless shrouds).

The mere reproduction or evocation, even recomposition, of the Zurbarán canvases is not, however,

Gautier's principal intent. The subject of the poem is, rather, the inability of the narrator to reconcile two extremes of emotion: revulsion and admiration. How can he balance his "Mais je ne comprends pas ce morne suicide" ("But I do not comprehend this gloomy suicide") with his vision of "Le vertige divin, l'enivrement de foi/ Qui les fait rayonner d'une clarté fiévreuse" ("The divine vertigo, the intoxication of faith/ Which makes them shine with a febrile brightness"). Toward the conclusion of the poem, the real source of this dilemma is revealed when the narrator (with the eyes of a painter) expresses his personal difficulty in conceiving of a totally spiritualized life, in which the physical world is a mere tribulation to be put up with—indeed, a matter of little import:

Forme, rayon, couleur, rien n'existe pour vous,
À tout objet réel vous êtes insensibles,
Car le ciel vous enivre et la croix vous rend fous.
(Form, light, color, nothing exists for you,
To every physical object you rest insensible,
For heaven intoxicates you and the cross has made you
   mad.)

How could the poet who once described himself as "un homme pour qui le monde extérieur existe" (a man for whom the external world exists) understand such transcendent spirituality, such unworldliness? For Gautier, the solid ground of reality lay exclusively in the perceived object, and he saw in the plastic arts the true medium for achieving permanence and endowing life with value. Literature, too, might approach the plastic, both in subject matter and in treatment. This was to be the goal of his final collection of verse, and the theory of art for art's sake was to be its foundation.

ENAMELS AND CAMEOS

Gautier's poetic practice was not always aligned, however, with his theoretical views, as is clear from the contents of *Enamels and Cameos*—nor, for that matter, was his poetic theory consistently formulated. All the same, as the critic P. E. Tennant has pointed out, Gautier *was* consistent about stating four basic principles: Beauty is defined by clarity of form (the *forma* of classical aesthetics), and form and idea are inseparable; pure art is autonomous, not to be held accountable to social, political, or religious evaluation; art is not natural but, rather, artificial—divine of effect, perhaps, but made by man; and, finally, although a certain irrational state ("inspiration") is functional in the creation of art, pure art is the product of calculation and hard work.

The appearance of *Enamels and Cameos*, in 1852, was a turning point in French literature, marking the shift away from Romantic lyricism to a more aesthetic, objective manner in which art would exist in a world of its own, apart from the mundane personal or social concerns of everyday life. Gautier labored over and corrected the contents of the collection for the last twenty years of his life, eventually enlarging its scope from the eighteen poems of the first edition to the forty-seven poems of the final edition of 1872. Once again, there is no rigorous thematic unity or structure (Richard Grant, in his study *Théophile Gautier*, makes a case for a loose thematic structure), nor is the disposition of the individual pieces of particular significance—with the exception of "L'Art" ("Art"), which Gautier specified as the final poem. As the title of the collection suggests, and as Gautier himself stated, the goal was "to treat small subjects in a restricted manner."

All but four of the poems are in octosyllabic quatrains, for Gautier had come to favor the more intimate eight-syllable line to the rhetorical twelve-foot Alexandrine. The almost exclusive repetition of a single stanzaic form does not preclude a surprising variety of subject matter—on the contrary, it emphasizes a richness of rhyme and a certain structural solidity.

Gautier does not wholly abandon the big Romantic themes; rather, he treats them in miniature. For example, a number of poems in the collection are openly personal in the Romantic manner: "Le Château du souvenir" ("The Castle of Remembrance") is clearly autobiographical, and several other poems celebrate Gautier's affairs with various mistresses. Yet, though Gautier avails himself of the confessional mode introduced by the Romantics, his "personal" poems are in fact curiously impersonal, conveying little sense of the familiar or intimate; in them, life is preserved in cameo.

"SYMPHONY IN WHITE MAJOR" AND "ART"

Gautier's two best-known poems are included in *Enamels and Cameos*: "Symphonie en blanc majeur" ("Symphony in White Major") and "Art." The latter is an openly didactic piece and a clear poetic statement of

Gautier's concept of literature as plastic art, its final stanza making this exhortation to his fellow poets: "Carve, burnish, build thy theme,—/ But fix thy wavering dream/ In the stern rock supreme."

"Symphony in White Major" is a tour de force of thematic variation, and a comparison with "In deserto" from the collection *España*, a poem that shares the same fundamental technical procedure, reveals the measure of Gautier's progress as an artist. Like "In deserto," "Symphony in White Major" is an evocation of a landscape, but the landscape evoked is that of a woman's body. That the woman of the poem existed in real life (she was the striking beauty Marie Kalergis, a student of Frédéric Chopin and a friend of Franz Liszt) is of little consequence. Gautier's aim is not a photographic image in the manner of "In deserto" but the re-creation, for the reader, of the associations and sensations produced within the artist by the sight of the woman.

There is clearly something not entirely human about such perfect beauty, for the first image is of a *femme-cygne* (swan woman) "from the Rhine's escarpments high." What follows is not so much a direct description of the woman's body as an enumeration of images, similes, and metaphors that relate the unique essence of her beauty: its pure, glacial whiteness. Much in the technique of the "transposition d'art," Gautier has analyzed the woman's beauty in order to retrieve its essential components, reconstructing not flesh and blood, but rather an effect:

> Of the marble still and cold,
>   Wherein the great gods dwell?
> Of creamy opal gems that hold
>   Faint fifes of mystic spell?
> Or the organ's ivory keys?
>   Her wingèd fingers oft
> Like butterflies flit over these,
>   With kisses pending soft.

It is a beauty that calls forth worship: "What host, what taper, did bestow/ The white of her matchless skin?" The woman's beauty is, in some sense, an abstraction of beauty itself. The heroine is barely present; the greater part of the poem avoids specific reference. Certainly, the final stanza refers directly back to the source of the artist's fantasy. Even here, however, personal experience is transformed and the passion of love expressed only indirectly. How much more satisfying is this ambiguity than the blunt, awkward "rocklike heart" of "In deserto":

> What magic of what far name
> Shall this pale soul ignite?
> Ah! who shall flush with rose's flame
> This cold, implacable white?

The technical and conceptual advances evident in "Symphony in White Major" can be found throughout *Enamels and Cameos*. There are inconsistencies with Gautier's aesthetic ideal of the cool, clear, nonsubjective work of art (his Parnassian successors, Leconte de Lisle and Heredia, would more consistently realize the goal of literature as a plastic art), but few readers have denied the integrity of the craftsman who labored over these poems. The poems may not affect the reader in his emotional being, but they please the intellect with their fluctuating colors, their wealth of rhyme, and their perfection of form.

OTHER MAJOR WORKS

PLAYS: *Une Larme de diable*, pb. 1839; *Le Tricorne enchanté*, pr. 1845; *La Fausse Conversion*, pr. 1846; *Pierrot posthume*, pr. 1847; *Théâtre de poche*, pb. 1855.

LONG FICTION: *Mademoiselle de Maupin*, 1835-1836 (2 volumes; *Mademoiselle de Maupin: A Romance of Love and Passion*, 1887); *Fortunio*, 1838 (novella; English translation, 1915); *Le Roman de la momie*, 1856 (*Romance of the Mummy*, 1863); *Le Capitaine Fracasse*, 1863 (*Captain Fracasse*, 1880); *Spirite: Nouvelle fantastique*, 1866 (novella; *Spirite*, 1877).

SHORT FICTION: *Les Jeunes-France: Romans goguenards*, 1833; *Nouvelles*, 1845; *Un Trio de romans*, 1852; *Avatar*, 1857 (English translation, 1900); *Jettatura*, 1857 (English translation, 1888); *Romans et contes*, 1863.

NONFICTION: *Voyage en Espagne*, 1843 (*Wanderings in Spain*, 1853); *Les Grotesques*, 1844 (2 volumes; *The Grotesques*, 1900); *Salon de 1847*, 1847; *Caprices et zigzags*, 1852; *Italia*, 1852 (*Travels in Italy*, 1900); *Constantinople*, 1853 (*Constantinople of To-Day*, 1854); *Les Beaux-Arts en Europe, 1855*, 1855-1856 (2 volumes); *L'Art moderne*, 1856; *Honoré de Balzac: Sa Vie et ses œuvres*, 1858; *Histoire de l'art dramatique en France depuis vingt-cinq ans*, 1858-1859 (6 volumes); *Abécédaire du Salon de 1861*, 1861; *Trésors d'art de la Russie ancienne et moderne*, 1861; *Loin de Paris*, 1865; *Quand on voyage*, 1865; *Voyage en Russie*, 1867 (*A Winter in Russia*, 1874); *Ménagerie intime*, 1869 (*My Household of Pets*, 1882); *Tableaux de siège*, 1871 (*Paris Besieged*, 1900); *Histoire du Romantisme*, 1874 (*History of Romanticism*, 1900); *Portraits contemporains*, 1874 (*Portraits of the Day*, 1900); *Portraits et souvenirs littéraires*, 1875; *L'Orient*, 1877; *Fusains et eaux-fortes*, 1880; *Tableaux à la plume*, 1880; *Les Vacances du lundi*, 1881; *Guide de l'amateur au Musée du Louvre*, 1882 (*The Louvre*, 1900); *Souvenirs de théâtre, d'art, et de critique*, 1883; *Victor Hugo*, 1902; *La Musique*, 1911; *Critique artistique et littéraire*, 1929; *Les Maîtres du théâtre français de Rotrou à Dumas fils*, 1929; *Souvenirs romantiques*, 1929.

BALLET SCENARIOS: *Giselle: Ou, Les Wilis*, 1841 (*Giselle: Or, The Wilis*, 1970); *La Péri*, 1843; *Pâquerette*, 1851; *Gemma*, 1854; *Sacountala*, 1858; *Yanko le bandit*, 1858.

MISCELLANEOUS: *The Works of Théophile Gautier*, 1900-1903 (24 volumes).

BIBLIOGRAPHY

Burnett, David. "The Destruction of the Artist in Gautier's Early Poetry." *Bulletin de la Société Théophile Gautier* 3 (1981): 49-58. A thoughtful analysis of the image of the poet whom society does not understand in Gautier's early poetry. Describes how Gautier's representation of the poet in his early work indicated his close affiliation with the Romantic movement.

Gosselin Schick, Constance. *Seductive Resistance: The Poetry of Théophile Gautier*. Atlanta, Ga.: Rodopi, 1994. Schick's exhaustive study begins with an analysis of the intextual repetition of Gautier's poetry, the citations, imitations and transpositions which make evident the poetry's displacement of the significant and the personal into aesthetic simulacra. The study covers each of Gautier's five major collections and deals with the contextuality, the fetishism, and the eroticism revealed in a miscellany of poems.

_____. "Théophile Gautier's Poetry as 'Coquetterie posthume.'" *Nineteenth-Century French Studies* 20, nos. 1/2 (1992): 74-84. Insightful study of the treatment of death in Gautier's late poetry. Describes the maturity that was generally lacking in his early poetry.

Grant, Richard. *Théophile Gautier.* Boston: Twayne, 1975. Remains one of the best introductions in English to Gautier's lyric poetry and to his more famous short stories and novels. Grant describes Gautier's originality in introducing fantastic elements into apparently realistic prose works. Contains an excellent annotated bibliography of important studies on Gautier's works.

Henry, Freeman. "Gautier/Baudelaire: *Homo Ludens* Versus *Homo Duplex.*" *Nineteenth-Century French Studies* 25, nos. 1/2 (1996/1997). Baudelaire dedicated his 1857 book of poetry *Flowers of Evil* to Gautier. This essay examines how both poets created complex poems that permit several levels of interpretation.

Hunt, Tony. "The Inspiration and Unity of *Emaux et camées* (1852)." *Durham University Journal* 73 (1980): 75-81. A short but thoughtful article on Gautier's most significant book of poetry. Hunt argues persuasively that this book contains Gautier's most finely crafted poems.

Majewski, Henry F. "Painting into Text: Theophile Gautier's Artistic Screen." *Romance Quarterly* 47, no. 2 (Spring, 2000): 84-102. Majewski examines one important aspect of the complex intertextual signs informing Gautier's poetry. He proposes to study the function of painting in Gautier's poetry as a kind of artistic screen.

Tennant, P. E. *Théophile Gautier.* London: Athlone, 1975. Largely a well-researched biography of Gautier, but Tennant also describes very well Gautier's importance in the development of lyric poetry and fantastic prose writings in nineteenth century French literature.

Theodore Baroody;
bibliography updated by Edmund J. Campion

JOHN GAY

Born: Barnstaple, North Devonshire, England; June 30, 1685

Died: London, England; December 4, 1732

PRINCIPAL POETRY

Wine, 1708

Rural Sports, 1713

The Fan, 1714

The Shepherd's Week, 1714

Trivia: Or, The Art of Walking the Streets of London, 1716

Poems on Several Occasions, 1720, 1731

To a Lady on Her Passion for Old China, 1725

Fables, 1727, 1738

Gay's Chair: Poems Never Before Printed, 1820

The Poetical Works of John Gay, 1926 (G. C. Faber, editor; includes plays)

OTHER LITERARY FORMS

John Gay's early reputation was based on his poetry, but he produced several dramatic pieces of note between 1712 and 1731. In fact, three of his plays were not published until after his death. His claim to lasting fame, however, was *The Beggar's Opera*, which opened at the Theatre Royal in Lincoln's Inn Fields, London, on the night of January 29, 1728. It ran for sixty-two performances between January and June of that year, thirty-two of which were consecutive. Produced under the direction of John Rich (1682-1761), manager of Lincoln's Inn Fields, the play supposedly made "Gay rich and Rich gay." Financial success aside, the piece wove together a number of popular modes: sarcasm against Italian opera, political satire, and social criticism that dared to compare the Court circle with the then-current underworld network. There is some evidence to support the contention that the opera was prompted by Jonathan Swift's suggestion to Alexander Pope (by way of a letter dated August 11, 1716) that Gay should write a series of "Newgate pastorals"—burlesques of the pastoral tradition that had succeeded so well in *The Shepherd's Week*. The problem with that theory, however, is that it seems unreasonable that Gay would have allowed the suggestion to remain in limbo for twelve years. Perhaps a more plausible source for *The Beggar's Opera* is the career of the famous highwayman, Jonathan Wild, who died at Tyburn Hill on May 4, 1725. Certainly, curiosity about Wild may well have motivated Gay to explore more deeply the workings of the London criminal element.

Polly (1729), a sequel to *The Beggar's Opera*, never graced the London stage during its author's lifetime. Sir Robert Walpole, the Prime Minister, had quickly recognized the assaults against himself and his party in *The Beggar's Opera*; thus, he ordered the Duke of Grafton, as Lord Chamberlain, to deny a license for the production of *Polly*. Obviously, he feared more of the same. Gay published his play, however, and sales were brisk because of the Whig ministry's refusal to permit a stage production—an event that did not take place until 1777. Shortly after Gay's death, his last opera, *Achilles* (1733), appeared on the stage for eighteen performances. However, its reception was cool, and general opinion held the piece to be hardly deserving of serious attention. The eight remaining plays published by Gay received varying degrees of critical response.

In May, 1711, Gay had published a two-penny pamphlet titled *The Present State of Wit, in a Letter to a Friend in the Country*, an account of contemporary periodical literature in England, with emphasis upon *The Tatler* and *The Spectator*.

ACHIEVEMENTS

John Gay's prominent stature within the literary and social circles of eighteenth century England requires no complex explanation. Indeed, his associations with his literary peers, especially among the outspoken Tory satirists of the early years of Sir Robert Walpole's ministry, were far deeper than mere political or professional ties. Alexander Pope, Jonathan Swift, and Dr. John Arbuthnot regarded him with the utmost love and respect. Even Walpole, whom he attacked, appointed him to the post of commissioner of lotteries, granted him an apartment at Whitehall Palace, and influenced Queen Caroline to offer him a household post. Lewis Melville, who fairly early in the twentieth century compiled a collection of Gay's letters and surrounded it with biographical bits and pieces, maintained that Gay's friends—Lord Burlington, Lady Suffolk (Henrietta Howard), the

duke and duchess of Queensberry—all placed their houses and their purses at the poet's disposal in an effort to compete for the pleasure of his company. Never, noted Melville, was a man of letters so pampered and petted.

Gay was, however, more to the Augustans than simply another social ornament or intellectual gadfly with a superficial talent for conversation and letters. Consider the degree to which his works held the interest of English readers and English theater audiences after his death in 1732. There were productions and revivals of his operas and recurrent editions of the *Poems on Several Occasions*, the *Fables*, *Trivia*, *The Shepherd's Week*, and even *The What D'ye Call It* (1715). Throughout the century, readers of his poems and plays realized the timelessness of his social criticism. What those same readers may have forgotten, however, is that as a poet Gay remained carefully within the outward conventions of his day, never extending his art beyond his interest or his ability. He turned his back on the epic and focused, instead, on burlesque—on minute descriptions, light satire, and jocular song. He seemed more interested in fol-

John Gay (Library of Congress)

lowing contemporary caricaturists than in emulating the strict Latin models of the first Augustan Age.

Gay gathered strength from the wit, the sparkle, and even the venom of his friend's personal dislikes and distastes, all of which helped him to refine his realistic humor. Thus, *The Shepherd's Week* reflects the bite of Pope's attack against Ambrose Philips's *Pastorals*, while there are more than coincidental associations between *Trivia* and Jonathan Swift's ultrarealistic "Description of the Morning" and "A Description of a City Shower," as well as some *Tatler* and *Spectator* fragments on the same general topic from Sir Richard Steele and Joseph Addison. Nevertheless, Gay never achieved intellectual or even poetic and satiric equality with Pope or Swift, principally because of his own poetic temperament. There are scholars of the period who maintain that he was only a songster—a very good one, to be sure, but still not a poet. Such a reaction may be too harsh, for he did hold his own among his contemporaries who sought to portray everyday life; he could harness current coffeehouse rumor and drawing-room gossip into readable poetry—with much the same success as the skilled novelists did later in the century. He knew the temper of the times: the city, its people, its activities. He read the weekly gazettes and news sheets that graphically reproduced the sounds, smells, and irrational moments of a supposedly rational age.

Gay thus catered to and transcribed the Augustan era. His poetry—as did that of Swift, Pope, Matthew Prior, John Dennis, and Thomas Parnell—provided a mirror for society; but his particular glass was polished bright and clear, perhaps not as prismatic as those of his colleagues. His poetry caught hypocrisy in mid-air and hurled it back in the face of his reader: the flattery, the filth, the amusement, the exaggeration. Again, he sought not the higher grounds of epic and lyric for his work, but chose to remain at eye level—to write *verse* about town, club, street, tavern, coffeehouse, theater, bear pit, drawing-room. As a poet, Gay was genuine, and the degree to which society accepted his verse indicates that he met the criteria for art and satisfied the demands of the intellect.

BIOGRAPHY

John Gay was born at Barnstaple, North Devonshire, on June 30, 1685. His father, William Gay, died in early

1695, while his mother, a Hanmer (and a relative of the speaker of Parliament and editor of Shakespeare, Sir Thomas Hanmer), had preceded her husband in death by only a few months (1694). An uncle, Thomas Gay (died 1702), took charge of both house and family, sending young John to the free grammar school at Barnstaple. There the boy received more than competent instruction in the classics and poetry from the Reverend Robert Luck, a young High Churchman from Westminster School, newly graduated from Christ Church, Oxford. After the death of his uncle, the boy set out for London to become an apprentice to a silk mercer, a vocation that quickly lost its appeal for him. In fact, he became so depressed that his health suffered, and so he returned, in 1706, to Barnstaple and the house of another uncle, the Reverend John Hanmer, a Nonconformist and a sincere Calvinist who died in July, 1707.

Upon Hanmer's death, Gay once more set his course for London, where he served his former schoolmate and fellow poet, Aaron Hill, as a transcriber and general secretary. His first poem, "Wine," came forth shortly thereafter; Gay announced that its sources were Miltonic, but the piece shows a strong influence of Ambrose Philips's most noteworthy labor of verse, *The Splendid Shilling*. Interestingly enough, the poem did not appear in the first edition of his *Poems on Several Occasions*.

At any rate, "Wine" sent Gay into the profession of letters. He formed an acquaintance with Alexander Pope, and his reputation rose when, in 1712, Bernard Lintot's *Miscellany* included his translation of one of Ovid's narrative poems from *The Metamorphoses* in close proximity to the first version of Pope's *The Rape of the Lock*. Early in 1713, *Rural Sports*, his georgic dedicated to Pope, appeared, followed, in the fall of that year, by a clever essay on the art of dress for Sir Richard Steele's *Guardian*.

Although Pope tried his hand at improving Gay's next major poetic effort, *The Fan*, the piece failed to engage the interest of its readers. Undaunted, Gay published *The Shepherd's Week*, a series of eclogues in which Pope also played a prominent role. Apparently the bard of Twickenham required some assistance in his attack upon Ambrose Philips and that poet's parodies of the pastoral form; Philips and Pope had published their separate volumes of pastoral poems in the same year

(1709). Gay's part in the conflict was to depict rustic life without the usual classical ornamentation; in other words, Pope wanted something in which cattle would be milked and pigs would stray from their sties. To his credit, however, Gay went beyond mere ridicule and managed to produce a series of eclogues containing interesting elements of pastoral folklore and accurate descriptions of rural scenes.

Shortly after the publication of *The Shepherd's Week*, Gay obtained a position as secretary to Lord Clarendon, probably as a result of Swift's influence; the poet then accompanied his employer to the court of Hanover in 1714. However, the death of Queen Anne within the same year terminated Clarendon's mission as well as his need for a secretary. Returning to England in September, 1714, Gay, acting on the advice of Pope and Arbuthnot, took to publishing poetry that would secure him some favor at Court. The most obvious of these pieces was an "Epistle to a Lady, Occasion'd by the Arrival of Her Royal Highness," written for the Princess of Wales, who came to England in mid-October, 1714. In that poem, he appealed directly for patronage and bemoaned the fact that he had been obliged to appeal for any type of employment.

The following year witnessed an upturn in the poet's fortunes. Lord Burlington sent him to Devonshire, and that journey found its way into a verse epistle titled "A Journey to Exeter." Then, in January, 1716, *Trivia* was published; Lintot paid him £43 for the effort, and he received at least £150 more from the sale of paperbound copies. Gay continued to serve the needs of the nobility and to compose verses in their honor. In July, 1717, William Pultney, soon to become earl of Bath, chose him as a companion for a trip to Aix. In 1718, he ventured to Cockthorpe, Oxfordshire, the seat of Lord Harcourt—which placed him near Pope, then hard at work on his translation of Homer's *Iliad*. Within two years, Lintot and Jacob Tonson published Gay's poems in two quarto volumes; more important to Gay at that point than the actual poems was the impressive subscription list, bearing witness to the extent of the nobility's willingness (at least at that moment during the reign of the first Hanoverian) to support its favorite men of letters. Gay allegedly earned in excess of £1000 from the two volumes, then lost it all (and much

more, perhaps) in the disastrous South Sea speculation (1720).

Fortunately, Gay was rescued from both spiritual and financial failure by two of the more prominent subscribers to his 1720 *Poems on Several Occasions*, Catherine Hyde and her husband Charles, third duke of Queensbury. They took him into their home and into their circle of influential friends, thus easing Gay's financial difficulties. He even managed to secure the post of lottery commissioner, for which he received £150 yearly from 1722 to 1731. His health continued to pose a problem, although his successful career as a dramatist was just beginning. By early 1728, with *The Beggar's Opera* ready for production, he had already gained a foothold with his tragedy *The Captives* and by nomination as gentleman-usher to the small Princess Louisa (which he declined to accept). By the time that *The Beggar's Opera* was halfway through its run of sixty-three days, Gay had already earned between £700 and £800. After the London season, the opera was performed widely throughout England and Scotland—and in Ireland where it was given twenty-four times consecutively. Even the sequel, *Polly*, although it never reached the stage during Gay's lifetime, brought the playwright between £1100 and £1200 from publication—far more than he could have achieved from actual performances.

Affluence, however, could not insulate Gay from sickness. In December, 1728, he suffered a serious attack of fever, and the duke and duchess of Queensbury took him to their country seat of Amesbury, in Wiltshire. There he remained, working on an expanded version of his *Fables* and producing several pastoral dramas, operas, and comedies that contributed little to his literary reputation. Late in November, 1732, he came to London to arrange for the production of his *Achilles*; he suffered an attack of inflammatory fever and died on December 4, 1732, attended by his friend and physician, Arbuthnot. He lay in state at Exeter Exchange and then was carried for burial to Westminster Abbey, where Queensbury had erected a handsome monument to his memory. The juvenile quality of the epitaph, written by Gay himself—"Life is a jest, and all things show it./ I thought so once, and now I know it"—hardly rises to the level of the writer's status in life and the fact that his personal fortune, at his death, was in excess of £6000.

ANALYSIS

To understand John Gay's poetry—both individual poems and the entire poetic canon—one must understand the role of the Augustan satirist: the persona, the mask, the complex writer-character that Jonathan Swift developed so naturally but so carefully and with such intensity in *Gulliver's Travels* (1726) and *A Modest Proposal* (1729). Of all Augustan prose writers and poets who flitted in and out of the persona, either to obscure or to sharpen their satiric bites, Gay employed the technique with the greatest variety. In his early poetry—"Wine," *The Fan, Rural Sports, The Shepherd's Week*—he donned the mask of sophistication and tradition, of the highly literate, classical, rural Virgilian, of the suburban citizen of the world. At the height of success—the 1727 *Fables* and *To a Lady*—he assumed an air of quiet but intense morality. Finally, in the later pieces added to the *Poems on Several Occasions* and the second version of the *Fables*, Gay donned the garb of directness and obvious simplicity, trying very hard to press home the moral of a tale or to meet at least halfway the intellectual and artistic tastes of his readers. Gay succeeded as a poet and a satirist, according to Patricia Meyer Spacks, when he learned to manipulate his persona rather than hide behind it.

"WINE"

Gay's first published poem, "Wine," written when the poet was only twenty-two, proved that he knew something about his subject and that he could at least imitate with the best of poets and imbibers. The blank verse, as well as the subject, reflects the influence of John Philips's *Cyder* (1708); the poem also demonstrates Gay's familiarity with the mock heroic form and his early command of humorous exaggeration. Most important, though, "Wine" suggests the potential of better poems to come. The reader recognizes that Gay has abandoned the traditional elegance of his more mature colleagues, turning instead to common scenes of lower-class life. Additionally, of course, the comic operas that would come later show the degree to which he sympathized with the poorer elements of London society. To the surprise of modern readers who take their poetry seriously (and perhaps fail to appreciate eighteenth century tastes), the authorized version of 1708 was pirated on no less than two occasions by one Henry Hills, a

London bookseller, which meant that the young poet's graphic descriptions of the seedier sides of London life proved attractive to more than a handful of his contemporaries. As all mere imitations (especially the immature ones) must fail, however, so did "Wine" fail to rise above the level of a schoolboy exercise.

THE SHEPHERD'S WEEK

The perils of imitation are still evident in a more accomplished work, *The Shepherd's Week* (1714). Writing under the influence of Alexander Pope, Gay had to keep a sharp eye on Pope's suggestion that he ridicule Ambrose Philips's pastoral poems, while at the same time expressing his own devotion to rural England and displaying his knowledge of the rustic aspects of English life. If he had had a third eye, Gay certainly would have attended more carefully to his model, Edmund Spenser's *The Shepheardes Calendar* (1579). At any rate, the result of his effort was a hodgepodge of all three influences. Gay must have realized what was happening, for the introductory "Proem to the Courteous Reader" stands as an apology for the entire set of pastorals, wherein the poet asserts that no English versifier heretofore has successfully produced a proper and simple eclogue after the true form of Theocritus. He then attacks Philips's outrageous conceits and proceeds to his own definition of the pastoral—an accurate imitation of the nature and manners of rustic life. In other words, Gay needed to tell his readers what he had done before they actually read the poem.

FABLES

Yet, Gay did not always have to apologize. In the fifty-one fables in verse composed for the five-year-old Prince William, Duke of Cumberland, and published a year before *The Beggar's Opera*, his performance was quite authentic and more than satisfactory. In fact, both for his own generation and for posterity, the *Fables* may well be Gay's most important poetic work. True, he had an adequate number of predecessors whom he could (and did) imitate—particularly Jean de La Fontaine, whose *Fables* were first published in 1668, then again in 1678-1679. He managed, however, perhaps for the first time as a poet, to generate an air of worldly wisdom and to give it substance through expressions of wit and lively verse. Obviously, Gay knew the state of the *polite* world—the same world that he had seen and felt during his "trivial" tour throughout London; but he also envisioned a moral world that might someday overcome the triteness and false elegance of his own age. The fables are light, genial, and even gay—of the stuff that would both interest and instruct a five-year-old child. Such pieces as "The Elephant and the Bookseller," "The Lion and the Cub," "The Two Owls and the Sparrow," "The Two Monkeys," and "The Hare and Many Friends" continue to make sense for the young and the old of the present century.

TRIVIA

The unfortunate aspect of Gay's most characteristic poem, *Trivia*, and his most important poetic work, the *Fables*, is that they leave the impression of a gentle, good-natured, and lovable man whose spiritual age never exceeded twenty-two. In a sense, the titles of the two works established forever Gay's reputation as the poet of the trivial and the fabled, sufficiently lacking in intellectual acumen to compete with his seriously motivated contemporaries. Such impressions are gleaned while reading Gay's poems together with Johnson's conclusion that Gay never went beyond the trivial; with Joseph Warton's contention (in his 1782 essay on Pope) that Gay was merely neat and terse; and with the correspondence of Pope and Swift, implying that Gay was a dear friend who needed to be loved and advised but whose poetry had little effect upon anyone. Consequently, not until recently has Gay's poetry been seen for what it is: a formal attack upon and a reshaping of the ideas, the values, and the very scenes of early eighteenth century England. In that sense, he stands pen-to-pen with his contemporaries, really no different in purpose from Matthew Prior, or Pope, or Swift. Thus, in *To a Lady on Her Passion for Old China*, he joins ranks with those who lashed out at grave philosophers poring over spiders and butterflies in the name of human contemplation; like moles, they dig for information known to and appreciated only by themselves. In criticizing the outwardly absurd, however, Gay departed slightly from his fellows in that he rarely became upset or overly bitter at what he knew and saw. Instead, he adopted the language and the tone of a civilized man who is rarely open in his criticism, but prefers detachment and only sufficient mockery to hold the attention of his reader.

MORAL CONDITION

If Gay can stand beside his fellow satirists and Tory comrades, he can also, on occasion, rise above them as a poet seriously concerned with the moral state of the world—the universal world, rather than the limited sphere of Augustan London. For example, in "A Thought on Eternity," he contrasts infinity to the pettiness of his own times, in which actions and events are measured in terms of specific chronological periods. The virtuous soul, he concludes, regards life (man's tenure upon earth) as a fleeting dream whereby the soul longs for freedom from earth and a flight into the wider span of eternity. In "A Contemplation on Night," published by Sir Richard Steele in his *Miscellany* of 1713, Gay looks to the heavens, a pure Newtonian sky, and enjoys the workings of an all-powerful Providence that nature has forced him to recognize. Even when the stars and the sun have passed from his view, he will, as a deeply moral man, understand the presence, the light, of the Creator. Even in the fairly early *Rural Sports*, in which Gay again takes advantage of the Augustans' drift toward Newtonianism, he does more than introduce countryside recreation into the georgic framework. The strength of the piece lies in his ability to combine vivid nature description with pure religious feeling; but the religious aspects aside, he still manages to create a poem that gives moral credence to the beauty of nature. He contemplates the sunset while also contemplating God, thus allowing the poetic soul to overflow with praise and declaration.

The same elements and combinations appear again in "Panthea" (1713), when a disappointed lady turns from the hateful town toward what she terms "some melancholy cave," a living grave in which she can cry and mourn forever. There she hopes to lose all sense of natural and man-contrived divisions of time. Another form of eternity emerges in "Araminta" (1713), a pastoral elegy set in a melancholy shade with such items as a croaking raven and an old ruin contributing to an atmosphere of human repentance.

Serious students of Gay's poetry may wonder why he never developed with more realism or intensity his respect for the creative power of God. Had he done so, he might have managed to contribute something to the growth and development of English hymnody. Gay, however, had little interest in and even less commitment to congregational worship. He evidenced little of the religious conviction demonstrated, for example, by Joseph Addison in the five *Spectator* hymns. The religious and moral elements that do appear in Gay's poetry are always rather ambiguous. For example, in the fable of "The Ravens, the Sexton, and the Earth-Worm," the ravens believe they smell a dead horse; however, the sexton informs them that the local squire has died and will be buried on this night. The sexton is obviously put out because of the ravens' inability to distinguish man from beast, although the birds reply that a dead horse smells as good as a dead human being. Upon the scene crawls an earthworm, the expert on carrion, to mediate. The worm essentially sides with the birds, but he does offer the advice that the essence of man is the soul, not the flesh. True virtue is seated in the immortal mind, the worm claims; thus, "Different tastes please different vermin."

The ambiguity of Gay's moral pronouncements takes the form of earnestness and cynicism combined. As an intellectual—or at least a member of an intellectual group of poets, dramatists, and aristocrats—he hid behind an intellectual hardness that he wanted very much to temper. Within his own moral composition, there was a struggle between the strong rustic and provincial elements to which he had originally belonged and the influence of those intellectuals whom he chose to join and whom he emulated in his art. Again, Gay could never be considered a religious person or a religious poet; nevertheless, he could not totally conceal the enjoyment and the legitimate spiritual uplift that came to him (as it certainly comes to all persons of sensitivity) when he saw the actual workings of a God-created and God-ordered nature.

LEGACY

It is interesting to note that Gay's reputation as a poet has held firm throughout almost two centuries of critical comment. Samuel Johnson, in 1781, could not rank Gay very high because he thought his subject failed to achieve a significant degree of genius. In 1959, Bonamy Dobrée thought that Gay lacked a "capacity for thought," which prevented him from treating the substance of his poems with any depth. Perhaps both of those observers placed too much emphasis on the surface content of what still remains Gay's most character-

istic poem, *Trivia: Or, The Art of Walking the Streets of London*. Certainly, the poem may be marred by the rapidity of a walking tour through too many disconnected (thematically as well as geographically) parts of town; and equally certain is Gay's imperfect command of the mock-epic style. Nevertheless, Gay could pump life into the trivial, cramming his scenes with more facts than the naked eye could perceive at a single glance: thirty-five separate localities, at least sixty different ways of earning a living, the signs of the weather, the accoutrements necessary for walking the streets. Gay, indeed, lacked originality and depth, but no scholar can ever accuse him of lacking versatility; he applied his pen to anything that he thought might gain him a patron or a pound.

Gay the poet never quite achieved the intellectual power or the substance of the first-rate Augustan minds and artists. There is even some merit to the argument that, during his lifetime, his friends, not his published works, were actually responsible for the establishment of his literary reputation. His charming and witty songs certainly contained sufficient depth and unity to merit recognition, and the same may be said for the operas. The remainder of his verse is readable, but it is also too imitative to be distinctive. His interest as both poet and dramatist centered upon everyday life, and the novelists, dramatists, and poets of the late Hanoverian period surely benefited from the force and the action of his descriptions and characterizations. There will always be, no doubt, some challenge even to that contribution, for Gay has long been attacked for superficiality. Still, literary history will continue to provide a place for Gay's poetry, for he contributed, if nothing else, a sharp engraving of his times. If readers cannot appreciate Gay as a poet, they can at least learn from him and envision the Augustan age because of him.

OTHER MAJOR WORKS

PLAYS: *The Mohocks*, pb. 1712; *The Wife of Bath*, pr., pb. 1713, 1730 (revised); *The What D'ye Call It*, pr., pb. 1715; *Three Hours After Morning*, pr., pb. 1717 (with Alexander Pope and John Arbuthnot); *Dione*, pb. 1720 (verse tragedy); *The Captives*, pr., pb. 1724; *The Beggar's Opera*, pr., pb. 1728 (ballad opera); *Polly*, pb. 1729 (ballad opera); *Acis and Galatea*, pr. 1731 (libretto; music by George Frederick Handel);

Achilles, pr., pb. 1733 (ballad opera); *The Distress'd Wife*, pr. 1734; *The Rehearsal at Goatham*, pb. 1754; *Plays*, pb. 1760; *The Plays of John Gay*, pb. 1923 (2 volumes).

NONFICTION: *The Present State of Wit, in a Letter to a Friend in the Country*, 1711; *A Letter to a Lady*, 1714; *The Letters of John Gay*, 1966 (C. F. Burgess, editor).

MISCELLANEOUS: *Poetical, Dramatic, and Miscellaneous Works of John Gay*, 1795, 1970 (6 volumes); *John Gay: Poetry and Prose*, 1974 (2 volumes; Vinton A. Dearing, with Charles E. Beckwith, editors).

BIBLIOGRAPHY

Bloom, Harold, ed. *Modern Critical Interpretations: The Beggar's Opera*. New York: Chelsea House, 1988. An important collection of critical essays on *The Beggar's Opera*. The essay by William Empson focuses on this opera as a fine example of the mock pastoral form. The introduction discusses Gay's sense of the absurd, combined with his sense of "potential punishment."

Dobrée, Bonamy. *William Congreve: A Conversation Between Swift and Gay*. 1929. Reprint. Folcroft, Pa.: Folcroft Press, 1969. A conversation between Jonathan Swift and Gay recorded at the house of the duke of Queensberry near London in 1730. They discuss Congreve's work with vigor, forthrightness, and wit. Of interest to scholars of both Gay and Swift.

Dugaw, Dianne. *Deep Play: John Gay and the Invention of Modernity*. Cranbury, N.J.: Associated University Presses, 2001. A critical and historical analysis of Gay's works. Includes bibliographical references and index.

Gaye, Phoebe Fenwick. *John Gay: His Place in the Eighteenth Century*. London: Collins, 1938. A full-length biography of Gay, useful as a source of information about his life and poetry, but full of assumptions.

Melville, Lewis. *Life and Letters of John Gay*. London: Daniel O'Connor, 1921. Reprints of Gay's letters, providing insight into the man and his life. Among Gay's correspondents were such notables as Jonathan Swift, Alexander Pope, John Arbuthnot, and the duchess of Queensberry. Includes previously unpublished letters that reside in the British Museum.

Nokes, David. *John Gay, a Profession of Friendship*. New York: Oxford University Press, 1995. A comprehensive biography with some previously unpublished letters. Nokes presents Gay as a complex character, torn between the hopes of court preferment and the assertion of literary independence. Includes bibliographical references and index.

Walsh, Marcus. *John Gay: Selected Poems*. Manchester, England: Carcanet Press, 1979. The introduction gives some critical commentary and background information on Gay's poems in this selection, noting that Gay has been in the shadow of Alexander Pope and Jonathan Swift. Argues that his neglect is partly due to his being an "ironist rather than a satirist." A brief but insightful criticism of Gay's works.

Warner, Oliver. *John Gay*. London: Longmans, Green, 1964. A brief overview of Gay's life and works, with critical commentary on the early poems and fables, and *The Beggar's Opera*. A readable account, well suited to introductory readers.

Samuel J. Rogal;
bibliography updated by the editors

STEFAN GEORGE

Born: Büdesheim, Germany; July 12, 1868
Died: Minusio, Switzerland; December 4, 1933

PRINCIPAL POETRY

Hymnen, 1890 (*Odes*)

Pilgerfahrten, 1891 (*Pilgrimages*)

Algabal, 1892 (English translation)

Die Bücher der Hirten- und Preisgedichte, der Sagen und Sänge und der hängenden Gärten, 1895 (*The Books of Eclogues and Eulogies, of Legends and Lays, and of the Hanging Gardens*)

Das Jahr der Seele, 1897 (*The Year of the Soul*)

Der Teppich des Lebens und die Lieder von Traum und Tod, mit einem Vorspiel, 1899 (*Prelude, The Tapestry of Life, The Songs of Dream and Death*)

Die Fibel, 1901 (*The Primer*)

Der siebente Ring, 1907 (*The Seventh Ring*)

Der Stern des Bundes, 1914 (*The Star of the Covenant*)

Das neue Reich, 1928 (*The Kingdom Come*)

The Works of Stefan George, 1949 (includes the English translations of all titles listed above)

OTHER LITERARY FORMS

Among the books written by Stefan George, only *Tage und Taten* (1903; *Days and Deeds*, 1951) contains writings other than poetry. The volume is a collection of miscellaneous small prose: sketches, letters, observations, aphorisms, and panegyrics. It was expanded to include the introductory essay from *Maximin, ein Gedenkbuch* (1906; memorial book for Maximin) for the eighteen-volume complete edition of George's works, *Gesamt-Ausgabe*, published between 1927 and 1934. In addition to his original works, George published five volumes of translations and adaptations: *Baudelaire, Die Blumen des Bösen* (1901); *Zeitgenössische Dichter* (1905; of contemporary poets); *Shakespeare, Sonnette*, 1909; and *Dante, Die göttliche Komödie, Übertragungen* (1909). *Zeitgenössische Dichter* contains George's translations of poetry by Algernon Charles Swinburne, Jens Peter Jacobsen, Albert Verwey, Paul Verlaine, Stéphane Mallarmé, Arthur Rimbaud, and others. Editions of George's correspondence with Hugo von Hofmannsthal and Friedrich Gundolf were published in 1938 and 1962, respectively.

ACHIEVEMENTS

Most of Stefan George's works were consciously addressed to a carefully selected and limited readership, and until 1898, his lyric cycles were published only in private, limited editions. Poems that appeared in early issues of *Blätter für die Kunst* (leaves for art) were initially ignored in Germany because of the journal's limited circulation, the general obscurity of its contributors, and the poets' lack of connections with accepted literary circles. On the other hand, George's early poems and translations were received very favorably by poets and critics in France and Belgium. In 1898, the first public edition of *The Year of the Soul*, still his most popular cycle of poems, brought George the beginnings of broader

recognition. Subsequent collections won him increasing acclaim for his originality and artistic virtuosity, until in 1927 he became the first, if reluctant, recipient of the Frankfurt/Main Goethe Prize. By 1928, when his collected works appeared, George was recognized internationally as the most gifted of the German Symbolist poets and the most influential renewer of the German language since Friedrich Nietzsche.

George's important contributions to modern German poetry resulted from his efforts to revitalize and elevate decaying artistic standards. His efforts in cultivating a new literary language took into account contemporary literary influences from other national literatures. While pursuing his goals, he actively encouraged other German poets, including Hugo von Hofmannsthal, Leopold von Andrian, and Karl Wolfskehl, to strive for a new idealism focused on truth, originality, and self-examination, rejecting the identification of poetry with the personality of the poet and his experiences that had long characterized the nineteenth century imitators of Johann Wolfgang von Goethe.

In 1933, when the Nazis endeavored to distort and exploit his artistic ideals, George refused their offers of money and honor, including the presidency of the German Academy of Poets. Nevertheless, after his death, misinterpretation of his ideas and attitudes regarding artistic and intellectual elitism established a link with Nazi ideology that reduced his literary stature and for many years deprived him of his rightful place in German literary history. Above all else, George was a poet of uncompromising artistic integrity, whose attempts to give German poetry a new direction of humanism and idealism were prompted by profoundly moral and ethical motives.

BIOGRAPHY

Stefan Anton George was born in Büdesheim near Bingen in the Rhine district of Germany. His ancestors were farmers, millers, and merchants. When George was five years old, his father, a wine dealer, moved the family to Bingen. Bingen had a lasting impact on the poet's imagination, and its landscapes informed much of his early poetry. In 1882, George began his secondary education in Darmstadt. He received broad humanistic training and excelled in French. While in school, he taught himself Norwegian and Italian and began translating works by Henrik Ibsen, Petrarch, and Tasso. When he was eighteen, he began writing poetry and published some of his earliest lyrics under the pseudonym "Edmund Delorme" in the journal *Rosen und Disteln* that he had founded in 1887.

Upon leaving school in 1888, George began the travels that later characterized his lifestyle. He went first to London, where he became acquainted with the writings of Dante Gabriel Rossetti, Algernon Charles Swinburne, and Ernest Dowson, whose poems he later translated and published in German. In Paris, in 1889, he met the French poet Albert Saint-Paul, who introduced him into the circle of Symbolist poets surrounding Stéphane Mallarmé. In this group of congenial literary artists, which included Verlaine, Francis Vielé-Griffen, the Belgian Albert Mockel, and the Polish poet Waclaw Rolicz-Lieder, George found needed personal acceptance and friendship as well as important poetic models. Verlaine and Mallarmé became his acknowledged masters and provided him with a sense of his own poetic calling.

After returning to Germany, George studied Romance literature for three semesters in Berlin. During this time, he experimented with language and even developed a personal "Lingua Romana" that combined Spanish and Latin words with German syntactical forms. In 1890, he published his first book of poems, *Odes*, in a private edition. Two years later, with Carl August Klein, he founded *Blätter für die Kunst*, which served as an initial focus for his circle of disciples and remained a major vehicle for his ideas for twenty-seven years.

Other encounters with contemporary writers and artists, with his own disciples, and with other personal friends had decisive formative influence on George's career. In 1891, he began a productive if frequently stormy friendship with Hofmannsthal, whom he viewed as his only kindred spirit among modern German poets. When Hofmannsthal refused to commit himself exclusively to George's literary ideas, their association broke off in 1906. George's only significant relationship with a woman, a friendship with Ida Coblenz (later the wife of Richard Dehmel), began in 1892 and influenced many of the poems in *The Year of the Soul*, which he originally intended to dedicate to her. After their association ended

in disappointment for George, he limited his emotional involvement to young male disciples, among whom Friedrich Gundolf and Maximilian Kronberger had profound impact on his mature poetry. Affection for Gundolf moved George to direct his creative attention toward molding German youth, while Kronberger, a beautiful adolescent who died of meningitis in 1904, provided him with a model for the divinely pure power of youth as an absolute force of life.

By 1920, most of George's poetic works had been completed. He spent his remaining years actively guiding his youngest disciples, working more as a master teacher than as a poet. When his health finally failed, he moved to Minusio near Locarno, Switzerland, where he died on December 4, 1933.

ANALYSIS

In the preface to the first issue of *Blätter für die Kunst*, Stefan George defined artistic goals for the journal that gave direction to his own poetry for the rest of his career. With its high literary standards, its personally selected group of contributors, and its carefully formulated program, *Blätter für die Kunst* was intended to be a force in the creation of a new German poetry. Its express purpose, specifically reflecting George's perception of his own poetic calling, was to foster a newly refined and spiritual form of literature based on a rejuvenation of classical ideals and a revival of pure literary language. Poetry thus engendered was to be a manifestation of a new way of feeling, furthering the quest for permanent values while rejecting any idea of literature as simple diversion, political instrument, or vehicle for naturalistic social criticism. George's ultimate goal was to provide artistic leadership for a generation that would build a new humanistic society embodying Platonic ideals of goodness, truth, and beauty. Everything that George wrote was directed toward the accomplishment of these purposes.

Intimate association with the French Symbolists in Paris was the formative experience of George's career. It provided him with models for his approach and technique, ideas concerning the poet's role in life, and a starting point for the lifelong exploration of his own poetic nature and its delineation in his works. From Charles Baudelaire, Stéphane Mallarmé, and Paul Verlaine, he learned to view the poet as a mediator between phenomena and literary art, who describes his perceptions using symbolism that is understood completely only by the poet himself. Through his symbolic creation, the poet thus isolates himself in a world to which his own spiritual identity provides the key, a key that the reader must seek in the poem. In this regard, it is important to understand that George completely rejected the idea of identity between the poetic and the personal self. The progressive revelations in his lyrics of the poet's role in life are therefore idealizations rather than reflections of experience.

A clearly defined process of strengthening, refinement, and crystallization of the poet's role emerges in the cycles that document George's development. His *Odes*, which belong within the frame of traditional idealism, examine such themes as the tension between reason and feeling, change as a basic force in life, and unhappy love and death; therein is revealed a personal struggle with self-examination and doubt. In *Algabal*, however, there is a new sense of personal validity; the title figure symbolizes the exclusive artist who creates a private realm in isolation from nature. A further objectification of poetic self appears in the prologue to *The Tapestry of Life*, in the figure of an angel. This alter ego of the poet appears not as a heavenly messenger but as a representative of life, announcing the colorful fabric of the artistic yet puzzling order of existence. George's attempts to refine and perfect the revelation of his poetic identity culminate in the Maximin poems of *The Seventh Ring* and *The Star of the Covenant*, in which Maximin becomes the ultimate symbol for the desired perfect fusion of body and spirit in self-awareness.

Central to George's view of the social role of the poet was the idea that the poet enjoys the special position of "master" within a circle of devoted disciples. This principle, which he saw modeled in the salon of Mallarmé, had significant impact on his poetry and the conduct of his personal life. The relationship of the poet to his disciples is reflected in poems dedicated to close friends and associates in *The Books of Eclogues and Eulogies, of Legends and Lays, and of the Hanging Gardens* and other cycles. It is also evident in the consistent emergence of the symbolic poet as a teacher figure. This casting of the poet in the role of educator is readily visible in poems from *The Year of the Soul* and in the "Zeitgedichte" ("Time Poems") section of *The Seventh Ring*, where the poet-teacher gives specific directions to his contemporaries, suggesting appropriate models for them to emulate. Developed to its ultimate in *The Kingdom Come*, the poet's role as teacher becomes that of a prophet who judges the age and sounds a warning.

From the standpoint of technique and approach, George considered the revitalization, refinement, and purification of literary language to be the most important aspect of his creative task. He protested against the debasement of language, advocating a revival of pure rhyme and meter with precise arrangement of vowels and consonants to achieve harmony in a distinctly musical poetic form. Creation of language became a basic principle of his writing. He followed the pattern of Mallarmé and rejected everyday words. Stressing the importance of sound and internal melody in his poems, he formed new, musically resonant words and imbued his verses with rich vowels, assonances, alliteration, and double rhymes. George's perception of the spoken and the written word as embodiments of the reality of the world extended even to a regard for the importance of the visual impression created by printed forms. In order to offer language that was unusual in this respect, he developed a special typeface and modified traditional orthography and punctuation for his publications. George undertook all of these measures because he believed that language alone can open hidden levels of mind, soul, and meaning.

While progressively modifying French Symbolist and other external influences to suit his own purposes, George succeeded at least partially in creating the new German poetry toward which he was striving. Patterning his poems after Baudelaire's perception of the symbolic structure of existence, he created works that reflected his personal attitudes of austerity and self-denial, while celebrating the ethical supremacy of the spirit over material existence. The poetic cycle became his characteristic form, and each of his collections exhibits the basic unity that it demands. In addition to genuine originality in the coining of words and in imagery, George's poems typically feature colorful calmness of motion, sensually intense metaphors and symbols, and remarkable simplicity. The unaffected wording and ordering of lines in *The Year of the Soul*, for example, anticipate certain tendencies in Surrealism, while the smoothly flowing verses of the "Gezeiten" ("Tides") section of *The Seventh Ring* and the utter clarity and lack of ambiguity in the poems of *The Star of the Covenant* reflect the complete creative control of words that George consistently demonstrated in his poetry. It is perhaps in that rare mastery of personal poetic language that George made his greatest contribution to German literature.

Even George's earliest, less successful cycles reflect searching attempts to define his poetic self. From the exploratory *Odes*, which focus on artistic experiences and on the mission and position of the artists in the world, George moved in *Pilgrimages* toward a more distinctly personal approach to self-examination, styling himself a wanderer in a manner somewhat akin to Goethe's poetic perception of himself. Not until *Algabal*, however, did he present a clearly cohesive symbolic representation of his own special nature.

ALGABAL

As George's first highly characteristic work, *Algabal* offers vivid examples of the new kind of poetic creation for which the poet pleaded in the first issue of *Blätter für die Kunst*. The poems of *Algabal* are replete with samples of the musical language that became such a critical part of George's works as a whole. In uniquely worded verses characterized by sonorous repetition of melodic vowel combinations, the poet transforms carefully chosen elements of reality into symbols for his internal world. In so doing, he gives them a different kind of existence, creating new levels of artistic revelation. He develops the central complex of symbols from the life of Elagabalus, the youthful Roman emperor and priest of Baal whose promotion of physically beautiful favorites and open homosexual orgies brought about his assassination. Transforming his eccentric model into Algabal, the lonely king of a personally created subterranean realm, George creates a haunting symbol for his poetic identity.

The first section of the cycle, "Im Unterreich" ("In the Subterranean Kingdom"), focuses on Algabal's domain as a major symbol for a new level of creative feeling. In an overwhelming intensity of visual impression, the components of external nature are transformed into precious gems that flash in bright colors, illuminating from within an edifice to which the light of day does not penetrate. Similarly, the natural smells of outside reality are replaced by peculiar, musty fragrances of amber, incense, lemon, and almond oil that infuse the artificial world. The most profound symbols of "In the Subterranean Kingdom" are the lifeless birds and plants of Algabal's garden. Amid stems and branches made of carbon, the black flower appears as a symbol for art, a conscious contrast to Novalis's blue flower of romantic longing.

In the other sections of *Algabal*, "Tage" ("Days"), "Die Andenken" ("The Memories"), and "Vogelschau" ("View of Birds"), George tightens the symbolic focus to elucidate the unique personality of the ruler of the underground palace and garden. Verses that stress the self-examination aspect of the creative process reveal George's perception of himself as a poet whose nature compels him to return alone to an ancient age in which other values predominate. New symbols are formed to treat traditional literary themes. Juxtaposed to the black flower of artificial life, for example, are images of death in vivid reds and greens. "View of Birds," the final poem of the cycle, underscores the idea that it is only through the poet's actively formative power of perception that life is given to the artistically constructed poetic world.

THE YEAR OF THE SOUL

Among all George's collections of poetry, the most popular yet least typical is the key cycle of his middle period, *The Year of the Soul*. Two factors in particular distinguish the poems of this group from his other major works. *The Year of the Soul* is George's only book that centers on love between man and woman. It is an important document of his relationship with Ida Coblenz. His poetic treatment of that ultimately unhappy emotional involvement contrasts markedly with the harmoniously warm and human love poems that he wrote for young men in *The Seventh Ring* and other later cycles. *The Year of the Soul* also differs from other George volumes in style and technique. The decorative stylization of diction and the boldness of ornamentation in nature imagery suggest a connection with the intentions and motifs of *Jugendstil*, whereas the pronounced simplicity of form that characterizes most of George's poetry reflects his tacit rejection of the *Jugendstil* tendency in art.

The poems of *The Year of the Soul* frame exploration of the problems of unfulfilled love in carefully controlled images of external reality. Modifying the traditional German nature poem, George symbolizes nature by a cultivated park that is organized and created by the gardener/poet. The parkscapes that he evokes offer individual natural phenomena as symbols for private experience and moods of the soul.

The first and most important of the book's three major sections presents the essence of the volume in concentrated form. It is divided into three subcycles, "Nach der Lese" ("After the Harvest"), "Waller im Schnee" ("Wanderer in the Snow"), and "Sieg des Sommers" ("Triumph of Summer"), each of which constitutes a rounded unit in its own right. Beginning with autumn, the poet employs the rhythm of the seasons to illuminate changing moods—hope, suffering, reflection, and mourning in an ever-renewing confrontation with the self. Special emphasis on color accents the varying moods evoked by the nature images, intensifying the dialogue between "I" and "you," newly perceived Faustian aspects of the poet's own soul which appear in the guise of the poet and a fictitious female object of his love. The motifs of "Wanderer in the Snow" augment the tension between the poet and the accompanying "you" as the wanderer traverses a winter of bitterness, austerity, and mourning. Sheer hopelessness radiates from the lines of the seventh poem, in which the poet declares that despite his faithful attention and patience, his love relationship will never bring him so much as a warm greeting. In "Triumph of Summer," a transition from the harsh emptiness of winter imagery to the anticipated warmth of summer promises a new approach to spiritual fulfillment. The ten poems of this segment dwell on the idea of joint creation of a "sun kingdom" with the "you" of the previous sections. The "sun kingdom," a symbol for the ideal realm for which George longed throughout his career, remains, however, a transitory vision as summer's end becomes a symbol for final parting.

The poems of the two other major parts of *The Year of the Soul*, "Überschriften und Widmungen" ("Titles and Dedications") and "Traurige Tänze" ("Sad Dances"), focus more precisely and personally on problems and themes introduced in the preceding section. In verses dedicated to friends, the poet again assumes the role of teacher, instructing his disciples concerning the inner spiritual encounter with love. Lyrics written specifically for Ida Coblenz give additional substance to the symbolic portrayal of George's painful love affair, while the beautifully songlike stanzas of "Sad Dances" elevate the volume as a whole to a single powerful symbol for his private experience of *Weltschmerz*.

THE SEVENTH RING

In 1907, George published the richest, most ambitious, and most complex collection of his career. *The Seventh Ring* represents the high point and culmination of his poetic development. It is especially fascinating for its presentation of a significant spectrum of George's stylistic possibilities, themes, and poetic perceptions, together with its clear revelation of his ultimate goals. In addition to the ever-present poems dedicated to members of his circle, the cycle contains the most important elements of the new tendencies that appeared in George's poetry after 1900. To be sure, the two later volumes, *The Star of the Covenant* and *The Kindgom Come*, are important for what they reveal of the final perfecting of ideas that are central to *The Seventh Ring*. Nevertheless, the sometimes sterile rigidity and flatness of *The Star of the Covenant* and the lack of uniformity in *The Kingdom Come* (which encompasses all of George's lyric creations written after 1913) render those two books anticlimactic.

Although *The Seventh Ring* is somewhat uneven in form, a fresh poetic emphasis on principles of mathematical order is evident in the highly visible relationships between special numbers, internal symbolism, and the formal organization of the work. There are obvious connections among the title, the division of the poems into seven groupings, the seven biblical creative periods, and the year of publication, 1907. In addition, the number of items in each subcycle is a multiple of seven, while the constitution of individual poems and their integration into units are governed by specific numerical factors. Especially important is the placement of the "Maximin" section. Positioned fourth in conscious reference to the year of the death of Maximilian Kronberger, the verses that he inspired form the thematic as well as the structural nucleus of the symmetrical collection.

Viewed in its entirety, *The Seventh Ring* is George's most comprehensive attempt to define his own position within his age. The "Time Poems" at the beginning permanently establish the poet in the chosen roles of teacher and judge which characterize all of his later writings. They attack the follies of the era, providing points of reference and standards against which to measure them as well as models for emulation in building a new, ideal, Hellenistic society. Goethe, Dante, Friedrich Wilhelm Nietzsche, and Leo XIII are among the examples of great human beings whom George glorifies. In "Tides," which contains some of the most impressive love poetry in the German language, George reveals as nowhere else the intensity and inner meaning of his feelings for Friedrich Gundolf and Robert Boehringer. Through the same lyrics, however, he comes to terms with the fact that those relationships have been replaced in importance by the more transcendent encounter with Maximin.

The so-called Maximin experience is commonly recognized as the key to George's mature poetry. In the "Maximin" section of *The Seventh Ring*, George transforms the life of his young friend into a symbol for the manner in which eternal, divine forces are manifest in the modern world. Deification of Maximin enables him to create a private religion as part of his quest for permanent values in the Hellenic tradition. The god Maximin is the embodiment of a primeval force, a universally present Eros. In lyrical celebrations of Maximin's life and death, George transforms the characteristic dialogues with self of earlier poems into conversations with divinity. In so doing, he elevates himself to the rank of prophet and seer. His prophetic calling then opens the way to new themes of chaos and destruction. While developing these themes, the poet creates the visions of Germany's fall that accompany the further revelation of Maximin's character in the other sections of *The Seventh Ring* and in *The Star of the Covenant* and *The Kingdom Come*.

OTHER MAJOR WORKS

POETRY TRANSLATIONS: *Baudelaire, Die Blumen des Bösen*, 1901; *Zeitgenössische Dichter*, 1905 (of contemporary poets); *Shakespeare, Sonnette*, 1909; *Dante, Die göttliche Komödie, Übertragungen*, 1909.

NONFICTION: *Blätter für die Kunst*, 1892-1919 (12 volumes); *Tage und Taten*, 1903 (*Days and Deeds*, 1951); *Maximin, ein Gedenkbuch*, 1906.

MISCELLANEOUS: *Gesamt-Ausgabe*, 1927-1934 (18 volumes; poetry and prose).

BIBLIOGRAPHY

Bennett, Edwin K. *Stefan George*. New Haven, Conn.: Yale University Press, 1954. A succinct critical study of George's works with a brief biographical background. Includes a bibliography.

Goldsmith, Ulrich K. *Stefan George*. New York: Columbia University Press, 1970. Biographical essay with bibliographic references.

Klieneberger, H. R. *George, Rilke, Hofmannsthal, and the Romantic Tradition*. Stuttgart: H. D. Heinz, 1991. Provides an introduction to the Romantic tradition in poetry and brief critical interpretation of the major works of Stefan George. Includes bibliographical references and index.

Metzger, Michael M., and Erika A. Metzger. *Stefan George*. New York: Twayne Publishers, 1972. Biography of Stefan George with a bibliography of his works.

Underwood, Von Edward. *A History That Includes the Self: Essays on the Poetry of Stefan George, Hugo von Hofmannsthal, William Carlos Williams, and Wallace Stevens*. New York: Garland, 1988. A very useful monograph on the comparative poetics of the four named. Bibliographical references, index.

Lowell A. Bangerter;
bibliography updated by the editors

GUIDO GEZELLE

Born: Bruges, Belgium; May 1, 1830
Died: Bruges, Belgium; November 27, 1899

PRINCIPAL POETRY

Dichtoefeningen, 1858
Kerkhofblommen, 1858
XXXIII Kleengedichtjes, 1860

Gedichten, gezangen en gebeden, 1862

Liederen, eerdichten et reliqua, 1880

Driemaal XXXIII kleengedichtjes, 1881

Tijdkrans, 1893

Rijmsnoer, 1897

Laatste verzen, 1901

Poems/Gedichten, 1971

OTHER LITERARY FORMS

Although known primarily as a poet, Guido Gezelle also wrote numerous essays on language, literature, art, and Flemish culture. These works were published during his lifetime in such Flemish journals as *Reynaert de vos*, *'t Jaer 30*, *Rond den heerd*, *Loquela*, and *Biekorf*. In addition, he published in 1886 a Flemish translation of Henry Wadsworth Longfellow's *The Song of Hiawatha* (1855) and, in 1897, a Flemish translation of Monsignor Waffelaert's Latin treatise *Meditationes theologiae* (1883). These translations, as well as his poetry and surviving letters, appear in the nine volumes of *Jubileumuitgave van Guido Gezelle's volledige werken* (1930-1939).

ACHIEVEMENTS

Although Guido Gezelle is one of Flanders's greatest poets and holds a prominent place in Netherlandic literature by being one of its leading nineteenth century poets and a significant forerunner of modern Dutch poetry, he won his fame primarily after his death. Some of his former poetry students helped to promote his art.

Especially instrumental in doing so was Hugo Verriest (1840-1922), who followed in Gezelle's footsteps by becoming a teacher and a priest. Verriest brought Gezelle's poetry to the attention of his own brilliant student Albrecht Rodenbach (1856-1880), a leader of a student group interested in preserving Flemish culture. While at the University of Louvain, Rodenbach became acquainted with Pol De Mont (1857-1931), a student-writer who had important connections with an artistic movement in Holland. This group of young artists, who called themselves the Men of the Eighties, was interested in setting new trends by breaking with the literary conventions of the past. They admired Gezelle and made the North (Holland) receptive to his poetry. De Mont was also involved with a group of artists in the South (Flanders), called Van Nu en Straks (of today and tomorrow). One of their goals coincided with that of the Men of the Eighties—that is, they wished to break with their past. Furthermore, they wished to revive Flemish consciousness in general and were, in fact, very successful in so doing. In their journal, *Van nu en straks*, they printed numerous articles on Flemish history, economy, and politics, as well as on Gezelle's poetry, giving it the highest praise.

Because this journal gained subscribers from all over the world, Gezelle's name was circulated far and wide. His poetry was printed not only at home but also abroad, and it became an inspiration to younger poets of note, especially Prosper van Langendonck (1862-1920) and Karel van de Woestijne (1878-1929) in the North. They picked up Gezelle's play with rhythm and sound, as well as his fresh and artistic use of the Flemish idiom. In a real sense, they not only owed Gezelle a literary debt but also helped to promote his art in their own modern verse.

As is true of so many great artists, Gezelle did not receive the recognition he deserved until after his death. Then, sculptors carved his statue, streets received his name, anthologies printed his verse, and translators recast some of his poems in various languages. Thus, Gezelle after his death accomplished what he had set out to do in his youth—to liberate Flanders and to inspire a "school" of writers. These writers, as well as Gezelle, are still read and studied today.

BIOGRAPHY

Born in Bruges on May 1, 1830, the year the kingdom of Belgium was established, Guido Gezelle was to become an important leader of and spokesman for the Flemish literary revival. Having inherited his father's literary sensibility and his mother's strong Roman Catholic devotion, Gezelle was destined to become a poet-priest. After he was graduated in 1846 from Sint Lodewijkscollege in Bruges, he continued his training in theological studies at the Minor Seminary in Roulers (1846-1849) and at the Major Seminary in Bruges (1850-1854). He was ordained to the priesthood on June 10, 1854.

In August, 1854, he was appointed to teach sciences and languages at the Minor Seminary in Roulers. Quickly thereafter, in 1857, he was promoted to professor of poetry, a position he held until August, 1859. These two years were marked by unusual creativity. Gezelle formed a eucharistic confraternity with some of his students in an effort to revive medieval devotion to Jesus Christ through adoration of Christ's Sacrament of Love. This confraternity provided both his students and himself with a poetic-mystical atmosphere enabling Gezelle to pursue his poetic goal—namely, to revive a kind of medieval Flemish "school" of poetry in an age when French was more prestigious and Flemish poetry virtually nonexistent. Gezelle was successful in encouraging some of these students to become poets, and during these years, he produced several collections of poetry himself: *Kerkhofblommen* (churchyard flowers), *Dichtoefeningen* (poetic exercises), *XXXIII Kleengedichtjes* (thirty-three small poems), and *Gedichten, gezangen en gebeden* (poems, hymns, and prayers).

Despite these early achievements, Gezelle met with criticism from all sides. His pedagogical approach ran counter to the rigid format of his day. By his unstructured classroom methods, he threatened an educational system which stressed adherence to uniformity of methods and conformity to previously set standards. Moreover, his close ties with students belonging to the confraternity raised eyebrows among those of his religious superiors who considered suspect any friendship between students and clergy. Hence, in 1860, Gezelle was relieved of his teaching assignment in Roulers and sent to Bruges. There, he was appointed director of the New English College and given a teaching assignment at the Anglo-Belgian Seminary. Gezelle's highly ineffective supervision of the college led to its demise within the year, while his teaching methods at the seminary continued to alienate colleagues and superiors alike. In 1865, Gezelle was discharged from all teaching duties and assigned the lesser post of curate at St. Walburgis parish in Bruges.

Gezelle's parochial duties as curate were so time-consuming that they brought his first poetic phase to an abrupt stop. Gezelle did, however, become active as a journalist, encouraged by his bishop, who recognized Gezelle's writing talents. After a period as a regular contributor to *Reynaert de vos*, a humorous political weekly based in Antwerp, he wrote for and then became editor of *'t Jaer 30*, an ultraconservative weekly concerned with local politics, which, under Gezelle's editorship, acquired a strong pro-Catholic and pro-Flemish tone. Finally, in 1865, he started his own journal, *Rond den heerd*, which contained everything from proverbs and jokes to essays on saints' lives, language, and the arts. In time, however, Gezelle's double workload as curate and editor became so exhausting that he began to suffer from increasingly bad health. Also, because he lacked sufficient time to scrutinize articles submitted to *'t Jaer 30*, he allowed into print too many pieces characterized by inflamed political rhetoric and a libelous tone. In addition, he was a poor manager of funds. Embroiled in political and financial problems, he suffered a mental collapse in 1872.

Gezelle was discharged from his parochial and editorial duties in Bruges and sent for recuperation to the quiet town of Courtrai in 1872. There he was assigned less time-consuming work as curate of the Church of Our Lady. Surrounded by friends and admirers of his verse, Gezelle slowly recovered and gradually resumed his poetic work. In 1873, he became a regular contributor to the *Westvlaamsch idioticon* (West Flemish lexicon). Gezelle poured all of his energies into this language study in an effort to revive the Flemish idiom, which had suffered from the increasing Frenchification in Flemish life and culture. This language study also spurred on his desire to restructure completely his early poetry collections and to publish them as his complete works in 1877. In addition, in 1880, he produced a collection of somewhat inferior poems, *Liederen, eerdichten et reliqua* (songs, elegies, and relics), and in 1881, he founded the language journal *Loquela*.

As a result of his renewed poetic and language interests, Gezelle in time won acclaim from all sides. He was elected founding member of the Royal Flemish Academy (1886), awarded an honorary degree from the University of Louvain (1887), honored with the papal decoration "Pro Ecclesia et Pontifice" (1888), knighted in the Order of Leopold (1889), and appointed to the Society of Dutch Letters in Leiden (1890). Moreover, his bishop gradually relieved Gezelle of all pastoral duties to provide him with the time required for private study and writing. These circumstances became the stimulus for Gezelle's second burst of poetic activity. He reached the peak of his poetic career with the publication of *Tijdkrans* (time cycle) in 1893 and *Rijmsnoer* (string of rhymes) in 1897. In their language impressionism, intricate cyclical structuring, and pure Flemish diction, these collections are the crowning achievement of his life. After his death on November 27, 1899, a final volume of poems was compiled, *Laatste verzen* (last poems).

ANALYSIS

DICHTOEFENINGEN

With *Dichtoefeningen*, Guido Gezelle made his literary debut. This collection contains the first public announcement of his literary-patriotic goal—to create a medieval Catholic and Flemish poetic program. In "Aanroeping" ("Invocation"), he establishes that its sources of inspiration are to be Christ, Mary, and nature. Its purpose is to render praise through the Flemish idiom, and the poet's role is to convert into verbal music and painting the sounds and sights nature supplies. In "Principium a Jesu" ("Beginning in Jesus"), Gezelle amplifies his views of inspiration by emphasizing that the poet has a greater responsibility than merely to paint and echo nature's sights and sounds: He also has the ethical obligation to reflect Christ in his lines in order thereby to instill Christian praise. To do so, Gezelle believed that the poet himself must first be sanctified through grace so that he might rightfully return nature's gifts to their source. Through the Christian muse, the poet can thus transform his own verbal music into Christian song. Poetry in this sense becomes a concomitant of grace as the poet cooperates with inspirational grace to return his poetic product to its ultimate source, Christ.

The earliest poems in *Dichtoefeningen* are essentially displays of the poet's own virtuosity as he chimes in his lines nature's sounds and vividly depicts nature's sights. Examples are "Boodchap van de vogels" ("Message from the Birds") and "Pachthofschildering" ("Farmyard Sketches"). The later poems turn these poetic exercises into spiritual exercises regarding the lessons residing in nature—lessons that lead the poet into the self and, hence, to a discovery of God. The poem "Het schrijverke" ("The Water Strider") is a meditation on an insect. The poet is puzzled by what the bug writes on the water as it skids along its surface. The bug teaches the lesson that it writes the name of God. The intellectual knowledge the poet gains from the bug's actions provides the basis for the experiential knowledge he acquires in "O 't ruisen van het ranke riet" ("Oh, the Rustling of the Slender Reed"). Here, the poet learns not only to intuit the meaning of the reed's "sad song" as the "sweet song" heard by God but also to hear his own sad pleas echoed in the rueful rustling of the reed. This self-identification with nature leads to further self-discovery in "De waterspegel" ("The Water Speculum"), where the poet sees reflected in creation not only his own image but also that of God, its "wonderous Artist." In "Binst het stille van de nacht" ("In the Quietness of Night"), he recognizes that, unlike the natural phenomena surrounding him, the poet himself assumes a very special place in creation, for he must do more than learn from, identify with, and admire nature and its Creator. The poet must also through his own verbal music transmit the spirit of God. The poem "Aan de leeuwerk in de lucht" ("To the Skylark in the Air") is the poetical and spiritual culmination of *Dichtoefeningen*. The poet no longer is the medium through which nature flows back to its original source, God; here, he transcends nature as his ecstatic poetic flight surpasses that of the lark. Through his ascent, the poet, unlike the lark, can ultimately bathe in God's peace.

GEDICHTEN, GEZANGEN EN GEBEDEN

Gedichten, gezangen en gebeden is a bittersweet collection containing poems about the ecstasies of Gezelle's triumphs and the agonies of his sadness experienced primarily during his Roulers years. It is the most personal of his collections, for the first time introducing the themes of sin, guilt, and friendship. In a significant way, this collection presents both the public and private voices of the poet-priest on the various meanings of the Cross. A number of these poems celebrate the Eucharist. Some of these follow the tripartite division of Ignatian meditational exercises, in which the memory prompts the imagination to see, the intellect analyzes what the imagination sees, and the will moves the affections to respond to God.

In "Bezoek aan het Allerheiligste" ("Visiting the Holy of Holies"), for example, as the persona partakes of the Eucharist, he pictures God's presence in Rome, Jerusalem, and Flanders. The imagination sees God descending everywhere, which prompts his intellect to ask why God would leave His angels to dwell here below. The answer, however, lies beyond the persona's grasp and only emphasizes the limitations of man's intellect. This in turn leads his will to adoration, to plead for God's acceptance, and to resolve to become more worthy of God's grace. While the persona in this poem is driven to his knees, in another meditation poem on the Eucharist, "Wie zijt gij" ("Who Art Thou"), he is moved to look up at the skies, to trace God in the stars, and to lift himself in songs and joy.

Others of the public poems were commissioned by Gezelle's bishop for the edification of Flemish-speaking people. The most moving of these are the Jesu poems, most notably "Jesu waar't de mens gegeven" ("Jesus, Were It Giv'n to Man"), "Jesu," and "Jesu liefste Jesu mijn" ("Jesu, Dearest Jesu Mine"). Though inspired by Gezelle's own sense of inadequacy, guilt, and shame, these poems are nevertheless public in intent. In them, as J. J. M. Westenbroek points out in *Van het leven naar het boek* (1967), the poet speaks foremost as the public priest, seeking to move others to pray. All of them have a two-part structure, the first part usually describing how sinful man resists God's grace, the second part depicting Christ as the patient wooer of ungrateful man. Strongly Christ-centered prayers, they are intended to move man to reflect on his guilt and sin in order to sue for grace. The soul-searching and penitent response these poems elicit belong to the essence of prayer.

The poetical highlights of *Gedichten, gezangen en gebeden*, according to Westenbroek, are three poems addressed to Gezelle's closest friend, Eugeen van Oye. They trace the various stages of that friendship between 1858 and 1859, when van Oye was wavering about his future vocation and Gezelle fervently tried to retain him for the priesthood. In "Een bonke kersen kind" ("A Bunch of Cherries, Child"), Gezelle uses the cherry cluster as a symbol in the opening and closing frame of the poem. The cluster of ripened cherries evokes an outburst of sensual joy at the beauties of creation as shared with the friend, but it also serves as a warning that such joys must not serve as selfish delights, but should be returned with thanks to their source. The temptation alluded to pertains to giving in to sensual pleasures as ends in themselves. In "Rammentati" ("Remember"), written after van Oye's decision to forego the priest-

hood, the earlier joy is replaced by the poet's fears and deep concern about the boy's spiritual welfare. The poem is a series of warnings to "remember" that the secular world is filled with much greater temptations than the sensual delights afforded by nature. Though not pressing van Oye to forego his secular ambitions, Gezelle instead seeks to fortify him for his journey into secular life by giving him concerned advice so that he might ultimately reach his heavenly home. In "Ik mis u" ("I Miss Thee"), written after van Oye had left the college, the poet pours out his grief over the boy's absence. A retrospective poem, it recalls various moments when van Oye was still one of his protégés. The poet misses his voice amid the chapel choristers and the poems he used to bring to his room, but most of all at the altar rail when the poet-priest used to feed him with Christ. Whereas "Remember" ended with warnings, this poem ends with uncomfortable questions: whether van Oye will remain steadfast in the faith, and whether Gezelle will ever see him again, even after death.

In the final analysis, nearly all of the contents of *Gedichten, gezangen en gebeden* are focused on the Cross, whether expressed as devotion to the Sacrament, the poet's own suffering in taking up Christ's Cross, or his priestly care for students. In all instances, they are indeed poems, songs, and prayers.

XXXIII KLEENGEDICHTJES

Toward the end of his Roulers days, Gezelle began to experiment with a new poetic form. The timing was not accidental. When it seemed inevitable that he would be separated from his confraternity, Gezelle could no longer rely on those student-poets allied with the confraternity to form the basis for his literary-patriotic platform. Hence he turned to a new poetic form which would have meaning in and of itself, rather than by virtue of the specifically Flemish-Catholic cause he wished to promote. Bernard F. Van Vlierden, in *Guido Gezelle tegenover het dichterschap* (1967), points out that by this time Gezelle was steeped in Arabian literature and had discovered some extremely brief poems. Some of them were condensations and crystallizations of rich thought, others no more than an interplay of sheer rhythm, cadence, and sound, splendid examples of *poésie pure*. Gezelle imitated and adapted this concise form and gave it its first expression in *XXXIII Kleengedichtjes*. All of these poems are quite brief, some only two lines of assonantal and alliterative chiming, chiseled artifacts of melody and sound, the meaning of which resides in the beauty of language itself. The majority, however, are short prayers. In fact, by the very title he chose for this collection, Gezelle explains that he meant to show the interrelatedness of poetry and prayer. The word *kleengedichtje* means "small poem," while the closely related word *kleingebedje* means "spiritual aspiration." Such brief, intense poems, Gezelle believed, are by their very nature nonverbal responses that arise from the heart, rather than the mind—outbursts that well up from the depths of one's being as it feels attuned to the rhythm and harmony of life itself. The *XXXIII Kleengedichtjes* thus demonstrate that poetry resides in prayer and that prayer resides in poetry.

Along with Gezelle's interest in this new poetic form came his desire to achieve an ideal structural form for the collection as a whole. Although it has no tight internal structure, *XXXIII Kleengedichtjes* is nevertheless a cohesive unit because all of its poems are brief and all demonstrate the interrelatedness of poetry and prayer. Furthermore, Gezelle purposely included thirty-three poems, not only because the number equaled the years of Christ's life, but also because it is a perfect number. Gezelle had already shown his fondness for perfect numbers when he had used the triad in the title of the earlier collection *Gedichten, gezangen en gebeden*. (This triad device is repeated later in the title *Liederen, eerdichten et reliqua*.) He had also already incorporated a unit of thirty-three poems in *Gedichten, gezangen en gebeden*. These, in fact, became the model for *XXXIII Kleengedichtjes*.

DRIEMAAL XXXIII KLEENGEDICHTJES

Not until 1881, however, when Gezelle wrote *Driemaal XXXIII kleengedichtjes* (three times thirty-three small poems), did he arrive at the circular pattern which characterizes the structure of the later *Tijdkrans* and *Rijmsnoer*. This expanded edition of *XXXIII Kleengedichtjes* consists of three units of thirty-three poems. Each unit has an internal structure, beginning with the poems on the cross and ending with poems about heaven. What dominates each unit, then, is the cross, whether as the cross of passion or the cross of triumph which opens the way to heaven. In its circularity, each unit resembles a set of Rosary prayers. Interestingly, as Gezelle explained in an article in *Rond den heerd*, the Flemish custom on Rosary Sunday was to pray a special Rosary of thirty-three Hail Marys in memory of Christ's life. In a sense, the *Driemaal XXXIII kleengedichtjes* repeats the circularity of the Rosary *three* times, in order to emphasize thereby the perfection of the overall structural pattern itself. The collection ends, appropriately, with the explanation of the number symbolism. In the last poem, "Die drieëndertig jaar" ("Who Three and Thirty Years"), Gezelle dedicates his heart, his hope, and all of these poems thirty-three times to Christ.

TIJDKRANS

In many of the *XXXIII Kleengedichtjes* Gezelle shows his interest in the poetical nature of language itself. This interest was an outgrowth of the philological study he was engaged in at the time and which resulted in his language journal *Loquela* in 1881. Both this philological interest and his growing concern with structural patterning paved the way for his last two, and greatest, collections, *Tijdkrans* and *Rijmsnoer*. In these final works, Gezelle demonstrates with great success the poetic potential of the Flemish language, and he did so in the perfect structural form these collections possess.

Written long after his emotional breakdown, *Tijdkrans* voices entirely new concerns. Here, Gezelle is no longer interested in imitating nature but rather in deciphering what it ultimately means. Whereas in his youth, as in *Dichtoefeningen*, he was drawn to the happy lark, in *Tijdkrans* he feels much more drawn to the sad nightingale, identifying with its mournful song. As he wonders if it sings of its own banishment, he is moved to reflect on his own life as a constant grave and to think of this earth as exile from the better world to come. The nightingale is mentioned several times in *Tijdkrans*, and in its song, Gezelle repeatedly hears expressions of his own sadness and chronic discontent. Having suffered from repeated setbacks in his youth, occasioned by somewhat envious colleagues and superiors who considered him a failure as a teacher, college director, and editor, he had gradually came to distrust humankind and to feel trapped by society itself. Hence, in *Tijdkrans* he feels constantly pursued by a vague enemy force he labels the world, and he lashes out at it repeatedly, accusing it of having pestered him too long. One major motif that emerges in *Tijdkrans*, then, is that life is constant strife, and the poet throughout adopts a combative stance to fend off both real and imagined attacks.

Such paranoia resulted in Gezelle's need for protection. Given his gloomy outlook, however, he could hardly turn to humankind for comfort. Hence, in *Tijdkrans* he often repeats his wish to die and, thus, to escape to eternity for safety and freedom. In these poems he is increasingly drawn away from the world, seeks solitary communion with nature, and ultimately through contemplation finds peace solely in God. Nature becomes the medium for those contemplative flights, and the best time to commune with it is at night, when the threatening world of men is asleep. Not only by night but also by day nature provides comfort in various ways, for it teaches worthwhile lessons which inevitably direct the poet's attention to God. Through nature Gezelle discovers, for example, the protection of God's omnipresence and constancy, for whether he poetically plumbs the depths of the ocean or scales the heights of the firmament, God is always there. Nature also provides the comfort of the Resurrection by its perennial renewal of springtime beauty and summer growth. Furthermore, it also instructs man how to live, for nature never does more than what it is appointed to be. As "O wilde en onvervalste pracht" ("Oh, Wild and Unadulterated Splendor") points out, simple flowers neither deceive nor pretend but in their untainted splendor reveal their naked truth, that they are what they appear to be. Man, by contrast, deceives, disguises, and dissembles. In its constancy of praise, beauty, and purpose, then, nature becomes the poet's faithful protector and friend.

The greatest protector and friend in *Tijdkrans*, however, is eternity itself. It alone offers the poet ultimate permanence and, hence, protection from the ravages of time. While Gezelle longed for this permanence outside of time, he also strove for it while alive and still part of time. This he did through the structural pattern he adopted for *Tijdkrans*. As its title suggests, *Tijdkrans* is concerned with time. In it, Gezelle not only writes *about* time, but he also directs himself *against* time by imposing on the collection a structural pattern which surpasses time. Within the boundaries of its three separate parts—"Dagkrans" (day cycle), "Jaarkrans" (year cycle), and "Eeuwkrans" (eternity cycle)—Gezelle was able to lock into permanent place all of those poems concerned with time. The year described in "Jaarkrans" is much more than a specific year, consisting of specific hours, days, and months; it essentially pertains to all years as they repeat the cyclical and oscillating patterns of the various months and seasons. Thus the year cycle in *Tijdkrans* is actually the time cycle of the collection as a whole. Moreover, the permanence of this universal year is absorbed by the permanence of eternity discussed in "Eeuwkrans." *Tijdkrans* thus possesses a meaningful progression of ideas throughout—the various stages of the typical day in "Dagkrans" spill over into the seasonal rhythms of the typical year in "Jaarkrans"; and both the day and the year in their predictable recurrence of hours, months, and seasons anticipate the static constancy of eternity in "Eeuwkrans." "Eeuwkrans," then, becomes the meaningful backdrop for both "Dagkrans" and "Jaarkrans"; for the stability inherent in the ever recurrent flux of time is absorbed in the permanence and constancy of eternity itself. In the structural pattern adopted for *Tijdkrans*, then, Gezelle was able to conquer the enemy time.

RIJMSNOER

Gezelle's last collection, *Rijmsnoer*, contains 216 poems, of which 204 were composed during the four-year span from 1893 to 1897, and reflects an inner peace he had found. While the majority of these poems are about nature, Gezelle no longer uses nature in them as the medium through which to voice his complaints. Rather, nature has become the symbol of God's grand design, and the poet simply bathes in the sheer joy of that design. Gezelle no longer reiterates his wish to die, or expresses a chronic discontent with the world, or feels dissatisfied with the enemy time. Rather, in *Rijmsnoer* he has found full satisfaction in the harmony which nature provides.

Paralleling the structure of *Tijdkrans*, *Rijmsnoer* also contains three basic sections—a short introduction of eight poems, called "Voorhang" (proscenium); a very large middle movement of 139 poems, divided into twelve units devoted to the months of the year; and a short conclusion of eight poems, titled "Aanhang" (appendix). Dominating the entire collection is the large middle movement. It is essentially an amplification of "Jaarkrans," the middle panel in *Tijdkrans*. Unlike the collection *Tijdkrans*, however, which includes a separate section devoted to eternity ("Eeuwkrans") and which by implication gives meaning to its middle panel "Jaarkrans," the middle panel of *Rijmsnoer* is suffused with Gezelle's awareness and assurance of eternity. Thus, in *Rijmsnoer*, the tension between time and eternity is nearly erased.

The most significant image in *Rijmsnoer* is the sun. For Gezelle, sunlight had become a symbol of eternal light. It not only makes flowers grope toward it, especially when the sun is darkened by clouds, but it also teaches men to reach toward light, especially when the shadows and clouds of daily existence seem to block out God's light. In a real sense, then, *Rijmsnoer* is filled with sun worship, the worshiper-poet progressing from seeing through a glass darkly to beholding God the Sun face to face. Living, for Gezelle, had in these final years become a ceaseless act of praying, a moving away from physical sight to increasingly greater spiritual insight. He had, as he says in "Zonnewende" ("Sun Searching"), come to see "with eyes closed" and "to breathe in the light of the sun." He had learned to conquer not only time but also death. He had come to experience within himself that like the sun, which appears anew each day, he too, despite the darker aspects of life and death, will eventually rise again and ultimately "shine eternally" ("Mortis Imago"/"Image of Death"). The culmination of this long search for light finds expression in "Ego Flos" ("I Am a Flower"), Gezelle's last great mystical poem, incorporated in *Laatste verzen*. Written shortly before his death, this poem pictures the poet as God's special flower and celebrates his one day surpassing all earthly flowers by growing in the full light of the Sun.

REVIVING FLEMISH LITERATURE

Ironically, though *Tijdkrans* and *Rijmsnoer* never refer even once to Gezelle's patriotic goal of reviving Flemish literature, it is precisely these two collections which stimulated that revival, especially after the poet's death. These collections were at first neither admired nor clearly understood, but later they were praised for their innovativeness in language and style. No longer resorting to those monotonous rhymes, conventional stanzaic patterns, and didactic techniques which characterize some parts of the earlier *Dichtoefeningen* and

Gedichten, gezangen en gebeden, the collections *Tijdkrans* and *Rijmsnoer* from beginning to end are truly inspired rather than consciously made. Their poems are fluid and varied, unforced and free, quickening and slowing their pace in accordance with the natural rhythms of colloquial speech. They are daringly innovative in their language as well. In them, Gezelle stretched his own Flemish idiom to its very limits, coupling contemporary words to medieval roots, transforming verbs into nouns and nouns into verbs, or simply combining different parts of speech. Through these two collections in particular, Gezelle became recognized far and wide.

OTHER MAJOR WORKS

TRANSLATIONS: *The Song of Hiawatha*, 1886 (of Henry Wadsworth Longfellow's poem); *Meditationes theologiae*, 1897 (of Monsignor Waffelaert).

MISCELLANEOUS: *Jubileumuitgave van Guido Gezelle's volledige werken*, 1930-1939 (9 volumes).

BIBLIOGRAPHY

King, Peter. *Gezelle and Multatuli: A Question of Literature and Social History*. Hull, England: University of Hull, 1978. A critical assessment of the works of Gezalle and his contemporary Multatuli, also known as Eduard Douwes Dekker. Includes bibliographical references.

Van Nuis, Hermine J. *Guido Gezelle, Flemish Poet-Priest*. New York: Greenwood Press, 1986. A brief biography and critical study of Gezelle's life and work.

Van Roosbroeck, G. L. *Guido Gezelle: The Mystic Poet of Flanders*. Vinton, Iowa.: Kruse, 1919. A short study of Gezelle's place in the history of Flemish literature.

Hermine J. van Nuis;
bibliography updated by the editors

KAHLIL GIBRAN

Born: Besharri, Lebanon; January 6, 1883
Died: New York, New York; April 10, 1931

PRINCIPAL POETRY

'Arā'is al-Murūj, 1906 (*Nymphs of the Valley*, 1948)

Al-Arwāh al-Mutamarridah, 1908 (*Spirits Rebellious*, 1948)

Al Ajnihah al-Mutakassirah, 1912 (*The Broken Wings*, 1957)

Kitāb Dam'ah wa Ibtisāmah, 1914 (*Tears and Laughter*, 1946; also known as *A Tear and a Smile*, 1950)

The Madman: His Parables and Poems, 1918

Al-Mawākib, 1919 (*The Procession*, 1947)

Twenty Drawings, 1919, 1974

The Forerunner: His Parables and Poems, 1920

The Prophet, 1923

Sand and Foam, 1926

The Earth Gods, 1931

The Wanderer: His Parables and His Sayings, 1932

The Garden of the Prophet, 1933

Prose Poems, 1934, 1962, 1971

Secrets of the Heart, 1947

Mirrors of the Soul, 1965 (Joseph Sheban, translator and editor)

Kahlil Gibran: A Prophet in the Making, 1991 (based on manuscript pages of *The Madman*, *The Forerunner*, *The Prophet*, and *The Earth Gods*)

OTHER LITERARY FORMS

Kahlil Gibran's collections include poetry, parables, fragments of conversation, short stories, fables, political essays, letters, and aphorisms.

ACHIEVEMENTS

As a poet, Kahlil Gibran made his greatest impact on Arabic literature. His Arabic publications broke new ground in poetic form and in the stridency of their exhortations. Barbara Young asserts in *This Man from Lebanon* (1945) that the West knows a soft Gibran while the East knows a Gibran who encased "steel in velvet."

While *Time* (January 22, 1945), in reviewing *This Man from Lebanon*, would only concede that Gibran's "poetry in Arabic was apparently more striking," Joseph Sheban in *Mirrors of the Soul* (1965) is more enthusiastic. Sheban claims that Gibran "created a new era in style, influenced by Western thought, and a revolution in

Kahlil Gibran (Kimberly Kurnizki)

the minds of the younger generation of his country." Annie Salem Otto concurs in *The Parables of Kahlil Gibran* (1981), saying that *Broken Wings* "was greeted by the Arab world as an innovation in that it was the first work" to break away "from the imitation of the old classics."

Gibran's writing in English is more prose than poetry. Gibran found his second language exceedingly inadequate for creating poetry and he frequently voiced his frustration to friends. Young claims that Gibran knew fifty Arabic words for the English word "love" and this was only one example of the way in which he felt inhibited when he attempted to render into English that which he conceived in Arabic. The fact is, as Sheban states, that Gibran actually has "very little poetry" among his voluminous works in English.

Nor have translations of Gibran's Arabic works done them justice. Sheban calls them "often inadequate" and Young attributes his "soft" image in America partly to the translation problem. What reads as angry and original poetry in Arabic tends to translate into what Stefan Kanfer, writing in *The New York Times Magazine* (June 25, 1972), calls "limp, mucid hooey." As a result, Gibran's English writings have made little impact on the

American literary tradition. In spite of this lack of literary recognition, Gibran's impact on the United States has been unparalleled by any other single poet, if sales are any indication. In 1965, *Time* reported that *The Prophet* was selling five thousand copies a week. In 1972, Nancy Wilson Ross in *Saturday Review* (LV, April 15, 1972) reported that it was still selling about half a million copies a year.

No biographer or critic seems completely able to explain Gibran's popularity. *Time* (August 13, 1965) says that *The Prophet* "appeals to the bereaved," can be used for "seduction," and "seems to provide a philosophy for the somewhat immature." Kanfer agrees, with a vengeance; if Americans come home "too pooped for Lear," they turn to Gibran as to a "tranquilizer." One critic, writing for *Masterplots* (1996), however, takes a more temperate view: ". . . *The Prophet* owes much of its popularity to the young, who find in Gibran's poetry the elusive quality of sincerity."

One cannot fail to mention Gibran's painting in speaking of his achievements. His paintings are sprinkled throughout his books and many were seen in public exhibitions during his lifetime. Gibran was a recognized portrait painter and painted many significant persons of his era; among them were Sarah Bernhardt, William Butler Yeats, and John Masefield.

The subject of his paintings was almost always the naked human form or the head and shoulders of a figure fading into mist. The paintings frequently superimpose a dominant figure on other vague figures so that a story is told or a theme implied. In this art, he was predominantly influenced by Leonardo da Vinci, one of his earliest heroes. Like the Renaissance painters, he used a complex background of a vast army of figures to broaden the meaning of the work.

During his lifetime, much of which was spent in New York City, Gibran was sought after as a speaker, reader, and socialite. He organized an academy of Arabic writers living in New York and published books in Arabic which incensed both the Maronite church and the Turkish rulers of the Near East. His personal charisma, his godlike image among his friends, is legend. Women were especially attracted to him and were willing simply to drop what they were doing with their own lives to support, help, or accommodate him. Barbara

Young, herself a poet, is the prime example. She served as his secretary for the last eight years of his life after hearing his work read once in a church.

Biography

Gibran Kahlil Gibran was born of Kamila and Khalil Gibran in Besharri, Lebanon. He had a half-brother, Peter, from his mother's previous marriage and two younger sisters, Marianna and Sultana. The Gibrans were moderately poor and eventually Kamila and her children emigrated to America when economic conditions in Lebanon worsened and it became more difficult to live with the reputedly indigent Khalil Gibran.

Tutored at home by his mother and befriended by one Father Yusef in his early years, Gibran learned Arabic, French, and English along with songs, folklore, and legends. He expressed a love for ancient villages and sacred grounds and an interest in God, angels, and another world. He demonstrated artistic talent early, sculpting in snow and building small stone cathedrals. He also wrote poetry and painted, though he destroyed these early efforts.

After arriving in Boston in June, 1894, the eleven-year-old Gibran entered an American school and was recognized by his teacher as possessing special talents and qualities. In 1896, Gibran returned to Lebanon, so that, according to Young, he could study Arabic literature; according to Andrew D. Sherfan, however, Kamila wanted to get him out of the clutches of an older woman who was influencing him in ways of which she disapproved. In Lebanon, he attended Madrasat Al-Hikma, School of Wisdom, where he was compelled to attend church twice a day. Otto indicates that he studied "medicine, international law, the history of religion and music" besides "classical Arabic literature." During this time, he first conceived of *The Prophet* in Arabic and edited a literary and philosophical magazine called *Al-Hakitat* (The Truth).

In 1901, at the age of eighteen, he was graduated with high honors and, according to Otto, traveled through Greece, Italy, and Spain to Paris, where he studied art and wrote his first book, *Spirits Rebellious*. Virginia Hilu's *Beloved Prophet* (1972) contradicts Otto's account, stating that Gibran went back to Boston in 1899 and remained there. In any case, the publication of

Spirits Rebellious in Arabic about 1902 caused the Turkish rulers to exile him, his church (the Maronite rite of Roman Catholicism) to excommunicate him, and the book to be publicly burned in Lebanon. The book cataloged the evils of the existing government and religion.

In 1903, all biographers agree, Gibran was in Boston, where his mother, Peter, and Sultana were dying of tuberculosis. He stayed with them through their ordeal and then, in 1904, held his first art show at the studio of Fred Holland Day. Also in 1904, Gibran met Mary Haskell, an acquaintance of Fred Day. Gibran apparently fell in love with her immediately; Mary later financed Gibran's study of art in Paris. In 1910, he returned to New York more deeply involved with Mary, proposing marriage and being turned down on more than one occasion. As their letters indicate, Mary felt his genius would thrive best if he were not married to her. They struggled several years over their final decision not to consummate their relationship sexually.

Gibran continued to write and paint. In 1914, he had his first New York exhibition at the Montross Galleries; his second was in 1917 at the Knoedler Galleries. In the same year, according to most biographers, he published a book called *Twenty Drawings*. After this period of greater concentration on art, he began to focus on writing with the help and encouragement of Mary Haskell, who apparently edited every line and helped him with English usage. He published a total of six books in English before his death of cancer in 1931, at the age of forty-eight. Two books that were almost complete were published posthumously.

His most famous and profitable book was *The Prophet*, published in 1923, and soon selling by the hundreds of thousands. His biographers indicate that it was the first of a projected trilogy: (1) *The Prophet* was to explore the relationship of man and man; (2) *The Garden of the Prophet* was to explore the relationship of man to nature; and (3) *The Death of the Prophet* was to explore the relationship of man and God.

In 1924, about the time that Mary Haskell became seriously involved with another man, Barbara Young became Gibran's secretary and remained devoted to him until his death. Upon Gibran's death, his will was read. It left his royalties to the town of Besharri, Lebanon, and his other possessions to his sister and Mary Haskell.

Barbara Young was named executor. A small funeral was held in Boston before the body was shipped to Lebanon. Heads of government and throngs of people met the body and it was buried in state with the highest possible honors, at a monastery near the Cedars of Lebanon outside of Besharri.

Going through his papers, Young and Haskell discovered that Gibran had kept all of Mary's love letters to him. Young admitted to being stunned at the depth of the relationship, which was all but unknown to her. In her own biography of Gibran, she minimized the relationship and begged Mary Haskell to burn the letters. Mary agreed initially but then reneged, and eventually they were published, along with her journal and Gibran's some three hundred letters to her, in Hilu's *Beloved Prophet*.

The early accounts of Gibran's life were mostly written by close friends who tended to make their reports accord with their feelings for Gibran. More objective viewpoints are found in Otto, Sherfan, and Hilu. Even so, there is sharp disagreement on some dates and events in Gibran's life and much diversity in emphasis and interpretation of events.

All agree, for example, that Gibran had an extraordinary number of female devotees. Claude Bragdon in *Merely Players* (1929) described the atmosphere in which Gibran lived as "pervasively, even oppressively, feminine." Some biographers stress his pen-pal relationship with May Ziadeh, a Lebanese writer, while others imply sexual relationships with many women, including two friends of Mary's, Charlotte Teller, and the somewhat mysterious "Micheline." In *Beloved Prophet*, Gibran's letters indicate the permanence of his celibate commitment to Mary, referring to their relationship as a "marriage"—as indeed hers do also.

ANALYSIS

Interest in Kahlil Gibran's biography and personality has largely preempted analysis of his writings for their own sake. The difficulties seem to be threefold: His personality and lifestyle were romantic and appealing; literary critics in America have basically deemed his writings beneath notice; and the diverse and unusual forms of his English writings are alien to American scholars.

To start with the last point, in 1957 Jean Lecerf, an expert in Arabic literature, defined the "prose poem" genre. He attributed two main qualities to it: first, parallelism, repetition, and refrain; and, second, imitation of the cadence of the sacred texts. Otto cites Lecerf's 1957 French article in *Orient* magazine, in which Lecerf places Gibran foremost among the founders of the prose-poem genre. This genre, apparently highly influential in Arabic literature, has not taken root in American literature; hence, Gibran has remained a "man without a genre" and has not received much serious attention by American literary scholars.

Gibran thought of himself as a poet-prophet-philosopher. This combination is a common one in Arabic literature and there is a word for it. No such word exists in the English language, and since Gibran cannot be easily placed in one of the recognized genres, the Occidental need to classify inhibits analysis. As Claude Bragdon writes, "*artist, poet, prophet* . . . they should be only one word, but this the English language fails to furnish."

Although the American tradition does not make it easy to analyze Gibran's Oriental/Western writing, some assessment can be made. Gibran can be evaluated in terms of theme, predominant images, and style. It is helpful to recognize that these may be inseparable with Gibran, who did not care about such things, and whose editors and publishers did not want to tamper with his words.

THE PROCESSION

The Procession has been praised as Gibran's highest poetic achievement in Arabic, as containing the essence of the message of his other books. It was issued at Gibran's own expense in 1918 (biographers disagree on the date), and George Kheirallah, one of its translators (1958), calls it the "hidden masterpiece of Arabic poetry." Bragdon describes the sense of the "procession" as a central metaphor of Gibran's when he writes that Gibran's works "represent the 'pilgrim's progress'" sequence. He adds that "each one contains and is the whole." A look at *The Procession* may be fruitful in the effort to identify themes, images, and form in Gibran's work.

That "each one contains the whole" suggests a dominant Arabic quality in Gibran's writings. As Otto explains it, "To the Oriental, all things suggest all things." Robert Hillyer's introduction to the 1974 edition of *A Tear and a Smile* describes the "Oriental method of personifying institutions and summarizing an entire situa-

tion into one symbol." He adds that Gibran liked to mass general statements "to emphasize concepts" of "ultimate reality." This ultimate reality, expressed by the forest youth in *The Procession*, is a complete and utter unity of all living things as they move outward/inward to the fulfillment of their beings. Instead of massing details to create unity as a modern realist would, Gibran piles generalizations upon generalizations, untested by harsh reality, with the certainty that they originate from God and thus possess the authority of sacred language.

The Procession is a dialogue or duet between a so-called sage and a youth in the forest. The sage laments the state of various categories of reality, such as religion, justice, and love. The youth denies the very existence of categories. He says categories themselves come from disunity and he sings of the unity of all things in the forest. The impact is achieved through the accumulation of the sage's repeated complaints and the youth's optimistic refrain.

Taking the concept of the procession as a central metaphor, one must see it as at least two-sided. The sage's words suggest the sorrowful march of humankind to an unknown destination. The youth disdains the notion of rank-and-file, horizontal, historical progress and reckons movement to be the "striving upward" equally of "the slender reed and oak tree." The youth sees glory only in natural things doing what they are naturally suited to do. If that natural "procession" toward self-fulfillment occurs, unity and bliss will follow.

THE FORERUNNER

In *The Forerunner*, Gibran compares the scholar with the serpent who crawls horizontally on the earth and knows the earth's secrets, and the poet with the songbird who flies upward and sings. These seem to represent two types of procession. The title *The Forerunner* indicates a procession, someone to follow someone else—in this case, a heraldic figure. The title may appear slightly misleading, for the book's message is that man is his own forerunner. The current self simply points to the coming of the greater self. This is the procession of the soul toward awareness of its greatness (Godness); it is not a historical procession.

THE PROPHET

This concept is repeated in *The Prophet*. The prophet says, "Like a procession you walk together towards your god-self." *The Prophet* has been called Gibran's greatest English work, and indeed it was his own favorite, conceived at the age of fifteen in Arabic, rewritten several times, and finally published in 1923. It is not unlikely that, as Gibran says, *The Procession*, published in 1918 in Arabic, was being drafted at the same time that *The Prophet* was germinating, in his pocket and at his bedside.

At any rate, there are similarities. The youth of the forest is like the youth, Almustafa, of *The Prophet*. Both offer wisdom to their elders. In each case, the format is arranged around areas of concern raised by those who are still in the grip of their lesser selves. In *The Procession*, the sage gives a summation of the state of each of the problem areas, but he is won over by the repeated discarding of the problems by the idealistic youth. In *The Prophet*, the elders do not attempt to tell the youth about the world as they see it; they simply ask for his comments. The youth, however, has lived twelve years with them, and they have come to love and trust his words. In *The Procession*, youth and sage meet briefly only once, so the sage naturally presumes upon his own age and wisdom as he speaks.

Both youths offer wisdom to their elders. Each book is compelling in a different way. The contrast of the realist and the idealist in the earlier book has some of the qualities of a joust and the reader waits to see which type of wisdom will triumph. In *The Prophet*, Almustafa reiterates in his monologues the blindness of the sage's position in the light of Truth. For example, the sage speaks of religion as a system of barter, of rewards and losses based on deeds done or left undone. The prophet does not agree. Speaking of religion he asks, Who can say that "this is for God and this for myself?" Later, he declares that "you cannot rise above your achievements nor fall lower than your failures." So, religion is not reward and punishment but revelation at the level of "procession" toward the greater self. The prophet harks back to the sage's complaint with some of his word choices, but he takes the whole issue far beyond quantitative measurement; he makes the sage's summary appear ludicrous before a God who does not make distinctions on the basis of merit.

THEMES AND CRITICS

Other themes which Gibran explores throughout his books are androgyny (Jesus being the ultimate of this spe-

cies), the plight of women, the supremacy of truth over human law, the significance of work, the importance of passion (associated with God and storms), the concept of love, the existence of the greater self toward which all are headed, and the possibility of reincarnation.

Much could be written about each of these themes, but since Gibran has been so thoroughly rejected by literary scholars in America, it seems important to spend considerable effort exploring the weaknesses which have so alienated this group. The apparent viciousness in the comments of some who have written about Gibran leads one to suspect that there must be an appeal or potential in Gibran's writing which is great enough to be hated. Perhaps, disillusioned romantics all, American critics are particularly harsh. The extensive portrait of one writer who retained his innocence in the face of World War I and the emerging notion of America as a spiritual "wasteland" must have been intolerable to some.

Gibran, it must be remembered, was not American enough to have picked up the cynicism and despair of that era in America. He fled a homeland that was held captive by alien rulers and regarded America as a mecca for his hopes and dreams. That America did receive him warmly and remunerate him adequately certainly did nothing to dispel his optimism.

Gibran does have some irritating qualities as a writer, best summarized by his strongest critic, Stefan Kanfer, who has accused him of "softheadedness," of an "unfocused, uncritical, tragically contagious view of man and God." Indeed it is an overwhelming lack of judgment regarding his own writings and ideas that is hard to accept. He blends the utterly trite with the incisively ironic and the sublimely wise—and seems not to realize the difference. This fuzzy judgment is most visible in *Sand and Foam*.

SAND AND FOAM

In this work, Gibran reveals talent for the short tale with an unusual twist at the end that leaves the reader thoughtful, amused, or even astonished. In a story of two pilgrims, the first asks the second the way to the Holy City. The second says with assurance, "Follow me." The first follows the second and they never reach the city. Gibran ends the story with the first pilgrim's understated comment: "What was to my surprise he became angry with me because he had misled me." The twist in the ending is unexpected but verifiable in ordinary human experience.

To find such bits of wheat in Gibran, unfortunately, one has to sift through enormous mounds of chaff. The same writer who said that "Poetry is a deal of joy and pain and wonder, with a dash of the dictionary" has also said: "One may not reach the dawn save by the path of the night." Both statements appear, nearly side by side, in *Sand and Foam*. This indiscriminate taste obscures some of Gibran's best qualities.

Those who knew him, for example, assert unanimously that Gibran had a wonderful sense of humor. Between pages of triteness rest some funny throwaway lines. "The lame should not break their crutches," he writes, "upon the head of their enemy." An exaggeration, he says, is "a truth that has lost its temper," and "A fact is a truth unsexed." Finally, in *The Forerunner*, he tells of three thirsty poets who sit philosophizing while a fourth poet drinks their punch: "The three poets with their mouths open, looked at him aghast and there was a thirsty yet unlyrical hatred in their eyes."

It may be safe to say that Gibran's writing will probably never affect American literature very seriously, though it will probably always be popular because it makes sense to the young. Youth predominates in his book; youth saves and redeems and is innocent of the evils of the elders. Gibran sees youth the way idealistic young people see themselves; he endows this self-concept with a religious right to be what it is and to assert itself over the collected wisdom of the culture.

Gibran has probably touched a part of each generation of Americans since 1940. Gibran crystalizes, Kanfer says, "a tendency that has always been present in American letters" to simplify, sentimentalize, and romanticize life to make it bearable. This weariness, naïveté, or lack of discipline in the struggle for meaning leads some to worship those like Gibran who explains everything in simple and authoritative language.

OTHER MAJOR WORKS

RELIGIOUS WRITING: *Al-ʿAwāṣif*, 1920; *Jesus, the Son of Man*, 1928.

NONFICTION: *Kahlil Gibran: A Self-Portrait*, 1959; *Wisdom of Kahlil Gibran*, 1966; *Beloved Prophet: The Love Letters of Kahlil Gibran and Mary Haskell*

and Her Private Journal, 1972; *Between Night and Morn: A Special Selection*, 1972; *Shuʾlah al-Zarqaʾ*, 1983 (*Blue Flame: The Love Letters of Kahlil Gibran to May Ziadah*, 1983); *The Book of Giving: A Tribute to Mother Teresa*, 1990; *The Beloved: Reflections on the Path of the Heart*, 1994; *The Vision: Reflections on the Way of the Soul*, 1994.

BIBLIOGRAPHY

Bushrui, Suheil B., and Joe Jenkins. *Kahlil Gibran, Man and Poet*. Boston: Oneworld, 1998. A biography of the poet and philosopher with a critical study of his writings. Bushrui, an authority on Gibran, and Jenkins, a research fellow at the University of Maryland, rely on new sources gathered during a ten-year study to capture Gibran's life. Includes bibliographical references and index.

Daoudi, M. S. *The Meaning of Kahlil Gibran*. Secaucus, N.J.: Citadel Press, 1982. This study is divided into three parts: The first contains biographical information, the second provides critical commentary on Gibran's works, and the third discusses his politics. An appreciative look at Gibran, noting that he was a prodigious author, not just the author of a single work as commonly supposed, and a philosopher of substance "whose themes are complex and inclusive, with deep social and political implications." The book concludes with an interesting essay, "Gibran and Arab Nationalism." Supplemented by a useful select bibliography.

Naimy, Mikhail. *Kahlil Gibran: A Biography*. New York: Philosophical Library, 1950. An intimate biography by Gibran's close friend and associate. Naimy dispels much of the myth that surrounded Gibran during his last years and reveals instead the human being who struggled and pulsated with life. Includes some hitherto unpublished writings and sayings by Gibran, as well as his last will and testament. An important biography for Gibran scholars.

Otto, Annie Salem. *The Parables of Kahlil Gibran: An Interpretation of His Writings and His Art*. New York: Citadel Press, 1963. This study concerns itself with those parables that Gibran wrote directly in English. Includes a description of his life, singling out the experiences that formulated his ideas on humankind and society and which are reflected in his writings and art. A useful addition to the Gibran scholarship.

Sheban, Joseph, and Joseph P. Ghougassian. *A Third Treasury of Kahlil Gibran*. Edited by Andrew Dib Sherfan. Secaucus, N.J.: Citadel Press, 1975. A full-length study of Gibran that looks at his formative years, his philosophy, his views on love—both poetic and analytical—and his political outlook. Included in the second book are extracts from Gibran's writings. Particularly noteworthy is Ghougassian's essay, "Love, the Quintessence of Human Existence," in which he explores Gibran's theory of love and relates it to those of other philosophers.

Young, Barbara. *This Man from Lebanon: A Study of Kahlil Gibran*. New York: Alfred A. Knopf, 1973. Written by a personal friend of Gibran who nevertheless attempts in this study to "stand aside from the personal relationship, and to explore the fabric of this man's genius with an impartial regard." Along with the story of the last seven years of Gibran's life, this volume contains some authoritative commentary on his work during this period.

Waterfield, Robin. *Prophet: The Life and Times of Kahlil Gibran*. New York: St. Martin's Press, 1998. Complete biography with bibliographic references and an index.

Anne Kelsch Breznau;
bibliography updated by the editors

ALLEN GINSBERG

Born: Newark, New Jersey; June 3, 1926
Died: New York, New York; April 5, 1997

PRINCIPAL POETRY
Howl and Other Poems, 1956
Empty Mirror: Early Poems, 1961
Kaddish and Other Poems, 1958-1960, 1961
The Change, 1963
Reality Sandwiches, 1963
Kral Majales, 1965

Wichita Vortex Sutra, 1966
T. V. Baby Poems, 1967
Airplane Dreams: Compositions from Journals, 1968
Ankor Wat, 1968
Planet News, 1961-1967, 1968
The Moments Return, 1970
Ginsberg's Improvised Poetics, 1971
Bixby Canyon Ocean Path Word Breeze, 1972
The Fall of America: Poems of These States, 1965-1971, 1973
The Gates of Wrath: Rhymed Poems, 1948-1952, 1972
Iron Horse, 1972
Open Head, 1972
First Blues: Rags, Ballads, and Harmonium Songs, 1971-1974, 1975
Sad Dust Glories: Poems During Work Summer in Woods, 1975
Mind Breaths: Poems, 1972-1977, 1977
Mostly Sitting Haiku, 1978
Poems All over the Place: Mostly Seventies, 1978
Plutonian Ode: Poems, 1977-1980, 1982
Collected Poems, 1947-1980, 1984
White Shroud: Poems, 1980-1985, 1986
Hydrogen Jukebox, 1990 (music by Philip Glass)
Collected Poems, 1992
Cosmopolitan Greetings: Poems, 1986-1992, 1994
Making It Up: Poetry Composed at St. Marks Church on May 9, 1979, 1994
Selected Poems, 1947-1995, 1996
Death and Fame: Poems, 1993-1997, 1999

OTHER LITERARY FORMS
Allen Ginsberg recognized early in his career that he would have to explain his intentions, because most critics and reviewers did not have the interest or experience to understand what he was trying to accomplish. Consequently, he published books that include interviews, lectures, essays, and letters to friends as means of conveying his theories about composition and poetics.

ACHIEVEMENTS
The publication of "Howl" in 1956 drew such enthusiastic comments from Allen Ginsberg's supporters and

such vituperative condemnation from conservative cultural commentators that a rift of immense proportions developed which has made a balanced critical assessment very difficult. Nevertheless, partisan response has gradually given way to an acknowledgment by most critics that Ginsberg's work is significant, if not always entirely successful by familiar standards of literary excellence. Such recognition was underscored in 1974, when *The Fall of America* shared the National Book Award for Poetry. In 1986 Ginsberg was awarded the Frost Medal by the Poetry Society of America.

The voice that Ginsberg employed in "Howl" not only has directed the style of several generations but also has combined the rhythms and language of common speech with some of the deepest, most enduring traditions in American literature. In both his life and his work, Ginsberg set an example of moral seriousness, artistic commitment, and humane decency that made him one of the most popular figures in American culture. The best of his visionary and innovative creations earned for him recognition as one of the major figures of the twentieth century.

BIOGRAPHY

The second son of Naomi Ginsberg, a political activist, and Louis Ginsberg, a traditional lyric poet and schoolteacher, Allen Ginsberg attended primary school in the middle-class town of Paterson, New Jersey. Except for his mother's hospitalization for mental stress, he grew up in a conventional and uneventful fashion. He entered Columbia University in 1943, intending to pursue a career in labor law, but the influence of such well-known literary scholars as Lionel Trilling and Mark Van Doren, combined with the excitement of the Columbia community, which included fellow student Jack Kerouac and such singular people as William Burroughs and Neal Cassady, led him toward literature as a vocation. He was temporarily suspended from Columbia in 1945 and worked as a welder and apprentice seaman before finishing his degree in 1948. Living a "subterranean" life (to use Kerouac's term), Ginsberg was counseled to commit himself to Columbia Presbyterian Psychiatric Institute to avoid criminal charges; there, in 1949, he met Carl W. Solomon, to whom "Howl" is dedicated. During the early 1950's, he began a correspon-

Allen Ginsberg (George Holmes, courtesy of Harper & Row)

dence with William Carlos Williams, who guided and encouraged his early writing, and traveled in Mexico and Europe. He was living in San Francisco when he wrote "Howl," and he read the poem for the first time at a landmark Six Gallery performance that included Gary Snyder, Philip Whalen, and Michael McClure. His mother died in 1956, the year *Howl and Other Poems* was published, and he spent the next few years traveling, defending *Howl* against charges of obscenity, working on "Kaddish"—his celebration of his mother's life—and reading on college campuses and in Beat venues on both coasts.

The growing notoriety of the Beat generation drew Ginsberg into the media spotlight in the early 1960's, and he was active in the promotion of work by his friends. He continued to travel extensively, visiting Europe, India, and Japan, and he published widely in many of the prominent literary journals of the counterculture. His involvement with various hallucinatory substances led to the formation of LeMar (Organization to Legalize Marijuana) in 1964 with the poet, songwriter, and publisher Ed Sanders, and his continuing disaffection with governmental policies took him toward active political protest. In 1965 he was invited to Cuba and Czechoslovakia by Communist officials, who mistakenly assumed that his criticism of American society would make him sympathetic to their regimes, but Ginsberg's outspoken criticism of all forms of tyranny and suppression led to his expulsion from both countries.

His political activity reached a peak in 1968, when he was arrested in Chicago at the Democratic National Convention with many other demonstrators, and in 1969, when he testified at the Chicago trials. In the early 1970's, he spent some time on a farm in rural New York, formally accepted the teachings of Buddhism from Chögyam Trungpa, who initiated him with the name "Lion of Dharma," and founded, with Anne Waldman, a school of literary inquiry at the Naropa Institute in Colorado. He was inducted into the American Institute of Arts and Letters in 1974, an indication of recognition as an artist in the mainstream of American culture, and he further confirmed this status by traveling with Bob Dylan's Rolling Thunder Review as a "poet-percussionist" in 1975. Continuing to combine artistic endeavor with a commitment to social justice, Ginsberg took part in protests at the Rocky Flats Nuclear Facility in 1978 and wrote the "Plutonium Ode," which expressed his concern about the destructive forces humans had unleashed.

During the 1980's, Ginsberg continued to travel, teach, write, and perform his work. The publication of his *Collected Poems, 1947-1980* in 1985 was received with wide attention and respect, and he was appointed distinguished professor at Brooklyn College in 1986, the year he published *White Shroud*, which includes an epilogue to "Kaddish" along with other poems from the 1980's. His ability as a teacher was clearly demonstrated in his appearance on the Public Broadcasting System series *Voices and Visions* in 1987. As the decade drew to a close, he was involved in a collaboration with Philip Glass on a chamber opera called *Hydrogen Jukebox* (a phrase from "Howl"), which was performed in 1990. Continuing to write with energy while teaching a graduate-level course on the Beats at the City University of New York Graduate Center, Ginsberg described his goals in the 1990's, in a poem called "Personals Ad," as similar to the ones he had always pursued: "help inspire mankind conquer world anger & guilt." It was an appropriate task for a "poet professor in his autumn years." He died on April 5, 1997, in New York City.

ANALYSIS

"Howl," the poem that carried Allen Ginsberg into public consciousness as a symbol of the avant-garde artist and as the designer of a verse style for a postwar generation seeking its own voice, was initially regarded as primarily a social document. As Ginsberg's notes make clear, however, it was also the latest specimen in a continuing experiment in form and structure. Several factors in Ginsberg's life were particularly important in this breakthrough poem, written as the poet was approaching thirty and still drifting through a series of jobs, countries, and social occasions. Ginsberg had been more heavily influenced by his father than was immediately apparent. Louis Ginsberg's very traditional, metrical verse was of little use to his son, but his father's interest in literary history was part of Ginsberg's solid grounding in prosody. Then, a succession of other mentors—including William Carlos Williams, whose use of the American vernacular and local material had inspired him, and great scholars such as the art historian Meyer Shapiro at Columbia, who had introduced him to the tenets of modernism from an analytic perspective—had enabled the young poet to form a substantial intellectual foundation.

In addition, Ginsberg was dramatically affected by his friendships with Jack Kerouac, Neal Cassady, Herbert Hunke, William Burroughs, and other noteworthy members of an underground community of dropouts, revolutionaries, drug addicts, jazz musicians, and serious but unconventional artists of all sorts. Ginsberg felt an immediate kinship with these "angel-headed hipsters," who accepted and celebrated eccentricity and who regarded Ginsberg's homosexuality as an attribute, not a blemish. While Ginsberg enthusiastically entered into the drug culture that was a flourishing part of this subterranean community, he was not nearly as routed toward self-destruction as Burroughs or Hunke; he was more interested in the possibilities of visionary experience. His oft-noted "illuminative audition of William Blake's voice simultaneous with Eternity-vision" in 1948 was his first ecstatic experience of transcendence, and he continued to pursue spiritual insight through serious studies of various religions—including Judaism and Buddhism—as well as through chemical experimentation.

His experiments with mind-altering agents and his casual friendship with some quasi-criminals led to his eight-month stay in a psychiatric institute. He had already had an unsettling series of encounters with mental instability in his mother, who had been hospitalized for the first time when he was three. Her struggles with the torments of psychic uncertainty were seriously disruptive events in Ginsberg's otherwise unremarkable boyhood, but Ginsberg felt deep sympathy for his mother's agony and also was touched by her warmth, love, and social conscience. While not exactly a "red diaper baby," Ginsberg had adopted a radical political conscience early enough to decide to pursue labor law as a college student, and he has never wavered from his initial convictions concerning the excesses of capitalism. His passionate call for tolerance and fairness has roots as much in his mother's ideas as in his contacts with the "lamblike youths" who were "slaughtered" by the demon Moloch—his symbol for the greed and materialism of the United States in the 1950's. In conjunction with his displeasure with what he saw as the failure of the government to correct these abuses, he carried an idealized conception of "the lost America of love" based on his readings in nineteenth century American literature, Walt Whitman and Henry David Thoreau in particular, and reinforced by the political and social idealism of contemporaries such as Kerouac, Gary Snyder, and Michael McClure.

Ginsberg brought all these concerns together when he began to compose "Howl." Yet while the social and political elements of the poem were immediately apparent, the careful structural arrangements were not. Ginsberg found it necessary to explain his intentions in a series of notes and letters, emphasizing his desire to use Whitman's long line "to *build up* large organic structures" and his realization that he did not have to satisfy anyone's concept of what a poem should be, but could follow his "romantic inspiration" and simply write as he wished, "without fear." Using what he called his "Hebraic-Melvillian bardic breath"—a rhythmic pattern similar to the cadences of the Old Testament as employed by Herman Melville—Ginsberg wrote a three-part prophetic elegy, which he described as a "huge sad comedy of wild phrasing."

"Howl"

The first part of "Howl" is a long catalog of the activities of the "angelheaded hipsters" who were his contemporaries. Calling the bohemian underground of outcasts, outlaws, rebels, mystics, sexual deviants, junkies, and other misfits "the best minds of my generation"—a judgment that still rankles many social critics—Ginsberg produced image after image of the antics of "remarkable lamblike youths" in pursuit of cosmic enlightenment, "the ancient heavenly connection to the starry dynamo in the machinery of night." Because the larger American society had offered them little support, Ginsberg summarizes their efforts by declaring that these people had been "destroyed by madness." The long lines, each beginning with the word "who" (which was used "as a base to keep measure, return to and take off from again"), create a composite portrait that pulses with energy and excitement. Ginsberg is not only lamenting the destruction of his friends but also celebrating their wild flights of imagination, their ecstatic illuminations, and their rapturous adventures. His typical line, or breath unit, communicates the awesome power of the experiences he describes along with their potential for danger. Ginsberg believed that by the end of the first section he had expressed what he believed "true to eternity" and had reconstituted "the data of celestial experience."

Part 2 of the poem "names the monster of mental consciousness that preys" on the people he admires. The fear and tension of the Cold War, stirred by materialistic greed and what Ginsberg later called "lacklove," are symbolized by a demon he calls Moloch, after the Canaanite god that required human sacrifice. With the name Moloch as a kind of "base repetition" and destructive attributes described in a string of lines beginning with "whose," the second part of the poem reaches a kind of crescendo of chaos in which an anarchic vision of frenzy and disruption engulfs the world.

In part 3, "a litany of affirmation," Ginsberg addresses himself to Carl W. Solomon, a poet he knew from the Psychiatric Institute; he holds up Solomon as a kind of emblem of the victim-heroes he has been describing. The pattern here is based on the statement-counterstatement form of Christopher Smart's "Jubilate Agno" ("Rejoice in the Lamb"), and Ginsberg envisioned it as pyramidal, "with a graduated longer response to the fixed base." Affirming his allegiance to Solomon (and everyone like him), Ginsberg begins each breath unit with the phrase "I'm with you in Rockland" followed by "where . . ." and an exposition of strange or unorthodox behavior that has been labeled "madness" but that is actually a form of creative sanity. The poem concludes with a vision of Ginsberg and Solomon together on a journey to an America that transcends Moloch and madness and offers utopian possibilities of love and "true mental regularity."

During the year that "Howl" was written, Ginsberg wondered whether he might use the same long line in a "short quiet lyrical poem." The result was a poignant tribute to his "old courage teacher," Walt Whitman, which he called "A Supermarket in California," and a meditation on the bounty of nature, "A Strange New Cottage in Berkeley." He continued to work with his long-breath line in larger compositions as well, most notably the poem "America" (1956), which has been accurately described by Charles Molesworth as "a gem of polyvocal satire and miscreant complaint." This poem gave Ginsberg the opportunity to exercise his exuberant sense of humor and good-natured view of himself in a mock-ironic address to his country. The claim "It occurs to me that I am America" is meant to be taken as a whimsical wish made in self-deprecating modesty, but Ginsberg's growing popularity through the last decades of the century cast it as prophetic as well.

Naomi Ginsberg died in 1956 after several harrowing episodes at home and in mental institutions, and she was not accorded a traditional orthodox funeral because a *minyan* (a complement of ten men to serve as witnesses) could not be found. Ginsberg was troubled by thoughts of his mother's suffering and tormented by uncertainty concerning his own role as sometime caregiver for her. Brooding over his tangled feelings, he spent a night listening to jazz, ingesting marijuana and methamphetamine, and reading passages from an old bar mitzvah book. Then, at dawn, he walked the streets of the Lower East Side in Manhattan, where many Jewish immigrant families had settled. A tangle of images and emotions rushed through his mind, organized now by the rhythms of ancient Hebrew prayers and chants. The poem that took shape in his mind was his own version of the Kaddish, the traditional Jewish service for the dead

that had been denied to his mother. As it was formed in an initial burst of energy, he saw its goal as a celebration of her memory and a prayer for her soul's serenity, an attempt to confront his own fears about death, and ultimately, an attempt to come to terms with his relationship to his mother.

"KADDISH"

The poem begins in an elegiac mood, "Strange now to think of you gone," and proceeds as both an elegy and a kind of dual biography. Details from Ginsberg's childhood begin to take on a sinister aspect when viewed from the perspective of an adult with a tragic sense of existence. The course of his life's journey from early youth and full parental love to the threshold of middle age is paralleled by Naomi's life as it advances from late youth toward a decline into paranoia and madness. Ginsberg recalls his mother "teaching school, laughing with idiots, the backward classes—her Russian speciality," then sees her in agony "one night, sudden attack . . . left retching on the tile floor." The juxtaposition of images ranging over many years reminds him of his own mortality, compelling him to probe his subconscious mind in order to face some of the fears that he has suppressed about his mother's madness. The first part of the poem concludes as the poet realizes that he will never find any peace until he is able to "cut through—to talk to you" and finally to write her true history.

The central incident of the second section is a bus trip the twelve-year-old Ginsberg took with his mother to a clinic. The confusion and unpredictability of his mother's behavior forced him to assume an adult's role, but without any previous preparation. For the first time, he realizes that this moment marked the real end of childhood and introduced him to a universe of chaos and absurdity. As the narrative develops, the emergence of a nascent artistic consciousness, poetic perception, and political idealism is presented against a panorama of life in the United States in the late 1930's. Realizing that his growth into the poet who is revealing this psychic history is closely intertwined with his mother's decline, Ginsberg faces his fear that he was drawing his newfound strength from her as she failed. As the section concludes, he squarely confronts his mother's illness, rendering her madness in disjointed scraps of conversation while using blunt physical detail as a means of showing the body's collapse—an effective analogue for her simultaneous mental disorder. There is a daunting authenticity to these details, as Ginsberg speaks with utter candor about the most intimate and unpleasant subjects (a method he also employs in later poems about sexual contacts), confirming his determination to bury nothing in memory.

This frankness fuses Ginsberg's recollections into a mood of great sympathy; he is moved to prayer, asking divine intervention to ease his mother's suffering. Here he introduces the actual Hebrew words of the Kaddish, the formal service that had been denied his mother because of a technicality. The poet's contribution is not only to create an appropriate setting for the ancient ritual but also to offer a testament to his mother's most admirable qualities. As the second section ends, Ginsberg sets the power of poetic language to celebrate beauty against the pain of his mother's last days. Returning to the elegiac mode (after Percy Bysshe Shelley's "Adonais"), Ginsberg has a last vision of his mother days before her final stroke, associated with sunlight and giving her son advice that concludes, "Love,/ your mother," which he acknowledges with his own tribute, "which is Naomi."

The last part of the poem, "Hymmnn," is divided into four sections. The first is a prayer for God's blessing for his mother (and for all people); the second is a recitation of some of the circumstances of her life; the third is a catalog of characteristics that seem surreal and random but coalesce toward the portrait he is producing by composite images; and the last part is "another variation of the litany form," ending the poem in a flow of "pure emotive sound" in which the words "Lord lord lord," as if beseeching, alternate with the words "caw caw caw," as if exclaiming in ecstasy.

By resisting almost all the conventional approaches to the loaded subject of motherhood, Ginsberg has avoided sentimentality and reached a depth of feeling that is overwhelming, even if the reader's experience is nothing like the poet's. The universality of the relationship is established by its particulars, the sublimity of the relationship by the revelation of the poet's enduring love and empathy.

The publication of "Kaddish" ended the initial phase of Ginsberg's writing life. "Howl" is a declaration of poetic intention, while "Kaddish" is a confession of personal necessity. With these two long, powerful works, Ginsberg completed the educational process of his youth and was ready to use his craft as a confident, mature artist. His range in the early 1960's included the hilarious "I Am a Victim of Telephone" (1964), which debunked his increasing celebrity, the gleeful jeremiad "Television Was a Baby Crawling Toward That Deathchamber" (1961), the generously compassionate "Who Be Kind To" (1965), the effusive lyric "Why Is God Love, Jack?" (1963), and his tribute to his mentor William Carlos Williams, "Death News" (1963), which describes his thoughts upon learning of Williams's death.

"KRAL MAJALES"

In 1965, after he had been invited to Cuba and Czechoslovakia, Ginsberg was expelled from both countries for his bold condemnation of their policies. In Prague, he had been selected by students (including the young Václav Havel) as Kral Majales (King of May), an ancient European honor that has lasted through centuries of upheaval; in the poem "Kral Majales" (1965), he juxtaposed Communist and capitalist societies at their most dreary and destructive to the life-enhancing properties of the symbolic May King—a figure of life, love, art, and enlightenment. The first part of the poem is marked by discouragement, anger, and sorrow mixed with comic resignation to show the dead end reached by governments run by a small clique of rulers. Yet the heart of the poem, a list of all the attributes that he brings to the position of Kral Majales, is an exuberant explosion of joy, mirth, and confidence in the rising generation of the mid-1960's. Written before the full weight of the debacle in Vietnam had been felt, and before the string of assassinations that rocked the country had taken place, Ginsberg reveled in the growth of what he thought was a revolutionary movement toward a utopian society. His chant of praise for the foundations of a counterculture celebrates "the power of sexual youth," productive, fulfilling work ("industry in eloquence"), honest acceptance of the body ("long hair of Adam"), the vitality of art ("old Human poesy"), and the ecumenical spirit of religious pluralism that he incarnates—"I am of Slavic parentage and Buddhist Jew/ who worships the Sacred Heart of Christ the blue body of Krishna the straight back of Ram the beads of Chango." In a demonstration of rhythmic power, the poem builds and builds until it tells of the poet's literal descent to earth from the airplane he took to London after his expulsion. Arriving at "Albion's airfield" with the exultation of creative energy still vibrating through his mind and body, he proudly presents (to the reader or listener) the poem he has just written "on a jet seat in mid Heaven." The immediacy of the ending keeps the occasion fresh in the poet's memory and alive forever in the rhythms and images of his art.

"WITCHITA VORTEX SUTRA"

The Prague Spring that was to flourish temporarily in events such as the 1965 May Festival was crushed by Soviet tanks in 1968. By then, the United States had become fully involved in the war in Southeast Asia, and Ginsberg had replaced some of his optimism about change with an anger that recalled the mood of the Moloch section of "Howl." In 1966 he was in Kansas to read poetry, and this trip to the heartland of America became the occasion for a poem that is close to an epic of American life as the country was being torn apart. "Witchita Vortex Sutra," one of Ginsberg's longest poems, combines elements of American mythological history, personal psychic exploration, multicultural interaction, and prophetic incantation. The poem is sustained by a twin vision of America: the submerged but still vital American spirit that inspired Whitman and the contemporary American realities by which "many another has suffered death and madness/ in the Vortex." A sense of a betrayal informs the narrative, and the poet is involved in a search for the cause and the cure, ultimately (and typically) discovering that only art can rescue the blighted land.

The first part of the poem depicts Kansas as the seat of American innocence, where the spirit of transcendental idealism is still relatively untouched by American actions in Vietnam. Whitman's dream of an open country and worthy citizens seems to remain alive, but events from the outside have begun to reach even this sheltered place. The land of Abraham Lincoln, Vachel Lindsay, William Jennings Bryan, and other American idealists is being ruined by the actions of a rogue "government" out of touch with the spirit of the nation. The poet finds himself trying to understand why this is happening and what consequences it has for him, for any artist. After this en-

trance into the poem's geopolitical and psychic space, the second part presents, in a collage form akin to Ezra Pound's *Cantos*, figures, numbers, names, and snatches of propaganda about the conflict in Vietnam. Following Pound's proposal that a bad government corrupts a people by its misuse of language, Ginsberg begins an examination of the nature of language itself to try to determine how the lies and deceptions in "black language/ writ by machine" can be overcome by a "lonesome man in Kansas" who is "not afraid" and who can speak "with ecstatic language"—that is, the true language of human need, essential human reality. Calling on "all Powers of imagination," Ginsberg acts as an artist in service to moral being, using all the poetic power, or versions of speech, that he has worked to master.

Ginsberg's "ecstatic language" includes, in particular, the language of the Far Eastern religions he has learned in his travels. To assist in exorcising the demons of the West, he implores the gods of the East (fitting, since the war is in the East) to merge their forces with those of the new deities of the West, whose incarnation he finds in such American mavericks as Bob Dylan. He summons them as allies against the Puritan death-wish he locates in the fanaticism of unbending, self-righteous zealots such as Kansas's Carry Nation, whose "angry smashing ax" began "a vortex of hatred" that eventually "defoliated the Mekong Delta." Through the poem, Ginsberg has cast the language artist as the rescuer, the visionary who can restore the heartland to its primal state as a land of promise and justice. In an extraordinary testament to his faith in his craft, Ginsberg declares, "The war is over now"—which, in a poem that examines language in "its deceits, its degeneration" (as Charles Molesworth says), "is especially poignant being only language."

THE FALL OF AMERICA

Other poems, such as "Bayonne Entering NYC" (1966), further contributed to the mood of a collection titled *The Fall of America: Poems of These States, 1965-1971*, but Ginsberg was also turning again toward the personal. In poems such as "Wales Visitation" (1967), a nature ode written in the spirit of the English Romantics, and "Bixby Canyon" (1968), which is an American West Coast parallel, Ginsberg explores the possibilities of a personal pantheism, attempting to achieve a degree of cosmic transcendence to compensate for the disagreeable situation on earth. His loving remembrance for Neal Cassady, "On Neal's Ashes" (1968), is another expression of this elegiac inclination, which reaches a culmination in "Mind Breaths."

"MIND BREATHS"

"Mind Breaths" is a meditation that gathers the long lines of what Ginsberg has called "a chain of strong-breath'd poems" into a series of modulations on the theme of the poet's breath as an aspect of the wind-spirit of life. As he has often pointed out, Ginsberg believes that one of his most basic principles of organization is his ability to control the rhythms of a long line ("My breath is long"). In "Mind Breaths," he develops the idea that the voice of the poet is a part of the "voice" of the cosmos—a variant on the ancient belief that the gods spoke directly through the poet. Ranging over the entire planet, Ginsberg gradually includes details from many of the world's cultures, uniting nations in motive and design to achieve an encompassing ethos of universality. Beneath the fragmentation and strife of the world's governments the poet sees "a calm breath, a silent breath, a slow breath," part of the fundamentally human universe that the artist wishes to inhabit.

"BIRDBRAIN"

The tranquillity of such reveries did not replace Ginsberg's anger at the social system but operated more as a condition of recovery or place of restoration, so that the poet could venture back into the political arena and chant, "Birdbrain is the ultimate product of Capitalism/ Birdbrain chief bureaucrat of Russia" (from "Birdbrain," written in 1980). Castigating the idiocy of organizations everywhere, Ginsberg's humor balances his anger, but there is an implication that neither humor nor anger will be sufficient against the forces of "Birdbrain [who] is Pope, Premier, President, Commissar, Chairman, Senator!" Yet in spite of his decades of experience as a political activist, Ginsberg has never let his discouragement overcome his sense of civic responsibility.

"PLUTONIAN ODE"

In "Plutonian Ode" (1978), Ginsberg offers another persuasive poetic argument to strengthen the "Mind-guard spirit" against the death wish that leads some to embrace "Radioactive Nemesis." Recalling, once again, "Howl," in which Moloch stands for the death-driven impulses of humankind gone mad with greed, Ginsberg surveys the history of nuclear experimentation. The poem is designed as a guide for "spiritual friends and teachers," and the "mountain of Plutonian" is presented as the dark shadow-image of the life force that has energized the universe since "the beginning." Addressing himself, as well, to the "heavy heavy Element awakened," Ginsberg describes a force of "vaunted Mystery" against which he brings, as always, the "verse prophetic" to "wake space" itself. The poem is written to restore the power of mind (which is founded on spiritual enlightenment) to a civilization addicted to "horrific arm'd, Satanic industries"—an echo of William Blake's injunctions at the dawn of an era in which machinery has threatened human well-being.

WHITE SHROUD

The publication of Ginsberg's *Collected Poems, 1947-1980* in 1984 secured his reputation as one of the leading writers of late twentieth century American literature, but it did not diminish his production. The appearance in 1986 of the collection *White Shroud* revived Ginsberg's political orations, identifying the demons of contemporary American life as he sees them: "yes I glimpse CIA's spooky dope deal vanity." There is a discernible sense of time's passage in this poem, which is a kind of postscript to "Kaddish." Once again, Ginsberg recollects the pain of his family relationships—his difficulties in dealing with aging, irascible relatives merging with his responsibility to care for those who have loved him, his feeling for modern America fusing with his memories of the Old Left past of his immigrant family. The poem tells how Ginsberg, in search of an apartment, finds himself in the Bronx neighborhood where his family once lived. There he meets the shade of his mother, still berating him for having abandoned her, but now offering him a home as well. There is a form of comfort for the poet in his dream of returning to an older New York to live with his family, a return to the "lost America," the mythic America that has inspired millions of American dreams.

COSMOPOLITAN GREETINGS

Ginsberg in the 1990's expressed his introspective side with lyric sadness in such poems as "Personals Ad" (1990), in which he communicates his quest for a "companion protector friend/ young love w/ empty compassionate soul" to help him live "in New York alone with the Alone." With the advent of his seventh decade, he might have settled for a kind of comfortable celebrity, offering the substance of his literary and social experiences to students at the Graduate Center of the City University of New York and to countless admirers on reading tours throughout the nation. Instead, he accepted his position as the primary proponent and spokesman for his fellow artists of the now-famous Beat generation, and he continued to write with the invention and vigor that had marked his work from its inception. Acknowledging his perspective as a "poet professor in autumn years" ("Personals Ad"), Ginsberg in *Cosmopolitan Greetings* remains highly conscious of "the body/ where I was born," but his focus is now on the inescapable consequences of time's passage on that body in poems that register the anxieties of an aging man trying to assess his own role in the cultural and historical patterns of his era.

The exuberance and the antic humor that have always been a feature of Ginsberg's poetry of sexual candor remain, but there is a modulation in tone and mood toward the rueful and contemplative. Similarly, poems presenting strong positions about social and governmental policies often refer to earlier works on related subjects, as if adding links to a chain of historical commentaries. While few of Ginsberg's poems are as individually distinctive as the "strong-breath'd poems" such as "Howl" or "Witchita Vortex Sutra," which Ginsberg calls "peaks of inspiration," Ginsberg's utilization of a characteristic powerful rhythmic base figure drives poems like "Improvisation in Beijing." "On Cremation of Chogyam Trungpa, Vidadhara," "Get It," and "Graphic Winces" offer statements that are reflections of fundamental positions that Ginsberg has been developing throughout his work.

"Improvisation in Beijing," which has been placed at the beginning of the book, is a poetic credo in the form of an expression of artistic ambition. Using the phrase "I write poetry . . ." to launch each line, Ginsberg juxtaposes ideas, images, data, and assertion in a flux of energetic intent, his life's experiences revealing the desire and urgency of his calling. From the explicitly personal "I write poetry to make accurate picture my own mind" to the overtly political "Wild West destroys new grass & erosion creates deserts" to the culturally connected "I write poetry because I listened to black Blues on 1939 radio, Leadbelly and Ma Rainey" to the aesthetically ambitious in the concluding line, "I write poetry because it's the best way to say everything in mind with 6 minutes or a lifetime," Ginsberg has gathered from a lifetime of reflection on the subject his responses to a request for his "sources of inspiration."

"On Cremation of Chogyam Trungpa, Vidadhara," a tribute to a spiritual guide, reverses the structural thrust of "Improvisation in Beijing" so that the lines beginning "I noticed the . . ." spiral inward toward a composite portrait built my "minute particulars," Ginsberg's term for William Carlos Williams's injunction "No ideas but in things." Ginsberg concentrates on specifics in tightly wound lines that present the observations of an extremely aware, actively thoughtful participant: "I noticed the grass, I noticed the hills, I noticed the highways,/ I noticed the dirt road, I noticed the cars in the parking lot." Eventually, the poet's inclusion of more personal details reveals his deep involvement in the occasion, which demonstrates his ability to internalize his guide's teaching. The poem concludes with a summation of the impact of the event, a fusion of awe, delight, and wonder joining the mundane with the cosmic. Typically at this time in his life, Ginsberg is acting from a classic poetic position, speaking as the recorder who sees, understands, and appreciates the significance of important events and who can find language adequate for their expression.

The collection, like Ginsberg's other major volumes, includes many poems that are not meant to be either especially serious or particularly profound. Ginsberg's forays into popular culture (singing with Bob Dylan or The Clash) are further indications of his playful side, including poems written to a musical notation ("C.I.A. Dope Calypso"), poetic lines cast in speech bubbles in a "Deadline Dragon Comix" strip, three pages of what are called "American Sentences" (which are, in effect, a version of haiku), and a new set of verses to the old political anthem, "The Internationale," in which Ginsberg pays homage to the dreams of a social republic of justice while parodying various manifestations of self-important propagandists and salvationists.

The poems in the volume that show Ginsberg at his most effective, however, occur in two modes. Ever since his tribute to Walt Whitman, "A Supermarket in California," Ginsberg has used the lyric mode as a means of conveying his deeply romantic vision of an idealized existence set in opposition to the social disasters he has resisted. These are poems of appreciation and gratitude, celebrating the things of the world that bring delight. "To Jacob Rabinowitz" is a letter of thanks for a translation of Catullus. "Fun House Antique Store" conveys the poet's astonishment at finding a "country antique store, an/ oldfashioned house" on the road to "see our lawyer in D.C." The lovingly evoked intricate furnishings of the store suggest something human that is absent in "the postmodern Capital." Both of these poems sustain a mood of exultation crucial to a lyric.

The other mode that Ginsberg employs is a familiar one. Even since he described himself as "Rotting Ginsberg" in "Mescaline" (1959), Ginsberg has emphasized physical sensation and the extremes of sensory response as means for understanding artistic consciousness, a mind-body linkage. Some of the most despairing lines Ginsberg has written appear in these poems—understandable considering the poet's ailments, including the first manifestations of liver cancer, which Ginsberg endured for years before his death. Nonetheless, the bright spirit that animates Ginsberg's work throughout is present as a counterthrust.

"In the Benjo," which has been placed at the close of the collection, expresses Ginsberg's appreciation for Gary Snyder's lessons in transcendent wisdom and epitomizes a pattern of affirmation that is present in poems that resist the ravages of physical decline ("Return to Kral Majales"), the loss of friends ("Visiting Father & Friends"), the sorry state of the world ("You Don't Know It"), and the fradulent nature of so-called leaders ("Elephant in the Meditation Hall"). In these poems, as in many in earlier collections, Ginsberg is conveying the spirit of an artistic age that he helped to shape and that his work exemplifies. As Snyder said in tribute, "Allen Ginsberg showed that poetry could speak to our moment, our political concerns, our hopes and fears, and in the grandest style. He broke that open for all of us."

OTHER MAJOR WORKS

NONFICTION: *The Yage Letters*, 1963 (with William Burroughs); *Indian Journals*, 1963; *Indian Journals: March 1962-May 1963*, 1970; *Notebooks, Diary, Blank Pages, Writings*, 1970; *Gay Sunshine Interview*, 1974; *Allen Verbatim: Lectures on Poetry, Politics, Consciousness*, 1974; *Visions of the Great Rememberer*, 1974; *To Eberhart from Ginsberg*, 1976; *As Ever: The Collected Correspondence of Allen Ginsberg and Neal Cassady*, 1977; *Journals: Early Fifties, Early Sixties*, 1977, 1992; *Composed on the Tongue: Literary Conversations, 1967-1977*, 1980; *Allen Ginsberg Photographs*, 1990; *Snapshot Poetics: A Photographic Memoir of the Beat Era*, 1993; *Journals Mid-Fifties, 1954-1958*, 1995; *Deliberate Prose: Selected Essays, 1952-1995*, 2000; *Spontaneous Mind: Selected Interviews, 1958-1996*, 2001.

EDITED TEXT: *Poems for the Nation*, 2000.

MISCELLANEOUS: *Beat Legacy, Connections, Influences: Poems and Letters by Allen Ginsberg*, 1994.

BIBLIOGRAPHY

Aronson, Jerry. *The Life and Times of Allen Ginsberg*. Videao. New York: First Run Icarus Films, 1993. An entertaining and informative documentary film.

Caveney, Graham. *Screaming with Joy: The Life of Allen Ginsberg*. New York: Broadway Books, 1999. A documentary of Ginsberg's zealous life and the Beat poets with more than 150 photographs and illustrations.

Ginsberg, Allen. *Spontaneous Mind: Selected Interviews, 1958-1996*. Preface by Václav Havel. Introduction by Edmund White. Edited by David Carter. New York : HarperCollinsPublishers, 2001. A generous selection of interviews that provide an introduction to Ginsberg's intentions as artist and public figure.

Hyde, Lewis, ed. *On the Poetry of Allen Ginsberg*. Ann Arbor: University of Michigan Press, 1984. This is a wide-ranging collection including critical evaluation from both ends of the spectrum (from extravagant praise to total condemnation), interesting historical information, interviews, and even excerpts from the Federal Bureau of Investigation's file on the poet. An excellent introduction to Ginsberg's work.

Kramer, Jane. *Allen Ginsberg in America*. New York: Random House, 1969. A detailed account of two years in the poet's life, showing him reading at universities, traveling, talking, and working on a variety of projects. Also provides revealing portraits of several other poets and an examination of Ginsberg's relationship with his father.

Landas, John. *The Bop Apocalypse.* Champaign: University of Illinois Press, 2001. An illuminating account of the religious aspects and elements of the work of Ginsberg, Kerouac, and Burroughs. Particularly good on the historical dynamics operating in the writers' lives.

Merrill, Thomas F. *Allen Ginsberg.* New York: Twayne, 1969. An essentially conventional, routine consideration of the poetry written during the first two decades of Ginsberg's life.

Miles, Barry. *The Beat Hotel: Ginsberg, Burroughs, and Corso in Paris, 1958-1963.* New York: Grove Press, 2000. A narrative chronicle of the Beats in Paris from the Howl obscenity trial to the invention of the cut-up technique. Based on firsthand accounts from diaries, letters, and many original interviews.

_____. *Ginsberg: A Biography.* New York: Simon & Schuster, 1989. An immense compilation of data concerning Ginsberg's life and work with a very extensive series of appendices and lists, but a book that does not effectively capture the man who wrote the poetry. A posture of objectivity prevents Miles from dealing with some of the most crucial questions of Ginsberg's creative life, but at the same time, the author's prejudices and distastes color much of the material. Valuable as research, not interpretation.

Molesworth, Charles. *The Fierce Embrace.* Columbia: University of Missouri Press, 1979. Contains an excellent chapter on Ginsberg and Robert Lowell which is one of the best critical evaluations of Ginsberg's work prior to 1979. See also Molesworth's essay in *The Nation,* February 23, 1955, pp. 213-215.

Portugés, Paul. *The Visionary Poetics of Allen Ginsberg.* Santa Barbara, Calif.: Ross-Erikson, 1978. Basing his study on Ginsberg's Blakean vision, Portugés provides a good guide to some of the early poetry and puts Ginsberg's visions into the context of other varieties of mystical experience. Somewhat erratic in focus and not always accurate on factual matters.

Schumacher, Michael. *Dharma Lion: A Biography of Allen Ginsberg.* New York: St. Martin's Press, 1992. Offers an incisive linkage of the poet's life with his writing.

Leon Lewis, updated by Lewis

DANA GIOIA

Born: Los Angeles, California; December 24, 1950

PRINCIPAL POETRY

Two Poems, 1982
Letter to the Bahamas, 1983
Summer, 1983
Journeys in Sunlight, 1986
Daily Horoscope, 1986
Words for Music, 1987
Planting a Sequoia, 1991
The Gods of Winter, 1991
The Litany, 1999
Interrogations at Noon, 2001

OTHER LITERARY FORMS

In addition to being an influential poet, Dana Gioia is one of the most controversial critics of his generation. His collection of essays *Can Poetry Matter? Essays on Poetry and American Culture* (1992) was a finalist for the National Book Award. He has edited a number of anthologies, coediting undergraduate literature textbooks with X. J. Kennedy and the *Longman Anthology of Short Fiction* (2001) with R. S. Gwynn. He also coedited *Poems from Italy* (1985) with William Jay Smith and *New Italian Poets* (1991) with Michael Palma. Gioia has translated "The Madness of Hercules" (1992) by Seneca and Eugenio Montale's *Mottetti: Poems of Love* (1990); he also translated several poems of Valerio Magrelli in his own collection *Interrogations at Noon* (2001). In addition, Gioia has composed an opera libretto, *Nosferatu* (pr., pb. 2001), with composer Alva Henderson, which had its concert premiere at West Chester College on June 7, 2001.

ACHIEVEMENTS

Dana Gioia is the most visible spokesperson for a movement in poetry variously called New Formalism, or Expansive poetry, which stresses the appropriateness of traditional forms for contemporary poetry as well as urging a return to storytelling in verse. *The Gods of Winter* (1991) was a quarterly choice of the English Poetry Book Society, and his collections are published by Peterloo in the United Kingdom as well as Graywolf in the United States.

BIOGRAPHY

Dana Gioia was born in Los Angeles, the first of four surviving children of Michael Gioia, a cabdriver and shoe-store owner, and Dorothy Ortiz Gioia, a telephone operator. One of his brothers, Ted Gioia, became a major jazz critic. The Gioia family was Sicilian, with most members living in the same neighborhood. Gioia's mother was of Mexican heritage, and thus Gioia grew up in a multilingual context, one that heightened his sense of language. When he won a scholarship to Stanford University, Gioia for the first time left behind both the security and the provincialism of a tight family structure. Gioia originally intended to study music, but his love of literature and his distaste for atonality directed him back to English, for which he was awarded a B.A. in 1973. Gioia then left to study comparative literature at Harvard.

While his work with Robert Fitzgerald and Elizabeth Bishop at Harvard confirmed his resolve to write poetry, Gioia became increasingly distressed at the direction that literary studies were taking in the academy; accordingly, he left Harvard with an M.A., having completed his Ph.D. course work, and returned to Stanford, in 1977 earning an M.B.A. degree. It was also at Stanford that he met Mary Hiecke, whom he married in 1980. After receiving his M.B.A., Gioia moved to New York and worked in business, eventually becoming a vice president of Kraft-General Foods. Though he was writing poetry and criticism regularly, he kept his two lives separate; in 1984, when *Esquire* magazine ran an article on forty men and women under age forty who were changing the country and listed Dana Gioia, businessman and poet, his associates in business were in complete surprise at his artistic accomplishments.

Gioia's *Daily Horoscope* was published in 1986 and attracted much attention for a first book. It was defended nearly as stoutly as it was attacked, even becoming the subject of a three-issue debate in *Northwest Review*. His second major collection, *The Gods of Winter*, appeared in 1991 and likewise stirred considerable debate, though many of the most vociferous critics had spent most of their energies denouncing the first volume. The collection was published simultaneously in the United States and Great Britain and was the choice of the Poetry Book Society in England, the first time an American poet was so honored. Also in 1991, Gioia's essay "Can Poetry Matter?" appeared in *The Atlantic* and elicited one of the largest responses the magazine ever received. Gioia's concerns for increasing the poetry public and thereby saving it from stagnation in the academy struck a nerve: Readers who felt closed off from contemporary poetry were as enthused as the M.F.A. free-verse establishment were threatened. Discussions of the article appeared in publications as various as the *Times Literary Supplement* and *The New Criterion* to *USA Today* and the *Washington Post Book World*. The piece became the title piece of Gioia's first collection of essays the following year.

Also in 1992, Gioia retired from the business world to dedicate himself full time to writing and editing, with an occasional guest professorship. In 1995 Gioia cofounded with Michael Peich the West Chester College summer conference on form and narrative, the nation's only conference focused on the traditional techniques of poetry. The conference grew steadily since its inception and began incorporating scholarly seminars and musical performances with creative-writing workshops. In 1996 Gioia returned to California, settling in rural Sonoma County with his wife and two sons. Gioia also organized a Teaching Poetry Conference in Santa Rosa, which first met in July of 2001. In 2001, Gioia published the full-length collection *Interrogations at Noon*.

ANALYSIS

Dana Gioia is a prominent spokesperson for New Formalism. As a critic of some discrimination, he has questioned many of the assumptions of postmodernism as well as the reputations of such figures as Robert Bly and John Ashbery. Yet Gioia's aesthetic positions are generally moderate; while the free-verse establishment has been particularly antagonistic toward New Formalism in general and Gioia in particular, he has never condemned the use of free verse, often writing it himself.

DAILY HOROSCOPE

Gioia's first major collection, appearing in 1986, was met with a great deal of controversy, yet it seems more as if critics were angry with his essays and reviews but decided to attack the poetry instead. While many of the poems are rhymed or metered, free verse is also common in the book; other poets had begun to return to traditional forms with a greater strictness than is shown in this collection, but Gioia's prominence made him a point of attack. Many of the poems deal with the business world and the sense of displacement of a Californian living in the Northeast; "In Chandler Country" contrasts with "In Cheever Country," "Eastern Standard Time" with "California Hills in August." The last poem considers how the Easterner might dislike the drought and brownness of the landscape, but Gioia, the Californian, ends:

> And yet how gentle it seems to someone
> raised in a landscape short of rain—
> the skyline of a hill broken by no more
> trees than one can count, the grass,
> the empty sky, the wish for water.

"Cruising with the Beachboys" catches the longing for lost youth, nostalgia stopping short of sentimentality, and "The Room Upstairs" is Gioia's first collected longer narrative poem. His musical interests are on display in "Lives of the Great Composers," written in the form of a fugue, and "An Elegy for Vladimir de Pachmann," as well as a tribute to the jazz musician Bix Beiderbecke. Some poems are set in airports, some in Europe—all reinforce the general sense of displacement in the volume. Gioia bided his time before entering into book publication, and the result is that *Daily Horoscope* seems far more advanced than the usual first book.

THE GODS OF WINTER

The Gods of Winter is a darker book than *Daily Horoscope*. It is dedicated to Michael Jasper Gioia, Gioia's infant son who died of sudden infant death syndrome (SIDS). Many of the poems are haunted by death: "Prayer," "All Souls,'" "Veterans' Cemetery." In "Planting a Sequoia," Gioia tells how "In Sicily a father plants a tree to celebrate his first son's birth—/ An olive or a fig tree—a sign that the earth has one more life to bear." In California, Gioia is planting a sequoia as a memorial to his dead first son in the hope that

> . . . when our family is no more, all of his unborn
>   brothers dead,
> Every niece and nephew scattered, the house torn down,
> His mother's beauty ashes in the air,
> I want you to stand among strangers, all young and
>   ephemeral to you,
> Silently keeping the secret of your birth.

There are also two narrative poems in the book, "Counting the Children" and "The Homecoming." The latter is a masterpiece and has even been dramatized and choreographed. The superb title poem ends,

> But if
> the light confides how one still winter must
> arrive without us, then our eternity
> is only this white storm, the whisper
> of your breath, the deities of this quiet night.

There are also lighter poems in the book, in particular "My Confessional Sestina," which parodies pseudo-formal practices of many creative-writing workshops, and "Money," which manages to take nearly every cliché about money and combine them into a poem that makes us see them afresh. *The Gods of Winter* was acclaimed on both sides of the Atlantic Ocean and was one of the finest collections of the late twentieth century.

INTERROGATIONS AT NOON

Appearing nearly a decade after *The Gods of Winter* (Gioia's previous collection), *Interrogations at Noon* was much anticipated. A substantial amount of the book consists of translations: Rainer Maria Rilke, two somewhat lengthy poems of Seneca, and six poems of Valerio Magrelli. Gioia is a fine translator, but the number of translations in addition to three excerpts from his libretto *Nosferatu* in a book that does not come to seventy pages suggest that the 1990's were not as poetically fertile as the previous decade. One wonders if Gioia's numerous other activities slowed his output of poems.

Still, there is some fine work in the collection. "The Voyeur" pictures a husband imagining himself a Peeping Tom as he watches his wife, seeking a new perspective on what he knows well. "The Litany" is a haunting litany-prayer "of lost things,/ a canon of possessions dispossessed." "Pentecost" is a moving poem to Gioia's dead son, ending, "Comfort me with stones. Quench my thirst with sand./ I offer you this scarred and guilty hand/ Until others mix our ashes." The first section of the book begins with an epigraph from Gustave Flaubert, which questions the efficacy of words when faced with ultimate meaning, and two poems expressly concern themselves with this theme: "Words" ("The daylight needs no praise, and so we praise it always—/ greater than ourselves and all the airy words we summon") and "Unsaid":

> So much of what we live goes on inside—
> The diaries of grief, the tongue-tied aches
> Of unacknowledged love are no less real
> For having passed unsaid. What we conceal
> Is always more than what we dare confide.

How fundamental the concern of the letters that people write to their dead is to Gioia is reinforced by the fact that "Words" and "Unsaid" are the first and last poems in the collection.

OTHER MAJOR WORKS

NONFICTION: *Can Poetry Matter? Essays on Poetry and American Culture*, 1992.

PLAY: *Nosferatu*, pr., pb. 2001 (libretto).

TRANSLATIONS: *Mottetti: Poems of Love by Eugenio Montale*, 1990; "The Madness of Hercules," 1992 (of *Seneca: The Tragedies*, edited by David R. Slavitt); *Juno Plots Her Revenge*, 1992 (of act 1 of Seneca's *Hercules furens*).

EDITED TEXTS: *The Ceremony and Other Stories by Weldon Kees*, 1983; *Poems from Italy*, 1985 (with William Jay Smith); *New Italian Poets*, 1991 (with Michael Palma); *Formal Introductions: An Investigative Anthology*, 1994; *An Introduction to Fiction, Seventh Edition*, 1995 (with Kennedy); *Certain Solitudes: Essays on the Poetry of Donald Justice*, 1997 (with William Logan); *An Introduction to Poetry, Ninth Edition*, 1998 (with X. J. Kennedy); *Literature: An Introduction to Fiction, Poetry, and Drama, Seventh Edition*, 1999 (with Kennedy); *Longman Anthology of Short Fiction*, 2001 (with R. S. Gwynn).

BIBLIOGRAPHY

Crosscurrents: A Quarterly 8, no. 2 (1989). Special issue, "Expansionist Poetry: The New Formalism and the New Narrative." A groundbreaking issue on the Expansive movement, with many essays essential to understanding the movement and Gioia. Gioia's contribution is the narrative poem "The Homecoming."

Feirstein, Frederick, ed. *Expansive Poetry: Essays on the New Narrative and the New Formalism*. Ashland, Oreg.: Story Line Press, 1989. This collection includes two of Gioia's essays, "The Dilemma of the Long Poem" and "Notes on the New Formalism," but also includes other perspectives on the Formalist movement, many of which offer insight into Gioia's aesthetic.

Gioia, Dana. "Paradigms Lost: Parts One and Two." Interview by Gloria Brame. *Eclectic Literary Forum*, Spring/Summer, 1995. This interview with Gioia stresses his influences and the effect on his life and work of the death of his first son to sudden infant death syndrome. Gioia also discusses the frequent misunderstandings of his ideas by supporters and critics alike.

Lindner, April. *Dana Gioia*. Western Writers series. Boise, Idaho: Boise State University Press, 2000. The most extensive consideration of Gioia's poetry. Lindner considers the Expansive movement in poetry and Gioia's criticism, translations, and poetry through *The Gods of Winter*. She also devotes considerable space to a discussion of Gioia's narrative work, an aspect of his poetry often overlooked.

Mason, David. "Dana Gioia's Case for Poetry." *The Poetry of Life and the Life of Poetry*. Ashland, Oreg.: Story Line Press, 2000. An excellent overview of Gioia's critical opus, this essay corrects many misinterpretations of Gioia's aesthetic and also makes clear the importance of Gioia's critical work in contemporary poetry. In the same volume is the essay "The New Formalism and the Audience for Poetry," which addresses many of the concerns of the New Formalist movement.

Robert Darling

NIKKI GIOVANNI

Born: Knoxville, Tennessee; June 7, 1943

PRINCIPAL POETRY

Black Feeling, Black Talk, 1968
Black Judgement, 1968
Black Feeling, Black Talk, Black Judgement, 1970
Re: Creation, 1970
Poem of Angela Yvonne Davis, 1970
Spin a Soft Black Song: Poems for Children, 1971,
    revised 1987 (juvenile)
My House, 1972
Ego-Tripping and Other Poems for Young Readers
    (juvenile)
The Women and the Men, 1975
Cotton Candy on a Rainy Day, 1978
Vacation Time, 1980 (juvenile)
Those Who Ride the Night Winds, 1983 (juvenile)
Knoxville, Tennessee, 1994 (juvenile)
Life: Through Black Eyes, 1995
The Genie in the Jar, 1996 (juvenile)
The Selected Poems of Nikki Giovanni, 1996
The Sun Is So Quiet, 1996
Love Poems, 1997
Blues: For All the Changes, 1999

OTHER LITERARY FORMS

Besides her volumes of verse, Nikki Giovanni has
made several poetry recordings. Some, such as *Truth Is
on Its Way* (Right On Records, 1971), have gospel music
accompaniment. Her recordings, as well as her many
public performances, have helped to popularize the
black oral poetry movement. Her two books of conversations with older, established black writers, *A Dialogue: James Baldwin and Nikki Giovanni* (1973) and
*A Poetic Equation: Conversations Between Nikki Gio-
vanni and Margaret Walker* (1974), offer the contrasting
attitudes of two generations of black American writers
on the aims of black literature in white America. The
first book is especially interesting for its spirited discussion about the changing relationships between black
men and black women, a topic of many of Giovanni's
poems. The second clarifies her literary development

and contains an impassioned plea for blacks to seize
control of their destinies.

*Gemini: An Extended Autobiographical Statement
on My First Twenty-five Years of Being a Black Poet*
(1971), which was nominated for a National Book
Award in 1973, offers scenes from her life as a child and
mother. While little is seen of the experiences and influences that shaped her art and thought, the book does
contain essays about the black cultural revolution of the
1960's that serve as companion pieces to her poems. She
has edited several texts, written syndicated columns—
"One Woman's Voice" (*The New York Times*) and "The
Root of the Matter" (*Encore American and Worldwide
News Magazine*); and contributed essays to many black
magazines and journals. *Sacred Cows . . . and Other Edibles* (1988) collects a number of her essays. A collection of her work has been established at the Muger Memorial Library, Boston University.

ACHIEVEMENTS

Nikki Giovanni has earned an impressive array of
honors throughout her literary career. In the late 1960's
she won grants from the Ford Foundation, National
Endowment for the Arts, and the Harlem Cultural Council. She was named one of ten "Most Admired Black
Women" by the *Amsterdam News* in 1969. In 1971 she
won an outstanding achievement award from *Mademoiselle*, an Omega Psi Phi Fraternity Award for outstanding contribution to arts and letters, and a Prince
Matchabelli Sun Shower Award; in 1972, a life membership and scroll from the National Council of Negro
Women and a National Association of Radio and Televi-
sion Announcers Award for her recording of *Truth Is on
Its Way*, and Woman of the Year Youth Leadership
Award from *Ladies' Home Journal*; in 1973, a National
Book Award nomination for *Gemini* and a Best Books
for Young Adults citation from the American Library
Association for *My House*. In the 1980's, she won a
Woman of the Year citation from the Cincinnati Chapter
of the Young Women's Christian Association, was
elected to the Ohio Women's Hall of Fame, received an
Outstanding Woman of Tennessee citation, won the
Post-Corbett Award, and was named Woman of the Year
from the National Association for the Advancement of
Colored People (Lynchburg chapter). In the 1990's, she

won the Jeanine Rae Award for the Advancement of Women's Culture and a Langston Hughes Award.

She has received numerous honorary degrees from academic institutions, including Wilberforce University, Fisk University, the University of Maryland (Princess Anne Campus), Ripon University, Smith College, Indiana University, Albright College, Cabrini College, and Allegheny College. Several cities have honored her with keys to the city, including Dallas, New York City, Cincinnati, Miami, New Orleans, and Los Angeles.

BIOGRAPHY

Yolande Cornelia Giovanni was born on June 7, 1943, in Knoxville, Tennessee, but grew up in Wyoming and Lincoln Heights, Ohio, suburbs of Cincinnati, where she currently resides. She described her childhood as "quite happy" in the poem "Nikki-Rosa," and her reminiscences in *Gemini* testify to her devotion to relatives, especially her sister Gary (who nicknamed her "Nikki") and her grandparents, John Brown Watson, one of the first graduates of Fisk University, and his wife Louvenia, whose strength of character she admired and emulated. Giovanni herself entered Fisk at sixteen and was graduated magna cum laude in 1967 with a bachelor of arts degree in history. At Fisk, her independent spirit led to her being expelled after one semester; but when she reentered in 1964, she immediately became involved in politics, reestablishing the university's chapter of the Student Nonviolent Coordinating Committee (SNCC). She also became greatly interested in literature and participated in John Oliver Killens's writers' workshop. She also briefly attended the School of Social Work at the University of Pennsylvania. It was black politics and black art, however, that held her interest. In 1967, a Ford Foundation grant enabled her to complete and publish her first book of poetry, *Black Feeling, Black Talk*, and its success led to a National Foundation of the Arts grant on which she attended Columbia University's School of Fine Arts in 1968. Instead of completing her proposed novel or work toward a graduate degree, she continued to work on a volume of poetry, *Black Judgement*, published through a grant by the Harlem Cultural Council on the Arts.

Her impact on black American literature was immediate and electric. Her celebration of blackness and her militancy placed her in the avant-garde of black letters. Hailed as the "Princess of Black Poetry," she began touring the United States, lecturing to college audiences, spreading her message of black cultural nationalism, "ego-tripping," and love. To raise black cultural awareness and to foster black art, she became an Assistant Professor of Black Studies at Queens College, Flushing, New York in 1968 and taught creative writing at Livingston College, Rutgers University, from 1968 to 1970. She organized the Black Arts Festival in Cincinnati in 1967, editing *Love Black*, a magazine of the people— "what the brother thought and felt"; participated in the 1970 National Educational Television program "Soul!"; and took part in the two-week black festival "Soul at the Center" at Lincoln Center in New York in 1972.

The core of Giovanni's life and work is love and service; the focus is the family: her own, the black community, humanity. In 1969, her son Thomas Watson Giovanni was born: Her concern for him—indeed for all children—was the springboard for her volumes of children's poetry, which include *Spin a Soft Black Song, Ego-Tripping and Other Poems for Young Readers, Vacation Time,* and *The Genie in the Jar.* She also worked with the Reading Is Fundamental (RIF) Program in Harlem, the Jackie Robinson Foundation, and the President's Committee on the International Year of the Child (1979). Her poetry reflects a life of meditation and domesticity. She is also an active member of black service organizations and an editorial consultant and columnist for *Encore American and Worldwide News Magazine*, a black news monthly with a Third World focus.

In the 1980's and 1990's she taught at a number of colleges and universities throughout the country, both as a faculty member and visiting professor, including College of Mount St. Joseph on the Ohio, Mount St. Joseph, Ohio, as professor of creative writing; Ohio State University, Columbus, as visiting professor of English; and Texas Christian University, as visiting professor in humanities. She started her long tenure as professor at Virginia Tech, Blacksburg, Virginia in 1987. She also contributes a great deal of her time to public service and directing a variety of art festivals and writing workshops. She directs the Warm Hearth Writer's Workshop, was appointed to the Ohio Humanities Council in 1987, served from 1990 to 1993 as a member of the board of directors for Virginia Foundation for Humanities and Public Policy, and participated in the Appalachian Community Fund from 1991 to 1993 and the Volunteer Action Center from 1991 to 1994. She was a featured poet at the International Poetry Festival in Utrecht, Holland, in 1991. She gives numerous poetry readings and lectures worldwide and appears on numerous television talk shows.

ANALYSIS

From the beginning of her career, Nikki Giovanni has combined private with public concerns, and her development has been toward the exploration of the inner life of one black female—herself—as a paradigm for black women's aspirations in contemporary America. An individualist who early admired Ayn Rand's concept of rational self-interest, Giovanni has a unique black identity. Her example of self-actualization embodied in her poetry has been not only influential but also inspirational, especially to black youth.

In *The Souls of Black Folk* (1903), W. E. B. Du Bois expressed the dilemma of the black American writer—a double consciousness of being both an American and a black. Nikki Giovanni, however, has never felt this division. In *Gemini* she asserts, "I've always known I was

colored. When I was Negro I knew I was colored; now that I'm Black I know which color it is. Any identity crisis I may have had never centered on race." The transition from Negro to black represents for her, as for LeRoi Jones and other adherents of the Black Consciousness movement, a transvaluation: black becomes a "sacrament." It is an outward and visible sign of an inward and spiritual grace, making a poetry reading a "service" and a play a "ritual." Rather than a mask that prevents the inner man from being seen, as in Ralph Ellison's *Invisible Man* (1952), color becomes a sign of worth itself. In her early poems and pronouncements, she proves herself a true Gemini, dividing the world into either/ or, into mutually exclusive categories. Everything is literally black or white: "Perhaps the biggest question in the modern world is the definition of a genus—huemanity. And the white man is no hueman." Her concerns, in her first two books of poems, like the audience she both addresses and represents, are exclusively black. Her early ideas about poetry are closely connected with her ideas about race. In her essay "The Weather as a Cultural Determiner" she elaborates on the thesis that black people are naturally poets: Indeed "we are our own poems": "Poetry is the culture of a people. We are poets even when we don't write poems; just look at our life, our rhythms, our tenderness, our signifying, our sermons and our songs." Her poems were originally composed for polemical, not lyrical, ends—for the black community: Poetry is "just a manifestation of our collective historical needs. And we strike a responsive chord because the people will always respond to the natural things."

POLITICAL POEMS

Throughout her poetry run two main themes, revolution and love—one destructive, the other creative. Even in her earliest verse both strands are evident: only the emphasis shifts from the former to the latter. For example, in an early poem, "Detroit Conference of Unity and Art (For HRB)," the "most valid" of the resolutions passed "as we climbed Malcolm's ladder" was "Rap chose me." The revolution that she calls for in *Black Judgement* is, on one

level, literal: In "Reflections on April 4, 1968," the date of the assassination of Martin Luther King, Jr., even her poetic structure collapses in the face of the need for violence:

What can I, a poor Black woman, do to destroy America? This is a question, with appropriate variations, being asked in every Black heart. There is one answer—I can kill.
There is one compromise—I can protect those who kill.
There is one cop-out—I can encourage others to kill. There are no other ways.

The revolution is also symbolic, striking out at the poisonous racial myths that have devalued blacks in America. In "Word Poem (Perhaps Worth Considering)" she writes: "as things be/come/ let's destroy/ then we can destroy/ what we be/come/ let's build/ what we become/ when we dream." The destruction here is of values and attitudes, seemingly in accord with the statement in *Gemini*: "Nobody's trying to make the system Black; we're trying to make a system that's human so that Black folks can live in it. This means we're trying to destroy the existing system." Giovanni's poems attack the American political establishment in a sweeping, generalized way; her analysis is simple—exterminate the white beast. Her real contempt is directed toward "Negroes" still in the service of white America: "The True Import of Present Dialogue, Black vs. Negro" is "Can you kill/ Can you kill a white man/ Can you kill the nigger/ in you." Her "Black Judgement" is upon ". . . niggerish ways." Aware that with children lies the future, she urges in "Poem for Black Boys" new revolutionary games:

Ask your mother for a Rap Brown gun
Santa just may comply if you wish hard enough
Ask for CULLURD instead of Monopoly
DO NOT SIT IN DO NOT FOLLOW KING
GO DIRECTLY TO STREETS
This is a game you can win.

Poetry of denial, vilification, and decreation (what she calls her "nigger-nigger" phrase) is essentially dead-ended; the main rhetorical problem of the new black poets was how to restore value to the black experience. Giovanni has accomplished such a restoration through the affirmation of her own life and the transforming

power of poetry. In her volume *Cotton Candy on a Rainy Day*, "The Beep Beep Poem" has a "song of herself" almost like Walt Whitman's:

i love the aloneness of the road
when I ascend descending curves
the power within my toes delights me
and i fling my spirit down the highway
i love the way i feel
when i pass the moon and i holler to the stars
i'm coming through

Such elation, however, is unusual. The tone of "Nikki-Rosa," "Mothers," and "Legacies" is more bittersweet. Giovanni gradually realized that writing itself is creative of value: She says in "Boxes," "i write/ because/ i have to." In the 1960's, writing appeared to be a luxury: In "For Saundra," she notes

maybe i shouldn't write
at all
but clean my gun
and check my kerosene supply
perhaps these are not poetic
times
at all.

MY HOUSE

In the 1960's, poetry was to be a witness of the times—"it's so important to record" ("Records"), but her poetry proved to be her house: *My House* shows her assimilation and transformation of the world into her castle. In "Poem (For Nina)" from that volume, she begins by asserting that "We are all imprisoned *in the castle of our skins*," though her imagination will color her world "Black Gold": "my castle shall become/ my rendezvous/ my courtyard will bloom with hyacinths and jack-in-the-pulpits/ my moat will not restrict me but will be filled/ with dolphins. . . ." In "A Very Simple Wish" she wants through her poetry to make a patchwork quilt of the world, including all that seems to be left behind by world history: "i've a mind to build/ a new world/ want to play."

In *My House* Giovanni began to exhibit increased sophistication and maturity. Her viewpoint had broadened beyond a rigid black revolutionary consciousness to balance a wide range of social concerns. Her rhymes had also become more pronounced, more lyrical, more gen-

tle. The themes of family love, loneliness, and frustration, which Giovanni had defiantly explored in her earlier works, find much deeper expression in *My House*.
Her change from an incendiary radical to a nurturing
poet is traced in the poem "Revolutionary Dreams":
from dreaming "militant dreams/ of taking over america," she

> . . . awoke and dug
> that if i dreamed natural
> dreams of being a natural
> woman doing what a woman
> does when she's natural
> i would have a revolution

This changed perspective accords with the conclusion of
"When I Die": "And if ever i touched a life i hope that
life knows/ that i know that touching was and still is and
will/ always be the true/ revolution." Love and sex form
the subject matter of many of her poems. She will
"scream and stamp and shout/ for more beautiful beautiful beautiful/ black men with outasight afros" in "Beautiful Black Men" and propose "counterrevolutionary"
sex in "Seduction" and "That Day": "if you've got the
dough/ then i've got the heat/ we can use my oven/ til it's
warm and sweet."

This bold and playful manner, however, is usually
modulated by the complications of any long-term relationship between men and women. While she explains
in *Gemini:* "to me sex is an essence. . . . It's a basic of
human relationships. And sex is conflict; it could be
considered a miniwar between two people," marriage is
"'give and take—you give and he takes.'" In "Woman"
her acknowledgment of the difficulty of a black man
maintaining his self-respect in America has led to her
acceptance of his failings: "she decided to become/ a
woman/ and though he still refused/ to be a man/ she decided it was all/ right."

COTTON CANDY ON A RAINY DAY

This poem, like many others in *Cotton Candy on a
Rainy Day*, bespeaks the tempering of her vision. When
Giovanni published *Cotton Candy on a Rainy Day*, critics viewed it as one of her most somber works. They
noted the focus on emotional ups and downs, fear and
insecurity, and the weight of everyday responsibilities.
The title poem tells of "the gray of my mornings/ Or the

blues of every night" in a decade known for "loneliness." Life is likened to nebulous cotton candy: "The
sweet soft essence/ of possibility/ Never quite maturing." Her attitude tired, her potential stillborn, she is unable to categorize life as easily as before, "To put a
three-dimensional picture/ On a one-dimensional surface."

One reason for her growth in vision seems to be her
realization of the complexity of a woman's life. The
black woman's negative self-image depicted in "Adulthood" was not solved by adopting the role of Revolutionary Black Poet. In "Woman Poem," "Untitled,"
"Once a Lady Told Me," "Each Sunday," and "The Winter Storm," the women with compromised lives are other
women. In "A Poem Off Center," however, she includes
herself in this condition: "maybe i shouldn't feel sorry/
for myself/ but the more i understand women/ the more i
do." A comparison of "All I Gotta Do" ("is sit and wait")
to "Choice," two poems alike in their subject matter and
their syncopated beat, shows that a woman's only choice
is to cry.

AFRICA AND BLACK MUSIC

Two other themes in her poetry also ally Giovanni
with the new black poets—Africa and black music. The
romantic and exotic Africa of the Harlem Renaissance
writers appears only in "Ego-Tripping," where Africa is
personified as a beautiful woman. Her own African experience has produced poems that give a balanced recognition of the African's separate identity. In "They
Clapped," Afro-Americans are treated like any other
tourists and African life is seen realistically.

> they stopped running when they learned the packages
> on the women's heads were heavy and that babies didn't
> cry and disease is uncomfortable and that villages are
>   fun
> only because you knew the feel of good leather on good
>   pavement.

Her conclusion—"despite the dead/ dream they saw a
free future"—opens the way for a new hope in "Africa":
"i dream of black men and women walking/ together
side by side into a new world/ described by love and
bounded by difference."

Black music forms the basis of many of her poems:
Aretha Franklin emerges as her personal idol, lines from

popular songs are woven into "Revolutionary Music" and "Dreams," and several of her poems are based on traditional black American music. She has written a blues tune, "Master Charge Blues," in which a modern woman lets her credit card cure her troubles, and a song which could be set to music, "The Only Song I'm Singing."

The use of the ballad stanza in "On Hearing 'The Girl with the Flaxen Hair'" is effective in building a narrative about white and black art: The girl with flaxen hair gets a song; the black woman does not because her man is tired after working. Her most successful adaptation of musical form comes in "The Great Pax White" which recalls gospel music (indeed, on her recording she read this poem to the tune of "Peace be still," which is also a refrain in the poem). Here Pax Whitie (a bitter parody of the Pax Romana) is described first in an inversion of the words beginning St. John's gospel: The word "was death to all life." Western history, its wars and brutality, is recounted with two alternating calls and responses: "ain't they got no shame?" and "ain't we got no pride?" Her historical account is heavily ironic:

> So the great white prince
> Was shot like a nigger in texas
> And our Black shining prince was murdered
> like that thug in his cathedral
> While our nigger in memphis
> was shot like their prince in dallas.

The irony here and in other political poems, such as "Oppression," will be directed in *Cotton Candy on a Rainy Day* toward herself in "Being and Nothingness" and "The New Yorkers."

HUMAN RELATIONSHIPS

As Giovanni's poems turned toward human relationships, there was a marked increase in her lyricism and especially in her use of imagery, both decorative and structural. Her lover's hands are compared to butterflies in "The Butterfly"; she feels like a falling leaf after a night of passion in "Autumn Poems"; getting rid of a lover is just so much "Housecleaning." "Make Up" sustains the image of cosmetics to talk about the life of pretense that a woman must live. On the whole, her verse descends from William Carlos Williams and Langston

Hughes, but her voice is her own. While she is not a stylistic innovator, nor a stunning image-maker, she has an ingratiating style, one that proceeds from the energy of her personality, and an increasingly sure command of phrasing.

In "The Wonder Woman (A New Dream—for Stevie Wonder)," Giovanni reviewed her life up to 1971: "i wanted to be/ a sweet inspiration in my dreams/ of my people but the times/ require that i give/ myself willingly and become/ a wonder woman." If her subsequent history has fallen short of this ideal, it is still her strong clear voice that one remembers after reading her poetry; her poems are ultimately the self-expression of a black woman who has discovered that "Black love is Black wealth" and who has brought many people, both black and white, to poetry.

CHILDREN'S POETRY

Giovanni devoted a great deal of her writing to children's poetry in the 1980's and early 1990's. She describes her writing for children as an opportunity to "share a bit of the past with children. Black kids deserve to hear their history. My kids books are serious but not dour." Her movement toward this type of poetry reflected her time spent as a mother and time spent enjoying her extended family. More than anything, the poems in her children's collection *Vacation Time* showcased her growing lightness of spirit and inner stability. Similarly, *Those Who Ride the Night Winds* revealed a new and innovative form and brought forth Giovanni's heightened self-knowledge and imagination. In *Those Who Ride the Night Winds*, she echoed the political activism of her early verse as she dedicated various pieces to Phillis Wheatley, Martin Luther King Jr., and Rosa Parks. A decade passed between the publication of *Those Who Ride the Night Winds* and her 1994 title *Knoxville, Tennessee*, a time during which she devoted energy to public causes and arts development, wrote essays, and contributed to edited texts.

THE MIDDLE YEARS

During the 1980's and the 1990's—Giovanni's "middle years"—her work continued to reflect her changing concerns and perspectives. *The Selected Poems of Nikki Giovanni*, which spanned the first three decades of her career, was lauded by critics as a "rich synthesis [that] reveals the evolution of Giovanni's voice and charts the course of the social issues that are her muses, issues of gender and race."

Her collection titled *Love Poems* has an interesting pop-culture twist to it. Ever an unwavering supporter of Black youth, Giovanni was devastated by the murder of rap singer Tupac Shakur in 1997 and had the words "Thug Life" tattooed on her left forearm in his honor. She then dedicated *Love Poems* to Shakur. "A lover whose love was often misunderstood," begins the dedication. Giovanni noted in an interview that she was frustrated with those who would confuse the message and the messenger:

> Rap is expressing the violence that's there, and we weren't even looking at that until rap came up and talked about it. It gave voice to the conditions that people are living under.

While there are somber, sociopolitical pieces here—the burning of black churches and the aforementioend role of "gansta rap"—most of the poems find Giovanni upbeat and domestic. Most of the poems are about friendship and sexuality, children and motherhood, loneliness and sharing, "beautiful black men" and "our faith and our energy and loving our mamas and ourselves and the world and all the chances we took in trying to make everything better." Her celebration of creative energy and the family spirit of African American communities dominates this collection.

BLUES: FOR ALL THE CHANGES

As the twentieth century came to a close, readers found a bit of the younger, more political Giovanni in several of the poems of her collection *Blues: For All the Changes*. While sociopolitical commentary in poetry often fails because it loses touch with humanity, Giovanni continues to keep focus on people: Here she spars with ills that confront Americans but every struggle has a human face. There is a real estate developer who is destroying the woodland adjacent to Giovanni's home in preparation for a new housing development ("Road Rage"). There is a young basketball star ("Iverson"), who, when harassed for his youth and style, finds a compassionate but stern sister in Giovanni. And there is President Bill Clinton, who is subject to Giovanni's forthcoming opinions ("The President's Penis"). Giovanni writes in this collection with an authority in-

formed by experience and shared with heart-stealing candor.

Pop culture and pleasure find a place in the collection as well. She writes about tennis player Pete Sampras and her own tennis playing; pays tribute to Jackie Robinson, soul singer Regina Belle, the late blues singer Alberta Hunter, and Betty Shabazz, the late widow of Malcolm X. She also writes fondly of her memories of going to the ballpark with her father to see the Cincinnati Reds.

Her battle with illness is captured in "Me and Mrs. Robin," which deals with Giovanni's convalescence from cancer surgery and the family of robins she observed with delight and sympathy from her window. Yet this gentle poem also revisits the real estate developer, who, the poem notes, has destroyed trees and "confused the birds and murdered the possum and groundhog." As she identifies with an injured robin, Giovanni's language invokes a gnostic cosmogony: God takes care of individuals; Mother Nature wreaks havoc left and right. "No one ever says 'Mother Nature have mercy.' Mother nature don't give a damn," Giovanni says; "that's why God is so important."

OTHER MAJOR WORKS

NONFICTION: *Gemini: An Extended Autobiographical Statement on My First Twenty-five Years of Being a Black Poet*, 1971; *A Dialogue: James Baldwin and Nikki Giovanni*, 1973; *A Poetic Equation: Conversations Between Nikki Giovanni and Margaret Walker*, 1974; *Sacred Cows . . . and Other Edibles*, 1988; *Racism 101*, 1994.

EDITED TEXTS: *Night Comes Softly: Anthology of Black Female Voices*, 1970; *Appalachian Elders: A Warm Hearth Sampler*, 1991; *Shimmy Shimmy Shimmy Like My Sister Kate*, 1996; *Grand Mothers: Poems, Reminiscences, and Short Stories About the Keepers of Our Traditions*, 1994; *Grand Fathers: Reminiscences, Poems, Recipes, and Photos of the Keepers of Our Traditions*, 1999.

BIBLIOGRAPHY

Baldwin, James, and Nikki Giovanni. *A Dialogue: James Baldwin and Nikki Giovanni*. Philadelphia: Lippincott, 1973. Based on a conversation aired by the Public Broadcasting Service as *Soul!* in 1971, this friendly, informal conversation sheds light on Giovanni's opinions regarding race and gender identity in America—foundational themes in much of her poetry. Includes a foreword by Ida Lewis and an afterword by Orde Coombs.

Bigsby, C. W. E. *The Second Black Renaissance: Essays in Black Literature.* Westport, Conn.: Greenwood Press, 1980. Bigsby analyzes many recent contributions to African American literature, including the work of Giovanni. Useful to any student of contemporary African American literature. Contains bibliographical references and an index.

Fowler, Virginia C. *Nikki Giovanni.* New York: Twayne, 1992. An introductory biography and critical study of selected works by Giovanni. Includes bibliographical references and index.

Giovanni, Nikki. *Conversations with Nikki Giovanni.* Edited by Virginia C. Fowler. Jackson: University Press of Mississippi, 1992. A collection of interviews with Giovanni containing invaluable biographical information and insights into her writing.

Giovanni, Nikki, and Gloria Naylor. "Conversation: Gloria Naylor and Nikki Giovanni." *Callaloo* 23, no. 4 (Fall, 2000): 1395-1409. Naylor and Giovanni discuss the importance of black people raising their tolerance of one another and resisting the stereotypes that suggest black men cannot be close to one another.

Gould, Jean. "Nikki Giovanni." In *Modern American Women Poets.* New York: Dodd, Mead, 1984. As treatments of this affable, self-confident poet are wont to be, Gould's discussion of Giovanni is warm and personal. Stresses her biography and particularly her precocious personal achievements; provides little direct examination of the poetry.

Madhubuti, Haki R. *Dynamite Voices.* Detroit: Broadside Press, 1971. Radical African American poet Madhubuti offers a history and criticism of some poets of the 1960's, of which Giovanni was one. Valuable, because he offers a contemporary look at the African American poetry scene. Contains a bibliography.

Walters, Jennifer. "Nikki Giovanni and Rita Dove: Poets Redefining." *The Journal of Negro History* 85, no. 3 (Summer, 2000): 210-217. The poetry of Nikki Giovanni and Rita Dove is discussed. Both women are examples of self-defined African American women who found a voice through writing.

White, Evelyn C. "The Poet and the Rapper." *Essence* 30, no. 1 (May, 1999): 122-124. Discusses Nikki Giovanni and cultural rapper and actor Queen Latifah, racism, rap music, and politics, topics which have abundantly influenced Giovanni's poetry.

Honora Rankine-Galloway,
updated by Sarah Hilbert

GIUSEPPE GIUSTI

Born: Monsummano, Tuscany (now in Italy); May 12, 1809
Died: Florence (now in Italy); March 31, 1850

PRINCIPAL POETRY
Poesie, 1848, 1877, 1962
Tutti gli scritti editi ed inediti di G. Giusti, 1924
Le più belle pagine di G. Giusti, 1934

OTHER LITERARY FORMS

Giuseppe Giusti's prose writings, though inferior to his poetic ones, must be regarded, nevertheless, as a complement to them, for like his verses, they bear the mark of constant, painstaking rewriting and polishing. While his writings in prose suffer from a belabored style, his poetry retains its appearance of streamlined spontaneity despite numerous revisions.

When Giusti's *Epistolario* (1904, 1932, 1956; correspondence) was published in its complete form, it confirmed his place in Italian literary history as a significant regional writer. Giusti's letters epitomize the distinct flavor of the Tuscan language as it was spoken by the common people of his time. In the vernacular that he cultivated with pride, perhaps even with a certain arrogance, Giusti depicted vignettes of everyday life in contemporary Tuscany.

A similar spirit informs *Raccolta dei proverbi toscani, con illustrazioni cavata dei manoscritti di G.*

Giusti ed ora ampliata ed ordinata (1853; illustrated collection of Tuscan proverbs from G. Giusti's enlarged and rearranged manuscripts), published three years after Giusti's death by his closest friend, Gino Capponi. The proverbs are a repository of Tuscan folkloric wit and wisdom, but, like Giusti's letters, they suffer at times from the linguistic excesses to which he was prone. "Memorie inedite" (unpublished memoirs), later published as *Cronaca dei fatti di Toscana* (1890; chronicle of events in Tuscany), as well as the introductory essay to *Della vita e delle opere di Giuseppe Parini* (1890; about Giuseppe Parini's life and works)—an introductory anthology of Parini's poems edited by Giusti himself—give a much better portrayal of him than do most of the letters or the sparse fragments of his autobiography.

Cronaca dei fatti di Toscana emerges as a truthful portrait of the author, as well as a faithful description of the political upheaval of 1847, when the Tuscan people were first given hope for resurgence by Pius IX's liberal concessions. Describing the Lucca festivals in those days of euphoric anticipation, Giusti interpreted them as a spontaneous popular symbol of the aspirations to freedom that the people of the region entertained. Turning out in droves "to rejoice at the ceasing of evil and at the beginning of good," men, women, children, and elderly folk from the countryside poured into the city. They came as out of a stifling closet into the fresh air, their parish priest leading them, waving their flags and carrying flowers while singing joyfully.

Although his choice of poems for the Parini anthology was far from excellent, in the accompanying essay Giusti reveals his affinity with that great Lombard poet, especially his appreciation for Parini's universal satire. Giusti, too, was to satirize the vices and corruption of society at large, rather than focusing on individuals in order to vent personal grudges. Another important aspect of his essay on Parini is his correct evaluation of eighteenth century Italian literature as the seedbed for the peninsula's resurgence in the nineteenth century. Nevertheless, even in his obvious admiration for, and agreement with, Parini's philosophical outlook, Giusti—as a "native" Tuscan writer—could not repress his sense of superiority over Parini in matters of language.

ACHIEVEMENTS

Giuseppe Giusti was a key poet of the Italian Risorgimento, and although the label of "minor poet" has been applied to his name, it does not minimize the important role he played in the literature and history of nineteenth century Italy. His greatest gift as an author was his keen common sense, exemplified in his use of the satiric traditions of his native Tuscany. While his regional standing may have limited his range, it also contributed to his instantaneous recognition and fame throughout the peninsula, as his *scherzi* (jokes) were circulated in manuscript form long before they became available in print. *Scherzi* are satirical poetic compositions often in short, quick-moving verses in the tempo of lively musical compositions also named *scherzi* by early nineteenth century composers. Structured in a great variety of meters and lengths, the *scherzi* were written to satirize events, mores, and public figures. Giusti's rapidly growing fame reinforced his belief that it was by the poetic word that he could contribute to his country's liberation.

With their sarcastic needling of police spies, princes, ministers, and courtiers, Giusti's *scherzi* became weapons of liberalism and symbols of the Italians' patriotic aspirations to unity and freedom. Although Niccoló Tommaseo, and even his friend Alessandro Manzoni, found Giusti unduly sardonic in matters of linguistic pride and purity, it was to Giusti that Manzoni went for advice in order to give the final, polishing touches to the language of his immortal novel *I promessi sposi* (1842; *The Betrothed*, 1951, a revision of the earlier *Gli sposi promessi*, 1827; *The Betrothed*, 1828). Manzoni's elegant Florentine language in that novel was to become the model for Italian prose.

Thus, if by his almost fanatical devotion to the Tuscan vernacular Giusti limited the scope of his poetic aspirations, he nevertheless helped to awaken the national conscience to the need for political and linguistic unity.

BIOGRAPHY

Giuseppe Giusti was born on May 12, 1809, in Monsummano, near Pescia in the Val di Nievole, of a well-to-do family. Giusti began his studies with a local priest, whose coarse and aggressive manners had a considerable influence on the boy's aversion for school. Reacting against his father's ambitious plans for him, the young Giusti continued to be a reluctant pupil in his brief residencies in boarding schools in Florence and in Lucca, and in a Pistoia seminary. When his father sent him to study law at the University of Pisa in 1826, the greatest attraction for the recalcitrant scholar was the Café of the Hussar along the Lungarno, where students gathered in informal merrymaking. It was in that carefree atmosphere that the poet began to be formed, as among his peers Giusti observed the various types and characters he was to make universal in his verse. The satirist in him did not fail to note with humor the hypocrisy that infiltrated even that joyful circle of student gatherings; it was from those early experiences, for example, that he later drew one of his most famous poems, "Gingillino" (1844-1845; "The Trifler").

Because of difficulties with his family, as well as a brief incident with the police, Giusti did not obtain his law degree until 1834, when he was twenty-five years old. His legal career, nevertheless, proved to be quite perfunctory; indeed, he gave it up before he had even started, lacking interest in the profession altogether. In 1836, he met Gino Capponi, who became his best friend and whose serenity was a positive influence on Giusti. Nevertheless, because of continuing family difficulties and a lack of physical vitality (only much later discovered to be the result of tuberculosis), he began to suffer from nervous disorders, alternating periods of depression and recovery.

A journey to Rome and Naples, where Giusti was welcomed enthusiastically by liberals in intellectual circles, did not help his recovery and indeed may have worsened his ill health. Sporadic short excursions took him outside Tuscany, to La Spezia and to Milan, where he was a guest of Alessandro Manzoni for a month. Between 1846 and 1847, Giusti lived alternately in his paternal home and at the Capponi residence in Florence.

When the Civic Guard was formed, Giusti happily joined it with the rank of a major. Having become officially recognized as a "very Tuscan writer," in 1848 he was named a resident member of the prestigious Crusca Academy. The same year, after the 1848 Revolution, he briefly held political office as a deputy in the first and second Tuscan legislative assemblies of Borgo Buggiano. With Capponi, he promoted the liberal cause, seeking a friendly agreement between the Grand Duke and the people, disregarding past grudges. In 1849, shortly before the restoration of the Grand Duke, Giusti was elected to the Constituent Assembly for the short time that it existed.

Giusti's satirical poems, needling the unemployed spies, the police *birri*, and the civil servants who were conveniently being retired, belong to this period of political upheaval, when the downfall of the old society was rapidly taking place. "A Leopoldo II" (1847; "To Leopold II") is a poem in which Giusti tried to see that ruler as a true prince and as a father of his region. It was an ephemeral enthusiasm, however, which was soon to be deflated by the Grand Duke's flight and the demagogues' seizure of power; when Leopold returned, he was accompanied by the Austrians.

Accused of having betrayed the cause of the people, disillusioned and bitter, Giusti at first sought refuge with his family at Pescia and Montecatini, and later at his friend Capponi's in Florence, where he died on March 31, 1850, of tuberculosis, the silent disease which had been undermining his health all along. Though deeply saddened by the failure of the Constituent Assembly and the triumph of reactionary forces, Giusti never lost hope for Italy's resurrection—for her Risorgimento.

ANALYSIS

Giuseppe Giusti's poetics should be sought in his concrete approach to life: Without searching for past utopias or making gigantic leaps into the future, Giusti's poems concentrate both in time and space on the present, on the topography, history, and mores of contemporary Tuscany. In one of his short prose writings, aptly titled "Dell'aurea mediocrità" (about golden mediocrity), Giusti evaluates human life in terms of a median condition residing between Heaven and Earth. Man's horizon should be sought, he suggests, at eye level, between the sky and the land, where the concreteness of life lies.

This amused acceptance of things as they are, not as they *should* be, had its roots in Giusti's native Tuscan traditions. Although his satirical mode has been traced to all sorts of Italian and foreign satirists, humorists, and caricaturists—his style has been compared, for example, to that of the lighthearted French folk poet Pierre Jean de

Béranger—his primary inspiration was the homely Tuscan folklore that extolled the virtues of moderation.

"THE BOOT"

The folkloric element in Giusti's verse is evident in the early poem "Lo stivale" ("The Boot"), written in 1836. Headed by an epigraph taken from Dante's rhymes, it is written in stanzas of six hendecasyllabic lines. The Boot is the narrator; it stands for Italy, whose safety resides in that unity which Dante so strongly advocated. Describing the Boot from top to toe, Giusti recalls the Boot's history and its ravaging by many who sought to rule it—"from one thief to the next." It is true, the Boot once "galloped" by itself and ruled the Roman world, but, wanting too much, it fell flat on the ground. While sketching the long, harrowing history of the peninsula, Giusti directs his sarcasm particularly against the Papacy. "The priests harmed me most/that truly malevolent race and indiscreet." In the end, the Boot asks only to be refurbished and given a solid form by a competent boot maker, yet should such a man of courage and energy appear, he would, as usual, "be kicked in his seat."

NOTABLE SCHERZI

Among Giusti's most famous *scherzi* of this first period are "L'incoronazione" ("The Coronation"), written in 1838, and three others, all of 1840: "Il brindisi di Girella" ("Girella's Toast"), "Umanitari" ("The Humanitarians"), and "Il Re Travicello" ("King Travicello"). "The Coronation" was written on the occasion of the coronation of the Emperor of Austria as King of Italy, but the satire is actually directed against Leopold II—the Emperor's brother—during whose tenure as Grand Duke of Tuscany the atmosphere in the region became more stagnant than ever. Identified in this poem as "il toscano Morfeo" ("Tuscan Morpheus") for the somnolence he caused among his subjects, Leopold became proverbially symbolic of complacency and ineptitude in government.

"Girella's Toast," "The Humanitarians," and "King Travicello" address what Giusti called, with much contempt, "our deepest wounds"—that is, the proliferation of cosmopolitanism, the opportunism of the weathercocks (those ready to change their loyalty to enter the ranks of the latest conqueror), and the obsequious role so many Italians played in order to gain favor, giving their allegiance to harsh or inept monarchs such as the

dull-witted King Travicello. All of those vices had to be eliminated if the country were to be rebuilt. Cosmopolitanism in particular went against Giusti's grain, for he believed that the Italians, being so divided among themselves, were hardly ready for the international scene.

It was this aversion to cosmopolitanism that prevented Giusti from siding with either the classicists or the Romantics in the battle between the two factions which had begun to rage in 1816, when he was a small boy. His posture on this all-important issue of his time was typically Giustian: He wanted to follow a middle road, preserving a balance between the old and the new. This eventually happened, though Giusti failed to understand how much the future of Italian independence was to be indebted to the spreading and absorption of European ideas within the peninsula.

"THE LAND OF THE DEAD"

"La terra dei morti" (1842; "The Land of the Dead") is Giusti's answer to a poem by the French poet Alphonse de Lamartine, "La Dernier chant du pèlerinage d'Harold" (1826; "The Last Song of Harold's Pilgrimage"), which had been reprinted in 1842. Recalling Lord Byron's exploits on behalf of the Greek struggle for independence from Turkey, Lamartine had contrasted Hellenic heroism with the Italians' resignation to their position as slaves of foreign rulers—a servility which lowered them to "human dust," the inhabitants of "the land of the dead." In 1826, Lamartine's insult to the Italian people had provoked strong reactions and had even embroiled him in a duel; since then, Giusti had been fueling his own patriotic sentiments. In "The Land of the Dead," he employed a seven-syllable line that imparted a spirit of urgency to the verse. There are great patriots in Italy today, Giusti replies to Lamartine, men such as Manzoni, Giuseppe Niccolini, and Gian Domenico Romagnosi, heirs to past glories. Will the ruins and monuments, vestiges of former greatness, be the Italians' cemetery or that of the barbarians, the invaders of the peninsula? Judgment Day will not be late in coming when the country is resurrected to life.

"THE SNAIL"

One of Giusti's most popular satirical poems, "La chiocciola" ("The Snail"), neatly sums up his outlook on life. In fast-moving lines of five syllables, "The Snail" dispenses the poet's Tuscan wisdom—a wisdom embedded in wit and practicality. Observing a snail during a walk in the country, Giusti realizes how far superior it is to man. A peaceful, home-loving, moderate creature, it never leaves its house in search of adventures or exotic foods. Unlike so many "teaching owls," who in fact can teach nothing to their peers, the snail excels above other living creatures. Even the hangman should take notice of this "exemplary" animal, which has been given by nature the prodigious ability of regrowing its head. Giusti's characteristic humor is particularly evident in the refrain: "Hail to the snail."

"THE TRIFLER"

Much has been written about "Gingillino" ("The Trifler"), an unusually harsh and relentless tirade against the "squandering" Tuscan bureaucrats that is quite unlike most of Giusti's satiric compositions. Gingillino is the symbol of all triflers, the host of civil servants who make up the slothful, spineless, and corrupt bureaucratic complex. As a baby, a child, a student, and finally as a graduate and an adult, Gingillino is "educated" to join the dalliers. He promptly learns to put into practice the dishonest teachings of peers and superiors and, in turn, goes on to flatter and please everybody by his deceit and sloth, but particularly the mighty, those in high places, in order to gain their favors.

"The Trifler" is a powerful, extended satire comprising 701 lines, including a prologue. The following stanzas, in various meters, consist of lines ranging from four to eleven syllables. This structural variety is meant to convey the various vices and tricks the dishonest bureaucrats must learn to master. From this large crowd of "demons," among whom even Judas would look like an inexperienced buffoon, the poet emerges, crazed and melancholy, wandering alone in the night's solitude to enjoy "the chaste embrace of your beauty, my deceived country."

"IN SANT' AMBROGIO'S"

Giusti's later poems, epitomizing the hopes and aspirations of the Italian people, belong to the years from 1846 to 1848. They are statements of the evolution of historical events to their dramatic apex; they also represent the poet's spiritual growth, greatly enhanced by his physical decline. Perhaps none of Giusti's compositions belonging to this last period of his life has been more quoted, lauded, and anthologized than "Sant' Ambrogio" (1846; "In Sant' Ambrogio's"). It is a poem that blends the lyric and satirical strands of Giusti's verse, relating an episode that the poet had witnessed when, in 1845, he was visiting Manzoni and his family in Milan. Doubtless Manzoni's religious fervor must have been felt by Giusti, whose Christian charity may well have been revived by his illness as well.

With subtle irony, the poet pretends to recount the incident with all due respect to a high-placed official of the Buon Governo—the Tuscan Grand Duke's police establishment—which regarded the poet's "little satires of no count" as dangerously anti-Austrian and subversive. Wandering about with Manzoni's son, Filippo, in Milan, he finds himself in the ancient fourth century Church of Saint Ambrose, the patron saint of the Lombard city.

At first, the poet is seized by a sense of revulsion, seeing the church invaded by a crowd of blondish, mustachioed, foul-smelling foreign military men, standing at attention before God. When the priest is about to consecrate the Host, the famous chorus "Va pensiero" ("Go forth my thought") is sounded by horns. The chorus, taken from Giuseppe Verdi's opera *I Lombardi alla prima crociata* (the Lombards in the First Crusade), has always been well known for echoing in its sad strains the unfulfilled aspirations of an oppressed people. No longer quite like himself, the poet is suddenly overcome by compassion for the Croatian and Czechoslovakian soldiers, who are forced to be away from their countries and their loved ones. "Those poor people" stand watch over the Italians, says Giusti. They are slaves of the Emperor of Austria, serving among people who hate them; they are the tools of a monarch who fears seditious revolts and loss of power. The spontaneous fraternal compassion of the patriotic poet heightens as the foreign soldiers begin a German chant. Is it not possible, Giusti asks, that in their souls, they resent "il principale" (the master) as much as the Italians do? "I may as well flee," he concludes; "otherwise I am liable to embrace a corporal."

Giusti's short life as a man and as a writer represents a landmark in Italian letters precisely because he was in tune with his times. Greatly desiring Italy's liberty, he nevertheless resisted fanaticism and intolerance, and his compassion and humor reflected the character of his people at their best.

OTHER MAJOR WORKS

NONFICTION: *Cronaca dei fatti di Toscana*, 1890; *Della vita e delle opere di Giuseppe Parini*, 1890 (includes poems by Parini); *Epistolario*, 1904, 1932, 1956.

MISCELLANEOUS: *Raccolta dei proverbi toscani, con illustrazioni cavata dei manoscritti di G. Giusti ed ora ampliata ed ordinata*, 1853; *Tutti gli scritti editi ed inediti di G. Giusti*, 1924 (includes all of his prose and poetry).

BIBLIOGRAPHY

Bossi, Maurizio Bossi, and Mirella Branca, eds. *Giuseppe Giusti: Il tempo e i luoghi*. Florence, Italy: L.S. Olschki, 1999. A collection of biographical and critical essays on Giusti. Published in Italian.

Horner, Susan. *The Tuscan Poet Giuseppe Giusti, and His Times*. Cambridge, Mass.: Macmillan, 1864. A biography of Giusti with some historical background.

Tusiani, Joseph. *From Marino to Marinetti*. New York: Baroque Press, 1974. An anthology of forty Italian poets including Giusti translated into English with some biographical notes on each.

Carolina D. Lawson;
bibliography updated by the editors

LOUISE GLÜCK

Born: New York, New York; April 22, 1943

PRINCIPAL POETRY

Firstborn, 1968
The House on Marshland, 1975
Descending Figure, 1980
The Triumph of Achilles, 1985
Ararat, 1990
The Wild Iris, 1992
The First Four Books of Poems, 1995
Meadowlands, 1996
The First Five Books of Poems, 1997
Vita Nova, 1999
The Seven Ages, 2001

OTHER LITERARY FORMS

Although known primarily for her poetry, Louise Glück occasionally publishes essays about her work and about other poets. Of most interest is "The Dreamer and the Watcher," published in *Singular Voices: American Poetry Today* (1985, edited by Stephen Berg), in which Glück writes quite personally about her poem "Night Song" and about her writing process. Discussing T. S. Eliot in a piece in *The Southern Review* titled "Fear and the Absent 'Other,'" Glück further identifies her literary affinities. *Proofs and Theories: Essays on Poetry* (1994) collects her thoughts on the writing of poetry.

ACHIEVEMENTS

With each book, Glück has deepened her range and her vision; each volume has gained for her additional recognition. Among her awards are Columbia University's Academy of American Poets Prize (1967), a Rockefeller Foundation grant (1968), a National Endowment for the Arts grant (1969-1970), the Eunice Tietjens Memorial Award (1971), and a Guggenheim Fellowship (1975-1976). Upon publication of her fourth book, *The Triumph of Achilles*, Glück received the 1986 Poetry Society of America's Melville Cane Award, the National Book Critics Circle Award for poetry, and the Boston Globe Literary Press Award for poetry. *Ararat*, her fifth book of poems, won the Rebekah Johnson Bobbitt National Prize for Poetry. In 1992 she won both the prestigious Pulitzer Prize and the William Carlos Williams Award for her collection *The Wild Iris*. Glück was also appointed Poet Laureate Consultant in Poetry in 1999-2000, along with Rita Dove and W. S. Merwin. All were named special bicentennial consultants. Her essay collection *Proofs and Theories* received the PEN/Martha Albrand Award for Nonfiction. Additional honors for her poetry include the Bollingen Prize and the Lannan Literary Award.

BIOGRAPHY

Louise Elisabeth Glück was born on April 22, 1943, in New York City, to a Wellesley-educated mother and a father who was a first-generation American businessman of Hungarian descent. The firstborn daughter of this family, who died before Glück's birth, is the acknowledged source of the poet's preoccupation with death, grieving, and loss that is a theme in her work. As a teenager, Glück struggled with anorexia, another experience that later was a theme in her poetry. She later worked with poet Stanley Kunitz, who became a major influence on her life as a poet. Glück attended Sarah Lawrence College in Bronxville, New York, and Columbia University in New York City. She married Charles Hertz, Jr., in 1967, and had one child, Noah Benjamin. Hertz and Glück later divorced and she married John Dranow in 1977, a writer and vice president of the New England Culinary Institute.

Since 1970 she has taught at numerous colleges and universities. Although Glück has indicated that she was somewhat hesitant about teaching, she later embraced it as a means of surviving the extended silences she endured when it seemed impossible to write poetry. She served as a poetry panelist or poetry reader at conferences and foundations, including Mrs. Giles Whiting Foundation and PEN Southwest Conference; she has also judged numerous poetry contests such as the Discovery Contest. In 1983, Glück began teaching as Scott Professor of Poetry at Williams College in Williams-

Louise Glück (© Star Black)

town, Massachusetts, and by 1984 had become a senior lecturer in English. In 1999 she was elected a chancellor of the Academy of American Poets.

ANALYSIS

Louise Glück's poetry has been remarkably consistent, both in its controlled, spare, laconic language and in its thematic interests. The universe, as portrayed in a poem such as "The Racer's Widow," is a violent assault, in which "spasms of violets rise above the mud," and the poet faces loss and estrangement in every human relationship. For consolation there is myth, art, language, and occasionally love between a man and a woman. With these consolations, however, there often comes either an oppressive permanence or an admission of terrible impermanence.

Another consistency seen in Glück's work is the refusal to romanticize one's predicament. There is a relentless vision in Glück's books as well as a gradual loosening of her tight syntactical grip. Glück can be relentless, sparse, and, in later works, vulnerable. The door to emotion has been set ajar. "Birth, not death, is the hard loss," Glück said in her first book. That remains true, but the poet has learned how to transform loss into art. In her career, Glück has consistently written with a spare tautness that has gained for her much respect among her contemporaries and among an older generation of poets and critics.

FIRSTBORN

Firstborn, Glück's first book, was published when the author was only twenty-five. The book is arranged in three sections: "The Egg," "The Edge," and "Cottonmouth Country." The titles of the book's sections give little clue to the book's subject matter: the squalor of both city and suburb, domestic and family tension, the coldness between people, and the bitter disappointment of marriage. Fully three-quarters of the volume consists of formal poems, often sonnet-like, which employ a tight, albeit "slant," rhyme scheme.

Typical of the first section is the opening poem, "The Chicago Train," which details the shocking sight of a couple with a child on a commuter train. The writer here spares no detail as she practically recoils from the smell and sight in recollection: "just Mister with his barren/ Skull across the arm-rest while the kid/ Got his head between his mama's legs and slept." The air is "poison," and the couple appear riveted in place, "as though paralysis preceding death/ Had nailed them there." Glück uses colloquial language to heighten the shock: "I saw her pulsing crotch . . . the lice rooted in that baby's hair."

Again and again the speaker is the onlooker, watching with a detachment that is both ironic and bitter. In "Thanksgiving" Glück details the holiday atmosphere in the suburbs where the speaker's sister is circled by "a name-/ less Southern boy from Yale" much the way a cat prowls the driveway outside, "seeking waste." Hardly festive, the day wears on toward "that vast consoling meal." The mother is seen with "skewers in her hands," and the turkey itself is a vision of "pronged death." Glück's vision here is relentlessly dark, the images those of waste and destruction. For this, by implication, the speaker is supposed to give thanks.

The second section, "The Edge," consists entirely of dramatic monologues spoken by various personas. The speaker might be a bride, a cripple, a nun, a child's nurse, or a man speaking about spring. Most powerful here (as well as typical) are "The Edge" and "The Racer's Widow." The former poem foreshadows much that is to come in Glück's work, especially the alienation of the female speaker from her husband. The speaker's heart is tied "to that headboard," and her "quilted cries/ Harden against his hand." The tension between them is palpable; the buried violence threatens to overwhelm the poem: "Over Mother's lace I watch him drive into the gored/ Roasts, deal slivers in his mercy." The speaker is trapped, "crippled with this house."

Also typical is the obsession with the physical body which gives "The Racer's Widow" much of its power. The speaker must face the loss of her husband, and she sees around her the ironic return of spring. Though she claims, "It is not painful to discuss/ His death," the poem's details belie her indifference. The widow states that "his face assaults/ Me, I can hear that car careen again." For consolation, she does not turn to a remembrance of love but to sharp observation and wry comment. Her last view of him was as he lay "draining there." No one can take him from her now, not even his adoring crowds: "And see/ How even he did not get to keep that lovely body." *Firstborn* shows the influence of Robert Lowell, John Berryman, and Sylvia Plath, and it has an obsessiveness that is both interesting and unnatural.

THE HOUSE ON MARSHLAND

Louise Glück's second book, *The House on Marshland*, is considered by many critics to mark quite an advance over her first book. A slim volume, the book is divided into two sections. Like the poems in *Firstborn*, the poems here are quite short, but the attention to formal qualities of rhyme and meter is now gone. The poems retain a spareness in language and imagery that continues to command respect. The book's subject is the twin loss of paradise and of innocence. The second section, "The Apple Trees," describes a journey away—physically and psychically—from a loved one.

The use of fairy tale and myth in *The House on Marshland* informs some of the book's strongest poems. In "For My Mother," for example, the speaker appears to be able to remember being in the womb, and this myth of Platonic oneness provides the poet with a reason to mourn, now, separateness and division: "It was better when we were/ together in one body." The father arrives, like a prince, and closes the mother's eyelids "with/ two kisses." What is there to mourn? The "absolute/ knowledge of the unborn" and the knowledge that there is no way back.

"Gretel in Darkness" uses a fairy tale to evoke its terror. The poet's method is not simply to retell the tale; the reader feels, and is meant to feel, that a personal story lies behind the retelling. The images here are straight out of Grimm: oven, witch, moonlight, and sugar. "This is the world we wanted," is the haunting first line. Lost in this horrifying world "far from women's arms/ and memory of women," the speaker is comforted by the presence of her brother, Hansel. Sadly, Gretel must admit, "But I killed for you." The end of Gretel seems to be a paranoiac madness from which she reaches futilely for Hansel. The nightmares recur: "We are there still and it is real, real,/ that black forest and the fire in earnest."

One change from *Firstborn* is the predominance of pastoral images in *The House on Marshland*. These images work well with the theme of the loss of Eden. Such images occur in "The School Children," in which "children go forward with their little satchels." The world the children face, however, is not a pastoral one. They hang their coats on "nails" and the fruit trees bear "little ammunition."

The journey that part 2 of *The House on Marshland* appears to describe begins, appropriately, with a poem titled "The Undertaking." The biblical images here, typical of Glück's work, provide the means for the speaker's escape. The first line, darkly ironic, makes this statement: "The darkness lifts, imagine, in your lifetime." The irony and darkness are discarded as the poem progresses and there seems to be hope, at last, in movement: "Extend yourself—/ it is the Nile, the sun is shining,/ everywhere you turn is luck." The hope, however, is short-lived. The speaker's journey is a lonely one; she must first don a widow's clothes and mourn the lost relationship. Her sole consolation is insight: "I think now it is better to love no one/ than to love you."

DESCENDING FIGURE

It is with her third book, *Descending Figure*, that Glück begins to consider possible ways of redemption. The images and themes, even the method, of *Descending Figure* are by now familiar: images of a garden, a lost world, the body, and lovers. The mood is one of cold appraisal. One must not mourn too easily; one must look around and find what it will take to go on. Glück here begins to use a new structure, a poem in several sections. Actually, she had used this structure in both earlier books, but now it is used more frequently and at what appear to be critical moments. "The Garden," "The Mirror," and "Lamentations" are the three sections of *Descending Figure*.

In the long title poem of the book's first section, "The Garden," the poet insists on further detailing the moments of being cast out of the biblical and mythical "garden." If the speaker can do nothing to prevent these losses, she will accurately detail what she sees—again, the impulse of the onlooker (the artist), who finds consolation in the recording of grief. The titles of the five sections of "The Garden" are "The Fear of Birth," "The Garden," "The Fear of Love," "Origins," and "The Fear of Burial." "The Fear of Birth" harks back to "For My Mother" in *The House on Marshland*, but there is the added resignation of these lines: "And then the losses,/ one after another,/ all supportable." The poet refuses to overdramatize her situation: Loss must be bearable; it will be borne.

Opening with "Epithalamium," the book's second section at first seems to contain poems with the most hope. The poems here bespeak a new beginning: marriage and new love. Almost immediately, however, the darkness intrudes. After the ceremony, there "begins/ the terrible charity of marriage"; the rightness of the word "charity" and its coldness keep the Glück tradition of spareness and relentless vision. The speaker's happiness is tinged with the sadness of former loves when her new husband must reassure her: "*Here is my hand that will not harm you.*"

The second section ends with a poem called "Happiness," in which two lovers lie in bed together. The speaker watches from a distance, watches how the "sunlight/ pools in their throats." The "I" here seems to be the alter ego of the female lover; when she opens her eyes, the "I" inhabits her rather than being outside her. This split between the conscious and unconscious self is another theme in Glück's work. There is also an interesting gentleness that the poems in *Descending Figure* begin to show. Perhaps the universe is not as hostile as formerly seen, the reader begins to think. "Happiness" ends with an image of the sun "the burning wheel/ passes gently over us."

Whatever hope the second section appeared to pose, the poet seems to find herself back in a world of loss and estrangement in the third section, appropriately titled "Lamentations." Here the poet begins to propose as possibilities for redemption both art and myth. She says as much in "Autumnal," which describes the harvest of fallen leaves and how they are carted off or burned: "So waste is elevated/ into beauty." There is also a bitter consolation to be found in the woman's role: "you give and give, you empty yourself/ into a child. And you survive/ the automatic loss." It is the woman who bends, accommodates, shapes herself to others: "At the grave,/ it is the woman, isn't it, who bends,/ the spear useless beside her." The descending figure of the book's title is, in one sense, God—who may take pity on those sorrowing down below. The poet longs for that vision, that distance from her suffering: "How beautiful it must have been,/ the earth, that first time/ seen from the air."

THE TRIUMPH OF ACHILLES

With her fourth volume, *The Triumph of Achilles*, Louise Glück reached a maturity of style and voice that is unusual for a poet of her age. Her vision of the world has remained constant in many ways, but there is a change in the poet's attitude toward herself and thus toward her readers. The poems proceed with much the same method—using myth and art to discuss one's life—but in this book the passion seems more evident, the loss more immediate, the stakes more critically viewed. If the previous volume has a cool tone, this volume is still hot from the artistic forge. There are three epigraphs at the beginning of *The Triumph of Achilles:* one is unidentified, one is from Saint Ignatius and focuses on being a prisoner to suffering, and the third is from Bruno Bettelheim and focuses on knowing good from evil. Clearly these identify the book's predominant themes.

"Mock Orange," the book's first poem, is the harrowing lament of a woman who finds the sex act to be humiliating and unsettling. Sex is an indignity which she hates, "the man's mouth/ sealing my mouth, the man's paralyzing body. . ." Once again, the poet is preoccupied with the body and with the inevitable alienation she feels from the lover. Yes, the lovers are momentarily "fused," but only by the "premise of union"; the "tired antagonisms" remain.

"Metamorphosis," another important poem, shows the poet's interest in finding, again, redemption. Perhaps suffering can be the means to a metamorphosis, in this case the suffering felt at watching a parent die. The poet's tenderness is reined in, by now something to be expected in Glück's work, but her restraint is more evident than in previous poems and books. The poem's third section, "For My Father," is surely meant to recall the piece to the mother in *Firstborn.* The remarkably parallel statement here is to the father: "I'm going to live without you/ as I learned once/ to live without my mother." The directness of Glück's utterance is newfound and hard-won; it shows in the rest of the poems as well.

The references to Greek myths are frequent and important. Glück alludes to Apollo, to Hyacinth, and to Patroclus and Achilles. The poems in which these references are made are some of the volume's finest: Glück is using the myths, the gods, to tell her stories and simultaneously is turning her suffering into its own "myth." For Glück, what is triumphant, finally, about Achilles is his feeling for another, a feeling which is both his doom and

his "triumph": "he was a man already dead, a victim/ of the part that loved,/ the part that was mortal."

Finally, however, it is Glück's long poem "Marathon" which is the crowning achievement of *The Triumph of Achilles.* It provides the book's focus; it shows the speaker being made mortal by suffering as Achilles was made mortal. Glück's vision is still relentless, but here her focus is turned on herself in the most personal of ways. The poems are not confessional—few personal details are given—yet they are deeply felt. For all of their distance, they seem torn from the heart. The process begins with "Last Letter" (section 1): "When I tried to stand again, I couldn't move,/ . . . Does grief change you like that?" The speaker longs to believe in such a transformation, but fears it is transitory, illusory, as is so much else: "What happens afterward/ occurs far from the world, at a depth/ where only the dream matters/ and the bond with any one soul/ is meaningless; you throw it away."

Such poems have come a long way from the wrenched syntax of the "sonnets" of *Firstborn.* Glück has reached a sophistication of theme and method that enables her to turn her vision to events of daily life and render them, truly, into art. What in *Firstborn* Glück struggled to say, in *The Triumph of Achilles* she writes of with grace and power. The poems in *Ararat,* Glück's next book, show a further extension of her talent.

ARARAT

Ararat, Louise Glück's fifth collection of poems, is also her most open, unguarded, and poignant book. A steady reader of Glück's work will find here, in a sense, no surprises: She continues to use classical and biblical references, she writes in a spare, lucid style, and she speaks in a disarmingly direct way that beguiles the reader with its starkness and simplicity. What is new is the personal subject matter: domestic scenes of childhood and what appear to be the speaker's adult life. Glück is always wise in her choice of book titles. Here the title's biblical reference has connotations of solid ground in the midst of floodwaters, and to the hope Noah found at flood's end. Perhaps Glück is signaling some bedrock consolation in the midst of life's tribulations.

Made up of thirty-two poems, presented with no section divisions, *Ararat* starts with "Parodos," a poem recounting an early "wounding." The book concludes, in rhythmic circularity, with "First Memory," also a poem about being wounded. Ironically, the concluding poem is also deeply affirmative, as the poet realizes that her pain meant she had feelings and was human. The poems between "Parodos" and "First Memory" describe domestic scenes in sparing detail. Family members move about, coldly, and the psychological tensions and distances between them are poignantly recalled. Glück refuses to beautify the moments. She writes, for example, at the start of "A Fantasy": "I'll tell you something: every day/ people are dying. And that's just the beginning." Yet despite the poet's refusal to accept easy consolations, her vision's sparingness becomes a beautiful, though stark, tribute to honesty and truth.

Some of the most moving poems in *Ararat* are ones describing the speaker's relationship with her father. Four that occur together in the book are "Snow," "Terminal Resemblances," "Lament," and "Mirror Image." The mundane opening of "Snow" describes a December visit to the circus with her father when she was a child. He holds the child on his shoulders, and the speaker recalls "staring straight ahead/ into the world my father saw. . . ." The moment of physical closeness (as well as shared sight) reveals the poet's deep love for her father.

Never sentimental, Glück's poems are raw and moving, each word carefully chosen. *Ararat* signals a significant advance in Glück's work; the poems are as spare as ever, but there is a new, loving, tenderness and sadness.

The work of Louise Glück has shown a steady unfolding. Its attention to language and theme has been consistent, as has its view of the world. As her work becomes more open, more lyrical, nothing of its austerity and perseverance has been lost. As Glück herself notes in "Song of Invisible Boundaries" (section 8 of "Marathon"): "Finally, this is what we craved,/ this lying in the bright light without distinction—/ we who would leave behind/ exact records." Later in *Ararat* she would write: "I was born to a vocation:/ to bear witness/ to the great mysteries." American poetry is greatly in debt to the poetic witnessing of Louise Glück.

MEADOWLANDS

In *Meadowlands*, Glück weaves a tapestry of mirrored words in which reader, writer, and marriage, husband, wife, and child reflect and are reflected by the mythic arc of Homer's *Odyssey*. However, Glück is less interested in the man and more intrigued by the people around him—Penelope, Telemachus, Circe—demonstrated stylistically by the fact that Penelope, Telemachus, and Circe all speak in the first person and Odysseus does not. As suitors swarm the house, cleaning out the cupboards and basically wrecking the place, Penelope stoically weaves. Observing his detached mother from a distance, Telemachus mopes and pitches fits to try to get her attention. When Circe's lover leaves her, she rages and grieves, vowing revenge. Unlike other Odyssean poems, however, is the fact that Glück highlights her own weaving: *Meadowlands* is a dualistic narrative that juxtaposes an ordinary contemporary marriage against Odysseus's famous one. By bridging the classical and the contemporary, Glück can consider the mundane details that constitute a marriage, as well as those that contribute to its dissolution, giving the book a rich, polyphonic texture.

Indeed, the organziation of the book is a textual weave using patterns of three. There are three sets of poems interwoven with each other throughout the book: poems centered on Penelope, Telemachus, and Circe, poems spoken by a "you" and "I" who are or have been married to each other in late twentieth century America, and poems titled "parables." This structural design seems to be a metaphor for the loom at which Penelope weaves and unweaves the work that delays her suitors indefinitely. The parables are the loom, the "Odyssey" poems are the warp (the lengthwise series of "yarns" extended across the loom) and the "you/I" poems form the woof, the filling thread in a yarn or weaving.

The parables constitute the most formal way the book has of directly addressing the reader and are indicators of Glück's most characteristic rendering of poetic voice. Yet readers are also able to grasp underlying themes and tensions through the character of Telemachus, who plays a critical role in the collection, Having withstood his father's absence and his mother's cold preoccupation, he is able to interpret their marriage from a distance not available to them. His monologues help to interweave the book's two marriages as they describe the dynamic between "husband and wife" as that of "opposing forces," at once "heartbreaking" and "insane" and "very funny." In many poems, his voice echoes the elegant detachment, the stoicism and clarity of one of

Glück's earlier collections, *Ararat*, where she observes her own parents.

VITA NOVA

Vita Nova picks up where *Meadowlands* left off: after a marital breakup, when single life in a new locale eerily recalls life before marriage. Here Glück explores that terrible interval between the loss of a love and the stirrings of new life and new emotions. Each poem is a meditation on spring, that is, on renewal, return, and reincarnation, and this endlessly poignant theme is expressed in Glück's resurrection of the timeless tales of ancient Greece and Rome. The title stems from Dante, who cited the Latin phrase "Incipit vita nova" at the opening of *La Vita Nuova*, in order to distinguish his innovative use of the Italian vernacular in the surrounding prose. Through the ensuing story of Dante's sublimated love for Beatrice, the phrase acquired connotations of religious conversion, the soul's awakening to a new life. Now Glück highlights her "vita nova" by employing the phrase as the title of two poems, which frame the volume at beginning and end.

The collection is resilient and full of surprise and light, sorrow and wisdom. Although her despair has a personal basis, it seems also to reflect the condition of a culture that has found the material world an inadequate substitute for the consolation that Dante found in the spiritual. She again employs mythic figures to comment on being human: the passions and sufferings of Eurydice and Orpheus, and the musings about love and loss of Aeneas and Dido find a place here. Readers find Glück as a pendulum: a goddess herself looking down on human folly and as a more earthly figure in poems about girlhood, an unforgiving mother, or the tough lessons cruel lovers teach. A dark humor is present here too, as when, in the narrative of "Vita Nova [2]," a dog named Blizzard becomes the child a couple never had and in the moment of final breakup, they face the absurd task of explaining it to him: "Blizzard/ Daddy needs you/ . . . the kind of love he wants Mommy/ doesn't have, Mommy's/ too ironic—Mommy wouldn't do/ the rhumba in the driveway."

OTHER MAJOR WORKS

NONFICTION: *Proofs and Theories: Essays on Poetry*, 1994.

BIBLIOGRAPHY

Bedient, Calvin. "Four American Poets." *Sewanee Review* 84 (Winter, 1976): 351-364. Bedient primarily reviews Glück's second book, *The House on Marshland*, though he discusses *Firstborn* (her first book) in passing, long enough to say that its poems "are brilliant but lack resonance." He identifies Glück's subject in the second book as "a romantic nostalgia for the absolute." He calls Glück's new poems "consummate."

Boruch, Marianne. "Comment: The Feel of a Century." *The American Poetry Review* 19 (July, 1990): 17-19. Reviewing *Ararat*, Glück's fifth book of poems, Boruch acknowledges that readers accustomed to Glück's earlier work might be surprised by the new poems. Boruch calls the change "both blinding and subtle." Glück's intention, in poems that are often vignettes of childhood experience, is clearly different. Her focus is death, solitude, and "the austerity of things."

Dobyns, Stephen. "Will You Listen for a Minute?" *The New York Times Book Review* 95 (September 2, 1990): 5. In his review of *Ararat*, Dobyns calls Glück's world one of "threat, competition, envy and grief." He sees the book almost as a single poem telling the story "of a wounding." Despite seeing the poems as relentless, often painful to read, Dobyns writes, "No American poet writes better than Louise Glück."

Dodd, Elizabeth Caroline. *The Veiled Mirror and the Woman Poet: H.D., Louise Bogan, Elizabeth Bishop, and Louise Glück*. Columbia: University of Missouri Press, 1992. An exploration of the lives and work of four women poets of the twentieth century. Dodd highlights the cultural forces in the personal and professional lives of these women that forced them to find a unique mode of expression in their poetry.

Hirsch, Edward. "The Watcher." *The American Poetry Review* 15 (November/December, 1986): 33-36. Hirsch's review of *The Triumph of Achilles*, Glück's fourth volume of poetry, focuses on the theme of the sleeper and the watcher. This theme introduces "oppositions" central to Glück's work: between waking and sleeping, consciousness and memory loss, present and future. Hirsch admires Glück's newly vulnerable voice, calling this book "her most moving collection of poems to date."

Upton, Lee. *The Muse of Abandonment*. Lewisburg, Pa.: Bucknell University Press, 1998. A critical and psychological analysis of the work of five American poets, including Louise Glück, that focuses on the issues of alienation, power, and identity. Includes bibliographical references and index.

Vendler, Helen. "Sociable Comets." *The New York Review of Books* 28 (July 16, 1981): 24-26. In a review of *Descending Figure*, Vendler compares Glück's writing to Sylvia Plath's. While Plath's rhythms are "spiky and hysterical," Glück's are "mesmeric, trancelike, almost posthumously gentle." Vendler identifies two strains in Glück's work, a "renunciatory one" of keeping by renouncing, and one of oppositions (dream versus finished art). Glück's "sternness" is much admired by Vendler.

Patricia Clark,
updated by Christine Steele and Sarah Hilbert

JOHANN WOLFGANG VON GOETHE

Born: Frankfurt am Main, Germany; August 28, 1749
Died: Weimar, Germany; March 22, 1832

PRINCIPAL POETRY

Neue Lieder, 1770 (*New Poems*, 1853)
Sesenheimer Liederbuch, 1775-1789, 1854 (*Sesenheim Songs*, 1853)
Römische Elegien, 1793 (*Roman Elegies*, 1876)
Reinecke Fuchs, 1794 (*Reynard the Fox*, 1855)
Epigramme: Venedig 1790, 1796 (*Venetian Epigrams*, 1853)
Xenien, 1796 (with Friedrich Schiller; *Epigrams*, 1853)
Hermann und Dorothea, 1797 (*Herman and Dorothea*, 1801)
Balladen, 1798 (with Schiller; *Ballads*, 1853)
Neueste Gedichte, 1800 (*Newest Poems*, 1853)
Gedichte, 1812, 1815 (2 volumes; *The Poems of Goethe*, 1853)

Sonette, 1819 (*Sonnets*, 1853)
Westöstlicher Divan, 1819 (*West-Eastern Divan*, 1877)

OTHER LITERARY FORMS

The unique significance of Johann Wolfgang von Goethe's contribution to German letters lies in the fact that his best creations provided models which influenced, stimulated, and gave direction to the subsequent evolution of literary endeavor in virtually every genre. Among more than twenty plays that he wrote throughout his career, several have special meaning for the history of German theater. *Götz von Berlichingen mit der eisernen Hand* (pb. 1773; *Götz von Berlichingen with the Iron Hand*, 1799) was a key production of the *Sturm und Drang* movement, mediating especially the influence of William Shakespeare upon later German dramatic form and substance. With *Iphigenie auf Tauris* (first version pr. 1779, second version pb. 1787; *Iphigenia in Tauris*, 1793), Goethe illustrated profoundly the ideals of perfected form and style, beauty of language, and humanistic education that characterized German literature of the classical period. His famous masterpiece *Faust* (published in three distinct versions, 1790, 1808, 1833; *The Tragedy of Faust*), with its carefully programmed depiction of the spiritual polarities that torment the individual, rapidly became the ultimate paradigm for the portrayal of modern man's fragmented nature.

Goethe's major narratives, including *Die Leiden des jungen Werthers* (1774; *The Sorrows of Young Werther*, 1779), *Wilhelm Meisters Lehrjahre* (1795-1796; *Wilhelm Meister's Apprenticeship*, 1825), *Die Wahlverwandtschaften* (1809; *Elective Affinities*, 1849), and *Wilhelm Meisters Wanderjahre: Oder, Die Entsagenden* (1821, 1829; *Wilhelm Meister's Travels*, 1827), are powerful illuminations of fundamental human problems. The monumental saga of Wilhelm Meister established the pattern for the German *Bildungsroman* of the nineteenth century, and it also had a substantial impact on Romantic novel theory.

A large portion of Goethe's oeuvre is nonfiction. He completed more than fourteen volumes of scientific and technical writings, the most important of which are *Versuch die Metamorphose der Pflanzen zu erklären* (1790; *Essays on the Metamorphosis of Plants*, 1863)

Johann Wolfgang von Goethe (Library of Congress)

and *Zur Farbenlehre* (1810; *Theory of Colors*, 1840). His historical accounts, specifically *Campagne in Frankreich, 1792* (1822; *Campaign in France in the Year 1792*, 1849) and *Die Belagerung von Mainz, 1793* (1822; *The Siege of Mainz in the Year 1793*, 1849), are vividly readable reports of firsthand experience. Writings that reveal a great deal about Goethe himself and his perception of his artistic calling are his autobiography, *Aus meinem Leben: Dichtung und Wahrheit* (1811-1814; *The Autobiography of Goethe*, 1824; better known as *Poetry and Truth from My Own Life*), and the many published volumes of his correspondence.

ACHIEVEMENTS

Johann Wolfgang von Goethe's overwhelming success as a lyricist was primarily the result of an extraordinary ability to interpret and transform direct, intimate experience and perception into vibrant imagery and symbols with universal import. In the process of overcoming the artificiality of Rococo literary tendencies, he created for the first time in modern German literature lyrics that were at once deeply personal, dynamically vital, and universally valid in what they communicated

to the reader. Beginning with the poems written to Friederike Brion, and continuing through the infinitely passionate affirmations of life composed in his old age, Goethe consistently employed his art in a manner that brushed away the superficial trappings and facades of existence to lay bare the essential spirit of man.

In his own time, Goethe became a world figure, although his immediate acclaim derived more from his early prose and dramatic works than from his lyrical writings. Even after the turn of the nineteenth century, he was still recognized most commonly as the author of *The Sorrows of Young Werther*, the novel that had made him instantly famous throughout Europe. Nevertheless, the simple power, clear, appealing language, and compelling melodiousness of his verse moved it inexorably into the canon of the German literary heritage. Much of his poetry was set to music by the great composers of his own and subsequent generations, and the continuing popularity of such creations as "Mailied" ("Maysong") and "Heidenröslein" ("Little Rose of the Heath") is attributable at least in part to the musical interpretations of Franz Schubert and others.

The real importance of Goethe's lyric legacy is perhaps best measured in terms of what it taught other writers. Goethe established new patterns and perspectives, opened new avenues of expression, set uncommon standards of artistic and aesthetic achievement, assimilated impulses from other traditions, and mastered diverse meters, techniques, and styles as had no other German poet before him. His influence was made productive by figures as different as Heinrich Heine and Eduard Mörike, Friedrich Hölderlin and Hugo von Hofmannsthal, Stefan George and Rainer Maria Rilke. As a mediator and motivator of the literary and intellectual currents of his time, as a creator of timeless poetic archetypes, as an interpreter of humanity within its living context, Goethe has earned an undisputed place among the greatest poets of world literature.

BIOGRAPHY

Three aspects of Johann Wolfgang von Goethe's childhood contributed substantially to his development as a literary artist. A sheltered existence, in which he spent long hours completely alone, fostered the growth of an active imagination. A complicated attachment to his sister Cornelia colored his perceptions of male-female relationships in ways that had a profound impact on the kinds of experience from which his works were generated. Finally, contrasts between his parents in temperament and cultural attitudes gave him an early awareness of the stark polarities of life upon which the central tensions of his major literary creations are based.

While studying law in Leipzig between 1765 and 1768, Goethe began to write poems and simple plays in the prevailing Anacreontic style. Although some of these productions relate to his infatuation with Kätchen Schönkopf, an innkeeper's daughter, they are more the product of his desire to become a part of the contemporary intellectual establishment than a direct outpouring of his own inner concerns. Among the important figures who influenced his education and thinking during this period were Christoph Martin Wieland, Christian Fürchtegott Gellert, and Adam Friedrich Oeser.

The experiences that resulted in Goethe's breakthrough to a distinctly individual and characteristic literary approach began when he entered the University of Strasbourg in 1770. Encounters with two very different people during the winter of 1770-1771 sharply changed his life. Johann Gottfried Herder introduced him to the concepts and ideals of the *Sturm und Drang* movement, providing him with new models in Homer and Shakespeare and moving him in the direction of less artificial modes of expression. Of equal consequence for the immediate evolution of his lyrics was an idyllic love affair with Friederike Brion that ended in a parting, the emotional implications of which marked his writings long afterward.

Upon his return to Frankfurt in 1771, Goethe was admitted to the bar. During the next five years, he fell in love with at least three different women. A painful involvement with Charlotte Buff, the fiancé of his friend Johann Christian Kestner, was followed by a brief attraction to Maximiliane Laroche. In April, 1775, he became engaged to Lili Schönemann, the daughter of a wealthy Frankfurt banker. Of the three relationships, only the interlude with Maximiliane Laroche failed to have a significant impact on his art. *The Sorrows of Young Werther* derived much of its substance from Goethe's experiences with Charlotte Buff, while the powerful internal conflicts generated by his feelings

for Lili gave rise to a small group of very interesting poems.

When the engagement to Lili became intolerable because of its demands and restrictions, Goethe went to Weimar, where he settled permanently in 1776. For the next ten years, he served as adviser to Carl August, duke of Weimar, whom he had met in Frankfurt in 1774. A broad variety of political and administrative responsibilities, ranging from supervision of road construction to irrigation, from military administration to direction of the court theater, left Goethe little time for serious literary endeavor. The resulting lack of personal fulfillment coupled with the prolonged frustrations of an unhappy platonic love affair with Charlotte von Stein caused him to flee to Italy in search of artistic and spiritual rejuvenation. While there, he perfected some of his most significant dramatic works.

The combination of exposure to Roman antiquity, classical Italian literature, and a uniquely satisfying love alliance with the simple, uneducated Christiane Vulpius formed the basis for renewed poetic productivity when Goethe returned to Weimar. In *Roman Elegies*, he glorified his intimate involvement with Christiane in imagery of the Eternal City. A second, more disappointing trip to Italy in 1790 provided the stimulus for the less well-known *Venetian Epigrams*.

In 1794, Goethe accepted Friedrich Schiller's invitation to collaborate in the publication of a new journal. There followed the most fruitful creative friendship in the history of German letters. Among the famous lyrical compositions that emerged from their relationship were the terse, pointed forms of the so-called Epigram War that they waged against their critics in 1796, and the masterful ballads that were written in friendly competition in 1797. Goethe regarded Schiller's death, in 1805, as one of the major personal tragedies of his own life.

The two specific experiences of later years which provided the direction for Goethe's last great productive period were exposure to the works of the fourteenth century Persian poet Hāfez and a journey to the places of his own childhood. While in Frankfurt in 1814, Goethe fell in love with Marianne von Willemer, the wife of a friend. The Hāfez-like dialogue of their intense spiritual communion is the focus of *West-Eastern Divan*, in which Goethe reached the culmination of his career as a lyricist. After it was published, only the final work on his immortal masterpiece *Faust* remained as a substantial task to be completed before his death.

ANALYSIS

In his famous letter to Johann Wolfgang von Goethe of August 23, 1794, Schiller identified the addressee as a writer who sought to derive the essence of an individual manifestation from the totality of natural phenomena. More particularly, he saw Goethe's goal as the literary definition of man in terms of the organization of the living cosmos to which he belongs. Only to the extent that Goethe viewed himself as representative of humanity in general does Schiller's assessment offer a valid approach to the understanding of his friend's lyric poetry. The focus of Goethe's verse is less humankind in the abstract than it is Goethe himself as a distinct, feeling, suffering, loving, sorrowing, longing being. From the very beginning, his works assumed the character of subjective poetic interpretations of his specific place in society, the implications of direct encounters with nature and culture, and the significance of concrete interpersonal relationships. He later described his creative writings as elements of a grand confession, pinpointing the fact that a major key to them lay in the penetration of his own existence.

Goethe's development as a lyric poet is clearly a continuum in which internal and external events and circumstances contribute to sometimes subtle, sometimes obvious modifications in approach, technique, and style. It is nevertheless possible to recognize a number of well-defined stages in his career that correspond to important changes in his outward situation and his connections with specific individuals. The predominant tendency of his growth was in the direction of a poetry that reaches outward to encompass an ever-broader spectrum of universal experience.

The Anacreontic creations of Goethe's student years in Leipzig are, for the most part, time-bound, occasional verse in which realistic emotion, feeling, and perception are subordinated to the artificial conventions and devices of the time. Typical motifs and themes of the collection New Poems are wine, Rococo eroticism, the game of love with its hidden dangers, stylized pastoral representations of nature, and a peculiarly playful association of love and death. Individual poems often move on the border between sensuality and morality, mirroring the prevailing social patterns. Especially characteristic is the employment of language that magnifies the separation of the world of the poem from experienced reality. In their affirmation of the elegant facades, the deliberate aloofness, the uncommitted playfulness of Rococo culture, these lyrics document Goethe's early artistic attitudes, even though they reveal little of his unique poetic gift.

STRASBOURG PERIOD

Under the influence of Herder in Strasbourg, Goethe began to move away from the decadent artificiality of his Leipzig songs. A new appreciation for the value of originality, immediacy of feeling, unmediated involvement in nature, and directness of approach is apparent in creations that are notable for their vivid imagery, plastic presentation of substance, force of expression, and power of language and rhythm.

Two types of utterance dominate the verse of this period. Highly personal outpourings of the soul, in which the representation of love is more passionate, serious, and captivating than in the Leipzig productions, are couched in formal stanzas that arose from Goethe's fondness for Friederike Brion. Free-verse poems that focus on *Sturm und Drang* ideals of individuality, genius, and creativity reflect the lyrical influence of Pindar and the dramatic legacy of Shakespeare in their form and tone. In what they reveal of Goethe's worldview, the love poetry and the philosophical reflections are deeply intertwined. Without love, Goethe's perception of life is empty; without the depth of awareness of individual responsibility in creation, love loses its strength and vitality. Love forms the basis for the experience of nature, while the external surroundings with their beauties, tensions, conflicts, and potential for joy give full meaning to love.

The most important new feature of the Strasbourg poetry is the visible emphasis on existential polarities in the description of the poet's relationship to people and things. Love and suffering, defiance and submission, danger and ecstasy are juxtaposed in the portrayal of a world of change, growth, and struggle. In endless variation, Goethe offers the intimate revelation of loneliness, longing, and lack of final fulfillment that are the fundamental ingredients of life viewed as a pattern of restless wanderings. The very acts of searching, striving, creating, and loving are communicated with an energy and a spiritual intensity that carries the reader along in a rush of emotional participation in universal experience.

THE LILI POEMS

Among Goethe's most interesting early works are the sometimes tender, often intensely painful lyric documents of his courtship of Lili Schönemann. Few in number, these writings illustrate the poet's cathartic use of his talent in a process of self-analysis and clarification of his position with respect to external events. At the same time, they underscore a growing tendency to come to grips with and master life through his art. Consisting of occasional pieces that are connected by recurring themes related to the tension between the attractions of love and the devastating torments of an accompanying loss of freedom, the Lili poems combine visions of joy with ironically biting yet dismal portraits of despair. A gem of the period is the famous "Auf dem See" ("On the Lake"), a vivid projection of both physical and spiritual flight from oppressive love, written in Switzerland, where Goethe had taken temporary refuge from the demands of life with Lili.

WEIMAR PERIOD

During Goethe's first years in Weimar, the frustrations of an unsatisfying association with Charlotte von Stein, the all-consuming responsibilities of the court, and his own inability to overcome completely the break with Lili contributed to his lyrics a new preoccupation with themes of melancholy resignation and self-denial. The heavy moods that characterize his works of this period inform short meditative poems as well as longer philosophical reflections, mournful love songs, and a few haunting ballads. Especially profound are two eight-line stanzas, each titled "Wanderers Nachtlied" ("Wanderer's Night Song"), in which the poet longs for and admonishes himself to courage, comfort, hope, belief, and patience. "Warum gabst du uns die tiefen Blicke?" ("Why Did You Give Us the Deep Glances?"), the most powerful of his poems to Charlotte von Stein, presents love as a mystical mystery. The two dramatic ballads, "Erlkönig" ("Elf King") and "Der Fischer" ("The Fisherman"), emphasize man's psychological subjection to the demonic power of his own impressions of nature.

ITALIAN JOURNEY

The experience of Italy completely changed Goethe's poetry. Among the most important developments which the journey inspired were the abandonment of suggestion and tone in favor of pure image, the transition from lyrical song to epic description, and the replacement of extended elaboration of worldview with terse epigrams and short didactic verse. During Goethe's classical period, his ballads achieved perfected form, while his depictions of nature attained their final goal in brightness and joyful plasticity. Where earlier poems feature colors that flow softly together, or points of color that invoke mood and an impression of the whole, the works created after 1790 are dominated by structure and the placement of objects in space. Ideas are presented in classical meters, especially hexameter, and as a result confessional poetry loses much of its melody.

ELEGIES, EPIGRAMS, AND BALLADS

Three groups of poems are particularly representative of the new directions in Goethe's lyrics: *Roman Elegies*, the epigrams, and the classical ballads. In their rich mural presentation of the poet's life in Rome, the *Roman Elegies* document the author's increasing tendency to circumscribe his own existence in verse, while their form, style, and combination of classical dignity with inner lightheartedness reflect the direct influence of Ovid, Catullus, and Propertius. The poems of *Venetian Epigrams* were similarly motivated by direct exposure to elements of classical Italian culture. They are especially notable for their rich imagery and their realism in depicting the emotional intensity of the poet's longing for Germany. In structure and style, they were models for the more famous epigrams written by Goethe and Schiller in 1796. Unlike the elegies and epigrams, Goethe's powerful ballads of 1797 arose out of materials that he had carried within him for a long time. The lyrical and melodic aspects that are absent from the other forms remain strong in rhythmic creations that emphasize passion and excitement while developing themes related to the classical ideal of pure humanity. Goethe viewed the ballad as an archetypal lyric form. His "Die Braut von Korinth" ("The Bride of Corinth") and "Der Gott und die Bajadere" ("The God and the Bayadere") are among the greatest German ballads ever written.

POETRY OF LATER YEARS

The erotic poetry of Goethe's old age had its beginnings in a group of sonnets that he wrote to Minchen Herzlieb in 1807. During the seven years that followed their creation, he wrote verse only occasionally. At last, however, the combination of stimuli from the deeply meaningful love affair with Marianne von Willemer and exposure to the works of Hăfez moved him to compose his greatest poetic accomplishment, *West-Eastern Divan*. In the framework of a fantasy journey of rejuvenation, Goethe entered a friendly competition with Hăfez while simultaneously declaring his own newly regained inner freedom. The central themes of the collection include longing for renewal of life, recognition of the need for spiritual transformation, coming to grips with Hăfez as a poet, love, wine, worldly experience, paradise, looking upward to God, and looking downward to the human condition. In some of the poems, Goethe returned to a kind of Anacreontic love poetry. In the heart of the cycle, he made of Hatem and Suleika timeless archetypal models for man and woman bound in the love relationship.

After *West-Eastern Divan*, Goethe wrote only a few poems of consequence. Among them, "Uworte, Orphisch" ("Primeval Words, Orphic"), in which he attempted to develop the core problems of human existence in five eight-line stanzas, and "Trilogie der Leidenschaft" ("Trilogy of Passion"), a tragic document of the state of being unfulfilled that was inspired by his final love experience, attained the power and stature of earlier lyrics. In these two creations, Goethe pin-pointed once more the essence of his own spiritual struggle between the light and the night of human existence.

"WELCOME AND FAREWELL"

While living in Strasbourg and courting Friederike Brion, Goethe created for the first time sensitive love poetry and descriptions of nature that exude the vitality of immediate experience. Perhaps the most characteristic of these works is the famous "Willkommen und Abschied" ("Welcome and Farewell"). The substance of the poem is a night ride through the countryside to Sesenheim and a joyful reunion with Friederike, followed by a painful scene of parting when morning comes. Significant elements include a new and plastic rendering of nature, fresh and captivating imagery, and melodic language that is alive with rhythm and motion.

A special power of observation is demonstrated in the poet's representation of that which cannot or can hardly be seen, yet the scenery is not portrayed merely for its own sake; rather, it is symbolic, for the uncanny aspects of the ride through the darkness are overcome by a courageous heart that is driven by love. Landscape and love thus become the two poles of the poem generating an inner tension that culminates in a peculiar equation of the beloved with the world as a whole. The portrayal of Friederike is especially notable for its psychological depth, while the expression of Goethe's own feelings of passion and eventual guilt lends the entire picture qualities of a universal experience of the heart.

"PROMETHEUS" AND "GANYMED"

Deeply personal yet broadly valid content is also typical of the so-called genius poems of Goethe's *Sturm und Drang* period. The intensity of emotional extremes is particularly vivid in the sharply contrasting hymns "Prometheus" and "Ganymed," which reflect the poles of Goethe's own spirit even more strongly than do his dramas. In depicting the two mythological titans, the poet concentrated on the creation of dynamic archetypes. "Prometheus" is a hard, even harsh portrait of modern man. The speaker of the lines is loveless and alone. Emphasis is placed on "I"; the focus is inward and limiting. In his defiant rejection of Father Zeus and the attendant process of self-deification, Prometheus champions the value of individuality and independence. Important themes of his declaration of emancipation from gods who are less powerful than man include faith in self, belief in the power of action, knowledge of the difficulty and questionability of life, and the divinity of man's creative nature. The tone of "Ganymed" is completely different. In the soft language of a prayer, the title figure proclaims his total submission to the will of the Father and his desire to return to the divine presence. A new side of Goethe's religiosity is revealed in the transformation of his sensitivity to nature into a longing for God's love. The central concern is no longer "I" but "you"; the direction is outward toward the removal of all boundaries in a coming together of deity and man. In the manner in which they play off the real world against the ideal realm, "Prometheus" and "Ganymed" are especially representative of the existential polarity lyrics that Goethe wrote during the pre-Weimar years.

ROMAN ELEGIES

Roman Elegies, the major lyrical product of Goethe's first Italian journey, comprises twenty confessional hexameter poems knit tightly together in a cycle that documents the poet's love for a fictitious young widow (Christiane Vulpius in Roman disguise). Two primary thematic configurations dominate creations that are among Goethe's most beautiful, most sensuously erotic works. The story of the tender love affair with Faustine, integrated into the Italian framework, is played off against the problems associated with renewal and adaptation of antiquity by the modern poet. Within this context, love becomes the key that makes entry into the Roman world possible.

Lively, direct reflection of the writer's enthusiasm for Rome sets the tone for the cycle. At the center of the introductory elegy, which forms an overture to the love adventure, there is a longing for the beloved who gives the city its true character. This yearning is followed in the next segment by a cynical glance backward at the boredom of Weimar society, which is in turn contrasted with the first report of the developing amorous relationship. An attempt to idealize the new situation, focusing specifically on the rapidity with which Faustine gives herself, leads to the elaboration of the described experiences in the light of ancient mythological gods. Through the creation of a new goddess, "Opportunity," as a symbol for the woman he loves, Goethe effectively connects the motifs of the sequence with classical themes. The fifth elegy provides the first high point in the poetic chain with its projection of the spirit of the author's existence in Rome as a blend of antiquity, art, and the erotic which mutually illuminate, intensify, and legitimize each other to yield a true "life of the gods." Other important sections of the cycle touch on questions of jealousy, gossip about the lovers, a Homeric idyll of the hearth, and a variety of encounters with Rome and its traditions, history, and secrets. Elegy thirteen is especially interesting for the tension that it establishes between the demands of lyric art and those of love for Faustine. A dialogue between Amor and the poet develops the idea that the former provides plenty of material for poetry but does not allow enough time for creative activity. Colorful pictures of the joys of love culminate in imagery of the couple's morning awakening together in bed. There is grand irony in the fact that the lament about not having enough time to write becomes a magnificent poem in itself.

Throughout the collection, love is the focus of polar conflicts on several levels. The intense need for unity with Faustine in the physical alliance is juxtaposed to the act of self-denial that provides the quiet enjoyment of pure observation and contemplation in the creative process. Within the social frame, the fulfilled love that is sought and attained cannot be brought into harmony with reality. Fear of discovery necessitates disguise of the beloved, deception of relatives, secret meetings, and isolation from the surrounding world. In the final elegy, however, Goethe is forced to conclude that the beautiful secret of his love cannot remain hidden for long because he himself is incapable of remaining quiet about it. The result is a many-faceted revelation of love as a timeless human situation.

BALLADS

Careful examination of Goethe's most representative ballads reveals a clear progression from verse stories in which man is at the mercy of a potentially destructive, magically powerful natural world to lyric accounts that proclaim the supremacy of the human spirit over the restrictions of mortal experience. Influenced by the popular pattern established in Gottfried August Bürger's "Lenore," Goethe's early ballads such as "Elf King" and "The Fisherman" describe the fatal resolution of inner conflicts in terms of individual surrender to seductive impressions of external reality. Later, philosophically more complex works ("The Bride of Corinth" and "The God and the Bayadere") portray death as a process of transcendence that purifies the individual while preparing the soul for joyful fulfillment on a higher plane of existence.

"Elf King" is somewhat similar to "Welcome and Farewell" in its representation of a night landscape's malevolent lure as it impresses its terror on the minds of those who encounter it. The substance of the narrative is the homeward night ride of a father and son; the darkness gives uncanny form and life to things that would appear harmless by day. The boy, who is ill with fever, believes that he hears the elf king enticing him, describes what he sees and feels to his father, and dies of fright when the older man's reassurances fail to convince him of the falseness of his delirious vision. Rhythmic language that conveys the beat of the horse's hooves through the countryside, immediacy created by dialogues involving the child, the phantom elf king, and the father, and moods evoked by contrasts between light and shadow, intimate fear and pale comfortings, all contribute to the psychological intensity of a presentation in which the poet attempted to find accurate formulation for the fantastic, indefinite problem of human destiny.

In "The God and the Bayadere," a confrontation with death is handled much differently. The legend of the prostitute who spends a night providing the pleasures of love to the god Siva in human form, only to awaken and find him dead on the bed, is a forceful lyrical statement about the redeeming properties of love. Denied her widow's rights because of her way of life, the bayadere makes good her claim by springing into the flames that arise from the funeral pyre. In response to this act of purification, Siva accepts the woman as his bride. Strong Christian overtones exist in the first stanza's emphasis on the god's humaneness and in the obvious parallels to the relationship between Christ and Mary Magdalene. The poem's thrust is that the divine spark is present even in a degraded individual and that even the lowest human being can be transformed and exalted through the cleansing influence of pure love.

WEST-EASTERN DIVAN

A major key to the literary productions of Goethe's old age is found in the notion of personal fulfillment through direct sensual and spiritual enjoyment of life. The implications of that approach to experience are most thoroughly and splendidly elaborated in *West-Eastern Divan*, a carefully constructed collection of verse that attempts to blend and join the artistic legacies of East and West in a book about love in all its manifestations. Both the pinnacle of Goethe's lyric œuvre and one of the most difficult of his creative works, *West-Eastern Divan* is a conscious declaration of the validity of man's unending search for joy in the world.

As revealed in the opening poem, the focal metaphor of the volume is the Hegira, which Goethe uses as an image for his flight from oppressive circumstances into the ideal realm of foreign art. Two central relationships dominate the twelve sections of his dream journey to the Orient. On one level, the individual poems are portions of a playful fantasy dialogue between Goethe and his Eastern counterpart Hăfez. The object of their interchange is a friendly competition in which the Western poet seeks to match the achievements of a revered predecessor. Conversations between two lovers, Hatem and Suleika, develop the second complex of themes, derived from elements of the love experience shared by Goethe and Marianne von Willemer.

"Buch des Sängers" ("Book of the Singer"), the most important of the first six cycles, sets the tone for the entire work. In the famous poem "Selige Sehnsucht" ("Blessed Longing"), Goethe explored the mystery of how one gains strength through the transformation that occurs as a result of sacrifice. Borrowing from a ghazel by Hăfez the motif of the soul that is consumed in the fire of love like a moth in a candle flame, he created a profound comment on the necessity of metamorphosis to eternal progress. The uniting of two people in love to generate the greatest possible joy is made to stand for the longing of the soul to be freed from the bonds of individuality through union with the infinite. The antithesis of "Blessed Longing" is presented in "Wiederfinden" ("Reunion"), a creation of extremely vivid imagery from "Buch Suleika" ("Book of Suleika"), the eighth and most beautiful section of *West-Eastern Divan*. Based on Goethe's separation from Marianne and their coming together again, the poem develops the idea that parting and rediscovery are the essence of universal existence. In a uniquely powerful projection of creation as division of light from darkness and their recombination in color, Goethe produced new and exciting symbols for love's power, rendered in lines that form a high point in German lyric poetry.

OTHER MAJOR WORKS

LONG FICTION: *Die Leiden des jungen Werthers*, 1774 (*The Sorrows of Young Werther*, 1779); *Wilhelm Meisters Lehrjahre*, 1795-1796 (4 volumes; *Wilhelm Meister's Apprenticeship*, 1825); *Die Wahlverwandtschaften*, 1809 (*Elective Affinities*, 1849); *Wilhelm Meisters Wanderjahre: Oder, Die Entsagenden*, 1821, 1829 (2 volumes; *Wilhelm Meister's Travels*, 1827).

SHORT FICTION: *Unterhaltungen deutscher Ausgewanderten*, 1795 (*Conversations of German Emigrants*, 1854); *Novelle*, 1826 (*Novel*, 1837).

PLAYS: *Die Laune des Verliebten*, wr. 1767, pr. 1779 (*The Wayward Lover*, 1879); *Die Mitschuldigen*, first version wr. 1768, pr. 1780, second version wr. 1769, pr. 1777 (*The Fellow-Culprits*, 1879); *Götz von Berlichingen mit der eisernen Hand*, pb. 1773 (*Götz von Berlichingen with the Iron Hand*, 1799); *Götter, Helden und Wieland*, pb. 1774; *Clavigo*, pr., pb. 1774 (English translation, 1798, 1897); *Erwin und Elmire*, pr., pb. 1775 (libretto; music by Duchess Anna Amalia of Saxe-Weimar); *Stella*, first version pr., pb. 1776, second version pr. 1806 (English translation, 1798); *Claudine von Villa Bella*, first version pb. 1776, pr. 1779, second version pb. 1788 (libretto); *Die Geschwister*, pr. 1776; *Iphigenie auf Tauris*, first version pr. 1779, second version pb. 1787 (*Iphigenia in Tauris*, 1793); *Jery und Bätely*, pr. 1780 (libretto); *Die Fischerin*, pr., pb. 1782 (libretto; music by Corona Schröter; *The Fisherwoman*, 1899); *Scherz, List und Rache*, pr. 1784 (libretto); *Der Triumph der Empfindsamkeit*, pb. 1787; *Egmont*, pb. 1788 (English translation, 1837); *Torquato Tasso*, pb. 1790 (English translation, 1827); *Faust: Ein Fragment*, pb. 1790 (*Faust: A Fragment*, 1980); *Der Gross-Cophta*, pr., pb. 1792; *Der Bürgergeneral*, pr., pb. 1793; *Was wir bringen*, pr., pb. 1802; *Die natürliche Tochter*, pr. 1803 (*The Natural Daughter*, 1885); *Faust: Eine Tragödie*, pb. 1808 (*The Tragedy of Faust*, 1823); *Pandora*, pb. 1808; *Die Wette*, wr. 1812, pb. 1837; *Des Epimenides Erwachen*, pb. 1814; *Faust: Eine Tragödie, zweiter Teil*, pb. 1833 (*The Tragedy of Faust, Part Two*, 1838).

NONFICTION: *Von deutscher Baukunst*, 1773 (*On German Architecture*, 1921); *Versuch die Metamorphose der Pflanzen zu erklären*, 1790 (*Essays on the Metamorphosis of Plants*, 1863); *Beyträge zur Optik*, 1791, 1792 (2 volumes); *Winckelmann und sein Jahrhundert*, 1805; *Zur Farbenlehre*, 1810 (*Theory of Colors*, 1840); *Aus meinem Leben: Dichtung und Wahrheit*, 1811-1814 (3 volumes; *The Autobiography of Goethe*, 1824; better known as *Poetry and Truth from My Own Life*); *Italienische Reise*, 1816, 1817 (2 volumes; *Travels in Italy*, 1883); *Zur Naturwissenschaft überhaupt, besonders zur Morphologie*, 1817, 1824 (2 volumes); *Campagne in Frankreich, 1792*, 1822 (*Campaign in France in the Year 1792*, 1849);

Die Belagerung von Mainz, 1793, 1822 (*The Siege of Mainz in the Year 1793*, 1849); *Essays on Art*, 1845; *Goethe's Literary Essays*, 1921; *Goethe on Art*, 1980.

MISCELLANEOUS: *Works*, 1848-1890 (14 volumes); *Goethes Werke*, 1887-1919 (133 volumes).

BIBLIOGRAPHY

Atkins, Stuart. *Essays on Goethe*. Edited by Jane K. Brown and Thomas P. Same. Columbia, S.C.: Camden House, 1995. A collection of seventeen essays by an eminent Goethe scholar, concentrating on the defense and clarification of the term "classicism" with regard to Goethe. Other subjects include Goethe's letters and the final scene of *Faust*.

Boyle, Nicholas. *The Poetry of Desire*. Vol. 1 in *Goethe: The Poet and the Age*. Oxford, England: Oxford University Press, 1991. The first volume of an acclaimed study of Goethe's life and work. Readings and interpretations of Goethe's writings through 1790.

_____. *Revolution and Renunciation, 1790-1803*. Vol. 2 in *Goethe: The Poet and the Age*. Oxford: Oxford University Press, 2000. A study of the most eventful years of Goethe's life. The emphasis is on the transformative influence of the French Revolution and of the German philosophical revolution on Goethe. Details Goethe's relationship with literary giant Friedrich Schiller and with the mother of his son, Christian Vulpius.

Croce, Benedetto. *Goethe*. Translated by Emily Anderson. Port Washington, N.Y.: Kennikat Press, 1970. Complete biography of Goethe by the premier philosopher of modern Italy.

Fairley, Barker. *A Study of Goethe*. Oxford, England: Clarendon Press, 1969. Biography of Goethe and a critical study of his works. Includes bibliographic references.

Gray, Ronald D. *Goethe*. London: Cambridge University Press, 1967. An introductory critical interpretation of Goethe's poetry and other works. Includes a bibliography.

Wagner, Irmgard. *Goethe*. New York: Twayne Publishers, 1999. Argues Goethe's contemporaneity and sees his works as reflecting a life shaped by the crises and developments of a changing epoch. Emphasis on Goethe as a man of imagination, especially as a poet. Examines *Faust* as the culmination of Goethe's life work. Chronology and bibliography.

Williams, John R. *The Life of Goethe: A Critical Biography*. Malden, Mass.: Blackwell Publishers, 1998. An extensive examination of the major writings, including lyric poems, drama, and novels. Also includes a discussion of epigrams, aphorisms, satires, libretti, and masquerades. Discusses Goethe's personal and literary reactions to historical events in Germany, his relationship with leading public figures of the day, and his influence on contemporary culture. Suggests that Goethe's creative work follows a distinct biographical profile. Large bibliography.

Lowell A. Bangerter;
bibliography updated by Margaret Boe Birns

ALBERT GOLDBARTH

Born: Chicago, Illinois; January 31, 1948

PRINCIPAL POETRY

Under Cover, 1973
Coprolites, 1973
Jan. 31, 1974
Keeping, 1975
Comings Back: A Sequence of Poems, 1976
A Year of Happy: Poems, 1976
Curves: Overlapping Narratives, 1976
Different Fleshes, 1979
Ink, Blood, Semen, 1980
The Smuggler's Handbook, 1980
Eurekas, 1981
Who Gathered and Whispered Behind Me, 1981
Faith, 1981
Original Light: New and Selected Poems, 1973-1983, 1983
Arts and Sciences: Poems, 1986
Popular Culture, 1990
Heaven and Earth—A Cosmology: Poems, 1991
The Gods, 1993
Across the Layers: Poems Old and New, 1993
Adventures in Ancient Egypt: Poems, 1996
A Lineage of Ragpickers, Songpluckers, Elegiasts, and Jewelers: Selected Poems of Jewish Family Life, 1973-1995, 1996
Beyond: New Poems, 1998
Troubled Lovers in History: A Sequence of Poems, 1999
Saving Lives: Poems, 2001

OTHER LITERARY FORMS

Albert Goldbarth brings the qualities of his poetry to his essays: They are reflective; poignant; both broadly philosophical and specifically autobiographical; learned in the physical, biological, and social sciences, as well as popular culture; cyclical and associational in form. Like his poems, these essays have individually won awards. His essay collections include *A Sympathy of Souls: Essays* (1990), *Great Topics of the World: Essays* (1994), *Dark Waves and Light Matter: Essays* (1999), and *Many Circles: New and Selected Essays* (2001).

ACHIEVEMENTS

Almost as important as Albert Goldbarth's various literary prizes for his poetry, including a nomination for National Book Award for *Jan. 31* and winning the National Book Critics Circle Award for *Heaven and Earth—A Cosmology: Poems*, is his representation in anthologies and standard reference works. His poetry is included in the prestigious anthologies *The Generation of 2000: Contemporary American Poets* (1984), *New American Poets of the 1990's* (1991), *Jewish American Poetry: Poems, Commentary, and Reflections* (2000), and several volumes in the annual *Best American Poetry* series, from 1993 onward.

BIOGRAPHY

Many details of Albert Goldbarth's life are referred to or featured in several poems or titles of his books. Indeed, the very young Goldbarth in his cowboy suit appears on the front cover of his chapbook *Keeping* (1975), while Goldbarth's signature is lithographically reproduced in the long verse epistle "Letter to Tony" in *Comings Back: A Sequence of Poems* (1976).

Born and raised in Chicago, Goldbarth was impressed by its cold climate and sometimes seedy urban environment. While growing up, the youth learned Yiddish from his first-generation American parents, as well as Hebrew from his not always diligent attention at Hebrew school. Both in youth and maturity, Goldbarth was impressed by the courage, industry, care, and love of his immigrant grandparents — Albert and Nettie Goldbarth, and especially Louis ("Louie") and Rose ("Rosie") Seligman. Also important were the Jewish culture and heritage transmitted by grandparents and parents. The extended family—aunts Regina, Sally, Hannah, Elena, Ceclia, Tillie, Dinah; uncles Lou, Abe, Morrie; cousins Alice, Izzy, Rebecca, DeeDee—have all figured meaningfully in Goldbarth's life and poems.

The hard work of his father, Irving ("Daddy Irv"), as an "insurance peddler," and of his mother, Fannie, who cared for not only the young Goldbarth but also his sister, Livia, plus the warmth of the household, helped foster Albert's ("Albie's") education, including his B.A. from the University of Illinois in Chicago in 1969. After completing an M.F.A. in poetry at the prestigious program at the University of Iowa in 1971, Goldbarth returned to Chicago and started a teaching career, ranging from Central YMCA Community College, Chicago; University of Utah, Salt Lake City; Cornell University, Ithaca, New York; and University of Texas, Austin to Wichita State University in Kansas, and the post there of distinguished professor of humanities. During his teaching career, Goldbarth has been moved by his students' lives outside the classroom, such as their deprived backgrounds or sometimes surprising off-campus jobs, such as that of exotic dancer.

From his youth, Goldbarth was interested in popular culture, such as comic books and science fiction, and involved in romance. Friendships, including those with fellow writers as Tony Sorbin and John Crisp, have been crucial in the adult life of Goldbarth, as have illnesses: Goldbarth's own high cholesterol and back trouble, sister Livia's cancer concerns, and especially the illnesses and deaths of Goldbarth's parents.

ANALYSIS

Partly following the New Formalist movement in modern American poetry, with sonnets, a sestina, and many poems in regular unrhymed stanzas in his oeuvre, Albert Goldbarth also has allegiances with modern confessional poets, making his life particularly important in its relation to several poems.

While Goldbarth warns in a few poems against too strictly literal an autobiographical reading of his poetry, he is explicit and specific in his poems about himself at all periods of his life, from youth to late middle age; his friends at the various periods of his life; and his various paramours, including their names. Overall, despite its wit (including puns and abundant, perceptive figurative language), humor, range both in language and subject matter, and liveliness, the poetry has an elegiac feeling because of the many poems that deal with the romantic or marital troubles and divorce of the author or of his friends, and especially illness and death among Goldbarth's loved ones, particularly his father and mother.

ARCHAEOLOGY AND PREHISTORY

Many of Goldbarth's poems deal with archaeology, prehistory, paleontology, and diverse associated subjects and themes. Goldbarth's skill at finding and making connections among apparently disparate things is evi-

Albert Goldbarth (© Betty Gottlieb)

denced in "Dialogue: Johann Joachim Wincklemann and Joseph Busch," intercutting monologues of the real eighteenth century German father of archaeology and an imagined twentieth century elderly German art restorer; ironically, while Wincklemann helps to re-create the past, Busch witnesses the reduction of Dresden to an archaeological ruin in the Allies' World War II fire-bombing, which seems repayment for the medieval massacre of Jews there, prefiguring the systematic German holocaust of them.

In "Ursus: Speech & Text," prehistoric archaeology is the subject, as often is the case in Goldbarth's poetry; the poem deals with the relationship between animals and humans through description of the various conceptions of bears, from the fearsome through Winnie the Pooh, as well as their manifestations in cave art, the visual arts being another of Goldbarth's recurrent interests. "The Story of Civilization" begins with the lack of communication between individuals in prehistory, Neanderthals, resulting in the killing of one by another with a dark sack, with killing "pervasive as weather." It moves through the development of agriculture, architecture, and extended lifespans, including Goldbarth's Grandpa Louie. It ends, in Goldbarth's typical circular, spiral form, with the communication through the modern invention, the telephone, to Goldbarth of the death of Grandpa Louie, who for a living carried sacks and now, with an irony emphasized by Goldbarth's figure of speech chiasmus, must be carried in Goldbarth's memory like a sack, almost empty but not devoid of the spark of Louie's life story.

Finally, "Khirbet Shema," based on the resemblance in photographs of the toppled columns of an ancient synagogue of the year 400 C.E. and unearthed pottery beads in a close-up, interrelates science, in an application of Albert Einstein's ideas about light and relativity (including the ending pun on whether a female synagogue attendee's cry on Yom Kippur is penitential or joyous being "relative"); Renaissance art, in the speaker's perception of an inversion of the theory of perspective, something farther away, the ancient synagogue, getting larger rather than smaller in his mind and mind's eye; and the Jewish culture connecting Einstein, the synagogue, Yom Kippur, and the female worshiper wearing the beads.

ROMANTIC LOVE

Facets of the romantic relationship are the focus of many of Goldbarth's poems. "Song for Longing" opens with anaphora, a recurrent stylistic device in Goldbarth's poetry—"Now you will," "Now we will," "Now anybody who"—tied to the poem's recurrent image, metaphor. He also uses synecdoche with "tongue," which comes in the poem to represent not only erotic contact between the lovers but also communication, language, and naming as related to romance. Both "Dynamics of Garbling" and "Codes" deal with the problems of communication in the romantic relationship, symbolized, respectively, by problems in the telephone line or the need to bypass through silent physical contact the world's distracting surrealistic phenomena and linguistic expressions like "the stork/ brings them."

Both "The World of Expectations" and "The Accountings," utilizing Goldbarth's repeated structural device of an incomplete beginning statement or reference, completed only at poem's end, deal, appropriate to their suspended structure, with adolescent erotic yearning. The former poem contrasts past and present, with at least one of the adolescents having fulfilled the yearning but now being divorced; the latter poem's same temporal contrast has the adult Goldbarth wanting to love of all those he has ever loved in his past, including his teachers and parents.

"Ellbee Novelty Company, Inc.," which profusely details all the popular-culture novelty items shown by Louie Berkie (after whom the company is named) in his warehouse tour, contrasts the plethora with the separate nocturnal lonelinesses of the owner and his cashier, Rosie. The joyousness in the poem's allusion to Christopher Smart's exuberant *Jubilate Agno* (1939) through the recurrent anaphora contrasts the implied sadness of Berkie's and Rosie's nights alone, without romantic love or lover.

RELIGION AND THE SUPERNATURAL

A repeated constellation of subjects in Goldbarth's poetry is religion, worship, the afterlife, the question of the existence of the supernatural, and the relationship between the supernatural and the material world, suggested in part by some of the titles of Goldbarth's collections: *Faith* (1981), *Heaven and Earth—A Cosmology, The Gods* (1993), and *Beyond* (1998). In *Heaven and*

Earth's "An Explanation," the speaker relays the report of an ecstatic female worshiper's speaking in tongues in a small rural charismatic church and then utterly disappearing, which he both implicitly and explicitly relates to an epileptic seizure witnessed in eighth grade (a transit to an ecstatic state) requiring the teacher's placing a spoon in the sufferer's mouth. The speaker asserts that the female worshiper was the universe's tongue, related to her speaking in tongues, which may have been swallowed by the universe itself. All of this is behind the explanation of the poem's title, of why the speaker threw himself across his lover when during sleep she began talking, in dream "tongues": He wanted to prevent her disappearance, which relates dreaming and sleep to a supernatural realm, along with Goldbarth's recurrent concerns about the disappearing and distancing in human life, relationships, and death.

In "A Pantheon," a Victorian world traveler encounters a variety of cultures and their deities—Egyptian gods, the God of Judaism, the Greek gods, Native American gods—which the speaker multiplies to the multitude of external entities that heterogeneous individuals and groups have imagined to heighten feeling, explain, comfort, or justify. In the three-part "Ancient Semitic Rituals for the Dead," composed of one section of poetry, one of drama, and one of prose, the speaker's drinking too much at a bar in section 1 is revealed to be a bolstering of his courage to visit his father's grave, with the distinctively Jewish wine Mogen David. At this visit, in section 2, the son, "Albie" (Goldbarth's nickname used by his family, as relayed in several poems) does commune with the spirit of his father, which helps reconcile the son to father, the father's death, and his own life.

Finally, "The Two Domains," representative of Goldbarth's fine extended-length poems, deals with the hiring by the female owner of a novelty catalog and warehouse of a male medium able to commune with and allay unhappy supernatural spirits, which are apparently disrupting her business. In this forty-five-page mixture of verse and prose, with the prose fiction components of plot and narrative are combined popular culture, romantic love, and the supernatural. The medium discovers that the unhappy spirits are frustrated lovers on the brink of fulfillment, and when he and the pragmatic business owner, representatives of the two domains of the other-

worldly and worldly, make love, they overcome the dead lovers' impeded act and in several senses lay the ghosts to rest.

ART AND COLLECTING

The visual arts—painting, painters, architecture, objets d'art—and collecting are recurrent subjects in Goldbarth's poetry. For example, the extended-length poem "Radio Pope" deals with the relationship between a father and a young daughter affected by the father's mania for collecting old radios, causing the nickname of the poem's title; the radios symbolize the communication, or lack of it, between parent and child. A key impulse behind both collecting and art, as suggested in "Acquisitions," is the assertion of self, the idea that "this is mine." The poem also contains Goldbarth's recurrent metapoetic comment on poetry (in this instance, the contrasting styles and perspectives of Elizabeth Bishop and Kenneth Koch) and scatology (a mentally disturbed modern painter uses his own excrement—symbolizing the idea that "this is mine"—for his medium).

The poems "In the Bar in the Bar" and "1880" show how the recurrent concept of layering in Goldbarth's poetry—related to archaeology, family, and time (one civilization or generation on top of another)—coincides with the poet's interest in art and science in the topic of the X-raying of paintings and the overpainting by painters of one work by another. In the former poem, the very different underpainting covered by *Portrait of Edward VI of England* suggests how an opposite self or perspective is inside many people, as in the case of the Goldbarthian speaker and his bride uttering "yes, yes" to the marriage vows, while already beginning to change to "no, no."

In the latter poem, a mysterious figure intruding in Pierre-Auguste Renoir's *At the Concert*, brought out by infrared examination, symbolizes or parallels the intrusion or beginning intrusion of the twentieth century—the telephone, Albert Einstein, Mark Rothko, Jackson Pollock—into the sedate Victorian world of the painting and of Renoir himself. The style of the poem, with its disjointed, intervallic, intruding stanzas of italics (with parts of some individual words broken off or fragmented from one italicized stanza to the next) of a conversation seemingly independent of the poem, helps convey the theme of fragmentation, as does the fragmenting pun on "brush" (the painter's brush or brushwork, the social brush or contact with another person) at the poem's end.

OTHER MAJOR WORKS

LONG FICTION: *Marriage and Other Science Fiction*, 1994.

NONFICTION: *A Sympathy of Souls: Essays*, 1990; *Great Topics of the World: Essays*, 1994; *Dark Waves and Light Matter: Essays*, 1999; *Many Circles: New and Selected Essays*, 2001.

EDITED TEXT: *Every Pleasure: The "Seneca Review" Long Poem Anthology*, 1979.

BIBLIOGRAPHY

Altieri, Charles. *Self and Sensibility in Contemporary American Poetry*. Cambridge, England: Cambridge University Press, 1984. An analysis of Goldbarth's "Song in One Serving" as poetry that combines a sense of lyric scene as well as self-consciousness, plus Goldbarth's management of connections within the work.

Baker, David. *Heresy and the Ideal: On Contemporary Poetry*. Fayetteville: University of Arkansas Press, 2000. Chapter 3, "Culture, Inclusion, Craft: On Albert Goldbarth, Jane Kenyon, Li-Young Lee, Wayne Koestenbaum, David Wojahn, Alice Fulton," aligns Goldbarth with this group; chapter 16, "Hieroglyphs of Erasure: Albert Goldbarth," argues that despite the apparent packing of Goldbarth's poetry with philosophy, information, and details, its ultimate meaning is the erasure of these.

Keller, Lynn. "The Twentieth-Century Long Poem." In *The Columbia History of American Poetry*, edited by Jay Parini and Brett Millier. New York: Columbia University Press, 1993. Uses Goldbarth's "novel/poem" *Different Fleshes* to exemplify the modern poet's use in an extended-length poem of varied lyric sequences in "nonlinear explorations of imagined history."

Logan, William. *Reputations of the Tongue: On Poets and Poetry*. Gainesville: University Press of Florida, 1999. Features a review, in chapter 9, "Chronicle at Home and Abroad," of Goldbarth's *Original Light*: "Many poets know one big thing, but Albert Goldbarth knows many little things."

Vendler, Helen. "Imagination Pressing Back: Frank Bidart, Albert Goldbarth, and Amy Clampitt." In *Soul Says: On Recent Poetry*. Cambridge, Mass.: Harvard University Press, 1995. Stresses the accomplishment of the faculty of imagination in these poets, and Goldbarth's omnivorous inclusion of history, details, and various branches of knowledge in his poetry.

Norman Prinsky

OLIVER GOLDSMITH

Born: Pallas, County Langford(?), Ireland; November 10, 1728 or 1730
Died: London, England; April 4, 1774

PRINCIPAL POETRY

"The Logicians Refuted," 1759
"An Elegy on the Glory of Her Sex: Mrs. Mary Blaize," 1759
The Traveller: Or, A Prospect of Society, 1764
"Edwin and Angelina," 1765
"An Elegy on the Death of a Mad Dog," 1766
The Deserted Village, 1770
"Threnodia Augustalis," 1772
"Retaliation," 1774
"The Captivity: An Oratoria," 1820 (wr. 1764)

OTHER LITERARY FORMS

Like Joseph Addison, Samuel Johnson, and other eighteenth century writers, Oliver Goldsmith did not confine himself to one genre. Besides poetry, Goldsmith wrote two comedies, a novel, periodical essays, a collection of letters, popular histories of England and Rome, and several biographical sketches. By the 1760's, literature had become a commercial enterprise, and successful authorship meant writing what the public would read. Goldsmith could write fluently on a wide variety of subjects, even when his knowledge of some of them was superficial. He was especially skillful at adapting another's work to his audience's interests: Many of his short poems are imitations of foreign models, and the collection of fictional letters, *The Citizen of the World* (1762), is an adaptation of Montesquieu's *Persian Letters* (1721). Both his collected works and his letters are available in modern editions.

ACHIEVEMENTS

Oliver Goldsmith used his fluent pen to write himself out of obscurity. Like many other eighteenth century writers, he progressed from hackwork to authorship—and along the way did something to raise the level of hackwork. His life and career demonstrate the transition that occurred in British literature as commercial publishing gradually replaced patronage as the chief support of writers.

Goldsmith is both one of the most characteristic and one of the best English writers of the late 1700's. His *The Vicar of Wakefield* (1766), for example, both reflects the taste of the period for sentimental fiction and maintains itself as a minor classic today. His *The Deserted Village* is likewise a typical pastoral of the period and a landmark of English poetry. In his own time, Goldsmith reflected an important new sensibility in English culture: an awareness of Britain as part of a European community with which it shared problems and attitudes. This new view is evident in *The Traveller*, which contrasts the great states of Europe in order to understand the character of each nation more than to trumpet British superiority; this cosmopolitan spirit also shapes the letters of *The Citizen of the World*, which analyze English society through a Chinese visitor's eyes.

Even without a historical interest, many readers still find Goldsmith enjoyable for his style and his comedy. Goldsmith is one of the masters of the middle style; no reader has to work hard at his informal, almost conversational prose and poetry. Although his pieces are often filled with social observation, Goldsmith's human and humorous observations of people make his work accessible and pleasurable even to those who never met a lord or made the Grand Tour. His characters and perceptions are rooted in universal experiences.

BIOGRAPHY

Although David Garrick's epigrammatic remark that Oliver Goldsmith "wrote like an angel, but talk's like poor Poll" exaggerates his social awkwardness, it does

Oliver Goldsmith (Library of Congress)

contain an important indicator. Before Goldsmith discovered authorship, his life had been all trial and mostly error.

As the second son of an Irish clergyman, Goldsmith could not look forward to independent means; most of the family resources went to increase the dowry of a sister. Nature seems to have been equally parsimonious toward him: Childhood disease, natural indolence, and physical ungainliness left him prey to his classmates' teasing and his schoolmasters' scorn. His later days at Trinity College in Dublin were no better: He got into trouble with administrators, ran away, but returned to earn a low bachelor's degree in 1749.

For the next ten years Goldsmith seemed at a complete loss for direction. He toyed with the idea of running away to America, but applied instead for ordination in the Church of England. Emphatically rejected by the local bishop, Goldsmith went in 1751 to study medicine at the University of Leyden. After mild attention to his studies, Goldsmith toured Europe, sometimes with the dignity of a "foreign student" and sometimes with the poverty of a wandering minstrel. Returning to London in 1756, he successively failed at teaching and at getting a medical appointment in the Navy. He found work as a proofreader for the novelist-printer Samuel Richardson and as a hack writer for the bookseller Griffiths. To raise money Goldsmith began writing *An Enquiry into the Present State of Polite Learning in Europe*, for which he found a publisher in 1759.

This lively account of the contemporary intellectual world won him attention from two literary entrepreneurs, Tobias Smollett and John Newbery, who gave him regular work on a variety of periodical papers writing essays, biographies, and a few poems. These labors brought him important acquaintances and the opportunity for greater success.

The year 1764 was a watershed for Goldsmith. First, he was admitted to the "Literary Club" which brought together such luminaries as the actor David Garrick, the painter Joshua Reynolds, the politician Edmund Burke, and the writer Samuel Johnson. Second, he published *The Traveller: Or, A Prospect of Society*, which established him in the public's mind as one of the foremost poets of the day.

The success of *The Traveller* brought Goldsmith the first substantial income of his career, but, since he never was capable of careful financial management, he continued to do piecework as well as to engage in serious projects. The last decade of his life saw a remarkable output of rapidly written general works, haphazardly compiled anthologies, as well as his best poem, a novel, and two plays. Whatever effort he put into a project, his name on the title page enormously increased chances for a brisk sale.

Goldsmith wrote practically until the hour of his death. His last effort was the poem "Retaliation," a verse response to Garrick's teasing epigram. Goldsmith died on April 4, 1774, the victim of both a fever and the remedy prescribed to cure it.

ANALYSIS

Eighteenth century poets viewed themselves primarily in relation to their audience. They acted as intermediaries between the audience and some higher truth: divine providence, the majesty of state, or the ideal world described by art. In his verse Oliver Goldsmith made two self-appointments: first as arbiter of literature for a society that had largely lost its ability to appreciate poetry, and second as commentator upon social changes.

Arbitrating poetic ideals and offering social commentary were not separate activities, Goldsmith thought, because readers who could not discriminate real feeling in poetry were likewise not likely to observe the world around them accurately. Again, like other eighteenth century poets, Goldsmith expressed his concerns in both comic and serious works. The comic efforts tease readers back from excesses; the serious ones urge them to return to the norm. These trends are clearest in Goldsmith's best poems, two mock elegies, the didactic *The Traveller* and the pastoral *The Deserted Village*.

COMIC ELEGIES

Thomas Gray's "Elegy Written in a Country Churchyard" (1751) had started a fashion in poetry for sentimental reflections upon occasions of death. This impulse, while quite natural, found further expression in lamenting the end of persons and things not traditionally the subjects of public mourning. (Gray himself parodied the fashion he had started with an ode on the death of a favorite cat who drowned while trying to snare a goldfish.) Goldsmith attacked this proliferation of laments in the *Critical Review* (1759). Citing the corruption of the elegy, Goldsmith judged that his peers thought flattery, bombast, and sorrow sufficient ingredients to compose a moving poem. He also teased the popular mode of elegies with several mock versions; the best of these are "An Elegy on the Glory of Her Sex: Mrs. Mary Blaize" and "An Elegy on the Death of a Mad Dog." No other poems so well illustrate Goldsmith's comic ability.

Adapted from an older French poem, "An Elegy on the Glory of Her Sex: Mrs. Mary Blaize" laments with tongue in cheek the passing of a one-time strumpet turned pawnbroker. The poem's narrator strives hard to attribute conventional virtues of charity and probity to her, only to admit in the last line of each stanza to some qualification of the lady's virtue:

> She strove the neighbourhood to please,
> With manners wondrous winning,
> And never follow'd wicked ways,—
> *Unless when she was sinning.*

"An Elegy on the Death of a Mad Dog," which first appeared as a song in *The Vicar of Wakefield*, makes a similar point about the perversion of elegiac conventions by telling of a "kind and gentle" man who befriended a dog "of low degree." At first they get along well until the dog "to gain some private ends" goes mad and bites the man. The townspeople lament that this good man must die a wretched death, betrayed by the ungrateful cur whom he has trusted. In the final stanza, however, the poet twists the reader's sentimental expectation of a tragic ending: Instead of the man, it is the dog that dies.

THE TRAVELLER

Goldsmith had more serious issues to lay before his audience. His first major poem, *The Traveller*, attempts a philosophic survey of European life, showing, he declared in the dedication, that "there may be equal happiness in states that are governed differently from our own; that every state has a particular principle of happiness, and that this principle in each may be carried to a mischievous excess."

Condensing observations made on his trip to Europe into one moment, Goldsmith describes himself seated on a mountaintop in the Alps, from which he can look across to the great states of Europe: Italy, Switzerland, France, Holland, and Britain. Each land reveals to the poet's eye its special blessing—and its liability.

Italy, bountifully supplied by Nature and once the seat of empire, has been exhausted by the pursuit and burden of wealth; now peasant huts arise where once imperial buildings stood. Switzerland, less endowed by Nature, produces a self-reliant and hardy race that has few wants but cannot develop "the gentler morals" which are a hallmark of a refined culture. France, dedicated to the graces of civilized life, has developed the most brilliant society in Europe but one which is prey to ostentation and vanity. Holland, claimed from the sea by an industrious people, devotes its energies to commerce and trade which now accumulates superfluous treasure "that engenders craft and fraud." England, which Nature has treated neither too richly nor too miserly, is the home of Liberty and Freedom which allow people to rule themselves; but self-rule in excess becomes party strife and colonial ambition.

Since every human society is imperfect, Goldsmith concludes, people must remember that human happiness is seldom regulated by laws or royal edicts. Since each of us is "to ourselves in every place consigned," the constant in life must be the "smooth current of domestic joy."

The Traveller echoes Goldsmith's favorite poets of the preceding generations and of his own time. Like Joseph Addison's "A Letter from Italy" (1704), it comments on England's political state by contrast with that of other European powers. Like Alexander Pope's *An Essay on Man* (1733-1734), it enunciates a philosophic principle in verse. Like Samuel Johnson's *The Vanity of Human Wishes* (1749), it concludes with the assertion that human happiness is determined by individual, not social experience. As derivative as *The Traveller* is, however, Goldsmith's poem is still his own. Less nationalistic than Addison's, less systematizing than Pope's, and less tragic than Johnson's, Goldsmith's poem possesses the graceful ease of the periodical essay whose tone is conversational and whose form mixes personal observation with public pronouncement. *The Traveller* is cast as an epistle to the poet's brother and as an account of the years of wandering which have led the poet to this meditation upon human experience. The interest moves easily and naturally from the poet's wanderings to his social meditations, observations, and finally to philosophic insight. In the dedication to *The Traveller* Goldsmith also laments the decay of poetry in a society verging on the "extremes of refinement." By echoing the themes and forms of earlier poets, Goldsmith offers his readers a return to the poetry of an age that brought the "greatest perfection" of the language. As he observed in *An History of England in a Series of Letters from a Nobleman to His Son* (1764), modern poets have only added finery to the muse's dress, not outfitted her anew.

THE DESERTED VILLAGE

The Deserted Village, 430 lines long, repeats the mixture of personal observation and public utterance. This time the topic is closer to home, the depopulation of the countryside because of a series of Enclosure Acts which turned formerly common village lands into private farms worked only for well-to-do landlords. Goldsmith observes that enclosure drives "a bold peasantry, their country's pride" into the city or away to the colonies. The poem is at once a lament for a lost way of life and a call to society to awaken to a danger.

The first 114 lines describe the poet's relationship to Auburn, the "loveliest village of the plain," an abstract, idealized version of Goldsmith's boyhood home. The poet recalls Auburn as a place of innocence where his youth was so happy that work and play were scarcely distinguishable. Now, like other villages, Auburn is "to hastening ills a prey"; these ills are trade, the growth of wealth, and the peasantry's departure from the land. The decline of Auburn darkens not only the poet's memory and civic pride but his hopes as well. Auburn was to be his place of retirement from life's cares where he might "die at home at last."

In the next 140 lines, the narrator surveys the buildings and inhabitants of Auburn: the church and the parsonage where the minister, "unpracticed he to fawn, or seek for power," kept a refuge to feed a hungry beggar, talk with an old soldier, and comfort the dying; the schoolhouse where the master, "a man severe and stern to view," shared with his pupils "the love he bore to learning"; and finally, the inn whose neat and trim interior played host to "greybeard mirth and smiling toil."

An equally long section then describes the present sad condition of Auburn. Imagining the village as a beautiful girl who turns increasingly to fashionable dress and cosmetics as her natural bloom fades, Goldsmith recounts how the "sons of wealth" force the peasantry off the land in order to build splendid estates with striking vistas. The displaced villagers trek to the cities, where pleasure seduces them from innocence or crime overcomes their honesty, or to the colonies, where a fiercer climate than England's threatens their lives. The section ends with a poignant description of families uprooted and friends or lovers separated as the people depart the village. With them "rural virtues leave the land."

The final section of the poem invokes "Sweet Poetry," which, like the inhabitants of Auburn, is being driven from the land. The poet hopes that poetry will nevertheless continue "to aid truth with [its] persuasive train" and teach humanity the age-old lesson that wealth ultimately destroys the simple virtues which bind people to the land and to one another.

The Deserted Village emphasizes that moral by a striking departure from literary convention. As a pastoral, the poem ought to persuade readers of the countryside's charms and goodness; as a pastoral it should express the ideals of peaceful virtue, harmony with nature, and productive use of the land that were commonplaces since classical Greek poetry. Goldsmith's poem presents these familiar ideas, but as a lament and a warning that the pastoral ideal is slipping away. Bound by tradition to use the conventions but unable to disguise the truth, the poet seeks to arouse rather than soothe the reader's imagination.

One of Goldsmith's most moving poetic devices in *The Deserted Village* is the catalog. At four crucial places the narrative slows to allow leisurely description; these descriptive catalogs are composed of grammatically and metrically similar lines. The device is an elaboration of the neoclassical practice of balancing and paralleling couplets; its effect is to intensify the emotional impact of the passage. The catalog of the inn's furnishings is the most vivid of these passages and illustrates Goldsmith at his best.

FLAWED EXPERIMENTS

Trying his hand at many different styles and pieces, Goldsmith inevitably failed at some. "Threnodia Augustalis," for example, a poem mourning the death of the Princess Dowager of Wales, falls victim to the bombast and pomposity that Goldsmith laughed at in other elegiac poems. It shows how increasingly difficult had become the task of making poetic praise of the aristocracy sound convincing in an age when middle- and lower-class life was providing rich materials for the essay and the novel.

Another flawed poem is "Edwin and Angelina," a ballad of the type becoming more popular as the century progressed. Readers were drawn to this genre of folk poetry for its mysterious happenings in remote and romantic locations. Goldsmith tried to mix these qualities with the didactic strain of *The Traveller* and *The Deserted Village*. He tells of young lovers, separated by a cruel parent, who later meet while both are in disguise. The joy of their reunion is delayed while each delivers a long moral dissertation on the necessity of steadfast virtue and trust in Providence.

"The Captivity: An Oratorio" is a more ambitious treatment of the same theme but equally unsuccessful. Goldsmith makes a promising start by using the Israelite bondage in Babylon—a subject hardly ever treated in the literature of the age—as the frame for his moral, but he simply does not have a poetic vocabulary capable of describing spiritual anguish. When, early in the poem, a prophet urges the Israelites to repent and "offer up a tear," the poem has reached its deepest point of profundity.

OTHER MAJOR WORKS

LONG FICTION: *The Vicar of Wakefield*, 1766.

SHORT FICTION: *The Citizen of the World*, 1762 (collection of fictional letters first published in *The Public Ledger*, 1760-1761).

PLAYS: *The Good-Natured Man*, pr., pb. 1768; *She Stoops to Conquer: Or, The Mistakes of a Night*, pr., pb. 1773.

NONFICTION: *An Enquiry into the Present State of Polite Learning in Europe*, 1759; *The Bee*, 1759 (essays); *An History of England in a Series of Letters from a Nobleman to His Son*, 1764 (2 volumes); *An History of the Earth, and Animated Nature*, 1774 (8 volumes; unfinished).

MISCELLANEOUS: *The Collected Works of Oliver Goldsmith*, 1966 (5 volumes; Arthur Friedman, editor).

BIBLIOGRAPHY

Dixon, Peter. *Oliver Goldsmith Revisited*. Boston: Twayne, 1991. A short critical analysis of selected works by Goldsmith. Includes bibliographical references and index. Good overview and introduction for students.

Ginger, John. *The Notable Man: The Life and Times of Oliver Goldsmith*. London: Hamish Hamilton, 1977. This well-documented biography emphasizes Goldsmith's milieu. In reference to Goldsmith's personality, Ginger stresses his loneliness late in life and tentatively tries to explain the social fool/literary genius paradox with references to his kindness and his recklessness. Discusses the works, especially *The Vicar of Wakefield* and *She Stoops to Conquer: Or, The Mistakes of a Night*.

Lucy, Sean, ed. *Goldsmith: The Gentle Master*. Cork, Ireland: Cork University Press, 1984. In this short volume, the editor offers a brief account of Goldsmith's life, which attempts to explain some ways in which his character has been misunderstood. Four commentaries follow on four genres. John Montague examines the poetry, especially *The Traveller* and *The Deserted Village* and discusses the themes of exile and prophesy in Goldsmith's writing. Includes an index.

Mikhail, E. H., ed. *Goldsmith: Interviews and Recollections*. New York: St. Martin's Press, 1993. A collection of biographical essays and interviews of Goldsmith by those who were associated with him. Mikhail has selected those recollections that have not been reprinted, as well as those that are not readily available. Arranged chronologically, the pieces cover most of Goldsmith's life.

Quintana, Ricardo. *Oliver Goldsmith: A Georgian Study*. New York: Macmillan, 1967. This volume in the Masters of World Literature series discusses Goldsmith's performance in each of the literary forms he practiced. Quintana views the poems as didactic, rhetorical works. He gives an account of Goldsmith among the Georgians, describing his friendships and social life, and how his contemporaries viewed him: as a writer of genius who was a fool in society.

Rousseau, George Sebastian, ed. *Goldsmith: The Critical Heritage*. London: Routledge & Kegan Paul, 1974. This anthology in the Critical Heritage series collects biographical and critical writing on Goldsmith published from 1762 to 1912. The first half contains discussions of his major works, including *The Deserted Village*. The second half is devoted to his life and works, gathering anecdotes and examples of the Goldsmith "legend." Much of the material would not be easily available elsewhere. Includes an introduction as overview and a bibliography.

Swarbrick, Andrew, ed. *The Art of Oliver Goldsmith*. London: Vision Press, 1984. This collection of essays in the Critical Studies series begins with a chronological table of the main events of Goldsmith's life. It includes a chapter each on *The Deserted Village* and *The Traveller*, as well as chapters on Goldsmith's plays, politics, classicism, and views of nature. Each section has thorough notes. Supplemented by an index.

Robert M. Otten;
bibliography updated by the editors

EUGEN GOMRINGER

Born: Cachuela Esperanza, Bolivia; January 20, 1925

PRINCIPAL POETRY

Konstellationen, Constellations, Constelaciones, 1953 (multilingual edition)

5 mal 1 Konstellation, 1960

33 Konstellationen, 1960

Die Konstellationen, Les Constellations, The Constellations, Los Constelaciones, 1963 (multilingual edition)

Das Stundenbuch, 1965 (*The Book of Hours, and Constellations*, 1968; includes translations from *Constellations*)

Worte sind Schatten: Die Konstellationen, 1951-1968, 1969

Einsam Gemeinsam, 1971

Lieb, 1971

Eugen Gomringer, 1970-1972, 1973

Konstellationen, Ideogramme, Stundenbuch, 1977

Vom Rand nach innen: Die Konstellationen, 1951-1995, 1995

OTHER LITERARY FORMS

As the leading theoretician of concrete poetry in Europe, Eugen Gomringer has also published essays, manifestos, and lectures, including the important and provocatively titled *Poesie als Mittel der Umweltgestaltung* (poetry as a means of shaping the environment). In addition, most of his theoretical texts were reprinted in his best-known collection of poems, *Worte sind Schatten*. Gomringer has also promoted the school of concrete poetry as an editor of journals and collections. In 1953, he cofounded the journal *Spirale* and served as the editor of its literary section. In 1960, he founded the Eugen Gomringer Press in Frauenfeld, Switzerland, serving as the editor for eleven issues of the journal *Konkrete Poesie/Poesia concreta*, which was published in Frauenfeld from 1960 to 1964. Gomringer has always been fascinated by nonrepresentational painters and artists whose "concrete" works he sees as being intimately connected to his own; in 1958, he edited a collection of essays in honor of the fiftieth birthday of sculptor, designer, and abstract painter Max Bill, and in 1968, he published monographs on the works of Josef Albers and Camille Graeser. He also collaborated with artists on books with "concrete" artistic themes.

ACHIEVEMENTS

In 1953, in Bern, Switzerland, Eugen Gomringer published his first concrete poems, in his newly founded magazine *Spirale*, earning himself the title "the Father of Concrete Poetry." Although another group of concrete poets (the "Noigandres" group) had organized in Brazil at about the same time, Gomringer's first poems appear to have predated those of the Brazilians, and it was Gomringer's poems and theoretical texts that served as the basis for the spread of this new school in Europe. More important, Gomringer's linguistic ingenuity showed the German-speaking world that literary innovation and creativity were still possible in the aftermath of the (linguistic) destruction of the Third Reich. He demonstrated that it was perfectly legitimate, and even a matter of great urgency, to question the adequacy of the building blocks of any new literature—namely, the language itself.

Gomringer's influence was enormous in Germany, Austria, and Switzerland. The experimental poet Helmut Heissenbüttel has openly admitted his indebtedness to Gomringer; indeed, the whole Stuttgart School of poets who gathered around the aesthetician Max Bense (including Heissenbüttel, Franz Mon, and Claus Bremer) would hardly have been conceivable had it not been for Gomringer's pioneering work. In Austria, the poets Friedrich Achleitner and Gerhard Rühm, who formed the nucleus of the short-lived but important neo-Dadaistic cabaret Die Wiener Gruppe (the Viennese group), were friends of Gomringer and transmitted his ideas to their own countrymen, including nonmembers of the group, such as the poets Ernst Jandl and Friederike Mayröcker. In Gomringer's own Switzerland, usually rather conservative in literary matters, his work acted as an impetus or signal for a new beginning. Although there was no "Swiss Concrete School" as such, poetic creation, which had been in the doldrums since the end of the war, began to accelerate, and one can discern Gomringer's influence in the poems of Kurt Marti, Peter Lehner, Ernst Eggimann, Hans Schumacher, and others. Even German-speaking writers whose primary interest is prose owe a debt to Gomringer, for he taught them to experiment with language within their texts. This is not to say that any of these authors slavishly copied Gomringer's works, but they did change or alter their language so that it would more adequately confront a highly industrialized and technological society. This broad trend toward linguistic restructuring lasted about twenty years and is one of the central components of postwar German literature.

BIOGRAPHY

Although he was born in Bolivia, Eugen Gomringer received his secondary education in the German-speaking part of Switzerland and studied economics and art history at universities in Bern and Rome. His study of art brought him into contact with modern nonrepresentational painting, which he emulated in his first poems in the early 1950's. At a meeting in 1955 with other poets who wrote in a similar fashion, Gomringer decided to term these poems "concrete." From 1954 to 1958, he served as secretary for Max Bill, who was then the director of the Hochschule für Gestaltung (institute of design) in Ulm, West Germany, a descendant of the famous Bauhaus School. Bill, who was also the head of the departments of architecture and product design at the institute, was greatly affected by constructivist principles and frequently used elementary shapes with almost mathematical precision in his paintings and sculptures. Gomringer was in turn influenced by Bill's works. It was also in Ulm that Gomringer met other artists of the abstract school, such as Josef Albers and Friedrich Vordemberge-Gildewart, as well as the influential professor of semiotics Max Bense and the poet Helmut Heissenbüttel.

After his stay in Ulm, Gomringer embarked on a decade of intense creative activity. He began publishing collections of the poems that he had been writing in the previous years; he founded his own press and his own magazine, *Konkrete Poesie*, in 1960; he served as business manager for a Swiss labor organization, the Schweizerischer Werkbund, from 1962 to 1967; and he began working as a design and advertising consultant for various firms, including a large department store and (since 1967) the famous Rosenthal concern.

The 1960's marked the high point for Gomringer's creative output and for the concrete school that he had fostered. By the end of that decade, one could discern several signs indicating that the peak of the movement had passed. Instead of writing poems, Gomringer began writing monographs and essays; an *Anthology of Concrete Poetry* appeared in 1967 (edited by Emmett Williams), firmly establishing Gomringer's role in the movement; an English translation of some of Gomringer's works appeared in 1968 (*The Book of Hours, and Constellations*, edited by Jerome Rothenberg); he published an anthology of his poems and theoretical writings in 1969 (*Worte sind Schatten*), and he edited two anthologies of concrete poetry in 1972. In that same year, Gomringer made a lecture tour through South America that perhaps served as his official farewell to the concrete movement, for since then he has done little creative writing. He has devoted most of his energy to his design and advertising career and in 1976, began teaching the theory of aesthetics at the art academy in Düsseldorf.

ANALYSIS

Although Eugen Gomringer's principal inspiration derived from the visual arts, he was also attracted in his university years to poets who emphasized the visual aspects of their works. He admired Arno Holz, who arranged the lines of his poems symmetrically on either side of an imaginary "central axis" running down the middle of the page. He enjoyed the idiosyncratic vocabulary and typography of Stefan George, and he was fascinated by the condensed elliptical style of Stéphane Mallarmé and the typographical pictures of Guillaume Apollinaire's *Calligrammes* (1918; English translation, 1980). These affinities, along with concrete poetry's resemblance to the reductive and destructive tendencies of late Expressionism and Dada, have led some scholars to see a direct link between prewar and postwar linguistic experimentation—a misleading connection, for Gomringer does not share the philosophical tenets (the search for the inner essence of man that lies beyond the grasp of reason) or the elements of shock and negation found in this earlier poetry. Instead, Gomringer affirms the economic recovery of postwar Europe and rejoices in technological progress. He argues that the modern industrial world requires a level of communication that is direct, simple, abbreviated, and universally intelligible. The irrationalism of the prewar years has no place in his work. In Gomringer's view, poetry today should resemble the signs in a large international airport, where travelers speaking a variety of languages must be able to find their way with a minimum of confusion. Poetry should be like contemporary advertising copy—straight to the point and easy to remember.

Gomringer chose to call his poetry "concrete" because his poems disregard the syntactical relationships of traditional verse. Isolated words are placed on a paper in such a way that the visual arrangement contributes to or even constitutes the field in which thoughts can move. The concrete poem is thus neither a statement nor a description but an assemblage of words that forms an object. That is, it is not an assertion *about* something, but rather its own *concrete* reality; it is not an abstraction from reality but a concrete object made of the reality of language. The development of this new form paralleled developments in what is generally called the "abstract" art of the first half of the twentieth century. A large group of abstract painters (Wassily Kandinsky, Paul Klee, Piet Mondrian, Hans Arp, and Kurt Schwitters, to name only a few) created aesthetic constructions that, like Gomringer's poetry, satisfy a natural desire for order. The aesthetic harmony characteristic of both the concrete poem and the abstract work of art is, however, basically different from the harmony of the natural world, and only the arrangement of the materials on the canvas or on the paper can make this harmony visible. Many of these artists claimed, too, that since they were dealing with the essential elements of reality, their paintings were not "abstract" at all but rather "concrete," much more concrete than traditional mimetic art. Theo van Doesburg wrote a manifesto in 1930 about concrete art, Max Bill termed an exhibit of his works in 1944 "concrete," and Kandinsky always maintained with great tenacity that his paintings were the only truly concrete works to have been created.

In order to call attention to the unique form of his poems, Gomringer uses the term "constellation." He defines a constellation as a grouping of a few different words on a page in such a manner that the relationship between the words does not arise through syntactic means but through the material, concrete, and spatial presence of the words themselves. Thus, the reader is

permitted to select, by experimenting and playing with the text, the interpretation that suits him best. The poet establishes the field of language from which meaning will emerge, but the reader is invited—indeed, obliged—to participate in the creation of the poem. Nothing is taught, narrated, or described: The poem is an autonomous product.

Such a process points to the most radical aspect of Gomringer's oeuvre. Through a confrontation with the language of the concrete poem, Gomringer hopes, the reader will gain a new relationship to the objects of the real world, because these objects are reflected in and represented by language. These new relationships should lead to insights about the tyranny of language over thought—that is, the reader should realize that inherited language systems are no longer adequate to communicate ideas in a highly technological age and that a new universal language must be developed in order to facilitate the understanding of complex, specialized data. Concrete poetry promotes the development of this language by designing models from various languages and testing their efficacy on the global community. In this search for a universal language, he anticipated later developments in the science of linguistics, such as generative-transformational grammar and theories of universals.

WORTE SIND SCHATTEN

Gomringer's most representative collection, *Worte sind Schatten*, includes examples of the four categories into which his constellations can be divided: visual constellations, or ideograms, whereby the arrangement of the words on the page constitutes the main impact of the poem; audiovisual constellations, which can be read either silently or aloud; constellations in foreign languages (Spanish, French, English, and Swiss-German); and constellations in book form, which require the reader to turn several pages in order to see the poem develop visually before his eyes, much like a film. The constellations in all categories generally employ a small number of words restructured or varied in the poem by means of combinations and permutations.

The visual texts have no real beginning and no real end, because words or letters are arranged on the page, not necessarily in lines, to form a linguistic picture. The eye of the reader must roam about the page until it has grasped the poem, both words and picture, as an entity. In this category, one finds a poem that contains the numeral 4 printed several times to form the shape of the Roman numeral IV (much like some types of computer pictures), a poem in which the letters of the word "wind" are arranged in a seemingly haphazard pattern on the page, perhaps to suggest leaves being blown by the wind, and the famous "Schweigen" poem, in which the word *schweigen* (silence) is printed fourteen times to form a box on the page with a space in the middle, the "silence" of the poem. Such poems are usually tautologies, in that the "picture" is an illustration of the semantic content of the word being used.

The audiovisual constellations are for the most part printed in traditional verse form—that is, individual lines and stanzas are recognizable even though the lexicon has been greatly reduced. An example is the poem titled "Vielleicht" (perhaps):

> vielleicht baum
> baum vielleicht
> vielleicht vogel
> vogel vielleicht
> vielleicht frühling
> frühling vielleicht
> vielleicht worte
> worte vielleicht.

(The other words translate to "tree," "bird," "spring," and "words.") The poem suggests the extent to which names for things are arbitrary, imprecise, or inaccurate.

Gomringer's constellations in foreign languages are similar in structure to the audiovisual poems, leading some scholars to view both categories as only truncated imitations of traditional verse. An example is a poem in English, "You Blue," which can be interpreted, variously, as a comment on the color spectrum, on racial discrimination, or on the scale of human emotions: "you blue/ you red/ you yellow/ you black/ you white/ you."

CONSTELLATIONS

The constellations in book form are perhaps the most innovative of Gomringer's works. An example of this type of poem is *5 mal 1 Konstellation*. Here, Gomringer prints various combinations of the words *mann* (man), *frau* (woman), *baum* (tree), *kind* (child), *hund* (dog), *vogel* (bird), *berg* (mountain), *land, wind, haus* (house),

wolke (cloud), and *see* (sea or lake). Each word has a set position on the page, but all the words are not printed until the final page: Sometimes only an individual word appears, and at other times the words are in groups of two, three, or four. Each page is like a part of a landscape painting, and when the pages are turned, the landscape seems to come to life. In another of these book-poems, *1 Konstellation: 15*, words and letters appear and disappear within a grid of fifteen squares printed in the center of the page. When one leafs through the poem, these words and letters seem to jump and skip about, much like the figures in an animated cartoon. A final example, *The Book of Hours*, is both the most profound and the longest (forty-three pages) of the poems, and it requires the most meditation on the part of the reader. Using a minimal vocabulary of twenty-four words, such as *freude* (joy), *wort* (word), *frage* (question), *ziel* (goal), *geist* (spirit), and the possessive adjectives *mein* and *dein* (my, your), Gomringer provides the reader with a quasi dialogue consisting of almost every possible combination of these words—for example, "dein geist, mein geist"; "dein geist, mein wort"; and "dein mein geist." The poem invites religious and philosophical interpretation on many levels.

A further analysis of these and similar poems is not possible, for as Gomringer states repeatedly, his concrete poems do not make a statement about reality but are their own reality. This brings one to the central dilemma of Gomringer's work: If the concrete poem has no content or theme and reaches fruition only when the reader projects his *own* meaning onto it, how can the reader hope to gain *new* information about the technological and scientific world from it? Does not the reader only interpret the poem in the light of knowledge *already present* in his own consciousness? The lack of syntactic structures in the poem, which supposedly allows words to form new relationships, does not appear to be an adequate device to overcome this handicap, because the reader can never escape the traditional semantic categories assigned to the words in natural language. Thus, Harald Hartung, in his book *Experimentelle Literatur und konkrete Poesie*, criticizes the words used in *The Book of Hours* arguing that they are but clichés taken from premodern and pretechnological nineteenth century poetry, of little value today.

Gomringer's followers (Heissenbüttel among them) recognized this predicament and attempted a more realistic solution. They reasoned that in order to change one's view of the world, which is filtered through language, one must change *all* the features of language, including syntax and morphology. Even these experiments were not successful, however, because the authors did not take into account the fact that communication must be based on some type of accepted norm. Drastic unilateral adjustments to the norm without the agreement of the other members of the language community can rarely have a tangible effect.

Gomringer's constellations have also been criticized for other reasons. It has been charged that, by avoiding social and political issues, the poems tend to affirm rather than censure the established order. Moreover, the detailed a priori theoretical matrix makes the poems elitist to a degree; the average reader, unaware of the manipulations he is "supposed to" perform, will dismiss the poems as unintelligible babblings. Finally, the reductive nature of the form is perhaps its most serious and inescapable liability: Solutions to complex contemporary problems cannot be achieved within such a simplistic format. Precisely because it offers an oversimplified aesthetic, concrete poetry still attracts a small number of practitioners, but Gomringer's more lasting legacy will be found in the work of writers who have turned his linguistic innovations to larger purposes—including writers who have no direct acquaintance with his work, who have nevertheless absorbed the critical attitude toward language that he fostered.

OTHER MAJOR WORKS

NONFICTION: *Manifeste und Darstellungen der Konkreten Poesie, 1954-1966*, 1966; *Camille Graeser*, 1968; *Josef Albers: Monographie*, 1968; *Poesie als Mittel der Umweltgestaltung*, 1969; *Der Pfeil: Spiel— Gleichnis—Kommunikation*, 1972 (with Anton and Joachim Stankowski); *Modulare und serielle Ordnungen*, 1973 (with Paul Lohse); *Konkretes von Anton Stankowski*, 1974 (with Anton Stankowski); *Theorie der konkreten Poesie*, 1997; *Zur Sache der Konkreten*, 2000.

EDITED TEXTS: *Max Bill*, 1958; *Konkrete Poesie: Deutschsprachige Autoren*, 1972; *Visuelle Poesie*, 1972.

BIBLIOGRAPHY

Dencker, Klaus Peter. "Visual Poetry, What Is It?" In *Translations: Experiments in Reading*, edited by Donald Wellman, Cola Franzen, and Irene Turner. Cambridge, Mass.: O.ARS, 1986. A comparison study of pattern poetry and concrete poetry genres, and an analysis of the theories of Gomringer.

Gumpel, Liselotte. *"Concrete" Poetry from East and West Germany*. New Haven, Conn.: Yale University Press, 1976. A critical and historical study of experimental poetry in Germany. Includes bibliographic references and an index.

Linnemann, Martina E. "Concrete Poetry: A Post-War Experiment in Visual Poetry." In *Text into Image: Image into Text*, edited by Jeff Morrison and Florian Krobb. Amsterdam, Netherlands: Rodopi, 1997. A comparative study of the concrete poetry of Gomringer and Claus Bremer.

Robert Acker;
bibliography updated by the editors

LUIS DE GÓNGORA Y ARGOTE

Born: Córdoba, Spain; July 11, 1561
Died: Córdoba, Spain; May 23, 1627

PRINCIPAL POETRY

Fábula de Polifemo y Galatea, 1627 (*Fable of Polyphemus and Galatea*, 1961)
Obras en verso del Homero español, 1627 (includes *Fábula de Polifemo y Galatea* and *Soledades*)
Soledades, 1627 (*The Solitudes of Don Luis de Góngora*, 1931; also as *The Solitudes*, 1964, Gilbert Cunningham, translator)
Obras poéticas de D. Luis de Góngora, 1921 (3 volumes; based on the Chacón manuscript of 1628)

OTHER LITERARY FORMS

During the Golden Age of Spain, drama was the most prestigious literary form. Lope de Vega had developed Spain's national *comedia*, and Luis de Góngora y Argote, like almost every other Spanish writer, tried his hand at theater. Góngora's plays met with little success. He completed two *comedias*: *Las firmezas de Isabela* (pr. 1610) and *El doctor Carlino* (pr. 1613). A third play, "Comedia venatoria," was left unfinished. Góngora's plays were unsuccessful because of their excessive difficulty; he was primarily a lyric poet, and therein lies his importance. Ironically, his greatest achievement in poetry constituted his main fault in drama: The dialogue was so complicated that the audience was unable to follow the plot, and the long lyrical sequences in the plays diverted attention from the main action.

ACHIEVEMENTS

The figure of Luis de Góngora y Argote has prompted critical polemics for the last three centuries. For a long time, critics divided his poetry into two categories: the easy-to-understand popular poems and the *culteranos*, complex works that are difficult to comprehend because of distorted syntax and a new poetic language. To quote a famous expression, Góngora became known as "Prince of Light, Prince of Darkness." Research indicates, however, that his poetry developed in one constant line, culminating in the integration of opposing stylistic tendencies. The year 1613 marked the beginning of a literary controversy, yet unresolved, when the first manuscript copies of *Fable of Polyphemus and Galatea* were distributed at court. Literary circles in Spain were shocked, and opinion was drastically divided. On one hand, Góngora's ardent admirers proclaimed him to be the prince of poets. On the other hand, his enemies accused him of destroying both language and poetry. It is important to mention that among his severest critics were two of the leading Spanish poets of the Golden Age: Lope de Vega and Francisco de Quevedo. With *Fable of Polyphemus and Galatea* and the first part of *The Solitudes of Don Luis de Góngora*, distributed in 1613, Góngora nevertheless became the central figure of Spanish poetry. The impact of his complex style, *culteranismo*, was so powerful that even his worst enemies were ultimately influenced by his poetry.

Góngora's reputation fluctuated in succeeding centuries. His Baroque vision horrified the classicist souls of the eighteenth century, who held him responsible for the decadence of Spanish poetry. Nevertheless, they admired the "easy" Góngora, the Prince of Light. This atti-

tude prevailed during the nineteenth century as well. The revaluation of Góngora's *culteranismo* did not begin until the end of the nineteenth century, when the French Symbolists, especially Paul Verlaine, praised Góngora's poetry as a brilliant attempt to create musicality and perfection. The most significant revaluation of his work, however, was initiated in 1927, when a group of young Spanish poets and critics joined to celebrate the third centennial of his death. The enthusiasm following the celebration led to the creation of the Generation of 1927, the most brilliant group of Spanish poets since the time of Góngora. Critics today credit Góngora with perfecting the poetic language in Spanish. His work did not constitute a break with Renaissance models, but rather a culmination of its ideals. In the words of scholar Dámaso Alonso, Góngora was Europe's foremost seventeenth century lyrical poet. A young generation of international critics seems to agree with Alonso's judgment.

BIOGRAPHY

Luis de Góngora y Argote was born in Córdova, Spain, on July 11, 1561. He was the son of Francisco de Argote and Leonor de Góngora. His use of his mother's surname before his father's, not an unusual practice in Spain, was a result of economic considerations and a desire to carry a more euphonic name (Góngora was extremely fond of proparoxytonic words). It seems that, coming from an aristocratic family, his father originally intended to make his son a lawyer and to place him, through various political connections, in the court of the Habsburg rulers. Consequently, the young Don Luis was sent to study at Salamanca, where he never completed his studies because he spent most of his time writing poems, flirting, and gambling. Góngora nevertheless was able to learn in depth Latin, Greek, and classical literature and mythology. His maternal uncle, who held a hereditary position at the Cathedral of Córdova, convinced the young poet to enter the church. Góngora became a deacon and in 1585 inherited his uncle's position; he was not ordained as a priest until almost thirty years later.

The young poet was uncomfortable in his role as a churchman. There is a letter extant from the Bishop of Córdova accusing Góngora of not fulfilling his ecclesiastical duties and of preferring bullfights to the chorus. Gónora was also accused of writing profane poetry. He replied sarcastically to these accusations, and a small fine was imposed upon him. Thereafter, Góngora devoted himself to writing poetry, and his name became famous throughout Spain, especially because of his romances, which are included in many of the important collections of the time, such as the *Flores* of Pedro de Espinoza and the important *Romancero general* of 1600.

In 1613, with his *culteranos*, he became the central, if controversial, figure of Spanish poetry. The polemics and debates that his poems aroused, together with their success, moved him to abandon his native Córdova to settle in Madrid in 1617. His hopes of obtaining favors from the government proved futile, and this circumstance, combined with his passion for gambling and a luxurious lifestyle, soon consumed his limited capital. Sad, destitute, and frustrated, he returned to Córdova in 1627, where he died on May 23 of that year.

ANALYSIS

Romances and *letrillas* constitute two important forms of popular Spanish poetry. The romance is customarily written in octosyllabic lines (although other metric forms are sometimes used). The rhyme is assonantic, or imperfect, meaning that after the tonic vowel, all other vowels are equal. This poetic mode has no stanzas, and only the even lines rhyme, usually with one assonance carried throughout the entire poem. The *letrillas* are generally written in octosyllabic lines and grouped in stanzas of either four, eight, or ten lines. The rhyme is consonantic, or perfect, meaning that all sounds after the tonic vowel are identical. The *letrilla* usually has a refrain. Both the romances and the *letrillas* were originally intended to be sung.

It would be a mistake to consider the romances and *letrillas* written by Luis de Góngora y Argote as "popular" or "easy" poems. His first dated poem (1580) is a romance; his last, dated 1626, is also a romance. This poetic form was basic to Góngora's work. Although the themes of the romances vary, they generally follow traditional Spanish subjects. Góngora wrote amatory, mythological, satirical, religious, and Moorish romances. Within the Moorish convention, some of his best romances correspond to the theme of the *cautivo*,

the Christian prisoner of the Moors, who dreams of his homeland. It is important to remember that this theme is also present in many other authors. For example, having once been a *cautivo* in Africa, Miguel de Cervantes included this theme in a long fragment of *Don Quixote de la Mancha* (1605, 1615). Hence, the situation described in the romances of captives is genuine. Góngora was able to re-create lyrically a popular feeling in a superior manner.

The *letrillas* are also numerous and cover a wide range of subjects. Many of them are satirical and were intended to make people laugh. It is interesting to note, though, that some of Góngora's most accomplished creations in this genre are not sarcastic but deal with religious themes. Indeed, his *letrillas* devoted to the Yuletide are among his best poems.

"THE FABLE OF PYRAMUS AND THISBE"

It is impossible to consider in detail the romances and *letrillas*. They total 215 compositions, with approximately forty-four additional ones attributed to the poet. One of the romances, however, deserves special attention: "Fábula de Píramo y Tisbe" ("The Fable of Pyramus and Thisbe"). The perfect conjunction of the two "styles" that critics noted in Góngora's poetry, it is a *culterano* poem in a popular form. Góngora took a mythological theme and inverted the topos into a cruel parody. This parody is also stylistic: Góngora took his own literary devices and converted them into a new form. "The Fable of Pyramus and Thisbe" is not "easy"; presupposing an extensive knowledge of mythology and Spanish Renaissance culture, the poem is a net of references, imagery, and ideas that captures in its lines the epitome of the Spanish Baroque. A work of 508 lines, it is a virtual encyclopedia of literary figures. The most prominent are metaphors of the first, second, and third degrees, metonymies, catachreses, and hyperboles. A typical example of the style of the poem is found in the description of Thisbe. Góngora follows all of the Renaissance topoi of beauty: Her face, for example, is a crystal vase containing carnations and jasmines. The inversion of the topos follows immediately. Since her face is made of flowers, her nose should also be floral, but it is described as an *almendruco*, a small almond. The ending *-uco* in Spanish (the base word is *almendra*) carries a pejorative connotation. This example shows the vision that Góngora is trying to capture in the text: It is a contrasting world of light and shadows, of beauty and ugliness—a Baroque worldview.

OCCASIONAL SONNETS

Góngora was the author of at least 166 sonnets; some fifty more are attributed to him. The sonnets, like the romances, span his entire literary life. It is important to remember that the sonnet form had not only a literary function in the Golden Age, but also a social one. Poets were expected to write for various special occasions, and most of the time the sonnet was the chosen form; it was short and had a flavor of enlightenment and culture. Thus, Góngora often was compelled to write occasional sonnets. Many such poems were written for special festivities, such as births, weddings, and hunting parties, or were merely encomiastic compositions to celebrate sayings or actions of the nobility. Góngora managed to overcome the limitations imposed upon him, composing masterpieces based on these stock themes. Not all of his sonnets, however, were occasioned thus; many were born in the soul of the poet and offer lyrical expressions of his persona.

It is impossible to consider the sonnets individually, but the "Inscripción para la tumba de El Greco" ("Epitaph for the Tomb of El Greco") deserves mention. Critics have noted that there is a relation between Góngora's poetry and El Greco's art. Both responded to a distorted vision of the world that was typical of the Baroque period. Góngora's admiration for El Greco's painting is easy to understand in the light of his poetry. Both artists were successful in creating a new code and a new mode of expression.

Góngora frequently employed traditional Renaissance topoi. The *carpe diem* and *brevitas vitae* themes combine in a sonnet written in 1582 to create a typically Baroque worldview. The poet describes a beautiful woman in the spring of her life; the Baroque spirit emerges in the last stanza, when the poet asserts that the gold of her hair will become silver, that the freshness of her face will become a crushed violet, that beauty, youth, and the lady herself will become "earth, dust, smoke, shadow, nothingness."

FABLE OF POLYPHEMUS AND GALATEA

Fable of Polyphemus and Galatea is Góngora's masterpiece. The text is a recreation of Ovid's fable of Acis and Galathea. Góngora transforms the 159 Latin hexameters into sixty octaves. The poem also contains an introduction of three octaves, for a total of sixty-three (504 hendecasyllabic lines). The argument of the poem is basically the same as Ovid's: The horrible Polyphemus loves Galathea, a beautiful nymph, but she falls in love with the young and beautiful Acis. In a jealous rage, the Cyclops grabs a gigantic rock and crushes Acis under it. The young lover is changed into a river by Galathea's mother, Doris.

In *Fable of Polyphemus and Galatea*, Góngora created a completely new poetic language. The border between everyday and lyrical language had never before been so clearly delineated. Góngora found his tools in the rhetorical devices of the classical Roman and Greek writers, learning from them not only a new vocabulary but also a new syntax. His use of this new grammar offered the best means of giving the language a new "sound": He intended that only a highly educated and select few would be able to understand his work. The main syntactical innovation introduced by Góngora was the hyperbaton. This grammatical inversion had indeed been used before in Spanish but never taken to the extremes to which Góngora carried it. He consistently separated the noun from its adjective and the subject from its object; furthermore, as in Latin, he placed the verb at the end of the sentence. In addition to these grammatical anomalies, Góngora introduced hundreds of neologisms. A further complication was his use of words whose meaning had evolved through the centuries. Góngora used these words in their original metaphorical sense. He was able to develop a complete code of metaphors, based on mythology and private associations. Once the code was established, he constructed his images accordingly, creating such difficult texts that even the learned Spanish speaker needed a prose "translation" of the poem. Hence, the first critics and commentators did exactly that, and, in the twentieth century, Dámaso Alonso's work in reviving Góngora began with a prose version of the most complicated poems.

In spite of its difficulties, *Fable of Polyphemus and Galatea* is not unintelligible. Góngora's art is completely organized and follows a rigorous pattern. Even the most difficult passages respond to a logic that takes notice of the most minute details. The obvious conclusion is that even in his "darkest" moments, Góngora is still the Prince of Light. *Fable of Polyphemus and Galatea* shines with the magical light of inner order and beauty. It reveals a Renaissance attitude hidden behind a Baroque mask.

THE SOLITUDES

Góngora originally conceived *The Solitudes* as four books, each being a long eclogue. Unfortunately, he completed only the first and a part of the second. Undoubtedly, the unfavorable reception of *Fable of Polyphemus and Galatea* and the *Soledad primera* (*First Solitude*) prompted his abandonment of the project. In the words of A. A. Parker, Góngora was too proud to cast any more pearls before swine. Although the poem is incomplete, Góngora left a substantial fragment. The *First Solitude* is composed of 1,091 lines, and the unfinished *Soledad segunda* (*Second Solitude*), of 979 lines. The external form of *The Solitudes* is the *silva*, a stanza combining seven- and eleven-syllable lines in a free pattern. After the rigid mode in which he composed *Fable of Polyphemus and Galatea*, Góngora probably thought that he could express himself more eloquently in a flexible stanza. Indeed, *The Solitudes* carry the difficulties of *Fable of Polyphemus and Galatea* to an even higher degree.

The argument of the poem is almost nonexistent. A young man survives a shipwreck and reaches the shore, where he is greeted by shepherds. The next morning he sets out on a walk and meets a group of people celebrating a rural wedding. The rest of the poem describes the festivities that follow the ceremony. At sunset, the newly married couple goes off to enjoy their first night together. The *Second Solitude* begins the next morning, when the young pilgrim meets a group of fishermen on the banks of a river. He accompanies them to a nearby island, and again there is a description of the rest of the day. Throughout the following morning, the group observes a hunting scene. Góngora was probably near the completion of the *Second Solitude* when he stopped abruptly. It has been suggested that Góngora planned to write "solitudes" of the country, of the shore, of the woods, and of the desert. The first two books follow a similar pattern: the journey; the arrival, followed by a soliloquy, festivities, a chorus; and, finally, evening games in the *First Solitude* and hunting in the *Second Solitude*.

It is clear that the nature of the poem is not heroic, but lyrical. What Góngora accomplished was to create a world that was both parallel to and removed from nature. In many ways, this new world was better than nature itself. At first, *The Solitudes* may appear to be superficial, without a "message" and preoccupied with only the technical aspects of poetry. Yet after the difficulties of the text are overcome, one sees that the poem offers an optimistic view of the world: Things are intrinsically beautiful. The world is infused with light. Nature is perceived in an instant and is captured in its purest form. Góngora, the magician of sounds and colors, became a daemon with the power to create a new world.

OTHER MAJOR WORKS

PLAYS: *Las firmezas de Isabela*, pr. 1610; *El doctor Carlino*, pr. 1613.

BIBLIOGRAPHY

Alonso, Dámaso. *Estudios y ensayos Gongorinos*. Madrid: Editorial Gredos, 1982. A collection of essays and critical studies of Góngora's works published in Spanish.

_____. *Góngora y el Polifemo*. Madrid: Gredos, 1980. A three-volume biographical and critical study of Góngora focusing on his *Fable of Polyphemus and Galatea*. Published in Spanish.

McCaw, R. John. *Transforming Text: A Study of Luis de Góngora's "Soledades."* Potomac, Md.: Scripta Humanistica, 2000. An extensive critical interpretation of *Soledades*. Includes bibliographical references.

Vilanova, Antonio. *Las fuentes y los temas del Polifemo de Góngora*. Barcelona: PPU, 1992. A two-volume, in-depth critical study of Góngora's *Fábula de Polifemo y Galatea*. Published in Spanish.

Woods, Michael. *Gracián Meets Góngora: The Theory and Practice of Wit*. Warminster, England: Aris & Phillips, 1995. A critical study of the use of humor in Baltasar Gracián y Morales and Luis de Góngora y Argote. Includes bibliographical references and indexes.

Francisco J. Cevallos;
bibliography updated by the editors

ENRIQUE GONZÁLEZ MARTÍNEZ

Born: Guadalajara, Mexico; April 13, 1871
Died: Mexico City, Mexico; February 19, 1952

PRINCIPAL POETRY

Preludios, 1903
Lirismos, 1907
Silénter, 1909
Los senderos ocultos, 1911
La muerte del cisne, 1915
El libro de la fuerza, de la bondad y del ensueño,
   1917
Parábolas y otras poemas, 1918
Jardins de Francia, 1919 (translation)
La palabra del viento, 1921
El romero alucinado, 1923
Las señales furtivas, 1925
Poemas truncas, 1935
Ausencia y canto, 1937
El diluvio del fuego, 1938
Tres rosas en el ánfora, 1939
Bajo el signo mortal, 1942
Segundo despertar y otras poemas, 1945
Vilano al viento, 1948
Babel, poema al margen del tiempo, 1949
El nuevo narciso y otras poemas, 1952

OTHER LITERARY FORMS

Enrique González Martínez's reputation rests entirely on his poetry. He was active as a journalist, and his only published fiction—three short stories—appeared in a provincial newspaper and in a magazine which he coedited early in his career. These stories show a marked influence of the Naturalist movement. The first one, "Una hembra" (a female), which appeared in *El heraldo de Mexico* in 1895, narrates the transformation experienced by a girl of the humblest class when the illicit love affair into which she is forced by the terrible circumstances of her life results in the birth of a child. The second story, "La chiquilla" (the girl), which was published in *Arte* in 1907, relates the sensual awakening of a young girl being reared in the house of a priest. In the third of the stories, "A vuelo" (ringing bells)—also pub-

lished in *Arte*, in 1908—a sick boy dies when he is unable to suppress his desire to ring his favorite bell in the church on the day of the town fiesta.

González Martínez's acceptance speech on his admission to the Mexican Academy of Language, "Algunos aspectos de la lírica mexicana" (some aspects of Mexican lyricism), examines the history of Mexican lyric poetry and draws the picture of its evolution, analyzing the best Mexican poets, pointing out weaknesses and virtues, and determining influences and trends. It has been considered one of his most refined prose pieces.

González Martínez wrote two autobiographical volumes *El hombre del búho* (1944; the man of the owl) and *La apacible locura* (1951; the peaceful madness). In these two books, written during the author's advanced years, he recalls the most important moments and events of his life in a plain and clear style, without literary pretentiousness. Sincerity and humility are perhaps the most impressive features of these two works, in which the poet talks about his contemporaries, describes his friends, and tells of his successes and his disappointments.

ACHIEVEMENTS

Enrique González Martínez achieved his first literary success at an early age. When he was fourteen years old, he won first prize in a contest organized by the English-Spanish newspaper of Guadalajara, *The Sun*, for his translation of an English poem about John Milton. Later in his life, he was Effective Member of the prestigious Mexican Academy of Language, president of the Athenaeum of the Youth of Mexico, member of the Seminary of Mexican Culture, Founding Member of the renowned National College of Mexico, and a professor of language and literature at various institutions of higher education. He received the 1944 Manuel Ávila Camacho Literary Award, was president of the organizing committee of the American Continental Congress of Peace, and, in 1949, was a candidate for the Nobel Prize in Literature.

BIOGRAPHY

Enrique González Martínez was born in Guadalajara, the capital of the state of Jalisco, Mexico, on April 13, 1871. He was the son of a schoolteacher, José María González, and his wife, Feliciana Martínez. González Martínez attended the grade school directed by his father, and in 1881, he entered the preparatory school run by the Church in the Conciliar Seminary of his native city. Five years later, when he was only fifteen, he entered the School of Medicine of Guadalajara.

González Martínez's fondness for poetry began at a very early age. As a child, he often amazed his parents and other adults with his achievements as a student as well as with his ability to write verse. Although he devoted himself with enthusiasm to the study of medicine during his student years, his interest in poetry grew. When he was graduated as a medical doctor in 1893, he had already published a number of poems in newspapers and magazines, earning for himself a reputation as a provincial poet.

Despite his appointment upon graduation as an adjunct professor of physiology in the School of Medicine in Guadalajara, González Martínez did not have much success practicing medicine in his native city. At this time, González Martínez's father was offered the post of headmaster in a school that was going to be opened in Culiacán, the capital of the state of Sinaloa. It was an excellent opportunity to improve the family's economic situation, and since González Martínez had yet to establish himself as a physician, he decided to move to Culiacán with his parents and his younger sister, Josefina. They arrived there at the end of 1895, and for the next six months González Martínez tried without success to establish his professional practice. After this time, he decided to move to the small town of Sinaloa, where he finally established himself and resided for the next fifteen years. In 1898, González Martínez married Luisa Rojo y Fonseca, a girl who had strongly impressed him when he had first seen her on his initial visit to Sinaloa. Their marriage produced four children— Enrique, María Luisa, Héctor, and Jorge—the youngest child, however, only lived sixteen months.

The fifteen years that González Martínez lived in Sinaloa were a period of intense professional activity as a doctor as well as of incessant literary production. For some time, the poet seemed to be content with publishing his poems in newspapers and magazines of the provinces as well as the capital, where he was beginning to be known. Nevertheless, in 1900, an event took place that prompted González Martínez to publish his first book of poetry. For reasons not yet fully understood, a

newspaper in Guadalajara published a false report of his death. Several publications in different cities expressed their sorrow for the early death of such a promising poet and reprinted poems of his that had previously appeared in their pages. One of González Martínez's friends published a long article lamenting the death of the poet, recalling his life, listing his successes, and praising his virtues as a physician, a man of letters, and a citizen. When all of this came to the attention of González Martínez in the small town where he lived, the poet rushed to deny the false information, and in a letter written in a joking tone he thanked his friend from Guadalajara for the informative and sorrowful article. After the uproar occasioned by this event had passed, the poet concluded that his poems must be good enough to be published in book form, and thus his first collection, titled *Preludios* (preludes), appeared in 1903.

Although González Martínez continued practicing medicine, his other activities seemed to multiply after the publication of his first book. In 1907, he published *Lirismos* (lyricisms), his second book of poetry, and between 1907 and 1909 he edited, along with his friend Sixto Osuna, the magazine *Arte*, which was published in

Enrique González Martínez (Instituto Nacional de Bellas Artes, Mexico)

Mocorito. Between 1907 and 1911, he occupied the position of Political Prefect in the districts of Mocorito, El Fuerte, and Mazatlán in the state of Sinaloa, and at the beginning of the Revolution of 1910, he was the Secretary General of the government in Culiacán, the capital of the state of Sinaloa. In 1909, he published another book of poetry, *Silénter* (silently), and was appointed Correspondent Member of the Mexican Academy of Language.

The year 1911 was of special importance in the life of González Martínez. It was during this year that he published his book *Los senderos ocultos* (the concealed paths). It was also the year in which he decided to abandon his medical career completely in order to devote the rest of his life to poetry, changing his residence and that of his family to Mexico City. There, he began to work as an editorial writer for the newspaper *El imparcial*. Finally, he was designated Effective Member of the Mexican Academy of Language and affiliated himself with the Athenaeum of the Youth of Mexico, whose president he became a year later. In 1912, he founded the magazine *Argos*, which appeared for only one year, and in 1913, he was appointed Under Secretary of Public Instruction and Fine Arts. After occupying this position for a year, he spent a year as Secretary General of the government in Puebla. In 1915, he returned to Mexico City to devote himself to teaching and was appointed a professor of Spanish language and literature and of general literature in the National Preparatory School, as well as in the Normal School for Women. He was also appointed a professor of French literature in the School of Higher Studies, later called the Faculty of Philosophy and Letters. He soon lost his professorial positions, however, for political reasons.

After 1915, the poetic production of González Martínez increased, and his books of poetry followed one another with a frequency uncommon even among the most prolific poets. Nevertheless, despite his constant dedication to poetry, in 1917 he went back to work for a newspaper, this time as an editorial writer for *El heraldo de México*, while at the same time acting as coeditor of the magazine *Pegaso*.

In 1920, González Martínez began his diplomatic career with an appointment as Minister Plenipotentiary to Chile, whence he was transferred to a similar position in Argentina two years later. After another two years, he was appointed Minister Plenipotentiary for Mexico in Spain and Portugal, and he held this position for six years, until 1931.

The relatively peaceful life of González Martínez suffered two serious disruptions. The first was the death of his wife, Luisa, in 1935, and the second was the death of his son Enrique in 1939. The poet expressed in his poems the sorrow and the solitude that these two deaths caused him.

In 1942, González Martínez was admitted into the Seminary of Mexican Culture. A year later, he was appointed Founding Member of the important cultural organization the National College of Mexico, and in 1944, he received the Manuel Ávila Camacho Literary Award. In 1949, he presided over the organizing committee of the American Continental Congress of Peace, and he was nominated for the Nobel Prize for Literature. He died as he was approaching his eighty-first birthday, on February 19, 1952.

ANALYSIS

Placing Enrique González Martínez in the global picture of the movements and tendencies of Hispanic literature is not an easy task. Among the factors contributing to this difficulty is the fact that the poet was active for more than a half century, during which time many styles and techniques succeeded one another. Nevertheless, although González Martínez was influenced by many poets, both from his own epoch and from other eras, he never permitted another poet's idiom to smother his own voice.

González Martínez began to write when the poetic environment in the Hispanic world was dominated by *Modernismo*. The great Nicaraguan poet Rubén Darío had succeeded in imposing his peculiar modality on this movement not only in Latin America but also in Spain. *Modernista* poetry was greatly influenced by the Parnassian and Symbolist schools of French origin, often featuring landscapes of ancient Greece or of eighteenth century France and including all kinds of exotic plants and flowers. The preferred fauna were animals known for their beauty, such as the peacock and the swan—especially the latter, which became a symbol of the movement. Metals and precious stones were used constantly as poetic motifs. The language of the *Modernistas* was musical and richly textured; adjectives were used profusely, and the imagery evoked strange impressions and sensations, synesthesia appearing with extraordinary frequency.

It was only natural that a movement so generalized and powerful as *Modernismo* had an influence on a young poet such as González Martínez, who had an expansive concept of poetry and who was well equipped for artistic creation to the most refined degree. In his poetry can be found Parnassian and Symbolist notes, Satyrs and beautiful animals, musically elegant adjectives and synesthesia—everything with the clear desire to produce a refined artistic creation. For these reasons, many would consider González Martínez a member of the *Modernismo* movement.

Nevertheless, González Martínez was never a *Modernista* in the style of Rubén Darío. His Satyrs and nymphs suffer from a lack of realism, and his fowls and stones—they are not always precious—do not function as mere ornaments in his poetry but contribute to the development of its ideas as well as communicate emotion. Closer connections could be found between González Martínez and *Modernistas* with the tendencies of the Cuban José Martí and the Colombian José Asunción Silva or with Darío in his later years, when his poetry was richer in insight and profundity. In González Martínez, interior concentration, simplicity of expression, and directness of communication are dominant characteristics.

"WRING THE SWAN'S NECK"

For these reasons, González Martínez fits better among the members of postmodernism. It is true that he was only four years younger than Darío and that he was several years older than the *Modernistas* Leopoldo Lugones, from Argentina, and Julio Herrera y Reissig, from Uruguay. Nevertheless, it must be considered that the Mexican published his first book of poetry in 1903, when he was already thirty-two years old, and that he reached his peak when *Modernismo* was fading and postmodernism was at its apex. In this connection, the sonnet "Tuércele el cuello al cisne" ("Wring the Swan's Neck") should be mentioned.

This is the famous poem in which González Martínez recommended the death of the swan, the symbol of *Modernismo*, and its replacement by the owl as less or-

namental but more wise and thoughtful. The poet himself said that his sonnet was not intended as an attack on Darío and the other first-class *Modernistas*; rather, it was directed against Darío's epigones. Nevertheless, González Martínez's poem was widely regarded as the death blow to *Modernismo* and the beginning of postmodernism. In any case, González Martínez's aesthetic was fundamentally different from that of the *Modernistas:* He was inclined toward meditation and the patient study of the mysteries of life, rather than toward verbal brilliance for its own sake.

PRELUDIOS

When González Martínez published his first book of poems, he was already an experienced poet, with perfect technical control. In each poem of his first book, *Preludios*, the formal perfection of a master craftsman can be observed, although the poet still had not found his direction. In *Preludios*, many different influences can be noted. The strongest is that of the *Modernistas*, which came to the poet through his compatriots Manuel Guitérrez Nájera and Salvador Días Mirón. Other influences were those of Latin poets, such as Horace, and of Mexican traditional poets, such as Manuel José Othon. Some of González Martínez's phrases have all the brilliance and elegance characteristic of *Modernismo*, as in "Ríe" (laugh)—"over the warm ermine of your shoulders,/ your laugh, fair blond, come forth/ as rainy gold"—or in "Baño" (bath), in which he says that the sculptural nude body of a girl is a "volcano of snow in an eruption of roses." His descriptions of nature, and of the love scenes that take place in it, have all the charm and delicacy of the classical or the national poets, as can be seen in the series of sonnets grouped under the title of "Rústica" (rustic).

The presence of these diverse influences and orientations clearly indicates that in *Preludios* the poet was still trying to find his voice and a more profound source of inspiration. The distinctive voice that would later be characteristic of the best of González Martínez's production is heard only in a few poems in *Preludios*, as when in "A una poeta" (to a poet) he exhorts a fictitious colleague to go to nature in search of "an ideal for your longings," telling him: "See the country, look at the sea, contemplate the sky:/ there is beauty there, inspiration and everything!" Likewise, when he talks of the healthy effects of night and silence, he says: "when the angel of the night spreads/ his sweet peace . . . under the blue silence the poet stretches/ his wings towards the world of dreams."

LIRISMOS

Lirismos, the poet's second collection, was a continuation of the search for himself which began in *Preludios*, and an intensification of his desire for formal perfection. The book is composed mostly of sonnets, and the influences of the *Modernistas* and the ancient classics continue, although somewhat mitigated by characteristics of the French Parnassian and Symbolist movements. Upon the appearance of this book, many praised the artistic perfection of its poems and, based on this perfection, considered the book superior to the first one. The poet, however, was not deceived by these opinions and noticed that the Parnassian coldness had frozen his own voice.

SILÉNTER

As a result, in his next book, *Silénter*, with the sonnet of the same title, he seems to advise himself to look for inspiration in self-intimacy, saying, "give forms to your desires, crystallize your idea/ and wait proudly for a distant dawn." In the first tercet of this sonnet, he calls upon himself to achieve interior silence, advising himself that "a sacred silence sets you apart from the uproar." In one of the central poems of *Silénter*, which is also one of the poet's best known, "Irás sobre la vida de las cosas . . ." (you will go over the life of things . . .), he persists with his idea of returning to nature and investigating silence. He extols nature—"the soliloquy of the fountain, as well as/ the weak blinking of the star"—and advises "that you refine your soul until you are able to listen to the silence and see the shadow."

In another of his best-known poems, "A veces una hoja desprendida . . ." (sometimes a fallen leaf . . .), González Martínez goes deeper in his understanding of nature, expressing a greater intimacy with it: "that star and I know each other,/ that tree and that flower are my friends." In this poem, his identification with nature becomes complete; the poet exclaims "Divine communion! . . . I finally know what you murmur, clear fountain;/ I finally know what you tell me, errant breeze." In "Soñé con un verso . . ." (I dreamed of a verse . . .), the poet tells of having dreamed of a vibrant, clear, and

strong verse; when, after waking, he attempts to relate his dream, he gives a fairly accurate description of his calm and peaceful way of writing poetry: "with mournful crepe my lyre veiled its cords/ and my verse was made of a soft melancholy/ like the steps that glide over the rug." In another poem, "En voz baja" (in a soft voice), the poet tells about his struggle to discover the secret of Nature. He begins by saying, "in all that exists/ I have heard many times your voice, nature"; then, describing his efforts to Nature, a woman, he tells her: "I pursue you and you escape; I adore you and everything is in vain./ Hermetically you hide the clue to the arcanum"; finally he asks when the moment will come in which "devoted lover . . ./ you will tell me in a soft voice the divine secret?"

LOS SENDEROS OCULTOS

In *Los senderos ocultos* González Martínez continues the process initiated in his preceding books—that is, of trying to understand and identify with nature. Here this process reaches its greatest intensity and achieves the most satisfactory results. Perhaps for this reason, *Los senderos ocultos* has been considered by many to be the poet's best work. In "Busca en todas las cosas . . ." (seek in all things . . .), the author adds "the soul of things" as a new objective of the poet's search. That is why he advises: "seek in all things a soul and a hidden/ meaning," adding later that "you will know little by little how to decipher their language . . ./ Oh divine colloquy of the things and the soul!" In the poem "Renovación" (renovation), the poet continues his search for identification, which now is not with the soul or the life of things, but with life itself, in its more universal and comprehensive sense. That same desire for identification includes the poet's beloved in the poem "A la que va conmigo" (to the one who goes with me), in which he tells her that "we will go through life identified with it" and that the "soul of things will be our own soul."

The pantheistic overtones of "Renovación" are even more evident in "Doux pays" (French for "sweet country"), in which the poet dreams of "a divine marriage between human life/ and the life of the world." Later, these thoughts will be embellished with a kind of Christian sweetness, as, for example, in "Cuando sepas hallar una sonrisa . . ." (when you learn how to find a smile . . .): "when you learn how to find a smile in the drop of water, in the mist,/ in the sun, in the bird, and in the breeze," then "like the Saint of Assisi, you will call brothers/ the tree, the cloud, and the beast"; then "you will reverently take off your sandals/ not to wound the stones in the road." In "Tiendo a la vida el ruego . . ." (I have a request for life . . .), the poet expresses his desire for total possession of and identification with life when he says that he does not ask for "the incomplete gift, but for the totality of life"; in the previously mentioned "Wring the Swan's Neck," he elevates life to the category of a goddess: "adore life intensely/ and let life understand your homage."

In the beautiful and well-known poem "Como hermana y hermano" (like sister and brother), the poet describes the peaceful way in which he and his beloved are traversing the road of life, and he admits that life has secrets and mysteries that man cannot discover. When, in the silence of the night, the poet and his beloved hear their hearts beating, he says, "do not fear, there are songs heard/ but we will never know who signs them. . . ." When she, upon feeling a strange sensation, asks if he has kissed her, his answer is, "you will never/ know who gives those kisses." Finally, when she feels a tear sliding down her forehead, she asks him if he is crying, but the poet says, "we will never know who sheds those nocturnal tears."

LA MUERTE DEL CISNE

Although González Martínez maintained his preoccupation with the themes of his early collections, in *La muerte del cisne* (the death of the swan), he began to show a desire for innovation leading to new themes and more varied formal techniques. The result is greater diversity, but also a loss of cohesiveness and the appearance of contradictions. In the poem "Ánima trémula" (trembling soul), the poet aspires to totality and wants to be, at the same time, "the viewer and the spectacle,/ and be the dreamer and the dream." In "A una alma ingenua" (to a simple soul) he shows a preference for what is simple and humble, asking "the soul without ideas," to whom he is talking, to "give me your eyes to see life." In "Iba por un camino" (I was going on a road), the poet shows a powerful desire for life: "Let's live, let's live, because life is escaping!" In "Hortus conclusus" (Latin for "the enclosed garden"), on the other hand, he chooses to detach himself from life; when life calls, his soul "quietly and taciturnly . . . has closed the door . . . and does not answer." A kind of pessimism now appears with some frequency. In "Los días inútiles" (the useless days), the poet, reconstructing his past, feels the awakening of "an immense desire/ to sob by myself and ask for pardon"; in "Mañana los poetas" ("Tomorrow the Poets Will Sing"), he says that the poets of the future, despite all of their successes, "will pick up the abandoned lyre from the floor/ and will sing with it our same song."

LATER POETRY

In his subsequent books, González Martínez continued to write his own very personal poetry, meditating in silence on his ideas, in intimate communion with nature, and expressing himself in his direct, simple, and polished language. He was for a long time the most admired poet of Mexico, and several generations of young poets considered him their guide and inspiration. In his later years, when he was no longer in vogue, his poetry suffered a radical devaluation, and he has never regained his former eminence. Nevertheless, he dominated an entire epoch in his country, and he wrote poems that will not disappear with the passing of time.

OTHER MAJOR WORKS

SHORT FICTION: "Una hembra," 1895; "La chiquilla," 1907; "A vuelo," 1908.

NONFICTION: "Algunos aspectos de la lírica mexicana," 1932; *El hombre del búho*, 1944; *La apacible locura*, 1951.

BIBLIOGRAPHY

Brushwood, John S. *Enrique González Martínez*. New York: Twayne, 1969. An introductory biographical study and critical analysis of selected works by Martínez. Includes bibliographic references.

Geist, Anthony L., and José B. Monleón, eds. *Modernism and Its Margins: Reinscribing Cultural Modernity from Spain and Latin America*. New York: Garland, 1999. A rereading of modernism and the modernist canon from a double distance: geographical and temporal. It is a revision not only from the periphery (Spain and Latin America), but from this new fin de siècle as well, a revisiting of modernity and its cultural artifacts from that same postmodernity.

Goldberg, I. *Studies in Spanish American Literature*. Port Washington, N.Y.: Kennikat Press, 1968. A critical study of Modernism in Latin American Literature.

Rogelio A. de la Torre
(including translations from the Spanish);
bibliography updated by the editors

JOHN GOWER

Born: Kent(?), England; c. 1330
Died: Southwark, England; October, 1408

PRINCIPAL POETRY

Cinkante Ballades, probably before 1374
Mirour de l'Omme, 1376-1379
Vox Clamantis, 1379-1382
Confessio Amantis, 1386-1390
Traitié pour Essampler Les Amantz marietz, 1397
Cronica Tripertita, c. 1400
In Praise of Peace, 1400
The Complete Works of John Gower, 1899-1902 (G. C. Macaulay, editor)
The Major Latin Works of John Gower: The Voice of One Crying and the Tripartite Chronicle, 1962 (Eric W. Stockton, translator)

OTHER LITERARY FORMS

John Gower is remembered only for his poetry. A fine craftsman, he holds a secure place in English poetry even when compared to his friend and the major poet of his time, Geoffrey Chaucer.

ACHIEVEMENTS

In his own lifetime and in the generations immediately following, John Gower's reputation as one of England's primary poets, second only to Geoffrey Chaucer himself, was secure and unquestioned. Gower wrote, and wrote competently, major poetic works in three languages: French, Latin, and English. With Chaucer, Gower was instrumental in adapting the polished French style to English poetry, and his preeminence is recognized by his successors from John Lydgate to Sir Philip Sidney.

Gower's critical reputation began to decline sharply, however, in the seventeenth century, and it has never completely recovered. There were at least three major reasons for this decline. First, because of certain revisions in his works reflecting the political situation of the late fourteenth century, Gower has often been considered a political opportunist and sycophant. Second, it has been conjectured that another revision in his *Confessio Amantis* is evidence that Gower had a bitter and unresolved quarrel with his friend Chaucer. Third, Gower's works have been considered to be rather dull. The first two of these charges have nothing whatever to do with the quality of Gower's poetry, and in fact are probably unfounded. The third charge is much more difficult to answer. It is certainly true that the *Mirour de l'Omme* and to some extent the *Vox Clamantis* are for the most part unpalatable to modern readers, though this is chiefly the result of a shift in taste away from the popular medieval mode of the *complaint*, which was generalized in content and moralistic in purpose. Gower's great English work, *Confessio Amantis*, is less overtly didactic and reveals the poet's real talent for imaginative storytelling.

Although Gower no longer receives the undeserved high praise of being placed second only to Chaucer, he is nevertheless recognized today as a poet of no small talent, though perhaps without Chaucer's genius. He was a superb craftsman, whose verses in both French and English have a smoothness and a polish which Chaucer never achieves, although the regularity may at times become monotonous. Furthermore, Gower the craftsman had a keen interest in unity and form. For example, he imposed a careful and rigid structure, whether based on the seven deadly sins or the three estates, upon his *complaint* material. There is also reason to believe that the many revisions he made in his major works during his lifetime were at least in part an attempt to forge them into a single, unified whole: John Fisher sees them as a three-part discourse on the nature of man and of society, and the need for each individual, but particularly the King, to follow reason and natural law for the common profit.

BIOGRAPHY

John Gower was born about 1330. That he was a Kentishman is indicated by several aspects of his English verse which were characteristic of the fourteenth century Kentish dialect. It has been suggested that he was descended from the Gower family of Langburgh, Yorkshire, and that he moved to Kent at an early age. All of this must remain conjecture, however, since no documentation exists, and little is known of Gower's early life. He was almost certainly a member of an upper-middle-class family, and perhaps was a retainer in some noble house.

During the period 1365 to 1374, Gower was involved in a number of speculative real estate transactions in Kent. He may have been a lawyer, since his works display a keen knowledge of the legal profession. Probably about this time Gower was writing the short love poems in French which would later be collected in the *Cinkante Ballades*. Gower could have become familiar with French courtly poetry had he been connected in his youth to a noble household. But the *ballades* show little influence of the contemporary school of French poetry, and John H. Fisher (in *John Gower*, 1964) has conjectured that he may have written the poems for the London *Pui*, a semireligious middle-class fraternal organization which held poetical contests at its feasts.

By the mid-1370's, Gower's literary career reached a turning point, as he became at once more ambitious and more sober. One influence could have been his association with Geoffrey Chaucer, which may have begun about that time, since by 1378, when Chaucer left for Italy, they were close enough for Chaucer to have given Gower his power of attorney. Gower now set his mind on a very moralistic and very long French poem, the *Mirour de l'Omme*. He followed this almost immediately by another moralizing poem, this time in Latin, called *Vox Clamantis*. In the first book of this poem, Gower presents a vivid and frightening picture of the Peasant's Revolt of 1381, from the perspective of a conservative, upper-middle-class landholder. He sees in the revolt the concrete epitome of the abstract evils of the world which he describes at length in the *Mirour de l'Omme* and the remainder of the *Vox Clamantis*.

By the late 1370's, Gower seems to have already begun his relationship with the Priory of St. Mary Overeys in Southwark. He was a major benefactor of the priory, and he possibly contributed largely to its restoration in 1377. He is known to have lived in a personal apartment in the priory by the late 1390's and may have been living

there for years, having been granted the living space in return for his charitable contributions. There is a strong possibility that many of the Gower manuscripts, which suggest authorial supervision in their excellence, may have been produced at the priory under Gower's watchful eye.

About 1386, King Richard II requested that Gower write something in English, and this marked a second turning point in his literary career, since in writing *Confessio Amantis* Gower was able to develop his real talent as a storyteller. But the different versions of *Confessio Amantis* also provide a good indication of Gower's relationship with the King. In the first version of *Vox Clamantis*, Gower had excused the young King from blame for the state of affairs in England, and exhorted him to follow after the example of his father, the Black Prince. The first version of *Confessio Amantis* in 1390 still presents the King in a good light. It also makes a flattering allusion to Chaucer as a poet of Venus. Later that year Gower revised the poem, leaving out his earlier praise of Richard's rule, and in 1393 he revised it again, rededicating the work to Henry, earl of Derby (later to become Henry IV), and, incidentally, leaving out the praise of Chaucer. This latter action has caused some to speculate that a quarrel had occurred between the two poets, perhaps over Chaucer's good-humored jibes in the Man of Law's prologue at the "moral" Gower's shameful stories of incest in *Confessio Amantis*. But the dropping of the Chaucer allusion may be explained in other ways. Gower may have left it out simply because he wanted to eliminate exactly the same number of lines as he was adding with his new dedication. He may even have dropped the lines because he knew that Richard would not like the revisions he had made, and Gower did not want to jeopardize Chaucer's favorable position with the King. On the other hand, Henry seems to have appreciated the dedication, for in 1393 he gave Gower a gift of a ceremonial collar.

Gower's opinion of Richard seems to have continued to deteriorate, for he also revised the *Vox Clamantis*, and replaced the passages excusing the King's youth with lines of stern admonition about the state of affairs in England. Gower welcomed the deposition of Richard and ascension of Henry IV in 1399 and wrote in the *Cronica Tripertita* a rather distorted history justifying Henry's assumption of royal power. Henry recognized Gower's loyal support, granting him an annuity of two pipes of wine on November 21, 1399.

By this time, Gower's health was failing. On January 25, 1398, nearly seventy years old, he married Agnes Groundolf, who was almost certainly his nurse. Perhaps Gower had been married before, but there is no record of it. During his final years while Agnes took care of him at St. Mary's, Gower was unable to do much writing, for he went totally blind in about 1401. Gower's will was attested on August 15, 1408, and proved on October 24 of that year. In it, he generously remembered Agnes and the canons of the priory, and gave his body to be buried in the churchyard there. The effigy can still be seen at Southwark Cathedral. It depicts Gower's head resting on three large volumes—the *Speculum Meditantis* (another name for the *Mirour de l'Omme*), the *Vox Clamantis*, and *Confessio Amantis*—upon which he wanted his posthumous reputation to rest.

ANALYSIS

Anyone who reads only a few lines of John Gower's poetry cannot help being struck by its intentional didacticism. Imaginative writing was typically didactic during the medieval age, but Gower's moralistic streak was so pronounced that it prompted his good friend Chaucer to apply the adjective that has been inseparable from the poet's name since it first appeared in *Troilus and Criseyde* (1382): "the moral Gower."

Since it seems clear that Gower thought of himself first as a moralist and only secondarily as a poet, any examination of Gower's poetry must concentrate chiefly upon theme. With Gower, the theme was nothing new or unusual; he was not an original thinker, but spoke with a voice rooted in tradition and mirroring the attitudes of the conservative, upper middle class to which he belonged. What is remarkable is the persistence of Gower's chief theme through his three major works, the *Mirour de l'Omme*, *Vox Clamantis*, and *Confessio Amantis*; with almost monotonous consistency Gower stresses the degeneracy of the contemporary world because of the perversion and distortion of love. The love of which Gower speaks is the universal, divine love which in medieval thought (particularly as popularized in Boethius's *The Consolation of Philosophy*, 523, and

Macrobius's *Commentary on the Dream of Scipio*, early fifth century C.E.) was regarded as binding the universe in an ordered harmony. This universal order is divine law; thus law and love are immutably connected.

It is society in which Gower is chiefly interested. The laws governing society—human or "positive" law—should reflect the love and order of natural law, which man's reason should recognize. John Fisher, who was first to realize the importance of this concept of nature and human law in Gower's three major works, calls those works a trilogy which takes its entire structure and meaning from this law/love idea. Thus Gower stresses the importance of individual reason and virtue in conjunction with legal justice that preserves the moral order for the common profit. For Gower, this meant preservation of the social order as well, and so the Peasants' Revolt of 1381, for example, becomes in the *Vox Clamantis* an illustration of man rebelling against reason and natural law.

In addition, this preservation of law and order meant that the King occupied a uniquely vital position. Gower constantly stresses the importance of the principle of kingship in an ordered society. The King is charged with the responsibility of preserving legal justice and order among all three estates (clergy, nobility, and peasantry), and maintaining the moral integrity of the entire nation. This belief goes far in explaining Gower's shifting attitude toward Richard II and his ultimate allegiance to Henry IV as a king more likely to fulfill this obligation. Important in Gower's evaluation of Richard was his absolute insistence on man's responsibility for his own actions. He consistently attacks fatalism and the idea of the "wheel of Fortune," stressing instead the responsibility of every individual, particularly the ruler, to follow the dictates of reason.

Gower's revisions of his main works reflect this disintegrating opinion of Richard, and link the three works to form a complete and systematic commentary on man and society. The encyclopedic nature of such an undertaking was typical of the Middle Ages, but Gower's concern for unity and form was rare. His moral theme and the influence of other didactic treatises of his day suggested to him two particular organizing formulae: the seven deadly sins and the three estates. While it may be argued that such formulae provide arbitrary and artificial patterns of organization, it cannot be denied that Gower's preoccupation with order and unity is strong; it may, in fact, reflect the theme of order so loudly proclaimed in the three works: form matches content.

MIROUR DE L'OMME

Gower's earliest major work is the *Mirour de l'Omme*, which he refers to in later life as the *Speculum Hominis* and, finally, the *Speculum Meditantis*, the alterations being an attempt to bring the earlier poem's title into harmony with *Vox Clamantis* and *Confessio Amantis* in order to suggest the close relationship of the three works. The *Mirour de l'Omme* survives in a single manuscript discovered in the Cambridge University Library in 1895 by Gower's great editor, G. C. Macaulay. The manuscript consists of 28,603 octosyllabic lines of French verse, although the absence of several leaves at the beginning and end indicate that the complete poem must have been some two thousand lines longer. The verse form is a twelve-line stanza known as a "Héliland Strophe," popular among French moral writers of the period. The lines rhyme *aabaabbaabaa*, and the stanzas generally contain a pause in the middle and a moral tag or summing up at the end, in the last two or three lines. Macaulay describes Gower's verse as strictly syllabic, while at the same time displaying a distinct English rhythm. He also stresses the uncanny regularity of the lines, finding only twenty-one of the more than 28,000 lines in the poem to be metrically imperfect.

Gower's main concern in the *Mirour de l'Omme* is his constant theme of the decay of the world and society because of man's turning from reason. He begins by calling sin the cause of all evils in the world, and in the first main section of the poem Gower presents a manual of vices and virtues and delineates the efforts of the Devil and Sin to conquer man. Sin, it is said, was conceived by the Devil, who, enamored of his own creation, engendered upon her Death. Death, following his father's lead, likewise intermarried with Sin and produced the seven deadly vices. The Devil then held a conference with his whole brood and with the World to plan how they might best defeat God's plan and circumvent man's salvation. The parallel between this and John Milton's *Paradise Lost* (1667) is of course striking, although it seems unlikely that Milton could have read the *Mirour de l'Omme:* As far as is known, there was no manuscript

available in his time. Still, no common source has been found, so the problem of the relationship of the two works is unresolved.

In Gower's work, the Devil is unsuccessful in his first attempt to win man over, since after much debate man follows the dictates of Reason. The Devil, however, increases his forces. After the seven daughters of sin marry the World, each has five daughters of her own, so that for some nine thousand lines, Gower delineates the five branches of each of the seven deadly sins. The entire progeny of vices then violently attack man, who comes completely under the power of Sin. God retaliates by sending seven virtues to marry Reason, and each of these has five daughters, to counter the thirty-five vices already described.

In the second main section of the poem, the next eight thousand lines, the author proposes to examine human society in order to determine whether the vices or the virtues are winning. Thus, Gower begins a complaint on the estates of man, reviewing every class of human society, beginning with the clergy, and moving through secular rulers, to the common people. Every rank of society is corrupt, according to Gower. The tone here is unrelentingly somber, yet this is probably the most interesting section of the *Mirour de l'Omme* because of the picture it gives modern readers of life in fourteenth century England. The descriptions are generally stock, but not necessarily untrue, and may be worth reading for the sake of comparison with Chaucer's estates-satire in the general prologue to *The Canterbury Tales* (1387-1400): Here Gower describes a gluttonous monk who loves hunting, a venal friar who abuses the office of the confessional by taking advantage of young women, a physician in collusion with the apothecary to bilk his patients, and shopkeepers who engage in any number of tricks to cheat customers—such as the tavern keeper who is able to get all the wines of Europe from a single cask. In Gower's world view, the order of society reflected the divinely ordained harmony of the universe. Reason and the law of love kept all in order. Thus rebellion was tantamount to revolt against God, and, because it perverted reason, turned men into beasts.

Having described the origin of sin and the effect of sin on society, Gower ends with a discussion of what man must do to be reconciled with God. Man must reform and pray to the Virgin to intercede for him; thus the poem ends with a Life of the Virgin. What is thematically most important in this section is Gower's insistence upon man's responsibility for his own actions. The condition of the world and society cannot be blamed on the stars, says Gower, nor are plants, birds, and fish at fault, since they follow the law of nature. Man is to blame: He is a microcosm and the chaotic state of the world reflects his sin.

In the final analysis, the *Mirour de l'Omme* is not a great poem. It is not even, by most standards, a very good poem. Its organization and versification are admirable, and it gives a useful picture of its age, and there are flashes of good poetry in the complaint on the estates, but the unity is destroyed by the poem's inordinate length and monotony. Perhaps its relation to Gower's other major works is of chief interest: written in French, the *Mirour de l'Omme* was intended as a "mirror" in which one of the cultivated French-speaking laity might examine his conscience. Personal virtue and individual responsibility are the themes, and from here Gower could expand into the areas of legal justice and royal responsibility.

VOX CLAMANTIS

Gower's second major work, the *Vox Clamantis*, is a poem in seven books, consisting of some 10,265 lines of Latin elegiac verse. Gower's Latin lacks the smoothness and regularity of his French and English compositions, and the style is further muddled by his extensive wholesale borrowings from other Latin poems. Eric Stockton, the poem's modern translator, enumerates thirteen hundred lines which were appropriated chiefly from Ovid, the *Aurora* (started c. 1170) of Petrus Riga, and the *De Vita Monachorum*; nevertheless, in spite of the patchwork of sources, Gower keeps the train of thought coherent, and the fact that the poem survives in ten manuscripts, four produced in Gower's lifetime, attest to the work's popularity.

This popularity, in contrast with the *Mirour de l'Omme*, is due in part to the more public nature of the *Vox Clamantis*. The subject matter—a critique of the three estates—is essentially the same as the second part of the *Mirour de l'Omme*, but the use of Latin suggests that Gower's concern is now not so much with the individual virtue stressed in the French poem as with the consequences of individual morality in human society. Thus he uses the universal language, and, by aligning himself through his title with the messianic prophets Isaiah and John the Baptist, he implies that his words are divinely inspired.

The poem begins with what has been justly praised as the most powerful part of the *Vox Clamantis:* a vivid allegorical description of the Peasant's Revolt of 1381. The revolt is seen as a concrete manifestation of the consequences of individual sin for society as a whole: disintegration and chaos, a society rushing madly toward its own apocalyptic destruction. This first book begins as a dream vision. The narrator, after a fearful night, has a dream in which he sees moving across the fields bands of people suddenly changed, through God's wrath, into the forms of beasts. Here Gower graphically pictures how the failure of man to follow the dictates of reason degrades him and makes him bestial. The men turn into asses, swine, frogs, and flies, and oxen who refuse to eat straw or to be subject to the yoke—a description corresponding closely to Gower's condemnation of the peasantry at the end of the *Mirour de l'Omme*. Wat Tyler is pictured as a jay skilled in speech, inciting the peasants, who bring chaos to society by upsetting the ordered hierarchy which reflects the harmony inherent in natural law.

Book I continues with a description of the ferocious sacking of London, called "New Troy," and the murder of the archbishop of Canterbury, Simon Sudbury. Although the historical accuracy of Gower's account may be questionable, it does present a clear picture of the horror that a middle-class Londoner must have felt at the time. The narrator flees to the forests but can find no refuge until he escapes aboard a ship, apparently the ship of faith. He lands in the isle of Britain, whose inhabitants have through violence done away with law and justice, though they could be the greatest people on earth if they could learn love. Gower again stresses love, the binding force of the universe, as the glue to hold society together.

How did society fall so low? Gower begins book II, apparently the original opening of the poem, by emphasizing once again man's moral responsibility: Men like to blame Fortune for their problems, but this is merely shirking responsibility. Man is to blame for all evil in the world. This Gower follows by four books criticizing the three estates (clergy, nobility, and peasantry) in a manner similar to that of the *Mirour de l'Omme*. Again, Gower presents an interesting picture of the age, but one that lacks the realistic detail of Chaucer's satire or Langland's. Lechery and avarice are the most common vices. The two most vivid sections are, first, the description of the smaller merchants and artisans of London— the bakers, butchers, jewelers, and the like, all in the service of fraud that make the bustle of the city real for the reader—and, second, the vehement condemnation of all connected with the law, for law is turned into a device to make money, rather than a reflection of divine order.

In book VI Gower specifically addresses the duties of the king, which are seen chiefly in terms of legal justice: The king should avoid sin and protect all laws and should rule peaceably and with love. It has been noted how Gower excused King Richard in the first version of the *Vox Clamantis* but indicts him in the second; in the final version, to which Gower appended the *Cronica Tripertita* (c. 1400), the fall of the king is portrayed as the direct consequence of the evils of his reign. Thus, Gower's conviction of the moral responsibility of the king for preserving the order of the state seems to have grown stronger as time went on.

After his address to the king, Gower returns to the general degeneration of the world from its former state. The theme of a golden past is brought out by a series of biblical and historical allusions which illustrate the world's decay. Book VII begins with a description of the statue of Nebuchadnezzar's dream the statue's golden head, representing the golden age, has been chopped off, and only the feet of iron and clay remain, symbolizing the iron-like hearts of the avaricious and the weak flesh of the lustful in the degenerate present.

The theme is not unlike that of Chaucer's "The Former Age." In fact, several of Chaucer's philosophical "Boethian" lyrics parallel parts of the *Vox Clamantis*: In book VI, chapter 14, Gower reminds the king that true nobility comes from virtue rather than birth—the theme of "Gentilesse." At the end of chapter 18, Gower begs the king to restore the laws and banish evil, in lines recalling the envoy to "Lak of Stedfastnesse." Since Chaucer translated Boethius in 1380, when Gower would have been writing this poem, it is interesting to speculate upon an exchange of ideas between the two poets.

The entire *Vox Clamantis* ends with a striking *memento mori*. Asserting again how man, the microcosm, perverts all creation when he sins, Gower gives the notion a gruesome twist by describing how the forms of putrefaction suffered by the flesh after death parallel the seven deadly sins: The avaricious man has now no coffer but a coffin; the wrathful man cannot now frighten away the worm devouring his heart. "As ye sin, so shall ye rot" seems to be the rule. Death comes to all; therefore, it is time now to repent. Gower ends by lamenting the condition of England, which not only is full of sin but as a result lacks justice. An apocalypse is in store unless the nation repents and finds its way back to justice.

Thus, the *Vox Clamantis* ends as it began—with a clear emphasis upon the social consequences of the individual sins enumerated in the complaint on the estates. Reform is needed in society from the top down and in each person, but particularly in the king himself. Gower now needed to elaborate upon royal responsibility and its relation to love, and that is the theme of Gower's last and greatest work.

CONFESSIO AMANTIS

When Gower began to write in English, he also changed his approach to his theme and made it more subtle. According to the prologue to *Confessio Amantis*, Richard II gave Gower a commission for the poem, so Gower decided to write "in oure englissh." Since the audience was the court, Gower took the fashionable courtly love tradition as his starting point. In the "religion of love" vein, Gower structured his book as a confessional manual for a lover, full of tales illustrating the various sins against love, in the framework of the seven deadly sins with Genius, priest of Venus, as confessor. Chaucer's *The Legend of Good Women* (1380-1386), a courtly love parody of the *Golden Legend*, may have sprung from the same royal command and may have been intended as a companion piece to *Confessio Amantis*. Gower, however, showed much more enthusiasm for the task, compiling a work of thirty-three thousand lines. The less moralistic approach and more accessible English language made this Gower's most popular work: Some forty manuscripts survive, and the book was printed by Caxton.

Yet *Confessio Amantis* is apparently only a retreat from moralism. That it is deliberately intended to begin where the *Vox Clamantis* leaves off is apparent when the statue of Nebuchadnezzar's dream that ended the *Vox Clamantis* reappears in the prologue to *Confessio Amantis*. Also in the prologue are stressed again Gower's favorite themes: the decay of society and the world because of moral corruption and the destruction of reason; the corruption of the three estates, for which man must take full responsibility; and the disorder in creation mirroring the disorder in the microcosm, man. It is further asserted that society is chaotic because love, the creative principle that brings unity, is gone.

Most readers have seen this prologue as irrelevant to the love theme of the confession itself. The intended connection, however, is obvious: The world is in decay because of a lack of love, of *caritas*. The confessor, through his exemplary tales, instructs the lover in governing his passion through reason. Even the casual reader cannot help noticing that most of the tales do not take romantic love as their theme. In the "Tale of Constantine and Sylvester" (book II), for example, Constantine recognizes that the urging of natural law, that universal principle of love, call for pity—treating others as you would have them treat you. This has nothing to do with courtly love, but reveals Gower's larger purpose. In the conclusion of *Confessio Amantis*, the lover is revealed to be too old for love—a poignant reminder of the transience of earthly love, *cupiditas*—and is advised to pursue instead the love (*caritas*) which does not end and which leads to the common profit.

The implication is that reason, in the end, has triumphed over blind passion and set the lover on the true course of love. This implies another of Gower's chief themes, delineated at length in the tales of *Confessio Amantis*: individual moral responsibility. Because man is endowed with reason, he must use it to direct his will to the good and not be overcome by passion, for this is disorder and sin. Derek Pearsall has shown that Gower's characters move in a world where human behavior has definite meaning, and where they are morally responsible for the consequences of their actions. Thus Gower's revisions of his sources often take the form of providing motives, or relating cause to effect. In the "Tale of Constantine," for example, Gower declares that charity never goes unrewarded, so Constantine's leprosy is cured. In the "Tale of Tereus" (book III), from Ovid, Tereus be-

comes enamored of Philomene "with all his hole entente," and when he rapes her "he no reson understod." He is compared to a wolf, a lion, a hound—Gower depicts the bestiality of man without Reason. Clearly Tereus is morally culpable, and Gower also adds Philomene's prayer to Jupiter, in which she states that the god suffers many wrongs to be done, but that the evil is not his will. The point Gower makes is that man, specifically Tereus, is responsible for the evil. Thus what in Ovid is a tale of blind lust and barbarism is in Gower a tale of moral retribution.

The general theme of the tales is man's moral responsibility for the world's disorder, but it must be remembered that the original audience was the king. More than anyone else, the king must be a responsible moral agent, since he is accountable for the stability of the whole realm. Thus Gower adds book VII, on the education of Alexander. G. C. Macaulay and C. S. Lewis both considered this a digression; its central importance, however, is clear, given the whole corpus of Gower's poetry. *Confessio Amantis* moves from a look at the chaos in the world because of the absence of love, to an indictment of individuals through the exemplary tales, to a specific exhortation to the king to be himself a morally responsible being and so return the discordant realm to harmony. A king should learn chiefly five points of policy: truth, largess, justice, pity, and chastity. Central to these is justice: The king must be subject to God and follow the law, and he must ensure that legal justice prevails. Most edifying in book VII is the tale of Lygurgius, Prince of Athens, who, having obtained his subjects' promise never to change the laws in his absence, left the city never to return, having established laws "only for love and for justice" to further "the comun profit."

Gower's concern with universal love and the common profit is presented rather abstractly in the *Mirour de l'Omme* and *Vox Clamantis*. In *Confessio Amantis*, however, where Gower must use exempla to illustrate different virtues and vices, his deep human compassion is manifest in his treatment of characters. Even in extreme cases, such as the "Tale of Canace" and her incestuous relationship with her brother (book III), Gower can be sympathetic: He excuses the lovers because they simply follow natural law—incest is forbidden only by positive (human) law. It is the father, King Eolus, whose wrath kills Canace and her child, and who must be seen as morally culpable. Gower's addition to the story of Canace's address to her brother and the pathetic detail of the baby playing in his mother's warm blood serve to sentimentalize the tale and win the reader's sympathy for the victims.

This streak of compassion in the moral Gower is what makes *Confessio Amantis* so appealing. Not only the characters in the tales, but those of the frame story as well are treated with sympathetic understanding. The lover, for instance, is very sympathetic: He is a pathetic and very human character who will obviously never win his love. He seems eminently real in his envy of his rivals, his eagerness to do little things for his lady, his practical aversion to going abroad to win fame in arms in order to impress his lady and possibly losing her to someone else while he is gone, and in the lover's humorous confession that he has never been late for a date with his love since she has never given him one.

Confessio Amantis, then, can be read for its own sake; one need not look in it only to find in the "Tale of Florent" (book I) or the "Tale of Constance" (book II), analogues of Chaucer's "The Wife of Bath's Tale" and "The Man of Law's Tale," or to read "Apollonius of Tyre" as the source of Shakespeare's *Pericles* (1608). It may be in the end that Gower turns out to be an artist in spite of himself. His verse is neither ornate nor ambiguous nor complex; he was rather a consummate craftsman whose English octosyllabic couplets are almost monotonously smooth and regular. C. S. Lewis called him England's first master of the "plain style," and Peter Fison noted that the verse deliberately avoids calling attention to itself. Perhaps Gower's aim was not to detract from the moral, which for him was poetry's most important aspect, but in *Confessio Amantis* this style serves very well to focus attention on the action of the tale. Furthermore, Gower's concern for cause and effect, for the consequences of moral actions, leads to well-plotted tales, even as his concern for charity as a motivating factor in human actions helps to make his characters sympathetic. Thus, the techniques which Gower cultivated to further his primary moral purpose contributed ultimately to his secondary, aesthetic ends. As a result, when Gower is read today, it is for his skill as a storyteller as demonstrated in some of the tales of *Confessio*

Amantis, and not for the very conscious morality of that or any other work.

BIBLIOGRAPHY

Bennett, J. A. W. "Gower." In *Middle English Literature*, edited by Douglas Gray. Oxford, England: Clarendon Press, 1986. Pieces together an important introduction to the life and works of Gower. Of major interest is the particular emphasis placed upon the exposition of classical elements found in Gower's works.

Bullón-Fernández, María. *Fathers and Daughters in Gower's "Confessio Amantis."* Rochester, N.Y.: Brewer, 2000. This volume in the John Gower Society's monograph series examines Gower's works from a feminist perspective. Bibliographical references, index.

Craun, Edwin D. *Lies, Slander, and Obscenity in Medieval English Literature: Pastoral Rhetoric and the Deviant Speaker.* New York: Cambridge University Press, 1997. Craun draws on manuscript sources to examine how the medieval clergy developed the authority and persuasive force to attempt to govern the day-to-day speech of Western Christians. An exploration of how Chaucer, Langland, Gower and the "Patience" poet presented and judged these attempts to label some political, social, and private speech as deviant and destructive as lying, slander, blasphemy and other sins of the tongue.

Harbert, Bruce. "Lessons from the Great Clerk: Ovid and John Gower." In *Ovid Renewed: Ovidian Influences on Literature and Art from the Middle Ages to the Twentieth Century*, edited by Charles Martindale. Cambridge, England: Cambridge University Press, 1988. Examines Gower's debt to the great poet Ovid. Comparisons between Gower's *Confessio Amantis* and Ovid show that Gower may have borrowed his technique and inspiration from Ovid, but not his content. Includes good end notes and an index.

Olsen, Alexandra Hennessey. "Literary Artistry in the Oral-Formulaic Tradition: The Case of Gower's *Apollonius of Tyre*." In *Comparative Research on Oral Traditions*, edited by John Mills Foley. Columbus, Ohio: Slavica, 1987. Argues effectively that Gower makes use of themes and type scenes, devices found in the oral-formulaic tradition. These survive in written texts after their purpose in orally composed works passes. It is perceived here that Gower does so for conscious literary artistry; Olsen uses evidence from Gower's *Appolonius of Tyre* to make her point. Contains thorough comparative notes and references.

White, Hugh. *Nature, Sex, and Goodness in a Medieval Literary Tradition*. New York: Oxford University Press, 2000. A thematic and historical examination of thirteenth and fourteenth century English and European literature, including, along with Gower, Guillaume de Lorris, Alanus de Insulis, Geoffrey Chaucer, and Jean de Meung.

Yeager, R. F. "The Poetry of John Gower: Important Studies, 1960-1983." In *Fifteenth Century Studies: Recent Essays*, edited by R. F. Yeager. Hamden, Conn.: Archon Books, 1984. Presents a complete overview of twenty-three years of critical studies of the works of John Gower. The essay includes sections devoted to editions and translations, bibliographies, bibliographies and portraits, language studies and stylistics, source studies, and critical studies. This excellent introduction to recent studies devoted to Gower contains a very complete set of notes for bibliographic reference.

_____, ed. *John Gower: Recent Readings*. Kalamazoo: Medieval Institute Publications, Western Michigan University Press, 1989. This book-length collation of criticism contains a good introduction and many illustrations appropriate to the study of Gower. Thirteen articles cover topics that range from the authorship of Gower's works to metaethics. Each essay contains extended notes, and the work is a valuable addition to the canon of studies of John Gower.

_____, ed. *Re-visioning Gower*. Asheville, N.C.: Pegasus Press, 1998. A collection of essays presented at the meetings of the John Gower Society at the International Congress on Medieval Studies, Western Michigan University, 1992-1997. Includes bibliographical references.

Yeager, R. F., and A. J. Minnis, eds. *John Gower's Poetic: The Search for a New Arion*. Rochester, N.Y.: Boydell and Brewer, 1990. Presents the idea that Gower was a serious student in the matter of language. To reinforce this claim, Yeager offers chapters that include studies of Gower's stylistics and transformations. Contains extensive footnotes and a complete index. This work offers a refreshing perspective of interest to any student of the literature of Gower.

Jay Ruud;
bibliography updated by the editors

JORIE GRAHAM

Born: New York, New York; May 9, 1951

PRINCIPAL POETRY

Hybrids of Plants and of Ghosts, 1980
Erosion, 1983
The End of Beauty, 1987
Region of Unlikeness, 1991
Materialism, 1993
The Dream of the Unified Field: Selected Poems, 1974-1994, 1995
The Errancy, 1997
Selected Poems, 2000
Swarm, 2000
Never, 2002

OTHER LITERARY FORMS

Jorie Graham is known primarily for her poetry.

ACHIEVEMENTS

In an era of lyric poetry in minor modes and moods, Jorie Graham's work is strikingly grand in scope. Her imagination is both galactic and intensely particular, at times more reminiscent of Dante than of her contemporaries. She is also an extremely self-demanding poet, one who attempts to think where thought cannot seem to go, and to feel what seems too painful to feel. The poem, Graham has said, should be an act in the *present* tense, which holds genuine risks (instead of risks invented for the sake of the poem) and thus holds the possibility of personal transformation.

After an apprentice volume in lyric moods and miniatures (poems, for example, about her mother's sewing box and her own pencil sketches of wildflowers) and after the superb volume *Erosion*, Graham began to write what she calls "books"—breathless, ferociously intelligent cascades of language—rather than individual poems. The sections of these volumes do have titles but are recursively structured so that they avoid self-containment. *The End of Beauty* and *Region of Unlikeness* flow like vigorous and troubled rivers of incalculable force. Their architecture as volumes, their substance, and their streaming prosody make these two volumes innovations of a high order.

Graham's creativity has secured her a MacArthur Fellowship, recognition from the Academy of American Poets, the Morton Dauwen Zabel Award from the American Academy of Arts and Letters, and several Pushcart Prizes for individual poems. *The Dream of the Unified Field* was awarded a Pulitzer Prize (1996). In 1997 Graham was elected a Chancellor of the Academy of American Poets, and in 1999 she was elected to membership in the American Academy of Arts and Sciences.

BIOGRAPHY

Though born of American parents, Jorie Graham grew up in Italy. Many of her poems reflect this background, especially those about Italian Renaissance paintings and European mystics, such as Saint Francis of Assisi, Saint Clare of Assisi, and Saint Teresa of Avila. She was educated at the Sorbonne, where she studied philosophy. She received a B.A. at New York University, where she studied cinema and began writing poetry. She received an M.F.A. at the University of Iowa in 1978 and later became a member of the permanent faculty in the Writers' Workshop, a program she directed for several years. In 1999, she began teaching at Harvard University as Boylston Professor of Rhetoric and Oratory.

ANALYSIS

Jorie Graham's first volume of poetry, published in the Princeton Series of Contemporary Poets, is in many respects unlike her later work. The poems are self-contained lyrics, densely figured and elaborately

Jorie Graham (Jeannette Montgomery Barron)

wrought. They have little of the impetuosity of style and subject and the rapidity and evasion of closure that characterize Graham's later work.

"THE GEESE"

The poems, though more slight, are often lovely in themselves and occasionally press upon the enigmas that evolve into the great intellectual labyrinths that Graham explores in her major works. "The Geese," for example, anticipates the theme of what Graham would eventually call, in her own distinctive metaphysical code, "hurry" and "delay"—which can be translated, but roughly, into the paradoxes of temporality and timelessness. Alternatively one might translate these terms as "flux" and "form," the changing temporal body and the permanent body of beauty, or as designations of the longing human beings have for change against their longing for fixity and stability.

In "The Geese" Graham incarnates the paradoxical terms with which people think their reality into simple, earthly activities and forms. While she is hanging out clothes, she sees geese flying overhead. Their flight becomes an "urgent" and "elegant" code for "hurry," for the flowing onwardness of time. Spiders that spin filaments between the clotheslines become an emblem for those forces in the world that hold things together—that bind, as the poem says, "pins to the lines, the lines to the eaves." More largely, the spiders on their clothesline loom signify the desire to keep human meanings intact and to mend the rifts and wounds of time. Between these two contending forces is an "astonishing delay": "And somewhere in between/ these geese forever entering and/ these spiders turning back,// this astonishing delay, the everyday, takes place."

Graham has been called a gnostic poet, and it is true that she presses thought against the secret places and conundrum points of the universe. She asks not only, "Why this strange process called time?" but also, "How do consciousness and flesh coincide?" The title of her first volume signals Graham's interest in these ontological questions. Friedrich Nietzsche's contention that even the wisest man "is only a discord and hybrid of plant and of ghost" provides a conjunction of incommensurables that stirs Graham's imagination.

In later volumes, *The End of Beauty* and *Region of Unlikeness*, Graham would extend these ontological concerns by undertaking to explore woman or the anima and its relationship to the animus through rewritings of the stories of Eve and Adam, Penelope and Ulysses, Eurydice and Orpheus, Daphne and Apollo. In recasting these cultural mythologies, Graham portrays woman as the will toward change and transformation that chooses against the stasis of paradise and perfection, and the overlords who would paralyze woman within the form of the beautiful. Eve's coming out of Adam's body is, for Graham, the tragedy that makes time and history, an ongoing tragedy that she embraces and loves, though with suffering. Similarly, Eurydice and Daphne are used to signify the will to change. Eurydice goes back to Hell because Orpheus tries to fix her form with his backward gaze. Daphne transforms herself when Apollo tries to snare her within the trammels of beauty. In Graham's rewritings of all these stories, woman becomes that principle of escape from fixities that makes time and history. "Gnosis," for Graham, will entail not only an explora-

tion of the unthinkable interface of body and soul but also an exploration of an archetypal Eve-life within and outside the body of Adam.

HYBRIDS OF PLANTS AND OF GHOSTS

The quest for knowledge of self and selfhood begins in *Hybrids of Plants and of Ghosts*. The self-portraits of this volume initiate an analysis that will become an analysis of "Selfhood," of the mystery of being. Three poems are notable in this respect: "Self Portrait," "My Face in the Mirror Tells a Story of Delicate Ambitions," and "On Why I Would Betray You." Graham's self-renderings in all of these are wonderfully ethereal. Their ghostliness comes from the fact that she depicts a generic, nongendered selfhood. Rather than painting herself as individual presence, Graham paints "the self" people share. Her self-portraits in this first volume and in later volumes are ontological rather than projections of a particularized identity.

In "Self Portrait," she draws herself as a field of snow she "makes tracks on" by merely looking out her window. At the end of the poem, she describes herself as a record whose delineations are made by the needle moving around and across the record surface. This record is, however, like the records Graham imagined as a child, an unmarked darkness that the needle must cut anew each time it is played. Such is her lovely, precise, haunting image of the self, with its simultaneous presentness and lack of presence.

Despite their alluring concretions, however, the ontological questings of these poems have caused some critics to describe Graham as an "intellectual poet," as if this were a fault. Were she to moderate her intellect, one wonders whether she would be adjudged a "merely personal poetess." Fortunately, the philosophical dimensions of Graham's poetry show no signs of shrinking to ladylike size and have actually grown with each new volume. In *The End of Beauty* and *Region of Unlikeness* Graham begins to paint herself at once in more intensely personal terms and more abstractly and philosophically: as "hurry" and "delay" in "Self-Portrait as Hurry and Delay" or the gesture between Adam and Eve. Growing more expansive, Graham's self-portraits begin to render not only the bare ontological bones of being but also the self as an individual and an archetypal gesture toward more being.

THE WORLD OF PAINTINGS IN EROSION

Hybrids of Plants and of Ghosts also prefigures what would become for Graham a major theater for thought: the world of painters and painting. In this first volume Graham writes poems for Paul Cézanne and Mark Rothko which pay tribute to these painters by distantly emulating their paintings in her images. In her next book, *Erosion*, painting figures much more largely. While one poem describes a Goya painting and another two paintings by Gustav Klimt, most address paintings from the Italian Renaissance. She often seems to want to argue with the paintings, to change them. Indeed, in an interview, Graham remarked that by being so fixed and immovable, paintings stimulate her rage to change. The repose of these aesthetic forms has the paradoxical effect of making her want to transform the image and its meanings.

In "San Sepolcro," the first poem of the volume, Graham invites the reader to look at *Madonna del Parto* by Piero della Francesca. Graham's description of the painting is like a film fast-forward. "And the dress keeps opening/ from eternity// to privacy, quickening. . . . each breath/ is a button// coming undone, something terribly/ nimble-fingered/ finding all of the stops." In the painting itself, Mary is notably tranquil, her hand reposing rather than unbuttoning. Clearly Graham has added to the painting the metaphysical force of "hurry." As if finding the "on switch" to this fixed aesthetic form, Graham injects temporality into the painting, making it come alive in her own era.

Similarly, Graham urges the figures of Adam and Eve in Massacio's *The Expulsion* to come alive. She tells the sorrowing couple to take their hands from their faces, to accept the lives, the process of change they have chosen by eating from the tree of knowledge. Although the repose of paintings holds great allure for Graham, their stillness is also a provocation to change and to a conception of art that emphasizes acts rather than objects.

THE END OF BEAUTY

Not surprisingly, Graham's next volume, *The End of Beauty*, adds the canvases of Jackson Pollock to her gallery of paintings. "The end of beauty" is, among other things, the end of poems as finished forms and the beginning of poems as tumultuous futural projections and acts of personal change. These aesthetic commitments of Graham are importantly linked to her ethical commitments, which become clearly enunciated in *Region of Unlikeness*. Here, in a series of poems about Eve, Graham endorses the step out of Eden, the moment when Eve seeks knowledge and in doing so initiates change, movement away from perfection. Graham's sense of the poetic enterprise might be compared to Wallace Stevens's idea of the Supreme Fiction, the aesthetic project that seeks not final form but to change as people change.

Although Graham embraces change—the Eve-acts that make history—she also values what her metaphysical lexicon terms "delay." "Delay" is the self when it looks in the mirror and sees a story of delicate ambitions. "Delay" is a mind-absorbing painting by Rothko or a Renaissance master. "Delay," as becomes clear in *The End of Beauty* and *Region of Unlikeness*, is the attempt to stay married. It is the attachment to one's particular backyard and its red birds. It is what people know of love.

"Delay" is also present in the depth of the world. Though Graham's advocacy of change links her to the open-ended aesthetic projects of postmodern art, the link is only partial. She obviously appreciates the writings of experimental postmodernists such as the "language poets," but her own aesthetic is far from the aesthetics of surface that many postmoderns embrace. Her images, for example, are nothing like Andy Warhol's soup labels, and her poetry makes everywhere evident a commitment to depth in both image and event. One senses that one could fall endlessly into any one of the "delays" she allures to her poetic world.

COMMITMENT TO DEPTH

Two poems in *Erosion*, "At Luca Signorelli's *Resurrection of the Body*" and "Two Paintings by Gustav Klimt," demonstrate with particular force Graham's commitment to depth. In the latter poem she writes of one of Klimt's last works, *The Bride*. An unfinished painting, it suggests that the glittering mosaic surfaces for which Klimt is famous may conceal mutilation scenes. As Graham describes it, after Klimt's death an incomplete painting was found in his studio. It pictured "a woman's body/ open at its point of/ entry," with "something like/ a scream" rising between her legs. The painter had begun to cover "this mouth/ of her body" with a garment rendered in soft, delicate brush strokes. *The Bride* makes Graham wonder whether even Klimt's landscape paintings, like his painting of beech trees called *Buchenwald*, conceal death scenes. The beech grove may be Buchenwald concentration camp, whose myriad dead may be lingering in the leaves of Klimt's forest floor, longing to come back.

"At Luca Signorelli's *Resurrection of the Body*" describes a resurrection painting of the Renaissance master in which skeletons crawl out of their graves and climb into physical bodies that await them on the earth's surface. Graham talks to the painting and asks its figures why they are in such a hurry to get bodies back. Then the poem flicks to a description of the painter cutting into the body of his son after his son dies. The way in which Graham enacts this scene is much too marvelous to be told. She describes the cutting as an act of love, a healing process for the father. He needs to see that his son's soul cannot be found in the body. Having awaited "the best/ possible light," the father begins cutting "with beauty and care." It is a slow, painstaking process that takes days. At the end of this "deep/ caress," the father's mind "could climb into/ the open flesh and/ mend itself." Although the father must, in terrible pursuit of gnosis, lovingly explore his son's body, he cannot cut deep enough to reach the spirit. It will always recede before him. Like the vanishing point used in painting with perspective, "the flesh/ open endlessly,/ its vanishing point so deep/ and receding// we have yet to find it."

The poem also embodies the thematics of discord and dissolve between the material and immaterial, the hybridization of plant and ghost that shapes Graham's first volume. This poem discovers, though, that the body is a depth that leads to a vanishing point for thought. The images in Graham's poetry seem similarly fathomless. The point at which mind and matter meet, meaning and image merge, cannot be finally thought: Thought can only disappear into the mystery.

EXPLORING THE TRAGIC

The other depth that grows larger and larger in Graham's poetry is the depth of the tragic. Graham is, as critics so often note, "relentlessly cerebral." As her corpus grows, it also becomes clear that she is relentlessly committed to feeling, and to feeling beyond the point at which one blacks out for the pain. It is this combination of intense intellect and growing depth and range of feeling that would cause one to compare Graham to Dante.

Like Dante's *Divine Comedy*, Graham's poems in *The End of Beauty* and *Region of Unlikeness* attempt to link disparate realms, the sublime and the hellish, the agonies of the personal life with cultural tumult at large. A montage strategy, which was at times disconcerting in her early work, is in these volumes fully mature and profoundly disturbing. The poems are often in two parts, the second seeming to be of a totally different substance; these two parts, though, by the end of the poem become a sort of liquid montage that blends the disparate and discordant experiences and implies without stating an endlessly reticulating realm of subterranean connections.

"Imperialism," the last poem of *The End of Beauty*, juxtaposes an acrimonious argument between a couple, one in which the form of marriage cannot seem to hold their feeling, to a childhood experience of being made to enter the Ganges River. The river is teeming with people washing their bodies and their personal effects; it is also thick with ashes and remains from funeral pyres that burn along the Ganges night and day. The child cannot contain her terror. In the hotel afterward, neither Demerol nor her mother's arms can console her. At first the two parts of the poem seem arbitrarily conjoined; as one thinks the poem and feels it, however, connections begin to appear. As the marriage form cannot hold the feelings of its partners, the mother-daughter relationship cannot absorb the terror of the child. Like many of Graham's poems, "Imperialism" deals with the fact that people's forms for experience—parenting, marriage, the idealistic phantasms of imperialists—are finally unable to absorb and hold their teeming reality. The poem leaves the reader with an awed and awful feeling that one is ultimately on one's own in a river of life turbulent with human suffering.

REGION OF UNLIKENESS

Region of Unlikeness begins with a poem called "Fission" that also forces disparate experiences into the montagelike structure described earlier. The poem's speaker is watching the Stanley Kubrick film *Lolita* (1962) when a man bursts into the theater announcing the Dallas shooting of John F. Kennedy. *Lolita*, as presented in the poem, makes the female body into a too-large and physical surface of desire, so that desire itself becomes obscenely grandiose and public. As the light of the theater, the projector light, the house lights, and light from a skylight beam into the room, the speaker begins to feel that the lights converge on her, the leprous gray of blended film light and daylight. The spotlight seems to be on her own body and its sexual potential. She feels stripped, torn from herself, and it is at just this moment that she must absorb Kennedy's death, with her father beside her crying. This collision of disparate realms of experience causes fission, an explosion of troubled energy that one psyche can hardly contain.

This process of fission moves through much of the volume. In "From the New World," for example, Graham painfully brings together "the story about the girl who didn't die/ in the gas chamber, who came back out asking/ for her mother" with her own family experience of placing a grandmother in a nursing home. The grandmother is "in her diaper sitting with her purse in her hand all day every/ day, asking can I go now." In these poems Graham seems to be dealing with the bad conscience of a whole people—how human beings have survived only by compartmentalizing the painful, glossing the tragic.

As *Region of Unlikeness* grows poem by poem, the sense of human temporality as a fragile surface to an immense tragedy also grows. Graham is, as she says, now writing books, not poems, and these books push and push toward a gnosis that is at once too painful and absolutely necessary.

Materialism is another work in which the book as a composition overarches its individual poems. It is the last of Graham's collections to precede her first retrospective gathering, *The Dream of the Unified Field*, which brings together a healthy sampling of twenty years' work. Earning Graham the Pulitzer Prize, this collection established her as a major voice of her generation.

THE ERRANCY

In other books of the 1990's, Graham continues to compose, much as a novelist, chapter-poems for longer works. *The Errancy* once again shows Graham exploring and exhibiting her immense learning. If the book has an overall conceit, it is one that has to do with the partially doomed nature of all quests, whether they be those of

the knight-errant or the poet. These poems explore all the etymological strands of the book's title. Errancy is the state of erring, but it is also (as errantry) the condition of wandering. The human desire to prove one's self, to test limits, leads us to stray out of bounds. Is error deviation or evil? Graham's complex, learned, and impassioned intellect finds poetic forms that ask this question in varied ways and that enact on an aesthetic level the deviant self-testing and self-definition of the knight-errant.

SWARM

Swarm also builds from a generative images, this time of bees reforming into a mass or colony or organic community before moving on to build a new dwelling place. The constant reconfigurations of parts and wholes is a way of seeing the various impulses that make up an individual, small-scale human relationships, and even tribal and national histories. Graham reverses one element in her poetic manner here. Her lines and sentences, so often open-ended and accretive, are in this collection much more terse. So often a poet of extension, for this book she comes closer to the "less is more" approach. Lacunae abound between sentence parts, utterances, and allusions. Both praised and damned as a difficult poet, in *Swarm* Graham offers readers even fewer guideposts, giving ammunition to those critics who have argued that the demands she makes on her readers can become counterproductive.

OTHER MAJOR WORKS

EDITED TEXT: *The Best American Poetry, 1990*, 1990 (with David Lehman); *Earth Took of Earth: A Golden Ecco Anthology*, 1996.

BIBLIOGRAPHY

Gardner, Thomas. "Jorie Graham's Incandescence." In *Regions of Unlikeness: Explaining Contemporary Poetry.* Lincoln: University of Nebraska Press, 1999. Gardner examines five collections (from *Erosion* to *The Errancy*) in order to map Graham's progress in responding to the limits of language and understanding. This piece expands upon an article first published in *The Hollins Critic* (October, 1987) that treats three of Graham's books.

Graham, Jorie. Interview by Ann Snodgrass. *Quarterly West*, no. 23 (1986): 151-164. An intense and highly illuminating interview in which Graham talks about many aspects of her poetry, from her poems about paintings to her aesthetic forebears to her ideas about the genders and their role in her self-portraits.

_____. "Some Notes on Silence." In *Nineteen New American Poets of the Golden Gate*, edited by Phillip Dow. New York: Harcourt Brace Jovanovich, 1984. This short essay is essential to understanding Graham's versification and her poetic commitments. She says that the way in which she places a poem on the page shows the pressure of silence against speech and the failures of language. She also talks about the poem as an act with genuine risks taken by the soul of the speaker. She says that choices in poems are not only aesthetic but also moral.

Longenbach, James. "Jorie Graham's Big Hunger." In *Modern Poetry After Modernism*. New York: Oxford University Press, 1997. Longenbach examines Graham's manner of bedecking innocent or insignificant actions with associative contemplation that charges them with grandeur. A reluctant and partial admirer, he observes the nonlinear nature of her compositions.

Vendler, Helen. "Jorie Graham." In *The Music of What Happens*. Cambridge, Mass.: Harvard University Press, 1988. Vendler focuses on a work's uniqueness rather than its meaning or ideology. Like French critic Roland Barthes, she insists that pleasure motivates writers.

_____. "Married to Hurry and Grim Song." *The New Yorker* 63 (July 27, 1987): 74-77. Two excellent commentaries, the first on *Erosion*, the second on *The End of Beauty*. Vendler, with her usual acuity for both placing a poet within tradition and defining his or her distinctive style and concerns, gives Graham the highest of praise. Of *Erosion*, she says, "This is a poetry of delicate and steady transgression, in which the spirit searches the flesh and the flesh the spirit, melting and dissolving the boundaries thought to separate them." About *The End of Beauty*, Vendler says that Graham has found a new way of passing from the beautiful to the tragic—the way of speculative thought.

Anne Shifrer,
updated by Philip K. Jason

ROBERT GRAVES

Born: Wimbledon, England; July 24, 1895
Died: Deyá, Majorca, Spain; December 7, 1985

PRINCIPAL POETRY

Over the Brazier, 1916
Goliath and David, 1916
Fairies and Fusiliers, 1917
Treasure Box, 1919
Country Sentiment, 1920
The Pier-Glass, 1921
The Feather Bed, 1923
Whipperginny, 1923
Mock Beggar Hall, 1924
The Marmosite's Miscellany, 1925 (as John Doyle)
Welchman's Hose, 1925
Poems: 1914-1926, 1927
Poems: 1914-1927, 1927
Poems: 1929, 1929
Ten Poems More, 1930
Poems: 1926-1930, 1931
To Whom Else?, 1931
Poems: 1930-1933, 1933
Collected Poems, 1938
No More Ghosts: Selected Poems, 1940
Work in Hand, 1942 (with others)
Poems: 1938-1945, 1946
Collected Poems: 1914-1947, 1948
Poems and Satires: 1951, 1951
Poems: 1953, 1953
Collected Poems: 1955, 1955
Poems Selected by Himself, 1957
The Poems of Robert Graves Chosen by Himself, 1958
Collected Poems: 1959, 1959
The Penny Fiddle: Poems for Children, 1960
Collected Poems, 1961
More Poems: 1961, 1961
The More Deserving Cases: Eighteen Old Poems for Reconsideration, 1962
New Poems: 1962, 1962
Ann at Highwood Hall: Poems for Children, 1964
Man Does, Woman Is, 1964

Love Respelt, 1965
Collected Poems: 1965, 1965
Seventeen Poems Missing from "Love Respelt," 1966
Colophon to "Love Respelt," 1967
Poems: 1965-1968, 1968
The Crane Bag, 1969
Love Respelt Again, 1969
Beyond Giving: Poems, 1969
Poems About Love, 1969
Advice from a Mother, 1970
Queen-Mother to New Queen, 1970
Poems: 1969-1970, 1970
The Green-Sailed Vessel, 1971
Poems: Abridged for Dolls and Princes, 1971
Poems: 1968-1970, 1971
Poems: 1970-1972, 1972
Poems: Selected by Himself, 1972
Deyá, 1972 (with Paul Hogarth)
Timeless Meetings: Poems, 1973
At the Gate, 1974
Collected Poems: 1975, 1975 (2 volumes)
New Collected Poems, 1977

Robert Graves (© Washington Post; reprinted by permission
of the D.C. Public Library)

OTHER LITERARY FORMS

Robert Graves published fifteen novels, including one
(*No Decency Left*, 1932) written in collaboration with
Laura Riding. His novels are usually based on historical
events or mythology. *I, Claudius* (1934) and *Claudius
the God and His Wife Messalina* (1934) borrow heavily
from Suetonius's *Lives of the Caesars* (c. 120 C.E.).
Count Belisarius (1938) concerns the brilliant general of
the Byzantine emperor Justinian. *Sergeant Lamb of the
Ninth* (1940) and *Proceed, Sergeant Lamb* (1941) fictionalize the life of an actual English soldier in the
American Revolution. *The Story of Marie Powell, Wife
to Mr. Milton* (1943) elaborates imaginatively on John
Milton's marital problems. *The Islands of Unwisdom*
(1949) is based on the abortive attempt by the Spanish in
the sixteenth century to colonize the Solomon Islands.
They Hanged My Saintly Billy (1957) is a minor work
about the notorious career and execution of Dr. William
Palmer for poisoning his friend, John Parsons Cook.

Biblical topics inspired two novels: *My Head! My
Head!* (1925), about Elisha and Moses, and *King Jesus*
(1946), his most significant attempt to fuse his ideas
about the Triple Goddess with Christian and Hebrew
myth. Greek mythology inspired *The Golden Fleece*
(1944, published as *Hercules, My Shipmate* in America)
and *Homer's Daughter* (1955), while *Seven Days in
New Crete* (1949, *Watch the North Wind Rise* in America) is an entertaining fantasy about a mythological future when the worship of the Goddess is reestablished in
Crete, the ancient stronghold of the Goddess cult.

Graves published more than fifty works in the nonfiction category, including literary criticism, books about
writing and language, an autobiography, a biography of
T. E. Lawrence, social commentaries, and studies in
Greek and Hebrew myths. In addition, he translated
such writers as Suetonius, Homer, Hesiod, Lucius Apuleius, Lucan Pharsalia, and Manuel de Jesus Galvan. He
was one of the most versatile writers of the twentieth
century, a persistent maverick often embroiled in intellectual arguments with other scholars because of his
sometimes eccentric views.

ACHIEVEMENTS

*The White Goddess: A Historical Grammar of Poetic
Myth* (1948), and Robert Graves's other studies in my-

thology, *The Greek Myths* (2 volumes; 1955), *Hebrew Myths: The Book of Genesis* (1964, with Raphael Patai) and *The Nazarine Gospel Restored* (1953, with Joshua Podro), together with his novels and poetry based on myth, have undoubtedly had a subtle and pervasive influence on modern literature. Their impact cannot be distinguished precisely from that of other writers, such as James Frazer, T. S. Eliot, Joseph Campbell, and others, who have contributed to the renewed interest in mythology and ancient patterns of belief. With the passing of the enthusiasm for social realism, the old patterns of myth have reasserted themselves with a surprising vigor—perhaps in direct proportion to current discomfort with the demythologized, purely practical bent of technological society. Graves contributed significantly to this rediscovery of the past.

For the novel *I, Claudius*, Graves received the Hawthornden Prize, the oldest of the famous British literary prizes, and the James Tait Black Memorial Prize, administered through the University of Edinburgh for the year's best novel. Collections of his poetry gained the Loines Award for Poetry (1958), the William Foyle Poetry Prize (1960), the Arts Council Poetry Award (1962), and the Queen's Gold Medal for Poetry (1968).

Graves held only one full-time salaried position in his life—in 1926, when he taught for one year at the Egyptian University of Cairo. He was Clark Lecturer at Trinity College, Cambridge, in 1954, however, and Arthur Dehon Little Memorial Lecturer at the Massachusetts Institute of Technology in 1963. He also lectured in California, Hungary, Israel, and Spain. In 1970, he became an Honorary Member of the American Academy of Arts and Sciences.

BIOGRAPHY

Robert Graves was born July 24, 1895, in Wimbledon, near London, to Alfred Percival Graves and Amalie von Ranke Graves. His father was an inspector of schools, a Gaelic scholar, and a writer of poetry of a conventional sort. His German mother was related to the historian Leopold von Ranke. Robert was one of ten children, five of them from his father's first marriage. The Graves household was conventionally religious, a tradition which Graves dispensed with in his maturity, but which left him, according to his autobiography,

Goodbye to All That (1929), with "a great capacity for fear . . . a superstitious conscience and a sexual embarrassment." To the age of twelve, Robert and the other Graves children sometimes visited their German relatives, including their aunt, Baronin von Aufsess, who lived in a medieval castle in the Bavarian Alps. These romantic environs undoubtedly colored his early poetry.

When Graves attended Charterhouse, where he was listed as R. von R. Graves, his German connections were an embarrassment because of the anti-German sentiment developing in England. Graves did not find his schoolmates particularly congenial until he won their respect by becoming a competent boxer. He did find one prominent friend in George Mallory, a famous mountaineer who later died climbing Mount Everest. Mallory introduced Edward Marsh, then secretary to Winston Churchill, to Graves's poetry. Marsh, a patron of the contemporary Georgian school of poetry, encouraged Graves in his writing; but, he said, Graves should modernize his diction, which was "forty years behind the time."

Graves joined the Royal Welsh Fusiliers when World War I began and went to France as a nineteen-year-old officer. He became a close friend of the well-known war poet Siegfried Sassoon. Graves's autobiography, *Goodbye to All That*, written when he was thirty-five, includes one of the best accounts of trench warfare to come out of the war. Both Graves and Sassoon survived the war, though they suffered physical and mental wounds in the process. Graves received multiple wounds from an exploding shell and was, in fact, listed among the casualties, but eventually someone noted that the "corpse" in the hospital tent had moved and Graves lived to fight again. One lung was seriously damaged, however, and he was soon brought back to England to serve in a training role.

The more lasting damage that Graves suffered from trench warfare however, was psychological, and helped to determine the nature of his poetry for nearly ten years. He suffered from war neurasthenia; he was prone to nightmares, obsessed with military strategy even in peaceful surroundings, and had waking hallucinations about comrades who had died in the war. He became acquainted with Dr. W. H. R. Rivers, a Freudian psychologist who was an expert in war neurasthenia and also interested in the role of the subconscious in poetic creativity. Under his influence, Graves became fascinated with dreams and developed a theory about poetry as a way of expressing and resolving mental conflicts. His poetry of this period was haunted by images of guilt, despair, and entrapment. Though he seldom wrote specifically about war experiences, he translated the emotions aroused there into more Gothic visions. Only years later, after he had achieved some distance from combat, could he treat it in both poetry and prose with a certain gritty objectivity.

In 1918, Graves married Nancy Nicholson, a painter, socialist, and ardent feminist who kept her maiden name. The couple had four children. Although it had seemed positive, the marriage failed in a shattering domestic crisis in which the American poet, Laura Riding, who had been staying with the Graves family, made a dramatic exit from a fourth-story window. She survived with a broken back and gradually recovered over a period of months. Graves and Riding were companions for the next thirteen years. They established the Seizin Press and later moved to Majorca, where Graves lived until his death in 1985 except when lecturing at universities or when political conditions forced the evacuation of British nationals. On one such occasion while Graves and Riding were living temporarily in the United States, Riding fell in love with and married the American poet Schuyler Jackson. Graves went back to England and eventually married Beryl Hodge, with whom he lived in Majorca until his death. He had four children from this marriage.

Laura Riding had a considerable influence on Graves's writing. She was more obsessed with "truth" than with emotional expression in poetry, and was fascinated with word-meanings. She encouraged Graves to forgo the gothic effects he was using when he looked upon poetry as emotional therapy. She insisted on more rigorous thinking and verbal precision. Perhaps she merely supported a development which was already under way in Graves's writing; in any case, his poetry became more philosophic and ironic. After Riding severed her association with Graves, he developed his fascination with the mythological White Goddess, which provided a pattern of images for almost all his subsequent poetry.

Some critics suggest that the White Goddess mythology universalized Laura Riding's personality, though Graves claimed that he simply discovered, and did not invent, the great Triple Goddess of moon, earth, and underworld who dominated preclassical religion. He became interested in the concept while doing research for a novel about Jason and the Golden Fleece, and studied such anthropologists as James Frazer, J. J. Bachofen, Jane Harrison, and Margaret Murray as well as recent archaeological studies. He finally worked out his theory while examining thirteenth century Welsh minstrel poems. These investigations culminated in *The White Goddess*, a unique combination of esoteric lore and inspired speculation. He was convinced (or claimed to be, at least) not only that the goddess cult once dominated the Western world, but also that most of the social evils of civilization stemmed from her overthrow and the subsequent domination by the male. The mythology of the goddess inspired much of Graves's subsequent writing.

ANALYSIS

Robert Graves was perhaps the most significant inheritor of the Romantic tradition in twentieth century poetry. After articulating his devotion to the White Goddess, he specialized in love poetry. He wrote significant poetry, however, at every stage of development, sometimes dealing with psychological or philosophical ideas as well as with mythological themes.

According to Graves, the art of poetry requires long experience with and attention to the meanings of words, a carefully developed craftsmanship, and an intuitive openness to what he called the poetic trance. He explained this process lucidly in one of his Oxford lectures, "The Poet in a Valley of Dry Bones" (published in *Mammon and the Black Goddess*, 1965):

A poet lives with his own language, continually instructing himself in the origin, histories, pronunciation, and peculiar usages of words, together with their latent powers, and the exact shades of distinction between what Roget's *Thesaurus* calls 'synonyms.'

The use of the English language depends largely upon precedent. One needs to know the precedents and when to deviate from them. Graves says that "The exact rightness of words can be explained only in the context of a whole poem: each one being related rhythmically, emotionally, and semantically to every other."

"THE NAKED AND THE NUDE"

This meticulous sense for shades of meaning is demonstrated in an ironic poem called "The Naked and the Nude." "Nude" is associated with sly seduction, showmanship, and mock-religious poses, while the state of nakedness is appropriate in contexts of love, medicine, and "true" religious devotion: "naked shines the Goddess when/ She mounts her lion among men." The poet warns that though the brazen nude may defeat the naked in life, in the world of the dead they shall be pursued by Gorgons with whips. There, in a final play on meaning, "How naked go the sometime nude!" Here, of course, "naked" means exposed in its actuality. Thus, in the poet's personal lexicography, "nude" implies exploitation and prostitution, while the term "naked" fuses connotations of love, beauty, and truth.

"THE COOL WEB"

Graves has other poems which explore in a more serious tone the function of language. One of the most perceptive is "The Cool Web," where language serves as a buffer between the speaker and the intensity of raw experience. It is one of the best poems written on the theme of language as a cocoon that protects but also embalms:

> There is a cool web of language winds us in,
> Retreat from too much joy or too much fear:
> We grow sea green at last and coldly die
> In brininess and volubility.

This state of insulation from the stark reality of experience contrasts with the clearer perception that he attributes to children: "Children are dumb to say how hot the day is . . . How dreadful the black wastes of evening sky. . . ." The poet suggests that one must either smother in a sea of words or throw off language and die of madness, "Facing the wide glare of the children's day." Besides being a unique expression of the function of language in controlling emotional reaction to experience, the poem also suggests a view of alternative fates somewhat analogous to Achilles' dilemma in Homer's *Iliad* (c. 800 B.C.E.). Achilles was supposed to have two possible destinies: a short life of violent action in obedience to his passions which would bring him everlasting fame, or a long, uneventful life if he chose to return home. Of course, the romantic traditionally prefers the short, intense life to the long, dull, conventional existence. Graves, however,

gives a new turn to the screw: The ferocious quality of reality is not a romantic illusion, but its true color. It is the dull, conventional life which is an error—an illusion of order conceived and perpetuated by language.

"THE PHILOSOPHER"

Although Graves had the romantic's distrust of cold reason uninformed by the heart, the poem called "The Philosopher" seems to entertain at least the possibility of some benefit derivable from logic—given a suitable environment. The ideal housing for the logical mind is, unfortunately, a barren prison cell where the mind might be "free" of all the usual distractions of living. There one might weave a more perfect web of thought, "Threading a logic between wall and wall,/ Ceiling and floor more accurate by far/ Than the cob-spider's." In this paradoxically ideal situation, one might attain "Truth captured without increment of flies." The poet imagines the cell becoming a

> spacious other head
> In which the emancipated reason might
> Learn in due time to walk at greater length
> And more unanswerably.

The poem achieves an ironic fusion of contradictory attitudes—although, only persons quite dead to the world are in a position to form a logically consistent philosophy. This may suggest an outright parody of philosophers, but one fancies that the poet would really like to reconcile the worlds of experience and thought if he could. Perhaps Graves was struggling with Laura Riding's rather obscure requirement that poetry express "Truth."

Graves meticulously avoided schools and movements in poetry. Having emerged from the Georgian school popular in his early youth, he deliberately disregarded T. S. Eliot and Ezra Pound, who were dictating poetic taste somewhat later. Graves maintained that one does not write good poetry by imitating popular fashions or even recognized geniuses in the genre. The style should always be one's own and the idea or experience itself should determine form, diction, and rhythm. He despised what he saw as the tendency in modern poetry to cultivate obscurity for its own sake or to throw out rhyme or rhythm simply to rebel against nineteenth century Romanticism. He did, however, modernize his diction, as Edward Marsh once told him to do, weaning himself away from all decorative elaboration that served no function in the poem. When the cult of Eliot and Pound was on the wane, Graves became a model to many younger poets for his craftsmanship and his ability to match rhythm and diction with content.

"THE PIER-GLASS" AND "THE LEGS"

Graves repeatedly displayed this versatility of language. During the time when he was haunted by his war experiences, he became adept at the Gothic mode. The collection called *The Pier-Glass* contains some of his best poems of that period. The title poem uses the ambience of a haunted house to convey the acute emotional trauma of its female persona, who returns obsessively to a deserted bedroom, "Drawn by a thread of time-sunk memory." She gazes at her pale reflection in a cracked pier-glass and at the curtained bed which is likened to a "puppet theatre where malignant fancy/ Peoples the wings with fear."

In spite of the gothic touches of such poems as "The Pier-Glass," Graves was soon writing other poems in an altogether different mode, as cool and ironic as anyone could wish. "The Legs," for example, is entirely original in subject matter, though surrealism may have inspired the wry humor and absurdity of the scene:

> There was this road,
> And it led down-hill,
> And round and in and out.
>
> And the traffic was legs,
> Legs from the knee down,
> Coming and going,
> Never pausing.

The persona is apparently feeling rather smug because he is standing firmly in the grass by the roadside, clearly self-possessed in the midst of this mindless activity of legs. Suddenly, his feeling of superiority becomes slightly clouded with doubt:

> My head dizzied then:
> I wondered suddenly,
> Might I too be a walker
> From the knees down?
>
> Gently I touched my shins.
> The doubt unchained them.
> They had run in twenty puddles
> Before I regained them.

The simplicity of diction, the clarity of the symbolic action, and the delicately modulated tempo make this poem delightful.

ORIGINS OF THE WHITE GODDESS

Graves became increasingly objective in his poetry as the urgencies of war and domestic upheavals receded, abandoning his notion of poetry as therapy, and writing more and more in a philosophic or ironic vein. With the disappearance from his life of Laura Riding and his subsequent fascination with ancient myth, he found a reservoir of symbols and metaphors that contributed to a burst of creative activity during which he wrote some of the best love lyrics of his age. As he affirmed in "To Juan at the Winter Solstice," one of the best-known of the poems inspired by the White Goddess mythology, "There is one story and one story only/ That will prove worth your telling." That is the love story between the Great Goddess of moon, earth, and the underworld (or a woman who embodies her) and her champion, who represents in ancient myth the Sacred King (the god of the waxing and waning year)—or, by extension, the poet inspired by his muse. As he explains his discovery in *The White Goddess*:

> The Theme, briefly, is the antique story, which falls into thirteen chapters and epilogue, of the birth, life, death and resurrection of the God of the Waxing Year; the central chapters concern the God's losing battle with the God of the Waning Year for love of the capricious and all-powerful Threefold Goddess, their mother, bride and layer-out. The poet identifies himself with the God of the Waxing Year and his Muse with the Goddess; the rival is his blood-brother, his other self, his weird.

The God of the Waxing Year is, of course, a variation of the primitive vegetation god. He suffers death in the fall but revives in the spring, like the Egyptian Osiris, murdered by his brother Set, god of desert and drought, only to be restored to life by his wife Isis. The poet sees himself in both creative and sacrificial roles, alternately inspired by the love of the Goddess Muse and suffering ritual death when her love grows cold.

The historical and religious origins of the goddess, nevertheless, have some purely literary precedents in the numerous fatal women of Romantic poetry—John

Keats's supernatural "La Belle Dame sans Merci," and Samuel Taylor Coleridge's weird women who dice with Death for the life of the Ancient Mariner. This is exactly the guise in which Graves often meets her, stressing her more frightening implications over her occasional gentleness. In "Darien," the poet tells his son about the Muse. "Often at moonrise I had watched her go./ And a cold shudder shook me/ To see the curved blaze of her Cretan axe." The Cretan axe is an emblem of the ancient Moon Goddess, having both convex and concave surfaces, suggesting different stages of the moon. The axe forebodes the price of being her chosen lover, for it is an instrument of sacrifice.

In the poem titled "The White Goddess," the persona also hints at the price of seeking the favor of the goddess. Spring, the poet suggests, always celebrates the Mountain Mother;

> But we are gifted, even in November
> Rawest of seasons, with so huge a sense
> Of her nakedly worn magnificence
> We forget cruelty and past betrayal,
> Heedless of where the next bright bolt may fall.

In ancient times, certain animals were associated with the Goddess, particularly the cat, bitch, cow, sow, owl, dove, and crane. (Her consort had other animal forms, such as the snake, bull, or the white roebuck.) In Graves's poem "Cat-Goddesses" the triad expands to nine (like the powerful ninefold-mountain mother of Parnassus whom Apollo reduced to nine little nymphs, the Muses). The poem speaks of the "perverse habit of cat-goddesses" who, "With coral tongues and beryl eyes like lamps/ Long-legged, pacing three by three in nines," offer themselves indiscriminately to "tatter-eared and slinking alley-toms." They do this simply to provoke jealousy. They promptly desert the "gross-headed, rabbit-coloured litters" that result from such casual unions. None of these careless offspring is the sacred child whom the Goddess bears to her chosen Sacred King, symbolizing the rejuvenation of spring and the fertility of the land.

"RETURN OF THE GODDESS" AND "THE SWEET SHOP AROUND THE CORNER"

In "Return of the Goddess," the Queen appears as a crane, reclaiming errant frogs who had unwisely crowned a king of their own devising. "The log they crowned as king/ Grew sodden, lurched and sank"; the frogs, "loud with repentance," await the Goddess's judgment day. At dawn, the Goddess returns as a "gaunt red-legged crane" to claim them, "Lunging your beak down like a spear/ To fetch them home again." This clever fable perhaps suggests that men, too, erred in transferring their allegiance to a male deity. Sooner or later, the impostor will sink, and the immortal Goddess will return.

Sometimes the Goddess is invoked only indirectly in a more realistic context. The excellent short poem "The Sweet Shop Around the Corner" tells of a little boy who, losing track of his mother in a crowd, grabs a strange woman's hand and drags her boisterously into a sweet shop, demanding candy. Only gradually does he realize with dread that something is wrong:

> Were Mother's legs so lean, or her shoes so long,
> Or her skirt so patched, or her hair tousled and grey?
> Why did she twitter in such a ghostly way?
> *O, Mother, are you dead?*
> 　　　　　What else could a child say?

It is, of course, unnecessary for the appreciation of this poem to realize the mythic quality of Mother turned Crone. The poem is a model of clarity and brevity, yet achieves a striking revelation. The child, so confident in himself and his world of indulgent Mother and animal joys, looks suddenly upon the face of old age and death.

Although Graves's long love affair with the White Goddess inspired many good poems, such exclusive attention to this mythic framework ultimately limited his further development. It was hard for even so expert a craftsman to go on telling the "one story only" in fresh and exciting ways. The change or deepening of perspective that one might expect from age never appeared. Moreover, sometimes the reader may yearn for a real woman with a distinctive personality to emerge from the repeated avowals of love. Nevertheless, Graves wrote some very good poetry at almost every stage of his long and devoted career. Through his investigations in mythology and his celebration of it in poetry, he reactivated a past which makes the present richer.

OTHER MAJOR WORKS

LONG FICTION: *My Head! My Head!*, 1925; *No Decency Left*, 1932 (as Barbara Rich, with Laura Riding); *I, Claudius*, 1934; *Claudius the God and His Wife Messalina*, 1934; *"Antigua, Penny, Puce,"* 1936 (also known as *The Antigua Stamp*, 1937); *Count Belisarius*, 1938; *Sergeant Lamb of the Ninth*, 1940 (also known as *Sergeant Lamb's America*); *Proceed, Sergeant Lamb*, 1941; *The Story of Marie Powell, Wife to Mr. Milton*, 1943 (also known as *Wife to Mr. Milton, the Story of Marie Powell*); *The Golden Fleece*, 1944 (also known as *Hercules, My Shipmate*, 1945); *King Jesus*, 1946; *Watch the North Wind Rise*, 1949 (also known as *Seven Days in New Crete*); *The Islands of Unwisdom*, 1949 (also known as *The Isles of Unwisdom*); *Homer's Daughter*, 1955; *They Hanged My Saintly Billy*, 1957.

SHORT FICTION: *The Shout*, 1929; *¡Catacrok! Mostly Stories, Mostly Funny*, 1956; *Collected Short Stories*, 1964.

NONFICTION: *On English Poetry*, 1922; *The Meaning of Dreams*, 1924; *Poetic Unreason and Other Studies*, 1925; *Contemporary Techniques of Poetry: A Political Analogy*, 1925; *Another Future of Poetry*, 1926; *Impenetrability: Or, The Proper Habit of English*, 1926; *The English Ballad: A Short Critical Survey*, 1927; *Lars Porsena: Or, The Future of Swearing and Improper Language*, 1927; *A Survey of Modernist Poetry*, 1927 (with Laura Riding); *Lawrence and the Arabs*, 1927 (also known as *Lawrence and the Arabian Adventure*, 1928); *A Pamphlet Against Anthologies*, 1928 (with Laura Riding, also known as *Against Anthologies*); *Mrs. Fisher: Or, The Future of Humour*, 1928; *Goodbye to All That: An Autobiography*, 1929; *T. E. Lawrence to His Biographer Robert Graves*, 1938; *The Long Week-End: A Social History of Great Britain, 1918-1938*, 1940 (with Alan Hodge); *The Reader over Your Shoulders: A Handbook for Writers of English Prose*, 1943 (with Alan Hodge); *The White Goddess: A Historical Grammar of Poetic Myth*, 1948; *The Common Asphodel: Collected Essays on Poetry, 1922-1949*, 1949; *Occupation: Writer*, 1950; *The Nazarene Gospel Restored*, 1953 (with Joshua Podro); *The Crowning Privilege: The Clark Lectures, 1954-1955*, 1955;

Adam's Rib and Other Anomalous Elements in the Hebrew Creation Myth: A New View, 1955; *The Greek Myths*, 1955 (2 volumes); *Jesus in Rome: A Historical Conjecture*, 1957 (with Joshua Podro); *5 Pens in Hand*, 1958; *Greek Gods and Heroes*, 1960; *Oxford Addresses on Poetry*, 1962; *Nine Hundred Iron Chariots: The Twelfth Arthur Dehon Little Memorial Lecture*, 1963; *Hebrew Myths: The Book of Genesis*, 1964 (with Raphael Patai); *Majorca Observed*, 1965 (with Paul Hogarty); *Mammon and the Black Goddess*, 1965; *Poetic Craft and Principle*, 1967; *The Crane Bag and Other Disputed Subjects*, 1969; *On Poetry: Collected Talks and Essays*, 1969; *Difficult Questions, Easy Answers*, 1972.

CHILDREN'S LITERATURE: *The Big Green Book*, 1962; *The Siege and Fall of Troy*, 1962; *Two Wise Children*, 1966; *The Poor Boy Who Followed His Star*, 1968.

TRANSLATIONS: *Almost Forgotten Germany*, 1936 (of Georg Schwarz; translated with Laura Riding); *The Transformation of Lucius, Otherwise Known as "The Golden Ass,"* 1950 (of Lucius Apuleius); *The Cross and the Sword*, 1954 (of Manuel de Jesús Galván); *Pharsalia: Dramatic Episodes of the Civil Wars*, 1956 (of Lucan); *Winter in Majorca*, 1956 (of George Sand); *The Twelve Caesars*, 1957 (of Suetonius); *The Anger of Achilles: Homer's "Iliad,"* 1959; *The Rubáiyát of Omar Khayyám*, 1967 (with Omar Ali-Shah).

EDITED TEXTS: *Oxford Poetry: 1921*, 1921 (edited with Alan Porter and Richard Hughes); *John Skelton: Laureate*, 1927; *The Less Familiar Nursery Rhymes*, 1927; *The Comedies of Terence*, 1962; *English and Scottish Ballads*, 1975.

MISCELLANEOUS: *Steps: Stories, Talks, Essays, Poems, Studies in History*, 1958; *Food for Centaurs: Stories, Talks, Critical Studies, Poems*, 1960; *Selected Poetry and Prose*, 1961.

BIBLIOGRAPHY

Bryant, Hallman Bell. *Robert Graves: An Annotated Bibliography*. Boston: G. K. Hall, 1986. Contains a select but good listing of primary sources and a thorough, annotated catalog of secondary sources. The latter are arranged alphabetically by author. The cut-off date is 1985. The index refers to authors, titles of critical works, journals in which they appeared, works by Graves dealt with, as well as significant themes in the writings of Graves.

Cohen, J. M. *Robert Graves*. New York: Grove Press, 1960. Though the biographical information in this book has been supplanted by recent biographies, Cohen's study remains a solid critical statement of Graves: His poetry is central and all other writings peripheral. Although Cohen undervalues the mythic poetry of Graves, his comments on the prose are very insightful.

Graves, Richard Perceval. *Robert Graves: The Assault Heroic, 1895-1926*. New York: Viking Press, 1986. Though primarily concerned with Graves's life, this book delineates the conditions that led him to write *Goodbye to All That* and leave England. The effect of World War I and his rejection of conventional morality appear largely in this study.

_____. *Robert Graves: The Years with Laura, 1926-1940*. New York: Viking Press, 1990. The second volume of Richard Graves's three-volume study. Looking closely at the relationship between Graves and the American poet Laura Riding, this volume provides information concerning the respective contributions of the collaborators. More so than in his first volume, Richard Perceval Graves is concerned with literary matters, though his fascination with the sensational aspects of the years Graves and Riding spent together is evident. Of much interest, as in the first volume, are the notes, which indicate the breadth of Graves's friendships and the variety of places in which his papers have been placed.

_____. *Robert Graves and the White Goddess, 1940-1985*. London: Weidenfeld and Nicolson, 1995. This concluding volume to Richard Graves's three-volume biography of Robert Graves lacks the savor and drama of the second volume, because it covers the relatively sedate life of an aged, lionized poet. Robert Graves had by age 45 settled into life with Beryl Hodge, his second wife. They took up residence in Majorca, where he was visited by an unending succession of disciples and young women whom Graves adopted as lovers and muses.

Graves, Robert. *Conversations with Robert Graves*. Edited by Frank L. Kersnowski. Jackson: University Press of Mississippi, 1990. This collection of interviews and recollections portrays Graves as a man and writer from early in his career in a diary entry by Virginia Woolf to shortly before his death in an essay by Jorge Luis Borges. The entries concern the life and friendships of Graves, his major themes and concerns, and his method of writing and revision. There is a very strong sense of the presence of Robert Graves.

_____. *Good-Bye to All That: An Autobiography*. Edited, with a biographical essay and annotations, by Richard Perceval Graves. Providence, R.I.: Berghahn Books, 1995. Graves traces the monumental and universal loss of innocence that occurred as a result of World War I. Written after the war and as he was leaving his birthplace, he bids farewell not only to England and his English family and friends but also to a way of life.

Mehoke, James S. *Robert Graves: Peace-Weaver*. The Hague: Mouton, 1975. This volume is one of the most thorough studies of Graves's fiction and its relationship to Graves's central myth: the White Goddess. The study of the critical reaction to Graves is invaluable.

Seymour-Smith, Martin. *Robert Graves: His Life and Work*. London: Hutchinson University Library, 1982. Though strongly biographical, this study places emphasis on the forces and occasions that shaped the writings of Graves and devotes much attention to Graves's friends and the historical events. Seymour-Smith relies heavily on the fact that Graves and many of his acquaintances attended the University of Oxford. The book deals pointedly with sensational events. The notes provide information not only about the author's sources but also about his relationship with Graves.

Snipes, Katherine. *Robert Graves*. New York: Frederick Ungar, 1979. Clearly an introductory study of Graves's life and writing, this book provides guidance through the major works and genres. The summaries of the novels are clear and helpful.

Katherine Snipes;
bibliography updated by the editors

THOMAS GRAY

Born: London, England; December 26, 1716
Died: Cambridge, England; July 30, 1771

PRINCIPAL POETRY

"Elegy Written in a Country Churchyard," 1751
Six Poems by Mr. T. Gray, 1753
Odes, by Mr. Gray, 1757
Pindaric Odes, 1758
Poems by Mr. Gray, 1768

OTHER LITERARY FORMS

Thomas Gray did not write a great deal of poetry, but he was a most prolific writer of letters. In the eighteenth century, the personal letter became so refined as an exercise in wit, description, and intellect that modern critics and literary historians now regard the letter as a minor art form of the period. Among the very greatest eighteenth century letter writers are Gray and his close friend Horace Walpole. The Gray of the letters sounds different from the poet. As he addresses his personal friends on a remarkably broad range of topics, there is a refreshing clarity and ease that his concept of poetry as an expression of ideals excluded from his verse. Especially famous are his descriptions of the Alps, which foreshadow the Romantic appreciation of nature's wilder aspects; but whatever the subject, the letters reveal that Gray was as much an artist in prose as in poetry.

ACHIEVEMENTS

Thomas Gray is usually viewed as the least significant major writer in an age that included such giants as Jonathan Swift, Alexander Pope, and Samuel Johnson, or as the most significant of such minor figures as James Thompson and William Cowper. That he enjoys such stature is the more amazing when it is remembered that, in his lifetime, he published less than one thousand lines of verse. Gray's immortality results from the quality of his work or, more accurately, the fine craftsmanship apparent in his every line. Poetry was only one of many subjects that interested Gray; indeed, critics and literary biographers often place him with John Milton and Johnson as one of the most learned poets in English literature. This

is not to say that his poetry was not important to Gray. He was sensitive to the critical response to what he allowed to be published, and he brought to his composition all of the learning and love for precision characteristic of the scholar. He wrote about things that mattered to him, things that moved him, and, like William Wordsworth, he recollected in tranquillity his overflow of powerful feelings before beginning to write. Because some of the things that moved him—Gothic castles, wild mountain vistas, the annals of the poor—were subjects that later moved the poets of the early nineteenth century, he has often been called a "pre-Romantic." This epithet, however, is less useful than usual when it comes to characterizing Gray, for Gray did not share the Romantic concern with everyday speech, nor was he moved to self-revelation. Gray intruded into his work only inasmuch as he did not hesitate to use his profound scholarship; thus, he spoke with complete intelligibility to a rather select audience. It is the achievement of this careful, intellectual, and most perfect poet, that the final products of his craftsmanship manage to transcend the intellect to communicate feelings that move his readers regardless of place or time.

BIOGRAPHY

Thomas Gray was born in Cornhill (London) on December 26, 1716. Of twelve children born to Philip and Dorothy Gray, only Thomas survived childhood. The family was fairly prosperous; Philip was a scrivener and exchange broker, and Dorothy operated a millinery. Dorothy was a loving parent, but Philip was an ill-tempered wife-beater who was reponsible for making young Thomas's childhood less than happy. It may well have been to remove the child from his father's influence that Dorothy arranged for her eight-year-old son to go off to school at Eton, where her brothers were masters. At Eton, Gray met Richard West and Horace Walpole, who became his closest friends, but with the exception of the happiness resulting from these friendships, the studious and solitary Gray found little pleasure in the company of the rowdy young men of Eton. In 1734, Gray and Walpole left Eton for Cambridge University. The death of his aunt, Sarah Gray, provided an income sufficient for his modest needs. Gray left Cambridge in 1738 with the intention of studying law at the Inner Temple. In 1739, however, his friend Walpole was ready to put the finish-

Thomas Gray (Hulton Archive)

been a writer of Latin poetry but now began to work with classical forms, such as the ode, in English. Gray's first major poems, "Ode on the Spring," "Ode on a Distant Prospect of Eton College," and "Hymn to Adversity," were composed in 1742, but the Eton ode was not published until 1747; the Spring ode and "Ode on the Death of a Favorite Cat" appeared in an anthology in 1748. In the meantime, Gray was awarded a bachelor of civil law degree in 1743 and settled into the life of a Cambridge scholar. His appetite for study was insatiable. His notebooks attest to his extensive knowledge of natural history as well as art, philosophy, and languages. The famous "Elegy Written in a Country Churchyard" was published on February 15, 1751. It was immediately popular, and Gray's printer had to produce five editions that year to meet the demand. In December, 1757, four months after the publication of the *Odes*, he rejected an offer to be poet laureate; it was an office which politics and poor poetry had caused to fall into low repute. The next decade was spent quietly at Cambridge, with frequent trips to London, Scotland, and Wales. In 1768, Gray was made Regius Professor of Modern History at Cambridge. His final years were plagued by attacks of gout, and he endured considerable pain until his death on July 30, 1771. He was buried beside his mother in the village of Stoke Poges.

ANALYSIS

In the spring of 1742, Thomas Gray turned his attention from writing Latin verse to composing in English. His first effort, "Noontide," later renamed "Ode on the Spring," was included with a personal letter to his dear friend, Richard West. The letter came back unopened, and soon Gray's fear was confirmed; the companion of his Eton days had died. Ironically, that poem which West never saw dealt with the brevity of life. Certainly, Gray had reason to ruminate on such a theme; eleven of his siblings had died in infancy, leaving him the sole survivor. Now, the death of West intensified his feeling of loss. The purpose of mortal existence became the theme which Gray was to address from a variety of points of view in nearly all of the major poems of his career.

"ODE ON THE SPRING"

While "Ode on the Spring" is an early effort, it is not unaccomplished. Gray simply did not produce careless

ing touch on his own education by taking the traditional Grand Tour of Europe. Walpole's father, the famous prime minister Sir Robert Walpole, believed that his son might benefit from the company of a good, sober companion and offered to pay all of Gray's expenses to take the Tour with Horace. For two years, Gray and Walpole traveled through France, Italy, and Switzerland. Gray was fascinated by the culture of Europe and vividly recorded his experiences and feelings in letters that are considered among the finest written in English. While touring Italy in May, 1741, Gray and Walpole quarreled. The reason for the disagreement is not clear—years later, after Gray's death, Walpole assumed the blame—but Gray returned to London alone and was not reconciled with his friend until 1745. In 1742, he settled again at Cambridge and, except for a brief residence in London (1759-1761), stayed there for the rest of his life.

On June 1, 1742, Richard West died; Gray never forgot the loss of his dearest friend. This same time marks a period of increased literary productivity as Gray turned from Latin to English as his poetic medium. He had long or unrefined poetry; he labored long and thoughtfully to achieve a precise result. Some critics, including the great Samuel Johnson, have attacked "Ode on the Spring." In his *Lives of the Poets* (1779-1781), Johnson objects that "the language is too luxuriant, and the thoughts have nothing new," and fundamentally Johnson is correct. The language is indeed luxuriant, and the content is by no means original. The poem is largely descriptive of the Buckinghamshire country where the poet, seated under a tree near the water, considers the brief lives of the insects as they frolic in the spring sun. The insects are a metaphor for the segment of humanity which, unlike the reclusive and scholarly poet, enjoys the sportive life of temporal pleasures. As the poet meditates on his *sic transit* theme, the insects are suddenly allowed to interrupt and "in accents low" answer the sober poet. They tell him that from their point of view it is he who is wasting his life: He is alone, without a beautiful female companion; he has hoarded no treasures to give him pleasure, and his being adds nothing to the beauty of the countryside. Moreover, the poet's spring flees as quickly as the insects'. Gray allows the poet no rebuttal to the insects' argument; their last words, "We frolic, while 'tis May," end the poem. Talking insects are unusual, but what they and the poet have to say is not. The figure of the poet as the detached observer who prefers to remain isolated from the affairs of humanity stretches back into antiquity. While "Ode on the Spring" is admittedly composed of highly conventional elements, it can be argued that the composition of those elements is unusually sophisticated and uniquely characteristic of Gray.

The persona in "Ode on the Spring" is very close to Gray himself: reclusive, scholarly, an observer more than a participant. The luxuriant language serves a double purpose. It creates an ideal nature, lavish and beautiful beyond reality, a nature before the fall in which the reader is not unduly shocked to find that humans can still talk to animals. Against this ideal, where beautiful May follows beautiful May without worry about time, is presented the fate of both the poet and the insects. Their concern, mortality, is very real; indeed, it is more real because it still exists despite the context of an unreal nature. The language, however, in addition to clarifying the external message of the reality of death, also satirizes.

The poet, speaking in the first person, creates through his elaborate language this beautiful, ideal nature, although he would prefer to remain divorced from the mortal humanity he contrasts with his creation. He would be unique and pompously states,

> With me the Muse shall sit, and think
> (At ease reclin'd in rustic state)
> How vain the ardours of the crowd,
> How low, how little are the Proud,
> How indigent the Great!

The Muse, however, refuses to cooperate, and the poet's ideal nature with its ideal talking insects includes him with the rest of mortal humanity. Not only do his insects remind him that "On hasty wings thy youth is flown," but they also challenge his very style of life and argue that contemplation and detachment are most wasteful of spring. Thus, "Ode on the Spring," while conventional and luxuriant, as critics have said, is still a very skillful handling of conventions and an accomplished example of how poetic language can communicate more than one message simultaneously.

The news of West's death motivated Gray to explore more deeply the theme of human mortality that "Ode on the Spring" had introduced. During the summer of 1742, a season of intense sorrow and intense creative energy for Gray, he produced two important poems: "Hymn to Adversity" and "Ode on a Distant Prospect of Eton College."

"HYMN TO ADVERSITY"

"Hymn to Adversity" is less concerned with mortality than it is with the quality of existence. Like the spring ode, this poem is also voiced in the first person, but the element of parody is gone, and there is no reason to suspect that the voice in the poem is not that of Gray himself honestly attempting to cope with his own unhappiness. The theme is simple. Adversity visits everyone, but, realizing this, humans can be led to forgiveness, generosity, and love for their fellows, with whom they are united by the common bond of affliction. The poet invites adversity to come to him, not in its more horrible form of disease, poverty, or death, but in the benign form of a teacher who can instruct him in what it means to be human. The critic and biographer of Gray, Morris Golden, has stated that to a modern reader "Hymn to

Adversity" is perhaps "the chilliest poem written by Gray." This seems to be an excellent description, for the piece represents precisely those poetic conventions which delighted eighteenth century audiences but which modern taste has discarded. The poem teaches a moral, an excellent Christian moral: humanity should endure and strive to profit from whatever is given to it and not rage against fate. The message is clarified by an extensive use of personification. Adversity is a definite, intelligent, and feminine entity. She is even given family relationships; she is "Daughter of Jove," sister and nurse to Virtue, companion of Wisdom (who dresses in sable), Melancholy (a silent maid), warm Charity, severe Justice, and weeping Pity. Her band includes screaming Horror, Despair, Disease, and Poverty; Laughter, Noise, and Joy flee from her frown. This is certainly an impressive cast for a poem of only forty-eight lines. While a modern reader might complain that personification can diminish the subtle ambiguities necessary for the reader's creative participation in the poem, the neoclassical reader would applaud the clarity of the lesson. Even Dr. Johnson was so impressed by the "moral application" of the ideas found in "Hymn to Adversity" that he refused to mention his "slight objections"—unusual for Johnson. Of course, Johnson himself frequently employed personification, and he must have recognized that "Hymn to Adversity" is a thematic cousin to his own *The Vanity of Human Wishes* (1749).

"ODE ON A DISTANT PROSPECT OF ETON COLLEGE"

The most enduring accomplishment of that fruitful summer of 1742 was "Ode on a Distant Prospect of Eton College." The theme is still the same: mortality and its consequences. Here, however, the poet relates his observations of the landscape without remarking on the quality of lifestyles as he did in "Ode on the Spring" and without preaching the Christian lesson of "Hymn to Adversity." In the Eton College ode, wisdom, the desired companion of Adversity in the hymn, is something that should not be courted but left to wait until its inevitable time. Likewise, happiness, which the poet of "Hymn to Adversity" made flee before the welcomed approach of adversity, is here lamented: "And happiness too swiftly flies." It is not surprising that, next to "Elegy Written in a Country Churchyard," the Eton College ode has sur-

vived as Gray's most popular poem. It does not trouble the reader with pompous poets and talking insects, nor does it try to persuade the reader to enjoy the taste of bitter medicine. The poet who watches the children at play on the fields of Eton is surely no less lofty in his diction or elaborate in his constructions than the poets who sang of spring and adversity. The Eton poet, however, appears more natural in this elevated stance. In relation to the children he is observing, he really is a voice of wisdom, and as it is clear that he takes no special pleasure in his relatively elevated state, he manages to avoid sounding pompous despite the baroque language. What does emerge is a sense of very deep and sincere sorrow, the more sincere to the reader familiar with Gray's life when it is remembered that he had been a student at Eton, and the writing of this ode in 1742 marked the severing of the last tie with those innocent days. He had lost the friendship of one school friend, Walpole, and now the last Eton friend, West, was gone too. Dr. Johnson objected to this ode because the subject "suggests nothing to Gray which every beholder does not equally think and feel." Actually, the same comment might be made to the poem's credit, but what is missing, and what an eighteenth century moralist would have expected, is a clearer statement of the lesson suggested by the subject being described. Gray, however, seems too personally affected to allow his meditations on the Eton landscape to follow to the expected lesson of Christian optimism, and he abruptly cuts himself off and concludes with one of the most famous lines in English poetry: "No more; where ignorance is bliss,/ 'Tis folly to be wise."

Viewed together, these three products of 1742, "Ode on the Spring," "Hymn to Adversity," and "Ode on a Distant Prospect of Eton College," make an interestingly unified trilogy. The spring ode introduces the two most obvious approaches to life: tranquil meditation and active pursuit of pleasure. No clear advantage is given to either, for one attitude is given to insects and the other to a pompous poet. "Hymn to Adversity" returns to explore in greater detail the life devoid of insect pleasures and steeled by trouble. In turn, the Eton ode focuses on the alternative, the life of innocent pleasure without the burdens of thought and hardship. None of these early works is distinguished by profundity or originality of thought, and while the adversity hymn and Eton ode do argue for particular lifestyles, clearly the trilogy of 1742 finally shows a Gray who has discovered no satisfactory answer to his questions.

"ELEGY WRITTEN IN A COUNTRY CHURCHYARD"

Gray's concern for the questions of human mortality and the proper conduct of life continued beyond the very productive year 1742. The poems written at that traumatic time clarified some of the questions but ultimately resolved nothing for the poet. Four years later, after Gray had had the opportunity to recollect in tranquillity the problems that West's death had forced on his attention, he returned to his theme in a poem that continues to be admired as a masterpiece of world poetry. "Elegy Written in a Country Churchyard" was probably begun in 1746, but, like all of Gray's efforts, it was carefully reworked many times, even after its first publication in 1751. Indeed, Gray allowed publication only after he learned that a copy of the poem had been obtained by the editors of the *Magazine of Magazines*, a journal of which Gray had a low opinion, and that that magazine was about to publish the verses without permission. Gray's edition, published on February 15, 1751, by Robert Dodsley, beat the *Magazine of Magazines* by only one day. The poem was immediately popular; since the first hurried printing, it has gone through countless editions and numerous translations. In fact, some literary historians have claimed that it is the most famous poem in all of English literature.

Like Gray's earlier efforts, the elegy is a product of its author's wide reading and knowledge of conventions. The poem is an excellent example of landscape poetry, a versified description of a rural scene incorporating the poet's reflections on the moral significance of what is observed. More specifically, Gray's elegy represents a then-popular species of landscape verse called graveyard poetry. These gloomy exercises, set in cemeteries and crypts, invariably reflected on the inevitability of death. While the ostensible purpose of the graveyard school was moral instruction, clearly some students of that school allowed sensational, grisly description to become an end in itself, with the moral lesson serving as little more than an excuse for cataloging every mortuary horror imaginable. Compared to such morbid works as

James Hervey's *Meditations Among the Tombs* (1745), a prose piece that went through several editions in the eighteenth century, Gray's elegy is mild stuff indeed. "Elegy Written in a Country Churchyard" is genuinely concerned with mortality and the quality of life, and its gothic trappings exist only to establish the appropriate somber mood for the first-person ruminations of the poet. That mood owes much to the great care which Gray took with the sound of his poem. Onomatopoeia and alliteration are expertly employed with a diction that includes a great many long vowel sounds in order to communicate the mood of the poet. "Elegy Written in a Country Churchyard" does not merely tell the reader about the dead; it allows each reader to share in the experience of thinking about them.

Again, those thoughts are not memorable for their originality; rather, the achievement of the poem is its sensitive collection of the reactions that thoughtful people have always had to the awareness of their mortality. "The 'Church yard' abounds with images which find a mirror in every mind, and with sentiments to which every bosom returns an echo," said Dr. Johnson. Perhaps the principal message of the poem is the effect of death as a reminder of the unity of the human species and, indeed, the unity of the species with all of nature. The social conditions that distinguish one person from another in life are, finally, superficial. Talent, sensitivity, love of knowledge, and of course death, are common to the human community and ignore the fleeting borders set up by temporal wealth and power. The poet is saddened that the poor are restricted in their ability to develop and share their talents, but finds comfort in the ultimate erasure of all differences by death.

"THE PROGRESS OF POESY" AND "THE BARD"

With "Elegy Written in a Country Churchyard," Gray reached an understanding of the human condition, but he did not stoically accept the tragedy of poverty and stifled talent brought about by misuse of power. The old theme of the quality and style of life appears once more in the two great Pindaric odes, "The Progress of Poesy" and "The Bard." Unlike the previous elegy, the Pindarics were written in anticipation of successful publication. Gray intended them as his crowning achievement and poured into them all of his skill as a master of poetic diction and classical forms, together with all of his vast knowledge of history. Unfortunately, even the well-educated poetry readers of the eighteenth century were unprepared for so learned a poet as Thomas Gray. The poems were greeted with charges of obscurity and unintelligibility, and in later editions Gray grudgingly provided notes to explain the references and allusions.

Both odes deal with poetry. "The Progress of Poesy" glorifies the art and demonstrates that poetry supports and contributes to political liberty. When tyranny establishes itself, poetry and the beauty and order it creates leave, for oppression and beauty cannot coexist. "The Bard" is a specific example of the idea expressed in "The Progress of Poesy." Here, the last Welsh bard to escape the purge ordered by the invading Edward I confronts the king with a historically accurate prophecy of the downfall of his royal line. The bard's words, his poem, actually create a reality; the prophecy will come about, and then poetry will have destroyed tyranny. Gray composed this poem with considerable enthusiasm and later declared: "I felt myself the Bard." The statement is significant in relation to the theme first introduced by "Ode on the Spring." The noblest life, that of the creating bard who combats oppression and levels the social barriers in the community of humanity, was Gray's own, and those carefully crafted poems that so elegantly explored what to do with life were themselves the best answer.

OTHER MAJOR WORKS

NONFICTION: *The Correspondence of Thomas Gray*, 1935 (Paget Toynbee and Leonard Whibley, editors).

BIBLIOGRAPHY

Bloom, Harold, ed. *Thomas Gray's "Elegy Written in a Country Churchyard."* New York: Chelsea House, 1987. Gray's elegy is probably the eighteenth century's single most celebrated poem, and it remains the subject of much critical debate. Brings together a number of important essays on the elegy, spanning several decades.

Downey, James, and Ben Jones, eds. *Fearful Joy: Papers from the Thomas Gray Bicentenary Conference at Carleton University.* Montreal: McGill-Queen's University Press, 1974. These essays, presented at Carleton University in 1971 (the two hundredth anniversary of Gray's death), provide an excellent "source book" for students of Gray. All aspects of Gray's life, times, and poetry are addressed. Included is a handsome series of early illustrations of his work, many by the great artist-poet William Blake.

Golden, Morris. *Thomas Gray.* New York: Twayne, 1964. An excellent introduction to Gray's life and work. A brief biographical chapter is followed by chapters discussing Gray's "literary views," his major and minor works, and the question of his status as classical or romantic poet. A chronology and bibliography are included.

Ketton-Cremer, R. W. *Thomas Gray: A Biography.* Cambridge, England: Cambridge University Press, 1955. A solid, well-written biography, very much in the "life and works" tradition. Clearly written and well researched, this remains the best account of Gray's life. Contains an impressive set of illustrations.

McCarthy, B. Eugene. *Thomas Gray: The Progress of a Poet.* Madison, N.J.: Fairleigh Dickinson University Press, 1997. Critical interpretation of selected works by Gray. Includes bibliographical references and index.

Mack, Robert L. *Thomas Gray: A Life.* New Haven, Conn.: Yale University Press, 2000. Mack expands our knowledge of this forefather of the Romantic movement by incorporating recent revisionary scholarship on Gray as well as original archival research on the poet's family and formative years. Mack casts new light on Gray's personality and on the psychological and sexual tensions that defined his compelling poetry.

Sitter, John. *Literary Loneliness in Mid-Eighteenth Century England.* Ithaca, N.Y.: Cornell University Press, 1982. Sitter's study of the major poetry and fiction of the "Age of Sensibility" is crucial to an understanding of the contexts within which Gray's poetry can be most productively read. Full of important insights into Gray and the historical period.

William J. Heim;
bibliography updated by the editors

ROBERT GREENE

Born: Norwich, Norfolk, England; c. July, 1558
Died: London, England; September 3, 1592

PRINCIPAL POETRY

Orlando furioso, c. 1588 (verse play)

Alcida: Greene's Metamorphosis, 1588 (poetry and prose)

A Looking Glass for London and England, c. 1588-1589 (verse play; with Thomas Lodge)

Friar Bacon and Friar Bungay, c. 1589 (verse play)

John of Bordeaux, c. 1590-1591 (verse play)

A Maiden's Dream, 1591

James IV, 1591 (verse play)

OTHER LITERARY FORMS

Robert Greene is known primarily for his comedies, prose romances, and pamphlets of London rogue life. Four plays are definitely his: *Orlando furioso* (c. 1588), *Friar Bacon and Friar Bungay* (c. 1589), *James IV* (c. 1591), and *A Looking Glass for London and England* (c. 1588-1589; with Thomas Lodge). A fifth, *John of Bordeaux* (c. 1590-1591), has been attributed to Greene because of its close similarity to his known work in theme, diction, and structure. Two more, *Alphonsus, King of Aragon* (c. 1587) and *Selimus* (c. 1587), both *Tamburlaine*-type tragedies, have also been attributed to him, but these bear little resemblance to his known plays.

Greene's romances made him England's most popular writer of prose fiction in the 1580's. Early works, showing Italian influence, include among others, *Mamillia: A Mirror or Looking Glass for the Ladies of England* (1583, 1593), *Morando: The Tritameron of Love* (1584, 1587), *Planetomachia* (1585), and *Penelope's Web* (1587). His pastoral romances, including *Ciceronis Amor* (1589, also known as *Tullies Love*), *Pandosto: The Triumph of Time* (1588), and *Menaphon* (1589), developed themes and forms popularized by Sir Philip Sidney's *Arcadia* (1590). Mantuanesque pastoral, with repentance as a major theme, predominates in later works, among them *Greene's Never Too Late* (1590), *Francesco's Fortunes* (1590), and *Greene's Mourning Garment* (1590).

In his last two years, Greene turned to another form, the rogue, or "connycatching," pamphlet, thereby creating a literary fashion. His *A Notable Discovery of Cozenage* (1591), *A Disputation Between a Hee Conny-Catcher and a Shee Conny-Catcher* (1592), *The Black Book's Messenger* (1592), and other small books in this series combined London street argot with satire of middle-class greed to produce a form that appealed to all levels of society.

Greene's death in 1592 sparked the publication of two alleged "deathbed" pamphlets, *Greene's Groatsworth of Wit Bought with a Million of Repentance* and *The Repentance of Robert Greene*, both usually attributed to him, but neither closely resembling his known prose, and thus probably spurious. The one surely authentic posthumous work, *Greene's Vision* (1592), follows the pastoral-penitent style of 1590 and was therefore likely written in that most fruitful year of his brief career.

ACHIEVEMENTS

The works for which Robert Greene is best known, his romances and his comedies, are largely poetic achievements, as well as milestones in the development of English prose and drama. What sets even his early fictions apart from those of his contemporaries (mainly

Robert Greene (Hulton Archive)

translations of continental stories) is his concern for the carefully crafted, rhythmic sentence, its meaning conveyed through striking images and comparisons. Though following English writer John Lyly to some extent in the development of this "euphuistic" style (after Lyly's *Euphues, the Anatomy of Wit*, 1579), Greene quickly learned to vary his forms, changing pace and tone to suit the demands of scene and character. By 1584, four years after the appearance of his first work, Greene was experimenting with other poetic modifications of his prose; he began to insert songs and emblematic poems to heighten description and further illuminate his characters. The songs, in particular, became a trademark of Greene's romances, achieving a remarkable variety of verse forms and moods in such works as *Tullies Love, Menaphon*, and *Greene's Never Too Late*. These and other later romances by Greene are so dense with verse, especially love songs, poetic love letters, and introspective lyrics, that it can be said that here Greene's primary vehicle of story development is poetry. This style made Greene England's most popular prose writer in the years 1588 to 1592, the year of his death.

To make his verse achieve both illumination and individuation of his characters, Greene was more or less forced to break ground untouched by any previous English poet. Particularly vivid in this regard are two poems from *Menaphon*: "Sephestia's Song to Her Child" and "Doron's Eclogue Joined with Carmela's." The first, a lullaby about the forced separation of a noble family, and the second, a humorous love poem, are written in low style, their images drawn from English domestic life; both violate poetic conventions of the time by achieving a pastoral mood in deliberate avoidance of the conceits and heightened atmosphere of works such as *The Shepheardes Calender* (1579) or the eclogues of *Arcadia*.

Greene's great influence on English dramatic comedy is principally owing to this same originality, this same enlivening and varying of mood through poetic device. Although his contemporaries appear to have thought most highly of him as a "maker of plots," Greene's plays immediately impress the modern reader by their verse. His best-known comedies, *Friar Bacon and Friar Bungay* and *James IV*, gain their power from that varying of image and verse form from character to character, scene to scene, that marks the romances. The same serious use of English rural imagery that Greene used in his later prose to create pastoral tones pervades his comedies as well and gives them those qualities that critics have called distinctly "festive" and "romantic." These qualities make Greene's plays as important in the development of comedy as are Christopher Marlowe's in the growth of tragedy.

Though poetry is a vital element throughout Greene's work, his influence as a poet has been far less great than his influence on the other genres, primarily because almost all his poems are incidental to his romances. In his time, several pieces were anthologized in collections of pastoral verse, but no scholar has detected in other poets' work the kind of influence that Greene's comedies exerted on William Shakespeare or his pamphlets on Ben Jonson and Thomas Dekker. This influence notwithstanding, the fact that some of his poems, such as "Doron's Description of Samela" (also from *Menaphon*) and "Sephestia's Song to Her Child," are now recognized as being the best of their type from the period.

It may be that Greene's poetic influence has merely been overlooked: Little systematic study of his poetry has been made; Greene's complete verse was not collected and published until 1977. Nevertheless, his influence was significant. It is clear, that in taking comedic lessons from Greene, Shakespeare followed his practice of varying structure (using rhyme, blank verse, prose, or song) to suit a speaker's rank or the tonal demands of a scene. The matching of verse to sense which is found in *As You Like It* (c. 1599-1600) or *The Winter's Tale* (c. 1610-1611) is an idea first embodied in English comedy in the plays of Greene. Likewise, Greene's poetic experiments with rural vernacular in his romances led to his cultivation of street talk in the connycatching pamphlets, their popularity inspiring the city-based works of Jonson, Dekker, and all those who followed them.

BIOGRAPHY

According to the most widely accepted speculation, Robert Greene was born to a saddler and his wife in Norwich, Norfolk, in 1558. There is no reliable evidence for this speculation, since the only mention of Norwich as his birthplace is found in the posthumous pamphlet *Greene's Groatsworth of Wit Bought with a*

Million of Repentance, its attribution to Greene probably spurious. Nevertheless, since it is known that Greene took his B.A. from St. John's (Cambridge) in 1580, the speculated birthdate is a likely one. Moreover, since Greene held a sizar's appointment at Cambridge—a type of work-study position in which middle-class students kept their places by serving students from noble houses—it is also likely that Greene came from the home of an artisan.

Nothing is known about Greene's life before he entered Cambridge and little is known of it after he left. Cambridge records reveal his baccalaureate degree and his M.A. from Clare in 1583, but neither his contemporaries nor Greene himself has left an account of his life there, notwithstanding the great practical importance Greene attached to his degrees, particularly the master's (and his second master's, from Oxford, in 1588); the words "Master of Arts in Both Universities" are prominently displayed on his title pages. Who exactly Robert Greene was or what he did besides write and publish is not known. Most of the available quasi-biographical remarks come from a friend, Thomas Nashe, a notorious exaggerator, from an enemy, Gabriel Harvey, even less trustworthy, and from pamphlets of spurious attribution, *Greene's Groatsworth of Wit Bought with a Million of Repentance* and *The Repentance of Robert Greene*. Of Greene's appearance and character, Nashe wrote:

> . . . a iolly long red peake, like the spire of a steeple, he cherisht continually without cutting, whereat a man might hang a Iewall, it was so sharp and pendant.

> A good fellowe hee was . . . and in one yeare he pist as much against the walls as thou and thy brothers [speaking to Harvey] spent in three.

> He made no account of winning credite by his works . . . ; his only care was to haue a spel in his purse to coniure up a good cuppe of wine with at all times.

Harvey, incensed over an inferred insult in Greene's last work, *A Quip for an Upstart Courtier*, vented his anger in the following exercise of his poetic talent: "a rakehell, a makeshift: a scribbling foole:/ a famous bayard, in City, and Schoole." Harvey went on to say that Greene had had a whore as mistress and by her a son, Fortunatus, who died in infancy. Certainly, no corrobo-

rating evidence has been found. Nevertheless, the posthumous pamphlets, both in the repentance mode, stress the supposed degradation of Greene's life by putting into the deceased writer's mouth self-accusations similar to those made by Greene characters in several romances.

Mitigating somewhat these views are remarks by poet "R. B." (probably Richard Barnfield), who wrote *Greene's Funeralls* (1593): "For iudgment *Ioue*, for Learning deepe, he still *Apollo* seemde:/ For fluent tongue, for eloquence, men *Mercury* him deemde./ His life and manners though I would, I cannot half expresse." Although this praise helps to balance the record, it provides no further fact. The only certain information about Greene's later life is the month and year of his death, September, 1592, the cause of death being a protracted illness, probably *not* brought on, as Nashe claimed, by a banquet of rhenish wine and pickled herring.

This veil over Greene's life is ironic in that he achieved great contemporary fame as a writer: Indeed, his popularity was so great that the titles of his works included his name. In fact, for ten years after his death, "Greene" continued to appear as a character in pamphlets and stories, his protean identity in these works reflecting the elusiveness of his actual biography.

ANALYSIS

To understand Robert Greene as a poet requires distinguishing among the three main categories of his verse: the ninety poems incidental to his romances, his memorial poem about Sir Christopher Hatton (*A Maiden's Dream*), and his verse comedies. The first illustrates the use of verse in the service of characterization in prose narrative; the third shows varied verse structure as the vehicle of character and mood. The second is Greene's only self-contained work in a conventional verse genre.

POEMS INCIDENTAL TO THE ROMANCES

The reader of Greene's incidental poems is doubly struck: first, by Greene's concentration on a single theme, the workings of romantic love; second, by the sheer diversity of Greene's forms, voices, and conceits. Whereas Sir Philip Sidney, William Shakespeare, and the other Elizabethan sonnet-cyclists explored the potential of a single form and voice to express the nuances of love, Greene's personae vary with his many character types, male and female, who "spoke" or "sang" poems of from four to eighty lines, in blank verse, ballads, quatrains, couplets, rhyme royal, and Petrarchan sonnet rhyme. Although rarely straying from English iambics, Greene did experiment with feminine endings and quantitative verse. His lines are predominately pentameter; but his many songs frequently call for use of tetrameter and the alternation of line lengths. He even composed several hexameters.

Despite his numerous ventures into different meters and lengths, Greene favored the six-line stanza (*ababcc, abbacc,* or *abcbdd*), the tetrameter couplet (particularly in his pastoral songs from 1588 onward), and the ballad. These forms, combined with his almost exclusive use of end-stopped lines, make it clear that Greene intended his verse to be sung—at least to be songlike. His usual introduction to a poem is typified by the following from *Greene's Never Too Late:* ". . . whereupon sitting downe, she [Isabella] tooke her Lute in her hand, and sung this Ode." In these introductions, Greene frequently calls his poems "ditties," "dumpes" (sad songs), "madrigals," and "roundelays," to emphasize their tunefulness. When he calls his poems "odes" or "sonnets," he does not use such terms to signify specific verse forms. "Ode" implied to Greene's readers a serious, measured expression of emotion; "sonnet" merely meant "song." The "ode" sung by Isabella is classical only in its mythological imagery; it is written in rhymed tetrameter couplets. Greene's sonnets range in length from twelve to more than thirty lines and are almost all balladlike, some with refrains.

Whether Greene actually intended his poems to be set to music is not known. Since most of his pieces are "written through" (without refrains) and contain a fairly complex image structure, it seems more likely that he meant them to remain on the page, to be considered at a more leisurely pace than music allows. A clear case in point is "Melicertus' Eclogue" from *Menaphon.* Influenced by Edmund Spenser, Sidney, and other contributors to the pastoral tradition, Greene here uses a song form to work out a complicated conceit that does not lend itself to singing. In the poem, Melicertus, a nobleman disguised as a shepherd, describes the beauties of his love, Samela. As Melicertus proceeds to show how the various features of his mistress were created to sat-

isfy particular fancies of the gods, the poem proceeds in ballad form; but the number of images in even one line, "And mounts to heauen on ouer leaden wings," demands a readerly pace, enabling one to review a stanza to gather missed ideas.

Sometimes, however, a Greene poem is fully suited to musical setting. One of these is "Sephestia's Song to Her Child"; the strong pauses in each line mark this "dittie" as intended for the voice and the lute. Like Thomas Campion's airs, it moves the reader by invoking a familiar mood through a few definite images within a simple narrative.

In terms of imagery, most of Greene's songlike poetry from his early romances (1583-1588) displays a self-conscious classicism, conforming to his early use of such settings as Olympus, Ithaca, and Troy, and his explicit following of such learned models as John Lyly and Baldassare Castiglione. From 1588 on, most of Greene's verse comes closer to what might be called the English folk spirit, as exemplified in Sephestia's lullaby. Greene's imagery in these poems tends to spring from the same native source as his rhythms and stanza forms. Ironically, this shift is first seen in a romance titled *Tullies Love,* a work outwardly classical in setting and character, since it deals with the courtship of Cicero and the patrician lady Terentia. This romance even includes a Vergilian pastoral setting, the "vale of Love"; nevertheless, the genius of this vale is distinctly English, almost Chaucerian.

ROMANTIC LOVE

Thematically, most of Greene's poems, like the romances in which they are contained, are about the workings of love, usually painful, in young men and women. As expressions of his characters' emotional states, the poems can be compared to soliloquies or set speeches in drama. What each poem says about love depends on the character's personality, station in life, and situation at the moment. Thus, the title character of *Menaphon,* a shepherd in love with a princess, joyfully proclaims his love in one poem and woefully exclaims on his rejection in another; his fellow shepherd, Doron, also sings about the lady, but his description is platonic, since he admires Samela, but does not dote on her affection. Greene creates love poems to fit an amazing array of character types: prostitutes, icy virgins, betrayed wives, arrogant princes, love-scarred travelers, love-starved rustics, and many others. Philomela's ode reveals the mind of the chaste wife of a jealous husband; in a completely different spirit is the song of Infida, the whore who inveigles the hero of *Greene's Never Too Late:* "Thine eyes like flames of holie fires,/ *N'oseres vous, mon bel amy,* Burnes all my thoughts with sweete desires."

Because most Greene romances lead to a main character's remorse for wrongs done in the name of love, many of his poems dwell on either the overwhelming power of the emotion or the horrors of infatuation. Greene frequently handles this allegorically, in narratives about Cupid, Venus, and other mythological figures, as in "Radagon in Dianem," from *Francesco's Fortunes.* At other times, he comes at the issue directly, as in Philomela's ode, or in Francesco's sonnet on his infidelity. The two approaches differ with the characters' differing moods and motives: where the unscrupulous Radagon wants to seduce the innocent Mirimida by impressing her with his inventive wit, Francesco, ravaged by such schemes, creates verse that exhibits his newly found peace of mind. The second poem, while less showy, presents a more fully elaborated image, that of the prison, within a form that demands more control than does that chosen by Radagon. These two poems typify the marriage of form and dramatic function which Greene achieves in his best incidental poetry.

DRAMATIC VERSE

Even casual scrutiny of Greene's work suggests a connection between his stage writing, which began in 1588, and the change in his poetic style that took place the same year. Certainly, his many poetic experiments in the romances before 1588 had made Greene a fluent versifier before he began writing for the stage. His first known play, *Orlando furioso*, of which only a partial text remains, shows Greene's ease in spinning long iambic sentences dense with mythology. Conversely, the more personal, vividly descriptive poetry in *Greene's Never Too Late* and *Francesco's Fortunes* owes something to the fast-paced, richly sensual dialogue of *Friar Bacon and Friar Bungay* and *James IV*.

Greene's plays probably had deeper influence on his incidental verse than did the verse on the dramatic style. Playwriting gave Greene a broader, generally less educated audience; drama also demanded greater diversity of diction and tone to suit the greater range of character types. The ephemerality and comparative informality of spoken verse demanded images that were vivid, yet simple enough to fit conversational discourse. That Greene learned these lessons quickly is shown by *Friar Bacon and Friar Bungay*, one year after *Orlando furioso*. The later play features crisp dialogue interrupted infrequently by the long set speeches of which the earlier play had largely consisted. Of particular note is Greene's brand-new imagery, drawn from the English countryside, not from the courts of Venus. When Greene's aristocrats declaim in this play, they use hyperboles drawn from the contemporary world of commerce, not from Ovid. The most immediate impact of this new technique on Greene's incidental verse is found in *Menaphon.* One year later, the pastoral story of Mirimida, which concludes *Francesco's Fortunes*, shows even more strongly the influence of this play, as characters of different ranks speak verse amazingly different in diction and style; most of these poems are invigorated by images of English country life.

A different type of influence, but equal to that of *Friar Bacon and Friar Bungay*, was exerted on Greene's incidental poems by *James IV*. Written substantially in rhymed verse of various schemes, *James IV* tested Greene's ability to compose in a highly demanding poetic form a work for the popular stage. This form allowed Greene to imbue with a songlike tone this semihistorical tale of an English lady married to, betrayed by, and reunited with a Scots king. Like the tetrameter narratives contained in his romances of 1590, the rhymed verse in *James IV* gives the play a folk quality that softens and distances the often harsh events. The "feel" of the play is similar to that of Shakespeare's late romances. *James IV* also influenced the meditative "odes" in such romances as *Philomela, Francesco's Fortunes*, and *Greene's Vision.* The most striking traits of these poems—the single, integrated image and the perspective of melancholy wisdom—appear in numerous passages in the play.

The quiet lyricism of many of the speeches in *James IV* rehearses the tone of the "odes"; the emphasis on "I" and on the image of the speaker's performing a simple act, whether playing the lute or embroidering, even as the poem proceeds, makes them highly personal. At the same time, each speaker moralizes on a familiar theme, thus making the emotions available to all. Since the moral reflects explicitly back on the speaker, not on the reader, the "odes" have a quietly salutary effect, neither accusing nor warning. The sprightly tempo of the ballad form of these "odes," influenced by *James IV*, helps the romances containing them to convey that gentle optimism which is the hallmark of Greene's art.

A MAIDEN'S DREAM

Greene's only extended, self-contained work in a traditional poetic genre is *A Maiden's Dream*, his eulogy for Lord Chancellor Sir Christopher Hatton, who died November 20, 1591. The 389-line poem holds a strange place in the Greene chronology, as it comes at the end of a year in which he may have published no other verse, either dramatic or incidental. In 1591, Greene had turned from the romance to the connycatching pamphlet, its characters being crooks and tradespeople, its setting the streets and haunts of London, its language slang and trade talk. How surprising, in this context, to read *A Maiden's Dream*, its rhyme-royal stanzas setting forth a young woman's vision of Hatton on his bier, "all in armour clad . . . a crown of Oliues on his helme . . ."; weeping Astraea holds his head in her lap, while tearful nymphs surround them. It is the sort of scene that Greene had not painted since his romance *Alcida: Greene's Metamorphosis*, which had featured three pairs of emblematic poems adorning the tombs of fallen lovers. Yet, after the allegorical stage is set and the characters introduced, *A Maiden's Dream* proceeds in a different manner from that of the earlier work. Whereas the *Alcida* poems had piled up mythological parallels to the miseries of the lovers in the story, *A Maiden's Dream* presents allegorical figures: Justice, Temperance, Religion, and so on, who speak about affairs of state in England and Hatton's record of service. The gods are mentioned once or twice, for atmosphere, but Greene's intent is to recount the dead Chancellor's deeds, and by so doing present his own vision of an ideal England.

Within the series of eulogies presented in turn by each of the arrayed Virtues, Greene comments on other issues: religion, foreign wars, the conflicts of classes; his views are typically moderate, his tone unembittered. As readers of the pamphlets or the plays might expect, his principal causes are charity and mercy, and Hatton be-

comes a convenient symbol of them both. Like his incidental poems from 1588 on, *A Maiden's Dream* was clearly influenced by Greene's playwriting. The later plays, particularly *James IV*, gave Greene fluency in composing dramatic rhymed verse, while his playwriting experience as a whole enabled him to present an idea graphically and concisely; thus, the allegorical frame. The plays also taught him to intensify emotion and change mood through the use of vivid images from everyday life, rather than through mythological hyperbole.

Although Greene would not again publish verse, whether extended, dramatic, or incidental, *A Maiden's Dream* gave him practice with a framework—the dream vision—and a mode—allegory—that he would employ the following year in another patriotic work, *A Quip for an Upstart Courtier*. This prose work is one more example of Greene's ability to apply in one genre the lessons learned in another.

OTHER MAJOR WORKS

LONG FICTION: *Mamillia: A Mirror or Looking Glass for the Ladies of England*, 1583, 1593 (2 parts); *Arbasto: The Anatomy of Fortune*, 1584; *The Mirror of Modesty*, 1584; *Morando: The Tritameron of Love*, 1584, 1587 (2 parts); *Planetomachia*, 1585; *Euphues His Censure to Philautus*, 1587; *Penelope's Web*, 1587; *Alcida: Greene's Metamorphosis*, 1588 (includes poetry); *Perimedes the Blacksmith*, 1588; *Pandosto: The Triumph of Time*, 1588; *Ciceronis Amor*, 1589 (also known as *Tullies Love*); *Menaphon*, 1589; *Francesco's Fortunes*, 1590; *Greene's Mourning Garment*, 1590; *Greene's Never Too Late*, 1590; *Greene's Farewell to Folly*, 1591; *Philomela: The Lady Fitzwater's Nightingale*, 1592; *Greene's Vision*, 1592.

PLAYS: *Orlando furioso*, pr. c. 1588; *A Looking Glass for London and England*, pr. c. 1588-1589 (with Thomas Lodge); *Friar Bacon and Friar Bungay*, pr. c. 1589; *John of Bordeaux*, pr. c. 1590-1591 (fragment); *James IV*, pr. c. 1591; *Complete Plays*, pb. 1909.

NONFICTION: *The Spanish Masquerado*, 1589; *The Royal Exchange*, 1590; *A Notable Discovery of Cozenage*, 1591; *The Second Part of Conny-Catching*, 1591; *The Third and Last Part of Conny-Catching*, 1592; *A Disputation Between a Hee Conny-*

Catcher and a Shee Conny-Catcher, 1592; *The Defense of Conny-Catching*, 1592; *The Black Book's Messenger*, 1592; *A Quip for an Upstart Courtier*, 1592; *Greene's Groatsworth of Wit Bought with a Million of Repentance*, 1592; *The Repentance of Robert Greene*, 1592.

MISCELLANEOUS: *Life and Complete Works in Prose and Verse*, 1881-1886. (15 volumes).

BIBLIOGRAPHY

Crupi, Charles. *Robert Greene*. Boston: Twayne, 1986. An excellent, readable work on Green's life and works. Two chapters are devoted to Greene's life, one to his prose works, and one to his plays. Supplemented by a chronology, notes and references, a selected bibliography, and an index.

Esler, Anthony. "Robert Greene and the Spanish Armada." *ELH: A Journal of English Literary History* 32 (September, 1965): 314-332. Focuses specifically on *The Spanish Masquerado* as war propaganda through its use of simple imagery and rhetoric. An interesting, if limited, analysis. Includes a bibliography.

Gelber, Norman. "Robert Greene's *Orlando Furioso*: A Study of Thematic Ambiguity." *The Modern Language Review* 64, no. 2 (April, 1969): 264-266. Argues about a historical influence on *The Historie of Orlando Furioso* in terms of classical and medieval perspectives. Carefully considers Greene's treatment of women in this perspective. Supplemented by a bibliography.

Harrison, George Bagshawe. "Robert Greene, 1558-1592." In *The Story of Elizabethan Drama*. Cambridge, England: Cambridge University Press, 1924. Assesses Greene's contributions to Elizabethan comedy. Provides a specific discussion of *The Honorable Historie of Frier Bacon and Frier Bungay* and compares it with Elizabethan drama in general.

Hoster, Jay. *Tiger's Heart: What Really Happened in the Groat's-Worth of Wit Controversy of 1592*. Columbus, Ohio: Ravine Books, 1993. Hoster attempts to separate fact from fiction as to the authorship of *Greene's Groatsworth of Wit Bought with a Million of Repentance*. Includes bibliographical references and index.

Jordan, John Clark. *Robert Greene*. Reprint. New York: Octagon Books, 1965. A fine study of Greene's life and works. Emphasis is placed on historical and cultural influences on Greene. Includes an analysis of Greene's poetry, as well as his prose work and plays. Complemented by a chronology, appendices, a bibliography, and an index.

Sanders, Norman. "Robert Greene's Way with a Source." *Notes and Queries* 212 (March, 1967): 89-91. Analyzes Greene's borrowings in his *Greenes Farewell to Folly*. Argues that it was originally intended for the stage but was later reworked into a romance. Contains a bibliography.

Senn, Werner. "Robert Greene's Handling of Source Material in *Frier Bacon and Frier Bungay*." *English Studies: A Journal of English Language and Literature* 54 (December, 1973): 544-553. Analyzes Greene's use of sources in *The Honorable Historie of Frier Bacon and Frier Bungay*. Compares *The Honorable Historie of Frier Bacon and Frier Bungay* to *James IV* in terms of themes. Supplemented by a bibliography.

Christopher J. Thaiss;
bibliography updated by the editors

FULKE GREVILLE

Born: Beauchamp's Court, Warwickshire, England; October 3, 1554

Died: Brooke House, London, England; September 30, 1628

PRINCIPAL POETRY

Mustapha, 1609 (verse drama)
Caelica, 1633
An Inquisition on Fame and Honour, 1633
A Treatise of Warres, 1633
A Treatise of Humane Learning, 1633
Alaham, 1633 (verse drama)
A Treatise of Monarchy, 1670
A Treatise of Religion, 1670

OTHER LITERARY FORMS

Fulke Greville wrote three verse dramas modeled on Seneca: *Mustapha, Alaham*, and *Antony and Cleopatra*. He destroyed *Antony and Cleopatra* because he feared that it contained material "apt enough to be construed, or strained to a personating of vices in the present Governors, and government." *Mustapha* exists in three different versions: one published without Greville's permission in 1609, two identical manuscripts which seem to have been written before the printed edition, and the 1633 version, which appeared along with *Alaham* in the collection of Greville's works titled *Certain Learned and Elegant Workes of the Right Honourable Fulke, Lorde Brooke*. It was probably the translation of Robert Garnier's *Marc Antoine* (1592) by Sir Philip Sidney's sister, Mary, the countess of Pembroke, that initiated the fashion of the "French Seneca" to which Greville's plays were a contribution.

Of Greville's titled prose works, the two most important are *A Letter to an Honourable Lady* (1633) and *The Life of the Renowned Sir Philip Sidney* (1652), containing a survey of international relations in the 1580's and a history of Elizabeth's reign as well as an account of Sidney's life. Of particular interest to the literary historian is Greville's discussion of the difference between his view of poetry and that of Sidney.

ACHIEVEMENTS

Fulke Greville's reputation as a poet has grown appreciably. In *Poetry* (1939), Yvor Winters announced that Greville was "one of the two great masters of the short poem." Commenting upon the great lyrics of the sixteenth century, Winters described them as "intellectually both profound and complex . . . restrained and direct in style, and . . . sombre and disillusioned in tone." While more recently critics have questioned the appropriateness of using the term "plain style" to describe Greville's verse, the poems in *Caelica*, his sonnet sequence, are now highly regarded.

His verse treatises, with the exception of G. A. Wilke's perceptive and informed comments (*Fulke Greville, Lord Brooke, the Remains: Being Poems of Monarchy and Religion*, 1965, G. A. Wilkes, editor), have received little attention. Didactic in tone, they are sententious and restrained in diction, but their very aus-

Fulke Greville (Hulton Archive)

terity can be moving to a reader interested in intellectual verse. Summarizing his own aesthetics in *A Treatise of Humane Learning*, Greville describes poetry and music as "things not pretious in their proper kind," but he adds that they can function "as pleasing sauce to dainty food . . . [c]ast upon things which in themselves are good" (stanza 12).

Greville has found some appreciative readers among men of letters and poets: Charles Lamb surprised his friends at a dinner party by selecting Greville and Sir Thomas Browne as the two writers whom he would most have liked to meet; Algernon Charles Swinburne, T. S. Eliot, and Theodore Roethke have praised Greville's works, but Samuel Taylor Coleridge paid him an especially high tribute when he imitated *Caelica*, "LXXXIV" in "Farewell to Love."

BIOGRAPHY

Fulke Greville, First Lord Brooke, supplied a structure for his own biography by having an epitaph engraved on his tomb at Warwick Castle that sums up his life in exemplary brevity: "Fulke Greville/ Servant to

Queen Elizabeth,/ Councillor to King James,/ And Friend to Sir Philip Sidney,/ Trophaeum Peccati [Trophy of Sin]." His father, also named Fulke, married Anne Neville, who came from a family with landed wealth and a titled past. The relationship to which Greville gave most prominence on his tombstone, his friendship with Sidney, began when they entered Shrewsbury grammar school on the same day, October 17, 1564. Before he was fourteen, Greville matriculated at Jesus College, Cambridge. Sidney went to Oxford, but they were reunited when they were introduced to Elizabeth's court in the late 1570's. Both young men joined the political party of Robert Dudley, the Earl of Leicester, Sidney's uncle and an old friend of the Greville family.

Leicester's radical Protestant party thought that religion should determine domestic and foreign policy and opposed the more conservative faction led by William Cecil, Baron Burghley, and his son Robert Cecil. Both Sidney and Greville wanted to engage in more adventurous activities than Elizabeth was willing to sanction. In their early thirties they ran away from court to join Sir Francis Drake on a voyage to the West Indies, but the Queen sent after them. After Sidney ignored the first messenger, the second messenger brought with him an offer of employment for Sidney under Leicester in the Low Countries. Greville remained in England, and Sidney's appointment ended tragically.

Sidney was wounded at Zutphen on October 12, 1586, and died three weeks later. The entire court went into mourning. Greville was overwhelmed. Later, he took upon himself the task of protecting his friend's reputation as an author. Rather than let an inferior version of *Arcadia* be made public, Greville interested himself in which manuscript was to serve as the source for William Ponsonby's 1590 quarto edition of the first two books and a part of the third. The chapter divisions, chapter summaries, and the arrangement of the eclogues were supplied by an "over-seer" who may have been Greville himself.

By 1594 Greville had joined the Essex circle, led by Robert Devereux, the Earl of Essex, nephew to Leicester and political heir of Sidney. Essex had both married Sidney's widow, Frances Walsingham, and established himself as the leader of the radical Protestant faction. The influence of Essex assisted Greville in obtaining his

first important political appointment as treasurer of the navy in 1598. By 1601, Essex had rebelled against the Queen and had been executed for treason; the death of Essex and disgrace of his party enabled Robert Cecil, Greville's great antagonist, to solidify his power. It was probably in 1601 that Greville destroyed his copy of *Antony and Cleopatra* because it might be interpreted as a political commentary on Elizabeth, Essex, and Cecil.

Prior to Elizabeth's death in 1603, Greville expected to be appointed to the Privy Council, but when James came to the throne, he lost his position as treasurer of the navy. Because Cecil regarded him as a dangerous political opponent, it was not until after his death in May, 1612, that Greville was able to enter the phase of his life that he himself labeled "Councillor to King James." Following Cecil's death, Greville shrewdly sought (and bought) the favor of all the leaders of the important political factions at court. On October 1, 1614, he became chancellor and under-treasurer of the Exchequer and Privy Councillor. After a decade of retired life, Greville entered the politically corrupt Jacobean court to serve for seven years as a prominent and powerful official. In 1621, an aging man, he lost his position as chancellor and under-treasurer, but the king created him Baron Brooke of Beauchamp's Court on January 29, 1621. Greville had requested two baronies so that he could leave two heirs, but the second, which he claimed on the basis of descent from Robert, Lord Willoughby de Broke, was denied.

Greville died on September 30, 1628, after having been stabbed by his servant Robert Hayward, a month earlier. The servant's motives remain in doubt, but Greville's contemporaries speculated that Hayward might have felt angered by Greville's will. He left Hayward only twenty pounds a year for life. Greville gave orders that if his assailant had escaped, no one should pursue him: He desired that no man "should lose his life for him." The doctors replaced the "kell," a fatty membrane around the intestines, with "fat thrust into the wound of his belly . . . which putrifying, ended him." Ronald A. Rebholz, Greville's modern biographer, has suggested that his "temperamental incapacity for a prolonged relationship with a woman" might have resulted from a "homosexual bias which he controlled or could not admit" (*The Life of Fulke Greville: First Lord Brooke*, 1971). A contemporary, Sir Robert Naunton, however, describes him as "constant courtier of the ladies." His descendants quarreled over his property, taking opposite sides in the Civil War that was to divide England during the reign of Charles I. The last phrase that Greville caused to be placed on his tombstone, "sin's trophy," suggests the degree to which his youthful idealism had given way in his last years to a grim disillusionment.

ANALYSIS

At fifty-eight, Fulke Greville wrote to Sir John Coke his much-quoted statement: "I know the world and believe in God." Critics have interpreted this comment as emblematic of Greville's thought. He is described as a worldly man whose experience led him gradually to reject this world as vain; these feelings of *contemptus mundi* are also supposed to have led him to attack human learning as a preparation for divine revelation. C. S. Lewis has described him as having the intellectual orientation of an Existentialist, the cast of mind of Sören Kierkegaard or Blaise Pascal (*English Literature in the Sixteenth Century Excluding Drama*, 1954). Greville's pessimism, however, may have been influenced by things external as well as internal. He outlived most of his contemporaries, but those who lived well into the seventeenth century shared his nostalgia for the Elizabethan court of their youth.

Greville's own analysis of his aesthetic intentions deserves careful attention:

> For my own part, I found my creeping Genius more fixed upon the Images of Life, than the Images of Wit, and therefore chose not to write to them on whose foot the black Oxe had not already trod, as the Proverbe is, but to those only, that are weather-beaten in the Sea of this World, such as having lost the sight of their Gardens, and groves, study to saile on a right course among Rocks, and quicksands.

His readers, then, will be those who want instruction and who do not need to be engaged by "the images of wit." The fiction or feigning which Sidney regards as the essential feature of poetry was not important to Greville. He wanted to present his ideas in restrained diction, preferring plain statement to the ornateness that was popular earlier in the sixteenth century.

It is misleading to speak of Greville's development as a poet because, except for a pirated version of the verse drama *Mustapha*, none of his work appeared during his lifetime. Since the Warwick manuscripts demonstrate that he revised his poetry and prose repeatedly, it is difficult to establish a reliable system of dating. Ronald Rebholz and G. A. Wilkes have each proposed plausible chronologies for composition and revision, but it is impossible to draw final conclusions because of the complexity of the manuscript evidence. Without suggesting that Greville moved from one phase to another, it is possible to differentiate three somewhat distinct literary styles: (1) the meditative style that Greville uses in *Caelica* (2) the strenuous, involuted manner of the verse dramas, which led Swinburne to compare Greville's work to that of George Chapman, and (3) the analytical and discursive verse of his poetical treatises, poetry containing some of Greville's most profound thoughts. Rather than viewing Greville's literary career as a progression from *Caelica* to the treatises, or, conversely, as a movement from success with the lyric to failure with the philosophical poem, one should assess each of these styles in terms of its own literary objectives.

CAELICA

Although frequently included in discussions of the sonnet sequences that became popular in the 1590's, *Caelica* might be more accurately described as a collection of short lyrics. In forty-one poems Greville uses the English sonnet form of three quatrains followed by a couplet, rather than the Italian form favored by Sidney, but he often breaks the poems before the sestet, as was customary in the Italian sonnet tradition. His other poems are usually composed of stanzas of four or six lines. Some evidence exists that the first seventy-six poems were composed prior to Sidney's death in 1586, and most scholars think that the sonnets are now arranged in the order in which they were composed.

Rebholz has described *Caelica* as evolving into a "series of anti-love poems." A large number of poems attack the inconstancy of women and men in a tone reminiscent of John Donne at his most cynical. The latter part of Greville's sequence is dominated by religious themes and images. His philosophical insights can be as moving as they are profound. In Sonnet LXXXVII, which C. S. Lewis singles out for special praise, Greville describes the soul as having fled the body: "To see it selfe in that eternall glasse/ Where time doth end and thoughts accuse the dead,/ Where all to come is one with all that was." Sonnets LXXXIV and LXXXV are companion poems which present a contrast between earthly love governed by Cupid and the heavenly love governed by a "Nature by no other nature knowne." These two contrasting poems illustrate the conflicting themes and unresolved tensions in *Caelica*.

MUSTAPHA AND ALAHAM

Greville's two surviving verse dramas, *Mustapha* and *Alaham*, both use plots derived from Eastern sources. In *Mustapha*, Soliman the Magnificent (1520-1566) murders his loyal and virtuous son Mustapha because Rossa, a freed bondwoman for whom he feels a destructive sexual passion, persuades him that his son is plotting against him. Rossa wants to make her own son the sultan's heir. Her daughter Camena tries to warn Mustapha, but he will not save himself if it means causing disorder in the state. Ironically, the people almost rebel over the murder, but Achmat, Soliman's chief adviser, decides that order must be preserved in the state even if it means allowing Soliman's wicked act to go unpunished.

Alaham, like *Mustapha*, examines sexual lust and lust for power within a political context. Alaham is the second son of a sultan, but he is so consumed by a lust for power that he is willing to burn his father, brother, and sister alive on a funeral pyre in order to seize the throne. Hala, his unfaithful wife, decides to revenge herself on Alaham for murdering her lover and plots a violent revenge. She contrives a suitable punishment for him by devising a poisoned crown and cloak. She tortures him further by killing their child in front of him while he writhes in agony. After murdering the child, she realizes that she has killed the baby she had by her lover, not by her husband. Then she kills her other child and rejoices that she is going to hell, where she can indulge her passion for excess.

TREATISES

Rebholz has suggested the following chronology for the composition of the treatises: *A Treatise of Monarchy* (1599-1604, pb. 1670), *An Inquisition on Fame and Honour* (1612-1614, pb. 1633), *A Treatise of Warres* (1619-1621, pb. 1633), *A Treatise of Humane Learning* (1620-1622, pb. 1633), *A Treatise of Religion* (1622-

1628, pb. 1670). Greville, however, seems to have intended to print the poems in the following order: (1) "Religion," (2) "Humane Learning," (3) "Fame & Honor," (4) "Warre." The order is given in Greville's hand in a manuscript of the treatises. The problem of chronology is complicated also by the omission of *A Treatise of Monarchy* and *A Treatise of Religion* from the first posthumous collection in 1633; these two treatises were published separately in 1670 as *The Remains of Sir Fulke Greville, Lord B*. In the case of *A Treatise of Religion*, Greville's antiprelatical stance probably led authorities to suppress the work.

The poems' titles accurately reflect their content. Greville the statesman and thinker presents his arguments in unadorned but powerful simplicity. As he observes in *A Treatise of Humane Learning*, he regards music and poetry as "ornaments to life," but only "whiles they do serve, and not possess our hearts." To interest oneself in art for art's sake would lead to a "disease of mind." Greville acknowledges that arts, like music and poetry, if they are used in church or military ceremonies, can "enlarge the mind" and suppress "passions of the baser kind." He, however, remains skeptical about the value of any knowledge other than the knowledge of God's grace.

By the end of his life, Greville felt the world to be so corrupt that reform was impossible. He had abandoned his faith in two of the basic tenets of Christian humanism: confidence that rational inquiry might result in the reform of institutions and conviction that each man was obligated to serve the state in order to promote the common good. In the last poem printed in *Caelica*, he prays for an apocalypse: "Rather, sweet Jesus, fill up time and come/ To yield the sin her everlasting doom."

OTHER MAJOR WORKS

PLAYS: *Mustapha*, pb. 1609 (verse drama); *Alaham*, pb. 1633 (verse drama).

NONFICTION: *A Letter to an Honourable Lady*, 1633; *The Life of the Renowned Sir Philip Sidney*, 1652; *Prose Works*, 1986 (John Gouws, editor).

MISCELLANEOUS: *Certain Learned and Elegant Workes of the Right Honourable Fulke, Lorde Brooke*, 1633; *The Remains of Sir Fulke Greville, Lord B.*, 1670.

BIBLIOGRAPHY

Alexander, Gavin. "Fulke Greville and the Afterlife." *The Huntington Library Quarterly* 62, nos. 3/4 (2001): 203-231. Alexander discusses Greville's preoccupation with his posthumous influence. It is characteristic of Greville to look back to the dead, but it is equally his habit to think forward beyond his own death.

Dwyer, June. "Fulke Greville's Aesthetic: Another Perspective." *Studies in Philology* 78 (1981): 255-274. Argues that Greville is essentially a religious poet. According to Dwyer, Greville's aesthetic involves his belief that the subject matter of poetry should be virtue, the tone should be moral, and the style should be restrained. Contends that Greville's *Caelica*, his sonnet sequence, must be interpreted in the context of his Calvinism.

Greville, Fulke. *Prose Works*. Edited by John Gouws. Oxford, England: Oxford University Press, 1986. The standard edition of Fulke Greville's prose. In addition to supplying an authoritative text, Gouws has carefully annotated difficult passages. This edition makes more accessible Greville's important biographical and political commentary in his *The Life of the Renowned Sir Philip Sidney*.

Hannay, Margaret P. *Philip's Phoenix: Mary Sidney, Countess of Pembroke*. Oxford, England: Oxford University Press, 1990. Greville regarded his close friendship with Sir Philip Sidney as a major influence on his life. This biography of Sidney's sister, Mary Sidney Herbert, countess of Pembroke, comments upon Greville and his contributions to and participation in the literary interests of the Sidney circle.

Klemp, P. J. *Fulke Greville and Sir John Davies: A Reference Guide*. Boston: G. K. Hall, 1985. Presents a chronological bibliography of works by and about Fulke Greville from 1581 to 1985. Each entry in the bibliography has been annotated. General studies of the political and literary contexts are also included in this useful bibliography.

Logan, Terence P., and Denzell S. Smith, eds. *The New Intellectuals: A Survey and Bibliography of Recent Studies in English Renaissance Drama*. Lincoln: University of Nebraska Press, 1977. This bibliographical summary covers Greville's closet dramas, especially *Alaham* and *Mustapha*, and includes an annotated discussion of studies written between 1928 and 1973.

McCoy, Richard C. *The Rites of Knighthood: The Literature and Politics of Elizabethan Chivalry*. Berkeley: University of California Press, 1989. This study of Greville and Sir Philip Sidney concentrates on the impact of chivalric codes and models of behavior on Elizabethan and Jacobean courtiers. McCoy offers insights into the philosophical issues that underlie courtly entertainments and pageants.

Mimura, Aya. "The Absent Reader: Tension in Fulke Greville's Prose and Tragedy." *Shakespeare Studies* 30 (1992): 1. There are three different versions of Fulke Greville's tragedy "Mustapha," while "Alaham" may also have been revised several times. The definitive and posthumous edition of his plays "Mustapha" and "Alaham," which illustrate his struggle between urge to write and fear of political danger, is examined.

Rebholz, Ronald A. *The Life of Fulke Greville, First Lord Brooke*. Oxford, England: Clarendon Press, 1971. The standard biography, this scholarly volume is thorough and meticulous. Rebholz divides Greville's life into four parts: "Friend to Sir Philip Sidney" (through Greville's youth); "Servant to Queen Elizabeth" (middle life, through his loss of office); "Councillor to King James"; and "Trophaeum Peccati" (in which the death of hope, Christian humanism, and Greville's own death are addressed). Appendices treat the dating of Greville's works, provide a foldout genealogical table, and reprint letters. The volume ends with a bibliography listing both primary and secondary sources, and an index.

Waswo, Richard. *The Fatal Mirror: Themes and Techniques in the Poetry of Fulke Greville*. Charlottesville: University Press of Virginia, 1972. This full-length study of Greville's life and works contrasts the poetics of Greville and Sir Philip Sidney. Major emphasis is given to *Caelica*. Waswo comments upon the Platonic and Petrarchan elements in Greville's sonnet sequence and analyzes the rhetorical texture of what is frequently described as his "plain style."

Jeanie R. Brink;
bibliography updated by the editors

EDGAR A. GUEST

Born: Birmingham, Warwickshire, England; August 20, 1881
Died: Detroit, Michigan; August 5, 1959

PRINCIPAL POETRY
Home Rhymes, 1909
Just Glad Things, 1911
Breakfast Table Chat, 1914, 1916
A Heap O' Livin', 1916
Just Folks, 1917
Over Here, 1918
The Path to Home, 1919
When Day Is Done, 1921
All That Matters, 1922
Poems of Patriotism, 1922
The Passing Throng, 1923
Rhymes of Childhood, 1924
Mother, 1925
The Light of Faith, 1926
Harbor Lights of Home, 1928
The Friendly Way, 1931
Life's Highway, 1933
Collected Verse, 1934
All in a Lifetime, 1938
It Can Be Done, 1938
Today and Tomorrow, 1942
Living the Years, 1949

OTHER LITERARY FORMS

Edgar A. Guest's prose works resulted largely from his readers' demands for information about his personal life. Thus, what he did produce in that genre tended to be heavily autobiographical and included such titles as *Making a House a Home* (1922), *My Job as a Father* (1923), and *What My Religion Means to Me* (1925). His autobiography, *Between You and Me*, appeared in 1938.

ACHIEVEMENTS

Although Princeton University undergraduates once voted Edgar A. Guest the world's worst poet, and the "serious" writers and readers of American poetry disdained to pay even the slightest attention to his work or even to utter his name—"I'd rather flunk my Wasserman test/ Than read a poem by Edgar A. Guest," complained a couplet supposedly contrived by Dorothy Parker—the transplanted poet-journalist from Birmingham, England, literally laughed at his critics all the way to the bank. With the Detroit *Free Press* as his launching pad, he saw, at the height of his popularity, his poems syndicated in approximately three hundred newspapers, his bound volumes of verse bought by almost three million people, and his personal income estimated at between $128,000 and $135,000 a year. His 1916 volume, *A Heap O' Livin'*, alone went through thirty-five printings and sold more than one million copies—fifty thousand of those in the first year. Henry Ford and William Lyons Phelps were among his close friends and admirers; he owned a large, colonnaded winter home in Detroit (complete with electronic gadgets, such as a garage-door opener, that did not become fashionable until some fifteen years after his death) and maintained a summer residence in Pointe aux Barques. With all of his personal, professional, and financial success, Guest never once claimed the title of poet. "I am a newspaper man who writes verse," he maintained; and the almost fifteen thousand separate pieces of carefully proportioned verse spanning a period of more than forty-three years amply bear him out.

Edgar A. Guest founded and established his own back-country island on the editorial pages of America's urban newspapers. He firmly declared a commonwealth for "jes' plain folkes": housekeepers, farmers, doctors, factory workers, and youngsters. He gave to that island-state a constitution based upon friends and friendships; God, faith, and public worship; and even his own immediate family—a wife and children so representative of middle America. The verse that appeared in newspapers throughout the country extolled the virtues of sitting on the back or front porch, bearing and rearing children, washing tablecloths, owning wood-burning stoves and wooden tubs, making sausages, and eating lemon and (especially) raisin pies. Rarely did Guest pay any attention to the negative aspects of daily existence—not that he thought crime or evil to be mere figments of the imagination; he simply refused to acknowledge their presence or their attempts to defeat the American way of life. Thus, death, for him, became "God's great slumber grove" or a "golden afterwhile." Guest saw no future for people to sit idly by, "in a dreary state," "growlin' that your luck is bad,/ An' that your life is extry sad. . . ."

More clearly than any of his critics, Guest knew his own limitations; he knew what he wanted to accomplish as a journalist and a writer of verse. Indeed, he once summarized that purpose with a typical example of "Eddie" Guest oversimplification: "I do the same kind of jingles as James Whitcomb Riley used to write. All he tried to be was sincere." No one could have doubted Guest's sincerity as he read his own verse on the radio and television, weeping with the sentiments that his lines actually aroused in him. Guest achieved popularity (as well as financial success) because millions of Americans recognized his sincerity and shared his emotions. A newspaperman who wrote verse, Guest became an American phenomenon—a writer who truly represented every person about and for whom he wrote.

BIOGRAPHY

The earliest phase of Edgar Albert Guest's life reflected the hard times that the poet tried to obscure from, or at least soften for, his readers. He was born in Birmingham, England, the son of Edwin Guest and Julia Wayne—the former a speculator and broker in copper. When the elder Guest's firm failed in the depression of the late 1880's, the father emigrated to America, settled in Detroit as an accountant for a brewery, and then brought his wife and children over in 1891. Edwin Guest, however, again lost his position, this time in the financial panic of 1893, making it necessary for his eleven-year-old son to perform a variety of after-school jobs—running errands for a butcher and a grocer and attending to soda fountains. In 1895, young Guest secured a part-time job as office boy in the bookkeeping department of the Detroit *Free Press*; thus began an association that would continue for the next sixty-four years and end only with the poet's death. Three years later, Edwin Guest died; this meant that young Edgar had to leave high school without a diploma and devote his full energies to assisting in the support of the family.

Fortunately for Guest, circumstances limited his tenure with the accounting department at the Detroit *Free Press*. A cub reporter's position became available and he began work at the news desk; then, on a temporary basis, he filled in at the exchange desk, where he clipped and filed light verse and feature items for future reprinting. Reacting to what he read—or, perhaps, *against* what he read—Guest began to compose his own filler verse, samples of which he submitted to the Sunday editor, Arthur Mosely. Thus, on December 11, 1898, "Eddie" Guest became a published poet. Other verses, all of a light and highly topical nature, followed; his pieces appeared regularly in a weekly column headed "Chaff," later to be titled "Blue Monday Chat." After a short term on the paper's police beat (which really conditioned him against the negative side of humanity), he moved to the feature desk and began to produce his own daily column of homespun verse and witty observations titled "Edgar A. Guest's Breakfast Table Chat" (obviously having been influenced by the work of the elder Oliver Wendell Holmes). The column became popular almost immediately; in fact, hundreds of readers began to collect the pieces and preserve them in scrapbooks, urging, at the same time, that they be published in book form. Thus, in 1909, Harry Guest, the columnist's brother and a printer, produced a limited edition (eight hundred copies) of the

Edgar A. Guest (Hulton Archive)

collection under the title *Home Rhymes*; two years later, another volume, *Just Glad Things*, came from the same printer—this time in an edition of fifteen hundred copies. Five years later, the Detroit Rotary Club assumed sponsorship of Guest's publications and promoted a third collection under the title *Breakfast Table Chat*—the success of which attracted commercial publishers and syndicators. Beginning with a reissue of *Home Rhymes, Just Glad Things,* and *Breakfast Table Chat* in 1916, Guest entered into an arrangement with Reilly and Britton (later Reilly and Lee) of Chicago as his publishers; the George Matthew Adams Syndicate assumed responsibility for distributing his pieces to major newspapers throughout the nation.

Guest married Nellie Crossman on June 28, 1906; she, their three children, and the family's general domestic activities became the major themes (and variations of themes) upon which the poet built his verses. During World War I, his rhymed messages cheered American doughboys on their way to France, while other rhymes provided special encouragement to those who remained on the home front. Further, thousands of copies of *Over Here* (again reflecting Guest's predilection for borrowed titles), specially bound in khaki, were dispatched to France for distribution in the camps and trenches. Guest produced his poetry at a steady rate, at least one effort a day, and he even devoted some time and attention to other forms of communication. During the 1930's, he hosted two radio programs, *It Can Be Done* and *Welcome Valley;* in 1951, he entered the homes of his faithful readers with a television show, *A Guest in Your Home.* After producing several phonograph recordings of his verse, Guest responded in 1935 to an invitation from Universal Studios to explore an acting career. He became very homesick, however, and even more distracted by the limitations of working from prepared scripts. Also, the $3,500 weekly contract had very little effect upon either his ego or his bank account, and after several months in Hollywood he returned to Detroit and to his beloved family.

Guest's popularity and financial success never really altered his folksy personality or dampened his enthusiasm for people and public activities. For example, from 1942 until his death, he served as the Protestant cochairman of the Detroit Round Table of the National Confer-

ence of Christians and Jews; he was seriously involved in the work of the Detroit Boys Club, the American Press Humorists, the Masonic Order, the Detroit Athletic Club, and the Detroit Golf Club—the last mentioned reflecting his favorite outdoor pastime. Although once a Swedenborgian, Guest joined the Episcopal Church after his marriage, while publicly announcing political affiliation with the Republican Party. Finally, although he never had the opportunity to complete his high school education and was never recognized by literary critics, Guest managed to collect his dues from the academic world in the form of honorary doctorates from Albion College (Litt.D.), Wayne University (L.H.D.), and the University of Michigan (LL.D.). He died in Detroit on August 5, 1959, two weeks before his seventy-eighth birthday.

ANALYSIS

Early in 1939, writing in the *Saturday Review,* an academician by the name of Arnold Mulder of Kalamazoo College complained to the world that, although Carl Sandburg had recently established legal residence in Michigan, "We haven't a single poet who is to Michigan what Robert Frost is to New England or Robinson Jeffers to California." For sheer quantity, lamented the professor, "we have to fall back on 'Eddie' Guest." Such a statement typifies the general critical reaction (although one is hard put to discover any critical reaction at all) to Edgar A. Guest's poetry, both during the height of his public acceptance and after his death.

Instead of poetry as the academics practiced and preached it, Guest wrote simple rhymes touched with "humanness." In easy, lilting verse he described to his readers the specifics of his wife canning pickles, baking raisin pie, falling prey to the glib tongue of a door-to-door salesman, and being afraid when alone during a thunderstorm. Those same readers browsed through the open book that contained domestic events within the Guest household: saw the daughter's new bonnet, heard her lisp her prayers, watched her turn aside a sparkling new doll at Christmas and run, instead, to her old ragged model. Through the poet's devoted eyes, those same readers watched the growth and development of a son, another Edgar Albert Guest ("Bud") from colic to college. Included in the family activities, and in turn transferred to the pages of the nation's major newspapers, were the garden and the joys of watching plants grow; tulips, for example, turned Guest from an observer of life to a backyard philosopher: "If it's fellowship you sigh for, learn the fellowship of daisies./ You will come to know your neighbor by the blossoms that he raises."

One can well imagine the professional legions rising in fits of apoplexy after being fed a dose of such rhyme, but "Eddie" Guest went forward, unmindful of any and all criticism. In fact, with such lines about the benefits of gardening, he expanded his audience to include scores of home gardeners, from those who tenderly coaxed their window boxes to fruition to others who ruled over an acre or more. Guest discussed with them, and sympathized with them, about their weeds and the stubborn yellow clay that he once mistakenly threw into a nearby alley, and again donned the philosopher's toga: "I believe in laughter and I believe in love,/ And I believe the daffodils believe in God above." Little wonder, then, that garden clubs all over America began and even ended their monthly gatherings with invocations and benedictions from the collections of Edgar Albert Guest.

One cannot analyze Guest's verse within the context of traditional critical criteria; one can only compile lists: examples of his sing-song rhythm ("The groom is at the altar, and the organ's playing low,/ Young and old your friends are waiting, they are sitting row by row"), of his end-rhymes (play-away, sight-right, room-bloom, sleep-deep, face-commonplace, alone-unknown, springs-things, fools-tools, text-next, world-curled, few-new, live-give), and of his obvious attempts to emphasize the colloquial elements of American English ("a heap o' livin'," "sun an' shadder," "Afore ye really 'preciate," "with 'em allus on yer mind," "gradjerly," "cornerin' life's riches"). In fact, one may even avoid reading the poetry entirely by simply compiling lists of titles by category; thus: "A Boy and His Dad," "A Boy and His Stomach," "The Boy and the Flag," "Boy o' Mine," "Boy or Girl?," "The Boy That Was," "Boyhood Memory," "A Boy's Hope for the Future," "Every Boy's Chance," "If I Were Sending My Boy Afar," "Father and Son," "Father to Son," "It's a Boy," "Little Master Mischievous," and so on through the alphabetized tables of contents of a dozen or so collections. The titles serve as splendid synopses of the poems themselves.

Edgar Guest has a just claim to a place in American literary history. Simply on the basis of sheer volume and wide public acceptance, he deserves some rank among the minor poets of twentieth century America. He left his mark on American popular culture and for that reason his poetry will continue to be read.

CANINE POEMS

Aside from the meter, the rhymes, and the language, Guest's poems are simple descriptive sketches, trite even for the times in which he composed them. For example, "The Joy of a Dog" begins with the mother's concern for scattered germs and dirt and hair upon her carpets, then moves to the moment when, as he well should, the poet's little boy "climbs a-straddle of my knee" and asks for a dog. Beneath it all lies the poet's firm belief that "every boy should have a dog."

In another piece, he writes about "The Yellow Dog"—described as homely, shinny, battered, and dirty. The animal serves as Guest's representative of every man and animal who "had to fight his way through life and carried many a scar." Continuing the moral of "The Joy of a Dog," Guest depicts the relationship between lonely dog and equally lonely boy, for "when some scrubby yellow dog needs sympathy and joy,/ He's certain of a friend in need, if he can find a boy."

Guest's dogs function at the same common, mundane, middle-class level as all of his human subjects. In "The Common Dog," he fashions a verse tale about a cur from the proverbial other side of the tracks who "envied nobler breeds," found the home of a rich man, yet had problems adjusting to a life of luxury and comfort. Again, the dog serves as a four-legged version of the common man who simply was not "bred for luxury" and, thankfully, contents himself with pursuing those "pleasures which belong to the commonest folks in town."

Finally, in a poem bearing the simplest title of all of Guest's simple canine poems, "The Dog," the versifier plods through thirty-two lines to explain what his reader has always known: namely, that the dog is humans' best (and, at times, only) friend. The point to be driven home is that Guest consumed considerable space relating the same throughts about the same subjects in the same words and through the same forms. Few, however, complained: His readers bought his books and recited his lines to one another with the same speed, precision, and regularity with which he composed them on the typewriter.

"HOME"

Guest's most noted and popular poem—titled "Home" and beginning with "It takes a heap o' livin' in a house t' make it home"—demonstrates exactly how easily he could manufacture popular verse. To begin, he developed absolute familiarity with the language of the new American middle class created by Warren Harding and Calvin Coolidge, left underworked and underfed by Herbert Hoover, and led out of the economic wilderness by Franklin D. Roosevelt. "Home" literally sinks from the weight of its own clichés: appreciate the things you left behind, the palace of a king, Death is nigh, Death's angel comes, scenes that grip the heart, pleasant memories, the roses around the porch that blossom from year to year, the early morning sun, and so on.

Practically every American adult (and even the children) who read the morning paper or subscribed to a popular magazine or listened to a radio knew Guest's "Home" before he or she ever saw it on the printed page. Guest's "Home"—his "heap o' livin'"—was the veritable castle that every middle-class American owned or hoped to own, and it appeared in the language and the imagery that every middle-class American recognized. Guest's vast reading audience seemed never to tire of the same words and phrases tapping none to gently upon their mental chamber doors: three "heaps o' livin'" and a single "heap o' sun an' shadder"; seven "homes"; eight "got t's"—all crammed into thirty-two lines. Consciously or not, Guest practiced what he preached as he advised his readers, "And gradjerly, as time goes on, ye find ye wouldn't part/ With anything they ever used—they've grown into yer heart."

The table of contents of Guest's collected verse could serve well as a general index to American life. The poet of dogs and boys and home and mince pie also turned to fishing, books, God, and Abraham Lincoln. The last item may well be the most interesting, principally because the reader observes Guest relying somewhat on his imagination rather then merely keeping his hand in his bag of tried and true phrases and references. In "Abe Lincoln," Guest tries to place his subject in a context meaningful to twentieth century America. The poet himself admits that the "Moral of it isn't much"; nevertheless, coming from him, it appears especially fresh; "greatness may be round about,/ But when seen from day to day men are slow to find it out." As always, Guest clings to clichés: Lincoln appears as "a fellow splitting rails" who lives in a "shabby sort of place," is "homely as a bale of hay." For Guest, it was but a short distance upward from the legal morality that Lincoln carved out of the rails of Illinois to the lakes, streams, and brooks created by God for the fishermen of America. In a piece titled "Fishing Nooks," he produced an angler's version of Genesis to identify the territory where "selfishness and greed and pride/ And petty motives don't abide."

RELIGIOUS THEMES

Although Guest could never be identified as a religious poet, religion still played an exceedingly important role in his work. He functioned, in his verse, as an evangelical spokesman for the morality and the way of life that his readers believed were thoroughly American and even more thoroughly Christian. Thus, for him and his followers, "Football is a manly game and I am glad he's not afraid"; success is "found in the soul of you,/ And not in the realm of luck"; music is reduced to the "wondrous joy" of the "concert when the kiddies and their mother start to sing." Even the drug store has it religiomoral hierarchy as the poet extolls the virtues of the "Little country drug store, not like those in town,/ Where is heard the rustle of many a silken gown."

"FAITH"

When Guest did attempt to tackle the subject of faith or religion, he avoided theological abstractions and complexities. Faith (in the poem of the same name) therefore can easily be applied to man at work, providing substance for his dreams, rules for his self-denial, and direction for his ideals. The tone of the poem rides the rhetoric of the pulpit and the locker room, the backslapping and the verbal harangue of the chancel cheerleader to "meet trouble and swiftly rout it,/ For faith is the strength of the soul inside,/ And lost is the man without it." In another "Faith" poem, Guest describes his beloved garden, where the sun shines brightly on both "saint and sinner." Faith, he has determined, "gleams, as the blossoms of spring to us,/ Lighting life's purpose and making it holy." Again, the source of Guest's popularity emerges with alarming clarity; he looked hard at the Constitution of the United States, underlined the part about the pursuit of happiness, and beat terribly hard upon those drums that sent Americans off in search of the joys of living within the bounds of a God-created republic.

OTHER MAJOR WORKS

NONFICTION: *Making a House a Home*, 1922; *My Job as a Father*, 1923; *What My Religion Means to Me*, 1925; *Between You and Me*, 1938 (autobiography).

BIBLIOGRAPHY

"Heap O'Rhymin'." *Time* 57 (March 19, 1951): 85-86. This is a portrait penned by an anonymous *Time* staff writer describing the poet and summarizing his career on the occasion of his seventieth birthday.

"Into God's Slumber Grove." *Time* 74 (August 17, 1959): 72-73. This obituary efficiently summarizes Guest's life and career. Though reviled by academics and fellow poets, Guest was incredibly popular in his lifetime. *Time* recalls how Guest's homespun poetry cheered American troops in both World War I and World War II.

McEvoy, J. P. "Sunny Boy." *The Saturday Evening Post* 210 (April 30, 1938): 8-9. This is an old source, but a valuable one, as it provides a view of Guest earlier in his career. He considered himself a newspaper reporter, and McEvoy describes how his column in the Detroit *Free Press* in 1904 titled "Chaff" evolved into his widely syndicated "Edgar A. Guest's Breakfast Table Chat" column. McEvoy points out that Guest's book, *A Heap O' Livin'*, sold more than one million copies when it came out in 1916.

Samuel J. Rogal

GUILLAUME DE LORRIS *and* JEAN DE MEUNG

Guillaume de Lorris

Born: Lorris(?), France; c. 1215
Died: Unknown; c. 1278

Jean de Meung

Born: Meung-sur-Loire, France; c. 1240
Died: Paris, France; 1305

PRINCIPAL POETRY

Le Roman de la rose (*The Romance of the Rose*, partial translation c. 1370, complete translation 1900)

OTHER LITERARY FORMS

Guillaume de Lorris is not known to have written anything other than the first portion of *The Romance of the Rose*. Jean de Meung, perhaps in connection with a scholarly career, undertook translations from a number of Latin works. He rendered Vegetius's fourth century *Epitoma rei militaris* as *L'Art de chevalerie*; also extant is Jean's translation of the letters of Abélard and Héloïse, but his versions of Giraud de Barri's *The Marvels of Ireland* and Saint Aelred of Rievaulx's *De spirituali amicitia* (early twelfth century) have not survived. This latter work had a discernible influence on *The Romance of the Rose*, particularly in the view of friendship presented by the character Reason. Jean was influenced most, however, by one other work he translated, Boethius's *De consolatione philosophiae* (c. 524; *The Consolation of Philosophy*). Boethius, as a character in his own work, is instructed in points of Neoplatonic metaphysics by Philosophy, and Jean adopts both this instructional mode and much of Philosophy's teachings in his portrayal of Reason.

Manuscript tradition assigns to Jean two other poems, a *Testament* (thirteenth century) and *Codicil* (thirteenth century). This ascription is uncertain, but it is worth mentioning that the *Testament* contains a retraction of certain "vain little poems," probably not intended to include *The Romance of the Rose*. As is also the case with Geoffrey Chaucer, such a retraction is problematic at best, and critics tend to divide into two camps, either questioning the sincerity of such last-minute penitence, or else imparting thereby a greater moral seriousness to even the apparently playful aspects of the author's works.

ACHIEVEMENTS

The Romance of the Rose is a major work of Old French literature and of the allegorical genre. Its popularity was immediate and widespread (as attested by the more than three hundred manuscripts which still survive), and the poem exerted a strong influence at least down to Elizabethan times. By 1400, interest in the poem had developed into a "quarrel," or debate, with one faction (including Christine de Pisan) decrying the misogyny and lasciviousness in the poem, and the other faction upholding the poem's aesthetic worth and moral soundness. Probably the most illustrious medieval author to be influenced by *The Romance of the Rose* was Geoffrey Chaucer, who translated part of the poem into Middle English. Dean Spruill Fansler considered Jean de Meung to have been Chaucer's "schoolmaster," in that Chaucer's first exposure to authorities such as Boethius and Macrobius was doubtless through *The Romance of the Rose*. Chaucer's first major poem, *The Book of the Duchess* (c. 1370), is a dream allegory much indebted to Guillaume de Lorris in its descriptive passages. Subsequently, *The Romance of the Rose* became for Chaucer but one of many Continental influences, but it is worth noting that Jean's portrait of the Old Woman is echoed in Chaucer's Wife of Bath. A major contemporary of Chaucer, the anonymous "Pearl-Poet," makes explicit reference to *The Romance of the Rose*, and the poem exerted a structural influence on his dream allegory *Pearl* (c. 1400).

The popularity of *The Romance of the Rose* continued into the Renaissance; as Alan Gunn notes in *The Mirror of Love: A Reinterpretation of "The Romance of the Rose"* (1951), twenty-one editions of the poem were printed between 1481 and 1538. Edmund Spenser, particularly in *The Faerie Queene* (1590, 1596), is the major figure of this period to have reaped benefits from a reading of Jean de Meung. From him, according to scholar Rosemund Tuve, Spenser learned how "to use large images in a huge design, philosophically profound if allegorically read."

In the following centuries, interest in the poem waned as allegory in general fell into disfavor. In the twentieth century, beginning perhaps with C. S. Lewis, critics and readers have once again found in *The Romance of the Rose* a work of complex artistry. Interpretations of the poem vary widely, however—so much so that scholars may even be said to have entered into a new "quarrel of the Rose."

BIOGRAPHY

Most of what is known of both authors of *The Romance of the Rose* is inferred from their works alone. Midway through the poem, the God of Love mentions two of his most faithful servants, Guillaume de Lorris and Jean Chopinel ("the lame") of Meung-sur-Loire. From the statement (line 10,588) that Jean will continue Guillaume's work forty years later, critics have worked back to a date of around 1230 or 1235 for Guillaume's portion and 1275 for that of Jean. Jean de Meung is otherwise known to have lived in Paris from 1292 until 1305. Presumably, he had left Meung-sur-Loire, a small village southwest of Orléans, for the intellectual climate surrounding the recently established University of Paris.

ANALYSIS

A sense of allegory has not been completely lost to the modern reader, who is likely to have come upon instances in George Orwell's *Animal Farm* (1945), if not in John Bunyan, Spenser, or medieval morality plays. Guillaume de Lorris imparted a major impetus to the popularity of one subgenre of allegory, the dream allegory. In contrast, to understand Jean de Meung's "exploded" approach, it is worth referring to the more encyclopedic style of allegory which Boethius had anticipated, and which was developing shortly before Jean's time in, for example, the *Complaint of Nature* by Alanus de Insulis. One other convention which may prove to be a barrier for the modern reader of *The Romance of the Rose* is that of courtly love, which was found earlier in Provençal lyrics and their reinterpretation of Ovid's *Ars amatoria* (c. 2 B.C.E.; *Art of Love*), and in the romances of Chrétien de Troyes. The relationship of this convention to medieval reality is widely disputed, but its signs are obvious enough: The Lover is struck by Cupid's arrows and undergoes a physically debilitating "lovesickness," which can be relieved only by the Lady's favors.

The first and most obvious feature to note about the text proper is that it is the work of two authors. Guillaume's portion, lines one through 4058, was left unfinished. In some manuscripts, a quick and inartistic close was provided, presumably by some enterprising scribe. Jean's massive continuation (to line 21,780), however, became a lasting part of the poem. The fact of dual authorship raises questions about the unity of the work—that is, whether Jean understood Guillaume's intentions.

THE ROMANCE OF THE ROSE

Guillaume establishes the pattern of versification for *The Romance of the Rose* Macrobius, author of the *Commentarii in somnium Scipionis* (fifth century) is cited as an authority. Since Macrobius categorized merely erotic dreams as meaningless "insomnia," some commentators have inferred that Guillaume must have intended his readers to delve beneath the first, erotic level of the dream allegory that follows.

One night, the author, "in the twentieth year of his life," fell asleep and dreamed what he would call *The Romance of the Rose*, in which may be found "the whole art of love." It is Love who commands him to retell the dream, in a poem undertaken "for she who is so precious and so worthy to be loved that she should be called Rose." These remarks can be examined closely for clues to the interpretation of what follows. If the dream is told at the urging of Love, it seems unlikely, as C. S. Lewis pointed out, that Guillaume intended to close with a "palinode" (or repudiation) of Love. The dedicatory remark indicates a clear affinity between the Rose and "the Lady," but a more precise allegorical interpretation is not given.

The Dreamer wakes to a fine May morning, dresses, and goes out from the town, led on by the sweet singing of birds. (The lyrical landscape through which he walks becomes a commonplace used by other writers in dream allegories.) He follows a river to a garden enclosed by high walls, upon which are depicted the first of the allegorical figures: Covetousness, with her clawed hands; Old Age with her mossy ears; and so on. (Symbolic details such as these recall the iconographic details of medieval paintings.) Apparently, these figures signify those qualities banned from the Garden of Delight, and perhaps from the courtly life in which young love may bloom. Inside the wall, the figures will be animated, and yet the static, pictorial sense with which Guillaume begins his allegory is consistent with the generally decorous tone of his work.

The Dreamer, hearing birdsong from within the garden, seeks out a doorway, which he knocks upon and which eventually is opened by Idleness. She exhibits all the qualities of beauty which are commonplaces in medi-eval literature, including sweet breath and clear skin (which is likely to have been rather rare in medieval reality). The Dreamer wanders on to the next group of allegorical figures: Diversion, Joy, Courtesy, and their company of dancers. All are lovely, elegant youths dressed in the most delicate fashions. Surpassing them, however, is the God of Love in his robe of many flowers, with all manner of birds flocking about him. The sweetness of these scenes and the sylphlike creatures who frolic about in them may fail to charm modern readers, especially those who encounter the poem in two English translations: Charles Dahlberg's prose version or Harry W. Robbins's very pedestrian pentameters. Readers who cannot approach the Old French might take a look at these passages in the Middle English version, or in Frederick S. Ellis's Victorian version, which goes a long way toward reproducing "the harmony . . . such as would cheer the saddest wight,/ And wake his soul to sweet delight."

The entrance of the God of Love gives way to another of Guillaume's decorative allegories, this time involving the God of Love's twin bows and ten arrows (named for encouragements and discouragements to love: Beauty, Despair, and so forth). This sort of schematic allegory appears in passages in Spenser's work but does not become a major part of Jean de Meung's repertoire in his continuation of the poem.

The Dreamer wanders off again, cataloging the varieties of fruit, trees, animals, and flowers he sees, until he arrives at the Fountain of Love, where Narcissus died. In the bottom of this pool, he sees twin crystals in which are reflected all of the garden, including, finally, a single rosebud which he must possess. At this moment, he is struck by Love's (encouraging) arrows; he becomes Love's vassal and is instructed in his commandments. It is in this section that Guillaume's poem is most clearly an art of love, and yet the simultaneous involvement of the Narcissus myth has yielded conflicting interpretations. The crystals are seen either as the Lady's eyes, reflecting the whole garden of her love, or as the Lover's own eyes, the narcissistic point of view from which his love will spring. In this view, what is ostensibly an art of love gives way on a deeper level to an allegory of misdirected (because it is not divine) love.

At this point in the text, the Dreamer becomes the Lover, and his quest of the Rose begins. The Lover attempts a direct approach with Fair Welcome but is snubbed by Danger. Reason instructs him of his folly, but the Lover tries again, counseled by Friend and Venus, and obtains a kiss. Jealousy erects a castle enclosing the Rose and imprisoning Fair Welcome, with the Old Woman set to guard him. The Lover laments this ill turn of Fortune's wheel. It is worth remarking that in these passages Guillaume's allegorical methods begin to incorporate monologues offered by various advisers, a technique which will be the dominant mode employed by Jean.

CRITIQUES OF JEAN'S CONTRIBUTION

In analyzing Jean's portion, it is perhaps best to begin with a short synopsis of his allegorical plot. Reason and then Friend reappear to give advice, after which the god of Love summons his barons for an assault on the castle. False Seeming and Abstinence overcome the gatekeeper Foul Mouth, whereupon the Old Woman panders to Fair Welcome. Danger interferes again, however, and Fair Welcome is again imprisoned. Venus, Nature, and Genius are enlisted as helpers; Venus shoots a flaming arrow through an aperture in the tower, through which the Lover then passes with his pilgrim's staff. After a few assaults on a narrow passage, the Lover scatters seed on the rosebud, plucks it, and then awakens from his dream.

C. S. Lewis believed that Jean was an inept allegorist and points to the redundant appearances of Reason, Friend, and Danger. He also faults Jean for lapsing out of allegory into "literal narration" in the Old Woman episode, but here he is clearly too prescriptive in his ideas of allegory. The development of allegory, as John V. Fleming argues, was in the direction of increased exemplification and thence to verisimilitude; William Langland's figures likewise slip over into the literal, and even Chaucer's seemingly realistic characters are in part allegorical representations of the occupations for which they are named.

More challenging are Lewis's other charges, that Jean has no sense of structure, is a popularizing "encyclopedist," and is uninspired even in his satires. These charges stem from the various "digressions" and soliloquies (not represented in the plot synopsis above) that stretch out Jean's portion to its unassimilable length. The advocates for the various approaches to love sum-

mon up wide-ranging sets of arguments that recall the exhaustiveness of Scholastic theologians and the comprehensiveness of the encyclopedic poets immediately preceding Jean. All manner of authorities are cited, any number of exemplary tales are retold, and a great deal of practical advice is dispensed. Guillaume had indeed cited Macrobius, told the tale of Narcissus, and given the ten commandments of love, but in nothing like the proportions exhibited by Jean.

To the charge that Jean was a popularist, Gunn counters that Jean in various passages asserts that his intentions are literary, not didactic, and that his is a handbook of love, and not of the various other disciplines from which illustrative matter is drawn. Jean fulfills his desire to popularize Boethius via a separate translation, rather than in the derivative passages in *The Romance of the Rose*. Gunn's defense of Jean's aims as being aesthetic rather than didactic, however, probably tips the balance too far in the opposite direction. Partway through her discourse, Reason states: "Your country is not on earth. You can easily learn this from the clerks who explain Boethius's *Consolation* and the meanings which lie in it. He who would translate it for the laity would do them a service." Shortly thereafter, the Lover interjects, "Ah, lady, for the king of angels, teach me by all means what things can be mine." Jean probably did not intend his work to be read as an encyclopedia, but as a Boethian work which, while not without aesthetic intentions, could be mined for *sententiae* or authoritative statements—and not only concerning love, for Reason here addresses the riches of the spirit.

As for the quality of Jean's satire, Lewis was clearly too dismissive of its merits, stating that of Jean's two main targets, women and churchmen, "neither is a novel subject for satire." Lewis was disgruntled, as most modern readers tend to be, by Jean's "general vice of diffuseness," which lulls one into inattentiveness through each "gallop of thousands of couplets." By taking a cue from the Dreamer, however, and strolling leisurely through Jean's labyrinthine garden, the reader will discover some flowers of wit. One of the more extended satires of women is found in Friend's discourse, and one may also find there many cynical observations on opportunistic love. The discourse of False Seeming has been read more profitably not as a vague satire on clerics, but as a specific attack on the contemporary development of the mendicant orders of the church. In addition to these satires, there can be found many amusing instances of an irony whereby Jean undercuts a speaker's view, or wherein the Lover exhibits a comical obtuseness. (Tuve's study singles out and illuminates many such passages.)

The charge that Jean's work is lacking in structure can best be considered in conjunction with the question of the poem's unity. Jean's narrative follows a more associative logic than that of Guillaume, with one subject leading to another in what sometimes seems like a nightmare of digressiveness. It is inconceivable that Guillaume would have gone on at such length. The two sections are also quite different in tone and allegorical method. In Guillaume's section, the tone is decorous, as emblematized in his pictorial, iconographic approach to allegory. With Jean, the tone is abstract and anarchical, as embodied in the *psychomachia* ("soul-battle" or war of abstractions) of the assault on the castle, and didactic, as achieved by means of Boethian technique of instruction. The differences are everywhere evident, but can Jean's section be read as in any way fulfilling Guillaume's?

Two main structural metaphors have been advanced as justifying the shifts that occur in Jean's section. The first of these is the threefold progress with which the Church fathers interpreted the Fall: the suggestion to the senses (Satan), delight of the heart (Eve), and consent of the reason (Adam). The Dreamer had already been seduced by the sensations of the garden, then shot through with the passions of Love; Jean, in addressing the third, intellectual seduction, sensibly enough takes an approach by way of the debates of the scholarly world. The second traditional framework cited is that of the *gradus amoris* or five "steps of love"; Guillaume provides the four preliminaries, and Jean gathers all of his faculties to address the final, climactic phase. These arguments depend on the assumption of traditions so pervasive as to preclude explicit references to them within the text—traditions simply taken for granted. While this assumption remains debatable, what can perhaps more easily be agreed upon is that Jean's section in itself is unified enough to provide at least a sustained commentary on Guillaume; a problem nevertheless remains in interpreting the precise stance taken by Jean on any of the individual issues he raises.

This problem recurs when one considers whether Jean's allegory is capable of a thoroughgoing religious interpretation or is ultimately secular in its outlook. It is by no means obvious how a reader should weight the various philosophies presented by the allegorical figures. The two figures who seem to have the most authority are Reason and Nature. Those who favor a Boethian solution to the poem's metaphysics feel that Reason comes closest to being Jean's spokesperson. Nature, however, outweighs Reason at least in the sheer bulk of text assigned to her, and so Jean has been said to advocate her brand of secular regeneration. That the poem closes with the attainment of the Rose lends support to this interpretation; Jean is then seen as a freethinker, ahead of his time, or as a clerkly satirist of the pretensions of courtly love. A perhaps more attractive view asserts that Jean ironically undercuts every philosophical system presented in the poem, leaving a series of negations and partial truths which the Lover, of his very (fallen) nature, cannot but fail to integrate. A parallel to Jean's technique can be found in the *via negativa* of some kinds of Scholasticism.

Running somewhat counter to these intratextual battles is the view, argued most extensively by Fleming, that *The Romance of the Rose* was not seen by its contemporaries as invoking any serious tensions with received Catholic thought. One medieval reader of the poem had declared that Dante's *La divina commedia* (c. 1320; *The Divine Comedy*) was a "copy" of *The Romance of the Rose*, and manuscript illuminations likewise seem to gloss the poem theologically. The poem was well received at first in conservative religious circles, and only toward the end of the Middle Ages did the "quarrel" as to its moral effects arise. In Fleming's view, Jean left himself open to such misinterpretation by letting some characters run on to such lengths that readers lost sight of his more orthodox pronouncements.

This stance has as its major strength an honest attempt to read the poem through the eyes of its contemporaries rather than from a twentieth century point of view. It is by no means certain, however, that medieval "criticism" had as its goal the impartiality to which modern critics ideally aspire. There is ample evidence of a countertendency to draw numerous contradictory readings from a given allegorical work, as a kind of speculative exercise. Furthermore, it seems presumptuous to dismiss the "quarrel" as belonging to an age which had forgotten how to read allegory correctly. The comparison to *The Divine Comedy* points equally to that work's greater sense of integration of courtly and religious ideals. In the end, it seems necessary to grant to *The Romance of the Rose*, as to Chaucer's *The Canterbury Tales* (1387-1400) and William Langland's *The Vision of William, Concerning Piers the Plowman* (1362, c. 1377, c. 1393), a profound and ultimately unresolvable ambiguity which reflects the questing and uncertain spirit of a sophisticated age.

BIBLIOGRAPHY

Arden, Heather M. *The Romance of the Rose*. Boston: Twayne, 1987. A general introduction to the work, including detailed outline and plot summary, discussion of cultural and literary contexts, and a review of critical approaches. Includes a chronology and a selected annotated bibliography.

Brownlee, Kevin, and Sylvia Huot, eds. *Rethinking "The Romance of the Rose": Text, Image, Reception*. Philadelphia: University of Pennsylvania Press, 1992. A collection of thirteen essays by distinguished critics of the poem, most written expressly for this volume. Three focus on Guillaume de Lorris, two on Jean de Meung, two on manuscript illuminations, and six on the early reception of the poem inside and outside France.

Fleming, John V. *The "Roman de la Rose": A Study in Allegory and Iconography*. Princeton, N.J.: Princeton University Press, 1969. Focuses on the interpretation of the illustrations that accompany numerous manuscripts of the poem, and the ways in which such a reading complements rhetorical and literary analyses.

Hult, David F. *Self-Fulfilling Prophecies: Readership and Authority in the First "Roman de la Rose."* Cambridge, England: Cambridge University Press, 1986. Offers a detailed analysis of Guillaume de Lorris's section of the work and argues that it is not fragmentary but finished, a complete artistic whole.

Huot, Sylvia. *"The Romance of the Rose" and Its Medieval Readers: Interpretation, Reception, Manuscript Transmission*. Cambridge, England: Cambridge University Press, 1993. Addresses the reception of *The Romance of the Rose* by French-speaking readers from the late thirteenth to the early fifteenth century, primarily through close study of the manuscript tradition.

Kay, Sarah. *The Romance of the Rose*. London: Grant & Cutler, 1995. A brief critical guide to the backgrounds and the most important formal and thematic approaches for study of the poem.

Kelly, Douglass. *Internal Difference and Meanings in the "Roman de la rose."* Madison: University of Wisconsin Press, 1995. Argues that the controversies and divergent critical interpretations raised by the work are best considered as the result of divergent meanings developed in the book itself: Different textual levels offer different meanings to different readers.

Luria, Maxwell. *A Reader's Guide to the "Roman de la Rose."* Hamden, Conn.: Archon, 1982. An introductory book for the general reader or student, including a survey of major critical approaches. Includes outlines, summaries, and glossaries to help orient readers; a number of sources and analogues; and a selective research bibliography.

Paul Acker;
bibliography updated by William Nelles

JORGE GUILLÉN

Born: Valladolid, Spain; January 18, 1893
Died: Málaga, Spain; February 6, 1984

PRINCIPAL POETRY

Cántico: Fe de vida, 1928, 1936, 1945, 1950 (*Canticle*, 1997)

Clamor: Tiempo de historia, 1957-1963 (includes *Maremágnum*, 1957; *Que van a dar en el mar*, 1960; and *A la altura de las circunstancias*, 1963; *Clamor*, 1997)

Cántico: A Selection, 1965

Homenaje, 1967 (*Homage*, 1997)

Aire nuestro, 1968 (includes *Cántico, Clamor*, and *Homenaje; Our Air*, 1997)

Affirmation: A Bilingual Anthology, 1968
Y otros poemas, 1973
Final, 1981
Horses in the Air and Other Poems, 1999

OTHER LITERARY FORMS

Jorge Guillén is a literary theorist and translator as well as a poet. His critical work *Language and Poetry* (1960) was first published in English translation, appearing in Spanish as *Lengua y poesía* the following year. Guillén edited the *Cantar de los cantares* of Luis de León and the Aguilar edition of the works of Federico García Lorca; in addition, he published volumes of correspondence and essays on García Lorca and Gabriel Miró.

Guillén's translations of poetry into Spanish are included in *Homage* under the heading "Variaciones"; among them are three of William Shakespeare's sonnets; "Torment," by the Portuguese Antero Tarquínio de Quental; poems by Arthur Rimbaud; "The Lake Isle of Innisfree," by William Butler Yeats; several poems by Paul Valéry; and others by Jules Supervielle, Saint-John Perse, Archibald MacLeish, and Eugenio Montale.

Huerto de Melibea (pb. 1954; the orchard of Melibea) is a short poetic drama re-creating the tragedy of the Fernando de Rojas play *La Celestina* (1499; *The Spanish Bawd*); it was later incorporated into *Clamor* in *Our Air*.

ACHIEVEMENTS

The most classical and intellectual member of the *generación del 27*, Jorge Guillén's rank among modern Spanish poets is high. The clean beauty of his lyrics has been recognized by contemporaries as diverse as García Lorca and Jorge Luis Borges, and Guillén is widely regarded as one of the greatest Spanish poets. He has been called the Spanish equivalent of T. S. Eliot and Paul Valéry. His greatness as a poet stems from the high quality of his verse rather than from the influence he has exerted.

Guillén's "Salvación de la primavera" ("Salvation of Spring") has been called one of the greatest love poems of the Spanish language. In the wake of a century of Spanish poetry that lacked interest in pantheism, Guillén and his friend Pedro Salinas are credited with creating a mode of poetry whereby hidden reality is disclosed by the contemplation of simple things.

Guillén was awarded the Etna-Taormina International Poetry Prize in 1961, and he received numerous other awards as well, including the Bennett Literary Prize (New York, 1976), the Miguel de Cervantes Prize (Alcaláde Henares, Spain, 1977), and several Italian literary prizes.

BIOGRAPHY

Jorge Guillén was the oldest of four children born to Julio Guillén Sáenz (1867-1950) and Esperanza Alvarez Guerra (1869-1923), both of Valladolid. In "Patio de San Gregorio," Guillén recalls his childhood as both happy and difficult, filled with duties, studies, and games. He attended high school in Valladolid and at the Maison Perreyve of the French Fathers of the Oratory in Fribourg, Switzerland. He pursued his university studies at Madrid and Granada, and he was graduated in 1913. Thereafter, he secured a teaching position at the Sorbonne, and he worked as a correspondent for the newspaper *La libertad* from 1917 to 1923. He received his doctorate from the University of Madrid in 1924, writing his dissertation on the *Fábula de Polifemo y Galatea* (1613) of Luis de Góngora y Argote.

In 1921, while in Paris, Guillén married Germaine Cohen, who bore him two children: Teresa in 1922 and Claudio in 1924. Germaine died in 1947, and in 1961, while in Bogotá, Colombia, Guillén married Irene Mochi Sismondi. Guillén reconciles his two marriages in the poem "Pasiones" ("Passions"), where he represents Germaine as France and Irene as Italy and proceeds to vow undying love for both countries, citing a vigorous confrontation with the future as the most effective way of keeping the past alive. The "In memoriam" section of *Clamor*, which became the central section of *Our Air*, is devoted to his love for Germaine, and the "El centro" ("The Center") section of *Homage* is devoted to his love for Irene.

Guillén assumed his first professorial chair at the University of Murcia in 1926. Three years later, he was offered a lectureship at Oxford, and from 1931 to 1938 he was a professor at the University of Seville. After being imprisoned in Pamplona for political reasons in 1938, he fled Spain, crossing the bridge between Irún and Hendaye on foot. He went to the United States, taught at Middlebury College in Vermont for one year, spent the following year at McGill University in Montreal, and then moved to Massachusetts, where he taught at Wellesley College until 1957. He taught one final year as Charles Norton Eliot Professor at Harvard, retiring in 1958.

In 1982, Guillén's native city of Valladolid staged a week-long tribute to him; scholars and fellow poets from Spain and from abroad came to honor the venerable poet, who had published his most recent volume, *Final*, at the age of eighty-eight. On February 6, 1984, Jorge Guillén died of pneumonia in Málaga, Spain.

ANALYSIS

Jorge Guillén was stigmatized early in his career as a cold, intellectual poet, and although that is almost the opposite of the truth, it took a long time for his reputation to recover. He strove after the ideal of *poesía pura* (pure poetry) and sought to distill from experience its barest essence, weeding from his verse the incidental and the ornamental.

Guillén's concern for *poesía pura* was obviously influenced by Juan Ramón Jiménez and Paul Valéry, while his pantheistic view of nature reveals the influence of José Ortega y Gasset. There was no such view of nature among the poets of nineteenth century Spain, and the radiance and intensity in Guillén's work hard back to the Neoplatonic tradition of the sixteenth century poet Luis de León. In technique, Guillén was influenced by Francisco Gómez de Quevedo (especially in the trenchant wit of his epigrams, which Guillén called *tréboles*) and Juan Meléndez Valdés, the great Spanish lyricist of the eighteenth century. In Guillén's classical Spanish rhythms and packed metaphors, he reveals the influence of Luis de Góngora y Argote, and there are also traces in his work of the creationism and Surrealism of the Chilean Vicente Huidobro.

Fond of assonance and short lines, Guillén uses a wide variety of meters. Often he uses the *décima* (with stanzas of ten octosyllabic lines) to express in simple form his ecstasy before the miraculous panorama of nature in a balance of rhythm, thought, and feeling. Contrary to the Spanish practice, he capitalizes the first word of each line of his poetry, and many of his poems have a

Jorge Guillén

circular structure, harking back in the last line to a key word in the first.

Nouns which stress essence predominate in Guillén's poems, and his lexicon is basic and relatively spare. As fond as he is of onomatopoeia, he uses nearly as many nouns that are expressive of sound (such as *baraúnda, batahola, guirigay, algarabía*) as he does verbs. In "Alamos con río" ("Poplars with River"), for example, *arrullar* (to coo) appears as "Poplars that are almost music/ Coo to him who is lucky enough to hear." In addition, Guillén is fond of elliptical sentences and exclamations, colloquial expletives (such as *zas* and *uf*), and rhetorical questions. Although his poetry is not easy reading, his vocabulary is not difficult.

Guillén was well grounded in Spanish and world literature quotations of and allusions to all periods abound in his work. His pieces are often headed by untranslated epigraphs in English, German, French, Italian, or Portuguese. He also makes moderate use of classical allusions, although often without encumbering the poetry with specific names.

CANTICLE

Many years of Guillén's poetic career were devoted to refining his *Canticle*, first published in 1928. The original collection included a mere seventy-five poems; in 1936, the poet added fifty more. The edition of 1945 contains 270 poems, and the 1950 volume contains 332.

First and foremost in *Canticle*, which, strictly speaking, is a "canticle" or "hymn of praise," Guillén wishes to communicate his ecstasy at the very existence of the created world. In the short poem "Beato sillón" ("Blessed Armchair"), for example, it is the armchair that gratefully puts him in touch with the physical universe and which allows him to transcend it ("The eyes do not see,/ They know"). He does not need magic to attain these heights, for he is fortunate enough to be able to savor the incidental properties of a world that, for him, is "well-made."

In *Canticle*, Guillén celebrates the perfection of the universe, ever grateful for its never-ending miracles. In a ten-line poem titled "Perfección" ("Perfection"), the poet submits to the beauty of one sunny day at noontime. He senses that the attributes of nature (the dense blue of the firmament "over-arching the day" and the sun at its zenith) reveal a superior order, which he perceives in architectural terms ("All is curving dome"). The sun reigns over the firmament, and its counterpart on Earth is the rose, man's perennial symbol of divine beauty. This moment so affects the poet that he feels time stop in a vision of the completeness of the planet. A corollary to this attitude is that death, as part of that natural order, is not to be feared, for without death, the perfect order of the universe would be impossible.

After the overwhelming optimism of *Canticle*, it comes as somewhat of a relief, as G. G. Brown notes, to see that the poet is capable of recognizing some of the more negative features of life in his next volume, *Clamor* (in Spanish, the word *clamor* has more the connotation of "plaint" or "cry" than it does in English). Here, Guillén undertakes to describe the baseness of a Satanized world, even alluding to the horrors of the Spanish Civil War, a subject previously avoided in his work. As the poet grew older, he found it more difficult to savor nature in self-absorbed tranquillity. Guillén himself, however, insisted that *Clamor* is not a negation of *Cántico*, but rather a further perceptual step.

CLAMOR

In *Clamor* there are such titles as "Dolor tras dolor" ("Pain After Pain"), "Zozobra" ("Anguish"), and "El asesino del planeta" ("The Murderer of the Planet"); the vehement political statement of "Potencia de Pérez" ("Power of Pérez"); and references to Avernus, pollution, the vulgarity of television and pornography, nuclear holocaust, and the biblical Cain, the first murderer. (In a much later poem, Guillén uses the neologism *cainita* to describe the agony of his struggle in Spain before he chose to become an exile). A unique feature of *Clamor* is Guillén's insertion among the poems of his *tréboles* (literally "shamrocks" or "clover"), three-line or four-line statements which variously resemble epigrams, haiku, and other brief forms (for example, "Yours is the dawn, Jesus/ Watch how the sun shines/ In an orange-juice sky").

HOMAGE

In *Homage*, there is somewhat of a reconciliation between the rapture of *Cántico* and the bitterness of *Clamor*, as the poet seeks consolation from art, which allows some of his earlier optimism to resurface. In the section "Al Margen" ("Marginal Notes"), Guillén documents his reactions to many of the world's great thinkers and writers, from Sappho to César Vallejo. Guillén expresses his appreciation of Aristophanes for making him laugh ("While I laugh, I do not die"), of the converted Spanish Rabbi Sem Tob for his wisdom, of the erudition of Alfonso Reyes, and of the Italian Communist Antonio Gramsci ("From the prison there flashes before the astounded/ Like a revelation, that incredible/ capacity for injustice that is man's"). There are also some less charitable observations (concerning Arthur Schopenhauer, for example). At the end of this section, under the heading "Al margen de un Cántico" ("Marginal Notes on a Cántico"), Guillén includes five poems of commentary glossing his own earlier poems, thereby reserving a place for himself in his own literary history.

This section is followed by the love poems of "The Center," written to Guillén's second wife, followed in turn by the section "Atenciones" ("Attentions"), which consists of verse portraits of writers ranging from Juan Ruíz to Rubén Darío. "Attentions" includes a five-poem cycle that honors the memory of José Moreno Villa, Pedro Salinas, Federico García Lorca, Emilio Prados, and Manuel Altolaguirre. The final section of *Homage* includes Guillén's translations of an impressive number of poems from world literature, as well as sundry poems of his own.

LOVE AND LOVERS

It comes as no surprise that a poet who is keenly aware of the miraculous should frequently concentrate on the nature of love. For Guillén, the love between man and woman suggests the larger relationship between man and cosmos and allows the individual to become greater than he is, to transcend the confines of time and space, of history and geography. In addition, love can give the assurance that death itself has been transcended, synchronizing the lovers with the natural cycle of the world. Moreover, the lover can be her beloved's salvation by protecting him from "phantoms" that might keep him from communicating with his own inner vitality.

For Guillén, the body of a woman is the epitome of perfect creation. In "Desnudo" ("Nude"), for example, the poet observes that the female body needs no embellishment, no backdrop to improve its perfection, for that perfection consists not in its "promise" but in its "absolute presence." Another example of a sensuous achievement is the epithalamium "Amor dormido" ("Love Asleep"). The poet and his beloved are together in bed, bathed by moonlight. He contemplates her as she sleeps. Without waking up, she embraces him, and the poet feels himself transfigured, drawn into the realm of her dream.

WOMEN

Guillén has a special tenderness for the company of women, and his students at Wellesley became the subjects of a number of affectionate poems such as "Muchachas" ("Girls"), "Poesía eres tú" ("You Are Poetry"), "Nadadoras" ("Swimmers"), and "Melenas" ("Hair"). He is emphatic about the need for a man to become a man in the total sense, through the welcome intercession of a woman, and in a short poem, "El caballero" ("The Gentleman"), Guillén writes contemptuously of the typical Spanish café scene ("All men, terrible world of men/ Life that way could not be uglier"). Here, he employs a humorous neologism, *machedumbre* (composed of *macho*, meaning "male," and *muchedumbre*, meaning

"crowd") to convey precisely how ridiculous and unthinkable such a world without women would be for him. The strong convictions that Guillén holds on this subject lead him to pontificate, in a later poem, "Sucesos de jardín" ("Garden Happenings"), that "He who never embraces [the other sex] is ignorant of everything."

Despite the foregoing quotation, Guillén is generally successful in avoiding clichés and seldom indulges in arrant nostalgia. In "Su persona" ("Her Person"), for example, the poet chides himself for attempting to feast upon the memory of an old love, a figment of mist not anchored concretely in his current physical reality. He refuses to allow "phantoms" to convert him into a phantom, and love as a memory is condemned as a "fictitious delight." According to Guillén, one can relive and enjoy the past most profitably by continuing to savor new experiences rather than by wallowing in memories.

HUMOR AND RELIGION

Humor and self-deprecation are not alien to Guillén. In "Perfección de la tarde" ("Afternoon Perfection"), for example, the poet depicts a garden setting in lofty imagery, complete with alliteration and ecstatic utterances. In the midst of this garden idyll, however, a robin's dropping lands smack on the poet's bald pate, and the poet stands humbled in his pomposity.

Guillén himself has characterized *Canticle* as a "dialogue between man and the world," wherein "man affirms himself in affirming creation," and there is a noticeable absence of traditionally religious subject matter in this volume. In *Clamor*, there is clearly a greater emphasis on the message of Christianity, as in "Epifanía" ("Epiphany")—in whose manger scene the helpless infant "says in silence: I am not a king,/ I am the way, the truth and life"—and in "Viernes santo" ("Good Friday"): "A centurion already understands./ The three Marys weep. Sacred Man./ The Cross." A poem in *Homage*, "La gran aventura" ("The Sublime Adventure"), may provide a more balanced view of Guillén's religious stance. In this poem, he speculates whether the creation of man by God or the creation of God by man is the worthier marvel, concluding that in either case, there is no escape from the miracle of creation—that "the earth is a sublime adventure."

Guillén's achievement as a poet stems from his rare ability to seize a fragment of time and transform it into a single, simple jewel of articulation. When his lapidarian stance became obsessive and threatened to dehumanize his poetry, he dared to change and strove for means to make his work more human. Nor was he oblivious to evil and suffering; rather, he sought to be attentive to the "well-made world" while in the shadow of the other, "badly made world." The words which Guillén once wrote in a dedicatory passage to his readers were true of himself as well: He was eager to share life like a fountain and to realize that life more fully through the power of words.

OTHER MAJOR WORKS

PLAY: *Huerto de Melibea*, pb. 1954.

NONFICTION: *En torno a Gabriel Miró*, c. 1959; *Federico en persona: Semblanza y epistolario*, 1959; *Language and Poetry*, 1960.

BIBLIOGRAPHY

Brown, G. G. *A Literary History of Spain: The Twentieth Century*, 1972.

Havard, Robert. *Jorge Guillén, Cántico*. London: Tamesis, 1986. A critical study of Guillén's *Cántico*. Includes bibliographic refences.

MacCurdy, G. Grant. "The Erotic Poetry of Jorge Guillén's *Homenaje*." *Hispania* 65, no. 4 (December, 1982): 586-593. A critical study of one of Guillén's poetic works.

_____. *Jorge Guillén*. Boston: Twayne, 1982. An introductory biography and critical study of selected works by Guillén. Includes bibliographic references.

Matthews, Elizabeth. *The Structured World of Jorge Guillen: A Study of Cantico and Clamor*. Liverpool, England: F. Cairns, 1985. Matthews analyzes Guillén's *Cántico* and *Clamor*. Includes bibliographic references.

Miller, Martha La Follette. "Self-Commentary in Jorge Guillén's *Aire Nuestro*." *Hispania* 65, no. 1 (March, 1982): 20-27. A critical study of on of Guillén's works.

_____. "Transcendence Through Love in Jorge Guillén's *Cántico*." *Modern Language Notes* 92, no. 2 (March, 1977): 312-325. A critical analysis of *Cántico*.

Sibbald, K. M., ed. *Guillén at McGill: Essays for a Centenary Celebration*. Ottawa, Canada: Dovehouse, 1996. A collection of critical essays on Guillén's works. Text in English and Spanish. Includes bibliographical references.

Jack Shreve; bibliography updated by the editors

THOM GUNN

Born: Gravesend, Kent, England; August 29, 1929

PRINCIPAL POETRY

Fighting Terms, 1954, revised edition 1962

The Sense of Movement, 1957

My Sad Captains and Other Poems, 1961

Selected Poems, 1962 (with Ted Hughes)

A Geography, 1966

Positives, 1966 (with photographs by Ander Gunn)

Touch, 1967

The Garden of the Gods, 1968

The Explorers, 1969

The Fair in the Woods, 1969

Poems, 1950-1966: A Selection, 1969

Sunlight, 1969

Last Days at Teddington, 1971

Moly, 1971

Poems After Chaucer, 1971

Moly and My Sad Captains, 1971

Mandrakes, 1973

Songbook, 1973

To the Air, 1974

Jack Straw's Castle, 1975

Jack Straw's Castle and Other Poems, 1976

The Missed Beat, 1976

Games of Chance, 1979

Selected Poems, 1950-1975, 1979

Bally Power Play, 1979

Talbot Road, 1981

The Menace, 1982

The Passages of Joy, 1982

Undesirables, 1988

The Man with Night Sweats, 1992
Collected Poems, 1993
In the Twilight Slot, 1995
Boss Cupid, 2000
Site Specific: Seventeen "Neighborhood" Poems,
2000

OTHER LITERARY FORMS

Thom Gunn is best known for his poetry as well as his essays that present criticism and autobiographical information. *The Occasions of Poetry: Essays in Criticism and Autobiography* (1982) collects Thom Gunn's reviews and essays on poets from Fulke Greville and Ben Jonson to Robert Creeley and Robert Duncan. It also contains four valuable essays on the composition and inspiration of Gunn's own poetry, including the autobiographical sketch "My Life up to Now" (1977).

ACHIEVEMENTS

Thom Gunn has been richly honored for his work during his lifetime. He won the Levinson Prize in 1955, the Somerset Maugham Award in 1959, the Arts Council of Great Britain Award in 1959, the American Insti-

Thom Gunn (© Ander Gunn, courtesy of Farrar, Straus and Giroux)

tute of Arts and Letters grant in 1964, the National Institute and American Academy Awards in Literature in 1964, and the Rockefeller award in 1966. In 1980, he was awarded the W. H. Smith Award, and in 1983 the PEN/Los Angeles Prize for poetry for *The Passages of Joy*. In 1988, he won the Robert Kirsch Award for body of work focused on the American West as well as the Sara Teasdale prize and the *Los Angeles Times* Kirsch award. He was honored with the Shelley Memorial Award of the Poetry Society of America in 1990 and the Lenore Marshall/*Nation* Poetry Prize in 1993 for *The Man with Night Sweats*. He held a Guggenheim Fellowship in 1971 and was a MacArthur Fellow in 1993.

BIOGRAPHY

Born Thomson William Gunn, Thom Gunn grew up in the London suburb of Hampstead Heath, "forever grateful" that he was "raised in no religion at all." During the Blitz, he read John Keats, Alfred, Lord Tennyson, and George Meredith, who have all influenced his verse in various ways. His parents—both journalists, although his mother had stopped working before his birth—were divorced when he was eight or nine. After two years in the British Army, Gunn went to Paris to work in the offices of the Metro. He attended Trinity College, University of Cambridge, during the early 1950's; there he attended the lectures of F. R. Leavis and began to write poetry in earnest, publishing his first book, *Fighting Terms* (1954), while still an undergraduate. He worked briefly on the magazine *Granta* and, as president of the English Club, met and introduced Angus Wilson, Henry Green, Dylan Thomas, and William Empson, among others. Here he also became a pacifist, flirted with socialism, hitchhiked through France during a summer vacation, and met Mike Kitay, his American companion, who influenced his decision to move to the United States.

After graduation, Gunn spent a brief period in Rome and Paris. At the suggestion of the American poet Donald Hall, Gunn applied for and won a creative writing fellowship to Stanford University, where he studied with the formalist poet and critic Yvor Winters. After a short teaching stint in San Antonio, Texas, where he first rode a motorcycle ("for about a month"), heard Elvis Presley's songs, and saw James Dean's movies, Gunn accepted an offer to teach at the University of California at Berkeley in 1958.

Gunn returned to London for a year (1964-1965) just as the Beatles burst upon the scene. Back in San Francisco he gave up tenure in 1966, only a year after it was granted, and immersed himself in the psychedelic and sexual revolution of the late 1960's. While teaching at Princeton University in 1970, Gunn lived in Greenwich Village when the first art galleries began to appear in SoHo. He moved to San Francisco and began his tenure at University of California at Berkeley, first as a lecturer and then, beginning in 1973, as an associate professor of English. He continues to teach on a part-time basis in order to allow him, as he says, to write relatively unfettered by academic demands.

ANALYSIS

Thom Gunn first achieved notoriety in England, as part of what was called "The Movement," an unofficial tag applied to some poets of the 1950's who were, in Gunn's words, "eschewing Modernism, and turning back, though not very thoroughgoingly, to traditional resources in structure and method." Poets of The Movement included Philip Larkin, Kingsley Amis, and Donald Davie, among others. Gunn continued to achieve critical acclaim by approaching a diverse number of subjects previously excluded from poetry, with a similar regard for structure and meter.

Having moved to the United States in the late 1950's, Gunn is somewhat of an amphibious poet. One might say that while his poetry has its formal roots in the English tradition, his subject matter has been taken largely from his American experience. He is known particularly for his exploration of certain counterculture movements from the 1950's to the 1980's. He is comfortable on the fringes of society, where popular culture thrives; rock music, motorcycle gangs, leather bars, and orgies have been his milieu. He is also considered one of the poets who deal most frankly with homosexual subject matter and themes. What distinguishes Gunn from other poets working with the same material is that he has refused to abandon structure and meter, preferring to impose form on chaotic subjects. Since the mid-1960's, however, Gunn has been increasingly influenced by American poets, notably William Carlos Williams; he turned first to the flexible meters of syllabic verse and subsequently to free verse, without sacrificing his demanding sense of form.

A poet interested in the possibilities of identity, Gunn is best known for his explorations into the existential hero, who takes many guises in his poetry, including the soldier and the motorcyclist. The greatest influence on his thought in these matters has been the existentialism espoused by Jean-Paul Sartre in his philosophical treatise *L'Être et le néant* (1943; *Being and Nothingness*, 1956). For Sartre, man is condemned to freedom to make his own meaning in an absurd universe. For Gunn, poetry has been the vehicle of this creation.

FIGHTING TERMS

Thom Gunn began his poetic career, while still at Cambridge, with the publication of *Fighting Terms*. The image of the soldier is first of all, Gunn has written, "myself, the national serviceman, the 'clumsy brute in uniform,' the soldier who never goes to war, whose role has no function, whose battledress is a joke," but it is also the "attractive and repellant" real soldier, who kills but also quests, like Achilles and Odysseus. Above all, the soldier is the poet, "an existential conqueror, excited and aggressive," trying to make sense of his absurd situation.

These poems show Gunn's propensity to try, not always successfully, to make meaning of action in the intervals between action. "The Wound" is a good example. While recuperating, a soldier remembers the engagement of battle. As "the huge wound in my head began to heal," he remembers the Trojan War, but it is unclear whether this was his actual experience or only a hallucination. It could be that he is a contemporary soldier reverting to myth in the damaged and "darkened" valleys of his mind. When he rises to act again, his wound "breaks open wide," and he must again wait for "those storm-lit valleys to heal." His identity is thus never resolved.

Similarly, in "Looking Glass" the narrator is a kind of gardener who observes his life under glass. He compares it to a Garden of Eden in which "a fine callous fickleness" sent him in search of pleasure, "gratification being all." Yet there is no God present in this world to give the world an a priori meaning: "I am the gardener now myself. . . . I am responsible for order here." In the absence of God, "risks are authorized"—a theme that will imbue Gunn's later poems of experience. He is also alienated from society and does not "care if villagers suspect" that his life is going "to seed." He takes a kind of pride in his status as outsider: "How well it goes to seed." The act of observing the wild garden of his life is a pleasure in itself, even though he is an outcast, "damp-booted, unemployed."

In "The Beach Head" the narrator is a would-be conqueror planning a campaign into his own society: "I seek a pathway to the country's heart." Again the alienated outsider ("I, hare-brained stranger") is heard making sense of his life, wondering whether to enter history through a fine gesture, "With little object other than panache / And showing what great odds may be defied." His alternative to action is to watch and "wait and calculate my chances/ Consolidating this my inch-square base." This conflict is at the heart of Gunn's poetry, early and late: whether to risk the heroic act or succumb to the passivity of contemplation. Yet the latter too has its risk—namely, that his failure to act may cause society's "mild liking to turn to loathing."

THE SENSE OF MOVEMENT

The Sense of Movement continues Gunn's exploration of the active versus the contemplative existential hero. Here the pose, poise, or panache of the hero is more important than the goal of the action, the movement constituting its own meaning. The volume introduces Gunn's idealized "American myth of the motorcyclist, then in its infancy, of the wild man part free spirit and part hoodlum"; his motorcyclist series is based on Andrew Marvell's mower poems. Gunn admits that the book is largely derivative ("a second work of apprenticeship"), partaking of Yvor Winters's formalism, William Butler Yeats's theory of the mask, and Jean-Paul Sartre's existentialist philosophy of engaged action.

The opening poem of the volume, "On the Move," explores the conflict between "instinct" and "poise." This is a key dichotomy in Gunn's work. The natural world of instinct is largely unavailable to thinking human beings, who, unlike birds, must create a kind of surrogate impetus for the meaningful movement. The motorcyclists become the focus for this conflict because of their assumed pose of wildness; yet it is a pose, a posture

that is only "a part solution, after all," to the problem. Riding "astride the created will," they appear "robust" only because they "strap in doubt . . . hiding it." The doubt has to do with their destination, as they "dare a future from the taken routes." The absurdity of action (a notion central to existential thought) is emphasized in that the person can appeal neither to natural instinct nor to metaphysics for the meaning he must himself create: "Men manufacture both machine and soul." Unlike "birds and saints," the motorcyclists do not "complete their purposes" by reaching a destination. The movement is its own excuse: "Reaching no absolute, in which to rest,/ One is always nearer by not keeping still."

"In Praise of Cities" affirms the disorderly evolution of human attempts to create meaning in the cityscape, which is personified as a woman, "indifferent to the indifference which conceived her." She withholds and offers herself to the one who wants to discover her secrets. "She wanders lewdly, whispering her given name,/ Charing Cross Road, or Forty-Second Street." Yet the city is really a mirror in which the narrator sees his "own designs, peeling and unachieved" on her walls, for she is, finally, "extreme, material, and the work of man." As in "On the Move," however, the narrator does not so much comprehend as simply embrace the city, with "a passion without understanding." His movement is its own excuse, but the communion with humankind, through his created cityscape, is real.

MY SAD CAPTAINS AND OTHER POEMS

My Sad Captains and Other Poems marks a turning point in Gunn's career, a border crossing that is evident in the book's two-part structure. The first half is concerned with the conflict between the "infinite" will and the "confined" execution, and the meter is suitably traditional. The epigraph from *Troilus and Cressida* (c. 1601) suggests that while "desire is boundless," "the act is a slave to limit." Limit is represented by the formalist quality of the poems in this first part of the book.

The second half of the book is much less theoretical, more concerned with direct experience, as its epigraph from F. Scott Fitzgerald suggests: "It's startling to you sometimes—just air, unobstructed, uncomplicated air." This thematic quality is reflected in the breathy technique of syllabic verse, in which the line is determined by the number of syllables rather than accents; the rhymes are random or, when regular, slant. The syllabic form is well suited to the direct apprehension of experience in such poems as "Light Among Redwoods," where "we stand/ and stare—mindless, diminished—/ at their rosy immanence."

Thematically, the volume continues to develop Gunn's "existential conqueror" motif in poems such as "The Book of the Dead" and "The Byrnies," while expanding his poetic repertoire to include snails and trucks as well as some more exotic familiars: Tattoo parlors in "Blackie, the Electric Rembrandt" and gay and leather bars in "Modes of Pleasure" (two poems, one title) and "Black Jackets."

"A Map of the City" is perhaps even more successful than "In Praise of Cities" in affirming the human chaos of the city by its treatment of the theme within a traditional form. The speaker stands on a hill at night, looking at the "luminous" city like a map below. Like William Blake's "London," Gunn's city is a maze of drunks, transients, and sailors. From this vantage point he can "watch a malady's advance," while recognizing his "love of chance." He sees the city's concrete boredom and suffering but also its abstract "potential" for both satisfaction and danger. From this perspective, he can, if only for a moment, get his bearings in relation to the city as a whole, as a map, so that when he descends into the maze again, he will be able to navigate his way through its dangers and flaws. He embraces the "crowded, broken, and unfinished" as the natural concomitants to the riches of city life, as he concludes: "I would not have the risk diminished."

The title poem, "My Sad Captains," is a tribute to all those friends who have inspired the poet, "a few with historical/ names." these men who were immersed in experience once seemed to him to have lived only to "renew the wasteful force they/ spent with each hot convulsion"; yet now they exist "apart" from life, "winnowed from failures," and indeed above life, "and turn with disinterested/ hard energy, like the stars."

Though this poem closes the volume, it can be profitably read together with any number of poems from the book, but especially the opening poem, "In Santa Maria del Popolo," which describes a painting of the "one convulsion" of "Saul becoming Paul" by the sixteenth century artist Caravaggio (Michelangelo Merisi). Here Paul becomes "the solitary man," "resisting, while embracing, nothingness." Yet it is to Caravaggio that Gunn looks for this revelation, the artist being one of his "sad captains."

Although Gunn did not do much more with syllabic verse after *My Sad Captains and Other Poems*, it was, he said, a way of teaching himself about "unpatterned rhythms," or free verse. From this point onward he worked in both traditional and "open" forms.

POSITIVES

Positives is written entirely in open forms. These poems were written to accompany his brother Ander's photographs of life in London. Poems about other works of art are common, especially in modern poetry. W. H. Auden's "Musée des Beaux Arts" (1939) and John Ashbery's "Portrait in a Convex Mirror" (1964) are examples of poems that interpret paintings from a distant time and place, as is Gunn's own "In Santa Maria del Popolo." In *Positives*, however, the collaboration is very much contemporary. The poems are written with the photographs, which seem to have taught Gunn to pay attention to the details of street life, pubs, construction sites, abandoned houses, and bridges in a way he never had before. As a result, Gunn gives up the symbolism of Yeats for luminous realities: "It is not a symbolic/ bridge but a real bridge;/ nor is the bundle/ a symbol." This quality makes *Positives* the least philosophical of his early works, even though the theme is large: the progress from birth and "doing things for the first time" to old age and "the terror of full repose." Written to face the photographs, the poems are freed of the burden of description, so that they have a transparent quality, a light touch, and, on the whole, a positive tone.

The poems and photographs depict the "memoirs of the body" in the lines of a face or a stance or gesture. In most cases, "an ambiguous story" can be read there: either as "the ability to resist/ annihilation, or as the small/ but constant losses endured/ but between the lines/ life itself!" These moments of activity in the present—human beings absorbed in the space between past and future—are Gunn's subjects: a child bathing, boys waiting to grow up, motorcyclists riding, a bride overwhelmed by the weight of lace, an old woman balancing a bundle on her head. Each has a history and a destiny, but these are components of their present hopes and fears.

TOUCH

Touch similarly reaches out to a real humanity. By making choices one may cut off other possibilities, but one also affirms a commitment to the individual experience. In "Confessions of the Life Artist" the narrator is "buoyant with the sense of choice." Having chosen, one finds that the death of possibilities unchosen only fortifies "one's own identity."

The opening poem addresses the "Goddess" of loneliness—Proserpine, the fruitful goddess confined away from human touch in the underworld. When she arises in a park, one of Gunn's ever-present soldiers is waiting for "a woman, any woman/ her dress tight across her ass/ as bark in moonlight." The final line seems to reject the idea that myth can enrich human lives; rather, it is persons, "vulnerable, quivering," who lend to myth their own "abundance."

The movement explored in previous volumes here becomes not linear motion through time but the spatial, encircling movement of the imagination wedded to emotion. In the "turbulence" of "The Kiss at Bayreuth" there is a paradoxical moment in which two "may then/ be said to both move and be still." The egotism of the "inhuman eye" of contemplation is overcome in the moment that two are able to "not think of themselves."

Similarly, in the title poem, touch is what Gunn's narrators seem to have been gravitating toward all along. As the narrator slips into the familiar space of a shared bed, he discovers an "enclosing cocoon . . . where we walk with everyone." This personal communion implies a larger community of sleepers who partake in the "continuous creation" of humanity.

There is not room here for a full discussion of the long poem "Misanthropos," but it is in this poem of seventeen sections that the theme of *Touch* is most fully explored. The protagonist is the last man on earth after a great holocaust, or at least he seems to be. The problem of identity in the absence of others to validate one's existence is explored as the man sheds old values, memories, and emotions as he sheds his former clothes. When he at last loses the distinctions of language, he encounters other survivors, and direct sensation, experienced anew, is shocking.

MOLY

The background informing *Moly* is Gunn's experience with LSD (lysergic acid diethylamide), which, he said, "has been of the utmost importance to me, both as a man and as a poet." Although he recognized the acid trip to be "essentially non-verbal," it was important and "possible to write poetry about any subject that was of importance to you." Unlike other drug-induced poetry, which tends to mimic the diffusion and chaos of the raw experience in free verse, the poems in *Moly* attempt to present "the infinite through the finite, the unstructured through the structured." These poems are highly controlled by structure and meter, while dealing with strange transformations.

The title poem, "Moly," is a dramatic monologue in the voice of one of Odysseus's men who has been turned into a pig by the witch Circe. Its rhymed couplets underscore the dual nature of man, part human and part beast, in search of the essential and magical "root" that will restore his humanity: "From this fat dungeon I could rise to skin/ And human title, putting pig within." The herb he is seeking is moly ("From milk flower to the black forked root"), which rhymes with "holy." The influence of Yeats's "Leda and the Swan" (1924) is evident, yet the swine-man of Gunn's poem is a typically contemporary twist on the mythological theme of the beast-god of Yeats's modernist poem.

Gunn's 1973 essay "Writing a Poem" discusses the conception and composition of "Three," but it is illuminating as a more general discussion of how a poem comes to be. Gunn says that he encountered a naked family on the beach and wanted to preserve them on paper as a kind of "supersnapshot," to find "an embodiment for my haunting cluster of concepts" about them. He calls his desire to perserve this feeling a sense of "decorum"—that is, a description that would be true to his direct experience of them, not the "pat" theme of "innocence and repossession."

JACK STRAW'S CASTLE AND OTHER POEMS

This idea of decorum seems to dominate the poems in *Jack Straw's Castle and Other Poems*. Here there is a kind of easy humor and simplicity of emotion only glimpsed in the earlier poems. In "Autobiography," perhaps influenced by Robert Creeley, the speaker desires (and achieves) "the sniff of the real." "Last Days at Teddington" tells of a return to a house that "smelt of hot dust through the day," and all sensation is clear and complete, like the garden that "fell back on itself."

The title poem, however, is a nightmarish version of a fairy tale, in which Gunn confronts his own worst enemy, himself: "I am the man on the rack/ I am the man who puts the man on the rack/ I am the man who watches the man who puts the man on the rack." Yet by confronting the demons of the imagination in this way, he seems to clear the air for a renewed apprehension of experience, to recognize that the "beauty's in what is, not what may seem." In this way, "Jack's ready for the world."

THE PASSAGES OF JOY AND THE VANITY OF HUMAN WISHES

The Passages of Joy is the world the poet of "Jack Straw's Castle" has readied himself for. In "The Menace," the speaker discovers "the stifling passages" of the mind, where "the opposition lurks" not outside himself, but within: "I am, am I,/ the one-who-wants-to-get-me." The joys seem less simple, more problematic after the decades of easy sex and drugs. This volume, in fact, contains Gunn's frankest expression of homosexual concerns in the era of acquired immune deficiency syndrome (AIDS), although its focus shifts away from leather bars and orgies to long-standing relationships of shared domesticity.

The title is taken from Samuel Johnson's *The Vanity of Human Wishes* (1749), a satire on the tragic and comic elements of human hopes and errors. One of the poems ("Transients and Residents") bears an epigraph from Johnson's poem:

> Time hovers o'er, impatient to destroy,
> And shuts up all the Passages of Joy.

The very personal poems of this volume show Gunn, now past fifty, dealing with the effects of age—in a person, in a generation, and perhaps in the race.

The three parts of the book show Gunn in a range of moods, from what might be called the meditative poems of the first and third parts to the hip pop-culture poems of part 2. Part 2 begins with a poem for Robert Mapplethorpe, the controversial photographer of the more dangerous elements of the gay scene. Another poem features a "dead punk lady," the murdered girlfriend of Sid Vicious of Sex Pistols fame.

The poet of "A Map of the City" still "would not have the risk diminished," for in the risks are to be found certain "passages of joy." In addition to the literal underground passages of "Another All Night Party," in which orgies occur, there are also the symbolic rites of passage of "Adultery" and "Talbot Road."

"Talbot Road" is a poetic treatment of Gunn's "year of great happiness" in London during the Beatles era, when, according to his almost-identical prose account in "My Life up to Now" (1977), "barriers seemed to be coming down all over." One of these barriers had to do with Gunn's own homosexuality. the centerpiece of the five-part poem is a return to Hampstead Heath, where he meets "my past self" in the form of a nineteen-year-old. "This was the year," he says, "the year of reconciliation," but it is unclear whether he means his own nineteenth year of 1964-1965; the ambiguity is intentional, for he means both. Hampstead Heath had been for him the scene of childish play and vague adolescent longings, where by day he "had played hide and seek/ with neighbor children"; in 1964, however, he could see the dark side that had always been there, since by night the Heath had long been a notorious venue for promiscuous sexual encounters, and there he now "played as an adult/ with troops of men whose rounds intersected/ at the Orgy Tree."

The central poem of the volume, however, is "Transients and Residents," in which these literal and figurative passages give way to the real passage of time. The four poems that make up this sequence stand in their own right as powerful and timely meditations on the passage of joy in the age of AIDS. Subtitled "An Interrupted Sequence," these four portraits of gay men in different roles explore the passing of a time of carefree sexual awakening and put the reader in the midst of sickness and death. The last portrait is of the poet himself at his desk, catching a glimpse of himself writing—which interrupts the sequence. This interruption perhaps provides a clue into the poet's view of the other portraits he has been drawing, for like the drug dealer in "Crystal," "he puts his soul/ Into each role in turn, where he survives/ Till it is incarnation more than role."

On the streets of "Night Taxi," a cabdriver takes his "fares like affairs/ — no, more like tricks to turn: / quick, lively, ending up/ with a cash payment." As in the earlier motorcycle poems, Gunn remains obsessed with movement. The cabdriver is intent on maneuvering his way gracefully through the maze of the city, one with his machine. There is still a sense of independence, yet there is also a sense of community; the driver's movement is dependent upon others, even subservient to the wishes of others: "It's all on my terms but/ I let them think it's on theirs." It is an appropriate poem to end this book that focuses mostly on the importance of other people.

UNDESIRABLES

Gunn's more recent poems, such as those in *Undesirables*, return to the gritty side of city life in the 1980's, observing characters and situations with an edge of black humor, like scenes reflected in a switchblade. He has not given up his preoccupation with Yeats— "Old Meg" is an incarnation of Yeats's Crazy Jane—but all sense of imitation is gone. Gunn has renounced the Yeatsian pronouncement for the rabbit punch and the belly laugh. "Punch Rubicundus," for example, is a ribald poem about an aging homosexual, in which the satire is all self-directed. The host, Mr. Punch, enters one of his "vaudeville of the sexual itch" parties, riding on a donkey, and says, "But this *can't* be Byzantium. (Though/ they do say Uncle Willie's ghost got an invite)." The irreverent reference to Yeats's "Sailing to Byzantium" (1927) and "Byzantium" (1932) is clear: Uncle Willie is William Butler Yeats, whose spirits were supposed to ride "astraddle on the dolphin's mire and blood" to "the holy city of Byzantium."

The poetry of Thom Gunn continues to develop as an up-to-the-minute report on the contemporary scene. Yet his roots in the tradition of poetry are deep, and his dialogue with the poets and forms of the past is as much a part of his evolution as a poet as is his keen eye for the realities of his time.

THE MAN WITH NIGHT SWEATS

Thom Gunn received critical acclaim for *The Man with Night Sweats*, recognized for its unsentimental examination of AIDS, death, and neglected members of contemporary American society. He wrote the poems during 1982 to 1988, a period when the AIDS epidemic was devastating the homosexual community and plaguing the global community with widespread homophobia and concerns over its transmission. Here the topic of AIDS seemed a theme to which Gunn could attach a particular passion and poetic craft, a place to offer heartbreaking poems of young men struggling with a disease

that consumes them with fear and its cruelty. The skepticism of his past poetry here gives way to elegy and lament, lyrical meditation, and a form of rage that is finely tooled with his poetic balance.

In this collection, Gunn acts as both a witness to the devastation of AIDS as well as one deeply involved with it. He writes in "The Renaissance," "You came back in a dream./ I'm all right now you said." His witnessing of the suffering also takes on a ferocity, a compulsion to attest to the wreckage of AIDS, almost as a way to provide a kind of defense:

> I shall not soon forget
> . . . .
> The angle of his head,
> Arrested and reared back
> On the crisp field of bed, . . .

One of the strongest poems of the collection is "Lament," an elegy of more than one hundred lines in which the speaker describes in great detail the slow dying of a close friend in a hospital ward. Rather than elevate the dying friend with praise and abstraction as does traditional elegy, this piece repeats that death is a "difficult enterprise" and chronicles the tedium and pain experienced by his friend—the "clumsy stealth" that has "distanced" him "from the habits of health." "Lament" is a perfect example of Gunn's tightly channeled, yet deeply felt elegies that form this collection.

BOSS CUPID

Boss Cupid echoes the elegiac style of *The Man with Night Sweats*, its three sections examining the loss of friends, lovers, and even, in one case, a lifestyle. Rather than focusing entirely on loss however, the collection also explores the sexual allure of youth, and renewal and recovery. Frank references to "the sexual New Jerusalem" of Gunn's younger years are here, and in "Saturday Night," he writes a genuinely affecting lament for the sex and drugs scene of the mid-1970's. It moves beyond the endpoints referenced in *The Man with Night Sweats* and his subsequent *Collected Poems* by pushing the boundaries of his poetry to include, in one loose whole, the makings of legend, myth, phantasmagoria, and autobiography. Historic, mythic figures such as Arachne and King David make appearances here, as well as the homeless, college students, and social deviants (as in his five "songs for Jeffrey Dahmer" grouped under the title "Troubadour"). His edgy wit, lyric versatility, and adept caricatures of personas help make this collection a powerful reminder that every life is "dense/ with fine compacted difference."

OTHER MAJOR WORKS

NONFICTION: "My Life up to Now," 1977; *The Occasions of Poetry: Essays in Criticism and Autobiography*, 1982, expanded 1985 (Clive Wilmer, editor); *Shelf Life: Essays, Memoirs, and an Interview*, 1993; *Thom Gunn in Conversation with James Campbell*, 2000.

EDITED TEXTS: *Poetry from Cambridge 1951-52: A Selection of Verse by Members of the University*, 1952; *Five American Poets*, 1963 (with Ted Hughes); *Selected Poems of Fulke Greville*, 1968; *Ben Jonson*, 1974.

MISCELLANEOUS: *Thom Gunn at Seventy*, 1999.

BIBLIOGRAPHY

Brown, Merle E. *Double Lyric: Divisiveness and Communal Creativity in Recent English Poetry*. New York: Columbia University Press, 1980. Brown argues that poetry is the result of the dialectic between the poet's thinking and speaking selves, the poem being a communal expression of that double consciousness. The theory bears fruit in the two chapters devoted to Gunn's work. The first explores the idea of "inner community" in the long poem "Misanthropos," the second the idea of "authentic duplicity" in Gunn's poetry up to *Jack Straw's Castle and Other Poems*.

Dodsworth, Martin. "Thom Gunn: Poetry as Action and Submission." In *The Survival of Poetry: A Contemporary Survey*, edited by Martin Dodsworth. London: Faber & Faber, 1970. A flawed essay that tries, with questionable success, to compare Gunn to George Gordon, Lord Byron and to relate his work to Sartrean existentialism.

Eagleton, Terry. "Myth and History in Recent Poetry." In *British Poetry Since 1960: A Critical Survey*. Oxford, England: Carcanet, 1972. Gunn's poetry up to and including *Moly* is, along with Donald Davie's poetry, the centerpiece of this discussion of the importance of myth to contemporary poets' relationship to history (and relative "histories"). Eagleton defines myth in the loose sense of Gunn's Sartrean existentialism, as well as the stricter, traditional sense of Greek mythology.

King, P. R. *Nine Contemporary Poets: A Critical Introduction*. London: Methuen, 1979. The chapter devoted to Gunn, "A Courier After Identity," discusses five distinct personas in Gunn's poetic development: the "embattled" stance of *Fighting Terms*, "a life of action and of pose" in *The Sense of Movement*, the "divided self" of *My Sad Captains and Other Poems*, the striving for "contact" with humankind and nature in *Touch*, and the "widening sympathies" of *Moly* and *Jack Straw's Castle and Other Poems*. An excellent overview.

Klawitter, George. "Piety and the Agnostic Gay Poet: Thom Gunn's Biblical Homoerotics." *Journal of Homosexuality* 32, nos. 3/4 (1997): 207-232. Examines the way in which Gunn has relied on biblical stories throughout his writing career to carry gay-themed poems.

Landau, Deborah. "'How to Live. What to Do.': The Poetics and Politics of AIDS." *American Literature* 68, no. 1 (March, 1996): 193. Examines the work of four poets—Thom Gunn, Timothy Liu, Paul Monette, and Mark Doty—to theorize their distinct aesthetic responses to the AIDS crisis.

Wilmer, Clive. "Definition and Flow: Thom Gunn in the 1970's." In *British Poetry Since 1970: A Critical Survey*, edited by Peter Jones and Michael Schmidt. Manchester, England: Carcanet, 1980. This study in influence examines the reasons for Gunn's drift away from the "monumental qualities" of metered and syllabic verse (Yvor Winters and Ezra Pound) to the modern "fluidity" of free verse (D. H. Lawrence and William Carlos Williams). Wilmer concludes that Gunn's compromise shows his capacity for change, the essential quality of "a living civilization."

_____. "Thom Gunn: The Art of Poetry LXXII." *The Paris Review* 37, no. 135 (Summer, 1995): 142. Uses an interview with Thom Gunn to analyze his writing method, his influences, and several poems.

Richard Collins,
updated by Sarah Hilbert

IVOR GURNEY

Born: Gloucester, England; August 28, 1890
Died: Dartford, England; December 26, 1937

PRINCIPAL POETRY

Severn and Somme, 1917
War's Embers, 1919
Poems, 1954 (Edmund Blunden, editor)
Poems of Ivor Gurney, 1890-1937, 1973 (Leonard Clark, editor)
Collected Poems of Ivor Gurney, 1982 (P. J. Kavanagh, editor)
Eighty Poems or So, 1997
Rewards of Wonder: Poems of Cotswold, France, London, 2000

OTHER LITERARY FORMS

Besides being a poet, Ivor Gurney is recognized as a gifted songwriter and composer of instrumental music. Of special interest are fine settings of poems by William Shakespeare, William Butler Yeats, Sir Walter Ralegh, Ben Jonson, John Clare, A. E. Housman, Wilfred Owen, John Masefield, and Edward Thomas. Gurney's musical work often exhibits the same erratic genius that distinguishes his poems, but this promising career was cut too short by the debilitating effects of military service and mental illness.

ACHIEVEMENTS

Ivor Gurney considered himself unjustly neglected and "one of Five War Poets." Both judgments are gradually being accepted by students of early twentieth century literature. His reputation is benefiting from the general recovery in critical esteem and cultural interest of the World War I poets. His work is associated with that of Wilfred Owen, Rupert Brooke, Siegfried Sassoon, Robert Nichols, Isaac Rosenberg, and others, as part of a significant chapter in modern literary history: the terrible interlude in which a conventional Georgian quietism was being replaced by new virtuosities of shock and disillusionment born in the trenches of war-ravaged Europe. Gurney's own poetry shares in that transformation of thought and technique. In many ways the most enigmatic and inconsistent of those soldier-poets, and still the least known, he forged out of his own waywardness innovations in diction, rhythm, and tone that often surpass the others in interest and effect. None evokes more intricately the modernist pathos of "two ditches of heartsick men;/ the times scientific, as evil as ever, again."

Gurney is also important as the first twentieth century writer to exhibit strongly the influence of Gerard Manley Hopkins, whose vigorous and technically daring verse appeared posthumously in 1916 and 1918. Specific resemblances of theme, language, and style suggest that Gurney responded immediately to the qualities in Hopkins now acknowledged as that Victorian poet's most energizing contribution to the voice of modern literature.

Since Edmund Blunden's 1954 edition of the poems, including many previously unpublished pieces of great merit, Gurney has been discussed in several studies of the War Poets and represented in anthologies of modern verse. Michael Hurd's biography, *The Ordeal of Ivor Gurney* (1978), and the Oxford *Collected Poems of Ivor Gurney* are signs of heightened contemporary interest in the underrated accomplishment of this poet. What more Gurney might have achieved were it not for his rapid psychological disintegration is not certain. There is justice, however, in William Curtis-Hayward's estimate that in Ivor Gurney "what we have is the ruins of a major poet."

BIOGRAPHY

The two pressing facts of Ivor Bertie Gurney's life and poetry were his grisly experiences as a signalman and gunner in the trenches during World War I and his subsequent (though not necessarily consequent) decline into insanity. He was already suffering "beastly nervousness" before the war and actually hoped that the rigors of military life might stabilize his mind. The conditions he endured in the battlefields of Europe would have shaken the steadiest constitution, yet Gurney's vivid poems and letters of this period are remarkably poised and ironic. There was even a kind of jauntiness about his amused image of himself as a "neurasthenic musician" in soldier's garb. He resorted seriously to poetry at this time as a substitute for music and as a therapeutic outlet for troubled feelings and observations. Some of these verses appeared in English magazines, and two small volumes, *Severn and Somme* and *War's Embers*, were published. After being gassed in 1917, however, Gurney went home disabled and soon began to be sporadically afflicted by the melancholic derangement that would haunt the rest of his life. Following several generally shiftless years of unhappiness and encroaching mental disorder, he was sent permanently to the asylum in Dartford, Kent. There he continued to compose poems and verse fragments of eccentric brilliance, mostly expressing baffled resentment and spiritual anguish or intensely reliving grim wartime experiences.

Counterpointing the fierce inspirations of war and madness were two other important influences in Gurney's life: natural beauty and music. His heart was always in the delightful rural byways of his native Gloucestershire, where his elemental need for country beauty and for rich associations rooted deep in local history was nourished. Nevertheless, it took the refining crucibles of battle and mental torment to transform the Severn and Cotswold landscape in Gurney's poetry into a sustained metaphor of joy and timeless sanity. Likewise, it was war and then psychological debility that turned his hand to poetry from his first love, music. He left the Royal College of Music to enlist in a Gloucestershire infantry regiment, and after the war was ultimately unable to resume the career that had been expected of him. Still, Gurney's accomplishment in music remains impressive. When he died of tuberculosis at Dartford in 1937, it was just a month too soon to see the tribute to his music in a special issue of *Music and Letters*. Nature and music, then, had formed his determination to "let beauty through" in the face of all that seemed ugly, brutal, and discordant in the world. Both recur as subjects in his poetry.

Among Gurney's acquaintances were many familiar names from the literary and musical circles of the day: Walter de la Mare, Ralph Vaughan Williams, Lascelles Abercrombie, John Masefield, Sir Edward Marsh, Herbert Howells, and others. Neither his sufferings nor his work was neglected by influential friends during his lifetime, although sad petitioning verses and letters from the asylum years sometimes accused "England" of shameful ingratitude. Altogether, it was Ivor Gurney's fate to make poetry out of the sorrows and rare consolations of a stricken consciousness.

Analysis

Ivor Gurney's most interesting poetry falls generally into three types or styles. In two of these his accomplishment is often of the highest quality. To some extent, the three modes represent a development in his manner and technique, though the trend toward increasing originality, urgency, subjectivity, and disruptiveness is far from consistent. If there is any chronological pattern, it perhaps reflects the emergence and then the fragmentation of a unique artistic personality.

Spare lyrics

The first category of poems consists of lucid lyrics notable for a spare and laconic modernity of expression. Usually short, these terse, cool pieces demonstrate a precise control of form and tone. Typical verses in this sardonically beautiful vein include "The Love Song," "Generations," "Old Tale," "The Songs I Had," "When I Am Covered," "To His Love," and even the sinister "Horror Follows Horror." As some of these titles suggest, Gurney's style here is songlike—a reflection of his strong musical talents and disposition. His thought, however, almost always has an elusive quality.

"Generations"

In the Blakean parable "Generations," for example, "The plowed field and the fallow field" alike sing a "prudent" song of fatalistic indifference to life's vicissitudes. The method of this poem is both unromantic and economical, with a disarmingly steady naturalness of idiom. Its amoral vision nevertheless seems to be slyly undermined by the poet's use of ambiguous connotative diction ("prudent," "reckoning," "power," and "brooding"), together with shifting values of the word "best." Rhythmic regularity reinforces this ambivalence of tone, and of course the relation of inanimate to human destinies remains an unasked question. Gurney's other poems of this type have much the same redolent simplicity. He achieves on these occasions the ironic distance that has since been considered the predominant perspective of twentieth century verse.

"To His Love"

One of the finest war poems of this sort is the elegiac "To His Love," addressed with subtle but bitter irony to a dead comrade's beloved. It is ostensibly a nostalgic reminiscence and a conventional tribute to the commemoration of patriotic sacrifice. This poem too, however, is discreetly ambivalent. The phrasing and imagery actually signal bleak indignation at the untruths about war and death that are perpetrated by sentimental attitudes and rituals. In particular, attention is increasingly focused on the soldier's shattered body itself ("You would not know him now . . .") and on the significance of burying as quickly as possible ("Cover him, cover him soon!") what is left of their friend ("that red wet/ thing").

The real meaning of those sickeningly dehumanized remains is obviously not what the State and customary sentiment demand. Hence the compulsion to conceal the ghastly evidence under "violets of pride" in memorial rites that transmute the soldier's memory into a romantic glorification of war. Without openly offending the bereaved, the sustained ironic potential of words such as "pride" illustrates Gurney's ability to let tone control the fury underlying a placid surface. A similar duality is expressed in the off-handedness and coy enjambment of "But *still* he died/ *Nobly*." Here the tone captures and undermines the cavalier outlook of those who pass over the ugliness of death in battle by summarily glamorizing it. The same effect is achieved in the brusque logic of the immediately following clause ("so cover him over/ with violets . . ."), which dismisses the victim by automatically according him the standard "poetic" formalities of interment amidst royal purple violets. Burial deep under "thickset/ Masses of memoried flowers" removes and idealizes a gruesome reality that, the poem implies, should in fact be confronted. Moreover, habitual sentiments and ceremonial gestures tend to supplant authentic personal expression of grief and dissipate any sense of official responsibility. The flowers must be especially "thick-set" in "Masses" (a pun on the eucharistic service) to conceal sufficiently the horror beneath from anyone who might rightly be angered or disillusioned by it. The unusual adjective "memoried" is richly connotative, hinting that the violets bring *memories* of happier days, are *commemorative* of military honor, *reminding* one of death, and perhaps capable themselves of *remembering* generations of other soldiers misrepresented and exploited even in death for the sake of pride.

Memory is indeed the poem's dominating idea. What impression of the dead should be retained? One possibility is the pastoral image of blithe youth in Gurney's opening stanzas, but that seems "useless indeed." Likewise, to make the soldier's death an instrument of nationalistic propaganda or romantic self-delusion is to perpetuate falsehoods that have, as his embittered fellows know, no connection with what really happened to him. The poem's final irony is the realization that even those aware of the truth yearn to escape it. A better use for a profusion of memorial flowers, it is urged, would be to hide from the poet himself "that red wet/ Thing I must somehow forget." It is nevertheless strongly implied that such immediate, excruciating knowledge cannot, and hence must not, be forgotten or betrayed. This complex and poignantly developed theme, found in other Gurney poems too, suggests the unsettling insights that England was being afforded by the War Poets.

PERSONAL NARRATIVES

The second strong vein in Gurney's verse is much more personal, tumultuous, and distinctive. The poems of this sort tend to be descriptive narratives that powerfully realize scenes, events, or sensations—usually stirring impressions connected with battle or with nature. Emphatic irregular rhythms and densely packed language show the influence of Hopkins and, to some extent, of Walt Whitman. Gurney first read these poets in the trenches, where, inevitably, his own manner was already being reforged into a more vigorous utterance.

The result was the emergence of a dramatic diction and syntax suited to the emotions and violent physicality of his new experiences: "wading/ Three feet of water past fire to the bones/ For Hell cold east of snow-sleeting Chaulness." The language energetically struggles with and overleaps grammar and traditional usage. It abounds in compound words, alliteration, striking inversions, breathless rhythms, onomatopoeia, and strikingly compacted visual and sensory effects. In many of the war poems raw, brutal, shocked action and feeling are reenacted with physical and psychological realism.

Sometimes it is sound that the thickly textured language indicates ("the thud of boots/ On duck-board wood from grate on rough road stone"); elsewhere it is a visual image ("Moonlight lying thick on frost spangled fleet foot sward"), and still elsewhere a terrible revelation of mental anguish. Occasionally Gurney juxtaposes styles, as in the black drollery of "The Silent One." There the "finicking accent" of an officer in the trenches is incongruous amid battle's "flashes" and "bullets whizzing." The poet-soldier is politely invited by his superior to crawl ahead to almost certain death. "Darkness, shot at: I smiled, as politely replied—/ 'I'm afraid not, Sir.'" Instead he keeps flat, thinking about music and swearing "deep heart's deep oaths/ (Polite to God)."

"CANADIANS"

In general, the war poems seek to catch directly the feel and mentality of battlefield life itself—the hours of waiting, the marching, the brief respites, and of course the squalor and violence. More than anything else, Gurney captures the pity and degradation. In "Canadians" the reader keenly senses the "infinitely grimed" faces, numbed weariness, and brutalization of "slouching" men "Dead past dead from the first hour" in a desolate place. A fifteen-line sentence of especially elliptical and interrupted syntax suggests the jumbled association of ideas raised in a fellow soldier's mind by such "iniquity of mere being," and biblical echoes and other religious allusions extend the situation's moral significance and lead the speaker to a bitter final reflection. He concludes that these Canadian volunteers, supposedly having come "finely" and freely and recklessly, must actually be victims that "Fate had sent for suffering and dwelling obscenely/ Vermin eaten, fed beastly, in vile ditches meanly."

The disillusionment felt by the poem's evidently Christian speaker enhances the force of the protest; to suggest that only a malevolent impersonal Fate could contrive such misery is to deny the right of Europe's Christian nations to make war in this fashion. That does not, of course, necessarily reflect Gurney's own view. As in the case of "Generations," discussed earlier, ideas different from the writer's own opinions may sometimes be dramatized in this way. In any event, the poem depicts one witness's emotional and intellectual reaction to the sordidness of modern mechanical warfare. The effect, as in other verses on related topics, is to deglamorize utterly a species of conflict that, ironically and ominously, makes men seem "Cave dwellers last of tribes."

NATURE POEMS

Gurney employs the same densely textured style for other subjects—notably in poems evoking "the love of Earth in me." What distinguishes those nature poems is an extraordinary fidelity to concrete particulars. Again like Hopkins, he is fascinated with specificity—real things that can be seen and named in catalogs of precise images. Poems such as "Cotswold Ways," "The Dearness of Common Things," "The Escape," and "Looking Up There" are typical. In such verses Gurney is drawn especially to creation's counterpointing of "strange" and "queer" beauties. He works at "breaking to sight" the hidden richness of "small trifles,/ Real, beautiful" and even of sensually tactile things such as the fabric of clothing. "How hard beauty hurts men," he cries, "with commonness and pangs and hurts them!"

There is also a dynamic vitalism, as in lines such as "The stars are sliding wanton through trees" or "The line of blue faint known and the leaping to white." The nature poems also express a personal devotion born of the need for engrossing antidotes to the distresses of battle and psychological suffering. Music figures similarly in the poems, occasionally being linked to the harmonies of nature; in one moment of dark humor, moreover, Gurney describes how he "learnt the machine gun, how it played/ Scales and arpeggios."

The poetry of this second type, then, divides Gurney's admirers from his detractors. The style is often undeniably knotted and cryptic—here and there virtually to the point of unintelligibility. Punctuation is haphazard, grammar deliberately tortured, allusions cryptic, and psychological impressionism pursued with such verisimilitude as to defy confident interpretation. The effect is to concentrate wonderfully Gurney's strenuous dramatization of consciousness, however, and to capture with distinctiveness what Hopkins would have called the "inscapes" of objects, action, or feeling. The peculiarity is not just the price paid for visual, aural, and semantic richness; it actually inheres in what Gurney is determined to elicit from the difficult materials of his experience. Success with such techniques is bound to be erratic, and there is a limit to what the power of suggestion by itself can express, but there are some splendid achievements in Gurney too. Indeed there is more than enough to justify the trouble of attending patiently to the poems—reading them aloud wherever possible—and perhaps valuing them as much for what they bravely attempt as for their relatively few sustained, unquestionable triumphs.

FLEXIBILITY IN VERSIFICATION

In formal versification, Gurney shows the flexibility that might naturally be expected of a musician. This is true of both the generally early simpler poems and the more rhetorically emphatic idiom of his second style. There is little inclination toward free verse or even blank verse and extraordinary versatility in rhyme patterns and cadences. Gurney's rhymes are usually rigid, yet remarkably unobtrusive—except when he attempts audacious pairings such as "coolish" with "foolish" or, within one line, "clangour" with "anger." Successful half-rhymes contribute to this effect of naturalness. The finely modulated poem "When I Am Covered," which may be Gurney's own epitaph, has four tercets that repeat twice an aba bab arrangement, while the following stanza from "To Crickley" shows the cumulative effect of more forceful rhyming:

> Then to you—deep in Hells now still-burning
> For sleep or the end's peace—
> By tears we have not saved you; yearning
> To accusation and our hopes loss turning.
> What gods are these?

The poet's rhythms, on the other hand, mark a decisive break from tradition. They tend toward the irregularity of passionate speech rather than the more or less consistent stress patterns of metrical law. Like Hopkins, he strove for the authentic accents of "speaking in high words," and wrote few pieces in standard rhythm that do not have a rather trivializing sing-song quality. The "To Crickley" stanza printed immediately above may serve also to illustrate Gurney's irregular cadence; each of the five lines is rhythmically different, only the last being standard, and the remaining stanzas of the same poem exhibit still other variations.

A MIND AT WAR WITH ITSELF

In turning to the third of the characteristic types of poem written by Ivor Gurney, technical analysis is difficult and perhaps out of place. Fascinating and moving as these strange poems are, they are bound to be incidental to the development of Gurney's critical reputation. Their form can be described as a peculiarly loose and discursive soliloquy sometimes reminiscent of William Wordsworth's procedure in *The Prelude* (1850). Most of these poems date from the asylum years

and are in fact repetitive and fragmentary. They tend also to be obsessive autobiographical laments in which Gurney strives courageously to make sense of his pain, disappointment, and shame. One or two, such as "The Lock Keeper," are more even and detached, though they do not surpass in power and pathos the ungainly personal utterances.

All the poems of this type do contain occasional lines or passages with the lucid beauty or Hopkinsesque strength of Gurney's other work, but the main interest of these pieces lies in their curiously gripping revelation of a sensitive mind at war with itself. For example, in "Chance to Work," addressed to the police authorities, Gurney begins with fervid recollections of a youthful joy in books, in music, in poetry, in love, and especially in natural beauty. Then come lines about strange illness, war, hospital, "evil forces," broken hopes, and the desperate therapy of hard physical exertion. Finally, there are the dreadful loneliness, suicidal longings, and complex recriminations of the asylum ward. The litany of real and imagined horrors concludes ruefully with the recurrent plea of Gurney's last years: "O if such pain is/ Not of account—a whole life's whole penalties/ To cancel . . . Grant pity, grant chance of Work." This poem, and others like it, are probably artistic failures, but they portray with unforgettable authenticity the hell of what is too readily called maddened consciousness.

A few excellent representative poems that have not already been cited are "Memory, Let All Slip," "Half Dead," "Darkness Has Cheating Swiftness," "Moments," and "What Evil Coil." Taken as a whole, Gurney's best poetry represents an imaginative and technical accomplishment at least comparable to that of the better-known War Poets. Doubtless he is less consistent, and much more often confusingly idiosyncratic. At the same time, his is in certain ways a more sensitive and stylistically original voice. One cannot help responding to what he called "the making's eager pain"—his urgent impulse to find adequate forms of utterance for thoughts and feelings that customary poetic modes would not accommodate. Admired more by fellow poets—Edmund Blunden, de la Mare, Jon Silkin, and others—than by academic critics, Gurney's verse is probably too frequently singular, febrile, disorderly, and experimental (and too notoriously that of a madman) for the popular or scholarly taste. He may have been right to cry with ghastly candor, "There is nothing for my Poetry, who was the child of joy./ But to work out in verse crazes of my untold pain." Yet Edmund Blunden is also correct in having said of him,

> He perished, one may say, war and consumption apart, from the merciless intensity of his spirit both in watching the forms of things moving apace in the stream of change and in hammering out poetic forms that should remain as their just representation and acclamation.

OTHER MAJOR WORKS

NONFICTION: *Collected Letters*, 1991.

BIBLIOGRAPHY

Gray, Piers. *Marginal Men: Edward Thomas, Ivor Gurney, J. R. Ackerley*. Houndmills, Basingstoke, Hampshire: Macmillan, 1991.

Gurney, Ivor. *Collected Letters*. Edited by R. K. R. Thornton. Manchester, England: Carcanet Press, 1991. Invaluable source of biographical details of Gurney's life and friendships.

Hill, Geoffrey. "Gurney's 'Hobby.'" *Essays in Criticism* 34 (April, 1984): 97-128. Hill explores Gurney's poetry and music, oddly enough finding his poetry to be his self-proclaimed "hobby." Examines Gurney's irony as evidenced in his poetry, the same irony that Gurney claimed he detested, much like Walt Whitman, the poet Gurney considered to be his mentor.

Hooker, Jeremy. "Honoring Ivor Gurney." *Poetry Nation Review* 7, no. 17 (1980): 16-19. Emphasizes the fact that Gurney's world was one of madness and incarceration, deeply affecting his poetry. Hooker honors Gurney as a poet and a man who, through a disintegrating life, managed to enliven the language with verse and was not fully appreciated in his period or in modern times.

Hurd, Michael. *The Ordeal of Ivor Gurney*. Oxford, England: Oxford University Press, 1978. The most quoted of all Gurney's sources, this book is an exhaustive study of his life and writings. In the course of the text, Hurd analyzes dozens of Gurney's poems while maintaining a chronological perspective. Supplemented by indexes and notes, this is a necessary source for the Gurney scholar.

Moore, Charles Willard. *Maker and Lover of Beauty: Ivor Gurney, Poet and Songwriter*. Introduction by Herbert Howelles and decorations by Richard Walker. Rickmansworth, England: Triad Press, 1976. Although issued in a limited edition, this biographical volume on the poet-musician is one of the few sources available.

Pilkington, Michael. *Gurney, Ireland, Quilter, and Warlock*. Bloomington: Indiana University Press, 1989. A reference guide to the songs of Gurney and three other songwriters of these turn-of-the-century composers.

Waterman, Andrew. "The Poetic Achievement of Ivor Gurney." *Critical Quarterly* 25 (Winter, 1983): 3-19. Waterman's primary focus is to show how Gurney modernized himself and his perspectives in his poetry between the war years and his incarceration in a lunatic asylum. Not only is Gurney's poetry analyzed, but his musical talent is also critically explored.

Michael D. Moore

H

———

H. D.

Hilda Doolittle
Born: Bethlehem, Pennsylvania; September 10, 1886
Died: Zurich, Switzerland; September 27, 1961

PRINCIPAL POETRY

Sea Garden, 1916
Hymen, 1921
Heliodora and Other Poems, 1924
Collected Poems of H. D., 1925
Red Roses for Bronze, 1931
The Walls Do Not Fall, 1944
Tribute to the Angels, 1945
The Flowering of the Rod, 1946
By Avon River, 1949
Selected Poems of H. D., 1957
Helen in Egypt, 1961
Hermetic Definition, 1972
Collected Poems, 1912-1944, 1983
Selected Poems, 1988

OTHER LITERARY FORMS

Although H. D. is known chiefly for her poetry, she did produce works in other genres, including novels, a verse drama, a screenplay, and a children's novel. The nonfiction trilogy *Tribute to Freud, Writing on the Wall, Advent* (1974) presents an account of her psychoanalysis with Sigmund Freud in the 1930's. *End to Torment* (1979) is a memoir of Ezra Pound.

Other posthumous publications have included *HERmione* (1981), an autobiographical novel that was written in 1927, and *The Gift* (1982), a memoir about her childhood that was written in London during the Blitz of World War II. *HERmione* contains fictionalized depictions of young Ezra Pound and others, and it lyrically describes young H. D.'s acceptance of herself as a woman and an artist. *The Gift*, as it shifts between recollections of childhood and descriptions of the destruction and

fear in London wrought by the bombing during World War II, presents revealing looks at H. D.'s view of life.

ACHIEVEMENTS

Hilda Doolittle, or H. D. as she signed her pseudonym, was at the center of the pre-World War I literary movement known as Imagism. It had a profound influence on twentieth century poetry, insisting on direct treatment through concrete imagery, freshness of language, economy of expression, and flexible versification. H. D. was a protégée of Ezra Pound, and the images in her poems best demonstrated Pound's definition of the image as "that which presents an intellectual and emotional complex in an instant of time." "Priapus" and "Hermes of the Ways," H. D.'s first Imagist poems, published in 1913, were hailed as innovative breakthroughs; with the publication of *Collected Poems of H. D.* in 1925, she came to be regarded as the finest of the Imagists. A number of these early poems, such as "Orchard," "Oread," "Heat," and "Sea Gods," have been repeatedly anthologized. (Unless otherwise noted, all poems cited are from *Collected Poems of H. D.*).

H. D.'s productive literary career spanned some fifty years. Her later poetry, somewhat neglected, included *Red Roses for Bronze*; the World War II trilogy, *The Walls Do Not Fall, Tribute to the Angels*, and *The Flowering of the Rod*; her long "epic" poem, *Helen in Egypt*; and *Hermetic Definition*.

H. D. has received less critical attention than others of her generation. Although her early Imagist poetry was highly acclaimed, critical response to her later work has been mixed. Some critics have argued that this later work is marred by patches of triteness and sentimentality and a too-narrow focus; others have praised its spiritual richness and the undeniable beauty of many of its passages, and later critics have called attention to its feminist aspects. Although she was awarded *Poetry*'s Levinson Prize in 1938, she was near the end of her life before there were signs of renewed interest in her work: She received the Harriet Monroe Memorial Prize in 1958; the Brandeis Award in 1959; and the prestigious poetry award of the American Academy of Arts and Letters in 1960—a prize given only once every five years. Several books appraising H. D. appeared in the 1960's, and since the mid-1970's numerous articles and

H. D. (Beinecke Rare Book and Manuscript Library, Yale University)

the first full-length biography have been published. Her *Collected Poems, 1912-1944* was published in 1983.

BIOGRAPHY

Hilda Doolittle was born in Bethlehem, Pennsylvania, the first Moravian community in America, on September 10, 1886. Her mother, Helen Wolle Doolittle, was artistic and musical; her father, Charles Leander Doolittle, was professor of mathematics and astronomy at Lehigh, later director of the Flower Observatory at the University of Pennsylvania. Hilda had a rich childhood in a setting of mystical Moravianism that exerted a lasting influence on her poetry.

At the age of fifteen she met Ezra Pound, the first of several extraordinary figures who profoundly influenced her life. Pound, then a precocious graduate student at the University of Pennsylvania, encouraged her to become broadly read, and together they studied Latin, Greek, the classics, yogic texts, and a great diversity of authors. Pound, according to their fellow student William Carlos Williams, "was wonderfully in love with her," but their relationship was somewhat stormy. In 1908, he pro-

posed that they elope to Europe, but her family ties and her suspicions of his other romantic liaisons deterred her. This estrangement was equivocal, however, and in 1911 Hilda joined Pound and his literary circle in London, never again to live in America. Her first Imagist poems were published in *Poetry* (January, 1913), under the signature that Pound suggested, "H. D., Imagiste." Active in the Imagist movement, she published her first collection, *Sea Garden*, in 1916.

The intense experiences of the World War I years forever after dominated H. D.'s life and art. Although still attached to Pound, in 1913 she married her fellow Imagist, Richard Aldington. Their marriage, initially happy, was troubled by infidelity and the turmoil of war. In 1914, H. D. met H. D. Lawrence. Their strong mutual attraction persisted through the war years, and their relationship was ever afterward present in H. D.'s life and work. In 1915 her first child was stillborn; in 1916 Aldington enlisted, and at the same time began an extramarital affair. In 1917 H. D.'s favorite brother was killed in France, and in 1919 her father died. In 1919, gravely ill with pneumonia, she gave birth to her daughter, Perdita; H. D. never revealed who the father was, and she and Aldington separated. Distressed by these events to the point of collapse, she was aided by a young woman from a wealthy English family, Winifred Ellerman, known by her pen name Bryher. For a time they lived together, and traveled to Greece, America, and Egypt. In 1922, H. D. settled near Zurich, with Bryher nearby, to rear her daughter and write. Her literary reputation established by the 1925 publication of *Collected Poems of H. D.*, she lived an active though secluded life, dedicated to her art.

In 1933, dissatisfied with her imperfect understanding of the events of her life and how they related to her art, she entered analysis under Freud. This experience, together with her experiences in London during World War II, permitted her to crystallize her own "legend," to expand upon the multiple meanings in her writing. She wrote much during the last fifteen years of her life, including her most ambitious long poem, *Helen in Egypt*, and the autobiographical novel, *Bid Me to Live* (1960). Following a brief visit to America to accept an award for her poetry, she was disabled by a stroke and died on September 27, 1961, at a clinic near Zurich, at the age of seventy-five.

ANALYSIS

H. D. was a lyric poet with one overarching dramatic theme: a heroine's quest for love and spiritual peace. Her poetry about this one central drama, although written in concise and crystalline images, is an evocative and often enigmatic reworking of scenes, a retelling of tales, where new characters fuse with old, where meanings subtle shift with the perspective, and where understanding interchanges with mystery.

"OREAD"

The early poem, "Oread"—one of the most often anthologized of H. D.'s poems—has been celebrated as the epitome of the Imagist poem. First published in February, 1914, this deft six-line poem not only illustrates the essence and freshness of the Imagist approach but also foreshadows and reflects many of the themes to which H. D. would turn and return in her art. The six lines of the poem rest upon a single image:

> Whirl up, sea—
> whirl your pointed pines,
> splash your great pines
> on our rocks,
> hurl your green over us,
> cover us with your pools of fir.

The image in this poem is a "presentation," not a representation; it is a tangible, immediate manifesting of a physical thing, not a description of a scene or an abstract feeling. On the immediate level, the poem is an image of a stormy sea whose wave crests are like forest pines as they crash against the shore and recede, leaving rocky pools in their wake. The image evokes a complex picture suggesting color, the beating of waves on a coast, sounds crashing and hushed, and even fragrance.

"Oread" has, as the Imagists insisted free verse should have, a rhythmic and linguistic development that is musical rather than metrical, corresponding to the sense of the poem. The first three lines describe an active, thrashing sea advancing on a rocky coast, and the last three suggest a lessening forcefulness, still powerful but withdrawing. The rising and falling movement is created in part by emphatic, initial-stress spondees and trochees in the beginning lines of the poem, which then give way to the more yielding dactyls, anapest, and iambic of the last two lines. These prosodic modifications

are paralleled by the vowel and consonantal sounds: rough plosives and fricatives dominate the first half; the last half employs liquid continuants to suggest waning flow and submarine calm. This shift in tone is also underscored by the appearance of back vowel sounds in the last three lines only, giving the lines a more sonorous and less frenzied sound.

Various devices give unity to the poem. It is set as one sentence, in lowercase. The imperative mood of the verbs that begin all but the fourth line emphasizes the thrusting force of the waves. Internal rhymes subtly reinforce the central metaphor, fusing sea and forest: the aspirated "h" and the liquid "r" and "l" of "whirl" are repeated in "hurl"; and the last word, "fir," is a partial assonantal echo of the first word, "whirl," and "green" similarly echoes "sea." Consonants are repeated with like effect. For example, the "h," "l," "p," and "s" of "whirl up, sea" are forcibly compressed in "splash," and quietly recapitulated in "pools of fir." Line 4 ("on our rocks"), which introduces character and location, is distinguished from the preceding lines by its lack of a verb, its use of back vowel sounds, and its triseme (or anapest); yet it is yoked to line 3 by enjambment, again subtly sustaining the fusion metaphor.

"Oread" has an elusiveness that is typical of H. D.'s poetry: The identity of the speaker is obscure, the location of the seacoast is unspecified. Who is "us"? Why are the rocks "our rocks"? The answers lie hidden in the title, which contains much that is enigmatic and unspoken. An oread is a nymph of Greek myth—in particular, a mountain nymph. Like naiads, nereids, dryads, sylphs—the nymphs of rivers, the sea, woods, air— oreads were usually personified as beautiful young girls, amorous, musical, gentle, and shy virgins, although occasionally identified with the wilder aspects of nature and akin to satyrs. The oread is one of the multiple forms that H. D. used to develop the central feminine consciousness in her writings. The oread inhabits the lonelier reaches of nature, rocky places of retreat; as H. D. put it in her children's novel, *The Hedgehog* (1936), "The Oreads are the real mountain girls that live furtherest up the hill."

CLASSICAL METAPHORS

Mountain nymphs were especially identified in myth as companions of the goddess Artemis, the virgin huntress associated with the moon; Artemis guarded the chastity of her nymphs as jealously as her own. It is one of the finer aspects of H. D.'s poetry that she can evoke the presence of things that are not mentioned yet shimmer ghostlike somewhere just out of poetic range: The goddess Artemis is an offstage presence in this poem, as in others. Her figure, white, distant, cold, virginal, yet passionate, is another of the complex manifestations of consciousness that appear in odd guises throughout H. D.'s poetry. In *Helen in Egypt*, for example, the moon goddess is symbolized by the white island in the sea where Helen encounters her lover Achilles. Artemis is embodied in the form of another island in "The Shrine" (subtitled "She Watches over the Sea," and dedicated to Artemis when initially published); it is an island whose difficult approaches can wreck mariners but can also reward those who reach "the splendor of your ragged coast": "Honey is not more sweet/ than the salt stretch of your beach." There is a sexuality, even a bisexuality, about this Artemis apparent in such lines as these, or as in the opening lines of "Huntress": "Come, blunt your spear with us,/ our pace is hot."

The title "Oread" is an allusion to both the moon goddess Artemis, the virgin huntress, and her nymph-companions, wild and free in the mountains. This allusion is but one of many in H. D.'s poems to the Greek world, which was, along with Egyptian, Roman, and other civilizations of antiquity, a frame of reference and an abiding source of inspiration for her. A reader with only a slight familiarity with H. D.'s writings will thus recognize in a title such as "Oread" resonances of the classical world. Virtually all of her poems and prose writings allude to it, either directly or by implication. Many of her early poems are explicitly set in the ancient world; others, such as "Sea Iris" and "Sea Lily," are located there only by reference to "temple steps" or "murex-fishermen," or, like "Oread" and "Lethe," have their settings implied solely by their titles.

In the classical world, H. D. found a metaphor for her own loneliness; as she once wrote to William Carlos Williams, "I am, as you perhaps realize, more in sympathy with the odd and the lonely—with those people that feel themselves apart from the whole. . . ." It was a far country of the imagination where she could find retreat both from the pain of love and from the strain of war and

modern life. Ancient Greece or Egypt is envisioned as a stark and beautiful world, a world of cold purity in harmony with nature, where an austere peace could be found in the harsher aspects of the natural landscape. Cities are squalid (as in "The Tribute"), crowded, hideous, and menacing (as in "Cities"); H. D. finds the starker elements of sea, rocky coasts and mountains, trees and wild flowers, storms and wind, the moon and stars, rain, snow and frost, to be sympathetic as well as remote. "I go," she says in the epigraph to *The Flowering of the Rod*, "where I love and where I am loved: Into the snow." The wild seacoast of "Oread" is a manifestation of this nameless land. Linked to the classical world, it appears and reappears throughout H. D.'s work, a dense metaphor for the mental landscape of the particular feminine consciousness present in her writings.

LAYERS OF MEANING

This piling up of associations to be evoked by allusion, as in "Oread," is a stylistic device that H. D. used in both poetry and prose. Her object was to create a many-layered work, dense with meaning, rich with metaphor, and evocative of mystery and legend. She labeled this style *Palimpsest* (also the title of her 1926 novel), a palimpsest being a parchment on which earlier writing has been erased but is still faintly discernible under new writing. H. D. thought of her writing as a superimposition of recurring, almost archetypal feelings and behaviors, like photographic negatives placed on top of one another, yielding a new yet old picture or pattern.

"Oread" illustrates this style. Against the background of rich allusion that is implied in the title, "Oread" is seen to have many layers of superimposed meaning. One step beyond the level of the surface imagery, the poem becomes an incantation, a prayer almost, spoken by the remote-dwelling oread on behalf of herself and her cloistered sisters. They seek, through communion with the elemental natural forces that sustain them in their retreat from the world of men, to be cleansed and strengthened, purified and rededicated to the harmonies of the natural world they have chosen for their refuge. There is also, in the call to the sea to "cover us with your pools," an implied wish to be suspended oblivious in the healing waters, to be reunited with the seamatrix. This hint is echoed in many poems, such as the similar plea found in "Lethe" for release from the pain of loveless existence: "The roll of the full tide to cover you/ Without question,/ Without kiss." The subject of women hurt and deserted by men whom they loved recurs throughout H. D.'s poems about goddesses, demigoddesses, and other women of antiquity (of whom there are many in her verse—Demeter, Simaethea, Circe, Leda, Phaedra, Helen, Thetis, Cassandra, Calypso, Eurydice, and more). These poems present passionate women ill-treated by men.

SEXUAL METAPHOR

Many of H. D.'s poems are about the foundering of a passionate impulse through indecision or rejection and the compensating retreat to colder climes that are clean and pure and white, yet haunted by memories of what was and what might have been. These poems are not only about retreat from the pitch and toss of emotion, but they are also poems about immersion in the salt flood of passionate entanglement.

This is the case with "Oread": At the same time that the poem invokes purification by a sort of baptismal rite, it is on yet another level wryly and compellingly sexual. In the first two lines of "Oread," the sea, traditionally a feminine metaphor, takes on masculine attributes as the image fuses sea and tree: "Whirl up, sea—/ whirl your pointed pines." (A reader familiar with H. D.'s Attic wit will not be surprised to note that "pines" is an anagram of "penis," although there is no direct evidence that H. D. intended this play on words—or the equally suggestive pun on "fur" in "pools of fir." She often referred to her poems, as in *The Walls Do Not Fall*, as "anagrams, cryptograms,/ little boxes, conditioned/ to hatch butterflies.")

The sea-crests, hardened by their fanciful merging with thrusting pines, are urged to "whirl up," to "splash," to "hurl" themselves against a rocky coast, to "cover us," as male animals cover the female, perhaps to inseminate (insinuated by the oblique reference to fertility in the word "green"). The natural rhythm of the poem, abetted, as previously noted, by various prosodic and grammatical devices, suggests arousal, climax, and commingled torpor. On an elementary level, "Oread" is about events in the natural world; on another level, the landscape pictured evokes the austere classical world to which consciousness may retreat; and, on still another level, the natural landscape becomes a metaphor for the landscape of the body.

The superimposition of sexual metaphor occurs again and again throughout H. D.'s poetry. For example, the pubescence implied by "pools of fir" is an echo of the earlier poem, "Hermes of the Ways," where Hermes is invoked in his original form as a god of fertility: "Hermes, Hermes,/ the great sea foamed,/ gnashed its teeth about me;/ but you have waited,/ where seagrass tangles with shore-grass." "Priapus" (later retitled "Orchard"), a poem addressed to the Greek fertility god usually represented with an exaggerated phallus, celebrates the bounty of nature in lines transparent with reference to female genitalia: "grapes, red-purple,/ their berries/ dripping with wine,/ pomegranates already broken,/ and shrunken figs/ and quinces untouched,/ I bring you as offering."

Feminine anatomy is also likened to coastal recesses or rocky chambers, as in the aforementioned "The Shrine," or in "Circe," a poem about the legendary enchantress who would "give up/ rock-fringes of coral/ and the inmost chamber/ of my island palace" for a glance from Odysseus. In H. D.'s metaphors for the sexual landscape, love and lovers meet where sea meets shore, on salt beaches, as in the refrain that haunts *Helen in Egypt*, on "the ledge of a desolate salt beach." This unusual coupling of rocky clefts with female sexuality and genitalia—perhaps suggested by the analogous promontory of the mons veneris—is typical of H. D.'s use of contrarieties and oxymora. Fire in ice, sweet in salt, soft and hard, male and female—these contrasts are used to create images of great vitality.

FEMININE CONSCIOUSNESS

As H. D.'s art evolved, she developed a central feminine consciousness through a variety of images and personas and events, each of which lent associational meaning to the others. This feminine spirit is both delicate and durable, beautiful but tough, capable of surviving great buffeting, much as the "weighted leaf" in the poem "Storm," broken off by the vaguely masculine storm, "is hurled out,/ whirls up and sinks,/ a green stone." This spirit or consciousness may appear as an oread, as Helen of Troy or other figures from classical myth, or as a green stone, a sea-shell, a worm on a leaf, a hardy sea flower, a chrysalis—or as meldings of several of these.

An image from *The Walls Do Not Fall* presents the poet as an "industrious worm" that survives calamity to tell its story, to "spin my own shroud," in *Helen in Egypt*, Theseus (the character modeled on Freud) calls Helen "Psyche with/ half-dried wings." The portrayal of Psyche—in Greek myth, the personification of the soul, beloved by Eros—as a newly formed butterfly is a complex image into which are telescoped links to the figure of the oread and to other chrysalis-like manifestations of H. D.'s poetic consciousness.

This consciousness grew out of the events and situations and characters of H. D.'s life, and each of her poems is a symbolic re-creation of some part of her life, thus giving a further, hidden meaning to the poetry. For example, the knowledge that the nickname bestowed upon H. D. by the green-eyed Ezra Pound was "Dryad" adds another dimension to "Oread." A dryad is a wood-nymph, and the nickname was perhaps a token of their early love among the apple trees of Pennsylvania, where H. D. was a virgin and Pound something of a satyr. Early poems such as "Oread" and "Priapus," with their bold sexual undercurrents, can thus also be read as amusing, half-mocking secret messages to the principal men in her life. Although not confessional poetry, H. D.'s work was intimately bound to her personal experiences, especially those of the period from 1911 to 1920, and though her poems may be grasped without knowing these circumstances, even a slight familiarity with them enhances the reader's pleasure and understanding. H. D. had no hesitation in acknowledging this autobiographical dimension: as she said of her thinly disguised autobiographical novel, *Bid Me to Live*, "It is a *roman à clef*, and the keys are all easy enough to find."

CREATING HER OWN LEGEND

By poeticizing the story of her life, H. D. was consciously attempting, as she indicated in *Tribute to Freud* (1956), to create her own legend, to universalize her own experiences and emotional states, not for idiosyncratic self-glorification, but rather to capture a timeless expression of an age-old quest—a quest through the labyrinth of memory for enlightenment and love, for the truth of the soul, for mystical union, for her womanhood, for the purpose of her art. The goal was to "justify all the spiral-like meanderings of my mind and body," as she said of

her analysis with Freud. She was concerned with preserving the intricate setting of her memories: "We wander in a labyrinth," she observed in *By Avon River*; "If we cut straight through, we destroy the shell-like curves and involutions." This quest motif furnishes a final, ontological, or even religious layer of meaning to "Oread" and other poems. The oread's venturing from her forested retreat to the sea-ledges can be interpreted as seeking the love of lover, mother, and father—and perhaps the godhead, since the image of merged sea and trees is suggestive of the Moravian doctrine of mystical union with Christ's body that influenced H. D. as a child and later as a poet.

H. D.'s poetry was original and manifested a new development in Western literature. Reversing the usual form of allegory, she drew images from the natural world and characters and situations from classical sources to transmute the story of her own life into poems expressing universal human experience. Exemplified by "Oread," her poems are like ideographic pictures or signs with many meanings coiled in single images—images that, in their distilled essence, contain the world seen by a gifted poet.

OTHER MAJOR WORKS

LONG FICTION: *Palimpsest*, 1926; *Hedylus*, 1928; *Kora and Ka*, 1934 (includes *Mira-Mare*); *The Usual Star*, 1934 (includes *Two Americans*); *Nights*, 1935; *Bid Me to Live*, 1960; *HERmione*, 1981.

SHORT FICTION: *The Hedgehog*, 1936.

TRANSLATIONS: *Choruses from Iphigeneia in Aulis and the Hippolytus of Euripides*, 1919; *Euripides' Ion*, 1937; *Hippolytus Temporizes*, 1927 (adaptation of classical text).

NONFICTION: *Tribute to Freud*, 1956; *Tribute to Freud, Writing on the Wall, Advent*, 1974; *End to Torment*, 1979; *The Gift*, 1982.

BIBLIOGRAPHY

Burnett, Gary Dean. *H. D. Between Image and Epic: The Mysteries of Her Poetics*. Ann Arbor, Mich.: UMI Research Press, 1990. This study deals with H. D.'s poetry between the wars (1916-1944). Burnett refers to this period as her middle period between the Imagist years and the later epics. Her concerns about her life, her response to the war, her research on ancient mystery cults, and her interest in the work of her contemporaries are traced and shown as a context for reading these poems. Includes a bibliography and an index.

Collecott, Diana. *H. D. and Sapphic Modernism, 1910-1950*. New York: Cambridge University Press, 1999. This critical study argues for recognition of H. D. as a key figure in the shaping of Anglo-American modernism. The development of a homoerotic strand within H. D.'s distinctively modernist poetics comes together in Collecott's central concept of sapphic modernism.

DuPlessis, Rachel Blau. *H. D., the Career of That Struggle*. Brighton, England: Harvester Press, 1986. This compact volume offers an overview of H. D.'s literary career informed by feminist criticism. The author defines four types of "authority" that H. D. confronted in her poetry: cultural authority, the authority of otherness, gender authority, and sexual or erotic authority. Using these concepts, she tries to explain why H. D.'s poetry is often difficult. Supplemented by primary and secondary bibliographies, and an index.

DuPlessis, Rachel Blau, and Susan Stanford Friedman, eds. *Contemporary Literature* 27, no. 4 (1986). This special issue on H. D. includes Ezra Pound's tribute to H. D. (1916) and a number of fine essays. The poet Alicia Ostriker discusses H. D.'s creation of a poetic role for herself as poet/mother; Adalaide Kirby Morris describes how H. D. lived outside the Western ethic; and Eileen Gregory provides excellent readings of many of H. D.'s early lyrics.

Friedman, Susan Stanford. *Psyche Reborn: The Emergence of H. D.* Bloomington: Indiana University Press, 1981. This important study charts the progress of H. D.'s career, especially her development from Imagist to a poet who adopted the epic form of quest-poetry. Her later poetry, grounded in feminism according to Friedman, celebrates the woman as author and hero who, with her word, will save a self-destructing civilization. Examines the impact of Sigmund Freud's theories on her art in transition, and H. D.'s own understanding of how gender influences literature.

Fritz, Angela DiPace. *Thought and Vision: A Critical Reading of H. D.'s Poetry*. Washington, D.C.: Catholic University of America Press, 1988. Fritz attempts to cover H. D.'s entire poetic canon, and in doing so reaffirms her eminence as a modernist and feminist poet. Ths study is intended to complement *H. D.: Woman and Poet*, and it suggests throughout that H. D.'s thought and vision are best defined in her poetry. Includes a bibliography and an index.

Guest, Barbara. *Herself Defined: The Poet H. D. and Her World*. Garden City, N.Y.: Doubleday, 1984. In this highly experimental biography, Guest ignores such conventions as footnotes and chronological tables. She includes no bibliography and few dates. Her tremendous scholarship, however, is evident, and her book is a successful evocation of the ambiance, the people, and the places that made up H. D.'s world. The book is thus a reliable account of H. D.'s life, even though critics such as Susan Stanford Friedman have pointed out that in Guest's book, H. D. herself remains a more shadowy figure than many of the people who surrounded her.

King, Michael, ed. *H. D.: Woman and Poet*. Orono, Maine: National Poetry Foundation, 1986. This anthology contains two dozen expert essays and a good annotated bibliography of works written about H. D. from 1969 to 1985. King's useful introduction outlines the concerns of each section of the book and summarizes briefly each essayist's ideas. Besides sections on H. D.'s place in poetic tradition, her poetry, and her prose, this volume contains an interesting chapter on her career in the theater. Part of the Man/Woman and Poet series. Includes an index.

Laity, Cassandra. *H. D. and the Victorian Fin de Siècle: Gender, Modernism, Decadence*. New York: Cambridge University Press, 1996. Argues that H. D. shaped an alternative poetic modernism of female desire from the "feminine" personas. An examination of female modernism to demonstrate extensively the impact of the Decadents on a modernist woman writer.

John Clendenin Townsend;
bibliography updated by the editors

PAAVO HAAVIKKO

Born: Helsinki, Finland; January 25, 1931

PRINCIPAL POETRY

Tiet etäisyyksiin, 1951
Tuuliöinä, 1953
Synnyinmaa, 1955
Lehdet lehtiä, 1958
Talvipalatsi, 1959 (*The Winter Palace*, 1968)
Puut, kaikki heidän vihreytensä, 1966
Selected Poems, 1968
Neljätoista hallitsijaa, 1970
Runoja matkalta salmen ylitse, 1973
Kaksikymmentä ja yksi, 1974
Runot, 1949-1974, 1975
Runoelmat, 1975
Viiniä, kirjoitusta, 1976
Rauta-aika, 1982 (*The Age of Iron*, 1982)
Kullervon tarina, 1983
Sillat: Valitut Runot, 1984
Toukokuu, ikuinen, 1988
Talvirunoja, 1990
Runot! Runot, 1984-1992, 1992

OTHER LITERARY FORMS

Paavo Haavikko is one of the most prolific Finnish writers; he has published more than fifty books in his native language and has written equally masterfully in every literary genre. He made his debut in the 1950's with collections of lyrical poems, and in the following decades he published novels, short stories, epic poems, and plays, in addition to which he has written two opera librettos, based on his plays: *Ratsumies* (1974; *The Horseman*, 1974) and *Kuningas lähtee Ranskaan* (1984; *The King Goes Forth to France*, 1984). The music for both operas was composed by Aulis Sallinen, and they were first performed at the Savonlinna Opera Festival in Finland. They have since been staged in West Germany, New Mexico, and London's Covent Garden.

History has provided some of the major themes for Haavikko's poetry and plays, and he has also published nonfiction in that field. His literary work includes collections of aphorisms, scripts for films, and radio and television plays. Some of Haavikko's work has been translated into English, French, German, and Swedish. Haavikko also published three volumes of memoirs and continued to write opera libretti. In 2000, he collaborated with the composer Tuomas Kantelinen on an opera about the early twentieth century Olympic long-distance runner Paavo Nurmi. This work, titled *Paavo Suuri, Suuri juoksu, Suuri uni*, was directed by Kalle Holmberg and received widespread exposure throughout Europe.

ACHIEVEMENTS

From the very start of his literary career, Paavo Haavikko never sought favor with the reading public; in fact, he rebelled against the thought that art and literature should be "pretty" or popular; for him, a poet's greatest achievement is the writing itself. His unique contributions in the forefront of post-World War II literature were early recognized, and consequently he was awarded the Finnish Government Literature Prizes for his work in the years 1958, 1960, 1962, 1964, 1966, 1969, 1970, and 1974. In 1966, Haavikko received the Aleksis Kivi Prize (which is named after the writer of the first Finnish-language novel, published in 1870), and in 1969 he was awarded the Finnish Government Drama Prize and an honorary doctorate from the University of Helsinki. A symposium was held in 1976 in Joensuu, Finland, at which the participants, who represented the academic disciplines of literature, history, political science, and economics, analyzed and examined Haavikko's work. In 1978, he received the Order of the White Rose of Finland for his literary achievements. Haavikko's four-part television drama, *Rauta-aika* (based on his poem), which has also been published in book form, won for him the Prix d'Italia as best European television series of the year 1982.

Only a sampling of Haavikko's poetry, plays, and other literary work have been translated into other languages. As Philip Binham, one of the English-language translators of Haavikko's work, has pointed out, Finnish is particularly difficult to render in translation the subtlety and rhythm of Haavikko's language; indeed, Haavikko's poetic expression has often posed problems even to native Finnish readers. In the 1960's, however, some of Haavikko's work began to appear in translations, and in 1984 Haavikko won the Neustadt Prize, administered by

Paavo Haavikko (© Irmeli Jung)

the University of Oklahoma, which is given to non-American writers for a particularly substantive and challenging body of work. He also won the Nordic Prize of the Swedish Academy in 1993. As of 2001, it seemed perplexing to observers that neither Haavikko nor his Swedish-Finnish contemporary, Bo Carpelan, had won the Nobel Prize, as both were almost universally commended as deserving of that honor. Nonetheless, it is hard to deny that Haavikko has, over the entire course of his career, been one of the world's leading poets.

BIOGRAPHY

Paavo Juhani Haavikko was born on January 25, 1931, in Helsinki, the capital city of Finland, a city in which the poet has lived all of his life and which he has always found attractive and exciting, and about which he also has written a book. Haavikko's father was a businessman, and after his high school graduation in 1951 and customary service in the Finnish Army, Haavikko also entered the business world, working as a real estate agent. Like many Finnish modern poets, Haavikko has consistently maintained a second profession alongside his literary career; in fact, he believes that an author who is solely occupied by writing loses touch with the reali-

ties of life. Indeed, in his poetry Haavikko never seems to be an observer on the sidelines; he appears to be in the middle of the events and freely uses concepts and imagery from commerce and the business world in his creative writing, most of which he has done on weekends. From the late 1960's, Haavikko has been the literary editor for a major Finnish publishing company and a literary consultant to several printing presses. In 1955, Haavikko married poet and writer Marja-Liisa Vartio (born 1924); she died in 1966. Haavikko and literary historian Ritva Rainio Hanhineva were married in 1971.

Haavikko has always, in his work, shown a great skepticism toward any political or philosophical ideology: "If the philosophy is wrong, all deeds become crimes." Varying political ideologies are much the same in Haavikko's eyes: "Socialism! so that capitalism could begin to materialize./ Capitalism! the Big Money!/ They spend their evenings in a small circle,/ hand in hand, fingers linked in fingers, and like to remember their youth." Haavikko's stand is that of an anti-utopian realist, to whom an individual's uniqueness and freedom are the highest values; in his view, man has "perhaps a two percent margin" in the maze of corporations, institutions, and governments and their bureaucracies, or simply in the complexity of life and in facing fate. To Haavikko, the most positive aspects of life are nature, the biological world, and the human mind.

In his own country, Haavikko is generally seen as a conservative and patriotic poet, who paradoxically has often through his work questioned some of his society's most cherished myths and values. Beginning in the 1980's, Haavikko was a regular columnist for the magazine *Suomen Kuvalehti*, and in the 1990's he started a small publishing press called Art House. By this point in his career, Haavikko had become a well-known figure in Finnish cultural life, even to people who did not particularly follow poetry. Gray-haired, distinguished-looking, and wearing thick eyeglasses, Haavikko had become a national sage without suffering the decrease in literary quality often associated with such a status.

ANALYSIS

Paavo Haavikko belongs to the generation of Finns who experienced World War II as children, growing into maturity in the immediate postwar years, a period which in many ways constituted a watershed for the Finnish society, in which a major, still ongoing culture change began in the 1950's. The largely rural society (seventy percent of the population lived in the countryside until the postwar years) had been a major source of literary themes for the prewar writers and poets. Finnish as a creative literary language was still relatively new, Finland having been part of the Swedish kingdom for six hundred years and of the Russian empire for one hundred years, during which time Swedish was the language of culture and education. In the nineteenth century, a smoldering nationalistic movement gained impetus, under the influence of the ideas of the German philosopher Johann Gottfried von Herder, and, in 1863, the Finnish language was granted equal status with Swedish. The following decades produced an abundance of writers of Finnish-language literature, which reflected Continental European trends and the "national neo-Romanticism." The latter was partly a product and a culmination of the struggle for the country's independence, which was gained in 1917.

World War II broke the continuity of Finnish literature. The war experience and the resulting circumstances and conditions caused a reevaluation of prewar ideas and ideology. It was a time of careful assessments of history and of the present possibilities for the country's political, economic, and cultural survival. New influences from the Anglo-Saxon world, especially in the form of translated literature, reached Finland, and in the late 1940's a new generation of poets entered the literary scene.

Many of the representatives of the new poetry experimented with a number of styles, not immediately finding one distinctly their own. Not so with Haavikko. His first poetry collection, *Tiet etäisyyksiin* (the roads to far away), published in 1951, when the writer was twenty years old, showed him following his own instincts and philosophy about the nature of poetry and of language, humankind, and the world. The poets of the new era of modernism strove for fresh forms of expression, rejecting the preexisting poetic structures and in their themes avoiding any sort of ideology or sentimental self-analysis. Haavikko took these aims further than anybody else. He constructed his poems in nonrhyming, rhythmical language, attempting to get as close as possible to the spoken idiom.

He set out to examine the "eternal issues" of love, death, the identities of man and woman and their relationship to each other, and the possibilities for the individual human being in an ever-changing world, in which the human character, man's psyche and behavior, and his actions and passions stay the same. Haavikko also set out to find linguistic expressions that would most clearly and honestly define and depict all these phenomena. Haavikko sees language as restricting humanity's perception of human processes and thoughts, even causing an estrangement from the realities of life. In an early poem, he speaks of the limitations of his native language: "Finnish isn't a language, it's a local custom/ of sitting on a bench with hair over your ears,/ it's continual talking about the rain and the wind." In another poem, he speaks of his own role as a poet in improving the existing modes of expression: "I'm on a journey into the language/ of this people." On the other hand, Haavikko has also realized the advantages of his mother tongue, whose structure allows a compactness and a poetic construction in which "the relations between one thing and another, the world picture, are the most important elements."

This last observation pertains to Finnish folk poetry, a rich warehouse of themes and frames for his work. Haavikko set out to clear from literary expression all empty rhetoric and pathos, taking words, which he perceives as "treacherous symbols," and using them to find the truth. In this never-ending search for truth—for ultimately there are no answers—Haavikko creates poetry in fluid combinations of images and concepts, taken from nature, everyday urban surroundings, mythology and tales, and classical antiquity as well as more recent history.

The structures of Haavikko's poems are complex, multifaceted, and multilayered. His lyrics have been compared to rich tapestries, to top rough-edged crystals, and to modern Finnish objets d'art. All these descriptions are fitting, and perhaps one more could be added, a concept taken from nature: Haavikko's poems could be seen as many items frozen in a block of ice; the block may melt, the ice become water and part of the continuous life cycle, and the pieces encased may become recognizable and identifiable, or the ice block may remain an enigmatic, opaque object, beautiful to contemplate but giving no answers to the viewer. Haavikko's poetry has also been likened to music, its sound obviously being most resonant in the original language. In the end, the responsibility for an interpretation and an understanding of the poet's ideas is left to each individual reader.

As Kai Laitinen and others have pointed out, Haavikko's writing is deeply rooted in a cultural and geographic area and its social and historical processes; the poet's perspectives are those of a European and of a citizen of a small European nation. The small size of the Finnish reading public (and, for writers in the Finnish language, a international public without much innate potential) has led Finland's writers to be unusually versatile, working in several forms and often having different identities in different genres or milieus. At times, the author's work reflects not only an individual's loneliness and feeling of being different but also an entire nation's sense of isolation and separateness.

Besides that, Haavikko has had much to say about the most central and universal issues of human existence—the identity of an individual, the relativity of values, and the difficulty of living—and about the concepts of society, history, and literature. He has said it through complex anachronisms, analogies, and "precise ambiguities," all the while refining and defining language, which in his work, especially in the opera librettos and the aphorisms, has become increasingly sparse and intense. He has moved freely between literary genres, letting the subject matter determine the form of his writing.

In an interview, Haavikko has stated that, when composing poems, he always lets the entire poem take shape in his mind, before writing it down, for fear that the words will take over and begin to lead a life of their own. He may use concrete images or paradoxes, weave the thread of human experience through several time periods, illuminating the present through the past and speaking about the future at the same time:

> The Greeks populated Mycenae,
> the poets of Rome in their turn
> filled Greece with shadowless beings,
>
> there is no night when no one wrote
> someone's writing into these rooms too,
> poem-dressed lovers, when we are not saying
>
> The room is not free but full of breathing
> and embraces, light sleeping, hush,
> be still, so we don't wake, someone's writing
> into the night.

For Haavikko, there is no separation of time and space; human existence, behavior, interactions, and in the end human fate, remain the same.

From the early metaphysical lyrical poetry through the plays, opera librettos, epic poetry, aphorisms, and historical analyses, Haavikko's work has continued to create lively debate, providing new perspectives and new insights through its oracle-like visions and presentation of world structures. In the meantime, Haavikko continues to search for "himself, woman, god, tribe, old age and the grave" and the uniqueness of things, "not wanting generalizations, either, but trying to make things concrete." For Haavikko, one who generalizes is a fool, and in his work the poet never pontificates. He merely invites the reader onto new paths, to which he has opened the way.

THE WINTER PALACE

The collections of poems published by Haavikko in the 1950's firmly established him as the most original and brilliant representative of the modernist group. The nine-poem collection *The Winter Palace* is a synthesis of all the themes which had preoccupied Haavikko in his previous work. The collection derived its name from the imperial Russian palace in St. Petersburg, and within this frame of a center for historical events, the poet examines the nature of art, poetry, love and death, and political power. The first poem begins: "Chased into silver,/ side by side:/ The images./ To have them tell you." The poet warns the reader to be alert, to enter this experience with an open mind, and through personal perception to organize the kaleidoscope, which will follow, into a comprehensible whole.

As an eighteen-year-old high school student, Haavikko had read T. S. Eliot, who without doubt pointed him the way "into the unknown." At about that time, Haavikko wrote a poem which served as a declaration of his intentions: "Bridges are taken by crossing them/ Each return is a defeat." From then on Haavikko continued crossing bridges, and *The Winter Palace* has been mentioned as the Finnish *Waste Land*:

> This poem wants to be a description,
> And I want poems to have
> only the faintest of tastes.
> Myself I see as a creature, hopeful
> As the grass.

These lines are almost improbable
This is a journey through familiar speech
Towards the region that is no place.

HISTORY, POLITICS, AND COMMUNICATION

After *The Winter Palace*, Haavikko turned to writing prose. He had already in his earlier collections of lyrical poetry, particularly in *Synnyinmaa* (native land) and *Lehdet lehtiä* (leaves, pages), dealt with the issues of the politics of the day, especially examining the events during the war and its aftermath, illuminating and assessing, through similar historical events, the actions and reasoning of the principal Finnish statesmen, as well as probing the Finnish national identity and attitudes. Historical themes in general increased in Haavikko's work considerably in the next two decades; seventeen of his plays are within a historical framework.

Haavikko continued questioning the essence of power, the motives and aims of those wielding it, and how they influence the world, in particular the fate of the individual, who is tied to a historical situation. Most of Haavikko's novels and plays deal with social problems and issues involving the state, the church, the judiciary and taxation systems, diplomacy, commerce, and the family unit. In these contexts, the writer examines the problem of communication, how different social roles are manifested in the speech act, and the ways in which language is used and manipulated by various interest groups and individuals.

For Haavikko, nonverbal communication is much less dangerous than verbal communication; generally, everything bad derives from words: "And so out of words grow war/ and war becomes real/ it eats men, horses, corn,/ fire devours houses, years gnaw on man." An individual's odds for survival, however, are increased if he is aware of and can master the largest possible body of the various ways of communicating and knows the requirements that certain social roles impose on speech. Women's language is different from that of men: "It is pleasant to listen to, difficult to speak,/ impossible to understand." One of Haavikko's themes is that of a woman's greater strength, compared with that of a man; men desire power, they plan and develop; women have more common sense and keep everything together, and they steer life along healthier lines. Haavikko's writing implies that the cruelties and injustices of the world usually derive from men's actions. There is a deep, underlying pessimism in his prose, but it is lightened by a special brand of humor, the Finnish "gallows humor," which is a mixture of absurdity and irony and which, alongside more classical satire, is embedded in all the poet's work.

AN ILLOGICAL WORLD

In 1966, Haavikko published his only collection of lyrical poems of that decade, *Puut, kaikki heidän vihreytensä* (trees in all their verdure), which in its direct and clear simplicity remains one of his major works, alongside the collections of 1973 and 1976, when he returned briefly to lyrical poetry, dealing with new and different subject matter. Haavikko's interest was turning increasingly toward economics and history, particularly Finnish history and toward Byzantium, both of which provided him with a background against which to examine the fate of rulers, political factions and their intrigues, and man's quest for power and riches. In short, Haavikko could study the entire world in microcosm. The world as expressed in Haavikko's poetry is illogical, it is a paradox, and it is merciless; once an individual comes to terms with this understanding of the world, however, "looking it into the eyes every moment," it is possible for him to live without fear and, characteristic of Haavikko, without hope.

NELJÄTOISTA HALLITSIJAA

Haavikko's epic poem *Neljätoista hallitsijaa* (fourteen rulers) consists of fifteen cantos, based on the events described in the chronicle of Michael Psellus, an eleventh century Byzantine court historian and philosopher. The first four songs are the poet's first-person prologue, after which he merges with Psellus, through whose eyes he draws the Byzantine worldview. The main themes are, as in much of Haavikko's work, the position of the individual, who cannot escape his fate though he himself also shapes that fate, and the frame of historical understanding, the historical process devouring the individual, who searches for permanence but finds it an illusion. In this cyclical world, however, in which everything is in flux, an individual must, in some way, influence the outcome of the events, and he must try to combat evil, which Haavikko includes in his term "fascism." The word represents to the poet, among some other aspects, all accumulated stupidity, in which an initially small, annoying amount may become dangerous. In Haavikko's terminology, the opposite of fascism is pragmatic caution in all human endeavor, perceiving realities, being prepared for the worst, all the while maintaining the ability to function and staying alive. Haavikko's interest in Byzantium links him to modernists such as the Irish poet William Butler Yeats and the Greek poet Constantine Cavafy. Like those two poets, Haavikko felt a concrete, historical sense of connection to the Byzantine Empire, as raiders from Finland had encountered Byzantine culture while on expeditions southward at the turn of the first millennium. Perhaps, Haavikko hypothesized, the famous "sampo" in the *Kalevala* was a Byzantine machine for producing coinage! The concrete historicism of *Neljätoista hallitsijaa*, combined with Haavikko's rigorously ironic view of history (his lack of credence in history's substantiality) endows it with both spectacle and skepticism.

KAKSIKYMMENTÄ JA YKSI

Haavikko's stylistic and thematic concerns and his preoccupation with human cognitive processes are expressed in the following lines: "Every house is built by many people/ and is never through,/ history and myth are told and told again/ contradicting halls lead to understanding." These concerns led the poet to begin telling old Finnish myths anew, by rewriting one of the central cycles of the *Kalevala*, a compilation of folk poetry which was collected and edited by Elias Lönnrot and first published in 1835. This compilation became the national epos and had a great impact on the national culture, inspiring writers, painters, and composers, such as Jean Sibelius. Haavikko's version of the Sampo cycle (which in folk tradition centers on a mythical talisman which brings good fortune), *Kaksikymmentä ja yksi* (twenty and one) takes place in Byzantium, where, according to the poet, Finnish Vikings went in search of a coin-minting machine, which they hoped to plunder.

FOLK POETRY

Haavikko continued following a partially economic point of view in his subsequent re-creations of the world of the folk poetry, which he inhabited with antiheroes, people modeled after those of modern times, while at the same time depicting the archetypal man. The poet

has acknowledged his indebtedness to his native oral traditions, which have provided him with an inheritance of the world of the epic, and he has interpreted that world in the language and with the techniques of the twentieth century.

OTHER MAJOR WORKS

PLAYS: *Münchhausen*, pr. 1958; *Nuket*, pr., pb. 1960; *Lyhytaikaiset lainat*, pr. 1966 (radio play); *Audun ja jääkarhu*, pr. 1966 (radio play); *Freijan pelto*, pr. 1967 (radio play); *Ylilääkäri*, pb. 1968 (*The Superintendent*, 1978); *Agricola ja kettu*, pr., pb. 1968; *Sulka*, 1973; *Harald Pitkäikäinen*, pb. 1974; *Ratsumies*, pb. 1974 (libretto, music by Aulis Sallinen; *The Horseman*, 1974); *Näytelmät*, pb. 1978; *Viisi pientä draamallista tekstiä*, pb. 1981; *Kuningas lähtee Ranskaan*, pr. 1984 (libretto, music by Sallinen; *The King Goes Forth to France*, 1984); *Lastenkutsut*, pr. 2000; *Paavo Suuri, Suuri juoksu, Suuri uni*, pr. 2000 (libretto, music by Tuomas Kantelinen).

TELEPLAYS: *Rauta-aika*, 1982 (adaptation of his poem); *Kirkas ilta*, 1995; *Korkein oikeus*, 1999.

NONFICTION: *Puhua, vastata, opettaa*, 1972; *Ihmisen ääni*, 1977; *Kan-sakunnan linja*, 1977; *Ikuisen rauhan aika*, 1981; *Pimeys*, 1984; *Yritys omaksuvaksi*, 1987; *Vuosien aurinkoiset varjot*, 1994; *Prospero*, 1995.

MISCELLANEOUS: *Romaanit ja novellit*, 1981 (novels and short fiction).

BIBLIOGRAPHY

Binham, Philip. "Dream Each Within Each: The Finnish Poet Paavo Haavikko." *Books Abroad* 50, no. 2 (1976): 337-341. A brief look at the first half of Haavikko's career, emphasizing its experimental aspect; does not give sufficient coverage of the poet's Byzantine and historical concerns but is otherwise reliable and insightful.

Haavikko, Paavo. "What Has the Kalevala Given Me?" *Books from Finland* 1 (1985): 65. The poet himself discusses his relationship to Finland's fundamental body of mythological legend and inferentially his stance toward story and history.

Ivask, Ivar, ed. *World Literature Today* 58, no. 4 (1984). This special issue was devoted to Haavikko's work on the occasion of his winning the Neustadt Prize in 1984. Includes not only reprints of some of Haavikko's work but rigorous and laudatory analyses as well.

Laitinen, Kai. *Literature of Finland: An Outline.* Helsinki: Otava, 1985. This source, now superseded by George Schoolfield's book, does provide a good overall placement of Haavikko within the literary tradition of Finland; particularly mentions his relationship both to earlier Finnish-language traditions and to Swedish-Finland literature.

Paddon, Seija. "John Ashbery and Paavo Haavikko: Architects of Postmodern Space in Mind and Language." *Canadian Review of Comparative Literature/Revue Canadienne de Littérature Comparée* 20, nos. 3/4 (1993): 409-416. This comparison of Haavikko to Ashbery is based not solely on observed similarities but also on Ashbery's lavish admiration for Haavikko's *Talvipalatsi.* Paddon is one of the leading scholars of Finnish poetry in North America, and this is one of the few articles on Haavikko in English to go into sustained analysis of his poetic techniques.

Schoolfield, George. *A History of Finland's Literature.* Lincoln: University of Nebraska Press, 1998. Provides a substantial overview of Haavikko's entire poetic career; also gives a sense of his comparative importance in the national literature and the cross-fertilizations between his work and that of his Finnish and Finnish-Swedish contemporaries.

Tuula Stark,
updated by Nicholas Birns

MARILYN HACKER

Born: New York, New York; November 27, 1942

PRINCIPAL POETRY

Presentation Piece, 1974
Separations, 1976
Taking Notice, 1980
Assumptions, 1985
Love, Death, and the Changing of the Seasons, 1986
Going Back to the River, 1990
The Hang-Glider's Daughter: New and Selected Poems, 1990
Selected Poems, 1965-1990, 1994
Winter Numbers: Poems, 1994
Squares and Courtyards, 2000

OTHER LITERARY FORMS

Marilyn Hacker has published translations, criticism, and reviews in *Grand Street, The Nation, Ploughshares,* and elsewhere. She has also translated the works of French poets.

ACHIEVEMENTS

Marilyn Hacker brings together a sophisticated and urbane intelligence, technical and verbal virtuosity, and a level of wit that is not always found in such a committed feminist and lesbian poet. Her work has been greeted with awards and grants since the publication of *Presentation Piece,* which received the National Book Award in 1975, and was a Lamont Poetry Selection of the Academy of American Poets in 1973. She was a Guggenheim Fellow in 1980-1981 and an Ingram Merrill Fellow in 1984-1985. *Winter Numbers* was awarded the Lenore Marshall Prize (1995), a Lambda Literary Award, the John Masefield Memorial Award of the Poetry Society of America, and the B. F. Conners Award from the *Paris Review.* Hacker has had considerable influence as an editor of literary magazines. She has been editor-in-chief of *Thirteenth Moon: A Feminist Literary Magazine* and editor of *The Little Magazine* and *Woman Poet: The East.* From 1990-1994 she served as editor of the highly regarded and venerable *The Kenyon Review.* Hacker also served as a guest editor for *Ploughshares.*

BIOGRAPHY

Marilyn Hacker was educated at the Bronx High School of Science, Washington Square College of New York University, and the Art Students League. She has lived in New York, Mexico City, San Francisco, and London and has come to divide her time between Manhattan and Paris. Her marriage to science fiction writer Samuel Delany did not survive their mutual acknowledgment of homosexuality, and Hacker has lived since the mid-1980's with her life partner, Karyn London. Many aspects of her life, especially the evolution of her relationship with her daughter, Iva, and her mother (whose death is the subject of the fine "Mother" and "Mother II" in *Assumptions*), her battle with breast cancer, her witness to the ravages of AIDS, as well as the intricacies of friendship, travel, and the vicissitudes of love, form the subjects of her poetic work.

ANALYSIS

In an interview published in the early 1980's, Marilyn Hacker defined her stance as a feminist poet: "We are reclaiming the idea that a poet is speaking to and for other people. . . . It doesn't assume a stance of isolation and defeat. It comes from the necessity for communication and reclamation." In this self-definition Hacker identifies some of the strongest features of her poetic work. From her earliest volume her commitment to freshness and originality in language distinguishes her. While the reader is always close to the specific and ordinary details of the life of a mid-twentieth century woman—the dark blue coffee mug, the horrors of transatlantic flights, and the struggles of rearing a daughter in New York City—this closeness to the everyday is never banal or prosaic. Things as usual as eating, arranging meetings, and the loss of a lover are refined and elevated by Hacker's remarkable technical and verbal skills.

In the interview cited above, Hacker observes that "any writing is composed of words. If we use the words that we have received, we will be talking about the same old things. . . . The subject may be new, revolutionary, but if it's the same old language, it's the same old language." At the heart of Hacker's work is the presentation of an intimately revolutionary life in a style that matches its subject matter in freshness. While she stresses innovation and reform in her view of society, and in particular the situation of women in that society, she nevertheless belongs to a poetic tradition that reaches back through W. H. Auden, James Wright, and Adrienne Rich to nineteenth century poets such as George Meredith, Robert Browning, and George Gordon, Lord Byron, and finally to troubadour and even earlier classical poetic forms and styles. Hacker's work affirms and reinforces the traditional poetic heritage and uses it as an in-

strument to call for political and personal redefinition. Her learning and political seriousness are nevertheless worn with a joyous, wry, and self-mocking air that honors the reader's intelligence.

Taken as a whole, Marilyn Hacker's books of poetry are an optimistic and richly comic version of a troubled and often doctrinaire period in American literary history. She takes strong and deeply felt positions as a feminist, a lesbian, and a formalist. Yet it is as if the very intensity of her commitment leads her to embrace the comic rather than the tragic vision, to cherish the possibility of a private life: "Life's not forever, love is precarious./ Wherever I live, let me come home to you/ as you are, I as I am, where you/ meet me and walk with me to the river." Having acknowledged that, one should not forget that virtually her first public act upon becoming editor of *The Kenyon Review* was to refuse a grant from the National Endowment for the Arts because of the threat of censorship from that body.

PRESENTATION PIECE

Presentation Piece is exactly that, an introduction of a poet with a distinct voice and a defined intellectual and emotional stance. The presentation is both formal and

Marilyn Hacker (© Layle Silbert)

intimate: "We are creatures of structure," she writes. Yet it is a structure that is far from singular. For Hacker, there is a diverse multitude of possible and intertwined structures. There are structures of language, culture, love, food, politics, nature, sexuality, and, perhaps above all, poetry: Hacker exploits the opportunity for freedom she gains by living fully in as many of these structures as possible.

The tongue comes to represent some of Hacker's most urgent concerns and most meaningful structures. The tongue is the organ of speech; it can stand for language itself (as in when one speaks of one's "mother tongue" or one's "native tongue"); it is the means by which one is able to "taste" food; and, finally, it is an element in erotic play. Each of the significations of the tongue plays a crucial part in Hacker's vision of the world, and it appears throughout her work. The first poem in the first volume ("Presentation Piece") establishes this motif: "Meet me tonight under your tongue./ There is no easy way up. Bite/ on your lip. . . . Let me live in your mouth."

The mood of *Presentation Piece* is defiant. Images of the mouth and tongue and tasting are vehement, even violent: "In an affluent society/ cannibalism/ is a sexual predilection." Language too, that most central structure, becomes problematic. While she can say on the one hand that "it is a privilege to learn a language/ a journey into the immediate/ morning. . . . the place of human wonder in a structure," she must, on the other hand, end the poem with, "I crushed privet leaves/ for the green sap and bitter smell/ and learned on broken weeds/ the pain of fire and water/ which is as real as any other/ language." Even here one notices the lushly sensual and vivid specificity of Hacker's writing, and there are interludes where the enjoyment of the lover seems to deflect anger. Here the mouth and tongue are speaking and being heard: "Dancing/ between moving limbs, the slow flowers/ of our friction opened/ together. So quickly/ you were salt and sweet/ on my tongue."

Hacker senses a danger in the background of individual human relations that is echoed and magnified in the danger and violence of the political world. In an important poem called "Iceplants: Army Beach," the two elements, the personal and the political, come together. Two lovers are sunbathing on the beach, "Your body

glistens like a new/ subway token. . . . Your/ wet shoulders incite me to spurious literature/ while jeweled ice spatters my belly and thighs." The "spurious literature" and the playful corporeality are overshadowed by the realization that the lovers are on a beach that has been used, presumably in World War II, as a line of defense against invasion from the sea. Inside the concrete fortress, contemporary lewd graffiti indicates the hostility and alienation of language and sensuality. The poem is an answer both to the obscenity of the inscription and to the obscenity of controlled, sanctioned violence: "There is," she writes, "a poem in touching/ or in not touching. The poem/ defines the tension between skin and skin,/ increasing, decreasing, rhythmically/ changing the space it defines."

The tension Hacker associates with her poetry comes (as she observes in an interview) "from the diction of ordinary speech playing against a form. When there is an internal or external form to be worked with and worked against, unexpected and illuminating things can happen in the piece of writing." "Forage Sestina" is, perhaps, the most impressive example of this illuminating tension in *Presentation Piece*. The sestina form is the most intricate of the forms devised by the troubadours in the twelfth century in southern France. It consists of six stanzas of six lines each, and the final word of each line appears in each stanza at the end of new lines and in a new regular order; the final three-line stanza is a coda that uses some of the repeated words. To call a sestina (the most sophisticated and premeditated of forms) a "*forage* sestina" is immediately to manifest the tension between formal intricacy and emotional spontaneity. Hacker has her lovers picking through a ruined house in what seems to be a ruined city: "This is for your body hidden in words/ moving through a crumbling structure." The two seem to be the ruin themselves: "I want to touch you, but you are the wall/ crumbling, the report over the wire/ service that there were no survivors." The elegant form of the poem does not erase the destruction. Indeed, language has had a part in the devastation: "Falling words" are responsible for erosion in a wall. Yet the breaking and collapse in the poem and of the poem open some new and living possibility in the last line: "Over the last beam/ keeping the sky from the walls, vines drip into the room."

Hacker's "Elegy: For Janis Joplin," which is addressed to the singer from the poet's exile, is a harsh and brutal evocation of a style of singing and an attitude of defiant self-destruction that resembles the poet's own. It follows the traditional elegiac form, beginning with a realization of the death of the young artist and working through the process of mourning and grief to some condition of reconciliation with the loss. It is written "from exile"—a motif that becomes increasingly important in Hacker's work: "A man told me you died; he was/ foreign." The awareness of Joplin's death allows the poet to see herself as an artist called upon to perpetuate the singer's message of pain and anger: "Stay in my gut, woman lover I never/ touched, tongued, or sang to; stay/ in back of my/ throat, sandpaper/ velvet, Janis." Joplin, with her combination of emotional authenticity, unabashed sensuality, poignant vulnerability, and singing style conspicuous for its stridently raucous assault on both her vocal cords and the audience, represents an important side of Hacker's own work. Hacker uses a Joplin-like emotional recklessness to animate and revivify inherited poetic forms. She writes in the final stanza of "Elegy": "You got me through/ long nights with your coalscuttle/ panic, don't be scared/ to scream when it hurts." Just as the tradition of the elegy focuses on the recovery of the poet from mourning, Hacker becomes herself the voice of the singer: "oh mother it hurts, tonight/ we are twenty-seven, we are/ alone, you are dead."

SEPARATIONS

Separations, the next volume of poetry, continues Hacker's concern with the condition of the female artist who follows the life of exile, erotic adventures, and artistic experimentation. The bohemian life followed routinely by male poets as an education in the ways of the world is much more problematic for a woman, as she suggests in "The Life of a Female Artist Is Full of Vicissitudes." The artistic creation is experienced as an explosion: In "oils thick as a sapling . . . seventeen/ shades of green, the crucified woman burgeons to power." The poem is a register of the alternating, changing social and biological dimensions that inevitably belong to the life of a woman. Like "Elegy: For Janis Joplin," however, this poem underscores the significant extent to which a woman artist's life continues to be the setting or background against which "vicissitudes," especially male vicissitudes, manifest their more significant activities: "Lucky if she doesn't/ die of cancer at fifty-two, a/ virgin, . . . and her Muse,/ bearded and placid, gets his wife pregnant again."

The dominant feature of *Separations*, however, is not only the exiled and uncertain condition of the woman artist; it is the larger and more universal array of separations and losses to which one is subject. In the series of remarkable sonnets called "Geographer: For Link (Luther Thomas Cupp) 1947-1974," Hacker is at her most desolate emotionally and at her most adroit technically. There are five numbered sonnets, four unnumbered, and a final coda of five lines. Each of the sonnets is patterned so that six of the fourteen lines end with a single word; each of these words reappears as the final line of the coda. In enumerating the five dominant words, one has named the theme and meaning of the sonnet series. The words are (in the order in which they are used): "death," "words," "child," "time," and "city," and the resonances Hacker achieves with these few words hold the poem together. Since "nothing rhymes with death," the poem seeks out other forms of order: "Richter plays Bach. My baby daughter plays with a Gauloises pack." The play on words, which is the stock in trade of the poet's craft, brings the poem back to the material of which it is made: "word, word, word: the cure/ for hard nights." So the form of the poem is going to be in the bare repetition and turning of language itself: "Sorry, I can't make any metaphors. . . . death is nobody, death is a word,/ dying happens." Link, whose death as a young man is the occasion of the poem, is associated with map making, with imaginary cities, with drawing and writing. It is as if one could, in drawing the world, imaginatively possess it. The poet remembers "the time/ we mapped an imaginary city/ on your graph pad. Shanghai, Leningrad, what cities/ we pored over in picture-books, marking time!" Now that the geographer is dead, the poet remembers his body as a kind of landscape: "Night after day after night, I mapped the city/ on the brown geography of its child." In the end, as in the Joplin elegy, Hacker is left with language: "From the gutted building, we salvaged words."

In the sonnet sequence that gives *Separations* its name, Hacker is at her most Byronic: "Satisfied lovers eat big breakfasts. I/ want black coffee and a cigarette/ to dull this cotton mouth." The less than romantic reality with which her poetry lives gives her room for her jaunty irony and tough-tender style. What she calls "a phthisic honesty" is a survival skill: "I like being alone and I like pain."

TAKING NOTICE

Taking Notice reveals a Hacker more intensely than ever engaged with representing her poetics to her reader. In the often-anthologized poem that opens this collection, "Feeling and Form," Hacker writes a letter to a painter friend and associates her ideas about poetry with the aesthetics of Susanne Langer (a philosopher who wrote a book on the subject, *Feeling and Form*, 1953). "Poetry," she writes, "dovetails contradictions." This image, which suggests the cabinetmaker's craft in wood, indicates Hacker's commitment to meticulous, respectful handling of the materials of her art. She explains not only her relationship with the words with which she works but also the comic and ironic form she adopts: "Recapitulate:/ tragedians accept the Status Quo/ as a Good Thing. . . . We/ will not be tragic heroes, love, okay?/ I think the status quo has had its day." Her conclusion links form and feeling: "Revolutions feed on comedy."

A substantial part of *Taking Notice*, "La Fontaine de Vaucluse," signals a theme that would become increasingly significant in Hacker's later work. The time she spends living in France grows in importance. The site of the fountains of the Vaucluse is a sacred spot where the fourteenth century Italian poet Petrarch lived and wrote of Laura, his mistress and muse. The Vaucluse becomes a similarly inspiring place for a twentieth century poet in exile, though it is now more an attraction for buses full of German and French tourists than a secluded grotto: "We came for the day/ on a hot bus from Avignon. A Swed-/ ish child hurls a chalk boulder." The distractions of modernity, the enormous distance between herself and the romantic past, are transcended, at least for a while, by the comradeship Hacker feels with her friend the writer Marie Ponset: "Marie/ and I, each with a notebook on her knee,/ begin to write, homage the source calls up/ or force we find here." The two poets are animated and inspired by each other; they function for each other as Petrarch's Laura functioned for him: "Our own

intelligent accord that brings/ us to the lucid power of the spirit/ to work at re-inventing work and love." The French landscape and culture connects Hacker with other historic women artists. "From Provence," for example, brings to mind the bohemian writer Natalie Barney as the poet watches two French women in the Hotel Regence: "I wonder, is the brain/ fed by the eye, or does it feed the eye?"

In "Canzone," which names a verse form that is intimately associated with Petrarch and with the Fountaine de Vaucluse, Hacker enlarges upon and develops the long-latent centrality of the tongue, celebrating the specific forms of human gratifications with which France is supremely blessed: "Consider the three functions of the tongue: taste, speech, the telegraphy of pleasure." The tongue is a gift that is, at the same time, the vehicle by which other gifts are given: "Sentient organ-/ isms, we symbolize feeling, give/ the spectrum (that's a symbol) each sense organ/ perceives, by analogy, to others." Language, gastronomy, and carnal sensuality are the triad of pleasures that have always ameliorated loss and disappointment in Hacker's poetry, and her increasing rootedness in France brings a new confidence to her work of the 1980's.

ASSUMPTIONS

Assumptions, in which Hacker encounters the deaths of her friend the poet James Wright and her mother, continues, deepens, and perhaps humanizes her voice. In the elegiac poems she writes on these occasions, however, she develops an expression that is less frantic than that of the earlier elegy on the death of Joplin, at the same time that it reaches more substantial and seasoned emotional ground.

In her memorial poem "Letter from the Alpes-Maritimes: I. M. James Wright" ("I. M." for "in memoriam"), Hacker evokes in considerable detail the simplicity and pleasures of her life in Vence. The wildflowers, the lucid air, and the creative freedom that are a part of life in the south of France fill the poem; she walks "out the French door,/ yellow exclamations of broom in scrub-wild" and makes her way down "to the ravine/ where a cold brook sings, loud as the nightingale's liquid vespers." Writing from the source of the Romance tongue, Hacker addresses her poet friend in Italian and Latin: "Carissima Joannissima, ave" (dearest James, hail). She has "exchanged upper-Manhattan Soave for Cotes de Provence," and even more significantly, she says that now "I watch the sky instead of television." Her life is almost monastic in its solitude; she goes out to dinner alone and writes "between courses, in a garden, where twilight/ softens the traffic." She worries, though, that "a woman alone/ must know how to be cautious when she gets drunk." The poem addresses the changes that have eroded the political hopes of the 1960's and 1970's: "Djuna Barnes and the Equal Rights Amendment/ died in the same month." She declines to join other Americans in celebrating the Fourth of July, which seems a mockery when women's rights are still not fully guaranteed by the Constitution. The erosion of political expectations has given as much as it has taken: "I didn't know I could change and choose/ another ambiance." The letter ends with light references to the possibility of a university job. Hacker concludes her letter with a line that, given the knowledge of Wright's death, must be construed a somber ambivalence: "I'll stop, hoping to see you in October/ face to face." When one removes the comma, the line indicates that Hacker will indeed need to stop hoping to see her friend, her "Carissima Joannissima."

Hacker's poems focusing on issues surrounding the death of her mother have little of the serenity and sense of reconciliation that one sees in "Letter from the Alpes-Maritimes." Some of the roughness from the Joplin poem is to be found, as well as perspectives that illuminate Hacker's relationship with her daughter, Iva. Like Joplin, Hacker's mother is flamboyant and associated with an extravagant use of language: "In the Bronx she/ rages, shrunken, pillow-propped in a rank/ room." A bedridden invalid, the mother is limited to "fictions, afternoon lies the nurse tells to a furious old woman, who will die." The banal fictions her nurses feed her contrast vividly with the urgent narratives her daughter can never tell her. In "Fifteen to Eighteen," Hacker tells of sneaking home late from a date, succeeding in getting into bed unobserved, and then hearing the "gargled cry, always 'God damn/ you to hell,' to start with." Her mother is in insulin shock, and her daughter must handle the strong and combative woman. When the mother has recovered, having no memory of what has happened, she turns to Hacker and asks ferociously what she is doing there and

why the bed is in a mess. The poem titled "1973" confronts Hacker's mother's reaction to her daughter's pregnancy. Hacker is Jewish, and the father of the baby is black. The mother writes one line in reply: "I hope your child is white." In "Mother II" and "Autumn 1980," the incendiary anger and resentment that characterized the earlier poems gives way to other, more resonant reflections. "No one," writes Hacker, "is 'Woman' to another/ woman, except her mother." The unshakable lineage of the body links mother and daughter: "Naked or clad, for me, she wore/ her gender, perpetual chador, her individual complex/ history curtained off by sex." Seeing her mother's body, even naked, draped in the Arab woman's robe of concealment, Hacker is able to begin to address her own daughter's lineage to her: "Am I 'Woman' to my water-/ dwelling brown loquacious daughter,/ corporeal exemplar of/ her thirst for what she would not love?" "Mother II" ends with this question unanswered. "Autumn 1980" brings Hacker to the occasion of her mother's death. The poet is traveling, giving lectures away from New York City, staying with friends in Saratoga Springs. The poem, in blank verse, is bound together by a repeated line: "I didn't know that she had died." The process follows the long bus trip back to New York, while Hacker envisions "a shrunken-souled old woman whom I saw . . . on a hospital/ slab in the Bronx." Hacker had earlier written (in "Fourteen"), "When I need a mother I still go shopping," so one is not surprised that her experience of her mother's death comes to a resolution when she rides "on the female wave, typically into Macy's." In this department store, she comes finally to know her loss: "[I] knew what I officially didn't know/ and put the bright thing down, scalded with tears."

Assumptions constitutes a major step forward for Hacker and prepares the way for what many critics take to be her major achievement, the novel in verse of 1986, *Love, Death, and the Changing of the Seasons*. The title of the book comes from a phrase she had used in "Untoward Occurrence at Embassy Poetry Reading" (a poem in *Presentation Piece*), which says that "the primordial subjects" of poetry are "love, death/ and the changing of the seasons," according to poet Robert Graves. In the 1986 work, using a lightly sketched narrative line that holds the sequence of sonnets and other forms together,

Hacker tells of the burgeoning of a love affair with a younger woman named Rachel, its ups and downs during travels and separations, and finally its demise. Elaborated on that story, however, is a complex and witty account of what Graves had called "the unique, the primordial subjects."

Hacker's work shares many features with George Gordon, Lord Byron's, *Don Juan* (1819-1824, 1826) and George Meredith's *Modern Love, and Poems of the English Roadside* (1862). Both of these nineteenth century poems operate out of a substantial romantic commitment, while at the same time they are able to take a gently mocking and ironic distance from their passion. In this and other respects Hacker resembles W. H. Auden, of whom she said in an earlier poem, "He was a genius who was often smart." Similarly, Hacker has learned to protect herself from the self-destructiveness of a romanticism unmediated by thought and distance. At the end of section 3, she writes, "A sense of humor is a state of grace." In "Symbiose II" one finds an especially good example of the effect that Hacker's use of rhyme has on the comic tone of the book as a whole: "We never begin drinking before seven./ We almost always have good appetites./ We always have good sex on Tuesday nights./ We like to give as good as we are given."

GOING BACK TO THE RIVER

Going Back to the River continues to stimulate critics to applaud "the depth and range of [Hacker'] emotional effects, her ability to elevate the ordinary and deflate the grandiose." Here Hacker returns to the shorter forms of the earlier volumes. There are the familiar themes of transatlantic living, whether she is telephoning between New York and Paris or physically traveling the distance; the vicissitudes of a woman poet's life; the efforts of reconciling (or discovering the impossibility of reconciling) with family; and the consequences of solitude. In "April Interval" she writes, "Now I'm an orphaned spinster with a home where spoils of these diurnal expeditions/ can be displayed in prominent positions."

In the poem from which the volume takes its name, "Going Back to the River," Hacker exhibits her mature gifts. There is as always the matching of high and low, the romantic and the tawdry: "Dusk, iridescent gasoline floats on the/ rain-puddles, peacock feathers on macadam." Like many of her poems, this one is a letter: "What will I say to your when I write to you?" The pleasure and simplicity she finds in her life is expressed when she writes, "Go to the river, take what it offers you."

WINTER NUMBERS

Winter Numbers squarely confronts, on both personal and societal levels, two scourges of the late twentieth century. The collection opens with "Against Elegies," an intense meditation on suffering, loss, courage, and indifference during the epidemics of AIDS and cancer that have felled or threatened the friends and associates of both the writer and her readers. Other poems reflect upon Hacker's own fight against breast cancer. At once private, public, and political, "Cancer Winter" may be the most powerful poem in the collection. Its great strength comes from Hacker's ability to speak not only for herself, but also for so many others.

SQUARES AND COURTYARDS

Squares and Courtyards establishes a public meeting place in verse for people (readers) to congregate in the company both of loss and perseverance, sorrow and affirmation. Hacker's formal skills are challenged by the emotional charges that explode against the walls of verse. Yet she is up to the task, once again, of her harrowing subjects: AIDS, HIV, and cancer.

OTHER MAJOR WORKS

TRANSLATIONS: *Edge*, 1996 (of Claire Malroux); *A Long Gone Sun*, 2000 (of Malroux); *Here There Was Once a Country*, 2001 (of Venus Khoury-Ghata).

BIBLIOGRAPHY

Campo, Rafael. "About Marilyn Hacker: A Profile." *Ploughshares* 22 (Spring, 1996): 195-199. An excellent, interview-based short biography that traces the contours of Hacker's career and causes with useful commentary on the tension between her roles as poet and editor.

Finch, Annie. "An Interview on Form." *American Poetry Review* 25, no. 3 (May/June, 1996): 23-27. Hacker is the interviewee in this fascinating discussion of how poetic forms work to engage the disenfranchised and more generally, the contemporary poet's relationship to formal traditions. The discussion has interesting political dimensions.

Hacker, Marilyn. Interview by Karla Hammond. *Frontiers: A Journal of Women's Studies* 5 (Fall, 1981): 22-27. In this thoughtful interview from the late 1970's Hacker makes a strong case for her formal and technical approach to writing. She discusses the poets from whom she learned and whose work has become a part of her own. Her early exposure to the classic male poets (John Donne, W. H. Auden, William Butler Yeats, E. E. Cummings, T. S. Eliot, and Ezra Pound) is complemented by her adult reading of modern and contemporary women poets.

Howard, Richard, and Marilyn Hacker. "The Education of the Poet." *Antioch Review* 58, no. 3 (Summer, 2000): 261-274. This transcription of a recorded conversation between Howard and Hacker covers such ground as their mutual regard for each other's work, the advantages and disadvantages of being an editor, why younger poets do not read very much poetry, and what goes into the effective education of a poet. The conversation took place in August of 1998.

Monaghan, Pat. Review of *Going Back to the River. Booklist* 86 (March 1, 1990): 1258. Monaghan calls Hacker a poet "whose books you can't put down," partly because of her poems' "steamy" sex but also because of her stellar mastery of poetic forms. She is, Monaghan says, "one of America's most authoritative poets."

Mutter, John. Review of *Love, Death, and the Changing of the Seasons. Publishers Weekly* 230 (September 12, 1986): 90. In this brief review, Mutter summarizes the content of Hacker's love chronicle and calls attention to her seemingly effortless achievement in breathing life into the sonnet form.

Saner, Reg. "Studying Interior Architecture by Keyhole: Four Poets." *Denver Quarterly* 20 (Summer, 1985): 107-117. In this review of *Assumptions*, Saner gives useful information on Hacker's use of classic and traditional verse forms. The piece offers a balanced assessment of her strengths and weaknesses in terms of mainstream critical approaches.

Sharon Bassett,
updated by Philip K. Jason

HAFIZ

Born: Shiraz, Persia; c. 1320
Died: Shiraz, Persia; 1389 or 1390

PRINCIPAL POETRY

The *Divan* was composed and edited by Hafiz, possibly as early as 1368; it contains much of the poetry that can safely be assigned to Hafiz. There are existing manuscript copies of his poems from the first quarter of the fifteenth century. The first printed collection in Persian appeared in 1791. The first English translations of individual poems were performed by Sir William Jones, in *A Grammar of the Persian Language* (1771), and other works published in 1797 and 1799. Other translators published selections from Hafiz's works in 1774, 1787, 1795, 1800, and in subsequent years. The first English-language compilation laying any claim to completeness, *The Divan*, was published by H. Wilberforce Clarke in 1891.

OTHER LITERARY FORMS

Apart from manuscripts he is known to have copied, the only existing works for which Hafiz's authorship has been established are poetry. Other Persian writers have referred to prose works by the author, but no such writings are extant.

ACHIEVEMENTS

In the hands of Hafiz, the lyric poem, or *ghazal*, reached its highest level of development as the author combined technical virtuosity with sublime poetic inspiration. With subtle, meticulous craftsmanship, this literary form, which otherwise could be reproached as stilted and artificial, reached under Hafiz the zenith of its expressive qualities. The author's spiritual and romantic quests are evoked in delicate tones that are admirably suited to the Persian metric forms. The exquisite aspects hidden in everyday experience merge with elements of the author's larger vision, which is tinged with mystical yearnings in places as well. It is a measure also of Hafiz's unexpected depth that simple odes, with their seemingly transparent imagery, upon closer examination reveal multiple patterns of meaning that reflect the timeless qualities of daily joys and sorrows. At its finest, the poetical raiment of Hafiz's work displays meticulous, seemingly effortless construction as the diverse, multicolored threads of thought and feeling are interwoven in bright and perennially appealing designs.

In addition to the odes, or lyric poetry, Hafiz wrote elegies (*qasa'id*), of which two are included in his collected verse; he also wrote a certain number of shorter works (*qita'*) and at least forty-two quatrains (*rubai'yat*). These forms, with their own harmonic and metrical requirements, demonstrate the author's attainments with other kinds of poetry. Although outwardly the entire corpus of Hafiz's known work does not exemplify a single unitary or holistic theme, the various elements of his poetical canon combine patterns and topics that are in keeping with the standards of versification upheld by classical Persian prosody.

During his lifetime, Hafiz earned the title *khwajah*, or learned man. It would appear that he was honored, as well as tolerated, by some of the rulers of his day. The claims of some writers that, possibly with the support of the shah, he was at one time a professor of Koranic exegesis at an institution of religious learning have not been confirmed. Hafiz never obtained an appointment as a court poet; while he gained some renown during his lifetime, the honor with which his name is held was conferred largely by subsequent generations of poets and literary men.

BIOGRAPHY

Little is known with exactitude about the life of the great poet, born Shams al-Din Muhammad. Even the outlines of his biography are uncertain, and rather few details may safely be accepted from the historical works and literary studies that deal with his age. Hafiz's own work has been examined for hints and allusions that would reveal more about his personal circumstances or his station in society. Some poems contain dedications, which would indicate some of the political figures to whom they were addressed; some works conclude with chronograms, by which numerical values assigned to characters yield certain dates. Nevertheless, such evidence may be gleaned only from some writings, mainly from the middle period of the author's life. The entire

problem has been exacerbated by the incompleteness of existing manuscript texts, the earliest of which were transcribed possibly twenty years after the poet's death; other texts date from thirty to sixty years or more after Hafiz's own time. In its turn, the lack of a single accepted body of work limits the usefulness of biographical research based on Hafiz's own writings. Tantalizing suggestions, which can be neither proved nor disproved, add an aura of the legendary to the rather sparse data that have been established beyond doubt.

It would seem that the poet's father was a merchant who moved from Isfahan to Shiraz under conditions suggesting family circumstances of relative poverty. The author was probably born about 1320, the date most often mentioned by the pertinent authorities, though some works cite 1317 and others suggest 1325 or 1326. When he was quite young, his father died; nevertheless, he evidently received a thoroughgoing education. To his given name, Shams al-Din Muhammad, was added the epithet Hafiz, which is bestowed upon those who have learned the Koran by heart. There are enough learned references in his poetry, to Arabic theology and Persian literature, to suggest that he gained familiarity with classical subjects relatively early in life.

During his youth, Hafiz is reputed to have served as a dough maker in a baker's shop and as a manuscript copyist. Some of Hafiz's poems were dedicated to Qiwam al-Din Hasan (died 1353), who served at times as vizier to a local ruler who had arisen during the waning years of the Mongol period of Persia's history. While Hafiz thus wrote some of his most important works by about the age of thirty, political upheaval, and the struggle between rival dynasties for the control of Shiraz, probably complicated the poet's life. During the reign of Mubariz al-Din Muhammad (died 1358), religious differences arose between the Sunni ruler and the Shiite citizenry; Hafiz still may have enjoyed protection from one of the shah's ministers.

The most important creative period for the author evidently occurred early in the reign of Jalal al-Din Shah Shuja' (died 1384); it would seem that Hafiz's renown spread across Persia, into the Arab lands, and as far as India. There is some evidence that he was invited to serve other rulers, though he declined, as he was notoriously reluctant to leave his native city. He may well have been married; one poem from 1362 or 1363 seems to have been meant as a eulogy for a deceased son.

It is thought that Hafiz lost favor at the Shah's court, and remained in some disgrace from 1366 to 1376; though the grounds remain obscure, it has been alleged that the author's exuberant celebration of the joys of wine and love disquieted those in political power. He may have spent a year or two in other Persian cities, such as Isfahan or Yazd. One account, which is generally deemed apocryphal, has the poet undertaking a journey to India, only to turn back at Hormuz, on the Persian Gulf, from fear of the open sea. Much of the rest of Hafiz's life, so far as is known, was spent in Shiraz. He may have regained some favor with patrons in the government; whether he held any academic position is unclear. There are no records, in any event, of his appointment to any educational institutions in Shiraz. Moreover, it is quite possible that the recurrent complaints about personal poverty, which appear at intervals throughout the *Divan*, actually did reflect the poet's own situation to some extent.

The last years of the author's life occurred during the unsettled period that followed Timur's invasion of Persia. While Hafiz may have been assisted sporadically by members of the earlier government who remained in Shiraz, by some accounts, which historical research has actually tended to confirm, he met with the great conqueror in 1387 and half-seriously set forth his justification for placing love's attractions above the control of provinces and nations. Hafiz died in 1389 or 1390, and subsequently his tomb became one of the most celebrated monuments in Shiraz, at which later generations of literary aficionados would gather.

ANALYSIS

While Hafiz's lyrics have widely been considered the most nearly perfect examples of this genre, his poetry has an ineffable quality which seemingly eludes exact analysis. For that matter, specialists have contested whether cohesiveness may be found in specific poems, and whether shifting levels of meaning may account for abrupt transitions in topical content. In a technical sense, however, the felicitous union of diction, metric length, emphasis, and rhyme is everywhere in evidence. Hafiz's appeal is veritably universal: Romantic, often light-hearted, and alive to the joys of this world, his poems reveal sublime attributes in the experiences and perceptions felt on this earth. It is from this point of departure that metaphysical or theological speculation may begin, but while concerns of this sort are taken up in the author's writings, they are far from obtrusive. Indeed, in some connections they may appear inscrutable. The poet's philosophical interests, though immanent, do not impede the measured, melodious currents that guide his thoughts across specific series of lines.

In some quarters Hafiz was reproached as a hedonist and a libertine; he has been charged as well with the use of blasphemous motifs, both in his attitude toward the clergy and for poetic symbolism suggesting affinities with mystical schools of thought. The cast of mind revealed in his verse is effulgent, and slightly irreverent; in calling for the wine bowl or in depicting woman's beauty, however, he shows little that is immoderate or overly indulgent. He may seem bedazzled, but he is not really helpless, in the face of love's charms or the lure of the tavern; at least the precision with which his verses are delivered would suggest controlled self-awareness. There are some rhetorical flights of fancy which most readers probably will tolerate. The features of women conjured forth in Hafiz's poems point to an idealized romantic conception, the embodiments of which would appear now and again before the writer.

The poet seems wistfully conscious that this life is fleeting; but unburdened by fatalism he has resolved to accept the world's pleasures where they may be found. Literary and theological references crop up here and there; they suggest the author's familiarity with learned works even as his own views on life's deeper issues are recorded. When they make their appearances, reflections on death and ultimate designs to this existence reveal a thoughtful, broadly tolerant outlook that, for all of its mystical, seemingly heterodox inspiration, complements and affirms the positive values the author has proclaimed elsewhere in his verse.

COMMAND OF IMAGERY

The enduring qualities of Hafiz's poetry are maintained in the first instance through his consummate use of imagery; indeed, memorable lines and passages are recalled specifically from these associations. Although classical Persian poetry to an extent depended upon specific, fixed points of reference—the roses and nightingales that make their appearances in Hafiz's works originated in prototypes handed down by generations of versifiers—his poetic vision placed these stock images in fresh and distinctively personal literary settings. The allegorical and the actual merge gracefully in the gardens where many of his poetic encounters take place; directly and through allusions, visions of orchards, meadows, and rose gardens are summoned forth. These settings, almost certainly taken from those in and around the author's own city, are typically flanked by box trees, cypresses, pines, and willows. The wind, likened sometimes to the breeze of paradise, wafts scents of ambergris, musk, and other perfumed fragrances; at times there is jasmine in the air.

Roses also figure prominently in many of Hafiz's lines, often as buds, blossoms, and petals; at other times hyacinths, lilies, violets, and tulips appear. The narcissus seems to have its own self-answering connotation. The nightingale, which at places alights upon the roses, provides musical accompaniment to the poet's fonder thoughts; at some junctures swallows or birds of paradise enter the poet's landscape. Celestial bodies often mark transitions to metaphorical passages: The Pleiades sparkle but sometimes provoke tears; at times Venus or Saturn is in the ascendant. The moon mirrors and hurls back images of the beloved's features.

Archetypal visions of women enter many of the lyrics, though generally by hints and partial references. Seemingly bemused by the eyebrows, the pupils of the eyes, the hair, the neck, or the moonlike visage of the loved one, the author must have readily conceived a host of similes. Tresses resemble a tree's leafy growth; lips recall roses in the fullness of their blossom. Perfumed winds mingle with the lover's soft voice. Hafiz seems to have been particularly entranced by the mole, or beauty spot (*khal*), to be found on the cheeks of some women. This fascination, and his willingness to place love above riches and power, led him to compose some of the most celebrated lines in all poetry: "If that beauteous Turk of Shiraz would take my heart in hand,/ I would barter for her dark mole Bukhara and Samarqand."

In other moods the author wrote from the standpoint of a *rind*, or vagabond; in this frame of mind the cares of this world are gently shunted aside for the tavern and the bowl of wine. Many such lyrics at the outset are addressed to the *saqi*, or cupbearer; sad tidings and glad are greeted with the thought that the rosy glow of drink will set matters in perspective. The intrinsic pleasures of fellowship around the bowl are evoked; at times there are melancholy images as well, as when the poet's heart-blood, or the ruby lips of an absent lover, are contrasted with the tawny drink before him. Poverty and the vicissitudes of romantic encounters could seemingly be offset by the mellowing reflections good wine could bring. There are occasions as well when the bowl suggests another quest, when the pursuit of enigmatic romance might be superseded by concern with the ultimate questions. Another image is introduced here and there, that of the cup of Jamshid from old Persian lore, which was supposed to provide magical visions of the universe. Another very famous ode begins with the lines

> Long years my heart had made request
> Of me, a stranger, hopefully
> (Not knowing that itself possessed
> The treasure that it sought of me),
> That Jamshid's chalice I should win
> And it would see the world therein.

This poem ends with speculation on the views of divinity propounded by thinkers and groups from various persuasions that were out of favor in the Persia of Hafiz's day.

RELIGIOUS THEMES

The religious themes developed in Hafiz's verse betray heterodox influences coupled with a broadly tolerant point of view. Some references merely bear the outward stamp of mystic ways of life: the dervish's cloak (*khirqah*) and the dusty, stony path of the spiritually inclined mendicant are featured in some notable lyrics; there are odd juxtapositions of the religious search and the meditations of the wine bibber. Although in some passages the author suggests that his innate liberality and profligacy precluded any commitments to the religious life, he seems nevertheless to have been struck by the free and open spiritual journeys of the peripatetic dervish, or *qalandar*. The impious, slightly scandalous regard with which Hafiz was held in some quarters was given added weight by his references to religious views that went beyond those officially upheld by the authorities.

Mystical currents in Islamic thought had been disseminated under the general rubric of Sufism; such habits of mind eluded the strict doctrinal categories of more orthodox thinkers. Sufi interpretations of philosophical and religious questions still had found adherents among important men of letters in Persia; the evidence from Hafiz's works suggests a more than casual acquaintanceship with mystical teachings. Indeed, though without conferring his entire approval, the poet refers to the distinctive spiritual orientation of the Sufis in many places. More controversial were his quotations from al-Husayn ibn Mansur al-Hallaj, who was executed in Iraq in 922 for his alleged personal identification with God. Hafiz apparently found some inspiration in the celebrated martyr's beliefs in love and manifestations of the divine all around in the world. Moreover, in keeping with the multiple sources of Sufism, where elements of several religious doctrines could be acknowledged in the continuing quest for spiritual guidance, Hafiz's lyrics also point to vital truths in Christianity and in Magian (Zoroastrian) traditions. Elsewhere the author quotes from the Koran, generally where matters of love and tolerance embracing diverse ways of life are involved.

Conflicting interpretations have been advanced on another level, however; it has been contended that hidden meanings lie within the outwardly simple and straightforward compositions of Hafiz. It has been averred, for example, that the vocabulary of mystical sects appears with enough regularity that two, or several, connotations were intended in many of the author's verses. This approach, which can be applied to certain Persian expressions, as well as to loan words from Arabic, assumes great depth in lyrics whose nominal subject matter already is handled through direct and metaphorical means. In this light, mentions of roses may be taken, specifically and obliquely, as references to love, but also (in Sufi usage) may denote initiates in a religious order. The common term *sihr* (magic), originally from Arabic, acquires numerous connotations where contexts involving both romantic and mystical-theological concerns arise. No single pattern of such underlying meanings, beyond those to be found in a literary language that is rich in poetic and theological usage, has been uncovered that may be used uniformly throughout Hafiz's works. On the other hand, it may well have been the case that the poet at certain junctures freely adopted semantic forms that would reflect the several concerns that at various times bemused him.

POLITICAL WORKS

Political concerns across the range of Hafiz's works may be considered briefly under two headings. In the first place there are a certain number of frankly panegyric poems, which openly were meant to gain or retain the benevolent attention of rulers during his age. Such works are useful largely in that they cast some light on the poet's position in society and may readily be assigned dates; most are from the 1350's and 1360's. Flattery here is couched in terms that to some extent recall the images from other verse. Other poems, however, disclaim interest in political controversies, and indeed regard power as one of the less desirable ends in this life. In some notable lines the reader is advised to practice kindness with friends and courtesy toward enemies; beyond this point the author evidently had little interest in the polemical issues of political philosophy.

POETIC CRAFTSMANSHIP

By inference and from direct references it may be learned that two of the most important literary predecessors of Hafiz were Nizami Ganjavi (c. 1140-c. 1202) and Saʿdi, from the thirteenth century. By his own time the *ghazal* had long been established as a major vehicle of poetic expression. It had become a standard form by which a certain number of distichs, or *bayt*, could be set to a single rhyme; the hemistichs also are made to rhyme. The final distich often contains the author's identifying name; in these lines Hafiz often addressed himself in self-congratulatory tones or in wry and self-effacing expressions. A set number of line feet are used in the verses of a single poem; emphasis follows a pattern that is strictly consistent throughout. To be sure, some variations may be observed among separate compositions. The number of lines may vary, generally between five and twelve; syllables may he emphasized in different patterns from one poem to the next. A notable feature in many of Hafiz's lyrics is the conclusion of each line with the same word; this practice, as a further demonstration of his virtuosity, lends added impact to many poems. Specific standards of emphasis and metric construction may also be found in other poetic forms, such as the elegies and quatrains Hafiz wrote; these works, while expressing some of the same concerns as the lyrics, are of interest largely as illustrating other facets of the author's poetic craftsmanship.

The troubled question of unity was raised by early critics, possibly including some readers from the poet's own lifetime. In discussing the works of the Persian author, Hafiz's first English translator, Sir William Jones, described his verse as "like orient pearls at random strung." One of the British scholar's contemporaries contended that Hafiz's works were utterly incoherent, although he nevertheless managed to produce Latin translations of some poems. Later writers have reached decidedly mixed conclusions on this vexed issue, which has also preoccupied leading Iranists of the twentieth century. Even when allowance is made for the diversity of themes and subjects in works composed possibly over a number of years, there are outward and rather conspicuous signs of inconsistency in individual compositions. Separate lyrics often enough will deal abruptly with two or more topics; sometimes transitions are not clearly made. This trait has given added credibility to theories of multiple mystical meanings in Hafiz's works, but even in this sense internal discrepancies arise. Although metaphorical usage may be considered to conjoin elements in the frankly romantic lyrics, in some poems the setting is transferred from the garden to the tavern with no specific mode of passage. Other lyrics, after the contemplation of worldly cares and joys, shift rather sharply to essentially philosophical or religious concerns. Apart from the poetic conventions of metric length, emphasis, and rhythm that unite the lines within specific compositions, some passages would not be incongruous if affixed or transposed to other works. At the same time, it should be noted that allegations of disunity have been made against only a certain number of poems; it may be argued that in the author's works as a whole, continuity of themes and outlook may readily be discerned. Moreover, where combined meanings are concerned, suggesting both a symbolic and an actual realization of the author's design, it may be contended that conceptual integrity is preserved where imagery and allusion are interwoven about issues of major concern to the poet.

INFLUENTIAL LEGACY

The influence of Hafiz has been very great. In Persia, though the example he set probably precluded yet further summits in the development of the classical *ghazal*, many later writers derived inspiration from his works; the most notable from the great early age of Persian poetry probably was Jami (1414-1492). A number of commentaries and transcribed manuscripts, as well as poetry composed along similar lines, attest the reception of Hafiz in the lands of the Ottoman Empire. Although it was several centuries before Hafiz's works were printed, translations eventually did much to acquaint important creative thinkers with the poems of the Persian author. Among writers in the English language, there are notable references to Hafiz in the works of Alfred, Lord Tennyson, and Ralph Waldo Emerson; even given the vagaries of translation and comparative availability, it has been maintained that among classical Persian authors only Omar Khayyám made a more definite impression in England and America. In continental Europe Hafiz's renown was spread particularly with the publication of a German translation of the *Divan* in 1812-1813, by the Austrian Orientalist Joseph von Hammer-Purgstall. Johann Wolfgang von Goethe utilized this work in according Hafiz pride of place in his *West-östlicher Divan* (1819; *West-eastern divan*, 1877). Later translations of Hafiz, eventually into a number of languages, assisted both in the scholarly assessment and the public availability of his works. In Russia a number of poets were notably influenced by Hafiz's lyrics, beginning probably with Afanasii Afanas'evich Fet (Shenshin) in the middle of the nineteenth century. It may be added as well that the modern Islamic world has also drawn inspiration from the Persian poet's works; here Sir Muhammad Iqbal, of Pakistan, might be mentioned in particular. In Iran itself, a spate of articles, studies, and scholarly editions of Hafiz's poetry have maintained his high reputation during the twentieth century.

BIBLIOGRAPHY

Bell, Gertrude Lowthian. *The Teachings of Hafiz*. London: Octagon Press for the Sufi Trust, 1979. This book includes a preface by E. Denison Ross with a detailed account of the fourteenth century historical and political setting in which Hafiz lived.

Cloutier, David. *News of Love*. Greensboro, S.C.: Unicorn Press, 1984. This book discusses the theme of separation and union in the process of love relationships.

Hafiz. *Drunk on the Wine of the Beloved: One Hundred Poems of Hafiz.* Translated by Thomas Rain Crowe. Boston: Shambhala Publications, 2001. This translation of some of Hafiz's poems includes a useful introduction and a section on the poet himself.

_____. *The Gift: Poems by Hafiz The Great Sufi Master.* Translated by David Ladinsky. New York: Penguin Putman, 1999. A well-known translator of Hafiz presents a major collection of English translations preceded by an introduction that surveys the life and work of Hafiz. Ladinsky's translations are playful, contemporary, and rich in surprising metaphors.

Hillman, Michael C. *Unity in the Ghazals of Hafez.* Minneapolis: Bibliotheca Islamica, 1976. This source is useful in understanding the *ghazal* as a unique lyrical form of Persian poetry.

Meisami, Julie Scott. "The World's Pleasance: Hafiz's Allegorical Gardens." *Comparative Criticism* 5 (1983): 153-185. Insights into one of Hafiz's major motifs.

Ordoobadi, Ahmad. *Hafez and Separation Anxiety.* Shiraz, Iran: S.N., 1979. Ordoobadi seeks connections between psychology and literature through the works of Hafez.

Pourafzal, Haleh, and Roger Montgomery. *The Spiritual Wisdom of Hafez: Teachings of the Philosopher of Love.* Rochester, Vt.: Inner Traditions, 1998. This source includes verse translations, explanations, bibliographical references, and an index.

Schimmel, Annemarie. "Hafiz and His Critics." *Studies in Islam* 16, no. 1 (1979): 1-33. Overview of Hafiz and his commentators.

Wilson, Peter Lamborn, and Nasrollah Pourjavady. *The Drunken Universe: An Anthology of Persian Sufi Poetry.* Grand Rapids, Mich.: Phanes Press, 1987. This is a collection of verse translations includes commentary and a chapter on biobibliographies. The commentary underscores that love poetry by Hafiz can easily be misunderstood when separated from its spiritual context.

J. R. Broadus;
bibliography updated by Mabel Khawaja

DONALD HALL

Born: New Haven, Connecticut; September 20, 1928

PRINCIPAL POETRY

To the Loud Wind and Other Poems, 1955
Exiles and Marriages, 1955
The Dark Houses, 1958
A Roof of Tiger Lilies, 1964
The Alligator Bride: Poems New and Selected, 1969
The Yellow Room: Love Poems, 1971
The Town of Hill, 1975
Kicking the Leaves, 1978
The Happy Man, 1986
The One Day, 1988
Old and New Poems, 1990
The One Day and Poems, 1947-1990, 1991
The Museum of Clear Ideas, 1993
The Old Life, 1996
Without: Poems, 1998
The Painted Bed, 2002

OTHER LITERARY FORMS

Donald Hall became well known not only for his poetry but also for his short fiction, his criticism, and his books on the writing of poetry. He has written or edited approximately one hundred anthologies, textbooks, books of poetry, prose, children's books, criticism, and essays. *Their Ancient Glittering Eyes: Remembering Poets and More Poets* (1992) brings together interviews with T. S. Eliot, Marianne Moore, and Ezra Pound as well as criticism on twentieth century poets. *Life Work* (1993) is a collection of essays about the vocation of being a writer and living in a rural area with people who work at hard physical jobs. *Death to the Death of Poetry: Essays, Reviews, Notes, Interviews* (1994) contains reflective essays on the craft of poetry and criticism. *Principal Products of Portugal: Prose Pieces* (1995) assembles the prose nonfiction that Hall published in a wide variety of periodicals on Henry Adams, Bob Cousy, Henry Moore, and many other topics. *I Am the Dog, I Am the Cat* (1994), *Lucy's Christmas* (1994), *Lucy's Summer* (1995), *When Willard Met Babe Ruth* (1996), and *The Milkman's Boy* (1997) are among his children's books.

ACHIEVEMENTS

Donald Hall, the son of a successful businessman and grandson of a farmer, is poet laureate of New Hampshire—a recognition he regards with bemused pride. His major book, *Exiles and Marriages*, announced his arrival in 1955 as a new voice in poetry and subsequently won the James Laughlin Award the same year; over the next several decades Hall continued to win praise for his poetry and many other kinds of books, including more than one hundred anthologies, textbooks, books of poetry, prose, children's books, criticism, and essays. Among the honors accorded him are the National Book Critics Circle Award, the *Los Angeles Times* Book Prize for *The One Day*, the Lenore Marshall Poetry Prize in 1987 for *The Happy Man*, and the Frost Medal in 1991. Hall's children's book *The Ox-Cart Man* (1979) won a Caldecott Medal. Among the magazines and journals that have published Hall's verse are *The New Yorker, The Iowa Review, The Atlantic, The American Poetry Review*, and *The Virginia Quarterly Review*. Hall's poetry has received generally positive criticism.

Hall has earned a number of prizes for individual works, including the Newdigate Prize of the University of Oxford for "Exile," the Academy of American Poets' Lamont Poetry Selection Award for *Exiles and Marriages*, and the Edna St. Vincent Millay Memorial Prize from the Poetry Society of America.

BIOGRAPHY

Donald Hall was born on September 20, 1928, in New Haven, Connecticut, the son of Donald Andrew Hall and Lucy (Wells) Hall. Hall's father ran a successful dairy business. Hall's early years were divided between the contrasting worlds of middle-class suburbia and a pastoral, sensory-laden life on his grandparents' farm in Danbury, New Hampshire. The Eagle Pond farm has remained in the Hall family for generations, and Hall now lives there, fulfilling a childhood dream to return. Hall has said that his whole intellectual and emotional life evolved from these conflicting cultures: the materialism and normalcy of his parents' world and the closeness to nature and the land of his grandparents' farm.

Spending time with his grandfather and doing farm chores as a boy gave Hall time to reflect. At the age of

Donald Hall

fourteen, he began to write poetry and yearn for a writing career. He also entertained ideas of a career as a great athlete or actor; his later adventures "trying out" for the Pittsburgh Pirates and giving many dramatic poetry readings show that for Hall these notions were not mere fantasies.

Hall entered Phillips Exeter Academy in Exeter, New Hampshire, not for social reasons but because his parents thought highly of the school's academics. He went on to Harvard University, because he believed that institution produced the best teachers. While an undergraduate, Hall dated Adrienne Rich, became friends with Robert Bly and Richard Wilbur, and was one of the founders of the Poet's Theatre in Cambridge, Massachusetts. He won the Garrison and Sergeant prizes and was graduated with his B.A. from Harvard in 1951. On September 13, 1952, he was married to Kirby Thompson—a marriage that produced a son, Andrew, and a daughter Philippa, before it ended in divorce in 1969. Hall was married to the poet Jane Kenyon on April 17, 1972. She died on April 22, 1995, at the age of forty-seven. The tumultuous experience of his wife's courageous struggle with leukemia is the topic of Hall's collection *Without*.

The first major milestone of Hall's academic life saw him going to the University of Oxford in England as a Henry Fellow; there he also won recognition for his first important book, *Exiles and Marriages*. Hall earned his B.Litt. in 1953, then attended Stanford University in 1953-1954 as a Creative Writing Fellow. Returning to Harvard from 1954 to 1957, Hall served as a junior fellow in the Society of Fellows.

Hall suffered two personal tragedies at the same time as his academic and writing careers began to flourish. His grandfather Wesley Wells died in 1953, and his father died in 1955 at the early age of fifty-two. Both deaths made an enormous impact on Hall's imagination; he wrote elegies in honor of both men and has continued to reflect on the convention of remembering the dead.

Meanwhile, Hall served as a broadcaster on several British Broadcasting Corporation television programs featuring poetry, recorded several albums of poetry, including that of Henry Wadsworth Longfellow and John Greenleaf Whittier, and received increasing praise for his own verse.

From 1957 to 1975, Hall served on the faculty of the University of Michigan, rising in the ranks from an assistant to a full tenured professor. Guggenheim Fellowships in 1963-1964 and 1972-73 allowed him to live and write in England, where he first discovered a love for Walt Whitman's poetry. At Michigan, Hall taught creative writing and literature courses, including an intriguing course on literary modernism featuring James Joyce, William Butler Yeats, and Edwin Muir. Some students considered Muir incompatible with the other two writers, but Hall managed to sway opinions through his ferocious energy, charm, wit, and performing skill as a teacher. Hall continued to write prose criticism and essays while in Ann Arbor, publishing *String Too Short to Be Saved*, *Henry Moore*, *Writing Well*, and *Dock Ellis in the Country of Baseball*.

Hall left the university in 1975 to pursue writing full-time and to return to the Eagle Pond farm in New Hampshire, where his grandmother and mother had been born. After his retirement from teaching, Hall published more essays and prose such as *Remembering Poets* and *Seasons at Eagle Pond*. His poetry books published after 1975 present his mature voice.

The most important event in the poet's elder years has been the death of his wife Jane Kenyon on April 22, 1995. They had originally met when she was a student at the University of Michigan. After their marriage, Kenyon and Hall lived and worked together for twenty years at the New Hampshire farm founded by Hall's great-grandfather. Kenyon was an accomplished author in her own right, the writer of four widely admired books of poetry and a translator of the Russian poet Anna Akhmatova. It was Kenyon who convinced Hall to give up his full-time teaching job to try the lifestyle of the freelance writer in the idyllic setting of rural New England. Hall fondly remembers the many years during which they worked together in the picturesque setting of the Eagle Pond Farm.

ANALYSIS

Donald Hall began his career writing formalistic, four-line stanzas with rhyme schemes. The poems' topics vary, but they tend to be emotionally distant reflections. "Elegy for Wesley Wells" in Hall's first major book, *Exiles and Marriages*, however, is marked by a more reflective and impassioned voice, anticipating a major Donald Hall theme in subsequent books: the celebration of life and the mourning of death.

Hall's general pattern of development as a poet begins with objectivity, moves to surrealism and diversity, and culminates with the use of multiple voices. Imaginative texture, experimentation with free verse, and the use of personas increase throughout Hall's work. He writes on a bewildering variety of topics: the changing nature of rural New England, the individual's relationship with history, the classical world of Greek myth, youth and old age, religious artifacts and ceremonies, the fragmentation of the modern world, the world of art, airplanes and crashes, sexuality and parenthood, patterns of thought, and the cycle of birth, life, and death. Hayden Carruth believes that Hall sees the past as better than the present—the values of Hall's grandparents were "more humane and reasonable than the values of their descendants."

Hall's poetry can be best appreciated through attention to five fundamental motifs that run throughout his work: grandfather, grandmother, father, Eagle Pond farm, and Mount Kearsarge. Each motif is a potent imaginative symbol for the past, present, and future.

This may suggest only a Freudian pattern of meaning in Hall's poetry; perhaps he desires to supplant his forefathers and mate with mother earth. Hall's overriding themes, however, are grief, celebration, and making sense of the cycle of life through ordering one's consciousness. He chooses to explore the cycle of life through this cluster of motifs associated with rural New England, but his poetry contains many other themes.

Hall's poems sometimes defy literal translation or easy paraphrase. His use of surrealism, stream-of-consciousness sequences, and primal archetypes prevents superficial descriptions of his work. At his best, he challenges himself and his readers, discovering many voices and points of view on fundamental human concerns. Hall can be lyrical, humorous, despondent, satiric, grim, and joyous all in the same book. In a book of interviews and essays, *Goatfoot Milktongue Twinbird* (1978), Hall explains his philosophy of poet as both word maker and mystic; the mystical or "vatic" voice provides inspiration and insight yet sometimes creates texts beyond the poet's own control. The poet sometimes says things he or she does not understand, because poetry approximates a preverbal response to the world.

EXILES AND MARRIAGES

Hall's first major book, *Exiles and Marriages*, explores the themes of loss, isolation, and renewal. The tone is somber and detached, slightly ironic. Already Hall is absorbed in one of the predominant themes of his career, reconstructing the past and comparing modern middle-class complacency and emptiness to the values of ancient Greece. In this collection he initiates a search for heroes; his grandfather, the Lone Ranger, and Oedipus are among those considered.

In the most philosophical of his early poems, "Exile," Hall writes of the modern self-destructive tendency to move on endlessly, constantly rearranging the furniture of the mind without reflecting on what it means. By distancing themselves and avoiding the pain of loss, Hall says, modern people become exiles and transients.

Hall seeks communion with the past in "Elegy for Wesley Wells," a poem written for his grandfather, who died in 1953. This poem explores the decaying world of a farm left without a farmer to watch over it; animals run awry and fields grow with weeds. Hall's mythic recreation of his grandfather's world presents the values

he learned from watching his grandfather work the fields. Wesley Wells was a man rich not in material wealth but in the experience of life—milking, cultivating, repairing. When young people take the place of men such as Wells, the poet believes, certain noble virtues die. Looking back at his childhood spent on his grandfather's farm, the poet considers that he has lost something beyond replacement. Yet he has already implied a path toward renewal that subsequent books will pursue.

THE DARK HOUSES

In *The Dark Houses*, Hall focuses on the loss of his grandfather and father. A certain homesickness and lyrical despair inform poems with topics ranging from the uncertainty of language to experiences of isolation to religious ceremonies. In "Christmas Eve in Whitneyville," Hall writes of his father's death in 1955, exploring an emotional attachment that made him a prisoner but a love that transcended stultifying suburban order.

Poems in *The Dark Houses* explore the themes of suffering, loss, decay, and a failure to overcome limitations. An experimental series of poems that take their titles from Edvard Munch paintings shows Hall's conversion from objective, private suffering to subjective, imaginary journeys. While most of *The Dark Houses* dwells on grief and loss, some poems point toward an increased spectrum of voices. Hall becomes more fascinated with artistic expression, creativity, and, by implication, renewal.

In fact, the major difference between *The Dark Houses* and *A Roof of Tiger Lilies* is Hall's increased reliance on surreal and fantastic images from the subconscious. He begins to reach out in a variety of directions, relying on references to sculptor Henry Moore and writers Charles Tomlinson, Henry James, and Edwin Muir, and an allusion to the Bronze Age Mycenean culture in one poem. Here he abandons the traditional verse forms of his first books and experiments with free verse, at times using humor in poems such as "Self-Portrait as a Bear" and "The Moon." Though he does not completely abandon his obsession with dead relatives and the New Hampshire farm, he takes new approaches toward them.

"THE DAYS"

A poem from *A Roof of Tiger Lilies* representative of Hall's new style is "The Days," in which the poet imagines himself as an old man contemplating the past from his easy chair in Connecticut. A portentous concluding stanza of this poem says that the days of this man's past lie buried underground; a huge chorus of voices and paintings from different points of view wait to be unearthed. The old man wishes that he could travel to this buried world like a tourist with a camera and then return to the earth's surface with scrupulous snapshots of lost experiences. This is precisely what Hall sets out to do in subsequent books of poetry; in fact, "The Days" is almost a prophecy of his later book *The One Day.*

THE ALLIGATOR BRIDE

In some ways Hall's next book, *The Alligator Bride*, is his most uncharacteristic. Reading *The Alligator Bride* gives one the impression that Hall has exhausted his own experience; he now looks outward into the realms of aircraft and art and inward into the language of dreams. The book shows an influence of the mystical poetry of Yeats. Hall creates an irrational world of associations, colors, and emotion without explicit meaning. The reader must "float" upon the images of these poems, not attempting to force a literal or abstract translation of meaning. Each reader of *The Alligator Bride* constructs an individual, idiosyncratic interpretation from its bizarre collage of images. The book does, however, include "Mount Kearsarge," a potent recollection of the lost childhood hours of rocking on Grandfather's porch, looking at the top of the blue, hazy mountain. *The Alligator Bride* also includes tender memories of Hall's grandfather in "The Table," where the poet recalls a voice that "talked forever" and wrapped him "with love that asked for nothing." Despite its foray into the surreal, this collection continues the great themes of his career.

THE YELLOW ROOM

In *The Yellow Room*, Hall shifts his focus to love poetry, describing the progression of a relationship from beginning to end. The surrealistic tone of *The Alligator Bride* seems momentarily overshadowed by an incipient psychological drama. Hall works with honesty in narrative free-verse forms in *The Yellow Room*, developing the theme of adjustment from the yellow room—the internal world of the lovers—to a remote island where the poet exiles himself after the affair ends. In the beginning stages, the poet's interest in celebrating the flesh and

making love all day long give a certain sentimentality and egocentric narrowness to some poems.

THE TOWN OF HILL

The Town of Hill finds Hall returning to some of the dreamlike images and topics of *The Alligator Bride*; the reader is constantly aware of a blurred line between fantasy and reality in these poems. The topics range from a humorous prose poem about a convocation of dead presidents to the sale of frozen rats in Detroit as pet food to the false praise and piety of poetry readings.

The title poem, "The Town of Hill," explores a New Hampshire town that was evacuated in a 1940's water-control project; the short lines and bald images emphasize abandonment and the remoteness of the past. This town, covered by water as if it had been a dream, resembles all forgotten memories—images that become unreal once one calls them to the surface again. This is a place to which Hall will return, but for now a door shuts under water, rendering the memories remote. Other poems such as "White Apples" raise the icon of Hall's father, calling him again from the past, causing the poet to sit up in bed and stare at another closed door.

Many of the poems in *The Town of Hill* border on the subconscious or mythic, being utterly nonrational or ineffable in content. At its best, Hall's impressionist verse can create a powerful visceral response in a reader, a feeling of kinship with a poet who has journeyed through the forbidding territory of the mind. Some poems in the book approach tongue-in-cheek satire of suburban middle-class values. In "To a Waterfowl," Hall pictures polite society women, wearing hats like pink ducks, who applaud timidly, avoiding the strangeness that lies within their own hearts. "Poem with One Fact" prowls around posh Detroit suburbs, cataloging the emptiness and cold-blooded consumerism running through the lives of common folk. "The Green Shelf" shows the speaker driving past a man who has suffered a heart attack while mowing his lawn; the speaker returns to his neatly ordered house to arrange his soup cans on the shelf. The overall tone of *The Town of Hill* is that of a tour guide who is introducing travelers to another dimension of reality, finding the horrors both within and outside normalcy.

KICKING THE LEAVES

Hall's next three major books in many ways transcend everything he wrote before them: *Kicking the Leaves*, *The Happy Man*, and *The One Day* each announce an important new phase in Hall's career. Each of these three was awarded more critical recognition than any of Hall's previous books.

Kicking the Leaves is the most accessible and emotionally profound of Hall's books, combining the weirdness and imaginative color of his surrealistic poems with the homeliness and honesty of his memory poems about his grandparents. *Kicking the Leaves* was occasioned by Hall's retirement from academic life and return to his grandparent's farm in New Hampshire; this phase of his life was therefore both a brave new venture into a full-time writing career and a nostalgic retreat into happy memories of childhood. This risk taking and sense of renewal allow Hall to respond fully to a barrage of emotions, ideas, memories, and themes. *Kicking the Leaves* contains only thirteen poems, but they are long, discursive reflections that attain a remarkable grace and intelligence.

Every poem in *Kicking the Leaves* in one way or another reflects on the theme of death and reconstructing the past. Many of the poems explore a process of loss, reflection, subconscious journeys, memories, and renewal. The poems are divided between those imaginatively remote from experience, such as "Eating the Pig" and "Wolf Knife," and those directly reflecting on Hall's ancestors, such as "Flies" and "Kicking the Leaves." Hall asks the reader to immerse himself or herself in his nostalgia for his grandparents, but one is not assaulted with trivia or sententiae. These poems are universal and resonant, even basic in their concerns: returning from a football game, driving back to a hometown, waiting at Grandmother's bedside, remembering horses that faithfully worked the land.

"Eating the Pig" describes how a pedestrian dinner party became in the mind of the poet a bizarre ritual of Communion. Hungry visitors eagerly devour a stuffed pig, feeling slight discomfort as they look at its intact head. Hall imagines himself speaking to the pig, imploring it to forgive this wanton destruction of its body. Suddenly the reader enters the realm of myth as Hall invokes the ancient Tigris and Euphrates rivers, and the party becomes a sort of eucharistic communion with the past as twelve participants take the body of the pig into

their own. A similar rich fantasy can be found in "The Wolf Knife" and "The Black Faced Sheep."

"Kicking the Leaves" and "Names of Horses" have both been widely anthologized in college poetry textbooks. In the title poem, Hall recalls primal memories of kicking colored leaves at the New Hampshire farm, celebrating the fall season and the sense of shelter provided by the closeness of the leaves and his grandparents' presence. The poet remembers carrying out the ritual of raking leaves with his own father and daughter, wondering as years pass where each subsequent autumn will find them. The leaves tell stories to the poet about remembering the past and attaching oneself to the earth. Finally, the poet accepts his place in the grand scheme of life and death, accepting the sensuous pleasures of leaves amid all the changes in life. The kicking of leaves lends a permanence to an otherwise brief passage through life.

"Names of Horses" is another celebration and coming to terms with death, this time remembering beasts of burden who faithfully dragged plows and wagons year after year. The poem makes a powerful statement about accepting the cycle of life and death—as does all of *Kicking the Leaves*—when Hall remembers putting one horse to death when it became too old to work. This is the fate waiting all living creatures: an anonymous pit in the ground. Yet one can go on in life comforted by the fact that others will remember. The survivors reflect on the past and in doing so create new meaning for their own lives.

THE HAPPY MAN

In *The Happy Man*, Hall opens up a new spectrum of topics and returns to the formal verse patterns of his earlier work. *The Happy Man* is more introspective and philosophical than *Kicking the Leaves*; Hall maintains a solemn, rather dark tone, contemplating many older men and women haunted by ambiguous ghosts from the past. Many characters in this book have suffered great disappointments. Hall uses some of his usual pastoral imagery, but *The Happy Man* struggles with a complexity and varied chorus of voices unanticipated by previous books. Hall brings the whole notion of happiness into question, working toward his own new definition.

The Happy Man is divided into four sections, titled "Barnyards" "Shrubs Burnt Away," "Men Driving Cars," and "Sisters." The major theme of the book is the process through which people decide to create their own happiness. The longest and most complex section, "Shrubs Burnt Away," describes the plight of an alcoholic man who confronts his past. An assortment of others also search for happiness—an elusive dream for people plagued by neglect, breakdown, and abuse. There is irony in the fact that the harder these characters search for happiness, the more difficulty they have in finding it.

In "The Twelve Seasons," Hall experiments with a twelve-line stanza, over the course of twelve stanzas blending imagery from barnyard, kitchen, farmhouse, and forest. He develops a passage through four seasons of weather and through seasons of the past; the poem contemplates growing old, brushes with death, and creating strength from meaningful work and remembering the dead. Dominant motifs from *The Happy Man* include building toward death and the image of Mount Kearsarge on the horizon, reminding the poet of lost values he seeks to replace with fresh insight into the state of his own happiness.

After numerous poems expressing confusion and suffering, *The Happy Man* concludes in a crescendo of faith and a positive statement about the meaning of life. Poems such as "Granite and Grass" and "A Sister by the Pond" show Hall's process of overcoming grief and despair through a determined celebration of life's positive qualities.

The last poem in *The Happy Man*, "The Day I Was Older," is another beautiful elegy for Hall's father. In ten-line stanzas the poet contemplates various artifacts from a domestic scene: a clock, a newspaper, a pond, a cup. Each brief section takes on a special meaning as the poet realizes that he has crossed a barrier between himself and death; the previous night he outlived his father. Now he remembers kissing the cheek of a dying man, and he writes "The Day I Was Older" in his father's honor, speaking to a presence that will never cease to exist in his imagination. Though Hall remembers his father in all the artifacts, the cup can never be completely emptied. As he himself approaches death, the poet continues to have this memory and the values his father taught him.

THE ONE DAY

The One Day, Hall's next book of poetry, is a departure in style and structure. This single, book-length poem resembles a work of fiction in its complex framework of characters, settings, and narratives. *The One Day* echoes with influences from the Bible, Vergil, Juvenal, Robert Frost, and Walt Whitman. It is less autobiographical and more ambitious than anything Hall had yet attempted; its seriousness and historical perspective have an explicit purpose—to enumerate notions of human multiplicity and define a house of consciousness that will allow for personal renewal.

In ten-line stanzas, *The One Day* focuses on a male and a female voice who tell stories about growing up, attempting to find meaningful work, suffering from disappointment, and growing old. The two major voices quote from others, and their stories freely intermingle. Multiplicity and imaginative richness give *The One Day* a dreamlike, intuitive organization somewhat reminiscent of poems from *The Town of Hill*.

The One Day is composed of three major sections, "Shrubs Burnt Away" (based on a section from *The Happy Man*), "Four Classic Texts," and "To Build a House." The style is stream of consciousness with many references to history, literature, and religion. With the background of this heterogeneous chorus of voices, Hall emphasizes the need to build a house in one's mind, to come to an understanding of the various conflicts and disappointments each person must face. According to Hall, in order to survive one must construct a place of solace in one's mind where one has the space to evaluate experience. In the end, *The One Day*, like *The Happy Man*, celebrates what life offers as the poet renews himself and foresees leaving this world in a happy frame of mind. *The One Day* makes a profound statement about preparing for death, enjoying love, finding meaningful work, and building toward self-knowledge and social order.

OLD AND NEW POEMS

Old and New Poems selects from Hall's previous books of poetry and adds twenty-two new poems. Collected for the first time are four of his older poems. In "The Hole," he writes of the emptiness of those who make their psychic houses into jails. Because the dying man in this poem (Hall's father) digs himself into an isolated well of suffering, he distances himself from the currents of life around him. *Old and New Poems* is an impressive documentation of the range and achievement of

Hall's career. He has said that he could not resist editing some of the lines he first set down at age eighteen, although many poems have not been altered substantially.

In some of the new poems, Hall experiments with a new step-down line, while others continue the narrative model and use of different voices of *The One Day*. In some of the new poems the reader senses a fear of convalescence and meaningless old age. Hall still looks to memories of friends and family as sources for inspiration. Echoes and allusions from previous books abound, as if he were attempting to survey and reiterate some of his classic themes. Yet he looks beyond autobiography in "Edward's Anecdote" and "Carlotta's Confession."

"Praise for Death" is another elegiac piece, this time in thirty-eight numbered stanzas of five lines whose sentences often leap across the white spaces. Hall combines his predominant patterns of thought (mourning and celebration) in this poetry slide-show of memories past. The poet proclaims his desire to die in a positive frame of mind. Through death each person will meet the great answer to a question pleaded out by the course of his or her whole life. Remembering those who have died and imagining the afterlife, the poet creates a lyrical song of praise. While the world appears to decay and meaningless new voices replace old, familiar ones, the poet takes comfort in this great equalizer. "Praise for Death" in many ways restates an idea that Hall began developing in his very first book, in his "Elegy to Wesley Wells."

THE MUSEUM OF CLEAR IDEAS

The Museum of Clear Ideas indicates the energy of Hall's poetic productivity even in the latter stages of his career, as many of the poems were originally published in periodicals such as *The Atlantic Monthly* and *Harvard Review*. Hall's book begins with "Another Elegy," a humorous and pathetic portrait of a fictional alcoholic poet named Bill Trout who lives a crazy life of traveling, fishing, and aspiring to be a minister. Approximately half the book is devoted to a series of poems, "The Museum of Clear Ideas," that take their inspiration from the classical Roman poet Horace, known for satires and epistles that used wry irony to mock the poet-persona as well as the ostensible victims of the satire.

Hall creates the persona of a Disney character, Horace Horsecollar, and pursues his satires on various topics such as celebrities, famous historical characters, and re-

ligion. Horace even recites an ode to a jet airplane. The book includes a nine-part poem called "Baseball" and three "Extra Innings," which constitute about a third of the book.

THE OLD LIFE

Hall's twelfth book of poetry contains several important lyrics, including "The Night of the Day," an account of two cows meandering on a road. The poem's title makes a thematic connection with Hall's earlier important book *The One Day*. "The Thirteenth Inning" creates a transition between this new book and the baseball reflections of *The Museum of Clear Ideas*. The ninety-six-page title poem is a strong autobiographical reflection on the ups and downs of a life characterized by joy and grief, celebration and defeat, youthful passion and the wisdom of old age, the vicissitudes of love, marriage, family, and the responses of the turbulent literary world. Hall's warm reflections on his conversations with his daughter and grandson build a beautifully complete description of life fully lived and love deeply felt. The final poem of the book, "Without," invokes one of Hall's favorite literary modes, the elegy, this time taking up a most personal subject, the death of the poet's wife Jane Kenyon.

WITHOUT

In some ways, Hall has been preparing his whole life to write this wrenching, poignant account about the death of his wife, the poet Jane Kenyon. It is a sad and anguish-filled book not unlike C. S. Lewis's *A Grief Observed* (1961). Hall chronicles the progress of his wife's illness, her medical treatments, and her courageous desire to face life and death without flinching. "Her Long Illness" is a poem that continues at intervals throughout the book, describing the many friends, doctors, nurses, and neighbors who play a role in the story that rings with grief. Readers also get a sense of the immense joy the couple knew during their years together, so that finally the book is not about despair as much as it is a celebration of a life together. The poem-letters that Hall writes to his wife after her death are unsurpassed in their honesty, passion, and emotional intensity.

OTHER MAJOR WORKS
SHORT FICTION: *The Ideal Bakery*, 1987.
PLAY: *The Bone Ring*, pr. 1986.

NONFICTION: *String Too Short to Be Saved*, 1961; *Henry Moore*, 1966; *Marianne Moore: The Cage and the Animal*, 1970; *Writing Well*, 1973; *Dock Ellis in the Country of Baseball*, 1976 (with Dock Ellis); *Remembering Poets: Reminiscences and Opinions*, 1978; *Goatfoot Milktongue Twinbird*, 1978; *The Weather for Poetry*, 1982; *Fathers Playing Catch with Sons: Essays on Sport (Mostly Baseball)*, 1984; *Seasons at Eagle Pond*, 1987; *Poetry and Ambition: Essays, 1982-88*, 1988; *Anecdotes of Modern Art: From Rousseau to Warhol*, 1990; *Here at Eagle Pond*, 1990; *Their Ancient Glittering Eyes: Remembering Poets and More Poets*, 1992; *Life Work*, 1993; *Death to the Death of Poetry: Essays, Reviews, Notes, Interviews*, 1994; *Principal Products of Portugal: Prose Pieces*, 1995; *Donald Hall in Conversation with Ian Hamilton*, 2000.

CHILDREN'S LITERATURE: *The Ox-Cart Man*, 1979; *I Am the Dog, I Am the Cat*, 1994; *Lucy's Christmas*, 1994; *Lucy's Summer*, 1995; *When Willard Met Babe Ruth*, 1996; *The Milkman's Boy*, 1997.

EDITED TEXT: *The Oxford Illustrated Book of American Children's Poems*, 1999.

BIBLIOGRAPHY

Davie, Donald. "Frost, Eliot, Thomas, Pound." *The New York Times Book Review* (February 19, 1978): 15, 33. Reviews Hall's book *Remembering Poets* and Hall's notion of the poet in contemporary culture. Praises him for humanizing the poetic endeavor, but takes issue with some evaluations.

Hall, Donald. *Donald Hall in Conversation with Ian Hamilton*. London: Between the Lines, 2000. This book reprints many interviews of Hall by Ian Hamilton originally published in periodicals.

_____. Interview by Liam Rector. *American Poetry Review* 18 (January, 1989): 39-46. The interviewer asks Hall to place himself in a scheme of literary generations, reflect on his youth, and talk about his career achievements. Hall talks candidly about his friendships with other poets and gives his own assessment of his work. The interview is included in Rector's edited collection on Hall.

Hansen, Tom. "On Writing Poetry: Four Contemporary Poets." *College English* 44 (March, 1982): 265-273. Focuses on *Goatfoot Milktongue Twinbird* and Hall's statement of faith in the poet's vocation. Explains his use of the title words in his psychomythology, his concept of the poet-priest-scholar, and the sensuous enjoyment of reading poetry.

Moyers, Bill. "A Life Together." Video in *The Moyers Collection/Bill Moyers Journal*, produced by David Grubin. Princeton, N.J.: Films for the Humanities, 1993. One hourlong interview with Donald Hall and Jane Kenyon about poetry, the creative process, and a life together.

Rector, Liam. "About Donald Hall." *Ploughshares* 27, nos. 2/3 (Fall, 2001): 270-274. Rector briefly profiles Hall's life and work.

_____, ed. *The Day I Was Older: On the Poetry of Donald Hall*. Santa Cruz, Calif.: Story Line, 1989. The first book-length study of Hall's work, this volume includes essays of criticism and commentary by Robert Bly, W. D. Snodgrass, and other contemporary poets. Contains fifteen of Hall's poems, photographs, an interview, book reviews, and an excellent bibliography of Hall's work.

Spencer, Brent. "The Country of Donald Hall: A Review Essay." *Poet and Critic* 12 (1980): 30-38. Spencer reviews *Goatfoot Milktongue Twinbird* and several poetry books, explaining how Hall's concept of the poet as maker and mystic grants him enormous freedoms. The essay contains some excellent discussions of individual poems and a general statement about the nature of Hall's poetry.

Ullman, Leslie. Review of *Without*, by Donald Hall. *Poetry* 173, no. 4 (February, 1999): 312-314. Ullman discusses *Without*, an autobiographical work dealing with the fifteen months during which Hall's wife, the poet Jane Kenyon, battled leukemia, and with the following year of mourning.

Jonathan L. Thorndike,
updated by Thorndike

ARTHUR HENRY HALLAM

Born: London, England; February 1, 1811
Died: Vienna, Austria; September 15, 1833

PRINCIPAL POETRY

Poems, 1830

Remains, in Verse and Prose, 1834 (Henry Hallam, editor)

Poems of Arthur Henry Hallam, 1893 (Richard Le Gallienne, editor)

The Writings of Arthur Hallam, 1943 (T. H. Vail Motter, editor, poetry and prose).

OTHER LITERARY FORMS

In addition to his poetry, Arthur Henry Hallam also wrote essays. Expository prose was probably more congenial to him than verse, and his most promising efforts were in that area.

ACHIEVEMENTS

Arthur Henry Hallam died at the age of twenty-two without having written any major poetry, yet he left behind unmistakable evidence of literary ability that, had he lived, might well have developed into lasting eminence (though probably in criticism rather than in poetry). While his verse displayed promise, none of his poems proved to be immortal; and his work does not appear in standard literary anthologies. For all its tantalizing possibility, Hallam's surviving literary output has interest chiefly as a revelation of the mind and personality valued by Alfred, Lord Tennyson above all others. Besides their relevance to Tennyson, however, Hallam's apprentice verses are still a minor literary achievement in their own right.

BIOGRAPHY

Arthur Henry Hallam, the son of a famous historian, was born in London on February 1, 1811. He spent the summer of 1818 abroad with his father, Henry, learning French. After two years of preparatory school at Putney, Hallam again traveled throughout the summer and then entered Eton, remaining for five years. While there, he was an active participant in debates on issues such as Catholic emancipation, the disarming of the Highlanders after Culloden, the merits of Thomas Jefferson, John Milton's political conduct, ancient versus modern writers, the character of Augustus, Greek accomplishments in history and drama, and many similar topics. Hallam left Eton, properly confirmed, in July,

1827, and then went on to Italy, where he remained for nine important months. Returning to England by way of Switzerland, he entered Trinity College, Cambridge, in October, 1828, and was soon recognized as an erratic but brilliant student who was already showing promise as a poet. In April, 1829, Hallam met Tennyson, thereby beginning the most eloquently celebrated friendship in English literature, and incidentally inviting a comparison of poetic talents that has never been to Hallam's advantage.

On May 9, 1829, Hallam was elected to membership in the Apostles, a debating society at Cambridge which included most of those whose fellowship and intellectual stimulation would be important to him, including Tennyson, for a time. Though Tennyson was relatively indifferent to the club and its disputations, Hallam relished this further opportunity for debate, and he presented several excellent essays to its members. Perhaps the most decisive addition to his own outlook gained from the Apostles was an appreciation for the poetry of Percy Bysshe Shelley, which quickly became a passion.

After illness, poetic defeat (by Tennyson), and summer travel in France and Switzerland, Hallam returned to Trinity in the fall of 1829 and arranged for the first English edition of Shelley's *Adonais* (1821). His friendship with Tennyson also deepened considerably. During Easter vacation in 1830, Hallam visited the Tennysons at Somersby in Lincolnshire and fell in love with Alfred's sister Emily. That May, a collection of his verses (*Poems*) circulated privately. Some of its lyrics had originally been intended to appear jointly with Tennyson's, but this plan was quashed by Henry Hallam; so when *Poems, Chiefly Lyrical* appeared in June, 1830, it contained Tennyson's work only. That summer Hallam and Tennyson were off to Spain on behalf of rebels opposing the Spanish monarchy. Tennyson always retained fond memories of this exciting and scenic venture, which he recalled in a poem of 1864.

In 1831, however, Hallam and Tennyson were together less often, for when the latter's father died in February, Alfred left Cambridge immediately. In March, Hallam's father forbade his seeing Emily Tennyson for a year. By that time, Hallam was beginning to relinquish his poetic ambitions, having been regularly overshadowed by his more promising friend. He acknowledged this disparity implicitly with a perceptive review of Tennyson's poetry, which was published that August in the *Englishman's Magazine*. It is Hallam's most important literary criticism. (A second essay by him on Tennyson, intended for the *Edinburgh Review* in 1832, has disappeared.) On October 29, Hallam read to the Apostles a striking review of his own religious opinions called "Theodicaea Novissima" that lastingly impressed and influenced Tennyson.

In January, 1832, after some confusion over residency, Hallam was graduated from Cambridge. By March, his father's prohibition had expired and Arthur (now of age) was free to announce his year-old engagement to Emily Tennyson, though the immediate result was only a tedious series of unsatisfactory financial negotiations between the Hallam and Tennyson families. Arthur, despairing and in bad health, was forced to work in a London law office copying documents. He spent much of his literary energies that year translating poems from Dante's *La vita nuova* (c. 1292; *The New Life*). There was a short journey up the Rhine with Tennyson in July, a visit to Somersby in August, and an ecstatic Christmas there at year's end. Just when Hallam's life promised some fulfillment, however, he became seriously ill, went abroad for one last summer with his father, and died unexpectedly from a brain hemorrhage in Vienna on September 15, having attained the age of twenty-two years, seven and one-half months. In an episode that Tennyson would later versify, his body was then brought back to England and buried at Clevedon, on the Bristol Channel, on January 3, 1834.

Remains, in Verse and Prose, edited by his father, appeared later that spring, circulating privately (the first public edition was in 1862). Tennyson himself then spent almost seventeen years meditating upon the significance of his brilliant friend's death and writing the poems that would eventually comprise *In Memoriam* (1850); he also named his son for Hallam. A selection of Hallam's poems, together with his essay on the poetry of Tennyson, were edited with an appreciative introduction by Richard Le Gallienne in 1893. An invaluable edition of *The Writings of Arthur Hallam* (1943) by T. H. Vail Motter has been superseded in part by the texts and notes in Jack Kolb's edition of Hallam's letters, containing many poems.

ANALYSIS

Arthur Henry Hallam's chief contribution to English poetry lies in his influence upon Tennyson, including their rivalry and friendship, their mutual literary and intellectual reflections, and the tragic questioning of Hallam's loss that resulted in Tennyson's *In Memoriam*. Both were aspiring poets prior to their meeting, but Hallam's kindred mind almost certainly deepened Tennyson's in certain respects and helped him to some liberating influences, those of Shelley and Italy in particular. Tennyson's lifelong commitments to political and religious freedom, scenic travel, and poetic concern with landscape and geology probably owed a great deal to Hallam. Anyone familiar with Tennyson's poems, moreover, is aware that Hallam inspired not only *In Memoriam* but also some shorter poems, such as "Ulysses," which was in large part a heroic response to the news of Hallam's death, and "Vastness," which was in part a poignant reminiscence of it. Tennyson's longest poem, *Idylls of the King* (1859-1885), an epic of King Arthur, is thought to reflect the idealized humanity that Hallam might well have achieved. Full discussion of Tennyson's poetry, then, would deal at length with Hallam as a literary influence.

POETRY AS BIOGRAPHY

The poems that Hallam left are especially valuable as biography. While still at Eton in 1827 he published some verses on a story connected with the Lake of Killarney in the *Eton Miscellany*, but these were not reprinted by his father. His nine-month stay in Italy that year resulted in a flourish of poetry, much of it inspired by a young woman of twenty-six named Anna Wintour, whose dark eyes and floating hair he found irresistible. Several of his poetic tributes to her were in Italian (as some letters between Emily Tennyson and himself would later be). Other poems concerning Italy celebrated *objects d'art* in the Pitti Palace in Florence and the graves of John Keats and Shelley in Rome. After returning to England in 1828, Hallam continued to think of Anna Wintour and wrote for her a long poem, full of Dante and William Wordsworth, titled "A Farewell to the South," which was published in 1830 but suppressed in 1834. It compares favorably with what other poets have written at the age of seventeen.

MEDITATIVE FRAGMENTS

In 1829, Hallam wrote (and published the next year) a series of "Meditative Fragments in Blank Verse," as he called them, which attest to his struggles not only with spiritual questions but also with desperate fears of approaching insanity, as his letters of that year attest. Another poem, called "Lines Written in Great Depression of Mind" (March, 1829), even expresses his wish for death. That April, in the first of three vain tries, Hallam attempted to win the Chancellor's Medal at Cambridge with a long poem on the required topic, "Timbuctoo"; it was published separately as a pamphlet in 1828, reprinted in *Poems*, and appeared again in the *Remains, in Verse and Prose*. In three important footnotes, Hallam cited Plato, Samuel Taylor Coleridge, and Shelley (whom he praised) as sources. The prize was awarded to Tennyson's poem instead. Though naturally disappointed not to have won himself, Hallam (who had written a sonnet "To A. T." in May) was ever afterward a firm admirer of Tennyson's poetry and preferred it to his own.

TRAVEL POEMS

Hallam's French and Scottish travels of 1829 resulted in further poems, some of which are little more than exercises in versification and dialect. Two poems from July, "Sonnet Written in the Pass of Glencoe" and another "Written in View of Ben Lomond," evince Hallam's interest in geology; they have been compared with similar passages in *In Memoriam*. That same month Hallam visited Glenarbach, formerly the seat of Lord Webb Seymour (a geologist and friend of Henry Hallam), the home of Ann Robertson, who had been born in Italy and was there to rival Anna Wintour (unsuccessfully) when Hallam was there in 1827. Seven of Hallam's poems were addressed to Ann and her family, especially "A Farewell to Glenarbach," which reveals the influence of Wordsworth and several other predecessors upon Hallam, who was then eighteen.

POETIC INFLUENCES

Many of the verses written by Hallam throughout 1829 (his most prolific year) are those of an aspiring young poet who was learning to expand his capacities by studying and imitating more accomplished predecessors. Thus, his Scottish poems were frequently Words-

worthian, including "Written on the Banks of the Tay," "Stanzas Written in a Steam-boat," "Sonnet Written at Fingal's Cave, on the Island of Staffa" (compare Wordsworth's) and, more obviously, "Sonnet Written in the Pass of Killiecrankie, and Alluding to That Written by Mr. Wordsworth in the Same Place." Hallam's "Stanzas Written After Visiting Melrose Abbey in Company of Sir Walter Scott" commemorated an aged author and his hospitality without fully realizing what a favor had been received, while "The Burthen of Istambol" revealed that George Gordon, Lord Byron's influence upon Hallam was still active.

At Malvern in September, 1829, Hallam wrote "Lines Addressed to Alfred Tennyson," the first clear indication of their intimacy. He also attempted "Wordsworth at Glenarbach: An Episode," recalling a conversation with Ann Robertson about the poet; strongly indebted to Shelley's "Julian and Maddalo," it suggests that Hallam was experimenting further with poetic diction and forms. Thus, in "To One Early Loved, Now in India"—for which read Italy—he tried nine-line Spenserian stanzas (rather than his more frequent eight-line ones) in a final poetic tribute, the last of eleven poems in all, to Anna Wintour. In December of the same year, Hallam wrote a less experimental but biographically significant sonnet full of his rapture at meeting Emily Tennyson.

POETIC DECLINE

Thereafter the Tennysons were prominent in Hallam's poetry, but its volume was decreasing. During the Easter vacation visit to Somersby in 1830, Hallam wrote one sonnet to Alfred Tennyson and three to Emily. There were then two further poems addressed to Emily and her sister Mary, love poems for Emily alone, a lament for the death of the Reverend George Clayton Tennyson, and one more sonnet for Alfred's brother Charles, who was also a poet worthy of attention. "Stanzas," one of the poems addressed to Emily, was published in the *Englishman's Magazine* in August, 1831, together with Hallam's review of Tennyson's poems.

By 1832 Hallam's poetic ambitions had subsided, largely unfulfilled; he wrote only a handful of poems thereafter. "Scene at Rome," in 155 lines of blank verse, is a dialogue (imitating Walter Savage Landor) between Raffaelle and Fiammetta in the former's studio; it is very much like prose. "Lines Spoken in the Character of Pygmalion" are better, anticipating Robert Browning; they were actually spoken by Hallam as part of a charade. In September, he offered a sonnet "on an old German picture of the three kings of Cologne" to *Fraser's Magazine*, where it was published five months later. Finally, in "Long hast thou wandered," a poem of uncertain date, Hallam bade farewell to poetic composition; with few exceptions, all of his important literary work after October, 1831, was in prose.

OTHER MAJOR WORKS

NONFICTION: *The Letters of Arthur Henry Hallam*, 1981 (Jack Kolb, editor).

BIBLIOGRAPHY

Chandler, James. "Hallam, Tennyson, and the Poetry of Sensation: Aestheticist Allegories of a Counter-Public Sphere." *Studies in Romanticism* 33, no. 4 (Winter, 1994): 527. An examination of late Romantic aestheticism in the works of Hallam and Tennyson.

Clausen, Christopher. "Arthur Henry Hallam and the Victorian Promise." *Sewanee Review* 101, no. 3 (Summer, 1993): 375. A discussion of the differences between Tennyson's *In Memoriam* and William Gladstone's essay "Arthur Henry Hallam."

Hallam, Arthur Henry. *The Letters of Arthur Henry Hallam*. Edited by Jack Kolb. Columbus: Ohio State University Press, 1981. This selection of Hallam's voluminous correspondence includes many responses from personages such as Alfred, Lord Tennyson, his sister Emily, William Ewart Gladstone, and Richard Monckton Milnes. Kolb's introduction argues for the importance of the correspondence as Hallam's means "to keep pure and limpid," in Hallam's own words, "the source of all generous emotions."

_____. *The Poems of Arthur Henry Hallam*. Edited by Richard Le Gallienne. London: Elkin Mathews & John Lane, 1893. Contains a selection of poems, as well as the essay "On Some of the Characteristics of Modern Poetry, and on the Lyrical Poems of Alfred Tennyson." Le Gallienne's introduction provides a biographical sketch that explores the bases of Hallam's aesthetic writings. The poetry remains largely unanalyzed.

_____. *The Writings of Arthur Hallam*. Edited by T. H. Vail Motter. London: Oxford University Press, 1943. Collects Hallam's poems, essays, reviews, and translations, as well as juvenilia, an evaluation of the critical writings, and a note on Hallam's voluminous correspondence. Also contains a useful chronology of Hallam's life. Motter explains in his preface that the collection attempts to correct the perception of Hallam as a "mere shadow" of Alfred, Lord Tennyson.

Kolb, Jack. "'On First Looking into Pope's Iliad': Hallam's Keatsian Sonnet." *Victorian Poetry* 29 (Spring, 1991): 89-92. This brief note argues that Hallam was versed in the "modern poetry" of John Keats, an important influence on his and Alfred, Lord Tennyson's poetry, at an earlier date than was previously believed. Kolb's evidence is a poem written at age fourteen to his sister in imitation of Keats's "On First Looking into Chapman's Homer."

Mansell, Darrel. "Displacing Hallam's Tomb in Tennyson's 'In Memoriam.'" *Victorian Poetry* 36, no. 1 (Spring, 1998): 97-112. Mansell argues that Tennyson's poem "In Memoriam A. H. H." is in error concerning some facts about Hallam's death.

Martin, Robert Bernard. *Tennyson: The Unquiet Heart*. Oxford, England: Clarendon Press, 1983. This authoritative and brilliant biography of Alfred, Lord Tennyson is equally excellent on his friendship with Hallam. While hardly a chapter fails to mention Hallam, three chapters are devoted to him and his influence on Tennyson. These focus on student life at Cambridge, Hallam's influence on Tennyson's publications, and Hallam's death.

Dennis R. Dean;
bibliography updated by the editors

THOMAS HARDY

Born: Higher Bockhampton, England; June 2, 1840
Died: Dorchester, England; January 11, 1928

Principal poetry

Wessex Poems and Other Verses, 1898
Poems of the Past and the Present, 1901
Time's Laughingstocks and Other Verses, 1909
Satires of Circumstance, 1914
Selected Poems of Thomas Hardy, 1916
Moments of Vision and Miscellaneous Verses, 1917
Late Lyrics and Earlier, 1922
Human Shows, Far Phantasies, Songs, and Trifles, 1925
Winter Words in Various Moods and Metres, 1928
Collected Poems of Thomas Hardy, 1943
The Complete Poetical Works, 1982-1985 (3 volumes; Samuel Hynes, editor)

Other literary forms

Besides his eight substantial volumes of poetry, Thomas Hardy published fourteen novels, four collections of short stories, two long verse plays, and a variety of essays, prefaces, and nonfiction prose. Although

Thomas Hardy (Library of Congress)

Hardy directed before his death that his letters, notebooks, and private papers be burned, much interesting material has survived in addition to that preserved in *The Early Life of Thomas Hardy* (1928) and *The Later Years of Thomas Hardy* (1930), both of which were dictated by Hardy himself to his wife Florence Hardy. A definitive seven-volume edition of Hardy's letters (1978-1988) was edited by Richard Little Purdy and Michael Millgate. In addition, Ernest Brennecke has edited *Life and Art* (1925). *An Indiscretion in the Life of an Heiress* appeared serially in 1878 and as a book in 1934; it is a story based on scenes from Hardy's rejected first novel, *The Poor Man and the Lady*, which he later destroyed.

Achievements

Although Thomas Hardy's poetic reputation has grown steadily since his death, critics seem unable to agree on the exact nature of his poetic achievement or even on a list of his best poems. Aside from a small group of frequently anthologized pieces, the bulk of Hardy's poetry goes unread. Part of the problem is of course the immense amount of his verse—nearly a thousand poems in eight substantial volumes. The other problem is the inevitable comparison between his poetry and his fiction and the tendency to prefer one or the other, instead of seeking continuities in his work. This is an unavoidable problem with a poet-novelist, particularly with a novelist as accomplished as Hardy, whose fiction is better known than his poetry.

Hardy began his career as a novelist rather than as a poet. He turned to poetry later in life, publishing little before 1898. Here, however, chronology can be misleading. Actually Hardy began composing verse early in life and continued to write poetry throughout the years when he was publishing his Wessex novels and tales. To a certain extent, economic pressures early led him to relegate poetry to a secondary place in his career. Once he had abandoned architecture, he turned to fiction in order to earn a livelihood. Had the means been available to him, he might have remained primarily a poet.

Yet even during his most productive years as a novelist, Hardy was putting aside verse that he would later publish. Sometimes these poems develop a lyrical twist to a scene or episode given fuller treatment in his novels, as in the case of "Tess's Lament," "In a Wood," or "At Casterbridge Fair." Moreover, Hardy was a lyrical prose stylist as well as a contemplative or meditative poet. The genres were fluid to him, and he moved easily from one to the other. Florence Hardy wrote in *The Later Years of Thomas Hardy* that "he had mostly aimed at keeping his narratives close to natural life and as near to poetry in their subjects as the conditions would allow, and had often regretted that these conditions would not let him keep them nearer still." Indeed, the same themes often appear in both the poems and the fiction: the capriciousness of fate, the cruelty of missed opportunities, and the large role of chance, accident, and contingency in human affairs.

Nor does chronology help much in understanding Hardy's development as a poet, since his verse shows only subtle variations in theme, subject matter, style, or treatment over more than six decades. There is a timeless quality in his verse, both early and late, with no discernible falling off in his creative power even in the late poems. Between 1898 and 1928, Hardy published eight volumes of lyrical poetry and two lengthy verse plays, which—even without the prior achievement of his fiction—would have made for an impressive literary career. That his poetry appeared after midcareer is a tribute to Hardy's undiminished creative imagination, especially when one remembers that the bulk of his poetry was published after he was sixty, with more than half of his lyrical poetry appearing after he turned seventy-four. *The Dynasts: A Drama in Three Parts* (1903, 1906, 1908) alone would have been a major accomplishment for a writer of his age. For his last volume, *Winter Words in Various Moods and Metres*, published posthumously, he wrote an unused preface in which he boasted that he was the only English poet to bring out a new volume of verse on a birthday so late in life. His ambition was "to have some poem or poems in a good anthology like the Golden Treasury." Thus the poems, though they are the work of a lifetime, are in their final form the product of Hardy's late career.

Yet these poems are not the serene and mellow harvest of a successful literary career. Hardy turned to poetry in mid-career after the hostile critical reception of *Jude the Obscure* (1895); after that, he resolved to write no more novels. Instead, his poems extend and concentrate the often bitter and fatalistic tone and mood of his fiction. His verse reflects the weariness and discourage-ment of his Wessex characters, who have faced the worst that life can offer and cherish no illusions about what the future may bring. Many deal with love entanglements and marital difficulties. Others are cynical poems about human failings or brooding meditations on aging, loss, and death. Even his nature poems are elegiac in tone, presenting a Darwinian view of harsh competition for survival in a brutal and indifferent world. One critic has remarked that Hardy's vision reflects "his sense of the irreconcilable disparity between the way things ought to be and the way they are: the failure of the universe to answer man's need for order."

Although Hardy may have lacked the buoyant optimism of Robert Browning or the sturdy faith of Alfred, Lord Tennyson, there is no lack of emotional depth in his poems. Hardy had an instinctive sense of the emotional basis of all good poetry. Temperamentally, he found the Wordsworthian formula of "emotion recollected in tranquillity" a continual source of creative inspiration. He had a keen emotional memory and even late in life he could recall the poignancy of incidents that had occurred a half century earlier. His range of topics may have been limited to a purview of Wessex, but he selected his poetic incidents or anecdotes on the basis of their emotional appeal and concentrated on evoking the essence of a mood or feeling. His wife recalled his remark that "poetry is emotion put into measure. The emotion must come by nature, but the measure can be acquired by art."

Hardy served his apprenticeship in Gothic architecture and the same careful attention to detail that marked his church designs is evident in his subtle metrical variations. Although he experimented with a variety of stanzaic forms—the villanelle, triolet, and sapphic—he was partial to the ballad form and the common measure of hymn stanzas. He affected simplicity in his verse, favoring a subtle irregularity and practicing "the art of concealing art." Florence Hardy writes:

> He knew that in architecture cunning irregularity is of enormous worth, and it is obvious that he carried on into his verse, perhaps in part unconsciously, the gothic art-principle in which he had been trained—the principle of spontaneity, found in mouldings, tracery, and such like—resulting in the "unforseen" . . . character of his metres and stanzas, that of stress rather than of syllable, poetic texture rather than poetic veneer.

Hardy is thus paradoxically the last of the great Victorians and the first of the moderns—at once traditional in style and modern in thought, attitude, and feeling. He laments the passing of the timeless relation of the countryman to the soil in his native Wessex and anticipates the confusion and bewilderment of the characters in his poems, who think in new ways but continue to feel in the old ways. Like Robert Frost, he writes of a diminished world, in which science has undercut traditional ways of thinking and believing. He shares much with the Georgian poets, who were younger than himself; their subdued lyricism, their dread of the Great War, their nostalgic pastoralism, and their sense of undefined loss and privation. What is unique in his vision is the compassion that he expresses for the victims of this changed world: his deep sense of their human plight and their loss of traditional sources of consolation. Hardy described himself once as less of a doubter or agnostic than "churchy" in an old-fashioned way: a person for whom the traditional sources of faith had disappeared yet who dreamed of "giving liturgical form to modern ideas." It is ironic that, when asked late in life whether he would have chosen the same career again, Hardy replied that he would rather have been "a small architect in a country town," so deep was his love of church architecture and the grace and ornateness of the gothic style.

BIOGRAPHY

Thomas Hardy was born on June 2, 1840, in a rambling, seven-room cottage in Higher Bockhampton, on the edge of Bockhampton Heath, near Dorchester. He was the eldest of four children, with a sister, Mary, born in 1841, a brother, Henry, in 1851, and a sister, Kate, in 1856. His father, also named Thomas, was a master builder and mason with a love of church music and violin playing, and his mother Jemima (née Hand) was a handsome, energetic woman of country stock who loved books and reading. At birth, their first child was so frail that he was supposed dead; but an attending nurse rescued the baby, and his mother and aunt nursed him back to health, although Thomas remained a small, delicate child, physically immature in appearance until well into adulthood. Despite his frail appearance, Thomas was a vigorous, active boy who relished village life and freely roamed the heath behind his home. As a child he so en-

joyed the country dance tunes and melodies his father played that he was given a toy accordion at the age of four and was taught to play the fiddle as soon as he could finger the strings. The Church of England service strongly moved him and sometimes on wet Sunday mornings he would enact the service at home, wrapping himself in a tablecloth and reading the morning prayer to his cousin and grandmother, who pretended to be the congregation.

At the age of eight, Hardy began his schooling at the local school in Bockhampton, recently established by the lady of the manor. The boy was a quick pupil and after a year he was transferred to Isaac Last's Nonconformist Latin School near Bockhampton. There he continued until the age of sixteen, when he was apprenticed to the ecclesiastical architect John Hicks. During this time he played at country dances with his father and uncle and taught Sunday School at the local parish. After his formal schooling ended, Hardy continued to study Latin and Greek with his fellow apprentices. Hardy also began writing verses about this time, being especially impressed with the regional dialect poetry of Reverend William Barnes, a Dorset poet. After continuing his apprenticeship in church architecture for almost six years, Hardy finally left Bockhampton for London at the age of twenty-one.

In the spring of 1862, Hardy arrived in London with two letters of introduction in his pocket, having decided to continue his study of architecture there. Through good fortune, he found temporary work with a London friend of Hicks, who was able to recommend Hardy to the noted ecclesiastical architect John Blomfield, with whom Hardy began work as an assistant in the drawing-office. Hardy persevered in his architectural training, and within a year he won a prize offered by the Royal Institute of British Architects for his essay on the uses of glazed bricks and terra cotta in modern architecture. Blomfield's office was within walking distance of the National Gallery, and Hardy soon began spending his lunch hours there, studying one painting carefully each day. He especially admired the landscapes of J. M. W. Turner and the Flemish masters.

Work was light under Blomfield and young Hardy found time to write his first sketch, "How I Built Myself a House," which he published in *Chambers's Journal* in

1865. He also continued writing poetry during this time, although little of his juvenilia has survived. In the evenings he continued his education at King's College in London, studying French. For a brief time he even considered applying to Cambridge to study for the ministry, but he gave up the idea as impractical.

The confinement of life in London gradually sapped Hardy's health, and within five years he was advised to return to Bockhampton to recuperate. There he assisted his former employer John Hicks with church restorations and soon regained his health. With time on his hands, Hardy turned to fiction and began working on his first novel, *The Poor Man and the Lady*. In 1870, he sent the manuscript to a London publisher, whose editor, George Meredith, praised the young writer but urged him to try something else with more plot ingenuity and suspense. This Hardy did, and ten months later finished his second novel, *Desperate Remedies*, which unfortunately was also initially rejected before it was published in 1871.

In the meantime, Hicks had sold his firm to another architect, G. R. Crickmay, who engaged Hardy to complete some church restorations in Cornwall. Hardy moved with the firm to Weymouth and in March, 1870, set off to Cornwall to inspect a dilapidated gothic church at St. Juliot. There he met Emma Gifford, the young sister-in-law of the rector, who was eventually to become his first wife. At this time Hardy was already engaged to his cousin Tryphena Sparks, a young schoolteacher, but their engagement was broken after he met Gifford.

Although Hardy did complete his supervision of the church restoration at St. Juliot, his interest was gradually shifting from architecture to literature, and he began writing fiction in earnest. *Under the Greenwood Tree* was published in 1872, followed by *A Pair of Blue Eyes* (1872-1873) and *Far From the Madding Crowd* (1874). He was now sure enough of his future to marry Gifford in London on September 17, 1874, and after their honeymoon in France, he settled down to begin *The Return of the Native* (1878).

The next ten years saw the publication of five more novels and a number of short stories, strengthening his reputation as a major writer. He also continued to write poetry but withheld most of it from publication until after 1897. As their means grew, the Hardys moved back to Dorchester and built their permanent home, Max Gate. Hardy began making notes for an epic treatment of the Napoleonic Wars, eventually to become *The Dynasts*. Unfortunately, the Hardys had no children. This may have put a strain on their marriage, for although Emma Hardy continued to serve as her husband's secretary, making fair copies of his manuscripts for publication, she gradually drew apart from him and became embittered, perhaps resenting his success. Their marriage became a cold formality of two people living in separate rooms and seeing each other only at meals. The difficulties of this first marriage may have been reflected in the bleakness of Hardy's outlook.

After the Hardys moved into Max Gate in June, 1885, he embarked on his last decade of fiction-writing. This period saw the publication of another five novels and approximately fifty short stories. *The Mayor of Casterbridge* (1886) was followed by *The Woodlanders* (1886-1887), *Tess of the D'Urbervilles* (1891), *Jude the Obscure* (1985), and *The Well-Beloved* (1897). The multivolume edition of the Wessex novels also appeared in 1895-1896. During this time, Hardy was writing virtually a novel a year.

Hardy had ventured to treat new material in *Jude the Obscure*, and the uniformly hostile critical reception accorded the novel led him to put aside fiction after 1897 and embark on a second literary career as a poet. For the next thirty-one years he would write only poetry. During that time, he published eight volumes of poetry, at least some of it early work, and the epic-drama *The Dynasts*. Hardy began to be recognized as a major English writer and received a number of awards, including honorary degrees from Aberdeen, Cambridge, and Oxford.

Emma Hardy died at Max Gate on November 27, 1912, and during his bereavement Hardy visited the scenes of their courtship. Two years later, he married Florence Emily Dugdale, a young admirer who had served as his personal secretary after his wife's death. By this time, he was universally recognized as the last great Victorian writer and the preeminent English man of letters, although his lack of reputation abroad prevented him from receiving a Nobel Prize. Despite personal misgivings, he spoke out patriotically for England during World War I. After the war, he lived quietly with his second wife at Max Gate during the last decade of his life. In 1923, he published a second verse play, *The Famous Tragedy of the Queen of Cornwall*, based on the romance of Tristan and Iseult. After a brief illness, Hardy died on January 11, 1928. His heart was buried in the grave of his first wife in their parish churchyard in Stinsford, and his ashes were installed in the Poets' Corner, Westminster Abbey. After his death, Florence Hardy published a two-volume biography that her husband had dictated to her. She died on October 17, 1937.

ANALYSIS

More than one critic has called the lyrics in *Satires of Circumstance* Thomas Hardy's finest achievement, although his most notable poems are probably distributed evenly among his eight volumes. Since there was no period of peak creative achievement for him—rather, a steady accumulation of poems over a long and productive career—the reader must search among the collected verse for those poems in which Hardy's style, vision, and subject matter coincide in a memorable work. Given the strength and originality of his vision, it is difficult to speak of influences on Hardy's poetry, although in many respects he carries forward the Romantic tradition of William Wordsworth and Percy Bysshe Shelley and the homey realism of George Crabbe. An obscure Dorset poet, William Barnes, whose poetry Hardy edited in 1908, may have first introduced him to the possibilities of writing regional poetry. Barnes was a clergyman and philologist with a keen interest in local dialects who introduced vivid scenes of Wessex life into his verse. Hardy read and admired Algernon Charles Swinburne and paid tribute to him on numerous occasions, notably in "A Singer Asleep," although his influence on Hardy appears to have been slight. Hardy's poetry is perhaps most akin in tone and spirit to Wordsworth's pastoral lyrics and odes, particularly "Michael," although Hardy's characters often lack the simple heroism and nobility of spirit of Wordsworth's protagonists.

WESSEX POEMS AND OTHER VERSES

The appearance of Hardy's first volume of poetry, *Wessex Poems and Other Verses*, was greeted by the critics with scarcely more understanding than that which had been accorded to *Jude the Obscure*. The fifty-one selections are a mixture of lyrics, sonnets, and ballads illustrated by the poet with thirty-one "Sketches of Their Scenes," designed to accompany the poems. The volume includes five historical poems in a ballad sequence about the Napoleonic Wars which anticipate *The Dynasts*; a series of four "She, To Him" love sonnets written in the Shakespearean manner; a number of lyrics on disillusioned love, of which "Neutral Tones" is probably the best; and a set of meditative nature poems, including the sonnet "Hap" and "Nature's Questioning." An additional group of lyrics enlarges upon scenes from the novels, including the lovely "In a Wood," which echoes a nature description from *The Woodlanders*, and "The Ivy Wife," a figurative portrait of a possessive wife that borrows its metaphor from a description in that same novel.

"Neutral Tones" is the most frequently anthologized of Hardy's *Wessex Poems*, and deservedly so. This four-quatrain lyric, rhyming *abba*, employs a series of muted winter images and a pond-side meeting to describe the death of a love affair. The implied confession by the beloved that she is no longer in love creates the dramatic occasion, and although the pronoun employed is "we," the point of view is clearly that of the forsaken lover. The poem possesses that haunting quality of a painful moment forever etched upon one's memory: The colorless imagery of the setting suggests an impressionistic painting of two lovers meeting against a dreary December landscape in which nature's barrenness ("starving sod," "greyish leaves") serves as a counterpoint to the death of love. Even the negations of Hardy's poetic syntax combine with the winter imagery and the bitter dramatic occasion to sustain the mood of "Neutral Tones." This poignant lyric about the failure of a love relationship was written, interestingly enough, just before Hardy's engagement to his cousin Tryphena Sparks was broken, perhaps because he discovered her infatuation with his friend Horace Maule. This theme of love's betrayal is of course also found often in Hardy's novels, although it achieves greater intensity and concentration in poems such as "Neutral Tones."

"Hap," a sonnet about the force that shapes events unpredictably, records Hardy's troubled response to evolutionary theory, with its view of natural selection operating impartially, without purpose or direction. The speaker would prefer a personalized universe, even with "some Vengeful god," who wills and controls the course of events, rather than "Crass Casualty," "dicing Time," and "These purblind doomsters" who mete out bliss and pain alike without reason. "Hap" is thematically related to "Nature's Questioning," which implies that the author of the universe is "some Vast Imbecility" unconscious of human pains. This poem was so often quoted against him as evidence of his alleged atheism and hostility to religion that Hardy finally decided to write a preface for his second volume explaining that his poems taken individually did not necessarily reflect his personal philosophy. He later restated this disavowal in the preface to *Winter Words in Various Moods and Metres*; still, many of his poems did seem to invite speculation about his personal views. "Heiress and Architect," for example, is a philosophical allegory cast in terms of a dialogue between two speakers representing romantic and realistic views of life. The heiress finds her elaborate plans diminished in each succeeding stanza as she submits them to the cold scrutiny of the architect. Her house designs progressively shrink in this allegory of human dreams crushed by realities, a theme familiar to Hardy's novels.

POEMS OF THE PAST AND THE PRESENT

Hardy's second volume, *Poems of the Past and the Present*, comprising a hundred poems, is nearly twice as long as *Wessex Poems*. Two major sections include "War Poems," dealing with the Boer War, and "Poems of Pilgrimage," about notable historical and literary shrines in Italy and Switzerland, where the Hardys had traveled in the spring of 1882; a third section was composed of "Miscellaneous Poems." The "War Poems" record Hardy's deep reservations about British imperialism and the cost of war to ordinary men; "Drummer Hodge" is about a boy drafted from Dorset and fated to lie after his death under southern constellations. Among the "Miscellaneous Poems," "The Last Chrysanthemum" and "The Darkling Thrush" are incomparably the best. The first describes a perennial blooming out of season, into the winter, past the time when it should have flowered. This curious natural event becomes the occasion for a lyrical meditation on the mysteries of growth and change that regulate the life of each organism. Hardy continues the English tradition of the nature lyric, although in a much more subdued form than, for example, Wordsworth's "I Wandered Lonely as a Cloud." Instead of drawing inspiration from a simple vernal scene, Hardy records a more complex response to a post-Darwinian natural world that can no longer be identified with a beneficent Creator. In the final stanza of "The Last Chrysanthemum," however, he seems unwilling to discard entirely the notion of a deliberate, shaping purpose, even though the poem's affirmation is tentative at best.

This metaphor of unseasonableness is carried forward in "The Darkling Thrush," perhaps Hardy's finest lyric. Here tone, mood, theme, subject, and setting coincide to shape a nearly flawless meditation on the dawning of a new century. Hardy's thrush is his solitary singer, the projection of the speaker's hopes and the spirit of his age, which in the midst of a bleak winter landscape, an image of the times, finds reason to fling his song against the gathering darkness of the coming age. Hardy employs the traditional formula of the romantic inspirational lyric: the speaker's despondency, the corresponding gloom of the natural landscape, then the sudden change of mood within the lyric, in this case in the third octave, after the glimpse of a seemingly trivial natural event, the sight of a single thrush singing in a copse against the winter twilight. Yet this poem does not achieve the triumphant resolution of Percy Bysshe Shelley's "To a Sky-lark" or John Keats's "Ode to a Nightingale"; instead, the concluding octave is curiously equivocal, even subversive of traditional consolations. The speaker still finds little cause for rejoicing; he simply pauses to marvel at the anomaly of the thrush's song against so bleak a setting. There is something so casual and disarming about the country setting, with the speaker leaning musingly on a "coppice gate" and quietly reflecting on the starkness of the December landscape, that readers may at first miss the implicit irony in his response to the thrush's "caroling." Was it merely an illusion to find cause for hope in the bird's song? The poem's deliberate ambiguity resists any easy interpretation, but it would be unlike Hardy to offer glib reassurances.

TIME'S LAUGHINGSTOCKS AND OTHER VERSES

Time's Laughingstocks and Other Verses includes ninety-four poems in four groupings: "Time's Laughingstocks," "More Love Lyrics," "A Set of Country Songs," and "Pieces Occasional and Various." Most of the selections are rustic character sketches and ballads of uneven quality, although Hardy considered one of the ballads, "A Trampwoman's Tragedy," to be perhaps "his most successful poem." It is a country tale of jealousy, murder, and a hanging that leaves the speaker alone in the world, without her "fancy-man," to haunt the hills and moors in which the deeds took place.

Satires of Circumstance

Satires of Circumstance continues the pattern of Hardy's earlier volumes of poetry, with 106 poems in four sections: "Lyrics and Reveries," comprising religious and philosophic meditations; "Poems of 1912-13," recollections of his courtship of Emma Gifford; "Miscellaneous Pieces"; and "Satires of Circumstance in Fifteen Glimpses." Two of the poems in the first section, "Channel Firing" and "The Convergence of the Twain," are among his most popular poems. Written three months before the outbreak of World War I, "Channel Firing" contains an ironic premonition of the impending conflict. The poem is narrated from the point of view of the dead in their coffins in a country churchyard, suddenly awakened by the "great guns" at sea. The nine stanzas in common measure present an ironic view of the futility and inevitability of war, with even God unable to prevent the ensuing bloodshed. All he can do is to reassure the frightened souls that "judgment-hour" is not at hand; the noise comes only from the naval guns practicing in the English Channel off the Dorset Coast.

Hardy wrote "The Convergence of the Twain" to commemorate the sinking of the luxury liner *Titanic* on April 14-15, 1912, after the ship collided with an iceberg on her maiden voyage across the Atlantic. He uses eleven stanzas of triplet rhyme with an extended third line to develop the theme and counterpoint of the human vanity ("Pride of Life") that boasted of building an unsinkable ship and "The Immanent Will" that prepared an iceberg to meet her by "paths coincident" on the night they were fated to collide. A retrospective narration in the first five stanzas pictures the sunken ship with her jewels and elegant furnishings now the home of grotesque sea-worms and "moon-eyed fishes." The final six stanzas recount the inevitable steps toward the final encounter as the two "mates"—ship and iceberg—move inexorably toward each other. A grim determinism seems to stalk this symbol of human arrogance and pride as the ship that even God "could not sink" goes down on her first voyage.

After the death of his first wife, Hardy wrote a series of elegies to Emma Gifford in his "Poems of 1912-13." The best of these may be "Voices," with its poignant recall of his first impressions of her as a young woman in Cornwall, its haunting dactylic tetrameters, and its lovely refrain. Here also Hardy projects much of his sadness and regret for their embittered relationship later in their marriage and for the series of misunderstandings that drove them apart. In "The Voice" he tries to recapture the joy of his earliest memories of his wife as she was during their courtship.

Perhaps the harshest portrait in *Satires of Circumstance* is Hardy's depiction of the hypocritical clergyman, who, "In Church," is discovered after the service by one of his Bible students, practicing before a mirror the flourishes and gestures that "had moved the congregation so."

Moments of Vision and Miscellaneous Verses

Moments of Vision and Miscellaneous Verses, with 159 poems, is Hardy's largest volume, including a substantial body of reflective personal poems and an additional seventeen selections about World War I titled "Poems of War and Patriotism." Several of these lyrics are worth mentioning: "Heredity," with its glimpse of family traits that leap from generation to generation; "The Oxen," a frequently anthologized poem narrating a common folk legend about how the barnyard animals were said to kneel in adoration of the nativity on Christmas Eve; "For Life I Had Never Cared Greatly," a confession of Hardy's personal disillusionment; and "In Time of 'The Breaking of Nations,'" about how life, work, and love continue despite the ravages of war.

Later poetry

Two more volumes were yet to appear during Hardy's lifetime. Now in his eighties, he published *Late Lyrics and Earlier*, a collection of 151 lyrical incidents and impressions; three years later *Human Shows, Far Phantasies, Songs, and Trifles* appeared, with 152 poems. His last volume, *Winter Words in Various Moods and Metres*, was published posthumously by Florence Hardy. There is a sameness about these late poems that makes it difficult to select particular ones for discussion. A few show sparks of creative novelty, but many are recapitulations of earlier themes or material gleaned from notebooks or recollections during the time that Hardy was dictating his two-volume biography to his wife.

In *Late Lyrics and Earlier*, "A Drizzling Easter Morning" records a skeptic's response to the Easter resurrection on a day when rain falls and rural life continues unabated. "Christmas: 1924" from *Winter Words in Various Moods and Metres* draws a stark contrast between man's perennial hopes for peace on earth and his use of poison gas in modern warfare; "He Never Expected Much" sums up the poet's personal philosophy; and "He Resolves to Say No More" expresses a tired old man's farewell to life, in which he refuses to offer any last words of insight. Perhaps this mood simply reflected his age and illness, but Hardy's last poem lacks the resoluteness of, for example, William Butler Yeats's "Under Ben Bulben."

THE DYNASTS

At one time *The Dynasts* was hailed as Hardy's major achievement, although critics have since revised their judgment of this massive verse drama, "in three parts, nineteen acts, and one hundred and thirty scenes," of the Napoleonic Wars. Hardy subtitled his work "An Epic-Drama of the War with Napoleon," although he meant to glorify the British role in checking the French emperor's dynastic ambitions. In the play, he presents an allegorical view of history as a relentless, deterministic pageant in which human beings, mere automatons, enact the designs of the Immanent Will. Ever since his youth Hardy had been planning a literary project involving the Napoleonic Wars, although he was unsure what form the work would eventually take. The final epic-drama, which he undertook in his sixties, is conceived on the grand scale of Shelley's *Prometheus Unbound* (1820), with the historical sweep of Leo Tolstoy's *War and Peace* (1865-1869), and though the work is unevenly executed, in places flawed by excessive allegory, and perhaps even inaccessible to the modern reader, it contains many impressive scenes.

From his early plans for an "*Iliad* of Europe from 1789 to 1815," Hardy evolved a dramatic form flexible enough to allow rapid panoramic shifts in scene that traced the paths of marching armies across the map of Europe and recorded the plots and intrigues of Napoleon as he schemed to strengthen his military domination. A chorus of Spirits or Phantom Intelligences introduce and conclude the scenes and interweave their comments with the human action below. What is most impressive, however, is Hardy's historical knowledge of the Napoleonic period, combined with his innate repugnance for war and his deep compassion for the victims of the clash of nations. His controlling vision, here and throughout his poetry, was of the continuity and sameness of the human spirit everywhere. As he observed about *The Dynasts:* "The human race [is] to be shown as one great network or tissue which quivers in every part when one point is shaken, like a spider's web if touched."

OTHER MAJOR WORKS

LONG FICTION: *Desperate Remedies*, 1871; *Under the Greenwood Tree*, 1872; *A Pair of Blue Eyes*, 1872-1873; *Far from the Madding Crowd*, 1874; *The Hand of Ethelberta*, 1875-1876; *An Indiscretion in the Life of an Heiress*, 1878 (serial), 1934 (book); *The Return of the Native*, 1878; *The Trumpet-Major*, 1880; *A Laodicean*, 1880-1881; *Two on a Tower*, 1882; *The Mayor of Casterbridge*, 1886; *The Woodlanders*, 1886-1887; *Tess of the D'Urbervilles*, 1891; *Jude the Obscure*, 1895; *The Well-Beloved*, 1897.

SHORT FICTION: *Wessex Tales*, 1888; *A Group of Noble Dames*, 1891; *Life's Little Ironies*, 1894; *A Changed Man, The Waiting Supper, and Other Tales*, 1913; *The Complete Short Stories*, 1989 (Desmond Hawkins, editor).

PLAYS: *The Dynasts: A Drama in Three Parts*, pb. 1903, 1906, 1908, 1910 (verse drama), pr. 1914 (abridged by Harley Granville-Barker); *The Famous Tragedy of the Queen of Cornwall*, pr., pb. 1923 (one act).

NONFICTION: *Life and Art*, 1925 (Ernest Brennecke, editor); *The Early Life of Thomas Hardy*, 1928; *The Later Years of Thomas Hardy*, 1930; *Personal Writings*, 1966 (Harold Orel, editor); *The Collected Letters of Thomas Hardy*, 1978-1988 (7 volumes; Richard Little Purdy and Michael Millgate, editors).

BIBLIOGRAPHY

Gibson, James, and Trevor Johnson, eds. *Thomas Hardy: Poems*. New York: Macmillan, 1979. Significant essays by Dyson, Larkin, Marsden, and Gunn are numbered in this collection, one of the well-known Casebook series. Contains an introduction that reviews all important critical works on the poetry, a select bibliography, and an index.

Hynes, Samuel. *The Pattern of Hardy's Poetry.* 2d ed. Chapel Hill: University of North Carolina Press, 1961. Hynes finds the basic patterns of Hardy's poetry in the conflict of irreconcilables. This generates the type of structure, diction, and imagery of the poetry. Hynes also seeks to distinguish the good from the bad and to analyze what makes the difference. Includes an index.

Kramer, Dale, ed. *The Cambridge Companion to Thomas Hardy.* New York: Cambridge University Press, 1999. An essential introduction and general overview of all Hardy's work and specific demonstrations of Hardy's ideas and literary skills. Individual essays explore Hardy's biography, aesthetics, and the impact on his work of developments in science, religion and philosophy in the late nineteenth century. The volume also contains a detailed chronology of Hardy's life.

Lanzano, Ellen Anne. *Hardy: The Temporal Poetics.* New York: P. Lang, 1999. An examination of Hardy's poetics in light of the temporal context out of which he wrote more than 900 poems. To a large extent, Hardy's struggle with the forms of time is a record of the nineteenth-century engagement with the relationship of consciousness to the new science and the loss of traditional beliefs.

Orel, Harold. *The Final Years of Thomas Hardy, 1912-1928.* New York: Macmillan, 1976. The author, vice president of the English Thomas Hardy Society, takes a biographical approach to the last phase of Hardy's poetry.

Paulin, Tom. *Thomas Hardy: The Poetry of Perception.* Basingstoke, England: Macmillan, 1975. Although Hardy seems to deny the possibility of revelation and vision, his poetry is full of references to it. Paulin seeks to work out this contradiction. Contains a select bibliography and an index.

Pinion, F. B. *A Commentary on the Poems of Thomas Hardy.* New York: Macmillan, 1976. The book complements the author's *A Hardy Companion.* Contains background notes on the majority of Hardy's

poems, arranged volume by volume, a chronology, a glossary, and indexes.

Taylor, Dennis. *Hardy's Metres and Victorian Prosody.* Oxford, England: Clarendon Press, 1988. Taylor asks why Hardy was so interested in metrical form and why the Victorians generated so many varieties of it. In seeking to answer these questions, Taylor moves to a deeper understanding of meter itself. Includes a bibliography and an index.

Weber, Carl J. *Hardy's Love Poems.* New York: St. Martin's Press, 1963. The book is divided in two halves, the first forming a biographical setting for the collection of 116 love poems to Emma, which comprises the second half. Includes a bibliography and indexes.

Andrew J. Angyal;
bibliography updated by the editors

JOY HARJO

Born: Tulsa, Oklahoma; May 9, 1951

PRINCIPAL POETRY

The Last Song, 1975
What Moon Drove Me to This?, 1980
She Had Some Horses, 1983
Secrets from the Center of the World, 1989
In Mad Love and War, 1990
The Woman Who Fell from the Sky, 1996
A Map to the Next World: Poetry and Tales, 2000
How We Became Human: New and Selected Poems, 1975-2001, 2002

OTHER LITERARY FORMS

Joy Harjo has published mainly volumes of poetry, though she also has written many essays. She edited, with Gloria Bird, *Reinventing the Enemy's Language: Contemporary Native Women's Writing of North America* in 1997. She also wrote a screenplay, *Origin of Apache Crow Dance* (1985). In 2000, Harjo published her first children's book, *The Good Luck Cat,* illustrated by Paul Lee.

ACHIEVEMENTS

Joy Harjo is known for her use of Native American mythology in her work and for her Native American heritage as a member of the Muskogee Creek Nation. Her work has earned many honors and awards, including the William Carlos Williams Award, the Josephine Miles Award, the American Book Award, the National Endowment for the Arts Fellowship in 1978, the New Mexico Governor's Award for Excellence in the Arts, the American Indian Distinguished Achievement Award, the Lifetime Achievement Award from the Western Literature Association, and the Lifetime Achievement Award from the Native Writers Circle of the Americas. Benedectine College conferred an honorary doctorate to her in 1992. Harjo also received the Woodrow Wilson Fellowship at Green Mountain College in Poultney, Vermont, in 1993 and the Witter Bynner Poetry Fellowship in 1994.

Besides being a talented poet, Harjo plays the saxophone and performs her poetry along with her band, Poetic Justice. In 1997, they produced an album titled *Letters from the End of the Century*. The recording won the Musical Artists of the Year award from the Wordcraft Circle of Native Writers and Storytellers.

BIOGRAPHY

Joy Harjo was born Joy Foster in 1951 in Tulsa, Oklahoma, to Allen W. and Wynema Baker Foster. Harjo's mother was of mixed Cherokee and French heritage, while her father was a full-blooded Creek Indian. Her mother was nineteen when Harjo was born and had three more children in the next six years. Harjo's childhood was not a happy one, as her father drank and had extramarital affairs. He abused his family physically and emotionally. Her mother divorced Foster and remarried another abusive man. Harjo eventually came into conflict with her stepfather and left the house.

Harjo spent her high school years at the Institute of American Indian Arts in Santa Fe, New Mexico. The school's population consisted of members of various tribes. Though the school did not provide the best edu-

Joy Harjo

cation, Harjo felt she benefited from the experience. She toured with an all-Native American dance troupe and became involved with a fellow student named Phil Wilmon. In 1968, the tour ended, and Harjo graduated, returned to Oklahoma, and gave birth to her son, Phil Dayn.

Harjo returned to Sante Fe without Wilmon and enrolled at the University of New Mexico. She eventually became an English and creative writing major. She also met poet Simon J. Ortiz. Ortiz and Harjo became lovers, and he fathered Harjo's daughter, Rainy Dawn. Harjo split with Ortiz and graduated in 1976.

Harjo next went to the University of Iowa's Writers Workshop. She faced difficulties as a single mother of two but eventually earned her M.F.A. She next studied filmmaking at the Anthropology Film Center in Santa Fe. She also taught at the college level, including at the University of New Mexico in Albuquerque. She later left New Mexico, living in Los Angeles and later Honolulu. Harjo took her last name when she became an enrolled member of the Muskogee tribe at the age of nineteen. Harjo was the surname of her paternal grandmother.

ANALYSIS

Harjo is usually classified as a Native American poet. A member of the Muskogee tribe, she uses Native American imagery, folktales, symbolism, mythology, and technique in her work. She writes about women and women's issues and takes political stands against oppression and government as well. Landscape and environment play an important part in her work. Many poems have a sense of location or place. Sometimes those places are specific, such as Kansas City or Anchorage. At other times, they are dreamscapes or psychic spaces the poet visits. Many of Harjo's poems detail journeys and finding a sense of place. This fits with both her personal history and the history of the indigenous Americans, such as the Muskogee, one of the tribes forced to relocate along the Trail of Tears.

Connected with landscape and place is memory. Harjo writes from personal and tribal memories, often connecting them with the places she has lived or visited.

Another recurring theme is her anger at being half Caucasian and fluent only in English, the "enemies'" language. Many of her poems articulate this anger.

WHAT MOON DROVE ME TO THIS?

Harjo's first book-length collection of poetry contained the ten poems from the chapbook *The Last Song*, as well as many other poems. The book is divided into two sections, "Summer" and "Winter." The poems contain images and themes that Harjo would develop more in her later works.

One of the characteristics of Harjo's poetry is the use of imagery from Native American mythology. Both coyotes and crows appear in this collection. Both animals are trickster figures, and Harjo uses them as such. "Kansas City Coyote" introduces a character who appears in two of the poems. The name later emerges in the poem "Old Lines Which Sometimes Work, and Sometimes Don't." In this second poem, Kansas City Coyote is an unreliable male figure.

> "I'll be back in ten minutes.
> Just going to get cigarettes."

> That was the last time I saw him,
> two years ago.

A more general male coyote reference appears in the poem "Lame Dear." Crows, or blackbirds, appear in several poems as well, though not always as gender specific as Harjo's coyote references.

The persona of Noni Daylight also appears for the first time in this collection. Some critics see the Noni Daylight persona as an alter ego of the poet. Also evident in this collection is an awareness of the problem of alcoholism among Native Americans, particularly males. For instance, in "Conversations Between Here and Home" we see

> Emma Lee's husband beat her up
> this weekend.
> His government check was held
> up, and he borrowed the money
> to drink on.

Other poems such as "The Lost Weekend Bar" and "Chicago or Albuquerque" show similar imagery.

SHE HAD SOME HORSES

Harjo's second full-length volume is divided into four uneven parts. Many of the poems in this collection use rhythms and beats influenced by Native American chants. The first section is titled "Survivors." There are twenty-five poems in this section, detailing survivors of a variety of things, such as Henry, who survived "being shot at/ eight times outside a liquor store in L.A." and "The Woman Hanging from the Thirteenth Floor Window." The woman in this poem may or may not survive as Harjo deliberately leaves the ending open-ended, not completing the story that could be told about many women.

The second section is titled "What I Should Have Said" and contains eleven poems. Since the last line of her previous collection was "That's what she said," this section of her second book could be considered a follow-up to the first collection. This section of the book contains poems about connecting or the difficulties of connecting in a long-distance relationship.

Section 3 is named "She Had Some Horses." Harjo uses the horse as a symbol in other poems as well. The horse is a powerful Native American symbol signifying strength, grace, freedom, among other characteristics.

The title poem begins this section. It repeats the line "She had horses" throughout the poem. The horses are varied and vivid: "She had horses who threw rocks at glass houses./ She had horses who licked razor blades." Later in the poem, Harjo states, "She had some horses she loved./ She had some horses she hated./ They were the same horses." The other four poems in this section continue to use and build on the imagery and symbolism of horses.

The fourth section is just one poem, titled "I Give You Back." In this poem, the speaker is giving fear back to those who caused it. It is a political poem, as Harjo gives the fear "back to the white soldiers/ who burned down my home, beheaded my children,/ raped and sodomized my brothers and sisters."

SECRETS FROM THE CENTER OF THE WORLD

In this book, Harjo wrote poems that were inspired by the photographs of astronomer Stephen Strom. The collection is almost solely prose poems of very short length. This book shows a great use of landscape since all the photos are of southwestern landscapes. Harjo uses what is in the photos as well as what she imagines may be in the photos for her poems.

> A summer storm reveals the dreaming place of bears. But you cannot see their shaggy dreams of fish and berries, any land signs supporting evidence of bears, or any bears at all.

IN MAD LOVE AND WAR

Harjo's fifth book is a mixture of styles. While some resemble traditional poems with line breaks and stanzas, just as many are prose poems. Several have brief explanatory notes or dedications, such as the poem "For Anna Mae Pictou Aquash . . . ," a poem written about a young Micmac woman who was murdered and her body dismembered by the Federal Bureau of Investigation. "Strange Fruit" is dedicated to Jaqueline Peters, a writer and activist murdered by the Ku Klux Klan.

As in previous books, Harjo divides this one into subsections—"The Wars" and "Mad Love"—after introducing the book with the poem "Grace." "Grace" speaks again of separation and the hurt and anger of a dispossessed people. These themes are continued through "The Wars" section. For instance, in the poem "Autobiography," Harjo says, "We were a stolen people in a stolen land. Oklahoma meant defeat."

"Mad Love" changes tone slightly with poems about Harjo's grandfather and daughter, as well as poems about musicians such as Nat King Cole and Billie Holiday. Harjo's growing interest in music is evident in this section. Both sections again contain poems rooted in place and landscape, such as "Climbing the Streets of Worcester, Mass." and "Crystal Lake."

THE WOMAN WHO FELL FROM THE SKY

In her sixth book, Harjo shows herself as much the storyteller as poet. The collection's prose poems are story centered, often retellings of Native American myths, such as the title poem and "The Creation Story." Each poem is followed by a brief story about how the poem was written. The book is again divided into two parts, "Tribal Memory" and "The World Ends Her." Harjo puts attention on the condition of Native Americans and other oppressed peoples in such poems as "Witness" and "A Postcolonial Tale." Other familiar themes such as love of music and Native American spirituality are also evident. As in her previous book, she looks at the atrocities committed by humans as well as the concept of love. She says in the explanation for "The Myth of Blackbirds," "I believe love is the strongest force in this world, though it doesn't often appear to be so at the ragged end of this century."

A MAP TO THE NEXT WORLD

A Map to the Next World is an ambitious collection containing forty-eight poems in 136 pages. Split into four sections, "Songline of Dawn," "Returning from the Enemy," "This Is My Heart; It Is a Good Heart," and "In the Beautiful Perfume and Stink of the World," the book lives up to its title. While again cataloging the horrors of history, Harjo also offers spiritual guidance to the next world. The poem "The End" describes the death of Pol Pot, the notorious leader of the Khmer Rouge in Cambodia. The next poem, "compassionate fire," links Pol Pot with Andrew Jackson, the "hero" of the American Indian wars, who later became president of the United States. This collection also contains the fourteen-part poem "Returning from the Enemy," a poem tracing her own coming to terms with her father. In "Preparations," Harjo says, "We should be like the antelope/ who gratefully drink the rain,/ love the earth for what it is—their book of law, their heart."

OTHER MAJOR WORKS

SCREENPLAY: *Origin of Apache Crow Dance*, 1985.

CHILDREN'S LITERATURE: *The Good Luck Cat*, 2000.

EDITED TEXT: *Reinventing the Enemy's Language: Contemporary Native Women's Writing of North America*, 1997 (with Gloria Bird).

NONFICTION: *The Spiral of Memories: Interviews*, 1996 (edited by Laura Coltelli).

BIBLIOGRAPHY

Lang, Nancy. "'Twin Gods Bending Over': Joy Harjo and Poetic Memory." *Melus* 18, no. 3 (Fall, 1993): 41-49. This article examines poetic memory in Harjo's poetry. Lang states that Harjo's poetry shows complex layers and voices of memory. These memories can be personal, ancestral, tribal, or mythical. Lang further studies the use of memory in conjunction with Harjo's use of urban landscapes and briefly discusses the Noni Daylight poems.

Pettit, Rhonda. *Joy Harjo*. Boise, Idaho: Boise State University Western Writer Series, 1998. Pettit's work takes an insightful look at the way Harjo uses technique, style, and symbol. She analyzes the use of edges in all of Harjo's major poetry except *A Map to the Next World*. Pettit includes biographical information on Harjo as well as analysis of her first four major books. Also included is a bibliography of secondary sources.

Scarry, John. "Representing the Real Worlds: The Evolving Poetry of Joy Harjo." *World Literature Today* 66, no. 2 (Spring, 1992): 286-291. As Scarry's title suggests, his article takes a look at the development of Harjo's style and themes. Scarry starts with the poems from the first chapbook, *The Last Song*, then discusses poems from *Secrets from the Center of the World* and *In Mad Love and War*. He also compares Harjo to contemporary poets Paula Gunn Allen and Wendy Rose.

Wilson, Norma C. "The Ground Speaks: The Poetry of Joy Harjo." In *The Nature of Native American Poetry*. Albuquerque: University of New Mexico Press, 2001. Wilson's book covers a variety of Native American poets including, Wendy Rose, Linda Hogan, Simon J. Ortiz, and others. In chapter 9 Wilson gives an overview of Harjo's life and poetry, discussing such themes as landscape, fear, and communication.

Womack, Craig S. "Joy Harjo: Creek Writer from the End of the Twentieth Century." In *Red on Red: Native American Literary Separatism*. Minneapolis: University of Minnesota Press, 1999. Womack provides a different perspective on Harjo and other Native American writers, being himself a Creek-Cherokee. His book looks at Native American literature with tribally specific concerns. In his chapter on Harjo, he recognizes the strength of Harjo's voice. He also shows the Creek content and use of Creek history in Harjo's work.

P. Andrew Miller

MICHAEL S. HARPER

Born: Brooklyn, New York; March 18, 1938

PRINCIPAL POETRY

Dear John, Dear Coltrane, 1970
History Is Your Own Heartbeat, 1971
Photographs: Negatives: History as Apple Tree, 1972
Song: I Want a Witness, 1972
Debridement, 1973
Nightmare Begins Responsibility, 1974
Images of Kin: New and Selected Poems, 1977
Rhode Island: Eight Poems, 1981
Healing Song for the Inner Ear, 1985
Honorable Amendments, 1995
Songlines in Michaeltree: New and Collected Poems, 2000

OTHER LITERARY FORMS

Michael Harper works almost exclusively as a poet, but, in collaboration with Robert B. Stepto, he has edited one of the most influential anthologies of African American letters since Alain Locke's anthology from the Harlem Renaissance, *The New Negro: An Interpretation* (1925). Like Locke's anthology, *Chant of Saints: A*

Michael S. Harper (© John Foraste)

Gathering of Afro-American Literature, Art, and Scholarship (1979) represents a substantial accomplishment in defining the importance of African American artists and writers to American culture. This was followed by *Every Shut Eye Ain't Asleep: An Anthology of Poetry by African Americans Since 1945* (1994) and *The Vintage Book of African American Poetry* (2000). In addition to his poetry and these anthologies, Harper has published several essays, including "My Poetic Technique and the Humanization of the American Audience," in *Black American Literature and Humanism*. Harper also edited *The Collected Poems of Sterling A. Brown* (1980).

ACHIEVEMENTS

Formal recognition of Harper's poetry has thus been consistent from the publication of his first collection of poems, *Dear John, Dear Coltrane*, which was nominated for the National Book Award in 1971. After *History Is Your Own Heartbeat*, his second collection, received the Poetry Award of the Black Academy of Arts and Letters in 1972, other grants and awards followed: a National Institute of Arts and Letters Creative Writing Award (1972), a Guggenheim Fellowship (1976), a Na-

tional Endowment for the Arts grant (1977), and the Massachusetts Council of Creative Writing Award (1977). In 1977, Harper's seventh book, *Images of Kin*, received the Melville Cane Award and was nominated in 1978 for the National Book Award. Harper was appointed the poet laureate of Rhode Island in 1988 and was named a Phi Beta Kappa scholar in 1990.

In accordance with his literary and cultural stature, Harper was invited to read in the bicentenary exchange with England in 1976, at the Library of Congress in 1975 and 1976, and, received an American Special Grant in 1977, in several of the African countries—Senegal, Ghana, Gambia, Zaire, Zambia, Tanzania, Botswana, and South Africa—as well as at numerous American universities.

Harper has been honored with visiting professorships at Harvard and Yale Universities and distinguished professorships at Carleton College and the University of Cincinnati. In 1970 he began his employment at Brown University. Promoted to full professor at the age of thirty-six in 1974, Harper received the endowed chair of the Israel J. Kapstein Professorship in 1983.

BIOGRAPHY

Michael Steven Harper was born on March 18, 1938, in Brooklyn, New York, and his birth brought with it particular pressures to succeed: He was the first male born on either side of the family, and he was delivered at his parent's home by his grandfather, Roland R. Johnson. His father, Walter Harper, was a postal worker and supervisor; his mother, Katherine Johnson, worked as a medical stenographer. While not wealthy, the Harper family did enjoy a middle-class income that permitted the acquisition of a good record collection, interesting the young Harper in music and serving as a source for his later development as a poet.

At thirteen, Harper and his family, including his younger brother Jonathan and his sister Katherine, moved to a predominantly white neighborhood in West Los Angeles, an area in which several black families were to have their houses bombed in the early 1950's. Enrolling shortly thereafter in Susan Miller Dorsey High School, Harper was assigned to an industrial arts course of study rather than to an academic one, presumably because he was black, and only his father's intervention with a counselor reversed the institutional assumptions about his abilities. Suffering from extreme asthma in 1951, Harper spent the summer confined to the house and, also because of his asthma, later refused to undress for gym class, for which he failed the class and was kept off the honor roll. Always having been encouraged to study medicine in the tradition of his grandfather and his great-grandfather Dr. John Albert Johnson, an African Methodist Episcopal Church bishop and missionary in South Africa from 1907 to 1916, Harper used the incident to escape the family's pressures and to turn his attention from the classroom and his interests in medicine, literature, and history to the ordinary life in the streets and neighborhoods around him. While not a disciplined student, he was a good test-taker, and he was graduated from high school in 1955.

From 1956 to 1961, Harper pursued a premedical course at Los Angeles State College (now California State University at Los Angeles) while at the same time working full-time as a postal worker. In college, a zoology professor discouraged his study of medicine, assuming that blacks were incapable of sustaining the rigors of medical school. On the job, Harper encountered well-educated blacks who were unable to advance—not because they lacked merit, but because they were black. Together, these two experiences of racism, experienced first hand, helped shape his sense that American society was essentially schizophrenic: It celebrated free competition based on merit, but it barred blacks from an equal chance to participate in the culture—color was too often more consequential than character.

While Harper was in college, two books in particular, *The Letters of John Keats* (1958) and Ralph Ellison's *Invisible Man* (1952), and a course, "The Epic of Search," which offered a historical view of the human quest for self-assertion from *The Odyssey* (c. ninth century B.C.E.) to *Invisible Man*, rekindled his desire to write. In high school, he had experimented with poetry, short fiction, and drama, but he had abandoned those early attempts. Deprived of encouragement to study medicine, Harper enrolled in the Iowa Writers Workshop in 1961. Restricted to segregated housing, he became increasingly aware of the fragmentation in American cultural life. As the only black enrolled in both poetry and fiction classes, Harper began to write poetry seriously, receiving en-

couragement from the writer Ralph Dickey and the painter Oliver Lee Jackson. In 1962, turning his attention to teaching, Harper left Iowa to teach at Pasadena City College, armed at twenty-four with a long-standing knowledge of black music and a newly developing expertise in black history, writing, and painting—all of which would come to inform his new commitment to his principal mode of expression: poetry.

The following year, 1963, Harper returned to Iowa and, although he had been in the Creative Writers Program, he passed the comprehensive examinations in English, receiving his master's degree. He taught then at Contra Costa College, San Pablo, California, from 1964 to 1968. After teaching the following year at Reed College and Lewis and Clark College in Oregon, he taught as associate professor of English at California State College at Hayward in 1969-1970. Although receiving a tenured appointment as an associate professor at Brown University in 1970, Harper spent 1970-1971 at the University of Illinois, pursuing a postdoctoral fellowship at the Center for Advanced Studies. In 1971, Harper began teaching at several universities as a visiting professor while being employed at Brown University, where he served as director of the Graduate Creative Writing Program from 1974 to 1983. He was appointed to an endowed chair at Brown in 1983, and he served as Rhode Island's poet laureate from 1988-1993.

ANALYSIS

Michael S. Harper's oeuvre has established his stature as a significant voice in contemporary poetry. As an African American poet, Harper explores the historical and contemporary duality of consciousness that was first expressed by Frederick Douglass in the nineteenth century and W. E. B. Du Bois in the early twentieth century: What it means to be both black and American, and how one survives as both. While using to a limited extent a narrative frame, Harper's lyricism pays homage to the heroic endurance of family members, unsung musicians, and historical activists through a consciously developed technique that affirms the African American literary tradition, grounded in the oral tradition of storytelling and the musical heritage of spirituals, blues, and jazz. Avoiding the sometimes strident, polemical tones of black poetry in the 1960's and 1970's, Harper nevertheless fashions an ethically powerful voice, marked not only by a passion in exposing the tragedy of black history in America but also by a compassion for the individuals who have sought to endure and to create out of the cauldron of racism. His distinctive voice and all-embracing vision have evoked praise from both black and white reviewers and critics.

In an interview with Abraham Chapman, Michael Harper identifies the poetic technique of much of his work as "modality," an abstract musical concept that he uses as a metaphor for his ethical vision as well as for his subjective principle of composition. Many of Harper's poems lend themselves to performance; they are meant to be read aloud. In hearing them, one hears, through a range of idiom, dialect, and individual voices, the past fused with the contemporary, the individual speaking forth from communal experience and the black American's kinship, simultaneously tragic and heroic, to the whole of American cultural values. Rooted in classic jazz patterns from such musicians as Duke Ellington, Charlie Parker, and John Coltrane, modality is "about relationships" and "about energy, energy irreducible and true only unto itself." As a philosophical, ethical perspective, modality is a "particular frequency" for expressing and articulating "the special nature of the Black man and his condition and his contributions" to the American synthesis of cultural values. As such, modality refutes "the Western orientation of division between denotative/connotative, body/mind, life/spirit, soul/body, mind/heart" and affirms a unity of being and experience: "*modality is always about unity.*" Consequently, Harper's poetry gathers fragments from private and public experience, past and present, and seeks to rejuvenate spiritual forces historically suppressed by bringing them to the surface in a poetry of "tensions resolved through a morality worked out between people."

DEAR JOHN, DEAR COLTRANE

In the early poems of *Dear John, Dear Coltrane*, Harper's modal experiments succeed in a variety of forms that nevertheless remain unified in the power of his particular voice. In "Brother John," Harper eulogizes Charlie Parker, the "Bird/ baddest nightdreamer/ on sax in the ornithology-world," Miles Davis, "bug-eyed, unspeakable,/ Miles, sweet Mute,/ sweat Miles, black Miles," and John Coltrane, who serves as a mythic cen-

ter for the poem and the volume as well as several later poems. Typical of Harper's multiple allusions in naming, however, both the poem and the volume also eulogize John O. Stewart, a friend and fiction writer; nor is Coltrane merely a mythic figure, for Harper maintained a personal friendship with him until his death in 1967; in addition, the name "John" also conjures echoes from Harper's great-grandfather, who spent several years in South Africa, and, further, evokes John Brown, who figures prominently in later poems by Harper. Thus, from early in his work, Harper uses modality to reconcile past and present, myth and history, and private and public; personal mourning becomes part of a universal experience and a communal celebration. Drawing inspiration from both the suffering and the achievement of jazz artists in this poem and in subsequent poems in his career, Harper establishes the modal wordplay that affirms his philosophical stance as an activist of the conscience, "I'm a black man; I am;/ black; I am; I'm a black/ man; I am; I am," and his own cry of being, refusing any limiting universality of humanness that is blind to ethnic heritage and experience: "I am; I'm a black man;/ I am."

In other poems from that first volume, Harper links past and present as well as private and public by exploring larger patterns of history. In "American History," Harper asserts the invisibility of black suffering to mainstream America by juxtaposing "Those four black girls blown up/ in that Alabama church" with "five hundred/ middle passage blacks,/ in a net, under water . . . so *red-coats* wouldn't find them." Concluding in an ironic but colloquial idiom, he asks: "Can't find what you can't see/ can you?" In "Reuben, Reuben," Harper uses the death of his own son to overcome his pain in the transcendence of creative energy, just as blues singers have always done when faced with the horror of loss: "I reach from pain/ to music great enough/ to bring me back . . . we've lost a son/ the music, *jazz*, comes in."

HISTORY IS YOUR OWN HEARTBEAT

Harper's early poems test the possibilities of modality, and, in such techniques as concrete imaging, literary allusions, sprung syntax, enjambment, blues refrains, idioms, variable line lengths, and innovative cadences, he discovers in modality a formalism strong enough to bear diverse experiments in free-verse forms and yet a visionary field large enough to draw from virtually any relationship, however intimate or distant, however painful or joyful, for individual affirmation. In his second collection, *History Is Your Own Heartbeat*, Harper uses modality to reconstruct personal history, integrating it with a mythic sense of spiritual unity. Divided into three sections, the book begins with a twenty-poem sequence, "Ruth's Blues," which employs his white mother-in-law's physical deterioration as an extended metaphor for the denial of black and white kinship. In tribute to Ruth's endurance in her quest for physical and psychological health, Harper shows the potential for a unified American sensibility, one which respects cultural differences yet realizes from the pain of division that American experience "is all a well-knit family;/ *a love supreme*," if one chooses to affirm multiple origins. The following two sections, "History as Personality" and "High Modes," pay homage, respectively, to influential personalities such as Martin Luther King, Jr., and Gwendolyn Brooks and, in the latter, to the painter Oliver Lee Jackson. Throughout these sections, Harper emphasizes the unity of a historical and cultural continuum that reaches back to Africa and comes forward to his own family, claiming his own past and an American history that is freed of its delusions, confronting its origins in the slavery of Africans and the genocide of Native Americans, to whom Harper also unearths literal kinship. In several ways, then, this volume, as the title suggests, builds from literal links of kinship with a diversity of races and cultures to a holistic view of American values, in contrast to the exclusive emphasis on European origins characteristic of traditional American history. By healing himself of narrow stereotypes, Harper offers "a love supreme" to his fellow citizens, asserting kinship even where citizenship has been denied and is diminished by racism.

SONG: I WANT A WITNESS

Subsequent books extend Harper's sense of kinship and develop the aesthetic of modality. In *Song: I Want a Witness*, he explores the black American religious heritage, using the metaphor of testifying, and conceptualizes the literary process as essentially one of an ethical affirmation of heroic character. Tracing American culture back both to Native America, by a link with a great-great-grandmother who was Chippewa, and to the Puritan legacies of Roger Williams and John Winthrop, by a

link to the spirit of place where he lives, Harper, in "History as Appletree," develops an organic metaphor that embodies history and family while also bringing the negative, through an extended photographic metaphor of those ignored by history, to present light and image. In this vision, the fruit of the tree, American culture itself, blossoms with the fertility of long-forgotten bones whose dust nurtures the root system.

DEBRIDEMENT

The collection *Debridement*, a medical term for cutting away the dead flesh of a wound so that it will not infect the healthy body and a metaphor for revising stereotyped versions of American history, honors the heroic actions of John Brown, Richard Wright, and the fictional John Henry Louis. Together, the three sections, each revolving around its respective persona, correct the myth that Americans who have fought against racism were insane, zealous, hysterical. Instead, Harper argues through the modality of these poems, they were—and are—themselves the victims of racism, surviving because they have pursued a truth that has for the most part been hidden from them.

NIGHTMARE BEGINS RESPONSIBILITY

In *Nightmare Begins Responsibility*, the poet extends a logic that runs through the previous two books. Once one realizes that the pejorative American myth is false, then one must act to overcome the cultural insensitivity of racism and the apathy toward the land, both as physical and cultural environment. Alienation and isolation yield only to courageous, often unpopular action, and the American Dream and manifest destiny are concepts of death riddled with literal exploitation and genocide unless one replaces them with the values of kinship and acts to establish historical knowledge and contemporary intimacy as the basis for defining oneself as an American.

IMAGES OF KIN AND HEALING SONG FOR THE INNER EAR

Harper's insistence that one accept both unity and diversity, both pain and love, continues in *Images of Kin*, which reverses the chronological order of the selections which represent an anthology of his earlier poetry. By beginning with new poems and working back to the earlier ones, Harper testifies to the imperative for reconstructing American myth and history. *Healing Song for the Inner Ear* expands the modality of celebrating friends, family, musicians, and poets by bringing them into Harper's constantly expanding vision of history. Functioning much like his first book, this collection moves both backward and forward, but it also moves toward a more international perspective than that found in any of his earlier collections. From the American perspective of "Goin' to the Territory," which salutes the influence of Ralph Ellison and witnesses his aesthetic endurance, and "The Pen," which gives voice to an oral tradition become literary artifact, embodying values inherent in both black American and Native American lives, a modality in which "patterns of the word fling out into destiny/ as a prairie used to when the Indians/ were called Kiowa, Crow, Dakota, Cheyenne," to a series of poems set in South Africa, Harper explores the complexity of image and story embedded in history and the enduring truth of experience excavated in modal expression.

"THE MILITANCE OF A PHOTOGRAPH . . ."

In the poem "The Militance of a Photograph in the Passbook of a Bantu Under Detention," Harper meditates on the history behind the photograph that identifies a black South African from Soweto, and he asserts "This is no simple mug shot/ of a runaway boy in a training/ film. . . ." Harper senses his own history here; the runaway might have been a nineteenth century slave, the training film could well serve as a powerful tool for the suppression of historical facts, and the mug shot suggests that color itself (since only blacks must carry passbooks) is the crime. Personally, Harper must also unite his great-grandfather's experience in South Africa with the strategies of apartheid, and, in uniting the past personal association with the contemporary public policies of racism, Harper affirms the courage of the oppressed: "The Zulu lullaby/ I cannot sing in Bantu/ is this song in the body/ of a passbook/ and the book passes/ into a shirt/ and the back that wears it." Perhaps the modality of such a link between Americans and South Africans, between forgotten language and forgotten people, serves as the celebration of Harper's enduring theme, as in the epigraph to the poem: "Peace is the active presence of Justice."

SONGS IN MICHAELTREE

In Harper's retrospective collection, which culls poetry from eight previous volumes, he returns to his characteristic progressive, improvisatory power that respects a variety of traditions in the arts. He celebrates the accomplishments of outstanding figures of the African-American community while also tenderly exploring the "Michaeltree," an emblem of his own life, with deeply felt poems about members of his family. Serving as figurative bookends to the volume is a poem of six stanzas, each line repeated three times, beginning with the triad, "when there is no history," followed by an image of "a blind nation in a storm," that is "belted in these ruins." Here Harper asserts a reclamation from silent and suppression of the many-centuried struggle of African Americans in the United States, and sets the tone for the collection.

Poems from past collections are balanced by Harper with additional material to assist the reader in understanding his life of teaching and writing. "Notes to the Poem" functions as a teaching text and provides background to Harper's familiar themes, elucidating his use of historical data that might be obscure to those who don't share his expertise. "To the Reader" invites the reader on a journey that explores the evolution of his creative consciousness. Here he acknowledges his debt to the "pioneering writers: Robert Hayden, Sterling A. Brown, and Ralph Ellison." He also notes the influences of family members and, through anecdotal notes, that of his experiences with publicly reading his poetry. Finally, "Notes on Form and Fictions" examines his poetic technique and the derivations of his innovations. He notes, "I began to write poems because I could not see those elements of my life that I considered sacred reflected in my courses of study: scientific, literary, and linguistic." The reader thus better understands his overriding attraction to African American music as a source for shape, language, rhythms, and the near-mythic hero-figures of his poetry.

OTHER MAJOR WORKS

EDITED TEXTS: *Chant of Saints: A Gathering of Afro-American Literature, Art, and Scholarship*, 1979 (with Robert B. Stepto); *The Carleton Miscellany: A Ralph Ellison Festival*, 1980 (with John Wright); *Every Shut Eye Ain't Asleep: An Anthology of Poetry by African Americans Since 1945*, 1994 (with Anthony Walton); *The Vintage Book of African American Poetry*, 2000 (with Walton); *The Collected Poems of Sterling A. Brown*, 1980.

BIBLIOGRAPHY

Antonucci, Michael. "The Map and the Territory: An Interview with Michael S. Harper." *African American Review* 34, no. 3 (Fall, 2000): 501-508. This interview refers back to Harper's statements in earlier interviews and allows for clarifications of his position on poets as historians and other matters. Comments on Robert Hayden, the legacy of John Brown, Ralph Ellison, African American cultural heroes, and several of Harper's own poems.

Breslin, Paul. "Some Early Returns." *Poetry* 134 (May, 1979): 107-114. In this review of *Images of Kin: New and Selected Poems*, Breslin admits to liking Harper's work—noting that his style is distinctive—but has reservations about his ability to realize each poem fully. Nevertheless, he appreciates Harper for the range of his voice and his desire for completeness.

Brown, Joseph A. "Their Long Scars Touch Ours: A Reflection on the Poetry of Michael Harper." *Callaloo* 9, no. 1 (1986): 209-220. One of the several pieces on Harper to be found in this particular journal, this one provides a succinct, useful overview of Harper's themes and sense of history.

Forbes, Calvin. Review of *Honorable Amendments. African American Review* 32, no. 3 (Fall, 1998): 508-510. Forbes questions the reasons for Harper's retreat to secondary status, feeling he is no longer numbered among the indispensable African American literary artists. He takes Harper's lack of literary awards as one kind of evidence. Forbes examines Harper's fondness for the iambic measure and wonders if this dimension of his work, along with Harper's admiration for general humanistic values like hard work, has somehow alienated him politically. Forbes concludes, "Harper at his best is the personification of the black literary mainstream poet doing his thing."

Jackson, Richard. *Acts of Mind: Conversations with Contemporary Poets.* University: University of Alabama Press, 1983. The interview with Harper, recorded here and titled "Magic: Power: Activation: Transformation," discusses, among other things, the lyricism in his poetry and his kinship with people. In this conversation, Harper explains how he constructs his poems and how magic and power shape the world. Useful in providing insight into Harper's motivations.

Lehman, David. "Politics." *Poetry* 123 (December, 1973): 173-180. On balance, this essay is an unfavorable review of *Debridement*, criticizing Harper for his lack of daring and even ghetto speech that does not work. Lehman notes, however, that Harper can and does "jolt us out of the ordinary" with his choice of words.

Lieberman, Laurence. *Unassigned Frequencies: American Poetry in Review, 1964-77.* Chicago: University of Illinois Press, 1977. In his commendable essay "The Muse of History," Lieberman reviews Harper's *Debridement* and considers it one of Harper's best works to date, calling him a poet of "musical richness and density of style in the short, compact lyric." Commends Harper for his restraint and freedom from emoting in contrast with the intensity of his subjects. The essay also critiques Derek Walcott's *Another Life* (1973), drawing parallels between the works of these two poets.

Turner, Alberta T., ed. *Fifty Contemporary Poets: The Creative Process.* New York: David McKay, 1977. Harper discusses how he wrote "Grandfather." He says: "I have always been a poet who had a pattern for a poem at conception. . . ." This volume contains some relevant background information about this poem, as well as some insights into Harper's approach to his art.

Michael Loudon,
updated by Philip K. Jason and Sarah Hilbert

JIM HARRISON

Born: Grayling, Michigan; December 11, 1937

PRINCIPAL POETRY
Plain Song, 1965
Locations, 1968
Outlyer and Ghazals, 1971
Letters to Yesenin, 1973

Returning to Earth, 1977

Selected and New Poems: 1961-1981, 1982

Natural World, 1982 (includes sculpture by Diana Guest)

The Theory and Practice of Rivers: Poems, 1985

The Theory and Practice of Rivers and New Poems, 1989

After Ikkyu and Other Poems, 1996

The Shape of the Journey: New and Collected Poems, 1998

OTHER LITERARY FORMS

Although Jim Harrison began his career as a poet, it was the publication of his fourth fiction title, *Legends of the Fall* (1979), that brought him national recognition. The book, which consisted of three novellas, two of which had previously appeared in *Esquire*, proved so successful that Dell Publishing Company reissued his previously published novels in paperback editions. Since that time he has published several other volumes of fiction. *The Boy Who Ran to the Woods* (2000) is his first book for children. Harrison's novels and novellas, like his other writings, are often violent, yet they are marked by a lyrical poetic voice.

Harrison has also written screenplays and published numerous essays dealing with sports and the out-of-doors; these articles complement the tone and thrust of his other writing and offer further evidence of his commitment to the natural environment and the code of ethics necessary for its maintenance. *Just Before Dark* (1991) is a collection of his nonfiction prose pieces.

ACHIEVEMENTS

Jim Harrison has long been recognized as a talented and important voice in American letters. He has combined a unique blend of elements, uniting the American vernacular with a distinctly Eastern metaphysics. He consistently fuses primitive and naturalistic images with the arcane and ponderous and draws upon both gothic and surreal conventions.

By refusing to limit himself to a single genre and by attending to "audible things, things moving at noon in full raw light," Harrison has been able to appeal to a diversified audience and to promulgate an integrated vision which embodies the subtler nuances of the physical and natural world. Relying on what T. S. Eliot called "the auditory imagination," he enables the reader to hear and feel simultaneously the meaning and motion of objects and experiences and to take part in the poet's personal journey toward self-discovery.

BIOGRAPHY

James Thomas Harrison was born December 11, 1937, in Grayling, Michigan, and has spent most of his life in and around northern Michigan, the land of Ernest Hemingway's Nick Adams stories. Perhaps because this area has become "largely mythical" in the wake of development, it has come to constitute Harrison's Yoknapatawpha County, peopled by figures drawn from both his German and Swedish ancestral lines.

More important than any particular biographical data is the spirit of the land and its people which Harrison has assimilated. Because the terrain "lacks drama," it has sensitized him to "particularities" and made him more aware of the unique flavor of various locales. It has also indelibly colored his allegiances. Significantly, after trying his hand at teaching at the State University of New York, Stony Brook, Harrison returned to Michigan and bought a nine-acre farm near Lake Leelanau. As he subsequently explained: "I feel much less isolated from people here than at the university."

As the allusions which pepper Harrison's writing make clear, he is a prodigious reader. Not surprisingly, his graduate work was in comparative literature and he considers himself an "internationalist," identifying Pablo Neruda, Rainer Maria Rilke, William Butler Yeats, Basil Bunting, Federico García Lorca, Walt Whitman, Hart Crane, Robert Duncan, and Ezra Pound as major influences.

ANALYSIS

It is difficult to envision Jim Harrison ever becoming a widely read poet. His poetry, while extremely tactile, is not easily apprehended. Using the natural world as a springboard, he infuses it with mystic correspondences and multiple layers of allusion. His preferred forms are the suite and the ghazal, both of which involve loose assemblages of stanzas which are related largely by free associations. Hence, what may appear to be arbitrary suspensions of narrative sequences are, instead,

highly crafted movements through the poet's preconscious mind.

Harrison is an iconoclast whose thought patterns,
even in his more traditional narratives, tend to be elliptical. In the suites and ghazals, this tendency culminates
in violent disruptions of linear connection and the com-
pounding of discordant images. His poetry requires that
the reader transcend the limits of the rational mind and
follow the poet on his personal explorations, which have
their own indigenous logic. Harrison is reaching directly
for the experiences he is rendering.

Plain Song is an uneven and underrated book which
attempts more than is readily apparent. Donald Jones,
one of the few reviewers to treat the book apart from
other collections, aptly applies the concept "numinous
surds" to convey the craftsmanship of the best of these
poems. What is most striking about this volume is Harrison's capacity to fuse his northern Michigan sensibility
with an almost mystic sense of cosmic unity and a host
of both classical and modern allusions. What reviewers
see as his devotion to "the thing-in-itself" is but the surface of the work. Behind all of these poems is an organic
consciousness unfettered by logical dictums and intent
upon immersing the reader in the elemental flux.

PLAIN SONG

Plain Song begins with a modest *ars poetica*,
"Poem," which reveals Harrison's poetic credo and his
affinity for the natural world. Using the woods as a correlative for poetic form and the stalking bobcat to represent content, Harrison pictures structures as mere backdrops which, by definition, "yield to conclusion they do
not care about or watch." Poems, "Word Drunk" explains, are living creatures "suffused with light," essences yielding their "own dumb form—weight raw,
void of intent." Herein lies the source of Harrison's pre-
disposition toward suites and ghazals; both facilitate experimentation with form and transport the reader into
"another field, or richer grain."

Already evident in these early pieces is his attention
to sensory detail. Quite overtly in such poems as "Exercise" and "Park at Night," Harrison invites the reader to
hear the almost muted sounds of nature: grass moving to
create passageways, soil shifting, and fire selecting new
wood. It is a keen ear, indeed, which can, as Harrison
does in "Sounds," communicate the "loud weight of

birds" capable of drowning out the carpenter's hammer,
and can, in "February Suite," convey the sounds of soldiers breaking "like lightbulbs in a hoarse cry of dust."
In other poems, such as "Northern Michigan" and "Returning at Night," he transforms what a casual observer
might see as unkempt properties into wildlife sanctuar-
ies. Often, as in "Dusk," what emerges is a gestalt of the
visual, the olfactory, and the auditory.

The dominant point of view, rather too baldly stated
in "Trees," is that man's utilitarian perspective senselessly discounts that which is superfluous to his materialistic ends. Clearly, Harrison's sentiments lie with the
victims of civilization's onrush. This is most blatant in
his depiction of the wolf in "Traverse City Zoo" and his
wry commentary in "Fox Farm," but also present in
"Kinship," which captures the nobility of the senile Uncle Wilhelm.

Jim Harrison (Library of Congress)

Harrison's romantic attachment to the woods and wilds is balanced by his capacity for irony and self-mockery. In "Lisle's River," for example, after establishing a resonance with the surroundings, he reverses himself, recounting a drunken violation of the spirit of place. In a very different vein, the persona that emerges from "Sketch for a Job Application Blank" is simultaneously self-abasing and proud. Compounded images of childhood and ancestry culminate in a series of oxymorons which transform sex into sacrament and darkness into a medium for growth. This tendency to shift gears and undercut his own affections is what saves Harrison from sentimentality.

Elemental images of darkness and death play a prominent part in these poems. The young boy in "David" can see through the antiseptic haze of words and the profusion of flowers which surround the father's casket and can confront the reality of death. In "John Severin Walgren, 1874-1962," a muted elegy to his maternal grandfather, Harrison describes death as an inevitable process "when the limit's reached" and yet captures the terror of "the blood of the young, those torn off earth in a night's sickness"—a terror which leads to the pronouncement of a bitter nihilistic credo in "New Liturgy" and a similarly virulent renunciation in "Malediction."

As a first volume, *Plain Song* is important; at its best it reveals Harrison's ability to forge connections between objects. It also hints at the techniques and philosophies which have come to characterize his work. It is not, however, a representative collection in that he seems to rein his imagination and content himself with presentation rather than probing.

LOCATIONS

The nascent strengths found in *Plain Song* come to fruition in *Locations*. Movement and process are dominant in these poems. Gone is even a residual tendency to focus on the "thing-in-itself"; instead, a single act or object is introduced and its implications unfolded through a process of accretion. "Walking," for example, fuses memories and immediate stimuli in such a way as to capture the incessant natural rhythms that enable nature to renew itself and man to perceive even the familiar as notable. That "Walking" calls to mind Henry David Thoreau's essay is not surprising; throughout the book

Harrison is, effectively, reconquering the land much as Thoreau suggested that the saunterer must.

The three poems which are labeled "suites" in this volume are most representative of Harrison's means of building upon the significance of an image. Just as "Suite to Fathers" employs an ambiguous and shifting sense of "fathers," so, too, do "Suite to Appleness" and "War Suite" convey multiple levels of meaning associated with the dominant image. The effect in all three cases is not to convolute, but to clarify through transmutation.

"Suite to Fathers," which constitutes a tribute of sorts to past masters in the field of arts and letters, is framed by two references to night as a "blind woman" and as a woman staring with a "great bruised eye." The "countless singulars" which the poem unveils are coupled with a pervasive sense of gothic horror culminating in the image of the poet's brain as a "glacier of blood, inching forward . . . silt covered but sweet." A similar movement pervades "Suite to Appleness," a poem which transforms the destruction of an apple into a working metaphor capable of suggesting the callousness which induces war atrocities, suicides, ecological disruption, and "all things bruised or crushed as an apple." This thread is continued in "War Suite," which interweaves references to various orders and kinds of wars, not to equate them but to distinguish those that are propelled by necessity and those that are gratuitous and often fought out of vanity. The slaughter of whales and hawks that is lamented in "Natural World" is clearly in the latter class.

"The Sign," though structured in a way similar to the suites, is less intense. Harrison indulges in a dream-induced reverie over the astrological significance of having been born under the sign of Sagittarius, situated between the eagle (Scorpio) and the seagoat (Capricorn), and contemplates the patterned luminosity that somehow makes the infinite black more poignant. Significantly, however, these are indulgences permissible only at night, and he therefore concludes this meditation with the sobering realities of digging a well and the certifiable majesty of a stag "bounding away into his green clear music."

"American Girl" is similarly playful and freewheeling. Beginning with references to Helen of Troy and other temptresses, Harrison shifts his focus to his own rites of passage, which dispelled his idealism and revealed that media's images of women were "calcined, watery, with air-brushed bodies and brains." The experiential elements in this piece as well as in "Night in Boston" and "Locations" are rendered with a levity absent in much of *Plain Song*, suggesting that Harrison has achieved a needed distance.

What lies at the heart of Harrison's perspective is a respect for the natural world. The majesty of the red-tailed hawks in "Cold August" has the capacity to restore his spirits despite the metallic cast that has transformed the once verdant fields. This and other poems demonstrate that he is keenly attuned to seasonal variations as they are manifest in both landscape and animal life. While in "Cold August" and "Thin Ice" he uses a single phenomenon as a touchstone against which to measure the change, in "A Year's Changes" he provides a catalog of sense experiences and registers the sounds and silences which characterize the various seasons.

OUTLYER AND GHAZALS

Outlyer and Ghazals marks a turning point in Harrison's poetic career. The first seven poems (the outlyers) continue themes and techniques found in the earlier volumes. The remainder of the pieces (the ghazals) are groundbreaking and infectious. The title of the opening piece, "In Interims: Outlyer," suggests the point of view employed throughout this volume. "Interims" suggests the breaking space needed to contemplate those phenomena which are too easily dismissed as peripheral, while "outlyer" can be translated as a reference to the poet who has the task of contemplating buried connections. There is also the sense of the poet as the marginal man inhabiting the proverbial outback in the company of the aborigines. With such a frame, it is not surprising to find the epigraph drawn from Guillaume Apollinaire, another innovator and iconoclast.

"In Interims: Outlyer" properly sets the tone for the volume; it testifies to the poet's refusal to take aim at institutional pretense, asserting the need for a higher ordering of principles. Most overtly in "In Interims: Outlyer," the poet is charged with celebrating the bittersweet in order to resurrect the animistic spirit, the "Numen of walking and sleep," an end which he accomplishes in "Hospital," which captures the archetypal

sounds of agony, and "Awake," which transforms a catalog of various anxieties and complaints into a workable backdrop against which to graft his ax-hewn wood metaphor.

Harrison is most effective when he discards the cowboy persona and allows his mystic sensibility to merge with his ironic wit. It is this that allows him in "She Again" to recast what was at best a simpering machismo in "Cowgirl" and "Drinking Song" into a gestalt of emotions which is winsome and lyrical. This combination also gives him the distance to explain that "in interims all journeys end in three steps with a mirrored door, beyond it a closet and a closet wall." Death is accepted as a constant, not as something to fear; it is celebrated as the completion of the circle and the prerequisite for the next procession.

At his best, Harrison's sense of relationships allows him to forge analogies which are surprisingly appropriate. Incongruities are blended in such a way that the shift from the "diamond head caught in crotch of branch" to his sister who died in an auto wreck debases neither phenomenon. This ability to relate dissimilar objects and events lies at the heart of the ghazals that dominate the book. In these sixty-five poems, Harrison gives his mind's eye full rein and repeatedly surprises his reader into taking a second look. Whether he is describing the screams of ecstatic stones becoming thinner, as in the opening poem, or exploring the implications of non-Euclidean geometry, as in the forty-fifth, his vision is always fresh and clear.

Ghazals, Harrison points out in his prefatory note, are essentially lyrics dating from the thirteenth century. They are akin to suites in that both proceed by means of metaphorical leaps of faith, but they are considerably shorter than suites, being limited to twelve couplets. Both the brevity and the couplet form serve Harrison well, allowing him "to regain some of the spontaneity of the dance, the song unencumbered by any philosophical apparatus, faithful only to its own music." Throughout the volume, poetry is equated with music, "scattered, elliptical, needing to be drawn together and sung," and thus it is appropriate that in the twenty-first ghazal Harrison assembles a series of universal sounds into a consciously orchestrated medley which is dissonant but captivating. Insisting that "Poetry must die so poems will live again," Harrison is constantly experimental, pushing back the strictures of his chosen form.

The tempo of these poems is brisk and the tone lilting. He fuses together the lyric and the gothic and ruthlessly burlesques human foibles in order "to be finally sane and bow to all sentient creatures," as he explains in the thirty-second ghazal. Yet, he recognizes that "Apollinaire fertilizer won't feed the pigs or chickens" and that poetry "won't raise the dead or stir the living or open young girls' lips to jubilance." Hence, he is often self-mocking, calling himself, in the second poem, "a poet and a liar," saying, in the sixth, that he "writes with a putty knife and goo" and lamenting, in the thirty-fourth, that the "modal chord I carried around for weeks is lost for want of an instrument." It is this kind of circumspection that prevents him from taking himself too seriously and disarms the reader.

Again, the tightest of these pieces are securely moored to rural embankments. The rural emerges not simply as a purifier, but as an essential antidote to the rapacity of the urban. Yet, he does not romanticize it; he rejects what he terms the "befouled nostalgia about childhood" and launches more than an occasional barb at the provincialism and hardships of rural life. In the second poem he imagines what might happen if there were poetry competitions at the county fairs, and in the third he captures the wearisome lot of a country girl who is hired out in the off-season.

These poems are replete with references to the slaughter of predators and other wild creatures; with quiet irony, Harrison debunks the logic of the rancher and the hunter alike. In the sixteenth poem, he neatly understates the plight of the "tamed" bear strapped to a bicycle "with straps of silver and gold straps inlaid with scalps." This image signals his overall moral stance which prompts him to envision Spiro Agnew, vice president during Richard Nixon's administration, "retired to a hamster farm" and the wild animals "spying on the geologists" in the fourteenth poem and to complain about "vicious horses kicking when I bite their necks" in the twenty-seventh.

He relentlessly lampoons the world of politics. Art becomes, in the fifteenth poem, a miracle needed "to raise those years which are tombstones carved out of soap by the world's senators," and, in the sixteenth, the

drama of "civic theater" emerges as "interminable with unconvincing geometric convulsions." In the eighteenth, the pathos of the migrant worker functions as a concertina, undercutting the pretense of literary groupies and the perniciousness of the Department of Defense. Still, Harrison eschews activism, refusing to become another "tremulous bulls-eye for hog fever" or "a poisoned ham in the dinner room of Congress."

As part of a disaffected generation, Harrison is wary of all institutions and, in the final analysis, holds nothing sacred other than the human capacity for wonder. Thus, religion emerges as a target because it has become institutionalized. Gone are the legends that were once central to an understanding of the cosmos. He rues the loss in both the fifty-second and fifty-third ghazals, implying that it is the magic—the "serpent becoming dragon and twelve moons lost at sea"—that has been sacrificed in the name of civilization. No longer does one find "Small people who hitch rides on snakes or ancient people with signs"; instead of being vital, religion has been sanitized and become entropic, as he suggests in the forty-ninth poem. The displacement of wonder by guilt leads him to note wryly in the first ghazal that "Jesus *will* return and the surprise will be fatal."

LETTERS TO YESENIN

Just how important wonder is for Harrison becomes clear in *Letters to Yesenin*. As he says in the twenty-seventh poem, "We learn to see with the child's delight again and perish." In this volume there is little of the youthful bravado that characterized his earlier works. He is deadly serious in this, his most consistently crafted book; his voice is honest and compelling. The disaffection evident in the ghazals has been sharply intensified as he does battle with the ghosts and killing realities of the past and present and tries to arrive at a credible reason for rejecting suicide as a proper response to life's absurdity.

The volume, which includes thirty meditative letters directed to Sergei Aleksandrovich Esenin, the Russian poet who hung himself after writing his farewell poem in his own blood, teems with mordant critiques of the human condition. As Harrison admits in the twenty-ninth letter, the poems "often resemble a suicide note to a suicide." What prevents the constant presence of death from overwhelming these poems is Harrison's indomitable wit, his capacity to draw away from his target and mock his own reveries. In the fifteenth letter he rhetorically asks whether this is a time for joking, and responds unequivocally: "Yes. Always." What results is a curious blend of backwoods and gallows humor which fuels Harrison's ironic perspective. For the most part, his attempts at levity are confined to parenthetical remarks that lighten his otherwise dark imagery, but he also includes a few extended spoofs of the "triumphs" that make life bearable. The most effective, the ninth letter, is a mock ode to paper clips.

Harrison's ironic perspective allows him to cut through the veneer and depict the Russian revolution as "a red tinged glory, neither fire nor sun, a sheen without irony on the land" in the thirteenth letter, and to debunk the romance associated with Esenin's career. Noting the way in which Esenin's displacement and despair fed on each other, and were exacerbated by his tumultuous marriage to Isadora Duncan, Harrison sums up the cost in the twenty-eighth poem: "One body and soul net, one brain already tethered to the dark, one ingenious leash never to hold a dog, two midwinter eyes that lost their technicolor."

In an effort to come to terms with Esenin's meteoric rise, which he compares to a "proton in an accelerator," and the motivation for his death, he alludes to countless others who were, to varying degrees, victims of their own genius. Among those he would like to "dream back to life" are Osip Mandelstam, Bella Akhmadulina, Waslaw Nijinski, Aleksandr Blok, and Hart Crane. Also present are Chief Joseph, who nobly "led a thousand with a thousand horses a thousand miles" during the Nez Perce War, and those who were senselessly slaughtered at the 1972 Olympics. Chief Joseph "was very understanding, incidentally, when the Cavalry shot so many of the women and children. It was to be expected"; Harrison has also become inured to the violence and destruction of contemporary life.

It is clear, especially in the nineteenth and twenty-seventh poems, that he is tired of putting on a show and contenting himself with "those pure empty days with all the presence of a hole in the ground," and yet, unlike Esenin, he refuses to allow circumstances to overwhelm him. He remains capable of "helpless sensual wonder" and readily partakes of the "libidinal stew that calls us to

life however ancient and basal," as he phrases it in the twenty-ninth letter. Further, as he makes clear in the twenty-fifth poem, he places a good deal of stock in the poet's mandate to speak for those who are condemned to suffer voicelessly. The poet emerges from the sixteenth poem as a "sorcerer bored with magic who has turned his attention elsewhere" and is capable of capturing "wonders that psilocybin never conceived of in her powdery head."

By the time he reaches the "Postscript," he has not only effectively vented the angst that threatened to dislodge his tenuous grip, but has also recast his view of Esenin's suicide, causing him to comment that it lacked the dignity of an animal's death and to announce his own decision to stay. The final piece, "A Domestic Poem for Portia," reaffirms this decision and acts as a completion of the circle begun in the first letter. It is not an optimistic piece by any stretch of the imagination, but the recurrent chorus of "nothing" which weighted the first piece has been replaced by variants of "This is all it is." He has, effectively, settled; what seemed about to overwhelm him has been accepted, leading him to conclude: "I'm hanging onto nothing today and with confidence, a sureness that the very air between our bodies, the light of what we are, has to be enough."

RETURNING TO EARTH

Returning to Earth which followed on the heels of *Letters to Yesenin* (the two were published in a joint volume in 1979) invites disappointment. While both works display the same finely honed poetic imagination, they are markedly dissimilar. *Returning to Earth* is a loosely structured compendium of poems and sense-impressions which is keynoted by an incessant playfulness and a tendency to scramble metaphors. While it is laced with telling insights, it is not as compelling as *Letters to Yesenin*. When Harrison says "I widowed my small collection of magic until it poisoned itself with longing," one cannot help feeling that he is referring to the time devoted to novels in lieu of poetry.

The title itself sets this work apart from *Letters to Yesenin*. The poet has left the literary realm and reentered northern Michigan. This meaning is suggested by his vignette about his fat pet bird with a malformed wing and a penchant for drink; when the bird, like the poet, drinks, he "flies in great circles miles wide, preferring bad days with low cold clouds looking like leper brains." After howling his pain, he "drags himself through air mostly landing near a screen door slamming, a baby's cry, a dog's bark, a forest fire, a sleeping coyote. The fabulous memories of earth!"

The point that is most insistently made in this volume is that life on earth is replete with agonies and events which leave scars that are only significant, finally, to the individual who suffered them. With a much more buoyant tone than that found in previous works, Harrison chronicles his own litany of complaints without dwelling on any particular one for too long. The net result is akin to reading a well-written journal which teems with insight but stops short of fleshing out the whole. That this may well have been Harrison's intent is suggested by his reference to the almost solipsistic nature of poetry—"brain moving as a river, governed precisely by her energies"—and by his desire to have his life "in cloud shapes, water shapes, crow calls, marsh hawk swooping over grass and weed tips." It is this desire that leads him to endorse the impressionistic and elliptical, claiming "No music in statement, the lowest denominator by which our fragments can't find each other."

SELECTED AND NEW POEMS

The publication of *Selected and New Poems* made much of Harrison's earlier work, which had gone out of print, readily accessible. The volume includes about half of the poems from *Plain Song*, all but four of the poems from *Locations*, and all but one of the "outlyers" found in *Outlyer and Ghazals*. It also reprints *Letters to Yesenin* and *Returning to Earth* in their entirety and includes about twenty pages of new poems. Both the editorial selection and the accompanying Imagistic drawings by Russell Chatham reveal the care that went into its production.

Because it includes all of Harrison's best poems, it highlights his range and complexity, establishing him as a major voice in American poetry. The new poems again demonstrate his ability to use form as a liberator, to resist the tendency to write stylized or predictable poetry; Harrison is a master of the double entendre and again revealed not only the breadth of his knowledge but also the volatility of his imagination. He moves back and forth between concrete and abstract images as he es-

chews the narcissism of so many of the meditative, confessional poets as well as the self-effacement of the formalists.

These poems do not fall neatly into any particular pattern. Harrison includes two ghazals, both of which reinforce the notion that this is a form that suits him well. "The Chatham Ghazal" includes in each couplet an objective observation, which is then confounded by an unexpected addition which acts back upon the initial image and casts it in a fresh light. "Marriage Ghazal" proceeds somewhat more sequentially with each couplet preparing the way for the next. In "Marriage Ghazal," Harrison moves from the image of a "sea wrack" seeking shore, through the image of a disembodied soul reentering its body and heading inland, and to an image of the drifter uniting with another, with whom he builds a new boat presumably to set sail on a different sea.

Operative in the best of these pieces is a multiple perspective which is explained in the final poem, "After Reading Takahashi." Beginning with the relatively mundane thought that "nothing is the same to anyone," Harrison energizes this idea with a series of counterpoints which leads finally to the resolve "to look at all creatures and things with a billion eyes, not struggling with the single heartbeat that is my life." The same point is more obliquely suggested in "Rooster." After an extended debate with himself, he realizes that "the worthless rooster" with his magnificent, wavering crow is "the poet's bird brother" (a sobering thought) and decides he cannot kill the bird without first sitting down and talking it over with him.

While poems like "Frog" are relatively straightforward and convey sensory memories economically and directly, the bulk of the new poems reach beyond the concrete, becoming almost ethereal. The opening poem, "Not Writing My Name," is a case in point. It begins with the poet's fantasy of etching his name in the snow with each letter being hundreds of yards long, but he dismisses this as the idea of a "star-crossed jock ego" and turns his attention instead to the visible signs and tactile sensations that accompany a northern Michigan winter. Following a series of conventional images, he suddenly introduces the mastodon floating through the trees, uses a metaphorical flashback to Africa, and thus lays the groundwork for the final image: "I have become the place the crow didn't appear." Similarly, in "My First Day as a Painter," he begins with a list of things to paint in which "nude women" initially seem to be an obsession but are abruptly transformed into a metaphor which encompasses both the regenerative powers of nature and the ethereal beauty resident in all things.

In several of the poems, he reverses the process by beginning with an abstraction and gradually grounding it with an infusion of concrete images. A variant of this technique is found in "Epithalamium," in which a gothic description of the wind blowing straight down from the heavens is used to signify a once-in-a-lifetime experience, a miracle of sorts. By the end of the poem, he has pulled away from this epiphany and begun to doubt that it ever occurred.

Absent in these poems is the whine which in previous volumes has crept into Harrison's voice. He has, "Walter of Battersea" suggests, chosen to dance rather than allow his complaints to overwhelm him or his poetry. Poems like "A Redolence for Nims," "Noon," and "Birthday" imply that he has come to accept the changes that accompany aging and the losses that punctuate life as part of a cyclical process through which the old skin is shed and a new set of dreams is formulated to provide the needed quotient of warmth. He has, in this sense, gained the necessary distance to transform private preoccupations into artistic statements and to transport the reader into his northern clime so as to share both the romance and the struggle of living in close contact with the environment.

NATURAL WORLD

Natural World, a collaborative venture between Harrison and Diana Guest, combines poetry and sculpture to celebrate the richness and diversity that is to be found beyond the beaten path. As in previous Harrison collections, however, the celebration is muted by acknowledgments of the waste and suffering that humankind has inflicted upon the animal kingdom and by references to the inherently painful process of natural selection. The majority of the poems included in this volume are reprinted from previous Harrison collections, most notably from *Plain Song* and *Locations*. In this volume, however, the poems assume an even more poignant resonance because of their juxtaposition with Guest's sculptures. The whales and hawks mourned in "Natural World," for example, emerge as creatures to be revered, as creatures that "alter the universe" and make life a little more livable. Similarly, the foxes of "Fox Farm" and the wolf in "Traverse City Zoo" invite the reader to question the ethics that allow humankind to exploit animals for the sake of vanity and commercial gain.

As in his other works, there is a tension between Harrison's naturalist proclivities and his tacit justification of humankind's sporting use of animals. This tension is clearly expressed in "Scrubbing the Floor the Night a Great Lady Died," an ode of sorts following the death of a three-year-old filly. On one hand, Harrison condones the use of animals in the sporting arena by noting that "A great creature died who took her body as far as bodies go toward perfection," but, on the other hand, he empathizes with the horse, noting that "if I cannot care about a horse, I cannot care about earth herself. For she was so surely of earth, in earth, once so animate, sprung in some final, perfect form. . . ."

THE THEORY AND PRACTICE OF RIVERS

Perhaps the clue to Harrison's apparent ambiguity lies in his belief in eternal essences and perpetual flux. These ideas, nascent in "Horse" and "Cobra," come to fruition in *The Theory and Practice of Rivers*, in which he muses that he will "assume the water mask, to finish my life disguised as a creek . . . to swallow myself in ceaseless flow." *The Theory and Practice of Rivers* is consummate Harrison. It reflects not only the breadth of his talent and interests but also his ability to control metaphors that would overwhelm lesser writers. The volume is made richer still by a liberal infusion of sketches by Chatham, who did the sectional illustrations for *Selected and New Poems*.

Dedicated to his deceased niece, the book opens with a wide-ranging poem dedicated both to her memory and to the possibility that her spirit continues to inhabit the rivers in which she once played. In this poem, Harrison uses water imagery as a recurrent metaphor, but he also broaches countless other subjects as he allows his mind's eye to reflect upon past adventures in all corners of the globe. Despite the diversity of subject matter, however, Harrison is constantly attuned to the mysterious ebb and flow that characterizes the life process, a process akin to a voyage across uncharted waterways. As with the other poems in this collection, the tone of the title poem ranges from the deadly serious to the playful. In fact, it is the vacillations of mood that make these pieces so compelling. Poetry, Harrison implies in the title poem, must shun equilibrium and systematic formulas, for these are not the things of life. "Life often shatters in schizoid splinters" and defies easy categorization.

Harrison's sardonic wit peppers this volume, as in "The Brand New Statue of Liberty," in which he describes a customized necklace made of representative skulls of those who have been sacrificed for the American Dream. Equally ironic are "Looking Forward to Old Age," "The Times Atlas," and "Rich Folks, Poor Folks, and Neither," each of which critiques the banalities and posturing that have come to characterize modern civilization.

As in his previous works, Harrison relies heavily upon allusions and stream-of-consciousness techniques which make the reader see commonplace phenomena in new lights. At the same time, however, he maintains a childlike capacity for wonder and occasionally, as in "My Friend the Bear," asks the reader to suspend disbelief and imagine a very different world, a world in which human being and beast form a tentative partnership that serves both their ends.

AFTER IKKYU AND THE SHAPE OF THE JOURNEY

The new poems in Harrison's volumes from the mid-1980's onward reveal his having spent less and less time working in this form. Still, many of them hold up quite well and suggest that there is much more that Harrison can yet accomplish as a poet. Most notable are the poems in *After Ikkyu*, a collection inspired by his many years of Zen practice. The influence of Ikkyu, the fifteenth century Zen priest and poet, has energized and freshened Harrison's vision and style. For new readers, the collected and new poems in his *The Shape of the Journey* provide a place to begin.

At his best, Harrison uses his elliptical thought patterns to make connections that would not otherwise be obvious, to force the reader to stretch intellectually. While his segues are not always easy to follow given the syntactical and grammatical liberties that he takes, they are generally insightful and worthy of pursuit, connecting not only with one another but with the reader as

well. His ability to capture the sounds and movements of the woods and rural environs, no less than his ability to translate the pathos of the dispossessed and disaffected, should surely earn him a hearing among all those who are concerned with what has been sacrificed in the name of civilization. Harrison, regretfully, represents a dying breed; he is a poet sufficiently attuned to the natural environment to tally the losses and to do it with a remarkable native wit.

OTHER MAJOR WORKS

LONG FICTION: *Wolf: A False Memoir*, 1971; *A Good Day to Die*, 1973; *Farmer*, 1976; *Legends of the Fall*, 1979 (collection of three novellas: *Revenge*; *The Man Who Gave Up His Name*; and *Legends of the Fall*); *Warlock*, 1981; *Sundog*, 1984; *Dalva*, 1988; *The Road Home*, 1998; *The Woman Lit by Fireflies*, 1990 (collection of three novellas: *Brown Dog*; *Sunset Limited*; and *The Woman Lit by Fireflies*); *Julip*, 1994 (collection of three novellas: *Julip*; *The Seven Ounce Man*; and *The Beige Dolorosa*); *The Road Home*; 1998; *The Beast God Forgot to Invent*, 2000 (collection of three novellas: *The Beast God Forgot to Invent*; *Westward Ho*; and *Forgot to Go to Spain*).

SCREENPLAYS: *Cold Feet*, 1988 (with Thomas McGuane); *Revenge*, 1989; *Wolf*, 1994 (with Wesley Strick).

NONFICTION: *Just Before Dark: Collected Nonfiction*, 1991; *The Raw and the Cooked: Adventures of a Roving Gourmand*, 2001.

CHILDREN'S LITERATURE: *The Boy Who Ran to the Woods*, 2000.

BIBLIOGRAPHY

Davis, Todd. "A Spiritual Topography: Northern Michigan in the Poetry of Jim Harrison." *Midwest Quarterly* 42, no. 1 (Autumn, 2000): 94-104. Examines the spiritual topography in the poetry of Jim Harrison, that is, how his quest for life's meaning is influenced by the natural world, particularly the landscape of Northern Michigan, and how that landscape figures in the poems.

Harrison, Jim. "Jim Harrison." In *Conversations with American Novelists*, edited by Kay Bonetti et al. Columbia: University of Missouri Press, 1997. Harrison discusses how the skills he developed writing poetry were transferred to his fiction and how university writing programs sometimes are negative in their influence.

_____. "Poetry as Survival." *Antaeus* 64 (Spring/Autumn, 1990): 370-380; "From the Dalva Notebooks: 1985-1987." *Antaeus* 61 (Autumn, 1988): 208-214. The pieces cited in this entry are companion pieces of a sort. The first does much to explain Harrison's affinity for the poetic process and for Native American art; the latter sheds insight into both *Dalva* and *The Woman Lit by Fireflies*. Taken together, the two pieces do much to remind the reader that the author remains a reflective critic and commentator, attuned to the forces of the late twentieth century.

Jones, Donald. "Numinous Surds." *Prairie Schooner* 40 (Winter, 1966): 366-367. One of the earliest reviews to recognize the range of Harrison's talents. While recognizing weaknesses in Harrison's earliest poems, Jones gives him high praise for "clear, strong, supple speech of reverberant passion along with a naked freshness of sense-data and diction."

Mueller, Lisel. "Versions of Reality." *Poetry* 117 (February, 1971): 322-330. Mueller identifies the abiding strengths that have made Harrison's poetry compelling, while at the same time identifying the stylistic conventions that make his work difficult for the novice or casual poetry reader to apprehend. She also touches on his biography and draws parallels between Harrison and Theodore Roethke.

Rosenthal, M. L. "Outlyers and Ghazals." *The New York Times Book Review* (July 18, 1971): 7, 18. Explains how Harrison avoids the bathetic traps that might befall a lesser writer and analyzes Harrison's choice and execution of the ghazal, demonstrating the manner in which he builds one couplet upon the next. Also shows appreciation for Harrison's infectious wit and his ability to infuse his work with a sensibility that transcends the regional and generational influences that his poems clearly reveal.

Siegel, Eric. "A New Voice from the North Country." *Detroit Magazine*, April 16, 1972, 19-20. A good article for those who want a sense of Jim Harrison, the person, replete with family obligations and biographical scars. The article also depicts Harrison's writing regimens and his various therapeutic diversions.

Taylor, Henry. "Next to Last Things." *Poetry* 176, no 2 (May, 2000): 96-106. As part of an omnibus review, Taylor applies his considerable critical skills to an appreciation of Harrison's *The Shape of the Journey*.

Veale, Scott. "Eat Drink Man Woman." *The New York Times Book Review* (January 3, 1999): 15. In this brief review of *The Shape of the Journey*, Veale finds this collection to have "a meandering feeling." He praises Harrison's grounding in the natural world, especially in those poems set in rural Michigan. He also values Harrison's colloquial style.

C. Lynn Munro,
updated by Philip K. Jason

TONY HARRISON

Born: Leeds, England; April 30, 1937

PRINCIPAL POETRY

Earthworks, 1964

The Loiners, 1970

From "The School of Eloquence" and Other Poems, 1978

Continuous: Fifty Sonnets from "The School of Eloquence," 1981

Selected Poems, 1984

The Fire-Gap: A Poem with Two Tails, 1985

Selected Poems, 1987

V. and Other Poems, 1990

The Gaze of the Gorgon, 1992

Black Daisies for the Bride, 1993

Permanently Bard: Selected Poetry, 1995

The Shadow of Hiroshima and Other Film/Poems, 1995

Versus Verse: Satirical Rhymes of Three Anti-bodies in Opposition to Practically Everything, 1995 (with Geoffrey B. Riddehough and Geoffrey A. Spencer)

Prometheus, 1998

Laureate's Block and Other Occasional Poems, 2000

OTHER LITERARY FORMS

Tony Harrison has strong, continuing connections with the theater and opera. His version of Molière's *Le Misanthrope* (1666; *The Misanthrope*, 1709) was produced by Great Britain's National Theatre in 1973, and his radical adaptation of Jean Racine's *Phèdre* (1677; *Phaedra*, 1701)—whose title, *Phaedra Brittanica*, suggests how far he took it away from its source—appeared in 1975. His adaptation of Aeschylus's *Oresteia* (458 B.C.E.) came in 1981. He has also worked in opera, both as a librettist (with Harrison Birtwistle in *Bow Down* in 1977) and as a regular translator and adaptor for the Metropolitan Opera in New York. He provided the English lyrics for Mikis Theodorakis's songs for the film *The Blue Bird* (1976).

Harrison has a wide range of interests as a translator, and the occasional translation often shows up in his volumes of poetry, but he also addresses himself to more substantial translation projects. While a lecturer in English in Nigeria, he collaborated with James Simmons on a translation of Aristophanes' *Lysistratē* (411 B.C.E.; *Lysistrata*) into the Pidgin English of a native tribe. He is also the translator of the work of the fourth century C.E. Greek epigrammatist Palladas, and the selection *Poems* appeared in 1975. In 1988, he wrote his first play, *The Trackers of Oxyrhynchus*, which was published in 1990.

ACHIEVEMENTS

Unusual in actually being able to make a living as a poet, albeit by adapting his talents to the theater, Tony Harrison is a major spokesman for that peculiarly British phenomenon, the educated, working-class intellectual, nostalgically loyal to the class from which he came while committed without hypocrisy to the primarily middle-to-upper-middle-class world of the arts with all of its comforts and civilities.

In 1969, Harrison won the Cholmondeley Award for Poetry, and in the same year the UNESCO (United Nations Educational, Scientific, and Cultural Organization) Fellowship in Poetry allowed him to travel as a representative of the international world of poetry to South America and Africa. Those journeys, through several countries, were to be used as subjects of several poems in his later publications. In 1972, *The Loiners*, his first full-length collection, won the Geoffrey Faber Memorial Prize.

He has held numerous fellowships, having been named a Northern Arts Fellow in Poetry at Universities of Newcastle and Durham in 1967-1968 and 1976-1977; a Gregynog Arts Fellow at University of Wales in 1973-1974, a UK/US Bicentennial Arts Fellow, New York, in 1979-1980; and a Fellow of the Royal Society of Literature in 1984.

BIOGRAPHY

Tony Harrison was born in Leeds, Yorkshire, to a working-class family, and his primary education was in the Cross Flatts County Primary School. A promising student, he moved from there to the Leeds Grammar School. (At the secondary school level, English education clearly differentiates between students with academic inclinations and talents and students likely to terminate their education in their teens, a separation which often has serious class implications.) Harrison went on to Leeds University, where he took a degree in classics and a diploma in linguistics.

Tony Harrison (© Peters, Fraser, and Dunlop)

Harrison was married in 1962 and has one daughter and one son. He also began his first career that year as an itinerant university lecturer, teaching for four years in Nigeria, and in Prague, Czechoslovakia, for one year. In 1967, he became the first Northern Arts Fellow in Poetry at the Universities of Newcastle-upon-Tyne and Durham. Between 1973 and 1978, he had close connections as a translator and adaptor of European dramas with Great Britain's National Theatre and served as resident dramatist with them in 1977-1978. He also developed a continuing relationship as translator and librettist with the Metropolitan Opera, while maintaining his personal connections with northern England by living in Newcastle.

In the late 1980's, Harrison's became directly involved as a theater director and as a playwright. He became a stage director at the National Theatre in London and was given the responsibility of bringing his first play, *The Trackers of Oxyrhynchus*, into performance, first at the ancient stadium at Delphi in Greece and then in London, with further presentations in Yorkshire and in Denmark. The play was originally written for one performance, but it proved to be strong enough for a major run.

He travels extensively, particularly in Third World countries under the sponsorship of UNESCO, and is widely known as a poet and commentator upon poetry in countries as far apart as Cuba, Brazil, Senegal, and Gambia.

ANALYSIS

It is generally accepted that Tony Harrison is not quite like his contemporaries in English poetry. That is true in more ways than one, although at the same time, seen from another angle, he is clearly aligned with many of the poets of postwar Great Britain. On the obvious level, he can be distinguished because of his use of his poetic gifts in the service of the theater. The role of translator and adapter is difficult to assess and is often unheralded. Indeed, it might be argued that the least obvious intrusion of the translator is the best indication of how successful that act of necessary manipulation of another's text is, since what is desired is a mirror image (in another language) of the original act of creation. Harrison, however, has not always confined himself to such gentle tumbling of art into another language, and it is of some value, when speaking of him as a writer, to look at a work such

as *Phaedra Britannica* in order to see just how "creative" he can be in the face of a foreign text, using a flexible, almost unhinged couplet to turn Racine's *Phèdre* into a play about the English and their personal and political involvement in India. The result is not Racine, and it would be silly to suggest that it is, but it is an interesting example of how a late twentieth century poet can make verse drama despite its unfashionableness, and make it without ascending to fulsome, pumped-up afflatus, which would be risible, at the least, and pompously inappropriate in an age of deliberately flattened rhetoric.

THE LOINERS

It is not, however, simply a matter of Harrison's ability to turn his poetic gifts to the theater which is meant in distinguishing him from other poets. There is, for various reasons, a tendency in British poets to confine themselves, with some considerable success, to a narrow thematic line. This is not always true, and it should not be taken as necessarily debasing the quality of their work. Harrison, on the other hand, perhaps partly because of his travels as an educator, itinerant poet, and theatrical journeyman, has a very wide range of interests in his poems. *The Loiners*, his first collected volume, is the best example of that breadth and includes poems not only about his native north of England but also about Africa, America, South America, Europe, and the once-called Iron Curtain countries—states that fell under the control of the former Soviet Union. In those poems his liberal-leftist political inclinations are joined to his mischievous enthusiasm for sexual high jinks in poems which set out to smash the linguistic and political barriers with some considerable sophistication and impropriety. The poem "The Bedbug" puts it succinctly:

> Comrade, with your finger on the playback switch,
> Listen carefully to each love-moan,
> And enter in the file which cry is real, and which
> A mere performance for your microphone.

Along the way, in a manner consistent with his education in the classics and linguistics, he plants elegant, teasingly relaxed translations of European poets from the classical period forward; he surprises with the economy with which he intrudes metaphysical tendencies into poems, seemingly without effort. In "The Nuptial Torches," men burning at the stake are seen thus: "Their souls/ Splut through their pores like porridge holes./ They wear their skins like cast-offs. Their skin grows/ Puckered round the knees like rumpled hose."

MISCHIEVOUSNESS OF "BRINGING UP"

The high-spirited cleverness of such imagery and the wit and sophistication with which Harrison interpolates allusions of intellectual (and technical) complexity into *The Loiners* bring him closer to American poets than one might expect of a writer who comes from the working class of Yorkshire, and at his deliberately flashy, improper best (see "Flying Down to Rio: A Ballad of Beverly Hills" in *From "The School of Eloquence" and Other Poems*), there are touches of James Merrill. Harrison knows that he has this sweet tooth for being naughty, and he sometimes makes poetry out of it.

In *Continuous*, the poem "Bringing Up" allows him to talk of his mother's reaction to some of the poetry in *The Loiners*: He ruefully remembers, at her death, his desire to put a copy of his poems in her hands before her cremation. "You'd've been embarrassed though to meet your God/ clutching those poems of mine that you'd like banned." He retrieves himself for a moment with the wry idea that they could both have their way: "I thought you could hold my *Loiners*, and both burn!" The poem continues, with Harrison determined to follow the idea with metaphysical doggedness in which he mingles (as he often does) wit with tenderness:

> And there together in the well wrought urn
> what's left of you, the poems of your child,
> devoured by one flame, unreconciled,
> like soots on washing, black on bone-ash white.
>
> May be you see them in a better light!
>
> But I still see you weeping, your hurt looks:
>
> *You weren't brought up to write such mucky books!*

TRACES OF METAPHYSICS

Perhaps something ought to be said about this word "metaphysical," which is usually applied to a group of late sixteenth and early seventeenth century poets including John Donne and Andrew Marvell, and is taken to mean that style of poetry, sometimes of philosophical theme (hence the word "metaphysical"), in which meta-

phors, images, and ideas, while often deliberately inappropriate, not only are used but also are explored rigorously in order to wring every association out of them, sometimes to a wildly ridiculous extent. There is a touch of swagger, of showing off, about this kind of poetry, even when it is tonally serious and thematically profound; when it is neither, it can still be aesthetically exciting. Harrison often attaches metaphysical structures to the most innocent metaphors, and his "riding" them with relentless enthusiasm is seen as informally connecting him to the "Martian" group (if it can even be called that), whose most obvious and successful practitioner is the British poet Craig Raine.

"THE SCHOOL OF ELOQUENCE" SERIES

Harrison is, however, much more formidable than such improvisatory zest for the startling image might suggest, and it is in his "The School of Eloquence" series that much of his best work has been done, and indeed may continue to appear, since the concept is open-ended. Appropriating a prosodic oddity which had previously been employed by George Meredith in his *Modern Love* (1862), a sonnet consisting of sixteen rhyming pentameter lines, Harrison has provided himself with a flexible form (with which he often deliberately tampers, committing "errors" to achieve spontaneity and tonal densities), and which serves as an ideal vehicle for his worldly-wise comments on modern society. Most important, the form provides him with a supple shape in which he can explore the dilemma of his worldly success with considerable range of feeling. Caught between his working-class background (which is still a potent force in British society), for which he has considerable affection, and his enviable position as an educated traveling man with reputation and connections in the glamorous world of the arts and the theater, he believes that he has, albeit innocently, betrayed his family. Educated out of his "clothed-capped" background and possessing artistic gifts far beyond the ambitions which his parents had for him, he uses these sonnets to try to make sense of what happened:

> The mams, pig-sick of oilstains in their wash,
> wished for their sons a better class of gear,
> wear their own clothes into work 'but not go posh,
> go up a rung or two but settle near.

The poems come together, a few at a time, and develop into a small autobiographical novel, ranging from memories of childhood to rueful anecdotes about his fragile relationship with his parents before their deaths. Sometimes the poems deal with the difficult times of the parents' last illnesses, attempting to discover why so much love was so ineptly expressed. Despite his determination to write simply and to use working-class and regional dialect when appropriate, the poems are not simplistic. The last verse of "Breaking the Chain," from which the quotation above was drawn, deals with the expensive draftsman's instruments which his father bought for him, hoping that he might end up close at hand: "This meant the 'drawing office' to the dads,/ same place of work, but not blue-collar, white." It ends in a way which ought to remind the reader of Harrison's metaphysical bent, and perhaps of John Donne's use of the compass image in "A Valediction: Forbidding Mourning." Harrison uses the idea with the lightest touch so that the smartness will not breach the plangent feeling:

> Looking at it now still breaks my heart!
> The gap his gift acknowledged then 's wide as
> eternity, but I still can't bear to part
> with these never passed on, never used, dividers.

There is some danger in this fusion of metaphysical imagery and deep feeling, the former threatening to fall into "cuteness," as it does occasionally (disastrously so in "Guava Libre," *From "The School of Eloquence" and Other Poems*), and the latter always a possible danger in the sonnets dealing with his family. Usually he knows how far to go, and his good taste allows him to decide what the mix of high intelligence, clever allusions, deliberately awkward usages, and native dialect ought to be and how far he can dare take them. The danger is most apparent when the poems get into the area of private feeling, where he chooses to divest himself of sophistication for simple tale-telling, where the flatness of the language and the lines teeters on the edge of sentimental excess:

> James Cagney was the one up both our streets
> His was the only art we ever shared.
> A gangster film and choc ice were the treats
> that showed about as much love as he dared.

That "choc ice" (from the poem "Continuous") may be a bit too cunning, a bit too much total recall of the language of the cinema house of his childhood. Yet a poem such as "Marked with D" gets much of its power from the way in which he strides into danger, taking his father's past job as a baker and indecorously describing his father's cremation in metaphysical images and puns baldly related to the baking of a loaf of bread:

> The baker's man that no-one will see rise
> and England made to feel like some dull oaf
> is smoke, enough to sting one person's eyes
> and ash (not unlike flour) for one small loaf.

In context, this kind of impropriety works not so much because it is so outrageously smart, but because, in a peculiar way, it enforces the simplicity of this working-class life, a world in which only the sparseness, the paucity of aspiration, exists in the crudest metaphor: The poetry comes out of its unpoetic rejection of appropriately sonorous language.

The family poems allow Harrison to enter into the continuing problems of the British working classes, the continuing limitations and disappointments of stunted lives, seemingly destined to be similarly confined in the future as the country goes on its inexorably threadbare way. The intrusion of the black and brown Commonwealth refugees into the working-class neighborhoods, already run-down and overcrowded, is the subject of a series of poems in which the wariness, the sense of the despair and helplessness of the lower class, seeing themselves as the victims of other people's problems, at and on the edge of racial prejudice that they hardly understand, is expressed through the eyes of his father. In these poems, Harrison can be most clearly identified as a working-class poet.

PASTORAL POEMS

He is, however, always more than one kind of poet, and he often uses the sonnet form to explore his continuing fascination with language and how it can be used, misused, and sometimes betray, not simply within a community but also on the wider scale of political chicanery and indifference. He is a poet of considerable range; the open-ended nature of "The School of Eloquence" series, both thematically and tonally, allows for personal intimacies, political comment, scholarly puzzles, and arcane jokes about high and louche lowlife. Harrison is a cosmopolitan poet in the very best and widest sense of that word: intelligent, lettered, witty, skeptical, and, sometimes, cheerfully rude. It is also interesting to see Harrison reacting to America, not only in his obviously satiric poems about urban excess but also in his pastoral mode, which was not strongly represented in his work until the early 1980's. Harrison has two lovely long poems, set in the rural fastness of central Florida, "The Fire-Gap: A Poem with Two Tails" and "Cypress and Cedar," which extend his range into thoughtful apprehension of man's relation to the natural world in ways which are reminiscent of Samuel Taylor Coleridge's conversation poems on one hand and haunting reminders of Robert Frost on the other.

V. AND OTHER POEMS

In 1987, Harrison was shocked into writing a major poem by his discovery that his parents' gravestones as well as those of many others in the cemetery on Beeston Hill in Leeds, Yorkshire, had been desecrated, not simply by being knocked about but also by the addition of obscene graffiti. The letter *v* appeared with some regularity in the sign-painting, indicating to Harrison that at least one of the vandals had an enthusiasm for football contests in which *v.*, standing for versus, signified team competition: Leeds *v.* Derby or, more seriously, black *v.* white, man *v.* wife, class *v.* class, or any of the other polarized conflicts which make life uncivilized. It is a disturbing poem, looking with considerable pessimism on the way in which young urban men in particular have descended to animalistic behavior, gratuitous violence, and aimless destruction. Given the nature of the usual market for poetry, the poem might well have been anthologized and forgotten, except for the fact that an English television program allowed Harrison to read the poem on prime-time television. The dismay expressed in the poem was understood, but Harrison had not restrained himself in the use of the language of the streets in the poem, and the flow of four-letter words caused considerable criticism of the television company and of the poet. It was, however, an interesting exception to the usual fate of poetry, since it not only articulated a public concern in art of considerable quality but also provoked the usually indifferent public, for perhaps the wrong reasons, into paying attention to an art form that it rarely, if ever, chooses to contemplate.

"LAUREATE'S BLOCK"

In the 1990's, Harrison merged a number of his talents to produce works that blended poetry with drama, film, and world news. His three filmed poems, *The Gaze of the Gorgon*, *The Shadow of Hiroshima*, and *Prometheus* attempted to explain the atrocities of the twentieth century: Nazism, nuclear war, imperialism, the unevenness of capitalism. Yet the poet also made an obvious turn from his stand-by themes of politics and issues of class to his personal life. His work seemed to center on settling old scores with figures in the literary establishment, as well as an apparent obsession to convey a message—whether personal or political—to the public at large. In a very public quarrel and debate, played out in his poem titled "Laureate's Block" (from his 2000 collection of the same name), Harrison openly defended his staunch refusal to be appointed Britain's poet laureate while publicly quarreling with British poet Andrew Motion: "I'd sooner be a free man. Free not to have to puff some prince's wedding," he wrote in the poem, and specifically attacked "toadies like Di-deifying Motion"—a reference to an elegy, "Mythology," that Motion had written upon Princess Diana's death.

In addition to his literary feuds, Harrison seemed to relish trumpeting details of his domestic life. Again in "Laureate's Block," he ends the poem with this quatrain:

> A poet's death fills other poets with dread,
> a king's death kings,
> but under my duvet is Queen Elizabeth,
> and off our bed slide these quatrains and all of Thomas
> Gray.

Harrison alludes to his bedding of the Queen, both literally and metaphorically, while also making reference to the status of his marriage: the lover in the poem is not his wife, Teresa Stratas, but the actress Sian Thomas. Here, Harrison's messy personal life is held out for public display, a remarkable event given that Harrison is a notoriously private man.

OTHER MAJOR WORKS

PLAYS: *Aikin Mata*, pr. 1965 (with James Simmons; adaptation of Aristophanes' play *Lysistratē*); *The Mis-*

anthrope, pr. 1973 (adaptation of Molière's play *Le Misanthrope*); *Phaedra Britannica*, pr. 1975 (adaptation of Jean Racine's play *Phèdre*); *Bow Down*, pr., pb. 1977 (libretto; music by Harrison Birtwistle); *The Passion*, pr., pb. 1977 (adaptation of the York Mystery Plays); *The Bartered Bride*, pr., pb. 1978 (libretto; music by Bedřich Smetana; adaptation of Karel Sabrina's opera); *The Oresteia*, pr., pb. 1981 (libretto; music by Birtwistle; adaptation of Aeschylus's play); *Dramatic Verse, 1973-1985*, pb. 1985; *The Mysteries*, pb. 1985; *The Trackers of Oxyrhynchus*, pb. 1990 (based on Sophocles' play *Ichneutae*); *Square Rounds*, pb. 1992; *The Common Chorus: A Version of Aristophanes' "Lysistrata,"* pb. 1992; *Plays: Three*, pb. 1996.

TELEPLAY: *The Big H*, 1984 (libretto; music by Dominic Muldowney); *The Blasphemers' Banquet*, 1990.

TRANSLATION: *Poems*, 1975 (of Palladas of Alexandra).

BIBLIOGRAPHY

Astley, Neil, ed. *Tony Harrison*. London: Bloodaxe Books, 1989. Much of the best criticism of Harrison is done in articles that appear either in literary journals or in literary reviews. As a result, these articles are often hard to find—particularly for an American reader. Astley has done a great service in bringing together the best articles written about Harrison, who has emerged as a major subject for scholars and poetry critics.

Byrne, Sandie, ed. *H, v., & O: The Poetry of Tony Harrison*. New York: St. Martin's Press, 1998. Critical interpretation of Harrison's poetry focusing on the three poems of the title. Includes bibliographic references and an index.

_____. *Tony Harrison: Loiner*. Oxford: Oxford University Press, 1997. Commemorates the sixtieth birthday of Harrison through an exploration of his work, including that of his best-known poem, "The Loiners." Includes personal recollections of working with Harrison and critical analyses of his techniques and themes.

Cunningham, Valentine. *British Writers of the Thirties*. Oxford, England: Oxford University Press, 1989. This book deals with a literary period before Harrison's time, but it has an excellent section on the problem of "class" in English literature, as well as a close investigation of the way in which the laboring class in England has been represented in poetry and the novel. The tendency for most English writers has been to steer cautiously through working-class themes, since most of these writers have middle-class backgrounds. The limitations this places upon them are carefully discussed. Harrison, originally working-class, educated himself into the middle class but continues to use his early background as a theme in his poetry.

Donoghue, Denis. "Venisti Tandem." *The London Review of Books* 7 (February 7, 1985): 18-19. The distinguished literary critic and university professor has a direct and uncomplicated style that can be understood without any particular training. In this article, he discusses *Selected Poems* with patient and fastidious attention to Harrison's themes, his use of tone, and those two rather opposing elements in Harrison's work: his occasional vulgarity and his use of his classical learning.

Dunn, Douglas. "Snatching the Bays." *Encounter* 36 (March, 1971): 65-71. Dunn, a poet himself, who often works in the same area of interest as Harrison, reviews Harrison's early book *The Loiners*, distinguishing with some care the various themes that would become common in the long run of Harrison's career and discussing his strengths and weaknesses. An interesting study in conjunction with later comments on Harrison's mature work.

Kelleher, Joe. *Tony Harrison*. Plymouth: Northcote House, 1996. A brief critical introduction to Harrison's work.

McDuff, David. Review of *Selected Poems*, by Tony Harrison. *Strand Magazine* 27, no. 1 (1985/1986): 73-76. McDuff tries to see the volume in the light of developing tendencies that can be traced from an early point in Harrison's career. He addresses the class theme in the poems and perceptively examines Harrison's use of form to reveal tone. He sees in Harrison clear lines of development from a kind of smart sophistication to a deepening gentleness, particularly in his poems on social themes.

Morrison, Blake. "Labouring." *The London Review of Books* 4 (April 1-14, 1952): 10-11. Morrison is a poet and a contemporary of Harrison; as such, he is able to see Harrison in the context of a range of poets working in England in the late twentieth century. This article is specifically concerned with the volume *Continuous*. Morrison, who is something of a narrative poet himself, is sensible on Harrison's strengths in narrative and how he makes stories out of innocent, working-class anecdote. He is also good on the theme of the price Harrison has paid in educating himself out of the working class.

Rawson, Claude. "Family Voices." *The Times Literary Supplement* no. 4266 (January 4, 1985): 10. Rawson is a professor of English literature with strong ties to the eighteenth century, but he is a sensitive reader of modern poetry, and in this article he discusses Harrison's family poems, his use of the sonnet form, and his attempts to blend the Yorkshire accent of his family with the higher style of his own literate, international background. He is also sensitive to the satirical edge which appears occasionally in the poems.

Reid, Christopher. "Here Comes Amy." *The London Review of Books* 8 (April 17, 1986): 20-21. Reid is a poet and contemporary of Harrison. This valuable review addresses the poem that caused so much public response, the notorious "V." Reid discusses Harrison as an artist of continually developing social conscience and comment, and he is also perceptive on Harrison's deliberately awkward usages in his poetry. Harrison has always felt obliged to use simple, sometimes unlettered, language in dealing with his working-class-themes, and Reid discusses the value and the dangers of such a practice.

Rowland, Anthony J. *Tony Harrison and the Holocaust.* Liverpool: Liverpool University Press, 2001. Argues that while some of Harrison's poems are barbaric, they can be evaluated as committed responses to the worst horrors of twentieth century history.

Thwaite, Anthony. *Poetry Today: A Critical Guide to British Poetry, 1960-1984.* London: Longman, 1985. Thwaite is a poet, critic, reviewer, and editor, particularly well equipped to discuss the whole range of contemporary English poetry, as well as those writers who still have allegiance to Wales, Scotland, and Ireland. Thwaite sees the resemblance between Harrison and Douglas Dunn—both working-class poets, one from Yorkshire, one from Scotland—and discusses the way in which their determination to keep their connections with working-class areas of Britain continues to affect their poetry.

Charles H. Pullen,
updated by Sarah Hilbert

HARTMANN VON AUE

Born: Swabia (now in Germany); c. 1160-1165
Died: Swabia (now in Germany); c. 1210-1220

PRINCIPAL POETRY
Die Klage, c. 1180
Erek, c. 1190 (*Erec*, 1982)
Iwein, c. 1190-1205 (*Iwein: The Knight with the Lion*, 1979)
Gregorius, c. 1190-1197 (English translation, 1955, 1966)
Der arme Heinrich, c. 1195 (English translation, 1931)

OTHER LITERARY FORMS

Although all extant works by Hartmann von Aue are in verse form, scholars have been tempted to consider the courtly epics *Erec, Iwein, Gregorius,* and *Der arme Heinrich* as prototypes of modern prose forms such as the novella and the novel. Nevertheless, Hartmann is first and foremost an epic poet. Because he and his contemporaries drew no such generic distinctions, neither shall this survey.

ACHIEVEMENTS

In *The Emergence of German as a Literary Language*, Eric Blackall describes the development of "an uncouth language into one of the most subtle literary media of modern Europe," attaining respectability, however, only after 1700. Blackall implies here that until the eighteenth century, German literature was essentially derivative struggling to define itself in the presence of other, highly developed European languages and literatures. Seen in this light, the modest oeuvre of Hartmann von Aue—often topically repetitive and linguistically naïve by modern standards—can be appreciated for its true worth: as a giant stride toward vernacular poetry of the highest stature.

Hartmann's language is a model of consistency and moderation. His sentences are clearly constructed, his rhymes are natural and unaffected, and his mastery of various verse forms is assured. His was a poetry of reflection and reason, and he frequently employed devices which clarified the theme for his audience, particularly parallelism and contrasting imagery. In his verse, he presented problematic situations that would be of interest and application to a broad audience, avoiding bizarre plots that would defeat his didactic purposes. The same concerns are reflected in his language: Hartmann pruned outdated expressions, dialect words, and foreign phrases in favor of a language accessible to a broader geographical audience. In this respect, Hartmann anticipated Martin Luther's efforts to promote a standard German language. Finally, Hartmann is credited with introducing the Arthurian romance in Germany.

For his innovations in style, form, and language, Hartmann was respected by his contemporaries, honored by patron and audience alike, and frequently imitated by his colleagues. With Wolfram von Eschenbach and Gottfried von Strassburg, Hartmann is regarded as one of the three literary trendsetters of his age—at once exemplary and inimitable.

Perhaps of greater significance than his stylistic innovations, however, was the attitude that Hartmann brought to his works. His personal experiences and reflections are presented in a serious, contemplative mood, ennobling both the man and his writing. Furthermore, an earnest involvement with the social and moral issues of his society are hallmarks of his poetry. Hartmann's thoughtful treatment of the tensions existing between society and religious devotion illuminated one of the most enduring concerns for German culture, a concern mirrored in works of later authors as diverse as Hans Jakob Christoffel von Grimmelshausen, the Brothers Grimm, and Thomas Mann.

Hartmann's popularity and literary success resulted in part from his attempts to unify form and content. He constantly strove to make his language appropriate to the experiences and emotions described in the text. The tales themselves, of Erec and Iwein, of Gregorius and Heinrich, were certainly not extraordinary for his time; many of his contemporaries created more adventurous, more bizarre stories to captivate their audiences. Hartmann, however, was able to engage his listeners in a more intellectual fashion, by stating problems inherent in his society and by examining them thoughtfully and intelligently, so that the listener understood their import for his own life.

BIOGRAPHY

As is the case with many medieval poets, documentary evidence attesting the life and deeds of Hartmann von Aue is sparse. The few tantalizing clues that have survived have become the topic of continuing scholarly debate and controversy. From brief statements within the works of Hartmann and his fellow courtly poets, from contemporary events, and from astute speculation, a plausible biography has been established. Hartmann's birth date, for example, can be surmised only by backdating—that is, by assuming that his earliest work was composed at approximately the age of twenty. Thus, since the first work attributable to Hartmann appeared around 1180, he was probably born between 1160 and 1165. His noble appellation "von Aue" indicates that he lived in the German territory known as Swabia, located in present-day northwestern Switzerland and southwestern Germany. From the introduction to *Der arme Heinrich*, in which Hartmann describes himself as "learned"—that is, able to read Latin (and presumably French)—one can assume that he enjoyed an education, most likely in a monastery school. As an adult, Hartmann became an unpropertied knight in the administrative service of a noble lord.

Hartmann's earliest works convey his involvement in courtly society and its chivalric conventions, but his failure at *Minne* (courtly love), the death of his beloved lord and patron, and his eventual participation in a Crusade reflect a gradual but fundamental change in his life. Hartmann forsook the conventions of *Minne* and his role as *Minnesinger*, placing himself in the service of Christ and composing instead songs of the Crusades and of renunciation. Although *Iwein* appears to have been the last secular work that Hartmann wrote, scholars now believe that this work was merely the completion of an earlier commission and thus does not accurately reflect Hartmann's mature stance. There is no evidence that Hartmann wrote anything during the last ten or more years of his life. The date and circumstances of his death remain a mystery to this day. Poets of the time implied that Hartmann was still living in 1210, but by 1220 he was mentioned as being among the deceased.

ANALYSIS

The period of courtly love poetry presents several insoluble problems for the modern reader. Little is known of the poets as individuals, of the circumstances in which their songs were created and performed, or of the melodies that accompanied the songs. Few manuscripts survive, and these were often copied down generations after the fact; by the time individual songs were committed to parchment, deviations from the original text were inevitable. These factors impose limits on any analysis of Hartmann von Aue's poetry. Although his surviving works are few in number—sixteen songs and five works of substantial length—they are rich in variety, reflecting his changing concerns and the gradual refinement of his style.

DIE KLAGE

The earliest work attributable to Hartmann is *Die Klage* (lament), a relatively youthful attempt at conventional courtly poetry. The title is somewhat misleading, for the content clearly represents disputation or rational debate. Here a young knight, unsuccessful in courtly love, engages the service of his "body" and "heart" to clarify their roles in this delicate struggle. This didactic piece, clearly a product of reflection and not of immediate personal suffering, recommends traditional chivalric qualities such as discipline, loyalty, and dependability; moderation and modesty; striving and denial. In spite of its relative superficiality and clumsy logic, *Die Klage* represents the first rational clarification of the redemptive and civilizing qualities required by courtly society. Hartmann's goal here was no less than to determine those qualities that allow the individual to find favor in the eyes of God and his fellow man. This question and the contemplative search for an appropriate answer characterize Hartmann's entire oeuvre.

In the same period in which he wrote *Die Klage*, Hartmann composed the first of his courtly love songs. These earliest poems also uncritically propagated the chivalric qualities necessary for attaining the favor of a noble lady, though Hartmann soon demonstrated his unwillingness to feign joy over the pains of unrequited love. Later poems reflected a greater sorrow that had befallen Hartmann—the death of his lord and patron. The poet had mentioned his failure to win the favor of a particular lady, but that was only a temporary disappointment when compared to the loss of his lord. (Although more recent scholarship questions the sincerity of the singer-patron relationship, suggesting that the poet's expression of gratitude was purely conventional, Hartmann was doubtless loyal and grateful to his patron. Obviously, the death of his lord had a lasting effect on Hartmann's life and thus on his poetry.)

In any case, Hartmann's failure in love prompted him to assess his position. While not questioning the conventions of courtly society in general or of courtly love in particular, Hartmann did come to the realization that he himself was not suited to such *Minne* service. As he wrote at the time: "True joy is never having loved." He was too honorable to place blame on the lady in question, reserving all culpability for himself. In truth, Hartmann was not made for such a contest. The protest against his personal suffering eventually grew into a denial of courtly love, couched in a typically objective critique. Hartmann no longer praised this idealized, unrequited love, celebrating instead a mutually harmonious relationship with a woman of less than noble stature beyond the stifling bounds of the court. At the same time, this shift in Hartmann's attitude toward courtly love was motivated by an intense spiritual reorientation: For the salvation of his and his patron's souls, Hartmann joined a Crusade, creating songs of dignified devotion as a religious stimulus to others of his class. These changes in Hartmann's outlook took place only gradually, and their development can be traced in his works.

EREC

Hartmann's *Erec* is German literature's first Arthurian romance, a genre that has retained its popularity to this day. Though Hartmann relied on an earlier work by Chrétien de Troyes for his source, he should not be accused of plagiarism: In the Middle Ages, it was assumed that authors would choose their themes from an established collection of plots; true *inventio*, or originality, appeared in the manner of presentation. One noticeable innovation in Hartmann's version is the role of the narrator; actual dialogue is subordinated to the third-person narrative, in which an objective distance from event and character is achieved.

While Chrétien had described the successes of a mature hero, Hartmann's story begins with an impetuous youth. Overwhelmed by his passion for the beautiful Enite, Erec ignores his obligations as knight and ruler, thus bringing dishonor on himself, his court, and his land. He can regain his honor only by renewed, mature striving within the dictates of courtly society; by doing precisely that, he, too, gains personally through a more mature and balanced relationship with his wife. Their love nurtures the well-being that now permeates their entire sphere of influence.

Hartmann's young Erec has failed abysmally and must undergo a lengthy and painful process of maturation, until he can prove himself worthy of being the leader of a court and the ruler of a kingdom. The major tension in this work is provided by the concepts of personal and social love. Personal, possessive love (that is, passion) must not prove destructive to the greater good represented by a harmonious, integrated society. The prevailing motif of beauty is subtly compared and contrasted to substantiate this point: Sensual beauty is destructive, for it lures the knight to thoughts and deeds of sexual excess, but beauty can also be the outward manifestation of inner harmony, as exemplified by Enite and the lovely ladies at King Arthur's court. Hartmann explores these conflicts to demonstrate how the individual can enjoy his personal life while remaining a constructive member of society.

Symmetrically placed episodes reinforce this theme: Erec's immature adventures at the outset of the work are paralleled by his mature successes at the conclusion. In tracing the development of the titular hero from a self-centered youth to a responsible ruler, Hartmann reminded his contemporaries of the responsibilities of the individual knight to others and to society as a whole; Hartmann saw the courtly social code calcifying into a set of rules for membership in an exclusive club.

IWEIN

Hartmann's *Iwein*, based on yet another tale by Chrétien, examines the responsibilities of the knight from a different point of view. Unlike Erec, Iwein is overly concerned with acquiring honor and, from a sense of rampant egoism, neglects equally important chivalric imperatives. Iwein is persuaded to leave his wife for a year (lest he end like Erec) to participate in jousting tournaments and adventures and thereby accumulate more honor. Iwein becomes so self-centered that he fails to return home at the end of the year's time and is consequently condemned before Arthur's court as unfaithful, having betrayed his wife's and society's trust. The accusation strikes Iwein so forcefully that he goes mad and lives in the wilderness as a wild man. Only through a number of painful learning experiences does he gradually regain his senses, his honor, his wife, and his position in society. The lion mentioned in the subtitle serves to accent the importance of loyalty; Iwein rescues a lion, which then becomes his faithful companion, truly a "noble" beast. The errant Iwein is also treated with kindness by others until he can learn to reciprocate their goodness unselfishly. In stages, Iwein learns loyalty, kindness, and consideration for others, and his selfless service is rewarded with honor and salvation.

From the large number of surviving manuscripts, it is evident that *Iwein* was Hartmann's most popular work. In recognition of its important theme and stylistic excellence, modern scholars have frequently referred to it as *the* classical work of the high courtly period. Nevertheless, *Iwein* is a problematic work, for it appears to have been written at widely separated intervals. The first one thousand lines exhibit characteristics of Hartmann's middle period, around 1190, while the remainder of the work is composed in a mature yet detached style. Scholars speculate that the work was commissioned while Hartmann was still involved in courtly service and attempting to accommodate himself to its demands; after a lengthy interruption, during which time Hartmann had disengaged himself from *Minne* conventions, he returned to the manuscript to fulfill, albeit mechanically, the commission. Since *Iwein* still accepts the precepts of courtly society unquestioningly, one can scarcely consider it as Hartmann's definitive statement on the subject, especially in the light of his mature personal convictions and the discrepancy in style. It is a tribute to Hartmann's artistry that he could complete such a work "mechanically" yet produce one of the most popular epics of the High Middle Ages.

GREGORIUS

Gregorius, Hartmann's courtly legend of the life of a fictive pope, was based on a contemporary French source, *Vie du Pape Gregoire*. Despite its explicit references to *Oedipus tyrannus* (c. 429 B.C.E.), *Gregorius* is an ingenious mixture of Asian and Occidental mythology and folklore, although Hartmann's version features a distinctly Christian accent with its traditional progression of innocence, sin and downfall, contrition, penance, and salvation. The plot itself is at once fascinating and convoluted. The devil succeeds in blinding two noble children, so that the brother seduces his own sister. The brother then dies on a pilgrimage, while the sister secretly nurses the child of the incestuous relationship. The child is set adrift at sea, accompanied only by a tablet on which is inscribed a message that explains his origin and begs that he pray for his parents' salvation. The foundling is raised by foster parents, educated at a monastery school, and named after the local abbot, Gregorius. All goes well until an argument reveals to the young man his parents' shame. Despite the Abbot's insistence that his namesake is predestined for the priesthood, young Gregorius flees to take up an adventuresome life as a knight. In his first encounter with the outside world, Gregorius frees a beleaguered city and claims the widowed queen as his bride. In all innocence, Gregorius has married his own mother, thus heaping incest upon incest. He now flees again, in complete despair. Taken to a remote island, he is chained to a rock, and the key to his bonds is thrown into the sea; thus, Gregorius spends the next seventeen years in bondage and isolation. In the meantime, a successor to the deceased pope is sought. The name of Gregorius appears in a dream to the electors, and two papal legates are dispatched to locate this holy man; they are led to the island, where, miraculously, the key to Gregorius's chains is found in the belly of a fish. Soon, the fame of the new pope draws the incestuous queen to Rome, in the hope of gaining absolution from her sins. Gregorius and his mother immediately recognize each other and are reunited and absolved of their mutual burden. The tale closes with an epilogue reminding the audience that all sins can be expiated through contrition and penance.

Aside from the titillating motif of incest, this work offers its audience several moral considerations to ponder: Is Gregorius somehow responsible for the sins of his parents? Should he be punished for unwittingly and unwillingly becoming a participant in incest himself? Despite the folklore surrounding such "sins," the church of Hartmann's day would have considered neither of these sins to be culpable. As several scholars have indicated, Gregorius's actual transgression is against himself and his God. In agreement with the mother's original request, the Abbot had insisted that the youth devote his life to prayer for his parents' salvation; Gregorius's defection was thus a betrayal of his sacred duty. In choosing to sally forth as a knight in search of adventure, courtly love, and honor—duties required of the chivalric class—he was placing personal gratification and *superbia* (ego or self) before his obligation to others and to his God.

In criticizing Gregorius for his blind devotion to *Minne* and honor, Hartmann was in fact questioning the entire structure of courtly society. He showed that the arch virtues mentioned above could lead to sin and downfall, and could be expiated only through a long and horrible penance such as that which Gregorius suffered, chained to his island rock. To be sure, Hartmann did not completely undermine the values inherent in the courtly system, but he did expose them as less than absolutes. Even supposedly courtly virtues can be tools of the devil to tempt innocents from their divinely chosen paths. It is significant that a story that begins badly in worldly society can end happily in the religious seclusion of Rome. This qualified renunciation of the profane in favor of the sacred was the most pronounced development in Hartmann's life and found its poetic culmination in the songs he composed for the Crusades.

DER ARME HEINRICH

Der arme Heinrich, in its own time perhaps the least appreciated of Hartmann's works (if the small number of surviving manuscripts is any indication), has ironically become the most popular. Scarcely fifteen hundred lines in length, it has been considered the prototype of the modern German novella. It was the poem's treatment of its theme, however, and not its formal aspect, that made it revolutionary in Hartmann's day. Heinrich is the epitome of a medieval nobleman. He possesses all the knightly virtues; he enjoys riches and honor, power and fame. Suddenly and inexplicably, he is struck down by leprosy, the most odious illness imaginable. The man who was once the ideal of social virtue is now cast out by that very society, for his beauty has turned to ugliness, his honor to dishonor, his fame to infamy. In search of a medical cure for his affliction, Heinrich travels first to Montpellier and then to Salerno, but he learns that he can be saved only by the blood from the heart of a pure maiden. In despair, Heinrich retires to the country, where he is welcomed and nursed by a family of loyal tenants. The daughter is especially drawn to Heinrich and asks why he has been so cursed. His answer is that he had been a worldly fool, accepting happiness and success as his just reward and not as a sign of God's grace.

Just as Heinrich had been obsessed with his worldly possessions, the daughter becomes equally fanatic in her desire to die for his salvation. In extended discussions with her parents, the girl proclaims her desire to depart this life. Eventually, Heinrich accedes to her wishes, and they leave for Salerno, but at the moment the doctor is about to make the initial incision, Heinrich glimpses the beautiful girl and experiences a change of heart. He releases the girl unharmed, knowing that he cannot accept such a sacrifice and must reconcile himself to living the remainder of his life as a leper. The girl, however, is in despair and curses Heinrich for depriving her of escape from this world. At this point, both are miraculously "cured" through God's mercy: Heinrich is restored to a youthful state of good health and beauty, while the girl regains a healthy desire to live out her life on Earth, as Heinrich's wife. Together, they live a full and happy life before entering Heaven.

In this didactic tale, Hartmann again warned of the dangers of *superbia*, of selfishly living only for worldly goals *or* of selfishly desiring a premature death. Both Heinrich and the girl must learn to live in this world while still recognizing the divine scheme of things. This moral was directly aimed at the courtly society of which Heinrich is representative. With his unrestrained and unquestioning appreciation for worldly values, Heinrich fails to realize that all things come from God: Heinrich's successes, his suffering, and his ultimate salvation are all the result of God's grace. That Heinrich must overcome the courtly values as limitations, that he marries a girl beneath his social standing, that he lives out the remainder of his life far from court—these developments would have seemed foreign to a courtly audience and as such were obviously viewed as unwelcome provocations. This would account for the contemporary reception of Hartmann's text.

BIBLIOGRAPHY

Hasty, Will. *Adventures in Interpretation: The Works of Hartmann von Aue and Their Critical Reception.* Columbia, S.C.: Camden House, 1996. A survey of criticism of Hartmann's work from the Enlightenment to postmodernism which concludes that the interpretations by modern readers have been shaped mainly by critical trends.

Jackson, W. H. *Chivalry in Twelfth-Century Germany: The Works of Hartmann von Aue.* Rochester, N.Y.: D. S. Brewer, 1994. A study of Hartmann's poetic representation of knighthood and chivalric values with consideration of historical, literary, and linguistic, influences.

Robertson, John George. "Hartmann von Aue." In *A History of German Literature*, by Dorothy Reich. 6th ed. Edinburgh: Blackwood, 1970. A brief analysis of Hartmann's work.

Wapnewski, Peter. *Hartmann von Aue.* Stuttgart, Germany: Metzler, 1979. Critical analysis of Hartmann's work with bibliographic references. Published in German.

Todd C. Hanlin;
bibliography updated by the editors

_____

ROBERT HASS

Born: San Francisco, California; March 1, 1941

PRINCIPAL POETRY
Field Guide, 1973
Praise, 1979

Human Wishes, 1989
Sun Under Wood, 1996

OTHER LITERARY FORMS

From 1977 to 1983 Robert Hass wrote critical essays and reviews commissioned by various journals and magazines. He notes that he was grateful for the opportunity to write these essays "because I learned about my art by writing about it." He also developed an interest in translating. In the early 1980's, Hass joined Robert Pinsky, Renata Gorczynski, and the Polish poet Czesław Miłosz in preparing a translation of Miłosz's *The Separate Notebooks* (1984). Hass maintained this working relationship with Miłosz, and together they translated five more books of Polish poems.

Hass also edited collections of the poetry of Robinson Jeffers and of Tomas Tranströmer; he coedited *The Pushcart Prize XII* (1987). In 1993 he edited *Into the Garden: A Wedding Anthology, Poetry and Prose on Love and Marriage*, and in 1994 he edited and translated *The Essential Haiku: Versions of Bashō, Buson, and Issa* (1994). After serving as poet laureate of the United States, he edited *Poet's Choice: Poems for Everyday Life* (1998).

ACHIEVEMENTS

Robert Hass received a Woodrow Wilson Fellowship (1963-1964) and a Danforth Fellowship (1963-1967). His first collection of poetry, *Field Guide*, won the Yale Younger Poets Prize in 1979. When Stanley Kunitz presented the award, he applauded Hass's awareness of the plant and animal worlds as well as his wedding of the natural and moral universes.

Hass's works continued to gain for him recognition as a leading poet of his generation. His second collection, *Praise*, garnered the William Carlos Williams Award. In 1984 he was awarded a John D. and Catherine T. MacArthur grant as well as the prestigious National Book Critics Circle Award for his *Twentieth Century Pleasures: Prose on Poetry* (1984). In 1989 he earned a Guggenheim Fellowship.

In 1996 his *Sun Under Wood* won for him a second National Book Critics Circle Award, as he served his two-year tenure as poet laureate of the United States (1995-1997). He also wrote critical articles and reviews,

Robert Hass in 1997. (AP/Wide World Photos)

edited, and turned to the translation of poetry, focusing on Japanese haiku masters and Miłosz.

BIOGRAPHY

Robert Hass was born in San Francisco, California, on March 1, 1941. He absorbed the literary culture of the West Coast, and although he initially intended to become a novelist or essayist, the poems of Gary Snyder and Allen Ginsberg excited him. In his mid-twenties, after trying fiction, he turned to poetry with a sense of vocation. As a native Californian, he absorbed California's Asian influence, its radical politics, and its dramatic landscape. His great-grandfather had settled in California in the 1800's, and Hass absorbed a sense of habitat from the natural beauty of Marin County. The ocean, the mountains, and the unique flora and fauna of the San Francisco Bay Area shape his poetry collections as well as his critical observations in *Twentieth Century Pleasures*.

He married Earlene Leif while an undergraduate at Saint Mary's College in California. Their three children, Leif, Kristin, and Luke, were born while both parents attended graduate school. Hass received his master's degree from Stanford University (1965), where he studied and sparred with poet and New Critic Yvor Winters. In graduate school, Hass edited a campus newspaper dedicated to investigating Stanford's research connection to the United States military; this helped to develop his leftist politics. He also established friendships at this time with other poets, including James McMichael and Robert Pinsky. Next Hass taught English at the State University of New York, Buffalo, and in 1971 was awarded his doctorate from Stanford. He then returned to his alma mater, Saint Mary's College, as a professor of English. In 1989 he accepted a teaching position at the University of California at Berkeley. He and his wife divorced in 1989, and in 1995 he married poet Brenda Hillman, who provided fresh impetus to his poetry. She helped him to write more inwardly through techniques of hypnosis and meditation as well as through a review of the poetry of Emily Dickinson and of Sylvia Plath.

ANALYSIS

The poetry of Robert Hass displays a range of emotion as well as a thoughtful meditative stance. His openness to the Asian aesthetic is evident in his poems, which offer a keen insight into a fleeting moment. He has acknowledged the influence of the poetry of Wallace Stevens, Walt Whitman, William Carlos Williams, and Ezra Pound. Also, influenced by California's rich natural showcase, Hass makes nature a primary theme in his poetry.

FIELD GUIDE

After reading works of Aristotle and Charles Darwin in his great-books course at Saint Mary's College in California, Hass was assigned to examine nature with field glasses and then write about these observations. This practice of close observation followed by written meditation soon became a pattern for his poetry. In fact, his first collection of poems is titled *Field Guide*. It introduces precise details of California's landscape. In "Fall," he tells of gathering "mushrooms/ near shaggy eucalyptus groves/ which smelled of camphor and the fog-soaked earth." This sense of smell is compounded with attention to the other senses as well in "San Pedro Road":

> Casting, up a salt creek in the sea-rank air
> fragrance of the ferny anise, crackle of field grass
> in the summer heat. Under this sun vision blurs.

The poet continues with mentions of rock crabs, mussels, black rocks, and white bass. Many of the poems in *Field Guide* offer a Walt Whitman-like joy in cataloging things seen, heard, touched, tasted, and felt. Also the influence of haiku is evident in the chaste brevity of image, as in "Maps": "Apricots—/the downy buttock shape/ hard black sculpture of the limbs/ on Saratoga hillsides in the rain."

In "Measure," Hass introduces his quiet, receptive narrative voice as he sits at his writing desk watching a plum tree in the sunset. He suggests that he belongs to the "idleness of attention" which finds quiet fulfillment in poetry. The next poem in the volume displays Hass's ability to satirize a self-important professor. He mocks the professor's egoism and his confidence in his fashionably complex observations. His sterile dream is to develop an "odorless narcissus." Foolishly self-centered, he does not notice the disinterest around him:

> There is a girl the self loves.
> She has been trying to study him for days.
> but her mind keeps
> wandering.

PRAISE

Praise is a collection of twenty-three poems and one longer poetic meditation. Again, Hass displays the quiet listening and reflective posture he developed in his first collection. "Meditation at Lagunitas" is the thematic center of the collection and one of Hass's best-known poems. The first-person narrator is troubled after talking with a friend who is anxious over the inadequacies of language: ". . . everything dissolves: *justice, pine, hair, woman, you* and *I*."

Pondering the word *blackberry*, the narrator regrets that "a word is elegy to what it signifies." However, the chill brought by this observation is erased when he recalls a loved woman's skin, a childhood river outing, "little orange-silver fish." Hass ends the poem incanting "*blackberry, blackberry, blackberry*," asserting his assurance in the power of words to retrieve and to convey meaning.

TWENTIETH CENTURY PLEASURES

Hass shows himself to be a subtle and insightful prose stylist in this volume on poets and poetry. *Twentieth Century Pleasures* is a collection of essays and reviews commissioned by journals from 1977 to 1983. In his warm, intimate conversational style, he explores the work of other poets, including James Wright, Robert Lowell, Thomas Tranströmer, Czesław Miłosz, and Rainer Maria Rilke. He comments on the power of the imagination and meditates on poetic form, rhythm, and image. In "One Body," he decries the distortions of excessive poetry analysis which he sees as "a huge body of commentary which has very little to do with the art of poetry." This volume also includes a memoir, "Some Notes on the San Francisco Bay Area as a Cultural Region," in which he recounts his coming of age as a boy in California. He also traces the influence of various writers on his own development.

HUMAN WISHES

Human Wishes, Hass's third collection of poems, consists of meditative lyrics and short prose pieces. In this work Hass abandons the short lyric poem with its focus on natural image. Instead, these thirty-two poems use a sentence-length line, and, in general, move closer to prose. In the title poem, taken from Samuel Johnson's verse satire "The Vanity of Human Wishes: The Tenth Satire of Juvenal Imitated," (1749), Hass ponders language's subjection to desire, which brings distortion, making words seem inadequate. In this volume, he is less concerned with recording tangible, immediate images; instead, he explores an ever-widening pool of social contexts and associations. In "Human Wishes," for example, he effortlessly links the sun, the Upanishads, a gardener, a television special on chimpanzees, his wife Earlene, her antique cupboard, and a shopkeeper's bet on horses.

The tone of this collection is more doleful than the earlier works, and the emotional range is more expansive than that offered by the spare quality of haiku. There are many voices and tones in these poems as the point of view shifts from his former preference for first person to that of "a man," "a woman," "they," and "you." Hass also makes more extensive use of ironic oppo-

sitions. In "Museum," he introduces a comfortably complacent young couple, smoking and reading in a museum coffee shop with their sleeping baby. Next to this cozy scene with which the narrator has "fallen in love" are artist Kathe Kollwitz's agonized carvings of people "who are suffering the numbest kinds of pain: hunger and helpless terror."

In "A Story About the Body," readers are given the longings of a young poet who thinks he is in love with a mature Japanese artist. The juxtaposition is made ironic when she indicates her interest and then asserts, "but I must tell you that I have had a double mastectomy." The poet withers and returns to his cabin; next morning, he finds a bowl from her on his porch. It seems to be filled with rose petals, but underneath are dead bees. Sections 3 and 4 of the collection continue with this theme of desire unfulfilled.

SUN UNDER WOOD

Hass was honored with his second National Book Critics Circle Award for *Sun Under Wood*. These twenty poems are his most frankly personal, recounting the disturbing stories of his mother's alcoholism, his father's death, his brother's drug addiction, and his own painful divorce. He approaches these difficult subjects in his private past without being sentimental; instead he makes use of his characteristic meditative form.

In "Layover," he turns from purely personal concerns to comment on a more international level. His point of view is that of the idle mind, looking from a plane window in Anchorage, Alaska, awaiting a change in planes. The scene is dreary and gray as he watches bundled bodies hoisting luggage in what seems a neverending "loading and unloading." From there the poem moves to a resigned economic and philosophical awareness that "the exhaust of turbine engines [is] the burnt carbons of pre-Cambrian forests, life feeding life/ feeding life in the usual mindless way." Passively, he goes on to note other signs of the "colonizer" and then expands to Iraq's 1991 military withdrawal from Kuwait, which he helplessly distrusts. The poem closes with four juxtaposed images: the imagined ties and underclothing contained in the suitcases outside, the three young Indians talking in a nearby seat, the mother soothing her small child, and the stale air shared by all those inside the plane.

This poem is followed by "Notes on 'Layover,'" which inventively plays with varied hypothetical alterations in the poem. The poet muses, "I could have said" a raven cried out in the cold or the consoling mother had had an ovarian cyst; the poem could have focused on airport arrivals or on salesmen's pitches. This prose poem then returns to the raven's cry and its flight, black against the white snow. However, the strong natural image does not have the impact that it delivers in the earlier poetry of *Field Guide* and *Praise*. The searching, the alienation, and the feeling of displacement ensure that Hass's poetry speaks truthfully of and for the postmodern world. He continues to move between concrete description and abstract statement or meditation, probing this intricate interaction for his readers.

OTHER MAJOR WORKS

NONFICTION: *Twentieth Century Pleasures: Prose on Poetry*, 1984; *An Unnamed Flowing: The Cultures of American Poetry*, 2000.

TRANSLATIONS: *The Separate Notebooks*, 1984 (of Miłosz; with Miłosz, Robert Pinsky, and Renata Gorczynski); *Unattainable Earth*, 1986 (with Miłosz); *Collected Poems: 1931-1987*, 1988 (with Miłosz); *Provinces*, 1991 (with Miłosz); *The Essential Haiku: Versions of Bashō, Buson, and Issa*, 1994; *Facing the River*, 1995 (with Miłosz); *Road-Side Dog*, 1998 (with Miłosz).

EDITED TEXTS: *Rock and Hawk: A Selection of Shorter Poems by Robinson Jeffers*, 1987; *The Pushcart Prize XII*, 1987; *Tomas Tranströmer: Selected Poems, 1954-1986*, 1987; *Into the Garden: A Wedding Anthology: Poetry and Prose on Love and Marriage*, 1993; *Poet's Choice: Poems for Everyday Life*, 1998.

MISCELLANEOUS: *A Story About the Body*, 1998; *Sounding Line: The Art of Translating Poetry*, 1999.

BIBLIOGRAPHY

Billington, James. "Writing for the Mind and the Heart." *Civilization* 3, no. 1 (January/February, 1996): 9l. Outlines Hass's agenda as poet laureate of the United States, 1995-1997, including his persuasion of newspapers to publish both old and new poetry in the belief that public poetry enriches the public discourse.

Davison, Peter. "The Laureate as Onlooker." *Atlantic Monthly* 279, no. 3 (March, 1997): 100-103. Offers an overview of Hass's four collections of poems, charging him with contemplative passivity and a "beautiful stillness" which, although charming and modest, suggest the posture of an onlooker rather than an energetic participant.

Lea, Sydney, and Jay Parini. "An Interview with Robert Hass." *New England Review* 2 (1979): 295-314. In a lengthy interview, Hass outlines the poet's job as that of reconnecting words to firm objects; he also discusses his early interest in poetry, his teachers and colleagues, and the social role of poetry. He decries the damage done by both academics and critics in distorting poetry. He also looks at the need for a poet to write for a known audience.

Moyers, Bill. "Robert Hass." In *The Language of Life: A Festival of Poets*. New York: Doubleday, 1995. In an interview with the poet, Moyers discusses Hass's indebtedness to Bashō, the great seventeenth century initiator of the haiku form, and to Issa, a later Japanese farmer poet. He also explores the poet's interest in Buddhist notions of balance and the influence of his parents' difficulties on his poetry.

Shapiro, Alan. "And There Are Always Melons." *Chicago Review* 33 (Winter, 1983): 84-90. Identifies in Hass's first two collections his simultaneous celebration of image and fragment with the ongoing continuity of rational tradition. Shapiro also outlines the poet's lack of resolution between sensual immediacy and the desire to repose in the intellect.

Shillinger, Kurt. "New Laureate Wields Bully Pen for Poetry." *Christian Science Monitor*, October 12, 1995, p. 1. Discusses the everyday detail that drives Hass's poetry. Also outlines his program to make poetry more accessible: give inner-city students the same kind of models he himself had found in the Beat poets; work to influence public-political thought through poetry; establish a series of annual awards for publishers, critics, and community figures who promote poetry; and make an effort to place both new and old poetry in daily newspapers.

Marie J. K. Brenner

ROBERT HAYDEN

Born: Detroit, Michigan; August 4, 1913
Died: Ann Arbor, Michigan; February 25, 1980

PRINCIPAL POETRY

Heart-Shape in the Dust, 1940
The Lion and the Archer, 1948 (with Myron O'Higgins)
Figure of Time: Poems, 1955
A Ballad of Remembrance, 1962
Selected Poems, 1966
Words in the Mourning Time, 1970
The Night-Blooming Cereus, 1972
Angle of Ascent: New and Selected Poems, 1975
American Journal, 1978
The Legend of John Brown, 1978
Collected Poems, 1985

OTHER LITERARY FORMS

Robert Hayden also edited two volumes of black literature: *Kaleidoscope: Poems by American Negro Poets* (1967) and *Afro-American Literature: An Introduction* (1971) with David J. Burrows and Frederick R. Lapides.

ACHIEVEMENTS

In 1976, Robert Hayden became the first African American to be appointed as poetry consultant to the Library of Congress. He twice won the Hopwood Award for Poetry at the University of Michigan and has been awarded the Academy of American Poets Fellowship, the Lenore Marshall Poetry Prize, the National Book Award for Poetry, and the Shelley Memorial Award. His strength as a poet lay in his convincingly ambivalent vision of the world, the consistent philosophical basis of that outlook, and the quietly effective language with which he renders it.

BIOGRAPHY

Robert Earl Hayden was born in Detroit, Michigan, on August 4, 1913, as Asa Bundy Sheffey. His natural parents divorced while he was young, and he was reared by William and Sue Ellen Hayden, taking their name and thinking that he had been legally adopted. His natu-ral mother sometimes lived next door to the Haydens, and he has described his childhood environment as angry and disrupted. Hayden suffered from extremely poor eyesight, and even as a child, he spent more time in reading poetry—and later in writing it—than in more physical activities.

From 1932 to 1936, Hayden attended Detroit City College (now Wayne State University). There he had the first of three important meetings with famous poets: Langston Hughes came for a reading, and Hayden was able to have the more established poet read and evaluate some of his work. After graduation, and while he was briefly married, Hayden met Countee Cullen; later, working on a master's degree at the University of Michigan, Hayden was able to study poetry under W. H. Auden.

During this period he married again, to Erma Morris, and in 1946, he and his family moved to Nashville, where Hayden began a twenty-two year teaching career at Fisk University. By this point in his life, he had published some of his most famous poems ("Middle Passage," for example) and had twice won the Hopwood Award for Poetry at the University of Michigan. He and his wife had also converted to the Baha'i faith, a worldview which underlies much of Hayden's poetry, especially in its reconciliation of the oneness of God with the multiplicity of his historical manifestations and in the sustaining faith that the dark side of man's existence, evidenced by such events as the assassinations of which Hayden writes in "Words in the Mourning Time," "are process, major means whereby/ oh dreadfully, our humanness must be achieved."

From the time he left Fisk in 1968 until his death in 1980, Hayden was a professor of English at the University of Michigan. In 1976, he became the first African American to be appointed as poetry consultant to the Library of Congress.

ANALYSIS

Suggesting a Neo-platonic world of faultless knowledge and harmony that human beings once possessed, and often casting a wistful backward glance toward that lost perfection, while at the same time dreaming of an equally perfect future harmony where the difficulties of this world can be transcended, Robert Hay-

Robert Hayden (Library of Congress)

den nevertheless focused his poetic attention on this world, on the shifting and equivocal present. Calling himself a "realist who distrusts so-called reality," Hayden wrote with a clear realistic bent: His work centers on the natural and human of this place and time. These he lovingly describes, yet he also distrusts them; for the present reality is, both factually and poetically, one that betrays the hopes and dreams of human beings.

Because of this ambivalence, Hayden's poetry has always a slightly distant, reserved quality, and although the tone gives way sometimes to simple weariness, other times to wistfulness, the dominant tone is ironic acceptance. Even though many of Hayden's poems are on specifically black themes, using such archetypal images of black literature as flight, and although many celebrate the historical heroes of black American life, Hayden's detachment was often at odds, particularly during the 1970's, with the dominant mood of black culture. Hayden's poetry may occasionally have a political subject, and it is always critical of the cruelties and hypocrisies of America's past, but it is not polemical or didactic, and Hayden's appeal resides perhaps more

among other artists and academicians than among a large popular audience. Indeed, despite the consistency of Hayden's output, he was not published by a major press in America until Liveright published *Angle of Ascent* in 1975.

DAEDALUS POEMS

In his early "O Daedalus, Fly Away Home" and the other later poem about Daedalus, "For a Young Artist," Robert Hayden describes his view of the task of poetry, its relationship to the reader, and the stance of the poet. "For a Young Artist," based on a story by Gabriel García Márquez, begins with a protagonist, the artist, trapped in a pigsty. His condition is a tragic one, but he subsists on the meager fare that he scavenges from nature, rejecting the charity of society. Much of the focus of the poem is on that society: It finds the fallen artist at once baffling and prophetic. The people curse him but ask for his blessing, unable to decide whether he is "actual angel? carny freak?"

The uncertainty of their vision is characteristic in Hayden's world, where one struggles to make sense of his drastically reduced and often deceitful surroundings. The artist himself, however, is proud, refusing charity, refusing to hide his nakedness. His struggle—and this is the distinctive motif in Hayden's poetry—is for ascent. His transformation from ugliness to beauty, his attempt at flight is a difficult one, but after many failures, he finally achieves the "angle of ascent" in a "silken rustling" of air. In "O Daedalus, Fly Away Home," a more impressionistic poem, the main character also makes for himself a set of wings; struggling there against the powers of night, he weaves together "a wish and a weariness" in order to rise above the evil spell and fly home.

TRANSFORMATIONS OF REALITY

Hayden's poetry is always about such transformations of reality. For him the world is confusing and contradictory. All that human beings can know is the darkness of this world: Their former and their future knowledge remain merely clouds. One knows only shadows, as in Plato's cave. The human attitude is thus a wish for the light that lies beyond, a weariness for the light that humankind has lost. The human need is a search to reconcile the two, to balance the two shadowy worlds or to transform this world.

In either case, Hayden's poetry is always dialectic: Each poem arises out of such conflicts as time and timelessness, art and history, dream and memory, past and present, flight and descent. What the artist must do is weave together those opposites into a set of poetic wings, synthesize the two into a oneness, itself a vision of the ultimate oneness, so that the reader understands better the necessary but frightening, terrible but beautiful position that human beings occupy in the world.

POETRY OF BALANCE

Hayden's poetry, with its careful balance between a world he loves and lives in and must describe and his dissatisfaction with its failures and limitations and with his vision of what life was and must be again, teases the reader with its doubled perspective and its delicate and supple language. The poems themselves are often traditional in their narrative structure and regular rhythm. Paradox and pun, both suggesting tension, are frequent devices, and irony, an attitude of approving distance, is the most common tone. Hayden's poetry is a world observed with wit and disappointment, with love and sorrow. His strongest work makes the reader reobserve the world, set in the context of history and art, of philosophy and poetics. Hayden is a black poet in his specific attention to black myths and heroes, if not in an attempt to capture the distinctive voices of black culture. He is also, however, simply a poet, for the themes he works through and the voices with which he speaks make real a universally human perception of this world.

A characteristic posture for Hayden's poetic figures is, then, one of balance. Hayden gives this theme witty representation in the poem "The Performers," where the persona watches literal balancers, "two minor Wallendas," who are washing windows seven stories up in space. The persona identifies with them and their dangerous situation until he sees himself falling. The window washers enter his office, thanking him for his understanding of their position, as he thanks them for making him see once more his own precarious yet protected location. They are like the poet-juggler in Richard Wilbur's poem "Juggler," and their job too, like that of Wilbur's poet-persona, is to make others see the world again in both its freshness and its gravity.

Although the balance may be between the two attractive opposites of past and future perfection, since they are but shadows, it is more frequently between present, human realities. In "Moose Wallow," for example, the protagonist feels the shadowy presence of moose watching him from either side, while he experiences both hope and fear. In "The Broken Dark," a rabbi describes "Demons on the left. Death on either side,/ . . . the way of life between." Within this world, the poet finds himself both alien and at home, both struggling to accept the world and attempting to flee it. The need for acceptance leads to the strong realistic feeling of Hayden's work: the attention to detail, the careful visual imagery, and the strong characterization and narration. Indeed, some of Hayden's most vivid poetry depends on the brilliant creation of character and on his storytelling ability.

ROMANTICISM VS. REALISM

The struggle to flee the world, however, leads to an equally pervasive attraction to myth, history, and art—alternatives to the time-drenched present—and to philosophical abstraction, as in the emphasis on Platonic reflections, that gives the poetry an equally consistent romantic quality. If in his realism Hayden resembles a poet like Wilbur, in his Romanticism he most resembles William Butler Yeats. There are specific similarities: The twelve-year-old girl of "The Peacock Room," who becomes a cadaver caught up in the folds of a fluttering peacock, recalls several of the poems about Maud Gonne. "Dance the Orange" concludes with a Yeatsian merging of the dancer and the dance. "Lear Is Gay" uses the metaphor of time as a scarecrow. The similarity is more than incidental, however: It is essential to Hayden's vision, and one of the powers of Hayden's poetry arises from this tension between his Romantic underpinnings and his realistic surface.

"MONET'S 'WATERLILIES'"

This tension is evident in "Monet's 'Waterlilies,'" the first section of which is a meditation on the "poisonous news" from Selma and Saigon. From this reality, the poet retreats to art, to the painting that he loves, where space and time are reconciled; then "The seen, the known/ dissolve in iridescence." Looking at the painting, the poet discovers the "aura of that world/ each of us has lost." Then reality gives way, and the painting becomes the "shadow" of the joy of that lost world. Indeed, several of Hayden's poems suggest his attraction to the static visual arts and his conviction that poetry is like painting: "Richard Hunt's 'Arachne,'" "Koda-chromes of the Island," "Butterfly Piece," "The Peacock Room"—these and several others have as their subject man's attempt to transform reality into something more nearly resembling the ultimate presence than its human and temporal manifestation.

"BUTTERFLY PIECE"

In "Butterfly Piece," the poet examines Brazilian butterflies that have been preserved and encased as works of art, and it seems he can find no higher praise than to compare them with Fabergé enamel work: Nature may mirror art, but the movement of the poem is away from this assurance. In the second stanza, Hayden focuses on how their bright colors resemble those of the human world, colors so bright that they burden, that they break. Finally then, he comments that this wild beauty has been killed and sold "to prettify," a distinct diminishment of the original implication. Thus art provides for Hayden one alternative to the human world, where lives are too often burdened, too often break. Yet if perfect art can in its serene reconciliation of time and space rekindle memories of a more perfect vision, it can also be a diminution of reality; even here, then, Hayden maintains the ambivalence of his vision.

HISTORICAL URGE

Like art, history provides an alternative to present patterns. Sometimes the history is personal, as in "Beginnings," the poem that opens *Angle of Ascent* and that itself opens simply with the names of Hayden's ancestors; this calling the roll suggests the search for identity that is another theme in Hayden's work, one obviously related to his own confused childhood identity. More often the history is public, as in the events of the American past, and particularly those of black American history, representing a time outside the uneasy present.

"MIDDLE PASSAGE"

The historical urge is most clearly seen in Hayden's narrative poetry, such as in "Middle Passage," a long poem in which the coming of slaves to America is told by a series of different voices. That poem, too—and it is among Hayden's finest—begins with a list of names: the hopeful and religious names of the slave ships, Hayden writes, bright and ironical compared with the grim cargo

of human beings they are delivering. The voices include that of the ship's log and of a deponent at a trial. Ariel's song from *The Tempest* (1611), a song used by T. S. Eliot for different purposes in *The Waste Land* (1922), suggests that those who have been drowned have been transformed, not into pearl or coral as in William Shakespeare's vision, but into New England pews and altar lights.

Hymns enter, as well as the voice of the slave trader himself. In the climactic third section, the poet himself speaks, first describing the horrible historic voyage "through death" and contrasting with the voice of a white slave trader who has survived the *Amistad* mutiny, when blacks did in fact mutiny and take over a ship. The self-justifying voice of that narrator counterpoints the bravery of Cinquez, the prince who led the mutiny and transformed the horror of confinement by using the terrible liberating force of rebellion. This is, the poet says at last, the "deep immortal human wish/ the timeless will"; it is that of transfiguration, of life out of death, a living death redeemed into new life. In this historical vision, Hayden creates his most powerful narrative image of humankind's potential transformation—for Hayden, all life is a voyage, all human beings are confined, all worthwhile acts are attempts to be free.

DREAM AND MEMORY

As well as the balance between the present reality and such timeless entities as myth, history, and art, Hayden presents the balance between dream, the longing for a perfect future, and memory, the dimly recalled past, as alternatives to the present. "The Dream (1863)," contrasts the dreams of liberation of a Southern slave who envisions her liberators as heroic and mythic figures with excerpts from letters of a Union soldier who is among her real liberators. Although the letters are often hackneyed and sentimental, their humor stale, they have a human bravery and modesty that is attractive. As always, Hayden's vision of them is ambivalent, but it is finally affirmative. The dreams, however beautiful in their abstract imaginings, are inappropriate to the reality, and the dreamer sinks to the ground at the end, attempting to rise, but failing.

Distrusting the present, Hayden creates in his poetry a tension between it and timeless worlds—art, history, myth, memory, and desire. Out of those tensions, he finds the movement of his poetry. Thus there is in his work, as in the human lives he describes, a constant choice, an alternation of poetic attention and human needs, so that his characters, like the poet, are always at once alien to and at home in this world, making an uneasy peace, living in delicate balance.

MOTIFS OF TRANSFORMATION

There is in Hayden another way of dealing with dialectical opposition: not the balancing of the two, but the movement from one to another. As often as his poems depict stasis and balance, so also do they suggest synthesis through process, an equal possibility for working through man's ambiguous place in the world. Thus transformation and metamorphosis become major motifs in his work. In "Theme and Variation," which—as the title suggests—indicates the large direction of Hayden's work, he writes that "all things alter . . . become a something more,/ a something less." In "Richard Hunt's 'Arachne,'" for example, he captures the movement downward. Here Arachne is caught in the moment of her transformation from human to arachnid—not yet changed to unthinking animal, no longer fully woman. Horrible as the surface is, however, Hayden's attitude remains detached: If she is on the one hand "dying," she is on the other "becoming."

"AN INFERENCE OF MEXICO"

The theme of transformation informs and unifies Hayden's long poem "An Inference of Mexico." Like many of his works, this poem involves travel. Hayden writes about "the migratory habits of the soul," but it is clear that the body migrates through the world as well. (The contrast with the settledness of Hayden's own adult life is interesting.) In this poem the light of Mexico, strange and savage, causes the persona to reexamine his world. The first section involves a burial, the putting away of the old life; as he watches a funeral, he looks upward to see "graveblack vultures," which are "transformed by steeps of flight." An anonymous voice urges him to flee, but when, in the second section, he looks at the mountains, they are equally dark and seem themselves to be "imploring a god." In the third section, "Veracruz," he looks at the ocean where tourists ignore "the bickering spray." Then at the center of this section, the poet indicates man's choices: flight and escape—"Leap now/ and cease from error"—or acceptance, a

turning shoreward, "accepting all—/ the losses and farewells,/ the long warfare with self,/ with God." For the persona, reality itself becomes a dream, and he chooses to escape; he turns to leap, to cease from error, and in the next section his heart turns heavenward in praise of pagan gods, followed by a section contrasting the Christian and pagan deities that coexist in the Mexican culture. The escape cannot last, however; the poet is inextricably tied to things of this world, and so in the sixth section he finds himself back in the market, where he is surrounded by tourists and beggars, asking for charity while the fire-king god looks blankly on. The last section, "La Corrida," contrasting bull and matador, sun and shadow, again suggests man's awful power and dilemma; it is the poet's own voice that now begs for charity, that all human beings be redeemed and delivered from what they are "yet cannot be" and from their past, all they know "and do not wish/ to know."

"An Inference of Mexico" also employs Hayden's two favorite images for the human predicament. The first is war. Superficially, "Locus," too, describes a landscape, and, like "An Inference of Mexico," it is rich in descriptive detail of flora and fauna, of people and events. The trees are those of "an illusionist," however, and the human position in this world is one of antagonism: spies watch Hernando de Soto's troops, runagates hide from Southern masters. Here nature thrives, but it thrives on spareness, nature itself doing what Hayden asks of man: accepting a world that gives one less than he needs and more than he can often bear. The flowers "twist into grace"; the houses are symbols of dreams dying prolonged and painful deaths. The past remains, then, "adored and/ unforgiven." It is not merely landscape, but "soulscape," and this soulscape is a "battleground/ of warring shades whose weapons kill."

Even in "On Lookout Mountain," where the Civil War battleground has been converted into an unimportant tourist spot, where choices once daring and dangerous have become selections of souvenirs and trivia, the cries of Kilroy, like those of Civil War soldiers and even those of the present, are concentric. Although on one level the present insignificance contrasts with the momentous past, on another they are only versions of the same story; the cries of past generations remain audible in "the warfare of our peace."

FLIGHT AND DESCENT

The image which recurs most frequently throughout Hayden's poetry, however, is flight, in tension with its opposite, descent, but also used as a pun for a further tension, the noun formed from both "to flee" and "to fly." Descent, that transformation to something less, is a dangerous alternative to flight. In "The Dream," Sinda, the dreamer, sinks to the ground at the end; in "The Performers," the observer of the window washers stays with them in his imagination until he sees himself falling with no safety strap to hold him up. In "The Ballad of Nat Turner" it is the dream of falling angels that confirms Turner's destructive but liberating vision. The poem which best exemplifies descent is "The Diver." It opens with the diver sinking through the sea's "easeful/ azure." That descent is an escape from the present, with its warring shadows, its balances and choices. The creatures that the diver sees remind him of "lost images," but he sinks beyond them. It is as "dreams of/ wingless flight." The goal of this descent is a ship, but the treasures that the diver finds there are "voracious life." His flashlight probing "fogs of water," everything seems eerie, a game of hide and seek. The diver's longing is to throw off everything, to yield to the rapturous deep, "have/ done with self and/ every dinning/ vain complexity." This deep, which once seemed so easeful, now becomes frenzied, canceling, numbing. Whether by reflex or by will, the persona begins to struggle. He escapes somehow, manages the "measured rise" to the surface. Like Robert Frost's "Stopping by Woods on a Snowy Evening," "The Diver" shows how restful the dark can seem, how the strange beauty of this deep and dark alternative can entice one to leave behind the promises and battles of his own disappointing world. Here, too, as in Frost's poem, although with considerably more effort, the poet-persona rejects escape; ascent for the diver is only a return to the surface of life, but it is as difficult as the ascent in any of Hayden's poems.

Another kind of escape may be fleeing—the flight, say, of an escaping slave, of another who flees a reality that certainly burdens and threatens to break him. This is the kind of escape that Hayden describes in "The Ballad of sue Ellen Westerfield" or "Runagate Runagate," an escape which is not the treacherous evasion of "The Diver" but the attempt to be free. The flight is thus a pun-

ning ascent, as in "Runagate Runagate," where slaves rise "from their anguish and their power," willing to be free. Sue Ellen Westerfield escapes slavery, a burning ship, and a white lover—all escapes that are necessary in her difficult attempt at freedom.

The final transformation, that which the soul aspires to and which the poet ultimately embraces, is what Hayden, in the title of his collected poems, calls "the angle of ascent." Flight is, of course, a prominent motif in black literature. For Hayden it is the most important of all images, for it suggests not merely escape, but meaningful escape, not merely transformation, but transfiguration, so that present reality becomes an image of the perfect reality for which human beings long. In both poems about Daedalus, Hayden aptly uses this metaphor, and what the poet-personae do is rise. After their struggle they achieve that angle of ascent in order to find a resting place where they are not at all alien. The treatment of the metaphor is sometimes less serious. In "Unidentified Flying Object" (UFO) the main character seems to have climbed aboard a UFO, leaving her life in total disorder, her face "transformed" into something that the man who observes her has never seen before. Although the poem ends with a hint that Mattie Lee may have suffered a darker fate, the ambiguous ending can only slightly modify the witty assertion of the earlier movement of the poem—an ascent that leaves behind radios and roasts, churches and suitors, gossips and sheriffs. In "'Summertime and the Living. . . .'" the living is not easy, and the characters' dreams and hopes contrast with the vividly depicted reality of their lives. The city dwellers find the summer a time for poor folks, when they can sit on stoops and talk, when they share their common dream, here a fantasy of Ethiopia, the Africa of remembered past and longed-for future, which spreads across them "her gorgeous wings." Their lives, too, are for a moment "transformed by steeps of flight."

OTHER MAJOR WORKS

NONFICTION: *Collected Prose*, 1984.

EDITED TEXTS: *Kaleidoscope: Poems by American Negro Poets*, 1967; *Afro-American Literature: An Introduction*, 1971 (with David J. Burrows and Frederick R. Lapides).

BIBLIOGRAPHY

Conniff, Brian. "Robert Hayden and the Rise of the African American Poetic Sequence." *African American Review* 33, no. 3 (Fall, 1999): 487-506. A discussion of Hayden's development in the poem "Middle Passage" of an experimental poetics that could examine racism by telling an episode of its history in a number of contending voices.

Davis, Arthur P. "Robert Hayden." In *From the Dark Tower: Afro-American Writers, 1900 to 1960*. Washington, D.C.: Howard University Press, 1982. This study emphasizes the craftsmanship of Hayden. Davis illustrates the variety of verse forms and techniques used in the later poems and discusses in detail a few poems. Although some of Hayden's best poems deal with racial subject matter, his technical mastery raises them above the level of protest.

Davis, Charles T. "Robert Hayden's Use of History." In *Modern Black Poets: A Collection of Critical Essays*, edited by Donald B. Gibson. Englewood Cliffs, N.J.: Prentice-Hall, 1973. This clear, well-illustrated study examines Hayden's lifelong preoccupation with African American history. Davis traces in individual poems the changing emphasis from physical to spiritual liberation, in subjects ranging from Nat Turner to Malcolm X.

Fetrow, Fred M. "Portraits and Personae: Characterization in the Poetry of Robert Hayden." In *Black American Poets Between Worlds, 1940-1960*, edited by R. Baxter Miller. Knoxville: University of Tennessee Press, 1986. This illuminating study approaches Hayden's poetry through his portraits of real and imagined persons. Two groups of African American historical figures are fighters for freedom and artists and entertainers. Fictional characters are also studied for insights into Hayden's personality.

_____. *Robert Hayden*. Boston: Twayne, 1984. The first book-length study of Hayden, this volume is a good introduction to his work. After tracing his life, Fetrow studies the poems chronologically according to subject matter: confession, description of people and places, black heritage, and spiritual transcendence. Supplemented by a chronology, notes, a select bibliography (including a list of secondary sources with brief annotations), and an index.

Gikandi, Simon. "Race and the Idea of the Aesthetic." *Michigan Quarterly Review* 40, no. 2 (Spring, 2001): 318-350. Gikandi discusses Hayden's lifelong struggle with the relationship between the question of race and the idea of the aesthetic, and with questions concerning how the moral lines and social boundaries of modernity are drawn.

Glaysher, Frederick, ed. *Collected Prose: Robert Hayden*. Foreword by William Meredith. Ann Arbor: University of Michigan Press, 1984. This excellent one-volume collection of Hayden's prose includes previously unpublished or inaccessible pieces. Four interviews are especially helpful in clarifying Hayden's intentions in specific poems.

Su, Adrienne. "The Poetry of Robert Hayden." *Library Cavalcade* 52, no. 2 (October, 1999): 8-11. A brief profile of Hayden and a critique of "Those Winter Sundays," "The Prisoners," and "Monet's 'Waterlilies.'"

Williams, Pontheolla T. *Robert Hayden: A Critical Analysis of His Poetry*. Foreword by Blyden Jackson. Urbana: University of Illinois Press, 1987. In one of the most thorough studies to date, Williams examines all aspects of Hayden's poetry. An opening biographical summary clarifies poetic influences and remaining chapters chronologically treat all published works. Supplemented by a comprehensive bibliography (including an unannotated list of secondary sources), copies of key poems discussed in the text, a chronology, notes, and an index.

Howard Faulkner;
bibliography updated by the editors

SEAMUS HEANEY

Born: Mossbawn, County Derry, Northern Ireland; April 13, 1939

PRINCIPAL POETRY
Death of a Naturalist, 1966
Door into the Dark, 1969
Wintering Out, 1972

Stations, 1975

North, 1975

Field Work, 1979

Poems, 1965-1975, 1980

Sweeney Astray: A Version from the Irish, 1984 (as *Sweeney's Flight*, 1992)

Station Island, 1984

The Haw Lantern, 1987

The Cure at Troy: A Version of Sophocles' "Philoctetes," 1990

New Selected Poems, 1966-1987, 1990

Seeing Things, 1991

The Midnight Verdict, 1993

The Spirit Level, 1996

Audenesque, 1998

Opened Ground: Selected Poems, 1966-1996, 1998

The Light of the Leaves, 1999

Electric Light, 2001

OTHER LITERARY FORMS

Preoccupations: Selected Prose, 1968-1978 (1980) is a collection of memoirs, lectures, reviews, and essays in which Seamus Heaney accounts for his development as a poet. *The Government of the Tongue: The T. S. Eliot Memorial Lectures and Other Critical Writings* (1988) similarly gathers later reviews and lectures, developing his subsequent views on the relationship between society and poetry.

ACHIEVEMENTS

Seamus Heaney's work has been recognized with some of the most prestigious honors in literary circles. Perhaps his most impressive award came in 1995, when he won the Nobel Prize for Literature. For *Death of a Naturalist*, he won the Eric Gregory Award in 1966, the Cholomondeley Award in 1967, and, in 1968, both the Somerset Maugham Award and the Geoffrey Faber Memorial Prize. He also won the Poetry Book Society Choice citation for *Door into the Dark* in 1969, the Irish Academy of Letters award in 1971, the Writer in Residence Award from the American Irish Foundation and the Denis Devlin Award, both for *Wintering Out* in 1973, the E. M. Forster Award, election to the American Academy and Institute of Arts and Letters in 1975, and the W. H. Smith Award, the Duff Cooper Memorial

Prize, and a Poetry Book Society Choice citation, all in 1976 for *North*.

In 1982 Heaney was awarded D.H.L. degrees by Fordham University and Queen's University of Belfast; the two universities noted particularly that his reflection of the troubles of Northern Ireland in his poetry had universal application. He then received the *Los Angeles Times* Book Prize nomination in 1984, as well as the PEN Translation Prize for Poetry in 1985, both for *Sweeney Astray: A Version from the Irish*. He won the Whitbread Award in 1987 for *The Haw Lantern*, the Lannam Foundation Award in 1990, a Premio Mondello (International Poetry Prize) from the Mondello Foundation in Palermo, Sicily, in 1993, the Whitbread Award in 1997 for *The Spirit Level*, and the *Irish Times* Award in 1999 for *Opened Ground*. He again won the Whitbread Award, in 1999, for poetry and book of the year for his translation of the epic Anglo-Saxon poem *Beowulf*, which was considered groundbreaking in its use of the modern idiom.

BIOGRAPHY

Seamus Heaney was born into a Roman Catholic farming family in rural Country Derry, Northern Ireland

Seamus Heaney (© Nancy Crampton)

(Ulster), the predominantly Protestant and industrial province of the United Kingdom in the island of Ireland. Much of his boyhood was spent on a farm, one border of which was formed by a stream that also divided Ulster from Eire, the predominantly Catholic Republic of Ireland. As a schoolboy he won scholarships first at the age of eleven to St. Colomb's College, a Catholic preparatory school, and then to Queen's University, Belfast, from which he graduated in 1961 with a first class honors degree in English. There he joined a group of young poets working under the direction of creative writers on the faculty.

He began his professional career as a secondary school English teacher, after which he went into teacher education, eventually joining the English faculty of Queen's in 1966. When civil dissension broke out in Ulster in 1969, eventually leading to martial law, Heaney, as a Catholic-reared poet, became increasingly uncomfortable. In 1972 he relocated to a manor in the Eire countryside to write full-time, although he also became a faculty member of a college in Dublin. Beginning in 1979, he adopted the practice of accepting academic appointments at various American universities and spending the rest of the year in Dublin. In 1986 he was appointed Boylston Professor of Rhetoric and Oratory at Harvard University, and in 1989 he became professor of poetry at Oxford University. To accommodate both positions, he split his time between a home in Dublin and one in Boston.

ANALYSIS

Almost from the beginning of his poetic career, Seamus Heaney gained public recognition for poems rooted deep in the soil of Northern Ireland and flowering in subtle rhythms and nuanced verbal melodies. In many respects he pursues a return to poetry's foundations in Romantic meditations on nature and explorations of the triple relationship among words, emotions, and the imagination. Heaney's distinctive quality as a poet is that he is at once parochial and universal, grounded in particular localities and microcultures yet branching out to touch every reader. Strangely, this unusual "here and everywhere" note remains with him even when he changes the basic subject matter of his poetry, as he has done frequently. His command of what William Blake

called "minute particularity" allows him to conjure up a sense of the universal even when focusing on a distinct individuality—to see "a world in a grain of sand." He makes the unique seem familiar. Because his success at this was recognized early, he was quickly branded with the label "greatest Irish poet since Yeats"—an appellation that, however laudatory, creates intolerable pressure and unrealizable expectations. Neoromantic he certainly is but not in William Butler Yeats's vein; Heaney is less mythic, less apocalyptic, less mystical, and much more material and elemental.

In many respects Heaney's art is conservative, especially in technique. Unlike the forms of the iconoclastic leading poets of the first half of the twentieth century—T. S. Eliot, E. E. Cummings, Wallace Stevens, Ezra Pound, William Carlos Williams, and Dylan Thomas—Heaney's meters, figures, diction, and textures are all relatively straightforward. Also in contrast, his poetry is not "difficult" as theirs was; his sentences generally employ standard syntax. Nevertheless, he is a master technician with an ear for fine and subtle verbal melodies. Instead of breaking with the past, his poems much more often depend on forging links; his music often harks back to that of William Wordsworth, John Milton, or Edmund Spenser. Yet his diction is common and Irish as well as formal and English. Colloquial speech patterns of the brogue often counterpoint stately cadences of British rhetoric. The combination produces a varied music, blending the different strains in his personal history and in the history of his people and his region. His best poems ring in the memory with echoes of modulated phrase and evocative sound patterns. He has probed the Irish conscience and discovered a way to express it in the English language, to render the Irish soul afresh.

DEATH OF A NATURALIST

Heaney's first book, *Death of a Naturalist*, laid the groundwork for his achievement. Centered firmly in the country scenes of his youth, these poems declare both his personal heritage from generations of Irish farm laborers and his emancipation from it, acquired by the mastery of a foreign tradition, the literature of the English. His art is Irish in origins and inspiration and English by training. The result is a surprisingly uniform and rich amalgam that incorporates much of

Ulster's complex mix of cultures. The poems become what Heaney at the time hoped was possible for his region: the preservation of both Irish and English traditions by a fusion that transcended either of them separately.

"Digging," a celebrated poem from this volume, illustrates this idea. It memorializes the typical work he associated with his father's and grandfather's generations (and, by implication, those of their ancestors): cutting turf, digging. He deliberately contrasts their tool of choice, the spade, with his, the pen: "I've no spade to follow men like them." By his instrument he can raise their labor into art, in the process ennobling them.

"Follower" similarly contrasts his labor with his father's. It captures in paced phrases and exact images his father's skill at and identification with plowing. This was the ancestral craft of the Heaneys; it makes his father what he is. As a result, it serves as the model of what young Seamus believed he should grow up to become. Sent instead to school, however, he was not reared to the plow and could never do more than hobble in his father's wake. The poem ends in a complex and disturbing image:

> But today
> It is my father who keeps stumbling
> Behind me, and will not go away.

The meaning is clear and manifold. His father stumbles intellectually—because the son has climbed beyond him—and culturally, for he will never be able to reach this point or even appreciate it. His father also stumbles merely physically, as the older generation does, and he must be cared for by his son when he cannot care for himself. Finally, his father is a clog at Heaney's heels, hindering him by his heritage: The poet will never be able to evade his father's influence.

DOOR INTO THE DARK

Three years later, *Door into the Dark* found Heaney continuing to explore this material from his upbringing, but it also showed him expanding his range and developing new moral insights. Increasingly he began sensing that the various pasts in his heritage—of family, race, and religion—were reincarnating themselves in the present, that the history of the people was recapitulating itself. This insight bound present and past indissolubly

together. What unfolded in the here and now, then, became part of a gradually evolving theme and variations, revealing itself in event and place.

Some of the poems in this volume accordingly focus on events and occupations illustrating continuity in the Irish experience. "Thatcher," for example, celebrates an ancient Irish craft: thatching roofs out of by-products and discards. The fabric of the poem beautifully reflects and incorporates its subject, for its rhythms and rhymes form parallel patterns that imitate one another and interlock, although the dovetailing is not exact. Left unstated in the poem is an implied theme: The craft of the poet is equally ancient and equally intricate. A similar interweaving of past and present occurs in "The Wife's Tale," in which the persona—a farm woman—re-creates simply the routine of laying out a field lunch for laborers during threshing. The narrative is matter-of-fact and prosaic, detached and unemotional, and unspecific in time: It could be almost anytime, a reiterative action. Her action thus binds the generations together, suggesting the sameness of human life regardless of time. The poem also subtly depicts the interdependence of husband and wife—he fights and plants, she nourishes and supports—and their failure to merge completely: "And that was it. I'd come and he had shown me,/ So I belonged no further to the work."

A number of the poems in this volume are simply musings on travels in Ireland and on the Continent. At first it is easy to pass over these pieces, because the simple, undramatic language and quiet tone do not attract much attention. In fact, however, these meditations are extremely important in the evolution of Heaney's poetic orientation, for they document his growing awareness of place as a determinant of sensibility. For Heaney, a person's surroundings, particularly the environment of his or her growing-up years, become the context to which he or she instinctively refers new experiences for evaluation. They become the norms of consciousness, the images from which the individual forms values. In "The Peninsula," for example, the persona spends a day touring the scenes of his youth. He discovers upon return that he still has "nothing to say," but he realizes that henceforth he will "uncode all landscapes/ By this." In "Night Drive" the speaker, driving through France and thinking of his love in Italy, finds his "ordinariness" renewed by simple things such as signposts and realizes that the same thing is happening to her. Environment forms and frames consciousness.

More important, it also frames historical consciousness, the intersection of the past with the present in the individual. In the poems that first document this idea, Heaney announces what is to be a major theme: the inescapable presence of the past. This emerges in "Requiem for the Croppies," a long-after-the-fact elegy for the insurrectionist Catholic peasants—designated "croppies" because in the 1790's they cropped their hair to indicate their support of the French revolutionaries—who were slaughtered by the thousands at Vinegar Hill at the end of the uprising of 1798.

The poem, a simple sonnet, quietly recalls the mood of that campaign, in which unarmed, uneducated plowboys terrorized the great estates of the absent English overlords until they were hemmed in and mowed down by cavalry and cannon. At first, for the rabble the rebellion was a romp; finally, it became a nightmare and a shame. The poem documents this in one encircling image: The ultimate harvest of the battle is the spilled barley, carried for food, which sprouts from the mass graves the following summer. A better symbol of futility and helplessness could hardly be found. Written in 1969, the year of the recurrence of the "trouble" (ethnic conflicts in Ulster between Protestant unionists and Catholic secessionists), the poem both marks Heaney's allegiances—he was reared Catholic—and records his dismay over the renewal of pointless violence. Significantly, Heaney left Belfast for good in that year, although his major motive was to devote his full time to writing.

"BOGLAND"

In the same year, Heaney encountered the book *The Bog People* (1969) by the ethnologist and anthropologist P. V. Glob. This account of a race of Iron Age peoples who inhabited the boglands of northern Europe in the dark past, before the Indo-European migrations of the first millennium B.C.E., was based largely on excavated remains of bodies that had been preserved by immersion in bogs. The photographs of these bodies particularly fired Heaney's imagination, especially because many of them had been ritualistically sacrificed.

Since the newspapers and magazines had recently been saturated with atrocity punishments and murders, often involving equally primitive rituals, Heaney postulated a connection between the two, forged by the history of terrorism between clans and religions in Northern Ireland: Modern Ulster, despite centuries of alterations in its facade and supposed progress in its politics and civilization, was populated by a race different only in accidentals from its Iron Age progenitors. The same elemental passions and atavistic fears seethed beneath a deceptively civilized surface. Furthermore, those ancient dark mysteries that precipitated the superstitious sacrifices had not been superseded by civilization; they had merely receded into the background. Unsuspected, they continued to be inherited in the blood. Although he nowhere uses the Jungian terminology, Heaney seems to subscribe to the idea of the collective unconscious, the reservoir of instinctive, intuitive behavior acquired genetically.

These ideas bear first fruit in "Bogland," in which he invents a powerful metaphor for another of his central themes. He visualizes his kind, his culture, as centered on a bog: "Our unfenced country/ Is bog that keeps crusting/ Between the sights of the sun." The bog simultaneously buries and preserves, destroys and reconstitutes. Through it the past becomes continuous with the present, *re*-presented in it. The bog records all generations of humanity that have grown up alongside it, disclosing continuous occupation: "Every layer they strip/ Seems camped on before."

The bog is also an analogue of the human mind, which similarly buries and preserves, and which inherits the entire weight of the past. Furthermore, both have fathomless depths, brooding pools, and nameless terrors bubbling up from unplumbed regions. The bog becomes the perfect image of the inexplicable in the self and in society as a whole. Further, it provides Heaney with a device for illustrating the force behind the violence and a means of distancing himself from it. The bog becomes a link with humankind's preconscious, reptilian past: "The bogholes might be Atlantic seepage./ The wet centre is bottomless."

WINTERING OUT

Heaney's third book, *Wintering Out*, secured his early reputation. Like his first two books, it is rooted in his homeland, but it also includes poems of departure. Places precisely realized play a large part in it; in particular, these places declare themselves through their ancient names. Heaney spins music out of them:

Anahorish, soft gradient
of consonant, vowel meadow,

after-image of lamps
swung through the yards
on winter evenings.

Brough, Derrygarve, Ballyshannon voice related melodies, weaving together past and present, counterpointing also with English names: Castledawson, Upperlands. The two languages together stitch the present out of the past.

The volume opens with "Bog Oak," which Heaney makes into a symbol for his bog world: It is a relic from the past, wood preserved in a bog where no oaks now stand, excavated to make rafters for new buildings. Furthermore, it is saturated with the bog, so that images of past centuries may be imprinted in it, as on film, to be released as the wood is used and thus to redirect the present. In one more way, then, the past is reincarnated. Dreaming that the oak images will bring him contact with the spirits of past poets, Heaney reminds his readers that the history of poetry is also a means of realizing the past in the present.

Other species of the Irish environment also participate in this process of continuity. "Gifts of Rain," for example, memorializes the omnipresent threat of rain in the Irish weather. Yet the poem also makes the rain into a stream flowing through everything, a liquid voice from the past: "Soft voices of the dead/ Are whispering by the shore." It becomes a solvent of the Irish experience.

This awareness of and openness to all aspects of life, especially the dark and the violent, leads Heaney to treat some topics in this volume that are quite different from his past choices. Among them is one of the more inexplicable incidents of human cruelty: infanticide by mothers, or maternal rejection of infants. "Limbo" considers an infant drowned shortly after birth and netted by salmon fishermen. Heaney dispassionately records the ironies, beginning with the simple suggestion that this child's baptism was in fact murder, the most extreme

sacrilege, although he fully sympathizes with the mother's agony. Still, the child died without baptism; hence, it is ineligible for Heaven and must be relegated to Limbo, a place of painless exile, according to orthodox Catholic doctrine. Such a conclusion, however, is so unjust that it seems incompatible with any God who claims to incarnate love: "Even Christ's palms, unhealed,/ Smart and cannot fish here."

Similarly, "Bye-Child" re-creates the perspective of a child shut up by his mother in a henhouse, without vital human contact. The inscription states that he could not speak. Heaney seems astounded that anyone could deny a human the possibility of communication: to be human is to communicate. This child, as a result, becomes in turn a curiosity, a rodent, an alien, a "moon man"—nothing human. Still, his response to his rescuers reveals an attempt to communicate, to reach "beyond love."

The experience that apparently enabled Heaney to contemplate such events took place through Glob's *The Bog People*. He was so struck by the images of some of the recovered bodies—particularly those sacrificed in earth mother rites and those punished for crimes—that he wrote poems about them. The first, the three-part "The Tolland Man," first published in *Wintering Out*, has become one of his most widely reprinted poems. Heaney first describes the body, now displayed at the State Museum at Århus, Denmark, and briefly alludes to his fate: Given a last meal, he was hauled in a tumbril to the bog, strangled, and deposited as a consort to the bog goddess, who needed a male to guarantee another season of fertility. In the second section Heaney suggests that the ritual makes as much sense as the retaliatory, ritualistic executions of the Troubles; the current practice is as likely to improve germination. The third section establishes a link between survivors and victims, past and present. It implies that all humans are equally involved, equally responsible, if only by complicity or failure to act. Heaney suggests that senseless violence and complacent acceptance of it are both parts of human nature.

STATIONS

Heaney's next book, *Stations*, marked both an advance and a setback. The advance was compound, both formal and topical. Formally, the book consists of a series of prose poems; topically, they all deal with the experience of growing up rural and Catholic in an industrialized, Protestant-dominated culture. The title *Stations* alludes to this: The events detailed here constitute the contemporary equivalent of the Stations of the Cross, the sufferings Christ endured in his passion and death; moreover, they are the way stations of modern education, the stopping points of the soul. The poems show Heaney returning to his childhood to identify and document his indoctrination into the complicity he finds unacceptable in *Wintering Out*. In all these ways the book celebrates gains.

Yet the individual poems of *Stations* are less successful and less uniform than his earlier work. They disclose an artificiality, a staginess, a contrived quality formerly absent. They also depend on a good bit of private information for comprehension. In some respects this is curious, because Heaney managed to avoid any hint of these weaknesses elsewhere, either in his poetry or in the retrospective prose that also dates from around this time. To an extent this uneasiness must be associated with his private uncertainty during this period, when he was trying to justify his leaving Ulster rather than staying to take a stand.

NORTH

Whatever the reason, it left the poetry of the same time intact. His second book of 1975, *North*, capitalized on his previous successes; significantly, the title indicates that all these poems still focus on the poet's Ulster experiences. The book includes more meditations on place and place-names, such as "Mossbawn"; there are also a few more nature pieces and reminiscences. Far and away the majority of the collection, however, deals with the cultural conflict of the North, the pagan heritage of Ireland, and the continuity of past and present through the mediation of the bog people. A series based on bone fragments from the past supplements the bog material. Practically all Heaney's best-known poems are found in this volume.

Furthermore, this is the first of Heaney's books which is more than a mere collection. The order and arrangement are designed to create an integrated reading experience; groupings reflect, refract, and diffuse patterns and themes. The basic structure of the book is twofold, with each part using distinctive verse forms. Part 1 focuses on the "North" of northern Europe from the time of its first population to the present. The basic verse is the taut, unrhymed or off-rhymed quatrain developed for *Wintering Out*; much of the diction is formal or archaic, and the atmosphere is solemn and austere. Part 2 takes "North" as contemporary Ulster. The root verse is the standard pentametric rhymed quatrain; the diction and tone are informal and playful. The polarity seems to reflect the two kinds of poetry Heaney describes repeatedly in *Preoccupations*: poetry that is "made" and poetry that is "given."

Some of the poems in part 1 actually fall partly outside this overly neat division. "Funeral Rites," an often-praised poem, joins the urgency of funerals during the Troubles with the legacy of pagan burials. The theme of the poem is that the frequent occurrence of funerals today has cheapened them: they lack the impact of ancient funerals, when death still meant something, still could be beautiful, and still could give promise of resurrection. The title poem also crosses the established border of the book. It centers on the imagination of the poet in the present, where he must work with what he finds—which falls far short of the epic standards of the past. Voices out of the water advise him to search the past of the race and express it through the roots of his language.

The center of part 1 is the past. Here the bog poems take precedence. There are six of them, all powerful. "The Grauballe Man" depicts another victim of the bog mother cult, this one written as if the persona were in the presence of the body. Heaney arranges a series of metaphors drawn from biology to create the image of the body, then inserts the line "The head lifts"—and the body seems to come alive before the mind's eye. The persona explicitly denies that this can be called a "corpse." Previously, seen only in photographs, the man seemed dead, "bruised like a forceps baby." Now he is "hung in the scales/ with beauty and atrocity"—he has taken on the life of enduring art yet also testifies to humanity's eternal and ongoing depravity. Violence creates beauty, and vice versa.

A second poem, "Punishment," portrays another category of victim among these people. According to the Roman historian Tacitus, the ancestral Germans punished women taken in adultery by shaving off their hair and immersing them naked in the bog, weighed down with stones and logs, until they drowned. This barely postpubescent girl of Heaney's poem illustrates the practice: undernourished, shaved, and blindfolded, she has no visible wounds. The persona sees her as a "scapegoat," a figure of terror: "her shaved head/ like a stubble of black corn." Yet she was also "beautiful," one who could arouse love. Nevertheless, he recognizes that had he been present, he "would have cast . . . / the stones of silence," in an allusion to the New Testament story of the woman taken in adultery. Heaney asserts that all human beings comply with the practices of their tribe, and then he finds the perfect modern parallel. In the early 1970's young Catholic women who consorted with British soldiers were punished similarly by the Irish Republican Army: they were shaved, tarred, feathered, and chained to public railings. Again all spectators comply, and the past, the primitive past, is present.

In "Strange Fruit" Heaney borrows the metaphor in the title from a black American civil rights protest song, in which "strange fruit" refers to the bodies of lynched blacks hanging from gallows. The fruit in the poem is ancient: an accidentally preserved severed head of a young woman. Here there is no justification in ritual; the woman is simply the victim of random violence or tribal conflict. Heaney, as before, suggests that exhuming the head from its bog grave is equivalent to restoring it to life and beauty. This time, however, he finds the consolation of art itself disturbing. He adds a new note, alluding to another Roman historian: "Diodorus Siculus confessed/ His gradual ease among the likes of this." Multiple atrocities generate complacency as well as complicity. Thus this girl stops short of beauty; far from attractive, she has "eyeholes blank as pools in the old workings." This is an image of the forlorn, the abandoned. These black eyeholes—lacking eyes—still outstare "what had begun to feel like reverence." Tolerating atrocities may not be the state human beings finally want to reach.

FIELD WORK

Heaney's next book, *Field Work*, poses a series of questions, mostly dealing with the relationship between art and social conscience. They thus cast doubts on both the attitude he had adopted toward contemporary violence and the resolution to which he had come about his life. Still, the answers he finds basically confirm his de-cisions. He chooses here the path of civilization, of art, the "field work" of the practicing artist. At the balancing point of this book rest the Glanmore sonnets, a series of ten sonnets reflecting his life at the country estate of Glanmore, County Wicklow, his retreat after Belfast. In terms of subject matter, he returns overtly to the natural settings and homely ways of his first two books. In this work, however, he is much more concerned with the poetic temperament, its influences, and its relation to society.

Accordingly, several of the sounds trace the parallels between Heaney and other figures who used rural solitude to comment on society: the Roman poets Horace and Vergil, the mythical Irish hero Sweeney, and the English poet William Wordsworth. The sonnets themselves are the densest, most intricate poems he had written to this point, rich and finely fashioned, delicate and subtle. Typical is sonnet 5, which commemorates the elderberry bush that served as refuge for the poet as a boy; he shapes it and his reminiscences about it into a symbol of his searches into the roots of language and memory.

Another major section of the book is devoted to elegies—three for victims of civil violence, three for fellow poets, and one for a relative killed in World War I. These are more conventional poems of mourning than his earlier meditations, which lamented but also accepted. They reflect a sense of absolute and final loss, the senseless wasting away that the pace of modern life leads people to take for granted, anger that so much good should be squandered so casually. Still, death is relentless and undiscriminating, taking the small with the great: "You were not keyed or pitched like these true-blue ones/ Though all of you consort now underground."

SWEENEY ASTRAY

After *Field Work* Heaney moved for a while in a different direction. *Sweeney Astray: A Version from the Irish* is an adaptation of the medieval Gaelic epic *Buile Suibhne*. Heaney had long been fascinated by the character of Sweeney, at once king and poet, and had used him as one of the persona's alter egos in *Field Work*. In the poem Sweeney fails in a quest and suffers the curse of Saint Ronan, the peacemaker, after repeatedly violating truces and killing one of the saint's clerics. Already nicknamed "Mad" because of his battle rages, Sweeney is now transformed into a bird and driven into the wilderness, doomed to be hunted by man and beast alike and to suffer delusions. The poem is more an anthology of rhapsodic songs and laments made by Sweeney in his exile than the standard heroic quest-poem. It is easy to detect the sources of Heaney's fascination, which include the easily overlooked rhyme of Sweeney's name with his own—the kind of thing he would spot immediately. Like Heaney, Sweeney is driven out of a violent society, though given to violence himself; he feels a natural kinship with animals, birds, trees, plants, and the things of the wild; he identifies with the places of his exile; and he senses the elemental divine pulse beating in and unifying everything. Furthermore, he represents the wounded imagination, in love with and repelled by the ways of humans in the world.

Although widely praised and honored, *Sweeney Astray* seems to have fallen short of Heaney's expectations. It did receive some hostile reviews, from Irish critics who did not really believe that English is a suitable medium for anything Gaelic and English critics who viewed Irish writers as plotting a hostile takeover of things British. The extent of Heaney's disappointment appears in the layout of *New Selected Poems, 1966-1987*, in which this book is the most scantily represented of his major works, being given only sixteen pages as against sixty-six for *Station Island* and forty-four for *North*. Clearly, it is more difficult to cull from a continuous sequence than from a collection; yet it is also true that ever since the publication of *North* Heaney had paid considerable attention to the organization of his books, so that, theoretically at least, excerpting should be difficult from any of them.

STATION ISLAND

Station Island is Heaney's amplest, most diversified, and most highly integrated book of poems. It consists essentially of three parts: a collection of separate lyrics, many family-centered and some combined into mini-sequences; the title sequence, centered on Station Island, also called St. Patrick's Purgatory, in west Ireland, a favorite Irish pilgrimage site; and a series named "Sweeney Redivivus," in which he creates new poems through the persona of the poet-hero brought back to life in himself and committed to reveal what remains of the past in the here and now. The lyrics show Heaney experimenting with new line lengths, new forms, and new approaches. They include meditations reminiscent of W. H. Auden, such as "Chekhov on Sakhalin," and a series on found objects called "Shelf Life"; both provide him with occasions for discovering unexpected epiphanies.

Similarly, the Sweeney poems disclose Heaney deepening his vision. The identification with his mythic predecessor required by the translation brings him to a new vantage point: He realizes that perceptive and imaginative as Sweeney was, deeply as he penetrated to the soul of things, he still remained alien from the bulk of the people, and he had not changed much. Heaney writes out of a new humility and also now out of relief. He concludes that he need not blame himself for having abandoned his people in the Troubles. They were not really his people, in retrospect; his values were not theirs. He could not accomplish much for them that would last. Better to pursue his poetry.

The title series also teaches him that lesson, though in a different way. It is Heaney's major triumph, consolidating and drawing on strengths he had been establishing since early in his career. It is the quintessential place-poem, for Station Island has many places and provides multiple occasions for poetry. Situated on Lough Derg in County Tipperary, Eire, the island was originally a primitive settlement; in the eighth or ninth century it became a locus of pilgrimage, renowned as a place of penitence. A number of foundation rings remain, the relics of either monastic cells or primitive dwellings. Devotees complete the act of repentance by making a circuit of these, kneeling and praying at each in turn, and by this act gaining remission of punishment for past sins.

Heaney bases his cycle on the persona's return to the island in middle age. Although by this point in his life an unbeliever, he finds the island well populated with souls eager to establish common ground with the living. For the devout, St. Patrick's Purgatory is a place of personal repentance, expiation, and rectification. For the literary, as a purgatorial site it has a forerunner in Dante's *Purgatorio* (c. 1320). Heaney uses the experience as a poetic examination of conscience, a Catholic devotional exercise: He reviews his career as a poet, attempting to determine once again the proper relationship between poetry and society. In this process he gains assistance and insight from the attendant ghosts, who include a number of figures from his private and literary past, notably including James Joyce. Heaney records their conversations, often weaving their voices together in terza rima, the verse form used by Dante. In the twelfth and last poem, Joyce advises Heaney to follow his lead in concentrating on art and ignoring the politics of the moment.

The Haw Lantern

The Haw Lantern continues in the direction mapped out in *Station Island*. In volume it is among the slightest of Heaney's collections: thirty-one poems in fifty-two pages. His topics, too, are rather commonplace in comparison: hailstones, alphabets, fishing lures, a peacock's feather, and (in the title poem) the fruit of the hawthorn. Heaney transforms this brilliant red winter fruit metaphorically into a lantern, an instrument for seeing and for measuring human values. Commonly used for hedging in the British Isles, this thorny shrub becomes a means of testing human integrity in the daily situations that finally count. The book also contains another of Heaney's trademark sequences. "Clearances," a set of eight sonnets written to commemorate the death of Heaney's mother, moves him to another stage in the definition of his poetic character. Symbolically, this constitutes Heaney's prayer at his mother's deathbed, bonding him to the past and committing him to the future. It also sets him apart from Joyce, his spiritual mentor, who made his refusal to pray at his mother's bedside a pivotal scene in *A Portrait of the Artist As a Young Man* (1916) and *Ulysses* (1922).

Reflections on aging

Despite being an active writer and continuing to produce published collections, Heaney seemed to move toward poetry that had a decidedly "later" feel about it in the 1990's and into the twenty-first century, as if the poet were consistently revisiting old scenes, revising opinions, refining thoughts once had, and critiquing versions of self presented in previous poems. In *Seeing Things*, Heaney appears to reach for a lightness, moving away from the thickets of alliteration and sensuality found in the early work or the harsh minimal realities of the bog period or even the casual sublimities of daily life found in both *Field Work* and, to a lesser extent, *The Haw Lantern*.

The Spirit Level and Opened Ground

The Spirit Level explores the themes of politics, humanism, and nature. It includes in its composition a plea for hope, innocence, and balance, and to seek eventually that "bubble for the spirit level." Here he balances the personal with the universal, as well as the process of life to death, in an attempt to seek an equilibrium. *Opened Ground* provides a comprehensive overview of his poetry from 1966 to 1996, with works from the 1990's heavily represented: Much of *The Spirit Level* is reproduced here. By chronologically following his progression as a poet, readers can discern Heaney's peculiar wistful and earthy mixture of rural reverie and high public speech and see how his interests broaden in the middle and later poems when the poet seeks out Greek myths, Irish epics, and Scandinavian archaeological digs to look for correlatives appropriate for his meditations.

Electric Light

Perhaps Heaney's most reflective collection during this period is *Electric Light*. Using a compilation of poetic genres and styles—including eclogue, elegy, epigram, yarn, meditation, and ecstatic lyric—Heaney meditates on the origins and inevitable ending of his life and art. His array of verse styles showcases Heaney's will and ability to speak of many kinds of experiences to many kinds of reader. Above all, his awareness of his aging, from which he turns away in memory and looks past in poems about death, gives the collection special coherence and expression. In "The Gaeltacht," modeled on a poem by Dante, he examines his literary fame, his desire for release from it, and a return to primal things. Heaney wishes he were in the Gaeltacht, a Gaelic-speaking region of northwestern Ireland, with one of his old pals "and that it was again nineteen sixty." Then other friends now old or dead would also be with them "talking Irish."

He also celebrates nature with a range of poems that explore landscapes, such as his birthplace of Northern Ireland, imprinted by human life, its meanings and violence handed down through the generations. Heaney's use of dialect and feeling-laden place-names distinctly help convey this theme. Notable literary figures make appearances here as well: He elegizes the Russian poet Joseph Brodsky, offers translations of Roman poet Vergil and Russian poet Alexander Pushkin, and has memorial poems for the Polish poet Zbigniew Herbert and American translator Robert Fitzgerald.

OTHER MAJOR WORKS

NONFICTION: *Preoccupations: Selected Prose, 1968-1978*, 1980; *The Government of the Tongue: The T. S. Eliot Memorial Lectures and Other Critical Writings*, 1988 (pb. in U.S. with the subtitle "Selected Prose, 1978-1987," 1989); *The Redress of Poetry*, 1995; *Homage to Robert Frost*, 1996 (with Joseph Brodsky and Derek Walcott); *Seamus Heaney in Conversation with Karl Miller*, 2000; *Sounding Lines: The Art of Translating Poetry*, 2000 (with Robert Hass); *Finders Keepers: Selected Prose, 1971-2001*, 2002.

TRANSLATION: *Beowulf: A New Verse Translation*, 1999.

BIBLIOGRAPHY

Burris, Sidney. *The Poetry of Resistance: Seamus Heaney and the Pastoral Tradition*. Athens: Ohio University Press, 1990. Burris has produced the first full-length study of Heaney's work, approached from the pastoral perspective, both classical and Romantic. It is a thorough scholarly analysis, providing an illuminating context for reading Heaney's poetry, but is rather heavy for the general reader. The notes and index are full, but there is no bibliography.

Deane, Seamus. "Seamus Heaney: The Timorous and the Bold." In *Celtic Revivals: Essays in Modern Irish Literature, 1880-1980*. London: Faber & Faber, 1985. A close personal friend of Heaney here provides a warm, congenial introduction to his poetry, paying particular attention to his relation to the Celtic movement of the twentieth century. Deane tends to fault Heaney, however, for not becoming the voice of the beleaguered Catholics.

Heaney, Seamus. Interview by John Haffenden. In *Viewpoints: Poets in Conversation with John Haffenden*. London: Faber & Faber, 1981. In this revealing interview with the poet, Haffenden asks effective questions, especially about childhood, the Ulster background, religion, nature, and place; he also knows how to nurse reactions. Heaney discloses qualities not immediately apparent in the poems.

Longley, Edna. "Poetry and Politics in Northern Ireland." In *Poetry in the Wars*. Dover: University of Delaware Press, 1987. This essay is not limited to Heaney, and it considers only the political implications of his work. Still, it is a thorough discussion of the way the political situation in Northern Ireland has affected literature in general and his poems in particular. It provides another necessary context.

Morrison, Blake. *Seamus Heaney*. Contemporary Writers Series. London: Methuen, 1982. Morrison's introduction is an indispensable first reference for the study of Heaney's life and works. He comments on the development of the poetry intelligently, and his account of the background is revealing. The book contains good notes and a solid starting bibliography but has no index.

Parkinson, Thomas. "Serious Work: The Poetry and Prose of Seamus Heaney." In *Poets, Poems, Movements*. Studies in Modern Literature. Ann Arbor: UMI Research Press, 1990. This brief essay is worth attention not because of depth or detail but because the insights of a major critic are always illuminating. Parkinson places Heaney clearly among the bewildering variety of contemporary writers.

Salmagundi 80 (Fall, 1988). This entire issue of this literary journal is concentrated on Heaney. It includes a bibliography, an interview, an essay by the poet, and studies by Helen Vendler, Mary Kinzie, Donald Davis, Jay Parini, and Barry Goldensohn. The various views presented here combine to create one of the most comprehensive surveys of the poet available.

Tobin, Daniel. *Passage to the Center: Imagination and the Sacred in the Poetry of Seamus Heaney*. Lexington: University Press of Kentucky, 1999. Tobin offers exceptional insight into the work of Heaney with an excellent overview and a fresh perspective on the deepest meaning of Heaney's poetry from 1965 to the present.

Vendler, Helen Hennessy. *Seamus Heaney*. Cambridge, Mass.: Harvard University Press, 2000. Whereas other books on Heaney have dwelt chiefly on the biographical, geographical, and political aspects of his writing, this book looks squarely and deeply at Heaney's poetry as art.

James Livingston,
updated by Sarah Hilbert

ANTHONY HECHT

Born: New York, New York; January 16, 1923

PRINCIPAL POETRY

A Summoning of Stones, 1954
The Hard Hours, 1967
Millions of Strange Shadows, 1977
The Venetian Vespers, 1979
The Transparent Man, 1990
Collected Earlier Poems, 1990
Flight Among the Tombs, 1996
The Darkness and the Light, 2001

OTHER LITERARY FORMS

Critical pieces by Anthony Hecht have been compiled as *Essays in Criticism* (1986). He has also worked as a translator, publishing a version of Aeschylus's *Seven Against Thebes* (1973; with Helen Bacon) and of Voltaire's *Poem upon the Lisbon Disaster* (1977).

ACHIEVEMENTS

An admirer of John Crowe Ransom, Allen Tate, and George Santayana, Anthony Hecht maintained the wit, precision, and intellectual rigor of the modernist voice for decades following World War II. He avoided a variety of trends in American poetry, including confessional poetry and didactic antiwar poetry, during the 1960's and 1970's. Yet his focus on issues surrounding art and human experience and on ethics—questions of human evil throughout \history—brought Hecht major recognition. In 1968 *The Hard Hours* received the Pulitzer Prize in poetry. In 1983 Hecht was a recipient of the Bollingen Prize, and from 1982 to 1984 he was U.S. poet laureate. He has won a variety of other awards, including that of the Academy of American Poets, the Prix de Rome, Guggenheim Fellowships, the Eugenio Montale Award for Poetry, the Frost Medal, and the Wallace Stevens Award. He has also received honorary doctorates from Bard College, Georgetown University, Towson State University, and the University of Rochester.

BIOGRAPHY

Anthony Hecht was born in New York City on January 16, 1923. He was graduated from Bard College in 1944 and spent the next three years in Europe and Japan as a rifleman in the U.S. Army. He was also briefly in the Counter-Intelligence Corps. With his unit, Hecht discovered the site of mass graves in an annex area of the Buchenwald concentration camp. This shattering experience would shape his worldview and influence the direction of his poetry.

Upon his return from Europe, Hecht took several teaching jobs, moving around from the Middle West to New England and finally back to New York. He spent a year at Kenyon College between 1947 and 1948 and studied with John Crowe Ransom, who was editing *The Kenyon Review* and published several poems by the young poet. Hecht embraced Ransom's New Critical perspective and soon afterward continued his tutelage under the Fugitives, working informally with Allen Tate. He went on to take a master's degree from Columbia University in 1950.

His first book, *A Summoning of Stones*, appeared in 1954, the same year as his marriage to his first wife, the mother of their two sons. In 1971 Hecht was married to Helen D'Alessandro, who bore his third son. Over several decades Hecht taught in a number of colleges and universities, including Kenyon College, the State University of Iowa, New York University, Smith College, and Bard College. At the University of Rochester he was the John H. Dean Professor of Poetry and Rhetoric from 1967 to 1982; during this time he also spent brief periods as a visiting lecturer at Washington University, Harvard University, and Yale University. Beginning in 1982, for two years, Hecht served as poetry consultant to the Library of Congress. He went on to join the graduate faculty at Georgetown University. His career also led him to spend some time abroad, as a Fulbright professor in Brazil and a trustee of the American Academy in Rome.

ANALYSIS

Terms such as "baroque," "neoclassical," "meditative," "realistic," "manneristic," "metaphysical," and "pessimistic" as well as "optimistic" have been used to describe Anthony Hecht's poetry. These varying descriptions reflect not so much transitions in the course of his poetry as the depth and complexity of his work. His poems are unpretentiously finely wrought, reflecting his interest in Greek and Roman poetry and seventeenth century poetry in addition to the work of the generation of poets that directly preceded him, including such writers as Ransom, Tate, and W. H. Auden. Hecht has also translated poems by writers including Joseph Brodsky, Charles Baudelaire, Guillaume Apollinaire, Voltaire, and Joachim du Bellay. His view of tradition is not unlike the one expressed in T. S. Eliot's essay "Tradition and the Individual Talent." Hecht is also very much aware of history, from the battles of the ancients to the wars of the twentieth century. Many of his poems are very serious, addressing such themes as death and carnage, while others are light and playful. His treatment of history and attention to the history of poetic convention set his work apart from that of many American poets of the latter part of the twentieth century.

A SUMMONING OF STONES

Selected poems from Hecht's first volume, *A Summoning of Stones*, reappear in his *Collected Earlier Poems*. Among these, "La Condition Botanique," "A Poem for Julia," and "Alceste in the Wilderness" have

Anthony Hecht (© Lotte Jacobi)

received considerable critical attention. "La Condition Botanique" treats the relationship between humanity and nature, especially the human attempt to order the natural world. The meditation is highly structured with a mirrored rhyme scheme, *abccba*. It moves great distances in time and space, from the Romans to Marie Curie, from Mexico to Brooklyn, from Ezekiel to the Buddha, suggesting the unending quest for order and stasis. Human endeavor is treated with some degree of humor. For example, the opening of "La Condition Botanique" is ironic:

> Romans, rheumatic, gouty, came
> To bathe in Ischian springs where water steamed,
> Puffed and enlarged their bold imperial thoughts, and
> which
> Later Madame Curie declared to be so rich
> In radioactive content as she deemed
> Should win them everlasting fame.

Some of the stanza breaks are rhymically counterpointed through the enjambment between the last line of one stanza and the first line of the next. Hecht's amusing catalog, which moves at a quick pace structurally and thematically, echoes the flux of the world.

"Alceste in the Wilderness" takes the main character of the seventeenth century comedy of manners and pursues the disillusionment of the misanthrope of Molière (Jean Baptiste Poquelin) in the heart of Africa, far removed from the pretense of French society. Alceste finds a monkey corpse as "heat gives his thinking cavity no quarter,/ For he is burning with the monkey's fever." His exile in the wild stands in ironic contrast to the affected manners of the world he rejected. This combination is furthered by the poet's adherence to poetic convention, employing an *abbaab* rhyme scheme and iambic meter for images of death and corruption.

"A Poem for Julia" is meditative, opening with a description of a painting of a madonna by Hans Memling, a fifteenth century Flemish painter. The name Julia has resonances in the course of poetry and calls to mind Proteus's beloved in William Shakespeare's *Two Gentlemen of Verona* (c. 1594-1595) and Robert Herrick's poems, including "Upon Julia's Clothes" and "Upon Julia's Voice." After addressing the painting by Memling, the speaker considers the human desire to transcend death.

On one level, then, the poem addresses the relationship between art and the world; it also treats the relationship between art and history. For example, "a small, foul-minded clergyman" considered that Michelangelo's *Last Judgment* was "a lewd and most indecent show/ Of nakedness, not for a sacred place."

Although Hecht celebrates artifice, like William Butler Yeats in "Byzantium," "A Poem for Julia" identifies its genesis in nature. Related to the theme of art as opposed to the real and physical is the subject of spirit and the eternal. To close six long stanzas of blank verse, the poet presents the perpetual balance of spirit and nature:

> The heart is ramified with an old force
> (Outlingering the blood, out of the sway
> Of its own fleshy trap) that finds its source
> Deep in the phosphorous waters of the bay,
> Or in the wind, or pointing cedar tree,
> Or its own ramified complexity.

Thus, the heart perceives nature as transcendent, but the persona makes no direct statement. Still, since the poem is for "Julia," the poet suggests that love is central to the painter's vision and the poet's craft. Through the name, the poet gracefully acknowledges the role of convention in art. Through the literary allusions and the description of a painting, "A Poem for Julia" ingeniously deals with art in self-referential metaphors.

The Hard Hours

Hecht opens his first book with a philosophical epigraph, quoting George Santayana: "To call the stones themselves to their ideal places, and enchant the very substance and the skeleton of the world." In contrast, he opens his second book, *The Hard Hours*, published thirteen years later, with a dedication to his two sons. Reflecting this difference, many of the poems in the latter book are thematically more personal and structurally less ordered than those in *A Summoning of Stones*. History is also treated with less distance and more emotion. A number of poems in *The Hard Hours* have been the subject of numerous critical discussions.

"Rites and Ceremonies," a ten-page meditation on the Buchenwald concentration camp and religious persecution through the ages, has received, possibly, the most attention of any of Hecht's poems. It illustrates many facets of his sensibility and orientation. The poem is structurally complex and is thematically immersed in human history—a history rife with accounts of cruelty. "Rites and Ceremonies" reveals the poet's personal exploration of major theological considerations. Finally, the poem echoes Eliot in places and thereby pays homage to a great modernist, but this also serves to highlight Hecht's perceptions as opposed to those of Eliot. Whereas Eliot presents the transcendent through images of the world and timelessness through temporal images, Hecht treats the human condition through references to historical events in which humanity is bound by its brutality. Whereas Eliot gives thanks for the divine sacrifice of love, Hecht mourns the sacrifice of human life and makes only ironic reference to the Bible. Hecht's Jewish background contributes to his perspective.

Like Eliot's *Four Quartets* (1943), "Rites and Ceremonies" is in four parts, and each is composed of statements, counterstatements, and variations. The second part is titled "The Fire Sermon," like a section in Eliot's *The Waste Land* (1922). Hecht's poem is also conversational in places and includes quite a few literary references. It differs from Eliot's poetry, however, in that no revelation is at hand, only words and prayers and the poet's acute attention to the problem of evil and the grim history of the Jews in Christian hands.

The persona, who seems very close to the poet, speaks in several tones. The first part, "The Room," opens in praise of God and is psalmlike in rhythm and diction. This prayer refers to a post-Holocaust world that is both the source of the poet's desire to pray to God and the cause of his skepticism. Biblical allusions in "Rites and Ceremonies" ring with irony. The poem begins, "Father, adonoi, author of all things," and alludes to the birth of the Messiah:

> Who was that child of whom they tell
>   in lauds and threnes?
> whose holy names all shall pronounce
>   Emmanuel,
> which being interpreted means,
>   *"Gott mit uns"*?

The allusion is highly ironic as it echoes Matthew 1:23, where an angel tells Joseph of Isaiah's prophecy and says that a virgin will bear a son to be called Emmanuel (which means "God with us"). The biblical allusion, punctuated by a question mark, is followed by a description of Buchenwald. In an understated tone, Hecht describes the signs of the millions killed and the method of extermination.

"Rites and Ceremonies" thereby opens with a contemplation of a place in twentieth century Germany where suffering was so great that questions are raised concerning the efficacy of language and prayer. Hecht then considers other events in previous centuries which also defy reason. In the second part, "The Fire Sermon," he treats several infamous incidents that took place in medieval Europe and considers the relationship between God and humanity—or perhaps more accurately, he questions the will of God as it is perceived by human beings.

Noting that a shipful of men died on Easter, the speaker asks, "Was it a judgment?" In reference to the death of hundreds of friars during Lent, he says that the Church decided that this was not a judgment. Finally, the speaker recounts the execution of Jews throughout Europe because two Jews had allegedly confessed, under torture, to poisoning the wells; it was believed that purging the Jews would end the plague. This belief, along with the Crusaders' slaughter of the heathen, was based on the assumption that people can discern God's will and help carry it out. The Church's position is rendered irrational—highly suspect, at best, and at worst self-serving. The tone here is matter-of-fact, and the images are unembellished—the speaker saying, for example, "Even as here in the city of Strasbourg,/ And the Jews assembled upon them [platforms],/ Children and all, and tied together with a rope."

The third part of "Rites and Ceremonies," "The Dream," begins, "The contemplation of horror is not edifying,/ Neither does it strengthen the soul," but continues by describing the death of three medieval saints—Lucy, Cecilia, and Lawrence. The speaker then switches to the public scourging of the Jews during Lent, which was described by the poet Joachim Du Bellay. Thus Hecht suggests that the history of brutality is a long one. "Rites and Ceremonies" is a version of the story of human tragedy updated by the grim addition of the Holocaust.

The final section, "Words for the Day of Atonement," confronts the troubling theological issue of the cause of human suffering. The accepted view, that it is a consequence of sin, has been challenged in the previous sections of the poem. The speaker now says, discursively, "Merely to have survived is not an index of excellence,/ Nor given the way things go,/ Even of low cunning." He goes on to ask, "And to what purpose, as the darkness closes about/ And the child screams in the jellied fire,/ Had best be our present concern." This is followed by an allusion to Eliot's "The Hollow Men" through the repetition of a litany: "The soul is thine, and the body is thy creation:/ O have compassion on thy handiwork./ The soul is thine, and the body is thine." Whereas Eliot contrasts the mundane world of humanity to the kingdom of Heaven, Hecht's focus is on the here and now. Even as he makes a reference to the Christian promise of salvation in Matthew 10:30 ("Even the hairs of your head are numbered"), Hecht's imagery remains rooted in human history." "Rites and Ceremonies" closes with a consideration of the Holocaust. The images have a tragic literal significance:

> Neither shall the flame
> Kindle upon them, nor the fire burn
> A hair of them, for they
> Shall be thy care when it shall come to pass,
> And calling on thy name
> In the hot kilns and ovens, they shall turn
> To thee as it is prophesied, and say,
> *"He shall come down like rain upon mown grass."*

The last line, from Psalm 72, is highly ambiguous, since the psalm itself has been interpreted in several ways. In the Anglican tradition it has been viewed as being messianic; therefore, the ending may be considered optimistic, as it makes a mystical leap to the promise of salvation. Yet this is rendered ironic by the graphic imagery of the Holocaust. The psalm, however, is most often interpreted in Jewish tradition as a prayer for a king's moral integrity and his just treatment of his subjects. The simile is taken to suggest, metaphorically, fertility resulting from his gentleness as a ruler. Thus, "Rites and Ceremonies" calls attention not only to the relationship between God and humanity but also to how humanity governs itself. The history of the treatment of the Jews is a grim reminder of a monstrous flaw in the makeup of humanity.

This is also dealt with in "More Light! More Light!"—a poem dedicated to Heinrich Blücher and his wife Hannah Arendt, author of *Eichmann in Jerusalem: A Report on the Banality of Evil* (1963). In rhymed couplets, "More Light! More Light!" juxtaposes a medieval heretic's death to the murder of a Pole and several Jews by the Nazis. The first stanza includes the heretic's prayer, "I implore my God to witness that I have made no crime." His death, however, is agonizing, because the sack of gunpowder does not ignite: "His legs were blistered sticks on which the black sap/ Bubbled and burst as he howled for the Kindly Light." Yet there is no sign of this light in the poem. The poet continues with an equally graphic description of the murder of a Pole, who was shot and left to bleed to death because he refused to kill two Jews. The absence of God is implied as the narrator says, "No light, no light in the blue Polish eye." Although the heretic may die with more dignity because of his faith, God does not appear to intercede for him or the Pole. Instead of a sign of salvation, "More Light! More Light" ends on a powerful image of death: "Ghosts from the ovens" settle on the dead Pole's eyes "in a black soot." The notion of transcendence is strictly limited to the heretic's vision. If there is any transcendent quality conveyed in the poem, it is evil. The title, quoting what are thought to be Johann Wolfgang von Goethe's final words, imbues the stanzas that follow with irony.

In "It Out-Herods Herod. Pray You, Avoid It," Hecht confronts the meaning of the Holocaust on a personal level; he confesses to his children as they sleep that he could not "have saved them from the gas." His inability to protect them from monstrous evil is contrasted with his children's feeling of security, for they think him omnipotent.

The title resonates on several levels. First, the extermination of children during the Holocaust is compared to Herod's slaughter of the innocents (Matthew 2) or possibly it "out-Herods" the ruler's brutality. The quotation comes from act 3 of *Hamlet, Prince of Denmark* (c. 1600-1601), where Hamlet advises the actors not to overact. The reference suggests that the speaker is reminding himself of his own limitations and his desire to avoid an exaggerated sense of power. In *The Hard Hours* Hecht considers the meaning of Buchenwald both intellectually and emotionally.

Other poems in this volume that have received considerable critical attention include "A Hill" and "The Dover Bitch: A Criticism of Life." "A Hill" is another poem in which little distance appears to separate the speaker from the poet. It subtly conveys the speaker's loss of innocence as he comes into contact with a world that has a troubling underside. Reminiscent of some of Robert Frost's poetry, "A Hill" is ambiguous. The speaker is in a setting that leads him to envision another setting; this in turn calls to mind a childhood recollection. Hecht suggests that there is a dynamic relationship between the objects of the world and human consciousness, since the speaker's view of a hill is related to a hill that he recalls from childhood. As in Frost's poetry, Hecht's settings reveal something about the speaker's consciousness and also something about the poet's philosophical perspective; both poets portray a post-Edenic world.

"The Dover Bitch: A Criticism of Life," on the other hand, is a light, whimsical poem and represents another dimension of Hecht's craft. It parodies Matthew Arnold's "Dover Beach." Whereas Arnold's speaker makes a series of profound observations on the nature of the world and fate and presents an idealized relationship with his love, Hecht's speaker informally discusses his relationship with the same woman. He claims that she treats him right and he gives her a good time. He concludes,

> and perhaps it's a year
> Before I see her again, but there she is,
> Running to fat, but dependable as they come.
> And sometimes I bring her a bottle of *Nuit d'Amour.*

"Dover Bitch" counters the idealism and philosophical abstraction of "Dover Beach" with realism. By parodying the masterly Victorian poet, who addresses the nature of reality, Hecht indirectly raises the question of the relationship between poetry and reality, including that in his own verse. Finally, Hecht comically yanks Arnold's poem from its Victorian context and into the second half of the twentieth century. Hecht's attention to the history of poetry has several different kinds of manifestations in his own work; it has steeped some of his poems with meaning, and it has been the source of the wit and humor in others.

MILLIONS OF STRANGE SHADOWS

Millions of Strange Shadows was published ten years after *The Hard Hours*. Although some critics consider this to be a transitional work, the poet's meditative stance endures. In addition, his preoccupation with the relationship between art and the world is expressed. "Dichtung und Wahrheit" (poetry and truth, or fiction and reality) wrestles with that very issue. The title is the one Goethe gave to his autobiography. The first part, written mostly in alternating tetrameter and trimeter lines, portrays two renderings of men: first, the famous sculpture of *The Discus Thrower*, and second, a photograph of several soldiers, including Hecht. The poet asks, "How can such fixture speak to us?" Both the sculptor's chisel and the camera "deal in a taxidermy/ Of our arrested flights." Here are philosophical questions going back to Socrates, including the relationship between stasis and motion, its rendering in art, and the ways in which the present is interpreted in art when it has become part of the past.

The second part of "Dichtung und Wahrheit" uses a longer line. It begins by invoking Wolfang Amadeus Mozart, whose music is often considered the measure of order and beauty. Hecht continues to pursue the relationship between the world and art. They are held in a dynamic balance as the speaker says, "We begin with the supreme donnée, the world," and quotes a person in a theatrical presentation who says, "We begin with the supreme donnée, the word." As in the poetry of Auden, the reader is left to question his or her own views, because the poem is intellectually challenging and presents no simple resolution.

"Apprehensions," which deals with Hecht's childhood, is according to several critics one of the best poems in *Millions of Strange Shadows*. It is written in blank verse in a conversational tone. Private and public worlds merge in "Apprehensions." Incidents in the poet's childhood are associated with cataclysmic world events, including the contemporaneous stock market crash and the Holocaust, which followed a decade later. As in many of Hecht's poems, there is an underlying symmetry. While the poem presents the child's and, ultimately, the poet's confrontation with painful reality, including his brother's illness, his father's suicide attempt, his governess's cruelty, and the brutality of the Holocaust, "Apprehensions" also presents the speaker's epiphanic perception of the beauty of the world—although a fallen one.

The strongest image is of the Teutonic governess, who craves lurid details in the popular press. She is "replete with the curious thumb-print of her race,/ That special relish for inflicted pain." "Apprehensions" closes with the speaker's dream of her, years after he knew her, in which their "relationship/ grew into international proportions." He envisions her as the infamous female concentration camp commandant, and he hears her say to him, "I always knew/ That you would come to me, that you'd come home." Although the poem appears to address childhood apprehensions, it reveals the American Jewish poet's empathy with the Jews of Europe, who were governed by rulers who created ghettos and camps that made the lurid stories of the tabloids look like tales for children.

THE VENETIAN VESPERS

Hecht's call for existentially responsible behavior also comes across in "Deodand," in *The Venetian Vespers*, published in 1979. On one level, it is a response to Pierre-Auguste Renoir's painting titled *Parisians Dressed in Algerian Costume*. The theme of the relationship between art and the world resurfaces. Based on the painting, the poet begins by describing a group of women in Paris who don exotic Arabic garments. They seem to be completely unaware of the inauthenticity of their antics. The speaker asks, "What is all this but crude imperial pride,/ Feminized, scented and attenuated,/ The exploitation of the primitive . . . ?" The second part of the poem switches to a description of the torturing of a French Legionnaire during the Algerian struggle for independence from France. The Algerians cut off his hands and feet, dressed him in a woman's wig and skirt, and paraded him through the streets.

The juxtaposition of these two descriptions and the role reversals convey the speaker's existentialism and refusal to embrace a political ideology. Although the young Legionnaire was involved in the French colonization of Algeria, he was a pawn in his own country's policy and in turn became the victim of terrible cruelty. Hecht examines some of the implicit cultural ramifications of the superficially pleasing images in Renoir's painting.

"The Venetian Vespers," a long six-part narrative in blank verse, also reveals the poet's compassion. Critics have compared it to Eliot's "Gerontion" in theme and have compared Hecht's speaker to Eliot's Prufrock. "The Venetian Vespers," a meditation on Venice, presents the psychological landscape of the speaker, a middle-aged American expatriate. He lost his parents long ago and is wifeless and childless. Through image motifs Hecht addresses the pain of aging and loneliness, the emptiness of contemporary life, the longing for transcendent meaning, and the particular history of one man. Humor is another dimension of human experience Hecht treats; the speaker notes that "the ochre pastes and puddings of dogshit/ Keep us earthbound in half a dozen ways,/ Curbing the spirit's tendency to pride."

In other places, however, the language and thought are elevated: "Morning has tooled the bay with bright inlays/ Of writhing silver, scattered scintillance." The speaker also describes landscapes from his past, such as his uncle's A&P store in Lawrence, Massachusetts. The reader learns that his parents were Latvian immigrants, and that his father went west and his mother died when he was six.

While "The Venetian Vespers" is a narrative poem, it includes numerous allusions to works by authors such as Thomas Mann, Marcel Proust, and George Gordon, Lord Byron, and references to artists and composers. Introduced by two epigraphs, one from Shakespeare's *Othello, the Moor of Venice* (1604) and the other from John Ruskin's *The Stones of Venice* (1879), "The Venetian Vespers" is yet another means by which Hecht explores art and its meaning.

Finally, the poem explores the meaning of human behavior. The speaker, a pacifist, served as a medic in the army. He saw the shooting of an acquaintance, which he describes in graphic terms: "Enemy machine-gun fire/ . . . had sheared away/ The top of his cranium like a soft-boiled egg." This soldier had carried with him a book of etiquette instead of sentimental mementos in the field, and the speaker confesses that "he haunts me here, that seeker after law/ In a lawless world." "The Venetian Vespers," therefore, is an extended effort rich in engaging philosophical and psychological perspectives.

THE TRANSPARENT MAN

The Transparent Man, published eleven years later, in 1990, includes several narratives. "See Naples and Die" presents an account of a marriage that dissolves as the couple vacations in Italy. The theme of loss is also pursued in "The Transparent Man," whose speaker is a young woman dying of leukemia. In the style of a dramatic monologue, she addresses a visitor, Mrs. Curtis. Completely aware of her bleak prognosis, she calmly reveals that her father does not visit her because the thought that she will predecease him is too painful. External and internal landscapes overlap in the poem through the poet's skillful presentation of unified imagery. For example, the speaker compares her disease to "a sort of blizzard in the bloodstream,/ A deep, severe, unseasonable winter." In turn, the physical landscape of autumn is compared to the brain. She says that the sycamores and beeches outside her window resemble "magnificent enlargements/ Of the vascular system of the human brain." In the conclusion of the poem, the speaker considers the trees outdoors and what they seem to suggest about the larger scheme of things. Hecht's treatment of nature again calls to mind the poetry of Frost, in which images of nature reflect human experience.

Hecht also presents love as a central force in human experience. In another monologue, "Devotions of a Painter," the speaker claims, "I am enamored of the . . . corrupted treasures of this world," and he concludes, "Against the Gospel let my brush declare:/ 'These are the anaglyphs and gleams of love.'" Sexual love is celebrated in a masquelike poem, "A Love For Four Voices: Homage to Franz Joseph Haydn." Here the two sets of lovers from Shakespeare's *A Midsummer Night's Dream* (c. 1595-1596) are identified with the four instruments in a string quartet, and they engage in a kind of musical dialogue. The epilogue directly relates art and love. Thus, on several levels Hecht associates these themes.

The poet refers to artistic convention in several humorous poems of this collection, including "Eclogue of the Shepherd and the Townie" and "Humoresque." Thus, *The Transparent Man* reveals both Hecht's consistency and his development over the course of his career. It reveals him as having a remarkable range, from the agonizing contemplation of genocide to the graceful construction of witty parodies. All his work is tempered by both his extensive knowledge of the history of poetry and his intellectual rigor.

THE DARKNESS AND THE LIGHT

Hecht moves into the twenty-first century with this collection, further displaying his range of style, emotion, intellectual cache, and modern-day references. Hecht culls from this range in a collection aptly titled *The Darkness and the Light*, in which he seems convinced that the sumptuous beauty he calls forth in a number of poems cannot compensate for the ravages of time. In "Memory," for example, a shaft of light striking some brass andirons in the late afternoon becomes "the dusty gleam of temporary wealth." These forty-four short lyrics are quintessential "later work" of a poet—alternatingly fiery and wistful, looking back over past darkness and strife to a promise of light and rest and to a personal pantheon (Charles Baudelaire, Horace, Johann Wolfgang von Goethe) represented here in nine translations. Hecht also creates poems from biblical stories—Lot's wife, Saul and David, the witch of Endor, and Abraham—and he speaks as Bible characters. These are not mere retellings, but ferocious reinterpretations. Haman, villain of the story of Esther, is frighteningly eloquent as a hangman serving the Third Reich. With ease, Hecht makes the reader feel terror, an emotion that few poets know how to convey.

Surprisingly, in a volume given to the acerbic, burning emotions of an aging man, it is notable that the showcase work is a love poem. "Rara Avis in Terris" is a dizzying display of a full range of tones, from adoration to sarcasm, fury to awe. "Hawks are in the ascendant," it opens, and he does mean "some jihad, some rash all-get-out/ Crusade" to which we perhaps are all too well accustomed in the twenty-first century. This gives way to a different scene, brilliantly pointed before rising to its own occasion: "But where are the mild monogamous lovebirds. . . ." Such is Hecht's art that the reader sees them: "Lightly an olive branch they bear,/ Its deathless leafage emblematic of/ A quarter-century of faultless love."

OTHER MAJOR WORKS

NONFICTION: *Essays in Criticism*, 1986; *The Hidden Law: The Poetry of W. H. Auden*, 1993; *On the Laws of the Poetic Art*, 1995; *Anthony Hecht in Conversation with Philip Hoy*, 1999.

TRANSLATIONS: *Seven Against Thebes*, 1973 (by Aeschylus; with Helen Bacon); *Poem upon the Lisbon Disaster*, 1977 (by Voltaire).

EDITED TEXT: *Jiggery-Pokery: A Compendium of Double Dactyls*, 1966 (with John Hollander).

BIBLIOGRAPHY

German, Norman. *Anthony Hecht*. New York: Peter Lang, 1989. This book-length study presents a chronological discussion of Hecht's books of poetry, beginning with *A Summoning of Stones* and ending with *The Venetian Vespers*. It also contains some useful biographical information and an index of subjects and poems.

Hecht, Anthony. *Anthony Hecht: In Conversation with Philip Hoy*. London: Between the Lines, 1999. This collection of interviews with Hecht provides biographical information and insights into his work. Includes bibliographical references.

Howard, Richard. "Anthony Hecht: 'What Do We Know of Lasting Since the Fall?'" In *Alone with America: Essays on the Art of Poetry in the United States Since 1950*. New York: Atheneum-Macmillan, 1980. The essay considers Hecht's style and focuses on language and imagery. Changes in the poet's work from volume to volume are noted.

Lea, Sydney, ed. *The Burdens of Formality: Essays on the Poetry of Anthony Hecht*. Athens: University of Georgia Press, 1989. This useful book includes new and previously published essays by critics and poets. "Rites and Ceremonies" and "The Venetian Vespers" receive extensive treatment in essays devoted to them. An appendix providing information on Hecht's life is followed by a bibliography of primary and secondary sources.

Lieberman, Laurence. *Unassigned Frequencies: American Poetry in Review, 1964-1977*. Urbana: University of Illinois Press, 1977. This collection includes a short essay on W. W. Merwin and Anthony Hecht which was originally published in 1968. The author focuses on Hecht's realism.

Whedon, Tony. "Three Mannerists." *American Poetry Review* 17 (May/June, 1988): 41-47. This article discusses the poetry of Larry Levis, David St. John, and Anthony Hecht. Autobiographical narrative poems are the central focus, with space devoted to Hecht's "The Venetian Vespers."

*Kathy Rugoff,
updated by Sarah Hilbert*

PIET HEIN

Born: Copenhagen, Denmark; December 16, 1905
Died: Fyn, Denmark; April 17, 1996

PRINCIPAL POETRY

Gruk, 1-20, 1940-1963 (as Kumbel Kumbell;
    Grooks, 1-6, 1966-1978)
Den tiende Muse, 1941
Vers i verdensrummet, 1941
Kumbels almanak, 1942
Vers af denne verden, 1948
Kumbels fødselsdagskalender, 1949
Du skal plante et træ, 1960
Husk at elske, 1962
Husk at leve, 1965
Lad os blive mennesker, 1967
Runaway Runes, 1968
I folkemunde, 1968
Det kraftens ord, 1969

OTHER LITERARY FORMS

While Piet Hein is known internationally for his aphoristic "grooks" (Danish *gruk*, his own coinage) and in Denmark is highly regarded for his more traditional strophic poetry as well, he also published collections of epigrams and prose aphorisms, expressing the same outlook which informs his poetry: *Man skal gaa paa Jorden–* (1944; one has to walk on the Earth); its sequel, *—Selv om den er gloende* (1950; even if it is glowing); and the volume *Ord* (1949; words). *Vis Electrica* (1962), a Festschrift treating the nature and manifold uses of electricity, includes grooks and conventional poems as well; the harmony between scientific and humanistic perspectives was characteristic of Hein's entire career.

ACHIEVEMENTS

Between 1940 and 1963, Piet Hein published twenty collections of grooks. Altogether, he wrote about ten thousand grooks, and by 1971 his publishing house would announce that the grooks had been printed in 1,250,000 copies. They are also available on two long-playing records, read by Hein himself. They have been set to music, have formed the basis for twenty short features on television (by Ivo Caprino), and have been made available in numerous translations, including Indonesian, Iranian, Japanese, and Chinese. One entire volume was published in Esperanto, and Hein himself personally re-created his grooks in German, French, Spanish, and, in particular, English. Several grooks have been written directly in these languages and are not available in Danish.

Writing, however, was only one of Hein's means of expression. Quotations from the grooks in newspapers, books, and lectures have spread to ashtrays, salt and pepper shakers, and ceramic plaques. Most of these objects have the distinctive shape of a rectangular oval or "superellipse": Hein, a mathematician, inventor, and designer as well as a poet, created this unique geometrical form. The superellipse merges the circle and the rectangle into a newly perfected form: It has solved the traffic problem in central Stockholm, joining two freeways in a roundabout system only 210 yards long in an aesthetically appealing design. Hein's innovative design has gained world recognition; he applied his superellipse to the structure of furniture and lamps, to the planning of Mexico City's Olympic Stadium and of the city center in Canada's Peterborough, and to architectural projects in France. Its three-dimensional version, the "superegg," can be found both as a sculpture and—in smaller sizes—as a drink-cooler and a stress-ball.

Hein's inventiveness and creativity were also evident in numerous other inventions and designs—especially in the design of board games and puzzles such as the Polygon Game and the three-dimensional SOMA Cube, which became favorite pastimes for thousands of grown-up children in Europe and the United States. The origin of these games was in Hein's fondness for "creative playing," which he shared with his friend Albert Einstein. In his essay "Et Menneske" ("A Man"), Hein quoted Einstein:

> There is a striking similarity, he said, between the usual games and the prime one: to discover the structure of nature. I cannot understand complicated things: therefore, I have tried to reduce the laws of nature to a simple formula. The great coherences in nature are simple. And when you see the perspective in things, nothing is small.

This holistic effort to find harmony in microcosm as well as in macrocosm was central not only to Hein's scientific achievements but also to his poetry.

For his literary and scientific achievements, Hein won a number of international honors, including the Alexander Graham Bell Silver Bell in 1968, the award Huitième Salon International du Lumière in 1973, and the International Aphia Prize in 1980. In 1970, he became a member of the British Society of Authors and won the Danish Design Council's Annual Award in 1989 and the Tietgen Medal in 1990. In 1972 he received an honorary doctorate in humane letters from Yale University. His speech of thanks attested to Hein's international outlook and humanist worldview:

> Science has a vital task in manifesting its own true nature: synthesis and openness, both in its own sphere and in the larger one of humankind. It must help both spheres to raise themselves above their present state of local habits in global worlds.

BIOGRAPHY

Piet Hein's creative versatility reflected his eclectic education. His father, civil engineer Hjalmar Hein, descended from a German-Dutch family; his mother, Estrid Hein, was a well-known Copenhagen ophthalmologist, a member of and prolific writer for the Danish women's movement, and a cousin to the writer Isak Dinesen. Hein's childhood home was located in Rungsted, north of Copenhagen, to which he returned to live for many years with his wife, Gerd Hein (1932-1968), an actress at The Royal Theater in Stockholm. Following her death in 1968, Hein moved to Poke Stoges in England; in 1976, he returned to Denmark and made his home at the Damsbo estate on the island of Funen.

Having received his high school and college education in Copenhagen, Hein passed his university entrance exams as a mathematics major in 1924. In 1925, however, after the obligatory examination in philosophy, he left Copenhagen for Stockholm to begin training as a painter at The Royal Academy of the Arts. In 1927, he returned to Copenhagen, where, until 1931, he studied philosophy and theoretical physics, both at the university and at the Niels Bohr Institute, without taking a degree. At the institute, Hein constructed a model that illustrated the principle of complementarity (formulated by Bohr in 1927), and his so-called atomarium, which, together with his participation in advanced colloquia concerning recent discoveries in atomic theory, earned him the greatest respect from his fellow scientists.

In the following years, Hein worked on various industrial designs and technical inventions, including an ingenious rotor engine. In 1947, he published *Helicopteren*, which was the result of an exhaustive study, and created a "coloroscope," a device to create light effects in which the spectrum could be moved from a spatial to a temporal state. During the 1930's, Hein began his creative authorship, concurrently joining a number of new liberal political movements. From 1935 to 1955, he was thus a member of the board of the Danish section of Open Door International, and from 1948 to 1949 president of the Danish section of the World Movement for World Federal Government. He has also been active in organizations such as the International PEN Club and numerous Danish groups promoting world peace and tolerance. His membership in the Adventurers Club testifies to his many travels and extensive stays in Europe and in North and South America. Likewise telling is Hein's membership in the Frensham Group—which he called "Ten-Wise-Men-and-Me"—an international organization furthering interdisciplinary research and contact between scientific and nonscientific groups. Hein died in 1996 in Denmark.

ANALYSIS

Throughout his entire career, Piet Hein strove for the harmony between scientific and humanistic perspectives. His dual perspective is apparent in *Kilden og krukken* (1963; the spring and the urn), a volume which intersperses brief philosophical prose texts, related to the classical fable, with some of Hein's numerous public lectures. The common theme is that while technology must serve humanity, the humanities must serve reason via the individual. Contemporary man, however, must first have his original synthesis restored—his balance of reason and emotion, of the objective and the subjective. Hein analyzes the disastrous split between the exclusively scientific, technological worldview on one hand and the exclusively humanistic worldview on the other.

Hein's life's work was given to a reconciliation of these opposing outlooks.

Piet Hein's vast literary canon—in particular, the grooks—is too multifaceted to be gathered under a single heading. A common denominator, however, was his precise, epigrammatic language. His speeches, aphorisms, grooks, and more conventional poetry were all informed by certain recurring themes which constituted his philosophy as well as his poetics. Thus, an aphorism from 1944, "Art is the solution to those problems which cannot be formulated clearly before they are solved," clearly expressed Hein's conviction that such scientific activities as the raising of new questions and the proving of new theories are fundamentally similar to the concerns of the artist. The natural sciences and the humanities have a common point of origin: human imagination. This insistence on the potential union of art and science was the subject of Hein's speech on having become an honorary member of the Danish Students' Association in 1970:

> In all areas it is a matter of seeing how the objects could be different from what we are used to, of generalizing the problem in a hitherto unnoticed dimension, and within the new, larger, more general multiplicity of choosing a specific case, a new and better solution. This process has been typical for all great innovations within science. This is the true form of imagination. Imagination is just a higher form of the sense of reality.

GROOKS

Hein insisted on viewing life's questions from new perspectives: "He on whom God's light does fall, sees the great things in the small." This point of view was precisely reflected, both in form and content, by the grooks:

> Infinity's taken
> by everyone
> as a figure-of-eight
> written sideways on.
> But all of a sudden
> I now apprehend
> that eight is infinity
> standing on end.

Hein began publishing short poems in Danish magazines and newspapers during the 1930's, in particular in one of the leading Copenhagen dailies, *Politiken*. Here the grooks were printed regularly after the German occupation of Denmark on April 9, 1940, often containing veiled allusions to the German forces. Originally, the grooks were published under the pseudonym "Kumbel Kumbell." Gradually, however, as their popularity grew, Hein used only the signature "Kumbel" on all his collections of grooks; his other poetry is published under his own name. An important feature of the grooks is that almost all are accompanied by a drawing. Even in his first collection, Hein worked as his own illustrator, placing himself in the center of the universe of the drawings as a little poet, usually with hat, bow tie, and lyre. His line is slim and elegant, and the illustrations are indispensable supplements to the text, which is set either in Hein's characteristic handwriting or in the corresponding typeface, Helvetica, in order to emphasize the graphic effect.

The grook found its way into Danish dictionaries, defined as a "small lyrical or intellectual aphorism in poetic form and with a point." Hein's grooks have their roots in the Old Norse Hávámál poems and share with them a wisdom about life expressed in concentrated form. With occasional sarcasm—yet free of any moralizing—they convey their message in a cathartic burst of humor, often based on paradoxical statements, puns, and other forms of wordplay, couched in sophisticated rhymes and rhythms. Underlying the grooks is always a cosmic and existential appeal—"As eternity is reckoned, there's a lifetime in a second"—as well as words to the wise on the art of living: "Love while you've got/ love to give./ Live while you've got/ life to live." Such injunctions to enjoy life here and now are frequently balanced, however, by warnings against intolerance and persecution: "Men, said the Devil,/ are good to their brothers:/ they don't want to mend/ their own ways, but each other's." Hein saw regimentation, ideology, and national and economic boundaries as barriers to human development. Since World War II, there has been no direct political sting in the grooks, but one would be hard-pressed to find a pithier warning to *Homo politicus* than Hein's rephrasing of Hamlet's "To be or not to be": "Co-existence/ or no existence."

DEN TIENDE MUSE

To his own generation, Hein was a traditionalist. His formal achievement lies in the turning of the common idiom toward the uncommon insight. Hein's intellectual and linguistic agility was most apparent in the grooks, but even in his more conventional poetry the emotional and potentially sentimental elements were subordinated to the speculative. Thus, when Hein rapturously described Danish landscapes, his impressions of nature became points of departure for philosophical reflections. He employed the same method in poetically sketching various writers and scientists, congenial spirits to whom he felt closely related, while actually presenting his own worldview. In his first volume, *Den tiende Muse* (the tenth Muse), Hein addressed poems to three of the most prominent humanistic spirits of modern civilization: Niels Bohr, who since his youth had been a friend; Albert Einstein, whom he frequently visited at Princeton; and Norbert Wiener, the founder of cybernetics, who wrote his last book while staying at Hein's home in Rungsted. In this volume, as well as in the collections *Vers af denne verden* (verses from this world) and *Du skal plante et træ* (you shall plant a tree), Hein presented the quintessence of his worldview: a cosmic perspective, a strong contempt for pretense and artificiality, and an adjuration to fight prejudice and to rescue the planet from the threat of annihilation.

It is this appeal to humane reason, this urgent request for universal solidarity, which gives Hein's work its timeless authority. Poet and designer, scientist and philosopher, Hein was an exemplary humanist who urged man to look to the future and the well-being of humankind.

OTHER MAJOR WORKS

NONFICTION: *Helicopteren*, 1947.

MISCELLANEOUS: *Man skal gaa paa Jorden–*, 1944; *Ord*, 1949; *—Selv om den er gloende*, 1950; *Vis Electrica*, 1962; *Kilden og krukken*, 1963.

BIBLIOGRAPHY

Claudi, J. *Contemporary Danish Authors*. Copenhagen: Danske Selskab, 1952. Contains a brief profile of Hein and his work up to 1950. Includes a historical outline of Danish literature.

Rossel, Sven H. *A History of Scandinavian Literature, 1870-1980*. Translated by Anne C. Ulmer. Minneapolis: University of Minnesota Press, 1982. History and criticism of Scandinavian literature of the ninteenth and twentieth centuries. Includes bibliographic references and an index.

_____, ed. *A History of Danish Literature*. Lincoln: University of Nebraska Press, 1992. A historical and critical study of Danish Literature. Includes bibliographic references and index.

Sven H. Rossel

HEINRICH HEINE

Chaim Harry Heine

Born: Düsseldorf, Germany; December 13, 1797
Died: Paris, France; February 17, 1856

PRINCIPAL POETRY

Gedichte, 1822 (*Poems*, 1937)

Tragödien, nebst einem lyrischen Intermezzo, 1823 (*Tragedies, Together with Lyric Intermezzo*, 1905)

Buch der Lieder, 1827 (*Book of Songs*, 1856)

Neue Gedichte, 1844 (8 volumes; *New Poems*, 1858)

Deutschland: Ein Wintermärchen, 1844 (*Germany: A Winter's Tale*, 1892)

Atta Troll, 1847 (English translation, 1876)

Ein Sommernachtstraum, 1847 (*A Midsummer Night's Dream*, 1876)

Romanzero, 1851 (English translation, 1859)

Gedichte, 1851-1857 (4 volumes; *Poems*, 1937)

Letzte Gedichte und Gedanken, 1869 (*Last Poems and Thoughts*, 1937)

Atta Troll and Other Poems, 1876 (includes *Atta Troll* and *A Midsummer Night's Dream*)

Heinrich Heine: The Poems, 1937

The Complete Poems of Heinrich Heine, 1982

OTHER LITERARY FORMS

Although Heinrich Heine is best remembered for his verse, he also made significant contributions to the development of the feuilleton and the political essay in Germany. Experiments with prose accelerated his rise to fame as a writer. Among the most important of his nonfiction works are *Reisebilder* (1826-1831; *Pictures of*

Travel, 1855), a series of witty essays that are spiced with poetic imagination and penetrating social comment; *Zur Geschichte der neueren schönen Litteratur in Deutschland* (1833; *Letters Auxiliary to the History of Modern Polite Literature in Germany*, 1836), which was later republished and expanded as *Die romantische Schule* (1836; *The Romantic School*, 1876) and constitutes Heine's personal settlement with German Romanticism; *Französische Zustände* (1833; *French Affairs*, 1889), a collection of sensitive newspaper articles about the contemporary political situation in France; and *Vermischte Schriften* (1854), a group of primarily political essays.

Heine's attempts to create in other genres were unsuccessful. During his student years in Berlin, he began a novel, *Der Rabbi von Bacherach* (1887; *The Rabbi of Bacherach*, 1891), but it remained a fragment. Two dramas, *Almansor* and *William Ratliff*, published in *Tragedies, Together with Lyric Intermezzo*, failed on the stage, although *William Ratliff* was later employed by Pietro Mascagni as the basis of an opera.

ACHIEVEMENTS

Second only to Johann Wolfgang von Goethe in impact on the history of German lyric poetry in the nineteenth century, Heinrich Heine was unquestionably the most controversial poet of his time. He was a major representative of the post-Romantic literary crisis and became the most renowned love poet in Europe after Petrarch, yet for decades he was more celebrated abroad than in Germany. Anti-Semitism and negative reactions to his biting satire, to his radical inclinations, and to his seemingly unpatriotic love of France combined to prevent any consistent approbation in Heine's homeland. Nevertheless, he became the first Jewish author to break into the mainstream of German literature in modern times.

Heine's poetic reputation is based primarily on *Book of Songs*, which went through twelve editions during his lifetime. The collection achieved immediate popularity with the public and was well received by critics; since 1827, it has been translated into more than fifty languages. Lyrics that became part of the *Book of Songs* were set to music as early as 1822, and within a year after the book appeared, Franz Schubert used six poems

Heinrich Heine (Library of Congress)

from the "Heimkehr" ("Homecoming") section in his famous cycle *Schwanengesang* (1828; "Swan Song"). Robert Schumann's *Dichterliebe* (1840; love poems) features musical settings for sixteen poems from *Tragedies, Together with Lyric Intermezzo*. By 1840, Heine's works had become prime texts for German Lieder. In all, more than three thousand pieces of music have been written for the creations of Heine's early period.

In 1835, four years after he went into self-imposed exile in France, Heine's works were banned in Germany, along with the writings of the social reform and literary movement Junges Deutschland (Young Germany). The critics rejected him as a bad influence on Germany's youth. His immediate popularity waned as conflicts with government censors increased. In the late nineteenth century, attempts to reclaim his works for German literature touched off riots, yet by then his enchanting lyrics had become so ingrained in German culture that it was impossible to expel them. The measure of Heine's undying significance for German poetry is perhaps the fact that even the Nazis, who formally prohibited his works once again, could not exclude his poems completely from their anthologies of songs.

BIOGRAPHY

The son of a Jewish merchant, Chaim Harry Heine spent his early years working toward goals set for him by his family. His secondary education ended in 1814 when he left the Düsseldorf Lyceum without being graduated. After failing in two apprenticeships in Frankfurt, he was sent to Hamburg to prepare for a career in commerce under the direction of a wealthy uncle. While there, he fell in love with his cousin Amalie. This unfulfilled relationship was a stimulus for verse that the young poet published in a local periodical. In 1818, his uncle set him up in a retailing enterprise, but within a year Harry Heine and Co. was bankrupt. Acknowledging that his nephew was unsuited for business, Uncle Salomon at last agreed to underwrite his further education.

Between 1819 and 1825, Heine studied in Bonn, Berlin, and Göttingen. His university years were very important for his development as a poet. While in Bonn, he attended lectures given by August Wilhelm von Schlegel, whose interest in his work stimulated Heine's creativity. In the fall of 1820, he moved to Göttingen. Besides law, he studied German history and philology until January, 1821, when he challenged another student to a duel and was expelled from the university. He continued his studies in Berlin and was rapidly accepted into prominent literary circles. Included among the writers with whom he associated were Adelbert von Chamisso, Friedrich Schleiermacher, and Christian Dietrich Grabbe. Rahel von Varnhagen helped in the publication of Heine's first collection of poems in 1822, and he quickly became known as a promising talent. During a visit to Hamburg in 1823, he met Julius Campe, who afterward published all Heine's works except a few commissioned essays that he wrote in Paris. Literary success persuaded him away from the study of law, but at his uncle's request Heine returned to Göttingen to complete work toward his degree. In the summer of 1825, he passed his examinations, though not with distinction. In order to facilitate a public career, he was baptized a Protestant, at which time he changed his name to Heinrich.

Travel was a significantly formative experience for Heine. Vacations in Cuxhaven and Norderney provided initial powerful impressions of the sea that informed the two North Sea cycles of the *Book of Songs*. Journeys through the Harz Mountains in 1824, to England in 1827, and to Italy the following year provided material for the *Pictures of Travel* series that elevated him to the literary mainstream of his time. Exposure to foreign points of view also aroused his interest in current political questions and led to a brief involvement as coeditor of Johann Friedrich von Cotta's *Politische Annalen* in Munich in 1827 and 1828.

When continued efforts to obtain permission to practice law in Hamburg failed, Heine moved to Paris in 1831, where he began to write articles for French and German newspapers and journals. Heine loved Paris, and during the next few years friendships with Honoré de Balzac, Victor Hugo, George Sand, Giacomo Meyerbeer, and other writers, artists, and composers contributed to his sense of well-being. When the German Federal Diet banned his writings, making it impossible for him to continue contributing to German periodicals, the French government granted him a modest pension.

The 1840's were a stormy period in Heine's life. In 1841, he married Cresence Eugénie Mirat (whom he called "Mathilde"), his mistress of seven years. Her lack of education and understanding of his writings placed a strain on their relationship and later contributed to the poet's increasing isolation from his friends. After returning from Hamburg in 1843, Heine met Karl Marx. Their association sharpened Heine's political attitudes and increased his aggressive activism. Salomon Heine's death in 1844 unleashed between the writer and his cousins a struggle for the inheritance. Eventually they reached an accommodation that guaranteed an annuity in exchange for Heine's promise not to criticize family members in his writings.

After a collapse in 1848, Heine spent his remaining years in unceasing pain. An apparent venereal disease attacked his nervous system, leaving him paralyzed. Physical infirmities, however, did not stifle his creative spirit, and from the torment and loneliness of his "mattress grave," he wrote some of the best poetry of his career.

ANALYSIS

Unlike many poets, Heinrich Heine never stated a formal theory of poetry that could serve as a basis for interpreting his works and measuring his creative development. For that reason, confusion and critical controversy have clouded the picture of his oeuvre, resulting in misunderstandings of his literary orientation and intentions. The general concept that he was a poet of experience is, at the very least, an oversimplification. To be sure, immediate personal observations of life were a consistent stimulus for Heine's writing, yet his product is not simply a stylized reproduction of individual encounters with reality. Each poem reveals a reflective processing of unique perceptions of people, milieus, and events that transforms seemingly specific descriptions into generally valid representations of man's confrontation with the times. The poet's ability to convey, with penetrating exactitude, feelings, existential problems, and elements of the human condition that correspond to the concerns and apperceptions of a broad readership enabled him to generate lyrics that belong more to the poetry of ideas than to the poetry of experience.

A characteristic of Heine's thought and verse is a purposeful poetic tension between the individual and the world. The dissonance between the artistic sensibility and reality is presented in unified constructs that represent qualities that were missing from the poet's era: unity, form, constancy, and continuity. By emphasizing condition rather than event, Heine was able to offer meaningful illustrations in the juxtaposition of antithetical concepts: sunny milieu and melancholy mood, pain and witticism, affirmation and negation, enchantment of feeling and practical wisdom of experience, enthusiasm and pessimism, love and hate, spirit and reality, tradition and anticipation of the future. The magic and power of his verse arise from his ability to clothe these dynamic conflicts in deceptively simple, compact forms, pure melodic sounds and rhythms, and playfully witty treatments of theme, substance, motif, and detail.

More than anything else, Heine was a poet of mood. His greatest strengths were his sensitivity and his capacity to analyze, create, and manipulate feeling. A colorful interchange of disillusionment, scorn, cynicism, rebellion, blasphemy, playful mockery, longing, and melancholy is the essence of his appeal to the reader's spirit.

The goal, however, is not the arousal of emotion but rather the intensification of awareness, achieved by drawing the audience into a desired frame of feeling, then shattering the illusion in a breach of mood that typifies Heine's poetry.

Although he was not a true representative of any single German literary movement, Heine wrote poems that reflect clear relationships to definite intellectual and artistic traditions. Both the German Enlightenment and German Romanticism provided him with important models. In matters of form, attitude, and style, he was a child of the Enlightenment. Especially visible are his epigrammatic technique and the tendency toward didactic exemplification and pointed representation. Gotthold Ephraim Lessing was his favorite among Enlightenment authors. Heine combined the technical aspects of Enlightenment literary approach with a pronounced Romantic subjectivity in the handling of substance, theme, and motif, particularly in the examination of self, pain, experience, and condition. The absolute status of the self is a prominent characteristic of his works. In the emancipation of self, however, he carried the thoughtful exploration of personal individuality a step beyond that of the early Romantics and in so doing separated himself from them. Other Romantic traits in his lyrics include a dreamy fantasy of feeling and a pronounced element of irony. Where Friedrich Schlegel employed irony to transcend the restrictive material world and unite man with a spiritual cosmos, Heine used it to expand the self to encompass the cosmos. The feature of Romanticism with which Heine most consciously identified was the inclination of Joseph von Eichendorff and others toward simple musical poems modeled on the German folk song. Heine specifically acknowledged the influence of Wilhelm Müller, whose cultivation of pure sound and clear simplicity most closely approximated his own poetic ideal.

In many respects, the polish of language and form that marked Heine's *Book of Songs* was never surpassed in later collections. At most a strengthening of intonation, an increase in wit, a maturing of the intellect subtly and gradually enhanced his writings with the passing years. Nevertheless, his literary career can be divided into four distinct phases with regard to material focus and poetic concern.

EARLY YEARS

Heine's initial creative period encompassed his university years and reached its peak in the mid-1820's. In *Poems*, the cycle of verse in *Tragedies, Together with Lyric Intermezzo*, and, finally, *Book of Songs*, the young poet opened a world of personal subjectivity at the center of which is a self that undergoes unceasing examination. Consciousness of the self, its suffering and loneliness, is the essence of melodic compositions that include poems of unrequited love, lyrical mood pictures, satires, romances, confessions, and parodies. Lines and stanzas deftly reflect Heine's ability to feel his way into nature, the magic of legend, and the spiritual substance of man, while the poetic world remains a fragmentary manifestation of the subjective truthfulness of the moment.

THE SELF AS A MIRROR OF THE TIMES

A major change in orientation coincided with Heine's move to Paris. The political upheaval in France and the death of Goethe signaled the end of an artistic era, and Heine looked forward to the possibility of a different literature that would replace the subjectivity of Romanticism with a new stress on life, time, and reality. He was especially attracted to the Saint-Simonian religion, which inspired within him a hope for a modern doctrine that would offer a new balance between Judeo-Christian ideals and those of classical antiquity. The lyrics in *New Poems*, the major document of this period, reveal a shift in emphasis from the self per se to the self as a mirror of the times. Heine's poetry of the 1830's is shallower than his earlier creations, yet it effectively presents the inner turmoil, confusion, and splintering of the era as Heine experienced it. Accompanying a slightly faded reprise of earlier themes is a new view of the poet as a heathen cosmopolitan who affirms material reality and champions the moment as having eternal value.

POLITICAL RADICALIZATION

The third stage in Heine's career is best described as a period of political radicalization. It most visibly affected his poetry during the mid-1840's, the time of his friendship with Marx. In the aggressively satirical epics *Atta Troll* and *Germany: A Winter's Tale*, he paired sharp criticism of contemporary conditions with revelations of his love for Germany, specifically attacking his

own critics, radical literature, militant nationalism, student organizations, the German hatred of the French, the fragmented condition of the German nation, and almost everything else that was valued by the establishment.

LAST OF THE ROMANTICS

Profound isolation and intense physical pain provided the catalyst for a final poetic reorientation after Heine's physical collapse in 1848. Some of the poems that he wrote in his "mattress grave" are among his greatest masterpieces, they reflect a new religiosity in spiritual penetration of the self. In *Romanzero* and other late poems, the poet becomes a kind of martyr, experiencing the world's illness in his own heart. The act of suffering generates a poetry of bleak glosses of the human condition, heartrending laments, and songs about death unequaled in German literature.

Although Heine styled himself the last of the Romantics, a significant difference in approach to substance distinguishes his early poems from those of the Romantic movement. Where Clemens Maria Brentano and Eichendorff celebrated existence as it opened itself to them, Heine sang of a life that had closed its doors, shutting him out. The dominant themes of his *Book of Songs* are longing and suffering as aspects of the experience of disappointed love. Combining the sentimental pessimism of George Gordon, Lord Byron, with the objective portrayal of tangible reality, he succeeded in exploring love's frustrations and pain more effectively, more impressively, and more imaginatively than any of his forerunners and contemporaries had done. In dream images, songs, romances, and sonnets that employ Romantic materials yet remain suspicious of the feelings that they symbolize, the poet transformed the barrier that he felt existed between himself and the world into deceptively simple, profoundly valid treatments of universal problems.

BOOK OF SONGS

The poems of *Book of Songs* are extraordinarily flexible, self-contained productions that derive their charm from the combination of supple form and seemingly directly experienced and personally felt content. Colorful sketches of lime trees, an ancient bastion, a city pond, a whistling boy, gardens, people, fields, forests, a mill wheel, and an old tower contribute to a world of great fascination and sensual seduction. The verse is often bittersweet, however, focusing not on the sunny summer landscape but on the sadness of the poet who does not participate in a beauty that mocks him. The forceful presentation of the individual's isolation and conflict with the times represented a fresh direction in poetry that contributed greatly to Heine's early popularity. At the same time, the carefully constructed tension between the poet and his surroundings established a pattern that became characteristic of all his works.

An extremely important feature of these early lyrics is the break in mood that typically occurs at several levels, including tone, setting, and the lyricist's subjective interpretation of his situation. The tone frequently shifts from emotional to conversational, from delicate to blunt, while the settings of the imagination are shattered by the banal reality of modern society. As the poet analyzes his position vis-à-vis his milieu, his positive feeling is broken by frustration and defeat, his hope collapses beneath the awareness of his delusion, and his attraction to his beloved is marred by her unthinking cruelty. There is never any resolution of these conflicts, and the poem itself provides the only mediation between the writer and a hostile world.

Among the most exquisite compositions in *Book of Songs* are the rustically simple lyric paintings from "Die Harzreise" ("The Journey to the Harz") and the rhythmically powerful, almost mystical studies from the two cycles of "Die Nordsee" ("The North Sea"). Filled with the fairy-tale atmosphere of the Rhine and the Harz Mountains, "The Journey to the Harz" poems exemplify Heine's ability to capture the compelling musicality and inner tone of the folk song and to combine these elements with an overwhelming power of feeling in the formation of an intense poetry of mood. In "The North Sea," he cultivated a new kind of language, anticipating twentieth century verse in free rhythms that sounded the depths of elemental human experience. Constant motion, changing patterns of light, play of wind, and movement of ships and fish combine as parts of a unified basic form. Heine pinpointed the individuality of the ocean in a given moment, reproducing atmosphere with precision and intensifying impact through mythological or human ornamentation. The rolling flow of impression is a consistent product of Heine's poetic art in its finest form.

NEW POEMS

Two years after moving to Paris, Heine published *Letters Auxiliary to the History of Modern Polite Literature in Germany*, his most significant theoretical treatise on literature and a work that marked his formal break with Romanticism. The major poetic document of this transition to a more realistic brand of expression is *New Poems*, a less integrated collection than *Book of Songs*, containing both echoes of early themes and the first fruits of his increased political commitment of the 1840's. *New Poems* attests strongly a shift in approach and creative concern from poetry as an absolute to the demand for contemporary relevance.

The first cycle of *New Poems*, "Neuer Frühling" ("New Spring"), returns to the motifs that dominate the "Lyric Intermezzo" and "Homecoming" segments of *Book of Songs* yet presents them with greater polish and distance. New variations portray love as a distraction, a nuisance that causes emotional turmoil in the inherent knowledge of its transitoriness. The tone and direction of the entire volume are established in the prologue to "New Spring," in which the poet contrasts his own subjection to the hindering influence of love with the strivings of others in "the great struggle of the times."

Among the other sections of the book, "Verschiedene" ("Variae"), with its short cycles of rather acidic poems about the girls of Paris, its legendary ballad "Der Tannhäuser" ("Tannhäuser"), and its "Schöpfungslieder" ("Songs of Creation"), is the least coherent, most disturbing group of poems that Heine ever wrote. Campe, his publisher, decried the lyricist's creation of what he called "whore and chamber-pot stories" and was extremely reluctant to publish them. Nothing that Heine wrote, however, is without artistic value, and there are nuggets of brilliance even here. Despite its artificiality and seeming inconsistency with Heine's true poetic nature, "Tannhäuser," for example, must be regarded as one of his greatest masterpieces. The deeply psychological rejuvenation of the old folk epic, which served as the stimulus for Richard Wagner's opera, reflects the poet's all-encompassing and penetrating knowledge of the human heart.

"Zeitgedichte" ("Poems of the Times"), the concluding cycle in *New Poems*, sets the pattern for Heine's harsh political satire of the 1840's. Some of the lyrics were written expressly for Karl Marx's newspaper *Vorwärts*. Most of them are informed by homesickness, longing, and the bitter disappointment that Heine felt as the expected dawn of spiritual freedom in Germany failed to materialize in the evolution of a more cosmopolitan relationship with the rest of Europe. Powerful poems directed against cultural, social, and political dilettantes anticipate the incisively masterful tones of his most successful epics of the period, *Atta Troll* and *Germany: A Winter's Tale*; irreverent assaults on cherished institutions, superficial political activism, and his own critics accent his peculiar love-hate relationship with his homeland.

ROMANZERO

Regarded by many critics as Heine's finest collection of poems, *Romanzero* presents his final attempts to come to grips with his own mortality. Rich in their sophistication, more coherent in tone than the lyrics of *New Poems* or even the *Book of Songs*, the romances, laments, and melodies of *Romanzero* reveal the wit, irony, and epigrammatic style for which Heine is famous in the service of a new, peculiarly transparent penetration of the self. Dominant in the poems is the theme of death, which confronts the individual in many forms. A new religiosity is present in the acknowledgment of a personal God with whom the poet quarrels about a divine justice that is out of phase with man's needs. Individual creations pass through the spectrum of human and religious history and into the future in the expectation of a new social order. Bitter pessimism unmasks the dreams of life, pointing to the defeat of that which is noble and beautiful and the triumph of the worse man over the better as the derisive law of the world. Voicing the mourning and bitter resistance of the tormented soul, Heine transforms personal confrontation with suffering and death into a timeless statement of universal experience.

Romanzero is divided into three main parts, each of which projects a substantial array of feeling: seriousness, despair, goodness, compassion, a longing for faith, bitterness, and mature composure. The first section, "Historien" ("Stories"), is composed of discursive, sometimes rambling narrative ballads and romances dealing with the tragedies of kings, heroes, and poets.

Some of them process through a temporal distance such typical Heine themes as the yearning for love, clothing them in historical trappings. Others, such as the cruel poem "Vitzliputzli" that ends the cycle, are profound discourses on man's inhumanity to man. The poems of "Lamentationen" ("Lamentations"), the second major section, are directly confessional in form: deeply moving cries of anguish, sublime expressions of horror, statements of longing for home. The "Lazarus" poems that conclude this portion of *Romanzero* are especially vivid documents of the poet's individual suffering in a world where God seems to be indifferent. In "Hebräische Melodien" ("Hebrew Melodies"), the last segment of the collection, Heine presented the essence of his reidentification with Judaism. Three long poems explore the broad dimensions of Jewish culture, history, and tradition, ending with an almost sinister medieval disputation between Christian and Jew that evolves into a tragicomic anticlerical satire. Thumbing his nose at irrational action, intolerance, and superstition, the poet offers a dying plea for humanism.

No other volume presents Heine so thoroughly in all his heights and depths, perfection and error, wit and seriousness. Captivating for the directness of despairing and contrite confession, repelling for its boastful, sometimes vicious cynicism, *Romanzero*, as perhaps no other work in the history of German lyric poetry, reveals the hubris of the problematic individual and penetrates the facade of the bright fool's drama that is life.

OTHER MAJOR WORKS

LONG FICTION: *Der Rabbi von Bacherach*, 1887 (*The Rabbi of Bacherach*, 1891).

NONFICTION: *Briefe aus Berlin*, 1822; *Reisebilder*, 1826-1831 (4 volumes; *Pictures of Travel*, 1855); *Die Bäder von Lucca*, 1829 (*The Baths of Lucca*, 1855); *Zur Geschichte der neueren schönen Literatur in Deutschland*, 1833 (*Letters Auxiliary to the History of Modern Polite Literature in Germany*, 1836); *Französische Zustände*, 1833 (*French Affairs*, 1889); *Der Salon*, 1834-1840 (4 volumes; *The Salon*, 1893); *Zur Geschichte der Religion und Philosophie in Deutschland*, 1835 (*On the History of Religion and Philosophy in Germany*, 1876); *Die romantische Schule*, 1836 (expansion of *Zur Geschichte der neueren schönen Literatur in Deutschland*; *The Romantic School*, 1876); *Über die französische Bühne*, 1837 (*Concerning the French Stage*, 1891-1905); *Shakespeares Mädchen und Frauen*, 1838 (*Shakespeare's Maidens and Ladies*, 1891); *Ludwig Börne: Eine Denkschrift von H. Heine*, 1840 (*Ludwig Börne: Recollections of a Revolutionist*, 1881); *Lutetia: Berichte über Politik, Kunst, und Volksleben*, 1854 (*Lutetia: Reports on Politics, Art, and Popular Life*, 1891-1905); *Vermischte Schriften*, 1854 (3 volumes); *De l'Allemagne*, 1855 (2 volumes).

MISCELLANEOUS: *The Works of Heinrich Heine*, 1891-1905 (12 volumes).

BIBLIOGRAPHY

Hermand, Jost, and Robert C. Holub, eds. *Heinrich Heine's Contested Identities: Politics, Religion, and Nationalism in Nineteenth-Century Germany*. New York: Peter Lang, 1999. A collection of essays concerning Heine's identity, which was formed and reformed, revised and modified, in relationship to the politics, religion, and nationalism of his era. The essays offer an understanding of Heine's predicaments and choices, as well as the parameters placed on him by the exigencies of the time.

Justis, Diana Lynn. *The Feminine in Heine's Life and Œuvre: Self and Other*. New York: P. Lang, 1997. Heine's literary representations of women and interactions with women vividly demonstrate his position as a marginal German-Jewish writer of the nineteenth century. Heine, like many Jews of that era, internalized the European cultural stereotype of the Jew as "woman," that is, as essentially inferior and marginal.

Nisbet, Delia Fabbroni-Giannotti. *Heinrich Heine and Giacomo Leopardi: The Rhetoric of Midrash*. New York: P. Lang, 2000. Nisbet provides a critical analysis of the similarities between the rhetorical strategies of Heine's text *Ludwig Börne*, Leopardi's "Il Cantico del Gallo Silvestre," and the midrashic process. In their texts, Heine and Leopardi interweave biblical references, historical events, and personal encounters with their narrative and juxtapose them to a contemporary situation, thus presenting the reader with their interpretation of an existential experience. These narratives are midrashic in inviting multiple interpretations of equal validity.

Pawel, Ernst. *The Poet Dying: Heinrich Heine's Last Years in Paris*. New York: Farrar, Straus and Giroux, 1995. In this biography of Heine, Pawel portrays a poet at the height of his creativity in the last eight years of his life when he was confined to his bed with a mysterious ailment.

Lowell A. Bangerter; bibliography updated by the editors

ROBERT HENRYSON

Born: c. 1425
Died: Near Dunfermline, Scotland; c. 1505

PRINCIPAL POETRY

Tale of Orpheus, 1508
The Testament of Cresseid, 1532
The Morall Fabillis of Esope, the Phrygian, 1570 (also known as *Fables*)
The Poems of Robert Henryson, 1906-1914 (3 volumes)
The Poems of Robert Henryson, 1981 (Denton Fox, editor)

OTHER LITERARY FORMS

Robert Henryson most likely did not write in any genre other than poetry.

ACHIEVEMENTS

For centuries the reputation of Robert Henryson rested on a mistake. His poem *The Testament of Cresseid*, which concludes or rounds out the events of Geoffrey Chaucer's *Troilus and Criseyde* (1382), was mistakenly credited to Chaucer and printed as Chaucer's (in an "Englished" version, smoothing out the Scottish dialect) for several generations. Thus, although his work drew admiration, the poet himself was little known.

Henryson was rediscovered by antiquarians in the eighteenth century, and for about one hundred years was a subject of interest among the Scottish literati, leading to the editions by David Laing (1865) and G. G. Smith (1906-1914). Today, Henryson is regularly studied, along with Gavin Douglas and William Dunbar, as one of the Scottish Chaucerians. Both Chaucer and John Lydgate can be seen to have influenced Henryson greatly. Although his own direct influence extends, perhaps, only to the English and Scottish lyricists of the early sixteenth century, he is now generally admired as a witty and learned man whose response to his sources (Aesop, Chaucer, classical myth) reveals an interesting mind at work and earns him the right to be included among early Renaissance humanists. He vies with Dunbar for the distinction of being the preeminent Scottish poet before Robert Burns.

BIOGRAPHY

Very little is known about Robert Henryson's life. Dunbar, listing dead poets in "Lament for the Makaris" (c. 1508), indicates that Henryson predeceased Stobo, who died in 1505. The other scant biographical evidence suggests that Henryson came from the area of Dunfermline (notable for its Benedictine abbey and site of one of the king's favorite homes); that he was admitted as a licentiate at the University of Glasgow in 1462; and that he served as a notary public and possibly as a schoolmaster. So little is certain about Henryson's life that scholars do not agree on the probable chronology of his works or even on the dates when he was most active as a poet. Nothing at all is known about Henryson's family life.

The range of knowledge displayed in the poems confirms that Henryson knew, at the least, a little about many subjects—law, medicine, astronomy, myth, and music—and at least a few books very well. His *Fables* adapt Aesop, whom Henryson read in Latin; his *Tule of Orpheus* is based on a passage from Boethius's *The Consolation of Philosophy* (523); he refers often to the Bible and frequently alludes to Chaucer.

ANALYSIS

Robert Henryson's work is often compared to Geoffrey Chaucer's and although he does not have the sweep and range of his English predecessor, Henryson does mirror, consciously or not, some of Chaucer's characteristics. Like Chaucer, he is interested in astrology, and in both *The Testament of Cresseid* and the *Tale of Orpheus*, the planets determine the fates of characters. In the *Fables*, his speaking animals sometimes have the comic and colloquial range of the Eagle in Chaucer's the *Hous of Fame* (1372-1380) or the birds in his *Parlement of Foules* (1380).

Henryson's most Chaucerian invention, however, is the narrative voice in *The Testament of Cresseid*. This narrative persona allows Henryson to present a morally complex situation with a degree of sophistication unmatched by his other works. Since the dates of Henryson's poems are uncertain, it would be wrong to view *The Testament of Cresseid* as a culmination of his narrative technique. Yet in this brief work he not only tells a story but also offers a series of moral perspectives on the action by allowing different characters, including the narrator, varying degrees of objectivity.

In the *Fables* and the *Tale of Orpheus*, he uses a more conventional method of achieving a mixed perspective. Each of the thirteen fables concludes with a separate section, labeled *moralitas*, which spells out the allegorical and moral implications of the fable itself. Similarly, the *Tale of Orpheus* concludes with an analytical *moralitas*, pairing each character and event with a specific allegorical function. Perhaps because formal allegory has long been an acquired taste, these two works show to a disadvantage beside the freshness and seeming modernity of *The Testament of Cresseid*.

MORALL FABILLIS OF ESOPE, THE PHRYGIAN

Henryson's longest work is a collection of thirteen Aesopic fables, each consisting of a beast tale followed by an explicating *moralitas*. Unanimity has not been reached on the question of the sources for Henryson's versions of the traditional fables, but most scholars agree that he depended on the Latin verse *Romulus* of Gualterus Anglicus for seven of the tales. He may also have used a French translation of Gualterus known as *Isopet de Lyon*, John Lydgate's *Isopes Fabules* (the first Aesopic collection in English), and William Caxton's *Fables of Aesop*.

Some editors, borrowing phrases from early manuscripts, call Henryson's fables the *Morall Fabillis of Esope, the Phrygian*, but Denton Fox, pointing out that Henryson evidently thought Aesop was a Roman, doubts the authenticity of the title and prefers simply *Fables* (see Fox's 1981 edition).

Henryson provides a prologue to his tales which echoes the Horatian dictum about delight and instruction. In general, the fables themselves are lively tales in a colloquial style, featuring anthropomorphic beasts wandering into error. Some of the errors are more blatantly human than others, but all are corrected in the *moralitas*, which often have a more formal level of diction than do the tales. The relationship between fable and moral is not always what the modern reader expects; sometimes the highbrow stiffness of the moral does not do full justice to the human (or bestial) complexity of the tale. The key word in the preceding sentence is "bestial," for clearly the animals of the stories, like Eurydice and Cresseid, represent aspects of man's appetitive nature.

An example of the gap between fable and *moralitas* may be taken from the first fable, "The Cock and the Jasp," in which a rooster, scrounging in a dunghill for food, comes upon a precious stone. Realizing that he, a cock, can have no use for a jewel, he casts it aside and continues the search for food. Now, to the reader, the rooster seems to have made a wise choice. Is it not better to attend to basic needs, like that for food, and ignore the useless material items? The *moralitas*, however, turns this perception inside out. Based on biblical tradition, the jewel is glossed as wisdom; suddenly, the cock can be seen as foolishly preferring dungy food to the intangible riches of knowledge. Henryson's intention, it would seem, is to shock the reader into recognizing his own similarity to the foolish cock.

The fables, then, are explicitly didactic, and they work by creating a gap between the formal "correct" view of a situation and the partial human/animal view. The tidy structure of "The Cock and the Jasp" is not, however, precisely paralleled by all the other fables. In fact, as the sequence progresses the fables themselves become harsher and bleaker, and the morals less pleasant. In the first seven, only blatantly evil characters are punished; in the latter six, however, the innocent begin to suffer. For example, in "The Wolf and the Lamb," the twelfth fable, a pathetic lamb argues for its life but, without any hope of justice, is killed and eaten. The *moralitas* compares the lamb to "the pure pepill" and the wolf to "fals extortioners and oppresouris" and warns powerful men not to be like the wolf. A moral universe divides fable twelve from fable one; Henryson has

moved from questions of personal governance, as in "The Cock and the Jasp," to address his fears about the contemporary political situation.

The thirteenth and final fable has a religious dimension; here a greedy mouse and a predatory paddock (toad) end up in a life-or-death water fight, and both are killed by a passing bird of prey. The mouse is allegorized by Henryson as man's soul, the paddock as man's body, and the whole tale as a parable for the difficulty of reconciling the two. Man is warned that unless he can reconcile body and soul he may become the victim of external predators. Henryson does not, however, offer a plan for effecting such a reconciliation. Although the early fables often surprise the reader, they do offer moral advice. The later fables, much darker, offer cautionary tales without explicit directions about how to avoid pitfalls oneself.

THE TESTAMENT OF CRESSEID

By far Henryson's best-known work, *The Testament of Cresseid* owes its popularity and vitality both to its link to Chaucer's *Troilus and Criseyde* and to its own conciseness, originality, and sincerity. The entire poem consists of 616 lines, in contrast to the eight thousand lines of the Chaucerian inspiration.

In *The Testament of Cresseid*, Henryson abandons the fable-moral structure characteristic of his other works. Instead, the poem itself stands as a suitable *moralitas* to *Troilus and Criseyde* itself. Henryson takes the events of Chaucer's poem, particularly the actions of Criseyde, and carries them out to what he sees as their morally logical conclusion. The justice meted out to Cresseid (as Henryson spells her name) is swift and cruel: Diomed abandons her, she contracts leprosy (generally then considered to be a venereal disease) and Troilus, resurrected by Henryson despite his death in Chaucer, kindly gives her alms, although her disease makes her unrecognizable. She dies willing her spirit to the goddess of chastity, Diana.

What was Henryson's intention in following Criseyde after Chaucer's poem ends? Some readers have accused him of a puritanical streak, seeing in him a fierce desire to punish the wicked. He may also have been playing into the hands of an interested public, who had known the legend of a promiscuous Criseyde before Chaucer ever took up the subject. Even if tradition had already branded Criseyde a whore, Henryson's treatment of her does seem, at first, to smack of moral judgment. He seems to want people to receive their just rewards in this world, rather than in Heaven or Hell. In his poem, Troilus, for example, is still alive, graciously donating alms and cutting a dashing figure. The reader is left with no doubt about the relative wages of sin and fidelity. Cresseid rots and dies; Troilus prospers.

The poem as a whole is admirably structured and has often been praised for its concision. It begins with a variation on the conventional medieval opening reference to spring. A Scottish spring, apparently, is a cold and "doolie" affair, an apt setting for the sorrowful tale. Henryson follows Chaucer in creating a kind of naïve narrator for the tale, one who is hopelessly sympathetic to Cresseid—a sympathy that neither Chaucer nor Henryson necessarily shares. Thus while Henryson the poet assigns Cresseid leprosy, Henryson the narrator weeps for her. The narrator, much like the narrators in Chaucer's dream visions, stays up one night reading *Troilus and Criseyde*, then turns to "another quair," another book, for the rest of the tale, seeking to answer the question of what happened to Criseyde when she left Troy and deserted her lover Troilus for the Greek Diomed.

The new story begins as Cresseid, cast off by Diomed, decides to come home to her loving father Calchas, whom Henryson depicts as the keeper of the temple of Venus. In this very temple Cresseid, on her knees in despair, blasphemes against Cupid and his mother by regretting that she ever sacrificed to them. The response to this blasphemy is swift; Cresseid has a dream vision in which "the sevin planetis" descend from their spheres. Earthly action is suspended while the planets debate Cresseid's punishment, with melancholy Saturn, "the hiest planet," being given responsibility for formulating the verdict. The narrator, true to his subjective affection for Criseyde, spends a stanza lamenting the "to malitious" judgment against Cresseid. The fate of the gods is nevertheless final, and the newly diseased Cresseid, after consultation with her father, moves into a nearby "spittail hous" to await death. At this point Henryson includes an inset poem (made up of nine-line stanzas as distinct from the poem's rhyme royal) in which Cresseid laments her fate, wishes for death, and

warns other ladies not to forget the pitfalls of sin and the fickle passage of time. This is her testament. Before Cresseid dies, she sends Troilus a ring. He suffers for her sake but stoically asserts that she brought her fate upon herself by her falseness.

The reader is left then with at least three verdicts on Cresseid: that of the planetary council, which condemns her for both her deed and her blasphemy of love; that of the narrator, who seems to see her (as she initially sees herself) as a wronged victim; and that of Troilus, who will always care for her but who accepts the inevitability of her fate. In the end, Henryson finds a way to offer multiple perspectives on a given action without resorting to the formal juxtaposition of fable and moral. The surprise of *The Testament of Cresseid* comes instead at the beginning, when readers realize that the apparently closed case of *Troilus and Criseyde* is suddenly subject to new evidence. Still, despite the resurrection of Troilus and the spectacular invention of Cresseid's leprosy, *The Testament of Cresseid* offers no final word on Cresseid's fate. She remains as lovable, and as wrong, as she was for Chaucer.

TALE OF ORPHEUS

The *Tale of Orpheus* is a poem in rhyme royal of about the same length as the *Troilus and Criseyde*. It is solidly based on a passage in Boethius's *The Consolation of Philosophy* (III, metrum xii) and on Nicholas Trivet's commentary on that passage. Despite its relative concision, Henryson's poem is encyclopedic and ambitious, containing, like Chaucer's *Hous of Fame*, a supernatural journey and an explanation of music based on the harmonious proportions of the universe.

Of Henryson's major works, the *Tale of Orpheus* is the least popular, perhaps because of the number of lines given over to a theoretical discussion of music and the genealogy of the gods. Modern readers, however, also find uncongenial the strange gap between the myth of the *Tale of Orpheus* and the *moralitas* offered, in which Eurydice, glossed as sinful affection, is said more or less properly to belong in Hell.

The poem opens with the genealogy of Orpheus, tracing his descent from the mating of Calliope, "of all musik maistresse," and Phebus Appollo, god of poetry and intellect. When Orpheus grows up, Eurydice, queen of Thrace, woos and marries him (the role reversal here will prove significant). He loves her dearly, and when she is snatched to Hell, furiously pursues her. Why does she "die"? While frolicking in a meadow she flees from a would-be attacker, the shepherd Arystyus, and is bitten by a snake. To understand why this series of events leads her to Hell, the reader must turn to the *moralitas*, which reveals that Orpheus, as "intellect," mates with Eurydice, "affection," at his peril. After all, Eurydice, rather than Orpheus, initiated the marriage. More oddly, Arystyus, who attacked Eurydice, is said to represent virtue, and in fleeing him, she exposed herself to sin, symbolized by the snake. Eurydice, then, represents a low passion for an intellectual creature like Orpheus and by implication all worthy human beings. Does Henryson rule out all human love? No, man may have it on one condition, the same condition on which Orpheus is allowed to lead Eurydice out of Hell: He must not look back, or downward, but always keep his eyes fixed on the celestial spheres.

Human love, then, is always in danger of backsliding, always on the verge of failure. This may seem like a dark message, akin to the darkness of Cresseid's fate, especially since Orpheus ultimately fails to win back Eurydice. The poem, however, offers some hope: Reason and affection can be brought together by the "harp of eloquence," the power of poetry. This power immobilizes Cerberus and the three fates, frees Tantalus, Ixion, and Ticius from their hellish punishments, and earns Orpheus the right to try to free Eurydice. Love depends on poetry (a cousin of celestial harmony) for survival.

Henryson's poem is itself an eloquent voice, both showing tender affection between Orpheus and Eurydice and hinting, with a touch of *contemptus mundi*, that human beings ought to focus primarily on higher things. With luck, one can have both affection and intellect; in this poem, however, poor Orpheus ends up with only his eloquence, his sad ballads. Bereft of affection, he does not seem to profit from his intellect.

In terms of overall technique, the *Tale of Orpheus*, like some of the fables, shows Henryson achieving a complex point of view by juxtaposing the vision of his essentially human lovers with the stern voice of the *moralitas*, in which they become the abstractions intellect and affection. If he is fierce about the wages of sin, he is also a persuasive portraitist of the appeal that the sin of human love inevitably holds.

SHORTER POEMS

The twelve shorter poems attributed to Henryson range across a variety of standard genres and include "Robene and Makene," a comic *pastourelle* (a dialogue between lovers); "Sum Practysis of Medecyne," a satire on doctors; and poems in which age debates youth and death debates man. The poems exhibit the variety of contemporary stanza forms, and do not, for the most part, speak in a voice that particularly echoes that of Henryson's three major works. Aside from the titles given above, the twelve include "The Annunciation," "The Abbey Walk," "The Bloody Serk," "The Garmont of Gud Ladeis," "Against Hasty Credence," "The Praise of Age," "Ane Prayer for the Pest," "The Ressoning betuix Aige and Yowth," "The Ressoning Betuix Deth and Man," and "The Three Dead Pollis." A thirteenth poem, "The Want of Wise Men," sometimes attributed to Henryson, has been rejected by Fox on the ground that no plausible proof of attribution exists. Indeed Fox suggests that proof of authorship is tentative for all of the shorter poems.

BIBLIOGRAPHY

Fox, Denton, ed. *The Poems of Robert Henryson.* Oxford, England: Clarendon Press, 1981. This fine collection is accompanied by a full introduction that reviews Henryson's life and reputation, the texts, the manuscripts, and the individual works. The poems are given extensive commentary and an excellent Middle Scots glossary makes reading easy and enjoyable.

Gray, Douglas. *Robert Henryson.* Leiden, Netherlands: E. J. Brill, 1979. This study begins with a background chapter on Henryson's world, but the bulk of the book (three chapters) is a detailed reading of the *Fables.* Contains separate sections on *The Testament of Cresseid*, "Orpheus and Eurydice," and the shorter poems. Includes illustrations and a good basic bibliography.

Kindrick, Robert L. *Henryson and the Medieval Arts of Rhetoric.* New York: Garland, 1993. A rhetorical study of Henryson's work which details Henryson's use of the *ars poetria, ars dictiminis, ars notaria,* and *ars praedicandi.* Provides an overview of medieval rhetorical traditions.

_____. *Robert Henryson*. Boston: Twayne, 1979. This analytic survey covers Henryson's personality as a writer, his times, and his literary tradition. He is characterized as a master of "wisdom literature," a brilliant stylist in both allegorical descriptions and realistic portrayals, as well as a possessor of a keen sense of humor. Such traits as his love and understanding of his fellow human beings, his portrayal of the dignity of the lower classes, his blunt yet clear diction, and his influences from rationalism and classical sources are discussed and examples are given. Includes a handy chronology and a short bibliography.

McDiarmid, Matthew P. *Robert Henryson*. Edinburgh: Scottish Academic Press, 1981. A biographical chapter dealing with the facts and speculations of Henryson's life is followed by a portrait of his times and the literary tradition he inherited. Detailed analyses of the three major poems as well as the shorter ones are accompanied by notes and a select bibliography.

McKenna, Steven R. *Robert Henryson's Tragic Vision*. New York: P. Lang, 1994. A critical analysis of the rhetoric used in selected works by Henryson. Includes bibliographical references and index.

MacQueen, John. *Robert Henryson: A Study of the Major Narrative Poems*. Oxford, England: Clarendon Press, 1967. This analysis discusses Henryson away from the Chaucerian tradition and characterizes him as a man of the early Renaissance rather than medievalism. MacQueen presents the carnal passions of fallen man, as represented by the animal characters, as the major theme in the three principal works. He traces the development of the poet's humanism through his education and literary background. Contains a fine discussion of style and diction and an appendix on the *Fables* in terms of the Aesopic tradition and the beast epic.

Stearns, Marshall W. *Robert Henryson*. New York: AMS Press, 1949. This monograph analyzes Henryson's reputation and his place in the social and cultural climate of his time. It explores his character as seen through the poetry and demonstrates his originality and his views on human beings and society. The author explores Henryson's sources and sheds light on several difficult passages. Contains an interesting chapter on Henryson's use and interpretation of astrology. This study hardly touches Henryson's merits as a poet and focuses on the political and social commentary in the poems. Includes a select bibliography.

*Diane M. Ross;
bibliography updated by the editors*

GEORGE HERBERT

Born: Montgomery, Wales; April 3, 1593
Died: Bemerton, England; March 1, 1633

PRINCIPAL POETRY

Musae Responsoriae, 1620, 1662 (printed)
Passio Discerpta, 1623
Lucus, 1623
Memoriae Matris Sacrum, 1627
The Temple, 1633
Poems, 1958, 1961

OTHER LITERARY FORMS

George Herbert's most important work besides *The Temple* is his prose treatise *A Priest to the Temple: Or, The Country Parson His Character and Rule of Holy Life*, written when he was in fact a country parson at Bemerton during the last years of his life, though not published until 1652. However idealized it may be, *A Priest to the Temple* gives a good picture of the life of humble service that Herbert offered to his God and his parishioners. The volume of *Outlandish Proverbs Selected by Mr. G. H.*, published in 1640, testifies to Herbert's lifelong interest in the proverb, a form of literary and moral expression that is prominent throughout the poems in *The Temple*. Other minor works include a translation of *A Treatise of Temperance and Sobrietie of Luigi Cornaro* (1634), and a series of "Briefe Notes" appended to, but indicating various disagreements with, *The Hundred and Ten Considerations of Signior Iohn Valdesso* (1638).

ACHIEVEMENTS

George Herbert has always been and perhaps will continue to be read somewhat in the shadow of John Donne, arguably the greatest and most influential of the seventeenth century Metaphysical poets. At the same time, however, Herbert has rarely lacked an audience well aware of his remarkable poetic abilities and unique voice. During his lifetime, Herbert's English poems were most likely circulated in manuscript, no doubt within a rather restricted circle of friends, and were evidently highly regarded. Upon publication in 1633, the year of his death, *The Temple* began to reach an ever-widening group of readers, the number and variety of whom say something about Herbert's appeal. It is not enough to note that Herbert was extremely popular, though he certainly was that: At least eleven editions of *The Temple* came out in the seventeenth century.

Perhaps more interesting is the fact that unlikely bedfellows shared an interest in Herbert and claimed him as

George Herbert (Hulton Archive)

their own. Members of the so-called High Church party found Herbert's deep attachment to Anglican ceremonial beauty particularly congenial, and they read *The Temple* as a record of how spiritual conflicts might evaporate in the face of simple faith, humility, and conformity. Several important poets, including Henry Vaughan and Richard Crashaw, along with a host of minor poets, including Christopher Harvey, Ralph Knevet, and Henry Colman, looked to Herbert as a guide in their devotions and a model for their poems. Other aspects of Herbert, however, appealed to many readers who could be called, for lack of a better term, Puritans. Though the Puritans are often criticized for a disinterest in, if not hostility to, art as an enemy of truth, Herbert's characteristic plainness, simplicity, and sincerity, coupled with his constant stress on the Bible as the center of the holy life, made him attractive to readers who were otherwise not greatly devoted to poetry. Richard Baxter and, later, John Wesley were extremely fond of Herbert, and it is no surprise that many poems from *The Temple* were subsequently adapted as hymns.

That Herbert could be appropriated so easily by such divergent readers indicates the richness of *The Temple*. Modern writers as varied as Gerard Manley Hopkins, T. S. Eliot, Dylan Thomas, Elizabeth Bishop, and Simone Weil have each in his or her own way learned from Herbert: as a poet who has a distinctive voice that nevertheless does not exclude other voices, particularly from the Bible and the Book of Common Prayer; as a man of purity and simplicity who is yet rarely naïve and often painfully sensitive to the intricacies of sin and self-deception; as a Christian, indeed a priest, wedded to humility but well aware that the resources of art can serve as resources of devotion.

BIOGRAPHY

George Herbert was born on April 3, 1593, into one of the most distinguished families of Montgomeryshire, active both in local politics and court service. The fifth son in a family of seven sons and three daughters, he was reared principally by his mother (his father died in 1596), by all reports a remarkable woman who left a deep impression on her children. Magdalene Herbert not only shrewdly managed an extremely large household—unlike the modern-day nuclear family, the upper-class household of the seventeenth century might contain upwards of a score of children, relatives, servants, and visitors—but also supervised the education of her children. Perhaps more important, as Donne relates in his commemorative sermon on her, she was a model of piety and took a great interest in the spiritual development of her family. Herbert's early childhood thus well prepared him for a life of distinction and devotion, two clusters of values that he later spent much time trying to reconcile.

Herbert's formal education began at Westminster School, and upon entering Trinity College, Cambridge, he soon established himself as a young man of great promise. Moving quickly through A.B. and A.M. degrees and positions as a minor, then a major fellow, Herbert became the university orator in 1620. Such an appointment not only indicates the great verbal and oral skills that Herbert must have demonstrated, skills that he would later use to great advantage as both a poet and a preacher, but also testifies to the high regard in which he was held. The orator was in some respects the public spokesperson for the university, constantly communicating with government officials and dignitaries, and it was only a small step to graduate from this office to a more prestigious position at court or in state service.

This was not, however, to be Herbert's path. Perhaps his attendance at two particularly troubling terms of Parliament (in 1624 and 1625) discouraged him from a life of secular employment. Perhaps the death of King James and the accession of Charles I left him without a strong group of supporters to back any possible ambitions. Perhaps as he grew older, passed through several serious illnesses, and deepened his devotions, he came to see that a secular career did not, in the long run, have nearly as much to offer as a life of holy service. For whatever reason, or, more likely, combination of reasons, Herbert chose to be ordained as a deacon by 1626, and four years later he became a priest. With his wife, whom he married in 1629, Herbert lived the remaining years of his life at Bemerton, a small parish near Salisbury. He died on March 1, 1633.

Herbert's poetry is often deeply personal, so that many readers insist on looking at *The Temple* as a kind of veiled autobiography. Surely the major themes of his life are indeed the major themes in his poetry: On one level, *The Temple* dramatizes Herbert's conflicting drives toward secular achievement and religious retreat, his search for a satisfying vocation, and his apparently constant self-doubts and worries about his unworthiness to be a lowly servant of God, let alone a priest. *The Temple* is ultimately, however, far more than autobiographical, and the reader should not assume that every statement made by Herbert the poet is literally true of Herbert the man. The persona who narrates and undergoes a variety of experiences in *The Temple* is very much like Herbert but also very much like the readers of *The Temple*. Herbert's purpose in writing his poems was not so much to express his personal concerns as it was to clarify and perhaps resolve certain important problems that all Christians—some would broaden this to include all thoughtful readers—share. The details of Herbert's life thus figure largely in his poems, but as part of a design that is much more inclusive.

ANALYSIS

The Temple is unquestionably one of the most inventive and varied collections of poems published in the seventeenth century, and a reader can go a long way toward appreciating George Herbert by studying this inventiveness and variety. At the same time, though, the full range of Herbert's intentions and impact may be missed if his technical virtuosity is seen as an end in itself. Everything known about Herbert suggests that he would not want to be described as a master craftsman or skilled technician of poetry unless it was also stressed that every effort of his artistry served a central purpose: helping him to know, love, and praise God, and to understand better his place in a world filled with sin but governed and redeemed by Christ. Such poems as "Jordan" (I) and (II) and "The Posie" are in fact critical of certain styles of poetry and show that Herbert is more than occasionally impatient with the subterfuge, indirection, and even pride that seem inevitable in producing a well-written work. Ultimately, however, poetic creativity and devotion are welded together in *The Temple*. As the title suggests, Herbert imagines himself to be a builder, and nearly all the details, both large and small, of the structure he raises show it to be a place of intricate beauty as well as sacred worship.

THE TEMPLE

Understanding the design of *The Temple* as a whole is no easy matter, in part because Herbert's natural inclination seems to be to "play" with structure, rather than to adopt a fixed schema as the pattern for the entire work. *The Temple* is divided into three parts, as though the reader is going to be led step-by-step through a physical temple. "The Church-porch," by far Herbert's longest single poem, offers a great deal of advice on moral matters to prepare a youth who is otherwise not yet ready for more serious devotions. After such an initiation, the reader is ready to enter the section called "The Church," a collection of lyrics that continues to describe various places or objects in the church (the altar, stained glass windows, and so on) but that in doing so dramatizes the spiritual conflicts of a believer trying to secure his faith. The final section, "The Church Militant," turns from the life of the individual believer to the corporate body of the church, which, like each individual, must endure a series of successes and failures throughout its history. While the tripartite structure of *The Temple* thus has a certain obvious coherence, there are limits to the usefulness of such a scheme. Though Herbert never completely drops his theme of tracing out the contours of the physical temple, he quickly shows that his main interest is in exploring the temple within the heart and mind of the worshiper.

Herbert's flexible and open-ended play with structure, his ability to make patterns that are stable enough to support a great weight of meaning but loose enough to avoid dull predictability, is seen to a great advantage in the way he arranges the poems of "The Church." Far from being a random miscellany, "The Church" is a carefully ordered collection in which the individual poems are placed in sequences and other kinds of groups, sometimes with poems that stand nearby in the volume, at other times with ones located many pages away. Although even a superficial reading of the poems soon advises the reader that he must watch closely how they relate to one another, Herbert provides a good description of his method and a clue to where he learned it in his poem "The H. Scriptures" (II). Despite its many parts, the Bible, he suggests, has a basic unity, and in order to understand any particular story the reader needs to trace how "This verse marks that, and both do make a motion/

Unto a third, that ten leaves off doth lie." Like the Bible, "The Church" has a basic unity, and the reader understands the poems fully only when he takes into account how they comment on and echo one another.

Sometimes the patterns and sequences of the poems are rather straightforward. "The Church" opens with a series that moves through the events celebrated during Easter Week, and the cumulative effect of such poems as "The Sacrifice," "The Agonie," "Good Friday," "Easter," and "Easter-wings" is to reinforce a sense of the importance of this part of the Christian calendar. In another group, the typical progress of a Christian life is reflected in the succession of titles: "Affliction," "Repentance," "Faith," "Prayer," and "The H. Communion." Even when Herbert does not fully develop a sequence, there are many examples of paired poems, where one answers, corrects, or otherwise responds to another. "Church-monuments," one of Herbert's most impressive poems even though its theme is the body's inevitable decay, is immediately followed by "Church-musick," which focuses on the high-flying freedom of the soul once it is released from the body. The desperate pleas that fill "Longing" are short-lived; by the first line of the next poem, "The Bag"—"Away despair! My gracious Lord doth heare"—the pleas have been answered.

Toward the end of "The Church," the speaker in the poem "The Invitation" calls out to God, inviting him to a feast; the following poem, "The Banquet," shows not only that the invitation has been accepted but also that the feast is far more glorious than the speaker had imagined. The more the reader follows the many links drawing the poems closer and closer together, the more apparent it becomes that one aspect of Herbert's design in "The Church" is to use the entire collection to trace a believer's gradual attainment not only of wisdom but also, more important, of peace. Read as one long, continuous sequence, the poems of "The Church" do seem to have a general plot, as the tribulations so much in evidence early in the work gradually give way to a more subdued questioning and heightened moments of bliss. Many commentators have noted that Herbert marks out this general plot very clearly for his reader: At the beginning of "The Church" the reader is invited to "approach, and taste/ The churches mysticall repast," and the final poem in the section, "Love" (III), concludes quite simply—

"So I did sit and eat"—showing that this task has been completed.

Without disregarding the broad movement in "The Church" from immaturity to maturity, pain to comfort, it is equally important to note that Herbert by no means presents a simple tale of easily achieved spiritual progress. The plot traced out by the lyrics in "The Church," while ultimately a hopeful one, is at the same time densely textured, complicated, filled with moments of weakness, backsliding, and lessons improperly learned. Numerous short sequences suggest that man's needs are answered by Christ, who is always nearby; for example, the momentary sense that Christ has vanished, and that even when he is near he is unapproachable, expressed in "The Search," "Grief," and "The Crosse," gives way to the blooming of joy in "The Flower"—joy that is both surprising and expected: "How fresh, O Lord, how sweet and clean/ Are thy returns! ev'n as the flowers in spring."

If comfort is predictable, though, so is despair, and many short sequences show how quickly man moves back again from wonder to worry; the exhilaration of "The Temper" (I), for example, is extremely precarious, over and done with, even by the time the next poem, "The Temper" (II), begins: "It cannot be. Where is that mightie joy,/ Which just now took up all my heart?" As confusing and frustrating as these constant oscillations may be, Herbert's purpose is not to undermine the reader's security. By linking his poems in a variety of ways, often teasing and challenging his reader, Herbert expands the limits of the lyric form, setting the entire collection up to do what no one lyric possibly could: to dramatize and analyze the various moods and rhythms of a faithful believer.

POETIC STRUCTURE

Herbert's structural skill is evident not only in the overall plan and order of *The Temple* but also in the individual poems. His playful sense of poetic structure, though, has often been misunderstood and held against him. Such obviously patterned poems as "The Altar" and "Easter-wings," both of which are typographically shaped to resemble the objects named in the title, often strike some readers as quaint at best. Eighteenth century critics, for example, viewed these poems rather condescendingly as typical of Herbert and did not hesitate to

consider him as a "false wit," incapable of more noble and creative effects.

Looked at more sympathetically, though, "The Altar" and "Easter-wings" are typical of Herbert only in suggesting how important poetic form is for him. Besides being a statement and a dramatization, a poem by Herbert is also an artifact, whose structure, sometimes simply, at other times subtly, reinforces a particular theme. At one end of the scale, there are directly imitative poems such as "Paradise," a poem about pruning in which the rhyme words are, in fact, pruned; "Heaven," in which the last word of the speaker's questions echoes in a following line as an answer; and "Trinitie Sunday," composed of a trinity of three-line stanzas. Other poems show more subdued but nevertheless effective pictorial designs: The shape of the stanzas in "The Agonie" suggests the image of the winepress mentioned in the poem, which calls to mind the association between Christ's sacrificial blood and sacramental wine; and each stanza in "The Bag" seems to contain an open space, literally like the bag mentioned in the poem used to take messages from man straight to God.

Such directly imitative devices help to prepare the reader for Herbert's far more challenging uses of poetic form in other places in *The Temple*. The structure of "Church-monuments," for example, is meant not so much to imitate a gravestone, as the title seems to suggest, as to help the reader imagine the decay described in the poem that will sooner or later overcome gravestones, bodies, and the entire physical world. Because the lines are only occasionally end-stopped, the rhythm becomes somewhat unsettling, even ominous, and since the word "dust" is repeated again and again, the entire poem momentarily becomes like the hourglass mentioned in the last few lines, "which holds the dust/ That measures all our time; which also shall/ Be crumbled into dust."

Similarly, the theme and mood of the speaker in "The Collar" are powerfully and immediately conveyed by its structure: The poem is apparently unshaped, with irregularly alternating lines of different length to suggest the disordered mind of a man who has lost all control. By the concluding lines, though, the structure of the poem communicates the achievement of order. As the speaker exhausts himself to a moment of calmness, "normal" poetic form also surfaces in the relatively stable *abab* rhyme scheme of the last four lines: "But as I rav'd and grew more fierce and wilde/ At every word,/ Me thoughts I heard one calling, *Child!*/ And I reply'd, *My Lord.*" Because he so often shapes his poems to have a visual impact, Herbert is compared with the emblem writers of his time, whose verses were either appended to illustrative plates or were at least meant to call to mind and interpret such illustrations. Such poems as "Church-monuments" and "The Collar," however, show that one of Herbert's particular skills is an ability to use the structure of his poems to imitate not only objects and static scenes but also dramatic processes.

LANGUAGE

Herbert's attention to structure is matched by his loving care for the language of his poems. Especially when compared to other works of his period, *The Temple* seems remarkably simple and direct, with little of the straining against meaning that characterizes so many of William Shakespeare's sonnets, and with hardly any of Donne's self-conscious roughness and almost inconsiderate obscurity.

As many critics have noted, though, Herbert's simplicity marks the triumph, not the abandonment, of art. The language of *The Temple* is that of the Bible (especially in the King James or Authorized Version, published in 1611) and the Book of Common Prayer: austere but resonant and multileveled. Herbert's delight in language reflects not only the deep influence of God's words, the Holy Scriptures, but also his awareness that human words, returned to God in prayer, praise, song, and poetry, are at least an acceptable celebration of God's Word made flesh in Christ.

Throughout "The Church," Herbert struggles with the dilemma that man in poetry, as in all things, can give to God only what God has already given him; but though this undermines any pretense of human self-sufficiency, it is an arrangement in which Herbert ultimately finds a great deal of comfort. The heartfelt simplicity of the three poems titled "Praise" and the two titled "Antiphon," among many others in "The Church," signifies not only a poetic choice but also an acceptance of man's subservient place in God's world.

At the same time, however, Herbert's humility allows him to exploit the richness of the English language. Modern readers who consider puns to be at best a low form of wit need to be reminded that Herbert, like most other seventeenth century poets, used puns and wordplay not only for comic effects but also for much more serious purposes: to indicate deep correspondences between various things in the world, between language and reality and between different levels of experience.

In "The Sonne" Herbert confesses "I like our language well," in part because it lends itself so easily to one especially significant pun: The reader is led quickly through the multiple meanings of the title word, from "son" to "sun," and finally to Christ, who combines these meanings as Son of Man, Son of God, and the guiding and warming light of Christians: their sun. There may well be even another concealed pun here; "The Sonne" is written in the form of a *sonnet*. The title "The Holdfast" is also a pun that takes the reader into the central conflict of the poem: A "holdfast" is something one can cling securely to, in this case God; in addition, "holdfast" is a term for a stingy, self-reliant man, such as the speaker of the poem, who must first relax his hold on himself before he can truly understand "That all things were more ours by being his," that is, Christ's.

Though it is sometimes difficult to determine where Herbert's wordplay leaves off and the reader's invention begins, the title "The Collar" sets off a series of associations that are relevant to the lines that follow: The collar is perhaps first and foremost the Christian's yoke of discipline and obedience from which the speaker flees; this word also suggests "choler," the anger and distress of the speaker as he raves on and on; finally, by a slight adjustment it also sounds like the "caller," alluding not only to the situation of the speaker calling out in anguish but also to the infinitely patient God who calls even his unruly servant "Child."

Herbert occasionally uses puns and wordplay to construct a puzzle, the explanation of which points the reader toward a comforting observation. In "Jesu," for example, the title word is "deeply carved" in the speaker's heart. When his heart is broken by "A great affliction," the letters become scattered, but even so they spell out an important message: the fragments *J* (often printed as *I* in the seventeenth century), *ES*, and *U* form the statement "I ease you," a welcome affirmation of the power of Christ. Not all Herbert's poems are puzzles, but his constant reliance on puns keeps his otherwise short and compact lyrics from one-dimensional simplicity. Even the smallest details in a poem are liable to expand into several important meanings. In "Christmas," for example, when he describes the "glorious, yet contracted light" of the Christ child, he not only marvels at how the greatness of God has taken the diminutive form of a baby, but also celebrates the fact that man is bound, by legal contract or covenant, to his God.

When Herbert questions, in the ominously titled poem "Discipline," "Who can scape his bow?" the various interpretations of the last word provide comforting associations. Besides being a weapon of war and traditional instrument of justice and wrath, the "bow" also calls to mind Cupid's bow and arrow, which are instruments of love; the rainbow, the sign after the Flood that God will change his ways of wrath; the bowlike cross, a common comparison found in many biblical commentators; and Christ's "bowing," taking human form in order to save humankind. Throughout *The Temple*, Herbert carefully avoids the two most common dangers of the pun—he is rarely ostentatious or ridiculous—and as a result his wordplay almost always adds a great deal of allusiveness and depth to his poems.

SPIRITUAL CONFLICT: "THE CHURCH"

What makes Herbert an enduring poet is not simply his structural and stylistic expertise but also the application of these technical skills to themes of great importance. The general subject of *The Temple* is, in Herbert's own words as reported by Izaak Walton, his seventeenth century biographer, "the many spiritual Conflicts that have passed betwixt God and my Soul." Knowing this, it should be no surprise to see that the poems in "The Church" are constantly dramatic, most often revolving around a dual focus: man's inevitable sins and misunderstandings, and the processes through which he is comforted, instructed, and corrected.

Before telling man's tale, however, Herbert places human life within the frame of one larger event, the Crucifixion. Christ's drama must be told first, and, accordingly, the poem on "The Sacrifice" is placed near the beginning of "The Church." Although this poem is in many respects unusual for Herbert—it is very long, and uses Christ not only as the subject but also as the speaker—its pattern recurs in many other places: Unlike such poets as Donne and Richard Crashaw, who often

try to sustain a high dramatic pitch for an entire poem, Herbert, here and elsewhere, normally works with quick, unexpected, striking dramatic moments. "The Sacrifice" has a startling immediacy as Christ narrates the humiliating events of his crucifixion, and yet the reader also senses a curiously triumphant detachment. Even though Christ's repeated refrain is "Was ever grief like mine?" his voice is calm and ironic as he lists in obsessive detail the incongruities of his situation, the Son of God tortured by the people he offers to serve and save. After more than two hundred lines showing Christ's rather impassive power, Herbert breaks his carefully established format: Christ suddenly cries out in anguish "*My God, my God—*," a broken, unfinished line that the reader presumably completes by adding, "why has thou forsaken me?" The refrain then changes in this stanza to the simple statement, "Never was grief like mine." Because of this sudden breakdown, the reader is drawn more surely into a fuller understanding of the sacrifice: Christ is not only serene and all-powerful but also, at least for one moment, vulnerable, human. Once "The Sacrifice" establishes to what extent Christ, despite his torment, is man's benefactor, the reader can realize more fully that the "spiritual Conflicts" in Herbert's poems are not truly between man and God but between man and himself.

Throughout "The Church," the focus is on the many ways that man finds to resist God. Like Donne, Herbert is convinced of man's basic and inescapable sinfulness, and some of his poems, like Donne's Holy Sonnets, explore arrogant intellectual pride ("Vanitie" [I] and [II]), disobedience ("Affliction" [I], "The Collar"), and the general blackness of the human soul ("Sinne" [I] and [II]). Beyond these themes, however, and in a manner that distinguishes him from Donne, Herbert is primarily interested in dramatizing far more intricate modes of self-deception and far less obvious subtleties of pride. The speaker in "The Thanksgiving," for example, seems genuinely moved by his meditation on Christ, and his exuberant plant to dedicate his life to charitable works probably strikes every reader as praiseworthy. In a turn that is characteristic of Herbert, however, the last two lines suddenly undermine all that has come before. At the height of his confident offering to Christ, the speaker stumbles: "Then for thy passion—I will do for that—/

Alas, my God, I know not what." Herbert is by no means ridiculing the speaker or banishing exuberance and charity from the devotional life, but he dramatizes very effectively how evasive one can be even when trying to dedicate oneself to following Christ's example.

"MISERIE" AND "THANKSGIVING"

A similar reversal occurs in "Miserie." Here the speaker clearly abhors sin and spends most of his time criticizing man's foolishness in choosing a filthy life of "strange pollutions" over the moral purity that might have been within reach. The accusations are extreme but compelling, and it takes little arguing to convince the reader that man is "A lump of flesh, without a foot or wing/ To raise him to a glimpse of blisse:/ A sick toss'd vessel, dashing on each thing." The last line, however, changes the focus of the poem entirely: After seventy-seven lines describing the "strange wayes" around him, the speaker suddenly realizes that "My God, I mean my self." In this way Herbert shows that abhorrence of sin, while perhaps admirable, may be a mode of pride unless one includes oneself in the indictment.

"The Thanksgiving" and "Miserie" are also good examples of how Herbert typically includes the reader in his dramatic revelations and reversals. Although it might be overstating the case to say that Herbert traps his readers, many assent to and often identify with his speakers from the start of a poem. Because they accept their premises—the statements in both "The Thanksgiving" and "Miserie" seem plausible, if not praiseworthy, until the very end—they also share in their fall. The self-deception and pride of the speakers in many of Herbert's lyrics are thus, in a certain sense, duplicated in the reader, and as the speakers are dramatized, explored, and corrected, so is he.

LYRICS OF COMFORT

Throughout *The Temple*, Herbert's subject is not merely the correction of man's numerous flaws: Equally dramatic are the lyrics of recovery and comfort where the speaker overcomes not pride but feelings of unworthiness, uselessness, and weakness. For all his moments of self-scrutiny and criticism, Herbert is a remarkably gentle poet, and he knows when to remind his readers how securely he feels that they are ground in God's mercy. Without God, he explains, human beings are nothing—a premise that many modern readers find ex-

tremely discouraging—but he goes on to add that human beings need not be without God. For Herbert, man is constantly cheered and renewed by God's presence: In "Aaron," feelings of worry about being a priest give way to calm confidence as soon as one sees that Christ "is not dead,/ But lives in me while I do rest"; in "The Flower," sadness about the fragility of life and poetry turns into a heightened sense of joy and beauty, truly "thy wonders"; and in "The Elixir," all human effort, as long as it is done "for thy sake," becomes "drudgerie divine," pleasant and ennobling.

"LOVE"

God's voice and presence appear throughout the volume, but nowhere so movingly as in the last poem of "The Church," "Love" (III). Here God and man meet face to face, and though a lesser poet might not have been able to withstand the temptation to overembellish the scene, Herbert's dramatic lyric is as understated as it is powerful. God is love, "quick-ey'd Love," whose every word and movement is meant to comfort an extremely shy human guest who is humbly aware that he is "Guiltie of dust and sinne." Man's unworthiness, however, is finally beside the point: Stated in its simplest possible terms, God knows, forgives, accepts, and redeems man.

Simple words of paraphrase, however, can never tell the whole story. "Love" (III) is not a statement but an enactment, not a bit of theological argument or explanation but a dramatization of a devotional gesture. From the beginning of "The Church," as he notes at the conclusion of "The Reprisall," one of Herbert's main tasks is to show how "In thee [Christ] I will overcome/ The man, who once against thee fought." The particular action and quiet tone of the last lines of "Love" (III)—"You must sit down, sayes Love, and taste my meat:/ So I did sit and eat"—confirm that the battle, against God and against himself, is over, celebrated by a meal that is simultaneously a lover's banquet, a communion service, and his first true taste of heavenly joy.

TODAY'S READER

Modern readers are justifiably impatient with and even suspicious of poets of belief. Generations of unskilled, moralizing, prescriptive, sanctimonious versifiers have spoiled the name of religious poetry, which despite its noble intentions, often seems to falsify and oversimplify life. Readers need not, however, be impatient with or suspicious of Herbert for these reasons. His faith encompasses and overcomes but does not exclude restlessness, doubt, and worry. *The Temple* records a wide range of spiritual experiences and moods, and Herbert flees from neither simplicity nor complexity, qualities which neither life nor art can long do without. Herbert's poems continue to strike readers as honest, perceptive, and compelling statements about his day-to-day affairs of the spirit and perhaps about their own as well.

OTHER MAJOR WORKS

NONFICTION: *A Treatise of Temperance and Sobrietie of Luigi Cornaro*, 1634 (translation); *Outlandish Proverbs Selected by Mr. G. H.*, 1640 (as *Jacula Prudentum*, 1651); *A Priest to the Temple: Or, The Country Parson His Character and Rule of Holy Life*, 1652.

MISCELLANEOUS: *The Works of George Herbert*, 1941, 1945 (F. E. Hutchinson, editor).

BIBLIOGRAPHY

Bloch, Chana. *Spelling the Word: George Herbert and the Bible*. Berkeley: University of California Press, 1985. The central book in Herbert's poetic and devotional life was the Bible, and Bloch explores the implications of this in fascinating detail. She examines not only Herbert's use of typology and his allusions to and direct quotations from the Bible but also subtler patterns of biblical influence in Herbert's poems of praise, thanksgiving, instruction, and affliction.

Charles, Amy M. *A Life of George Herbert*. Ithaca, N.Y.: Cornell University Press, 1977. Charles's extensively documented biography usefully corrects the oversimplified view of Herbert common since Izaak Walton's unreliable *Life of Mr. George Herbert* (1670). Charles organizes her book around the key places of Herbert's life, especially Cambridge, London, and Wiltshire, and supplements the sparse details of his life with rich commentary on his family, university career, and final years as parish priest in Bemerton.

Clarke, Elizabeth. *Theory and Theology in George Herbert's Poetry: Divinitie, and Poesie, Met*. Oxford, England: Clarendon Press, 1997. Explores the relationship between George Herbert's poetry and the notion of divine inspiration rooted in devotional texts of his time. Includes bibliographical references and indexes.

Fish, Stanley. *The Living Temple: George Herbert and Catechizing*. Berkeley: University of California Press, 1978. Fish attempts to resolve the apparent contradiction that Herbert's poetry appears both calm and unstable by linking *The Temple* to catechizing. Like a catechism, Herbert's poems surprise and test readers, but they are framed within a larger pattern of firm knowledge and faith. Using this model, Fish offers teasing examinations of how the poems constantly undermine themselves.

Hodgkins, Christopher. *Authority, Church, and Society in George Herbert: Return to the Middle Way*. Columbia: University of Missouri Press, 1993. A critical analysis in which Hodgkins demonstrates that George Herbert's poetry is predominantly nostalgia for old English social, political, and religious customs. Identifies the changes in his poetry as reflections of the changing times.

Stewart, Stanley. *George Herbert*. Boston: Twayne, 1986. In this brief study, Stewart surveys Herbert's life and writings in both poetry and prose and counters emphasis on Herbert's Protestantism by emphasizing his close connection with medieval Catholicism and High Anglican devotion. He concludes with a fine chapter on Herbert's influence on other seventeenth century poets and a helpful annotated list of key critical works on Herbert.

Strier, Richard. *Love Known: Theology and Experience in George Herbert's Poetry*. Chicago: University of Chicago Press, 1983. Strier offers penetrating critical readings of many of the key poems of *The Temple*, examining in particular how they confirm Herbert's deep debt to Protestant theology, especially that of Martin Luther. For Strier, Herbert's poems focus repeatedly on the unreliability of reason and the drama of human unworthiness rendered inconsequential by divine love.

Summers, Joseph H. *George Herbert: His Religion and Art*. 1954. Reprint. Cambridge, Mass.: Harvard University Press, 1968. This biographical and critical study is the best starting place for a study of Herbert. Individual chapters focus on such topics as Herbert's life and times, his religious Anglicanism as a generous mediation between Puritan and Catholic beliefs and practices, his poetic language and metrical inventiveness, and his innovative use of traditional poetic and musical forms.

Vendler, Helen. *The Poetry of George Herbert*. Cambridge, Mass.: Harvard University Press, 1975. While Vendler does not completely disregard the theological context of Herbert's poems, her focus is on close readings that stress poetic and emotional complexity. Her model is the "reinvented poem," one that constantly questions itself and ends inconclusively. She comments on nearly all Herbert's lyrics and sees him at his best when he is ceaselessly analytical, dramatic, and wrought by conflict.

Sidney Gottlieb;
bibliography updated by the editors

ZBIGNIEW HERBERT

Born: Lvov, Poland; October 29, 1924
Died: Warsaw, Poland; July 28, 1998

PRINCIPAL POETRY

Struna światła, 1956
Hermes, pies i gwiazda, 1957
Studium przedmiotu, 1964
Selected Poems, 1968
Napis, 1969
Poezje wybrane, 1970
Wiersze zebrane, 1971
Pan Cogito, 1974 (*Mr. Cogito*, 1993)
Selected Poems, 1977
Raport z oblężonego miasta i inne wiersze, 1983
   (*Report from the Besieged City and Other Poems*,
   1985)
Elegia na odejście, 1990 (*Elegy for the Departure*,
   1999)
Elegy for the Departure and Other Poems, 1999

OTHER LITERARY FORMS

Zbigniew Herbert was primarily a poet, but he was also a prose writer of considerable originality and distinction. A collection of essays titled *Barbarzyńca w ogrodzie* (*Barbarian in the Garden*, 1985) appeared in Poland in 1962; these essays are a unique combination of personal, richly poetic, firsthand description with analytical, scholarly research. Herbert also wrote several plays, including radio plays as well as works for the stage; a collection of his dramatic works was published in 1970 under the title *Dramaty* (plays).

In addition, Herbert published works in a genre of his own invention, his "apocryphas." These prose pieces are a synthesis of the short story and the essay; they contest traditional accounts or interpretations of major historical events and present the very different ("apocryphal") interpretations of the author. Although most of Herbert's apocryphas take their subjects from Western European history, some go farther afield—to Chinese history, for example. A collection of these works, "Narzeczona Attyli" (Attila's fiancé), has been awaiting publication in Poland for some time.

ACHIEVEMENTS

Zbigniew Herbert exerted great influence as a poet and as a moral force both in Poland and Western Europe. He was above all the spokesman of the individual conscience. He excited interest as a political poet, but although his poems addressed major political issues, they went far beyond immediate issues and encompassed a broad range of problems that are both philosophical and personal. Herbert resisted categorization and never represented a group or school of any kind. He gave the impression of being entirely alone, answerable only to his conscience—yet he managed at the same time to pitch his voice in such a way that he was one of the most authentically public poets of the age. This was the paradox of Herbert that gives his poetry its particular stamp.

Although Herbert was an antirhetorical poet, it is difficult to separate the content of his writing from his style. His poetic forms and rhythms exerted a powerful influence on other poets. One of the two greatest living Polish poets (the other, Czesław Miłosz, has translated a number of Herbert's poems into English), his influence has been acknowledged not only by younger Polish poets such as Ryszard Krynicki, Stanislaw Barańczak, and Jacek Bierezin but also by a wide range of poets in America and throughout the West.

His influence was also recognized with several awards throughout his career. In 1958 he won the Polish Radio Competition Prize and in 1964 he received the Millenium Prize from the Polish Institute of Arts and Sciences (United States). For his contribution to European literature, he was awarded the Nicholas Lenau Prize (Austria) in 1965. In 1973 he received both the Alfred Jurzykowski Prize and the Herder Prize. He also won the Petrarch Prize in 1979, the Bruno Schulz Prize in 1988, the Jerusalem Literature Prize in 1991, and a Jurzykowski Foundation Award.

BIOGRAPHY

Zbigniew Herbert grew up in the Polish city of Lvov; in 1939, when he was fifteen years old, this part of Poland was invaded by the Soviet Union. Herbert began to write poetry during World War II, and the war permanently shaped his outlook. The face of postwar Poland was permanently changed, socially, physically, and politically: Herbert's native city became part of the Soviet Union.

In 1944, Herbert studied at the Academy of Fine Arts in Krakow—he was always interested in painting, sculpture, and architecture—and a year later he entered the Academy of Commerce, also in Krakow. In 1947, he received a master's degree in economics and moved to Toruń, where he studied law at the Nicolas Copernicus University. He received the degree of master of laws in 1950. Herbert stayed on in Toruń to study philosophy and was influenced by the philosopher Henryk Eizenberg. In 1950 he lived briefly in Gdańsk and worked there for the *Merchant's Review* before moving to Warsaw, where for the next six years he held a variety of jobs: in the management office of the peat industry, in the department for retired pensioners of the Teachers' Cooperative, in a bank, in a store, and in the legal department of the Composers' Association.

Herbert's poems began to appear in periodicals in 1950, but no collection was published in book form; during the increasing social and cultural repression of the Stalinist years, several of the magazines publishing Herbert's work were closed by the government. It was only after the "thaw" of 1956 that his first two collections of poems were published, almost simultaneously. The event of publication after enforced silence is poignantly described in Herbert's poem "Drawer."

In the late 1950's, Herbert made his first trip to Western Europe. His collection of essays, *Barbarzyńca w ogrodzie*, reveals the impact of this experience. Herbert spent the years from 1965 to 1971 abroad, based in West Berlin but traveling to many countries, among them Greece, Italy, France, and the United States. He spent the 1970-1971 academic year teaching at California State University, Los Angeles. After returning to Poland to live in 1971, Herbert moved to West Berlin again in 1974, staying there intermittently until 1980, when he returned to Warsaw. He again left Poland in 1986 in protest of Communist policies but returned to Warsaw once communism was ended around 1990. Around this time his health began to deteriorate and when, in 1996, the Nobel Prize was awarded to Wislawa Szymborska (only seventeen years after another Pole and adopted Californian, Czesław Miłosz), the joy of this deserved distinction was mixed with a touch of regret for Herbert. For

Zbigniew Herbert

many, Herbert's achievements equaled those of his two honored compatriots, and there were those who considered him superior to both. He died in Warsaw on July 28, 1998.

ANALYSIS

Zbigniew Herbert was a member of the generation of poets who came to maturity during World War II. They are known as the War Generation, but they are also referred to in Polish literary criticism as *Kolumbowie* (Columbuses), because it was they who first "explored" the new postwar reality. This generation proved to be one of the most talented in twentieth century Polish literature, including, in addition to Herbert, such varied figures as Tadeusz Różewicz, Miron Bialoszewski, Tymoteusz Karpowicz, Wislawa Szymborska, and Anna Świrszczyzyńska. The war left an indelible imprint on all of them; as late as 1969, in the poem "Prologue," which introduced Herbert's fourth collection of poems, he wrote about those who took part in the war: "I must carry them to a dry place/ and make a large mound of sand/ before spring strews flowers for them/ and a great green dream stupefies them."

LESSONS FROM THE WAR

Few assumptions about the world and about civilization—what it is and what it is not—survived the war unscathed. The sense of continuity was broken, and many shared the vantage point of what might be called the "rubbish heap" of the present. Herbert's poem "Przebudzenie" ("Awakening"), from *Wiersze zebrane*, is a fine description of this attitude. It begins:

> When the horror subsided the floodlights went out
> we discovered that we were on a rubbish-heap in very
>   strange poses
>
> . . . .
>
> We had nowhere to go we stayed on the rubbish-heap
> we tidied things up
> the bones and sheet iron we deposited in an archive
> We listened to the chirping of streetcars to a swallow-
>   like voice of factories
> and a new life was unrolling at our feet.

The common experience of wartime destruction and of starting a "new life" united Herbert and the other members of his generation, and gave them their unique temporal perspective. They drew very different conclusions from their experiences, however, and there is no consensus of attitude or ideology among them. Herbert is sometimes linked to Tadeusz Różewicz, another poet who lived through the war, because they were close in age and were both moralists. Their values, however, were in fundamental conflict. Różewicz's poetry after the war denied all previous values and emphasized purely personal experience, whereas Herbert arrived at entirely different conclusions. He wrote:

> Something makes me different from the 'War Genera-
> tion.' It seems to me that I came away from the war
> without accepting the failure of the earlier morality. It
> is still attractive to me most of all because I painfully
> feel the lack of tablets of values in the contemporary
> world.

Herbert was a more positive poet than many other members of the War Generation, although rarely have positive values been won against greater opposition and with greater struggle.

USE OF THE PAST

One of the most striking features of Herbert's poetry was the manner in which he used the past. It was remarkably alive for him; historical figures frequently appeared in his poems with the vividness of our contemporaries. In Western Europe and the United States, poetry that invokes the great traditions of Western culture is often associated with reactionary values. In Poland during the decade after World War II, however, a paradoxical situation arose in which some of the writers who had most completely rejected the prewar culture found that they had little basis for rebelling against the Stalinist present; on the other hand, a poet such as Herbert, who strived to repossess the culture of the past, was able to express revolt in one of its most intense and radical forms.

It is a mistake, however, to call Herbert a "classicist," as he was sometimes labeled. For him, the past was not a static source of value; he is not an antiquarian, as his poem "Classic" made clear. For Herbert, the past represented living experience rather than lifeless forms. He did not adhere to the past at the expense of the present; instead, the past is the ally of the present. The distinction is a useful one and even crucial, for Herbert's use of the past was the opposite of that of a genuine classicist such as the contemporary Polish poet Jaroslaw Rymkiewicz. Herbert felt the dead are alive, made of flesh and blood. If there was a division between the past and the present, it was often spatial rather than temporal. In Herbert's famous poem "Elegy of Fortinbras," he assumed the persona of Fortinbras, who addresses Hamlet as his immediate contemporary; the poem ends by translating death into terms of spatial distance: "It is not for us to greet each other or bid farewell we live on archipelagos/ and that water these words what can they do what can they do prince." The ever-present tension and dialogue between past and present did not restrict Herbert's poetry; in fact, the reverse is true: He confronted the world in all its breadth, and his experience is placed in a seamless historical continuum.

INFLUENCES

Herbert was influenced both by the Catastrophists, such as Czesław Miłosz, who stressed philosophical and historical themes in their poetry, and by the avant-garde poets of the 1920's and the 1930's, such as Józéf Czechowicz, who eschewed punctuation. Several other poets of Herbert's generation who lived through the war also turned to the avant-garde in their search for poetic forms that were capable of rendering their experience. Many of Herbert's early poems shared the phenomenological preoccupations of the avant-garde; at the most fundamental level, poets were asking: How can one describe the world? How can one describe one's experience? Herbert's poems "I Would Like to Describe," Attempt at a Description," "Voice," "Episode in a Library," "Wooden Bird," "Nothing Special," and the later "Mr. Cogito Thinks About the Voice of Nature and the Human Voice" all approached this concern from different angles.

UNIQUE PUNCTUATION

Herbert's phenomenological preoccupations are particularly apparent in his handling of punctuation. Conventional punctuation was not automatically accepted by serious poets in Poland after the war, and Herbert was by no means alone in questioning its use. Prewar avant-garde poetry still enjoyed a high esteem among poets, and punctuation also had a political coloring: Lack of conventional punctuation became associated with revolt and with individualism. Herbert's first collection of po-

ems, *Struna światła* (chord of light), which represented work done during the first postwar decade, eschewed conventional punctuation, particularly the use of periods. In a prose poem written somewhat later, titled "Period," he placed punctuation in a very broad historical and social context; the poem ends: "In fact the period, which we attempt to tame at any price, is a bone protruding from the sand, a snapping shut, a sign of a catastrophe. It is a punctuation of the elements. People should employ it modestly and with proper consideration, as is customary when one replaces fate." In other words, for Herbert, the "period" marked a hiatus in the texture of the world and of reality. Its thoughtless use is presumptuous and even destructive, violating the living tissue and the continuities of the real world.

In England and America, the traditional use of punctuation was—with notable exceptions—maintained after the war; accepted practice had not been put into doubt by new experience. In Central and Eastern Europe, however, especially in those countries which had experienced the worst destruction during the war and which had suffered under Nazi occupation, conventional punctuation was sharply questioned, along with other inherited poetic practices. Indeed, punctuation became one of the major topoi, or themes, of postwar Eastern European literature—a theme that has yet to receive sufficient critical attention.

USE OF PROSE

Parallel to Herbert's radical reduction of punctuation (he frequently employed dashes, as well as occasional parentheses and question marks) was his development of the prose poem; much of the prose poetry written in Poland since 1957 was influenced by Herbert's explorations in the genre. While his first collection of poems was restricted to largely punctuation-free verse, his second, *Hermes, pies i gwiazda* (Hermes, dog and star), had a separate section of prose poems, comprising sixty of the book's ninety-five poems. Originally, Herbert intended these prose poems to constitute a separate volume, and he called them *bajeczki* (little fairy tales). His project was thwarted by an editor, however, and they were included in his second volume of poems. In subsequent volumes, Herbert intentionally interspersed prose poems among his punctuation-free verse poems, and this became his regular practice.

In his third collection, *Studium przedmiotu* (study of the object), the ratio of prose to verse poems is eighteen to twenty-eight; in his fourth collection, *Napis*, fourteen to twenty-six; and in his fifth, *Mr. Cogito*, five to thirty-five. The choice to use one form or the other was always highly deliberate with Herbert, depending on his attitude toward the subject of the poem, his distance from it, and his tone, as well as the rhythms he used. The more reflective poems, especially those that assume considerable distance from the subject and those that use strong irony, were frequently written in prose. The various modulations of these two basic forms were always carefully worked out. This is only one of the ways, but an important one, in which the form of Herbert's poetry is related to its content, and the resulting range of forms is astonishingly broad.

INANIMATE OBJECTS

Herbert's many poems about inanimate objects should be seen in the context of his attempt to explore the relationship between experience and reality. Herbert wrote fine poems (and again, his practice has been imitated by many younger Polish poets) about a pebble, a stool, a watch, armchairs, a clothes wringer; indeed, the title of one of Herbert's collections of poems means "study of the objects." Some readers have wondered why a poet such as Herbert, who was so consistently concerned with life and human experience, should write about lifeless objects. The poems were part of Herbert's attempt to separate what is subjective from what is objective and to see clearly. In the poem "I Would Like to Describe," Herbert wrote: " . . . so is blurred/ in me/ what white-haired gentlemen/ separated once and for all/ and said/ this is the subject/ and this is the object." Herbert was always interested in inanimate objects, but not *because* they are inhuman. On the contrary, he tended to find human traits in objects (rather than vice versa) and to discover a community of interest between humans and objects. In a conversation in 1969, Herbert said that he was fascinated by objects because

they are so completely different from us, and enigmatic. They come from a totally different world from ours. We are never sure that we understand them; sometimes we think so, other times we don't, depending on how much of ourselves we project on them. What I like about them is their ability to *resist* us, to be silent. We can never really conquer them or tame them, and that is good.

Thus, while Herbert humanized objects, he also respected their fundamental opacity. At the same time, there was no abyss between man and inanimate objects—on the contrary, there is a sense of identity with them, based on the realization of human fallibility and imperfection. Herbert was engaged in breaking down the barrier between the human and the inanimate and in extending the limits of the human.

ENDURING THEMES

Herbert's first volumes contain most of the themes that interested him throughout his career; certainly, his enforced silence during the Stalinist decade in Poland, from 1946 to 1956, contributed to the ultimate strength of these poems. Others of his generation, such as Różewicz and Szymborska, adapted to the Stalinist demands and were permitted to publish; as a result, their books that appeared during this period are inferior to their later work. Herbert wrote for a long time without a public audience, but his poems assumed a firm core of consistency and strength as he developed his themes. First among them was the imperative to resist, to listen to the individual conscience; he was willing to suffer for his ideals. The moral demand to direct one's gaze at reality itself is present in Herbert's first volume, as is his gift for infusing the past with life. Some of these early poems are about the difficulty of writing after the war, about the loss of ideals; at a profound level, they reflected Herbert's formal training in philosophy—not because the poems are explicitly "philosophical" but because they are informed by an intense, overriding concern for truth and clarity. Herbert consistently directed his attention outward, at the world as it exists. It was this stance that also makes it possible to consider Herbert as a "public" poet. The lines in these early poems are relatively short; they often seem to follow the rapidity of thought, and they already display the great agility that is typical of Herbert's style.

HERMES, PIES I GWIAZDA

Herbert's second volume, *Hermes, pies i gwiazda*, is marked by the sudden infusion of prose poems in the second section. Irony becomes more prominent, and the poet's tone is increasingly mordant. The individual lines of poems are sometimes longer in this volume, although there is the same agility and rapid spontaneity of association that marked the first volume.

STUDIUM PRZEDMIOTU

Herbert's third volume, *Studium przedmiotu*, carried his dialogue with objects to its furthest point. The volume is also among his most critical, taking aim at contemporary social and political reality. As he did this, however, Herbert evidently felt the need to assume a greater distance—critical distance—from the reality he sought to describe, and thus he adopted a variety of personas in this volume, giving his critique greater depth and historical reverberation.

NAPIS

Herbert's fourth book, *Napis* (inscription), shows a greater concern for textures, and the lines have become somewhat longer. This volume has been called Herbert's "expressionist" volume; in it, he gave full rein to his delight in dramatic metaphor. He developed further many of his previous themes, but the reader senses that there is a shift in the target of Herbert's sense of revolt. Focusing less on immediate social and political realities, the poet was increasingly concerned with the universal and the archetypal, extending back into the past and into the subconscious.

MR. COGITO

In Herbert's fifth collection of original poems, *Mr. Cogito*, the dominant theme is the identity of the self, explored through the title figure. Sometimes the persona of Mr. Cogito is entirely playful; at other times, he allows the poet to confront painful personal matters without obtrusive emotion. The volume contains a number of poems of striking philosophical depth, among them "Georg Heym—the Almost Metaphysical Adventure" and "Mr. Cogito Tells About the Temptation of Spinoza." Many poems in this book have longer lines than those of earlier volumes and are more meditative. They require a longer, deeper breath to read aloud, and some are very close to prose. A few are quite long and have a highly developed logical structure.

REPORT FROM THE BESEIGED CITY AND OTHER POEMS

Report from the Beseiged City and Other Poems marks a sharp return to topicality and contemporary events—in this case, the coup d'état of General Jaruzelski and the imposition of martial law. Again, events are seen in the context of a broad historical framework, but they are observed in the present, taking place under one's very eyes, as the title indicates. There are two major themes in this new collection. The first is the necessity to "bear witness" to the truth. Herbert assumed the role of chronicler of the "siege," and although he said this role is secondary to that of the people who are fighting, it is really of the utmost importance. Knowledge of the true nature of the war, the reality of the lives of those who take part in it, and even their very identity depend on the chronicler, the poet. The second major theme is suffering and the need for suffering, never presented fatalistically but rather combined with the imperative to revolt no matter how hopeless the situation. Rarely in contemporary literature has the need for resistance been stated so clearly, so forcefully, and with so few illusions.

The collection begins where "The Envoy of Mr. Cogito," the last poem in Herbert's previous volume, ended. In that poem, Herbert wrote that even if "the informers executioners cowards . . . will win," the individual must still revolt:

> go upright among those who are on their knees
> among those with their backs turned and those toppled
>   in the dust
> you were saved not in order to live
> you have little time you must give testimony
> . . . .
> go because only in this way will you be admitted to the
>   company of cold skulls
> to the company of your ancestors: Gilgamesh Hector
>   Roland
> the defenders of the kingdom without limit and the city
>   of ashes
> Be faithful Go

ELEGY FOR THE DEPARTURE

Elegy for the Departure was first published in Polish under the title *Elegia na odejście* in 1990. This volume brings together work uncollected in English from throughout Herbert's career, culling from his early works of 1956-1969 and from the 1990 volume. Its four sections draw chronologically from his writing, and a more depoliticized Herbert is evident in the selected poems. Darkness was certainly pouring into Herbert's poetry, and possibly into his life, around the time when most of the poems from the 1990 collection were composed, but it was present in his verse from the beginning, especially in his early poems, in which he bid farewell to the ghosts of his friends fallen during the war.

The English volume opens with one such poem, called "Three Poems by Heart," which originally appeared in "Chord of Light." The first of its three movements is a search for a person, or rather for a language, in which the memory of that person can be extracted from among horrifying images of wartime destruction:

> I can't find the title
> of a memory about you
> with a hand torn from darkness
> I step on fragments of faces
> soft friendly profiles
> frozen into a hard contour.

Readers will discern that here Herbert's voice is growing more personal, his irony more astringent. His stoicism seems to falter in the face of very human and basic fear, as in "Prayer of the Old Men," that ends on a mournful, pleading note:

> but don't allow us
> to be devoured
> by the insatiable darkness of your altars
> say just one thing
> that we will return later

The book's last section, focused on Herbert's late poetry, contains some of his most spacious work, a groundspring of vitality and variety. There is a tarantella of a poem about Leo Tolstoy fleeing family and keepers at the end "with great bounds/ his beard streaming behind." There is a somber, perfectly tuned image of Emperor Hirohito, history's wildness departed, laboring over a *tanka* (a genre of Japanese poem) about the state railroad. There is the unsparingly registered loss of "Prayer of the Old Men":

> when the children women patient animals have left
> because they can't bear wax hands
> we listen to sand pouring in our veins
> and in our dark interior grows a white church
> of salt memories calcium and unspeakable weakness.

The book ends with the expansive "Elegy for the Departure of Pen Ink and Lamp," in which Herbert laments the three objects presented in the poem both as companions of studious childhood and as symbols of the three ideas most often associated with "the Herbertian" vision: the critical mind, a "gentle volcano" of imagination, and "a spirit stubbornly battling" the darker demons of the soul. The tone of the poem is cryptic, and readers are unable to discern the nature of the personal catastrophe that seems to lie at its center. One learns only that the departure of the objects was caused by an unspecified "betrayal" on the part of the speaker and that it leaves him feeling guilty and powerless. The book ends with last words of the poem: "and that it will be/ dark." With that, the door closed on the work of Zbigniew Herbert.

OTHER MAJOR WORKS

PLAYS: *Jaskina filozofów*, wr. 1950's, pb. 1970 (*The Philosophers' Den*, 1958); *Dramaty*, pb. 1970 (collection of four plays).

NONFICTION: *Barbarzyńca w ogrodzie*, 1962 (*Barbarian in the Garden*, 1985); *Martwa natura z wedzidlem*, 1993 (*Still Life with a Bridle: Essays and Apocryphas*, 1991); *The King of the Ants: Mythological Essays*, 1999.

BIBLIOGRAPHY

Alvarez, A. *Beyond All This Fiddle: Essays, 1956-1967*. New York: Random House, 1969. A collection of critical essays on various authors including Herbert.

Barańczak, Stanisław. *Ironia i harmonia: Szkice o najnowszej literaturze polskiej*. Warszawa, Poland: Czytelnik, 1973. Introduction to Polish literature of the twentieth century by one of the premier scholars of Polish literature. In Polish.

Carpenter, Bogdana. "The Barbarian in the Garden: Zbigniew Herbert's Reevaluations." *World Literature Today* 57, no. 3 (Summer, 1983): 388-393. Excellent coverage in English.

Carpenter, Bogdana, and John Carpenter. "The Recent Poetry of Zbigniew Herbert." *World Literature Today* 51, no. 2 (Spring, 1977): 210-214. Two students of Herbert review his poems of the mid-1970's.

_____. "Zbigniew Herbert: The Poet as Conscience." *Slavic and East European Journal* 24, no. 1 (1980): 37-51. Covers themes and issues in Herbert's works.

Carpenter, John, and Bogdana Carpenter. "Zbigniew Herbert and the Imperfect Poem." *The Malahat Review* 54 (April, 1980): 110-122. On Herbert's poetics.

Levine, Madeline. *Contemporary Polish Poetry, 1925-1975.* Boston: Twayne, 1981. An introduction to and overview of Polish literature of the mid-twentieth century. Includes index and bibliography.

Sandauer, Artur. *Poeci czterech pokoleń.* Kraków, Poland: Wydawnictwo Literackie, 1977. A critical introduction to the history of Polish poetry. In Polish.

Wisniewska, Lidia. *Miedzy biegunami i na pograniczu: O Bialym malzenstwie Tadeusza Różewicza i poezji Zbigniewa Herberta.* Bydgoszcz, Poland: Wyzsza Szkola Pedagogiczna w Bydgoszczy, 1999. Criticism and comparison of the works of Herbert and Tadeusz Różewicza. Published in Polish with summaries in English, French, and German.

John Carpenter,
updated by Sarah Hilbert

ROBERT HERRICK

Born: London, England; baptized August 24, 1591
Died: Dean Prior, England; October, 1674

PRINCIPAL POETRY

Hesperides: Or, The Works Both Humane and Divine of Robert Herrick, Esq., 1648 (includes *Noble Numbers*)

The Complete Poetry of Robert Herrick, 1963, 1968

OTHER LITERARY FORMS

The vast majority of Robert Herrick's poetic works are included among the approximately fourteen hundred pieces contained in *Hesperides,* Herrick's only known published book of verse. There are about forty poems from contemporary manuscripts and poetic miscellanies that have at various times been attributed to Herrick, but their authorship is not certain and has been the subject of much editorial speculation.

Herrick is known exclusively for his poems. All that survives of his writing apart from his poetry are some fifteen letters he wrote when he was a student at Cambridge University (1613-1620) and a few pieces of official correspondence. The only other piece of writing with which he has been linked is a manuscript of poems and prose of topical interest, part of which has been said to be in his handwriting; his role in its authorship and compilation, however, is not yet firmly established.

ACHIEVEMENTS

In the more than three and a half centuries during which Robert Herrick's poems have circulated, his reputation has fluctuated widely. The earliest reference to him places him as a young poet in the company of the much esteemed Ben Jonson and Michael Drayton. One of his editors, J. Max Patrick, argued in *The Complete Poetry of Robert Herrick* (1968) that there is evidence to believe that Herrick was sufficiently well regarded in certain circles to warrant a relatively copious first printing of his collected works in 1648. What does not seem in doubt, however, is the oblivion into which his poems appear to have fallen within fifty years of their publication. References to Herrick are scant in the eighteenth century, and it was only in 1796 that an inquiry about him in a literary magazine began to stimulate the interest that would lead to his poetic exhumation. In 1810, an edition of about three hundred of his poems restored Herrick to public attention, providing a preview of the public response that his work would generate throughout much of the nineteenth century. Herrick came to be read and extolled for his numerous delicate and euphonious lyrics, while his satiric and "gross" epigrams proved offensive to Victorian sensibilities and went largely unpublished.

Modern critics have attempted to assess Herrick's achievements in a more balanced and integrated way; if they have generally been less rhapsodic over the "prettiness" and "sweetness" of his lyrics than the Victorians, they have also paid closer attention to the technical virtuosity and poetic acumen at work in the numerous forms and modes that *Hesperides* exhibits. In

Robert Herrick (Hulton Archive)

lucidity to suggest precisely what T. S. Eliot once claimed that Herrick's verse lacked: the "continuous, conscious *purpose*" characteristic of all major poets. Moreover, in his intermingling of ostensibly sensuous and erotic poetic experiences with religious, elegiac verse and political poems on the English Civil War, Herrick is increasingly coming to be seen not as a poetic trifler of exquisite sensibilities and superficial concerns but as a man very much of his war-torn, "troublesome" times. His "book" forms a significant poetic testament to a critical period in the evolution of English society and English poetic art.

BIOGRAPHY

What is actually known and documented of Robert Herrick's life forms a rather skeletal outline and can be readily summarized. Christened in London on August 24, 1591, Herrick appears to have been the seventh child of Nicholas and Julian Herrick. Nicholas, a goldsmith, fell to his death from an upper story of his house on Goldsmith's Row on November 9, 1592, just two days after he had recorded his will. Obvious questions were raised concerning the possibility that Herrick's father had committed suicide, and they appear never to have been resolved. The nature of Herrick's boyhood education is not known, but in 1607 he was apprenticed for ten years to his uncle, Sir William Herrick, a wealthy goldsmith and merchant. The venture, however, was aborted, when, in 1613, at the relatively old age of twenty-two, Herrick was enrolled with his uncle's consent in St. John's College, Cambridge. It was during his years at Cambridge that Herrick wrote the series of letters to his uncle cited above, all of which are variations on the timeless theme rehearsed by innumerable students: Send more money. Herrick received his A.B. degree in 1617, his A.M. in 1620, and in 1623 he was ordained an Anglican priest, serving in 1625 as chaplain in the Duke of Buckingham's abortive military expedition to the Isle of Rhe. In 1630, Herrick left London and its cultural life to assume the vicarage of Dean Prior in rustic Devon, a position he held until 1647, when, because of his loyalties to the king and the Church of England, he was expelled, an event that was the catalyst for his return to London and the publication of his works in the following year. Nothing else is known of him until the restoration of the

the modern "rediscovery" of the excellences of seventeenth century poetry, Herrick has fared well, ranking with John Donne, George Herbert, Andrew Marvell, and John Milton, as among the most widely read poets of the period; his "To the Virgins, to Make Much of Time," "Corinna's Going A-Maying," and "Delight in Disorder" are among the most often anthologized seventeenth century poems. At the same time, comparisons with his prominent poetic contemporaries—although occasionally invidious—have not only confirmed Herrick's stature but also helped to define the nature of his poetic achievement and appeal. To be sure, Herrick's poems do not have the dramatic intensity and immediacy of Donne's, and his one published volume may appear to lack the polyphonic self-scrutiny and structural rigor at work in Herbert's *The Temple* (1633). Still, from the concerns and images that recur throughout the *Hesperides*, there emerges a sense of a unifying poetic sensibility molding and transforming the disparate materials of the real world to reflect a coherent aesthetic vision. This vision is of sufficient strength and monarchy in 1660, when he successfully petitioned the Crown to be reinstated as vicar of Dean Prior, where, with no evidence of strife, he resided until his death in 1674 at the age of eighty-two.

That the documentary detail of Herrick's life is so easily reducible to a thumbnail sketch has made the task of relating Herrick's biography to his writings a difficult one. Indeed, early commentators tended, understandably, to approach Herrick's poems as if they were authorized and unexpurgated autobiography, attempting to fill in the gaps in what was known of his life from the evidence of his works. Such a modus operandi runs the obvious risk of confusing the poetic persona that Herrick creates in his verse with the person whom the persona masks, ultimately doing little to elucidate either the works or his life. Here is one example of this kind of mythobiography: In his poetry, Herrick projects himself as a discriminating analyst of feminine charms addressing a great number of meditations on beauty to personages such as Corinna and Perilla, Julia and Dianeme. This projection, however, does not in itself suggest that Herrick necessarily led the life of a libertine during his years in London nor that indeed Corinna and Perilla, Julia and Dianeme, ever existed. Nor, for that matter, is there any evidence to suggest that Herrick wrote such poems to while away the idle moments he supposedly endured after leaving the high life of London for the rustic seclusion of Dean Prior.

Still, invalid as it may be to take Herrick's poetry as the true mirror of his life, one can see, even from the sketchy biographical information available, how from the diverse strands of his background he wove the richly textured tapestry one encounters in his verse. His poems bespeak the deep immersion in the classics that he would have experienced at Cambridge, along with a full acquaintance with the poetic conventions current in the poetic circles of London in the 1620's. At the same time, his verses are steeped both in the biblical learning that any moderately educated person at the time would have imbibed and in the tenets of Anglican doctrine with which an Anglican cleric—especially one eager to demonstrate his steadfast affiliation with the Church of England—would have been conversant.

More important, Herrick draws upon the various elements of his life to create a complex and engaging poetic persona. The Herrick one meets in the poems is a character who bestrides different and potentially opposed worlds, seeking to reconcile them in the alembic of his verse. Classicist and divine, he pretends to be not merely the priest of both Apollo and the Christian God but also their poetic priest who aspires to serve the interests of both with one poetic vision and one poetic vocabulary—"Part Pagan," as he puts it in "The Fairie Temple: Or, Oberons Chappell," and "part Papisticall." Poetic priest of Bacchus and Eros as well, Herrick celebrates sensual experience for its physical value and for its intimations of a higher truth. Portraying himself as a votary of urban delights, Herrick asserts his contempt for the unrefined elements of country life but labors to articulate the ways in which country customs—like urban refinements—have their part to play in his poetic universe.

Above all, Herrick's poetic persona would have his readers believe that his life is embodied in his volume of verses, that his "book" is all that he has been and all that he hopes, in the face of encroaching mortality, "Times trans-shifting," to be. In that fictive sense his works are, indeed, "autobiography." In fact, though the literary record of the turbulent mid-seventeenth century is far from closed, there is no more eloquent testimony to the degree to which Herrick appears to have made his "book" his "Pillar" than the total literary silence into which he seems to have fallen after the publication of his verse, and in which the final twenty-five years of his life are enveloped. Vexing as this silence has been to critics and biographers trying to learn more about the man, it has had the effect of underscoring the point of one of Herrick's epigrams: "Seldome comes Glorie till a man be dead."

ANALYSIS

Robert Herrick is a poet of numerous modes and moods, whose poetic pleasure it appears to have been to present his readers with a world of abundance and variety. One need look no further than the opening poem in *Hesperides*, "The Argument of His Book," to get a sense not only of the dimensions of this plenitude but also of the underlying concerns that give Herrick's world its coherence, as well as of the style in which his poetic vision is mediated.

"THE ARGUMENT OF HIS BOOK"

Ostensibly, "The Argument of His Book" is a mere inventory, a poetic table of contents to the diverse "topics" treated in the hundreds of poems to follow, from the simple things of nature, "Brooks, Blossomes, Birds, and Bowers," to the grand themes of divinity, heaven, and hell. In its construction, the poem bespeaks simplicity, with the various categories to be treated in Herrick's ensuing poems neatly itemized in a series of seven rhymed, end-stopped couplets, each beginning with the unpretentious declaration "I say" or "I write." Yet the incantatory power that builds with the sonorous reiteration and skillful alternation of "I sing" and "I write" gives aural hints of an art that merely counterfeits artlessness and transforms a "simple" and potentially monotonous list into something like a litany, a ritualized—some have said liturgical—chant. As a result, the overtly commonplace and profane subjects, the things of nature, the country customs, the affairs of youth and the heart, acquire a heightened significance and a semblance of parity with the explicitly spiritual themes. The things of this world and those of the next, "The Argument of His Book" would suggest, do not entail essentially opposed visions of experience but, when apprehended with the heightening power of art, are revealed to be complementary constituents of one coherent universe. In "The Argument of His Book," Herrick brings together the contrarieties of existence but does so to reveal their intrinsic harmony and point to their ultimate reconciliation.

What art heightens, it changes; and so "metamorphosis," both as theme and as the image of art's heightening power, is central to "The Argument of His Book" and remains so throughout Herrick's verse. Thus, the "Blossoms" to which Herrick alludes in the opening lines of "The Argument of His Book" are of interest not only as flowers but also as emblems of a continuous process of mythopoeic creation and transformation, as parts of the story of "How Roses first came Red, and Lillies White." In this way, nature heightened by art becomes art. The liquids of nature, the "Dewes" and "Raines," are fused and merged within the closure of one of Herrick's couplets with liquids refined by art "piece by piece" into cosmetic artifacts: "Balme," "Oyle," "Spice," and "Amber-Greece." In the sensual delights "of Youth, of Love" the poet finds the "access" to sing, not of sensuality or wantonness but, in the phrase that has come to be synonymous with Herrick's personal signature, "cleanly-Wantonnesse."

What is "cleanly-Wantonnesse"? At once a figure of oxymoron, or paradox, and pleonasm, it is nothing less than the seminal conceit of Herrick's verse. On one hand, it evokes a wantonness in all its pejorative senses of lasciviousness, unruliness, and extravagance rendered "cleanly," chaste, and orderly; on the other hand, it suggests a "wantonnesse" in the less opprobrious sense of innocent playfulness that by its very definition must be "cleanly." In the very "play" of the conceit, Herrick suggests the way in which nature unrefined and base can be redeemed and shown to be "cleanly" by the power of poetic language.

"Cleanly-Wantonnesse," however, denotes not only nature heightened by art but also nature preserved by art from the destructive forces to which it is subject: time, decay, dissolution. For all of their sensuous appeal and connotations of fecundity, the "Dewes" and "Raines" that Herrick includes in his poetic repertoire are also conventional metonyms of transience and mourning and anticipate the presence in his verse of a strong elegiac impulse. Indeed, in Herrick's poetic world, of which "The Argument of His Book" is an epitome, the metamorphosis of art and the mutability of nature are inseparably linked, the former arising from and responding to the latter, even as the stories of "How Roses first came Red, and Lillies White" are immediately preceded in the same couplet by the theme of "Times trans-shifting." As natural phenomena, the sensual delights "of Youth, of Love" are as ephemeral as blossoms; yet the "cleanly-Wantonnesse" that Herrick envisions in these experiences is proof against mortality and, in the world of his verse, as enduring as the "Heaven" that Herrick hopes to have, "after all."

"THE AMBER BEAD"

The images and issues introduced in "The Argument of His Book" recur in much of Herrick's verse and are particularly conspicuous in the works for which he is best remembered. One thinks immediately, for example, of "The Amber Bead," Herrick's delicately terse four-stanza, four-line adaptation of one of Martial's epigrams. Its very size a reflection of the theme it articulates, "The Amber Bead" affirms the victory of art over the corruptive processes of nature. By being "cleanly" encased within a bead of amber, a common fly acquires a permanence and significance in death that it could never have attained in life. In turn, the congealed amber becomes a medium of art that derives its function from the heightening it imparts to a thing of nature. Within the metamorphosis of the poem, the bead becomes a chamber, and, as if to accentuate the triumph of art over decay, the poet notes in the closing distich that though as "Urne," as an emblem of death, the bead may be "little," as "room," a place more often associated with living things, it is "More rich than Cleopatra's Tombe."

THE JULIA POEMS

The dialectic encapsulated in "The Amber Bead" is explored in varying tonalities and degrees of resolution over a wide range of Herrick's poems and is evident even in the many ostensibly frolicsome compliments that Herrick pays to his poetic mistresses, chief among whom is Julia. Most of these unfold as celebrations of some particular part or aspect of the lady's person: "Julia's Clothes," "Julia's Ribbon," "Julia's Breath," "The Candor of Julia's Teeth," to name a few. All are exercises in synecdoche and in extolling the part they celebrate the personage the part adorns. Each, in turn, is a piece of hyperbole, investing the item in question with miraculous properties, the reader is led to believe, simply because the item is an extension of Julia. Heightened in the process, then, are Julia herself and all that belongs to her, and nature as well, which is at once surpassed and enriched by Julia's very presence.

Were all these poems on Julia straightforward variations on this formula, they would not have engendered and sustained the interest they have. Instead, they are exercises in discovery, and by indirection and implication lead the reader to infer what is never explicitly stated. Consider, for example, the distich on Julia titled "Another upon her weeping." At a glance the poem would appear to belabor the obvious and in none too artful a manner. Told merely that Julia "by the River sate; and sitting there,/ She wept, and made it deeper by a teare," the reader wonders why it need be said twice in one line that Julia was sitting by the river and may ask why, if the consequence of Julia's weeping is merely the addition of

one tear to the river, the poem needed to be written at all. It is only when one considers the secondary sense of "deeper" that the experience of the poem and the game of the poet become clearer. The dropping of a tear has made the river not merely physically deeper but also metaphysically deeper, more significant. The poet does not know, or, at least, does not say how this change has been accomplished; it is a mystery, and mysteries, as supernatural phenomena, are not to be solved but contemplated as manifestations of a higher power. Hence the deliberation with which the poet twice mentions where Julia was sitting: By protracting the line, he prolongs the experience and calls attention to the nub of the mystery, that Julia's mere presence enhances the value of the river. The poet has stated nothing of the kind; indeed, he could insist slyly that he was only describing a physical occurrence. Rather, it is Herrick's art here, as elsewhere, to immerse his reader in the process of discovery and permit him to recognize firsthand the power of poetic art to transform the commonplace into something extraordinary and imperishable.

"JULIA'S PETTICOAT"

Herrick's success in implicating the reader in the experience and interpretation of a poem is very much in evidence in another work involving Julia, the longer and more prominent "Julia's Petticoat." An apt illustration of "cleanly-Wantonnesse," the poem makes it clear that "cleanliness" and "wantonnesse" are in the eye of the beholder, both the poet who observes and describes the movements of Julia's gown and the reader who observes the poet and participates vicariously in the poet's experience.

From the very outset, however, it would appear that the experience in which the reader is invited to participate vicariously is itself vicarious and rather disingenuous. Unlike "Another upon her weeping," this piece is explicitly addressed to Julia, and by exploiting the rhetorical figure of synecdoche the poet can hide, as it were, behind Julia's petticoat and pay her compliments without being so bold as to address them to the person herself. In this way the interests of both parties are served: Julia can be flattered without blushing or having her modesty impugned, and the poet has license to fantasize as sensually as he pleases while feigning detachment.

The poem opens with the poet making an effort in good faith to keep his mind on "cleanly" things. Julia's garment is not merely any common blue petticoat, but an "Azure," therefore, heavenly blue, "Robe." Lest anyone suspect that the poet is paying more attention to Julia herself than to the gown she is wearing, he describes the notion of the garment as "ayrie," as if to suggest that it is animated either by its own power or by some force independent of Julia. Yet the poet's efforts to maintain a distinction between the movements of the petticoat and the movements of its wearer seem less and less successful, and the more "wanton," the more playful and unruly the motions of the skirts, the more "wanton," the more lasciviously suggestive grows the language of the poet. In the space of only two lines, the poet applies the words "erring," "wandring," and "transgression" to the undulations of the gown, all words associated with moral levity and sufficiently synonymous to suggest that the poet may find their suggestions delectable enough to linger over them and turn them over in his mind. Moreover, the animation of the skirts becomes more and more like personification, as the gown is said to "pant, and sigh, and heave," with obvious sensual connotations.

Still, who is finding titillation in the petticoat, the poet or the reader? After all, the poet could claim that those questionable words "erring," "wandring," and "transgression" are in their root meanings simply words of motion and direction and can be taken to imply moral lapse only by those susceptible sorts who would read such meaning into them. As for the poet, the more sensually and erotically suggestive the gyrations of Julia's petticoat grow, the more energetic he becomes in finding images for the experience that transcend the physical and carnal. Thus, when at one point the gold-spangled gown moves with especial freedom and makes "a brave expansion," the poet likens it to a "*Celestiall* Canopie," leaving it to the more corrupted mind of his reader to ponder the perspective from which the unfurling of a canopy is normally viewed.

In fact, the poet would lead the reader to view the experience with dual vision, if the reader has the imagination to transcend his own "wantonnesse." On one hand, the poet lets the reader take in every sensual nuance the scene evokes; on the other, he asks the reader to cele-brate the poetic vision that has brought the petticoat so suggestively to life. This is evident in what could be called, in more than one sense of the word, the climax of the poem, when the petticoat swirls so "wildly" that it clings to Julia's "thighs," thus forcing the poet to acknowledge for the first time the body beneath the garment that he has pretended to ignore all along. The poet responds very much as other poetic voyeurs of the period do, by being melted down, "As Lovers fall into a swoone." Here, though, the word "as" and the simile it introduces are significant. For ultimately, though the poet may be "like" a lover and feel "as" a lover might, he is *not* a lover. Unlike his poetic contemporaries, though he may lie "Drown'd in Delights," he could not "die," in the Renaissance sense of attaining sexual consummation. Nor was it sensual rapture that melted the poet down, but a "conceit," an idea, a fancy, a "conceitedness."

In short, what Herrick celebrates in "Julia's Petticoat," more than the petticoat itself, more than Julia herself, is the poetic apprehension, the "conceit," that makes the petticoat so seductive. Nor is this to suggest that the physical experience in the poem has been nullified or minimized. Rather, the poet insists, the physical experience has been perfected because as aesthetic vision it will always yield pleasure and never be consumed. Such is the sense conveyed in the poet's closing declaration that were the vision of Julia's petticoat to move, like the cloud guiding the Israelites in the desert, to "Life Eternal," he could still love. He could love because his sensual experience has been refined and made imperishable by art, and will endure long after Julia and her petticoat have ceased to move so enchantingly.

"DELIGHT IN DISORDER"

The ascendancy of art over nature, the making "cleanly" by art of what is "wanton" in nature, is virtually formalized as an aesthetic principle in what is probably Herrick's most familiar poem, "Delight in Disorder." Another of Herrick's meditations on feminine attire, the poem owes much to the song, "Still to be neat, still to be dress'd," from Ben Jonson's *Epicœne: Or, The Silent Woman* (1609); even so, in the particular terms and style in which it delineates the relationship of art and nature, "Delight in Disorder" is distinctly Herrick's poetic credo and a centerpiece of his verse.

On the face of it, the poem would appear to illustrate without qualification what its title professes: delight in disorder, preference for the unruliness of nature unregulated and unrestrained by art. Assuming the part of voyeur he had played in "Julia's Petticoat," the poet takes obvious delight in enumerating the various possibilities of "disorderliness" in a lady's attire, in envisioning a ribbon out of place, a cuff undone, a shoelace only loosely knotted. Moreover, the language in which these traces of untidiness are couched is of that suggestive sort that either reveals in the poet or elicits from the reader questions prompted by decidedly libertine impulses. These deviations from order and art are seductive, and when the poet concludes that they "bewitch" him more than when art is "too precise in every part," it would seem that for once Herrick permits the claims of nature to hold sway. A closer look at the texture and language of the poem, however, suggests that the poet himself is being quite precise when he objects not to art but to an art that is "too precise," too rigid, too artificial, too obviously artful, and that the "disorder" so esteemed in the poem is but a sensuously alluring illusion kept under firm control by a poetic art "neatly" disguised.

A hint of this control lies in the care with which the poet casts the experience in the form of a tightly structured argument, inscribed within one fourteen-line rhymed couplet sentence. Its central premise is stated in the opening couplet and illustrated by a series of five examples presented in the next five couplets, followed by a summation in the final two lines. Each example of disarray is introduced as if it were one more item on a checklist: "A Lawne," "An erring Face," "A Caffe neglectfull," "A winning move" in the "tempestuous" petticoat, "A careless shoe-string." The orderliness with which these items are listed seems modified by the sensuous turbulence that they arouse in the poet, but the more one perceives the excitation these examples produce, the more one is compelled to acknowledge the logical validity of the poet's main point and the rhetorical artistry with which he has presented it: Disorder, at least when packaged this way, is, indeed, delightful.

The last qualification is crucial. It is not just any kind of "disorder" that pleases, but a certain kind, a "sweet disorder," even as the "distraction" produced when the lady's "Lawne" is thrown errantly about her shoulders is

a "fine distraction." Such phrases as "cleanly-Wantonnesse" and, for that matter, the title of the poem, are rhetorical figures, oxymora, coupled antitheses, suggesting that what pleases the poet most about the carelessness he describes is the reconciliation it embodies of the abandon of nature and the purposefulness and girding control of art.

This "girding" control is literally evident in the fact that the seemingly uninhibited play of the various pieces of the lady's clothing does not prohibit them from performing the binding and restraining functions for which they are designed. The "Lawne" cast into "distraction" still envelops the shoulders "about" which it is "thrown." The "Lace" errs, strays, only to "Enthrall" yet another girdling item, the stomacher. The cuff, though "neglectfull," still encircles the wrist within it, while the "winning wave" produced by the "tempestuous" petticoat provides but a passing hint of expression and freedom in a garment intended to conceal and bind. Lastly, the shoestring is not so "carelesse" as to be unknotted, and in that "tye," that final reconciling of disparates, the poet transforms the "sweet disorder" he had set out to elucidate into its inverse, a "wilde civility," as the spontaneity of nature ultimately finds its most eloquent expression as a triumph of art.

"To the Virgins, to make much of Time"

Herrick's best art is a playful art but not escapist. In celebrating the virtues of artful playfulness, of "cleanly-Wantonnesse," Herrick does not avert his eyes—nor does he allow his readers to do so—from the darker side of nature, particularly the issues of transience and mortality. What gives Herrick's greatest poems their force is their sense of urgency in the face of temporal encroachment.

One familiar form assumed by urgency is that of the invitation or petition, an exhortation to participate in the poet's artfully playful world before it vanishes. Herrick is the foremost English poetic heir to the classical elegists and their recurrent theme, *carpe diem* (seize the day): Take advantage of the time. Such is the sole message of "To the Virgins, to make much of Time," best known for its opening line, "Gather ye Rose-buds, while ye may." A wholly unambiguous piece, the poem drives its point forcefully home through the poet's dexterous exploitation of rhyme. Using a feminine rhyming pattern in alternate lines, the poet creates an illusion of constant motion in order to persuade the virgins whom he is exhorting to marry, that their prime cannot endure, and that the only constant in life is the relentless motion of time and decay. Hence, time's "flying" today is coupled with "dying" tomorrow, while the closer to its apex the sun seems to be "getting," the nearer, in fact, it is to its "setting." To resist the opportunity to "marry" now is inevitably, the poet tersely concludes, to "tarry" forever.

"CORINNA'S GOING A-MAYING"

The *carpe diem* theme so succinctly intoned in "To the Virgins, to make much of Time" acquires a much fuller resonance and richness in "Corinna's Going A-Maying," one of the greatest of "invitational" poems, and Herrick's most profound scrutiny of the relationship between "cleanly-Wantonnesse" and transience, "Times trans-shifting." As it is in so many of Herrick's poems, the "wantonnesse" of "Corinna's Going A-Maying" is readily apparent. Cast in the conventional form of an aubade, a dawn song of a lover to his beloved, the poem presents a numinously sensual landscape and a speaker who has obviously thought of a wide array of rhetorical ploys with which to tease and cajole his mistress into going out with him to frolic and "fetch in May." Obviously of the persuasion that the best defense is a good offense, the poet anticipates any objections Corinna might raise about the moral propriety of what he is asking by impugning the morality of her reluctance. Corinna is a "sweet Slug-a-bed" for being so indolent as to stay in bed when all of nature has already risen and commenced its daily tasks. Nor can Corinna hide behind her virgin innocence when "A thousand Virgins on this day,/ Spring sooner than the Lark, to fetch in May." Is it not immoral to engage in such sensual delights? It is sacrilege not to; the birds have already said matins and sung hymns. Hence, Corinna is urged to "put on your Foliage" and join the rest of creation, for to do so is natural, and to do what nature ordains is holy.

That "cleanliness" is inherent in the "wantonnesse" in which the poet wishes Corinna to participate is, then, the central premise of the poet's argument. To be sure, that sensual pleasure is a sacred duty may seem an argument born of expediency and self-interest, and that the poet has to elaborate on this theme for four of the poem's five stanzas may suggest that Corinna, for one,

has not been readily persuaded. Still, one comes to admire not only the ingenuity of the poet's reasoning but also the scope of his vision. The workings of the entire world are cited as proof that the sacred and profane respond to the same laws. The universe he describes is one in which country and city are interpenetrated with the same divinity to form one all-encompassing temple in which each porch and door, "An Arke or Tabernacle is/ Made up of white thorn neatly enterwove." All humanity, the poet would have Corinna believe, participates in the same sacred rites of love, both those who formalize their love in the religiously and legally sanctioned customs, plighting their troth and finding a priest, and those who proceed directly to consummation. In the face of such evidence, can Corinna possibly maintain that the poet's invitation to go "A-Maying" is anything worse than "harmless follie"?

The poet does not wait for Corinna's reply—poets who issue such invitations, it seems, rarely do. Rather, as if to imply that enough time has been spent on polite discussion, the poet turns urgently in the last stanza of the poem to the *carpe diem* argument to confront Corinna with the imminence of their dissolution. Harsh and jarring as this concluding picture of existence is, it only follows logically from the vision of nature presented in the preceding parts of the poem. Corinna had been urged to partake of the sensual rites enjoyed by all of creation because she is part of that creation, but as a part of it she must share both in its joys and in its inevitable decay and disintegration.

Had Corinna been paying close attention to the poet's imagery, she might have anticipated this turn in the argument. The flowers with which the poet had exhorted her to bedeck herself flourish and fade with the seasons. The "gemmes" which, near the beginning of the poem, the poet had promised Corinna would be strewn "in abundance" upon her if she came forth, were but crystallized dewdrops, the illusion they conveyed of time standing still lasting only until the sunbeams melted them away. By the end of the poem the solidified dews have evanesced and liquefied in the poet's imagination into a vast sea in which "All love, all liking, all delight/ Lies drown'd with us in endless night." His sportiveness turned somber, the poet renews his appeal to Corinna to enjoy the "cleanly-Wantonnesse" of nature's rites while there is still time, "and we are but decaying," an ambiguous phrase which could be taken to mean not only that the poet and Corinna have not fully decayed yet, and so still have some time, but also that life itself is "but" a process of decay, which makes the injunction to seize the moment all the more imperative.

NOBLE NUMBERS

The elegiac apprehension of mortality that dominates the ending of "Corinna's Going A-Maying" informs much of Herrick's verse and recurs even in his explicitly Christian devotional verse. Found in *Hesperides*, this grouping of "divine" poems is referred to as his *Noble Numbers*. These poems present the idea that theological belief in an everlasting spiritual life is not forceful enough to dispel the emotional certainty with which Herrick ponders the dissolution of nature. Thus, in the poem titled "Eternitie," the poet thinks of how all "times" are "lost i'th Sea/ Of vast Eternitie," and if Corinna and her poetic lover had had to look forward to being drowned in "endless night," the poet in "Eternities" defines spiritual immortality as being "Drown'd in one endlesse Day."

"TO BLOSSOMS"

The hope to which Herrick always returns is art and the celebration of artistic vision. Art alone can freeze or at least arrest the processes of natural decay to prolong and preserve sensual beauty. Such is the lesson of one of the loveliest and most thoughtful of Herrick's meditations on mortality, "To Blossoms." Opening with the central question of all elegies, the poet looks at some falling leaves and asks simply, "Why do yee fall so fast?" Consolation comes only when the poet looks again and sees the leaves as pieces of art, as leaves of a book in which one can "read" a valuable lesson: "How soon things have/ Their end, though ne'r so brave." The recognition that even falling leaves, if viewed artfully, have a lesson to teach permits the poet to see the dropping of the leaves in a new way; instead of "falling fast," they now "glide," their descent softened, the pleasure they afford prolonged.

"THE PILLAR OF FAME"

The hope that reposes in Herrick's verses is epitomized in the poem that stands at the end of *Hesperides*, "The Pillar of Fame." A figure poem, its lines are arranged in such a way as to form the shape of a funereal

monument, "Charm'd and enchanted" to endure all the ravages of mortality. If the evidence of time has any weight, Herrick's art has not betrayed its maker's confidence.

BIBLIOGRAPHY

Berman, Ronald. "Herrick's Secular Poetry." In *Ben Jonson and the Cavalier Poets*, edited by Hugh Maclean. New York: W. W. Norton, 1974. Berman uses "A Nuptiall Song" to illustrate his thesis that the *Hesperides* contains ostensibly secular poems that embody an intellectual tension between the sensual life and the Christian view of that life. For Berman, Herrick's "secular" poetry, as expressed in "The Hock Cart," transforms natural objects by making them symbols of a spiritual state.

Coiro, Ann Baynes. *Robert Herrick's "Hesperides" and the Epigram Book Tradition*. Baltimore: The Johns Hopkins University Press, 1988. Coiro argues for the structural integrity of *Hesperides*, insisting that the collection of poems be read as a whole. After exploring the cultural, political, and generic implications of the title of the book, she provides a history of the epigram tradition and concludes with chapters on the epigrams of praise, mocking, and advice. The copious notes provide a rich bibliography to Herrick's criticism.

De Neef, A. Leigh. *"This Poetic Liturgie": Robert Herrick's Ceremonial Mode*. Durham, N.C.: Duke University Press, 1974. De Neef reads *Hesperides* as "a kind of dialectic" in which different personae or voices, which are nevertheless united by a common attitude, address the reader. These voices—the pastoral, courtly, realistic (epigrammatic), and artistic— suggest that there is a ritualizing, ceremonial process that unifies the *Hesperides*. Contains some excellent close readings of several of Herrick's poems.

Guibbory, Achsah. *Ceremony and Community from Herbert to Milton: Literature, Religion, and Cultural Conflict in Seventeenth-Century England*. New York: Cambridge University Press, 1998. Offers new and original readings of Herbert, Herrick, Browne, and Donne in an examination of the relationship between literature and religious conflict in seventeenth century England.

Low, Anthony. *Love's Architecture: Devotional Modes in Seventeenth-Century English Poetry*. New York: New York University Press, 1978. In his chapter on Herrick, Low discusses, with frequent quotations, his subject's Epicureanism and devotion to pleasure, even in the sacred poems in *Noble Numbers*. For Low, even the meditative poems reflect a religion of pleasure, and the goal is often the place, heaven, not God.

Marcus, Leah S. *The Politics of Mirth: Jonson, Herrick, Milton, Marvell, and the Defense of Old Holiday Pastimes*. Chicago: University of Chicago Press, 1986. Marcus devotes a chapter of her book to Herrick's *Hesperides*, which she discusses in terms of their relationship to the revelry and holiday moods associated with the monarchy. Marcus regards Herrick as the Cavalier poet-priest and finds in *Hesperides*, particularly in "Corinna's Going A-Maying," the sexual energy associated with her thesis.

_____. *Robert Herrick*. Rev. ed. New York: Twayne Publishers, 1992. Updated in the light of later scholarship. A comprehensive critical study of Herrick's work. Includes bibliographic references and index.

Rollin, Roger B., and J. Max Patrick, eds. *"Trust to Good Verses": Herrick Tercentenary Essays*. Pittsburgh: University of Pittsburgh Press, 1978. Contains an introductory essay concerning trends in Herrick's criticism, as well as essays on the love poetry, on visual and musical themes, on the political poetry, and on the evolving of Herrick's literary reputation. A welcome feature is the inclusion of a selected, thoroughly annotated bibliography of Herrick's criticism.

Swardson, H. R. *Poetry and the Fountain of Light: Observations on the Conflict Between Christian and Classical Traditions in Seventeenth-Century Poetry*. Columbia: University of Missouri Press, 1962. Acknowledging the tension between the pagan and the Christian in poems in both *Hesperides* and *Noble Numbers*, Swardson states that Herrick is not a religious poet. In a few poems, such as "Corinna's Going A-Maying," Swardson believes that the ceremonial or ritual in nature elevates the pagan subject matter.

Thomas Moisan;
bibliography updated by the editors

HESIOD

Born: Ascra, Greece; flourished c. 700 B.C.E.
Died: Ozolian Locris, Greece(?); unknown

PRINCIPAL POETRY

Theogonia, c. 700 B.C.E. (*Theogony*, 1728)
Erga kai Emerai, c. 700 B.C.E. (*Works and Days*, 1618)

OTHER LITERARY FORMS

Hesiod is remembered only for his poetic works. A number of poems are erroneously attributed to Hesiod, among them *Shield* (c. 700 B.C.E.) and *Catalogue of Women* (c. 700 B.C.E.).

ACHIEVEMENTS

Hesiod was respected, next to Homer, as a leading poet-teacher of the early Greeks, and his reputation stood all but unchallenged throughout Greco-Roman antiquity. For lack of a better term, he is sometimes described as a didactic poet, although neither of his poems follows the strict definition of a genre that took shape more than four centuries later in the Hellenistic age. Hesiod adapted the formulaic style, meter, and vocabulary of the Homeric epic to two ancient genres from the Near East. The *Theogony* is Hesiod's version of the type of creation epic found in the opening chapters of the biblical Genesis, and it had a formative influence on the great classical poets from Aeschylus to Ovid, similar to the hold that the book of Genesis has had on poetic imaginations in the Christian era. The *Works and Days* springs from an equally ancient genre, the protreptic "wisdom literature" that influenced several books of the Old Testament and that can be traced back as far as the third millennium B.C.E. In Greece's more secular civilization, Hesiod's works never attained the status of holy writ; it was never supposed that the *Theogony* or the *Works and Days* was divinely inspired (save in a general way by the Muses) or that the myths contained in them were canonical. Hesiod's writings have a religious and moral fervor, however, and his version of Greek mythology, although far from complete, remains the most important systematic account of the Olympian deities to the present day.

BIOGRAPHY

Most of the available information about Hesiod's life comes from his own poetry. In the *Works and Days*, he says that his father came from Cyme, an Aeolian Greek town on the west coast of Anatolia about thirty miles southeast of Lesbos, and worked as a merchant seaman until hard times forced him to relocate to a homestead across the Aegean, in poor country northeast of Mt. Helicon, in Boeotia. Hesiod was born and reared on his father's farm in Ascra, which he describes as "nasty in winter, disagreeable in the summer, and never good." In the *Theogony*, he describes his investiture as a poet by the Muses while he was herding sheep at the foot of Mt. Helicon. The parallels to this scene are Eastern, recalling the shepherd Moses, called by God away from his sheep, and Amos, summoned from his herds to prophesy. Another passage in the *Works and Days* tells of winning a trophy for a hymn at a festival in Chalcis on the nearby island of Euboea. Several references to

Hesiod (Hulton Archive)

a dispute with his brother Perses in the *Works and Days* indicate that Perses bribed the authorities when their father's estate was divided and took more than his share, but squandered his ill-gotten gain and came begging back to his brother. In the *Works and Days*, Hesiod uses the occasion of Perses' unjust behavior as the context for his discussion of *Dikē* (justice) and *Hybris* (violence).

The traditional belief that Homer and Hesiod once met in a poetry contest and a supposed text of the contest (the *Agon*) are rejected by modern scholars. Thucydides adds that Hesiod was killed in Ozolian Locris, just west of Delphi, by local inhabitants in the precinct around the temple of Nemean Zeus; Hesiod was taken off guard because an oracle had told him he would suffer this fate at Nemea, a prophecy that he had interpreted literally as meaning the city itself. Pausanias and other sources say that a tomb of Hesiod could be seen at Orchomenos, in northwest Boeotia.

Much of this, even the autobiographical passages in Hesiod's works, must be approached with reservations. Greek and Roman tourists would pay well to see "Hesiod's tomb," and the story of his death conforms to standard features of the cult of the poet-hero (such as the death of Orpheus). The dispute with Perses is impossible to reconstruct clearly, although its literary function is easily understandable. That Perses was an actual individual living in Hesiod's day has sometimes been questioned; his name may be fabricated from the root *perth-, pers-* to suggest "waster" or "spoiler." The meeting with the Muses of Mt. Helicon speaks for itself, and even the name "Hesiod" may be a generic nom de plume, "he who emits the voice" (as "Homer" may be interpreted as "he who fits [the song] together").

What remains of the life of Hesiod is probably better founded in truth. One of the few ancient poets who came from humble origins, Hesiod grew up in poverty; it is speculated that he adopted the trade of a rhapsode, reciting and composing poetry in central Greece. Unlike his fellow Boeotian Pindar (518 B.C.E.-c. 438 B.C.E.), Hesiod never embraced the values of the nobility with their contempt for the peasant, although in the *Theogony*, he acknowledges the Muses' scorn of rustics. Throughout his two masterpieces, Hesiod retained the little man's distrust of corrupt "kings," the peasant's grim view of life's realities, and a democrat's belief in an abstract justice that is indifferent to social rank.

ANALYSIS

Judged purely as literature, Hesiod's work falls short of the highest rank. His writing is rambling and structurally undisciplined; his values are sometimes quaint, his lists of gods or seasonal farm chores tedious. Hesiod was more than a compiler of myth and wisdom, however; his lofty ideals, connecting justice with a vision of growing divine order, break through the catalog form with striking force; his unsentimental view of life, in which just behavior and hard work are the chief determinants of every man's destiny, is forceful and intentionally inspirational. Hesiod's writing is less graceful than robust; much of its power is derived from a vision that made it a cornerstone of Greek thought and an influential component in the classical reading of neoclassical poets from the Renaissance through the Romantic era.

Because nothing is known of Hesiod's immediate literary context, it is hard to say how much is new in his two poems. It is sometimes rashly said that he was the first Greek to make a systematic account of divine mythology, the first to introduce Eros as a divinity, the first to engage in philosophy, and the like. There is no evidence for such claims, and although it may be reasonable to speculate with scholar G. S. Kirk that Hesiod came "near the beginning of a Boeotian poetical renaissance," it is hard not to see him as the culmination of a long oral tradition in Greece. His adeptness with formal battle pieces, tales of giants and monsters, and catalogs (a form often linked to Boeotia in particular), his self-consciousness in his vocation as a poet and his emphasis on the Muses and the poet's craft mark him as the practitioner of an already well-established and popular art. Attempts to link him with the subsequent development of philosophy in Ionia should be qualified by the fact that Hesiod's thought is still more theological and mythical than rational. Indeed, it fits the character of his thought better to study him as a theologian, although it is a matter of speculation which theological constructs are uniquely his.

It is also appropriate to perceive Hesiod as an essentially oral poet in the sense that (like Homer's) his style is formulaic to a high degree and his manner of organizing material is paratactic, "being often based" as Kirk says, "on the exploitation of casual associations rather than on the principle of strictly logical development." In *The Winged Word: A Study in the Technique of Ancient Greek Oral Composition as Seen Principally Through Hesiod's "Works and Days,"* Berkley Peabody explores the ramifications of the allegedly oral composition of Hesiod's poems, but because the rigid distinctions that Milman Parry and A. B. Lord attempted to draw between oral and literary compositions have been found inapplicable in other traditions, it is no longer considered possible to define orality with absolute rigor. Hesiod's tradition and style are undeniably oral, but he may have used writing, and, as Eric Havelock has long since argued, the permanence of the written word (introduced to Greece in about 750 B.C.E.) may well have inspired him to compose the kind of works he left behind.

THEOGONY

The earlier of Hesiod's poems, the *Theogony* (genealogy of the gods) gives an account in about one thousand lines of dactylic hexameter of the origin of the world and the forces that control it: gods, Titans, monsters, and personified abstractions, down to the establishment of Zeus's world order. Although the original shape of Hesiod's poem has been confused by later additions to the text, it was clearly his intention to represent as his main theme the progressive emergence of order from disorder. G. S. Kirk states that through a rambling and digressive narrative the reader can detect "some idea of a gradual progress, not only from more abstract cosmogonical figures to more concrete and anthropomorphic ones, but also from cruder and more violent gods to cleverer and more orderly ones." The core around which Hesiod's divine order forms is the succession of three generations: the first parents Uranus (sky) and Gaea (earth), then Cronus, then Zeus. Friedrich Solmsen has suggested an additional theme:

The series of events which make up the history of the divine dynasty from the birth of Uranus and Gaea to Zeus's advent to power has been determined by, and owes its intrinsic unity to, the idea of guilt and retribution. It forms one great conception.

After a long poem in the form of a hymn to the Muses, Hesiod starts his account with a brief cosmogony beginning with Chaos (void) and after him Gaea, Tartarus, and Eros (the primal generative force). Here and throughout his poem, Hesiod does not distinguish clearly between places (Tartarus), conditions (Chaos), physical entities (Gaea), and forces (Eros). Following a common instinct of Greek thought, Hesiod admits them to his narrative as characters first and in addition whatever else that their names, genealogy, or actions might imply. Cosmogony therefore quickly fades into theogony as the process of generation takes over. Chaos gives birth to Erebus and Night, who in turn couple and beget Aether and Day. Gaea gives birth to Uranus, the Hills, and Pontus (the sea) before coupling with her son Uranus (in the primordial union of earth and sky) to produce six male and six female Titans, three Cyclopes, and three Hundred-Handers. As Uranus tries to prevent the birth of these last three, Gaea conspires with Cronus, the youngest of her Titans, who cuts off his father's genitals as Uranus attempts to couple once more with Gaea. The blood from this mutilation falls to earth to beget the Furies, the Giants, and the tree nymphs. Cronus hurls his father's severed genitals into the sea, where the foam that spreads around them produces Aphrodite (the foam-, or *aphro-*, born goddess), who steps ashore at Cyprus attended by Eros and Himeros (longing).

There follows a catalog of some three hundred gods descended in two separate lines from Chaos and Gaea: from the former, the troublesome children of Night; from the latter, the three sons and three daughters of Pontus, who, in turn, spawn some fifty nymphs and a variety of other gods, sprites, and monsters. The catalog culminates in the birth of Zeus, son of the Titans Cronus and Rhea. Fearing a predicted overthrow by one of his children, Cronus swallows his offspring until their mother contrives to feed him a stone in the place of her youngest child, Zeus, who is kept safe in a Cretan cave. When Zeus comes of age, he forces Cronus to disgorge his three sisters Hestia, Demeter, and Hera and his brothers Hades and Poseidon. He also frees his uncles the Cyclopes, who in gratitude give him the thunder and lightning with which to win and maintain his rule.

Hesiod's genealogy concludes with an account of the progeny of the Titan Iapetus, with particular attention to the story of Prometheus, a trebly etiological myth, explaining first, why the gods are served the bones and fat of a sacrifice rather than the good meat; second, how Prometheus stole fire for man; and third, how Zeus contrived woman for mortals as a curse to offset the Promethean blessing of fire. The general lesson of the Prometheus myth, with the chaining of the trickster-Titan who dares to match wits with Zeus, is the impossibility of escaping the wrath of Zeus. This intimation of Zeus's knowledge and power leads to an account of the great battle by which Zeus established his power in the world, the Titanomachy, a showpiece of action poetry that became the prototype of John Milton's War in Heaven. As earlier in the poem Zeus had freed the three Cyclopes, so he now frees the Hundred-Handers to fight as his allies against the Titans. The blazing, crashing, thundering battle that ensues has a Wagnerian quality and may well have been a great crowd pleaser at Hesiod's recitations. It is followed by an equally impressive vision of the underworld to which Zeus consigns the conquered Titans. In a final battle (perhaps composed as a kind of encore to the Titanomachy), Zeus overcomes the last challenge to his power, the monster Typhoeus, a storm god who is defeated and, like the Titans, thrown into Tartarus. The poem concludes with Zeus's dispensation of titles and privileges to the Olympian gods and a series of seven marriages that consolidate his regime. In this genealogical coda, numerous younger gods are born, including the motherless Athena and the fatherless Hephaestus. At some point after this, perhaps with the list of goddesses who have lain with mortal men, the genuine work of Hesiod is believed to give way to the work of post-Hesiodic redactors intent on grafting the *Catalogue of Women* onto the *Theogony*. Although it is not agreed exactly where the break comes, the composition becomes looser near the end, and scholar Kurt Von Fritz states: "The text constantly deteriorates, till at the end it just dissolves."

LITERARY AND MYTHIC INFLUENCES

It is likely that theogonic poetry was well established in Greek oral tradition for generations before Hesiod, possibly as early as the Mycenaean age. Accounts of the origin of the world, the birth of the gods, and the establishment of the present order occur in archaic cultures from Iceland to the Pacific. More specifically, according to M. L. West, Hesiod's "succession myth," tracing the transfer of power from Uranus to Cronus to Zeus, "has parallels in Oriental mythology which are so striking that a connection is incontestable." A Hurrian succession myth, preserved in Hittite texts four centuries before Hesiod, and the Akkadian Enuma Elis (early second millennium B.C.E.), the official theogonic text used in the Babylonian New Year festival, provide mythic parallels so close as to justify the conclusion that the core of Hesiod's *Theogony* is a synthesis of Eastern stories known to the Greeks since the Minoan-Mycenaean period or somewhat later. This is not to say that Hesiod merely imitated Eastern poetry; like everything else that the Greeks borrowed, it was refashioned into a document of Greek culture.

WORKS AND DAYS

The same is true of the *Works and Days*, which might be called "The Wisdom of Hesiod" because of its affinity with works of exhortation and instruction attested in Sumeria as early as 2500 B.C.E., with Akkadian and Babylonian texts from c. 1400 B.C.E. and with Egyptian Middle Kingdom "instruction" texts from about the same time. In fact, "wisdom literature" is nearly as widespread in world cultures as is theogonic poetry. Hesiod's *Works and Days* shows a particular affinity with Eastern parallels: The myth of the five races of man has counterparts in Persia, India, and Mesopotamia; instruction in Hesiod's poem comes from a victim of injustice, as in a number of Egyptian wisdom texts, one of them more than one thousand years earlier than Hesiod; and the fable of the hawk and the nightingale points to the Near East, where the animal fable goes back to the Sumerians. These affinities, among others, argue that the *Works and Days* is not only cognate with Near Eastern poetic themes but was actually influenced by them.

The *Works and Days* is not narrative in outline, as is the *Theogony*. Instead, it is presented as a miscellany of advice and instructive stories to Perses, the poet's wastrel brother, who had bribed the "kings" and cheated him in the division of their father's estate. Its two themes are justice and work, and Hesiod makes it his business to show how they are intertwined in the life of a successful man. After a short poem to Zeus, Hesiod corrects what he had said in the *Theogony* about Eris, or Strife, daughter of Night. There are not one but two types of strife—one evil, the other good. Good strife is the healthy competition that urges men on to greater efforts in their work. Hesiod repeats the story of Prometheus to explain why man has to work for his livelihood, elaborating the account of Pandora as if to imply that woman is the ultimate and definitive curse upon humanity.

As an alternative explanation of the wretched lot of man, Hesiod next offers the myth of the five races of man. This entropic version of human history, each generation being of a baser metal than its predecessor, contrasts significantly with the progressive history of the divine world in the *Theogony* and emphasizes the sense of hopeless distance between men and gods which runs through much Greek poetry, especially tragedy. The fable of the hawk and his helpless victim, the nightingale, points to the supremacy of force in the animal world; as for the human world, Perses is asked to consider how justice wins out over violence because of the actions of Zeus. The role of Zeus as a punisher of injustice can be seen early in the *Iliad* (c. 800 B.C.E.; English translation, 1611), and a passage in the *Odyssey* (c. 800 B.C.E.; English translation, 1614) contains the idea that good crops and abundant livestock are rewards given to a just ruler. What is remarkable in Hesiod is the forcefulness with which he links justice, prosperity, and the role of Zeus as the embodiment of a just providence. It is justice that separates human life from that of the beasts: This *nomos*, or sacred law, is the decree of Zeus, and the success or failure of a man's life is the final proof that nothing escapes the eye of Zeus.

If this assertion seems more a statement of religious belief than an observation of fact, it is tempting to look anachronistically forward to some of the teachings of Calvinism, especially those that associated virtue with prosperity. A significant comparison can also be made with biblical wisdom literature, where the association of virtue with prosperity is standard, as in Proverbs 13:22, 13:25, and 14:11, for example. The next section of the *Works and Days* may seem a step closer to such a comparison: Hesiod preaches a work ethic in his famous exhortation to Perses, which represents hard work as the virtue that brings prosperity and idleness as the vice that brings ruin (see Proverbs 6:6-11). In the world that Hesiod depicts, therefore, justice and hard work are the route to success, violence and idleness the guarantors of disaster.

Obviously, the latter precept concerning work versus idleness is less religious than pragmatic, and the poem perceptibly shifts its emphasis at this point from the mythical, moral, and metaphysical to the practical. The lines that follow are a series of proverbs on how to keep what you have, beginning with moral and religious maxims and ending with prudent social and personal advice, such as that against sweet-talking women who are after a man's barn. The rest of the poem consists of specific advice to the farmer, a sketchy kind of almanac telling when to plow and reap and what equipment to use, Hesiod outlining farming techniques, winter procedures, and other seasonal chores. He offers advice to the farmer who goes to sea to sell his goods; on when and how to marry; and on social, personal, and ritual hygiene. Finally, there is a list of good and bad days of the month.

Judged as a purely literary performance, the *Works and Days* is uneven, especially in the latter sections containing advice on farming, but students of the poem see a unity of conception and a dour kind of vigor which offsets some of its literary shortcomings. Occasioned by an act of injustice, the poem adheres to a single theme: Good farming is as much a part of justice as good statecraft would be for Plato in the *Politeia* (388-368 B.C.E.; *Republic*, 1701). Moreover, Hesiod's qualified pessimism and the vividness with which he reveals the harsh life of the farmer are an essential background to the stern values he preaches; there is little of the "pastoral" here. Hesiod lacks the aristocratic magnanimity of Homer and never achieves the smooth, leisurely expansiveness of Homeric narrative. In this respect, Hesiod's curt style is suited to the bleak life he represents. On the other hand, the explicit force of Hesiod's ethical vision surpasses anything in Homer. This is partly because the political context is more real to the modern reader: Instead of the "feudal" society of warrior-kings and their dependents, whose chief virtues lie in loyal service, Hesiod depicts independent men whose dignity lies in their ability to take care of themselves, their households, and their farms. The *Works and Days* is a moral and political tract that contrasts the justice of work not only with the idleness of fools but also with the corruption of "gift-devouring kings" who enjoy indolence at the expense of others. The poem is thus more than an interesting glimpse of eighth century B.C.E. Boeotian farm life; it is a valuable cultural document. Its significance for the Hellenic civilization then taking shape lies in the assertion of a divine and impersonal justice working for the common man as well as for the great. The ideal of a universal, evenhanded law was essential not only to the political life of the Greeks but also to the idea of early Greek tragedy, where *Dikē* is as inevitable as the other workings of nature.

BIBLIOGRAPHY

Gotshalk, Richard. *Homer and Hesiod: Myth and Philosophy.* Lanham, Md.: University Press of America, 2000. A study of the nature and function of the poetry of Homer and Hesiod when their work is considered in historical context as developments of poetry as a distinctive voice for truth beyond religion and myth.

Janko, Richard. *Homer, Hesiod, and the Hymns.* Cambridge, England: Cambridge University Press, 1982. Aimed principally at specialists in classical languages. Discusses Hesiod's poetics in light of general trends that can be traced in works by predecessors, especially Homer, and successors. Explains how philological study can help ascertain dating of individual works from a period about which there is limited historical record.

Lamberton, Robert. *Hesiod.* New Haven, Conn.: Yale University Press, 1988. Written for the general reader with interest but no expertise in Greek literature. Reflects an understanding of Hesiod's works as important documents illuminating the customs and concerns of the ancient world. Comments on Hesiod's influence on the ancient world as well as his importance to the medieval and Renaissance literary traditions. Concentrates on interpreting the poetry rather than on assembling scholarly critiques of individual works.

Lawton, W. C. *The Successors of Homer.* New York: Cooper Square, 1969. Includes two chapters on Hesiod's major works, *Theogony* and *Works and*

Days. Links him with other Greek writers who preserved and expanded on the work of Homer in detailing Greek life, values, and customs. Identifies Hesiod's influence on later writers.

Marsilio, Maria S. *Farming and Poetry in Hesiod's "Works and Days."* Lanham, Md.: University Press of America, 2000. Marsilio demonstrates how Hesiod and Virgil viewed the farming lifestyle as a system of belief unto itself. Includes a translation of *Works and Days* by esteemed translator David Grene.

Solmsen, Friedrich. *Hesiod and Aeschylus.* Ithaca, N.Y.: Cornell University Press, 1949. Includes a lengthy chapter on *Theogony* and a shorter one on *Works and Days.* Attempts to distinguish what in these poems is original to Hesiod and what was commonplace in Greek myth and history. Identifies those parts of Hesiod's works that influenced the Greek dramatist Aeschylus, especially in *Prometheia* and *Eumenides.*

Thalman, William G. *Conventions of Form and Thought in Early Greek Poetry.* Baltimore: The Johns Hopkins University Press, 1984. Concentrates on literary conventions that appear in Hesiod's major works. Links him with other Greek poets who make use of dactylic hexameter as the principal meter for their work. Provides close readings of individual passages. Contains a useful bibliography.

Daniel H. Garrison;
bibliography updated by Laurence W. Mazzeno

WILLIAM HEYEN

Born: Brooklyn, New York: November 1, 1940

PRINCIPAL POETRY

Depth of Field, 1970
Noise in the Trees: Poems and a Memoir, 1974
The Elm's Home, 1977
The Swastika Poems, 1977
Long Island Light, 1979
The City Parables, 1979
The Bees, 1981
Lord Dragonfly: Five Sequences, 1981
Erika: Poems of the Holocaust, 1984
The Chestnut Rain, 1986
Brockport, New York: Beginning with "And," 1988
Pterodactyl Rose: Poems of Ecology, 1991
Ribbons: The Gulf War, 1991
Falling from Heaven: Holocaust Poems of a Jew and a Gentile 1991 (with Louis Daniel Brodsky)
The Host: Selected Poems, 1965-1990, 1994
Crazy Horse in Stillness, 1996
Diana, Charles, and the Queen, 1998
Host: Selected Poems, 1965-1990, 1998

OTHER LITERARY FORMS

A Profile of Theodore Roethke (1971) and *The Generation of 2000: Contemporary American Poets* (1984) are works collected and edited by William Heyen. Heyen has also written a novel, *Vic Holyfield and the Class of 1957* (1986), and numerous essays on American poetry and the environment. *Pig Notes and Dumb Music: Prose on Poetry* (1998) offers Heyen's thoughts on the writing life and the creative process.

ACHIEVEMENTS

William Heyen's work has been greeted by critical acceptance and acclaim from many quarters. In 1965, Heyen won the Borestone Mountain Poetry Prize from the *Prairie Schooner* for "Boy of Gull, Boy of Brine." During 1971-1972, he traveled to West Germany on a Senior Fulbright Lectureship and lectured at the Universities of Freiburg, Tübingen, Hannover, and Oslo, among others. He has been the recipient of three State University of New York Research Foundation Fellowships for poetry, two National Endowment of the Arts Creative Writing Fellowships (1973-1974 and 1984-1985), a John Simon Guggenheim Memorial Foundation Fellowship for Poetry (1977-1978), the Eunice Tietjens Memorial Award from *Poetry* (1978), the Witter Bynner Prize for Poetry (1982), and the New York Foundation for the Arts Poetry Fellowship (1984-1985). *Noise in the Trees: Poems and a Memoir* was chosen by the American Library Association as one of thirty Notable Books of 1974. *The Generation of 2000: Contemporary American Poets* was chosen by the American Library Association's *Booklist* as an Outstanding Book of 1984. *Crazy Horse in Stillness* won the 1997 National Small Press Book Award for Poetry.

BIOGRAPHY

Though William Heyen was born in Brooklyn, New York, in 1940, he was reared in Suffolk County on Long Island. His father, Henry Jurgen Heyen, had emigrated from Germany to the United States in 1929 and worked in the United States as a bartender and carpenter. Heyen's mother, Wilhelmine Auguste Else Wormke, had come to the United States from Germany in 1934.

Heyen's memories of his childhood experiences on Long Island fuel many of his poems. The same must be said, however, about his link by birth to Germany. When his father emigrated from Germany, he left his entire family behind. Two of the poet's uncles were killed during World War II, fighting on the German side. Wilhelm, an infantryman for whom Heyen was named, died on the day of the poet's birth. Hermann—whom Heyen describes as "a rabid Nazi"—was shot down over Russia.

In 1961, Heyen was graduated with a bachelor's degree in education from the State University of New York College at Brockport. He was an outstanding athlete who had been twice selected as an All-American in soccer during his undergraduate years at Brockport and who had starred as well on his high school and college basketball teams. After teaching English for a year at Springfield (New York) Junior High School, Heyen was married to Hannelore Greiner, with whom he has two children, William and Kirsten. He earned a master's (1963) and doctoral degree (1967) from Ohio University and taught English from 1963 to 1965 at the State University of New York College at Cortland. From 1967 until his retirement in 2000, Heyen taught at the State University of New York at Brockport, where he served as both professor of English and writer in residence.

ANALYSIS

William Heyen has written, "The most meaningful word in the language for me is 'home.'" This statement best summarizes the themes running throughout his poetry, for home can be located in a variety of places for Heyen. In *Depth of Field*, *Noise in the Trees*, and *Long Island Light*, Heyen is involved in intense recollection of his boyhood home in Suffolk County, Long Island. *The Swastika Poems* and *Erika* show Heyen longing for better understanding of the way his German ancestry influences his sense of belonging. Even his *Crazy Horse in Stillness* volume was generated by a sense of connection to the Algonquin culture that once flourished in what became Suffolk County.

Heyen is a writer whose purposes are clear: He believes that his poems should bear witness to the diminishment and desecration of the environment (including the environment of other people) and, by addressing this theme, empower people to act to prevent destruction of one another and of the earth. Though this aesthetic has resulted in unromanticized poetry, its purpose is essentially romantic—using art to inspire action. Heyen's concerns with his childhood home, with finding his place among his German ancestors, his spiritual home in Brockport, or his worldly home in an environment safe for all living things result in poems that serve as reminders of what human beings have lost and a prayer for what we may still be able to save.

In his first volume, *Depth of Field*, Heyen explores his concern for the shared home, the planet and its environment. Yet this focus on home intensifies greatly in his later books. Many of the poems in *Lord Dragonfly*, *Brockport, New York: Beginning with "And," The Chestnut Rain*, and *Pterodactyl Rose* reflect the poet's exploration of the environment and the relationship between his view of the environment and his aesthetic principles. He says, "As I open the gate into our next century, memory is my balancing pole." What does this mean to the poet-environmentalist? "Now, for the first time in our history, esthetics is a matter of life and death," Heyen writes. The result of this view is poems that reflect an effort to see environmental responsibility as a moral and ethical imperative.

One should not be surprised to see in Heyen's earliest works the search for his relationship to his various notions of home. These early works contain seeds of an aesthetic position the poet was only later able to verbalize. He has called it an "art of realization and commitment" that "will insist we change our lives by way of its presence and witness." An examination of Heyen's concerns over the years, from *Depth of Field* to *Pterodactyl Rose*, will show the evolution of his sense of responsibility as a poet and planet-dweller.

DEPTH OF FIELD

Depth of Field, in the light of Heyen's later works, offers glimpses of a growing Heyen aesthetic. Intuitively, he leaned heavily on themes of home, place, and ancestry. *Depth of Field* is broken into two sections, "The Spirit of Wrath" and "The Dead from Their Dark," arranged to suggest two of many possible ways of viewing experience. In "The Spirit of Wrath," Heyen explores a spectrum of experiences that are centered on loss or the threatening potential for loss, taken from his family and nature, both remembered experience and imagined.

Not surprisingly, given this range of subject matter, Heyen's lost Nazi uncles, Wilhelm and Hermann, enter this section of the book, foreshadowing the poet's more complete exploration of his German ties in his later poems of the Holocaust. Heyen addresses his uncles directly. As images of Wilhelm's life and sudden death are cinematically/ spun out on the screen of the page, Heyen writes, "Wilhelm, your face is a shadow/ under your helmet." To Hermann, he writes: "Hermann, you received the letters/ my father still talks and wonders about/ the ones in which he told you to bail out/ over England and plead insanity." In these moving pieces, Heyen calls upon memory to help him explore his relation to his family. Even in their differences, Heyen claims identity, finding his place among other Heyens.

The message of "Birds and Roses Are Birds and Roses" is quite simple: There are no satisfactions for the poet, when confronted by the threat of devastation, in the transcendent romanticism that sees "the timeless in the temporal." When confronted by "the remains of a thrush," Heyen recognizes his impotence: "I would flesh this one bird's feathers,/ resume its quick eye and lilting trill./ But these were not the mystics' flowers:/ their bush cast a shadow like a bell." Still, this is not the language of the cynic. Rather, this is a hopefulness, perhaps a longing to believe such miracles possible. Clearly, the world of a Heyen poem draws attention to the need for miracles, demands that humankind observe the simple requirement of leaving things alone and permitting them to undergo natural healing.

In "The Spirit of Wrath," it is clear that regardless of human efforts to control the natural and personal worlds, each person can hope to do only "what can be done," nothing more. The shark of the poem is simultaneously within one and abroad: "What it is you're after/ feeds at the bottom/ below the reach of your anchor." The shark-snagging adventure in "The Spirit of Wrath" is the promise of the poet's confrontations both within himself, in self-understanding, and outside himself, in the environment. This shark also sets up other mythopoeic interludes in the first section of *Depth of Field*.

Like the horse in "A Man Is a Forked Animal," which "does not think well enough to know/ his waking from his standing sleep," Heyen seems to suggest that as a species humans are not always able to differentiate the fearful elements of waking observation from the fears they imagine. On one hand, in "I Move to Random Consolations," Heyen rises at the poem's conclusion "to rock the crane's death." On the other hand, he envisions a dreaded insect that "never touched earth" and a spider that "hovers always/ just above the land." Confronted by fear-provoking environments, personal as well as natural, real as well as imagined, people are much like the eel in "Existential" that "can't or won't remember/ the small way out it entered."

A clue to an understanding of the second section of *Depth of Field* comes from an epigraph from Theodore Roethke:

> But when I breathe with the birds,
> The spirit of wrath becomes the spirit of blessing.
> And the dead begin from their dark to sing in my sleep.

"The Dead from Their Dark" offers the recompense William Wordsworth discovered in "Lines Written a Few Miles Above Tintern Abbey" (1798): the ability to "hear the still, sad music of humanity." The world is portrayed in "The Dead" as art, since only in and through art can one find the ideal, that moment of perfect anticipation. Heyen writes as if humanity were on the verge of something, some breakthrough, some deeper understanding but always suspended on the cliff of epiphany: "What was it I/ was thinking of saying?/ I can't remember." Perhaps from their dark, he urges, the dead know, like Roethke in Heyen's "Memoriam," that "whatever cripple seeks a Lord,/ however slowly,/ a Lord finds." In the end, Heyen seems to suggest, are not all human beings crippled seekers?

There is affirmation—though it arises from a certain unromanticized appraisal of the human condition—in this section of the book: "Today, unfolding a flower,/ the sun kindles, spreads/ the wren's feathers," Heyen writes in "The Fourth Day," the day "different" from those recounted in "The Spirit of Wrath" section. In "Depth of Field," he asserts that one affirms one's existence by attending carefully to the details of natural events that surround one. In the moment of such intense concentration, one achieves the kind of transcendence that the young Wordsworth promised but few modern writers have achieved. The reward for such transcendence and participation in this higher level of consciousness may, for Heyen, be the image. He writes with care and commitment to the transcendent moment: "It is the harp/ of the curved sun that orchestrates the morning." It was inevitable, given this view, that Heyen's aesthetic would change, moving from a young man's frenzied perception to the recollection of a mature poet. "This matter of memory" he writes in "To Live in the World," "runs deep/ as earth." Later, his intuition leads him to the question he continues to answer in later works: "And how will spirit want to say it?"

NOISE IN THE TREES AND LONG ISLAND LIGHT

In *Noise in the Trees* and *Long Island Light*, in which poems originally published in the earlier volume are deepened and extended by the publication of thirty-one new poems, the "spirit" is the spirit of Long Island as Heyen recollects it, or, more precisely, the spirit wavering behind natural phenomena. In either case, these poems are mythopoeic. "Legend of the Tree at the Center of the World" tells of the first spring morning. "Dog Sacrifice at Lake Ronkonkoma" describes a ritual performed when "the sacred lake laps shore/ with syllables of approaching spring." These poems promise an ancient, mystical spirit in nature. Yet Heyen offers more modern ritual in "Smith's Ride," describing a monument to the man who in 1660 rode bareback on a bull to claim as much of Long Island as he could. Now, each Halloween, the statue is desecrated. A troubling image in this poem brings change into focus: "the bull, whose spirit is metal,/ . . . now stares at the traffic below him,/ these

cars that climb the hill like deer,/ trucks that lurch his wilderness like bear."

In the same spirit, Heyen portrays the Long Island of his youth, "before the influx of the machine and cars and smoke and soot and dust." In *Noise in the Trees*, the poet is in love with this planet, this place of his youth. Yet simple recall is temporary: "the herds, of course, were doomed" ("The Trail Beside the River Platte"); "the pigeons avalanched/ down the boughs, and had not room to fly,/ and died by the thousands" ("The Pigeons"). In the first section of *Noise in the Trees*, Heyen addresses nature in the Whitman tradition, recalling its potential and mourning its loss. A significant outcome of Heyen's compare-and-contrast strategy is the inevitable effort to find his place, as T. S. Eliot says poets must, among other writers: Theodore Roethke, Mark Twain, and Theodore Dreiser, to name but three. To this end, experiences in nature become more than ritual, become a matter of spirit and redemption in "Clamming at St. James Harbor," "This Island," and "Tonging at St. James Harbor."

The memoir that separates the two sections of poems is a rich and poetic effort to show, as Wordsworth does in *The Prelude: Or, Growth of a Poet's Mind* (1850), the "growth of the poet's mind." It seems well suited for placement in the midst of the poems, as a break in the effort of recollection. No doubt originating from journals, by its very nature such writing enables one to reach certain subjects unreachable through the poetic imagination and to express them differently. The writer speaks more authoritatively, if not more authentically, in the language of journals. "Some aestheticians believe the lyric impulse begins with a crisis," Heyen explains. Of perhaps greater importance to a writer seeking his place among other writers, however, memoir and journal writing is squarely in a literary tradition, best exemplified for Heyen by Henry David Thoreau, who would "require of every writer, first or last, a simple and sincere account of his own life." Heyen's memoir describes the land—made distant because it is filtered and purified by memory—that he has inhabited.

In section 3, Heyen connects nature and its well-being to his own, preferring the safety of remembered nature. In "The Odor of Pear," he remembers pears, not as they exist, often imperfectly shaped and bruised, but pears "globed to rust and gold" that will "never/ rot and fall." The very next poem, however, offers a necessary contrast, a suggestion of dialectic. In "Cow, Willow, Skull, Cowbell," an old cow is soon to die. Among those who violently manipulate nature are humans. Wenzel in "The Lamb" acts out this violence almost mindlessly, with a stunning inability to recognize the impact of his behavior. In an effort to bear witness to the time when he first saw nature abused and treated as an "other," Heyen is unsparing of painful detail: "Both hind legs wrapped with rope,/ Wenzel's chosen lamb hung head down/ . . . Its throat slashed, the lamb drained." Heyen recalls the animal "skinned, . . . emptied of its blue/ and yellow organs," and himself, the horrified child: "I forgot my knees,/ and entered the deep kingdom of death." A similar pairing of his own life and the life of nature is seen in other poems of section 3, including "Pet's Death" and "The Swan." His recollection of adolescent hunting adventures ends with the certainty that he will always carry with him "the dark light, the foxfire/ of all my dead."

THE SWASTIKA POEMS AND ERIKA

In *The Swastika Poems*, Heyen explores a second element of place, among ancestors, as he does again later in *Erika: Poems of the Holocaust*, which includes many pieces from *The Swastika Poems* and again uses a memoir to separate two sections of verse. The epigraph to each collection, from Susan Sontag, offers one rationale for writing these poems:

> Ultimately, the only response is to continue to hold the event [the murder of the six million European Jews] in mind, to remember it. . . . This moral function of remembering is something that cuts across the different worlds of knowledge, action and art.

Another reason for writing these poems is personal; Heyen and his wife both have German ancestry. For the poet, an examination of his place among his ancestors is an inevitable extension of his obsession with home.

Heyen explains in his title poem the connection between the poems and his memory of being a German American during World War II: "They appeared, overnight,/ on our steps like frost stars/ on our windows." The poems in both *The Swastika Poems* and *Erika* are generally divisible into those presenting historical

events and those showing the poet's place among such events. Poems that relate history, often by use of extensive quotations from primary sources or references to events presented through other media, are "Blue," "A Visit to Belzec," and "The Uncertainty Principle." "Blue," a poem prefaced by Elie Wiesel's moving firsthand account of "the little faces of the children" whose bodies he "saw turned into wreaths of smoke beneath a silent blue sky," benefits (as do other poems in this collection) from Heyen's skillful use of rhythm to punctuate the experience of witnessing such a horror. As in "Darkness," Heyen uses enjambment to leave the reader with a sense of the hysterical, the measure of some act performed repeatedly, meticulously, mechanically, without conscience. "A Visit to Belzec" similarly relies on quotations in stanzas 2 and 4, in this case from Richard Grumberger's *Hitler's SS* (1970). "The Uncertainty Principle" attempts to re-create and comment upon Jacob Bronowski's "whole hour of film," a television presentation in which Bronowsky walks into the pond at Auschwitz, the mud of the dead. These poems, however, lose much of their effectiveness by their juxtaposition to primary and, as a result, more powerfully moving sources.

When Heyen places himself among these events, however, and performs the work most critical to his growing understanding of his ancestral home, the poems rise dramatically in effectiveness. Naturally, his Nazi uncles appear in these poems, as does his father-in-law. Alongside them for contrast, in "A Snapshot of My Father, 1928," there is Heyen's description of his father "on his way now,/ . . . on his way to America." Simple recall serves Heyen well as a tool for locating himself among family members. "The Numinous," however, is a record of a more immediate experience, one that renders a different kind of meaning. He leaves much unsaid in this poem: with whom he walks and where. "We are walking a sidewalk/ in a German city." Such a walk, in any German city, is trance-provoking for Heyen, producing the impression of a dreamed or an imagined experience. This impression holds only until "something/ bursts into the air," startling the walkers, who calm themselves by reminding one another that it is only pigeons, "only an explosion/ of beautiful blue-gray pigeons." As they continue their walk, he repeats, "Beautiful blue-gray pigeons," and concludes, "We will always remember." Nature will be a constant reminder, for in this volume human mortality is confronted by nature, a theme that Heyen carries into poems of what might be called his third phase, ecological concern, in which he continues his search for a home and seeks a sense of belonging. "Stories" from *Erika* helps make it clear: Stories abound, stories of ancestors and of the war, but they "solve nothing," he writes, "lead nowhere." Yet there is a Wordsworthian recompense: "but the spruce/ appears again,/ . . . its own true story, yours,/ mine, ours to tell." Many of these stories resurface in Heyen's 1991 poetic interchange with Louis Daniel Brodsky, *Falling from Heaven: Holocaust Poems of a Jew and a Gentile*.

LORD DRAGONFLY

Though stories fade, the natural world lives on, Heyen seems to say. The association in "The Numinous" between the explosion of pigeons and the imagined-terror-made-fact for the walkers shows the connections he perceives between the life of nature and the life of the individual. This connection is one that Heyen, who has searched thus far in his poetry for his true home, must inevitably explore, as he does in *Lord Dragonfly*, *The Chestnut Rain*, and *Brockport, New York*. These collections show most clearly the evolution of aesthetic as ethic in Heyen's work, in which the act of making a poem is an act of insisting upon action and change.

As is the case with *Long Island Light* and *Erika*, many of the poems in *Lord Dragonfly* and *The Chestnut Rain* have previously appeared in print, often in chapbooks. Perhaps as much as Whitman, who revised his work continuously to refine and understand his evolving literary message, Heyen tries to understand the patterns of poems, why they continue to surface as they do long after he thinks that he has finished with a subject. Naturally, the poems choose the poet. Yet Heyen consciously solves the puzzle of such visitations, seeing the different ways each poem may be connected to others he has written, often forming an interesting matrix of connections between his search for home, his ancestry, and his concerns with the environment. He often uses the same poems in different volumes and among other poems in an effort to tell the whole story, the truth that rests in multiplicity.

The five sequences of *Lord Dragonfly*, all of which underline Heyen's growing concerns with the environment, were published between 1976 and 1979 in limited-edition chapbooks by various small and fine presses. According to Heyen in a note to the volume, the five are placed "not chronologically, but in an order that itself forms . . . a sequence of sequences, each a consciousness defining its crisis, straining to know, coming to something it can hold to." The crisis of the first sequence, "The Ash," is the seasonal death of the ash and the death of a friend. In only six poems, Heyen manages to tell the entire story of the ash and of the man whom he comes to understand through "the snow-sheathed tree," seeing the man-versus-nature problem less as dialectical than as a potential and much-needed unification. The second sequence, "Lord Dragonfly," is thirty-six short imagistic poems, perhaps intended as haiku—balanced by the thirty-six short poems of the fifth sequence—that suggest that dependence on nature is more critical to humankind than dependence on any human being or any machine: "I am safe here,/ not a friend in sight," Heyen writes in one of these poems. In the third sequence, "Of Palestine," Heyen celebrates nature in the Middle East as a kind of language-maker or communicator that is always present (like pigeons in "The Numinous") to remind humankind of its history as a warring and forgetful species. Nature here seems sufficient, in and of itself, especially when these poems are followed by the "XVII Machines" of the fourth sequence. These poems enable the reader to imagine what humanity's blind dependence on machines might do, ultimately, to our lives. Heyen writes of machines that kiss people good night, collect butterflies, mend birds' nests, and even treat other machines. The final section again offers three dozen short imagistic poems, these focusing on the unseen world of deeper consciousness, the nature inside one, behind one's eyes: "there is a life, this one,/ beyond the body."

THE CHESTNUT RAIN

Similarly concerned with the larger sense of place, *The Chestnut Rain* is a long poem, in fifty-two sections, that effectively affirms natural order in the world. Heyen connects his childhood experiences with nature, and his sense of well-being during those days is balanced against "the mysterious chestnut blight" to communicate his sense of the fragility of humankind and nature alike. Throughout, Heyen shows preference for those, like Wenzel, who live close to nature; in fact, he portrays this boyhood mentor in a far more favorable light than in earlier volumes. Wenzel is natural man, Wordsworth's rustic, who now represents to Heyen, through the filter of recollection, man most nearly perfect. Wenzel is elevated to magician in "The Snow Hen": "Wenzel, as he often did, made magic, pulled an egg/ out of his Adam's apple/ under his beard." He assumes the role of prophet in "The Ewe's Song": "Wenzel said 'Come,' and I followed him." In "Blackberry Light" he is the symbolic last good man, comforted by Heyen: "Old Man Wenzel, try to forget the yellow manure/ seeping from under your sick ewes,/ the mucus and cheesy matter/ coughed up by tubercular cows." The world Heyen associates with Wenzel is a "frail and perishable home." Wenzel understood it and taught others its secrets, as in "That Socket": "Wenzel sucked a fresh egg through a pinhole./ This makes life, he said, and handed me the shell."

Undoubtedly, Wenzel is the central character and hero of *The Chestnut Rain*. Yet the image of light, of a certain kind of light, is equally heroic. Light in this volume symbolizes consciousness of the human world and the natural. In "The Light" Heyen maps out its course, from "light of a child you love" to "light of trains rocking the last chestnut ties" to "light of half-moons drifting your father's nails" to "light of the abandoned farm." His memory and imagination flow freely in this Whitmanesque poem, in the process offering the reasons that "we praise and grieve."

BROCKPORT, NEW YORK

Poems in *Brockport, New York* express Heyen's yearning for a transcendent and spiritual home, a place otherworldly, one deep inside but "beyond the body." In "Brockport Sunflowers," Heyen describes an imagined visit of sunflowers to his home. Like the people who reside in this spiritual home, they are easygoing and relaxed. "They would love the children," writes Heyen, "and listen to them,/ all day long, until the children were ready for bed." In the title poem, he admits "lives here in this port town/ vanish, but slowly, but vanish." Here, in "The Language," man can observe the natural world, as Heyen does the snake, "until, for a few beats/ of its

heart,/ I joined it on its leaf." This is a place where Wordsworth might say that man is perfectly suited to the planet on which he lives.

PTERODACTYL ROSE

No doubt Heyen has eschewed the time-worn observation of John Keats, that "themes are ugly clubs," because in *Pterodactyl Rose: Poems of Ecology* his new aesthetic arises from his ecological and conservationist concerns. Some explorations in irony are needed, as in "Harpoon": "Now that blue whales are as few as two hundred,/ I want the last one dead." He often addresses his poems to creatures, such as the dodo and the whale, that may be known one day only through what is written about them—animals either extinct or on the verge of extinction. He makes sense of experience usually unnoticed, as in "Redwings": "Maybe you've noticed that around here/ red-winged blackbirds aren't rare,/ but aren't seen often, either, and then, at distance."

RIBBONS: THE GULF WAR—A POEM

In *Ribbons: The Gulf War—A Poem*, Heyen once more enters contemporary history, this time a piece of history that is fresh from the news magazines and television screens as the poet relives its details and meanings with his readers. The power of reported events and personalities of popular culture is one part of Heyen's concern here, though perhaps his more important targets are the national psyche that makes possible such wars and the condition of war itself. This latter concern links *Ribbons* with Heyen's holocaust poems. Like George Orwell, Heyen explores the politically tinged language that hides the truth, that covers over the true horrors of humankind's motives and behavior. He writes (in part 34 of this long poem): "I've twice heard a general use the word 'ripple,'/ 'a ripple of bombs.' Half my childhood/ at ponds. A ripple of bombs."

DIANA, CHARLES, AND THE QUEEN

While it is a far cry from the battlefield to the public humiliations of a royal family, Heyen's *Diana, Charles, and the Queen* looks carefully and feelingly at what the popular media have trivialized while offering blazing insights about the culture that needs to know of these events. Who are Diana, Charles, and the queen to us? And why? Heyen, in this sequence of approximately three hundred eight-line poems, captures a fresh reality and human urgency that lies beneath the media myths.

CRAZY HORSE IN STILLNESS

In between his books on these two contemporary subjects, Heyen published his most intriguing book-length sequence, the monumental *Crazy Horse in Stillness*. Reaching back to another time and another sensibility, Heyen provides a splendid conjuring. This work, a series of short poetic bursts organized into chapter-like sections, examines and compares the essential humanity of Crazy Horse and Custer, two figures who have been reduced, rather than truly enlarged, to mythic stature. As in so much of his work, Heyen is concerned with the nature of the warrior. He writes as if invaded and empowered by the same spirits that nourished Crazy Horse himself. While each of the poems in this collection can stand in isolation, the larger work gains power and clarity as the pieces cohere and coalesce: Heyen builds his epic like a pointillist in verse.

OTHER MAJOR WORKS

LONG FICTION: *Vic Holyfield and the Class of 1957*, 1986.

NONFICTION: *Pig Notes and Dumb Music: Prose on Poetry*, 1998.

EDITED TEXTS: *A Profile of Theodore Roethke*, 1971; *American Poets in 1976*, 1976; *I Would Also Like to Mention Aluminum: A Conversation with William Stafford*, 1976; *The Generation of 2000: Contemporary American Poets*, 1984; *The Pushcart Prize XV, 1990-1991: Best of the Small Presses*, 1990 (with Elizabeth Spires); *Dumb Beautiful Ministers*, 1996.

MISCELLANEOUS: *From This Book of Praise: Poems and a Conversation with William Heyen*, 1978 (Vince Clemente, editor).

BIBLIOGRAPHY

Dodd, Elizabeth. "A Living Past." *Tar River Poetry* 36, no. 1 (Fall, 1996): 45-48. This review of *Crazy Horse in Stillness* is perhaps the most penetrating and properly appreciative discussion of a Heyen masterpiece.

McFee, Michael. "The Harvest of a Quiet Eye." *Parnassus* 10 (Spring/Summer, 1982): 153-171. This substantial review essay considers *Lord Dragonfly*, *The Bees*, *The City Parables*, *Long Island Light*, and *The Swastika Poems*.

Manassas Review: Essay on Contemporary American Poets 1, nos. 3/4 (1978). This entire issue, edited by Patrick Bizzaro, is devoted to discussion of Heyen's works up to and including *The Swastika Poems*.

Parmet, Harriet L. *The Terror of Our Days: Four American Poets Respond to the Holocaust*. Bethlehem, Pa.: Lehigh University Press, 2001. Parmet includes a long chapter, "The Confessional Poetry of Sylvia Plath and William Heyen: Searching for Expiation, Identification, and Communion with the Victims," that is the most extensive and substantial consideration of Heyen's Holocaust poetry. Other poets treated in this book are Gerald Stern and Jerome Rothenberg.

Patrick Bizzaro,
updated by Philip K. Jason

JOHN HEYWOOD

Born: London(?), England; c. 1497
Died: Louvain(?), Spanish Netherlands; October, 1578

PRINCIPAL POETRY

A Dialogue of Proverbs, 1546, 1963 (Rudolph E. Habenicht, editor)
The Spider and the Fly, 1556

OTHER LITERARY FORMS

In addition to writing poetry, John Heywood wrote dramatic works that can be divided into two groups: debates and farces. The four debates include *The Play of Love* (pr. c. 1528-1529), *Witty and Witless* (wr. c. 1533), *The Play of the Weather* (pb. 1533), and *Gentleness and Nobility* (1533, attributed to Heywood). The farces include *The Pardoner and the Friar* (pb. 1533), *Johan Johan* (pb. 1533, attributed to Heywood), and *The Four P. P.* (pb. 1541-1547). Two other plays, *Calilsto and Melibaea* (1530) and *Thersites* (1537), have been ascribed to Heywood but with insufficient evidence. Although Heywood was known in his own day primarily as the author of witty epigrams, modern criticism has tended to focus on his contributions to the evolution of English drama.

ACHIEVEMENTS

Many elements of John Heywood's work—comedy, bawdry, wordplay, and lyricism—reflect the various ways poetry was developing during the Renaissance in England. Heywood experimented with all these poetic devices, although his contemporaries saw him mainly as a "mad wit."

BIOGRAPHY

John Heywood's date of birth can only be calculated by a remark he made in a letter to Lord Burghley on April 18, 1575. He then claimed to be seventy-eight years old, which would place his birthday before April 18, 1497. There are even fewer direct indications of his birthplace. Bishop Bale and John Pitts, a friend of Heywood's son, both claim that he was born in London, and this is generally accepted for lack of any evidence to the contrary. Because of his long associations with the court, biographers often assume that as a boy Heywood entered the Chapel Royal as a chorister, but this is mere speculation. Nor is much known about his education. Anthony à Wood claimed that Heywood was a student at Broadgates, Oxford, for a short time, "But the crabbedness of logic not suiting with his airy genie, he retired to his native place, and became noted to all witty men." Broadgates did not begin to keep records until 1570, so this statement cannot be verified.

The first direct reference to Heywood's stay in Henry VIII's court occurs in 1515 when the *King's Book of Payments* records the payment of eight pence a day to a "John Heywoode." Even this reference raises more questions than it answers: It does not indicate what the money was payment for and, since the next reference to Heywood does not appear until 1519, some critics even assume that the first entry is for a different Heywood entirely. In June, 1519, however, Heywood received an allowance of one hundred shillings, and in August he is listed as a singer in the court. His associa-

tion with the court continued throughout Henry's reign, although his duties are not always listed in the payment book. Presumably he was involved in court entertainments of some sort. In 1526, he is referred to as a "player of the virginals," and in 1528 he was made steward of the royal chamber, a post he also held under Edward and Mary.

Thomas More entered Henry's court in 1519 and Heywood's association with More's circle is well known: Sometime in the 1520's he married Eliza Rastell, the daughter of John Rastell and More's sister, Elizabeth. Heywood's strong Catholicism, in fact, almost led him to the same fate that More met at Henry's hands; he was imprisoned in 1543. The cause was an accusation made by Heywood and others against Archbishop Cranmer, a Protestant. They charged that Cranmer was not reporting violations of the Six Articles which were issued in 1539 and which were strongly Catholic. Heywood escaped death by recanting, although it is indicative of his reputation as a wit that Sir John Harington attributed Heywood's release to his "mirth" even though no direct evidence appears to support the contention. Heywood's political associations were better documented than his personal life: He had two sons (Ellis and Jasper) and one daughter, who later married John Donne and became the mother of the poet; yet in William Rastell's will there is mention of two more daughters, Johanna Stubbs and Elizabeth Marvin, about whom nothing is known. It is perhaps appropriate that an artist whose life revolved around the court should be remembered primarily through his relations with that court.

When Henry died in 1547 with Edward as his heir, Heywood's position did not change: He continued to present plays in court. Mary's accession in 1553 would have seemed to assure Heywood a bright future. As a good Catholic himself, he had always admired the young princess, even writing a poem praising her in 1534, a year when Mary's Catholicism put her out of Henry's favor. Heywood gave a Latin and English oration during Mary's coronation and later celebrated her marriage to Philip in a poem. Mary, in turn, kept Heywood as steward of the queen's chamber and, when he resigned this post in 1555, granted him a forty-year lease on a manor and some lands in Yorkshire.

Heywood's associations with the court after Mary's death are not entirely clear. Although he died in exile in Louvain, he appears in records of Elizabeth's court during the first year of her reign. A comment made by Thomas Wilson is especially intriguing: He reports that he saw Heywood when he was in exile in Malines and brought him Elizabeth's forgiveness, saying that "the Queen was never so precise that she could not bear with men's weaknesses for their conscience in religion, and only misliked overt acts and rebellious practices." The phrasing of this message raises the possibility that Heywood might have been driven into exile because of a plot to restore Catholicism to the English throne. In any case, Heywood finally fled to Antwerp, where his son Ellis was in religious exile and, from there, went to Louvain, where he died in October, 1578.

It would be difficult to overestimate the influence which his years at court had on Heywood. As a dramatist, he must have benefited from the court masques and interludes which he directed. As a poet, he would have been in a position to benefit from as well as influence the development of English as a vehicle for poetic expression. He also found subject matter for his longest poem, *The Spider and the Fly*, in the enclosure laws and religious questions that would have been talked about in court at various times.

ANALYSIS

John Heywood's contemporaries knew him mainly as a writer of witty epigrams: John Florio, William Camden, and Gabriel Harvey comment on his skill in using this literary form. One of Heywood's epigrams opens with the question "Art thou Heywood with the mad merry wit?" and this wit emerges in the wordplay of which Heywood is so fond. His poems abound with puns and verbal quibbles and in this way he anticipates euphuism; in fact, John Lyly's work uses many of the proverbs that Heywood collected in his *A Dialogue of Proverbs*.

In addition to wordplay there is a minor substratum of lyricism in Heywood that antedates the sonnets and lyrics of later Renaissance poetry. "Green Willow" most obviously illustrates this strain in Heywood, introducing the typical despondent Petrarchan lover and using alliteration to lend smoothness to the lines. Alliteration also became a hallmark of euphuism.

Another important aspect of Heywood's work is his comic realism and bawdy humor. He constantly provides a dramatic context for his poems, and this context, be it the mock-heroic descriptions of warfare in *The Spider and the Fly* or the fast-paced marital arguments of *A Dialogue of Proverbs*, usually provides comic overtones to his work. When describing people—the old wife in *A Dialogue of Proverbs*, for example—he focuses on their imperfections to provide comedy. This comic realism, along with the bawdry found in many of Heywood's poems, has prompted critics to place him in the Chaucerian tradition of English poetry, a tradition carried on through the Renaissance by poets such as John Skelton.

A DIALOGUE OF PROVERBS

Heywood's first poetry to appear in print was *A Dialogue of Proverbs*, an attempt to bring together "the number of the effectual proverbs in the English tongue" within a dramatic context. That context is a dialogue between the narrator and a young friend concerning the latter's marriage: He must choose between marrying a beautiful but destitute young woman and an ugly and old but wealthy widow. Collecting proverbs was by no means an innovation in the sixteenth century. William Caxton's *The dictes or sayengis of the philosophres* (1477), Erasmus's *Adagiorum Chiliades* (1500), and Udall's *Apophthegmes* (1542), to name just a few, are all collections of proverbial lore. That Heywood worked specifically with English proverbs and attempted to provide a plot for them shows him to be a poet concerned with exploring the possibilities of the English language while giving a dramatic framework to his poem. Heywood was, after all, a playwright as well as a poet.

The strengths of *A Dialogue of Proverbs* are twofold—dramatic and verbal—and its weaknesses emerge in Heywood's inability to sustain the high standards that his best writing achieves. The dramatic structure of the work is complex, and such complexity does much to alleviate the tedium that a dialogue consisting mainly of proverbs might produce. Thus, after listening to his friend's dilemma and debating with him his marriage choices (Part I, Chapters I-VI), the narrator proposes to tell the young man about two unions he has known: one a marriage of young people for love and one a December-May marriage between a rich woman and a poor young man. The first story takes up the rest of Part I and chronicles the various ways the couple try to rise above their poverty; it ends when the wife and husband must part to make their separate ways in the world. The history of the December-May match takes up Part II and shows the gradual deterioration of a marriage undertaken on the young man's part only for money. The introduction of these two stories within the frame of the debate between the narrator and his friend shows Hewyood's fondness for elaborate plot structure.

He also delights in providing detailed descriptions of the secondary characters of the narrator's two stories, and often these descriptions are humorous. When the poor young wife goes to her aunt's house to beg forgiveness for her rash marriage, she meets another "kinswoman," Alice, whose "dissimulation" frightens the young wife. Alice is described in broadly humorous terms: "She is *lost with an apple, and won with a nut*;/ Her *tongue is no edge tool, but yet it will cut*./ Her cheeks are purple ruddy like a horse plum;/ And *the big part of her body is her bum*." While the wife is begging at her aunt's house, her husband is trying his luck with his family. After being refused aid by one uncle, he goes to another only to find him out and his wife leery of indigent relatives: "She was within, but he was yet abroad,/ And straight as she saw me she swelled like a toad,/ *Pattering the devil's Pater noster* to herself:/ God never made a more crabbed elf!"

Unfortunately, descriptions such as these are the high points of the work and are by no means common. Much of Part II is devoted to arguments between the old woman and her young husband and, while some of these are humorous, others are simply weighted down with proverbs. In addition, there are some strange lapses in dramatic structure for a poet who is also a playwright. Halfway through Part II, the December-May couple invite the young couple described in Part I to dine with them. During the dinner, the two husbands think to solve their emotional and financial problems by changing wives: As the young man in the December-May marriage begins to "cast a loving eye" on the young wife, her husband casts a loving look "to his plate," bought with the old wife's money. This comic dramatic situation, suggestive of a fabliau, is never developed by Heywood, and the young couple passes out of Part II with no effect on the story. It seems odd that Heywood went to the trouble of developing this dramatic situation only to leave it unresolved.

A similar ambiguity surrounds the narrator. In many ways his presence lends drama—and occasionally dramatic irony—to the work. His steadiness contrasts with his young friend's impulsiveness: After hearing the tale of the first two lovers, the young man would immediately hasten off to marry the old wealthy woman before even hearing about the December-May marriage. When he finally agrees to listen to the story of the second couple, he is so impatient that he will scarcely let the narrator pause for supper. Within the stories he tells, the narrator's role as confidant to both the young husband and the old wife provides humor as both come to him to complain of their marriage: "Out of doors went she herewith; and hereupon/ In at doors came he forthwith, as she was gone." The split-second timing of these entrances and departures shows Heywood's dramatic sense translated into comedy.

The narrator by no means provides a consistent focal point for the work, however, and his attitudes toward the December-May couple are not well defined. When the wife complains about her husband's numerous adulteries, she notes that they are not even necessary since "To tick and laugh with me he hath lawful leave." The narrator remarks that "To that I said nought, but laughed in my sleeve." If the narrator's callousness is used by Heywood to show the humor of the wife's predicament, he seems to change in the next chapter when he upbraids the husband for his behavior. Heywood seems to change the narrator's character as dramatic—or comic—propriety demands; in many ways, then, the narrator remains a cipher.

Heywood's verbal skill emerges in his play on words, a style that anticipates euphuism. Thus, when the uncle of the poor young man in Part I upbraids him for marrying against his family's wishes, he plays elaborately on the word *will*. Heywood often uses earthy images in his poetry, and this is true of *A Dialogue of Proverbs*. At one point there is a play on the words *purse,* purgation, and *laxative*. The arguments between the young husband and the old wife are especially rich in bawdy humor.

EPIGRAMS

Heywood's contemporaries saw him primarily as a writer of epigrams, and his output in this genre is enormous: He published collections of epigrams in 1550, 1555, 1560, and 1562. If, by an epigram, one means a short poem with a witty turn, then some of Heywood's epigrams do not even qualify as such. Epigram 92 of his first hundred, for example, is a long comparison of books and cheese, the point being that people differ in their tastes in both; it is hardly a startling display of wit. Similarly, he has several epigrams that are simply miniature sermons on some moral maxim.

At their best, however, Heywood's epigrams are lively examples of jest-book humor, drawing on animal fables, flytings, and colloquial dialogue for their effectiveness. Many of them involve invective between husband and wife; in fact, one almost suspects that Heywood considers marital arguments intrinsically amusing. Many of these colloquies, however, do contain humor in the form of puns and verbal quibbles. Occasionally one feels that, had Heywood worked in a longer form, he could have been a first-rate satirist. Epigram 30 of the first hundred is called "A Keeper of the Commandments" and is a relatively long epigram—forty-four lines—in which the narrator addresses a young rake and congratulates him on how well he "obeys" the Ten Commandments: For example, he has no more gods than one "for God thou hast none." The ironic play on the meaning of the Ten Commandments continues throughout the epigram, providing sardonic humor.

THE SPIDER AND THE FLY

If Heywood's canon may be judged by the amount of time he put into composing his poems, then surely *The Spider and the Fly* is his most important work: It did not appear until 1556, but Heywood says at the end that he had been working on it for more than twenty years. This time span may help to explain some of the ambiguity of the poem's allegory, for Heywood explicitly tells his audience in the preface that it is a parable. The story concerns a fly who wanders into a spider's web and is captured. This first leads to a debate between the spider and the fly as to the fly's legal rights and finally to an all-out

war between the nations of spiders and flies. At the end of the poem, all the forces having been spent, a maid comes into the room and brushes down the remaining cobwebs and kills the spider.

Finding a sustained allegory in this plot is difficult. The first part of the poem, setting forth the legal haggling of the two opponents, seems to be only a generalized satire on the legal practices of the day. In Chapter 27, however, the spider argues that "kings and peers" can be identified with spiders and flies. Obviously, Heywood has some topical reference in mind. Later, in Chapter 44, the fly and the spider talk heatedly about rents, and the whole issue of the fly's right to be on the windowpane seems to hint at the enclosure laws. If the poem is in part about those laws, then the spider would have to represent the nobles and the fly the peasants. This seems out of keeping, however, with the spider's earlier assertion that he and the fly represent kings and peers. Furthermore, the ending of the poem seems to shift ground toward religious allegory. In the conclusion of the poem, Heywood identifies the maid as Queen Mary. Most critics, therefore, see the spiders as representing Protestants and the flies Catholics: The maid's killing of the spider may be a reference to the execution of Archbishop Cranmer. The problem is that the conclusion, in which Heywood supposedly explains the poem's meaning, offers only generalized praise of Mary as a monarch "whose sword, like a broom . . . sweepeth out filth clean." Even Heywood's near-contemporaries had trouble with the poem's meaning: William Harrison, in his *Description of England* (1587), discusses "One [who] hath made a booke of the *Spider and the Flie*, wherein he dealeth so profoundlie, and beyond all measure of skill, that neither he himself that made it, neither anie one that readeth it, can reach unto the meaning thereof."

In a sense, the allegory of the poem is unimportant, for Heywood is at his best describing his characters on a very human level: He shows the mother spider's obvious pride in her "babe," who, at only eight weeks, wants to eat "some part of that flesh fly's brain." Similarly, the battle scenes define the mock-heroic nature of the poem as ants and flies prepare for glorious combat. Heywood also uses the witty puns and verbal quibbles of which he is so fond, especially in the legal debates between the spider and the fly. The fact remains, however, that the poem is simply too long: Once the reader has savored the initial incongruities that give the poem its mock-heroic tone, the speeches of the spiders and flies become tedious. There is also a curious lack of shaping in the plot, since, after the long war between the spiders and flies, the reader is left exactly where he or she was as the poem opened: Chapter 83 begins with the spider and the fly again debating the fly's fate. Perhaps this stalemate is necessary for the introduction of the maid (Queen Mary), whose wisdom finally solves the conflict, but it makes the main events of the poem seem curiously superfluous.

SHORTER POEMS

Heywood's shorter poems are strikingly different in content and poetic skill. Some are merely didactic, with little aesthetic leavening: "I desyre no number of manye thinges for store"; "Man, for thyne yll life formerly"; "The harme that groweth of idlenes." On the other hand, the short emphatic lines of "A ballad against slander and detraction" give the poem a vigor and forcefulness lacking in many of Heywood's other moralizing works. His most striking poems either commemorate a specific person or event or are on less serious themes.

Of the first group, the poems about Queen Mary, while uneven in quality, do have some excellent lines. The imperative that opens "A song in praise of a Ladie" imparts an energy to the poem that some of the later rather tame compliments seem to undermine. His metrical craftsmanship is also noticeably lacking: The stanzas vary markedly in their metrics and the two extant versions of the poem show Heywood making changes in phrasing that seem to disregard the meter of his lines. The poem celebrating Mary's marriage to Philip relies mostly on heavy alliteration to achieve its effects, while the central metaphor of lamb (Mary) and eagle (Philip) seems strained and awkward.

The poem "A breefe balet touching the traytorous takynge of Scarborow Castell" contains individual lines that are striking: "Ye thought ye tooke the castell at your landyng,/ The castell takyng you in the selfe whyle." Yet the didactic element perhaps keeps the poem from achieving what it might otherwise have done. The second stanza, for example, opens with a labored explanation that Scarborow Castle is simply a symbol of all royal lands, as if Heywood fears that an unobservant reader might be led by the poem to attack other property of the Crown. Furthermore, although the poem opens with an almost sympathetic picture of the gallant invaders, it does not go on to explore the ambiguity of seemingly heroic men caught in an ill-conceived venture: By the end of the poem they have become total villains. Heywood's most successful lyric, "All a grene wyllow is my garland," contains some lovely lines, while others occasionally fall flat. Nevertheless, its lyricism and Petrarchan conventions make it a fine example of early Renaissance love poetry.

Although Heywood is rather limited in poetic form—doing most of his work in epigrams or narrative poems—and is not always totally successful even in those forms, his work does show the sort of wit that later writers would develop more fully. His love of puns, wordplay, and alliteration seems to foreshadow writers such as Lyly, while his bawdry and comic realism align him with John Skelton and others. Thus his writing shows, in embryo, the beginnings of two very different—but typically Renaissance—types of writing. In this sense, his wit was certainly eclectic.

OTHER MAJOR WORKS

PLAYS: *The Play of Love*, pr. c. 1528-1529; *Witty and Witless*, wr. c. 1533, pb. 1846 (abridged), 1909 (also known as *A Dialogue on Wit and Folly*); *The Pardoner and the Friar*, pb. 1533 (possibly based on *Farce nouvelle d'un pardonneur, d'un triacleur, et d'une tavernière*); *Johan Johan the Husband, Tyb His Wife, and Sir Johan the Priest*, pb. 1533 (commonly known as *Johan Johan*; adaptation of *Farce nouvelle et fort joyeuse du pasté*); *The Play of the Weather*, pb. 1533; *Gentleness and Nobility*, pb. 1535 (attributed to Heywood); *The Playe of the Foure P.P.: A Newe and a Very Mery Enterlude of a Palmer, a Pardoner, a Potycary, a Pedler*, pb. 1541-1547 (commonly known as *The Four P.P.*; possibly based on *Farce nouvelle d'un pardonneur, d'un triacleur, et d'une tavernière*); *The Dramatic Writings of John Heywood*, pb. 1905 (John S. Farmer, editor).

MISCELLANEOUS: *Works*, 1562 (epigrams and poems); *Works and Miscellaneous Short Poems*, 1956 (Burton A. Milligan, editor).

BIBLIOGRAPHY

Bolwell, Robert W. *The Life and Works of John Heywood.* New York: Columbia University Press, 1921. This biography covers Heywood's early life, his years as a court entertainer, then as the queen's favorite, and finally his exile from England. The final chapter reviews his nondramatic writing, including poetry. The analysis tends to overlook personal and social influences, dwelling on his political career in court. A good but hardly definitive look at Heywood's life and works. Includes a chronology, original source material, and a bibliography.

De la Bere, Rupert. *John Heywood, Entertainer.* London: Allen & Unwin, 1937. This balanced, conservative analysis of Heywood's life and writing includes a short biographical introduction and special sections on the lesser known *A Dialogue of Proverbs* and *The Spider and the Fly.* Several texts are included as well as a bibliography.

Henderson, Judith Rice. "John Heywood's *The Spider and the Flie:* Educating Queen and Country." *Studies in Philology* 96, no. 3 (Summer, 1999): 241-274. Heywood's *The Spider and the Flie* has been one of the least appreciated of many neglected poems of mid-Tudor England. Henderson claims that Heywood's purpose for writing the poem was not only to instruct but also to exhort commoners, professionals, magistrates, and the monarch to fulfill their obligations to the commonwealth.

Heywood, John. *John Heywood's Works and Miscellaneous Short Poems.* Edited by Burton A. Milligan. Urbana: University of Illinois Press, 1956. A sound textual edition of Heywood's works with detailed notes throughout. The introduction reviews his literary reputation through the ages and ends with a reappraisal of Heywood as a unique though minor poet in the popular tradition of proverbs, fables, and other verse forms. The author characterizes Heywood as a satirist-without-malice with a colorful and colloquial English style.

Johnson, Robert Carl. *John Heywood.* New York: Twayne, 1970. This in-depth study explores Heywood's place in English literary history. A helpful chronological table accompanies a historical and biographical sketch which highlights Heywood's commitment to Christian humanism. A lengthy analysis of the poetry and the plays portrays Heywood as a comic poet rooted in the traditions of Tudor England. This book is an excellent source and contains a useful annotated bibliography.

_____. *Minor Elizabethans Bibliography.* London: Nether Press, 1968. This list is designed to update the earlier bibliography by Samuel A. Tannenbaum and Dorothy R. Tannenbaum and to aid in finding more detailed and specific references.

Tannenbaum, Samuel A., and Dorothy R. Tannenbaum. *John Heywood: A Concise Bibliography.* New York: S. A. Tannenbaum, 1946. This valuable bibliographic listing is divided into four sections: primary works, selections, biographies, commentaries, and bibliographical data. An important source for Heywood materials.

Walker, Greg. *The Politics of Performance in Early Renaissance Drama.* New York: Cambridge University Press, 1998. Interesting for its insights into Heywood in the context of the sociopolitical culture of Elizabethan England, this study examines the relationship between politics and drama in Heywood's day, exploring the complex relationships among politics, court culture, dramatic composition, performance, and publication. Heywood is addressed in a chapter titled "John Heywood and the Politics of Contentment."

Carole Moses;
bibliography updated by the editors

NAZIM HIKMET

Born: Salonika, the Ottoman Empire (now Thessaloníki, Greece); January 20, 1902
Died: Moscow, Soviet Union; June 3, 1963

PRINCIPAL POETRY
Güneşi içenlerin türküsü, 1928
835 satır, 1929
Jokond ile Si-Ya-U, 1929
Varan 3, 1930

1 + 1 = bir, 1930

Sesini kaybeden şehir, 1931

Gece gelen telgraf, 1932

Benerci kendini niçin öldürdü?, 1932

Portreler, 1935

Taranta Babu'ya mektuplar, 1935

Simavne Kadısı oğlu Şeyh Bedreddin destanı, 1936
    (*The Epic of Sheik Bedreddin,* 1977)

Moskova senfonisi, 1952 (*The Moscow Symphony,*
    1970)

Poems by Nazim Hikmet, 1954

Piraye için yazılmış saat 21-22 şiirleri, 1965

Şu 1941 yılında, 1965

Kurtuluş Savaşı destanı, 1965 (expanded as *Kuvayı
    Milliye,* 1968)

Dört hapisaneden, 1966

Rubailer, 1966 (*Rubaiyat,* 1985)

Yeni şiirler, 1966

Memleketimden insan manzaraları, 1966-1967 (5
    volumes; *Human Landscapes,* 1982)

Selected Poems, 1967

The Moscow Symphony and Other Poems, 1970

Son şiirler, 1970

The Day Before Tomorrow, 1972

*Things I Didn't Know I Loved: Selected Poems of
    Nazim Hikmet,* 1975

Kerem gibi, 1976

The Epic of Sheik Bedreddin and Other Poems,
    1977

Selected Poetry, 1986

OTHER LITERARY FORMS

Although he is remembered primarily for his poetry, Nazim Hikmet also became known early in his career for his plays; among the most notable of these are *Kafatası* (pb. 1931; the skull) and *Unutulan adam* (pb. 1935; the forgotten man), which deal with the practice of psychology and the conflict between worldly recognition and inner dissatisfaction. Other works in this genre, however, have been criticized for a facile identification of personages with political and social standpoints which they were meant to represent. Hikmet subsequently moved in other directions in his dramatic writing, first with works such as *Bir aşk masalı* (pb. 1945; a love story), which attempted a modern interpretation of traditional Middle Eastern characters; other plays involved experiments with old and new technical forms, as a part of the author's effort to adapt classical literary themes to contemporary concerns. Among later plays, by far the most widely known was *İvan İvanoviç var mıydı yok muydu?* (was there or was there not an Ivan Ivanovich?), which was written in exile and was first published in a Russian translation in 1956. In this contribution to the literary "thaw" in the Soviet Union, the author took issue with the personality cult and rigid, unswerving norms of criticism that had dominated creative writing under dictator Joseph Stalin.

Hikmet's narrative fiction is rather uneven; there is some moving and effective writing in *Sevdalı bulut* (1968; the cloud in love), which brings together short pieces, including children's stories, written over many years. His novels tend to display his ideological concerns; of these perhaps the most interesting is *Yeşil elmalar* (1965; green apples), which deals with crime, corruption, and penal detention. Also of interest as a semiautobiographical effort is *Yaşamak güzel şey bekardeşim* (1967; *The Romantics,* 1987). Works of political commentary furnish direct statements of the author's views on leading issues of his time; his treatises on Soviet democracy and on German fascism, both originally published in 1936, are particularly revealing in this regard. Other insights into the writer's thought may be gathered from his collected newspaper columns and compilations of his personal letters.

ACHIEVEMENTS

Throughout his creative lifetime, Nazim Hikmet was regarded as a politically controversial figure whose poetry expressed ideological concerns that situated him well to the left among Turkish writers of his generation. Although officially he was almost invariably out of favor in his own country—indeed, much of his adult life in Turkey was spent in prison, and work from his later years was composed under the shadow of Soviet cultural standard-bearers—his experiments with versification produced poetic forms that, more than any other works, announced the introduction of modern techniques into Turkish writing in this genre. During the last years of the Ottoman Empire, major innovations had been attempted by leading literary figures; language reform movements

Nazim Hikmet in 1950 in Istanbul, Turkey. (AP/Wide World Photos)

case against him. In 1950, the Soviet Union conferred its World Peace Prize upon Nazim Hikmet, an award he shared with Pablo Neruda. During the last years of Hikmet's life, he made a number of public appearances in Moscow, Warsaw, and capitals of other Soviet bloc countries. After his death, his work became the subject of lively discussion, much of it favorable, in his native Turkey, and important writings once more were published. Students of and specialists in Turkish literature have widely acknowledged his leading position among modern poets.

BIOGRAPHY

On January 20, 1902, Nazim Hikmet was born in Salonika, the port city in Thrace which was then part of the Ottoman Empire. His father was a physician who had held government appointments; his mother was a painter, and his grandfather, Nazim Paşa, was a poet and critic of some note. As a boy, Hikmet was introduced to local literary circles. His first poems were written when he was about seventeen. He was educated in Istanbul, at the French-language Galatasaray Lycée and at the Turkish Naval Academy. Although poor health precluded a military career, he went on to Moscow during the early period of Soviet-Turkish friendship; between 1922 and 1924 he studied at the University of the Workers of the East. He derived inspiration from the events of the Russian Revolution and probably was influenced as well by the bold new literary ventures of Soviet poets such as Sergei Aleksandrovich Esenin and Vladimir Vladimirovich Maiakovskii. Upon his return to his native country, Hikmet joined the Turkish Communist Party, which by then had been forced into a clandestine existence; in Izmir he worked for a left-wing publication and was sentenced to fifteen years in prison. He fled to the Soviet Union and returned only after a general amnesty was proclaimed in 1928. By that time his first book-length collection of poems had been published in Soviet Azerbaijan. In Turkey the Communist Party had been formally outlawed, and Hikmet was arrested forthwith.

proceeded alongside the development of literary vehicles suitable for wider circles of readers among the masses. Enlarging upon the earlier efforts of Mehmet Tevfik Fikret and other important writers, Nazim Hikmet devised new and strikingly resonant verse patterns that in their turn pointed to the possibilities that could be achieved with the use of free verse. Moreover, while admittedly experimental, his verse was distinctive in the unusual confluence of models chosen: Hikmet's poems show the influence of Soviet postsymbolists while, in some notable works, recalling classical Islamic traditions in modern, reworked guises. Hikmet's poetry is alternately strident in its political declamations and intensely personal in its evocations of the writer's sufferings and innermost wants. Many of his prose works, while never really descending to the level of Socialist Realism, are somewhat more narrowly symptomatic of the ideological persuasions that guided him.

Apart from his literary fame, Hikmet became well known from the political charges for which he served an aggregate of seventeen years in Turkish prisons. In 1949, an international committee was formed in Paris to press for his release; among others, Jean-Paul Sartre, Pablo Picasso, Louis Aragon, and Paul Robeson petitioned for the reopening of the Turkish government's

Nevertheless, Turkish publishers brought out verse collections such as *835 satır* (835 lines) and others; his works were deemed inflammatory by the authorities, who claimed that they incited workers against the government. He was imprisoned twice and later was able to find work mainly as a proofreader, translator, and scriptwriter. Indeed, some of his early poems refer to the tedious routine of his daily work, to which he was effectively restricted because of his political convictions. Although his plays won critical recognition, and some acclaim, for their introduction of new, unconventional dramatic forms—here Hikmet may in some ways have followed the technical innovations of Bertolt Brecht—political writings and newspaper columns had to be published under a pseudonym. He turned to historical topics, which nevertheless allowed range for his leftist populist outlook: The last work published in Turkey during his lifetime was *The Epic of Sheik Bedreddin and Other Poems*, which includes a long poem narrating events surrounding the life and death of the leader of a fifteenth century peasant revolt.

In January, 1938, new charges were brought against Hikmet; because copies of his poems were found in the possession of military cadets, he was arraigned for inciting unrest in the armed forces. A military court found him guilty, though the original sentence of thirty-five years was reduced to twenty-eight. During his imprisonment in Bursa, Hikmet embarked upon his poetic magnum opus, *Human Landscapes*, which was to be published only after his death, in a five-volume edition of 1966-1967. This monumental, and sometimes disjointed, work was circulated in parts among the poet's friends, family, and confidants; some portions of it were confiscated by the Turkish police or otherwise disappeared. Much of the writing Hikmet produced in prison has a musing, poignant, indeed bittersweet quality that was not so pronounced in his earlier works. On the other hand, some poems alight upon world events of which he had heard in passing: Germany's invasion of the Soviet Union, in 1941, and the United States' use of an atom bomb against Hiroshima at the end of World War II, are discussed in his verse from this period. In 1949, in spite of having suffered a heart attack, Hikmet undertook a hunger strike that lasted seventeen days. In response to international pressure, the Turkish government released him from prison in 1950, but shortly thereafter, in order to curb the expression of his political views, he was made liable for conscripted military service. The following year, Hikmet fled the country alone in a small fishing boat; he was taken on board a Romanian ship in the Black Sea and eventually made his way to Moscow.

During his years in exile, the last period of his life, Hikmet lived for some time in the Soviet capital and in Warsaw; he took out a Polish passport under the name Borzęcki, after a family to which he had traced some of his ancestors. Sometimes he also used the added surname Ran. He traveled widely and attended literary congresses in other Soviet bloc countries; he also spent much time in Paris. He visited China, Cuba, and Tanganyika. Once he was refused a visa to enter the United States. Although he was not a literary conformist, he continued to uphold Soviet positions on international security. Some of his works from this period did him little credit, though they dealt with issues similar to those of his earlier activist poems. He suffered from angina pectoris, which had developed during his longest prison term, and other chronic health complaints arose later as well. While he lived in Turkey he had married three times; his imprisonment had made settled family life impossible. In Moscow he took up residence with a fetching young "straw blonde" Vera Tuliakova. Some of his later poems wistfully call back images of the women in his life or point to the hopes he still cherished in spite of his advancing age and his problematical physical state. After a final heart attack, Nazim Hikmet died in Moscow on June 3, 1963. Homage was rendered him from leading literary figures in many countries. Since his death his reputation among Turkish writers has grown apace.

ANALYSIS

According to some estimates, the poetry of Nazim Hikmet has been translated into at least fifty languages. Perhaps more than any other Turkish writer, his work transcended the bounds of stylized Ottoman versification; at their best, his poems call to mind settings the author knew well, while extending a universal appeal on behalf of his social beliefs. Lyrical and rhetorical passages occur alternately in some of his major works;

his epics exhibit narrative powers which in some segments are used to depict events from the distant past or to evoke those from the author's lifetime.

Moreover, though early in his career he came to be known as much for his outspoken ideological positions as for his literary achievements, Hikmet's poetry conveys the sudden dramatic impact of historical occurrences; social issues are depicted in ways that can be felt beyond the strict limits of party politics. On a more personal level, romantic yearnings, whimsical observations of street scenes and travel, and indeed nature and the weather are discussed in simple yet deeply felt lines that complement Hikmet's more directly expressed political concerns. Some of his poems communicate the loneliness and anxiety he felt as a political prisoner, without indulging particularly in self-pity. On the whole, he cannot be classified purely as a rationalist or a romantic; rather, his works combine elements of both inclinations.

LANGUAGE

From the outset, Hikmet's poetry was brash, vibrant, and politically engaged; defiantly casting aside traditional poetic styles, the author's work exuberantly mixed ideology and amorous inclinations in lines that at first glance resemble dismembered declarative sentences punctuated by crisp, staccato repetitions of phrases and nouns. Statements begun on one line are carried forward, with indentations, to the next, and sometimes further indentations are inserted before the thought is concluded. Question marks and exclamation points enliven stirring passages in which the author seems to be carrying on a dialogue with himself, if not with nature or society.

The vowel harmony characteristic of the Turkish language is used to impart added force and velocity to some passages; moreover, the author's writing drew from folk songs, time-honored national sagas, and other sources in eclectic and distinctive combinations. Colloquial expressions, lower-class idioms, and outright vulgarisms appear from time to time. This approach, which seems ever fresh and lively in the hands of a talented practitioner, is notably well suited to Hikmet's subject matter. One early poem, evidently composed in a devil-may-care mood, contrasts the author's straitened and difficult circumstances—his many monotonous hours as a lowly proofreader were rewarded with a pittance—and the effervescent sensations of springtime, with Cupid urging him after a comely girl.

JOKOND ILE SI-YA-U

Considerable powers of creative imagination were called upon in early poetry of a political character. In the long poem *Jokond ile Si-Ya-U* (the Gioconda and Si-Ya-U), various narrative transitions are conjoined with abrupt changes of setting, from Paris to the open sea to Shanghai under the white terror; eventually the author's summary is presented from his vantage point in Europe. Some of Hikmet's experiences during his travel—he had met Chinese revolutionaries during a visit to France—appear in an ultimately fictional and somewhat fantastic form. The author, who is bored and chafing at what he regards as hidebound aesthetic classicism in the Louvre, comes upon a modern Gioconda in a most unusual guise. Her modern incarnation is exotic and remote, but deeply concerned about mass upheaval that aims at the transformation of traditional Asian society. Still inscrutable, she is made to stand by as the soldiers of nationalist leader Chiang Kai-shek execute a Chinese Communist spokesman. Ultimately the Gioconda is tried and found guilty by a French military court; hers is a fate quite different from spending centuries on canvas as a creation of Leonardo da Vinci. Other works express Hikmet's proletarian views of art: Beethoven's sonatas, he maintains, should be played out on wood and metal in the workplace. The raw power of the industrial age is reflected in his taut descriptive lines about iron suspension bridges and concrete skyscrapers. Yet the workers in his native Turkey were invariably badly off: They were bound to an unthinking routine and could afford only the lowest quality of goods.

TARANTA BABU'YA MEKTUPLAR

One early composition took up the cause of striking transportation workers in Istanbul in 1929. At times Hikmet considered events that were not too far removed from his own experience; his sojourns in Russia during the early years of the Soviet government probably furnished impressions recaptured in verses about the revolutionary events of 1917. Poems collected in *Taranta Babu'ya mektuplar* (letters to Tarantu Babu) raised another problem in world politics; they are letters in verse purportedly written by a young Italian to a native woman caught up in the Ethiopian war launched under Benito Mussolini. The author's commentary on the brutal excesses of fascism reveals a measure of political prescience as well as an expanded sense of solidarity with like-minded people in many nations.

THE EPIC OF SHEIK BEDREDDIN

Historical dimensions of class struggle are explored in *The Epic of Sheik Bedreddin*. Although government pressure by this time had restricted his choice of subject matter, making it almost impossible for him to publish work on contemporary issues, the author turned to more remote ages with the avowed intent of rescuing major events from the antiquarian dust that had gathered around them. This epic, based upon a book he had read during one of his early prison terms, was given added intensity by the author's experience of seeing a man hanged outside the window of his cell. While set in the early fifteenth century, Hikmet's work underscores the solidarity that brought together Turkish peasants, Greek fishermen, and Jewish merchants; in places he suggests that though historical works had depicted this era as the prelude to an age of imperial greatness, it in fact was rife with social unrest and discontent provoked by inequality and injustice. Ten thousand common people took up arms to oppose the sultan before the rebellion was finally put down. The eventual execution of his protagonist, one of the insurgents' leaders, was a grim, bloody business that Hikmet recounts in unsparing detail but with impassioned sensitivity. This long poem, one of the most celebrated in Turkish literature of the twentieth century, is also notable for the author's broadening concern with different verse techniques, which reached fruition with his works combining modern usage with classical Persian meters.

PRISON POEMS

During Hikmet's longest period of imprisonment, between 1938 and 1950, works displaying other facets of his poetic consciousness were composed; his outlook seemed to become more deeply personal, though perhaps not so brash and self-assertive as in some of his first poems. His meditations on the springtime reveal a sense of yearning and melancholy that was previously absent. For a time he was held in solitary confinement. He wrote of singing to himself and watching shadows on the wall; simple things began to matter more to him.

There are a number of touching passages in prison poems that he addressed to Piraye, his second wife; brief, bittersweet phrases recall their shared joys together, aspects of her appearance, and simple pleasures that mattered most to him.

The long period of his incarceration led to some brooding reflections on the transitory and changeless issues of this life. In some poems there is speculation on the seasons that have come and gone, children who have been conceived and grown since he entered prison; mountains in the distance, however, remain fixed points separated by specific spatial intervals. There are also some ironic musings on the fates of common criminals from among his fellow prisoners: One of them was held for murder but was paroled after seven and one-half years; after a second, much shorter, sentence for smuggling, he was released for good and eventually married. The couple's child would be born while much of Hikmet's term, as a political prisoner, still remained to be served.

Angina pectoris, followed by a heart attack, aroused uncertainty about the author's physical condition. He wrote poems reaffirming the necessity to go on living, particularly with half his heart devoted anyway to social concerns in Turkey or to political struggles in Greece and China. Some works that begin by marking the passage of time in prison contain brief but intense reactions to events of World War II, including bombing raids, the liberation of concentration camps at Dachau, and the dawn of the nuclear age.

RUBAIYAT

One collection of poems, *Rubaiyat*, written in 1945 but published posthumously in 1966, reveals the author's search for further literary forms that would express the ideological and philosophical content of his thought. Beginning with the example of the Sufi poet and religious thinker Jalāl al-Dīn Rūmī (1207-1273), Hikmet took up the position in effect that mysticism is merely a veiled means of approaching material and social reality. Hikmet purposely adopted the quatrain, on a pattern similar to that used by Omar Khayyám, specifically to take issue with the Persian poet's supposed hedonism. In some lines, counsel to take wine and be joyful is contrasted with the harsh, inescapable routines of working-class life. Elsewhere the philosophical idealism of classical writers is challenged by Hikmet's own commitment to dialectical materialism; in poems dedicated to Piraye, the poet asks whether the images he retains of her correspond to the material reality he remembers. On a technical level, this work is notable as well for the author's provocative insertion of colloquial language in passages that otherwise conform to time-honored standards of versification.

HUMAN LANDSCAPES

Contemporary history on a panoramic scale is taken up in *Human Landscapes*, which was written during the author's prison years but was only published several years after his death. Beginning with the project for an epic study of Turkish history during the twentieth century, at intervals the poet's narrative also turns to major events in adjoining regions, notably naval action of World War II in the Mediterranean and the work of Soviet forces against Nazi invaders. His commentary on the Turkish War of Independence (1919-1922) stands in stark contrast to the heroic national themes repeatedly invoked by other writers of that period. In Hikmet's view, it would seem that the people as a whole contributed to final victory but only through an inchoate mass rising that did not also lead to a social revolution. Indeed, many passages suggest that class differences remained acute but were altered by Turkey's changed status in the world economy. There are a number of brief sketches of individual lives, both from the wealthy and from the lower orders, often to state unpleasant truths about the people's living situation. Some characters, it is recorded, died of disease at early ages; farmers retained their land but lost all means of production. Many of the personages are war veterans from one conflict or another. There is much attention to dates, but not in the sense of commemorating events with patriotic connotations; important occurrences in individual lives are accorded the same emphasis as major developments in the nation's history. There is also a fair amount of random, seemingly senseless violence: Family quarrels lead to murder; after a man kills his wife, children use the head as a ball in a macabre game. A wrenching, gripping scene records the lynching of a Turk who had collaborated with the British occupation forces. There are some sardonic religious references which call to mind folk superstitions; in some later passages, Turks of a pro-

German inclination speculate about whether Adolf Hitler could be a Muslim. Leading Turkish statesmen and thinkers figure as portraits on the walls of business offices; the memories associated with them are quirky bits of characterization that are far from flattering.

The work as a whole darts about and circumambulates historical epochs as they affected different, indeed opposing, social classes. After nearly fifteen years of national independence, homeless and desperately hungry men are to be found outside a newspaper office; if wealthy businessmen cannot turn a profit in some branches of the export trade, because of government restrictions, they move readily to other sectors where their fortunes can be augmented. Some of them end up dealing with both the Allied and the Axis powers during World War II. The incidence of suicide on either side of the class divide is fairly high; among the poor, childbirth is difficult, painful, and sometimes ends in tragedy. Although this exercise in historical realism, based on the author's own observations of Turkish life, does not seem to hold out any immediate hopes for a better future, the poet's descriptions of nature and simple joys serve to leaven an otherwise grim and unsentimental saga.

Some later segments of this work are essentially similar to portions of *The Moscow Symphony and Other Poems*, an imaginative lyrical reconstruction of German-Soviet fighting which in the first instance was probably based upon news stories that Hikmet received in prison. After allowance for the different languages, it may be argued that some passages would do credit to a Soviet wartime poet: the anxiety of the war's first year, the vast human drama of armies locked in combat, and the camaraderie of soldiers brought together in common struggle are evoked in brisk, telling lines. Hikmet's own allegiances are discussed in another section, which depicts the execution of an eighteen-year-old Russian girl for partisan action against the Nazis. He wrote, "Tanya,/ I have your picture here in front of me in Bursa Prison," and, before returning to the Turkish settings where his epic had commenced, he added:

> Tanya,
> I love my country
>   as much as you loved yours.

LAST POEMS

Nazim Hikmet's last poems in some ways chronicled the tribulations of exile; many works had to do with his travels about the Communist world, as well as into Switzerland and to Paris. The impression arises that he considered many of his destinations as way stations; hotel balconies, train depots, arrivals and departures are recorded repeatedly and almost mechanically. His political works from this period, albeit written in countries that were openly receptive to his views, were lacking perhaps in the combative spirit that had distinguished the poems written in Turkey. Among such productions there may be found some caustic observations in verse on the Korean War—he deplored Turkey's participation in that conflict—as well as more positive and uplifting efforts composed for May Day celebrations or in response to the Cuban revolution. One poem was meant to commemorate the fortieth anniversary of the foundation of the Turkish Communist Party. His personal concerns, perhaps, were handled more effectively in his later works. One poem describes his meeting with a young blonde woman in an express train; as the sights pass by outside afterimages of her hair and eyelashes and of her long black coat repeatedly appear before his eyes. Some poems expressed his desire to be reunited with his lover, Vera Tuliakova, after journeys about various East European countries. In other works there are somewhat sour comments on his physical condition, which continued to deteriorate during his years in exile. Although he continued to cherish the values of this existence, some passages became dour and premonitory. Toward the end of his life he speculated:

> Will my funeral start out from our courtyard?
> How will you take me down from the third floor?
> The coffin won't fit in the elevator,
> and the stairs are awfully narrow.

LEGACY

For many years, Nazim Hikmet was regarded as Turkey's best-known Communist; his conspicuously partisan poetry on behalf of the working classes created more controversy than the pronouncements of many political figures. His importance as a poet, however, may be measured by the extent to which his works have been read even as interest in his ideological agitation, the long-standing scandal of his imprisonment, and his life in exile have become past concerns. While it is possible to distinguish major phases in his career as a poet—and arguably within those periods he was subject to variable moods—there are also elements of continuity which in their turn point to the enduring features of his work. Although some of his efforts may have aged more gracefully than others, his concerns with social justice, and with the struggle against fascism in Europe, certainly would find sympathy with many subsequent readers. He maintained that Marxism interested him largely for its literary possibilities and that his work was involved largely in the basic human issues of his time. His poems are quite possibly the most readily recognized of those from any Turkish writer of the twentieth century. Aside from his political fame, or notoriety, it may be contended not only that he had discovered forms by which modern free verse might be composed in Turkish but also that he had come upon themes and techniques which have been found to be intrinsically appealing on a much wider level.

OTHER MAJOR WORKS

LONG FICTION: *Kan konuşmaz*, 1965; *Yeşil elmalar*, 1965; *Yaşamak güzel şey bekardeşim*, 1967 (*The Romantics*, 1987).

SHORT FICTION: *Sevdalı bulut*, 1968.

PLAYS: *Ocak başında*, pb. 1920; *Kafatası*, pb. 1931; *Bir ölü evi yahut merhumun hanesi*, pb. 1932; *Unutulan adam*, pb. 1935; *Bir aşk masalı*, pb. 1945; *İvan İvanoviç var mıydı yok muydu?*, in Russian pb. 1956, in Turkish pb. 1971; *Enayi*, pb. 1958; *İnek*, pb. 1958; *İstasyon*, pb. 1958; *Yusuf ve Zeliha*, pb. 1963; *Sabahat*, pb. 1966; *Yolcu*, pb. 1966; *Damokles'in kılıcı*, pb. 1971; *Fatma, Ali ve başkaları*, pb. 1971; *Her şeye rağmen*, pb. 1971.

NONFICTION: *Sovyet demokrasisi*, 1936; *Alman faşizmi ve ırkçılığı*, 1936; *İt ürür kervan yürür*, 1965; *Cezaevinden Mehmet Fuat'a mektuplar*, 1968; *Kemal Tahir'e mahpusaneden mektuplar*, 1968; *Oğlum, canım evladim, Memedim*, 1968; *Bursa cezaevinden Va-Nu'lara mektuplar*, 1970; *Nazim ile Piraye*, 1975.

MISCELLANEOUS: *Bütün eserleri*, 1967-1972 (8 volumes; collected works).

BIBLIOGRAPHY

Des Pres, Terrence. "Poetry and Politics: The Example of Nazim Hikmet." *Parnassus: Poetry in Review* 6, no. 2 (1978): 7-25. A study of the political aspects of Hikmet's poetry.

Göksu, Saime, and Edward Timms. *Romantic Communist: The Life and Work of Nazim Hikmet.* New York: St. Martin's Press, 1999. The authors propose in this biography of Nazim Hikmet that his life and career form a microcosm of twentieth century politics. Göksu and Timms explore Hikmet's life chronologically through ten well-researched chapters. The clear structure helps the narrative to flow from one chapter to the next and allows the reader to grasp both the detail and the broad picture. Includes bibliographical references and index.

Kinzer, Stephen. "Turkish Poet Is Lauded, but Stays Exiled in Death." *The New York Times*, February 27, 1997, p. A4. As Turkey settles into what is likely to be an extended confrontation between secular and pro-Islamic forces, symbols take on exagerrated political importance for both sides. Perhaps no individual crystallizes the conflict better than Nazim Hikmet, atheist and Communist and also one of the greatest literary figures ever to emerge from this country.

J. R. Broadus;
bibliography updated by the editors

GEOFFREY HILL

Born: Bromsgrove, Worcestershire, England; June 18, 1932

PRINCIPAL POETRY

For the Unfallen: Poems, 1952-1958, 1959
King Log, 1968
Mercian Hymns, 1971
Somewhere Is Such a Kingdom: Poems, 1952-1971, 1975 (includes previous three collections)
Tenebrae, 1978
The Mystery of the Charity of Charles Péguy, 1983
Collected Poems, 1985
New and Collected Poems, 1952-1992, 1994
Canaan, 1996
The Triumph of Love, 1998
Speech! Speech!, 2000
The Orchards of Syon, 2002

OTHER LITERARY FORMS

Lords of Limit: Essays on Literature and Ideas (1984) is a collection of literary criticism and essays, including work on rhythm in poetry, George Eliot, and Tory radicalism. *The Enemy's Country: Words, Contexture, and Other Circumstances of Language,* (1991) is a monograph on the language of judgment, chiefly focusing on the poet John Dryden. It is a revision of Hill's Clark Lectures at Trinity College, Cambridge, in 1986. Geoffrey Hill also translated Henrik Ibsen's *Brand,* in 1978.

ACHIEVEMENTS

Since his attendance at Oxford in the early 1950's, Geoffrey Hill has won recognition as a significant poet; in the late 1960's and 1970's many critics, notably Donald Hall, Christopher Ricks, and Harold Bloom, championed him as a major poet of the twentieth century. His verse is characterized by mastery of difficult patterns of rhyme and allusions to historical and literary figures. His most frequent themes are religion and tradition, which he portrays in complex, often-contradictory ways. Some critics attack him for obscurity; others defend his dense style as perfectly suited to the difficulty of the thought he conveys. He has won many awards, including the Eric Gregory Award for Poetry (1961), the Geoffrey Faber Memorial Prize (1970), and the Whitbread Award (1971). He received the Loines Award of the American Academy and Institute of Arts and Letters in 1983 and in 1996 became a fellow of that academy. *The Triumph of Love* was cowinner of the Royal Society of Literature's Heinemann Award in 2000, and in the same year, Hill received the Ingersoll Foundation's T. S. Eliot Award for Creative Writing.

BIOGRAPHY

Geoffrey Hill was born on June 18, 1932, in the small market town of Bromsgrove, in Worcestershire,

England. He grew up in a nearby village, Fairfield, in which his father worked as a policeman. He was a lonely, introspective child who often went for solitary walks.

On these walks, he sometimes recited to himself poetry that he had learned from Oscar Williams's *A Little Treasury of Modern Poetry, English and American* (1946), a popular collection stressing such modernists as Ezra Pound, T. S. Eliot, and William Carlos Williams. Hill continued his devotion to poetry after his enrollment at Kelbe College, Oxford, in 1950. He was not among the most active members of the young Oxford literary set. Quite the contrary, he concentrated on his studies in English, gaining a thorough knowledge of English literary and intellectual history.

Under the aegis of Donald Hall, a well-known poet and translator of Japanese literature, Hill did publish a few poems. Hill's work at once attracted attention, but he did not sway from his intention to become a university teacher and scholar of English.

After graduation, he accepted a post in the English department of Leeds University. Here he benefited from contact with G. Wilson Knight, generally regarded as the foremost twentieth century Shakespeare critic. Knight, like Hill, was a polymath interested especially in the religious and symbolic aspects of poetry. Perhaps under the stimulus of Knight, among others, Hill continued to write verse. He also won a reputation as a difficult and immensely learned lecturer.

Hill's career since the 1950's has in essence continued the pattern laid down in his early adulthood. The continued attention his verse has received has transformed him from an academic who writes poetry into a poet who also works as a scholar. He was elected fellow of Emmanuel College, Cambridge, in 1980; this college is famous for its English faculty, which has included F. R. Leavis, among the most formidable and controversial of twentieth century critics. In 1988, he became university professor and professor of literature and religion at Boston University. Hill was married to Nancy Whittaker in 1956, and the couple has four children.

ANALYSIS

From his earliest work, religion and history have dominated Geoffrey Hill's poetry. Although a religious poet, he does not defend any particular orthodoxy. Instead, he explores various positions, often incorporating later poems in a sequence to reject positions upheld earlier. He often meditates on World Wars I and II, concentrating especially on Adolf Hitler's murder of the Jews.

Hill's work since *For the Unfallen* has rung the changes on a few constant themes. He has bitterly criticized the modern world: Its power and might have led to senseless slaughter, culminating in the Nazis' mass murder of Jews. Hill would like to find solace in premodern society and religion but is unable to do so. He can muster no more than critical interest in Christianity: He refuses consolation. His difficult rhymes and obscure diction mirror his pessimistic frame of mind.

FOR THE UNFALLEN

Many of these themes surfaced in Hill's first major collection, *For the Unfallen: Poems, 1952-1958*. The book begins with "Genesis," one of the few poems Hill kept from a small pamphlet published while he was in college. The poem describes a series of walks taken in

Geoffrey Hill (Alice Goodman, courtesy of Houghton Mifflin)

Worcestershire. In part 1, Hill dreams of creating a god-like language through poetry. Just as Adam was given authority to name all the animals of creation and thus to rule over them, so the poet can bring his own world into existence through verbal artifice.

Hill makes this suggestion only to withdraw it in part 2. He now portrays the poet as a skeptic withdrawn from the world. The reader might at this point think that Hill has pictured the poet as creator in order to denounce this view for undue pride. Hill once again proves elusive, as later parts hint that a poet who acknowledges humanity's lapse from perfection can return strengthened from a confrontation with sin and disillusion. He can then create a harmonious world that evokes Eden before the Fall; the difference from the initial claim to mastery is that the poet realizes the precarious nature of his vision.

For the Unfallen also includes a six-part sequence, "Of Commerce and Society," presenting a pessimistic attitude toward history. Hill criticizes the development of European society since the Renaissance. Commercial values have gained control of the major European states. The pursuit of money and power is inimical to art. The last poem in the sequence, "The Martyrdom of Saint Sebastian," describes a Jamesian artist whose devotion to high artistic standards leads to conflict with the public and their rejection of his work. The poet's fate is compared to Christian martyrdom.

The attitude so far described fits with Hill's devotion to the Tory Radicals of the nineteenth century. The "Young England" movement rejected the business values of the Industrial Revolution. Instead, figures such as Benjamin Disraeli preached return to the standards of medieval England. The Oxford philosopher T. H. Green, the subject of an essay in Hill's *Lords of Limit*, criticized capitalism for its undue accent on the separation of individuals. The Christian socialist F. D. Maurice was another key figure in this antibusiness tradition.

One might expect Hill to support a return to tradition, but, as always, the poet refuses to be pinned down. In "The Lowlands of Holland" he declares Europe dead because of its paralysis by tradition. Folk songs, used throughout the sequence, do not serve to support a return to "Merrie Old England"; they instead suggest the

weight of the past. Holland, the earliest center of European capitalism, is also a great center of art and culture, but its achievements are insufficient to stave off decay. Like Ezra Pound, Hill dislikes finance with savage intensity.

Perhaps the artist can redeem society, as another poem in the sequence, "The Death of Shelley," suggests. Throughout most of his short life, Percy Bysshe Shelley was devoted to the French Revolution. He thought that the overthrow of superstition and barbarous customs would inaugurate a new era for humanity. The biblical promises of a new world would be fulfilled by human effort alone; no supernatural intervention was needed. In this hoped-for transformation, poets, the "unacknowledged legislators of mankind," would play a key part.

Though Hill treats Shelley's hopes with sympathy, he rejects them. The sequence makes evident Hill's belief that twentieth century events make millenarian optimism impossible. In particular, Hitler's murder of several million Jews, as well as other horrors of the twentieth century, compel Hill to reject belief in progress. Even a society run by artists cannot blot out the historical record of the world wars.

KING LOG

Hill's next major collection, *King Log*, appeared a decade later, in 1968. It included the contents of a beautifully printed pamphlet, *Preghiere*, issued four years previously, as well as other poems.

Preghiere is an Italian word meaning "prayers." The poems in this sequence suggest that the artist is a priest who can overcome political oppression through ascetic devotion to art. As an example, "Men Are a Mockery of Angels" is spoken in the voice of the sixteenth century poet and philosopher Tommaso Campanella. Campanella was a Platonist who believed in rule by an intellectual and artistic elite. He devised an elaborate utopia, described in *La città del sole* (1602; the city of the sun). Hill depicts Campanella as a joyous person in spite of his imprisonment by the Spanish Inquisition. While he is jailed, he thinks about his philosophy and thus gains a certain detachment, so that his grim physical surroundings do not drag him into despair.

As one might by now expect, Hill's endorsement of this view of the artist is at best equivocal. This becomes clear in a later poem in the sequence, "Domaine Publique," which commemorates the death of Robert Desnos, a French poet who perished at the Nazi death camp of Terezin. Hill imagines Desnos mocking the Christian practice of asceticism. The charnel house created by the Nazis was not a means of spiritual purgation. When millions are murdered, asceticism loses its significance. So, at any rate, Desnos contends in the poem; yet although Hill seems largely in agreement, there is an undertone of detachment, hinting that perhaps the case for asceticism has not been altogether overcome.

The poems in *King Log* not included in the 1964 pamphlet center on two sequences: "Funeral Music" and "The Songbook of Sebastian Arrurruz." The first consists of eight sonnets in blank verse about the English Wars of the Roses. The initial sonnet describes the execution of John Tiptoft, Earl of Worcester, at Pomfret Castle in 1470. Tiptoft was a Christian Platonist and welcomed death: He could now ascend to a higher spiritual state. (Christian doctrine forbade suicide, as the initiative had to come from others.) Tiptoft arranged the details of his own execution. He asked for, and received, three blows of the executioner's ax to symbolize the three persons of the Trinity.

Hill finds the ascetic ideal appealing, even in the extreme form practiced by Tiptoft. The flesh-and-blood world, in this view, conceals reality: It is like the cave in Plato's *Politeia* (*Republic*, 1701), from which one must escape to gain genuine knowledge. Yet an attitude like Tiptoft's may conceal a strong will to power. Far from seeking exit from the world, Tiptoft's aim might be to secure fame: Other people will acclaim him for his discipline.

Hill does not claim that this reduction of spirit to power is true. As always, he merely suggests possibilities instead of affirming a definite line. The reader remains caught in the world's ambiguity—and this is Hill's principal message: The world is incapable of penetration by human beings.

The two positions sketched in the initial sonnet remain locked in struggle throughout "Funeral Music." Several of the poems show strong interest in Averroës, an Arab philosopher whose work influenced Thomas Aquinas and other Christian philosophers of the Middle Ages. Averroës followed the teaching of Aristotle. He emphasized contemplation as the highest aim of life, doctrine taught in book 10 of Aristotle's *Ethica Nicomachea* (*Nicomachean Ethics*, 1797). More controversially, Averroës came down firmly on one side of a famous Aristotelian dispute. According to Averroës, Aristotle thought that human minds are not really distinct. The "active intellect"—that is, the power of thought—is a single entity. Only will, emotion, and perception belong to individuals.

Hill finds this view congenial. The aim of ascetic discipline is to sink the person into the Universal Mind: One's individual personality does not count and is sloughed off. What prevents Hill from full commitment to this position, besides his liking for ambiguity? The answer lies in the subject matter of the sequence dealing with the Wars of the Roses. The violence and destruction of the wars, among the bloodiest in English history, prevent him from affirming humanity's goodness. Human beings are rapacious animals, according to Hill's sonnet on the Battle of Towton, the most destructive engagement of the wars. Much of the poem consists of diary entries by a soldier who believes that the real world lies elsewhere. Death in battle is a means to enter a higher realm. Hill makes clear through ironic language that the soldier has not grasped the reality of the battle. Far from a spiritual exercise, the struggle is an evil display of lust for power and plunder. The soldier has used philosophy and asceticism to conceal what is taking place, both in the world and in his own soul.

The death and destruction of war form the principal subject of another poem in *King Log*, "Ovid in the Third Reich." An artist living in Hitler's Germany claims that by the pursuit of spiritual values he can remain immune from the horrors of the Third Reich and its führer. By the speaker's use of cliché, it is apparent that here, for once, Hill takes a firm stand. He repudiates the standpoint of the artist. His alleged withdrawal is in fact complicity with the Nazis, since it turns a blind eye to crime and disguises the pursuit of physical safety under the mantle of ascetic withdrawal from the world. Hill's poem does not deal with a "made-up" attitude. Many writers and artists responded to the Third Reich by practicing "inner emigration." Although Hill strongly sympathizes with asceticism, he thinks that the position just sketched is an untenable dualism. "Ovid in the Third Reich" is probably Hill's most unequivocal political statement.

The reader will by now have the impression that Hill paints a grim and sour picture of the human race. While this is to a large extent true, Hill yet again cannot be easily captured by formula. The second major sequence of *King Log*, "The Songbook of Sebastian Arrurruz," manifests a different mood.

Arrurruz is an imaginary Spanish poet who lives at the end of the nineteenth and beginning of the twentieth century. The years of his maturity coincide with a period of ferment among Spanish intellectuals, resulting from Spain's disastrous defeat by the United States in 1898. Although Arrurruz does not directly concern himself with Spanish politics, he faces a sadness of his own. His wife has recently died, and he mourns her death.

What should he do? He considers asceticism: Perhaps he ought now to abandon sexual desire as a vain thing. This solution appeals to Arrurruz, but cheerfulness keeps breaking in, and the Spanish poet finds that he cannot abandon women. He remembers his wife not only with sorrow but also with delight, and the poem ends in a witty rather than an elegiac stance. Poetry itself has erotic force, and indulgence in wordplay is a form of sexual pleasure. The sequence differs in style as well as content from Hill's usual practice. It is direct and easy to read, rather than complicated and historically allusive. It won high praise from critics such as Martin Dodsworth who are normally inclined to criticize Hill for obscurity.

MERCIAN HYMNS

The poet had not abandoned his difficult style, as his next book, *Mercian Hymns*, made evident. The thirty poems in this book are written in a ritualistic language that is meant to be chanted as much as read. The "versets" of which the work is composed manifest Hill's knowledge of Anglo-Saxon bardic rhythms. The entire work constitutes an epic describing the reign of King Offa, an eighth century ruler from Mercia and the first Anglo-Saxon monarch able to bring most of England under unified control. Not coincidentally, Hill is himself from Mercia, and the epic is also an account of his childhood.

Although the verse forms imitate a typical Anglo-Saxon song of praise for a king, *Mercian Hymns* is by no means a celebration of King Offa. Quite the contrary, Hill satirizes the king's vanity and lust for power. The name "Offa" suggests "offal," a parallel Hill is not slow to exploit.

Naturally, a poet of Hill's depth has much more in mind than pricking the boasts of a fatuous monarch. Hill intends the poem to be an analysis of a certain type of power. As a boy, the king dreamed of being in command, and his attitude when he gains the throne reflects his youthful preoccupations. His subjects are like a child's toys, to be played with and manipulated as he wishes. He lacks a genuine sense for the reality of other people.

The indictment extends beyond King Offa. The poet himself views words as his creation: He too seeks power, though of a less immediately destructive kind than that of the king. One cannot respond to the dangers of political power by aesthetic retreat. Once more a leitmotif of Hill's work has come forward: Rejection of the real world for a spiritual or aesthetic quest cannot entirely succeed. All human beings bear the burden of original sin, and escape from this dire condition cannot come from human effort.

One of the poems in *Mercian Hymns*, "Crowning of Offa," reveals more fully Hill's attitude toward the past. Hill notes the splendor of the coronation and the church; he does not view these altogether ironically and in fact has a genuine admiration for them. He points out, however, that eighth century Anglo-Saxon society rested on *wergild*. If someone was killed, his family or retainers were expected to avenge him. If the killer paid *wergild*, he could save himself and end the feud. The amount paid depended on whether the killing was accidental or deliberate and on the rank of the victim.

Hill draws attention to this practice to show that Anglo-Saxon society was based on money. People varied in the amounts they were worth: A peasant had almost no value compared to a noble. Thus, it is entirely incorrect to contrast the modern capitalistic world with an idealized medieval past in which money was kept in its place. Medieval society was just as mercenary.

Hill's jaundiced view of the Anglo-Saxon world is in part directed at an unlikely target. In *Notes Toward the Definition of Culture* (1945), T. S. Eliot called for a return to an organic society. In Eliot's view, twentieth century society encouraged unlimited pluralism and toleration. Instead, a society needs to share a common way of life, founded in religion. Hill does not altogether reject this view but suggests that Eliot has oversimplified the relation between present and past. By accenting the commercial elements of King Offa's realm, Hill indicates that salvation cannot be found in return to a premodern utopia.

"Hymn XXV," the last of the "Opus Anglicanum" series, takes aim at another critic and artist, John Ruskin. Ruskin, a leading Victorian social critic and authority on painting, denounced the nineteenth century for abandoning craftsmanship. Workers who lived before the Industrial Revolution, he said, took pride in their work. Ruskin used as an example of his point the art of nail making. He noted in a famous letter in *Fors Clavigera* (1855-1859) that nails are not a purely utilitarian product. Far from being easy to make, they are the product of immense skill.

Hill's poem indicts Ruskin for romanticizing this craft. He does not deny Ruskin's point that the craft requires great skill; instead, he recalls his grandmother, who spent her life as a nail-maker. She practiced her trade in appalling poverty; her life was a struggle to survive, not the pursuit of a skill undertaken for its own sake. Just as in the poems about King Offa, the dark side of precapitalist society is laid bare by Hill.

Another of the poems of *Mercian Hymns* best sums up Hill's attitude to the state. In an imaginary meeting between King Offa and Charlemagne, Charlemagne gives Offa a sword as a present. (Although the two kings never actually met, Charlemagne did send Offa presents, including several swords, in 786.) The gift epitomizes the nature of kingship: The gift is an instrument of slaughter.

Hill himself is a character in the poem; he is portrayed driving his car in an area where Offa and Charlemagne might have met. As he drives along, he recalls battles of World War I, which mingle in his mind with Charlemagne's battles fought in the same area. He also thinks of the torture and execution of the philosopher

Boethius by Emperor Theodoric. However dubious Hill may be about the merits of asceticism, it is clear that political power is much worse.

TENEBRAE

After *Mercian Hymns* was published, Hill spent several years preparing a translation of Ibsen's *Brand* (1866). As a result, it was not until 1978 that he published his next volume of poetry, *Tenebrae*.

As the title suggests, this volume offers no respite from Hill's customary dark brooding. Here he takes over certain forms used in Spanish Baroque poetry and uses a principal subject of that era as the work's theme. Spanish mystics such as Saint John of the Cross and Saint Teresa of Avila often used sexual imagery to depict their religious struggles and visions; Hill does so as well. He extends the portrayal of the struggle between flesh and spirit to other historical periods. William Butler Yeats, the French religious thinker Simone Weil, and the German theologian Dietrich Bonhoeffer are among the persons depicted in *Tenebrae*.

Tenebrae is a Roman Catholic ceremony that commemorates the "harrowing of Hell"—Christ's descent into the underworld after his burial and prior to the resurrection. The rite is rarely performed, but attraction to the obscure is Hill's hallmark. He composed the poems in *Tenebrae* in a ritualized language intended to evoke the Catholic ceremony.

The first series in the book, "The Pentecost Castle," consists of fifteen short poems modeled on Spanish Baroque lyrics. One, based on a lyric by the poet Juan del Encina, pictures a heron pierced by the blade of physical love. The bird uses the experience to rise to a higher spiritual level.

Although Hill imitates the forms and themes of the Spanish Baroque, his attitude differs from the views of his Spanish exemplars. Though strongly attracted to mysticism, he is doubtful about the reality behind visions. He believes it very difficult to distinguish between true and false mysticism, and he thinks of God not as a savior but as a power that has withdrawn from the world, leaving humankind to its own devices. In "The Pentecost Castle," Hill's attitude toward the mystics about whom he writes is detached. He believes in a principle of compensation: A loss in sexual interest becomes a gain in spiritual insight, and vice versa. What spiritual insight means, however, is not a matter on which he is able to pronounce.

Another section of *Tenebrae*, called "Lachrimae: Or, Seven Tears Figured in Seven Passionate Pavans," takes a more negative attitude toward mysticism than the Pentecost sequence. Hill describes techniques of contemplation in detail, claiming that they have been deliberately designed to inflict pain. Do they offer any compensatory rewards? Hill, at least in this sequence, does not think so. One of his poems imitates an anonymous Spanish lyric; in contrast to the original writer, however, Hill denies that he has ever had contact with Christ. The final poem in "Lachrimae" is a translation of a verse by Lope de Vega, a sixteenth century playwright strongly inclined to skepticism. Hill's version closely parallels his model without altering its meaning: He finds Lope's doubt more congenial than the affirmations of the mystics.

Hill's challenge to conventional piety goes much further. He does not think Christ himself immune from hostile questioning. One of the poems pictures Christ on the cross; rather than gaze at him in wonder and with praise, Hill would like to question Jesus. One suspects that the horrors of the world wars, though not explicitly mentioned, are on Hill's mind.

Hill's jaundiced view of Christ does not indicate conversion to atheism. He is, as always, exploring a perspective to which he is attracted but not fully committed. "Christmas Trees," a tribute to the German pastor and theologian Dietrich Bonhoeffer, adopts a quite different point of view. Bonhoeffer was a Lutheran pastor from a well-connected German family with ties to the aristocracy. Having achieved fame at a young age for a brilliant doctoral dissertation, he had the potential to be a leading academic theologian. The rise of Hitler to power in 1933, however, changed Bonhoeffer's plans. He strongly opposed the Nazis and was a leader of the faction of the Protestant church that refused to recognize the leadership hand-picked by Hitler's minions. Bonhoeffer was involved in the July, 1944, plot to assassinate Hitler; after the plot's failure, he was arrested, imprisoned, and eventually executed.

Hill treats Bonhoeffer with unreserved admiration. His willingness to risk his life to overthrow Hitler is likened to the sacrifice of Christ. In order for the compari-

son to convey Hill's meaning, Christ's death itself must be regarded favorably. Though in the other poems he is uncommitted, Hill here displays no doubts about the meaning of Christ's redeeming death. Bonhoeffer is a true Christian who had imitated the life and works of his Master.

Perhaps even here, however, there is an undertone of religious skepticism. Bonhoeffer's participation in the plot and his resulting death were a sacrifice for the sake of the secular community, not the church. Bonhoeffer believed that if Hitler survived, Germany would face ruin; it is his attempt to act on this belief that earns Hill's praise. Further, while in prison Bonhoeffer wrote a number of letters that teach "religionless Christianity," in which God no longer intervenes in the world but requires people to act for themselves. This is exactly Hill's own belief.

THE MYSTERY OF THE CHARITY OF CHARLES PÉGUY

Hill's next major work, the last to appear in the 1980's, moves more in the direction of orthodox religion, although his characteristic ambiguity is fully present. The work in question is *The Mystery of the Charity of Charles Péguy*, a poem of one hundred quatrains, which appeared in 1983.

Péguy was a Frenchman of unusually forceful personality who lived from 1872 to 1914. He was both an ardent Catholic and a socialist. During the Dreyfus Affair, the controversy involving a Jewish army officer falsely convicted of treason, Péguy championed Dreyfus and allied himself with the socialist leader Jean Juares. He broke with the position of Juares, however, after France entered World War I in August, 1914, for Juares had sought a peaceful resolution, while Péguy was firmly anti-German. Péguy enlisted in the French army, although he was over the age at which he would have been drafted. He was killed in the first months of the war.

Through most of the poem, Hill presents Péguy with unfeigned admiration, even though many of Péguy's views differ sharply from ones that Hill has elsewhere supported. As Hill shows, Péguy created a myth of the French peasant as devoted to the soil. Before the depredations of capitalism, French rural life formed an ideal community. This view seems quite like the one Hill excoriated when it was professed by Ruskin; nevertheless, he presents it in straightforward fashion, without his usual ambiguity and irony.

Along with his devotion to the French nation went Péguy's religion. Church and state were for him not separate entities but united into an amalgam to which he gave allegiance. The foremost expression of his union of throne and altar was his cult of Joan of Arc; he portrayed Joan as the heroine of the nascent French nation. It was largely because of Péguy's efforts, along with similar endeavors by other French nationalists, that Pope Benedict XV elevated Joan to sainthood in 1920.

Hill views saints with much less enthusiasm than Péguy, but he presents Péguy's activities on Joan's behalf fully and fairly. Probably what he admires about Péguy is not his particular religious stance but his self-less devotion to what he considered right. It is this that constitutes the "charity" of Péguy mentioned in the title.

Hill goes further in his presentation of Péguy's assault on the values of the modern world; he wholeheartedly endorses Péguy's criticism of the power of the machine. In doing so, Hill does not reverse the position of his earlier work. He does not agree with Eliot and Ruskin (or, for that matter, with Péguy) that an ideal world existed before the rise of capitalism. Yet it does not follow from Hill's rejection of premodern nostalgia that he disagrees with these writers' criticism of the modern world.

Like Péguy, Hill believes that machines endlessly repeat motion without purpose. People are forced to adjust themselves to a fixed routine; they sooner or later fall victim to the implacable rhythm of industrialism. Hill, like Péguy, was strongly influenced in these views by the philosopher Henri Bergson. Bergson's doctrine of time receives considerable attention in the poem.

THE TRIUMPH OF LOVE

Like *The Mystery of the Charity of Charles Péguy*, *The Triumph of Love* is one long "poem" comprising a large number (150) of smaller items, a structure echoing the 150 psalms of the Psalter. Like *Mercian Hymns*, the poem's locale is Hill's West Midland childhood home, and the focus is the events of World War II. However, where *Mercian Hymns* uses the figure of King Offa—a

secular ruler—as a focal point, *The Triumph of Love* focuses on the figure of Saint Kenelm, also a member of ancient Mercia's royal family renowned not for his rule but for his martyrdom, and underneath, a repeated return to the figure of the Virgin Mary, to whom the poem is dedicated. Perhaps the most significant departure from Hill's previous work, however, is the extent and degree of satire, even of farce, in *The Triumph of Love*.

Hill's poetic voice switches tone and mood often and abruptly throughout the poem, at one point commenting of another poet ("Rancorous, narcissistic old sod— what/ makes him go on? We thought, hoped rather,/ he might be dead") and elsewhere characterizing the poetic form *Laus et vituperativo* ("praise and opposition") as

> . . . public, forensic,
> yet with a vehement
> private ambition for the people's
> greater good—Joannis
> Miltoni, Angli, pro Populo Angli-
> cano Defensio: this and other tracts,
> day-laboured-at, under great imposition
> Laus et vituperatio, lost, rediscovered,
> renewed on few occasions this century

Veering from the colloquial to the Latinate, Hill also puns, excoriates, and inserts editorial comments and mock "errata" into his verse. This chorus—or cacaphony—of voices echoes a new tolerance of disorder in Hill's poetry, a millennial embrace of postmodernism that nonetheless continues to express Hill's ongoing concerns with the aftermath of World War II's destruction of landscapes and peoples: "What is he saying;/ why is he still so angry?"

OTHER MAJOR WORKS

NONFICTION: *The Lords of Limit: Essays on Literature and Ideas*, 1984; *The Enemy's Country: Words, Contexture, and Other Circumstances of Language*, 1991.

TRANSLATION: *Brand*, 1978 (of Henrik Ibsen).

BIBLIOGRAPHY

Bloom, Harold. *Figures of Capable Imagination*. New York: Seabury Press, 1976. Bloom, a leading advocate of Romantic poetry, champions Hill's verse strongly. He claims that Hill is a poet of the sublime, a position other critics have rejected. Hill has a view of imagination based on affirmation of the body and recognition of its limits. This, Bloom thinks, has enabled Hill to write poetry ranking among the best in the twentieth century.

Hall, Donald. *The Weather for Poetry.* Ann Arbor: University of Michigan Press, 1982. Hall, an outstanding poet himself, has been a friend of Hill since Hill's Oxford days. Hall considers Hill's language to be beautiful; its subtle balance of movement and countermovement, he says, recall the quartets of Ludwig van Beethoven. Hill's poems achieve a blend of unity amid diversity.

Hart, Henry. *The Poetry of Geoffrey Hill.* Carbondale: Southern Illinois University Press, 1986. This is a comprehensive study of all Hill's work to the mid-1980's. It includes a full discussion of the early poems, many of which were not included in Hill's first collection. Hart offers detailed guidance to the allusions in the verse.

McNees, Eleanor Jane. *Eucharistic Poetry: The Search for Presence in the Writings of John Donne, Gerard Manley Hopkins, Dylan Thomas, and Geoffrey Hill.* Cranbury, N.J.: Associated University Presses, 1992. Includes an analysis of some of Hill's poetry with an emphasis on the religious symbolism that it contains.

Milne, W. S. *An Introduction to Geoffrey Hill.* London: Bellew, 1998. Critical analysis of Hill's poetry with bibliographic references.

Ricks, Christopher. *The Force of Poetry.* Oxford: Clarendon Press, 1984. Ricks, an outstanding English critic, is a master of close reading. He stresses the details by which Hill achieves his poetic effects, and he pays considerable and rewarding attention to Hill's punctuation.

Sherry, Vincent. *The Uncommon Tongue.* Ann Arbor: University of Michigan Press, 1987. Comparable to Henry Hart's book as a comprehensive study. Places less emphasis on thematic criticism than does Hart and more on poetic technique. Offers an analysis of each of Hill's major works through the mid-1980's.

Bill Delaney,
updated by Leslie Ellen Jones

EDWARD HIRSCH

Born: Chicago, Illinois; January 20, 1950

PRINCIPAL POETRY

For the Sleepwalkers: Poems, 1981
Wild Gratitude: Poems, 1986
The Night Parade: Poems, 1989
Earthly Measures: Poems, 1994
On Love: Poems, 1998

OTHER LITERARY FORMS

Although Edward Hirsch built his literary reputation on the basis of his stately neo-Romantic poetry, he widened his reading audience with the publication of two collections of essays in 1999. *Responsive Reading* is a collection of essays and book reviews analyzing the work of internationally renowned artists (mostly writers) who influenced Hirsch's development as a poet. The best-seller *How to Read a Poem: And Fall in Love with Poetry* is both an argument on behalf of the lyric as a significant mode of poetry and a textbook of poetic terms, movements, and subgenres.

ACHIEVEMENTS

Edward Hirsch's first books of poems, *For the Sleepwalkers*, received the Lavan Younger Poets Award from the Academy of American Poets and the Delmore Schwartz Memorial Award from New York University. His second book, *Wild Gratitude*, received the National Book Critics Circle Award. His third and fourth books, *The Night Parade* and *Earthly Measures*, were listed as notable books of the year in *The New York Times Book Review*. In addition, Hirsch has received numerous awards and grants, including the Prix de Rome, a Guggenheim Fellowship, a National Endowment for the Arts Award, and, in 1998, the American Academy of Arts and Letters Award for literature. Hirsch also received a MacArthur Fellowship in 2000.

BIOGRAPHY

Edward Hirsch was born to Irma and Kurt Hirsch in a suburb of Chicago, Illinois, in 1950. He attended Grinnell College in the late 1960's and won the Selden

L. Whitcomb Poetry Prize for three consecutive years (1970-1972). He also won the Academy of American Poets First Place Award three consecutive years (1975-1977). Hirsch received his Ph.D. in folklore in 1978. In 1979 Hirsch was hired by the department of English at Wayne State University, Detroit, Michigan. There he became friends with a young film studies assistant professor, Dennis Turner, whose death in 1984, the year Hirsch left Wayne State for the University of Houston, inspired one of Hirsch's best-known elegies, "Fast Break," collected two years later in his second book, *Wild Gratitude*.

Over the next decade of his residence in Houston, Hirsch's third and fourth books of poems would appear (*The Night Parade* in 1989; *Earthly Measures* in 1994). As the opening and closing poems—"Memorandums" and "Proustian"——indicate, the third collection is a book of memories, moving largely between recollections of his family (there are poems about almost all the members of his immediate family) and his birthtown of Chicago, bound by their mutual sturdiness amid tragedy. *Earthly Measures* celebrates art and artists but culminates in a celebration of ordinary people and life.

In the late 1990's Hirsch turned his attention largely to the essay as a way of explaining and celebrating the poetry he had come to love. He began writing a column for the influential magazine *American Poetry Review*, became a poetry editor of Robert Coles's magazine *Double Take*, and began writing occasional reviews for magazines such as *The New Yorker* and *The Nation*. Much of this material would wind up comprising the two books of essays that appeared in 1999, *Responsive Reading* and *How to Read a Poem*, along with a fifth book of poems, primarily dramatic monologues, titled *On Love*.

ANALYSIS

In an interview with Tad Marshall for the spring, 2002, issue of *The Kenyon Review*, Edward Hirsch discussed his attraction to twentieth century Eastern European poets in general, and Polish poets in particular, citing their desire to both escape and embrace the world. Hirsch attributes this vacillation to the historical pressures under which so many Eastern European poets

Edward Hirsch (© Miriam Berkley)

wrote during the twentieth century, lending their poetry an urgency and immediacy lacking in most American poetry. This lack may be even more apparent in the work of poets who come from relatively privileged backgrounds. For Hirsch, his privileged upbringing was tempered by his ethnicity, providing a foundation for what he called his "democratic ethos." Hirsch's narrators are never seriously tempted by the "transcendental" world of traditional religions or utopian politics (in the same interview Hirsch acknowledged his distrust of "didactic" political solutions to the problem of injustice), but they are drawn to the timeless permanence art seems to offer. This tendency to see art as immortal is as old as the creative process. What is new—and American—in Hirsch is how he weds this desire for aesthetic permanence to democratic values. His poems, particularly those from the first three books, shift back and forth between artistic lives and the ordinary lives of working people. This movement parallels the poem's internal vacillations, saying yes and no to the world, saying yes and no to "art," even as they dream of their own permanence.

INSOMNIA

The dream of permanence haunts all of Hirsch's poetry, but it manifests itself in the first two collections, *For the Sleepwalkers* and *Wild Gratitude*, as a psychosomatic illness, a form of anxiety: insomnia. However, this affliction becomes a useful malady, a way for the poet to live out the democratic ethos. To embrace America means, for Hirsch, embracing nocturnal existence: "For all the insomniacs in the world/ I want to build a new kind of machine/ For flying out of the body at night," he writes in "I Need Help" from *Wild Gratitude*. Indeed, Hirsch's first two books of poetry make much of their desire to sing for the night, for those Americans who may be "invisible" to mainstream society. Hirsch's work celebrates some of those marginal members known collectively as the working classes. One can find this working-class ethos in numerous American poets, such as Walt Whitman, Langston Hughes, and Carl Sandburg, and in this regard Hirsch's work is not exceptional. His first two books contain poems about a seamstress ("The Sweatshop Poem"), a waitress ("At Kresge's Diner in Stonefalls, Arkansas"), and a garbage man ("Garbage"). There are also poems for "Poets, Children, Soldiers," "For the Sleepwalkers" whose bodies have "so much faith in the invisible/ arrow carved into the carpet, the worn path/ that leads to the stairs instead of the window." As these lines indicate, the night stands not only for wayward or marginal Americans but also for the subconscious will to live that, for example, keeps a parking lot attendant at his job even as he half-resents, half-admires, a former classmate who has achieved success and fame ("In the Underground Garage," from *The Night Parade*). For Hirsch, the insomniac is a conduit of impulses and drives, giving himself over to rapture and despair, like the poet. In short, the nightwalker, like the artist, always risks melodrama for the sake of drama.

THE LYRIC

Melodrama is a generic hazard of the lyric mode of poetry, but it is a hazard Hirsch's poetry has insisted upon from his first book. Although the two books of poems published in the 1990's, *Earthly Measures* and *On Love*, are largely departures from this subgenre of po-

etry, the lyric mode is present in each of his books published in the 1980's and 1990's.

The lyric is privileged by Hirsch as a model of poetry per se because it is the most personal, the most subjective, the most emotional, of the poetic modes. Like all the Romantic poets, in particular Christopher Smart and John Clare (characteristically, Hirsch pays homage to the lesser-known Romantic poets), Hirsch believes that human relationships are essentially emotional, preserved primarily in family histories and cultural artifacts. As he writes in "Memorandums," the opening poem of *The Night Parade*, the poet puts "down these memorandums of [his] affections/ To stave off the absolute." Art, like family, is a buffer against oblivion and mortality.

There are many kinds of lyrics, and Hirsch has created some of his most stirring poems using the device of epiphany, a sudden revelation of meaning during an encounter or experience. Typically, in a Hirsch poem, revelation occurs when there is a failed or half-failed encounter or experience. Both "Scorched" (*Earthly Measures*) and "Infertility" (*The Night Parade*) concern that most intimate of failed encounters—the inability of a couple to have children of their own—while half failure is poignantly captured in "My Grandfather's Poems" (*The Night Parade*). Here the narrator recalls his childhood when he would fall asleep to the rhythm of his grandfather's voice reciting poetry in Yiddish, a language he could not understand. Since no one valued his grandfather's poems, they no longer exist except as the narrator's imperfect memories of certain rhythms, certain sounds.

ELEGIES

As a poet unafraid to risk sentimentality and melodrama, Hirsch wrote some of the most fully realized elegies in twentieth century American poetry. Three of the most moving ones concern a former colleague. These poems appear in *Wild Gratitude* and *The Night Parade*. The death of Hirsch's close friend, film scholar Dennis Turner, at the age of thirty-six inspired three published poems: "Omen," "Fast Break" and "Skywriting," the first two in *Wild Gratitude*, the third in *The Night Parade*. All three poems are marked by Hirsch's characteristic clarity of language and his unflinching glimpse at "the absolute." As its title suggests, "Omen" concerns the narrator's realization that his "closest friend// Suffering from cancer in a small, airless ward/ In a hospital downtown" is "going to die."

"Skywriting" focuses on the day of Turner's death, the vigil the narrator keeps as his "friend's dream/ Of health [drifts] further and further away." Though it too portends his friend's death, "Fast Break" honors the healthy athleticism of the body, the way sports are themselves a kind of art. Written as a single sentence, this poem is an ironic celebration of the good luck that attends a great basketball play. The narrator can hardly believe that, "for once our gangly starting center/ boxes out his man and times his jump." By the poem's end, after the ball has been passed from one player to another, the narrator's friend gets to score the basket. However, he pays a price:

. . . the power-forward explodes past them
in a fury, taking the ball into the air

by himself now and laying it gently
against the glass for a lay-up,

but losing his balance in the process,
inexplicably falling, hitting the floor

with a wild, headlong motion
for the game he loved like a country

and swiveling back to see an orange blur
floating perfectly through the net.

ORPHEUS RESURRECTED

Hirsch's last two collections of poems in the twentieth century, *Earthly Measures* and *On Love*, suggest a reorientation, or shift in emphasis, from the lyric to dramatic monologue and philosophical argument. In his first three books of poetry, both modes of poetry are present, but the lyric is clearly privileged. However, 1994's *Earthly Measures* is akin to 1981's *For the Sleepwalkers*, inasmuch as both concern the fate of art and artists struggling against mutability and mortality. Overseeing them all is the figure of Orpheus, haunting the alleys, roads, and streets of the American Midwest as often as the galleries and museums of London, Paris, and Rome. Still, it is the narrator of these poems, not a god, who gets the last word in "Earthly Light." Having

admired the seventeenth century Dutch painters, the narrator turns away and heads down to a busy street teeming with arguments, laughter, smells, and sights, all because,

. . . it is not heaven

but earth that needs us, because
it is only earth—limited, sensuous
earth that is so fleeting, so real.

On Love marks another step beyond the autobiographical self of the narrator. The bulk of the book consists of dramatic monologues spoken by philosophers, painters, and writers, ranging from Denis Diderot and Colette to Margaret Fuller and Zora Neale Hurston. In the fifteen monologues, some dramatic, some odes, the narrator imagines, considers, and defends the various types, forms, and values of love. Given the nature of many of these odes and monologues, it is not a great leap of faith to imagine them being recited, or sung, in the voice of Orpheus, who is better acquainted than most with the seeming timelessness of loss, yearning, and exile. In many respects, love was always the subject of Hirsch's poetry in the twentieth century, the love of art, the love of family, the love of friends, and, most important, the love of strangers—who are thereby transformed into neighbors.

OTHER MAJOR WORKS

NONFICTION: *Responsive Reading*, 1999; *How to Read a Poem: And Fall in Love with Poetry*, 1999.

BIBLIOGRAPHY

Ferguson, Suzanne. "'Spots of Time': Representation of Narrative in Modern Poems and Paintings." In *Word and Image: A Journal of Verbal/Visual Enquiry*. London: Basingbroke, 1988. In this article Ferguson discusses the Romantic epiphany "spots of time" and its relationship to the still life in the paintings of the Dutch painter Pieter Bruegel the Elder, the American painter Edward Hopper, and the American poets William Carlos Williams and Edward Hirsch.

Hirsch, Edward. "An Interview with Edward Hirsch." Interview by Kevin Boyle. *Chicago Review* 41, no. 1 (1995): 19-27. In this interview Hirsch discusses the relationship of academia to his work, the procedures he employs when writing poetry, the problem of literary theory, and the twentieth century poets he admires.

_____. "The Question of Affirmation and Despair: Interview with Edward Hirsch." Interview by Tod Marshall. *The Kenyon Review* 22, no. 2 (2000): 54-69. In this interview Hirsch discusses his democratic ethos in relation to modern American poetry, the problem of transcendence in art and religion, and the influence of literary theory on contemporary poetry.

Hirsch, Edward, and Adam Zagajewski. "Edward Hirsch and Adam Zagajewski." *Partisan Review* 66, no. 1 (1999): 70-77. In this conversation between the two poets Edward Hirsch and Adam Zagajewski, set at a festival in honor of the Czech poet Czesław Miłosz, Hirsch and Zagajewski read poems of theirs influenced by Miłosz.

Longenbach, James. "Poetry in Review—Edward Hirsch: Eating the World." *The Yale Review* 86, no. 3 (1998): 160-173. The author argues that the 1998 book of poems by Edward Hirsch, *On Love*, represents a triumph of art over mortality as Hirsch's aesthetic sensibility inhabits and transcends the various artists it honors.

Tyrone Williams

JANE HIRSHFIELD

Born: New York, New York; February 24, 1953

PRINCIPAL POETRY
Alaya, 1982
Of Gravity and Angels, 1988
The October Palace, 1994
The Lives of the Heart, 1997
Given Sugar, Given Salt, 2001

OTHER LITERARY FORMS
Besides her work as a poet, Jane Hirshfield has written a major work on the craft and philosophy of poetry:

Nine Gates: Entering the Mind of Poetry (1997). *Nine Gates* treats the gates through which readers and writers pass as they learn what poetry brings to life and how it works. Patricia Kirkpatrick considers this volume of essays as addressing "not only ways to read and write, but a way to live." *The Ink Dark Moon: Love Poems by Ono no Komachi and Izumi Shikibu, Women of the Ancient Court of Japan* (1988, expanded 1990) is a series of translations from the Japanese with cotranslator Mariko Aratani, and *Women in Praise of the Sacred: Forty-three Centuries of Spiritual Poetry by Women* (1994) is an anthology of women writers from 2300 B.C.E. to the twentieth century, writers of various spiritual traditions. Both of these collections are attempts to make more widely known the works of historical women poets whose work has often been neglected and marginalized. They are attempts to contradict the lingering myth that women throughout history have not written significant poetry.

ACHIEVEMENTS
Jane Hirshfield's honors include the Poetry Center Book Award, fellowships from the Guggenheim and Rockefeller Foundations, Columbia University's Translation Center Award, the Commonwealth Club of California Poetry Medal, and the Bay Area Book Reviewers Award.

BIOGRAPHY
Jane Hirshfield was born in New York, New York, to Robert and Harriet Hirshfield. Her father was a clothing manufacturer, and her mother was a secretary. From her childhood Hirshfield wanted to be a writer. After her first book was published her mother showed Hirshfield a note written on large lined paper from the first grade in which the young Hirshfield had written, "I want to be a writer when I grow up." Her first poem was published in 1973 after she graduated magna cum laude from Princeton University with an independent major in creative writing and literature in translation. She was part of Princeton's first graduating class to include women. Despite early publication, she withdrew from the writing life for eight years as she entered study at the San Francisco Zen Center. In 1979 she was lay-ordained in the lineage of Soto Zen and left the life of withdrawal. After

that time, Hirshfield devoted her life to writing, translation, and editing, earning numerous awards and grants. From 1991 to 1998 she served as lecturer in creative writing at the University of San Francisco and served as visiting associate professor at the University of California, Berkeley, in 1995. In 1999 she began serving on the core M.F.A. faculty of Bennington College. In 2000 she was appointed Elliston Visiting Poetry Professor at the University of Cincinnati.

ANALYSIS

Jane Hirshfield became a distinct voice in poetry at the turn of the twenty-first century through her sensitive observation of the significance of ordinary details of daily life. Unlike most poets of the Western tradition, Hirshfield tends not to be human-centered in her poetry. In other words, her poetry usually does not deal with human relationships, character, or direct interaction. Instead, her poetry objectifies the material of existence and relates matter to the individual or abstracted human nature. A typical poem of Hirshfield's mature work, for example, will note an utterly mundane object such as a grouping of broken seashells, the concept of rooms, crickets, cucumbers, or the nature of leather, and then proceed to relate it all to the human soul. Her poetry, in short, resembles Impressionist still-lifes.

While her work as translator and editor of women's poetry indicates Hirshfield's strong feminist nature, little of her poetry is political in the usual sense of direct comment on specific issues, but all her work is political in the sense of integrating the stirrings of the heart, one of her favorite images, with the political realities that surround all people.

Undoubtedly, the source for these characteristics of her poetry and for her very concept of what poetry is, "The magnification of being," derives from her strong Zen Buddhist training. Her emphasis on "compassion, on the preexistent unity of subject and object, on nature, on the self-sufficient suchness of being, and on the daunting challenge of accepting transitoriness," Peter Harris notes, are central themes in her poetry derived from Buddhism. Hirshfield does not, however, burden her poetry with heavy, overt Zen attitudes. Only occasionally is there direct reference to Buddhism.

Hirshfield considers herself an eclectic poet not tied to any one tradition. Her earliest influences developed from English sonnets and Latin lyrical verse, but early on she developed an interest in Japanese poetry, first through haiku, and later in Aztec, Eskimo, and court poetry of ancient India. She has mentioned her chief American influences as Walt Whitman, Emily Dickinson, Galway Kinnell, Elizabeth Bishop, Gary Snyder, and Robert Hass.

ALAYA

Jane Hirshfield's first book of poetry was part of the *Quarterly Review of Literature* poetry series of 1982. "Alaya" on one hand means "home" but also is, Hirshfield has said, "a Buddhist term meaning 'the consciousness which is the storehouse of experience,' of memory . . . the place where seed-grain is kept."

"The Gift" from *Alaya* points in the direction of Hirshfield's tendency in her later work to objectify all reality, even the personal: "From how many hands/ your body comes to me,/ and to how many will I pass it on." Here the body comes, not "you come to me," and the speaker will pass "it," the body, on, instead of passing on such things as his memory, his influence, or even his love. The poem is remarkable for its early mature handling of imagery and phrasing. The person addressed, for example, exaggerates "nothing" and leans "into the wind" and is "lost/but like a flock of geese." However flocks of geese do not really get lost. The poem ends as many of Hirshfield's poems do, and as many poems written in writing workshops often do, with a significant metaphor to draw meaning from the experience of this poem: "Slowly now,/ lift the lid of the box:/ there is nothing inside./ I give this to you, love."

The movement of the poem, then, would ordinarily be seen as a movement from the physical, the body, to the immaterial, the soul, but a Hirshfield poem, perhaps because of the poet's Zen beliefs, will not distinguish between physical and immaterial. The soul and body are indistinguishable. Despite the objective displacement of the self in "The Gift," however, much of Hirshfield's early poetry maintains a personal point of view, both in *Alaya* and in her next book.

OF GRAVITY AND ANGELS

Jane Hirshfield's second book of poetry, published in 1988, continues to demonstrate her mastery of language, yet nearly half of the poems in this volume include the pronoun "I." For most of the poems, the self remains integral to the text.

At her public readings and in her interviews, the poet talks frequently of her love for horses and her use of horses in her poems. "After Work" is a typical Hirshfield horse poem. The poem takes a straightforward description of a habitual moment in her life, the after-work feeding of the horses, and transforms the experience into meaning:

> I stop the car along the pasture edge,
> gather up bags of corncobs from the back,
> and get out.
> Two whistles, one for each,
> and familiar sounds draw close in darkness—

The horses come and eagerly devour corncobs brought by the speaker. However, despite the personal nature of this ordinary experience, Hirshfield objectifies it. The horses do not "just" come. They come "conjured out of sleep"; they come with "each small noise and scent/ heavy with earth, simple beyond communion."

One of the more memorable poems from *Of Gravity and Angels* is "Dialogue," which begins: "A friend says,/ 'I'm always practicing to be an old woman.'" Another friend considers herself differently: "'I see myself young, maybe fourteen.'" The speaker, however, identifies with neither friend.

Another often read poem is "The Song." In it, Hirshfield implies that all material nature has its own spirit. Here the spirit leaves the tree but never completely. In the same way that the tree will grieve its lost spirit, "the wood, if taken too quickly, will sing/ a little in the stove," still remembering her.

THE OCTOBER PALACE

In *The October Palace* Hirshfield reveals herself a fully mature poet, no longer a developing talent. She moves beyond the formulas of writers' workshop poems and finds the unique voice and range of experiences that has brought her the prizes and grants necessary for a sustainable poetic career.

Perhaps the overall theme of *The October Palace* is that every moment of one's life possesses its own meaning. This theme can be seen, perhaps most obviously, in "Percolation." The speaker is in the midst of wasting a

day confined inside because of the rain. As she meditates upon her confinement, and as she becomes aware of a frog croaking "a tuneless anthem," she develops serenity from the conviction that: "surely all Being at bottom is happy:/ soaked to the bone, sopped at the root." She discovers that life-giving peace must be wrung out of all experience, "yielding as coffee grounds/ yield to their percolation, blushing, completely seduced,/ assenting as they give in to the downrushing water."

In many of her poems Hirshfield enjoys relating narratives from various folk and historical legends. For example, in "A Plenitude" she considers the nature of fullness, completeness—plenitude—by relating a common story from Renaissance art:

> But there is the story, too,
> of a young painter meeting the envoy of a Pope.
> Asked for a work by which his art
> could be weighed against others', he dipped his stylus—
> with great courtesy, according to Vasari—
> in red ink, and drew a single, perfect O.

THE LIVES OF THE HEART

In her 1997 collection of poetry, Hirshfield develops fully a new imagery of the lion and of the heart. Lions appear with mythic power in such poems as "Knowing Nothing," "Spell to Be Said Upon Waking," "Lion and Angel Dividing the Maple Between Them," and "Each Happiness Ringed by Lions." In an interview with Katherine Mills, Hirshfield explained her idea about the lions: "The lion is fierceness and beauty; undeniable presence; danger; power; passionate love; transformation. Perhaps, for me . . . lions are the earthly answer to Buddhism." Thus, in "Knowing Nothing," "The lion has stalked/ the village for a long time." However, it does not want a goat in a clearing; "The goat is not the reason." Instead,

> The reason is the lion,
> whose one desire is to enter—
> Not the goat, which is
> only the lure, only excuse
> but the one burning life
> it has hunted for a long time
> disguised as hunger. Disguised as love.
> Which is not the reason.

Here the paradox of the lion's ferocity and its longing to assert itself—of its love—keep the reader searching but not finding the reason of life experience: "Love is not the reason./ Love is the lure."

In a similar way, these poems celebrate the heart, the center of human nature that keeps all people at the core of their existence. Hirshfield explained to Katie Bolick of *The Atlantic* "that for some years a central task in my life has been to try to affirm the difficult parts of my experience; that attempt is what many of the heart poems address. . . . At some point I realized that you don't get a full human life if you try to cut off one end of it, that you need to agree to the entire experience, to the full spectrum of what happens." For example, in "Secretive Heart" at its center, the heart, is one of the most mundane material objects, an old Chinese cauldron "still good for boiling water" but evidently not for much else. "The few raised marks/ on its belly/ are useful to almost no one."

GIVEN SUGAR, GIVEN SALT

Hirshfield's fifth volume of poetry continues with the old themes but proves her most expansive volume: "As water given sugar sweetens, given salt grows salty,/ we become our choices." Thus *Given Sugar, Given Salt* explores choices for meaningful living. In "Bone," for example, the speaker's dog unearths an old bone, the toy of her previous dog—for whose memory she still grieves. The new dog knows nothing of the old dog:

> My memories,
> my counting and expectations,
> mean nothing to her;
> my sadness, though,
> does puzzle her a moment.

However, the new dog does not remain puzzled for long. She just keeps chewing and then readies herself for a game of catch.

Choices control all people's lives. In "Happiness Is Harder" Hirshfield considers even happiness a choice. Sadness can be cured perhaps: "A person has only to choose./ *What* doesn't matter; just *that*-." However, "Happiness is harder."

Jane Hirshfield has, then, developed a unique voice among contemporary American poets. Her work has the quiet yet persistent vision characteristic of Zen. Life often is a question with no answer, but the question must be asked. Hirshfield continually asks.

OTHER MAJOR WORKS

NONFICTION: *Nine Gates: Entering the Mind of Poetry*, 1997.

TRANSLATION: *The Ink Dark Moon: Poems by Ono no Komachi and Izumi Shikibu, Women of the Ancient Court of Japan*, 1988, expanded 1990 (with Mariko Aratani).

EDITED TEXT: *Women in Praise of the Sacred: Forty-three Centuries of Spiritual Poetry by Women*, 1994.

BIBLIOGRAPHY

Harris, Peter. "About Jane Hirshfield: A Profile." *Ploughshares* 24, no. 1 (Spring, 1998): 199-205. Particularly valuable is Harris's study of the Zen influence in Hirshfield's work.

Hirshfield, Jane. "Some Place Not Yet Known: An Interview with Jane Hirshfield." Interview by Katie Bolik. *The Atlantic* 280 (September 18, 1997). A penetrating interview based on the ideas Hirshfield expresses in *Nine Gates* and their application to her own poetry.

Hoey, Allen. *Contemporary Women Poets*. Detroit: St. James Press, 1997. Hoey considers Hirshfield's career from a variety of perspectives. Perhaps most valuable is his examination of the influence of the poet James Wright on Hirshfield's poetry.

Kirkpatrick, Patricia. "The Magnification of Being." *Hungry Mind Review*, Winter, 1997-1998. Hirshfield defines poetry as "the magnification of being," and Kirkpatrick develops this idea as a thesis for her review of *Nine Gates*.

Paul Varner

DANIEL HOFFMAN

Born: New York, New York; April 3, 1923

PRINCIPAL POETRY
An Armada of Thirty Whales, 1954
A Little Geste and Other Poems, 1960

The City of Satisfactions, 1963

Striking the Stones, 1968

Broken Laws, 1970

The Center of Attention, 1974

Able Was I Ere I Saw Elba: Selected Poems, 1954-1974, 1977

Brotherly Love, 1981

Hang-Gliding from Helicon: New and Selected Poems, 1948-1988, 1988

Middens of the Tribe: A Poem, 1995

OTHER LITERARY FORMS

Daniel Hoffman is as well known for his literary criticism as for his poetry. He began his scholarly career by exploring myth and folklore, primarily in American literature. In *Paul Bunyan* (1952), he examines the effect of folk materials on literary forms. The story of the master-logger Paul Bunyan is interesting to Hoffman because for such writers as Robert Frost, Carl Sandburg, W. H. Auden, and Louis Untermeyer it has served as a national myth. Hoffman's brilliant *Form and Fable in American Fiction* (1961) demonstrates the shaping role of folklore in nineteenth century American romances and tales, including Nathaniel Hawthorne's "The Maypole of Merry Mount" and *The Scarlet Letter* (1850), Herman Melville's *Moby Dick* (1851) and *The Confidence Man* (1857), and Mark Twain's *The Adventures of Huckleberry Finn* (1884). Hoffman chose these authors because they wrote in the formative period of the American literary identity. In this book, he attempts to delineate the generic American folk hero, one who reflects the culture of the New World—a man without a past or a family or a life cycle, one with all the virtues and defects of youth, who never matures but metamorphoses into stronger versions of the self. Hoffman is interested in the moral or cultural meaning of folkloristic motifs. In his analysis of *The Poetry of Stephen Crane* (1957) and his assessment of *Poe Poe Poe Poe Poe Poe Poe* (1972), Hoffman uses both biographical and psychological interpretation to elucidate the religious and sexual conflicts at the heart of Stephen Crane's verse and to explore the many masks of Edgar Allan Poe throughout his oeuvre. Because of Hoffman's obvious closeness to the subject, his Freudian interpretations, and his variety of styles, ranging from reverie to colloquial asides to invec-

Daniel Hoffman

tive, the Poe book is an eccentric though exciting tour through Poe's works and an insight into Hoffman's enthusiasms.

His study of the poetry of William Butler Yeats, Robert Graves, and Edwin Muir in *Barbarous Knowledge: Myth in the Poetry of Yeats, Graves, and Muir* (1967) shows how, in order to fill the vacuum left by the de-emphasis on Christianity, these poets turned to archetypes or myths. This book offers excellent material on Yeats's use of Irish folklore and balladry, Graves's monomyth in *The White Goddess* (1948), and Muir's archetypes, but it is obvious that Hoffman found these three congenial to his own thematic and formal concerns in verse. Hoffman's many essays on American poetry, in particular "Poetry Since 1945" in the *Literary History of the United States* (1974) and "Poetry: After Modernism," "Poetry: Schools of Dissidents," and "Poetry: Dissidents from Schools" in *The Harvard Guide to Contemporary American Writing* (1979), testify to his encyclopedic knowledge of twentieth century verse.

Zone of the Interior: A Memoir, 1942-1947 (2000) marked a departure for Hoffman, being a memoir of his service in the U.S. Army Air Force during World War II. This service formed the unlikely apprenticeship for his vocation as a poet and literary critic, for his duty was to write airplane instruction manuals and abstract aeronautical research for the *AAF Technical Data Digest*. His unusual memoir illustrates the opportunities to develop craftsmanship that may be found in the most unexpected places and circumstances.

ACHIEVEMENTS

Daniel Hoffman has received many awards for his verse, among them the Yale Series of Younger Poets Award in 1954 (for *An Armada of Thirty Whales*) and the U.S. National Institute of Arts and Letters Award in 1967. In 1972, he became chancellor of the Academy of American Poets, and from 1973-1974 he was the poet laureate of the United States. From 1988 to 1999 he was poet in residence of the cathedral of Saint John the Divine in New York City. *Brotherly Love* and *Poe Poe Poe Poe Poe Poe Poe* both were finalists for the National Book Award, and *Hang-Gliding from Helicon* received the Paterson Poetry Prize.

BIOGRAPHY

Daniel Gerard Hoffman was born in New York City on April 3, 1923, and was reared in Larchmont and New Rochelle, New York. He started writing poetry in high school and became interested in the origins of poetic form—folk song, especially African American music, and folk art, such as ballads. He entered Columbia University in 1940, but his studies were interrupted by World War II. After serving in the Army Air Corps from 1943 to 1946 as editor of its *Technical Data Digest*, he returned to Columbia, receiving his B.A. degree (Phi Beta Kappa) in 1947, an M.A. in 1949, and a Ph.D. in 1956. At Columbia, his studies concentrated in English and American literature. There he perfected his writing style under the tutelage of Mark Van Doren. He also pursued his interest in folklore through anthropology courses with Ruth Benedict, his special concern being myth, magic, and religious ritual.

A critic, editor, and teacher as well as poet, Hoffman has been a professor of English at Columbia University, Swarthmore College, and the University of Pennsylvania, where he has been poet in residence since 1978

and is Felix E. Schelling Professor Emeritus of English. His long residence in the Philadelphia area (in Swarthmore, Pennsylvania, since 1965) has lent both familiarity and feeling to his work, *Brotherly Love*, based on William Penn's establishment of a colony in the New World. From 1956 to 1957, Hoffman was a visiting professor at the Faculté des Lettres in Dijon, France: The poems of *The City of Satisfactions*, Part II, reflect his experience there. He has also been a fellow in the School of Letters, Indiana University; the Elleston Lecturer in Poetry at the University of Cincinnati; and a lecturer at the International School of Yeats Study, Sligo, Ireland.

The persona of Hoffman as critic and teacher rarely enters his verse: Some notable exceptions are in "The Princess Casamassima," a poignant evocation of a young revolutionary and former student, and "Filling the Forms," a humorous meditation on academic bureaucracy. His private life is reflected in his love poems to his wife, Elizabeth McFarland (his "Musebaby"), and his celebration of his daughter Kate and son Macfarlane in "Ode" and "The Blessings," respectively. His verse in general, however, is neither confessional nor autobiographical; his personal testament is emblematic of a sensitive and intelligent witness of life in contemporary America.

ANALYSIS

In *The Harvard Guide to Contemporary American Writing*, Daniel Hoffman describes postmodern American poets as

> ripples on the great groundswell of the Romantic movement which nearly two centuries ago established the oppositions of feeling to thought, of self to institutions, which separate modern man from his past. The chief difference between the contemporary and the Romantic and modernist generations is, we now recognize the past as lost.

As a postmodern poet, Hoffman can be considered a conservative who believes in eternal human verities and the ability of literature both to discover and to preserve them. For Hoffman, modern life continues the Romantic thrust that places the poet at the center of the poem. He has fused his meticulous observations of nature and the human condition into a poetry that is personal yet always a form of public discourse. Like many poets of his generation, he began in the wake of Robert Frost, T. S. Eliot, and Wallace Stevens, trying to adapt conventional meters and verse forms to contemporary themes. Indeed, his early verse exhibits real verbal flamboyance with a recondite vocabulary, difficult syntax, and dazzling sound effects. His later books reflect a modulation in style, although he has never become a true adherent of William Carlos Williams's aesthetic of "poetry as speech." In the words of "The Poem," he now casts his message "in a sort of singing" (*The Center of Attention*). Hoffman's "song" is not of himself but of the epiphanies of unchanging reality that he has experienced. He avoids solipsism not through a unifying vision but through his use of gnomic verse, ballads, myths, folklore, and, most recently, through a historical poetic sequence. In poetry that is serious and responsible, yet personable and engaging, he has tried to meet Walt Whitman's challenge of the open road: "Clearly, the challenge is to face this reality, this life of junk, and in it, or out of it, somehow discover or recover the transcendence that Whitman had announced as our birthright."

In his preface to Daniel Hoffman's first volume, *An Armada of Thirty Whales*, W. H. Auden designated him as a modern-day nature poet, intent on recovering nature's "numinous" quality. This judgment would prove to be only partly correct. The most important animal in Hoffman's bestiary is man, and his relation to nature is problematical: The poems in his first book show nature as an analogue or as a foil to man—nature is always other. In *A Little Geste and Other Poems*, as Richard Howard has pointed out, man's kinship with nature's brutality and irrationality forms a terrifying undercurrent to his civilized verse. Nature, in Hoffman's poems, can provide astonishment and elevation: these glimpses, cherished but fleeting, form the substance of two early poems, "At Provincetown" and "The Larks" (*An Armada of Thirty Whales*). In the former, after an evocation of the "aerial carousel" of a swooping gull, the poet comments:

> Over the wharves at Provincetown
> the gulls within our arteries soaring

> almost complete the great mobile
> that all but froze the gullsblood to steel.
> Other wings across the harbour
> flash like swords and dive for garbage.

Here man and bird become united in the perception of the beautiful, but the fusion is only "almost" complete, and the last word of the poem, "garbage," brings the poet down to earth.

"THE LARKS" AND "EAGLES"

In "The Larks," "An exaltation of larks arising/ With elocutionary tongue/ Embellish sound on morning air/ Already fringed with scent of dung." From the "matin's golden dong" to the "scent of dung," there is a perfect tracing of movement in the poem, from "arising" in the first line to "descend" in the last. The diction in the poem is fancifully elevated, but the "dung/dong" is a clear call to the mundane present. Two other early poems from the same collection, "That the pear delights me" and "Ephemeridae," both display Hoffman's keen observation and verbal art, but their message is the same: Man is outside nature, alien to its harmonies. In the first, the poet's delight in the pear is deemed "inconsequential" and "incidental" "for the flower was for the fruit,/ the fruit is for the seed." The poet's conclusion is rendered in Latinate diction, the fruit of intellection; the activity of nature is sensuously evoked: the bees "nuzzle, gnash, & guzzle/ nectar of the pear"; "Pears plop down"; "pearpits feast and feed/ and stir, & burst, & breed."

The poet admires eagles in "Eagles" (one of a series of poems in *The Center of Attention* in which the poet attempts to encapsulate the essence of a tree or a mackerel or a dogfish through closely rendered observation of its natural ritual) for their fidelity to one another, for their perfect representation of freedom, and for their true—not symbolic, like the poet's—dominion. This poem clearly holds the natural world up to human scrutiny to the impoverishment of the human sphere. Hoffman knows that his reading of nature might be the imposition of his version of reality upon natural fact; two poems from *The City of Satisfactions*, "Natural History" and "Fables," make this very point. In the end, he can only ask nature's blessing "In a Cold Climate" for help in living.

Urban man has created a landscape filled with "shapes that no/ familiarity breeds . . . things/ whose archetypes/ have not yet been dreamed . . . facts/ burdened with nothing/ anticipating/ unhappened memories,/ visionary things" ("On the Industrial Highway," *Striking the Stones*). It is a place where bird song, the symbol of pure poetry in "Awoke into a Dream of Singing," has been replaced by a "convivial Rock-box," the ubiquitous radio ("O Sweet Woods," *The City of Satisfactions*). It is a world where the past is dead: "In the Graeco-Roman Room," only the bronze mouse, not the many Aphrodites or Hercules, has relevance. It is the future that Henry Adams divined at the turn of the twentieth century ("To Henry Adams at the Paris Exposition"). Hoffman has called the modern world "The City of Satisfactions," "where all that is desired can be supplied" ("Banished," *Striking the Stones*). In the poem "The City of Satisfactions," the reader is taken on one of Hoffman's nightmare train rides: This one begins "As I was travelling toward the city of satisfactions/ On my employment, seeking the treasure of pleasure." The traveler, however, gets off the allegorical track onto a "bleak siding" in the great American desert, and there proceeds through a ritual of smashing open a series of boxes to get to the treasure. His quest will become how, through his craft, to return to nature that which was found, and the poem ends by suggesting the enormity of the task: "If I could only make this broken top/ Fit snug back on this casket." The poet's destiny is caught up with America's, and Hoffman does not supply easy answers.

"AFTER GOD" AND "A NEW BIRTH"

In "After God" (*The Center of Attention*), he directly addresses the crisis of faith: If man has replaced God, "Who keeps His ceaselessly attentive eye/ Upon the light and fall/ Of each Polaris through the wide feast-hall/ Of the sky"? Where does authority lie? How does man define himself? What is the meaning of suffering? The "vacant hour" at the end of the poem that calls for a new "sacrifice" is the space that Cotton Mather claims would prove divinity; Hoffman seems to be calling for modern man's atonement as a prerequisite to lawful power.

Many of Hoffman's poems concern the writer's craft, and, not surprisingly, the difficulty of making stones sing. "A New Birth" (*The City of Satisfactions*) suggests that literary tradition can no longer serve the poet: "What patrimony I come by/ Lies, an empty sack,/ Shrivelled fables at my back." In fact, Hoffman has not discarded literary conventions in his verse. He has always been aware of the tensions between felt life and literary form. In "The Sonnet (Remembering Louise Bogan)," it is clear that for him poetic form does imply a civilizing grace; this is a "bad time" for poetry because modern culture cannot conceive a sonnet's "shape or know/ its uses" (*The Center of Attention*).

Hoffman has been called an intellectual poet; he writes, however, under the banner of imagination rather than intellect. True poetry springs from "intuition's blaze" ("Sources," *A Little Geste and Other Poems*), just as truth is not ensnared "by thought's glazened glare" but by cleaving "the dark around my bower/ Wayward as joy's arrow" ("Three Jovial Gentlemen," *The City of Satisfactions*).

This celebration of "intuition's blaze" is reflected in Hoffman's deep attachment to themes and forms from folk art. In "Another Country," "the great creatures on that sacred dome" (*Striking the Stones*) represent archetypes that he will incorporate in his work. The "ancestral memory" of the night heron in "Summer Solstice" (*Broken Laws*) is parallel to the myths and rituals found in human culture. *A Little Geste and Other Poems* contains two poetic sequences based on folk origins: "Taliesin," in which a Welsh hero turned modern bard laments: "Popularity's encomium:/ 'The hiatus of singular eminence'/ Repels; th'Elect rise on the piety/ Due those images which reflect/ The multitude's/ homogeneity"; and "A Little Geste," a retelling of the Robin Hood story as a fertility legend, a poem considered by Richard Howard to be Hoffman's masterpiece. Alternating songs, chants, lays, ballads, carols, and assonant verse, Hoffman elliptically recounts the coming and sacrificial death of a fertility god, "a presence, huge, horn-helmed, green-clad," destroyed by the Prioress—the Church. "As I am made of flesh and blood/ God send me my right food," sings "The Aubade." The "right food" or "sacramental meal" is the sexual revel in the forest in which Robin Hood, Maid Marian, and the crew participate. Robin's sexuality brings man in tune with the world's rhythm; he is "The God in Man whose name/ we cry at last has come/ His marriage rite to claim." Copulation releases man's divinity, but this blessed state is not sustained. The institutional Church intervenes: Robin's wounds will not stain Marian's thighs; his wounds are fatal. Blood becomes "transubstantiated" and "runs thin." The result is the world's impoverishment: "The green world turns to stone./ No sacrifices made,/ Sacred trees hewn down." All the sexual imagery that runs through Hoffman's poetry points back to this original green world.

BROTHERLY LOVE

Brotherly Love fuses Hoffman's talents as poet and scholar and provides a historical framework for his contemporary prophecy. In many ways, this is an optimistic book. The spirit of Philadelphia, the City of Brotherly Love, Penn's Holy Experiment in the New World, may point to a promising American future. The poetic sequence affords Hoffman the scope to examine Edenic America and America's fall from grace. His train ride back in time contains three parts: "Treating with Indians," the culture of the Leni-Lenape, from their *Walam Olum*; "An Opening of Joy," Penn's conversion to Quaker tenets and his vision for the colony; and "The Structure of Reality," the attempt and failure to translate the ideal into the real.

There are elaborate parallels in the text between the Native Americans and the Quakers: In Hoffman's view of American history, "the destination of two journeys meet," each with similar visions for the future. The epigraph from Ralph Waldo Emerson's "History"—"Who cares what the fact was, when we have made a constellation of it to hang in heaven an immortal sign?"—point to Hoffman's judgment: the possibility of a peaceable kingdom still exists because it was attempted in Philadelphia and was briefly successful. The seeds of its downfall—the displacement of the Delawares and the conflict between settlers and proprietors—are described just before two encomiums, Penn's own prayer for his city (now inscribed on City Hall in Philadelphia) and Voltaire's delight in the noble experiment. The conclusion to the book is optimistic:

> —Here possibilities of grace
> like fragrance from rich compost cling
> to leaves where our each deed
> and misdeed fall. The Seed
> stirs, even now is quickening.

The fertility myth has been raised to a history of the possibilities of the spirit. The natural round now promises grace.

MIDDENS OF THE TRIBE

Poem and novella mix in Hoffman's 1995 work, *Middens of the Tribe*. Once again the poet draws on his scholarly, academic background in history, folklore, and anthropology, but in a 1998 essay, "Narrative Strategies in *Middens of the Tribe*" that appeared in *Sewannee Review*, Hoffman reveals the fragments of personal experience (chance facts remembered from dinner-party conversations, memories of working for a year in Margaret Mead's office, visits to archaeological sites), family history (the life of his grandfather, a family doctor who was almost, but not quite, the doctor in the poem), and literary precedents (Geoffrey Chaucer's assemblage of pilgrims providing the paradigm for Hoffman's "tribe") on which he built to create the work. He reveals this information as part of a rejection of literary theories that "deny authorship to authors, or attribute authors' choices to the hegemony of dominant social classes, or maintain that the language writes the text."

In his attempts to create authentic voices for his characters, Hoffman feels free to switch between poetry and prose as fits the mood and subject matter being addressed. The old man musing on his scientific research speaks in poetry:

> can the middens
> of the tribe I study tell if family
> strife always reveals a culture's dynamics,
> if, amid bones, flints, sufferings are the same?

Yet elsewhere, when his musing becomes "materialistic," the voice switches to prose:

The litany of their names sustained him.

The noble numbers of that nomenclature summoned the titans and the heroes, the outsized, triumphant corporate bodies whose offices occupied entire floors of downtown skyscrapers, whose executives were domiciled therein with private, ample, many-windowed chambers looking out from upper stories upon the widespread bustling world invisibly governed from the buzzer-buttons and telephones upon their desks.

The modern "tribe," composed of the doctor's patients, contrasts with the anthropological analysis of the Cromlech tribe studied by the archaeologist. The messiness and self-centeredness of modern couplings, for instance, lead to unhappiness and loneliness for the modern characters, while the Cromlech's superficially impersonal (from a modern point of view) mating rituals in fact lead to a sense of partaking in the processes of nature. The modern experience of death is devastating, whereas the ritualized mourning of the Cromlechs offers the prospect of the dead still firmly enveloped in the web of tribal history. These contrasts reflect an overly romanticized view of "tribal" societies, in which community retains its primeval and mythical wholeness in contrast to a decidedly postlapsarian modern world. However, Hoffman's goal is not the historically accurate depiction of a society, whether ancient or modern, but to express a "principle of contrast [that] must be deeply imprinted in the mind, in the imagination, embodying as it does both repetition and opposition, both similarity and difference." To this extent, *Middens of the Tribe*, consciously or unconsciously, depicts the underlying principle of "binary opposition" that anthropologist Claude Lévi-Strauss detected in the structure of mythology composed by the "savage mind," the basis of the folklore that has inspired Hoffman throughout his career.

OTHER MAJOR WORKS

NONFICTION: *Paul Bunyan: Last of the Frontier Demigods*, 1952; *The Poetry of Stephen Crane*, 1957; *Form and Fable in American Fiction*, 1961; *Barbarous Knowledge: Myth in the Poetry of Yeats, Graves, and Muir*, 1967; *Poe Poe Poe Poe Poe Poe Poe*, 1972; *Others: Shock Troups of Stylistic Change*, 1975; *Faulkner's Country Matters: Folklore and Fable in Yoknapatawpha*, 1989; *Words to Create a World: Interviews, Essays, and Reviews of Contemporary Poetry*, 1993; *Form and Fable in American Fiction*, 1994; *Zone of the Interior: A Memoir, 1942-1947*, 2000.

EDITED TEXTS: *The Red Badge of Courage and Other Stories*, 1957; *American Poetry and Poetics: Poems and Critical Documents from the Puritans to Robert Frost*, 1962; *English Literary Criticism: Romantic and Victorian*, 1963 (with Samuel Hynes); *New Poets, 1970*, 1970; *University and College Prizes, 1967-1972*, 1974; *The Harvard Guide to Contemporary American Writing*, 1979; *Ezra Pound and William Carlos Williams*, 1983.

BIBLIOGRAPHY

Breslin, Paul. "Four Poets." *The New York Times Book Review*, March 22, 1981, 14, 31. In reviewing *Brotherly Love*, Breslin notes some reservations: One is regarding Hoffman's alliance with Voltaire's idealization of the Quakers' relationship with the Native Americans; the other is the poet's uneven treatment of the poems. Nevertheless, Breslin commends Hoffman on his distinguished writing, some of which is "deeply moving."

Cotter, James Finn. Review of *Brotherly Love*, by Daniel Hoffman. *America* 145 (July 25, 1981): 37-38. Cotter calls this poem a "true epic waiting to be explored and absorbed." He comments favorably on *Brotherly Love*'s concluding message of hope (letting the seeds remain on fertile ground), and says that this gives all that could be hoped for from a poet.

Howard, Richard. *Alone with America: Essays on the Art of the Poetry in the United States Since 1950*. New York: Atheneum, 1980. The essay on Hoffman, titled "A Testament of Change, Melting into Song," provides commentary on *An Armada of Thirty Whales* and *The City of Satisfactions*. Also includes reviews of *Broken Laws* and *The Center of Attention*. Recommended reading for its useful insights into Hoffman's work.

Rosenthal, M. L. "Critical, Lyrical, Literal, and Rapt." *Saturday Review* 51 (June 22, 1968): 72-73. Reviews *Striking the Stones*, citing "Testament" as the most effective with its simplicity and grace. If only Hoffman could put together all his poems as he did in "Testament," Rosenthal asserts, noting, however, that much of Hoffman's work does not match this standard. Discusses other poems from this collection, in particular "This Day" and "A Marriage."

Honora Rankine-Galloway,
updated by Leslie Ellen Jones

HUGO VON HOFMANNSTHAL

Born: Vienna, Austria; February 1, 1874
Died: Rodaun, Austria; July 15, 1929

PRINCIPAL POETRY

Ausgewählte Gedichte, 1903
Die gesammelten Gedichte, 1907 (*The Lyrical Poems of Hugo von Hofmannsthal*, 1918)
Loris, 1930
Nachlese der Gedichte, 1934
Gedichte und lyrische Dramen, 1946 (*Poems and Verse Plays*, 1961)

OTHER LITERARY FORMS

Hugo von Hofmannsthal's outstanding poetry forms only a very small portion of his literary legacy. During the 1890's, when his best poems were written, editions of his early lyric plays also appeared. They include

Hugo von Hoffmannsthal

Gestern (1891), *Der Tor und der Tod* (pb. 1894; *Death and the Fool*, 1913), *Die Hochzeit der Sobeide* (pr., pb. 1899; *The Marriage of Sobeide*, 1913), and *Theater in Versen* (1899). After 1900, he devoted most of his creative energy to the stage and published more than twenty additional books of dramatic writings before his death. Such works as *Elektra* (pr. 1903; *Electra*, 1908), *Jedermann* (pr., pb. 1911; *Everyman*, 1917), *Der Schwierige* (pb. 1920; *The Difficult Man*, 1963), and *Das Salzburger Grosse Welttheater* (pr., pb. 1922; *The Salzburg Great Theatre of the World*, 1958) became very popular. Hofmannsthal achieved his greatest theatrical success, however, as librettist for the operas of Richard Strauss. Because of his lyric virtuosity, *Electra*, which he revised for Strauss, *Der Rosenkavalier* (pr., pb. 1911; *The Cavalier of the Rose*, 1912; also known as *The Rose Bearer*), and *Arabella* (1933; English translation, 1955) received lasting acclaim. Hofmannsthal also wrote a few excellent short stories, parts of a novel, scenarios for several ballets, and more than two hundred essays, all of which have been published. Since his death, his notebooks and diaries have been edited, as have some twenty volumes of his extensive correspondence.

ACHIEVEMENTS

Unlike most poets, Hugo von Hofmannsthal did not go through a period of gradual literary development leading to eventual mature control of his art. Rather, he emerged at the beginning of his career as an accomplished lyricist and immediately became an enigma to the Austrian literary establishment. His earliest poems quickly caught the attention of critics and writers alike, especially the young Viennese moderns. His combination of youth and poetic genius was unparalleled in German letters, and many of his contemporaries found it very hard to reconcile the artistic power of his works with the teenage poet who had written them.

Among those most impressed with the young Hofmannsthal's creative facility was Stefan George. Much of Hofmannsthal's poetry appeared for the first time in *Blätter für die Kunst*, the literary organ of George and his circle. As a result, Hofmannsthal is often associated with the German Symbolists. Although he shared with George the desire to achieve the greatest possible perfection and purification of literary language and expression, his own lyrics are far more closely related to those of his friends Hermann Bahr, Arthur Schnitzler, and Richard Beer-Hofmann. As a part of this group, Hofmannsthal mediated ideas and prosody from a broad range of European models and traditions, created some of the most sensitive poems in modern German literature, and received acclaim in his own time as the greatest of the German Impressionists.

Hofmannsthal resisted the idea of compiling his poetry until years after he had turned his creative attention almost exclusively to drama. Only two collections were published in his lifetime, yet during a brief decade he had contributed to Austrian literature poems of beauty unequaled in the German language since the time of Johann Wolfgang von Goethe. The wider recognition that he later enjoyed as a dramatist and librettist came in no small measure as a result of his utter mastery of poetic language and lyric technique.

BIOGRAPHY

The only son of a Viennese bank director, Hugo Laurenz August Hofmann Edler von Hofmannsthal came from a mixed heritage of Austrian, Italian, and German-Jewish elements which were vitally important to his cultural and intellectual development. He was educated by private tutors until he was ten; then he entered secondary school in Vienna. An avid reader, he assimilated an astounding amount of knowledge in a very short time. His precocious intellect set him apart from the young people around him, contributing to a sense of loneliness that remained with him throughout his life.

In 1890, Hofmannsthal published his first poem, "Frage," under the pseudonym "Loris Melikow." That summer, he became acquainted with the actor Gustav Schwarzkopf, who introduced him to Hermann Bahr, Arthur Schnitzler, and Felix Salten. Within the next few months, Hofmannsthal published additional poems, his first essay, and his first lyric play, *Gestern*, in periodicals in Vienna and Berlin.

One of three important friendships that strongly influenced Hofmannsthal's creative career began in December, 1891, when he met Stefan George, who had come to Vienna to seek him out. A productive, if often stormy, relationship with George lasted for fifteen years and generated a correspondence which in its significance for German literature has been compared to that between Goethe and Friedrich Schiller. Although Hofmannsthal initially felt comfortable in George's group, differences in temperament and creative outlook caused severe tension. Hofmannsthal soon removed himself from active participation in George's literary ventures, even though their association did not break off completely until 1906.

During the 1890's, Hofmannsthal traveled extensively, met a variety of people, and set patterns that informed the remainder of his life. His first trip to Venice in 1892 was of special importance for his work as a whole. Venice became his second home and the setting for some of his later dramas. In 1892, he enrolled at the University of Vienna, where he briefly studied law. Between 1895 and 1899, he successfully completed a doctoral program in Romance philology. The late 1890's were especially productive years. While in Italy in 1897, he composed more than two thousand lines of poetry and lyric drama in one two-week period. By 1900, he had already written and staged several plays.

After marrying Gertrud Schlesinger in 1901, Hofmannsthal moved to Rodaun. During the years that followed, he devoted his time to mastering the drama, entering into enormously productive relationships with producer Max Reinhardt and composer Richard Strauss. In 1903, Reinhardt encouraged him to create a free rendition of Sophocles' *Electra* (418-410 B.C.E.), the production of which brought Hofmannsthal his first major theatrical success. After the play attracted the attention of Strauss, Hofmannsthal revised it, creating a libretto which when set to music was even more successful than the original drama. During the next twenty-three years, the two artists collaborated in the creation of five additional operas and several ballets.

For Hofmannsthal, World War I and the death of the old Austrian regime were a personal disaster from which he never recovered. After the war, he dedicated himself to the revival of Austrian and German culture. In 1917, he participated in the founding of the famous Salzburg Festival, and in the early 1920's he edited and published several collections of writings by earlier authors. Beginning in 1920, however, his health began to fail, and he suffered recurring illness until his death. He died of a cerebral hemorrhage two days after the tragic suicide of his older son Franz.

ANALYSIS

In the essay "Der Dichter und diese Zeit" ("The Poet and This Time"), written in 1907, Hugo von Hofmannsthal outlined the key concepts which informed his poems. From his perspective, the principal responsibility of the modern poet was to provide the reader with access to the whole spectrum of human experience. If nothing else, Hofmannsthal's poetry reflects his overriding desire to participate in and become a part of everything that he saw, felt, or dreamed, and to share with others the intensity of his impressions of life. He envisioned the poet as one who unites past, present, and future into an eternal "now," recording, preserving, and analyzing everything that moves his era. A human seismograph that responds to living realities, the poet awakens his audience to the inner meaning of their own unexamined experience.

Hofmannsthal's view of the poet's relationship to his times explains the diversity of his lyric creations and the complexity of themes, moods, and ideas that inform his literary art. His poems are like fragments of a vast mosaic, in which each carefully positioned element exposes the beholder to a small yet powerful aspect of the human condition. Hofmannsthal sought to reveal the broad range of possibilities to be found or generated within the individual, while moving people in the direction of cogent answers to basic existential questions: What is man? How can man perceive his own nature and actively create, refine, and perfect the features of his unique inner world? He did not wish to impose upon the reader a finished worldview but rather to offer raw materials, tools, and stimuli that might enable another person to awaken, expand, and mold his own perceptions. While giving direction to those searching for meaning, he sounded the abyss of his own soul, exposing to the public eye the sensitive observations, the multicolored dreams, and the speculative visions that constituted his innermost self. The poems thus engendered reflect his encounters with beauty and loneliness interwoven with feelings of love and defiance, with landscapes, people, and the material things of external reality.

As an Impressionist, Hofmannsthal sought a faithful reproduction of subjective sensual experience and precisely noted mood. His lyrics are remarkable for their acute awareness of the incidental, the transitory, the matchless spiritual state in all its peculiarities and narrow differentiations, nuances, shades, and halftones. His treatment of visual themes was especially effective; he wrote with a painter's eye. He saw mastery of language as the essence of poetic creation, and systematically cultivated an elevated literary diction.

"PREEXISTENCE" AND THE LYRIC DECADE

During his so-called lyric decade, Hofmannsthal capsulized in verse the most important aspects of his philosophy of life. His poems contain in embryonic form all the major ideas that he later expanded, modified, and refined in his dramas, librettos, and prose fiction. In combinations of vision and interpretation of the world and its phenomena, he developed a unified view of the internal harmony of present, past, and future reality, basing his approach on a concept he called "preexistence." According to Hofmannsthal, existence has two points of reference: mortal life and preexistence. Preexistence is man's state when he is removed from mortal life. It is the state from which he comes at birth, to which he goes at death, and to which he travels temporarily in dreams or similar experiences. In this system, preexistence is absolute existence, while mortality is a transitory situation with little meaning outside the framework of preexistence.

The idea of preexistence is central to Hofmannsthal's explorations of basic human problems such as death, transitoriness, and the search for personal identity. Filtered through the lens of preexistence, life itself becomes an infinite process of creative transformation and refinement through which the person achieves oneness with all reality by concretely and spiritually experiencing an endless series of modes of being. In one of his earliest poems, "Ghaselen II" ("Ghazel II"), written in 1891, Hofmannsthal captured the essence of his notion of preexistence in lines that describe life as a wandering of the spirit through the hierarchy of beings, a process of changing and growing. While the course of transformation is one of purification, it does not always proceed upward. The transition may be from worm to frog or from poet to vagabond.

METAPHORS FOR THE MORTAL STATE

In harmony with the representation of life as a realm of continually changing roles, Hofmannsthal developed three poetic metaphors for the mortal state, each of which—the dream, the drama, and the game—represents a brief, sharply framed, experience. Although these metaphors are certainly not original and reflect a clear bond to a broad range of models in European literary tradition, Hofmannsthal's treatment of them is especially characteristic for his lyric poems. He used the dream to explore life as a creative process occurring completely within the person. Mortality perceived as drama, a direct outgrowth of the preexistence concept, allowed him to portray man as an actor passing through a series of external identities which in turn emerge as Faustian aspects of the individual spirit. Hofmannsthal was especially fond of the drama metaphor. He styled himself a spectator and from that perspective wrote the poems that most powerfully illuminate life as a stage production. The game metaphor is the least emphasized of the three and is less fully developed in his poetry. Later, Hofmannsthal centered dramas and stories around adult games, highlighting the figure of the adventurer/gambler. His lyrics, however, focus on the child's game as an aspect of the created inner self. His representations of the internal world are often populated with game-playing children who are at once formed in the image of the poet and subject to him as their creator.

"STANZAS IN TERZA RIMA"

In 1894, almost at the midpoint of his lyric decade, Hofmannsthal wrote a series of four poems in iambic tercets. He labeled them simply "Terzinen" ("Stanzas in Terza Rima"). Collectively, they provide excellent illustrations of his treatment of the basic human experiences of transitoriness and death, clearly elucidating his approach to these problems in the light of the theory of preexistence. A year later, in "Ballade des Äusseren Lebens," he would stress the emptiness of a world unaware of preexistence, questioning the relevance of mortality and dwelling on the transience, absence of coherence, and consequent lack of enduring value of earthly things. In "Stanzas in Terza Rima," however, he affirmed the permanence of all things perceived in absolute spiritual terms, providing a positive alternative for the person who is conscious of preexistence.

The first of the four poems, subtitled "Über Vergänglichkeit," questions the idea that the past can be borne away and lost forever without a trace. Central to the poet's deliberation is the stark awareness that his own essence is in a state of change and that it has metamorphosed from its former existence as a child. Consciousness of the past, however, also extends before childhood, in the realization that the poet existed before his mortal birth as an elemental part of his ancestors. Within the absolute realm of preexistence, his dead forebears are likewise a living part of the poet.

Hofmannsthal's approach to death is an extremely important facet of the doctrine of preexistence. In his poetry, he illuminated two clearly defined aspects of death as a basic experience of the individual spirit's eternal progression. The poem "Erlebnis" ("An Experience"), which he wrote two years before the "Stanzas in Terza Rima," focuses on death as a vehicle of transfer from mortality to preexistence. In beautifully vivid imagery, filled with powerful sensual impressions of light and sound, the poet describes death as a drowning in a translucent, light-weaving ocean, followed by an immediate longing for the mortal life that has been lost. The yearning itself is compared to that of a ship's passenger who sails past his hometown, unable to cross to the land that represents his childhood.

In "Stanzas in Terza Rima II," as in "An Experience," death is presented not as a feared unknown, but as something that is clearly understood. In the terza rima poem, however, stress is placed on the second aspect of the death experience, the flow of life from one form to another. In harmony with the notion of a continual passing through a hierarchy of beings, as developed in "Ghazel II," the poet points to the conveying of vital energy from one entity to another in the image of life fleeing from pale little girls into trees and grass. Death is nothing more than an outward manifestation of the bond that pervades all existence, linking life into a great whole.

"Stanzas in Terza Rima III" is the first of Hofmannsthal's poems to employ his characteristic metaphor of life as a dream. This lyric emphasizes the creative power of dreams: Because the stuff of which man is made has properties like those of dreams, man is able to merge and become one with his dreams. Like death, then, the dream becomes a vehicle by which one attains ultimate definition within the sphere of absolute existence. "Stanzas in Terza Rima IV" expands the dream metaphor to its final dimensions by placing within its scope external relations with other people, internal longings, the structure and perception of the material world, and the conclusive penetration and understanding of life and self.

POEMS AND VERSE PLAYS

From the very beginning of his literary career, Hofmannsthal felt himself drawn to the theater. That fact is especially relevant to his amplification of the "life is a drama" metaphor in his poetry. Although he employed stage-related imagery in a variety of lyric contexts, the most representative poems in this category appear in the volume *Poems and Verse Plays* under the collective heading "Prologe und Trauerreden" ("Prologues and Elegies"). This set of lyric creations reveals the deeply personal nature of the drama metaphor, clarifying Hofmannsthal's self-appointed role as spectator in the theater of life.

"PROLOGUE TO THE BOOK 'ANATOL'"

One of the most famous poems in the group is "Prolog zu dem Buch 'Anatol'" ("Prologue to the Book 'Anatol'"), which was written to introduce a work by Arthur Schnitzler. It begins with a powerful, seemingly directionless, heterogeneous array of impressions from the domain of the theater. Latticework, artificial hedges, escutcheons, sphinxes, creaking gates, and waterfalls are artistically jumbled together. Throughout the first section, props, backdrops, and scenery are interwoven with bits of plays, apparently unconnected actors and actresses, and fragments of color and mood. The result is a vivid mosaic of constituents related only through their mutual association with the stage.

The second portion of the poem presents the reasons for the visible turmoil and disorder. The theater stands for the multiformity of mortal existence. The dramas that are performed proceed from natural personal impulse without effort, premeditation, or constraint, arising from within the players themselves. Hofmannsthal

enlarges the metaphor to encompass himself and the reader among the actors and summarizes their involvement by depicting life as "plays that we have fashioned" and "comedies of our own spirit." He thus gives his own version of William Shakespeare's "All the world's a stage."

"ZUM GEDÄCHTNIS DES SCHAUSPIELERS MITTERWURZER"

In the elegiac poems, Hofmannsthal presented more intensely the relation between the drama metaphor and his concept of preexistence. The elegies, some of which are dedicated to the memory of real people, focus on the actor as symbolic man. "Zum Gedächtnis des Schauspielers Mitterwurzer" (in memory of the actor Mitterwurzer) is very representative of the poet's development of this particular theme.

"Zum Gedächtnis des Schauspielers Mitterwurzer" examines the implications of the actor's death with respect to absolute existence. When the player dies, it is quickly apparent that something extraordinary has perished: With him have disappeared all the figures to whom he gave life. The characters no longer live because the special essence that this actor gave them could come only from him. Another actor playing the same part would somehow give a different nature to the role, and the character, in spite of mask and props, would be a new one. Because of the feeling of final loss, the poet seeks to penetrate to Mitterwurzer's true identity and learns that the dead actor is essentially one with the dreamer. He molds and forms the existence that surrounds him. Like the dreamer's world, the realm created by the actor comes from within himself. Hofmannsthal portrays Mitterwurzer's body as a magic veil that houses everything, a veil from which the actor could conjure up not only various animals and people, but also, more importantly, "you and me."

Briefly stated, the actor gives life. In Hofmannsthal's framework, the actor is a conduit through which individual souls can bridge the gap between preexistence and mortality. The death of Mitterwurzer represents the loss of such a conduit. More profoundly tragic, therefore, than the passing of characters already portrayed is the untimely preclusion of those as yet unborn. The substance of the poem's final lament is that Mitterwurzer's death has caused the departure of inhabitants from our own internal world and has prevented the arrival of others who might have had their birth within us. In dying, the actor has deprived those left behind of precious elements of their own being.

"DER JÜNGLING UND DIE SPINNE"

"Der Jüngling und die Spinne," a two-part existential work written in 1897, near the end of Hofmannsthal's lyric period, is one of a very few poems that develop in detail his representation of man as a player of games. Like the metaphors of the dream and the drama, the metaphor of the game is important to the definition of the internally formulated world of the individual. Creating a self-contained world, the artist "teaches" the "citizens" of that world certain games which then characterize both them and their creator. In the first segment of "Der Jüngling und die Spinne," a young man reveals himself as a representative Hofmannsthal figure, aware of his place in the middle of a universe, of which fate's decrees have made him master. While observing his "subjects," he notes their peculiar relationship to himself. Many have his own features. More important, they play games that he, as their originator, has taught them. For the youth, the process of looking inward is one of learning to understand not only himself but also life in its absolute sense. The transformation that occurs in the dawning of awareness is Hofmannsthal's ultimate symbol for the kind of impact that he intended his poetry to have on the reader. The timeless role of the poet—a synthesis of dreamer, actor, and player of games—is to teach actively by providing others with the needed personal keys to themselves.

"WHERE I NEAR AND WHERE I LAND . . ."

In the famous poem "Wo ich nahe, wo ich lande . . ." ("Where I Near and Where I Land . . ."), a powerful example of depth in simplicity, Hofmannsthal describes in greater detail the rapport that he wished to achieve with his public. Unlike the young man of "Der Jüngling und die Spinne," the "I" of "Where I Near and Where I Land . . ." is completely cognizant of his responsibility to elevate his world's inhabitants to spiritual planes beyond their present state. The teacher who has the capacity to communicate with the deepest levels of the soul, causing such levels to unfold in inner comprehension of self, might achieve the goal of Hofmannsthal's poetry, uplifting both himself and the world around him.

OTHER MAJOR WORKS

LONG FICTION: *Andreas: Oder, Die Vereinigten*, 1932 (*Andreas: Or, The United*, 1936).

SHORT FICTION: *Reitergeschichte*, 1899 (*Cavalry Patrol*, 1939); *Erlebnis des Marschalls von Bassompierre*, 1900 (*An Episode in the Life of the Marshal de Bassompierre*, 1952); *Das Märchen 672: Nacht, und andere Erzählungen*, 1905 (*Tale of the Merchant's Son and His Servants*, 1969); *Lucidor*, 1910 (English translation, 1922); *Drei Erzählungen*, 1927; *Das erzählerische Work*, 1969.

PLAYS: *Gestern*, pb. 1891; *Der Tor und der Tod*, pb. 1894 (*Death and the Fool*, 1913); *Das kleine Welttheater*, pb. 1897 (*The Little Theater of the World*, 1961); *Der weisse Fächer*, pb. 1898 (*The White Fan*, 1909); *Die Frau im Fenster*, pr., pb. 1898 (*Madonna Dianora*, 1916); *Der Abenteurer und die Sängerin*, pr., pb. 1899 (*The Adventurer and the Singer*, 1917); *Die Hochzeit der Sobeide*, pr., pb. 1899 (*The Marriage of Sobeide*, 1913); *Theater in Versen*, pb. 1899; *Der Kaiser und die Hexe*, pb. 1900 (*The Emperor and the Witch*, 1961); *Elektra*, pr. 1903 (*Electra*, 1908); *Das gerettete Venedig*, pr., pb. 1905 (*Venice Preserved*, 1915); *Kleine Dramen*, pb. 1906; *Ödipus und die Sphinx*, pr., pb. 1906 (*Oedipus and the Sphinx*, 1968); *Vorspiele*, pb. 1908; *Christinas Heimreise*, pr. 1910 (*Christina's Journey Home*, 1916); *König Ödipus*, pr., pb. 1910; *Alkestis*, pb. 1911; *Der Rosenkavalier*, pr., pb. 1911 (libretto; *The Cavalier of the Rose*, 1912; also known as *The Rose Bearer*); *Jedermann*, pr., pb. 1911 (*Everyman*, 1917); *Ariadne auf Naxos*, pr., pb. 1912 (libretto; *Ariadne on Naxos*, 1922); *Der Bürger als Edelmann*, pr., pb. 1918; *Die Frau ohne Schatten*, pr., pb. 1919 (libretto; *The Woman Without a Shadow*, 1957); *Dame Kobold*, pr., pb. 1920; *Der Schwierige*, pb. 1920 (*The Difficult Man*, 1963); *Florindo*, pr. 1921; *Das Salzburger Grosse Welttheater*, pr., pb. 1922 (*The Salzburg Great Theatre of the World*, 1958); *Der Unbestechliche*, pr. 1923; *Der Turm*, pb. 1925 (*The Tower*, 1963); *Die ägyptische Helena*, pr., pb. 1928 (libretto; *Helen in Egypt*, 1963); *Das Bergwerk zu Folun*, pb. 1933 (*The Mine at Falun*, 1933); *Arabella*, pr., pb. 1933 (libretto; English translation, 1955); *Dramatische Entwürfe*, pb. 1936; *Silvia im "Stern,"* pb. 1959.

NONFICTION: *Gespräch über Gedichte*, 1904; *Unterhaltungen über literarische Gegenstände*, 1904; *Die Briefe des Zurückgekehrten*, 1907; *Der Dichter und diese Zeit*, 1907 (*The Poet and His Time*, 1955); *Wege und die Begegnungen*, 1913; *Reden und Aufsätze*, 1921; *Buch der Freunde*, 1922 (*The Book of Friends*, 1952); *Augenblicke in Griechenland*, 1924 (*Moments in Greece*, 1952); *Früheste Prosastücke*, 1926; *Richard Strauss und Hugo von Hofmannsthal: Briefwechsel*, 1926 (*Correspondence of Richard Strauss and Hugo von Hofmannsthal*, 1927); *Ad me ipsum*, 1930; *Loris: Die Prosa des jungen Hugo von Hofmannsthal*, 1930; *Die Berührung der Sphären*, 1931; *Festspiele in Salzburg*, 1938; *Briefwechsel zwischen George und Hofmannsthal*, 1938 (letters); *Selected Prose*, 1952; *Selected Essays*, 1955.

EDITED TEXTS: *Deutsche Erzähler*, 1912 (4 volumes); *Die österreichische Bibliothek*, 1915-1917 (26 volumes); *Deutsches Epigramme*, 1923 (2 volumes); *Schillers Selbstcharakteristik*, 1926.

MISCELLANEOUS: *Gesammelte Werke in Einzelausgaben*, 1945-1959 (15 volumes); *Selected Writings of Hugo von Hofmannsthal*, 1952-1963 (3 volumes); *Hofmannsthal: Gesammelte Werke*, 1979 (10 volumes).

BIBLIOGRAPHY

Bangerter, Lowell A. *Hugo von Hofmannsthal*. New York: F. Ungar, 1977. A critical analysis of selected works by Hofmannsthal. Includes an index and a bibliography.

Del Caro, Adrian. *Hugo von Hofmannsthal: Poets and the Language of Life*. Baton Rouge: Louisiana State University Press, 1993. Del Caro argues that Hofmannsthal was an early opponent of aestheticism and was an heir of Friedrich Nietzsche in his search for a legitimate source for values. Includes bibliographical references and index.

Hammelmann, Hanns A. *Hugo von Hofmannsthal*. New Haven, Conn.: Yale University Press, 1957. A short introductory biography of Hofmannsthal. Includes bibliographic references.

Kovach, Thomas A. *Hofmannsthal and Symbolism: Art and Life in the Work of a Modern Poet*. New York: P. Lang, 1985. A biographical and critical study of Hofmannsthal's life and work. Includes bibliographic references and an index.

Vilain, Robert. *The Poetry of Hugo von Hofmannsthal and French Symbolism*. New York: Oxford University Press, 2000. Vilain suggests that Hofmannsthal's early interest in the works of the French Symbolists had an inhibiting effect on his own poetry. Includes bibliographical references and indexes.

Lowell A. Bangerter;
bibliography updated by the editors

LINDA HOGAN

Born: Denver, Colorado; July 16, 1947

PRINCIPAL POETRY
Calling Myself Home, 1978
Daughters, I Love You, 1981
Eclipse, 1983
Seeing Through the Sun, 1985
Savings, 1988
The Book of Medicines, 1993

OTHER LITERARY FORMS

Linda Hogan has published critical and personal essays and has written or coauthored books on Native American life, culture, and literature, as well as the environment and ecofeminism. Her work has been reprinted in numerous anthologies and edited collections.

ACHIEVEMENTS

Teaching and publishing represent major achievements for Linda Hogan, who has said that as a young girl she did not plan to attend college because, "I didn't know what college was." Yet by what Hogan might call a combination of love and defiance, she overcame the many oppressive conditions blocking those whom she characterizes as society's less privileged. Deliberately aimed at readers who may lack a formal education in literary forms, Hogan's writing often challenges accepted standards of literary taste.

Her achievement and potential have been formally recognized in her many awards: an American Book Award from the Before Columbus Foundation for *Seeing Through the Sun* (1985), a Minnesota State Arts Board grant, a Newberry Library D'Arcy McNickle Memorial Fellowship (1980), a Yaddo Colony Fellowship (1982), a National Endowment for the Arts fiction grant (1986), a Guggenheim Fellowship (1990), and a Lannan Award (1994). Her play *A Piece of Moon* (pr. 1981) received the 1980 Five Civilized Tribes Playwriting Award. Hogan's novel *Mean Spirit* (1990) received the Oklahoma Book Award for Fiction and the Mountains and Plains Booksellers Award (1990) and was a Pulitzer Prize finalist (1991). *The Book of Medicines* received the Colorado Book Award and was a National Book Critics Circle Award finalist.

BIOGRAPHY

Linda Hogan's ancestors include pioneer workers and farmers who had settled in Nebraska and Winchester

Linda Hogan

Colbert, a nineteenth century head of the Chickasaw nation. Growing up in Denver and later Colorado Springs, Hogan also spent much of her childhood on her grandparents' farm in Oklahoma. The former experiences introduced Hogan to a multicultural, working-class environment, the latter to rural poverty and hardship as well as the beauty of nature and strong ties to the land. Leaving school at fifteen to begin work as a nurse's aide, Hogan worked at a series of low-paying jobs before and during her first years in college. She earned a bachelor's degree from the University of Colorado at Colorado Springs and master of arts degree in creative writing from the University of Colorado at Boulder (1978).

During the period of her self-education and formal education, Hogan began to write, looking for a sense of pattern and significance in her existence. Since publishing her first book in 1978, Hogan has been an active writer and teacher: as a poet in the schools in Colorado and Oklahoma (1980-1984) and as a member of the faculties of the University of Colorado (1977-1979), Colorado Women's College (1979), the Rocky Mountain Women's Institute of the University of Denver (1979-1980), and the University of Minnesota, Twin Cities (1984-1989). Since 1989, Hogan has been a professor in the American Indian Studies Program and the English department at the University of Colorado.

As well as writing on issues relating to colonialism, other forms of oppression, and human rights, Hogan has been politically active. She participated with her family in an antinuclear encampment in the Black Hills of South Dakota during 1980, an experience later commemorated in the poems collected in *Daughters, I Love You* and reprinted in *Eclipse.*

Since the late 1980's, Hogan's work has focused increasingly on environmental and spiritual issues and on the nature of the animal-human connection. She seeks to reintegrate her Native American heritage and call to her readers' attention human beings' shared responsibility for the stewardship of the earth.

Hogan is the mother of two adopted daughters and has one granddaughter.

ANALYSIS

Linda Hogan's development as a poet demonstrates her lifelong commitment to certain ethical and emotional themes: problems of justice and injustice, the beauty and significance of the lives of ordinary people, strong bonds of family love, and a nurturing care for the natural world. Her style moves from very tightly structured, imagistic lyrics, focused in personal expression and feeling, outward to embrace geopolitical and ideological issues. At times her concerns are less immediately personal and more philosophical in their focus. Hogan favors a poetic form involving very brief to moderate-length first-person free-verse lyrics. In her later work, her imagistic intensity has given way to more discursive expression, looser construction, and more focused impact.

CALLING MYSELF HOME

Linda Hogan's first collection of poems, *Calling Myself Home* demonstrates her considerable promise as a writer. The ambiguous title reflects the complexity of themes that the author explores: While "calling myself home" signifies a journey back to origins, it can also be taken to mean that true home can only be found within the self. Both these meanings resonate in these poems; in fact, this tension is found in much of Hogan's work as well as her relationship with her family and ancestors.

"Landless Indians" Hogan's term for Chickasaw and other Oklahoma Indians, are typified by her grandparents and relatives, who lost their land to failed banks, swindlers, and periods of economic depression. Thus for Hogan and other members of her tribe, returning "home" carries with it in the act of reconnecting with the land—with home—and the painful awareness of what had once been. In response, Hogan turned to her inner resources to create a psychological and spiritual homeland capable of maintaining both individual and collective identity. She draws on her own experience in Oklahoma, the disjuncture felt by a racially mixed person living in an urban environment that is far removed from her homeland.

Calling Myself Home consists of two sections: "By the Dry Pond" and "Heritage." The first section offers reflective meditations on an arid, materially impoverished landscape, memories displaying a reverent attention to the details of landscape, and a sense of historical connectedness to the near and the prehistoric past. Frequent mention of an ancient turtle in a now-dry pond, for example, expresses both patient endurance and survival

and the image of the great tortoise, which, in many Native American mythologies, supports the world on its back. The title poem, "Calling Myself Home," weaves these themes together, imaginatively re-creating "old women/ who lived on amber" and danced to the rattles they made of turtle shell and pebbles. The speaker draws a connection between herself, her people, and the ancient ones: "we are plodding creatures/ like the turtle." Such affinity between people—especially women—and their land creates great strength. The generations of female forebears whom Hogan celebrates become a part of the earth's strength. Paradoxically, the speaker ends the poem on a note of farewell, stating that she has come to say good-bye, yet the substance of the poem indicates that the speaker, like the turtle, will carry her "home" with her always.

The book's second section focuses both on Hogan's personal and family experiences and also on larger themes of her heritage as a Chickasaw and as a Native American woman. Its title poem, "Heritage," alludes specifically to events Hogan described elsewhere involving her great-grandparents and other relatives: a plague of grasshoppers that destroyed her great-grandfather's farm in Nebraska, her uncle who carved delicate wood and bone objects and passed on traditional Chickasaw lore, her silent grandfather, and the counsel and practice of her grandmother. She alludes to secret wisdom, suppressed knowledge, and the sense of "never having a home."

Other poems celebrate metamorphosis and transformation, pervasive themes in Hogan's work: the natural transformation in the birth of a colt in "Celebration: Birth of a Colt"; the close observation, in "The River Calls Them," of tadpoles transforming into frogs; the speaker of "Man in the Moon" identifying with the Moon's phases, at times emaciated and nearly invisible and at other times fat with a house that will "fill up with silver." "Rain" describes fish both falling from the sky and being revived by the rain to feed the exuberant children—echoing "Calling Myself Home," in which women's bones transform into the Earth's calcified, tortoiselike skeleton.

ECLIPSE

The poems in *Eclipse* spiral outward from personal memory and family history to encompass wider philosophical and topical issues. *Eclipse* contains the poems from *Daughters, I Love You* and new sections of animal poems: "Landscape of Animals" and "Small Animals at Night." Other poems are grouped in sections titled "Who Will Speak?," "Land of Exile," and "Morning's Dance."

The poems of the first section affirm the affinity and continuity of the natural world. In some poems, this affinity represents a spiritual, almost mystical union, as in "Landscape of Animals." The poem "Ruins" wonderfully evokes the atmosphere of vanished life within ruins of ancient peoples of the American Southwest, while "Oil" reminds the reader of the fragility of the natural world: "The earth is wounded/ and will not heal." The poems of "Small Animals at Night" and "Land of Exile" center on the theme of continuity and on the interdependence that the speaker asserts connects herself, all human life, and the lives of animals.

DAUGHTERS, I LOVE YOU

In this collection Hogan addresses the threat of nuclear holocaust as well as historical and imminent guilt, fear, and danger. While most of the poems allude to the atomic bombing of Japan at the end of World War II, one poem, "Black Hills Survival Gathering, 1980," focuses on an accident at an atomic reactor in Idaho, and one poem grew directly out of Hogan's experiences at a peace encampment protesting the presence of nuclear weapons near the sacred Black Hills of South Dakota. Although the poems can be labeled "protests," the stronger unifying theme of *Daughters, I Love You* is its underlying spiritual message: Hogan sees that the most significant response she can make to answer the threats of power and poison is "a prayer that enters a house" to protect "the sleeping men and the gentle work/ of women."

The section "Who Will Speak?" explores the history of Native American peoples in the United States. "A Place for the Eagle" evokes a sense of the ancient oral traditions, showing creation as the joint work of animal and spirit shapers. In "Stone Dwellers" the speaker gazes at a museum display of historic and prehistoric artifacts, reconstructing the vanished life of the people on the earth. "Houses" re-creates family history, exploring the cruel injustice caused by the removal of the five southern nations from their homelands to the Oklahoma Indian Territory.

SEEING THROUGH THE SUN

Seeing Through the Sun groups its poems into four sections: "Seeing Through the Sun," "Territory of Night," "Daughters Sleeping," and "Wall Songs." The third section echoes and continues themes opened in the earlier *Daughters, I Love You* but focuses on a more personal vision of motherhood, moving at times into myth. "Tiva's Tapestry: La Llorona" evokes the Mexican legend of La Llorona, the Weeping Woman, said to walk neighborhoods at dusk, weeping for her children, whom she has killed, and seeking to kidnap replacements. The speaker talks of the sewing or embroidering of a picture that suggests the tragic mother: "She comes dragging/ the dark river/ a ghost on fire" who transforms into a cosmic figure "on the awful tapestry of sky/ just one of the mothers/ among the downward circling stars."

"Bees in Transit: Osage County" reflects themes addressed in Hogan's novel *Mean Spirit*, which depicted life in Oklahoma during the 1920's, when a number of Native American holders of oil rights were murdered under suspicious circumstances. Thorough investigations were not undertaken, and the killers were not brought to justice. The Osage murders, as they were called, were but an extreme manifestation of pervasive bigotry and oppression. A major theme of *Mean Spirit*, the suffering of women in those circumstances, emerges in "Bees in Transit: Osage County":

> dark women, murdered for oil
> . . . still walk in numbers
> through smoky dusk.

The poem combines Hogan's feeling for history with a spiritual outlook that has emerged more explicitly in *Seeing Through the Sun* and later works.

Hogan's range and subject matter expands in *Seeing Through the Sun*. "Death, Etc." offers a brittle, tightly rendered dialogue full of witty ambiguity: The speaker characterizes Death as a "Latin lover" who calls her Señorita and invites her to dance; she responds to his erotic advances by admonishing that "I am a taxpayer,/ I tell him,/ you can't do that to me." Other poems in the section titled "Territory of Night" move toward more outspoken erotic themes. A few of these, such as "Linden Tree," are tightly constructed, almost like haikus in their compression.

SAVINGS

In *Savings* Hogan expands on the themes raised in her earlier poetry and fiction in poems that are often more discursive in style than the tightly formulated images of *Calling Myself Home*. Many of these later poems are longer, and there is some experimentation with form, as in the loose unrhymed couplets of "The New Apartment: Minneapolis."

Hogan's thematic preoccupations move from the sense of hardship endured and overcome in her personal, family, and tribal history to wider consideration of global issues of justice, care, and responsibility. Her characteristic method of building from image to image is sometimes attached to a more abstract idea: In "The Legal System," an ambiguous voice suggests that the person's internalized "legal system" reflects and predicts both individual and collective judgments and prejudices.

In *Savings* Hogan's poems move out from Chickasaw history and the Oklahoma landscape to more global contemporary injustices, including the abuse of women, alcoholism, class hostility, the Holocaust, political refugees, undocumented immigrants, poverty, and bigotry. These poems differ from the focused topicality of those in *Daughters, I Love You*. The strategy of the earlier collection wove related images around a central theme; for example, in "Black Hills Survival Gathering, 1980," the image and feeling of sunrise is connected to Hiroshima, to a Buddhist monk protesting nuclear war and a bomber flying overhead. In contrast, *Savings* is often both more discursive and more allusive. In "The Other Voices" the speaker attempts to come to terms with an overpowering evil by contrasting unspecified refugees fleeing a police state with the commonplace, unthreatening lives of domestic animals.

THE BOOK OF MEDICINES

Hogan powerfully invokes the elemental forces in *The Book of Medicines*, expressing the affinity she feels with animals, plants, and weather. These natural forms serve as her totem: "power symbols offered as a source of healing . . . for the world . . . and for humans . . . as a means to reconnect with and show reverence for all things." The perspective is strongly Native American, contrasting vividly with the wasteful, rapacious attitude toward nature expressed by the European American exploitation of nature and natural resources.

In these poems, women are strongly allied with the "natural" force of the universe—like animals and plants, more firmly connected with and attuned to the world's natural rhythmic cycles and more viciously assaulted by forces now run amok, squeezing the life out of nature in the name of profit and progress. Hogan's poem "Fat" exemplifies greed out of control, describing a whaling town where "we sleep/ on a bed of secret fat," the debris of dead whales. Yet this is also a place where the speaker still hears the voice of Mother Earth, the whale, and the spirits:

> I hear it singing
> . . . it is a mountain rising
> . . . I want light.
> I am full
> with greed.
> Give to me
> light.

In this cosmology, the feminine principle as well as the more balanced and respectful attitudes of the Native American worldview hold out the greatest promise for a return to a more healthy natural equilibrium.

More assertively than in her earlier books, Hogan focuses on the natural world, examining and decrying the damage humans have done to the planet and to each other. Hogan's has become a powerful voice in the ecofeminist movement. The poems are presented in two sections: The first, "The Hunger," paints troubling pictures of human life and nature; "The Book of Medicines," offers a presecription for healing. The world of the first section is bleak, unsettling, and wasted: a place where "War was the perfect disguise" and "When [men] met a spirit in the forest/ it thought they were bags of misfortune/ and walked away/ without taking their lives" ("Skin"). In contrast, the second section describes growth, renewal and rebirth. As the poet notes in "The Origins of Corn," this world has become somewhere:

> you can't stop trading gifts with the land,
> putting your love in the ground
> so that after the long sleep of seeds
> all things will grow
> and the plants who climb into this world
> will find it green and alive.

With *The Book of Medicines*, Linda Hogan has become a true visionary and healer.

OTHER MAJOR WORKS

LONG FICTION: *Mean Spirit*, 1990; *Solar Storms*, 1995; *Power*, 1998.

SHORT FICTION: *That Horse*, 1985.

PLAY: *A Piece of Moon*, pr. 1981.

NONFICTION: *Dwellings*, 1995; *From Women's Experience to Feminist Theology*, 1997; *The Woman Who Watches Over the World: A Native Memoir*, 2001.

EDITED TEXTS: *The Stories We Hold Secret: Tales of Women's Spiritual Development*, 1986 (with Carol Bruchac and Judith McDaniel); *Intimate Nature: The Bond Between Women and Animals*, 1998 (with Deena Metzger and Brenda Peterson); *The Sweet Breathing of Plants: Women Writing on the Green World*, 2001 (with Peterson).

MISCELLANEOUS: *Red Clay*, 1991 (poems and short stories).

BIBLIOGRAPHY

Allen, Paula Gunn. *The Sacred Hoop: Recovering the Feminine in American Indian Traditions*. Boston: Beacon Press, 1986. Allen discusses contemporary Native American women poets and novelists, including Linda Hogan, in a context of woman-centered tribal values.

Bell, Betty Louise, ed. *Studies in American Indian Literature* 6 (Fall, 1994). Special issue on Linda Hogan; provides multiple points of view on Hogan's work.

Bruchac, Joseph. *Survival This Way: Interviews with American Indian Poets*. Tucson: University of Arizona Press, 1987. Aims at distinguishing a characteristically Native American identity and point of view as distinguished from a Western European perspective. Bruchac interviews a number of Native American authors, including Hogan.

Crawford, John, William Balassi, and Annie O. Eysturoy. "The Story Is Brimming Around: An Interview with Linda Hogan." Interview by Carol Miller. *SAIL: Studies in American Indian Literatures* 2, no. 4 (1990): 1-9. Miller's discussion with Hogan focuses to a large extent on Hogan's novel *Mean Spirit*, which is based on the historical experience of Osage Indians in the 1920's. In spite of entitlement to extraordinary wealth from newly activated oil wells, they were powerless to prevent a series of murders and other depredations committed by envious and avaricious interlopers.

_____. *This Is About Vision: Interviews with Southwestern Writers*. Albuquerque: University of New Mexico Press, 1990. Places Hogan in context with other Native American writers through parallel interviews with Joy Harjo, N. Scott Momaday, and Luci Tapahanso. Hogan's interview, by Patricia Clark Smith, includes discussion of early life, fiction, poetry, and work at a wild animal shelter.

Hogan, Linda. "A Heart Made Out of Crickets: An Interview with Linda Hogan." Interview by Bo Scholer. *The Journal of Ethnic Studies* 16, no. 1 (1988): 107-117. Focuses on her major social and literary concerns: working-class people, the accessibility of her texts to many people, her work and its relationship to the Chickasaw experience of the past and to contemporary colonialism and oppression.

Jaskoski, Helen. Review of *Calling Myself Home*. *SAIL: Studies in American Indian Literatures* 6, no. 1 (1986): 9-10. Sees the themes of metamorphosis and transformation as central to Hogan's vision.

Smith, Patricia Clark. "Linda Hogan." In *This Is About Vision: Interviews with Southwestern Writers*, edited by William Balassi, John F. Crawford, and Annie O. Eysturoy. Albuquerque: University of New Mexico Press, 1990. Provides good background on Hogan's early life and her view of her craft and her role as a writer. Includes discussion of her early life, fiction, poetry, and environmental work.

Helen Jaskoski,
updated by Melissa E. Barth

FRIEDRICH HÖLDERLIN

Born: Lauffen am Neckar, Germany; March 20, 1770

Died: Tübingen, Germany; June 7, 1843

PRINCIPAL POETRY

Nachtgesänge, 1805
Gedichte, 1826 (*Poems*, 1943)
Selected Poems, 1944
Poems and Fragments, 1966

OTHER LITERARY FORMS

The deep love for Greek culture that marked Friedrich Hölderlin's lyric poetry also had a profound impact on his other literary endeavors. Aside from his verse, he is most remembered for the epistolary novel *Hyperion: Oder, Der Eremit in Griechenland* (1797, 1799; *Hyperion: Or, The Hermit in Greece*, 1965). In the story of a disillusioned Greek freedom fighter, the author captured in rhythmic prose much of his own inner world. The novel is especially notable for its vivid imagery and its power of thought and language. Fascination with the legend of Empedocles' death on Mount Etna moved him to attempt to re-create the spirit of the surrounding events in the drama *Der Tod des Empedokles* (pb. 1826; *The Death of Empedocles*, 1966), which exists in three fragmentary versions. After 1800 he began translations of Sophocles' *Oedipus Tyrannus* (c. 429 B.C.E.) and *Antigone* (441 B.C.E.); his highly successful renderings were published in 1804. Among various essays on philosophy, aesthetics, and literature written throughout his career, his treatises on the fine arts in ancient Greece, Achilles, Homer's *Iliad* (c. 800 B.C.E.), and the plays of Sophocles are especially significant. Only a small portion of his correspondence has been preserved.

ACHIEVEMENTS

Unlike the great German lyricists with whom he is compared, Friedrich Hölderlin did not attain substantial literary recognition in his own time. This lack of recognition was in part a result of his own misperception of his audience. While he directed his poems to the broad following of the spiritual and intellectual renewal engendered by the French Revolution, his contemporaries, excepting a special few, did not penetrate beyond the surface of his particular revelation of the rebirth of idealism's golden age.

Friedrich Schiller's early patronage gave Hölderlin access to influential editors and other promoters of mainstream literature, enabling him to publish in important journals and popular collections of the time. His work appeared in Gotthold Stäudlin's *Schwäbisches Musenalmanach auf das Jahr 1792* (1792) and *Poetische Blumenlese* (1793), as well as Schiller's *Thalia* and other periodicals. Neither Schiller nor Johann Wolfgang von Goethe, however, fully recognized Hölderlin's true gifts as a writer. Eventually, they distanced themselves from him, and Hölderlin fell into obscurity.

After his death, Hölderlin remained forgotten until his work was rediscovered by Stefan George and his circle. George acclaimed him as one of the great masters of the age, pointing especially to the uniqueness of his language and the expressiveness of his style. In the modern poets whose works reflect a keen inner struggle with the meaning of existence, he at last found a receptive audience, capable of appreciating his contribution to the evolution of the German lyric. Among those whose writings give strong evidence of his productive influence are Georg Trakl, Rainer Maria Rilke, and Hugo von Hofmannsthal.

For his special mastery of form, his naturalization of classical Greek meters and rhythms in the German language, and his unique ability to clothe prophetic vision in verse, Hölderlin now stands alongside Goethe as one of the great poets of German idealism.

BIOGRAPHY

The untimely deaths of both his father and his stepfather determined the course of Johann Christian Friedrich Hölderlin's childhood and youth. His mother, a devoutly religious Lutheran, insisted that he prepare for a career in the clergy. While attending monastery schools at Denkendorf and Maulbronn, he began writing poetry that reflected the suffering of a sensitive spirit under the rigors of traditional discipline and an inability to reconcile the demands of practical reality with his inner sense of artistic calling. Youthful love affairs with Luise Nast (the "Stella" of his early poems) and Elise Lebret exacerbated the tension between the two poles of his existence.

In 1788, Hölderlin entered the theological seminary at the University of Tübingen. Although he completed his studies and received a master's degree that titled him to ordination, the years spent in Tübingen eased him away from any desire to become a pastor. With his friends Christian Ludwig Neuffer and Rudolf Magenau, he founded a poetry club patterned after the Göttinger Hain. He also joined a secret political organization with Georg Friedrich Wilhelm Hegel and Friedrich Wilhelm Joseph von Schelling and openly advocated social reforms inspired by the ideals of the French Revolution. The true key to his rejection of a life of service in the church, however, was neither purely artistic inclination nor political commitment but rather deep spiritual conflict within himself. Concentrated exposure to the literature, art, and philosophy of classical antiquity caused him to develop a worldview that placed the ancient Greek gods, as vital natural forces, next to Christ in importance for the dawning of a new, humane era of enlightenment and harmony. The tension between the old pantheon and Christian dogma made it impossible for him to feel comfortable in total dedication to institutionalized religion.

Among his contemporaries, Hölderlin's most important role model was Schiller, whose poetry had a strong impact on both his early Tübingen hymns and his later classicistic creations. In 1793, Hölderlin met Schiller for the first time. Their friendship remained rather onesided; Schiller did not reciprocate the warmth and devotion of his awestruck protégé. Through Schiller's mediation, Hölderlin obtained the first of a long series of positions as a private tutor. These situations, despite their repeated failure, enabled him to avoid the necessity of accepting an appointment as a pastor.

Hölderlin's most significant assignment as a tutor began in 1795, when he entered the service of a wealthy banker in Frankfurt. A love affair with his employer's wife, Susette Gontard, provided the stimulus for a newfound sophistication in his poetry. Much of the substance that he treated in verse while in Frankfurt was later refined and presented in more perfect form in the exquisite odes, elegies, and hymns of his late period. Susette herself became the model for Diotima in his novel *Hyperion* and the poems related to it.

After an unpleasant scene with Susette's husband in 1798, Hölderlin fled to Homburg, where he remained until 1800 with his friend Isaak von Sinclair. Hölderlin continued to see and correspond secretly with Susette, but he was unsuccessful in establishing himself in a permanently meaningful way of life. An endeavor to edit a new journal and make his living as a free-lance writer foundered. Plagued by an increasing inner isolation, he was compelled to return home to his mother.

From an artistic point of view, the years immediately after 1800 were the most important of Hölderlin's career; emotionally and spiritually, they were years of progressive devastation. New tutorial positions in Switzerland and France collapsed rapidly. In 1802, Hölderlin left Bordeaux and traveled home on foot. He arrived in Nürtingen mentally and emotionally disturbed after learning of Susette Gontard's death. In 1804, temporarily recovered from his nervous breakdown, he returned to Homburg, where Sinclair arranged for him to work as a librarian. When Sinclair was arrested for subversive political activities, Hölderlin's mental condition deteriorated drastically, and he was placed in a sanatorium. In 1806, he was declared incurably ill and given into the care of a carpenter and his wife. He spent the remainder of his life living in a tower room overlooking the Neckar, where he wrote occasional, strangely simple lyrics, played the flute and the piano, and received curious visitors.

ANALYSIS

In the final stanza of his famous poem "Die Heimat" ("Homeland"), Friedrich Hölderlin captured the essence of his personal artistic calling and its lyrical product. The pairing of love, the divine fire that stimulates creativity, with suffering, the holy reward that the gods give to their poet-prophet, defines the poles of existential tension that were a primary focus of his life and works. A peculiar mixture of the poetry of experience and that of ideas, his early hymns and his mature odes, elegies, and hymns in free rhythms are at once the offspring of intense adoration—of beauty, nature, Greek antiquity, an idealized world of tomorrow—and profound spiritual pain resulting from recognition of the abyss between the poet and the things that he cherishes. The result is a constant duality of mood: on one hand, deeply elegiac longing for the elements of a lost golden age; on the other, overwhelming joy in the message of love that is the joint legacy of the Greek world and the Christian tradition. Oscillating between hope and despair, anticipation and resignation, tragic darkness and powerfully prophetic vision, his verse documents the continuing struggle of a spirit that needs to belong to society yet remains alone as a priest who serves no church, a singer of a people no longer or not yet there.

Despite the concentrated projection of the deeply personal strivings of his own soul into his writings, Hölderlin's lyrics were based firmly in an age-old and broadly recognized tradition to which he gave new life. At the same time, they represent a mating of impulses from the German classical and Romantic movements that dominated the literary mainstream of his own time. His interpretation of models ranging from Plato to Spinoza, from Homer and Hesiod to Schiller and Goethe, and including Friedrich Gottlieb Klopstock, Johann Jakob Wilhelm Heinse, Christian Friedrich Daniel Schubart, and Ludwig Christoph Hölty generated a multisided literature that mixes a glowing sense of freedom with enthusiastic, unfettered pantheism and celebration of the highest human ideals with *Weltschmerz*.

SCHILLER'S INFLUENCE

The influence of Schiller upon Hölderlin's early creations is especially noticeable. Scholars often point to the melancholy longing for the beauty and glory of Greece, the lost spiritual homeland, as a defining characteristic of Hölderlin's early verse. His various elaborations of this theme, particularly his emphatic presentations of the ancient gods as living elemental forces, give remarkable evidence of having been motivated directly by Schiller's well-known poem "Die Götter Griechenlands" ("The Gods of Greece"). Moreover, his acclaim of a new humanistic age in hymns to freedom, humanity, harmony, friendship, nature, and other abstract concepts was clearly inspired not only by his infatuation with the ideas of the French Revolution but also by a deep reverence for Schiller, whose treatments of those same subjects are key building blocks in the poetry of German idealism. Even the meter and syntax of Hölderlin's first lyric efforts are obvious products of his familiarity with Schiller's language and forms.

INTROSPECTIVE MOODS

Hölderlin's Alcaic and Asclepiadean odes on nature, landscape, and love, written in Denkendorf and Maulbronn, are strongly subjective and self-oriented, weighed down by an almost oppressive intensity of reflection. The moods of *Sturm und Drang* are clearly visible, as is Klopstock's basic tone, in which personal experience is raised into a suprapersonal religious sphere. Amid trivial occasional verse, sentimentally broad discourses on life, and curiously sad love poems written to Luise Nast, there are already glimmerings of the elements that eventually informed Hölderlin's more characteristic lyrics. For example, "Die Unsterblichkeit der Seele" ("The Immortality of the Soul"), an ode that bears all the marks of Klopstock's manner, anticipates in direction and perception the later "Hymne an die Unsterblichkeit" ("Hymn to Immortality"), which was written in Tübingen. In the long hexameter poem "Die Teck" ("The Teck"), a glorification of a local mountain area, important themes of the late hymns appear: the Dionysian festival of the grape harvest, the sublime nature of dead heroes, the magnificence of the forested landscape saturated with the traditions of the fatherland, and the celebration of friendship.

A POETIC CALLING

An important focus of the works created in Tübingen is Hölderlin's growing preoccupation with the awareness of a personal poetic mission. From the rejection of seminary life's inhibiting restrictions in "Zornige Sehnsucht" ("Angry Longing") to the magnification and praise of Greece, the Muses, and his personal gods in a first formal cycle of hymns, Hölderlin's formulations stress his belief in a calling to reinterpret Christian and classical ideals within the framework of his own era. He saw himself as a kind of prophet in a time of special revelation that needed poetic amplification. Accordingly, he presented in the hymns aspects of a holy message based on the eternal example of antiquity. A pantheistic view of nature as a complex of ethical and emotional forces unified by a grand, divine essence charges the poems with living, vital myth in the creation of an ideal, harmonious realm that is the final goal of the poet's longing, both for himself and for all humankind.

ANCIENT GREECE

The evocation of Greece as Hölderlin's spiritual homeland, which begins in earnest in the Tübingen hymns, is fleshed out, solidified, and given its ultimate direction in the verse that emerged alongside *Hyperion* in Frankfurt. Peculiarly combined with the reincarnation of the ancient Greek spirit in Diotima (Susette Gontard), the poet's priestess of love and embodiment of eternal beauty, is a new, no longer effulgent picture of Hellas that contains sorrow, suffering, and tragic elements. Intense passion is intertwined with philosophical thoughtfulness in poetry characterized by its hearty enthusiasm, expression that is still youthfully immature, and fantastic, sensitive landscapes that are painted with fine feeling. Special emphasis is placed on quiet loveliness and the constancy of nature in a worldview that perceives life as originating in and striving toward childlike harmony. The most representative poems of this period are "Diotima," the first lyric fruit of a newly gained perception of love as a power that can suspend the continuity of time and bring to pass the rebirth of man, and "Hyperions Schicksalslied" ("Hyperion's Song of Destiny"), a penetrating treatment of the fathomlessness of existence that calls to mind Plato's separation of the realm of ideas from the world of phenomena.

DARK THEMES OF LATER YEARS

To a large extent, the significant poetic works that were written prior to Hölderlin's hasty departure from Frankfurt in 1798, and even those created shortly thereafter in Homburg, served as preliminary studies in language, form, and theme for the magnificent odes, elegies, and hymns that he wrote after 1800. It is somewhat ironic that his most sublime and deeply profound poems are the darkly mythological, prophetically intuitive visions of a mind on the brink of insanity. The ever-increasing emotional strain and existential pressure of his life without Susette Gontard served as a catalyst for the final refinement of ideas and structures that are the very essence of the night ode "Chiron," the wonderful elegy "Brot und Wein" ("Bread and Wine"), and the richly mysterious hymn "Patmos." In these and other masterworks of his final productive years, Hölderlin revealed more than ever before his quiet sensitivity, his pure and free view of nature, his precise sense of landscape saturated with the spirit of creative life force.

Despite their diversity, the mature poems are linked together in a fusion of classical and Christian traditions that places the gods of ancient Greece and Christ on nearly equal footing. The twofold experience of the proximity of the divine and man's difficulty in understanding it forms the core of a poetry that is remarkable for its combination of tangible and ethereal elements.

Important aspects of the integral system that is perfected and presented in these late writings include a hierarchical chain of genius-beings who govern absolute existence—Christ, the gods of Olympus, biblical prophets and patriarchs, apostles, Greek Titans, heroes, philosophers, great contemporary figures, spirits of nature and love; stress on the relationship of man to Mother Earth; a poetic landscape that is saturated with powers that point toward the divine origins of life; and constant awareness of the prophetic task of the singer's art and of the conflict between suffering and joy. All these are expressed in language and rhythms that are pregnant with expectation, careful preparation, and unspoken faith. In many respects, it is not so much the imparted vision as the clarity, musicality, and exactness of diction and the expressive perfection and beauty of form that elevate the lyric works of Hölderlin's last creative surge to the level of true greatness.

TÜBINGEN HYMNS

A mélange of the revolutionary spirit of the times and interpretation of the basic Christian humanist tradition as mediated by Klopstock and Schiller, Hölderlin's Tübingen hymns are all variations on the same feeling: an endless willingness of heart to accept eternal values. The celebration of inalienable human rights—freedom, equality, friendship, honor—is filled with the youthful impetuousness of the poet's faith blended with a certain naïve tenderness and grace. Although not especially original in vocabulary, meter, and imagery, clearly influenced by models such as Schiller's "An die Freude" ("Ode to Joy"), these early poems convey the charm of their creator's exuberant enthusiasm, the animating tension that is central to his later works, and the love-oriented metaphysical basis of his worldview.

While the hymns do not belong to the poetry of experience, they can be described only loosely as idea poems. To be sure, they are thematically abstract, but their focus is not thought and allegory, as in Schiller's philosophical lyrics. Rather, it is a kind of fundamentally religious perception of the universe in which theoretical principles are given semidivine status. Various common symbols are employed with significant frequency. The mountain typically represents freedom or pride; the eagle stands for courage. Humility and the eternal flow of life appear as valley and river respectively. All nature thus becomes a boundless ideal whole which is the object of intense longing and the source of repeated spiritual ecstasy.

In each of the hymns, the glorification of a concept that has been elevated to godhood is presented in a clearly defined structure. First, the poet approaches the chosen divinity. A central portion of the poem then elaborates the abstract deity's sphere of operation. A triumphant view of the addressed entity's power and domain is climaxed by the poet's humble retreat into recognition of his own inadequacy.

Especially representative of the Tübingen songs are "Hymn to Immortality" and "Hymne an die Freiheit" ("Hymn to Freedom"). The former begins with the flight of the prophet-singer's spirit, powered by love, to the divine realm of endless life. The first stanza evokes two of the major themes of Hölderlin's oeuvre: the poet's godly mission as a seer who penetrates the revelation of creation, and love as the driving force, sacred center, and unifying essence of the world. The joyful intoxication of the vision, however, gradually recedes, leaving in the final lines only emptiness in the realization that man's mortality makes it impossible for him to grasp and describe in song the unspeakable fulfillment of the immortal soul. "Hymn to Freedom" develops the idea that humankind can be completely free within the context of its intended holy life only if it remains true to the blessed laws of love that govern pure existence. By falling away from these divine ideals, man subjects himself to the shame of hell. Anticipating the hope-filled resolution of the late hymns, the poem ends with the suggestion of a final attainment of freedom in the eternity beyond death.

NACHTGESÄNGE

In 1805, Hölderlin published a small collection of nine poems under the title *Nachtgesänge*. Although this group constitutes less than a third of his mature odes, it forms the core of his late production of Alcaic and Asclepiadean forms. The individual lyric creations are carefully refined renderings of Hölderlin's characteristic themes: the eternal existence of the Greek soul that still governs human action; the glorious mission of poets as magi ordained by the gods to be mediators of divine truth; the pain of separation and the never-ending tension between man and deity; spiritual reconciliation of the homeless singer's sorrow; and anticipation of the

dawning of a new age in the gods' return. Accentuation of formal precision dominates a presentation that varies musically between lightly melodic language and dynamically passionate rhythms with heavily resounding vowels. Although love still appears as the binding force of extended nature, the motivating principle that gives these poems their special depth and flavor is an awareness of the tragic dominance of night.

Symbolically, night is the time of God's absence. It is the predominant feature of the entire era following the decline of classical civilization and the appearance of Christ. Ordained by the gods, it is endowed with sacred meaning and purpose, yet the poet longs for it to end in a bright revelation of light and for that reason faces its darkness with feelings that fluctuate between humble resignation and profound distress and pain.

Especially notable in the development of key odes is Hölderlin's tendency to frame his ideas in less demanding works, then to allow them to evolve in more complex versions that give full substance and direction to his message. Significant examples include "Der blinde Sänger" ("The Blind Singer") and its reinterpretation in "Chiron" and "Der gefesselte Strom" ("The Chained Stream"), rewritten as "Ganymed." "The Blind Singer" is an Alcaic ode that couches the theme of night in the problem of the poet's loss of sight. In the darkness, his creations lack inspiration, regained only when the gods restore his vision in new revelation. In "Chiron," the sightless singer-seer is transformed into a different symbol, the centaur Chiron, a healer who is struck by the arrow of the gods. The product of his wound is at once torment and ecstasy in apocalyptic visions of the cosmos. Like the blind poet, he is visited by the gods in a storm and sees a strong light break forth that gives everything order and harmony. "The Chained Stream," one of Hölderlin's most powerful celebrations of natural forces, is comparable to Goethe's "Mahomets Gesang" ("Mahomet's Song") in its vibrant imagery and pure musicality. The icebound stream, awakened from the night of winter by spring, arouses all nature to joy-filled life. In "Ganymed," the stream evolves into a symbol for the poet's feeling of aloneness in the world of mortals. It becomes the half-divine stranger Ganymed, whose only place of fulfillment and belonging lies in reconciliation with the gods in the arms of Zeus.

MOURNFUL ELEGIES

Hölderlin's most pronounced merging of classical Greek and Christian elements occurs in mournful elegies that combine lament for the passing of the golden age with deeply felt disappointment at the hollowness of contemporary reality. Overwhelming resignation is only partially offset by hope for the spiritual regeneration of man. In tone, these poems are closely related to the mature odes, especially in their emphasis on night as the bridge between past and future. Their main thrust is to justify the poetic act in a dark age that destroys the very foundation of lyric art. Employing various approaches to the problem, Hölderlin examines the violent spiritual conflicts that characterize the situation of the modern lyricist. He is presented as being kept from fulfilling his divinely appointed mission by a cold era that needs his uplifting mediation more than ever. Notable is the acute awareness of the poet's homelessness in his own time; this condition is caused at least in part by his inability to forsake the Greek tradition in favor of pure belief in Christ as the only redeeming force in the world.

Two elegies stand out as representative examples of Hölderlin's mastery of this particular verse form. The most famous is "Menons Klagen um Diotima" ("Menon's Laments for Diotima"), a creation that is dominated by the experience of the author's separation from Susette Gontard. Equally powerful is the intensely mysterious "Bread and Wine," in which the figure of Christ is merged with elements of Greek gods and heroes and transformed into the wine god Bacchus at the center of a Dionysian vision of ancient Greece.

"Menon's Laments for Diotima" is a cyclical drama of the soul that begins with the separation of lovers, vacillates between the poet's resigned acceptance of the situation and longing for reunion, and ends with a prayer of thanksgiving for the hope of fulfillment in a new union beyond death. As the poem crescendos in the third section, the music of total isolation and loneliness gives way to harmonies of belief in an indissoluble relationship. The mystical conception that within the absolute context of existence true lovers can never lose each other leads in the final segments to the victory of a faith whose eternal beacon is Diotima.

In "Bread and Wine," Hölderlin comes to grips with night and emptiness in a deeply mystical revelation of the poet's role in bringing to pass the return of the gods. The invocation of darkness allows a hidden light to shine forth. From within its fire, a bright manifestation of Greece emerges, and the poet becomes a priest of Dionysus who prepares the way for a new encounter between man and the divine. Special power arises from those parts of the poem in which concrete reality (images of evening in a small town) merges with images reflecting the fulfillment of the past and the promise of the future.

The tension between classical Greek and Christian traditions which animates all Hölderlin's mature lyrics is balanced in his Pindaric hymns by a strong mood of reconciliation and striving for harmony. Written in free verse but subject to complex structural rules, these poems are triadically arranged songs of prophetic awareness and dark, mythological, symbolic language. They treat the mysteries of life, death, and the gods in apocalyptic revelations of strange majesty that touch upon all Hölderlin's major themes. Perhaps nowhere else in his work did he couch his view of the poet's relationship to eternity in such strong imagery of commitment, obedience, and worship.

EMPHASIS ON CHRIST

Especially significant in the late hymns is a more pronounced emphasis on Christ as the center of metaphysical contemplation. At this point in his life, Hölderlin's attitude toward the Messiah was extremely complex. The Savior figure of his poetic visions is therefore something of a composite of Germanic hero, Greek Titan, and embodiment of the eternal principle of love in which the everlasting presence of God is manifest anew. Particularly noticeable characteristics of the Christ who triumphs over suffering are a sensitive look of naïve piety, peaceful radiance of bearing, and a sense of mythic uniqueness.

In one of the crowning achievements of his artistic career, the profoundly beautiful hymn "Patmos," Hölderlin embarks on a haunting journey to the scene of St. John's revelation in search of lingering evidence of the living Christ. The poem focuses on the stark tragedy of the Crucifixion as a symbol for the terror of divine absence which is overcome only in a process of sharing. The key concept is that of community, of the impossibility of grasping God alone. Musical cadences, forceful individual words, and rhythmic presentation of ideas are among the structural features that illuminate the landscape of the poet's spiritual universe.

Despite the victorious tone of most of the hymns, none of them documents total resolution of the dilemma generated by the poet's continuing allegiance to both the Greek gods and Christ. This fact is hammered home most dramatically in "Der Einzige" ("The Only One"), in which Christ's position of unique godhood clashes with the singer-prophet's desire to glorify all the gods because he cannot reconcile successfully their conflicting claims. By proclaiming Christ the brother of Bacchus and Hercules, Hölderlin attempts to make visible the painful conflict that arises from the very essence of the dual European heritage of his own origins. In so doing, he also creates a deeply personal symbol for a worldview that stands at the center of a lyric oeuvre which is matched in importance for the history of German poetry by the creations of few other writers.

OTHER MAJOR WORKS

LONG FICTION: *Hyperion: Oder, Der Eremit in Griechenland*, 1797, 1799 (*Hyperion: Or, The Hermit in Greece*, 1965).

PLAYS: *Antigone*, pb. 1804 (translation of Sophocles); *Oedipus Tyrannus*, pb. 1804 (translation of Sophocles); *Der Tod des Empedokles*, pb. 1826 (*The Death of Empedocles*, 1966).

MISCELLANEOUS: *Sämtliche Werke*, 1846 (2 volumes); *Sämtliche Werke: Grosse Stuttgarter Ausgabe*, 1943-1977 (8 volumes).

BIBLIOGRAPHY

Constantine, David. *Hölderlin*. Oxford: Clarendon Press, 1988. Substantial introduction to Hölderlin's life and work. The author seeks to write about Hölderlin chronologically and in an accessible way and to explore his life as a resource in the explication of his writing. Emphasizes Hölderlin as a poet of religious longing.

Fioretos, Arts, ed. *The Solid Letter: Readings of Friedrich Hölderlin*. Stanford, Calif.: Stanford University Press, 1999. Includes essays on philosophical and theological aspects of Hölderlin's work, his theory and practice of translation, and his poetry, ranging from early poems to uncompleted late hymns.

George, Emery. *Hölderlin's "Ars poetica."* The Hague, Netherlands: Mouton, 1973. An exhaustive critical analysis of Hölderlin's late hymns. Includes a bibliography.

Heidegger, Martin. *Elucidations of Holderlin's Poetry*. Translated by Keith Hoeller. Amherst, Mass.: Humanity Books, 2000. Six essays on Hölderlin by the major twentieth century philosopher Heidegger, with an introduction by the translator. The goal is to be of use to the public as well as the scholar, and includes the German as well as the English versions of the four poems to which Heidegger has devoted his essays. Emphasis is on the relationship of Hölderlin's poetry to modern European philosophy.

Henrich, Dieter, ed. *The Course of Remembrance and Other Essays on Hölderlin*. Stanford, Calif.: Stanford University Press, 1997. A collection of essays on the ideas and the works of Friedrich Hölderlin offering a glimpse of the early formation of German idealism. Contains a translation of Henrich's book devoted to Hölderlin's poem, "Remembrance." A vital resource for specialists and enthusiasts of the German Enlightenment and Romantic traditions.

Lernout, Geert. *The Poet as Thinker: Hölderlin in France*. Columbia S.C.: Camden House, 1994. A comprehensive historical survey of the reception of the poet's work by French critics and writers. Includes chapters on Heidegger's reading of Hölderlin, the French Revolution in Hölderlin's thought, and psychoanalytic theories about Hölderlin's illness. Also includes a chapter on the influence of Hölderlin on such important French authors as Albert Camus, Louis Aragon, and Philippe Sollers.

Ungar, Richard. *Friedrich Hölderlin*. Boston: Twayne Publishers, 1984. A basic and useful introduction to Hölderlin. Includes summaries and paraphrases of Hölderlin's poetry together with interpretations. Intended to assist readers who are encountering Hölderlin for the first time and to provide an understanding of the texts at the most elementary level. Chronology and annotated bibliography.

Lowell A. Bangerter;
bibliography updated by Margaret Boe Birns

JOHN HOLLANDER

Born: New York, New York; October 28, 1929

PRINCIPAL POETRY

A Crackling of Thorns, 1958
Movie-Going and Other Poems, 1962
Visions from the Ramble, 1965
The Quest of the Gole, 1966
Philomel, 1968
Types of Shape, 1969
The Night Mirror, 1971
Town and Country Matters, 1972
The Head of the Bed, 1974
Tales Told of the Fathers, 1975
Reflections on Espionage, 1976
Spectral Emanations: New and Selected Poems, 1978
In Place, 1978
Blue Wine and Other Poems, 1979
Powers of Thirteen, 1983
In Time and Place, 1986
Harp Lake, 1988
Selected Poetry, 1993
Tesserae and Other Poems, 1993
The Gazer's Spirit: Poems Speaking to Silent Works of Art, 1995
Figurehead and Other Poems, 1998

OTHER LITERARY FORMS

John Hollander has edited several anthologies, including *Selected Poems* by Ben Jonson (1961), *The Oxford Anthology of English Literature* (1973, with Frank Kermode), and *The Essential Rossetti* (1989). Among his well-regarded books of literary criticism are *The Untuning of the Sky: Ideas of Music in English Poetry, 1500-1700* (1961), *Vision and Resonance: Two Senses of Poetic Form* (1975), *The Figure of Echo: A Mode of Allusion in Milton and After* (1981), and, with Harold Bloom, *Poetics of Influence: New and Selected Criticism* (1988). Hollander has also written or edited several books for younger people, such as *The Wind and the Rain* (1961, with Harold Bloom), *A Book of Various Owls* (1963), and *The Quest of the Gole* (1966).

ACHIEVEMENTS

John Hollander is a scholar, professor, editor, and formalist poet who frequently combines the rigors of traditional meter and rhyme with far-ranging topics and imaginative energy. Hollander's interdisciplinary learning permits him to conjure up a host of allusions from philosophy, mathematics, music, science, religion, and the visual arts into his poetry. With his superb command of poetic tradition from ancient Greece to T. S. Eliot, Hollander's books build on existing forms and reinterpret them for the contemporary reader.

His first book of poems, *A Crackling of Thorns*, was chosen by W. H. Auden as the 1958 entry in the Yale Series of Younger Poets. Among Hollander's outstanding achievements are the Poetry Chap-Book Award in 1962 for *The Untuning of the Sky*, a National Institute of Arts and Letters grant for creative work in literature in 1963, the Levinson Prize from *Poetry* magazine in 1974, a Guggenheim Fellowship in 1979, the Bollingen Prize in Poetry (with Anthony Hecht) for *Jiggery-Pokery* in 1983, a MacArthur Foundation Fellowship in 1990, and an Ambassador Book Award in 1994. Among the magazines and journals that have published Hollander's verse are *The New Yorker*, *The New Republic*, *The New York Review of Books*, *Poetry*, *The Times Literary Supplement*, and *Harper's*.

BIOGRAPHY

John Hollander was born on October 28, 1929, in New York City, the son of Franklin Hollander, a physiologist, and Muriel (Kornfeld) Hollander. Hollander traces his family roots to the Kabbalist Rabbi Loew of Prague, Czechoslovakia, in "Letter to Jorge Luis Borges" from *The Night Mirror*. He was graduated from Columbia University with a B.A. in 1950 and an M.A. in 1952, and he completed his Ph.D. at Indiana University in 1959. Hollander was married to Anne Loesser on June 15, 1953; the couple were divorced in 1977. He has two children, Martha and Elizabeth.

After earning his master's degree, Hollander went to Harvard University as a junior fellow in the Society of Fellows (1954-1957). His academic career continued when he accepted the post of lecturer in English at Connecticut College (1957-1959). Having begun at Yale University as an instructor (1959-1966), he taught at

Hunter College (1966-1967) and was visiting professor at the Salzburg Seminar in American Studies (1965). He served as associate editor for poetry for the *Partisan Review* in 1970-1971 and was a contributing editor for *Harper's* during the same period. Hollander returned to Yale in 1977, gradually moving up the academic ranks until, in 1987, he was appointed A. Bartlett Giamatti Professor of English, a position he held through the 1990's.

ANALYSIS

As strongly as contemporary poets tend to resist labels, John Hollander in book after book confirms himself as a scholastic formalist, a proponent of elevated style, learned allusions, and highly systematic language. Yet he is not beyond satirizing staid literary conventions, even in his own poetry. Hollander is not a poet for beginners—most of his books include notes and require an encyclopedia and some previous knowledge of prosody.

Hollander is a poet of New York and the urban intellectual quest for reassurance and order in a chaotic world. Predominant Hollander themes are the struggle between freedom and restraint, the capacity of language to express truth, the search for one's roots, and reality viewed through worlds of art. His books constantly challenge the reader and reinvent themselves as he experiments with wit, satire, elegy, panegyric, Pindaric odes, Renaissance sonnet cycles, spy narratives, and a host of other topics and forms. His writing carries echoes of his academic training and Jewish heritage. Hollander relies on abstract and philosophical language combined with vivid, rich imagery. He respects tradition and aims for perfect architecture and unity of purpose and design in every book, although he sometimes ventures far afield in search of new modes of expression.

Many poets write only about personal experience in purely expressive language, but Hollander's knowledge of classical Greek and Roman literature as well as English literature allows him to manipulate a wide spectrum of genres, voices, topics, and allusions. He avoids the fashionable directness of autobiographical poetry and is more likely to imitate Andrew Marvell, Alexander Pope, or Ben Jonson. His favorite classical Roman

poet is Catullus, known for hendecasyllabic lines, fresh love poems, and satirical epigrams. In "West-End Blues" from *Visions from the Ramble*, Hollander adapts a Catullus poem to celebrate New York City bars catering to college students.

Hollander often juxtaposes a hierarchical sense of order and decorum to wildly inventive modern argot, including shocking discussions of sexuality. A self-absorbed, tortured persona struggling with conflict sometimes emerges from beneath the superficial appearance of order. Also known for his shaped poems, Hollander displays a playfulness and wit that often transcend the form he has chosen or invented for his purposes. A formidable presence in contemporary poetry, Hollander produces work that calls attention to itself without pandering to fashionable ideas or popular topics.

A CRACKLING OF THORNS

Hollander's publishing career began with a splash when Auden selected *A Crackling of Thorns* for the Yale series. In this collection the reader immediately notices the technical skill and attention to form. The book divides itself into three sections, "For Actors," "For Tellers

John Hollander (© David Rumsey)

of Tales," and "For Certain Others." Some poems seem inspired by literature of the seventeenth century such as "The Lady's-Maid Song," which uses octosyllabic lines with an interlocking rhyme scheme. Others, such as "For Both of You, the Divorce Being Final," resound with modern dilemmas.

"The Great Bear" uses hendecasyllabic lines arranged in six stanzas to develop another characteristic Hollander theme: how perception creates reality. In this case, a group of children search the night sky for constellations they cannot really make out. Only their innate sense of form, the mind's ability to find order in chaos, allows the viewers to obtain the image of the bear. Hollander puns on the title word throughout the poem, pointing at the need for some tradition to shape human understanding of the world.

MOVIE-GOING AND OTHER POEMS

The tone of *Movie-Going and Other Poems* is panegyric and reflective, less prone to poetic effusion. In the title poem, Hollander remembers the glory days of New York cinema when a little money would allow one access to an ever-expanding world of fantasy. Adolescents attending double features could imagine other worlds, looking at the Moorish proscenium with its painted stars. The poem concerns itself not so much with enjoyment of films as with the theme of transformation—allowing a bit of exotica, mystery, and splendor into the everyday world.

In "Aristotle and Phyllis," the poet draws on material from French poet Stephane Mallarmé to retell the story of Aristotle's amorous encounter when a girl walked past his writing desk. The Greeks' reliance on reason and their motto of "nothing in excess" provides the background for this narrative ode. The speaker first explains away his infatuation, but his stoic eloquence fails him. The poem moves from the world of academic decorum and clarity to a spirited romp in the garden, where Aristotle's passion gets the best of his reason.

One long poem in the book, "Upon Apthorp House," gives Hollander a historical-descriptive forum to document passing seasons and people in Cambridge, Massachusetts. Reconstructing the past of the famous Harvard residence allows Hollander to philosophize on human learning: "What we feel/ At points of being seems more real/ Than what we can reflect upon." Apthorp House,

like T. S. Eliot's Little Gidding, is a place where men were given free reign with books and ideas in a peaceful solitude of learning and spirit. If one is given a place such as Apthorp House, boundaries of time and place can be overcome.

VISIONS FROM THE RAMBLE

The strongest and most thematically consistent of Hollander's early collections is his third book, *Visions from the Ramble*, a sequence of poems about coming of age in New York. "The Ramble" refers to a densely wooded section in Central Park from which none of the city is visible. Hollander uses this as a metaphor, extricating himself from the oppressive crowding, noise, and smells of New York throughout the book. Perceptive readers will note a later poem from *The Night Mirror*, "New York," in which he satirizes and celebrates his city. He beautifully balances the recurring images of three pools of water and three naked girls in "From the Ramble" as he recalls fond memories of growing up there. In this long title poem, the poet tries to lose himself in the domesticated wilderness of Central Park at the same time that he wishes to return to the glorious days of youth. A dazzling vision of rippled swirls of light and three undressing girls captivates him. Like William Wordsworth on the banks of the river Wye in "Lines Composed a Few Miles Above Tintern Abbey" (1798), the poet takes in this natural scene and reflects on the nature of memory and perception. The disappointed poet later finds the three pools of water nearly vanished and realizes that he must replace the Ramble with a garden inside his mind.

A series of poems in *Visions from the Ramble* center on the Fourth of July and other summer rituals. "Fireworks," "The Ninth of July," and "Humming" all feature adolescent narrators in search of miraculous transformation. Looking at flashes of light in the sky or girls through a hole in an outhouse, the speaker searches for a secret elixir of life to hurry him along into adulthood. Often the stifling world of New York drives the speaker to find fulfillment elsewhere; several poems focus on the bimodal life of summers at the lake and schooldays spent in the city. *Visions from the Ramble* is a watershed in Hollander's career, allowing him to transform biographical material and relish the affirmation of nostalgia.

TYPES OF SHAPE

Types of Shape presents twenty-five shaped poems in the tradition of seventeenth century English poet George Herbert. Hollander's range of topics evident in titles such as "Eskimo Pie," "Skeleton Key," and "Swan and Shadow," the latter being a much-anthologized poem that shows a clearly outlined bird gliding on a lake above its mirror image. Hollander's shaped poems are intriguing experiments, but their inflexible forms undermine the power of his writing.

JIGGERY-POKERY

A more successful experiment is *Jiggery-Pokery*, a book of light verse in which all the poems begin with a double-dactyl nonsense line such as "higgledy-piggledy" or "jiggery-pokery," followed by a famous name and more double dactyls. Hollander's sense of mock-form playfulness makes each poem function as a rhythmical story complete with punch line conclusion.

THE NIGHT MIRROR

The Night Mirror, Hollander's sixth collection, employs surrealism, dream-sequence poetry, and impressionistic rendering of experience. Here he returns to his strengths, using various four- to six-line stanza patterns and experimenting with end rhyme. Yet the book lacks the sound focus of *Visions from the Ramble* and *Powers of Thirteen*. Two of the best poems in the book are "Letter to Jorge Luis Borges," an Argentinian writer known for founding the Magical Realism literary movement, and "Damoetas," a pastoral elegy dedicated to Hollander's former teacher Andrew Chiappe. "Damoetas" recalls John Milton's "Lycidas" with its pastoral conventions of green meadows, swans, and shepherds, but Hollander uses the style to memorialize the classroom style and impressive mind of his Shakespeare teacher.

In "Letter to Jorge Luis Borges," the poet explains he translated a Borges poem on the golden age of Prague using the same *abba* rhyme scheme. Borges's poem about Prague opens a Pandora's box of memories and associations for Hollander, whose ancestors came to the United States from that city. The poet conjures up a dream about his grandfather Rabbi Loew, who made a golem in a mysterious, smoky room. *Golem* is a Hebrew word originally meaning "embryo" but later becoming "monster" or "robot," a sort of Frankenstein creation myth. The golem goes after the rabbi's daughter and tries to steal away innocent children, but other stories about how he helped save the Jews of Prague echo in the poet's mind. Hollander thanks the Argentinian writer for animating his memory and giving him occasion to reflect on his ancestors.

TOWN AND COUNTRY MATTERS

Hollander uses another set of literary conventions to brilliant effect in *Town and Country Matters*, composed of "erotica and satirica." "Sonnets for Rosebush," a marvelous neo-Renaissance sequence, anticipates *Powers of Thirteen*. "Sonnets for Rosebush" combines the poet's penchant for literary allusion with modern ribaldry and urbane bawdiness. Probably one of the best poems of Hollander's entire career is "New York" from *Town and Country Matters*. Inspired by the classical Roman poet Juvenal and the eighteenth century poet Samuel Johnson, "New York" uses heroic couplets throughout. After his friend leaves New York, the speaker stays behind to ruminate over the pleasures and pains of the city, moving among the Broadway theaters, city parks, coffee shops, cinemas, operas, museums, and apartment buildings. Following the example of his friend, the poet leaves to reflect on the city from behind "dilapidated walls in cold Vermont," a noxious world of fireman's balls, vagrant handymen, and long drives to find a conversation. The poem's turning point comes midway, when the speaker stages his homecoming, realizing that the world always seems worse than one remembers it as a youth. Hollander moves to celebrate New York with all its crowds and cultural diversity, a world in which dreams are easily made and broken. Most important is the sense of identity and heritage the city provides. Hollander concludes by saying that New York provides a tragic beauty well worth enduring for all of its discomforts.

REFLECTIONS ON ESPIONAGE

Reflections on Espionage, Hollander's eighth book of poems, takes the form of a long narrative of 101 radio transmissions from a master spy code-named "Cupcake." Hollander relishes in the intricate game of editing and deciphering "intercepted" messages sent in complex code. The dated entries begin in January and end in October, varying in length from one to almost one hundred lines, all written in precise hendecasyl-labic form. Hollander creates for himself a supreme fiction of this spy writing in cipher to his friend, the agent "Image," his director "Lyrebird," and a host of various double agents involved in secret missions. Although few of the plot details become clear to the reader, the poet clearly thrives in the context of an encoder of messages (poetry) sent out to other agents (readers and fellow poets).

One critic, Louis Martz writing in *The Yale Review*, went as far as saying that Hollander's community of spies in *Reflections on Espionage* represent various contemporary poets. If Hollander uses Cupcake as his persona, then "it does not take much of a 'grid' to decipher Kilo as Pound, or Puritan as Eliot. . . . there is certainly a candid appraisal of Anne Sexton." The secondary level of meaning certainly does concern the nature of poetry as a secret language and the challenges of relating to other poets and readers. The primary narrative vehicle of Cupcake and his network of informants, however, remains in the foreground. The reader watches a somewhat reflective though happily employed agent slowly descend to the status of victim. Cupcake becomes more removed from the inner workings of his missions until a definitive message comes down from Lyrebird, "Terminate Cupcake." Hollander writes this final entry in cipher, but he also gives instructions on translation, allowing the reader to enter personally into the process of decoding messages.

The most moving sections of *Reflections on Espionage* have nothing to do with spies. The reader sympathizes with Cupcake as he writes of the thrills and disappointments of trying to create a perfect language. Cupcake vacillates among telling stories, analyzing other spies, describing visits to a museum, and writing self-analytic journal entries. During his best moments, Cupcake transcends this fiction by asking the hard questions: Why is telling the truth so difficult? Why does language emasculate as much as it reveals? As it turns out, Cupcake is no power broker, only a minor cog within a larger machine. He remains a middleman, an agent trapped by circumstances beyond his control, at the mercy of a higher power who determines that he can no longer serve the organization. Hollander also uses Cupcake to discuss the nature

of language, the process of writing, and the community of poets and readers who provide little feedback or support for struggling writers. The elaborate rules of this game Hollander creates for himself sometimes overshadow the more important, implicit message—that only through careful use can language reveal hidden truth.

TALES TOLD OF THE FATHERS

Tales Told of the Fathers is one of the few Hollander books without a compendium of notes at the back, perhaps because here the poet abandons some of his classical forms and takes more personal journeys. The title poem is a sequence of five sections in which Hollander deals with the metaphysical experience of death. The poet tries to deny his own mortality while constantly seeing signs—shadows, a skull floating in water, and the cold earth—suggesting finality. *Tales Told of the Fathers* refers to Hollander's own father in "Eine Kleine Nachtmusik," "Given with a Gold Chain," and "Kranich and Bach," as well as to his literary forefathers; the book contains elegies for James Wright, W. H. Auden, and I. A. Richards.

In "The Head of the Bed," Hollander uses dream imagery in a prose prelude and fifteen cantos of five triadic stanzas. The poet says that only after writing the long sequence did he realize that the two countries in the poem are "sleep" and "waking," showing the division between the conscious and subconscious quest for meaning. The poem divides itself between male and female identities, using the mysterious female characters "Lady Evening" and "Miss Noctae" to create a myth of womankind as elusive and dangerous. Like the poetry of Wallace Stevens, "The Head of the Bed" pushes the boundary of accessibility because of its obscure and difficult pattern of images.

"Kranich and Bach" refers to a brand of piano no longer made. In tightly constructed tercets, Hollander writes about his "poor father, who/ With forgotten fingers played as best he could" while the poet listened passively. The sound of his voice and music remind the speaker that he needs to reacquaint himself with his father, who waits at the end of some journey of the mind. The piano becomes a surrogate casket and emblem for all that is old and faded. The experience of hearing this music, however, allows Hollander finally to accept death. This final poem in the book summarizes the values the speaker hopes have been passed from father to son.

SPECTRAL EMANATIONS

Hollander dedicated his next book to his father, Franklin Hollander. *Spectral Emanations: New and Selected Poems* contains nine new poems in addition to selections from seven previous books. With characteristic Hollander precision, the title poem divides itself into seven sections each with seventy-two lines, thus totaling a factorial seven (504) lines in the poem. The sections are subtitled "Red," "Orange," "Yellow," "Green," "Blue," "Departed Indigo," and "Violet" to correspond to Philo of Alexandria's colors on a golden candelabrum representing planetary orbits. Each poem is followed by a prose section.

The poem is a kind of Jewish American odyssey in search of the sacred menorah, the seven-branched iconographic symbol of the seven days of creation used by Jews during Hanukkah. Hollander uses each color and planetary influence to represent a different kind of consciousness, ranging from a violent cry of battle to a joyous celebration of life. He wants to combine the radiance of all seven colors to reveal the intense "white light of truth." In fact, the central section of the poem, "Green," unfolds like an archeological adventure, describing the search for and restoration of the sacred lamp. The poem is one of Hollander's most challenging and intriguing with its interplay of various modes, moods, styles, and stanzas.

BLUE WINE AND OTHER POEMS

Blue Wine and Other Poems takes up a number of recurring themes and motifs, including sculpture, music, journeys, and death. The predominant theme of *Blue Wine and Other Poems* is the artist's view and how perception shapes one's understanding of the world. "Lyrical Interval," a series of somber poems in the middle of the book, paraphrases purely instrumental music. *Blue Wine and Other Poems* embraces a range of poems from exuberant, mock-Homeric odes to elegiac stanzas to the light verse of poems such as "The Notebook Labeled 'Jealousy.'" In this book, Hollander especially interests himself in the problem of perspective and the visual artist's relationship to things apart from himself or herself. He presents verbal responses to abstract expressionist painters' work, showing how perception shapes one's appreciation of art. Several poems on the theme of journeys, such as "The Train" and "Just for the Ride," show Hollander dealing with artistic rendering of experience. "The Train" combines dreamlike imagery and a trip to the 1939 World's Fair as background for two sleepers who are attempting to understand the journey from childhood into maturity.

The title poem shows another Hollander trait, wild inventiveness and range of emotion. The poet writes of visiting a friend's house and discovering what appears to be wine in bottles bearing mysterious labels. The poem dilates on how wine has inspired philosophers and epic heroes throughout history. The important feature of the mysterious blue wine is that it promotes a change of consciousness and new points of view; it matters little what kind of wine the bottles hold. Like all art, the wine actually becomes shaped by how the human mind perceives it in all its responses, theories, reflections, and ideas: "I will never forget the moment when/ It became clear . . . that the famous blue/ Color of the stuff could come to mean so little." The wine's glory comes not from special taste or ingredients but from the depth of one's love for it.

POWERS OF THIRTEEN

Hollander's next book, *Powers of Thirteen*, has the mathematical precision of a Leonardo Fibonacci series; this thirteenth book in the career of Hollander (whose full name has thirteen letters) is composed of a sequence of 169 (factorial 13) modified sonnets. The poet alters the sonnet form into a lyric of thirteen lines with thirteen syllables in each line. The sequence addresses itself to an unidentified "you" and has the focus of a Renaissance sonnet cycle such as Sir Philip Sidney's *Astrophel and Stella* (1591).

In addition to working as a long poem, the book contains several series of related poems. The theme of *Powers of Thirteen* may be found convincingly expressed in a subsequence titled "Thirteen." Hollander traces the roots of triskaidekaphobia, or abnormal fear of the number thirteen, in history, religion, and myth, arguing that although the number casts a foul shadow, the power of meaning invested in it overcomes the weight of negative association. Hosts avoid thirteen guests seated for dinner, boys dread their thirteenth year, and a thirteen-tone scale in music creates dissonance, but the poet finds solace in the unusual, exotic space of the number. The power of thirteen is the true expression of intense love, among other things, shared between the speaker and his lover. It may be best to think of the speaker's "you" as a range of various persons (including the object of sexual desire and an extension of the poet himself) who allow the poet to share dialogue on many topics. *Powers of Thirteen* encompasses a whole calendar of various celebrations, including poems about May Day, Labor Day, and winter holidays. Typical poems within the sequence showing Hollander's skill are 69, titled "Lepidoptery," and 99-106, "Speaking Plainly." Critics sometimes deride Hollander as being too literary, witty, and inventive. *Powers of Thirteen* responds directly to this criticism with irreverence, language-play, obfuscation, allusion, myth, and metaphoric might. When the world wants blunt simplicity, Hollander gives it complexity and grace, as he demonstrates in "Speaking Plainly."

IN TIME AND PLACE

In Time and Place is composed of three disparate books. Part 1 ("In Time") presents thirty-five poems in the *abba* rhyme scheme and octosyllabic lines of Alfred, Lord Tennyson's *In Memoriam* (1850) stanza. Like Tennyson, Hollander attempts to understand and work his way through various stages of grief following the loss of a loved one. Part 2 ("In Between") is a prose journal of seventeen pages in which the speaker returns to an old house filled with memories, searching for some "turnabout" in his writing at the same time that he satirizes serious journal-keepers such as Henry David Thoreau. Part 3 ("In Place") consists of thirty prose poems showing Hollander continuing his search for "life after verse" in the same house.

This poet, skilled in the tradition of formal verse, experiments with many foreign and exotic narrative modes. In *In Time and Place* he writes, "We had learned thereafter to mock that stiff way of walking, and after that, to replace it with our own little dances and gallops." Taken together, this collection's two sections of prose and opening sequence of poetry show Hollander testing the limits of formal verse and exploring concepts of space, landscape, time, and memory. The prose is admirable for its metaphoric clarity and

range of emotion, but it fails to build on the coherent theme of the first section with the intense grief of poems such as "Vintage Absence" and "Half-Empty Bed Blues."

Section 2 is a Joseph Conrad-like journey into the self, wavering between the trivial and the philosophical. It is the most difficult to appreciate, since it appears unrelated to the themes of grief and loss. Yet Hollander skillfully transcends his limitations, parodying himself as he writes in invisible ink while dwelling on the inadequacies and ambivalences created through writing. A series of aphorisms on how to misuse a notebook informs the middle section; Hollander wants to undermine the smugness and precision of the same poetic language he carried off expertly in the first section.

Section 3 contains thirty independent prose poems, all reflecting on the theme of place, memory, and resolution. Hollander continues the metaphor of returning home in "About the House," this time cataloging the house's infirmities without feeling trapped by them as he had in previous pages. The sense of place, he realizes, is not so much in the place itself as in the person who perceives it. The book's final poem, "In Place of Place," finds a resolution of or a replacement for the grief experienced in section 1. The poet realizes that no experience is ever given back; everything that follows, each replacement, represents an opportunity for new meaning in one's life.

HARP LAKE

Harp Lake, Hollander's seventeenth book of poems, casts off the experiments of *In Time and Place*, returning to the formalism of earlier books. *Harp Lake* is driven by a spiritual search that has antecedents in earlier Hollander books. The major themes of *Harp Lake* are the search for one's heritage (also apparent in *Spectral Emanations*) and the perception of meaning viewed through worlds of art (also apparent in references to worlds of painting, sculpture, and music in *Blue Wine and Other Poems*). Hollander even includes a shaped poem, "Kitty and Bug," reflecting back on *Types of Shape*.

Harp Lake's title poem, "Kinneret," refers to the Sea of Galilee. The earliest Hebrew name for the sea was Chinnereth, also meaning "harp," because of the shape of the body of water. A cluster of poems including

"Kinneret," "From the Old City," and "From the Inner City" allude to a visit to Israel, where Hollander renewed his connection to his Jewish heritage. "Kinneret" is composed of forty stanzas using the Malaysian *pantun* quatrains; the two couplets seem unrelated but become associated through various hidden rhymes, puns, and sounds. Like some ancient prophet gazing over the lake, Hollander mines his stores of memories and associations to arrive at a deeply personal spiritual awakening. In "From the Old City," he conducts a similar search for holy land and places of wisdom, replacing false fables with new truth. As a wanderer, the poet finds that arriving at resolution is not as easy as traveling to a physical locale. Hollander's interest in gardening and sculpture leads to "The Mad Potter," a dramatic monologue written by an artisan who surveys the breadth of his career and concludes that he has produced nothing useful. The potter finally looks at his occupation as positive, though, because it has given him a voice, a truth to leave behind for others.

FIGUREHEAD

The world of art makes another strong appearance in Hollander's *Figurehead and Other Poems*. Meditations on the relationship between art and memory ("the tapestry is what the thread/ Was for") are balanced by an instinctive playfulness ("Poetry must either become insane or/ Shun the strictly literal like the—should we/ Say?—the plague"), as well as wordplay itself. All kinds of punning—visual and verbal—abound here, underscoring Hollander's theme of "double-dealings/ With ourselves."

He delights in all kinds of rhymes and slant rhymes in the manner of Lewis Carroll or Gerard Manley Hopkins, like this sequence in "Getting from Here to There": "dawn, darn, dark, dirk, disk, dusk." This poem takes as its inspiration a word game invented by Lewis Carroll. By changing one letter at a time, a player transforms, for example, "dawn" to "dusk" in six steps, or "east" to "west" in eight. In the eleven stanzas of this poem, the reader is directed through various metaphysical journeys.

He misdirected us, and so we came
By a long route, which took us through a cave
Filled with the lapping of a distant wave.

Our confidence already on the wane
We wandered, wondering, ever more in want
Of knowing where the true way really went.

Hollander's fascination with painting is ever-present here. *Figurehead* contains meditations on the works of such masters as Diego Rodriguez de Silva y Velazquez, Saul Steinberg, René Magritte, Edward Hopper, and Charles Sheeler. There is a long poem about hyperrealist Sheeler, "The Artist Looks at Nature," a poem about a painting that is itself about painting. Hollander's observations suggest that he could be one of the greatest art critics if he so chose. Yet in his poems he goes further, trying to find words to reproduce, rather than describe, the effect of a work. "Variations on a Table-Top" was inspired by Steinberg, "whose carved and painted balsa table-tops were sculpted drawings of the table-tops they were drawn upon."

Pursuing a similar theme, "Then All Smiles Stopped Together" allows the subject of an imaginary painting in a poem to have her say. Robert Browning's "Last Duchess" explains how the facial expression that supposedly drove her husband to do away with her was, actually, a figment of the portrait painter, "wrought for the sake of shadowing alone,/ The false depiction of his pencil." The poems of this collection further Hollander's ability to disarm, charm, and intrigue his readers with witty and imaginative wordplay and tributes, making all the more apparent his affinity for intelligent humor and well-channeled creativity.

OTHER MAJOR WORKS

NONFICTION: *The Untuning of the Sky: Ideas of Music in English Poetry, 1500-1700*, 1961; *Modern Poetry: Essays in Criticism*, 1968; *Images of Voice*, 1970; *For I. A. Richards: Essays in His Honor*, 1973 (with R. A. Brower and Helen Vendler); *Vision and Resonance: Two Senses of Poetic Form*, 1975; *Literature as Experience*, 1979 (with Irving Howe and David Bromwich); *The Figure of Echo: A Mode of Allusion in Milton and After*, 1981; *Rhyme's Reason: A Guide to English Verse*, 1981; *Melodious Guile*, 1988; *Poetics of Influence: New and Selected Criticism*, 1988 (with Harold Bloom); *The Work of Poetry*, 1997; *The Poetry of Everyday Life*, 1998.

CHILDREN'S LITERATURE: *A Book of Various Owls*, 1963; *The Quest of the Gole*, 1966; *The Immense Parade on Supererogation Day and What Happened to It*, 1972.

EDITED TEXTS: *The Wind and the Rain*, 1961 (with Harold Bloom); *Selected Poems*, 1961 (of Ben Jonson); *The Untuning of the Sky: Ideas of Music in English Poetry, 1500-1700*, 1961; *Jiggery-Pokery: A Compendium of Double Dactyls*, 1966 (with Anthony Hecht); *Poems of Our Moment*, 1968; *American Short Stories Since 1945*, 1968; *Images of Voice: Music and Sound in Romantic Poetry*, 1970; *I. A. Richards: Essays in His Honor*, 1973; *The Oxford Anthology of English Literature*, 1973 (with Frank Kermode); *Literature as Experience: An Anthology*, 1979 (with Irving Howe and David Bromwich); *The Figure of Echo: A Mode of Allusion in Milton and After*, 1981; *Rhyme's Reason: A Guide to English Verse*, 1981; *Melodious Guile: Fictive Pattern in Poetic Language*, 1988; *The Essential Rossetti*, 1989; *Animal Poems*, 1994; *Garden Poems*, 1996; *Committed to Memory: One Hundred Best Poems to Memorize*, 1996; *War Poems*, 1999; *Sonnets*, 2001.

BIBLIOGRAPHY

Davie, Donald. "Gifts of the Gab." *The New York Review of Books* 22 (October 2, 1975): 30-31. Discusses *Tales Told of the Fathers* and *Vision and Resonance*, with the thesis that Hollander's learning frequently comes between the poet and his best work. Hollander's metaphysical language, says Davie, alienates the nonacademic reader.

Howard, Richard. *Alone with America: Essays on the Art of Poetry in the United States Since 1950*. New York: Atheneum, 1969. Argues that Hollander seeks an escape from the tyranny of memory through perfectly embodying the traditions of English poetry he knows so well.

McClatchy, J. D. "The Fall Guy." *The New Republic* 196 (February 9, 1987): 44-46. A discussion of *In Time and Place* with an excellent survey of the range of response to Hollander's books throughout his career. Hollander has been misunderstood or ignored by most critics, according to McClatchy.

Martz, Louis. "Recent Poetry: Mending Broken Connections." *The Yale Review* 76 (Autumn, 1976): 114-129. Reviews *Reflections on Espionage* with a general discussion of Hollander's method of working within confining poetic forms. Martz says that Hollander includes the whole human power of imagination inside each poem.

Pettingell, Phoebe. "Hollander's Poetic Playfulness." *The New Leader* 82, no. 4 (April 5, 1999): 15-16. Pettingell discusses poet Hollander's poetic playfulness and how it illuminates the brave pathos of human endeavor.

Warren, Rosanna. "Night Thoughts and Figurehead." Review of *Figurehead and Other Poems*. *Raritan* 20, no. 2 (Fall, 2000): 11-24. Warren demonstrates how *Figurehead* extends and complicates the poetic devices and themes Hollander used in *Movie-Going and Other Poems*.

Wood, Michael. "Calculated Risks." *The New York Review of Books* 25 (June 1, 1978): 27-30. A review of *Spectral Emanations*, arguing that Hollander's poetry tends toward imitation and artifice without underlying meaning. Although he is extremely talented, says Wood, Hollander's skills overshadow his actual achievement.

Jonathan L. Thorndike,
updated by Sarah Hilbert

ANSELM HOLLO

Born: Helsinki, Finland; April 12, 1934

PRINCIPAL POETRY
Sateiden Valilla, 1956
& It Is a Song, 1965
Faces and Forms, 1965
The Coherences, 1968
Tumbleweed: Poems, 1968
Waiting for a Beautiful Bather: Ten Poems, 1969
Maya: Works, 1959-1969, 1970
Message, 1970
Gee Apollinaire, 1970

Sensation 27, 1972

Alembic, 1972

Smoke Writing, 1973

Spring Cleaning Greens, from Notebooks, 1967-1973, 1973

Some Worlds, 1974

Black Book 1, 1975

Sojourner Microcosms: New and Selected Poems, 1959-1977, 1977

Heavy Jars, 1977

Lingering Tangos, 1977

Lunch in Fur, 1978

Curious Data, 1978

With Ruth in Mind, 1979

Finite Continued: New Poems, 1977-1980, 1980

No Complaints: Poems, 1983

Pick Up the House: New and Selected Poems, 1986

Outlying Districts: Poems, 1990

Near Miss Haiku: Praises, Laments, Aphorisms, Reports, 1990

Space Baltic: The Science Fiction Poems, 1962-1987, 1991

Blue Ceiling, 1992

High Beam, 1993

West Is Left on the Map, 1993

Survival Dancing, 1995

Corvus: Poems, 1995

AHOE (And How on Earth), 1997

rue Wilson Monday, 2000

Notes on the Possibilities and Attractions of Existence: Selected Poems, 1965-2000, 2001

OTHER LITERARY FORMS

Anselm Hollo early established himself as an important literary translator, bringing into English the works of Russian, Finnish, and Swedish poets in the 1960's and 1970's. Specific authors he translated included Andrei Voznesensky, Aleksandr Blok, and Paul Klee, and the genres he has translated range the gamut: fiction, nonfiction, plays, and screenplays. He also translated into Finnish and German the works of such varied authors as Allen Ginsberg, Gregory Corso, William Carlos Williams, and John Lennon. In his translations into German, he several times collaborated with Josephine Clare.

In collaboration with Gregory Corso and Tom Raworth, he wrote parodies collected in *The Minicab War* (1961). His essays, including an autobiographical essay, appeared in *Caws and Causeries: Around Poetry and Poets* (1999). Hollo has edited both literary journals and anthologies, including a guest stint with the London magazine *Horde* (1964), and the anthology *Modern Swedish Poetry in Translation* (1979), with Gunnar Harding.

ACHIEVEMENTS

Anselm Hollo has repeatedly received the praise of his fellow poets, including such notables as Ted Berrigan and Andrei Codrescu. The latter has called him "indispensable." While often identified with Language Poetry, a movement sometimes seen to have antiacademic and antiauthoritarian leanings, Hollo has nevertheless earned notable awards from both academia and formal poetry and arts organizations. In 1976 he was awarded the New York State Creative Artists' Public Service Award. This was followed in 1979 with a National Endowment for the Arts Fellowship in poetry, in 1989 and 1991 with the Fund for Poetry Award for Contributions to Contemporary Poetry, and in 1996 with the Gertrude Stein Award in Innovative American Poetry. For his work as translator, he was awarded, in 1981 and 1989, the American-Scandinavian Foundation Award for Poetry in Translation, and, in 1996, the Finnish Government Prize for Translation of Finnish Literature.

His poetry has been translated into Finnish, French, German, Hungarian, and Swedish.

BIOGRAPHY

Anselm Hollo received his early education in Finland and first spent time in the United States on an exchange scholarship during his senior year, attending a high school in Cedar Rapids, Iowa. He subsequently attended Helsinki University in Finland and the University of Tübingen in Germany. His early employment in the 1950's included working as commercial correspondent for a lumber export company in Finland and as an interpreter for the United Nations Atomic Energy Agency in Vienna, Austria. By the mid-1950's he was acting as translator and book reviewer for both German and Finnish periodicals, while also serving as secretary to his grandfather, Professor Paul Walden of the University of Tübingen. In 1958 he accepted employment by the British Broadcasting Corporation's European Services in London. He became program assistant and coordinator, remaining through 1966.

Beginning in 1967, Hollo accepted a series of positions as visiting lecturer, visiting professor, and visiting poet at universities in the United States, including, in the late 1960's and 1970's, the State University of New York, Buffalo; Bowling Green University, Ohio; Hobart and William Smith Colleges, Geneva, New York; Michigan State University, East Lansing; the University of Maryland, Baltimore; Southwest State University, Marshall, Minnesota; and Sweet Briar College, Virginia. This period included his serving as head of the translation workshop at the University of Iowa in Iowa City, in 1971-1972. In 1981, Hollo began a long association with the Naropa Institute at Naropa University in Boulder, Colorado, which would lead to his being named associate professor in the graduate department of writing and poetics in 1989. During the period 1981-1983, he also served as lecturer at the New College of California, San Francisco.

Throughout much of his career, Hollo has been associated with literary movements often seen in opposition to academe, including the Beat, New York, and Language schools of American poetry. Simultaneously he has held academic positions, initially as lecturer and later as professor. That Hollo felt the tension inherent in this pairing of professions may be indicated by his long tenure at Naropa, a Buddhist-inspired yet nonsectarian alternative college.

He married Josephine Wirkus in 1957, with whom he had one son and two daughters. In 1985, he married the artist Jane Dalrymple. She has provided artwork for several of Hollo's books.

ANALYSIS

Anselm Hollo's poetry has a light and airy appearance, with short and sometimes abrupt lines of verse arranged sparingly upon the page. While spare, the poems often demonstrate remarkable depth, and while often short, they are richly endowed with humor, intelligence, and imagination.

Anselm Hollo (© Miriam Berkley)

Against the tradition in which poets become best known for their longest works, Hollo first established and then maintained a reputation for short poems. This emphasis is a conscious one, reflected in the way he has presented individual poems in more than the usual number of retrospective and summary collections. The appearance of "bouzouki music" in successive books, including the major early compilations *Maya* and *Sojourner Microcosms*, for example, helped give the short poem a prominence it might have lacked if Hollo had not actively kept it before his readers.

Hollo has also used the context of the different compilations to give new perspective on his poems. He offered his collection *Space Baltic*, for example, as a collection of his "science-fiction" works. The inclusion of many poems within this book broadened the ways in which they could be read. A poem such as "Old Space Cadet Speaking," which earlier might have been taken as a purely metaphorical exploration of unrealistic ambitions, lent itself to a more literal, narrative reading within this new context.

As might be expected of a poet involved in translation work, and whose own career took him far beyond the borders of his native country, Hollo has demonstrated a deep concern with European literary traditions. At the same time, as a longtime U.S. resident, his poems have become deeply interwoven with the literature of his adopted country. In his frequent dedications of poems to contemporary writers and in his frequent allusions to writers of other times, however, he reveals his true allegiance, which is to a literary world whose borders transcend political lines.

While the seriousness of his poetry has never been in question, neither has Hollo's sense of humor, much of which is based upon his observations of modern life. On occasion his poems take a turn toward black humor, as in "manifest destiny." Others draw their humor from his observations of the literary world. Whether using situational humor or wordplay, Hollo has managed to steer clear of the coy and artificial.

"MANIFEST DESTINY"

Anselm Hollo's shorter poems often have a more distinctively assertive character than his longer poems. Some of this distinctiveness may arise from the pointed emphasis on the intersection of the personal and political worlds. The short "manifest destiny," first published in *No Complaints*, ranks alongside such other poems as "t.v. (1)," "t.v. (2)," and "the terrorist smiles," from *Finite Continued*. In "manifest destiny," Hollo initially creates a vision of a comfortable middle- or upper-class life, "in pleasantly air-conditioned home with big duck pond in back,/ some nice soft drinks by elbow, some good american snacks as well." Hollo explicitly evokes the wealth of the privileged: "at least four hundred grand in the bank, & that's for checking." The evocations of comfort and wealth ground the reader in a reality that becomes unreality by the end of the poem, when the meaning of the poem's title becomes clear. The unspecified people who "arrive in front of a large video screen" in the poem's first line spend "a copacetic evening" at the end of the poem,

> watching the latest military *techné*
> wipe out poverty everywhere in the world
> in its most obvious form, the poor.

The poem is notable not only for its concision and effectiveness but also for its prescience in making a point which would remain undiminished in its accuracy during succeeding decades.

"BOUZOUKI MUSIC"

Originally written and published in the late 1960's, "bouzouki music" is a poem that demonstrates the poet's ease with classical or mythological subject matter. Introducing the figure of Odysseus in its first line, the poem can be read as an incantatory exploration of this particular character or of the kind of character Odysseus represents. Written in five brief sections, the poem includes some of Hollo's finest lines:

> a man's legs grow
> straight out of his soul
>
> who knows where they take him

A light touch and glancing vision, as opposed to a possessive grip and direct stare, give the poem expansive force. Other poems, such as "on the occasion of becoming an echo," which invokes Gaia, and even "the new style western," which draws upon a modern, media-created mythology, give similar demonstrations of Hollo's approach.

"OLD SPACE CADET SPEAKING"

One of Hollo's "science-fiction," or speculative, poems, "old space cadet speaking" explores notions of reality and unreality. While a poem without the political dimension of "manifest destiny," it similarly begins by presenting an unreal world in terms to establish it as real, and similarly concludes by exposing its empty underpinnings. After beginning with a storyteller's opening phrase, "let me tell you," Hollo introduces the character of a spaceship captain possessed by the sensual vision of union with his lover. Although his physical destination goes unmentioned, the Captain dwells upon

> exactly what he would do
> soon as he reached the destination
> he would fuse with her plumulous essence
> & they would become a fine furry plant.

The adventure of space travel is reduced to the entirely personal dimensions of an erotic dream, the "ultimate consummation of long ethereal affair." Above and beyond the erotic episode, moreover, the Captain envisions a kind of transcendence, in which "he would miss/ certain things small addictions/ acquired in the colonies." This dream of transcendence seems his destination: "he was flying high/ he was almost there." Hollo then dissolves the image, in the manner of someone turning away from an entertaining show or absorbing story:

> & that is where
> we leave him to go on hurtling through the great warp
> & at our own ineffable goals.

In its final few words, the poem expands to include the reader. Like the Captain's, our goals, too, may be "ineffable." We long for that "ultimate consummation of long ethereal affair" and participate in the same fantasy of "hurtling through the great warp."

RUE WILSON MONDAY

A major work, *rue Wilson Monday* presents the daybook in verse of a period of time Hollo spent in France. His ruminations on events and personalities past and present, enriched by an ironically conscious Surrealist approach, combine with sensory passages to make *rue Wilson Monday* among Hollo's most rewarding efforts. "When I was invited to spend five months in France, in an old hotel long frequented by artists and writers, I decided to write something that would NOT be your typical 'sabbatical poem,'" he writes in a prefatory note. He calls the work a "hybrid of day book, informal sonnet sequence (though more 'simultaneist' than chronological), and extended, 'laminated' essay-poem." He credits the influence of Guillaume Apollinaire's 1913 poem "Lundi rue Christine," "a Cubist work composed almost entirely out of verbatim speech from various conversations in a café."

Hollo's work draws not upon living conversations he overhears at the Hotel Chevillon but instead upon conversations "in and around my head during that stay." For longtime readers of Hollo, many participants in the "conversations" are decidedly familiar to the territory, while some, such as Robert Louis Stevenson, appear as figures specially connected to the French hotel. The familiar figures, who help make these informal sonnets resonate with Hollo's earlier work, include such diverse individuals as Ted Berrigan, Gertrude Stein, John Lennon, Oscar Wilde, Heraclitus, Robert Bly, and "Archy the Vers Libre Cockroach." In a move some readers might regard as overly self-conscious, Hollo includes footnotes to help the reader participate in the "conversations" of the poems. While the poems themselves are lucid, these notes distinctly augment the reader's pleasure.

Early in the sonnet sequence, in poem number 2, Hollo positions himself as poet, by warning against "beautiful thoughts": "beware of those who write to write beautiful thoughts." He then establishes parameters: "upper limit: poet as brain in jar/ lower limit: poet as hectoring moralistic asshole." His preference for "gamesome pasquinade" suggests that Hollo's playfulness will come to the fore, in the course of the sequence of poems, even against the influence of "Mister Intellectual Rigor."

Many of the poems reflect Hollo's own experience in the world of poetry and serve occasionally as poetic defenses. In poem number 9, he answers the charge, "thou art too elliptical" with a response appropriately elliptical: "but what's not foible anymore?" In poem number 15, he makes an even more pointed statement of his position:

> give up your ampersands & lowercase i's
> they still won't like you
> the bosses of official verse culture
> (U.S. branch) but kidding aside
> I motored off that map a long time ago.

The imaginary conversations pervade these poems in unexpected ways. In poem number 56, Hollo quotes from a Kerouac School workshop led by Ted Berrigan in 1978 and then notes,

> yes Ted yes it is very much like it
> but you are the master of intelligent conversation
> and no emotional slither.

In his footnote, Hollo notes how his interior conversation with Berrigan also includes Ezra Pound, whose words he appropriates.

While the inspirational Apollinaire poem is directly quoted within the numbered sonnets, perhaps its most striking echo appears in poem number 21, which is literally cobbled together out of the words of other poets, as if overheard in Apollinaire's café. In his footnote, Hollo states that he composed the poem out of lines drawn from Philip Sidney; Alfred, Lord Tennyson; Michael Drayton; and Thomas Wyatt, among others.

OTHER MAJOR WORKS

NONFICTION: *Cows and Causeries: Around Poetry and Poets*, 1999.

TRANSLATIONS: *Kaddisch*, 1962 (of Allen Ginsberg's poem); *Red Cats: Selections from the Russian Poets*, 1962; *Some Poems*, 1962 (of Paul Klee); *In der flüchtigen Hand der Zeit*, 1963 (of Gregory Corso's poetry); *Selected Poems*, 1964 (of Andrei Voznesensky's poetry); *Paterson*, 1970 (with Josephine Clare; of William Carlos Williams's poem); *The Twelve and Other Poems*, 1971 (of Aleksandr Blok's poetry); *Modern Swedish Poetry in Translation*, 1979 (with Gunnar Harding); *The Czar's Madman*, 1992 (of Jaan Kross's novel); *And Still Drink More! A Kayankaya Mystery*, 1994 (of Jakob Arjouni's novel).

EDITED TEXTS: *Jazz Poems*, 1963; *Negro Verse*, 1964.

MISCELLANEOUS: *The Minicab War*, 1961 (parodies; with Gregory Corso and Tom Raworth).

BIBLIOGRAPHY

Cline, Lynn. "Anselm Hollo's Poetry Speaks Volumes." *The Santa Fe New Mexican* (May 13, 2001). In the "Pasa Tiempo" section. Cline writes about the poet's views on "life outside the box," based on Hollo's lectures.

Foster, Edward Halsey. *Postmodern Poetry: The Talisman Interviews*. Hoboken, N.J.: Talisman House, 1994. In Foster's interview with Hollo, the poet discusses his work and influences. Foster places Hollo alongside such figures as Alice Notley, Ron Padgett, and Rosemarie Waldrop.

Weatherhead, A. Kingsley. *The British Dissonance: Essays on Ten Contemporary Poets*. Columbia: University of Missouri Press, 1983. Kingsley discusses Hollo in terms of his status as a poet once active in England, alongside such figures as Basil Bunting, Charles Tomlinson, and Tom Raworth.

Mark Rich

OLIVER WENDELL HOLMES

Born: Cambridge, Massachusetts; August 29, 1809
Died: Boston, Massachusetts; October 7, 1894

PRINCIPAL POETRY
Poems, 1836
Songs in Many Keys, 1862
Songs of Many Seasons, 1875
The Iron Gate and Other Poems, 1880
Before the Curfew and Other Poems, 1888

OTHER LITERARY FORMS

A remarkably versatile writer, Oliver Wendell Holmes produced not only five volumes of poetry but also three novels (*Elsie Venner*, 1861; *The Guardian Angel*, 1867; and *A Mortal Antipathy*, 1885); several collections of essays, including *The Autocrat of the Breakfast-Table* (1858), *The Professor at the Breakfast-Table* (1860), and *The Poet at the Breakfast-Table* (1872); biographies of John Lothrop Motley (1879) and Ralph Waldo Emerson (1885); and a large number of essays dealing with medicine, including the classic study "The Contagiousness of Puerperal Fever" (1843).

ACHIEVEMENTS

Along with William Cullen Bryant, John Greenleaf Whittier, Henry Wadsworth Longfellow, and James Russell Lowell, Oliver Wendell Holmes has come to be known as one of the so-called Schoolroom Poets. The label is an unfortunate one: Half affectionate and half patronizing, it indicates that for the last 150 years these poets have been regarded as the creators of verse so simplistic in theme, rhyme, and meter that it is ideally suited to memorization and recitation by grade school children; indeed, until recently it was not uncommon to find the portrait of at least one of these five men gracing the wall of the average American grade school classroom.

In the final analysis, however, the amenability of a poem to memorization and recitation is not indicative of its intrinsic worth (or lack thereof). An objective reconsideration of Holmes's poetry reveals that he did indeed produce verse worthy of the admiration of serious readers of poetry. Such poems as "Old Ironsides," "The Last Leaf," "Dorothy Q.," "The Deacon's Master-piece," and "The Chambered Nautilus" are still thought-provoking and entertaining works, and it is doubtful that future generations of poetry readers will find them any less so.

In addition, Holmes's collection of essays *The Auto-crat of the Breakfast-Table* is still studied, and his novel *Elsie Venner*, so curiously modern in its psychological and ethical dimensions, could very well enjoy a revival of sorts in the present age of Freudian and Jungian approaches to human behavior.

BIOGRAPHY

Oliver Wendell Holmes was born on August 29, 1809, in Cambridge, Massachusetts, a town which had already become established as a major American cultural center by virtue of Harvard College and nearby Boston—"the hub of the solar system," as Holmes would note only half jokingly in Essay VI of his *Autocrat* papers. Holmes's father, Abiel Holmes (1763-1837), was a Congregational minister in Cambridge who had already established his reputation as a writer with *The Annals of America* (1805; revised 1829), generally regarded as the first attempt at an exhaustive compilation of American historical data beginning with 1492. Holmes's mother, Sarah Wendell, was a descendant of the noted Puritan poet Anne Bradstreet; indeed, like Bradstreet, Sarah Wendell was unusually liberal on religious issues, and her son—far from following in the devout footsteps of his clergyman father—had little patience with religious orthodoxy.

From an early age, Holmes was fascinated by natural science, and he is reported to have devoted the playtime of his childhood to analyzing the snails and insects which he found in the family's garden, but his decision to pursue a career in medicine—which, contrary to popular belief, probably was not due to his passion for driving horse carriages at illegal speeds

through the streets of Boston—would not come until much later. After a year (1824-1825) at a Calvinist preparatory school, Phillips Academy at Andover, Holmes entered nearby Harvard College and was graduated in 1829 as Class Poet.

Still undecided as to how best to use his unusual talents, he entered Dane Law School in Cambridge and remained there for one year (1829-1830); he then enrolled at Boston's Tremont Medical School, which he attended until 1833. This training was followed by two years of intensive study in Paris, a city which in the 1830's was noted for its superb facilities for medical research and which attracted the brightest medical students in the United States. In 1836, Holmes received his M.D. degree from Harvard and immediately commenced his extraordinary career as a physician, research scientist, and teacher.

In 1836 and 1837, Holmes won three Boylston Prizes for his essays titled "The Nature and Treatment of Neu-

Oliver Wendell Holmes (Library of Congress)

ralgia," "Facts and Traditions Respecting the Existence of Indigenous Intermittent Fever in New England," and "The Utility and Importance of Direct Exploration in Medical Practice." His 1843 essay "The Contagiousness of Puerperal Fever," generated widespread controversy in its day, and it was not until 1861 that the Hungarian obstetrician Ignaz Philipp Semmelweis confirmed Holmes's theory that the deadly "childbed fever" was spread by contagion—that, in fact, it was often transmitted by the midwives and physicians who attended births. Holmes also was a pioneer in the use of microscopes in scientific research, in the establishment of histology as a legitimate branch of science, and in the improvement of surgical procedures; in fact, it was Holmes who in 1846 suggested the name "anesthesia" for the physiological condition induced by Dr. William Morton in a demonstration at the Massachusetts General Hospital in October of that year.

Even at this early stage of his career, Holmes was teaching as well as doing extensive research; he was a professor of anatomy at Dartmouth College (1839-1840), and from 1847 to 1882 he served as the Parkman professor of anatomy and physiology at the Harvard Medical School. Between his teaching and research, Holmes tended not to continue his early practice as a family doctor. Part of the problem was his appearance. Boyish-looking and short (five feet four inches), Holmes found it difficult to instill confidence in his patients; more important, they apparently did not much appreciate his lighthearted manner, his sense of humor, or his reputation as—of all things—a poet.

Holmes had become famous as a poet at the age of twenty-one when, in response to a newspaper notice that the American frigate *Constitution* was to be demolished, he quickly wrote "Old Ironsides"—an enormously popular poem which is held to have been responsible for saving the famed warship. A collected edition of his poetry appeared in 1836, and Holmes (like Ralph Waldo Emerson) was very successful both as a public lecturer in the 1850's and as the remarkably obliging author of "occasional" verse (including a poem titled "For the Meeting of the National Sanitary Association").

In the minds of many nineteenth century Americans, however, Holmes was famous not as a physician, college professor, or poet, but as an essayist. When he was only twenty-two years old, Holmes published in the short-lived *New England Magazine* two brief, witty essays titled "The Autocrat of the Breakfast-Table" (November, 1831; February, 1832). A quarter of a century later, Holmes decided "to shake the same bough again, and see if the ripe fruit were better or worse than the early windfalls" ("The Autocrat's Autobiography"), and so in the first issue (November, 1857) of a new magazine titled the *Atlantic Monthly*, he printed the third "Autocrat" essay. The twelve essays serialized in the *Atlantic Monthly* were phenomenally popular; collected in book form, they reportedly sold ten thousand copies in three days and have been in continuous print ever since.

While his fame as an essayist was spreading, Holmes also tried his hand at long fiction, producing three self-proclaimed "medicated novels": *Elsie Venner*, *The Guardian Angel*, and *A Mortal Antipathy*. Of the three, *Elsie Venner* is the best. Finally, Holmes wrote two biographies. *John Lothrop Motley* (1879) focuses on the noted historian and United States minister to Austria (1861-1867) and to Great Britain (1869-1870); *Ralph Waldo Emerson* (1885) was written for the American Men of Letters series.

By the time Holmes died in 1894, his name was a household word in the United States; in fact, his name lived on well into the twentieth century, not only because of his writings but also because of his distinguished son, Supreme Court Justice Oliver Wendell Holmes, Jr. (1841-1935). In many respects, it would be difficult to appreciate nineteenth century American life and thought without having some understanding of Holmes and his achievements. Not only did he lead a rich and productive life that spanned nearly the entire nineteenth century, helping to train several generations of American physicians, but he also produced half a dozen popular and enduring poems and a series of essays which clearly found responsive chords in the collective American psyche. In fact, it is questionable whether literary scholars and historians have even begun to determine the extent to which Holmes influenced and reflected American thought and literature in the nineteenth century.

Although S. I. Hayakawa and Howard Mumford Jones are probably correct in maintaining that Holmes either was unaware of, or simply chose not to acknowledge, the mill towns proliferating in New England, the slums in the larger cities, and the squandering of human and natural resources which made possible the remarkable growth of America in the nineteenth century, it is nevertheless also true that this conservative Boston Brahmin, this American Samuel Johnson, this Renaissance man of medicine and literature was a spokesman for the majority of middle-class Americans of the nineteenth century.

ANALYSIS

Of the hundreds of poems which the prolific Oliver Wendell Holmes produced, at least six are still being given serious attention by students of American literature: "Old Ironsides," "The Last Leaf," "Dorothy Q.," "The Deacon's Masterpiece," "The Chambered Nautilus," and "The Living Temple." The six poems are surprisingly varied in theme, depth, and technical expertise, although generally speaking they do reveal Holmes's lifelong interest in historical, scientific, and spiritual matters.

"OLD IRONSIDES"

"Old Ironsides" was written virtually extempore in 1830 when the twenty-one-year-old Holmes read in the Boston *Daily Advertiser* that the American frigate *Constitution* was to be demolished. Launched in 1797, the forty-four-gun *Constitution*—better known as "Old Ironsides" because cannon balls allegedly would bounce off her sides—had served with great distinction in the Tripolitan War and the War of 1812. The *Constitution* was especially honored for its victories over two British vessels, the *Guerrière* (off Newfoundland) and the *Java* (off Brazil), in the War of 1812. Holmes's poem so aroused public sentiment against the demolition of the *Constitution* that the ship was ordered saved and rebuilt. A rather brief poem (three octaves), "Old Ironsides" is still a powerful work which moves organically from a skillfully ironic opening ("Ay, tear her tattered ensign down!") to an impassioned plea to let the ship be destroyed by "the god of storms" rather than by "the harpies of the shore." Generally speaking, the imagery is neither imaginative nor well developed ("the battle shout," "the cannon's roar"), but there are some vivid, highly emotional images ("Her deck, once red with heroes' blood") which tend to compensate for the commonplace nature of so much of the poem. More important, "Old Ironsides" shows Holmes to be a master of psychology: Nowhere does he plead overtly that the ship be saved; nowhere does he mention its proper name or catalog its many victories. Rather, by manipulating tone and imagery, Holmes produced a poem which is above all intensely emotional; indeed, those universal emotions upon which it plays—the honoring of the dead of war, the veneration of the old, the love of military glory—are probably as potent today as they were in the 1830's. It is difficult to imagine that either the poem or the ship—now carefully preserved and lying at anchor in the Charlestown Navy Yard—will be treated with anything less than the deepest respect for generations to come.

"THE LAST LEAF"

The poem "The Last Leaf" also reveals Holmes's tendency to handle aspects of American history in an emotional fashion, although this poem also embodies a more personal dimension. The subject, a "Sad and wan" old man who walks the streets dressed in "the old three-cornered hat,/ And the breeches, and all that," was Major Thomas Melville, the grandfather of Herman Melville. Of "The Last Leaf," Holmes wrote in a prefatory note to the Riverside edition of his writings that it "was suggested by the appearance in one of our streets of a venerable relic of the Revolution, said to be one of the party who threw the tea overboard in Boston Harbor," and that the smile with which Holmes (the poem's persona) greeted him "meant no disrespect to an honoured fellow-citizen whose costume was out of date, but whose patriotism never changed with years." Holmes goes on to note proudly that the poem was copied down by Edgar Allan Poe and memorized by Abraham Lincoln. "The Last Leaf" is not simply of historical or patriotic interest; it focuses upon the resiliency of the human spirit and, more precisely, the need and desire to cling to life despite the loneliness and physical infirmities of old age. In this regard, the poem is something of a tour de force; it is rather remarkable to find someone so young (twenty-two) writing with such tenderness and empathy of old age. On the other hand, the poem may be seen as a reflection of Holmes's extraordinary personality; for only someone as imaginative, compassionate, and observant as the author of "The Last Leaf" would be able to succeed in two such diverse pursuits as medicine and literature. One wonders whether the poem, first published in 1831 when Holmes was a medical student, was reread by him or his son as they approached old age (Holmes lived to be eighty-five; his son died in 1935 at ninety-four). Like Major Melville, each of them "live[d] to be/ The last leaf upon the tree/ In the spring."

"DOROTHY Q."

"Dorothy Q." also shows Holmes's imaginative response to an actual person of the past, but in this charming poem the subject is one of his own ancestors: Dorothy Quincy, Holmes's great-grandmother on the maternal side. The premise of the poem is simple enough: The poem's persona (Holmes himself) regards a portrait of Dorothy made when she was only thirteen years old. The portrait itself was not painted with exceptional skill, and the canvas had been damaged by "a Red-Coat's rapier-thrust," but the girl, "a lady born," reveals in "her slender shape" the "Hint and promise of stately mien." Holmes realizes that he owes to Dorothy a "Strange" gift, for she gave him "All my tenure of heart and hand,/ All my title to house and land;/ Mother and sister and child and wife/ And joy and sorrow and death and life!" Here Holmes reveals, as he seldom does in his poetry, his deep interest (by both training and temperament) in human heredity; for by her acceptance of Edward Jackson's proposal of marriage (the "tremulous question"), young Dorothy ultimately helped to create not only Holmes but also Amelia Jackson, the distant relative of Holmes whom he married in June, 1840 (hence the paradoxical line "Mother and sister and child and wife"). Holmes speculates on heredity by questioning what he would have been like had she declined Jackson's marriage proposal; "Should I be I, or would it be/ One tenth another, to nine tenths me?"; and, touching upon the rather serious issue of the degree to which people are to be held morally responsible for creating new human life, Holmes wonders, "Shall I bless you, Dorothy, or forgive/ For the tender whisper [that is, her saying "Yes"] that bade me live?" The hint of unhappiness which pervades that final couplet is uncharacteristic of Holmes. It evidently does not reflect Holmes's personal dissatisfaction with being alive, for apparently he was a singularly contented man; however, it does

seem to reflect his realization that many people certainly do regret having been born because of their physical or emotional problems. This unfortunate state of affairs, which would have been especially apparent to Holmes in his capacity as a physician, gave rise to two of his most enduring concerns. Is it not true that in large measure we are simply the victims of genetic factors beyond our comprehension or control? Furthermore, as "victims," should we—or our parents, or no one—be held morally responsible for our behavior? Several decades before the rise of naturalism in American literature, Holmes was confronting the power of human sexuality and the problem of determinism. Virtually all of that confrontation took place in Holmes's "medicated novels" (most notably *Elsie Venner*). In such poems as "Dorothy Q.," one sees but a glimmer of Holmes's deep interest in sex and genetic determinism.

"THE DEACON'S MASTERPIECE"

More widely known than "Dorothy Q." are "The Deacon's Masterpiece: Or, The Wonderful 'One-Hoss Shay'" and "The Chambered Nautilus," both of which were originally published in Holmes's Autocrat papers, but which can be read outside that context. "The Deacon's Masterpiece," one of Holmes's longest poems (120 lines), is also one of his most controversial. The story line is extremely simple: A deacon in 1755 sets out to build a "one-hoss shay." Mindful of the belief that in building a *chaise* "There is always *somewhere* a weakest spot" which is responsible for its eventual destruction, he constructs the carriage of the finest materials using the soundest technical knowledge available. One hundred years to the day after its creation, this ostensibly perfect carriage literally falls to pieces "in a heap or mound,/ As if it had been to the mill and ground!" The controversy resides in the poem's meaning: Is it a story about logic, a parable suggesting that any theoretically airtight system of beliefs is doomed to collapse simply because it cannot accommodate changes in context, attacks from without, or the passage of time? Or, is the poem (as is believed by many commentators) specifically a parable on the demise of Calvinism? The latter interpretation was first proposed in 1900 by Barrett Wendell, and the details in the poem upon which this reading is based are rather convincing. As Hyatt

Waggoner points out in his *American Poets: From the Puritans to the Present* (1968), the shay is specifically "a 'deacon's' masterpiece, and it disappeared just as the parson got to 'fifthly' in his sermon." The religious element in the poem is insistent, and although Calvinism as such is not mentioned, "those who wanted to take the hint could do so."

Even more convincing is Holmes's emphasis on the fact that the shay was constructed in 1755, a singular year in the history of Calvinism, or, more precisely, in its decline. In 1755 came the death of Jonathan Edwards, the author of the Calvinist tract *The Freedom of the Will* (1754), as well as the great Lisbon earthquake, an event which raised serious questions concerning free will and original sin. Between Edwards' death and the earthquake, Calvinism suffered blows from which it never recovered, and by 1855 that inflexible system of religious beliefs was perceived as being so inappropriate for the rapidly changing American way of life that it was simply rejected wholesale. Further support for this reading of "The Deacon's Masterpiece" is to be found in Holmes's personal attitude toward Calvinism: He felt that it was "not just mistaken but vicious." As Waggoner further reveals, Holmes felt that Calvinism not only

> denied man his dignity, it denied God his sublimity, reducing him to an unjust Oriental potentate. But most of all it offended the moral sense, especially in its doctrine of Election. "Any decent person," he once wrote, "ought to go mad if he really holds . . . such opinions."

Several other interpretations of "The Deacon's Masterpiece" have been offered (including the theory that it is an allegory about manufacturing), but in the light of Holmes's personal contempt for Calvinism and various details in the poem, it seems most reasonable to agree with Barrett Wendell's reading. The poem can be enjoyed even without accepting or rejecting it as a religious allegory. Its rollicking couplets, thick New England dialect, and lively humor still make interesting reading; it helps to explain why Holmes is regarded today as a master of light verse.

"THE CHAMBERED NAUTILUS"

Even better known than "The Deacon's Masterpiece" is "The Chambered Nautilus." The controlling image of the poem is the shell of a type of cephalopod native to the South Pacific and Indian oceans. The shell, a "ship of pearl," fancifully believed to sail about in the depths of the ocean, has been washed ashore and split open—"Its irised ceiling rent, its sunless crypt unsealed!" The splitting has revealed the internal structure of the shell: a spiral consisting of the progressively larger chambers which the cephalopod constructed, occupied, and abandoned as it grew to maturity. The image of that broken shell with its spiraling chambers is interpreted as conveying a "heavenly message": "Build thee more stately mansions, O my soul,/ As the swift seasons roll!" The poem, with its carefully controlled movement from poetic fancy (the shell as the "venturous bark" which sails where "the cold sea-maids . . . sun their streaming hair") to science (the observation and analysis of the beached shell) to spiritual faith, demonstrates that the didactic impulse which was so potent a force in early American poetry was still evident in Holmes's verse in 1858.

Evident it was, but not necessarily predominant. Although Holmes was enough of a proper Boston Brahmin not to question anyone else's religious beliefs overtly (witness the veiled allegorical attack on Calvinism in "The Deacon's Masterpiece"), he was much more a man of science than a man of faith, and in that respect he embodied the increasing tendency on the part of nineteenth century Americans to place their trust in technology rather than in religion. True, the persona of "The Chambered Nautilus" sees a "heavenly message" in the structure of the shell, but this does not qualify his obvious interest in conchology.

"THE LIVING TEMPLE"

Holmes's preference for science over faith is especially evident in his poem "The Living Temple" (1858). Working from the biblical statement that "your body is the temple of the Holy Ghost," Holmes provides a surprisingly effective paean to human physiology. It is true that in the first of the seven stanzas he indicates that the poem is intended to prove that God's "Eternal wisdom" may be detected as clearly in man's "wondrous frame" as it is in "the world of light" and "in earth below," but the fact remains that for the next five stanzas God is quite forgotten in the elaborate, neoclassical discussion of the human body and its functions. The second stanza focuses on breathing: "The smooth soft air with pulse-like waves/ Flows murmuring through its hidden caves"; the third deals with the circulatory system, that "woven net" at the center of which is the "throbbing slave . . ./ Forever quivering o'er his task"; the fourth focuses on muscles and bones, the "living marbles jointed strong/ With glistening band and silvery thong"; the fifth discusses vision (the eyes as "lucid globes") and hearing ("Hark how the rolling surge of sound,/ Arches and spirals circling round"); and the sixth deals with the human brain ("the cloven sphere") and, more abstractly, the mind ("Think on the stormy world that dwells/ Locked in its dim and clustering cells").

Holmes's excitement over the wonders of the human body is palpable in this poem, so much so that the final stanza—with its apostrophe to the "Father" to "grant thy love divine/ To make these mystic temples thine," and its request that when the marvelous human body dies its "poor dust" may be "mould[ed] . . . into heavenly forms"—sounds more than a little forced and artificial. One may, in fact, be reminded of the poetry of Holmes's Puritan ancestor, Anne Bradstreet, who often undercut the powerful personal emotions in her verse by introducing religious doctrine (see, for example, "Some Verses Upon the Burning of Our House," where her agony over the loss of her home is ostensibly nullified by the thought that she has "an home on high erect;/ Framed by that mighty Architect"). Even though "The Living Temple" has its origins in a biblical text, and even though the first and last stanzas introduce matters of religious faith, the fact remains that this is far more a poem of physiology than of religious orthodoxy. Unfortunately, the tension generated between the real and the ostensible subject weakens the poem significantly.

OTHER MAJOR WORKS

LONG FICTION: *Elsie Venner*, 1861; *The Guardian Angel*, 1867; *A Mortal Antipathy*, 1885.

NONFICTION: *The Autocrat of the Breakfast-Table*, 1858; *The Professor at the Breakfast-Table*, 1860; *The Poet at the Breakfast-Table*, 1872; *John Lothrop Motley*, 1879; *Medical Essays, 1842-1882*, 1883; *Ralph Waldo Emerson*, 1885.

BIBLIOGRAPHY

Brenner, Rica. *Twelve American Poets Before 1900*. New York: Harcourt, Brace, 1933. In the thirty-page chapter on Holmes, Brenner quotes from a number of Holmes's poems in order to picture his life through his poetry. The author examines the poetry, using it to chart Holmes's growth as a poet and transformations in his method and style. This volume has chapters on Holmes's contemporaries, many of them his friends—Ralph Waldo Emerson, Henry Wadsworth Longfellow, John Greenleaf Whittier, James Russell Lowell, Walt Whitman, and Emily Dickinson—which help situate him in the cultural and literary era to which he belonged.

Broaddus, Dorothy C. *Genteel Rhetoric: Writing High Culture in Nineteenth-Century Boston*. Columbia: University of South Carolina Press, 1999. A historical survey of rhetoric in nineteenth century Boston: how it was taught and its use in the promotion of culture and intelectual argument. The rhetorical technique of Oliver Wendell Holmes is discussed with those of Thomas Wentworth Higginson, James Russell Lowell, and Ralph Waldo Emerson. Includes bibliographical references and index.

Carter, Everett. "The Typicality of Oliver Wendell Holmes." In *Themes and Directions in American Literature: Essays in Honor of Leon Howard*, edited by Ray B. Browne and Donald Pizer. Lafayette, Ind.: Purdue University Studies, 1969. Carter's premise is that Holmes's work should be examined not in a search for literary originality and uniqueness but using an approach that recognizes his literary virtues as typicality and representativeness of his culture. Holmes's work, though currently unfashionable, Carter says, embodies the conventional beliefs of his times and was given form by these beliefs. Includes notes and bibliographic references.

Howe, M. A. De Wolfe. *Holmes of the Breakfast Table*. 1939. Reprint. Mamaroneck, N.Y.: P. P. Appel, 1972. This 172-page, illustrated biographical study divides Holmes's life into four periods. Each chapter uses his poetry in part to help describe his endeavors and illuminate his life. Contains an index.

Hoyt, Edwin Palmer. *The Improper Bostonian: Dr. Oliver Wendell Holmes*. New York: William Morrow,

1979. This definitive biography is thorough and well researched, with generous notes on each chapter. All twenty-nine chapters are short, well focused, and readable. Holmes as a literary figure is studied primarily in chapters 16-20, which quote a number of poems in full and in part. Supplemented by illustrations and a good index.

Small, Miriam Rossiter. *Oliver Wendell Holmes.* New York: Twayne, 1962. Small looks at Holmes's work in three groups: the Breakfast-Table series, the novels, and the poems for Harvard occasions. Her biocritical study follows a chronology established by the autobiographical echoes in his prose and poetry. In addition to six chapters, the book includes a chronology, references and notes, a select bibliography, and an index.

Sullivan, Wilson. *New England Men of Letters.* New York: Macmillan, 1972. By showing how their lives resulted in their work, Sullivan hopes to bring his ten subjects alive for a contemporary audience. The problems they explored in their work—social, philosophical, moral, religious—are explored for their relevance to current readers. The short chapter on Holmes uses his poetry to enliven an overview of his life and accomplishments.

Alice Hall Petry;
bibliography updated by the editors

MIROSLAV HOLUB

Born: Pilseň, Czechoslovakia; September 13, 1923
Died: Prague, Czech Republic; July 14, 1998

PRINCIPAL POETRY
Denní služba, 1958
Achilles a želva, 1960
Slabikář, 1961
Jdi a otevři dveře, 1962
Tak zvané srdce, 1963
Zcela nesoustavná zoologie, 1963
Kam teče krev, 1963

Selected Poems, 1967
Ačkoli, 1969 (*Although,* 1971)
Notes of a Clay Pigeon, 1977
Sagittal Section: Poems New and Selected, 1980
Interferon: Or, On Theater, 1982
On the Contrary and Other Poems, 1984
The Fly, 1987
Syndrom mizející plíce, 1990 (*Vanishing Lung Syndrome,* 1990)
Poems Before and After, 1990
Intensive Care: Selected and New Poems, 1996
The Rampage, 1997

OTHER LITERARY FORMS
Miroslav Holub's literary reputation rests primarily on his poetry, but he also published several collections of prose as well as more than one hundred scientific papers and the monograph *Immunology of Nude Mice* (1989). He has also produced essays on mostly scientific, autobiographical, and cultural topics.

ACHIEVEMENTS
A widely renowned immunologist as well as an acclaimed literary figure, Miroslav Holub successfully combined the two seemingly disparate careers of scientist and poet. He is generally regarded as one of the most important poets of Eastern Europe to emerge after World War II and is widely praised for his ability to integrate scientific fact and human experience in his poetry. His poetry, as well as his essay collections, has been translated and published in many languages, and he has been widely acclaimed outside his homeland, especially in the English-speaking world.

During the 1960's and 1970's, Holub was a highly sought after reader of his poetry, performing at such locations as the Spoleto Festival in Italy, the Lincoln Center Festival in New York, the Harrogate Festival in England, Poetry International in Holland, and the Cambridge Poetry Festival in England. He was a writer in residence at Oberlin College for a semester in 1979 and again in 1982 and was also awarded an honorary doctorate.

Because of his success as a scientist, Holub was able to travel widely even during the Cold War days of the Iron Curtain, conducting research and presenting papers at scientific conferences. His most notable scientific achievement was the development of a strain of nude (hairless) mice that were used to study various diseases.

BIOGRAPHY

Born in Pilseň, Czechoslovakia, Miroslav Holub was the son of Josef Holub, a lawyer who worked as a railway clerk, and Františka (Dvoráková) Holub, a language teacher. By the time Holub completed secondary school, Nazi occupation had closed down Czech universities. As a conscripted worker in a warehouse and at a railway station, he was writing and publishing poetry by the end of World War II.

In 1948 in a national student competition, he was selected as winner of the third prize for poetry and fifth prize for prose, but the communist student leader dissolved the students' union rather than award the prizes. The only permissible poetry was in the Socialist Realist vein, a style that advocated communist ideals and adhered to narrow political and moral mores, which Holub viewed as a cover-up of reality. As a result, Holub became silent for a period, devoting himself to science and receiving his M.D. in 1953 from Charles University. That year he also became editor of *Vesmír*, a popular science magazine, and he eventually returned to writing poetry as a kind of defense against the absurdity of the social order. In 1954, he became an immunologist on the staff of the Institute of Microbiology in Prague and also began work on his doctorate in immunology, completing the degree in 1958, the same year he published his first collection of poetry, *Denní služba*.

During the 1960's, Holub published several volumes of poetry in Czech which officials generally disregarded, but after he began to participate actively in the reformist movement by publishing essays in major Czech cultural and literary periodicals, he lost his job at the Institute of Microbiology in 1970. In addition, like many other Czech writers at the time, he was prohibited from publishing his work, and his books were removed from libraries. A new poetry collection ready for publication was destroyed, and Holub had to publish his compilation of selections by Edgar Allan Poe anonymously.

Miroslav Holub

In 1973, the Czech press published a self-criticism in which Holub affirmed loyalty to the communist authorities. Although this action later caused negative reaction by fellow writers and the Czech public, freedom to work as a scientist was crucial to Holub. Subsequently he was allowed to continue his scientific research at the Institute for Clinical and Experimental Medicine in Prague, where he remained until his death in 1998. He was nevertheless unable to publish his poetry in Czechoslovakia except "under the table," where his works sold quickly. Meanwhile, Holub's work had been introduced to the English-speaking world in 1967 with the publication of *Selected Poems* by Penguin as part of its Modern European Poets series.

Although Holub spoke fluent English and read widely in it, he continued to write poetry in Czech. In periods of repression in Czechoslovakia, the English translations actually appeared before the Czech originals and brought him international acclaim. Yet Holub considered poetry a pastime. According to Holub in a 1967 interview by Stephen Stepanchev in *New Leader*, the Czech Writers Union offered him funding to be able to devote two years to poetry, but he refused, indicating his love for science and noting, "I'm afraid that, if I had all the time in the world to write my poems, I would write nothing at all." Though his literary friends were suspicious of his scientific profession and likewise his scientific colleagues questioned his poetic side, Holub himself disavowed a real conflict between science and poetry. He acknowledged, however, that for him science and poetry endured an "uneasy relationship," but he continued work in both until his death in 1998.

ANALYSIS

Beginning with his earliest poems, Miroslav Holub was clearly affected by what he viewed as the absurdities of life in a socialist regime. In his essay "Poetry Against Absurdity," he declared that following the communist takeover in Czechoslovakia there could be "No more words. Just sharp, concrete, viable, bleeding images, partly inherited from the surrealist imagery of the thirties." In an interview in *The Economist*, Holub indicated that lyrical poetry would have been impossible for him to write given the psychological conditions under which he lived:

> When you live in a time that forbids you to say anything that you wish to say, when you are obliged to conceal part of yourself, it is better not to speak about the self at all. It is better not to express inner feelings because, frankly, you cannot flow about your feelings. The conditions are so terrible that the only thing possible is plain statement.

Therefore, from his earliest days as a poet, Holub rejected the Czech lyrical and romantic tradition. He regarded American Imagist and physician William Carlos Williams, another scientist/poet, as a major influence, but most critics note that Holub moved beyond the simplicity of Williams's verse to write complex, intellectual poems with layers of meaning. Holub's poetry reflects his incisive mind, his scientific bent toward detailed examination, and his rational, analytical approach toward a subject. Scientific metaphors dominate, even in Holub's definition of poetry as "some sort of infection."

Holub's poetic style, with its closeness to prose and with its terseness and objectivity, made his poems extremely well suited for translating into English, and these translations brought Holub international acclaim. Nevertheless, some critics have bemoaned the "nightmarish mesh of translations" that exists. In English, for example, significant variations occur in different translations of the same poems. Still, as readers repeatedly confirm, Holub's poetry communicates effectively even in translation.

DENNÍ SLUŽBA

In his first collection of poems, *Denní služba* (day duty), Holub set the tone, subject matter, and style that he was to follow with only limited expansions and variations throughout his career. Although this work has not been translated in English as a collection, many of the individual poems are available in one or more of the English collections.

"In the Microscope" functions as a metaphor for all his poetry, with its implicit comparison of the poet and the scientist and its emphasis on getting to the essence of life. Holub the poet chooses to examine life in the same way as Holub the scientist—through a microscope. Under the microscope, what first appear to be "dreaming landscapes,/ lunar, derelict" turn out to be full of "tillers of the soil" and "fighters/ who lay down their lives/ for a song."

Holub explores another of his major concerns in the form of a modernized version of the traditional fairy tale "Cinderella." The heroine spends her life dutifully, resignedly, solitarily carrying out her work of sorting peas, knowing that "she is on her own./ No helpful pigeons; she's alone./ And yet the peas, they *will* be sorted out." On one level Holub comments, as he so frequently does, on the repression of totalitarianism, but the poem moves on to comment on the mundaneness of life in general.

SAGITTAL SECTION

The first collection of Holub's poetry to be published in the United States, *Sagittal Section* had a bisected skull as its cover illustration. The illustration, as well as the poems themselves, emphasizes Holub's scientific point of view and his often expressed desire to lay things bare. The allusive, elliptical, ironic, and surrealist quality of his works is demonstrated repeatedly but nowhere better than in "The Fly." A female fly during the battle of Crécy mates with "a brown-eyed male," meditates "on the immortality of flies," lays "her eggs/ on the single eye/ of Johann Uhr,/ the Royal Armorer," and is then "eaten by a swift/ fleeing/ from the fires of Estrés."

INTERFERON

As David Young notes in his introduction to *Interferon: Or, On Theater*, this collection of poems functions through "two major metaphors, one from the world of immunological research that constitutes Holub's other profession, and one from the history of human attempts to understand the world by artificial and imaginative representations of it." Although the work is divided into four sections—"Biological Poems," "Towards a Theory of the Theater," "The Merry Adventures of the Puppets" and "Endgames"—both metaphors run throughout the work and are intermingled in various poems.

The ten-page title poem "Interferon" serves as a focal point for the collection by showing that the medical and theatrical metaphors are actually one. As Young says,

Interference on the cellular level corresponds to the presence of theater in our lives; both are attempts to arrest and mesmerize destructive forces, disease and history, attempts that may succeed in the short run and fail in the long.

Clearly, the work reflects the experiences of postwar Eastern Europe with poetry that is impersonal, detached, reduced to the basics. Yet some personal elements emerge in love poems like "Landscapes" and "United Flight 412." As forecast by the title, theater plays a significant role; in fact, some of the pieces might more aptly be called drama rather than poetry. Punch and Judy and Faust are major players, and myth and allegory predominate.

VANISHING LUNG SYNDROME

Perhaps Holub's finest collection of poetry translated into English, *Vanishing Lung Syndrome* covers vast areas of space and time with numerous historical, mythical, and contemporary references from a wide range of cultures. The poet moves rapidly from the Aztecs to Josef Bozek (one of the founders of Czech mechanics) in Bohemia in 1817 to a pedestrian who "slips into Wendy's" (the fast-food restaurant chain) in late twentieth century New York. Medical metaphors and ironic

paradoxes abound as evidenced in the poem "Yoga": "What would they [poets] be without their disease./ The disease is their health." The opening poem, "1751," focuses on insane asylums and officious fools, while the concluding poem "The Fall from the Green Frog," presents "Mommy/ drowned in her lung edema" and Dad "cremated with ribbon of vomit in the corner/ of his mouth."

One of many overtly political poems written while Czechoslovakia was still under the constraints of communist rule, the 1988 poem "Wenceslas Square Syndrome" captures the sense of the poet on the tightrope. The poem opens in the dead of a winter's night while police patrol the square in the mists that hug the ground, the "smog of silence." Into this image of cold and "unreal" Holub inserts an image of the life-force, but one that is "schizophrenic" in the totalitarian cold:

> But from the linden that forgot
> to lose its leaves resounds a blackbird's mighty voice,
> . . . .
> song of the only December schizophrenic blackbird,
> mighty, everlasting song of the only
> schizophrenic blackbird,
> yes, of course,
> a song.

POEMS BEFORE AND AFTER

A valuable collection, *Poems Before and After* contains selected works from eleven of Holub's Czech volumes. Although most of the poems have been published in other English collections, such a large selection together in a single volume provides readers with an excellent overview of Holub's career. The "Before" and "After" of the title refer to poems written (though not necessarily published) before or after the 1968 Prague Spring, the liberal period of January-August, 1968, under the first secretary of the Czechoslovak Communist Party Alexander Dubček during which liberal reforms were instituted but which ended with the Soviet-led invasion of the country on August 20. The poems show Holub's development as poet both in complexity and in tone, and the "After" poems tend to reflect a darker, more pessimistic view of life, though not one without hope.

INTENSIVE CARE AND THE RAMPAGE

Holub's last two English-language collections include poems from throughout his career interspersed with some new ones. The additions reflect how science, history, and myth continued to dominate Holub's poetry until his death. His tone remains skeptical and ironic, even reflecting a wariness about the newly gained freedom that came with the Velvet Revolution (the end of communist rule in Czechoslovakia). In "The Moth," Holub says,

> Freedom makes
> the moth tremble
> forever, that is,
> twenty-two hours.

In acknowledging the extreme brevity of the moth's life, Holub signifies his fears that freedom will also be short-lived.

Likewise his poem "At Last" celebrates newly gained intellectual and political freedom and expresses his anxieties about the future. He worries that "someone might cast/ a spell on us" or, perhaps worse, that, not knowing how to handle this freedom, "We might even/ be hostage/ to ourselves."

With poems like "Head-Smashed-In" and "The Slaughter-House," the final section of *The Rampage* suggests that life is violent, irrational, and full of paradoxes, but the poems are usually tempered with a sense of compassion and the slightest note of hope, as in "Landscape with poets":

> and there will be
> either a new form of life
> or, possibly,
> nothing.

OTHER MAJOR WORKS

NONFICTION: *K principu rolničky*, 1987 (*The Jingle Bell Principle*, 1992); *Immunology of Nude Mice*, 1989; *The Dimension of the Present Moment: Essays*, 1990; *Ono se letelo: Suita z rodného mesta*, 1994 (*Supposed to Fly: A Sequence from Pilsen, Czechoslovakia*, 1996); *Shedding Life: Disease, Politics, and Other Human Conditions*, 1997.

BIBLIOGRAPHY

Eagle, Herbert. "Syntagmatic Structure in the Free Verse of Miroslav Holub." *Rackham Literary Studies* 3 (1972): 29-49. Using a theory of free verse based on writings by the Formalists and Structuralists, Eagle provides a detailed, technical analysis of specific poems by Holub. Eagle uses the term "sytagmatic balance" to define the intonational principle that he believes unifies much of Holub's free verse.

Heaney, Seamus. "The Fully Exposed Poem." *Parnassus* 11, no. 1 (1983): 4-16. An excellent review of Holub's *Sagittal Section* and *Interferon: Or, On Theater* and a discussion of the effectiveness of Holub's poetry in translation.

Holub, Miroslav. "Poetry Against Absurdity." *Poetry Review* 80 (Summer, 1990): 4-8. Based on a lecture given by Holub at the Conference on Czech Literature, 1890-1990, at New York University in March of 1990, this essay effectively recalls the attempts by Holub and fellow Czech poets to record "the feeling of human responsibility in the overwhelming absurdity" of life following the Communist takeover in Czechoslovakia.

Walker, David, ed. *Poets Reading: The FIELD Symposia*. Oberlin, Ohio: Oberlin College Press, 1999. This collection of brief but excellent essays on Holub's poetry was originally published as a symposium on Holub in *FIELD* magazine. Dennis Schmitz's essay "Half a Hedgehog" and Tom Andrews's study "Hemophilia/Los Angeles" are particularly effective analyses of individual poems.

Young, David. Introduction to *Interferon: Or, On Theater*. Oberlin, Ohio: Oberlin College, 1982. A brief examination of the role of science and theater in Holub's poems.

Verbie Lovorn Prevost

ARNO HOLZ

Born: Rastenburg, East Prussia; April 26, 1863
Died: Berlin, Germany; October 26, 1929

PRINCIPAL POETRY

Klinginsherz, 1883
Buch der Zeit, 1884
Phantasus, 1898, enlarged 1916, 1925, 1929, 1961
Dafnis, 1904

OTHER LITERARY FORMS

Literary history recognizes Arno Holz as the cofounder and first important author and theorist of Naturalism in Germany. In the novella, *Papa Hamlet* (1889; coauthored with Johannes Schlaf, under the pseudonym Bjarne P. Holmsen), Holz contrasts the horrid living conditions and death of an unemployed Shakespearean actor and his family with the idealistic verses which the actor constantly recites. His play, *Die Familie Selicke* (pr., pb. 1890), is a bleak tragedy, ridiculed by traditional critics as "primitive animal grunts of an ape theater," which presents the misery of an impoverished family, on Christmas Eve, bitterly awaiting the arrival home of the drunken father with his already spent paycheck, while the youngest child is dying.

Holz's significant theoretical writings are *Revolution der Lyrik* (1899), which rejects rhyme, meter, and all artificial stratagems of traditional poetry in favor of the natural rhythms of Holz's own *Mittelachsendichtung* (central-axis poetry), which is based "on the natural rhythms of things themselves"; and *Die Kunst: Ihr Wesen und ihre Gesetze* (1891-1893), which seeks to develop and present a new "natural-scientific" aesthetic.

Holz also wrote four monumental plays: *Sozialaristokraten* (pb. 1896), one of the few successful Naturalistic comedies; *Die Blechschmiede* (pb. 1902; the sheet metal workshop), a 754-page satirical verse-drama with a *dramatis personae* of more than 3,200 characters; *Sonnenfinsternis* (pb. 1908; eclipse of the sun), the tragedy of a Naturalist painter who has mastered the "most complex precision-machinery of artistic technique" but cannot produce a masterpiece until his insight is heightened by the breakup of his marriage; and, finally, *Ignorabimus: Tragödie* (pb. 1913), an epistemological tragedy that pits natural-scientific positivism against Haeckelian cosmic monism.

ACHIEVEMENTS

In nonlyrical genres, Arno Holz is firmly established as the cofounder, with Johannes Schlaf, of Naturalism or "consistent realism," which sought to reproduce reality with photographic precision, neutrally and without structure and emphasis; he was also the coinventor of the technique known as *Sekundenstil*, which meticulously registers every detail and change in an event "from second to second." On the stage, this technique is manifest in the seemingly unedited, undramatic dialogue, enabling dramatic time and performance time to coincide.

Holz's theoretical writings on lyric poetry have a certain permanent value insofar as he was the first theorist in Germany to break with the old notion of metrics; in a broader perspective, he pioneered the quest for the "essential" innate laws of artistic materials, a quest which Impressionism, Expressionism, abstract art, Surrealism, and all modern art movements have pursued. He was wrong, however, in believing that his *Mittelachsenlyrik* (central-axis lyrics) would be the one universal form of all future poetry. Despite feeble attempts at imitation by other poets, including Rainer Maria Rilke, this central-axis poetry never became generally accepted, and today it is regarded as an interesting but merely idiosyncratic approach.

Recent critical appreciation has shifted from Holz's Naturalist contributions to the elaborate later versions of his great lyric masterpiece *Phantasus* (the short proto-*Phantasus*, 1898, although considerably less brilliant, has both intrinsic and hermeneutic value). This work did not, however, fulfill Holz's ambition to create a work which would be for the twentieth century what Homer's epics were for classical antiquity, or what Dante's *La divina commedia* (c. 1320; *The Divine Comedy*, 1802) was for the Middle Ages. *Dafnis*, written in the language and style of late-sixteenth century Baroque poetry, although generally acclaimed for its antiquarian virtuosity, seems thematically limited to a kind of Naturalist pansexualism. *Buch der Zeit* expresses the new *Zeitgeist* within traditional forms.

BIOGRAPHY

Arno Holz, the son of a druggist, was born on April 26, 1863, in Rastenburg, East Prussia. His family moved to Berlin when he was twelve. After his parents' divorce, he stayed in Berlin with his mother and attended high school but was not graduated. After a short period as an editor of a local newspaper, he spent the rest of his life in Berlin as a free-lance writer, mostly in relative poverty. For about two years, he shared a room with Johannes Schlaf, and together they introduced Naturalism into Germany. Gerhart Hauptmann dedicated his epochal *Vor Sonnenaufgang* (1889) to Bjarne P. Holmsen, their joint pseudonym. In the literary club *Durch*, they associated with the other leading Naturalists. Later, Holz broke with Schlaf, and his dogmatic intransigence led him to engage in bitter disputes with Schlaf and others. For a time, Holz's plays enjoyed a limited success. He also earned some money from toy patents, but he never attained a secure financial existence. His complete works in ten volumes were published during his lifetime. He died in Berlin on October 26, 1929, a bitter and forgotten man.

ANALYSIS

Arno Holz's masterpiece in the lyric genre is *Phantasus*, a poem-cycle on which he worked for more than thirty years, and which developed from two tiny fifty-page booklets (1898) to several successive expanded editions (1916, 1925, 1929), ultimately resulting in a final version sixteen hundred pages long (published posthumously in 1961). In the first edition, the poems were short, only one being more than one page long, and so scantily developed as to be almost outlines rather than poems—the term "telegram poetry" has since been applied to them. By the 1916 edition, however, more by a process of internal germination and luxuriation than by cumulative addition, the book had reached monumental proportions. A single line could have as many as thirty-five words, and one poem in book 6 is 372 pages long and contains one of the longest sentences on record in the German language— a single sentence occupying seventy pages. Thus, an author who first became known as a cofounder of the Naturalist movement in Germany climaxed his literary career with a work which, in its Baroque virtuosity, at first sight seems to represent the very opposite of Naturalism.

PHANTASUS, 1898

The poem-cycle *Phantasus* aims to be a modern *Divine Comedy*, a cosmic embodiment of the twentieth century "scientific" worldview, largely as understood in the evolutionary writings of the monist philosopher Ernst Haeckel. The Haeckelian conception of the embryonic repetition of phylogenetic evolutionary stages underlies Arno Holz's self-interpretation: "Just as before my birth I passed through the entire physical development of my species, at least in its main stages, so since my birth through its psychic ones. I was 'everything' and the numerous and variegated residues of this [evolution] are stored up in me."

The lyrical technique by which the vast panorama of world reality is deployed in *Phantasus* is, basically, the detailed elaboration of introspective contents, whether from the real world or imaginary worlds, and the identification of the lyric self with each and all. In Holz's own words: "The ultimate secret of the . . . *Phantasus*-composition consists in my incessantly splitting myself up into the most heterogeneous things and forms." Many short poems of proto-*Phantasus*, which are lengthened only moderately in later editions, identify the lyrical self with particular beings: natural objects, such as a star ("I am a star, I shine") or a lake (". . . my heart is this lake. . . . Purple fishes swim through my dark water"); real human beings ("I am the richest man on earth"); mythical figures ("I am the dwarf Turlitipu"); imaginary creatures ("Every thousand years I grow wings. Every thousand years my purple dragon body rushes through the darkness"); a cultural artifact, such as a Greek statue ("Corinth created me. I saw the sea") or an Oriental idol ("At night around my temple grove, seventy bronze cows stand watch"); or God himself, in caricature ("My silver cloud-beard floods the sky. I snore").

Holz's aesthetic dicta, "Art equals nature minus x," and "Art has a tendency to become nature again," are thus not meant in the sense of a meticulous Naturalistic copying of external reality. For Holz, the location of detailed "nature" is in the inner experience, memory, thought, and aspirations of the individual consciousness, where *all* reality is concentrated. The Holzian postulate that makes it possible for the lyric consciousness to become coextensive with the entire universe and with each item in it is the phenomenological view that reality exists neither centrifugally in a transcendental realm beyond things nor centripetally in a quasi-substantial subjective self but on a middle ground in the phenomena themselves. One poem begins: "Do not listen beyond things. Do not brood over yourself. Do not seek yourself. You do not exist." The poem then identifies the self: "You are the dispersing smoke that curls from your cigar," "the raindrop on the window-sill," the "soft crackling" of a kerosene lamp. The subjective-objective dichotomy is overcome in the phenomena which are understood as the contents of consciousness, where the lyrical self and the universe coincide—which accords with the psychology of Ernst Mach.

In *Phantasus*, this self reaches to the outer limits of time and space, ranging from the infinite to the infinitesimal, open-endedly in either direction. The objects in space are, moreover, not static and inert but dynamic and changing: "tattered planet-systems" mark late stages of stellar development; "glacial primal suns" have not yet ignited to full life. An organic metaphor depicts the prolific genesis of new reality in the cosmos: beyond "red fixed-star forests which are bleeding to death" [that is, dispersing their energy] . . . beyond worlds of night and nothingness, grow glimmering new worlds—trillions of crocus blossoms." An organic metaphor also succinctly affirms the paleontological antiquity of the lyric self in a "telegram-poem," which later became the first poem of the entire expanded cycle:

> Seven billion years before my birth
> I was a sword-lily.
> My seeking roots
> suctioned
> into a star.
> On its dark water
> floated
> my huge blue blossom.

Stylistically, this organic metaphor which structures Holz's cosmic imagination is made even more evident in the lexical and syntactical profusion of the 1925 *Phantasus* version. In that version, the genesis of the stars and galaxies is visualized in the metaphor of a plant scattering its sparkling spores into interstellar darkness. From a relatively static impressionistic snapshot, the poem has developed into a sinewy, twisting vine sprouting forth lexical tendrils out of its plant-like syntax. This is typical: In the later versions of *Phantasus*, the proliferation of verbs, adverbs, adjec-

tives, and pages-long prepositional phrases destabilizes the images by inundating the nouns in a flood of less substantial parts of speech. In proto-*Phantasus*, Holz's central-axis poetry served to capture momentary static impressions; in the expanded versions it evolves into a syntactic image of the pervasive organicism of all reality.

PHANTASUS, 1929

The idea of the cosmic universalism of the lyric self is developed in five very long poems of the 1929 *Phantasus*. In addition to the two-page introductory "Seven Billion Years" poem, book 1 consists entirely of two very long cosmic poems totaling 180 pages. The first, "Machtmythus" (myth of power), which uses a seven-line poem from proto-*Phantasus* as its point of departure, describes with meticulous precision the gradual rise and ultimate decadence of a vast Asiatic empire under a mighty leader (symbolizing the lyric self). Built on deceit and cruelty, this empire nevertheless made Buddha a cultural possibility. Sometimes "at night in dreams" this monstrous "beast of power" that had overrun the whole earth like a deadly global catastrophe seeks to break free again. The second, "Pronunciamento," follows human history and evolution backward from the storming of the Bastille to the "tiny clump of protoplasm" that made the first hesitant transition from inanimate to animate reality. The "pronouncement" asserts the eternal recurrence of the self: "I have always existed" in the men and women of all cultures and in all living creatures, and so also "I will never die." Some stages along the journey backward in time—all experienced as a primary participant by the lyric self—are a seventeenth century witch-burning, the discovery of America by Christopher Columbus, the Children's Crusade, the raids of the Muslims and Vikings, the lascivious excesses of the Roman Empress Messalina, the crossing of the Alps by Hannibal, the survival of the battle of Salamis by an oarsman, the fighting off of a huge python by a prehuman, and the engagement of dinosaurs in mortal combat in the Jurassic age on terrain that is now the bed of the Indian Ocean.

All book 3 is a single 467-page poem called "Das tausandundzweite Märchen," which developed from a fifteen-line poem in proto-*Phantasus*. The framework situation of the poet's attic room, his tobacco pipe, and his occasional drink of brandy, is recalled at intervals throughout the poem. The "story" falls into two parts. The first is a journey to Asia, partly on an imaginary zeppelin, partly on foot through a variety of wild landscapes and deserts, including the Himalayas. The second part is a surrealistic twelve-course banquet, a sequence of Herculean ordeals in which various repulsive figures present disgusting foods for the "lyric self" to eat. Each hideous presenter and each nauseating food is described most graphically, and the "lyric self" overcomes its revulsion and succeeds in downing each disgusting course by dwelling imaginatively on the charms and qualities of the Princess Gülnäre in twelve different dialectically positive elaborations which always begin with the words "She has thick, three-yard long, five-braided pigtails that weigh four pounds." Symbolically, the whole sequence represents physical revulsion for organic matter, which is then overcome by the great organic beauty and delight represented by the female body.

Comprising most of book 4, "Grosser Dichter-mittwochnachmittag in meiner Feuerstuhlbude" is a complex literary satire based on a nineteen-line proto-*Phantasus* poem. Finally, a 109-page poem of book 5, titled "Die Hallelujawiese" ("The Alleluia Meadow"), grew from a ten-line "telegram-poem."

On its merry Alleluia Meadow
my joyous heart tolerates no shadow.
Red, laughing Rubens-saints
dance the cancan with Viennese laundry maids.
Under almost breaking liverwurst trees
Corregio kisses Io.
No one is embarrassed.
That ass Goethe lies aslant fat Caroline's lap.
Little winged rascals call "Prost,"
Jobst Sackmann [Johannes Schlaf], my darling, chugs
    down a caraway brandy.

The first phrase alone, "On its merry Alleluia Meadow," is expanded to more than three full pages (125 lines) by the addition of numerous adjectives and phrases in clusters that define Holz's realm of creative imagination, symbolized by the Alleluia Meadow. On one hand, it is Naturalistic, seeking to embrace all reality without any

moralistic scruples or condemnation; it is, among many other things, "wanton, hilarious, madcap," "pan-cosmic, ownspheric, kaleidoscopic, gigantic"; "this-earthly, Utopian, other-worldly, Atlantean"; "faunic, mischievous, phrynically bacchantic, orgiastic, fantastic, cynically corybantic"; "unrestrained, . . . unaffected, untrained, undegenerate, hyperanimalic"; in short, it is "unashamedly amoral." On the other hand, it is idealistic, embracing all the most subtle and sublime contents and aspirations of human subjectivity "in most exquisite . . . delicate, pure"; "most aetherial, legendary, chimeric"; "most prismatic, jubilatic [sic], ecstatic"; "most irridescent, rainbowlike heavenly colors . . . with Arcadian, El-Doradan, Scheherazadan Paradise-wonders"; and it longs for the "most phantasmagoric, hallucinatoric, fairytalesplendorifloric, . . . most seraphic, sublime, cherubic enchantments." In this poem, the poetic imagination "tolerates no shadow," in the sense that it exercises the utopian function of excluding all unhappiness and torments, whether inherent in life itself or inflicted by man and society, and endorses absolutely every desire of the human heart.

In the original short poem, this utopian vision is symbolized by disparate persons and cultural figures engaging in sexual activity or drinking together. In the vastly elaborated version, all men, animals, and birds participate in a vast cosmic orgy with the sex act represented by three and a half large pages of three-word rapturous sexual exclamations in primitive dialect mingled with onomatopoeic bird calls to represent the satisfaction of a primary urge. The wellspring of all this activity is "every desire . . . every lust that ever was vibrant in man, Satan, God, or animal." The jungle of verbal-proliferations builds up to frenzied heights; copulation covers the whole earth; all languages and nationalities, all territories and dwellings are involved; countless historical figures and lesser persons are all engaged in a great sexual concatenation. Four of these long poems, "Machmythus," "Pronunciamento," "Das tausand-undzweite Märchen," and "The Alleluia Meadow," are among Holz's finest works.

PROTO-PHANTASUS BOOKLETS

The two small proto-*Phantasus* booklets supply the primary intuitive substratum on which the great sixteen-hundred-page *Phantasus* is erected. This early version can be characterized as Impressionist, with *Jugendstil* and Symbolist motifs. This form of Impressionism works with little dabs of color, little strokes of intuited accuracy. In addition to the broad cosmic motifs, numerous small proto-*Phantasus* poems center on the Impressionist themes of the children's paradise, the small German town, exotic or mythical lands, dreams, love and sex, gods and demons, the poetic mode of existence—themes which provide the spark to ignite the volatile poetic imagination. One childhood poem specifically describes the Holzian process of poetic fantasizing: "I lie on the old herb-deck and 'simulate'"; Holz pictures two neighbors as "God" and the "devil." God is the baker Knorr, who wears a white hat and has liqueur bottles displayed in his window. When the sunlight shines through them, the pastry looks yellow, red and blue. The devil is the chimney sweep Killkant in his black cylinder hat and dirty shoes, who rolls his eyes—making them look white—whenever he passes by "God's" liqueur bottles. This kind of "simulation" on a boyish level gives an idea of the symbolic truth-structures in Holz's sensory images. The *tertium comparationis* here is the have/have-not category. The boy, the chimney sweep, and the devil are have-nots. An image of desire is portrayed without protest and with great economy, using color ciphers—the object of desire bathed in beautiful colors, the frustrated desire imaged in the empty white of the eyes—but the sensory level also has beauty for its own sake, apart from any symbolic values, since reality resides in the phenomena as the content of consciousness.

Some of the childhood poems suggest that the move from East Prussia must have been traumatic for the young Holz. The sentence, "Far away on the island Nurapu blooms the tree Bo" combines the exotic with nostalgia for childhood; memory of the "other world" of Grandmother's porcelain figurines and tulips reminds the poet how bleak his present existence is: "Here no cuckoo-clock calls, no lavender-pot smells." Hearing a bird, the poet remembers what he had had as a child "and then—forgot." Small-town Germany is also linked with the childhood-paradise motif: "Red roofs! Out of the chimneys here and there, smoke, up high in sunny air . . . now a hen cackles. The whole town smells of coffee." The exotic, the erotic, the childlike fantasy blend

together in *Jugendstil* poems of palaces, temples, parks, and naked girls. Peering through a window of "a little palace in an old park" he sees "a rose-patterned tapestry, a blue divan, and a naked lady feeding a cockatoo." One poem describing a group of chic boarding-school girls ends with the narrator catching the most beautiful one by the waist and exclaiming in a *Jugendstil Marseillaise*: "Girls, disrobe and dance naked between swords." A similar sex-wish motif occurs in the mythical form of a shaggy faun catching a naked girl, or, comically, God himself snapping up "a little *fin de siècle* girl—black stockings, yellow silk waistcoat, and lily-underpants." In one dragon-demon poem, the creature observes the rabble's baseness and rapacious greed; without conjunction or transition the last line follows: "My claws glimmer, my eyes glow." The entire threat of retaliation by a violated moral order is contained in these luminous traces.

PHANTASUS, 1961

The later editions of *Phantasus* add little to the primary intuitive base. Despite its fifteen hundred additional pages, the final edition contains only about forty new poems; all the rest are expanded from the one hundred one-page poems of the 1898 proto-*Phantasus*. The additional length results not from the discovery of new basic motifs, but from the elaboration and explication of detail, from linguistic acrobatics and analytical cerebration, from the attempt—under the influence of Walt Whitman—to inject ever more circumstantial reality into the discourse, often with cascades of synonyms and sentences that are thirty or forty pages long. The compact cultivated gardens of the originally impressionistic poems have been overtaken, as it were, by a linguistic tropical jungle of spoken rhetoric, an encyclopedic effort to capture every detail and nuance of external reality in a manner compatible with the modern "natural-scientific" worldview.

OTHER MAJOR WORKS

SHORT FICTION: *Papa Hamlet*, 1889 (as Bjarne P. Holmsen; with Johannes Schlaf).

PLAYS: *Die Familie Selicke*, pr., pb. 1890; *Sozialaristokraten*, pb. 1896; *Die Blechschmiede*, pb. 1902; *Sonnenfinsternis*, pb. 1908; *Ignorabimus: Tragödie*, pb. 1913.

NONFICTION: *Die Kunst: Ihr Wesen und ihre Gesetze*, 1891-1893; *Revolution der Lyrik*, 1899; *Die befreite deutsche Wortkunst*, 1921.

MISCELLANEOUS: *Das Werk von Arno Holz*, 1924-1925 (10 volumes).

BIBLIOGRAPHY

Burns, Rob. *The Quest for Modernity: The Place of Arno Holz in Modern German Literature*. Bern, Germany: Lang, 1981. A critical study of Holz's work. Includes bibliographic references.

Domandi, Agnes, ed. *Modern German Literature*. New York: Ungar, 1972. Includes a short biographical and critical essay on Holz and his work.

McFarlane, J. W. "Arno Holz's 'Die Sozialaristokraten': A Study." *Modern Language Review* 44, no. 4 (October, 1949): 521-533. A critical assessment of a poem by Holz.

Oeste, Robert. *Arno Holz: The Long Poem and the Tradition of Poetic Experiment*. Bonn, Germany: Bouvier, 1982. An analysis of the poetic works of Holz and the historical background of epic and experimental poetry. Includes an index and a bibliography.

Wrasidlo, Barbara J. *The Politics of German Naturalism: Holz, Sudermann, and Hauptmann*. Ph.D. thesis. San Diego: University of California, 1986. Examines Naturalism in the works of Holz, Gerhart Hauptmann, and Hermann Sudermann.

David J. Parent
(including original translations);
bibliography updated by the editors

HOMER

Born: Possibly Ionia, Asia Minor; early ninth century B.C.E.

Died: Greece; c. late ninth century B.C.E.

PRINCIPAL POETRY

Iliad, c. 800 B.C.E. (English translation, 1611)

Odyssey, c. 800 B.C.E. (English translation, 1614)

OTHER LITERARY FORMS

Homer is noted only for his magnificent epic poems.

ACHIEVEMENTS

Homer's extant poetry consists of the *Iliad*, an epic of about sixteen thousand hexameter lines, and the *Odyssey*, a twelve-thousand-line poem in the same meter. A number of other poems attributed to Homer in late antiquity—the epigrams (twenty-six short poems contained in the *Life of Homer* that were attributed to Herodotus), *Margites*, *Batrachomyomachia* (battle of the frogs and mice), and the *Homeric Hymns* (thirty-three narrative hexameter poems in honor of various Greek divinities)—can be shown on the basis of style to postdate him. These latter poems may be either imitations or independent compositions in the general epic mode of the *Iliad* and the *Odyssey*.

Despite minor inconsistencies of detail—"even Homer nods," explained the Roman poet Horace—both the *Iliad* and the *Odyssey* give the impression of being complete compositions, unified in theme and elaborate in structure, which combine the powers of dramatic narrative poetry with the delicacy and nuance of lyric. Their aim is nothing less than to offer to posterity the world of the heroic past. This they accomplish with such force and conviction that the imaginative representation of the Trojan War and its aftermath becomes a kind of immortality: Just as the heroes of the *Iliad* and the *Odyssey* predict that they will become the subject of song, so Homer's song lives on. The supreme self-confidence of the genre, which exhibits heroes battling in order to gain the glory of being mentioned in epic poetry, must have been built upon the facts of social life in a highly critical, reputation-conscious culture. Homer was the ultimate representative of that culture. More than anything else, literacy may have caused its decline. It was Homer's achievement, then, to have composed so well that his work survived the onset of a new order, in which the poet's status as arbiter of the heroic, repository of tradition, and sole source of history, was drastically reduced. In terms of intellectual history, Homer may have been the genius who translated what was essentially "oral poetry" into a new medium: the written word.

Although his art is on a much larger scale, Homer still resembles the bards whom he portrays: Demodocus, Phemius, and Odysseus himself in the *Odyssey* and Achilles in book 9 of the *Iliad*. Like Achilles, who sings the heroic deeds of the ancestral heroes while sitting in his tent, Homer produces commemorative poetry. The naming of all the combatants in the Trojan conflict, in book 2 of the *Iliad*, is a relic of the sort of "catalog poetry" which must have been predominant in the traditional poetry of Greece before Homer. Comparative study has shown that the long and detailed battle scenes of the middle books in the *Iliad* represent a poetic genre that is paralleled by the heroic verse of many other cultures. Who fought a particular battle, which side won, and what the exploits were that brought about victory—these are the main concerns of such epics. Homer surpasses these martial epics. In the *Iliad*, he produces a poem which, while commemorating the fall of Troy (a historical event well known to ancient Greeks), he dwells more on the problem of human mor-

tality and its ramifications than on national pride over victory. One senses a profound and sympathetic poetic intelligence at work as Homer portrays the deaths of Hector and Patroclus and prefigures the death of Achilles. This universal sympathy extends even to the minutiae of the incessant killings in Iliadic battle scenes. There, no one dies without remark: One warrior is described as handsome, another's wife and children at home are mentioned, a third is an only son. It is difficult to judge Homer's achievement because nothing of his predecessors' poems survives, but it is clear from other epic verse, ancient and modern, that the *Iliad* is a masterpiece of the genre precisely because it goes beyond generic constraints and refuses to be mere praise of battle glory.

Like Odysseus, who narrates his adventures for the pleasure of the Phaeacian court in the *Odyssey*, Homer also delights his audience. In this, he surpasses comparable "adventure" narratives in both complexity and tone. His art lies in his ability to combine the themes of revenge, escape, initiation, and reunion in the *Odyssey*, in the same way that Demodocus, the Phaeacian bard, recounts epic tales (the Trojan Horse story) as well as amatory tales (the Ares and Aphrodite story). The *Odyssey*, then, shows that side of Homeric poetry which most resembles Odysseus himself, the "man of many turnings." It weaves multiple plots, centered on three major characters (Telemachus, Odysseus, and Penelope), whereas the *Iliad* concentrates on the single theme of Achilles' wrath and its consequences. The tone, also, of the *Odyssey* distinguishes it from the folktales, romances, and picaresque tales of travel with which it is often compared. The Odyssean sense of purpose gives moral value to the poem: Odysseus must return home to affirm the value of Greek culture. His slaying of the suitors, often criticized as excessive in Homer's rendering, is justified as divine retribution for the mistreatment of strangers (Odysseus himself being the "stranger" in his

Homer (Library of Congress)

own land). Thus, the poem is aesthetically and culturally satisfying, although in a different mode from that of the *Iliad:* Odysseus, and by implication Greek intelligence, is seen to be invincible.

Versatility in approach, attention to detail, control and seriousness of tone, the ability to incorporate and exceed earlier generic elements of his tradition—these are only a small part of Homer's achievement. More than this, Homer may be credited with crystallizing for later generations of European poets the genre of epic, regardless of whether those poets imitated him. In fact, many did. His influence on later Greek, Latin, and vernacular literature is enormous, a fact well documented by such scholars as Gilbert Highet. Apollonius Rhodius, Ennius, Vergil, Dante, Ludovico Ariosto, Pierre de Ronsard, Edmund Spenser, John Milton, and Ezra Pound are among the epic poets in his debt. Drama from Aeschylus on, lyric poetry, history, and the modern novel often reflect the brilliance of Homer's creations. This is not surprising; Aristotle had seen that the poems exemplify certain universal tendencies of plot, which he classed in the *Poetics* (probably between 334 and 323 B.C.E.) as tragic (*Iliad*) and comic (*Odyssey*). A writer in any mode that touches these two views of life, therefore, could conceivably use Homer as a model.

In terms of his own culture, Homer's achievement is best illustrated by the paucity of epic poetry *not* contained in the *Iliad* or *Odyssey* that survives today. Various literary and critical sources, among them Attic tragedy and Alexandrian commentaries, make clear the existence in ancient Greece of a body of traditional epic concerning the Trojan War and surrounding events. Of this wealth of material, only fragments under the collective title of the Epic Cycle survive. Clearly, the prestige of Homer's compositions eventually effaced all other poetic treatments of the Trojan War story, leaving only hints in the works of some ancient authors that there had once been other stories told of Achilles, Odysseus, and the other heroes of Homeric epic.

BIOGRAPHY

Nothing is known about the poet (or poets) of the *Iliad* and *Odyssey*. It should be noted that in ancient times, as well as in modern scholarship since the nineteenth century, opinion has varied on whether both epics were the creation of one poet. In Alexandria during the third and second centuries B.C.E., a group of critics known as the *Chorizontes* (separators) denied that one person composed both poems; at the same time, Aristarchus, one of the most influential editors of the text of the poems, maintained that the cross-references from the *Odyssey* to the *Iliad* do show the epics to be the work of one poet. It is not impossible that the works are by different poets, each a master; it is perhaps wiser to side with Aristarchus and the majority opinion of antiquity in attributing the *Iliad* and the *Odyssey* to one composer. The British scholar D. B. Monro demonstrated in the nineteenth century that the *Iliad* and the *Odyssey* never describe the *same* minor incidents relating to the Trojan War but instead form a series of *similar* vignettes. "Monro's Law," as this phenomenon has come to be called, might indicate that Homer consciously sought to avoid repeating himself; on the other hand, one could argue that the two poems represent narrative traditions so well known in the world of early Greece that any composer, while working on one poem, would automatically avoid a topic which he knew to be in the other one. Thus, the question of authorship remains open to debate, part of the larger Homeric Question which continues to fascinate students of these poems.

The dearth of biographical detail which might have explained the genesis of these remarkable works, although perplexing to scholars since antiquity, may actually have helped the poems to survive, for it enabled Greeks of all city-states to adopt them as their own "history"—one which clearly did not favor one region at the expense of another, or the traditions of one city-state exclusively, but rather attempted to integrate all the various versions of the Trojan War. Homer could never be dismissed as a biased observer whose local associations led him to trim the truth.

The anonymity of Homer is that of the epic genre itself. Evolving over generations of oral performance before an audience which knew poetry well, the art form which culminated in the *Iliad* and *Odyssey* conventionally made no mention of its performers. It is not accidental that even the name of Homer soon became a subject of speculation among the Greeks. Some ancient sources equated *Homeros* (the Greek form of the poet's name) with a noun meaning "hostage" and appended a story about the poet's early life to support the etymology. Others said that the word meant "blind." There is no evidence to support either guess. Indeed, the traditional picture of the blind bard is exactly that: a tradition—which is to say that it is still important "evidence," but not an established fact. It may reflect an ideology which conceives of the poet as "blind" to all contemporary, external influence, one who depends instead on what he "hears" from the Muse whom Homer addresses in the prologues of both poems. The Muse (another obscure word, perhaps related to the Greek root meaning "to remind" or "to remember") embodies and transmits Greek traditional stories through the epic poet. In the final analysis, then, for both Greeks and moderns, *who* Homer was is not important; what he transmits, is. Freed from the biographical method of criticism, the student of Homer can concentrate on the poetry itself.

The tradition of Homer's blindness can also be interpreted on another level—the social. The composition and performance of poetry was perhaps one of the few crafts available to the sightless in early Greek society. The figure of the blind bard Demodocus in the *Odyssey* (sometimes taken to be Homer's "self-portrait") could reflect a real situation: Such poets may have sung for aristocratic courts. Therefore, a conventional picture of the blind bard or an actual description (in general terms) may lie behind the story of Homer's handicap.

The problem of convention versus actuality (or individual observation of reality) is the main critical problem of Homeric poetry. How much is actually Homer's "invention" and how much belongs to the long tradition which he inherited? To what extent does Homer defy the tradition? The question is partially unanswerable, since Homer's predecessors have not survived. Nevertheless, some light is shed on Homeric innovations in traditional motifs by the comparative study of epic poetry. Thus Albert B. Lord, in his *The Singer of Tales* (1960), is able to bring parallel motifs from modern Serbo-Croatian heroic songs to the interpretation of certain episodes in the *Iliad* and *Odyssey*. The absence and return of Achilles, for example, can be seen as a "story pattern" that Homer has conflated with another pattern, the "death of the substitute"—in this case, Patroclus.

Such studies have increasingly shown that the poems are almost entirely "traditional" in their themes and motifs; at the same time, they exhibit a distinctive dramatic control which has modified themes so as to develop essential meanings. Thus, while Homer may have inherited the story of Achilles' wrath or Odysseus's wandering, only his own arrangement must be responsible for final narratives which, by a sophisticated counterpoint of themes—war and peace, life and death, fathers and sons—create complex worlds of significance. Although one knows nothing about the poet, his presence is immanent in the poems.

ANALYSIS

Before proceeding to analyze the poems themselves, something must be said about the nature of the poetry. That the *Iliad* and the *Odyssey* bear the marks of oral traditional poetry is now generally admitted, although opinions differ concerning the way in which this "oral" poetry was transcribed and transmitted. An understanding of oral poetics helps one to appreciate certain features of Homeric epic, such as repetition, which might be faulted were the poetics of written literature applied to the texts.

The origin of Homeric verse in oral poetry, composed before the art of alphabetic writing was brought to Greece (probably in the eighth century B.C.E.), has been the subject of academic discussion since the time of German philologist Friedrich A. Wolf, whose *Prolegomena ad Homerum* of 1795 began the modern era of Homeric study. Scholarship in the century after Wolf, however, chose to mine the larger vein which Wolf had opened in his work—namely, the thesis that the Homeric poems, as they exist, represent a collection of shorter lays on simple themes such as the wrath of Achilles which were edited or expanded early in antiquity. Thus, following Wolf, "analyst" criticism (as it came to be known) developed in response to the bulk and complexity of Homer's poems.

A highly literate society's Romantic ideas of the "primitive," illiterate bard did not accord well with these elaborate epics, so it was denied that one masterful poet produced both the *Iliad* and the *Odyssey*, or even one of them, alone. It is true that about a third of the poems, taken together, are repeated lines. Nineteenth century analyst criticism explained these internal repetitions as "borrowings" done by a series of editor-poets who had read other parts of the poems when those parts existed as individual lays. In a way, analyst criticism foreshadowed modern work on oral poetics, which can show that individual themes develop distinctive phraseological patterns that are then repeated whenever the theme recurs (although sometimes in modified form): a scene of sacrifice, for example, or the launching of a ship; a scene of taking a bath or giving a gift—all contain similar language whenever they appear in the poem. Such occasions were nearly ritual or, often, *were* ritual; it is only to be expected that traditional language describes them repeatedly, and it is no artistic fault. Analyst critics, however, having no field experience of living oral traditions, did not realize that heroic poems of a great many verses are attributable to single poets (Kirghiz bards, for example, have produced 125,000-line epics), nor did they realize that repetition is a key element in the effects of heroic epic, where it produces a rhythm in the composition parallel to the rhythm of the audience's own world.

It was left to a young American philologist, Milman Parry, to explain the real significance of such Homeric phenomena as repeated whole verses, scenes, and phrases. His demonstration, now more than fifty years old, showed that one class of repeated elements, the "formulas" or "groups of words regularly used under the same metrical conditions to express an essential idea," formed a system. Parry made detailed comparisons of noun-epithet combinations ("wily Odysseus"; "swift-footed Achilles"). His classifications showed that adjectives with proper names were determined by the demands of Homeric meter rather than by sense in a particular passage. In other words, "cloud-gathering Zeus" differs from "Zeus who delights in thunderbolts" or "Zeus, father of men and gods" not because Homer, in any one line, intends a different picture of the supreme Olympian god, but because the three noun-phrases can fill up different positions in the highly complex dactylic hexameter verse. His system demonstrated that almost every major figure in the poems has a set of adjectives to modify its name (with minute exceptions), but that only one noun-adjective combination exists for any given metrical position.

Parry concluded that such a widespread but economical system must have evolved over a long period of time. A single poet in a literate culture—Vergil, for example—would have no need to devise such a system, even if he could, but oral poets, under the pressure of improvised composition, might be expected to create just such aids to their art. Parry, with help from his assistant, Albert Lord, was able to find modern analogies for his theory in the coffee houses of Muslim communities in Yugoslavia, where oral poets entertained. "Formulas" could be identified in the Serbo-Croatian songs which Lord and Parry heard; singers discussed their art with them. In short, the analogy with modern oral poetry, used with caution, adds immensely to a study of Homer. The ability of oral poets to transmit, combine, and modify inherited themes, as well as language, seems perfected in the poet of the *Iliad* and the *Odyssey*.

ILIAD

"Sing, goddess, the ruinous anger of Achilles, Peleus's son"—the *Iliad*'s opening lines contain in essence the plot of the following twenty-four books of the poem. It is Achilles' wrath at being deprived of the woman Briseis, his prize of war, by the Greek commander Agamemnon, which causes Achilles' withdrawal from the fighting before Troy and the subsequent death of many of his companions. Among these is his beloved, Patroclus, who dies in Achilles' stead, attempting to ward off destruction from the Greeks while Achilles, defending his own standard of honor as a hero, waits for Agamemnon to make suitable recompense for the stolen woman. Only Patroclus's sacrifice is able to stir Achilles to fight. He proceeds to kill Hector, the mainstay of Troy and the slayer of Patroclus, and thereby chooses his own destiny: death at a young age, with undying fame.

The anger causes ruin, then, for thousands of Greek and Trojan warriors, for Patroclus (whom Achilles least expects to harm) and ultimately for Achilles himself. His death, though not described within the narrow time-limits of the *Iliad* (the main actions occur within the space of a few days), is rehearsed in the precisely delineated killing of his comrade. Apollo plays a supporting role in causing Patroclus's death in book 16, as he will when Achilles later is fatally wounded by Paris, whose abduction of Helen from Greece precipitated the Trojan War. Hector, in his own death speech, foretells the scene. Thus, the three deaths are inextricably linked: Anger kills the angered.

Achilles' anger might first be mistaken for youthful impetuosity or even childish resentment, but as Achilles' speeches to the entreating embassy of book 9 show, the hero's anger is fundamental to his nature as hero. Achilles rejects his society with an idealist's moral clarity—rejects that world in which a young man must war for an older man's stolen wife, under the command of an inferior man (Agamemnon) who takes "by right" the young man's own woman. This is the *Iliad*'s tragic irony. It is compounded by the irony that the wrath of the hero is sanctioned and justified by Zeus, who has agreed to further Achilles' request for compensatory honor; yet not even Zeus can save Achilles from the consequences of being born half divine and half human. His latter heritage ensures that Achilles must grieve and die.

Achilles, son of the divine sea-nymph Thetis and the mortal Peleus, is genetically unfit to live in either world, and the *Iliad* depicts his magnificent attempt at integration. His heritage, in the form of the father-son theme, is prominent throughout the poem. The opening line, with its patronymic "son of Peleus" hints at the theme; the ending in book 24 makes the theme explicit. In this regard, the *Iliad* moves from the influence of the mother to that of the father. Thetis is the one who, in book 1, persuades Zeus to honor her son by making the Greek warriors feel his need as they are hard-pressed in the fight. Yet this possibility of winning the highest glory, of being recognized as best of the Greeks—the divine stature akin to Thetis's divinity—fails to take into account the hero's humanity. Once he realizes that it is time to die, Achilles is dominated by the remembrance of his father.

In this reading of the poem, fathers are the lowest common denominators of the human. With increasing insistence, the theme recurs in the *Iliad*: Book 6 contains two examples. First, Glaucus and Diomedes, despite opposite affiliations, can find in their fathers and grandfathers common friends. This inherited bond becomes their reason for avoiding the slaying of each other. Next, in the same book, the completely mortal

Trojan counterpart of Achilles, Hector, meets his wife Andromache on the city wall. Hector's doomed infant son, Astyanax, is also present, and the poet arranges the scene so that the fate of Troy finds its symbol in the baby. He will not grow up to be "lord of the town" as his name signifies (and as his father is) but will be taken when the town falls, and both Hector and his wife know this. In this, their final conversation, the relationship of Hector with his son is placed in the wider context of paternal relations, as each partner recalls a father: Andromache mentions Eetion, killed in a raid by Achilles early in the war; Hector says that he is fighting not only for his own but also for Priam's glory, although he knows that the effort is in vain. This consciousness of genealogy and relation gives the *Iliad* much of its impression of depth, revealing as it does inherited motivations.

The heroic imperative, always to excel, is partly motivated by competition with fathers—filial piety is only part of the reason why heroes fight—and this side of the theme is not neglected. A father's example or instructions shame several heroes to join battle. Agamemnon goading Diomedes in book 4 and Odysseus goading Achilles in book 9 make use of the theme; Nestor, in book 11, unwittingly uses it to send Patroclus off to his death. In the final book of the poem, Priam also uses the common experience of fathers: On a night mission to the Greek camp to retrieve his son's corpse, the old man prompts Achilles to remember Peleus, his father. This time the purpose of the reminder is peaceful, and it succeeds; the poem ends in reconciliation, at least on the level of the individual. Achilles' new realization of his own mortality enables him humbly to accept a father's wish—in pointed contrast, no doubt intentional, to Agamemnon in book 1.

If the father-son theme emphasizes Achilles' mortal side, the theme of anger, from the poem's beginning, emphasizes the divine. The interaction of human and divine is one of the most important Homeric themes; Achilles is a paradigm for the way in which such interaction occurs. A Greek audience would have been attuned to the word which Homer uses to describe Achilles' state. *Mēnis* (the first word of the poem) is not ordinary anger; it connotes divine wrath. In fact, Achilles is the only mortal of whom it is used. There is, then, inherent antagonism between Achilles and the divine. Achilles, like any man, will inevitably lose in this contest because he must die. Gregory Nagy has shown that the theme of god-hero antagonism underlies the Greek concept of the hero in both poetic narratives and actual cult practices. Achilles' death, therefore, can be seen not only as the result of his human commitment but also as the logical result of his near-divine status, his encroachment upon divine prerogatives when he indulges his ruinous wrath. This explains why Apollo joins Paris in the killing of Achilles (as Hector predicts in book 22).

For many readers, the role of the gods in both the *Iliad* and the *Odyssey* is problematic. If events are predetermined, as the poet seems at times to say, how can a hero such as Achilles choose his destiny? Again, there appear to be levels of divine necessity. The will of Zeus is carried out in the poem, according to the prologue in book 1; yet Zeus himself must bow to restraint in accepting the predetermined death of his son Sarpedon later in the poem. The great span of time which led to the crystallization of Homeric poetry could account for the variant notions in the poems, from meteorological gods to moral forces: Zeus can thus without contradiction be both the "cloudgatherer" and the god who punishes the violators of guest-host relations. Then again, Homer is free to choose to emphasize whatever aspect of divinity best suits his poetic needs at a given point: He is not bound by a theology. In fact, the mention of "fate" can often be taken as the poet's way of saying "This is the way in which the plot goes"; the epic poet has Zeus's omniscience, thanks to the Muses.

Actually, the Homeric picture is remarkably consistent in one aspect: Gods act as mortals. They drink, deceive, laugh, love, hold grudges, have favorites; they merely do not die. Homer repeatedly develops the dramatic possibilities of this basic contrast, especially in "interlude" portions which do not significantly advance the plot. (The key plot-forwarding books are 1, 9, 11, 16, 19, 22, 23, 24.) Thus, book 5 contains episodes of deadly serious fighting as Diomedes has his heroic hour at the Trojans' expense, but the book ends with the comic assaults on Ares and Aphrodite. The effect is only to underscore how much mortals stand to lose in war.

At times the parallelism of divine and human worlds means that many actions appear to be caused by both human desires and divine will. For Homer, this is not a contradiction; the gods play a part in the world of men, but human beings are still free to make up their own minds—these are self-evident facts to the poet. This "double-motivation," the dual point of view which perceives events from both divine and human perspectives, creates in the epic a sense of heightened pathos balanced by impersonal tragic resignation. In a way, the duality reproduces that of the divinely inspired and objective poet as he sings, again and again, the one-time, life-or-death crisis of his hero.

The special beauty, then, of traditional poetry like the *Iliad* emerges in even such a brief analysis as this, where it has been shown that even the first line of the poem plunges one into thematic depths. Because of the nature of the medium, the same could be said of almost any line in the epic.

ODYSSEY

Homer's *Odyssey*, when contrasted with the *Iliad*, might well appear to be the work of another poet. It represents another world, the world of peaceful existence. In space and time it is the *Iliad*'s opposite, ranging widely over twenty years and dozens of locales, rather than describing only a few days. Its hero, Odysseus, is also the polar opposite of Achilles; a hero of intelligence rather than might, he survives the war and the homecoming, unlike Achilles or even Agamemnon. Whereas in the *Iliad* one manifestation of the hero's character predominates—his wrath—the *Odyssey* presents Odysseus as the possessor of a number of qualities and abilities. It is not accidental that more epithets beginning in the Greek word for "many" (*poly-*) attach to Odysseus than to any other figure in the epics. His "many turnings" are at one time essential to the plot of the poem (the many turns he takes) and to his disposition (as a man of much-turned thought) and so make a proper subject for the first line of the *Odyssey:* "Tell me, goddess, the man of many ways who was much buffeted after he sacked Troy."

The main plot of the poem—the return of the absent husband to his faithful wife, despite the odds—must have existed in folktale form before Greek epic appropriated it for the story of the homecoming Odysseus. The story can be paralleled in tales of many cultures, ancient and modern. Subplots, such as the encounters with the giant (Cyclops) and the witch (Circe), are also clearly from the common stock of popular narratives. Homer's fashioning of these materials is what makes the *Odyssey* unique.

First to be noticed is the small scope actually given such adventure motifs in the poem as a whole. They occur only in Odysseus's own narration of his experiences, books 9 through 12. His relationship with Calypso, the divine nymph who wished to detain him and make him immortal, is described not as a wonder-tale but in natural terms. The only unusual aspect of her island home, Ogygia, is its lush vegetation, symbolic of the excessive life she offers. The hints of Elysium in the description of the island (the land of the dead), and of her own darker nature (Calypso means "the hider" and connotes burial) are only undertones, subtly managed by the poet. Similarly, Scheria, the island of the Phaeacians who send Odysseus back to Ithaca on the last leg of his voyage, is described as a believable, realistic social setting—albeit for an unusual society. The reader is far from the nightmarish world of Cyclops, Circe, the Lotus Eaters, Scylla, and Charybdis. The primary distinguishing mark is the absence of danger; Ogygia and Scheria pose more spiritual temptations, offers to abandon the centripetal voyage home. For Odysseus's temperament such dangers equally threaten extinction. Without establishing his place as ruler of his Ithacan home, the hero has no reason to live. He must keep in motion until that rest.

Another unique feature of the *Odyssey* is tied to the adventure tales: Odysseus, not the poet, tells them. As noted earlier, Odysseus acts as a bard in the poem about him, and in so doing he creates a curious doubling of narrators. Two effects follow: First, time is artfully disarranged, so that a composite picture of Odysseus—past and present—emerges; second, irony enters the poem. By distancing the events through a second narrator, the poet leaves open the possibility that the tales of Odysseus are tailored by him, a possibility which gains credibility when the reader sees Odysseus tell at least five lies during the tale-telling in the second half of the poem.

If the irony of the device is admitted, it can be seen to accord with other artful displacements in the structure of the *Odyssey*, such as the so-called *Telemacheia*, or "story of Telemachus" (books 1 through 4). Why, in a poem about Odysseus, does the hero not appear until book 5? Why does his son hold the stage? Again, the answer lies in Homer's desire for sophisticated and ironic narration. The reader sees Telemachus setting out on his own odyssey, starting the process of initiation into manhood; at the same time, one sees the final step in his father's voyage back. From the divine prologue to this tale of crossed paths, the audience knows that Athena has arranged both the miniature odyssey of the son to Pylos and Sparta in order to learn of his father, and the journey of Odysseus himself. Yet neither participant in the plan knows about it. What seems to them to be hazardous appears to the audience as divine providence. The technique is, in fact, comic.

The "happy" ending of the *Odyssey* also reminds readers of comedy: The bad are punished (the suitors killed), the good rewarded, and a wedding of sorts takes place. It might be noted that Homer once again uses the father-son theme to accomplish the poem's final reconciliation: Not only is Odysseus reunited with Telemachus (and thus the beginning of the poem is joined with the end), but also Laertes, Odysseus's father, joins in the final battle. There is no better definition of what survival meant to a Greek: the reintegration into a social setting of family and community. The *Odyssey* is thus aesthetically and culturally satisfying.

Although it is often compared unfavorably with the *Iliad*—one ancient critic compared the *Iliad* to the sun at midday and the *Odyssey* to sunset, claiming that the latter was composed in Homer's old age—the *Odyssey* is perhaps less restricted by the presuppositions of Homeric Greek culture. The *Iliad* has had few successors in outlook; the *Odyssey*'s are legion. Both poems present a complete view of life: one as tragic, one as transcending tragedy.

BIBLIOGRAPHY

Alden, Maureen J. *Homer Beside Himself: Para-Narratives in the "Iliad."* New York: Oxford University Press, 2001. Advises students and others new to the

Iliad on how to read, understand, and absorb it, and then offers an analysis.

Bowra, Cecil M. *Homer.* New York: Scribner, 1972. A classic introductory critical analysis of Homer's works with bibliographic references.

Carlisle, Miriam, and Olga Levaniouk, eds. *Nine Essays on Homer.* Lanham, Md.: Rowman & Littlefield, 1999. A collection of essays exploring Homeric poetry with a variety of approaches including cultural anthropology, linguistics, philology, textual criticism, sociology, and archaeology. Intended for scholars and students of oral poetry and classical literature.

Ford, Andrew Laughlin. *Homer: The Poetry of the Past.* Ithaca, N.Y.: Cornell University Press, 1992. Focuses on the moment in Western literature when the Greek oral tradition began to be preserved in writing. An inquiry into the function of ancient poetics without exhaustive scholarship making it accessible to the informed general reader.

Lord, Albert B. *The Singer of Tales.* 2d ed. Cambridge, Mass.: Harvard University Press, 2000. This second edition offers a new introduction and a CD-ROM containing audio and visual material from the original research in the Balkans by Milman Parry. Parry began recording and studying a live tradition of oral narrative poetry in order to find how Homer had composed his two monumental epic poems. Lord's book, based on Parry's research, intends to demonstrate the process by which oral poets compose.

Nagy, Gregory. *The Best of the Achaeans.* Baltimore: The Johns Hopkins University Press, 1999. Revised edition of Nagy's analysis of Homeric heroic characters. Includes extensive bibliography.

Parry, Milman. *The Making of Homeric Verse: The Collected Papers of Milman Parry.* New York: Oxford University Press, 1987. Parry, considered one of the leading classical scholars of modern times, produced many articles and French dissertations which until now have been difficult to obtain. The collection includes Parry's unpublished M.A. thesis and extracts from his Yugoslavian journal.

Richard Peter Martin;
bibliography updated by the editors

GARRETT KAORU HONGO

Born: Volcano, Hawaii; May 30, 1951

PRINCIPAL POETRY

The Buddha Bandits down Highway 99, 1978 (with Alan Chong Lau and Lawson Fusao Inada)
Yellow Light, 1982
The River of Heaven, 1988

OTHER LITERARY FORMS

Nisei Bar and Grill, a play, was written in 1976 and performed in Seattle and San Francisco. Its revised version became a workshop production at the Kilauea Theater (1992). The play depicts interactions among veterans of World War II and the Korean conflict. *Volcano: A Memoir of Hawai'i*, his memoir of growing up on Hawaii, was published in 1995. Garrett Kaoru Hongo also has written literary essays appearing in *Agni Review*, *The New York Times Book Review*, *New England Review*, *Ohio Review*, and elsewhere. He edited the landmark anthologies *The Open Boat: Poems from Asian America* (1993) and *Under Western Eyes: Personal Essays from Asian America* (1995).

ACHIEVEMENTS

Garrett Kaoru Hongo's poetry is notable for its immediacy of voice, clear evocation of place, and poignant negotiation of both ethnic and temporal boundaries. He typically employs memory to compile imagistic pastiches that re-create an emotional state. Many of his poems are quests—for a synthetic cultural identity, for a true personal history, for a unique and satisfactory voice. Traversing landscapes from the volcano of his birthplace to the volcanic experience of living in a mainland metropolis (primarily Los Angeles), Hongo explores the brutality of contemporary life as it assaults the tenderness of the spirit. Alienation, discrimination, cruelty, violence, loss, and isolation permeate the poems as insults to the soul.

Hongo has received high acclaim and support through several prizes and fellowships: the Thomas J. Watson Travelling Fellowship, 1973-1974; the Hopwood Poetry Prize, 1975; the Discovery/*The Nation* Award,

1981; National Endowment for the Arts Fellowships, 1982 and 1988; Pushcart Prize selection, 1986; the Lamont Poetry Prize, 1987; and a Guggenheim Fellowship, 1990-1991. In 1989 he was a finalist for the Pulitzer Prize in poetry and the *Los Angeles Times* Book Award.

BIOGRAPHY

A fourth-generation Japanese American, Garrett Kaoru Hongo was born in Volcano, Hawaii, in 1951. His parents are Albert Kazuyoshi Hongo, who died in 1984, and Louise Tomiko Kubota Hongo. Until he was six years old, he and his family lived in Kahuku and then Hauula on the island of Oahu. Hongo learned at this time to speak Pidgin English and Japanese. From the ages of six to eighteen, Hongo lived with his family in and around Los Angeles, where he began to experience the harshness of city life (in contrast to the easy rhythms of life on the island) and the prejudices and injustices of a multicultural society. He attended an inner-city high school, which was an integration pilot combining whites, Asian Americans, African Americans, and Hispanic Americans in the same classes. Some of his poems, "Morro Rock" in particular, evoke conflicts experienced for the first time in his teenage years.

Hongo's beginnings as a poet came when he was eighteen and started writing love poems to a European American girl, celebrating a relationship that they felt pressured to keep secret. She awakened in him an intellectual camaraderie with "books about adolescent yearning and rebellion, about 'the system' not understanding you," notably William Golding's *Lord of the Flies* (1954), J. D. Salinger's *The Catcher in the Rye* (1951), Hermann Hesse's *Siddhartha* (1951), J. R. R. Tolkien's *The Lord of the Rings* (3 volumes, 1954-1955), and Ken Kesey's *One Flew Over the Cuckoo's Nest* (1962). His first serious poetry came when he was twenty and a student at Pomona College in Claremont, California. There as a freshman he read the early fiction of James Joyce, who made him aware of links between language and culture and the literary divisions of loyalty that an artist might feel.

As a sophomore he progressed to the poetry of Ezra Pound and William Butler Yeats, whom he began to revere as sages who had reinvented English according to their own inner voices. He immersed himself in listening to the language of poets by attending actual readings by Philip Levine (who was to become a mentor), Gary Snyder, Seamus Heaney, and Galway Kinnell. He studied Japanese and Chinese formally, and, as Hongo himself relates, "practiced calligraphy every night, and, afterwards, my mind tight and cluttered with bristling ideograms, read the great translations of Tang Dynasty Chinese poetry by Pound, Arthur Waley, Witter Bynner, and Kenneth Rexroth." Through this process he began to have confidence in his own authentic voice, what he calls his "inner speech," later encouraged by poet-teachers Bert Meyers, Charles Wright, C. K. Williams, and Philip Levine.

Garrett Hongo (© Ellen Foscue Johnson)

At the age of twenty, Hongo returned to Hawaii and began to try to reclaim that portion of his own past, his heritage. Here he discovered in a garage his father's library, consisting primarily of works of realistic fiction, and he established a connection with his uncle, Robert Hongo, who was a novelist. The first "real" poem Hongo wrote was called "Issei: First-Generation Japanese American." The poem relates an ancestral explanation of how he received his own middle name and thus reveals the close link between name and identity, between name and heritage. Writing the poem was a turning point for him, a moment that confirmed his calling. Hongo describes this experience in terms that represent the matter and spirit of much of his poetry:

It was a childhood recollection of my grandfather reading a Japanese book—a sort of bound scroll of folded paper stitched together in a way that reminded me of the lacing on a fishing pole. It was about descent, heritage, and his injunction to me to remember it. I wrote the lines quickly after practicing ideograms all night once, in cadences I imitated from translations of Chinese poetry. After I was done, I felt my life had changed—that I had said a *true* thing, that I was a *poet*. I remembered the feeling, the new conviction, and tried for it every time I wrote thereafter. It was a standard I used to test authenticity and depth of feeling.

Working to combine the early literary influence of "the fiction of John Steinbeck, the poetry of Dylan Thomas and Robinson Jeffers, the lyrics of Hawaiian songs, and Motown," Hongo entered the Watts Writers' Workshop. There he was primarily an observer while more experienced writers debated many of the same questions that plagued the young Hongo: voice, authenticity, ethnic fidelity and literary sophistication, legitimacy, genuineness. He began to connect the forms and methods of music and poetry, striving for the avant-garde mastery of jazz pianists McCoy Tyner and Cecil Taylor in his own writing, and finding a fascination with the representative possibilities of theater—*Macbeth* with an all-black cast, for example.

After being graduated cum laude in 1973 from Pomona College, Hongo journeyed to Japan on a quest for an understanding of where he might belong; he spent

a year there, traveling and writing poetry. He then commenced graduate study of Japanese language and literature at the University of Michigan. Returning to the West Coast, Hongo lived in Seattle from 1976 to 1979, where he worked as a professor and a poet. Ultimately he returned to California to study and receive, in 1980, an M.F.A. in English from the University of California at Irvine, where he continued in doctoral study in critical theory for two more years.

Although he finds himself more attuned to dialogue with poets than with professors, more at home in the artistic world than in the academy, Hongo negotiates the common ground with grace and intelligence. His critical training is apparent in his experimentation with various poetic forms, as well as in the metapoetic nature of some of his writings. Hongo is aware of the myriad poetic influences that have helped to define him. He pays homage to his predecessors by emulating their forms and by injecting himself into their situations or embedding their poems within his, as in "To Matsuo Basho and Kawai Sora in Nirvana," where the persona of the poem visits the pond of the famous frog haiku and invites the ghosts of the masters to return to him and speak, "before the fog rolls in." In his later poems Hongo often includes a dedication to other poets in a kind of ongoing literary conversation. His connection to other working poets helps to sustain his own writing; those who have figured in this dialogue include Mark Jarman ("Morro Rock"), Gerald Stern ("Nostalgic Catalogue"), Edward Hirsch ("Ancestral Graves, Kahuku"), and Charles Wright ("Volcano House").

Even though Hongo enjoys thinking critically about his own and others' poetry, he found deconstructionist theory to be debilitating rather than enabling and thus left his doctoral program in 1984, taking a position as an assistant professor of English at the University of Missouri, where he was also poetry editor of *The Missouri Review*. Meanwhile Hongo had married Cynthia Thiessen, a violinist, and his first son, Alexander, was born (a second son is named Hudson). In Missouri, Hongo began daydreaming about Hawaii, about California, about his own and his family's past. Instead of producing a doctoral dissertation, he wrote *The River of Heaven*—a decision that salvaged his spirit in an alien landscape and confirmed his allegiance to creativity rather than to scholarship. After a year's sojourn at the University of Houston, Hongo accepted a position at the University of Oregon and directed the creative writing program there from 1989-1993. He divides his time between Eugene and Volcano, a place for which his spirit hankers and where the ghost of his grandfather is evident. Hongo has become an active literary presence in his hometown and is the leader of a theater group. He speaks of his connection with place, of how the volcano itself informs his poetry:

> My poems speak now of the fragility of all things— culture, inheritances, loyalties—and the great vulnerability of love of them. I look out the window here and see myrtle trees with their red-crest blossoms–*o'hia lehua* in Hawaiian—and feel sad to think that there might only be sixty years left for this forest, for the *apapane* and *i'iwi* honeycreepers which live among these trees. Mostly, though, I still write from an ancient human sadness for existence and for eternity, a feeling Japanese aesthetics defined as *sabi*—a kind of serene worry or melancholy about the universe.

ANALYSIS

Garrett Kaoru Hongo's poems in *Yellow Light* and *The River of Heaven* offer a chronological narrative of his life and of his development as a poet. By reading the poems in the order of their presentation, one becomes immersed in the external details of life in the modern metropolis, exotic locales, and a multicultural community, as well as in the resulting internal emotions and reflections of the writer. A recurring theme in his work is the search for a personal identity that is unique, separate, and autonomous but also continuous with one's heritage. There is a sense of the need for separation and then return; the poems trace a journey of discovery.

YELLOW LIGHT

The title poem of *Yellow Light* sets the tone for the rest of the collection. These earlier poems reflect the writer's concern with the sensibility of his father's soul, which was brutalized by his necessary manual labor and the hardship of making a living in an alien society. The sensations, the impressions, of his father's condition were indelibly etched on the consciousness of the poet

as a young child. The conflict and compromise that he knew his father felt become abstracted into larger, less personal issues and then reparticularized into observable details of the environment and projections into the lives of observed people.

In "Yellow Light," a woman returns to her apartment after work and shopping. In her walk through the city, the poet juxtaposes images of nature to the trappings of city life. The contemporary urban environment has as its "natural" images children reenacting war games, sounds of domestic squabbles, noisy machinery, polluted air, and unsightly barriers separating yard from yard, protecting material property. These contrast with vivid sensations of a truly natural environment, appearing here as flowers that would be colorful, fragrant, and profuse.

The contrast continues in descriptions of the light the woman experiences. Light is often used in poetry to indicate truth or clarity of vision. The city offers only ugly, glaring, artificial light—false illumination. It is revealed in searchlights from car lots and the fluorescent and neon lights of commerce and trade. By offering as an alternative to this light the warm and mellow glow of a kitchen lamp, the poet hints that each individual may establish his or her own "natural" territory domestically: a place where one is in control and one's values and priorities are proper. Later poems indicate that poetry itself may be one's private territory, where a corrective vision can be offered as an alternative to the flawed world "out there." Hongo carries forth the kitchen image, and its associations with sustenance and nurturing, in the overpowering natural light of the moon, a larger version of the mellow kitchen lamp, here compared to the rich yellow of onions. The light of the moon proves ultimately victorious, as it blankets the horrors of the city and renders invisible the lesser metropolitan lights. The act of writing poetry, the poet suggests, may itself be redemptive.

The remaining poems in the volume continue with similar themes and may be grouped accordingly. Several of them focus on domestic life, often employing the idea of a return to the haven of home and family. In "Off from Swing Shift," a father returns home from the sapping drudgery of his assembly-line job to the comforts of his humble apartment and the pleasures of the idle pastime of gambling. In "Preaching the Blues," a young man returns from a time away from home to find his brother waiting for him at the airport. They reestablish the patterns of their childhood relationship by enacting the ritual of playing basketball in the parking lot. As they drive home, memories of their youth and the growth and patterns of their relationship engulf the narrator. He is filled with empathy for the life of his brother, which is linked with his, yet of an entirely different essence and identity.

Empathic projection is also apparent in two other domestic poems, "Stay with Me" and "The Hongo Store." In the former, the poet depicts a gesture of kindness between strangers. A woman on a bus is filled with emotional suffering. As she cries silently and unobtrusively, a young black man reluctantly bridges the gap from polite concern to a true sharing of her pain, as he comforts her by holding her. In the latter the poet projects himself into a photograph taken just after the family home and store had survived the eruption of a volcano, and he recaptures the entire episode from an adult perspective.

Several of the works could be labeled "identity poems," as they reclaim the poet's personal heritage and ethnic history. "Roots" and "Issei: First-Generation Japanese American" are obviously in this vein. The poem "Stepchild" moves out of the concern with personal identity to retrace the troubled history of Asian Americans in the first half of the twentieth century. The form of this poem is also unique, for it actually incorporates accounts by other writers of life in the internment camps and after World War II. The suffering of others like him, the narrator implies, is also part of who he is.

A major work in this collection could be labeled a "quest poem." "Cruising 99" is a poetic version of the influential Beat-generation book *On the Road* (1955) by Jack Kerouac. In this poem, the narrator and two friends travel Highway 99 in California, looking for something to make sense of their lives but also simply content with movement, at least the illusion of making progress, of seeking, of "getting there." The poem chronicles the details observed on the trip, again juxtaposing the natural and the artificial; that made by nature and that produced by humankind. Separate sec-

tions in various experimental forms re-create the human sounds, the sights, and the events of the trip: a chant to pass the time; a dialogue; a philosophical meditation about the purpose of travel; a palm-reading incident; haiku-like versions of postcard messages mailed home; an encounter in a café while the car is being repaired that leads to a realization of the fleeting nature of the travelers' youth; the surprising discovery of a Japanese community that brings them, ironically, back to themselves, back to where they began; and a final stanza on the patterns of running away and returning, patterns that can be remedied by a process of incorporation. By the end of this quest, the narrator realizes that one may become a landscape composed of all of one's heritage and experience: One becomes able to carry the journey within one rather than to move, constantly seeking something outside oneself.

Part of the quest in Hongo's case was to return to the ancestral homeland of Japan. Several of the poems recount the experience as "outsider poems." The visitor feels part of the culture yet alien to its sources. "Who Among You Knows the Essence of Garlic?" is an immersion into the culinary details of the Japanese ecosystem, ultimately becoming a microcosm of Japanese philosophy and culture that cannot include the American observer. In "To Matsuo Bashō and Kawai Sora in Nirvana," the poet visits a site frequented by two of the most famous of Japanese poets and attempts to speak with their ghosts, to become part of their literary tradition. Even if he can recapture their vision for a moment, he still senses that time and his own distance from their realities will continue to separate them.

The other categories of poems contained in this volume are portraits, meditations, and love poems, as well as an important set of pieces that might be called poems about art. "What For," in particular, reveals Hongo's concern with the value of capturing reality and giving it a name that occurs in writing poetry. This poem traces the child-poet's attraction to work rituals in his early life: the magic of incantation in Hawaiian natural mythology, family oral lore and storytelling, and singing. All these contributed to the making of the poet, yet they are contrasted to the adult death of the spirit that the child perceives in his father. As he sees the exigencies of modern life drag his parent down, the child-poet desires to use his own word magic to soothe the pain and cure his father's suffering.

THE RIVER OF HEAVEN

Hongo's second volume, *The River of Heaven*, takes its title from a line in "The Unreal Dwelling: My Years in Volcano," which is the death poem of the poet's grandfather. Here he imagines the last year of his ancestor's life in the town of Hongo's own birth. The title indicates the centrality of ancestral heritage and the image of the volcano itself in all the poems. Yet in this collection of poems, much of the restlessness of *Yellow Light* is gone. "Mendocino Rose," a poem of prologue to the collection, establishes a new tone of synthesis, wholeness, and peace. Indeed, the tenor of this poem is the harmonies that one can both find and impose on music, landscape, heritage, and a transplanted identity.

The collection is divided into two distinct parts, the first chronicling the poet's initial return to Hawaii after leaving at the age of six, and the second his moving to the mainland. There is a developmental movement to the first part. At the beginning the narrator simply tries to recapture the experience of coming home in all its sensuous detail, as in "Nostalgic Catalogue." There follows an immersion into the memories that are stimulated by the new sensuous stimuli, as in "Village: Kahuku-*mura*." He begins to experience a reclaiming of authentic selfhood in poems such as "Ancestral Graves, Kahuku" and "Hilo: First Night Back" and recognizes his kinship to relatives who remained in Hawaii. Then there is the self-scrutiny that results when he writes poetic stories of his ancestors and applies the lessons to himself, as in "*Jigoku*: On the Glamour of Self-Hate." The center of this section is Volcano itself and its landscape, which is real, as the birthplace of the poet, but also metaphorical, as the representation of fragility, destruction, and re-creation, which occur in poetry as in life.

The mainland poems of the second section are introduced by a quotation from Albert Camus to establish their predominant tone. Camus speaks of "this desire for unity, this longing to solve, this need for clarity and cohesion," at which Hongo has already hinted as being the process of poetry. These poems are more intellectual and literary, such as "Portrait of a Lady" (a title used by other famous writers such as T. S. Eliot, Ezra Pound, and Henry James). Hongo modernizes and individualizes both the form and the content of the tradition, offering a portrait of a contemporary ethnic woman in a free verse style that resembles a prose poem.

The elements present in both volumes of poetry remain, however they may be transformed or altered in tone. Hongo's persistent interests in identity, heritage, beauty, sadness, and the power of poetry lend a satisfying unity to the entire body of his work.

OTHER MAJOR WORKS

PLAY: *Nisei Bar and Grill*, pr. 1976, rev. pr. 1992.
NONFICTION: *Volcano: A Memoir of Hawai'i*, 1995.

EDITED TEXTS: *The Open Boat: Poems from Asian America*, 1993; *Songs My Mother Taught Me: Stories, Plays, and Memoir*, 1994 (by Wakako Yamauchi); *Under Western Eyes: Personal Essays from Asian America*, 1995.

BIBLIOGRAPHY

Evans, Alice. "A Vicious Kind of Tenderness: An Interview with Garrett Hongo." *Poets & Writers Magazine* 20, no. 5 (September-October 1992): 37-46. Hongo's writing stems from his need to be part of a "corrective process in American history." Useful comments on craft, family, and Asian-Pacific culture.

Filipelli, Laurie. *Garrett Hongo*. Boise, Idaho: Boise State University, 1997. A critical survey of Hongo's work with bibliographic references.

Kaganoff, Penny. Review of *The River of Heaven*. *Publishers Weekly*, no. 233 (February 12, 1988): 81. Earliest published review of Hongo's second collection of poetry.

Muratori, Fred. Review of *The River of Heaven*, by Garrett Hongo. *Library Journal*, no. 113 (May 1, 1988): 81-82. Slightly longer review of Hongo's second volume.

Sandra K. Fischer,
updated by Philip K. Jason

THOMAS HOOD

Born: London, England; May 23, 1799
Died: London, England; May 3, 1845

PRINCIPAL POETRY

Odes and Addresses to Great People, 1825 (with John Hamilton Reynolds)

Whims and Oddities: In Prose and Verse, 1826-1827

"The Plea of the Midsummer Fairies," "Hero and Leander," "Lycus the Centaur," and Other Poems, 1827

The Comic Annual, 1830-1839, 1842 (poetry and prose)

The Epping Hunt, 1829

The Dream of Eugene Aram, the Murderer, 1831

Hood's Own: Or, Laughter from Year to Year, 1839

Miss Kilmansegg and Her Precious Leg, 1840

Whimsicalities: A Periodical Gathering, 1844

OTHER LITERARY FORMS

As a journalist, Thomas Hood contributed prose as well as poetry to such periodicals as the *London Magazine*, *The New Monthly Magazine*, and *Hood's Magazine and Comic Miscellany*. He also wrote drama criticism for *The Atlas* for several months in 1826, before trying to write dramatic pieces of his own. In 1828, he wrote an ill-fated farce, *York and Lancaster: Or, A School Without Scholars*, for the theater manager Frederick Henry Yates, and followed this unsuccessful attempt with at least two more burlesques which have been lost in whole or in part. He wrote two closet dramas that were not published until after his death: *Lamia: A Romance* (pb. 1852) based on John Keats's poem of the same title, and *Guido and Marina: A Dramatic Sketch* (pb. 1882), a romantic dialogue.

Hood did numerous etchings and drawings for his publications, and had others executed under his direction. His best-known engraving, "The Progress of Cant," a large Hogarthian-style work published in 1825, shows a rag-tag parade of Lon-

doners bearing signs and banners to proclaim their favorite causes and philosophies, meanwhile exhibiting their contrary actions.

Encouraged by the early success of his first volumes of comic verse, Hood published a two-volume collection of short stories titled *National Tales* in 1827; unfortunately, just as his attempts to write drama demonstrated his lack of dramatic skill, the stories exhibited that he had no real talent for prose fiction. Hood imitated the Italian *novella* form used by the Elizabethans, without writing a single story of literary value. He also wrote two novels—*Tylney Hall* (1834) and *Up the Rhine* (1840)—with somewhat better popular success, although the novels were nearly as lacking in literary merit. *Tylney Hall* went through numerous printings in England and America, but owed its success to the humorous portions; the serious plot and major characters are rather insipid, manifesting the same contrivance and shallowness that afflicted his short stores. *Up the Rhine* was a success in the bookstalls—in England, America, and, predictably, in Frank-

Thomas Hood (Hulton Archive)

furt. A travelogue-novel similar to Mark Twain's *Innocents Abroad* (1869), *Up the Rhine* draws upon Hood's "exile" years in Germany (1835 to 1839). It is light and enjoyable reading, but far from "quality" fiction. In both novels Hood gave free vent to his punning genius, which adds humor but detracts from the overall temper of both stories. Another novel, *Our Family*, remained incomplete at Hood's death, although several chapters were published serially in *Hood's Magazine* (it was eventually published in 1861). There is no evidence that Hood's aspirations to be a novelist would have produced a better book. His many letters, though often delightful and always sparkling with wit and humor, are difficult to read. Hood's main difficulty as a prose writer was his inability to sustain a smooth, readable text that is not chopped up by distracting wordplay; in addition, he was simply not a good storyteller. Both problems greatly handicapped his ability to write long poetic narratives as well.

ACHIEVEMENTS

Thomas Hood's position in the generally overlooked period between the end of the Romantic movement and the beginning of the Victorian era has caused his true importance to be greatly underestimated. Although he can scarcely be called one of the giants of English poetry, his achievements are far from insignificant. His primary contributions to English letters have been fourfold: the refinement of English poetic humor, the popularization of poetry, the sympathetic portrayal of common English domesticity, and the arousal of humanitarian sentiments on a popular level.

Hood's comic verse—of which the amount is greater than and the quality superior to the work of any other English or American poet—evolved into what J. C. Reid calls "a highly individual amalgam of the farcical and the sinister, the pathetic and the ghoulish, that has few ancestors but many heirs." Hood's peculiar style did not preclude his diverse experimentation, whereby he often imitated and improved upon earlier comic techniques. He remains without rival in the use of the pun. He left a legacy of humorous poetry so varied that it not only provides a smooth transition from the often acrimonious wit of the eighteenth century—with none of the acrimony—but also often anticipates comic

techniques and themes that died with Hood until they were resurrected in the twentieth century, especially in the dark or grotesque humor of writers such as Franz Kafka.

Because Hood made poetry relevant to everyday life and wrote in a highly entertaining style, verse once more became something that the common people could enjoy. Since the death of William Shakespeare, who also catered in his drama to popular tastes, poetry had become an almost purely academic art form. The neoclassical movement isolated poetry from the common person to a great extent through various formulary restraints and elevated diction. The Romantic movement sought to reestablish the language of life as the language of poetry, but the philosophy and ideals of many Romantics were inaccessible to the masses. Hood popularized poetry by brilliantly expressing commonplace ideas in common words.

Writing for a popular audience meant being free to explore popular themes. Hood's treatment of domestic scenes merits special attention. Ordinary housewives and mothers, with their squalling babes in arms, domestic servants, husband-wife or parent-child relations, all of the accoutrements of home and hearth (especially cookery) receive sympathetic treatment from the pen of this devoted family man. Hood takes the reader into mansions, but through the servant's entrance, and takes the butler's perspective or leaves the reader in the kitchen. What William Hogarth did with engraving, Hood did with poetry. Not afflicted by pretension or ambition, but sensitive to both, he remained the poet of the common folk throughout his career.

In his later years, this sympathy for the proletariat led to some of the first and finest advocacy of basic human rights ever to be expressed in verse. Hood echoed the faint cries of social protest sounded by William Blake, amplified them, and added his own passionate appeals for reform. Never a revolutionary, Hood sought to inspire the upper middle class to extend a hand of true charity and compassion to the needs of the poor, sought to influence industrialists to pay a decent wage, sought to influence a notoriously competitive society to reassess its values. Hood was a voice crying somewhat in vain in the wilderness, but those he inspired were able to induce many notable social reforms in the second half of the nineteenth century.

Biography

Thomas Hood's father, also named Thomas, was a partner in the book-selling and publishing firm of Vernor and Hood, which produced *Poetical Magazine*, *Lady's Monthly Museum*, and the *Monthly Mirror*. His mother, Elizabeth Sands, was the daughter of an engraver. Both occupations determined the future career of Thomas Hood, one of six children in the Hood family to survive infancy. Hood's early education was at an Islington preparatory school, then at the Alfred House Academy at Camberwell Green. The deaths of his father and elder brother in 1811 left Thomas the man of the family, so he took a job clerking to supplement the family income. Poor health forced him to move from clerking to engraving for his uncle, but because his constitution continued to suffer, he was sent in 1815 to live with relatives in Dundee, Scotland, where he continued his apprenticeship in the engraving trade. At Dundee Hood began writing seriously. His health improved, and he returned to London in the autumn of 1817, where he worked as an engraver until he was hired in 1821 by John Taylor, a former employee of Hood's father and then editor of the *London Magazine*. Within a few months his mother died, leaving Hood the responsibility of providing for four sisters, one of whom also died a short time later.

At the *London Magazine* Hood was plunged into the company of many of England's prominent writers—Charles Lamb, Allan Cunningham, T.G. Wainewright, and John Hamilton Reynolds. Hood's friendship with Reynolds brought him into close contact with the circle and work of the recently deceased John Keats, and Hood strove for several years to imitate the great Romantic's lush and effusive style. Indeed, he was thought by many (including Cunningham) to be the logical successor of Keats, but Hood's collaboration with Reynolds on a book of comic verse in 1825 did more to further his literary career than any of his attempts to imitate the Romantics. During the same year, Hood married Reynolds' sister Jane and settled into the domestic life that would later inspire much of his poetry. Since he had ceased to edit the *London Magazine* during the pre-

vious year, Hood was obliged to publish in earnest for an income.

Hood's first daughter was born and died in May, 1827, inspiring Lamb's famous elegy "On an Infant Dying as Soon as Born." Hood's repeated exposure to the death of those closest to him was having a profound impact on his poetry, in which death figures so prominently. The following year an attack of rheumatic fever left Hood in the weakened condition that plagued him for the rest of his life. Hood continued writing, even while ill, since it was his sole means of support. He produced the first of his *Comic Annuals* in 1830, the year that his daughter Frances Freeling was born. Although his comic verse was popular, the Hood family never advanced beyond a lower-middle-class lifestyle. In 1832, they moved into their own home—Lake House in Wanstead—but the failure in 1834 of an engraving firm in which Hood had heavily invested, together with his own financial mismanagement, forced them to relinquish the house and accept the more economical life of the Continent. After the birth of his only son, Tom, Hood moved his family to Coblentz, Germany, to begin an "exile" that lasted until 1840.

In 1841, Hood assumed the editorship of *The New Monthly Magazine*. In and out of illness, financially struggling, and changing residences almost annually, Hood began to write his poems of social conscience. In 1843, he ceased editing *The New Monthly Magazine* to found *Hood's Magazine*, which he edited until early in 1845, although he was seriously ill during the entire period. A Civil List pension was granted his wife in November, 1844, when Hood was confined to what would be his deathbed. He continued writing almost to the very end. He died in May, 1845, and is buried at Kensal Green, London. Perhaps the finest tribute to his poetry is found in a letter from Hood to Frederick Ward, written in the summer of 1844: "Though I may not have reflected any very great honour on our national literature, I have not disgraced it. . . ." Such humility was typical of Thomas Hood.

Analysis

Primarily because he lived to write and wrote to live, Thomas Hood managed to publish a staggering amount of poetry in a relatively short time. Unfortunately, the pressure to keep the creditors at bay and the bacon on his table rendered much of his poetry unworthy of regard; he often failed to edit poems for which he could hardly afford enough time to write. He was seldom more than a hack writer, churning out journalistic doggerel and meanwhile maintaining an apparently voluminous correspondence, editing his annuals and magazines, executing his engravings, and trying to establish a reputation as a novelist. The mystery of his life is that he accomplished all this as a frequently bedridden invalid.

As a consequence of his need to offer original and entertaining poetry to the public on a regular basis, Hood wandered widely through the realm of possibilities to produce a profusion of experiments in form and content, in theme, rhythm, and rhyme—perhaps covering a wider range than any other English poet. In Hood one can find examples of such peculiarities as initial rhyme, various metrical arrangements of anapests and dactyls, all the major English stanza forms, and imitations of numerous styles—from those of Geoffrey Chaucer, Edmund Spenser, John Milton, Alexander Pope, Percy Bysshe Shelley, Lord Byron, Keats, and Shakespeare, to a host of lesser lights. Hood's imitations are often well-executed; his originals are even better. Omitting what is merely topical, trivial, childish, or deplorable, one finds that the remainder of Hood's canon contains a considerable quantity of poetry, some of it brilliant.

Hood began writing poetry as a pastime about 1814, during the period when he supplemented the family income by working as a clerk. In "Literary Reminiscences" (1833), Hood recalls how he stole moments from his employer, uninformatively identified as "Bell & Co.," to "take stray dips in the Castalian pool." A year later, after removing to Dundee, Scotland, to improve his health, Hood started writing a satirical *Dundee Guide*, the manuscript of which was unfortunately lost by 1820, although enough lines survived in a letter to show that it was nothing brilliant. As early as 1816, however, Hood began making anonymous contributions to Dundee periodicals, and thus first began to see his work in print. This fired him with a thirst to sell himself to "that minor Mephistopheles, the Printer's Devil." Hood was at this time being influenced by William

Wordsworth and Samuel Taylor Coleridge, Byron, and Shelley; to a lesser extent by Charles Lamb, George Crabbe, Robert Southey, and Leigh Hunt; and most of all by Sir Walter Scott, "The Great Unknown." The narrative manner of Byron's *Childe Harold's Pilgrimage* (1812-1818), *The Giaour* (1813), *The Bride of Abydos* (1813), *The Corsair* (1814), and *Lara* (1814) tempered by the influence of Scott's *The Lay of the Last Minstrel* (1805), *Marmion* (1808), *The Lady of the Lake* (1810), *Waverley* (1814), and *Rokeby* (1815) combined to foster Hood's first major poem, *The Bandit*, probably written between 1815 and 1817 but not published until forty years after his death.

THE BANDIT

The Bandit is a relatively long poem (some 820 lines divided into three cantos), a narrative about Ulric, the earl of Glenallen, who, as a result of treacherous circumstances, has been forced into the role of "Chieftain" to a band of outlaws. Although a cunning and brave leader, Glenallen secretly despises the mischievous deeds he has done, yet "Repeated wrongs had turned his breast to steel,/ And all but these he had forgot to feel." In the first canto, Glenallen discloses the plans of his final act as chief of the bandits, "To 'venge the wrongs he suffered from the world!" Heedlessly, he discloses to the outlaws his true identity as earl of Glenallen, proclaimed a traitor to the throne of Scotland. All the bandits except Wolf, Glenallen's rival, depart with the chieftain to take revenge on Glenallen's former friend, Arden, at the latter's wedding to Glenallen's former betrothed, Adelaide. In the second canto, Glenallen disrupts the wedding and announces his intention of murdering Arden before he can consummate the marriage; but after the pitiful pleadings of "trembling Adelaide," he repents and orders his bandits to disperse. Just at this moment Wolf arrives with another band to take Glenallen for the reward on his head. In the ensuing swordplay, Arden makes several attempts to save the life of Glenallen, who is finally wounded into unconsciousness after killing Wolf. Before the bandits can deal with the wedding guests, however, the castle is mysteriously set afire. The bandits take up the unconscious Glenallen and flee. Canto three opens with Glenallen already in the custody of the authorities, locked away in a tower and awaiting execution. In his bitterness of soul, he eagerly awaits the release that death will bring him. The keeper enters and proves to be a former confederate: "Is it Donald! or a mocking dream?/ Are these things so, or do they only seem?/ Am I awake?" Donald, after failing to convince Glenallen to escape, and in haste for what seems to be the sound of an approaching guard escort, lends his dagger to the captive so that he might dispatch himself honorably. Glenallen perishes just as "Pardon! Pardon!" echoes on the walls and Arden rushes into the cell.

The puerility of the plot and the verse fails to disguise the influences of Romanticism. Glenallen is a typical Romantic hero, arraigned in a stock melodramatic situation, pausing at the appropriate times to brood over his cruel alienation from humanity and life, more ready to die than to live. His is the childish fantasy of "after I'm dead and gone, then they'll be sorry they hurt me," but, after all, it is the same childishness of vision that pervades much of Byron and Shelley. The significance of *The Bandit* lies in Hood's ability to use language well and to exercise a healthy imagination in verse that accommodates at least the superficial elements of Romanticism at a time before he has seriously devoted himself to writing poetry.

KEATS'S INFLUENCE

Although there were Romantic tendencies in Hood's own writing before Keats's death, one can find in his verse a pronounced identification with the style of Keats that extends about five or six years after 1821, beginning with Hood's introduction to the Reynolds family through his work at the *London Magazine* that same year. John Hamilton Reynolds and his sisters had enjoyed a close friendship with Keats, and entertained fond memories of the young Romantic. Hood entered an atmosphere in the Reynolds household suffused with intimacies from the life and work of the relatively unknown Keats. To this period belongs most of what is often called Hood's "serious" poetry.

The Romantic movement had peaked and already begun to decline into the commonplace sentimentality and melodrama from which Robert Browning and Alfred, Lord Tennyson were destined to rescue it momentarily. Shelley and Byron's best works had already been published; indeed, Shelley died soon after Keats. Coleridge had graduated to philosophy, Wordsworth had defected to the establishment. Keats's final

volume–*Lamia, Isabella, The Eve of St. Agnes, and Other Poems*—had appeared in 1820 (Hood's closet drama *Lamia*, based on Keats's poem, was written in 1824, but not published until after Hood's death). With friendly critics encouraging and applauding the growing likeness of Hood's poetry to that of Keats, it was an easy time for Hood to begin imagining himself to be Keats's successor.

"THE SEA OF DEATH"

Perhaps a sense of identification with Keats's illness and death led Hood to give death such a preeminent place in his serious and even in his comic verse. Hood seems to accord death a place of passive acceptance, at times even to embrace it. For example, "The Sea of Death," which appeared first in the *London Magazine* (March, 1822) and later in *"The Plea of the Midsummer Fairies," "Hero and Leander," "Lycus the Centaur," and Other Poems*, makes the somewhat trite comparison of death to an "oceanpast" that erases the sand tracks of life "like a pursuing grave." This idea, however, is developed into a passively beautiful scene, where "spring-faced cherubs" also are asleep in "the birth-night of their peace." For contrast, Hood adds "neighbour brows scarr'd by the brunts/ Of strife and sorrowing"; and with the dead, Time itself "Slept, as he sleeps upon the silent face/ Of a dark dial in a sunless place." It is a typical Romantic eschatology; death is a place of silence and repose, a dreamlike eternity. Although Hood's view of death acquired a more theologically sound dimension during the next twenty years, his attitude of resignation to the inevitable did not change. His awareness of the closeness of death permeates all of his poetry; death, dying, and corruption tinge nearly every poem with sobriety and cause his humor to wax dark. Living in continual ill health as he did, this could hardly be called a Romantic affectation.

SONNETS

Hood's important poems from this period include a number of sonnets, many deserving more attention than they have received. The sonnets also reflect the influence of the Romantic poets. "Midnight," the pair "On a Sleeping Child" (all three in the *London Magazine*, December, 1822), and the eulogistic "Sonnet: Written in Keats's 'Endymion'" (the *London Magazine*, May, 1823) are among his very best. Another, beginning "It is not death . . . ," reveals not only Romantic, but also direct Shakespearean influence. It was included, along with most of his other "serious" poetry, in the volume *"The Plea of the Midsummer Fairies," "Hero and Leander," "Lycus the Centaur," and Other Poems.*

"THE PLEA OF THE MIDSUMMER FAIRIES," "HERO AND LEANDER," "LYCUS THE CENTAUR," AND OTHER POEMS

Most of the poems in this book (twenty-two out of thirty-seven) had been previously published, many in the *London Magazine*. The book constitutes the evidence offered by many that Hood was a thwarted Romantic, so pervasive is the influence of Keats. The title poem consists of 126 Spenserian stanzas (except that the final lines are pentameters), celebrating, "by an allegory, that immortality which Shakspeare has conferred on the Fairy mythology by his *Midsummer Night's Dream*."

Hood had previously written a fairly long Romantic allegory, "The Two Swans" (1824), and so had prepared himself to create what he no doubt hoped would be considered his masterpiece. Charles Lamb, to whom the poem was affectionately dedicated, likened the poem to "the songs of Apollo," but few others have felt it to be so. Although the poem abounds in the lush sensual imagery characteristic of Keats, it sags hopelessly throughout, mainly because the story is too skimpy and the monologues too substantial for a narrative of that length. The narrator, who happens upon a circle of accommodating but unhappy fairies (including Titania, Puck, Ariel, and Queen Mab), learns from Titania that they are unhappy because their "fairy lives/ Are leased upon the fickle faith of men." Her complaint lasts through nearly eight stanzas, after which the "melancholy Shape" of time (Saturn, Mutability) appears with "hurtful scythe" to harvest the wee folk. After an argument between the fairies and Saturn that lasts seventy-five stanzas (nearly sixty percent of the poem), the ghost of Shakespeare arrives just in time to save the fairies, who express their affectionate gratitude by crowning the Bard with a halo "Such as erst crown'd the old Apostle's head." As an allegory defending the importance of imagination (fancy) above reason in poetry, the significance of human feeling, the allurements of nature, and the mysterious, "The Plea of the Midsummer Fairies" fails; seeking to establish the principles of the Romantic movement, Hood offended through employment of its excesses.

The second poem in the volume, *Hero and Leander*, while certainly not lagging as a narrative, nearly approaches *The Bandit* in its tendency toward melodrama. Written in the sestina form of Shakespeare's *Venus and Adonis* (1593), the poem has a loveliness of its own but it is not brilliant. By far the better is the third poem, *Lycus, the Centaur*, first published in 1822. Dedicated to Reynolds, it employs the strikingly unusual rhythm of anapestic tetrameter couplets that give the impression of fast-paced narrative; it is a galloping rhythm, suitable to horses and centaurs. The 430 lines of the poem are rich in sensuous detail, a feature that lies nearly dormant in poetry from Keats to A. C. Swinburne. *Lycus, the Centaur* must be read aloud to be thoroughly appreciated. Admittedly, Hood's poetry did not achieve anything near perfection. The poem has flaws, as when Lycus complains of his loneliness: "There were women! there men! but to me a third sex/ I saw them all dots—yet I loved them as specks"; or when several successive closed couplets begin to give the feel of "The Night Before Christmas," but *Lycus, the Centaur*, for all its faults and its Keatsian imagery, is original and beautiful.

Most critics agree that the best poems in *"The Plea of the Midsummer Fairies," "Hero and Leander," "Lycus the Centaur," and Other Poems* are the lyrics, most of which are definitely Keatsian. Hood's "Ode: Autumn" at times provides an interesting contrast to Keat's "Ode to Autumn," but there is more to compare than to contrast. Two other short poems on autumn are included in the volume, as are three poems on the loss of innocence ("Retrospective Review," "Song, for Music," and "I Remember, I Remember"), a decent "Ode to Melancholy," and some of Hood's best sonnets. Pervasive throughout the book is the awareness, without terror, of death and corruption. Although the volume of serious poems caused some readers to see Hood as a worthy successor to Keats, *"The Plea of the Midsummer Fairies," "Hero and Leander," "Lycus the Centaur," and Other Poems* met with a generally poor critical and public reception and failed to sell out even a single printing.

ODES AND ADDRESSES TO GREAT PEOPLE AND WHIMS AND ODDITIES

The apparent cause of this cool reception to is that during the years immediately preceding its publication Hood had captured the public's attention as a writer of comic verse. In 1825 he produced *Odes and Addresses to Great People* (in collaboration with Reynolds), and in the following year the first series of *Whims and Oddities*. The time for humor in poetry had come—not the incisive, often caustic wit of the eighteenth century, but an inoffensive, wholesome humor to help people laugh their way through the oppressively industrial times at the beginning of the nineteenth century. The reading public wanted a humor that appealed to people of low estate without being vulgar. It found in the humorous verse of Thomas Hood exactly what it sought, and came to expect nothing more nor less than that from him.

The success of Hood's early comic publications depended heavily upon his skill as a punster, examples of which are so abundant that they need not be dwelt upon at length. Most commonly cited in this regard are the two ballads, "Faithless Sally Brown" and "Faithless Nelly Gray." In the first, two lovers go out for a walk that is interrupted by an impress gang from the Royal Navy; "And Sally she did faint away,/ While Ben he was brought to." After Ben's tour of duty is finished, he returns to find Sally is another man's sweetheart; he laments, "I've met with many a breeze before,/ But never such a blow." In the opening stanza of the second poem, "Ben Battle was a soldier bold,/ And used to war's alarms:/ But a cannon-ball took off his legs,/ So he laid down his arms!" Although these are not the best examples of his craft, there is no question that Hood was the best punster of his century (perhaps the best in English letters); most of his puns are exceptional. Unfortunately, much of Hood's humor is topical; many of his puns and jokes cannot be grasped by the modern reader without an understanding of the times and a knowledge of the idiom of the 1820's and 1830's. Even so, many of Hood's poems retain an appreciable humor for today because they present general observations on the human condition. The most notable include "An Address to the Steam Washing Company" in *Odes and Addresses to Great People*; "A Valentine," "The Fall of the Deer,"

"December and May," "She Is Far from the Land," "Remonstratory Ode: From the Elephant at Exeter Change. . . ," "The Sea-Spell," and the darkly humorous "The Last Man," all in *Whims and Oddities* (First Series); and "Bianca's Dream," "A Legend of Navarre," "The Demon-Ship," and "Tim Turpin" in *Whims and Oddities* (Second Series). In "The Demon-Ship" Hood does a masterful job of creating a terrifying situation that is reversed in the humor of the closing lines; in "The Last Man," the wry ending cannot shift a much longer poem into the comic mode, so that the overall effect is far from humorous. As a serious poem, "The Last Man" offers a brilliant description of a postapocalyptic world.

Hood continued writing "serious" poetry during the remainder of his life, but until the last few years, his comic verse claimed the limelight. With the failure of the engraving firm in 1834, and the subsequent "exile" to Germany, however, financial and physical hardship weighed heavily upon Hood and his family, and his comic verses began to acquire a certain note of sobriety. There had always been a loosely didactic element, a flexible moralizing, in his humor. Without gross distastefulness, Hood amused his audience by good-naturedly ridiculing people and institutions that were newsworthy or offensive to the public—in a way that often seemed to "teach a lesson." One of the most consistent objects of his humor was human greed; another was impoverishment. Employee displacement caused by unjust laws or advancements in technological efficiency also provoked his satirical wit. Since Hood no longer entertained hopes of succeeding Keats, his "serious" poetry began to develop an originality and power of its own, as Hood became a voice of the people's protest against those institutions. Hypocrisy and ambition became primary targets of his comic verse, which also developed a morbid, often sadistic, grotesqueness. Poems such as "Death's Ramble," from *Whims and Oddities*, in which a morality play is effected through pun after pun, led to "Death in the Kitchen" (1828), in which the puns are ingenious but the philosophizing about death unhumorous; to "Gog and Magog" (1830), with its hints of judgment and violence; to "Ode to Mr. Malthus" (1839), wherein the double standard of the well-to-do is satirized; and, finally, to *Miss Kilmansegg and Her Pre-*

cious Leg (1840). Each poem outdoes the last in taking a more caustic, albeit humorous, view of humanity or some of its elements.

MISS KILMANSEGG AND HER PRECIOUS LEG

Beginning with *Miss Kilmansegg and Her Precious Leg*, the serious side of Hood sought to reassert itself again, this time with a vigor and force of wit that it had manifested only in comic verse, but with a simplicity of expression unencumbered by flowery Romantic or Elizabethan rhetoric. During the final years of his life, Hood produced his greatest impact on English poetry in the songs of social protest–*Miss Kilmansegg and Her Precious Leg*, "The Song of the Shirt," "The Bridge of Sighs," and others—and his artistic masterpiece, "The Haunted House," which alone, said Edgar Allan Poe, "would have secured immortality for any poet of the nineteenth century."

Miss Kilmansegg and Her Precious Leg is a long satirical narrative of almost 2,400 lines. The central character is born into a family of great wealth:

> When she saw the light—it was no mere ray
> Of that light so common—so everyday—
> That the sun each morning launches—
> But six wax tapers dazzled her eyes,
> From a thing—a gooseberry bush for size—
> With a golden stem and branches.

After separate passages dealing in detail with her pedigree, birth, christening, childhood, and education, the reader learns that one day, while riding, Miss Kilmansegg lost control of her horse, which bolted at the sight of a ragged beggar, and in the ensuing accident "Miss K" lost her leg. Because she had been educated to a lifestyle of conspicuous consumption and hatred for the ordinary, she insists fanatically on replacing her natural leg with a golden one: "All sterling metal—not half-and-half,/ The Goldsmith's mark was stamped on the calf." (The pun on "golden calf" is intentional.) After she receives the expensive leg, the poem pursues her through her career as a fashionable debutante, her courtship, and her subsequent marriage to a foreign count of questionable origin. Their honeymoon is spent at a country estate, where she learns that her husband's sole interest is gambling. After several years of tumultuous living that exhausts all of "Miss K's" resources, the count murders

her in the night, using her expensive leg as a bludgeon. Hood concludes the poem with a moral reminiscent of the "Pardoner's Tale" from Chaucer: "Price of many a crime untold;/ Gold! Gold! Gold! Gold:/ Good or bad a thousand fold!" The poem is very funny throughout, but the humor is accompanied by an undercurrent of bitterness against the rich, and the moralizing stanza at the poem's conclusion seems to affirm its serious didactic intention.

"A TALE OF A TRUMPET"

Eight months later *The New Monthly Magazine* published Hood's "A Tale of a Trumpet," another long satirical poem, this time about a deaf woman to whom the devil supplies a trumpet through which she can hear all manner of scandalous gossip. Again, the poem ends in a moral against rumormongering. In November, 1843, *Punch* published Hood's "A Drop of Gin," a poem reminiscent of Hogarth's famous engraving "Gin Lane." The following month *Punch* published "The Pauper's Christmas Carol" and "The Song of the Shirt," poems of social protest which probably better express Hood's mind than any other poems of his last fifteen years.

"THE SONG OF THE SHIRT"

"The Song of the Shirt," with its driving, mechanical rhythm, is based on the plight of a poor widowed woman with starving infants who was arrested while trying to pawn some of her employer's garments to obtain money for food (she was a seamstress for seven shillings a week). Touched by the newspaper accounts and always sensitive to the exploitation of the poor, Hood wrote what his wife considered to be his finest poem. In it, a woman sits sewing, and as she sews she sings the "Song of the Shirt": "Work! work! work!/ While the cock is crowing aloof!/ And work—work—work,/ Till the stars shine through the roof!" The poem calls to mind the protest movements and revolutions which were soon to plague Europe in the wake of the Industrial Revolution—and the publication of Karl Marx's *Communist Manifesto* in 1848 and *Das Kapital* in 1850. The woman's lament is a desperate appeal born of the most abject misery: "Oh! God! that bread should be so dear,/ And flesh and blood so cheap!"

"THE HAUNTED HOUSE"

"The Haunted House" (*Hood's Magazine*, January, 1844), over which Poe became ecstatic, is indeed a powerful artistic creation: a descriptive, camera-eye narrative that builds an atmosphere of terror—which dissipates in the absolute meaninglessness of the poem. The reader can learn nothing of the source of the mystery, other than that a murder has apparently been committed, and that the house is haunted. The conclusion of the poem could be transplanted to any other part of the poem without disrupting the internal logic. It is as if Hood had left "The Haunted House" unfinished, perhaps to add to the sense of mystery and terror, but more likely through a lack of inspiration.

RETURN TO SERIOUSNESS

The artistic achievement represented by "The Haunted House" notwithstanding, Hood's heart in these last years was more concerned with the suffering of others. Having spent so many years in sickness and pain, laboring feverishly to meet endless deadlines, striving in spite of his own sufferings to make others laugh, he had acquired a true compassion for the poor and unfortunate that sought to be expressed in his verse. His last years of writing produced "The Lady's Dream" (February, 1844), a song of regret for a life not spent ministering to the needs of others; "The Workhouse Clock" (April, 1844), an "allegory" that fires its blistering sermon at a leisurely middle class: "Christian Charity, hang your head!"; and "The Lay of the Labourer" (November, 1844), a panegyric to the working class.

WHIMSICALITIES

A final volume of comic verse–*Whimsicalities: A Periodical Gathering*—appeared in 1844, but besides "The Haunted House," Hood's most regarded publication of that year is "The Bridge of Sighs." Often anthologized or cited as an example of dactylic verse, it concerns a young woman who commits a desperate suicide by leaping from a city bridge. Journalistic, as most of Hood's verse was, "The Bridge of Sighs" is based on an actual case; whatever the circumstances of the original suicide were, however, Hood turns the incident to good use in expounding a favorite theme:

> Alas! for the rarity
> Of Christian charity
> Under the sun!
> Oh! it was pitiful!
> Near a whole city full,
> Home she had none!

Hood continued to write even as he lay upon his deathbed, where, among other poems and letters, he produced "Stanzas" (March, 1845): "Farewell, Life! My senses swim;/ And the world is growing dim;/ . . . Strong the earthy odour grows—/ I smell the Mould above the Rose!" Hood's farewell to life concludes with the same homely, cheerful philosophy that infused so much poetry written in pain, the same positive outlook that inspired him to ask for reform rather than revolution: "Welcome, Life! the Spirit strives!/ Strength returns, and hope revives;/ . . . I smell the Rose above the Mould!" The juxtaposition of the stanzas intimates that Hood's source of hope and strength was his willingness to embrace death without terror. Nine years after his death, a monument was erected over his grave, paid for by public subscription. Beneath the bust of Hood is engraved a simple coat of arms: on the shield is a heart pierced by a sewing needle; under it, the scroll reads, at Hood's request, "He sang the Song of the Shirt."

OTHER MAJOR WORKS

LONG FICTION: *Tylney Hall*, 1834; *Up the Rhine*, 1840; *Our Family*, 1861.

SHORT FICTION: *National Tales*, 1827.

PLAYS: *York and Lancaster: Or, A School Without Scholars*, pr. 1829 (wr. 1828); *Lamia: A Romance*, pb. 1852; *Guido and Marina: A Dramatic Sketch*, pb. 1882.

MISCELLANEOUS: *Hood's Magazine*, 1861; *The Works of Thomas Hood*, 1869-1873 (10 volumes; Thomas Hood, Jr., and Mrs. Frances Freeling Broderip, editors), 1882-1884 (11 volumes), 1972 (8 volumes).

BIBLIOGRAPHY

Brander, Laurence. *Thomas Hood*. London: Longmans, Green, 1963. Discusses Hood's early and later poems, as well as the public poems, for which Hood is remembered the most. A valuable resource for beginning readers of Hood.

Bush, Douglas. "Thomas Hood." In *Mythology and the Romantic Tradition in English Poetry*. New York: W. W. Norton, 1963. A perceptive although brief account of Hood's works. The commentary on "Lycus, the Centaur" and "Hero and Leander" are worth reading.

Clubbe, John. *Victorian Forerunner: The Later Career of Thomas Hood*. Durham, N.C.: Duke University Press, 1968. A scholarly and important contribution to the literary criticism available on Hood's later poems. Clubbe asserts that Hood wrote many of his most memorable poems in the last decade of his life.

Edgecombe, Rodney Stenning. "Ransom's Captain Carpenter and Hood's Faithless Nelly Gray." *The Explicator* 58, no. 3 (Spring, 2000): 154-155. Edgecombe examines two poems, one by Hood and another by John Crowe Ransom, which offer a critique of violence and of the ballad form. Hood primes the satire of "Faithless Nelly Gray" with the subtitle "A Pathetic Ballad."

Jeffrey, Lloyd N. *Thomas Hood*. New York: Twayne, 1972. This introduction to Hood's poetry argues for the intrinsic value of his work despite his being overshadowed by the Romantics. Views the study of Hood's poems as an important lead into nineteenth century literature. Discusses his poetry selectively and devotes one chapter to the macabre and grotesque in his works.

Jerrold, Walter. *Thomas Hood: His Life and Times*. New York: Haskell House, 1968. A full account of Hood's life with critical commentary of his poems. Some inaccuracies about Hood's life are corrected here, particularly in his early period. An important work for Hood scholars.

_____, ed. *Thomas Hood and Charles Lamb: The Story of a Friendship*. London: E. Benn, 1930. The introduction is useful in its appraisal of Hood's "Literary Reminiscences," which reveals much about Hood's contemporaries and his early life.

Lodge, Sara. "Hood, Clare, and the 'Mary' Chain." *Notes and Queries* 45, no. 2 (June, 1998): 205-208. Lodge argues that Thomas Hood's disturbing piece "A Lay of Real Life" is a literary response to a poem by John Clare, titled "My Mary."

Reid, J. C. *Thomas Hood*. London: Routledge & Kegan Paul, 1963. A full-length biographical and critical study of Hood. Well researched and sympathetic in its approach to this poet.

Larry David Barton;
bibliography updated by the editors

A. D. HOPE

Born: Cooma, New South Wales, Australia; July 21, 1907

Died: Canberra, Australian Capital Territory, Australia; July 13, 2000

PRINCIPAL POETRY

The Wandering Islands, 1955
Poems, 1960
A. D. Hope, 1963
Collected Poems, 1930-1965, 1966
New Poems, 1965-1969, 1969
Dunciad Minor: An Heroick Poem, 1970
Collected Poems, 1930-1970, 1972
Selected Poems, 1973
The Damnation of Byron, 1973
A Late Picking: Poems, 1965-1974, 1975
A Book of Answers, 1978
Antechinus: Poems, 1975-1980, 1981
The Age of Reason, 1985
Selected Poems, 1986
Orpheus, 1991
Selected Poems, 1992
Selected Poetry and Prose, 2000

OTHER LITERARY FORMS

A. D. Hope distinguished himself as poet, critic, and editor. His collections of lectures, essays, and reviews addressed English and Australian literature, and he also edited anthologies. He wrote one play, *Ladies from the Sea* (pb. 1987).

ACHIEVEMENTS

While Australia has yet to produce a poet with a lasting influence on world literature, A. D. Hope has perhaps come closest to attaining an international reputation. Since the publication of his first collection in 1955, he emerged as the dominant figure in Australian poetry.

Hope stands outside the mainstream of much modern poetry in his strict formalism and outspoken disdain for much of the poetry and critical theories of his contemporaries, or what he called in *The New Cratylus:*

Notes on the Craft of Poetry "Heresies of the Age." In his carefully balanced wit and in the lucidity of his use of such neoclassical forms as the heroic couplet, he seemed much closer in his attitudes and manner to Alexander Pope than to T. S. Eliot. While early compared to W. H. Auden in his sometimes scathing denunciations of twentieth century life, Hope possessed a distinctive voice with a wide range; his satirical poems have been no less admired than his passionate love poetry. In all of his work, the notion of poetry as a learned craft is preeminent. Unlike many of his contemporaries, he remained content to express his vision in the traditional patterns of accentual-syllabic meter and rhyme.

Hope's first collection was published when he was nearly fifty; thereafter, his reputation grew rapidly. He was the recipient of numerous awards, including Grace Leven Prize (1956), the Arts Council of Great Britain Award for Poetry (1965), the Britannica Award for Literature (1965), the Myer Award for Australian Literature (1967), the Ingram Merrill Award for Literature (1969), the Levinson Prize (1969), and the Robert Frost Award (1976). He was elected Ashby Visiting Fellow of Clare Hall, Cambridge, and Honorary Fellow of University College, Oxford. In 1972, he was named Officer, Order of the British Empire, and Companion of the Order of Australia in 1981. He traveled and lectured extensively, especially in the United States.

BIOGRAPHY

Alec Derwent Hope was born in Cooma, New South Wales, Australia, on July 21, 1907, the firstborn of the family. His father, Percival Hope, a Presbyterian minister, moved the family to Tasmania when Hope was four years old. In the rural area where Hope's father's new congregation was located, school was rudimentary at best, often being held in the local sheepshearing shed. Hope, like many middle-class children, received much of his primary instruction at home. His mother, who had been a schoolteacher, taught him to read and write, and his father later instructed him in Latin. The family library was large, and the parents took turns reading classics of English literature aloud to the five children. Hope began to write poems in ballad stanzas when

A. D. Hope (Coward of Canberra)

he was seven or eight, and by the time he was in his early teens, he had published his first poem, a translation of Roman poet Catullus's *Phasellus ille quem videstis, hospites.*

When Hope was fourteen, he was sent to the Australian mainland for his secondary education, first at Bathurst High School and later at Fort Street High School, one of the best schools in Sydney. Upon graduation, he was awarded a scholarship designated for sons of Presbyterian clergymen and matriculated at St. Andrew's College of the University of Sydney. He had originally intended to study medicine, but low science marks forced him to read for an arts degree instead. During his undergraduate years, he published poems in university magazines and in the Sydney *Bulletin*. He was graduated in 1928. Hope distinguished himself in his undergraduate work in philosophy and English and won a scholarship for further study in England.

He entered University College, Oxford, in the fall of 1928, shortly after the graduation of Auden, Louis MacNeice, and Stephen Spender. Poor and underprepared, Hope had difficulty with the tedious Oxford English curriculum, which at that time leaned heavily toward philological studies. Despite his admiration for such notable scholars as C. S. Lewis, he managed no better than a third-class degree, which he completed in 1930.

He returned to Sydney just as the Depression was deepening and became a public-school teacher and vocational psychologist for several years before obtaining a position as a lecturer in education at Sydney Teachers' College in 1937. In 1938, he married Penelope Robinson and was appointed lecturer in English at Sydney, where he remained until 1944. In 1945, he became the senior lecturer in English at the University of Melbourne, where he taught courses in English and European literature. In 1951, he became the first professor of English at Canberra University College (now the Australian National University), a chair which he held until 1968, after which he was Library Fellow for three years and, later, Professor Emeritus. Hope, who long suffered from poor health, passed away on July 13, 2000, in Canberra.

ANALYSIS

In his introduction to a selection of his poems in 1963 as part of the Australian Poets series, A. D. Hope stated that "all theories about poetry are inadequate and that good poetry has been written on many assumptions which actually appear to be incompatible with one another." That claim notwithstanding, Hope did admit to several "comfortable prejudices" that allowed him to ignore poetical practices with which he had no sympathy. "The chief of these," he said, "is a heresy of our time which holds that by excluding those things which poetry has in common with prose, narrative, argument, description, exhortation and exposition, and that, depending entirely on lyric impulse or the evocative power of massed imagery one can arrive at the pure essence of poetry." This remark is central to any understanding of Hope's work, for he consistently lamented the impoverishment of twentieth century poetry when comparing it to the "great variety of forms practised in the past." The remark also reveals the strong influence of Latin studies on Hope's work, for his list includes most of the common topics of classical rhetoric. Of

those he mentions, narrative and argumentation are important techniques that he consistently employed in his best poems.

Hope's second complaint was with "the notion that poetry can be improved or its range extended by breaking down the traditional structure of English verse by replacing its rhythms by those of prose." Hope, who studied at Oxford with C. L. Wrenn, editor of *Beowulf*, wrote learnedly on the origins of English poetic meter, particularly on the transition from accentual meters to accentual syllabics, which took place in the century after Geoffrey Chaucer's death (the 1400's), and on the metrical practices of John Dryden and Alexander Pope. Like Robert Frost, Hope credited the tension between meter and sentence rhythm as the key to the successful iambic pentameter line, of which Hope was a master. Given his mastery of meter, Hope had little patience with theories of "open form" or "projective verse" that were forwarded in defense of free verse.

According to Hope, another of the modern "heresies" stemmed from "that irritable personalism which is partly a heritage of the Romantics, the view that poetry is primarily self-expression." Even though Hope stated his disagreement with the poetical theories of Edgar Allan Poe, he would seem to agree with the primacy of a poem's effect on its audience: "The poem is not a feeling, it is a structure of words designed, among other things, to arouse a certain state of feeling." Similarly, Hope seems to have agreed with T. S. Eliot ("a poet whose poetry I cannot bring myself to like at all") in the need for a poet to find "an 'objective correlative' for the transmission of the poet's state of heart and mind to his readers."

It should be apparent from these comments that Hope had little sympathy for the confessionalist tendencies of much modern poetry, which, according to Hope, provide many poets with "an adoring cannibal audience waiting for the next effusion of soul meat." He added that the emotions in poems should not necessarily be equated with the emotions of poets: "The delight of creation and invention is their proper emotion and this must be in control of all other feelings."

Finally, Hope's personal preferences in the language of poetry were that it be "plain, lucid, coherent, logically connected, syntactically exact, and firmly based in current idiom and usage." To a large degree, Hope remained true to this dictum; his poetry is remarkable for its avoidance of needless obscurity and ambiguity. As he said, "A poem which can be parsed and analysed is not necessarily a good poem, but a poem which cannot is almost certainly bad." He did, however, allow himself the option of a certain elevation of language, what has been disparaged in recent decades as "poetic diction." With William Wordsworth, Hope agreed that "a poet should certainly be a man speaking to men in a language common to all," but that does not mean that the debased vocabulary of conversational speech should be the poet's sole resource. For Hope, whose learning and therefore vocabulary were far-ranging, the "word-hoard" of the poet should be ample enough to include terms from a great range of interests which, in his own case, included numerous historical and literary references, classical allusions, and scientific terms.

AUSTRALIAN COLONIAL LITERATURE

Australian literature, like all colonial literatures, including that of the United States, has been throughout much of its short history in search of an identity. During the nineteenth century, Australian poets fell into two general classes: those who imitated the poetic styles of the English Romantics and Victorians, and those who carried on a lively body of "bush poetry," largely anonymous balladry derived from the folk traditions of Great Britain. Of the first group, Oscar Wilde, reviewing an 1888 anthology of Australian writing, could find "nothing but echoes without music, reflections without beauty, second-rate magazine verses, arid third-rate verse for Colonial newspapers, . . . artless Nature in her most irritating form." Hope made two revealing comments regarding the situation of the Australian writer of his generation: The first was that his father's library, while amply supplied with the classics of English literature, contained no Australian poets; the other was that, as late as the early 1950's, Hope had to struggle to obtain credit-status for the course in native literature that he instituted and taught at Canberra University College. Thus, Australian poets are caught in an uncomfortable dilemma: They may wish to create a truly "national" poetry, but they lack a tradition upon which to build it.

Hope himself identified, in *Native Companions*, the three main stages of a colonial literature. In the first, the work of colonial writers is simply part of the literary tradition of the homeland. In the second, writers born in the new land but educated in the tradition of the mother country attempt to create a literature of their own. In the final stage, this self-consciousness disappears, and writers emerge who can influence the whole literary tradition, including that of the mother country. Though Hope believed that Australian literature was in the middle stage, one could argue, with the publication of Judith Wright's *The Moving Image* and James McAuley's *Under Aldebaran* in 1946, the publication of Hope's first collection, *The Wandering Islands*, in 1955, and the novelist Patrick White's winning of the Nobel Prize in Literature in 1973, that Australian writing has clearly moved into its maturity.

THE WANDERING ISLANDS

Though Hope had been publishing poetry and criticism since the late 1930's, *The Wandering Islands*, which appeared when he was forty-eight, was his first full collection. In a cultural climate that was still marked by parochialism and censorship, Hope's first book was something of a *succès de scandale*. The sexual explicitness of the title poem, his lightly worn learning, and his unsparing satire caused many critics to accuse him variously of academism, obscurity, misogyny, and even anti-Australian sentiments. Certainly, "Australia" would not have pleased the nationalistic poets of the Jindyworobak movement, at whose expense Hope had on occasion been mercilessly critical in his reviews. In this outwardly bitter poem, Hope sees his homeland as "without songs, architecture, history." Despite the fact that Hope later characterizes himself as one who turns "gladly home/ From the lush jungle of modern thought" to a country which has not yet been overwhelmed by "the chatter of cultured apes," the poem gave his early critics an abundant supply of ammunition with which to attack him.

In the book's title poem, Hope also delineates another constant theme of his work: the attractions and disappointment of love. For Hope, "the wandering islands" are the isolations of individual sexual identities, which are always, like the sundered beast in Plato's analogy of the two sexes, frustrated in their attempts at complete union:

An instant of fury, a bursting mountain of spray,
They rush together, their promontories lock
An instant the castaway hails the castaway,
But the sounds perish in that earthquake shock.

In these brief seconds of orgasmic loss of self lies "all that one mind ever knows of another,/ Or breaks the long isolation of the heart."

Commenting on Hope's recurrent motifs in a review of *The Wandering Islands*, S. L. Goldberg notes that "the attitude from which his themes arise is Dionysian or tragic, disturbed, romantic, existentialist at least in its premises; on the other hand, the sense of tradition and order implicit in his art . . . is decidedly Apollonian or classical, and intellectual rather than freely organic." In this sense, Hope seems closest to the tradition of the English Metaphysical poets, John Donne in particular, who saw no divorce between passion and intellect, the "dissociated sensibility," to borrow Eliot's phrase.

SEXUAL IMAGERY

A significant number of Hope's best poems deal with the sexual theme, by turns satirically and seriously. In "Conquistador" he sings "of the decline of Henry Clay/ . . . a small man in a little way," who is mashed flat in a sexual encounter with a "girl of uncommon size," who uses "him thereafter as a bedside mat." The poem, which is not without its darker side, bears comparison with Auden's "Ballad of Miss Gee." In "The Brides," Hope, in an impressive piece of social satire, works an extended conceit comparing for the smartest model in the sexual showroom, is lured to the altar by promises of

> every comfort: the full set
> Of gadgets; knobs that answer to the touch
> For light or music; a place for his cigarette;
> Room for his knees; a honey of a clutch.

That the majority of contemporary marriages last not much longer than a new car's extended warranty period is at least implicit in this witty poem.

"IMPERIAL ADAM"

In other poems Hope expands the sexual theme to include larger observations of nature and human history. "Imperial Adam," one of his most widely reprinted poems, retells the story of the Fall as a sexual fable. Having partaken of the "delicious pulp of the forbidden fruit,"

Adam and Eve immediately experience the awakening of sexual desire:

> Sly as the snake she loosed her sinuous thighs.

> And waking, smiled up at him from the grass;
> Her breasts rose softly and he heard her sigh—
> From all the beasts whose pleasant task it was
> In Eden to increase and multiply

> Adam had learned the jolly deed of kind:
> He took her in his arms and there and then,
> Like the clean beasts, embracing from behind
> Began in joy to found the breed of men.

In lines that are reminiscent of William Butler Yeats's "A shudder in the loins engenders there/ The broken wall, the burning roof and tower . . . ," Hope foreshadows the whole violent future of humanity in the "sexual lightning stroke" of the first embrace. The poem closes with Adam witnessing the consequences of his act:

> Adam watching too
> Saw how her dumb breasts at their ripening wept,
> The great pod of her belly swelled and grew,

> And saw its water break, and saw, in fear,
> Its quaking muscles in the act of birth,
> Between her legs a pigmy face appear,
> And the first murderer lay upon the earth.

RESISTING ROMANTICISM

It is significant that Hope, in a later poem titled "The Planctus," offers "another version of the Fall" in which Eve escapes the Garden and is provided with another helpmate, "While Adam, whose fellow God had not replaced,/ Lived on immortal, young, with virtue crowned,/ Sterile and impotent and justified." In Hope's view, a purely hermetic retreat from the moral perplexities of life is equivalent to a living death.

One other early poem comments, at first satirically, on those who see the "standardization" of the modern age as somehow unnatural, in particular the typical "Nature Poet" who "from his vegetable Sunday School/ Emerges with the neatly maudlin phrase" to protest the "endless duplication of lives and objects" which the American poet Theodore Roethke decried in "Dolor." Against this romantic assumption, Hope weighs the evidence of Earth herself, whose procreative fecundity "gathers and repeats/ The cast of a face, a million butterfly wings." Hope argues persuasively that such "standardization" is, in fact, the essence of the reproductive forces that rule nature and human life. As he says, it is love that "still pours into its ancient mould/ The lashing seed that grows to a man again."

Even in those poems that seem purely lyrical, Hope resists the romantic temptation to find in love any easy solutions. In one of his finest short poems, "As Well as They Can," he combines the twin demands of art and love in lines that ironically echo the conceit of Donne's "The Bait":

> As well as he can, the poet, blind, betrayed
> Distracted by the groaning mill, among
> The jostle of slaves, the clatter, the lash of
>   trade,
>   Taps the pure source of song.
>
> As well as I can, my heart in this bleak air,
> The empty days, the waste nights since you went,
> Recalls your warmth, your smile, the grace and
>   stir
>   That were its element.

DIALECTICS AND HISTORY

Hope's poetry is founded on dialectical premises—between the sexes, between assertion and counterargument, between art and life, even between the living poet and his predecessors. In "Moschus Moschiferus," which is on first glance conventional in its subtitle, "A Song for St Cecilia's Day," he contrasts "the pure, bright drops of sound" of Tibetan hunters' flute music with the ends to which it is put, ensnaring the hapless mouse-deer of the title, hunted almost into extinction for their precious musk glands. As a footnote to the twentieth century which has seen, in Nazi Germany to cite only one example, the powers of music set to evil uses, Hope can offer the saint little more than a sardonic gift:

> Divine Cecilia, there is no more to say!
> Of all who praised the power of music, few
> Knew of these things. In honor of your day
> Accept this song I too have made for you.

Similarly, in carrying on a continuing debate with the writers and literature of the past, Hope takes a revisionist view of personalities and characters that must now be seen from a contemporary perspective. In "Man Friday" he writes a sequel to Daniel Defoe's *Robinson Crusoe* (1719) in which Friday, having had his fill of life in a country where

> More dreadful than ten thousands savages,
> In their strange clothes and monstrous mats of hair,
> The pale-eyed English swarm to joke and stare,
> With endless questions round him crowd and press
> Curious to see and touch his loneliness,

makes his escape home by a last, suicidal swim. "Faustus," informed by the devil that "Hell is more up-to-date than men suppose" and that his soul has long since been in hell, "reorganized on the hire-purchase plan," avoids living further in his purely material world by killing both Helen and himself. George Gordon, Lord Byron, who boasted of thousands of seductions, in "The Damnation of Byron" is condemned to a "Hell of Women" where, at last satiated by endless "wet kisses and voluptuous legs agape// He longs for the companionship of men, their sexless friendliness."

In all these poems, as well as in many others from *A Book of Answers* and *The Age of Reason*, Hope's collection of verse epistles and narratives concerning leading figures, both historical and fictional from the Augustan Age, one is always aware of an intellect passionately involved in a dialogue with the past.

ORPHEUS

When Hope's wife predeceased him, his dialogue with the past took final form as a five-part conversation with her shade. These "Western Elegies" immediately follow the title poem in Hope's last collection of verse, *Orpheus*. They are written in classical hexameter, a measure rarely used to good effect in English verse. They climax in a vast meditation on language and time, "The Tongues," in which Hope celebrates the flowering of Indo-European languages, then reviews his personal acquaintance and love for tongues as diverse as Latin, Norse, and Russian:

> The man who has only one tongue lives forever alone on
>   an island
> Shut in on himself by conventions he is only dimly
>   aware of,
> Like a beast whose mind is fenced by the narrow extent
>   of its instincts.

At the end of "The Tongues," Hope anticipates his own imminent translation, in the other sense of that word:

> How shall I tell her the world is simpler than men imagine,
> For those set apart by God speak a tongue used only by
>   angels;
> That the distance from East to West is no more than its
>   word for 'I love you'?
> And perpetual pentecost springs and renews itself in that
>   message,
> Which blesses the gifts of tongues and crowns, the
>   venture of Babel.

Even though Hope has stressed, perhaps ingenuously, that his own poems are "hardly ever 'confessions' and [are] usually written in a spirit of 'as if' highly misleading to any unwary commentator or putative biographer," it would be a mistake to assume that his poetry is impersonal in any sense. Eliot, who said that poetry should be "an escape from personality," went on to add that one must first have a personality to be able to escape from it. In "Hay Fever," a late poem which is one of the few clearly autobiographical works in Hope's oeuvre, the gentle memory of an Edwardian summer spent mowing hay in rural Tasmania moves the mature poet to speculate on the abundant harvest of a life's work:

> It is good for a man when he comes to the end
>   of his course
> In the barn of his brain to be able to romp
>   like a boy in the heap . . .
> To lie still in well-cured hay . . . to drift
>   into sleep.

A. D. Hope's voice, so distinctive in its ability to match the orchestra's full range, is truly remarkable.

OTHER MAJOR WORKS

PLAY: *Ladies from the Sea*, pb. 1987.

NONFICTION: *The Structure of Verse and Prose*, 1943; *The Study of English*, 1952 (lecture); *Australian Literature, 1950-1962*, 1963; *The Cave and the Spring: Essays on Poetry*, 1965; *The Literary Influence of Academies*, 1970 (lecture); *A Midsummer Eve's Dream: Variations on a Theme by William Dunbar*, 1970; *Henry Kendall: A Dialogue with the Past*, 1971; *Native Companions: Essays and Comments on Australian Literature, 1936-1966*, 1974; *Judith Wright*, 1975; *The Pack of Autolycus*, 1979; *The New Cratylus: Notes on the Craft of Poetry*, 1979; *Poetry and the Art of Archery*, 1980 (lecture); *Chance Encounters*, 1992.

EDITED TEXTS: *Australian Poetry, 1960*, 1960; *Henry Kendall*, 1973 (with Leonie Kramer).

BIBLIOGRAPHY

Argyle, Barry. "The Poetry of A. D. Hope." *Journal of Commonwealth Literature* 3 (1967): 87-96. One of the early but still relevant studies of Hope, this article places his work outside the Australian poetic tradition. Argyle argues that through its formal style and classical subject matter, the work transcends nationality and is far different from the often parochial verse of Hope's fellow Australians. Argyle concludes that Hope can be read the world over because he "does not demand that the reader be a specialist in Australian botany, marsupials, or [aboriginal] dialects."

Brissenden, R. F. "Art and the Academy: The Achievement of A. D. Hope." In *The Literature of Australia*, edited by Geoffrey Dutton. New York: Penguin Books, 1976. The discussion first corrects the idea that Hope's poetry is primarily satiric in nature. Instead, Brissenden argues, Hope's double role as a professor-poet lends his work learning and clarity. Through the analysis of several poems, Brissenden concludes that Hope invokes through his poetry the entire history and culture of Western civilization, thus making him far more than an Australian poet.

Darling, Robert. *A. D. Hope*. New York: Twayne, 1997. Reviews the whole of Hope's poetic work in the context of modernist and contemporary poetry, particularly Australian poetry.

_____. "The Mythology of the Actual." In *International Literature in English: The Major Writers*, edited by Robert L. Ross. New York: Garland, 1991. Hope's interest in science and his belief that the poet and the scientist share attributes form the basis of this essay, which analyzes fully several poems making use of scientific imagery. Supplemented by biographical information, a list of Hope's published poetry, drama, and criticism, and an extensive annotated bibliography of secondary sources.

Hart, Kevin. *A. D. Hope*. New York: Oxford University Press, 1992. Brief biography and critical interpretation of Hope's work. Includes bibliography.

King, Bruce. "A. D. Hope and Australian Poetry." *The Sewannee Review* 58 (1979): 119-141. King calls Hope "perhaps the best [poet] writing in English." The essay is of special interest, first, for placing Hope's work within the context of the overall development of Australian poetry, and second, for providing an overview of the directions that Australia's contemporary poetry was taking.

Paolucci, Anne, and Henry Paolucci. "Poet Critics on the Frontiers of Literature: A. D. Hope, T. S. Eliot, and William Carlos Williams." *Review of National Literatures* 11 (1982): 146-191. Because Hope was an accomplished poetry critic and theorist, this article is of special interest. It compares the critical and theoretical views of these three major contemporary figures and raises intriguing questions on whether the various English-language national literatures (such as Australian) will someday evolve into an international literature with English the only boundary, an outcome that Hope long predicted and promoted.

R. S. Gwynn,
updated by Alan Sullivan

GERARD MANLEY HOPKINS

Born: Stratford, England; July 28, 1844
Died: Dublin, Ireland; June 8, 1889

PRINCIPAL POETRY

Poems of Gerard Manley Hopkins, Now First Published, with Notes by Robert Bridges, 1918
Poems of Gerard Manley Hopkins, 1930, 1948, 1967
The Poetical Works of Gerard Manley Hopkins, 1990

OTHER LITERARY FORMS

Gerard Manley Hopkins's letters and papers were published in six volumes that appeared between 1935 and 1959: *The Letters of Gerard Manley Hopkins to Robert Bridges* (1935, 1955; C. C. Abbott, editor), *The Correspondence of Gerard Manley Hopkins and Richard Watson Dixon* (1935, 1955; Abbott, editor), *The Notebooks and Papers of Gerard Manley Hopkins* (1937; Humphry House, editor), *Further Letters of Gerard Manley Hopkins* (1938, 1956; Abbott, editor), *The Journals and Papers of Gerard Manley Hopkins* (1959; House and Graham Storey, editors), and *The Sermons and Devotional Writings of Gerard Manley Hopkins* (1959; Christopher Devlin, editor). A selection of letters from the three volumes edited by Abbott, *Gerard Manley Hopkins: Selected Letters*, was published in 1990. Edited by Catherine Phillips, the letters include many analyses of the work of other poets and artists; they also reveal his bouts of "melancholy," or depression, and implicitly show his internal struggles between his religion and his work as a poet. In addition to the published material, there are significant unpublished lecture notes and documents by Hopkins at the Bodleian Library and the Campion Hall Library at Oxford University.

ACHIEVEMENTS

Although Gerard Manley Hopkins saw almost none of his writings published in his lifetime, he is generally credited with being one of the founders of modern poetry and a major influence on the development of modernism in art. Many of his letters reflect a sense of failure and frustration. "The Wreck of the *Deutschland*," which he considered to be his most important poem, was rejected by the Jesuit magazine *The Month*. As a professor of classical languages and literature, he was not a productive, publishing scholar. As a priest, his sermons and theological writing did not find popular success. Yet in 1918, some thirty years after his death, his friend Robert Bridges published a collection of his poems. By 1930, when the second edition of this volume appeared, Hopkins began to attract the attention of major theoreticians of modernism: Herbert Read, William Empson, I. A. Richards, and F. R. Leavis. They acclaimed Hopkins as a powerful revolutionary force in poetry. Interest in his poetry led scholars to unearth his scattered letters and papers. Here, too, modern readers found revolutionary concepts: inscape, instress, sprung rhythm, underthought/overthought, counterpoint. Since about 1930, an enormous amount of scholarly analysis has combed through Hopkins's poetry and prose, establishing beyond doubt that he is one of the three or four most influential forces in modern English literature.

BIOGRAPHY

Gerard Manley Hopkins was the first of eight children born to Manley Hopkins, a successful marine insurance agent who wrote poetry and technical books. The family was closely knit and artistic. Two of Hopkins's brothers became professional artists, and Hopkins's papers contain many pencil sketches showing his own talent for drawing. He was devoted to his youngest sister Grace, who was an accomplished musician, and he tried to learn several musical instruments as well as counterpoint and musical composition. The family was devoutly Anglican in religion. When Hopkins was eight years old, they moved from the London suburb of Stratford

Gerard Manley Hopkins (Library of Congress)

(Essex) to the more fashionable and affluent Hampstead on the north edge of the city. From 1854 to 1863 Hopkins attended Highgate Grammar School. Richard Watson Dixon, a young teacher there, later became one of Hopkins's main literary associates. Hopkins studied Latin and Greek intensively, winning the Governor's Gold Medal for Latin Verse, as well as the Headmaster's Poetry Prize in 1860 for his English poem "The Escorial." His school years seem to have been somewhat stormy, marked by the bittersweet joy of schoolboy friendships and the excitement of a keen mind mastering the intricacies of Greek, Latin, and English poetry. He was such a brilliant student that he won the Balliol College Exhibition, or scholarship prize. Balliol was reputed to be the leading college for classical studies at Oxford University in the 1860's. Hopkins attended Balliol from April, 1863, until June, 1867, studying "Classical Greats," the philosophy, literature, and language of ancient Greece and Rome. The first year of this curriculum required rigorous study of the structure of the Latin and Greek languages. This linguistic study terminated with a very demanding examination called "Moderations." Hopkins earned a grade of "First" in his Moderations in December, 1864. The remaining years of "Classical Greats" involved the study of the philosophy and literature of ancient writers in their original tongues, concluding with the "Greats" or final honors examination. Hopkins concluded his B.A. (Hons.) with a "First in Greats" in June, 1867. A double first in Classical Greats is a remarkable accomplishment. Benjamin Jowett, the Master of Balliol and himself a famous classical scholar, called Hopkins "The Star of Balliol" and all who knew him at this period predicted a brilliant career for him. Hopkins loved Oxford—its landscapes and personalities, the life of culture and keen intellectual striving—and always looked back to his college days with nostalgia. His schoolmate there was Robert Bridges, who was to be his lifelong friend and correspondent.

These years were not peaceful, however, for the promising young scholar and poet. The colleges of Oxford University were then religious institutions. Only Anglicans could enroll as students or teach there. For some thirty years before Hopkins entered Balliol, Oxford University had been rocked by the "Oxford Movement." A number of its illustrious teachers had questioned the very basis of the Anglican Church, the way in which the Church of England could claim to be independent of the Roman Catholic Church. Many of the leading figures of the Oxford Movement had felt compelled to leave Oxford and the Church of England and to convert to Roman Catholicism. Among the converts was Cardinal John Henry Newman, whose *Apologia pro Vita Sua*, or history of his conversion from the Anglican to the Roman Church, was published in 1864, the year Hopkins was preparing for his Moderations at Balliol. To follow Newman's lead meant to give up hope of an academic career at Oxford, and perhaps even the hope of completing his B.A. Nevertheless, by 1866 Hopkins was convinced that the only true church was the Roman. In October, 1866, he was received into the Roman Catholic Church by Newman himself. It is hard for modern readers to imagine the pain and dislocation this decision caused Hopkins. His family letters reveal the anguish of his father, who believed that his son's immortal soul was lost, not merely his temporal career. Hopkins was estranged from his family to some degree ever after his momentous conversion. After he had completed his B.A. at Oxford, Hopkins taught in 1867 at Newman's Oratory School, a Roman Catholic grammar school near Birmingham. There he decided to enter a religious order. In May, 1868, he burned all manuscripts of his poems, thinking that poetry was not a fit occupation for a seriously religious person. Fortunately, some of his early writing survived in copies he had given to Robert Bridges. He wrote no further poetry until "The Wreck of the *Deutschland*."

In the summer of 1867 he went on a walking tour of Switzerland. In that September he entered the Jesuit Novitiate, Manresa House, London, for the first two years of rigorous spiritual training to become a Jesuit priest. There he followed the regime of the Spiritual Exercises of St. Ignatius Loyola (1491-1556), taking vows of poverty, chastity, and obedience. From 1870 to 1873 he studied philosophy at St. Mary's Hall, Stonyhurst, in the North of England. Although Hopkins had been a brilliant student of classical philosophy at Oxford, he seems not to have pleased his Jesuit superiors so well. Perhaps part of the problem was an independence of mind which could be disconcerting. At Stonyhurst he first read the medieval philosopher John Duns Scotus, who had an unusually strong influence on Hopkins's ideas. He then returned to Manresa House for a year as professor of rhetoric. From 1874 to 1878 he studied theology at St. Bueno's College in Wales. There he began to write poetry again when he heard of the wreck of a German ship, the *Deutschland*, and the death of five Catholic nuns aboard.

It is the custom in the Jesuit order to move priests from one location to another frequently and to try them out in a variety of posts. In the next few years, Hopkins tried many different kinds of religious work without remarkable success. He was assigned to preach in the fashionable Farm Street Church in London's West End, but he was not a charismatic or crowd-pleasing performer. Parish work in the Liverpool slums left him depressed and exhausted. When he was assigned temporarily to the Catholic parish church in Oxford, he seemed to have had trouble getting along with his superior. Finally, he was appointed professor of Greek and Latin literature at University College, Dublin, Ireland. He held this post until his death in 1889. The Catholic population of Ireland at that time was in near-revolt against English oppression. Hopkins felt a conflict between his English patriotism and his Catholic sympathies. Although he had been a brilliant student as a young man, the University College duties gave him little opportunity to do gratifying scholarly work. Much of his time was spent in the drudgery of external examinations, grading papers of hundreds of students he had never taught. His lectures were attended by only a handful of students. He projected massive books for himself to write, but never was able to put them together. In this period he wrote many sonnets which show spiritual desolation, unhappiness, and alienation. He died of typhoid in 1889 at the age of forty-five. Not until a generation later did the literary world recognize his genius.

ANALYSIS

In 1875 a number of Roman Catholic religious people had been driven out of Germany by the Falck Laws. In the winter of that year, five exiled nuns took passage on the *Deutschland*, which ran aground in a snowstorm near the Kentish shore of England. The ship gradually broke up in the high seas and many lives were lost, including the nuns'. Their bodies were brought to England for solemn funeral ceremonies and the whole affair was widely reported in the newspapers. At this time Gerard Manley Hopkins was studying theology at St. Bueno's College in Wales. He read the reports in the press and many details in his poem reflect the newspapers's accounts. He seems especially to have noticed the report that, as passengers were being swept off the deck into the icy seas by towering waves, the tallest of the five nuns rose up above the others just before her death and cried out for Christ to come quickly to her. Hopkins discussed this fearful catastrophe with his rector, who suggested that someone should write a poem about it. Taking that hint as a command, Hopkins broke his self-imposed poetic silence and began to write again. The experience of the tall nun at her moment of death captured his imagination. How frightening and cruel it must have been to be on the deck of the shattered ship! Yet she was a faithful Catholic servant of God. How could God torment her so? What did she mean when she cried out for Christ to come to her as the fatal waves beat down on her?

"THE WRECK OF THE DEUTSCHLAND"

"The Wreck of the *Deutschland*" is a very difficult poem. Unlike the smooth sentences of Tennyson's *In Memoriam* (1850), for example, Hopkins's elegy is contorted, broken, sometimes opaque. When Robert Bridges published the first volume of Hopkins's poems in 1918, he warned readers that "The Wreck of the *Deutschland*" was like a great dragon lying at the gate to discourage readers from going on to other, more accessible poems by Hopkins. The thread of the occasion, however, can be traced in the text. The dedication of the poem to the memory of five Franciscan nuns exiled by the Falck Laws drowned between midnight and morning of December 7, 1875, gives the reader a point of reference. If readers skip to stanza twelve, the story goes ahead, following newspaper accounts of the events reasonably clearly. Stanza twelve relates that some two hundred passengers sailed from Bremen bound for America, never guessing that a fourth of them would drown. Stanza thirteen explains how the *Deutschland* sailed into the wintry storm. Stanzas fourteen and fifteen tell how the ship hit a sandbank and people began to drown. Stanza sixteen depicts an act of heroism in which

a sailor tries to rescue a woman, but is killed; his body dangles on a rope for hours before the eyes of the sufferers. Stanzas seventeen through twenty-three are about the tall nun. In stanza twenty-four the poet contrasts his own comfortable setting under a safe roof in Wales with that of the nuns who were in their death struggle on the stormy sea. He has no pain, no trial, but the tall nun is dying at that very moment. Rising up in the midst of death and destruction, she calls, "O Christ, Christ, come quickly." Stanzas twenty-five through thirty-five contemplate that scene and ask, "What did she mean?" when she called out. What was the total meaning of her agony and life? The poem therefore can be divided into three sections: Stanzas one to ten constitute a prologue or invocation, stanzas eleven through twenty-five depict the agony of the shipwreck and the tall nun, and stanzas twenty-five through thirty-five contemplate the meaning of that event. The middle section, describing the shipwreck and the tall nun's cry, is reasonably clear. Difficult details in this section are mostly explained in the notes to the revised fourth edition of *Poems of Gerard Manley Hopkins*. There are some additional perspectives, however, which are helpful in grasping the total work.

"The Wreck of the *Deutschland*" is related to the Jesuit contemplative "composition of place" and "application of the senses." As a member of the Society of Jesus, Hopkins's daily life and devotions were shaped by the *Spiritual Exercises* (1548) of St. Ignatius Loyola. Moreover, at certain times in his career he withdrew from the world to perform the spiritual exercises in month-long retreats of an extremely rigorous nature. One objective of the spiritual exercises is to induce an immediate, overwhelming sense of the presence of divinity in our world. The contemplative is directed by the *Spiritual Exercises* to employ the technique of "composition." For example, to get a sharper sense of the divine presence, one might contemplate the birth of Christ. First one must imagine, or compose, the scene of the Nativity in all possible detail and precision. When Christ was born, how large was the room; what animals were in the stable; where was the holy family; were they seated or standing; what was the manger like? The imagination embodies or composes the scene. The contemplative then applies his five senses systematically to the composition. What did it look like, sound like, smell like, feel like, and taste like? Such a projection of the contemplative into the very situation induces a very powerful awareness of the religious experience. "The Wreck of the *Deutschland*" is similar to such a contemplative exercise. Hopkins is trying to experience the religious truth of the nuns's sacrifice. The middle of his poem is a composition of the scene where the tall nun died. It is constructed systematically to apply the five senses. Stanza twenty-eight depicts the struggle of the poet to put himself in the nun's place, to feel what she felt, to suffer as she suffered, to believe as she believed. At her death, she saw her Master, Christ the King. The poet tries to participate in her experience. The poem should be read in comparison with other poems of the religious meditative tradition—for example, the poetry of George Herbert, Richard Crashaw, and Henry Vaughan. Louis L. Martz in *The Poetry of Meditation: A Study in English Religious Literature of the Seventeenth Century* (1962) is the best introduction to this aspect of Hopkins's work.

COMPLEXITIES OF SPRUNG RHYTHM

In addition to the religious complexities of the poem, there are aesthetic complexities. Hopkins claimed to have discovered a new poetic form, "sprung rhythm," which he employed in "The Wreck of the *Deutschland*." Despite intense scholarly investigation of Hopkins's metrics, there is no clear agreement as to what he means by "sprung rhythm." "The Wreck of the *Deutschland*" contains thirty-five stanzas, each with eight lines of varying length. If one counts the syllables in each line, or if one counts only the accented syllables in each line, there is a rough agreement in the length of a particular line in each of the stanzas. For example, line one has four or five syllables in almost all stanzas. Line eight is much longer than line one in all stanzas. What makes lines of varying length metrical?

It is sometimes thought that Hopkins was isolated in the Jesuit order and did not know what he was doing when he created unusual poetic forms. That is absurd, for he was a professor of classical literature and in correspondence with leading literary scholars. The best way to look at sprung rhythm is to see what Hopkins's associates thought about meter. Robert Bridges, his college friend and lifelong correspondent, studied the iambic pentameter of Milton and wrote a major book on the prosody of Milton. Bridges thought that Milton built his lines out of iambic feet, units of two syllables with the second syllable pronounced more loudly than the first. An iambic pentameter line therefore had five iambic feet, or ten syllables with the even-positioned syllables stressed more loudly than the odd-positioned ones. Lines in Miltonic pentameter which do not fit this pattern follow a few simple variations defined by Bridges. Bridges's study appears to be accurate for Milton, but clearly Hopkins is not writing poetry of this sort. The number of unstressed syllables differs widely in his lines, a condition that Bridges shows never occurs in Milton.

Another of Hopkins's correspondents, Coventry Patmore, was a leading popular Catholic poet who wrote a study of English metrics based on time, similar to the prosody of hymns. Hopkins's sprung rhythm seems more consistent with such a musical time-based pattern than with the accentual-syllabic pattern of Milton as defined by Bridges. Hopkins, as a professor of classical languages, knew the advanced linguistic work going on in that area. Greek poetry was thought to be quantitative, based on the length of vowel sounds. As a schoolboy, Hopkins had to practice translating an English passage first into Latin, then into Greek poetry, arranging the long and short vowels into acceptable feet. (Some of his Latin and Greek poetry is collected in *Poems of Gerard Manley Hopkins*.) Modern readers are not often trained to understand these models in classical languages and so do not appreciate how important they are to Hopkins's patterns in English verse. In Hopkins's unpublished papers, there are lines of Greek poetry interlined by drafts of his English poems, sometimes with arrows and doodles matching up the English and Greek phrases. It seems possible that Hopkins based his distinctive rhythms on Greek models, especially the odes of Pindar, a topic that has been partially explored in Todd K. Bender's *Gerard Manley Hopkins: The Classical Background and Critical Reception of His Work* (1966). Essentially, however, the key to sprung rhythm remains to be discovered.

PRIEST VERSUS POET

"The Wreck of the *Deutschland*" was submitted to the Jesuit magazine *The Month* and, after some delay, rejected for publication. Hopkins said that they "dared not" print it, although there is no need to imagine a dark conspiracy among the Jesuit authorities to silence Hopkins. It is likely that the editors of *The Month* simply found "The Wreck of the *Deutschland*" baffling in form and content. The rejection dramatizes, however, a peculiar condition in Hopkins's life. His unquestionable genius for poetry found almost no encouragement in his immediate surroundings as a Jesuit priest. His poetry is, of course, shaped by Roman Catholic imagery and is mainly devotional in nature. Without his Church and his priestly calling, he never could have written his poems. On the other hand, what he wrote was largely unappreciated by his closest associates. Ironically, this highly religious poet became famous in the twentieth century because of the praise of readers who were frequently anti-Roman Catholic. There was a central anguish in Hopkins life, a conflict between his priestly duties and his artistic creativity. Many scholars have tried to explain how Hopkins's poetry and his priesthood fit together. One of the best such studies is John Pick's *Gerard Manley Hopkins: Priest and Poet* (1942). Roman Catholic critics usually tend to say that the Catholic faith made Hopkins a great writer. Readers who are hostile to Catholicism tend to think that Hopkins was a serious writer in spite of extreme discouragements and restraints placed on him by his faith. The truth is probably somewhere in the middle. If Hopkins had not been severely troubled, he would have had little motivation to write. His poems show all the commonplaces of religious imagery found in much less powerful Catholic poets, such as his friend Coventry Patmore. Hopkins rises above the average religious versifier because of his original genius, yet this originality is what the Jesuit editors of *The Month* did not understand.

"THE WINDHOVER"

Stung by the criticism of his major poem, not only by the Jesuit editors but also by his friend Robert Bridges, Hopkins never again tried to write something so long and elaborate. He retreated into the most traditional form in English prosody, the sonnet. After "The Wreck of the *Deutschland*," Hopkins's most famous work is the sonnet "The Windhover." More has been written about these fourteen lines than about any other piece of poetry of comparable length in English. All of Hopkins's sonnets are related to the Petrarchan model, but he alters the

tradition to fit his peculiar genius. The poem employs line-end rhymes *abba abba cdcdcd*. In addition to the repetition of sound at the end of each line, there is also thickly interwoven alliteration and assonance within each line. This internal rhyme is related to the *cynghanedd* or consonant chime of Welsh poetry. Hopkins tried to learn Welsh when he was a student at St. Bueno's College in Wales and he actually wrote a bit of Welsh poetry in the form called *cywydd*. The meter of "The Windhover" is the so-called sprung rhythm, allowing great variation in the length of lines. The Petrarchan sonnet uses its rhyme scheme to define two parts of the poem: *abba abba* is the octave or exposition in the opening eight lines, *cdcdcd* is the sestet or commentary in the concluding six lines. Hopkins explained in his letters that the essence of a sonnet is balance and proportion. The octave asserts a situation or condition and then a surprising commentary comes back in the sestet to reply to the octave. Since the sestet has only six lines, it must be correspondingly "sharper" or more forceful if it is to balance the initial statement. The key to the sonnet is this proportion. Hopkins wrote some sonnets longer than the usual fourteen lines and a few shorter, "curtail" or cut-short, sonnets. In all his sonnets, however, he maintains the proportion of octave to sestet, eight to six, and forces the shorter conclusion to a higher pitch of intensity.

In its octave, "The Windhover" describes the flight of a hawk of a kind commonly used in falconry or hunting circling against the dawn sky. The sestet begins with the description of the hawk diving, plummeting earthward, as it "buckles." The sure, steady circling of the hawk in the octave is astonishing, but the sudden buckling downward is even more thrilling. It is beautiful and breathtaking. In the sestet the increased beauty of the hawk as it dives is compared to a plough made to shine as it is driven through sandy soil, and to an ember coated with ashes that sparkles when it falls and breaks.

"The Windhover" illustrates one of the key terms in Hopkins's aesthetic vocabulary: "inscape," a word he coined for the inner nature of a thing which distinguishes it from everything else in creation. Hopkins's reading of Franciscan philosopher John Duns Scotus is pertinent to his concept of inscape. *Qualis* in Latin means "what." When we look at the *qualities* of things, we examine *what* they have in common with other members of their class. The *qualities* of a good racing horse are those features that it has in common with other good horses. Duns Scotus imagines that there is an opposite to *quality*. *Haec* means "this" in Latin. Duns Scotus coins the word *haecceitas*, the "thisness" of a thing, which sets it apart from everything else, making it unique and different—the principle of individuation. Hopkins frequently celebrates the rare, unusual, or unique in nature. He turns away from the universal quality and toward the individual. The octave of "The Windhover" can be seen as the poet's description of a natural event: the flight and dive of a falcon. In that movement, he seeks to find the inscape, the innermost shape as evidence of God's presence in the created world. He tries to see into the form of the thing, to find what makes it original, unique, special, strange, striking. Like the sacrifice of the tall nun in "The Wreck of the *Deutschland*," the act of the hawk is "composed" so as to be the object for a religious meditation.

Paradoxically, the only way to grasp the unique inscape of a thing is to compare it with something else. The tension of this paradox is evident in the striking, surprising comparisons which Hopkins employs in "The Windhover," comparing the dive of a hawk with a plough shining in use and a burning coal sparkling as it collapses. The poem says that these three events are comparable or analogous in that in each case when the object *buckles* it becomes brighter and more glorious. When the hawk buckles in its dive, it is a thousandfold more lovely than in its stately circling. When the rusty plough buckles to its work, the abrasion of the sandy soil makes the ploughshare shine in use. When the ash crumbles or buckles, its inner brightness shows through the gray, outer ash-coating. Hopkins gave "The Windhover" the dedication, "To Christ Our Lord." The Jesuit order sees itself as the chivalry or the Knights of Christ. Ignatius advises the novice to buckle on the armor of Christ. To become a Jesuit, to buckle on the armor of a true Christian knight, is the proper and glorious activity of a man who would follow his nature, or unique calling. In like manner, a hawk follows its true nature, it *is* what it was *made to be*, when it sails in the wind and dives. A plough was made to work the earth, a coal to burn, and these things do what they were intended to do when they buckle. The activity of buckling may be painful or dan-

gerous, but it produces glory, brilliance, grace, and beauty. The discipline of accepting the vows of the Jesuits may be painful in some earthly way, but it brings the glory of Christ's service. Christ, too, accepted the pain and duty of his earthly incarnation. He was buckled to the cross. He did what he had to do and so was brought to glory through pain and humiliation. The structure of "The Windhover" appears to be a set of analogies or comparisons all coming together in the word *buckle*. Such a structure is also to be found in the odes of the Greek poet Pindar, which Hopkins studied intensely in school. Pindar's poems praise a great athlete or hero by linking together a series of seeming digressions in one key image or figure, sometimes called a "constellation," such as the "golden lyre," a "beacon fire," a "horse," or a "tree." Hopkins's poetry unites the Christian tradition of anagogical interpretation of the created world and the Classical Greek tradition of the Pindaric ode.

THE SONNET FORM

Most of Hopkins's shorter poems are sonnets, yet within the confines of this form, Hopkins displays great originality in his metrical structure, his repetition of sound in alliteration and internal rhyme, and his changes in the length of the sonnet while maintaining the crucial eight-to-six proportion of the octave/sestet division. Like the form of the sonnet, the subjects of most of Hopkins's poems are extremely traditional: (1) elation at the sight of some particular bit of nature; (2) personal dejection, desolation, and despair; (3) celebration of the inner worth of an outwardly ordinary human being. These three topics are commonplaces of Romantic and post-Romantic literature. Hopkins's originality lies in treating these subjects with unusual power and perception. Romantic poets such as William Wordsworth and Percy Bysshe Shelley often looked at nature and said that they felt their hearts leap up to behold the beauty of spring or autumn. For Hopkins, every little corner of nature was evidence of the divine presence of God. His Christianity reinforces the Romantic sentiment. The confluence of the Romantic and the Christian tradition produces unusually powerful statements.

Consider, for example, the sonnet "Hurrahing in Harvest." Like "The Windhover," this poem is an Italian sonnet, rhymed *abba abba cdcdcd*. Lines six and seven end with an unusual rhyme device. "Saviour" is rhymed with the next line, but in order to hear the complete rhyme, one must continue to the "r" sound that begins line eight: "gave you a/ Rapturous." This extended rhyme is common in Hopkins and illustrates his predilection for unusual twists within the framework of rigid traditional expectations. The subjects of "The Windhover" and "Hurrahing in Harvest" are also similar. In both poems, the speaker looks up at the sky and finds nature breathtakingly beautiful. "Hurrahing in Harvest" declares that the summer is now ending. The *stooks*, or shocks of bundled grain, are now stacked in the fields. The technical and regional term *stooks* is characteristic of Hopkins's vocabulary. The word is not commonly known, but it is exact. The speaker looks up at the autumnal skies and sees the clouds. With the bold verbal comparisons which the poet prefers, he compares the skies to "wind-walks"—they are like alleyways for the winds. The clouds are like "silk-sacks"; they are soft, dainty, and luxurious. The movement of the clouds across the sky is like "mealdrift" or flour pouring across the heavens. In that soft, flowing beauty, the speaker walks and lifts up his eyes. He sees the glory of the natural scene and then recognizes that beyond the heavens, behind all the created universe, there stands the Savior. He at first rejoices in the sheer beauty of nature, but such earthly beauty leads him to the unspeakable inner beauty of Christ's immediate presence in the natural world. In the sestet, the speaker sees the azure hills of autumn as strong as the shoulder of a stallion, majestic and sweet with flowers, like the shoulder of God bearing the creation in all its glory. The speaker realizes that all this is here for him to see, and the realization makes his heart leap up as if it had wings; his spirit hurls heavenward.

NATURE SONNETS

Hopkins wrote many poems celebrating nature in sonnet form. "God's Grandeur" states in the octave that the grandeur of God's creating has been obscured by the Industrial Revolution, trade and toil. The sestet replies that there is a spark of freshness deep in nature which will spring up like the sun at dawn because God broods over the earth like a bird over its egg. "The Starlight Night" begins with a powerful octave describing the beauty of the stars in the night sky. The sestet replies that the stars are like a picket fence separating us from

heaven through which we can glimpse a bit of what is on the other side. "Spring" typically gives an excited picture of the juice and joy of the earth stirring in springtime and compares it to the youthful, primal goodness of children, a hint of sinless Eden.

"PIED BEAUTY"

"Pied Beauty" is one of Hopkins's most important philosophical poems on nature. It reflects his study of Duns Scotus and his notion of inscape. The poem is a "curtail" or cut-short sonnet, only ten and a fraction lines long. Hopkins explained that this poem maintained the eight-to-six ratio, which he felt was the key to the sonnet form. The exposition, which occupies the first six lines, states that God is especially to be praised for the irregular, dappled, serviceable parts of creation. The sestet generalizes that whatever is contradictory, strange, or changeable originates in God.

In Platonic thought, a material thing is beautiful insofar as it approaches its unchanging ideal. For example, a beautiful circle is one that approaches—as nearly as possible in our world—the perfection of an ideal circle. Because the things of our world are always struggling to become like their perfect forms, our material world is always changing. It is sometimes called the mutable world of "becoming." The ideal world cannot change, however, because when something is perfect, any change would make it imperfect. The world of Platonic ideals is therefore unchanging. It is sometimes called the world of permanent "being."

"Pied Beauty" makes a striking statement about the nature of beauty. It asserts that things are not beautiful because they approach the perfect type, but because they are various, changing, contradictory. Hopkins seems to be praising the very aspect of the material world that Platonic philosophy connects with degeneration and decay. Somehow God, who is perfect and unchanging, has fathered a universe of imperfection, contradiction, and decay. Nevertheless, this created world reflects his praise: Duns Scotus maintained that God's perfection must be manifest somehow in the constant change and variety of his creation.

"DUNS SCOTUS'S OXFORD"

Hopkins's admiration for Duns Scotus is expressed in "Duns Scotus's Oxford," which combines the nature-sonnet and the celebration of a famous man. Its octave depicts the ancient university town of Oxford. The sestet comments that this was the very city that Duns Scotus knew when the subtle doctor taught there in the thirteenth century. Now Hopkins finds Scotus to have the best insight into philosophical problems, even more comforting to him than Greek philosophers such as Plato, or Italian philosophers such as St. Thomas Aquinas. All of the nature sonnets give an extremely sharp picture of some relatively common event or situation in nature: a hawk in flight, the landscape of Oxford, the rebirth of the countryside in springtime, the clouds and fields of autumn. The poet reflects on the source of all this beauty. The scene itself uplifts his spirits, but the awareness of God's creative force glimpsed behind the material world brings even more elation.

THE HEROIC SONNET

A second group of poems is in the tradition of the heroic sonnet. These poems examine a person's life and define what is noteworthy in an ordinary man's career. "The Lantern Out of Doors" is typical. The octave tells of seeing a lantern moving at night. There must be someone behind that light, but he is so far off that he passes in the darkness and all that can be seen is a little spark. We have trouble knowing other people, and death is soon upon us. The sestet replies that Christ knows every person; Christ is the first and last friend of every man.

"Felix Randal," one of Hopkins's best sonnets, is about a blacksmith who fell ill and died. The once powerful man wasted away, but he finally came to accept Christ. Paradoxically, in the weakness of his death he became more blessed than in the pagan power he was so proud of in the days when he forged and fitted horseshoes with his fellow workers.

"The Soldier," "Tom's Garland: Upon the Unemployed," and "Harry Ploughman" all fit into the category of poems celebrating the inner worth of ordinary people. Perhaps the pattern of this kind of sonnet is best displayed in "In Honour of St. Alphonsus Rodriguez: Laybrother of the Society of Jesus." Alphonsus Rodriguez performed no noble deeds. For forty years, however, he faithfully carried out his duty and filled his station as doorkeeper. It is not his exploits, but his humanity, that Hopkins celebrates. Humility, obedience, and simple faith have their reward. The poem is in the tradition of

Milton's theme of the faithful Christians: "They also serve who only stand and wait."

SONNETS OF TERROR

The third major theme of Hopkins's sonnets is spiritual desolation and terror. These poems constitute the dark, opposite side of Hopkins's view of reality. In the nature poems, the poet looks at some part of the created universe and feels that God is in every corner of our world. His joy, already aroused by the pure beauty of nature, rises to an ecstatic pitch when he realizes that God is behind it all. The poems of desolation, sometimes called the "terrible sonnets," on the other hand, imagine a world without God—all joy, freshness, and promise withdrawn. They depict the dark night of the soul.

Many readers think that these poems are directly autobiographical, indicating that Hopkins in the last years of his life was devastated by despair. This view is probably not sound. The sonnet is a highly dramatized form; sonnets are traditionally constructed like little plays. Thus the speaker of one of Shakespeare's sonnets is no more Shakespeare, the man himself, than is Macbeth or Hamlet, and the persona or mask through which a sonneteer speaks is not to be confused with the real author. The *Spiritual Exercises* of Saint Ignatius, moreover, follows a spiritual progression which every Jesuit would imitate in his retreats and private worship. In a long retreat, lasting about a month, the exercitant is called upon to drive himself gradually into a state of extreme desolation into which a renewed sense of God's presence finally bursts like Easter into the dormant world.

The sonnets of terror may be as artificial as Elizabethan love sonnets. They may be, to some degree, virtuoso exercises in imagining a world devoid of spirituality and hope. The real feelings of Hopkins may be quite separate from the imagined feelings of the persona who speaks these sonnets. On the other hand, we can hardly imagine that Hopkins could write these poems unless there were some wrenching personal feelings motivating his creative act.

The sonnets of terror appeal to readers today because they mirror a cosmic despair or alienation. The feeling that modern man is a stranger in a strange land, that he is alienated from the profit of his own productivity, that he is caught in a meaningless or absurd activity like Sisyphus rolling his stone endlessly up a mountain in Hell, is extremely widespread. It is doubtful that Hopkins felt alienated in exactly this way. His religious belief promised him a future life and salvation. When he speaks of despair, it is always hypothetical: Think how unbearable life would be *if* there were not hope.

"CARRION COMFORT"

"Carrion Comfort," among the best of Hopkins's dark sonnets, considers despair, which is itself a sin, depicting the struggle of the Christian with his own conscience. It begins a series of six sonnets of unusual power which treat the struggle of the soul. These poems should be read in sequence: (1) "Carrion Comfort," (2) "No Worst, There Is None," (3) "To Seem a Stranger Lies My Lot," (4) "I Wake and Feel the Fell of Dark, Not Day," (5) "Patience, Hard Thing," and (6) "My Own Heart Let Me Have More Pity On." Read in sequence, these sonnets constitute a short psychodrama or morality play.

The Christian speaker confronts his own doubt, weakness, and unworth, and is terrified of God. In five scenes he is seen writhing and twisting in mental contortions of guilt and terror. At the conclusion of "My Own Heart Let Me Have More Pity On," the sestet provides the dramatic release, as God's smile breaks through, like sunlight on a mountain guiding the traveler. This sonnet sequence corresponds to the progress of the seeker through the final stages of his spiritual exercises. The same progress of the mind, through terror to elation at the Resurrection, is outlined in "That Nature Is a Heraclitean Fire and of the Comfort of the Resurrection." The first segment of this poem looks at the changing natural world. Like a bonfire, everything around us is changing, decaying, being consumed. Man seems so pitifully weak and vulnerable among these flames. The only hope is Christ's promise of salvation, which comes to man like a beacon. Man will pass through the fire and, even when all else is destroyed, his soul will endure like an immortal diamond.

HOPKINS'S VOCABULARY

A striking characteristic of Hopkins's poetry is his rich vocabulary. As he sought to find the inscape or unique form in the created universe, he also attempted to find in language the original, spare, strange, exactly right word. He was one of the best trained linguists of his age, working at the research level in Latin and Greek, while studying Anglo-Saxon and Welsh. His notes and journals show him repeatedly developing elaborate etymologies of words. He belonged to a widespread movement in the Victorian era, spearheaded by Robert Bridges and his Society For Pure English, which glorified the archaic elements in modern English. He records in his notes dialect words, and the special words used by workers for their tools or by country people for plants and animals. This attention to the texture of language pours forth in his poetry in an unusually rich, eccentric vocabulary.

LEGACY

Despite the orthodoxy of his religious views, Hopkins is known as one of the founders of modernism in literature. He is frequently compared with Walt Whitman, Emily Dickinson, and the French Symbolist poets as a great revolutionary who rebelled against the sterile forms of Victorian verse and brought a new urgency, freshness, and seriousness to poetry. He revolutionized the very basis of English meter with his experiments in sprung rhythm. He revitalized the bold metaphor in the manner of the English metaphysical poets. He created a whole new lexicon, a poetic vocabulary constructed from dialect, archaic, technical, and coined words.

The critics who initially praised his work in the 1920's and 1930's tended to see him as a cultural primitive, a man isolated from the corruption of society and so able to return to a state of nature and get to the core of language more easily than writers, such as Alfred, Lord Tennyson, who seemed corrupted by false traditions. Although Hopkins was undoubtedly a great innovator, he was certainly not a cultural primitive. He was a highly trained professor of Latin and Greek language and literature. In addition to his "Double First in Greats" from Oxford University, he undertook years of rigorous philosophical and theological training with the Society of Jesus. He was at the center of a group of correspondents who were as powerful intellectually as any group we can find in his era: Bridges, Dixon, Patmore, and other less frequent scholarly correspondents.

Hopkins was not a naïve writer; on the contrary, he was an extremely sophisticated writer. His poetry is revolutionary, not because he was ignorant of tradition, but because he brought together many powerful threads of tradition: the contemplative practice of the *Spiritual Ex-*

ercises, with their "composition of place" and "application of the senses"; the conventions of the Petrarchan sonnet; the complicated metrical studies of Bridges, Patmore, and the classical scholars; the classical philosophical background of Oxford University; and the medieval thought of the Jesuit schools, especially of John Duns Scotus. These traditions met, and sometimes conflicted sharply, in Hopkins. From that confluence of traditions he gave modern readers the unique gift of his poems.

OTHER MAJOR WORKS

NONFICTION: *The Letters of Gerard Manley Hopkins to Robert Bridges*, 1935, 1955 (C. C. Abbott, editor); *The Correspondence of Gerard Manley Hopkins and Richard Watson Dixon*, 1935, 1955 (Abbott, editor); *The Notebooks and Papers of Gerard Manley Hopkins*, 1937 (Humphry House, editor); *Further Letters of Gerard Manley Hopkins*, 1938, 1956 (Abbott, editor); *The Journals and Papers of Gerard Manley Hopkins*, 1959 (House and Graham Storey, editors); *The Sermons and Devotional Writings of Gerard Manley Hopkins*, 1959 (Christopher Devlin, editor); *Gerard Manley Hopkins: Selected Letters*, 1990.

BIBLIOGRAPHY

Bergonzi, Bernard. *Gerard Manley Hopkins*. New York: Macmillan, 1977. This volume, one in the Masters of World Literature series, contains five chapters of biography, followed by a sixth chapter which seeks to give a general account of Hopkins's poetry as linked to his life. Includes a select bibliography and an index.

Bloom, Harold, ed. *Gerard Manley Hopkins*. New York: Chelsea House, 1986. Includes a number of significant essays on Hopkins, a chronology, a bibliography, and an index.

Brown, Daniel. *Hopkins' Idealism: Philosophy, Physics, Poetry*. New York: Oxford University Press, 1997. Offers new readings of some of Hopkins's best-known poems and is the first full-length study of Hopkins's largely unpublished Oxford undergraduate essays and notes on philosophy and mechanics.

Downes, David Anthony. *Hopkins' Achieved Self*. Lanham, Md.: University Press of America, 1996. The first book to explore, in depth, the hermeneutics of Hopkins's notions of the self and to apply his ideas of "selving" to his poetry. Intended for scholars of Victorian literature and of Hopkins's work.

Gardner, W. H. *Gerard Manley Hopkins, 1844-1889*. 3d ed. 2 vols. New York: Oxford University Press, 1958. This third edition of the first really major study of Hopkins's poetry (originally published in 1944) is still one of the best. The first volume deals extensively with Hopkins's development of the sonnet form, his themes and imagery, and then seeks to place him in relation to modernism. Volume 2 goes through his poems more chronologically, but also deals with development of rhythm and critical theory. Contains appendices, a bibliography, and indexes.

Robinson, John. *In Extremity: A Study of Gerard Manley Hopkins*. Cambridge, England: Cambridge University Press, 1978. Traces the nature of Hopkins's religious experiences as they receive poetic expression. The latter was intense because the former was out of extremity. The philosophy of John Duns Scotus is seen as a vital bridge between experience and expression. Includes notes and an index.

Schneider, Elisabeth W. *The Dragon in the Gate: Studies in the Poetry of Gerard Manley Hopkins*. Berkeley: University of California Press, 1968. Still an excellent introduction to Hopkins's major poetry, dealing specifically with the development of style and rhythm. Includes an index.

Sulloway, Alison G. *Gerard Manley Hopkins and the Victorian Temper*. New York: Columbia University Press, 1972. Places Hopkins firmly in the Victorian context. Two appendices refer to the Tractarian wars. Includes notes, a selected bibliography, and an index.

Weyand, Norman, ed. *Immortal Diamond: Studies in Gerard Manley Hopkins*. New York: Sheed & Ward, 1949. Reprint. New York: Octagon Books, 1969. A series of essays by Jesuit scholars that represents the widest and clearest Jesuit commentary on the poet available to the time. Includes appendices, bibliography through 1946.

Todd K. Bender;
bibliography updated by the editors